Psychology Today
An Introduction

Second Edition

CONTRIBUTING CONSULTANTS

*Rudolf Arnheim, Ph.D., *Harvard University*
Joel Aronoff, Ph.D., *Michigan State University*
R. Freed Bales, Ph.D., *Harvard University*
J. Merrill Carlsmith, Ph.D., *Stanford University*
*Stephen Cohen, Ph.D., *Harvard University*
Morton Deutsch, Ph.D., *Teachers College, Columbia University*
Roger L. Dominowski, Ph.D., *University of Illinois, Chicago Circle*
*Edmund J. Fantino, Ph.D., *University of California, San Diego*
John C. Fentress, Ph.D., *University of Oregon*
*Kurt Fischer, Ph.D., *University of Denver*
Donald W. Fiske, Ph.D., *University of Chicago*
Daniel X. Freedman, M.D., *University of Chicago*
Stephen E. Glickman, Ph.D., *University of California, Berkeley*
Richard L. Gregory, Ph.D., *University of Edinburgh*
Calvin S. Hall, Ph.D., *University of California, Santa Cruz*
*Charles M. Hampden-Turner, D.B.A., *Cambridge Institute*
Jerry Hirsch, Ph.D., *University of Illinois*
*Matina Horner, Ph.D., *Harvard University*
Robert L. Isaacson, Ph.D., *University of Florida*
Douglas N. Jackson, Ph.D., *University of Western Ontario*
Samuel S. Komorita, Ph.D., *Indiana University*
Leonard Krasner, Ph.D., *State University of New York, Stony Brook*
*Dennis Krebs, Ph.D., *Harvard University*
Jonas Langer, Ph.D., *University of California, Berkeley*
Donald B. Lindsley, Ph.D., *University of California, Los Angeles*
*Joseph Lipinski, M.D., *Massachusetts General Hospital*
**Abraham H. Maslow, Ph.D., *Brandeis University*
Rollo May, Ph.D., *William Alanson White Institute*
James V. McConnell, Ph.D., *University of Michigan*
William J. McGuire, Ph.D., *Yale University*
*Alastair McLeod, (*doctoral candidate*)
Elton B. McNeil, Ph.D., *University of Michigan*
Neal E. Miller, Ph.D., *Rockefeller University*
Conrad G. Mueller, Ph.D., *Indiana University*
Edward J. Murray, Ph.D., *University of Miami*
Harry G. Murray, Ph.D., *University of Western Ontario*
Donald A. Norman, Ph.D., *University of California, San Diego*
Robert E. Ornstein, Ph.D., *Langley Porter Neuropsychiatric Institute*
*L. Anne Peplau (*doctoral candidate*)
Herbert L. Pick, Ph.D., *University of Minnesota*
*N. Dickon Reppucci, Ph.D., *Yale University*
*G. S. Reynolds, Ph.D., *University of California, San Diego*
Carl R. Rogers, Ph.D., *Center for Studies of the Person*
*Zick Rubin, Ph.D., *Harvard University*
*Brian Sarata (*doctoral candidate*)
Bertram Scharf, Ph.D., *Northeastern University*
Dan I. Slobin, Ph.D., *University of California, Berkeley*
*Carol Smith (*doctoral candidate*)
*Ted Steiner, Ph.D., *San Francisco State College*
S. S. Stevens, Ph.D., *Harvard University*
*David Tresemer (*doctoral candidate*)
Leona E. Tyler, Ph.D., *University of Oregon*
Robert I. Watson, Ph.D., *University of New Hampshire*
*Robert Watson, Jr. (*doctoral candidate*)
*David Wood, Ph.D., *Harvard University*

Advisory Board, Second Edition
Kurt Fischer, Dennis Krebs, George Reynolds, Zick Rubin, David Wood

Chapter Introductions written by Isaac Asimov.

**Contributors to Second Edition.*
***The late Dr. Maslow contributed to the First Edition.*

Psychology Today
An Introduction

Second Edition

CRM BOOKS
Del Mar, California

Library of Congress Catalog Card Number: 75-189836

Standard Book Number: 87665-131-7

Manufactured in the United States of America

Second Edition, First Printing

Foreword

How many academic psychologists remember what drove them originally to the study of psychology? It was the same impulse that the new student of the subject feels today: the quest for meaning and the search for understanding both of himself and of his world: "The proper study of mankind is man."

At a time of extraordinary change, when the shape of the new social landscape is not yet apparent, it is of crucial importance that all concerned men and women search for better understanding of the nature of human experience and the scope of human potential. Good textbooks teach students. This book tries to do something more. It has been designed to stimulate curiosity, to excite imagination, and to help in that search for understanding. This is why our graphics are so dramatic and why the Preface by Rudolf Arnheim deals with the role of pictures in learning. And why we have included two records as part of the text.

The book cannot pretend to provide all the answers, any more than psychology itself can, but it should start the reader on his own journey of exploration.

This new edition of *Psychology Today: An Introduction* is unique in publishing history. Thousands of students and professors who used the first edition—and for the most part liked it—told us how it could be improved. We listened, acted upon the advice we were given, and are proud to share the result with you.

Richard Holme

Richard Holme,
President and Publisher, CRM BOOKS

Preface
Learning by Pictures

How can a book help anybody learn or teach psychology? This is itself a psychological problem—and not a simple one. For good reasons, books are late arrivals in the history of civilization. They are preceded by learning through direct evidence: what a fish is you learn by seeing and handling it and by watching it go through its motions. What love is you learn by feeling it and doing it. There is no replacement for the efficacy of this most direct learning through the senses. Yet something more is needed.

A book appeals to the sense of sight, but it does so by a collection of meaningless signs, by scribbles arbitrarily connected with things known from elsewhere. A printed page is an assembly of hermetic reminders. No more indirect communication can be conceived than that leading from the sign 本 to the word *hon,* which is Japanese for *book,* and from there to the weighty, black rectangular object you are holding in your hands. Exactly the same is true for our English letters and words, although we are less immediately aware of it.

And yet, once the user is initiated, the words go straight to the point. You read *freedom,* and in your mind your senses leap through unblocked space, to images of a man weeping with joy at the liberation of Paris, of chains broken, of the Declaration of Independence. But more than that, the written word suggests what all these images have in common: the essence of freedom, the concept. And is it not concepts one wants to study in psychology?

Even thirty years ago, if Polonius had asked a student enrolled in an introductory psychology course, "What do you read, my lord?" the truthful answer would have been, "Words, words, words." And if Polonius had insisted, "What is the matter, my lord?" the student might well have answered with Hamlet, "Between who?" The book from which I learned psychology contained not a single illustration.

One might argue that this is an advantage—not only because words seem to nail down the generality of concepts with a precision no picture can provide but also because psychology aims at invisible things. Learning psychology is not like learning how to build a boat. To be sure, it also starts, as all knowledge must, with what the senses tell us. We watch a child hesitating to touch a rabbit. But this is only the beginning. What we really need to know is the constellation of attracting, propelling, and refraining forces that move the limbs of the child, and we need to know how these forces got into the child. What is there to illustrate?

Since the days of the pictureless textbooks, much has changed in psychology and elsewhere. For one thing, psychologists have begun to take professional notice of how tellingly the mind is mirrored in the outer appearance and conduct of man and animal. The school of behaviorism is only a systematized sector of this much broader new awareness, which makes psychologists watch how babies act in the company of their peers, how people sit on chairs, how the members of discussion groups take cues from each other's stances, how birds behave when they are frustrated. It is hard to tell to what extent this development in psychology was stimulated by the universal picture-consciousness of our century, which was made possible by the photographic techniques of taking instantaneous snapshots and printing them in faithful halftone or transmitting them electrically in black and white or natural color. For better or worse, words without pictures are becoming a distinctly incomplete experience for child and adult, and with the demand for visual information goes a growing expertise in reading pictures quickly and profitably.

The puritan notion that there is something slightly sinful about pictures has broken down with a vengeance in the field of psychological study. What strikes us first when we leaf through the new textbook is the enormous variety of illustrations. There are several reasons for this variety. It mirrors, first of all, the different views a psychologist has to face as he digs his way through the layers of the organism toward the inner sanctum of the mind. The quest starts, as I mentioned before, with what the senses observe about the appearance and behavior of things. The snapshot of a weeping child who seems to have touched a hot burner goes a long way toward giving flesh and blood to the sort of fact John B. Watson described rather opaquely sixty years ago: "Again, we could have a kinesthetic unlearned response when the infant reacts by crying to a long-sustained twisted position of the arm." We understand the theoretical message, but the photograph helps give us the full experience of the kind of event that the statement drew attention to.

The same is true for the inner sights of the body, for which the psychologist relies on dissection and microscopy. There was and still is something immediately enlightening about those simple, stark outline drawings describing the principal sections of the brain or the shapes of rods and cones in the retina. But the knowledge remains as anemic as the picture unless it makes contact at some point with the messy, moist texture of the real tissue, which a good photograph or full-color painting will convey.

Photograph versus drawing—the virtues and the vices of the two media reflect the many levels of abstraction that the scientist must mentally handle and reconcile. He starts with the full complexity of the individual case, its intriguing mixture of accidentals and essentials, nicely illustrated, for example, by a photograph on which an experimenter's hand turns the switch of a recording instrument. The skin of the hand is wrinkly and hairy—does this matter? Probably another hand would do as well; but you can never be sure, and the student of psychology must be challenged from the beginning by the scientist's task of finding the relevant principle in its accidental, "noisy" embodiment. Does the photograph of a person experiencing the so-called startle effect represent any living organism, any human being, any woman, or a particular middle-aged lady with short hair, earrings, and a striped dress? Once you know what is of the essence and what not, your problem is half solved.

If instead of showing the particular lady the picture presents the drawing of a mere stick figure, the reader is freed from solving the problem. The picture itself has selected the proper level of abstraction for him and gives him the answer: It does not matter who is startled—any person will do. This can be a great help in learning, and the choice of the appropriate level of abstraction can make all the difference between confusion and enlightenment. If an illustration reduces the system of interconnected endocrine glands to a network of disks and straight-line pipes, it may give more, not less, than a faithfully detailed picture would. Leonardo da Vinci knew this when in his superb anatomical drawings he replaced muscles and tendons with cords in order to show their function clearly.

Contrary to common belief, a remarkable feature of abstraction is that it never loses the connection with sensory imagery. This is evident in the highly abstract likeness of the glandular network: severely simplified though the picture may be, it is still an analogue of the bodily pattern of organs and ducts. But what kind of picture is, say, a learning curve? Here a series of experiments has been stripped to two sets of numbers: how often the task was accomplished and how long it took each time. No visible trace is left of rat, cage, dials, experimenter; however, the data, deprived of their original body, have been given a new one. They come to life again in the Cartesian world of pure spatial distances; and by means of nothing but a profile of ups and downs, they display the story of gradual training or sudden insight with dramatic simplicity. Nothing could be more abstract and more concrete at the same time. Or look at the graceful symmetry of the so-called normal curve. Can the lawfulness of nature be shown more visibly?

To draw such diagrams seems an easy job and therefore used to be entrusted to draftsmen who could handle a ruler and a compass but did not know how to see. Only recently it dawned on the producers of visual aids, such as textbook illustrations, that even the least "artistic" tasks of visual communication call for the imagination of the artist-designer—not just to make the book look beautiful but to make it readable.

The traditional textbook figures pretended to be without art, but inevitably they conformed to a style. They derived from the pale outline drawings of neo-classicism or from the realism of nineteenth-century lithographs and woodcuts. By now, the style of illustrations has become much more conspicuous—partly by reflecting the eclecticism of our century, which accepts the artistic styles of all times and places. Now we see an anatomical painting of the human brain glow in the somber light of a Rembrandt while on another page the tidy illusions of a Magritte have inspired an arrangement of surrealist symbols. Even the mere coloring of the dots in a scattergram transforms the statistical graph into an abstract painting in the manner of Larry Poons. To be sure, the powerful idiosyncrasy of the original artistic creator is processed in each case in order to become a normalized product, relying on standard meanings and decorative shapes. It is the easy art of magazines and record albums, of posters and wall decorations—an extension of the student's environment that will make him feel at home between the covers of the book.

This invasion of worldliness raises, of course, the problem faced by all teaching and learning today. How immediate should be the "relevance" of what the sciences offer? To what extent are the rigor of attitude, the severity of standards, the remoteness from the appeals of the marketplace prerequisites for any genuine concern with science and, in addition, a valuable training ground for the human personality? What happens when, say, the psychological difference between recognition and recall is illustrated by an encounter of Beardsleyan dandies and beasts? Does it make the reader approach an austere laboratory problem with an attitude of leisurely enjoyment? And if so, what is the outcome?

One thing is certain. The practice of any science goes beyond the acquisition of data, facts, and theories. There is a mood, an aura surrounding the phenomena to be studied and the way of studying them. These feeling tones of the subject can be valid or foolish—in psychology they reach from the mad brain surgeon of the horror movies to the sense of neat mastery provided by experimental learning theory—but they certainly guide the student as he approaches the subject and determine the attitude of the professional during his lifetime. It makes all the difference, for example, whether the dynamics of unconscious drives is approached with the uncompromising rationalism of Sigmund Freud or with the shiver of mystery it arouses in romantic minds.

Pictures are excellently qualified to suggest the mood of a subject. Their function in a textbook is not limited to the visualization of scientific data, because the study of the science itself is not limited to the data either. Illustrations establishing a mood are bound to be quite influential and therefore can be responsible for setting the tone in an entire area of study. If, for example, the visual theme of masks is chosen to introduce a chapter on impression formation and implicit theories of personality—in keeping with the original meaning of the word *persona*—the key concepts of hiding and of discrepancy between outside and inside will tinge everything the text says in words on the subject.

Pictures are no mere decoration, nor are they only stimuli for pedagogical releaser mechanisms. They represent the primary channel of all human understanding, the evidence of the senses. They are indispensable.

Rudolf Arnheim
Professor of the Psychology of Art
Department of Visual and Environmental Studies
Harvard University

Contents

Psychology Today
An Introduction

Second Edition

1 Introduction: Philosophy of the Science of Psychology

Editors' Note: This introductory chapter is meant to give you a broad base for your study of the text. You need not memorize the terms or learn the definitions in order to understand how philosophy underlies science. In the course of your reading of this text, you will see that there are several major theoretical approaches to the study of psychology. This chapter sets out the philosophical point of view that serves as the foundation for each approach (although it focuses on the contrast between the roots of behaviorism/experimentalism and the roots of cognitive/phenomenological approaches.)

The editors debated whether to put this chapter first or last in the book. It can be illuminating in either place, for different reasons. As it is—an introduction—it serves to show you how the data, the experiments, the theories of psychology are related to each other as a result of shared philosophical roots.

Reading it after you have read about the diverse areas of study in psychology (from, say, the physiological study of the brain to the investigation of interpersonal attraction) will enable you go gain an overview of their organization. The philosophical perspective will let you see both strong similarities and sharp contrasts.

The debate among the editors ended, as you can see, in making "The Philosophy of the Science of Psychology" an introductory chapter—and in adding this note. You may, perhaps, wish to read it both before *and* after the rest of the book, to see how your understanding of the concepts of this chapter has changed and whether you found it more helpful in preparing you beforehand for the study of psychology or in organizing what you had learned.

And you might let us know what you think—on the student response card bound into the book.

The vast majority of psychology textbooks open with the question, "What is psychology?" They go on to answer this question in various ways. "It is the science of *behavior,*" says one. "It is the study of mental activity and cognitive functioning," another contends. "It is the science of brain functioning," asserts a third. In truth, there is little agreement.

What psychology is, and what it can be, is for you to decide in the course of studying it. If you decide to take the subject seriously, you will probably have to commit yourself to an *assumption* about the nature of psychology. You may have to gamble a year or a whole career on that assumption.

Your teacher is probably less qualified than you to decide which basic assumptions about psychology should guide *your* search. The reason for this is that your teacher once stood at the intersection of several paths, where you stand now, and chose a particular *epistemology,* or path to knowledge. What he subsequently found was the direct result of taking that path, but because he chose that path, there were things—along the other paths—that he did not find. He can probably tell you a lot about the path he did choose but less about the ones he didn't. Also, most people have strong feelings about their own decisions. It is not unknown for a teacher to urge students to follow in his footsteps so that his initial choice of epistemology will appear justified—or to warn them off his path, if he has found it disastrous. So investigate the possibilities, but try, while you do so, to keep an open mind.

Assumptions about the path to knowledge, about how and where to look when searching for evidence, constitute a *philosophy of science.* There is a kind of philosophy of science we do *not* mean—the tradition of *reconstructing* scientific achievements. After a scientific breakthrough has been made, philosophers of science in that tradition attempt, like military historians, to reconstruct the victory on paper. They schematize the tactics used to win it, and they formalize, idealize, and simplify the victory. Because they weren't on the spot while the battle was raging, they cannot tell us that the victory was only gained because the incompetent colonel fell into a shell hole so no one heard his order to retreat.

By philosophy of science, we do mean *the logic of discovery in the minds of scientists while they are in the process of investigating.* This kind of philosophy exists in the minds of all scientists, whether or not it is consciously articulated. In fact,

its power to direct a person's thought may be even stronger when it is not actually expressed. When a scientist does start out to examine his philosophy of science, he asks himself the following kinds of questions: Why do I see as I do? How am I processing experience? What kinds of questions do I ask? What experimental methodologies and measurements do I use to answer those questions, and how does use of these tools and methods affect how I perceive things and the knowledge that I gain?

Many scientists may not call the answers to such questions a philosophy; they would say that having defined their procedures with such terms as "scientific," "strictly controlled," "well-designed," "a functional view," or "operational," they have adequately explained their approach. But all these terms rest on numerous *a priori* assumptions, some of which are examined in this chapter. Consider also that the scientist chooses a segment of nature to study. Like all of us, he orders and interprets his experience. His *in*tention regulates his *at*tention.

As an example of how an initial decision to view something in a certain way can make all the difference, consider the white object in the figure that opens this chapter. It is a vase, isn't it? If you do see a vase, the reason may be that you were directed to look at a "white object." The author of those directions *chose* to regard the black as a background and the white as an object set against the background. If the directions had said, "Consider the two black forms in the figure," you would probably have seen two human faces. Referring to "a white object" seems a very neutral, objective, and unbiased statement, but its impact is to narrow our vision immediately and sharply. It is not too hard to imagine spending a lifetime searching for vases and never seeing black faces—or seeing them occasionally but consigning them to the background. One tends to see either the vase or the faces. One view obscures the other.

The same thing happens in psychology. There are various ways of viewing the subject, and one way can obscure the others. If you study the psychology of groups, you will have difficulty focusing on individual processes; if you investigate mental disorder, you may exaggerate signs of disorder and fail to recognize signs of health. One basic set of alternative psychological perspectives is the following: You can examine *what caused a person to behave,* or you can look for *his reasons for behaving.* If you do one, chances are you will not do the other. The "causes perspective" focuses on a person's environment; the "reasons perspective" looks at that environment by means of the person's own perceptions. Each of these perspectives characterizes a main school, or approach, within the field of psychology. *Behaviorism* is the best-known "causes perspective." *Phenomenology* is one approach that looks at reasons. Phenomenology can be defined as the study of how an individual organizes his perceptions.

Behaviorism is familiar to almost everyone, for it has dominated modern Ameri-

can psychology; but there are many important approaches in psychology today that share the basic perspective of phenomenology. The cognitive-developmental approach, as set out, for example, by Jean Piaget, sees the developing organism as actively involved in structuring his environment. That is, the environment is not considered the primary shaper of the person's personality. The humanist viewpoint, as developed by theorists like Carl Rogers and Abraham Maslow, sees in human beings the potential for actualizing themselves, despite environmental irritations. Physiological approaches to psychological functioning lie somewhere between the phenomenological and behaviorist viewpoints; they see behavior as arising from internal forces, but those forces are not much under the individual's control.

All these approaches are represented in this text. But the discussion in this chapter will focus on behaviorism and on phenomenology because these two philosophies provide the sharpest contrast on a number of issues.

THE RULES AND DISCIPLINE OF OBSERVATION

You have probably heard the old story of the blind men and the elephant. Each man groped his way toward the elephant and encountered a different part. The one who found the tail announced that the elephant was like a rope. The one who found a leg said it was like a tree trunk, and the one who touched its side pronounced it wall-like. The one who found its trunk thought the animal so obviously serpentine that the man who had grasped a tusk and was crying, "A spear!" had to be out of his mind. The world looks different if we examine it from different angles—and the angle depends on where we stand.

Where to Stand

As we said before, behaviorism takes its stand in the environment surrounding the human or animal subject being investigated. It asks: if we change the environmental conditions (called stimuli and reinforcements), how will the subject *respond?* Notice the quite arbitrary selection of the environment as the *independent variable,* to be systematically manipulated by the investigator, and of the human subject as the *dependent variable,* which will change in response to environmental changes.

One kind of phenomenology takes its stand, just as arbitrarily, within the subject's perceptual field. It asks: how does this subject organize, interpret, and construe the things that appear in his field of vision? And with what results? With behaviorism looking from the outside in and phenomenology looking from the inside out, it is hardly surprising that they reach different conclusions.

Psychologists also differ on where they choose to *intervene* in the total system of the person and his environment, and they differ in what part of the system they see as dominating the others. Consider how psychologists holding various viewpoints would deal with an agitated patient. A specialist in psychiatric medicine administers a drug with a *calming* effect on the central nervous system, which may make the patient *perceive* the environment as less threatening and therefore help him obtain *rewards* from the environment. A phenomenologist tries to help the patient *perceive* the environment as less threatening so that he can get *rewards* from it, which will *calm* his central nervous system. A behaviorist manipulates the *rewards* in the environment, which will *calm* the patient's nervous system and lead him to *perceive* less threat.

The Idea of Objectivity

Whatever his viewpoint, the investigator is expected to be objective. What is objectivity?

Early scientific tradition separated the mind from matter, or things of the spirit from the material universe. To be objective was to see physical events as separate from oneself, as nonspiritual objects in a material universe, independent of man's desires. For centuries the realm of spirit and mind was the province of the Church, while scientists were free to explore the material universe of the "objectively real." At that time it would have been impolitic to claim that material reality was filtered through human perspectives—men's eyes were mirrors humbly reflecting the Great Machine, which God had wound up and set in motion.

Although the idea that our eyes merely reflect the material world has been demolished by many experiments in perception, scientists still emphasize the importance of objectivity, redefined in modern terms. Most social scientists still believe that what reality *is* must be kept separate from what one would like or imagine it to be. This belief is behind the ideal of scientific neutrality or value freedom. The ideal of scientific neutrality says that an investigator must make his assumptions, gather his data, make his observations, and state his conclusions without being influenced by his emotions, likes and dislikes, family or colleagues, patriotic feelings, greed, tastes or distastes. Results of studies that are conducted with scientific neutrality are then said to be value free. Scientists say they search for an *is,* not an ought; a *de*scription, not a *pre*scription. In addition, the notion of science as the *discovery* of things previously unknown, even undreamt of, suggests that scientists' own current values and preferences should be disregarded because they are limiting.

Behaviorists have a tendency to champion objectivity. Environmental variables, stimulus, and reinforcement are explicitly separated from the response of the subject. The response is a discrete, measurable entity—not unlike an object. Behaviorists point out that primitive man filled his universe with projections of his own animism. Spirits dwelt in caves, gods on mountains, a man in the moon. This anthropomorphic subjectivism still haunts psychology, they say. For example, Freudian psychiatrists see homunculi (little men) in the form of ego, id, and superego, inhabiting the mind. Presumably each ego has its own homunculus and so on in an infinite regress. This, behaviorists argue, is what happens when psychologists invent metaphors instead of focusing on *objectively describable behavior.*

The possibility that total objectivity may not be attainable is no excuse for failing to try. A scientist should make as strict a separation as possible between subjective biases and the world "out there." Hence, behaviorists tend to treat experiments that show high degrees of perceptual selectivity and the influence of values upon observation primarily as demonstrations of the need for more rigorous objectivity.

Phenomenologists have much more difficulty separating mind from matter and subjective from objective, because they regard matter as appearing in a *phenomenal field organized by the subjective mind.* But it is possible, they think, to identify principles of organization that different subjects share, and to separate phenomena that appear in the investigator's field of vision from phenomena that appear in the fields of the subjects being investigated. Here, then, objectivity takes on a somewhat different meaning. It is the capacity to move from perspective to perspective, observing similar patterns yet respecting the integrity and coherence of each viewpoint.

What makes moving among perspectives difficult is that two perspectives often focus upon the same objects but organize them differently, depending on the predilection of the subject. A collector of pottery would probably see the vase in the chapter-opening figure, and a portrait painter would be more likely to see the faces. An "objective" phenomenological investigator would see both and would try to understand why his subjects focused on one in preference to the other.

This meaning of objectivity calls into question the continued usefulness of value freedom and neutrality. It is doubtless foolish for an investigator to project his own life and spirit into, say, a study of the physical characteristics of the moon; it is less foolish to assume that a human psychologist and his human subject have something in common. An attraction or feeling between them, instead of being a temptation or a distraction that obstructs scientific discovery, may be a valuable clue. To the phenomenologist, a *mixture* of sympathy and detachment may produce better results than treating another person like an object.

Whatever the differences between behaviorism and phenomenology, they agree on the need for a *discipline of observation* that allows a psychologist to see beyond subjective appraisal. People often seem to believe that when they have evaluated something or someone, they have disposed of the subject. Instant evaluation—"John did that because he's a creep"—shuts out not only what *caused* him to behave, from the point of view of the behaviorist, but what John saw as his *reasons* for acting as he did, which is one viewpoint that the phenomenologist would want to uncover.

Verification and Admissible Evidence

On no issue do psychologists disagree more vehemently than on the kinds of data that are admissible as evidence. Behaviorism was born as a strong reaction against the introspective method of investigation. Introspectionists believed that a person could be trained to reflect upon his own feelings and inner experiences in such a way that two trained persons could compare feelings, and if they both said "I feel happy," that constituted valid data from which conclusions could be drawn. Behaviorists said no—there was no way of *verifying* that people's notions of happiness were even remotely comparable.

To establish their position, the behaviorists turned to the philosophy of *logical positivism,* which holds that we can know positively only what can be verified unambiguously by observation. One can *see* behavior, that is, a subject's physical response. A response usually has such measurable qualities as strength and frequency. So do the stimuli and reinforcements administered by the environment. If a certain pattern of reinforcements under certain stimulus conditions enables us to predict and control a person's behavior, then, behaviorists ask, *why speculate about his mental state?* His behavior can be seen by all observers, who can usually agree on a description of it. But his mental state can only be (unreliably) reported by him or (also unreliably) inferred by observers.

Phenomenologists would also criticize introspection—but from their own point of view, which is usually based on the philosophy that William James called *pragmatism.* Pragmatism holds that our beliefs, and the actions based on them, can be judged only by their practical consequences. Therefore, phenomenologists examine how a person perceives, construes, and organizes his environment so that they can see what practical consequences these perceptions, constructions, and schemes *have on the person himself*—on what he says, what he does.

Let us take a simple observation—Tom is stamping his foot—and see how behaviorists and phenomenologists would deal with it. Someone might infer from his act that "Tom is angry." That inference may be incorrect. Perhaps his right foot is cold; perhaps he is squashing a bug. But, behaviorists say, if we study Tom's foot stamping under various carefully controlled conditions, we will eventually be able to predict and specify the conditions under which different strengths and frequencies of foot stamping will occur. Once we can do that, we have identified the "causes" of the behavior, and inferences about angry feelings are unnecessary.

Some critics of this view, especially phenomenologists, argue that it is as much of an inference to assume that no feeling has intervened between an environmental event (say, the late arrival of Tom's girlfriend) and a behavioral response (the stamping of the foot) as it is to assume that a feeling *has* intervened. They say that to explain a person's behavior in terms that avoid reference to what the *person* may regard as its central characteristic is at best inadequate. They maintain that an explanation involving Tom's anger at his friend's tardiness may be less *precise* than a behaviorist explanation, but it would be more *accurate: If Tom perceives his reaction as one of anger, then that perception will have practical consequences for Tom.* These critics compare the behaviorist's concern with observable events to The

Drunkard's Search—he looked for his lost wallet under the lamppost because the light was better there.

Behaviorists vary a great deal in the strictness with which they judge the admissibility of evidence. Those who interpret the rules liberally are often called neo-behaviorists. Neo-behaviorists frequently allow for a number of intervening factors in the stimulus-response-reinforcement chain. They may investigate how environmental influences are mediated by a person's sex, race, socioeconomic class, personality traits, and so on. They might conclude that Tom stamps his foot chiefly because his friend is late but also because he is a male and has an extrovert personality.

Sometimes new techniques make it possible to measure something that behaviorists once ignored because it was "mentalistic" and unobservable. An example is the internal state of anxiety, which can be observed by measuring physiological variables like skin conductance, heart rate, and respiration. If these measures were used, the hypothesis that Tom stamped his foot as a result of mounting anxiety triggered by his friend's lateness would be acceptable to even a strict behaviorist.

There is a third philosophy that underlies some psychological perspectives—*operationalism.* It holds that the meaning of a proposition is simply the particular set of "operations" required to measure, implement, or verify it. Psychologists holding this point of view say, for example, that the meaning of human intelligence is what the IQ test and its scoring procedures measure. Like logical positivism, operationalism is dedicated to fighting subjective bias. It is important to understand, however, that psychologists do this only within the framework of their philosophies. No philosophy escapes from the *initial* bias of emphasizing only certain elements.

Levels of Study and Observation

Behaviorism and phenomenology "look past one another" not only because they examine their subject from different viewpoints but because they do so at different levels of human activity. For example, one can study a slice of cake at the level of cake baking: How much sugar, flour, eggs, milk, water, and baking powder went into it? How long was it cooked? Or one can study the cake chemically: What are the constituents of sugar and baking powder? How do they interact under heat? Or one can study the process at the level of atomic physics: What activity do the electrons display at 350° F.?

Similarly, psychology can be studied at the level of organized, or *holistic,* activities like "writing a book" and "baking a cake"; phenomenologists' studies are at this level. Or it can be studied at the level of single, or *atomistic,* variables like "lateness" and responses like "foot stamping"; behaviorists' studies are at this level. In fact, many behaviorists say that phenomena like cake baking and book writing are composed of thousands of increments of stimulus-response sequences and that describing the increments is sufficient to explain the larger phenomenon. This kind of approach is called *reductionist.* For example, a reductionist explanation of thunder would be a series of reactions that occur when gases are heated and expand. The *perceived phenomenon* of a thunderstorm is thus reduced to its constituent parts and interactions. The success of reductive explanations in the physical sciences has led to widespread attempts to use them in the social sciences; in fact, the popularity of explanation by division-into-parts has cast into doubt—as "unscientific"—explanation of wholes.

The assumption that the whole phenomenon *cannot* be reduced into parts without serious loss of meaning is known as *holism.* Holists argue that to fragment a phenomenon is to destroy its organizing principles. You can duplicate all the chemicals in a human body, shake them up, and all you will have is a gray puddle. Life is organization. Rats that have been taught to run a complex maze by reward and punishment have then had different legs paralyzed. Yet, they still know their way through the maze, even though they must use a totally different series of movements than they used before. If learning were simply the chaining together of hundreds of learned responses and movements, the paralyzed rats could not have negotiated the maze. Only if we give the rats credit for having an organized perception of the maze and their activity in it can their accomplishment be understood.

In opposition to these examples, behaviorists have demonstrated again and again that complex series of movements (for example, a rat rings a bell that opens a door that leads to a trolley on which he rides down a ramp to eat food) can be taught by incremental steps of response and reinforcement. We shall see in the following section how each school succeeds in "proving" its case.

THE TESTING OF HYPOTHESES

A cornerstone of the scientific method is that you do not dictate to nature; if you do, you will not find out how nature works but will merely get a reflection of your own domination or influence. Instead, you ask questions by formulating hypotheses. You put yourself "at risk," that is, you give your subject matter a fair opportunity to say "yes" or "no"—to confirm or disconfirm your hypothesis.

Putting Oneself "at Risk"

If you wish to test the hypothesis that male students will score higher than females on a mechanical-aptitude test, then you must be careful to avoid shouting "Come on, boys!" at intervals during the test. If you do shout it, the test results will probably only reflect your own prejudices about the sexes. One way to try and ensure that you do not prejudice your results is to formulate, expressly, the *null hypothesis;* in this case, it would be, "There is no statistically significant difference between male and female students on tests of mechanical aptitude." Then, if males do score higher, on the average, you have established a correlation between masculinity and mechanical aptitude, which *disproves the null hypothesis.* But you must keep in mind that this device to reduce bias only works *within* the hypothesis. You still have to consider why you asked that particular question in the first place. All the objectivity, neutrality, and value freedom of your *method* does not prevent you from asking questions that seek to bolster a prejudiced position.

There are two forms of reasoning—*deduction* and *induction*—and they differ in the extent to which they place an investigator "at risk." To deduce is to think from the general to the particular. With our mechanical-aptitude test, how do we use deduction to formulate a hypothesis? First, given these *general* conditions: students of both sexes, of equal overall intelligence, but with males more interested, on the average, in mechanical matters, then what *particular* concrete scores do I predict each group will make, on the average? I hypothesize, first, that males will score ten points higher, on the average; second, because their higher scores will be a function of their higher interest, I hypothesize that uninterested males will score

no higher than uninterested females. Formulating a question in this way is called the *hypothetico-deductive method.* It makes you predict that a concrete event will occur under *specified conditions;* if you fail to control the conditions, however, then the test of your hypothesis will be invalid—if, for instance, you did shout encouragement to the males. Scientists have traditionally been unwilling to accept ideas without some concrete demonstration of their truth. They skeptically say, "Show me!" The hypothetico-deductive method is a means of demonstration.

By contrast, *inductive* thought goes from the particular to the general, extracting from several clues some general propositions. It may be just as useful and quite as brilliant as deduction. Indeed, people think both ways, but induction is more prone to error—and, where possible, it is checked against deduction. Suppose that a male student takes several females out individually in his car and on each occasion simulates a breakdown on a lonely road. None of the females challenges the genuineness of the event. He therefore concludes (deduces) that "girls are not very mechanical." He came to this conclusion only *after* the events; because he had no chance to specify the conditions or control extraneous factors, his conclusion could be false for many reasons. Perhaps he preselected unmechanical and unintelligent girls because he only feels adequate in such company. Perhaps the girls were unable to believe that anyone could pull so old a gag. Perhaps they feared having to walk home alone if they challenged him. Perhaps all the girls were really members of Sisters against Sexism and will this very night kidnap him and dump him in an automobile junkyard, with the advice to practice his repairs and repair his practices!

Prediction and Control in Laboratory Experiments

The hypothetico-deductive method in its purest form is used in laboratory experiments. In the laboratory scientists can create the general conditions governing a predicted event and can fully control and vary them. Of course, the great advantage of laboratory experiments is that they allow an investigator to create the specific conditions in which he is interested instead of waiting—sometimes for years—for certain combinations of events to occur naturally in the environment. He can create conditions as they occur to him and "fill in" his theory like a tapestry. Behaviorism as a methodology was devised with the hypothetico-deductive method and the controlled experiment as its ideals. The general conditions behaviorists create are various contingencies of stimuli and reinforcements, and, within the laboratory setting, the result is prediction and control of the concrete response of the subject.

When we say that the investigator running an experiment puts himself "at risk," we are *not* saying that he *risks his philosophy of science.* Let us examine two series of experiments—one by a behaviorist, one by a phenomenologist—to illuminate this point. E. L. Thorndike, a behaviorist, put a series of cats in a cage and did not let them out until they had licked their own fur, whereupon the door was opened. In behaviorist terms, then, failure to lick was punished by confinement, and licking was reinforced by release. These cats, then, learned to "lick their way out" of confinement. In contrast, Adams, a phenomenologist, confronted each of his cats with a tasty piece of meat hung from the ceiling by a string, but the meat itself was surrounded by a cage, which barred direct access. The cats, which had presumably never before faced this particular problem, surveyed the scene for a few moments, then leaped quickly on top of the cage and without hesitation pulled the string up through the bars and ate the meat at the end of it.

The reason that both experimenters found what they wanted was that the experiments were designed to prove their philosophy and to ward off rival philosophies. If you wanted to prove that cats learned by chance reinforcement from the environment, then what better scheme could you devise than to reward them for licking their fur? No human genius—much less an insightful cat—would ever *perceive* that licking oneself would open a cage! Similarly, if you wanted to prove that cats do have organized perceptions that affect their actions, dropping a string and meat through the bars of a cage will provide a good opportunity to do so. (And if either of these sets of cats had not done what their experimenters expected of them, would we have been able to read about it?)

Such contradictory findings about animal behavior drew a wry comment from Bertrand Russell. Observing that behaviorism was strongest in America while phenomenology was strongest in Germany, Russell summarized the dispute as follows:

> One may say broadly that all animals that have been carefully observed have behaved so as to confirm the philosophy in which the observer believed before his observation began. Nay, more, they have all displayed the national characteristics of the observer. Animals studied by Americans rush about frantically with an incredible display of bustle and pep, and at last achieve the desired result by chance. Animals observed by Germans sit still and think, and at last evolve solutions out of their own inner consciousness.

And as the philosopher Abraham Kaplan once noted, "We are forever asking nature if it has stopped beating its wife." The questions we ask, the experiments we design are heavily loaded in favor of the answers we seek.

One serious question about the laboratory experiment and the hypothetico-deductive method must be asked when we think of their application, as in psychology, to human and animal subjects (rather than to chemicals, say, or to particles of matter). Do they retain their logical beauty and lack of bias? Remember that the justification for these methods was that they permitted nature to say "no" to a question. But if you lock a hungry animal in a cage or invite a human subject into a strange (to him) laboratory setting where *you* control nine-tenths of all the variables in advance, then have you *really* avoided dictating to nature?

This problem is not so serious for the behaviorist because he assumes that people are shaped by their environment in any event, so why not the laboratory environment. But experiments do pose problems in the phenomenological perspective. Can the investigator "create the specific conditions in which he is interested" without cutting across and even destroying the natural behavior *of his human subject?* An experimental technology that exactly fits the perceptual world of the investigator can be thought of figuratively as a cage in which the subject is trapped.

Suppose, for example, that a psychologist wished to study creativity—to discover the personality traits of certain artists, writers, scientists—in order to confirm or deny his hypothesis that certain traits, say, high IQ and introversion, are common to all creative persons. He devises an experiment to take place in his laboratory in which, after the subjects take IQ tests, they are approached by some confederates of the experimenter, who talk to them in a way designed (by the experimenter) to elicit their degree of introversion or extroversion. First, the definition of introversion is the experimenter's; the subject's perceptions of what constitutes an inward-looking person are never asked. Second, the subject may not act gregarious for any number of reasons: he finds the chair uncomfortable; he is afraid that he'll be late to a cocktail party; he perceives that the confederates are acting in an unnatural manner but he does not know why; he hates IQ tests. The experiment does not allow for these perceptions of the subject's reality. The problem is not only one of unequal power and unequal grasp of the situation but of the *unilateral right of labeling reality.* Alfred Schutz compared the investigation of inanimate things with the investigation of thinking creatures:

> It is up to the natural scientist and to him alone to define, in accordance with the procedural rules of his science, his observational field, and to determine the facts, data, and events within it which are relevant for his problem or scientific purpose at hand. Neither are those facts and events pre-selected, nor is the observational field pre-interpreted. The world of nature as explored by the natural scientist does not "mean" anything to molecules, atoms, and electrons. But the observational field of the social scientist—social reality—has a specific

meaning and relevance structure for the human beings living, acting, and thinking within it. By a series of common-sense constructs they have pre-selected and pre-interpreted this world . . . The thought objects constructed by the social scientist, in order to grasp this social reality, have to be founded upon the thought objects constructed by the common-sense thinking of men . . .

Psychologists must be aware of the problems inherent in borrowing the admittedly successful methodologies of physics; it would be a mistake simply to assume that these will be equally successful in probing human affairs.

Technique, Detachment, and Replication

One way of distinguishing science from magic is that the magician claims to have secret powers *undetachable* from his own personality and therefore unusable by others. In contrast, the scientist devises techniques that he can pass on to others so that they can replicate his work, achieve similar results, and see for themselves. It is best if the technique allows for replication that is *precise* and *invariable.*

In psychology it is usually the behaviorists who have the most detachable and replicable techniques. Some phenomenologists must reckon with the problem that each man perceives in ways that may have unique features, so that "ways of seeing" cannot always be passed on as easily as behavioral technology. For example, a good psychotherapist may use methods that work best for him, and if other therapists wish to adopt his methods, they will probably have to adjust them to fit their own personalities.

Means and Ends

Aristotle said that a science should seek no greater precision than its subject matter contains. Even this axiom can mislead us, because it assumes a *pre-existing amount of uniformity* that is "out there," waiting to be discovered. In contrast, many phenomenologists see man as an *order-imposing creature,* so that, what is "out there" can be ordered in different ways and in different degrees.

If you are to choose a philosophy of science, among the questions you must ask yourself are: How much ordering is desirable? How much control and precision? *And to what end?*

The question as to the ends of psychology is too seldom asked. Sir Francis Bacon said that knowledge was power, and that men besieged by nature sought power over her. It is easy to see that if person *A* learns how to harness a waterfall and develops a technique that is precisely replicable by persons *B, C, D,* and *E,* then all five persons will have more power in relation to the waterfall than they had before. But suppose that *A* learns how to control *B,* precisely and predictably, and gives his technique to *C,* who so perfectly replicates it that he then controls *D* and *E.* Can we say that the five persons have more power collectively than before?

You might object to the use of the terms power and control here—to mean only power *over* people. If so, if you say that people really seek power in the sense of potency *through* each other—to love, to understand, and to influence each other—then we may have to face the fact that influence is not a precise, predictable, and replicable process because it depends upon the other's willingness to be influenced. So we are back to the original question. Psychologists, or those who are planning to become psychologists, must ask themselves how much precision and uniformity they think is "out there" and how much precision they think they ought to impose. These are not only philosophical questions but moral ones. We can always increase order by screening out the disorderly and ambiguous. But can this selectivity keep us from seeing some of the best possibilities for man?

THEORIES AND THEIR CONSTRUCTION

A discussion of how theories are constructed must begin with a look at data. Webster's defines a datum as "something upon which an inference or an argument is based or from which an intellectual system of any sort is constructed." Data literally means "givens." But what are we given?

Effect of Data on Theory Construction

A very common way of looking at data is to treat them as discrete "pieces" of evidence, as if they were mutually exclusive. The data-gathering procedure in this case is to collect as many pieces as possible and then to laboriously study each piece and note its joint occurrence with other pieces. If two or more pieces occur together so often that it is unlikely to have happened by chance (that is, they correlate at a level of statistical significance), then the investigators posit some logical connection between them. Note that tests of statistical significance *assume* independence or "no relationship" between pieces of data until it is statistically proven otherwise. The idea is that data should *themselves* point to some connectedness between them, rather than that the investigator should impose his own conception of connectedness on the data, doing violence to nature.

The snag is that the violence may already have been done by assuming that data are "individualized"—especially when this conception of "pieces" is forced upon human nature. Such a conception presupposes a *monadic theory,* one in which *the pieces themselves will reveal the connection between them.*

There is a totally different possibility, namely, *a field theory,* which presupposes that the *nature of organization among parts reveals how the parts themselves should be defined.* The collection of discrete pieces of data may, in fact, shatter the organization of a field theory. There is an old story about the researcher who diced a piece of cheese with a kitchen gadget and then wrote a learned treatise on the cubic property of the cheese!

The conflict between monadic theory and field theory is part of the old dispute between atomists and holists, which we discussed earlier. If you favor a field theory, it is no use collecting many separated observations because these data only have meaning within a context. When the context alters, the pieces serve different functions. For example, the sentence *What is for supper, mother?* conjures up cozy visions of domesticity, whereas, *What is for supper? Mother.* might signify cannibalism. The words have not changed—only the punctuation—which specifies the organization of the words. With the change in organization come different functions for the same words.

Many behaviorists and other empiricists collect data *as if* a monadic theory were going to emerge from them. An analogy would be a task of collecting pieces of a jigsaw puzzle, each of which contains a clue as to how it is joined to the other pieces. Anyone undertaking such a task would find that the pieces of the puzzle did reveal the solution to the puzzle, as would be expected from monadic theory.

There are other possible analogies for the organization of data, however. Perhaps the pieces are interchangeable, so that, depending on how they are arranged, a number of pictures can be formed. The particular arrangement determines the picture that emerges. There may be no one correct picture but rather different pictures depending upon the preconceptions that the psychologist carries with him. Then the psychologist's theory would determine the behavior of the people whom he investigates. Theories with different images of mankind would produce people who behaved very differently. In that case, the psychologist would have to take responsibility for the behavior that he produced. A theory that assumed that people were aggressive would produce war-like people and societies, but one that assumed that people were gentle and cooperative would produce peaceful people and societies.

Theory and Paradigm

A scientific *theory* is an interconnected set of propositions that are intended to explain a body of specific observations, but it is more than that! As our discussion has indicated, scientific theories are not pure ivory-tower enterprises that are objective, eternal truths. To the contrary, every theory assumes a particular viewpoint, and from that viewpoint follow many practical implications, sometimes unrecognized by the scientists that hold the theory. T. Kuhn, a historian of science, has suggested the notion of a scientific *paradigm* to emphasize this point. When a science adopts a theory, it also adopts a paradigm, a way of thinking that extends the assumptions behind the theory into research method, scientific and professional institutions, and even beyond them into values and forms of organization in society at large. It is a kind of professional game-plan that includes the total strategy of professional scientists in dealing not only with nature but with students, colleagues, government agencies, foundations, and various groups of people. If the theory is successful and the science is important, the paradigm may extend into many parts of the society. Darwin's theory of evolution, for example, has had wide ramifications, influencing people's most basic conceptions of themselves and their societies.

Once a paradigm has become established, scientists work within it for a number of years, working out details of the paradigm and extending its boundaries into new domains. After a period of time, anomalies appear within the paradigm, problems that do not seem to yield to the accepted forms of methodological treatment. Finally, as the anomalies accumulate, a crisis develops and a conceptual revolution occurs: the original paradigm is replaced by an alternative paradigm that alters the previous philosophy of science and with it the entire game-plan. In physics the paradigm that grew out of the work of Sir Isaac Newton lasted for over two hundred years. For a long period various anomalies were largely ignored. Then, around the beginning of the twentieth century, an enormous conceptual revolution occurred. Albert Einstein and others developed a new theory, which treated Newtonian physics as only a special case of a more general theory. The new theory produced a *paradigm shift,* remaking the entire field of physics and thereby bringing changes in much of Western society.

PSYCHOLOGY AND SOCIETY

Although psychology is too young a science to have a paradigm as advanced as that of physics or biology, there is a case to be made that psychology now faces a

conceptual revolution. People look to the social sciences for help in understanding and solving human problems. Racism in the United States appears to be an intractable problem. Mental illness seems to grow in our society rather than diminish. Social justice seems to recede, and some people doubt the capacity of man to survive an endlessly accelerating technology. Wars continue to be fought and to get more murderous all the time. While all these crises appear at the *macro,* or holistic, level, much of the study psychologists do is at the *micro,* or atomistic, level. Psychologists are trying to build upward toward the macro level, but so far, their success has been rather limited.

In psychology today there tends to be a dichotomy between the ambition to be a science, largely championed by behaviorists, and the ambition to be *relevant,* championed by some, although by no means all, phenomenologists. In claiming virtue, behaviorists typically refer to their precision, thoroughness, and technique and repeatedly lay sole claim to the mantle of science within the field. Phenomenologists counterattack by emphasizing their humanism, their respect for man's greatest endowments, and their concern with human values. The practitioners of "hard" science and basic research claim that little is wrong with psychology that time and progress will not solve. The exponents of a "softer" science stress the failure of the field to respond to immediate human needs and crises.

The challenge, of course, is to construct a thorough and systematic body of thought that is *also* relevant. We can rush to heal society, but if we have no reliable body of knowledge, we will be of little help. We can learn to condition rats' responses with a marvelous precision and exactitude, while the country slowly comes apart before our eyes. There has to be another alternative, and you may have to find it.

SUGGESTED READINGS

COMBS, A. W., AND SNYGG, D. *Individual Behavior: A Perceptual Approach to Behavior.* New York, Harper & Row, 1959. Contains good philosophical discussion of *levels of analysis* by two of America's pioneer phenomenologists.

HAMPDEN-TURNER, C. *Radical Man: The Process of Psychosocial Development.* Garden City, N.Y., Anchor Books, 1971. Presents a convincing case in the opening chapter that the ramifications of behaviorism in social life are conservative and antidevelopmental.

HOMANS, G. C. *The Nature of Social Science.* New York, Harbinger, 1967. A small gem of clarity and conviction by a pro-behaviorist sociologist.

KAPLAN, A. *The Conduct of Inquiry: Methodology for Behavioral Science.* San Francisco, Chandler Publishing, 1964. Probably the best-written, most coherent and comprehensive review in the English language of methodological and philosophical issues by one of America's greatest teachers. He demonstrates the close connection between behaviorism and the most fruitful axioms of the physical sciences.

KOESTLER, A. *The Act of Creation.* New York, Macmillan, 1966. A *tour de force* on human and even animal creativity. Very critical of behaviorism.

KUHN, T. S. *The Structure of Scientific Revolutions.* Chicago, University of Chicago Press, 1970. The historian of science who argues that science proceeds by periodic conceptual revolutions in its philosophy of science. The implication is that we are due for one!

NATANSON, M. (Ed.). *Philosophy of the Social Sciences: A Reader.* New York, Random House, 1963. A most skillfully excerpted book that presents the conflicting views of Jonas, Nagel, Winch, Hempel, Shutz, Ayer, and Merleau-Ponty.

WANN, T. W. (Ed.). *Behaviorism and Phenomenology: Contrasting Bases for Modern Psychology.* Chicago, University of Chicago Press, 1964. An intellectually brilliant and exciting confrontation between "heavies" of both schools, including Skinner, Koch, MacLeod, Rogers, and Scriven. Quite the best book on this debate.

5

The Development of Intelligence, which details Piaget's first stage of cognitive development, relates to the description in Chapter 4 of a well-learned action. One important characteristic of a well-learned action is the learning of a contingency between what the organism does and what happens in its sensory world as a result of its action—the action is sensorimotor. Piaget calls his first stage of development the sensorimotor period.

6

The Development of Higher-Order Intelligence, after describing Piaget's three later stages of cognitive development, discusses the role of environment in cognitive growth. Its statement that intelligence involves an active interaction between the person and his world is an extension of the discussion of learning and the organization of behavior in Chapter 4.

7

The Development of Language continues the discussion of communication, begun in Chapter 2 with descriptions of how animals communicate. The two chapters offer a wealth of discussion that attempts to answer the question, "What is language?"

8

Social Development: The Case of Morality offers several views of how people grow into social beings. One explanation reflects the behaviorist learning principles of Chapter 3; another, developmental, explanation reflects Chapter 4's view of learning and the Piagetian theory of Chapters 5 and 6.

Learning and Memory provides both traditional and modern approaches to how people remember or forget. The traditional approaches relate to the theory of learning in Chapter 3; the hypotheses about the organization of memory relate to the view of learning in Chapter 4.

10

UNIT I Learning

As a student, one of your main concerns is the enterprise of *learning.* For most of your life you have probably been attending institutions whose main purpose is to help you learn. When you were a child, you learned how to eat, how to walk, how to speak, how to use a pencil. You learned your first-grade teacher's name, the capital of the United States, the shape of the earth. You learned social attitudes: what you were supposed to act like as a girl or a boy, how you were supposed to react to members of other ethnic groups. In fact, is there anything that you can do or say that you have not learned? The concept of learning is often used to explain everything that people do. Any concept that can explain everything is in danger of explaining nothing. Saying that a behavior

Chapter 2, Instinctive Behavior, provides an important sense of perspective for beginning the study of psychology because it views human beings as members of the species *Homo sapiens.* It looks at behavior in terms of Darwin's theory of evolution and examines how the behavior of members of a species is determined by the inherited characteristics of the species.

11

Problem Solving deals with the many forms that problems take and with the study of problem-solving behavior as a means of formulating and testing theories about human thought and its relation to behavior. Chapter 4 postulates that the process of solving certain kinds of problems involves four successive phases, with complete solution achieved only in the final phase.

The Biological Organism decribes the biological bases of behavior in humans and so extends the discussion of Chapter 2, which deals with these bases in nonhuman animals. Both chapters contain a discussion of the roles of heredity and environment in development—Chapter 2 for animals, Chapter 16 for humans. It also discusses recent findings—even on the level of a single nerve cell—of physiological correlates of kinds of learning, such as habituation, discussed in Chapter 2.

16

is learned does not explain the behavior; a more specific analysis is required. How is it acquired? What factors speed up or slow down its acquisition?

Many psychologists have attempted to answer these questions. One of the main focuses of psychology throughout the twentieth century has been the study of learning. Chapter 1 pointed out that any topic in psychology can be approached from many different viewpoints, and this unit will present three of the most important viewpoints toward learning. Each provides a general framework that extends far beyond the analysis of learning and will recur throughout the book.

Chapter 3, Conditioning and Learning, presents the behaviorist view of learning, which is the cornerstone of behaviorist theory. Behaviorism, one of the most influential theories in American psychology, sees behavior as controlled by external events, especially reinforcement and punishment. Learning is explained in terms of the conditioning of responses to specific stimuli.

Chapter 4, The Organization of Behavior, provides an introduction to one facet of cognitive psychology. The organization of behavior is carefully analyzed as a means of understanding how new learning is based upon past learning and present knowledge.

33

Psychotherapy II discusses at length the therapies—behavior modification and others—based on the principles of learning discussed in Chapter 3.

31

Bases of Disorder offers several explanations of how mental disorder arises, one of them being based on the principles of learning described in Chapter 3: maladaptive behaviors are learned because they are reinforced.

25

Patterns of Social Behavior: The Case of Sex Roles presents several possible explanations of how roles are acquired, one of them being the learning and conditioning approach of Chapter 3; another is the cognitive-developmental approach, which reflects the approach of Chapter 4.

18

Elementary Concepts of Motivation describes at length the concept of drive and its relation to reinforcement, which is discussed in Chapter 3.

Other Theories of Personality presents Chapter 3's learning approach to the concept of personality; in fact, many behaviorists challenge the whole notion of personality, and that challenge is presented in Chapter 22.

22

2 Instinctive Behavior

I HAVE WRITTEN a number of stories about robots: complex, artificial, manlike structures, with a "brain" sufficiently developed to allow them to speak, understand, and perform human functions in a human way. I supplied them with the *three laws of robotics,* which totally governed their behavior. My robots were machines designed to do useful work and would naturally have built-in safety factors, and the three laws were those safety factors. The robots, but not humans, had to obey the three laws:

1. A robot may not injure a human being or, through inaction, allow a human being to come to harm.
2. A robot must obey the orders given it by human beings except where such orders would conflict with the First Law.
3. A robot must protect its own existence as long as such protection does not conflict with the First or Second Laws.

I had supplied my robots, you see, with a set of *instincts* firmly imprinted on their "brains" at the moment of manufacture.

In one of my stories, a robot was constructed that could somehow read minds. The designers could not imagine how that could have been possible, and the robot was retained in the factory for study. Those who worked with it could not resist asking what was in the minds of other men or women, in connection with whatever it was that excited the desires or ambitions of the questioner. Since the robot could not injure a human being, it would tell the questioner not the truth, where that would cause grief or disappointment (which its telepathic powers would allow it to detect), but the kind of lie that would cause relief or joy. Naturally, with each person acting confidently under mistaken beliefs, there was soon wild confusion.

Finally, there was a bitter argument between two of the men, based on the false information each had been fed by the telepathic robot. They confronted the robot and demanded resolution. The robot faced a situation where it either had to say something (call it A) which would injure the self-love of at least one of the questioners or *not* say A, which would also injure the self-love of at least one of the questioners. The strongest instinct it possessed, the First Law, could not allow it to injure human beings either by doing something (saying A) or through inaction (not saying A).

So it collapsed—burnt-out, useless, dead.

Instincts that work well under some conditions are deadly under others. The light-hunting instinct of the moth, when natural sunlight is not involved, will carry it into an open candle flame and kill it. The harm-avoidance instinct of the robot, when subtle psychological factors are involved, will present it with an insoluble dilemma and kill it. I.A.

After the great biologist Charles Darwin published *The Origin of Species* in 1859, man's conception of himself underwent a fundamental change. No longer was man a unique kind of creature, completely different from animals; instead he was part of the animal kingdom—a species that had evolved by natural selection in the same way that all other animal species had evolved. To be sure, man was unique in some ways, but at the same time he was similar in many ways to other species, especially apes and other primates. By placing man firmly within the animal kingdom, Darwin laid the foundation for the field of psychology. In fact, publication of *The Origin of Species* is regarded by some people as marking the beginning of psychology as a legitimate field.

Although all of psychology has been influenced by Darwin's theory, one approach can be singled out as the most direct descendant of Darwin's work: *ethology,* the study of human and animal behavior from a biological point of view. Ethologists are especially concerned with describing and understanding *species-specific behavior* —that is, behavior that is characteristic of a particular species of animal. In *The Expression of the Emotions in Man and Animals* Darwin assumed that the behavior

Figure 2.1
Charles Darwin. Although not a psychologist, Darwin had a profound impact upon psychology. In addition to his contributions discussed in this chapter, his concept of natural selection has influenced psychologists in their study of the adaptive function of behavior; one direct result of this influence has been the formulation of principles relating to reinforcement (see Chapter 3).

Figure 2.2
Konrad Lorenz. Lorenz is a European ethologist whose study of animals in their natural environments has contributed to the area known as comparative psychology. His recent book, *On Aggression,* relates man's aggressive behavior to the aggression shown by lower species.

patterns of an animal are as characteristic of its species as the shape of its body. With this assumption he essentially founded ethology.

The first stage of most ethological studies is detailed field observation of a particular species, under unrestricted, natural conditions. After obtaining a fairly complete record of the behaviors that normally occur, the ethologist can begin to analyze them—to investigate the relationships among different behavior patterns and to determine how those patterns are influenced by events in the animals' environment. Ethological research has confirmed Darwin's assumption that particular behavior patterns are as specific to a particular species as its bodily characteristics. The discussion that follows includes many examples of these species-specific behavior patterns.

One step in the analysis of a behavior pattern is to identify its components. What actions make up a response? What stimuli must be present for a response to occur? But ethologists do not limit themselves to this kind of dissection. They see behavior not as a static collection of components but as an ongoing process, usually a very complex one. At different times the same stimulus may evoke very different responses; also, different stimuli may produce the same response. That is, changes in the environment alone do not fully account for behavior. Events occurring within the organism must be taken into account.

It may be helpful to think of an organism as an ongoing system. The system can produce many different outputs (responses) in reaction to many different inputs (stimuli). But since it is an ongoing system, a complete description of it must deal with more than just inputs and outputs. The organization of the behavioral system as a whole needs description. This chapter includes all three kinds of descriptions: it discusses systems of responding, systems of sensory input, and more complex behavioral systems that cannot be analyzed only in terms of either output or input. Before turning to those matters, it is necessary to consider one of ethology's central concepts—instinct.

THE CONCEPT OF INSTINCT

Because ethology is a direct descendant of Darwin's evolutionary theory, much ethological research has been devoted to the study of hereditary influences on behavior. In early ethological writings, the concept of *instinct* received much attention. Ethologists were impressed by the fact that different species behave differently and that certain behaviors are characteristic of (specific to) a given species. It was obvious, furthermore, that many species-specific behaviors are not learned in any direct sense. J. C. Fentress reports that a young wolf will howl and pounce in a characteristic way even if it has not had a chance to see other wolves do so (Figure 2.3). A baby rhesus monkey raised in a human family will produce the calls and facial expressions typical of rhesus monkeys even if it has never seen another monkey. As K. Lorenz pointed out in his book *Evolution and Modification of Behavior,* a striking amount of species-specific behavior occurs even under very unfavorable environmental and developmental conditions. Many species-specific behaviors seem to be part of very complex sequences, and unlike simple reflexes that are apparently automatic responses evoked by outside stimuli, they appear to originate largely within the organism. The concept of instinct is an attempt to account for these facts.

Instinct Versus Intelligence

In common parlance, instinct is often contrasted with intelligence. Man acts intelligently whereas animals, particularly organisms near the bottom of the evolutionary scale, are thought of as instinctive automatons. People also use the word "instinctive" to describe automatic behavior that human beings develop through long practice. A professional baseball player instinctively makes the right play, for exam-

Figure 2.3

A young wolf that has been reared from birth by humans will howl and pounce, even though it has never seen other wolves performing these behaviors and so cannot have learned them. Howling and pouncing, then, can be classified as instinctive behaviors.

ple, and an experienced driver instinctively steps on the brakes if a child darts into his path. Similarly, the phrase "maternal instinct" is usually not taken to mean that human mothers engage in a series of purely automatic (and unconscious) behaviors. Instead it indicates merely that love of children is a basic tendency common to most human mothers. Most people would not rule out the possibility that learning plays a major role in its development.

Another aspect of the suggested contrast between intelligence and instinct is illustrated by the behavior of the hunting wasp, shown in Figure 2.4. N. Tinbergen has observed that this animal digs a nest, flies once or twice around the nest site, and then heads off in search of food. The wasp can find its way back flawlessly, something that many people would not be able to do. It obviously learns landmarks extremely rapidly—and rapid learning is something we tend to think of as indicating intelligence. If the landmarks are moved a little, however, the wasp becomes hopelessly disoriented even though the nest is in clear sight. Here is an instance of a behavior pattern that clearly depends on learning but that, once learned, is extremely inflexible.

As a general though not perfect rule, the farther one moves up the phylogenetic scale, the more approaches a species can take to a given problem—that is, the more flexible its behavior is. In a series of experiments described by D. O. Hebb, a simple discrimination between a circle and a triangle (Figure 2.5) was taught to rats, chimpanzees, and two-year-old human children: In the different species the ability to generalize the concept of the triangle to new tasks varied greatly. When the triangle was rotated, the rat had to relearn the problem, whereas the chimp and the child generalized from the previous solution. In a more difficult test, a triangle made of circles had to be discriminated from a circle. The chimp failed to discrimi-

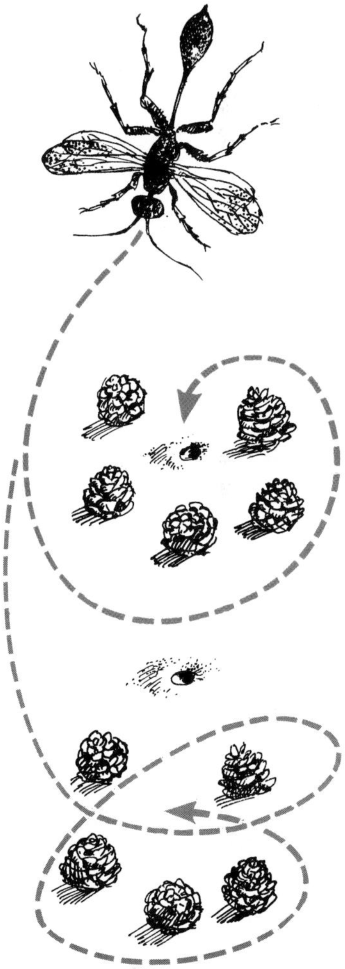

Figure 2.4

The hunting wasp learns where it has dug its nest by circling it a few times and observing the arrangement of prominent landmarks. If the landmarks are moved slightly, the wasp will not be able to find the nest, even if it is in plain sight.

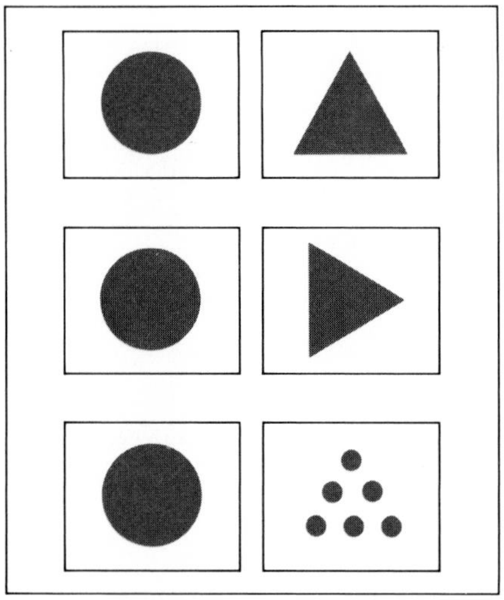

Figure 2.5
The shapes used by D. O. Hebb to study intelligence. He tried to teach a rat, a chimpanzee, and a two-year-old child to discriminate between the pairs of objects shown. Although the rat learned to discriminate between the circle and triangle shown at top faster than the chimp or child, it could not generalize that discrimination when the triangle was tilted, as in the middle pair. Only the child could discriminate between the bottom pair of forms.

nate between these two figures, but the child did so easily. Apparently the chimp could not abstract the overall triangular form from the group of circles that composed it. Again, flexibility of behavior and the ability to reorganize features of the environment appear to be roughly correlated with phylogenetic position.

The intelligence of a species is hard to define with precision, for one's conclusions depend on which aptitudes and behavioral propensities are examined. For example, Fentress found that it was very easy to train a young timber wolf to shake hands (three trials), but it took many hours to teach the animal to sit (see Figure 2.6). These observations say little about whether wolves are smarter or dumber than dogs. Timber wolves typically make pawing movements during play, so the shake-hands response was already there. It simply had to be brought under the control of a vocal command. On the other hand, timber wolves rarely sit, particularly if they are excited; consequently this behavior was more difficult to teach.

Heredity Versus Environment

A central issue for the definition of instinct is the relative importance of hereditary and environmental factors to the development of a behavior. Heredity must contribute a great deal to the behavior of the digger wasp, which can learn nothing from its parents—they die before the young wasp emerges from its pupa in the spring. In contrast, higher animals, especially human beings, usually undergo a long period of tutelage by parents and siblings. Despite the apparent implications of extreme examples, however, no behavior can be classed as completely hereditary (that is, completely uninfluenced by the environment) or as completely environmental (that is, completely uninfluenced by hereditary endowment). Every behavior is influenced by both factors.

The relative contributions of hereditary and environmental factors are difficult to unravel. For example, a female rat displays normal maternal behavior with its

Figure 2.6
This young timber wolf has easily learned the handshaking response because similar actions (pawing movements) are already a part of its behavioral repertoire. The wolf's rapid learning of this response might suggest that it is an animal of high "intelligence." Conversely, the much greater number of practice trials required before a wolf can learn to sit on command might lead one to conclude that it is an animal of little intelligence. Both conclusions are mistaken; the key factor is how much of the new, desired response is already present in other forms of the animal's behavior.

first litter even if it has been raised alone, with no opportunity to learn the behavior directly from other rats. This fact would seem to show that maternal behavior in the rat is instinctive. But H. G. Birch has reported other findings that contradict this conclusion. By placing a wide collar around the necks of female rats shortly after they were born, he prevented them from licking themselves. Later on, these rats failed to care for their young. These data are somewhat controversial, but they do show that it is risky to rule out experiential influence completely, even if a given behavior pattern persists in an impoverished environment or if the mechanism of experiential influence is not immediately obvious.

There is a better way to attack the heredity-environment problem than by trying to rule out one influence or the other. For example, animals with a similar hereditary endowment (like those born in the same litter) can be reared under different environmental conditions. If they then show systematic differences in behavior, the differences can be attributed to environmental influences. And if animals with different heredities are reared under identical conditions (which can be a tricky thing to arrange), then any differences in behavior can be attributed to genetic factors. In other words, differences in behavior between groups that are similar in all ways but one can be attributed to the one way in which the groups differ, even though no particular behavior pattern can be attributed solely to heredity or solely to environment. (Chapter 16 offers a detailed discussion of behavior genetics.)

Figure 2.7
Niko Tinbergen is a European ethologist who has studied extensively the behavior of animals in their natural environment. Two of his major interests have been instinctive behavior and imprinting. He has written several influential volumes on instincts, which have increased scientific interest in this area; among the many aspects that he has investigated is the nature of the stimulus that "releases" the animal's instinctual response.

SYSTEMS OF RESPONDING

Careful observation of any species of animal shows that much of its behavior consists of relatively stereotyped and frequently repeated patterns of movements. Lorenz and Tinbergen both developed the concept of the *fixed action pattern* to emphasize this fact. Much of the motor behavior of any species can be described by specifying only a few dozen fixed action patterns. Locomotor behavior, for example, consists of only a handful of patterns for each species. In the horse, P. R. Marler and W. J. Hamilton report, there are three: walking, trotting, and galloping. Each of these fixed action patterns is a distinct series of movements that varies little from one horse to another (Figure 2.9, page 24), and all normal horses display the patterns.

Displacement Activities

Fixed action patterns are merely descriptions of stereotyped sequences of movements. They do not fully describe the systems of responding that an animal possesses. One way of moving toward a fuller description is to examine not only individual patterns but the relationships among them. *Displacement activity*, for example, involves several fixed action patterns. Suppose that a tern is sitting on a nest of eggs. When it sees a man approaching, the bird begins to vacillate between escaping and staying on the nest with the eggs. At some point the bird is likely to stop vacillating and carry out a fixed action pattern that appears to be irrelevant to the situation: it preens its feathers. In a similar study, J. van Iersel and A. Bol found that when a tern is vacillating between attacking another bird and incubating its eggs, it may show another pattern of displacement activity, standard nest-building movements. The word "displacement" was originally used to suggest that behavioral energy was displaced from the conflicting behaviors (such as escaping versus incubating eggs) onto a seemingly irrelevant activity (such as preening), but the energy interpretation has been called into question by many investigators. It is best to think of the term merely as indicating the occurrence of an activity that seems irrelevant to the situation.

Figure 2.8
Preening or grooming is a form of instinctual behavior in many species; here an egret preens its feathers. Preening is an example of a fixed action pattern, which is a relatively stereotyped species-specific behavior. Also, preening commonly occurs as a displacement activity: a bird that is in conflict between two opposing fixed action patterns will suddenly begin to carry out an apparently irrelevant pattern, such as preening.

Displacement activities are very common in many species. Rats show displacement reactions similar to those described in the tern. Human beings, under moderate levels of conflict or tension, often perform simple stereotyped movements such as drumming their fingers or scratching their heads. And both people and other

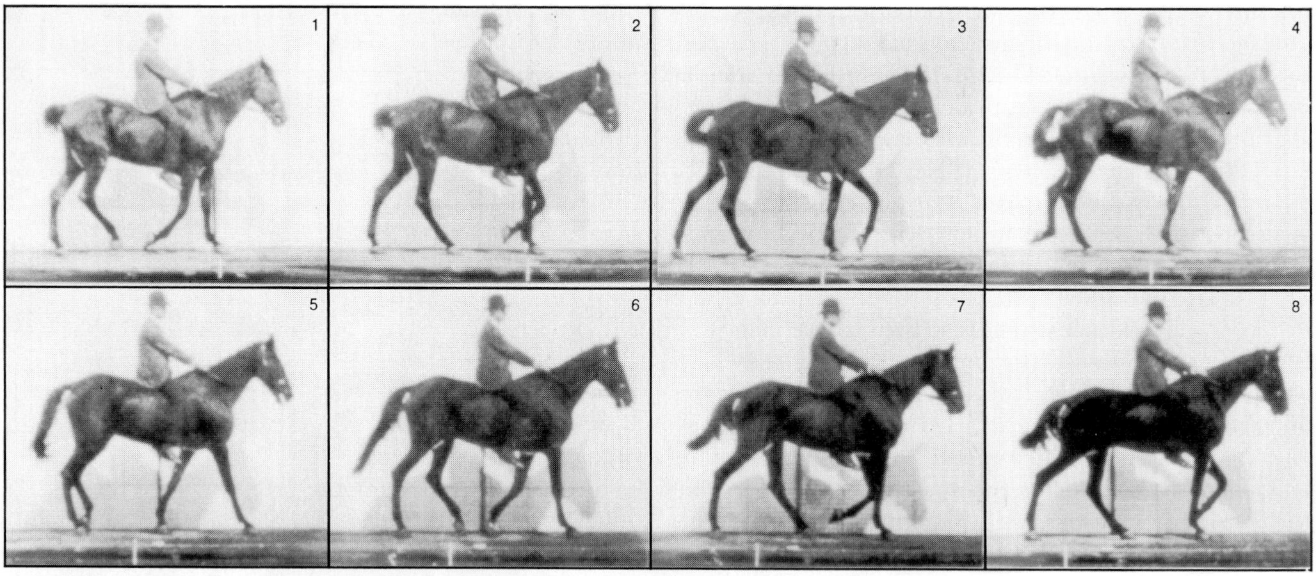
1
2
3
4
5
6
7
8

1
2
3
4
5
6
7
8
9
10

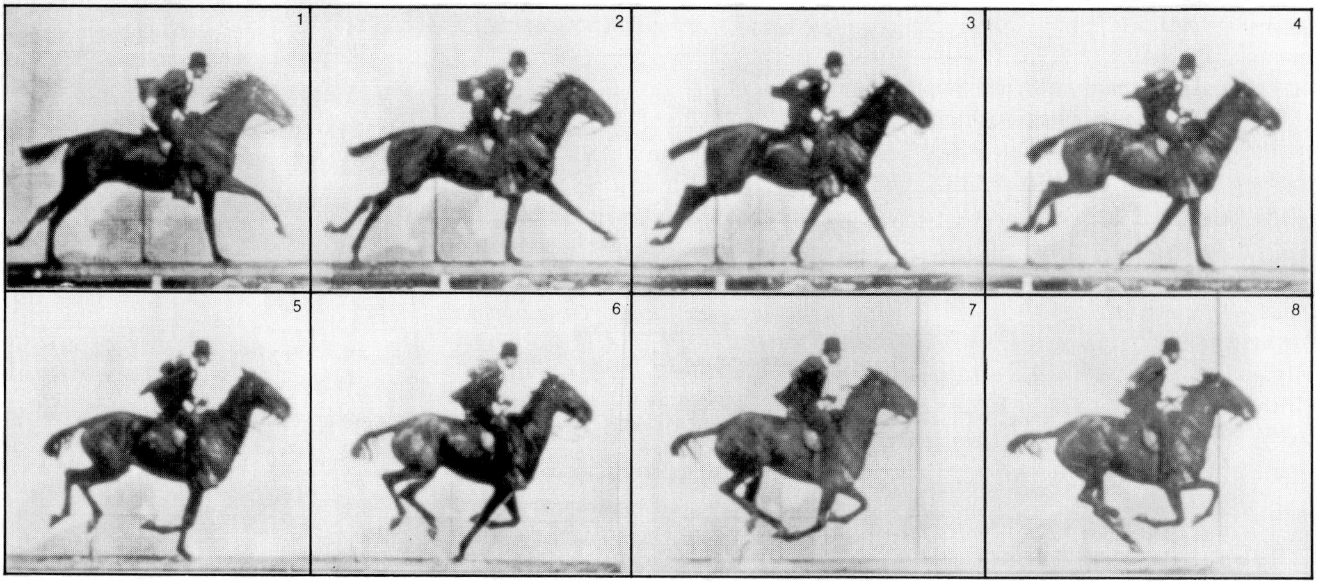
1
2
3
4
5
6
7
8

primates, in frustrating situations, may displace their aggression onto targets that are not the source of the frustration. For example, K. Fischer raised a baby female rhesus monkey in his home like a child. She would never threaten or attack Fischer, who was her human "mother," but when he punished her she would frequently threaten or attack someone else who happened to be nearby.

Figure 2.9 *(opposite)*
The three locomotive *fixed action patterns* of a horse are walking (top), trotting (middle section) and galloping (bottom). The series of movements involved in completing each pattern varies only a little from horse to horse. The series showing galloping are the famous photos by E. Muybridge, which proved that a horse does simultaneously lift all four feet from the ground when it gallops.

Neural Stimulation of Fixed Action Patterns

Recent investigators have found that fixed action patterns can be produced by electrical stimulation of the brain. E. von Holst and U. von St. Paul used this technique to study systems of responding in chickens. The area of the brain that von Holst and von St. Paul stimulated is called the brain stem, or diencephalon. They placed electrodes in various places in the brain stem and electrically stimulated each place. In some places, stimulation produced a specific behavior pattern, and different places often yielded different patterns. With a large number of electrodes, a large number of different patterns could be elicited. Stimulation of some areas produced simple actions—the chicken stood up, or sat down, or turned its head to one side. Other areas elicited more complex patterns—grooming, attack behavior, fleeing behavior, eating, or courtship.

Once von Holst and von St. Paul had specified exactly which fixed action patterns were produced by which areas, they began to examine the relationships among the patterns. To do this, they simultaneously stimulated two different areas that would normally evoke two different fixed action patterns and then observed how the two patterns interacted. In a natural setting, simultaneous evocation of two different fixed action patterns sometimes produces displacement, and electrical stimulation did the same. When von Holst and von St. Paul simultaneously stimulated an area that alone produced aggressive pecking and a second area that alone produced fleeing with feathers smoothed down close to the body, for example, the result was that the hen ran excitedly back and forth, giving piercing cries—a displacement activity. This is similar to the situation that occurs naturally when a hen is in conflict between protecting its nest and escaping from a dangerous enemy.

Several other types of interaction between fixed action patterns also occurred. Stimulation of one area alone caused the animal to stretch out its neck and flatten its feathers, while stimulation of a second area made it fluff up its feathers. When both these areas were stimulated simultaneously, the animal would stretch out its neck and flatten its feathers; after the stimulation stopped, it would fluff its feathers. That is, it showed first one fixed action pattern and then the other. In other instances, both action patterns occurred at once. Simultaneous stimulation of the area that produced looking to the left and the one that evoked sitting, for example, led the hen to sit and look to the left at the same time.

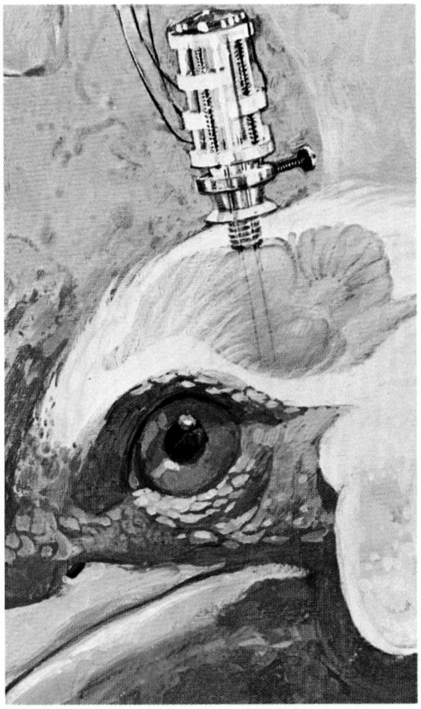

Figure 2.10
An electrode has been implanted in the brain of this chicken; the apparatus shown holds the electrode in place, and the electricity that stimulates the brain passes through it.

Motivation and Drive

Displacement and the other responses studied by von Holst and von St. Paul are relatively simple systems. They involve fairly straightforward interactions among two

Figure 2.11
Electrical stimulation at the appropriate site in its brain stem while a chicken is eating will elicit a "disgust reaction." What appears to be a complex behavior is actually a series of discrete simple behaviors: the chicken stops, spits out whatever food is in its beak, shakes its head rapidly back and forth, and finally rubs its beak on the ground.

Figure 2.12
Migration is a behavior that is determined by both genetically controlled physiological rhythms and external stimuli such as climatic changes. The Monarch butterfly *(Danaiis plexippus)* is thought to be the only species of butterfly that performs a seasonal two-way migration. The same individuals that fly south in the autumn return in the spring, after being inactive from November through March. During their southward migration and while in the south, these butterflies congregate by the thousands each night in certain trees and may remain there for weeks at a time. This massing (illustrated here) discourages intruders. Birds and whales also migrate each year; some patterns of their migration are shown in Figure 2.17, page 31.

or three fixed action patterns. Usually, when we speak of systems, we refer to a more complex interaction of a larger number of response patterns. For example, an animal's sensitivity to particular stimuli and the responses it makes in a given environmental context are not always the same. They shift with the animal's internal state. Birds migrate only at certain times of year; the praying mantis is most receptive to prey when it has gone some time without eating; and a major feature of human life is that our behavior is controlled partly by changes in emotion and moods.

Behavior that is influenced by changing inner states has traditionally been investigated under the general heading of *motivation,* and psychologists have frequently tried to explain motivational changes by invoking the concept of *drive.* A drive has generally been thought of as a source of energy that builds up in the organism over time until it reaches a point at which responding has to occur, thereby reducing the stored-up energy. In some cases, behavior does fit this description. In his book *Studies in Animal and Human Behavior,* Lorenz described the behavior of a well-fed starling that was deprived of the opportunity to catch flies for a long period of time. The bird occasionally went through elaborate fly-catching movements even though no flies were around. This kind of behavior is called *vacuum activity.* It is a striking example of how motivational forces seem to build up inside an animal and can lead to a behavior even in the absence of normally necessary cues. On the other hand, we do not gain much if we merely *invent* a drive to account for every instance of behavior that is influenced by inner motivational factors.

Because of the complexity and subtlety of the behavioral changes it brings about, motivation has been one of the most elusive concepts in psychology. Many biologically oriented psychologists think that a valid way to sneak up on an understanding of motivation is to study relatively simple animals with small behavioral repertoires, such as insects and crustaceans. In such animals one can investigate a functional behavior system such as sexual activity or feeding and then ask the question: what factors, both inside and outside the organism, influence the behavior in that system?

Feeding in the Blowfly V. G. Dethier studied feeding behavior in the blowfly, trying to construct a model of the mechanisms that govern the insect's feeding. He began by describing the nature of the feeding cycle.

As the time since its last meal becomes longer, the blowfly increases its locomotor activity, flying in a random course until it encounters the smell of food. At that point it flies toward the food, lands near it, and begins walking about in a random manner. If it encounters a drop containing sugar (its natural food), it extends its proboscis (a sort of hollow tongue) and, when the proboscis touches the solution, begins to suck. Over a period of about ten minutes, the animal takes one long drink and perhaps a few short ones. It then remains immobile for a few hours before it resumes its random flight.

Dethier began his search for an explanation of this behavioral cycle by examining in more detail what happens when a fly encounters a sugar solution (Figure 2.14). The blowfly, like many other insects, has taste receptors in its legs. When a group of these receptors is stimulated by sugar, the fly turns toward the area of stimulation and extends its proboscis downward. When the sugar receptors at the tip of the proboscis are stimulated, the animal begins sucking the sugar up into its esophagus and gut. Dethier found that, after a minute or two, the receptors lose their sensitivity to sugar. As a result, the animal stops feeding.

The receptors become sensitive again a few minutes after feeding has stopped, but the animal does not eat for several more hours. What keeps it from doing so? The easiest way to answer this question is to determine what will make the animal continue eating. Dethier found two nerves that, if cut, affected eating. Severing one of them caused the animal to eat much more than usual; severing the other made the fly eat so much that it actually burst. Later investigation showed that the first

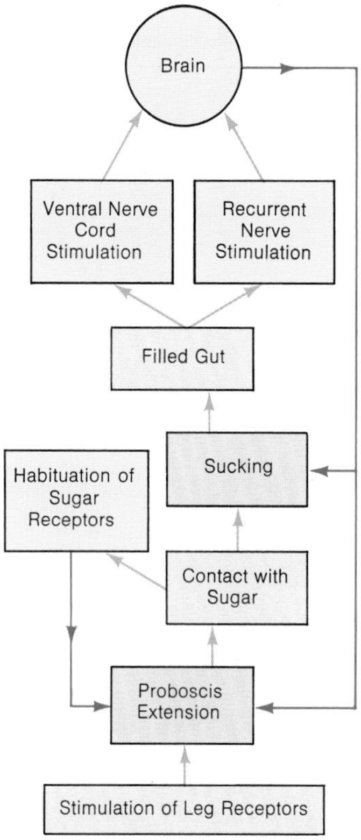

Figure 2.13
Diagram of the three feedback loops that control feeding behavior in the blowfly.

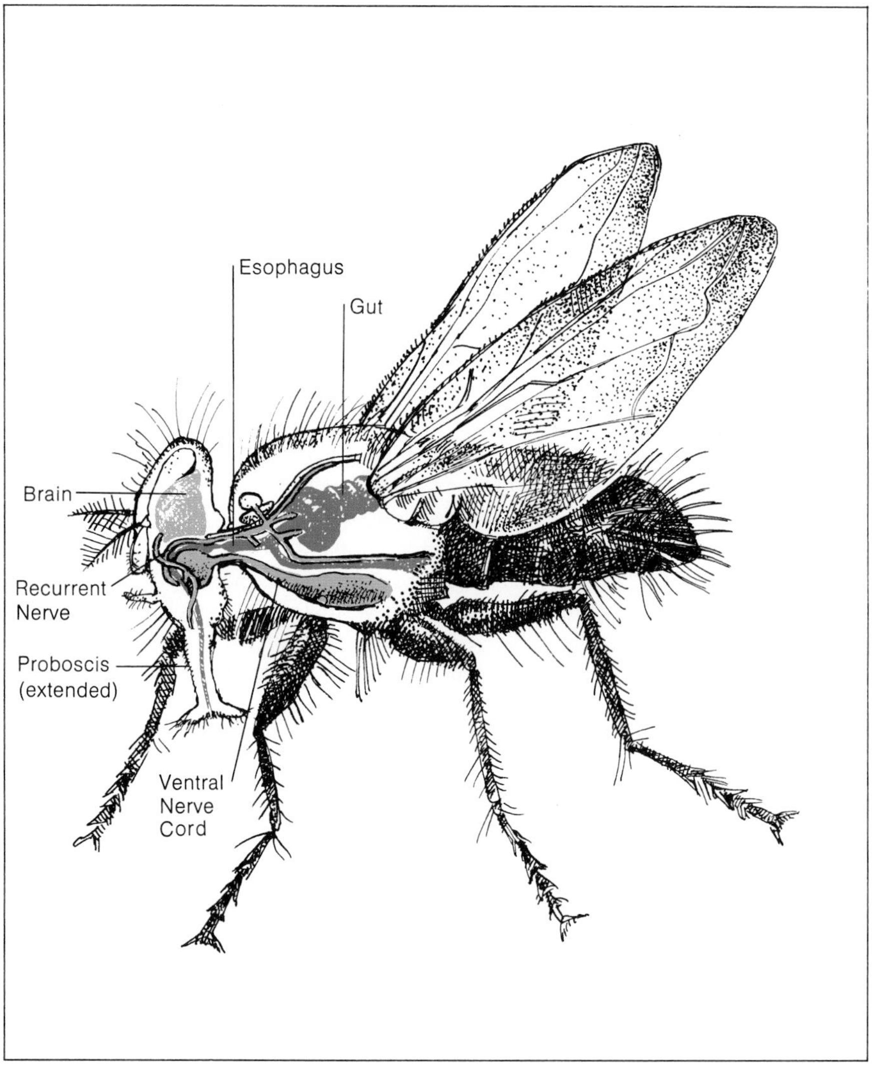

Figure 2.14
The blowfly.

nerve, called the recurrent nerve, receives impulses from receptors that measure the distention of the foregut. This nerve tells the brain when the foregut is full. The second nerve, called the ventral nerve cord, receives impulses from stretch receptors in the fly's body wall and tells the brain when the body wall is becoming distended with food. As Figure 2.13 shows, the blowfly's feeding system includes three "feedback loops" for controlling the amount of food eaten. Each loop uses a different source of information, but all of them influence the same behavior.

As this description indicates, the fly's eating behavior depends on several internal as well as external factors: not only on the presence of a source of food but on the periodic sensitivity of the external sugar receptors, the distention of the foregut (as measured by the recurrent nerve), and the pressure of the gut against the body wall (as measured by the ventral nerve cord). In addition, there are many poorly understood aspects of the behavior system that need further investigation. Dethier particularly stressed the important role of the fly's brain, whose activity may be a kind of "mental factor" in any model of motivation.

SYSTEMS OF SENSORY INPUT

We know from our daily lives that the sensory world stimulates and guides much of our behavior. The same is true for the nonhuman animals, but the world they experience through their senses may be quite different from ours. In many animals, only a few stimuli produce observable effects on behavior. The European naturalist J. von Uexküll painted a vivid verbal picture of the behavior of the mated female tick, which will climb into the branches of a tree and wait for weeks, if necessary, for a mammal to pass directly beneath her. As she waits, the tick seems unresponsive to the barrage of sights, sounds, and odors about her. The stimulus that signals an approaching meal and leads the tick to drop on her host is the smell of butyric acid generated by mammalian skin glands. In Uexküll's words, the tick is like a gourmet who picks the raisins out of a cake.

Sign Stimuli

Ethologists were quick to realize the importance of such observations. Different animal species live in different sensory worlds. Indeed, many species can be classified according to the stimuli they attend to, in much the same way that they can be compared in terms of fixed action patterns. Highly specific cues in the external environment often seem to serve as signals for complex sequences of behavior. Ethologists call these cues *sign stimuli.*

For example, Tinbergen reports that the male stickleback fish will attack a crude model of another stickleback if the model has a red belly. The general appearance of the model is unimportant so long as it has a red belly. The stickleback ignores models that seem very fishlike to human beings and quickly attacks other models that seem unfishlike but have a red underside (Figure 2.15). For a male robin protecting its territory, red breast feathers are a sign stimulus for an attack. In young herring gulls, the feeding response of pecking is affected more by the presence or absence of a red patch on the lower bill of a model "parent" than by distortions that to human beings make the model look very unbirdlike.

Although color is a key element in many sign stimuli, it is not always important. Tinbergen reports a remarkable example in which size is the key element. Many sign stimuli elicit a response only if they are about the right size. But a bird called the oystercatcher, offered a model egg several times larger than one of its own eggs, prefers the larger egg—even when the model egg is so large that the bird cannot assume a normal brooding position.

Because sign stimuli are so specific, ethologists at first interpreted them as indicating the existence of an *innate releasing mechanism.* The sign stimulus was assumed to release a fixed action pattern because the animal inherited a neural connection between the sign stimulus and the fixed action pattern.

Later research has shown that this early formulation was oversimplified. The

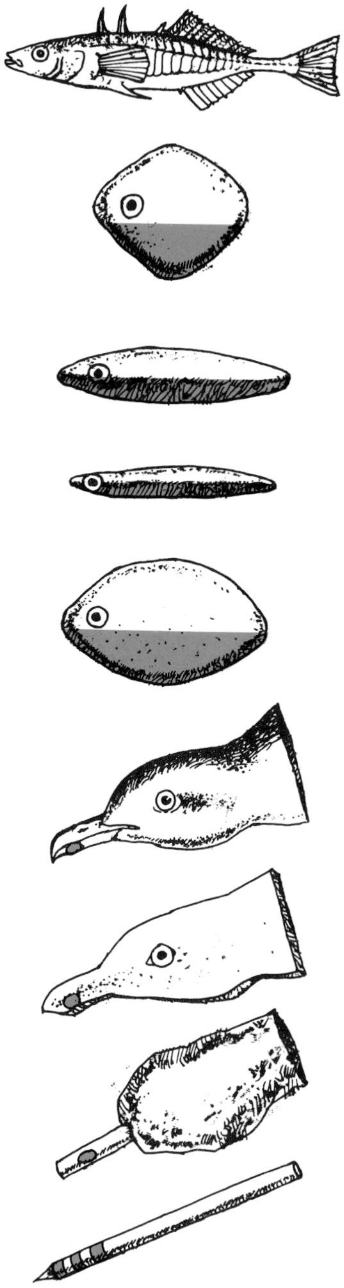

Figure 2.15
Tinbergen's ethological research showed that the male stickleback will attack all of the models shown above except the top one, which lacks a red belly, a characteristic of the male that appears only during mating season. (Lower series) young herring gulls were found to peck most frequently at the bottom model of those shown here. Young gulls apparently respond to the red patch as the sign stimulus for feeding behavior because the adult gull, which feeds them, has a red patch on its bill. (Left) a herring gull attempting to brood a supernormal egg.

difficulties with it are evident in a phenomenon discovered by Tinbergen. A cardboard model was moved through the air above the heads of young barnyard turkeys. When the model was moved in one direction, the shadow that it cast had a short neck and a long tail and looked like a flying hawk. If the model was moved in the opposite direction, the shadow had a long neck and a short tail and resembled a flying goose. The turkeys showed vigorous escape responses when the model cast the hawk shadow but few escape responses when it cast the goose shadow. Because the turkeys had never seen any hawks, it was tempting to conclude that the escape response to hawks was inborn and unlearned. That is, the shape of a hawk seemed to be a sign stimulus that automatically released the fixed action pattern of escape in the turkey.

Habituation

W. Schleidt has demonstrated that this interpretation seems to be incorrect. He showed that turkeys try to escape from any unfamiliar object of an appropriate size that is moving overhead, whether it is shaped like a natural enemy or not. When he exposed turkeys to circles or rectangles moving overhead, for example, they showed the same initial alarm reactions that they did to an overhead silhouette of a hawk. As the turkeys became familiar with the shapes, their alarm reactions decreased. This phenomenon, in which an animal responds in a particular way to a stimulus when it is first presented but gradually stops responding as the stimulus is presented over and over, is called *habituation.*

In each case, Schleidt found, the habituation of the turkeys' fear reaction was specific to the shape that was repeatedly presented. Turkeys that repeatedly saw a hawk silhouette but not a circle eventually stopped reacting to the hawk but did show fear in response to the circle. Conversely, animals that were repeatedly exposed to the circle but not to the hawk silhouette showed no alarm reactions to the circle but many reactions to the hawk. Schleidt concluded that the apparently innate fear of hawks that Tinbergen observed occurred because Tinbergen's turkeys had never seen hawks. If they had never seen flying geese, they probably would have shown a similar reaction to that shape as well because the fear response would not have had an opportunity to become habituated. (See Figure 2.16.)

Although interpreting the meaning of sign stimuli is a difficult task, the general point remains. The sensory apparatus of a particular species is characteristic of that species, and the meaningfulness of objects and events in the world of an animal are determined partly by the capacities and limitations of his sensory apparatus. Man cannot tell whether light is polarized, but bees and many other invertebrates can; they use polarization as an important cue for locomotion and orientation. For the

Figure 2.16
The number of alarm calls given by young turkeys is plotted across days of testing with various silhouette models. The novel stimulus, whether it was a disc, goose, or hawk shape, initially elicited fear responses in the turkeys, but eventually habituation occurred, and the alarm calls diminished accordingly. Note that beginning on day 3, the goose shape was shown ten times as often as the hawk one, which explains the greater habituation to it.
(After Tinbergen, 1951.)

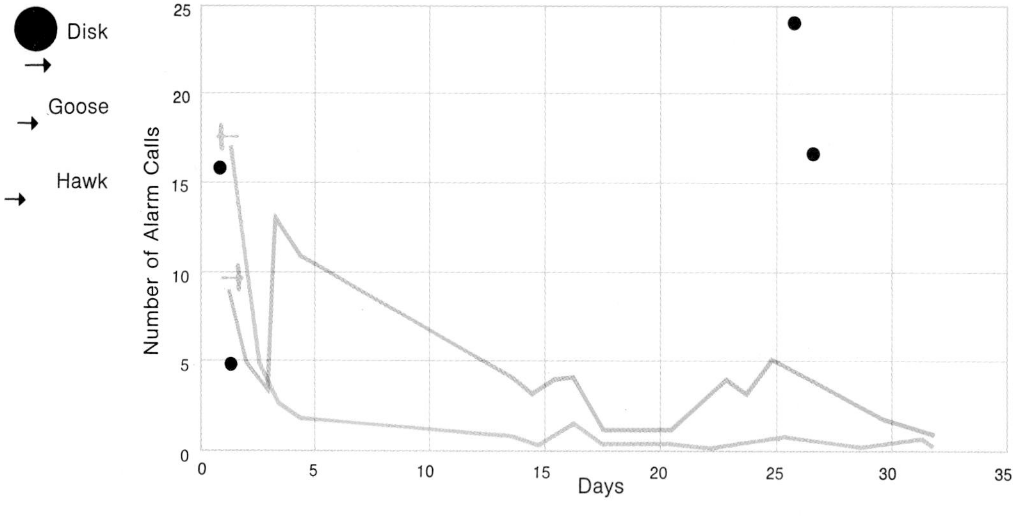

female tick, the significant stimulus is butyric acid, in concentrations that the human olfactory system cannot ordinarily detect. The upper limitation of auditory sensitivity in man is about 20,000 cycles per second, but some rodents can hear up to 100,000 cycles per second. Mice and rats show a definite startle response to hand claps, but they do not do so if the hand claps are recorded on tape, because tape recorders cut off the high-frequency components to which the rodents are particularly sensitive. Bats, which navigate by means of echolocation, can detect frequencies considerably above those that human beings respond to.

COMPLEX SYSTEMS OF BEHAVIOR

In our discussion so far, we have considered motor output and sensory input as if they were separate phenomena. This division, revealing as it is, is somewhat arbitrary and can be misleading if carried too far. To understand the functioning of an organism, it is not enough to analyze action patterns and sensory systems, outputs and inputs: the whole, as represented by an animal's natural behavior, always seems to be greater than the sum of the parts. Indeed, one of the virtues of ethology is that it attempts to describe entire systems of behavior and to deal with the full array of influences on what an animal does. Two of the most interesting kinds of behavior that ethologists have studied as ongoing systems are the migration of birds and the dance language of honeybees.

Migration

Many animal species migrate over vast distances. Alaskan fur seals, for example, breed only on the Pribilof Islands in the Bering Sea. I. Eibl-Eibesfelt reports that during the winter, the females and young seals swim some 3,000 miles to the coast of southern California, while the males travel to the southern Aleutian Islands (a much shorter journey). In the spring, the sexes join each other again in the Pribilofs. Eels born in the Sargasso Sea find their way to the coasts of North America and Europe; salmon return to their home streams to spawn after journeying hundreds of miles into the ocean; and both the nighthawk and the barn swallow of North America fly from as far south as Argentina to breed in the cold reaches of the Yukon and Alaska, a trip of about 7,000 miles (Figure 2.17).

The exact cues used by various species during their remarkable trips have been under investigation for many years, but because of the difficulties of studying migration in the field, no more than the bare outlines of the behavior have become clear. Birds, the most thoroughly studied migratory animals, seem to use the sun and the stars as guides as well as various landmarks. It has also been found that homing and migration do not necessarily follow a fixed course. G. V. T. Matthews

Figure 2.17
The migration patterns of green sea turtles, gray whales, Alaskan fur seals, and barn swallows and nighthawks are traced on this map of the Western hemisphere. Recent research on how migrating birds navigate has shown that no single factor can be said to account for their ability to unerringly make such long journeys. Night-flying birds do use the stars for navigation, but they also *learn* to take account of the rotational motion of the night sky; fledglings who were reared in a planetarium with artificial star patterns that had been rotated to a new axis chose to migrate north rather than south in the autumn.

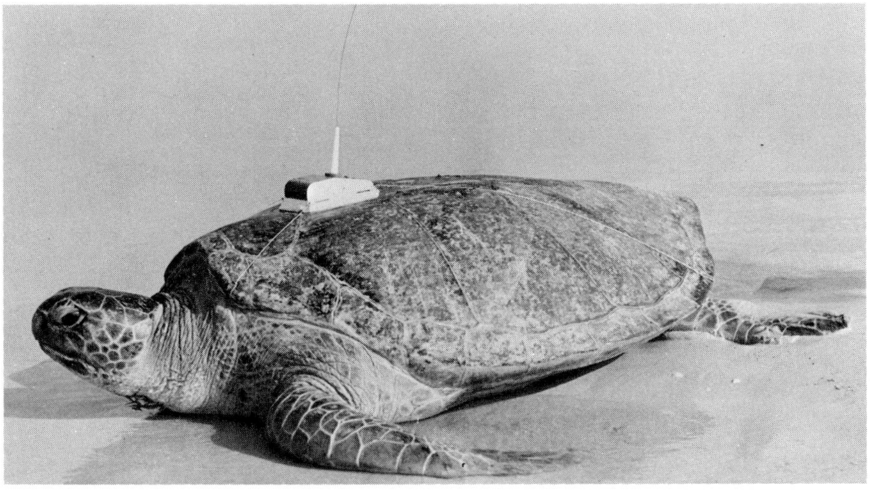

Figure 2.18
Migration patterns of animals like the green sea turtle can sometimes be traced by means of radio transmitters attached to their shells.

describes experiments in which birds were transported over large distances and then released. Many species still found their way home.

The Dancing of Honeybees

Honeybees are social insects. They live in colonies that include one egg-producing queen, a few males called drones, and many workers, which are females that have not developed genitals. The insects eat flower nectar and pollen, fertilizing plants by spreading pollen from one to another as they forage for food. Only a few bees, called scouts, leave the hive to search for food. When they find it, they collect some—on their bodies and in their stomachs—and return to the hive. Shortly thereafter, many other workers fly to the place where the scouts found food and begin gathering it. How do the workers find the food? The scouts do not lead them to it; they somehow tell the workers where it is when they return to the hive.

The communication process in bees is the subject of a long series of observations and experiments by K. von Frisch. His work is particularly impressive if one tries to imagine the difficulties he had to face both in recording the honeybees' behavior and in analyzing his observations.

In an early experiment, von Frisch demonstrated the precision with which worker bees locate a food source that the scouts have found. He fed some scout bees with food that he had placed on a particular group of flowers at a botanical garden. The plants were a kind not usually visited by the scouts, but within minutes after they had left the garden, many workers from the hive arrived. The workers lighted only on the species of flower where the scouts had been fed, ignoring the 700 other kinds of flowers in the garden.

How could one go about determining the nature of a communication process that works so precisely? Ideally, the bees' communication medium—their "language"—would have to convey information about the type of flower the scouts had found, its quality and abundance, and its distance and direction from the hive.

An obvious possibility is that the first factor, the type of flower, is communicated by odors the returning bees carry. The scout returns with flower odors on its body, and its stomach is filled with fragrant nectar, some of which it gives to the other bees. Through careful experimentation, von Frisch determined that bees use both these odors in finding the food source. In addition he found that they use a specific scent that the scouts themselves (by means of a scent gland) leave at the food source.

The odor of a flower alone would help a bee locate food near the hive, but it would not suffice for telling workers about the abundance of food or for locating distant sources—and bees often forage over a mile from their hives.

Von Frisch found that scouts returning to the hive from nearby food sources (fifty yards or less away) perform a circular movement called a round dance, illustrated in Figure 2.19. Bees in the hive follow the dancing bee, touching it with their antennae. When von Frisch varied the richness of an artificial food source he found that the bees danced more vigorously when the source was richer. The bees in the hive learned about the richness of the source from the vigor of the dance.

But the round dance apparently tells nothing about direction, as von Frisch showed in another experiment. He fed scouts from a lavender-scented dish near the hive, around which he had placed a number of similarly scented but empty dishes. After the scouts went back into the hive, he removed the full dish and put an empty scented one in its place. When the bees emerged from the hive to find the food, they did not settle on that dish but distributed themselves equally among all the dishes. Apparently the scouts had told the other bees that food was nearby but had not told them exactly where to look for it.

Later on, von Frisch repeated the experiment but put the dishes farther away from the hive. This time something entirely different happened. At about 200 yards, almost all the bees went to dishes very near the one where the scouts had eaten.

Figure 2.19
The dance language of bees. A scout bee that finds a rich source of food returns to the hive and performs a specific dance within the hive on the vertical surface of the comb. The scout performs the round dance only when the nectar source is close at hand; this dance signals the workers to search in the general area of the hive.

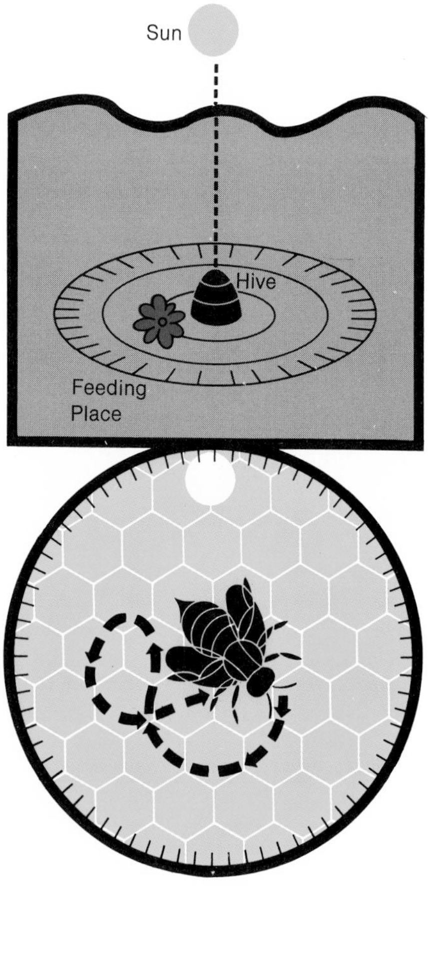

Why? Von Frisch noticed that the scouts did a different dance when the food source was far from the hive than when it was nearby. Instead of the round dance that conveyed no information about direction, they did a "wagging" dance. In the wagging dance a bee runs straight forward a little way, turns 360 degrees to the left, runs again, turns 360 degrees to the right, and repeats that sequence several times. (You might want to pause at this point and try to imagine yourself in von Frisch's place. What do you think the wagging dance means, and how would you find out if you were right?)

The distance from hive to food source, von Frisch managed to show, is indicated quite precisely by the speed of a scout's 360-degree turn. The direction of the straight run between turns indicates the angle of the path of flight. The bees "calculate" the angle by using the line connecting the hive and the sun, as shown in Figure 2.20. The calculation does not require direct sunlight—bees are sensitive to polarized light, which results from the scattering of the sun's rays in the atmosphere and is transmitted by blue sky, indicating the position of the sun even when it is out of sight behind a cloud or a hill. Polarized light is not transmitted when the sky is completely overcast, but bees can see the sun through a thicker cover of clouds than human beings can.

Bees' language, then, is highly complex. It involves at least three senses—smell, sight, and touch—and conveys information not only about the type and quality of the food the scouts have found but about how far the food source is from the hive and, if it is not nearby, in what direction.

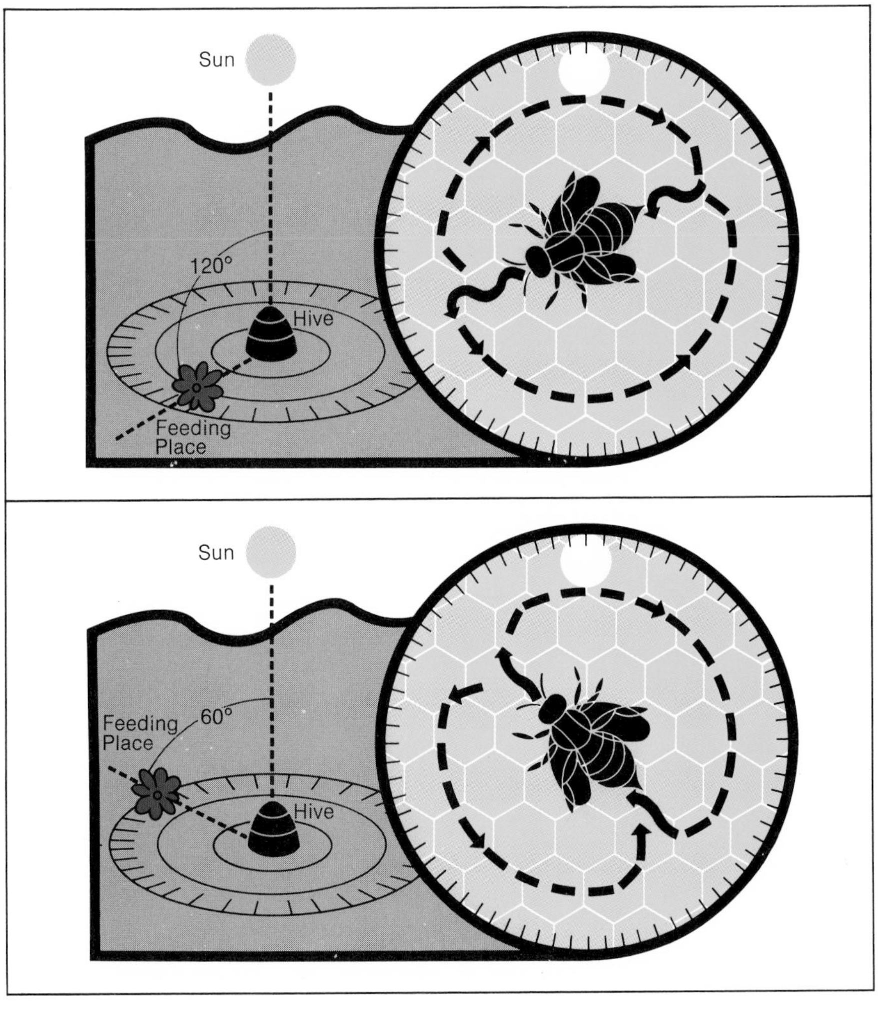

Figure 2.20

(Top) the bee's figure 8 dance, with the tail-wagging runs in the middle, is traced at approximately a 120-degree angle to the sun; the scout wags its tail rapidly in this case, signaling that the source is relatively close. (Bottom) this figure 8 is traced at a 60-degree angle to the sun, and the scout wags its tail slowly, signaling a more distant location.

Von Frisch spent many years studying the behavior of bees, and his work is an excellent illustration of ethological research. Even to decide which variables to compare requires a thorough knowledge of the behavior and physiology of the species under study. Beyond that, one must design an experiment that employs scientific controls without destroying the ecological validity of the situation—that is, without preventing the organism from behaving as it normally would. Combining careful naturalistic observation and careful experimentation and analysis is the essence of the ethological approach.

THE DEVELOPMENT OF BEHAVIORAL SYSTEMS

One of the most fruitful ways to study complex behavior is to observe its development in young animals. The importance of developmental studies for understanding the influence of learning on instinctive behavior has already been mentioned and is further discussed in Unit II. Let us turn now to two specific developmental phenomena that ethologists have studied: the early attachments that infants of some species form through a process called imprinting, and the species-characteristic songs that emerge as birds mature. Young animals seem to learn in different ways at different ages. As you read about imprinting and the development of bird songs, try to get an impression of the extent to which hereditary factors seem to control what an animal learns (and when), and also of the extent to which an animal's particular experiences can modify the behavioral tendencies it was born with.

Imprinting

Imprinting is one of the most striking examples of the interaction of complex hereditary factors with learning. Lorenz brought to the attention of ethologists the interesting fact that a newly hatched duckling or gosling, at a certain early age, will follow almost any moving object—a human being, a wooden box on wheels, a bird of a different species. A slightly older duckling or gosling (sometimes only a few hours older) will not follow these objects. This observation suggests that there are certain times in the life of these animals when they are particularly susceptible to attachments. It is not difficult to see the importance of these attachments for young birds. As the saying goes, birds of a feather flock together, and early attachments to particular moving objects—in the wild usually other birds of the infant's own species—seem to be the first stage of participation in many avian social structures.

Even though the objects that are followed do not have to look like members of the animal's own species (Figure 2.21), imprinting seems to be a primary mechanism for the early development of social bonds. In fact, Lorenz argued in his early writings that these first social bonds, once formed, are difficult if not impossible to break. For example, he mentions a barnyard goose that not only followed its keeper but, upon reaching sexual maturity, actually attempted to mate with him.

Imprinting was initially considered to be a special process by which objects presented during a highly restricted time period were stamped in (imprinted), and the imprinting was thought to be totally resistant to later modification. The time

Figure 2.21
This apparatus was designed to study imprinting. The chick has been exposed to the blue ball at a period in its young life when it is particularly susceptible to forming an attachment. During this period (when it ordinarily would attach itself to its mother), it will form an attachment to virtually any moving object—as to this blue ball—and will follow it. After no more than a few hours from the time this chick was photographed, the sensitive period ended, and it would probably not have followed the blue ball.

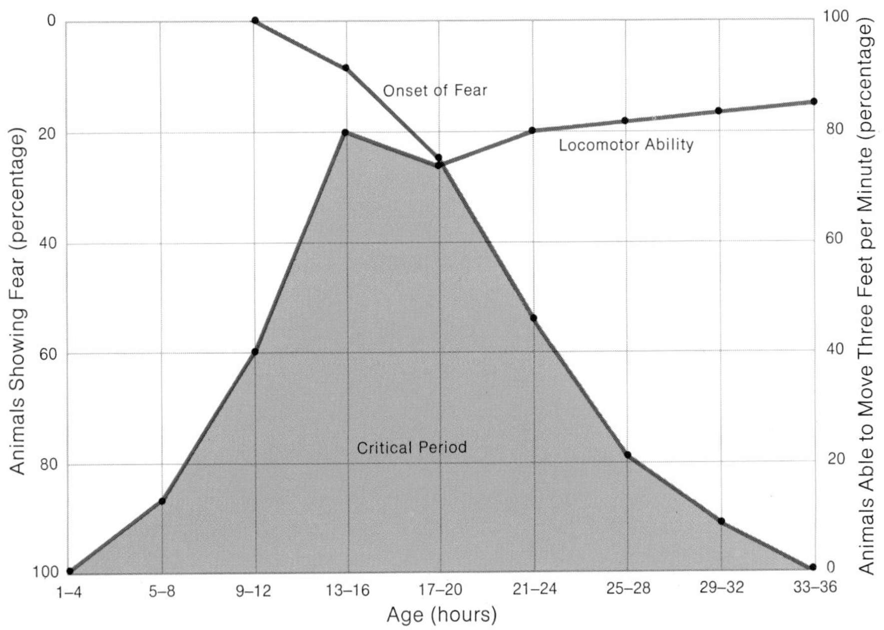

Figure 2.22
The sensitive (or critical) period for imprinting can only begin when the animal has attained a high enough level of locomotor ability so that it can follow the stimulus. Chicks, as shown in this graph, gain quickly in locomotor ability until they reach thirteen to sixteen hours of age. This factor sets one limit on the critical period; animals cannot follow a moving object until they can walk well. The other delimiting factor is the onset of fear of novel stimuli, which occurs when animals have become familiar with a certain environment. Although this period of shyness soon ends, it too limits the critical period for attachment; animals are afraid of a novel moving object during this time. The period of shyness in chicks begins between the ninth and twelfth hour of life and ends at about the thirty-fifth.
(After Hess, 1959.)

period was called a *critical period,* but laboratory studies have shown that the period is not quite as critical as early observations made it seem. Attachment can sometimes be modified or reversed, at least in a laboratory setting, and some learning relevant to the attachment can occur before and after the critical period. In addition, the period can often be prolonged or shortened by an experimenter. With a slight modification in terminology, we can retain the essence of imprinting without the exaggeration that was present in the original interpretation. Instead of *critical period,* we can use the more accurate phrase, *sensitive period.*

One interesting feature of development that has shown up clearly in studies of imprinting is that, once animals are familiar with a given set of environmental surroundings, they often avoid stimuli that are unfamiliar. Indeed, one factor that defines the end of the sensitive period during which imprinting can occur is the development of a fear of novel objects (Figure 2.22). It is as if an animal builds up an internal representation of certain features of its environment and then avoids stimuli that do not match that representation. In a similar way, many children and other young mammals, such as the wolf, go through a very shy period. In some cases, as R. Melzack has shown, a slight change in environment (for example, moving an object from one place to another) results in extreme avoidance reactions, and in others, as J. Bowlby and others have shown, the animal or child shows a fear of strangers for a while. Children's emotional reactions to novel objects will be discussed more fully in Chapter 4.

Bird Songs

How do birds learn to sing the songs characteristic of their species? An American child who grows up in a foreign country usually learns at least a bit of the foreign tongue even if his parents never speak anything except English, but a cardinal sings like a cardinal even if its parents have nested in a yard full of robins and sparrows. Is bird song perhaps not learned at all, but simply something that is developed through the maturation of inherited physical capacities?

Ethologists are very much interested in the effects of experience on bird song. As with imprinting, the relations between environmental and hereditary factors seem to be complex, and extremely subtle. They also vary from species to species.

In studying the vocalizations of birds, it is useful to have the assistance of sound spectrographs, which record sound graphically, as shown in Figure 2.23. Many

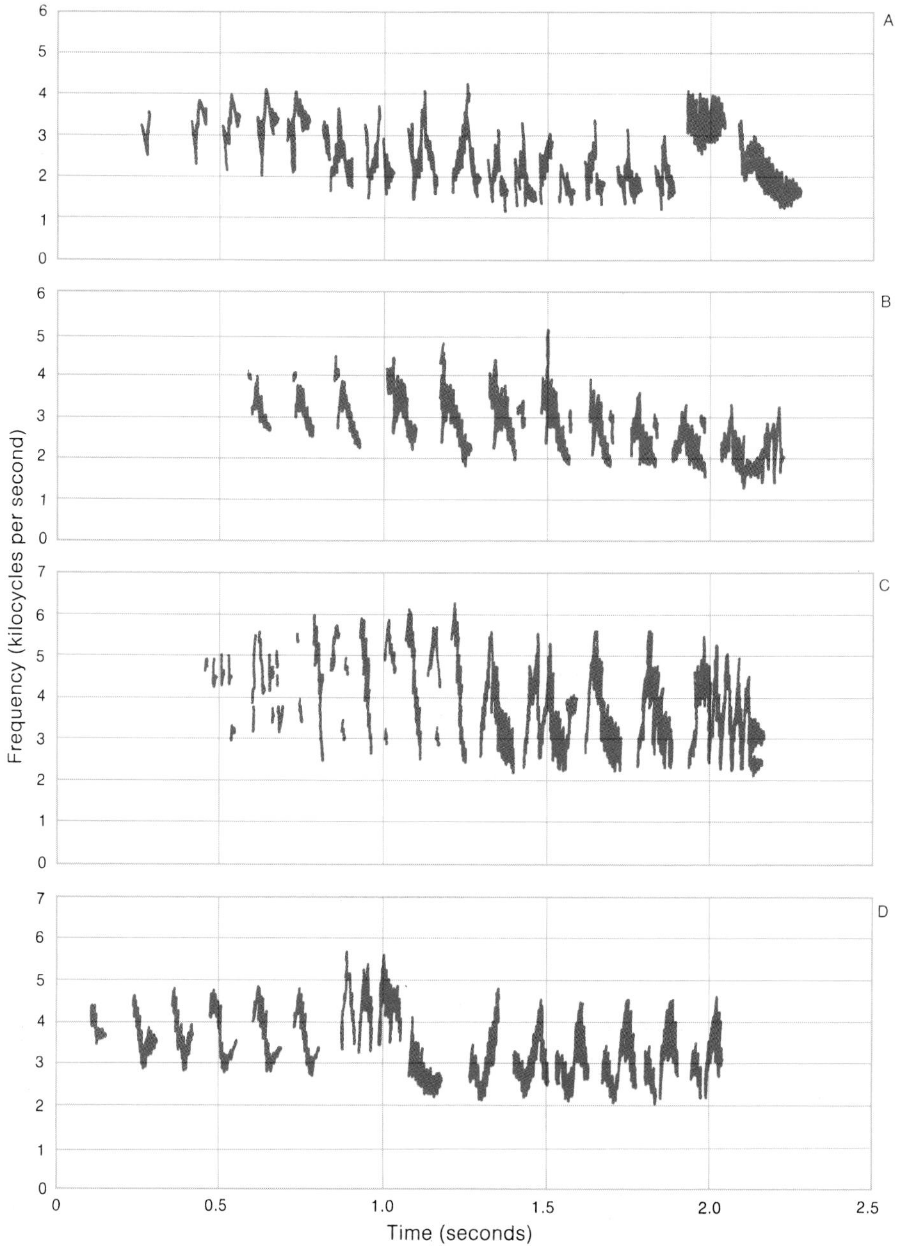

Figure 2.23
Sound spectrographs of the songs of chaffinches under varying circumstances. (A) The song of the normal adult chaffinch. (B) The song of a bird that has been hand-reared from birth in isolation, able to hear only itself sing. (C) The vocalization pattern of a bird removed from a group of other young birds at an early age and then reared in isolation. (D) The song of a bird reared in isolation but tutored with a recording spliced so that the ending of the normal chaffinch song came in the middle. This experiment seems to show that auditory experience other than hearing the normal adult song can affect the development of songs in young birds.
(After Thorpe, 1961.)

songbirds make the sounds of individual call notes normally, even when reared in isolation from other birds, but their species' full songs, which are sequences of the individual notes, often do not develop normally. W. H. Thorpe has shown that chaffinches hand-reared in isolation from other birds developed only very simple types of songs. But if the young chaffinches were exposed to the calls of other immature birds, their songs became somewhat more complex, and if they were exposed to the songs of adult birds, their songs became completely normal.

Chaffinches (and some other birds) are known to imitate the songs of neighboring birds of their species, for local dialects have been found that cannot be attributed to genetic differences. But the extent to which they imitate other sounds is limited. For example, Thorpe found that tape recordings of pure tones did not change the notes sung by chaffinches raised in isolation, although tape recordings containing chaffinch songs did—even if the recordings were played backwards.

P. R. Marler and M. Tamura found that white-crowned sparrows also develop local dialects from listening to the songs of nearby members of their species. Young sparrows kept in isolation develop a full song, but the song is abnormal in important ways and fails to show the local dialect of the area in which the birds were captured. Although these birds do not sing their full song until they are 200 to 250 days old, the dialect is acquired much earlier—between about ten and one hundred days of age. That is, there is a sensitive period for the acquisition of the dialect; interestingly, it occurs long before the birds can sing their song in fully developed form.

Because birds reared in isolation can still hear *themselves* sing, there is a chance that the species that develop normal songs in isolation might do so because they listen to themselves. To investigate that possibility, M. Konishi used surgically deafened Oregon juncos, which develop normal songs when reared in isolation without deafening. When he deafened the juncos at an early age, they developed many normal features of adult song, but there were more deviations from normal patterns in the songs of the deafened birds than in those of the undeafened birds.

Even in this extreme case of a bird that develops the ability to sing normally when it has never heard a sound from another member of its species, experience—in the form of auditory feedback—is crucial to the full development of behavior that obviously has a large instinctive component.

SUGGESTED READINGS

DARWIN, C. *Expression of the Emotions in Man and Animals.* Chicago, University of Chicago Press, 1965. With this book, originally published in 1872, Darwin developed the assumption that an animal's behavior is characteristic of its species, in the same way that its bodily characteristics are.

EIBL-EIBESFELT, I. *Ethology. The Biology of Behavior.* New York, Holt, Rinehart and Winston, 1970. A useful, up-to-date introductory survey on the field of ethology, written by a student and colleague of Konrad Lorenz.

FRISCH, K. VON. *The Dance Language and Orientation of Bees,* L. E. Chadwick (Tr.). Cambridge, Mass., Belknap Press of Harvard University Press, 1967. Von Frisch's most recent and most extensive treatment of his lifetime of work with honeybees.

LORENZ, K. *Evolution and Modification of Behavior.* Chicago, University of Chicago Press, 1965. In this short book, Lorenz analyzes the meaning of the term "innate" as applied to behavior and discusses controversies over the heredity of behavior.

——— *King Solomon's Ring.* New York, Thomas Y. Crowell, 1952. A light, easy-to-read book of essays about Lorenz's many interesting experiences with animals.

——— *Studies in Animal and Human Behavior,* Vol. I. Cambridge, Mass., Harvard University Press, 1970. Lorenz's most important papers are being brought together in English translation in several volumes.

MARLER, P. R., AND HAMILTON, W. J. *Mechanisms of Animal Behavior.* New York, Wiley, 1966. A thorough, well-written summary and integration of major areas of research on animal behavior.

ROE, A., AND SIMPSON, G. (Eds.). *Behavior and Evolution.* New Haven, Conn., Yale University Press, 1958. A collection of papers by important researchers in the field of behavior and evolution.

THORPE, W. H. *Learning and Instinct in Animals* (2nd ed.). Cambridge, Mass., Harvard University Press, 1963. An important treatment of ethological research on the nature of learning in different species of animals.

TINBERGEN, N. *The Study of Instinct.* New York, Oxford University Press, 1969. A stimulating discussion of instinctive behavior by one of the most important modern ethologists.

3 Conditioning and Learning

MOST PEOPLE SEEM TO FEAR and resent behaviorist notions. They seem to think it denies man freedom of will and makes of him merely a machine. I heard William Buckley discuss *Beyond Freedom and Dignity,* a book by B. F. Skinner, and he referred to Skinner's theories as implying a "dehumanization" of man. But does behaviorism dehumanize a man or merely *describe* a man?

Frankly, I tend to accept behaviorist notions. I find the behavior of people quite predictable; and the better I know them, the more predictable I find their behavior. They sometimes surprise me, I admit, but I have the feeling that this is because I don't know enough about them and not because they are capable of free will.

And, of course, my own behavior is most predictable of all; at least, to me. For instance, I respond favorably to praise. It has an extraordinary reinforcing effect on me. All my publishers and editors find this out at once. It is their profession, of course, to study the weaknesses of writers and use those weaknesses to manipulate those writers. So they carefully begin to praise the quickness with which I complete my work; the speed with which I read galleys and prepare indexes; the cooperativeness with which I make (reasonable) revisions, and so on and so on.

All this I lap up with avidity; no one has ever handed out praise in larger servings than I can swallow. What's more, in order to get still more of it, I complete my work more quickly than ever, read galleys and do indexes with still greater speed, make *reasonable* revisions with at least a trace of a smile, and the result is that over the last six years I have averaged nine books a year.

Came the time when I was supposed to work on the introductions to these chapters. I was in New York; the editorial staff was in California. I sent off some introductions and heard nothing. Whereupon I grew sad and sulky and found that I didn't feel like doing any more. When I was nudged very politely by the editors, I wrote a long letter, saying that unless I knew that they liked those I had already written, I could do no further work. Whereupon the staff, suddenly enlightened, promptly sent me a letter telling me that my introductions were great and that everybody loved them. At once I sat down to write more. Periodically, they sent me kind words and I sent more introductions. It was very neat and efficient.

But does that mean I'm just a robot? That I have buttons that need pushing? That I point them out, that they push them, and that all is well? Well, I guess so. I like to be praised and that's what I work for. Maybe we all have our buttons, and maybe we all know where they are, and maybe we all do our best to get them pushed.

Could the behaviorists be saying that it's love that makes the world go round? I. A.

One hundred years ago, most people believed that the mind and the body were completely separate. Darwin's theory of evolution was still new and highly controversial, and even those who accepted it usually made a sharp distinction between the body and the mind. The human body may have evolved, but not the human mind. The mind was thought to be an expression of the soul, and because the soul was not composed of matter, it could not be part of the material body. At that time psychology, which people were just beginning to consider a field of study in its own right rather than a subdivision of philosophy, was defined as the study of the mind.

Because most people believed that the mind was independent of the body, psychologists were continually faced with religious, philosophical, and methodological problems. How could they hope to do a systematic, scientific analysis of something that might not even be subject to physical laws? This difficulty had a profound impact on the kind of research that early psychologists did. Many of them used the so-called *introspective method:* they tried to notice and analyze the contents of

Figure 3.1
Wilhelm Wundt. Wundt is generally recognized as the first experimental psychologist; in 1879 he set up a laboratory in Leipzig to study the contents of conscious experience.

Figure 3.2
John B. Watson. Behaviorism, as formulated by Watson, had impact upon child-rearing practices and other applied areas, as well as upon academic psychology, especially in operant conditioning research.

Figure 3.3
Clark Hull. Hull's stimulus-response learning theory was the most comprehensive and ambitious psychological theory of his period. It was exactingly formulated and rigorously tested.

whatever crossed their consciousness. E. Boring describes how men like W. Wundt and E. B. Titchener made many important discoveries using this approach; however, they also tended to neglect people's overt actions, their outward behavior.

In the United States, discontent with this *mentalistic* psychology eventually produced the very different approach called *behaviorism,* which originated with J. B. Watson around 1913 and was carried on later by such well-known psychologists as C. Hull and B. F. Skinner. Watson argued that it is impossible to study in a scientific way phenomena that can be known only through subjective reports. If psychology was to be a science, he said, psychologists would have to concentrate on *observable behavior,* such as movements and speech; they should stop attempting to study mental phenomena such as consciousness and thought, except insofar as those phenomena were revealed in behavior. It was not that Watson had no interest in so-called mental phenomena. In fact, during the early days of behaviorism, he formulated a theory that explained thinking as *subvocalization*—as movements of the vocal cords that were so slight as to be inaudible. This theory, if it had been correct, would have allowed behaviorists to study thinking by analyzing the movements of the vocal cords. As P. Bridgman, the operationalist, soon pointed out, however, some thinking occurs so rapidly that the subvocalized sounds would have to be made at frequencies well beyond the physical capacity of the vocal cords.

LEARNING AND PERFORMANCE

From the very beginning of behaviorism, one of the main interests of behaviorists has been the study of learning. But the concept of learning comes very close to being a mental phenomenon. Consequently, behaviorists have sought to define learning precisely in terms of observable behavior. To begin with, they carefully distinguish between *performance,* which is what a person or animal actually does, and *learning,* which has to do with *changes* in what he can do. Some behaviorists, then, attempt to describe performance only, avoiding the use of the concept of learning. But the majority try to infer the process of learning from careful analysis of changes in an individual's performance.

Inferring changes in learning from changes in performance is not as simple a matter as it may seem. Improvements in performance are not always a result of learning. A football player may play better this week than last week for many reasons. He may have had a cold last week, or he may have had a fight with the coach, or perhaps this week's game is especially important. And when performance changes for the worse or does not change at all, one cannot assume that something learned earlier has been forgotten or that nothing has been learned.

In the laboratory, the psychologist can study animals that he is certain have had no previous experience with the task to be learned. For example, a hungry rat can be taught to run a maze for a food reward. If it runs the maze faster on Trial 20 than on Trial 1, the experimenter can tentatively conclude that learning has taken place, because he knows the past history of the rat. Once the animal has eaten its fill, however, it may be reluctant to run the maze as fast as it did before. Its performance is impaired, but what it has learned is not—when the animal is hungry again, it will demonstrate the learned response in as lively a fashion as before. Similarly, outside the laboratory, it is safe to assume that a person who successfully negotiates an advanced ski slope has learned how to ski. But the mere fact that he knows how to ski does not mean he will ski as well as he can on all slopes at all times. He may, for example, ski better (or worse) when people are watching than when they are not.

Another important goal of behaviorism, in addition to precise description of observable behavior, has been precise description of simple experimental techniques that can be used to *control* behavior. If one can specify that, under certain conditions, a particular experimental technique has a consistent effect on performance, then one does not necessarily have to be concerned about whether the performance is a result of learning. By using the technique with an animal or a person, the psychologist can produce the desired performance. In this way the psychologist can control much of behavior by simple manipulations of the environment. B. F. Skinner has been the most influential proponent of this type of behaviorism. His approach has been called *psychological engineering* because he is more interested in determining how to control behavior than in devising theoretical explanations of the processes that underlie behavior. This approach is reflected in behavior therapy, which is discussed in Chapter 33.

But even behaviorists who are not sympathetic to Skinner's approach prefer explanations of behavior that remain as close as possible to the experimental manipulations made. They usually explain learning by relating it to two well-established experimental techniques: classical conditioning and operant conditioning.

Figure 3.4
B. F. Skinner. The work and impact of B. F. Skinner cannot be summarized briefly. Various chapters in this volume discuss his contributions to experimental methodology, philosophy of psychology, operant conditioning, and behavior modification. In his recent book, *Beyond Freedom and Dignity,* he advocates the use of social control of behavior for humanistic purposes. His views have been debated heatedly for over thirty years. Irrespective of one's agreement or disagreement with Skinner's views, no one disputes his tremendous influence.

CLASSICAL CONDITIONING

Classical conditioning (sometimes called Pavlovian conditioning or respondent conditioning) involves reflex behavior. A reflex is an involuntary response that is elicited by a specific stimulus. For example, a sharp puff of air on the eye evokes a blink of the eyelid; a tap on the patellar tendon produces the knee jerk; the prick of a thorn causes reflexive withdrawal of the hand or foot. In classical conditioning, a new stimulus comes to elicit the response. For example, if several times in a row a buzzer is sounded just before a puff of air is blown at your eye, you will probably blink the next time you hear the buzzer, whether the puff of air follows or not.

The noted Russian physiologist I. P. Pavlov discovered classical conditioning in the course of a series of studies on the physiology of digestion, for which he won the Nobel Prize in 1903. Pavlov was originally concerned with the preparatory reflexes of the stomach—that is, how the stomach prepares itself, by secreting digestive juices, for food that is placed in the mouth. He found that the mouth also prepares itself, by secreting saliva, for food that is merely seen or smelled. This is a learned response; when an animal first sees or smells an unfamiliar type of food, it does not salivate. The fundamentals of conditioning that Pavlov unraveled in studying the conditions under which an animal learns to secrete saliva have had an extraordinary influence on nearly every theoretical position in the psychology of learning.

Strictly speaking, however, Pavlov was not the first to study the conditional reflex. That honor goes to a little-known American psychologist named E. B. Twitmyer. About the turn of the century, Twitmyer was a graduate student at the University of Pennsylvania. For his dissertation experiment he chose to work with the patellar reflex, or knee jerk. Twitmyer rigged up a small hammer that, when released, would strike the subject's patellar tendon. As a warning that he was about to release the hammer, he always sounded a bell beforehand. One day while he was testing a subject, he accidentally hit the bell. Although the hammer did not drop, the subject's knee jerked anyway. When Twitmyer asked him why, the subject said he didn't know—the response was involuntary. Twitmyer, recognizing that he had stumbled onto something very interesting, abandoned the original plan for his dissertation in order to study this fascinating new type of learned response. Although he reported his findings at the annual meeting of the American Psychological Association in 1904, none of the scientists there saw the significance of his work. In fact, it was the first published description of what we now call classical, or respondent, conditioning. Twitmyer, disappointed in the reception the scientific world gave his experiments, abandoned them entirely.

Figure 3.5
Twitmyer first discovered classical conditioning of reflexes quite by accident. While studying people's patellar reflexes, he discovered that the ringing of a bell, which always preceded stimulation of the subject's patellar tendon could elicit the knee jerk in the absence of stimulation. If he had persisted in his research, what we now call "Pavlovian conditioning" might have been called "Twitmyerian conditioning."

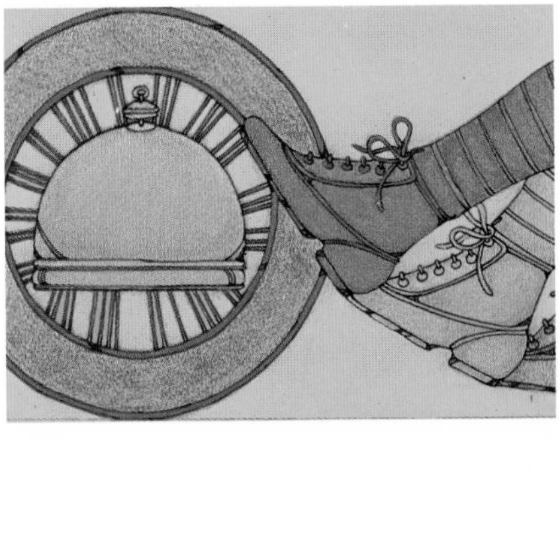

Within a year or so, Pavlov made essentially the same discovery working with dogs that Twitmyer had made with human beings. The scientific world gave Pavlov little encouragement at first either, but he was an established investigator—a Nobel

Prize winner with his own well-equipped laboratory—and he persevered. Finally, other scientists saw the importance of his work. So Pavlov's name, not Twitmyer's, is associated with the discovery. Because his work was more complete and more elegant than Twitmyer's, we shall discuss it in detail.

The salivary reflex, like all other reflexes, consists of a stimulus—food in the dog's mouth—that elicits a response—salivation. Pavlov discovered that, if a previously neutral stimulus regularly occurs just before food is placed into the dog's mouth, the neutral stimulus itself gradually comes to elicit salivation. In Pavlov's terms, the food in the mouth is an *unconditional stimulus.* It elicits the *unconditional response* (or unconditional reflex) of salivation. The term "unconditional" is used because the response does not depend on the organism's previous experience with the stimulus. In other words, an unconditional reflex is innate, not learned. The new stimulus that comes to elicit salivation is called the *conditional stimulus.* The salivation that it evokes is called the *conditional response,* or conditional reflex—conditional upon the animal's previous experience. In other words, a conditional response is learned. Any one of a large variety of stimuli can serve as a conditional stimulus for salivation: the sight of food, the sound of a metronome or a bell, the flash of a light. (Sometimes the words condition*ed* and uncondition*ed* are used instead of condition*al* and uncondition*al,* but the latter terms are more accurate translations of Pavlov's Russian.)

Figure 3.6
Ivan Pavlov. This Russian physiologist pioneered the investigation of classical conditioning. Like Skinner, his research opened a major branch in the psychology of learning and also has led to practical applications in the area of behavior modification.

Establishing a Conditional Response

The experimental apparatus that Pavlov used is illustrated in Figure 3.7. Before the experiments began, each dog underwent minor surgery: a tube was inserted in its cheek so that saliva would flow from the duct in the dog's salivary gland into a glass container. The mechanical device on the far left of the drawing kept track of the number of drops secreted. In front of the dog was a food tray from which the animal could eat. The unconditional stimulus was food in the dog's mouth. The conditional stimulus was one of several: either a ticking metronome, a light, or a brush that stimulated the animal's skin.

In a typical study, the experimenter presented a stimulus—say, the light—for about five seconds, then dropped a piece of food into the dog's tray. The dog picked up the food and salivated as a result of the food in its mouth; this was the unconditional response. As the pairing of light and food continued time after time, the light itself began to elicit salivation; this was the conditional response. Once every few trials, the light was presented alone, without food. As Figure 3.8 shows, the light alone soon came to elicit saliva—in this case, between ten and thirteen drops.

Figure 3.7
Pavlov's original apparatus for classically conditioning salivation in the dog. Note the harness to restrict extraneous movement by the subject, the food (the unconditional stimulus) and the tube running from the dog's cheek to a container for the saliva. The saliva dropping into the container activates the recording device, the kymograph. Interestingly, Pavlov's studies had been on the physiology of digestion, and he came upon the phenomenon later termed classical conditioning quite by chance. Pavlov first noted that the sound of his footsteps in the laboratory would activate the salivary response in the dog even though no food was present. Psychologists now understand that this sound had become a conditional stimulus because of previous associations of Pavlov's presence with feeding.
(After Pavlov, 1927.)

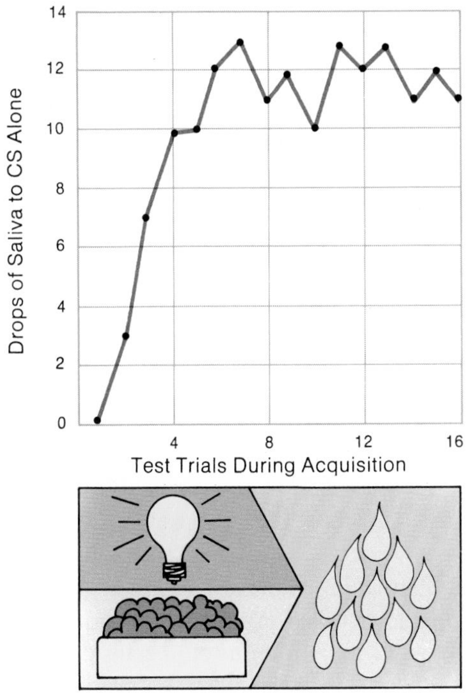

Figure 3.8

A plotting of the data from one of Pavlov's experiments in classical conditioning. The dog was simultaneously presented both food (unconditional stimulus) and a light (conditional stimulus) until it responded—by salivating—to the light alone. The curve connecting the points of data is a typical learning curve.

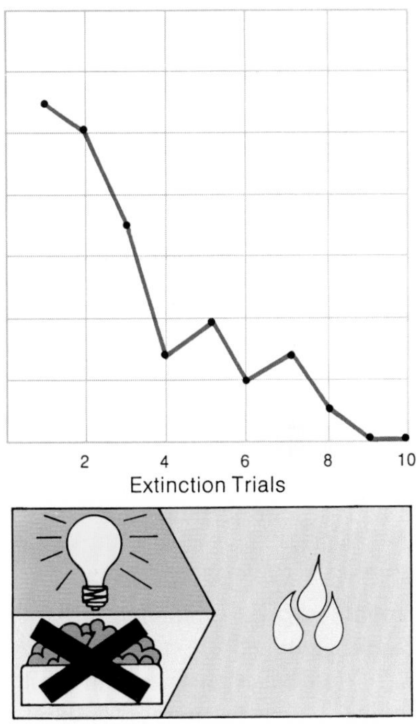

Figure 3.9

During the extinction phase of the same experimental paradigm, food (the UCS) no longer follows the presentation of the light (the CS). Over trials the number of drops of saliva elicited by the light declines rapidly. Zero responding was achieved on the ninth trial with this particular dog. Ideally, extinction training should be carried out beyond the ninth trial to ensure the relative permanence of the nonresponding.

(After Pavlov, 1927.)

Pavlov and his colleagues used a similar procedure to condition other reflexes. For example, an electric shock to a dog's forepaw causes a withdrawal reflex—the dog pulls its paw away from the location of the stimulus, although he cannot actually avoid or escape it. If the unconditional stimulus (the shock) is regularly preceded by some other stimulus, such as the ticking of a metronome, the dog soon pulls its paw away in response to the sound alone.

Experimental Extinction

A conditional reflex continues to occur, Pavlov found, only if the conditional stimulus is occasionally presented in conjunction with the unconditional stimulus. For example, if a dog has been conditioned to salivate in response to light and then, on a number of successive trials, a light is presented but food (the unconditional stimulus) is not, the amount of saliva elicited by the light gradually declines toward zero, as shown in Figure 3.9. Similarly, if a dog hears the ticking of the metronome on a number of occasions but receives no shock, it gradually stops lifting its paw

Figure 3.10

Among the involuntary behaviors that can be classically conditioned is blushing; like salivation, it is mediated by the autonomic nervous system. This sequence illustrates the paradigm, or formal procedure, of classical conditioning. Prior to conditioning, a trench coat is a neutral stimulus for the young woman (USC); male nudity, however, even in a statue, elicits blushing (UCR) in our subject. During the active conditioning phase she encounters a man in a trench coat, who holds it open, exposing himself; she blushes at the combination of trench coat and male nudity (CS + UCS). After conditioning, then, the sight of a trench coat makes her blush (CR).

in response to the ticking. This procedure is called *experimental extinction:* the conditional reflex gradually wanes and is *extinguished.* Unless it is occasionally strengthened by elicitation of the unconditional reflex, it ceases to occur.

In addition, extinction sometimes occurs spontaneously. Even though the conditional response of salivation to a light is often followed by food, the dog stops salivating when the light is presented alone. Pavlov was an excellent observer as well as a careful experimentalist, and early in his research he uncovered this enigma. It is called *spontaneous extinction.* Today it still has not been adequately explained.

Pavlov's findings had an enormous impact on American psychology in general and on behaviorism in particular. He so carefully worked out the factors that influence classical conditioning that many of the standard terms used to discuss conditioning and learning derive from him. J. B. Watson was so impressed by Pavlov's work that he based his entire behaviorist analysis of learning on it. All learning, he argued, could be explained in terms of classical conditioning. Although few behaviorists believe that today, most of Pavlov's findings have proved applicable to both types of conditioning.

OPERANT CONDITIONING

Around 1930 B. F. Skinner in the United States and J. Konorski and S. Miller in Poland described *operant conditioning* (sometimes called instrumental conditioning). Most behaviorists explain most everyday learning in terms of operant conditioning. There are a number of differences between classical and operant conditioning, but one of the most basic is that classical conditioning applies to reflexes, whereas operant conditioning applies to what is usually called voluntary behavior. When an animal salivates in response to food in its mouth, that is a reflex; in behaviorist terms, the reflex response is *elicited* from the organism by the stimulus. Operant behavior, by contrast, is said to be *emitted* by the organism; there is no identifiable stimulus that provokes it. No particular stimulus is needed to induce a rat to sniff and move about in its cage, for example. Such behavior is as natural for a rat as flying is for a bird or swinging through trees is for a monkey. The babbling of babies is another example of operant behavior. It is not normally elicited by external stimuli; it simply happens.

The occurrence of operant behavior is, however, influenced by events in the environment—in particular, by *rewards* and *punishments.* Generally, operant behavior that results in the appearance or attainment of something that is liked will be repeated, and behavior that results in something that is disliked will not be repeated. This is what operant conditioning is all about.

Reinforcement and Punishment

The environmental consequences of behavior can be classified according to their effect on the behavior. A consequence that results in the repetition of the behavior that produced it is called a *reinforcement,* or a reward; a consequence that results in the suppression of the behavior that produced it is called a *punishment,* or an aversive stimulation. Money, for example, is classed as reinforcement for people, because behavior that accumulates money tends to be repeated. Loss of friendship and pain are classified as punishment, because behavior that produces them tends not to be repeated. In fact, if a person is exposed to punishment, any behavior that ends the punishment tends to be repeated. In other words, the termination of aversive stimulation can itself be a reinforcer.

In each case, a behavior is followed by a consequence, and the nature of the consequence modifies the organism's tendency to engage in the behavior in the future. Behavior that is reinforced tends to be repeated; behavior that is punished tends not to be repeated. A reinforcer is defined as a stimulus or event that *increases* the frequency of occurrence of the behavior that it follows. A punisher is defined

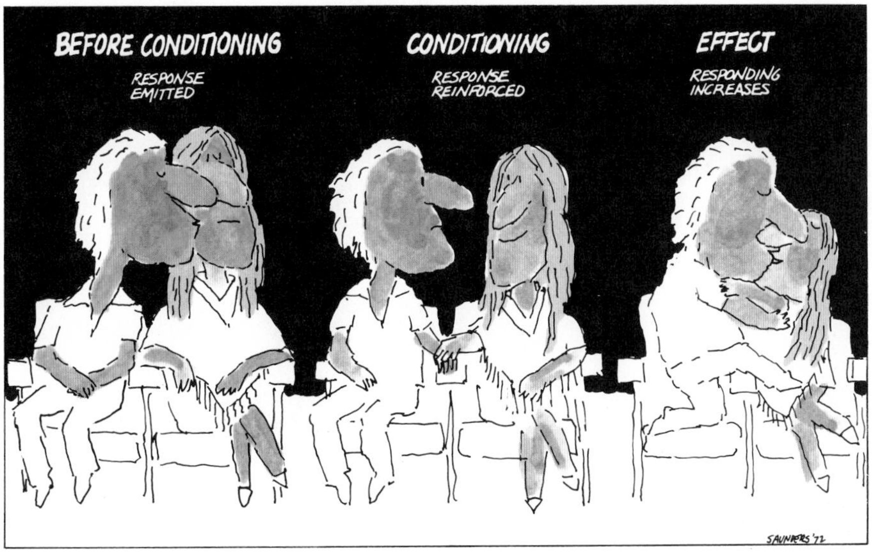

Figure 3.11
This sequence illustrates the paradigm, or formal procedure, of operant conditioning. The man has emitted a purposeful, voluntary response; his kissing behavior, an operant response, is controlled by its consequences. The woman then delivers positive reinforcement, such as smiling and holding his hand contingent upon his kiss on her cheek. Following such reinforcement of behavior, his responding increases, as can be seen in the frame at the right. Note also that these later responses show increased vigor and general activity.

as a stimulus or event that *decreases* the frequency of occurrence of the behavior that it follows.

Besides increasing the frequency of occurrence of the behavior that it follows, reinforcement has another effect of equal importance: it brings the reinforced behavior under the control of the stimuli prevailing at the time of reinforcement. That is to say, the behavior tends to occur predominantly in the presence of stimuli that in the past have set the occasion for its reinforcement. This effect of reinforcement is referred to as *stimulus control*—both because the stimulus controls the behavior and because the psychologist can control the behavior by controlling the stimulus. w/o reinforcement

Stimulus control can be observed when you speak with a slightly deaf person. If he fails to react to what you say, you speak more loudly, until he hears and reinforces your behavior. The next time you meet that person, you will probably speak more loudly than usual. In this case, the deaf person is a stimulus controlling louder speaking, because the louder speaking was reinforced at your earlier meeting.

Stimulus control is not always so reasonable, however. At times it results in *superstitious behavior*—behavior that persists because, purely by *chance*, it preceded reinforcement in a particular situation. Styles of putting in golf are influenced in this way. Although certain movements are essential to good putting, no one style guarantees success. If a player happens to use a particular stance on several excellent putts, that stance tends to remain because it has been reinforced. In fact, players often change their styles after a sequence of particularly bad putts. When they are again successful, they keep using the style that worked—until things go wrong.

The Acquisition and Shaping of Behavior

In order to see how operant conditioning is studied, let us trace a hungry rat's career in a piece of laboratory equipment evolved by B. F. Skinner and called a *Skinner box*. Our rat is going to be trained to press a bar for a food reward. The type of box used to study this behavior is shown in Figure 3.12; its essential parts are a bar, a light or a buzzer, and a food cup. The light or buzzer is used in the establishment of stimulus control after a behavior has been acquired.

When the rat is first put into the box, it acts uneasy and cautious until it has had an opportunity to explore for perhaps half an hour, sniffing and touching everything in the box. After that, the first part of operant conditioning can begin: the rat can be taught that the food cup sometimes contains food. This is done through a procedure called *magazine training*. Regardless of what the animal hap-

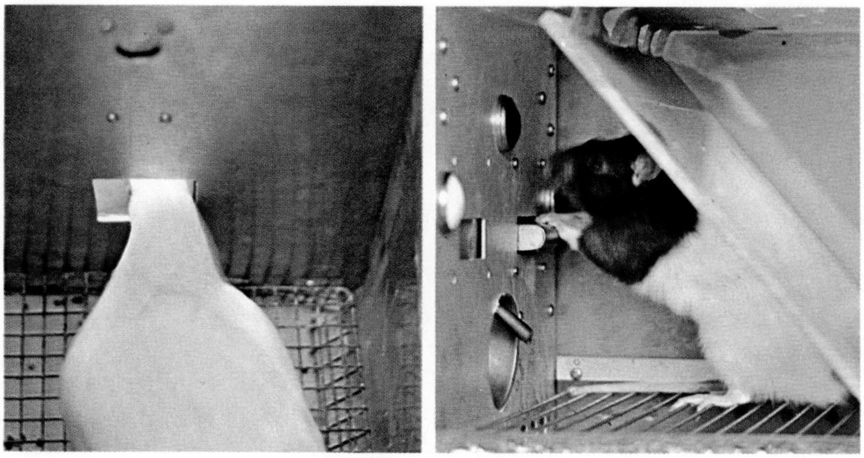

Figure 3.12
Apparatus used in animal operant-conditioning research. Because of the enormous contributions made by B. F. Skinner to research in animal learning, many psychologists refer to these training boxes as "Skinner boxes." These devices usually contain a lever for the animal to press or a disc to push or peck, so there is a discrete, readily observable, and measurable response for the experimenter to use as a performance index. Most operant-conditioning research with animals has been conducted with pigeons and white rats.

pens to be doing, the experimenter periodically drops a few pellets of food into the food cup—known as a food magazine—through plastic tube. The procedure is illustrated in Figure 3.13.

The purpose of magazine training is to make sure that the rat's bar presses will be reinforced immediately after the rat performs them. Since it takes time for an animal to get food into its mouth, food alone is not a good immediate reinforcer—the food may reinforce some other behavior than the bar press, such as moving its head in a certain way, if there is time for that to occur between pressing the bar and eating the food. What magazine training does is turn the sights and sounds that accompany the delivery of food, such as the click sound made when the food drops into the cup and the sight of the food, into signals for the reinforcer. Because such signals reach the animal instantly, they provide for immediate reinforcement. Stimuli of this sort are called *conditioned reinforcers* (or, sometimes, secondary reinforcers). Magazine training can stop when the rat runs to the food cup and eats as soon as the food has arrived. This behavior indicates that the sights and sounds accompanying the food are well enough established to act as conditioned reinforcers for bar pressing.

At this point the experimenter can begin to train the rat to press the bar. Operant behavior, as has been pointed out, is *emitted* by an organism rather than

Figure 3.13
These drawings depict the magazine training of a water-deprived rat. At first the rat ignores the click of the water dipper or may even be frightened by it. But being thirsty, it is active and eventually discovers the water. After repeated presentations the rat learns that the clicking sound signals the availability of water, and it will leap to the dipper with no delay.

elicited by a particular stimulus. That is, there is no stimulus that will force the rat to press the bar. If the experimenter waits long enough, however, the rat will probably press the bar by chance and that behavior can be reinforced. Or, to save time, the experimenter can *shape* the animal's natural behavior into the form of the desired response.

In order to press the bar, the rat must approach it, rise up on its hind legs, put its front paws on the bar, and push the bar down toward the floor. Before training begins, the rat has in its behavioral repertoire all the behaviors necessary for bar pressing, but they rarely occur in the required sequence. Shaping begins by reinforcing the first response in the desired behavior sequence—in this case, approaching the bar. After a few reinforcements, the rat begins to interrupt its other behavior in order to approach the lever. Now reinforcement can be withheld until the rat not only approaches the lever but rises slightly off the floor in front of it. At first, the experimenter may have to settle for reinforcing the mere lifting of one paw off the floor; later, he will reinforce only lifting both paws high enough to reach the bar. Next, reinforcement is withheld until the animal puts its paws on the bar. At that point, bar pressing is practically guaranteed. The experimenter simply withholds reinforcement until the lever is actually depressed, and he has finished shaping bar pressing. The procedure is illustrated in Figure 3.15.

Shaping, then, is the reinforcement of closer and closer approximations to a desired behavior. The reinforcement of successive approximations is a powerful technique, but it often assumes the status of an art rather than a science, for it takes a skilled trainer to know which approximations to reward and which to ignore. Furthermore, each successive approximation must be only a small step beyond what the animal was previously doing. If the steps are too large, the procedure fails.

There is nothing magical about bar pressing as a response, although it is the one most often studied in experiments with rats. The reason for its popularity is that it is a well-defined act, easy for a rat to perform and easy to record automatically. If reinforcement were made dependent on another operant response, such as smelling in the corner, that behavior too could be shaped and the rat would soon do little else. Any response that procures food will tend to be emitted by the animal—almost to the exclusion of everything else—in the simple environment of a Skinner box.

Several other kinds of apparatus are also frequently used in the study of operant behavior. Foremost among these are mazes; several popular types are shown in

Figure 3.14
Operant-conditioning methods have been applied to training a variety of animals. This killer whale has been trained at Sea World in San Diego, California, to perform a variety of new responses, such as a grateful kiss to the "doctor" who just "examined" her. The doctor rewards his patient with fish.

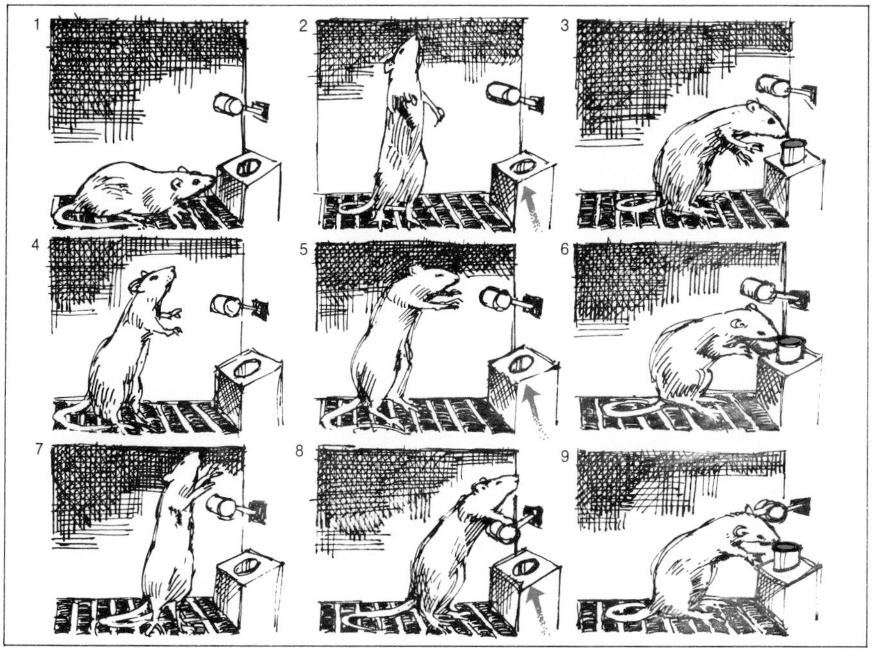

Figure 3.15
In shaping the rat to press the bar, the experimenter watches the rat and at first rewards it for any activity near the bar. As this activity occurs more frequently, he can restrict reinforcement to behaviors that are nearer putting weight on the bar. Usually the experimenter wires the apparatus so that when a true bar press does occur, it is automatically and immediately reinforced. Immediacy of reward is essential for effective shaping.

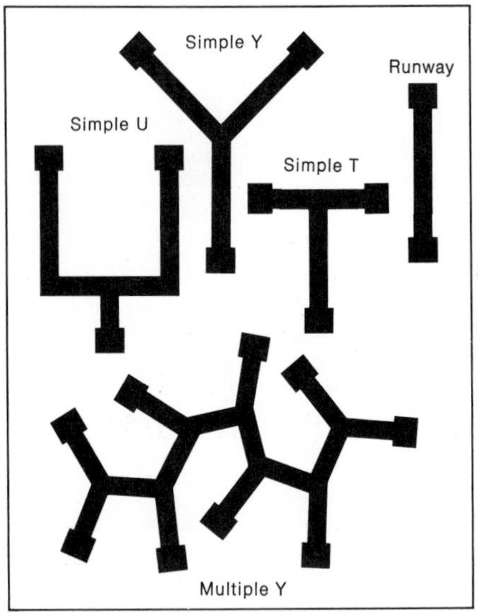

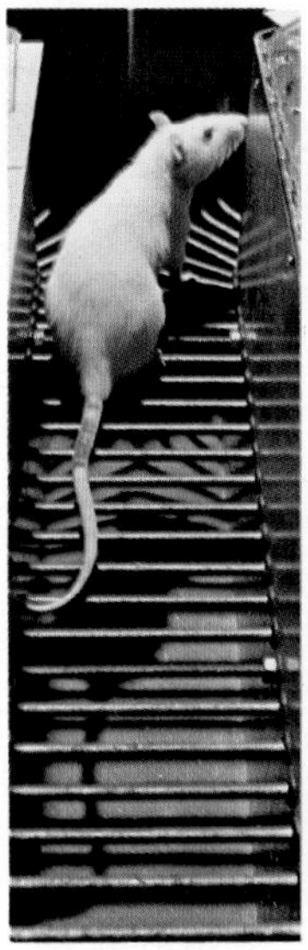

Figure 3.16
Since 1899 mazes have been used in the study of animal brain physiology and learning. One direction of research with mazes has been to identify which sensory cues are required by the animal to learn the maze. Sight, hearing, smell, and the other senses can be systematically rendered inoperative (by surgery or other means) to test whether that sense is essential. It has been found, for example, that although rats will use any sensory cue still available to them, generally no single one of the senses is required for rats to learn a maze successfully. The simple straight alley and the T-maze are two of the most common laboratory mazes. The U-maze is a T-maze modified so that an extra corner conceals each alley from the animal at the choice point. In the Y-maze the paths simply diverge at a smaller angle than in the T-maze. The multiple Y-maze involves a series of double-choice points for the animal along the route to the goal box.

Figure 3.16. In a maze, the rat runs or swims along the paths that lead to a goal box containing food. Figure 3.17 shows a typical rat's running-times on successive reinforced trials in the simplest of mazes, a straight alleyway. In a more complicated maze, not only the running-time but the number of incorrect turns that the animal makes would be recorded.

Another piece of apparatus is the jump stand, shown in Figure 3.18. The jump stand was invented by the late K. Lashley, an eminent physiological psychologist. It is used to train a rat to jump through a door that is marked in a particular way—with an X, for example. The rat's task is always to jump toward the door marked X, whether the X appears on the right door or on the left one. It usually takes some pressure, such as a squeeze of the tail, to get the rat to jump at all, but the animal usually learns which door to jump toward more quickly than it learns to run a maze. The reason is that punishment as well as reinforcement is used: The "wrong" door is locked, so that when the rat jumps toward it, it bumps its nose and falls into a net. The combination of food for jumping toward one stimulus and punishment for jumping toward the other is a very effective way to establish a discrimination rapidly.

Extinction

During shaping, why do we find a closer approximation to the desired response? Why doesn't the organism merely give up and return to whatever it was doing before

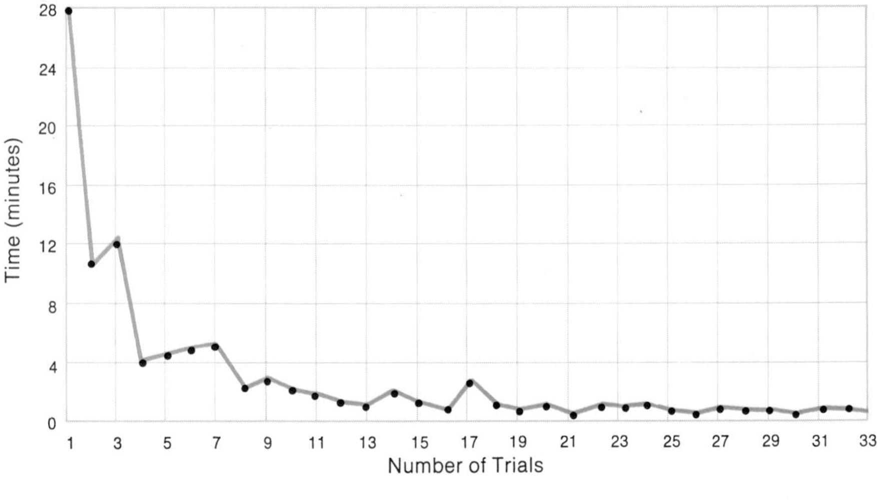

Figure 3.17
This learning curve depicts the increasingly brief periods of time required for a typical rat to traverse a simple straight alley maze. The plotted points form a decelerated, decreasing function. Note that the curve only approaches zero and will never reach zero because some time will always be consumed by the rat's running down the alley, however fast it moves.
(After Woodworth, 1921.)

Figure 3.18
(Top left) In this version of Lashley's jump stand, a puff of air from a tube leading up to the platform is used to make the rat jump, and the rat's task is to jump through the vertically striped door.

Figure 3.19
(Top) *Karl Lashley.* Lashley's work extends far beyond the invention of such apparatus as the jump stand. He is famous for his studies of the effects of cortical damage on learning in the rat.

shaping began? The behaviorist's answer to these questions involves an understanding of the effects of *extinction.*

The extinction of a behavior is brought about by withdrawing reinforcement. The main effect of withdrawing reinforcement is a decrease in the probability that the previously reinforced behavior will occur. Behavior that is no longer reinforced gradually dies out. But it does not die quietly: although the behavior gradually becomes less frequent, it is usually also executed more forcefully and in a wider variety of ways. For example, if a rat has been reinforced for lifting its forepaws slightly off the floor and then reinforcement is withdrawn, the rat lifts its paws less and less often. But the lifts that do occur are more variable and more forceful than before. Some will be high enough off the floor for the rat to press the bar, providing the experimenter with a closer approximation to the desired response.

These effects occur whenever a previously reinforced response is no longer reinforced, for people as well as for rats. Suppose a door that usually works well suddenly refuses to open. Your previously reinforced response of grasping the knob and turning it is no longer rewarded by the opening of the door. Within a few minutes, you will stop trying to get the door open. But in the meantime your responses will become more variable and more forceful than your first attempt. You

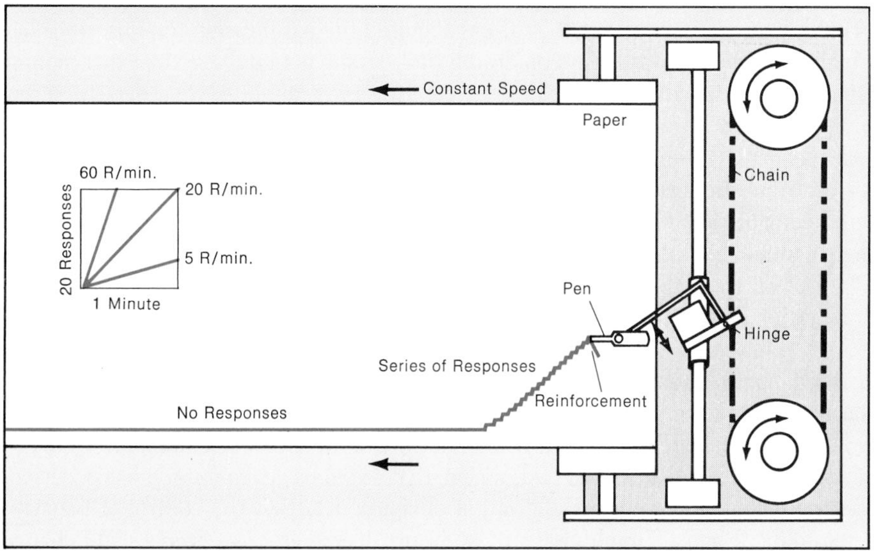

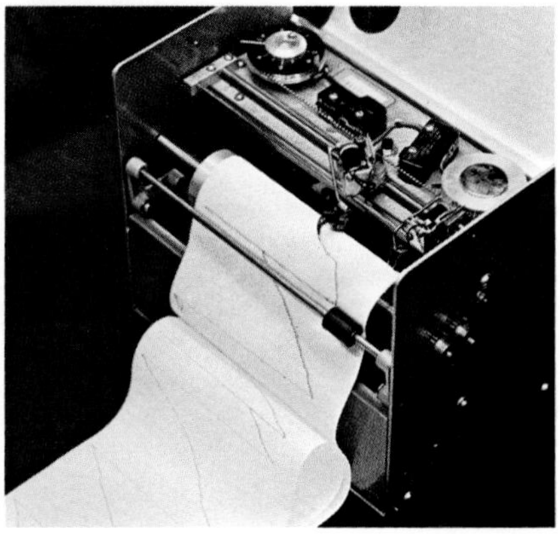

Figure 3.20
The photograph is of a cumulative recorder, widely used in operant conditioning research to record response rates. As can be seen in the diagram, each response causes the pen to step up a constant amount. Because the paper moves at a constant rate, the rate of responses determines the angle, or slope, of the recording. The inset graph in this diagram, and in the graphs on the following pages, is used to give the scale and show sample slopes corresponding to various response rates. In this example, if the inset graph were placed over the sample recording it would indicate a response rate of approximately 20 responses per minute (20R/min.)

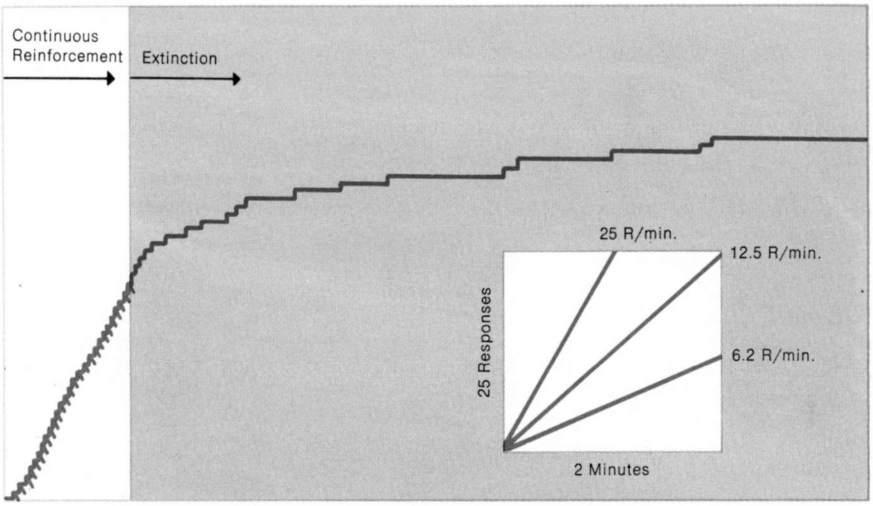

Figure 3.21
This is a record of responding made on a cumulative recorder. It shows that responses were continuously reinforced for a time and then were no longer reinforced. The withdrawal of reinforcement is called extinction, and these curves show how response rate declines in extinction. The rate can be seen from the overall angle, or slope, of the record. While reinforcement was continuous, responses were made at a high rate; the record here is steep, corresponding to the line in the inset indicating 25 responses per minute. As extinction progresses, the rate decreases. The slope of the record changes steadily toward a horizontal line, which has no slope and therefore indicates zero responding.

will probably turn the knob harder, perhaps with both hands. You may kick the door, or even go to another one—an extreme instance of variable responding. If any of these responses succeeds in getting you into the room, it will tend to persist. If none is successful, you will stop trying to open the door.

Figure 3.21 shows a typical *extinction curve:* the gradual decrease of unreinforced responding over time. Up to the point indicated by the blue line, responding was invariably rewarded with food. Then reinforcement was withheld. The responses became less frequent and eventually stopped altogether.

If an animal is removed from the experimental chamber for a while after a response has been extinguished and then put back in again, responding will occur again. This phenomenon is called *spontaneous recovery:* responding seems to recover from the effects of extinction spontaneously during the rest period outside of the chamber. The reason this happens may be that the animal is responding to situational cues. In the past it has always been reinforced for a certain behavior when it has been placed into the chamber; why not this time? Similarly, you may try the stuck door again the next time you want to get inside, even if last time you had to use a different entrance.

Stimulus Control

It was mentioned earlier that one effect of reinforcement is to bring behavior under the control of the prevailing stimuli. Extinction can also be used in establishing stimulus control. Assume that a rat has acquired the bar-pressing response and that the light in his box was always on during the training period. Now the experimenter changes the procedure so that the box is lit for a few minutes, then dark for a few minutes, then lit again, and so on, and he reinforces only bar presses that occur during periods of illumination. The rat quickly stops pressing the bar during periods of darkness. Because lever presses are not reinforced then, the response is extinguished. But the rat continues to press the lever for food when the light is on. The light comes to control responding because pressing of the bar is reinforced when it is on. In this way, reinforcement and extinction together can be used to bring a behavior under the control of specific stimuli (here, the light).

Discrimination and Generalization Now consider a pigeon whose key pecking has been reinforced in the presence of a red light. We present a green light and see whether the pigeon responds. If it does not, we say that it is *discriminating* between the two colors. If it does respond, we say that *stimulus generalization* has occurred. Both discrimination and generalization obviously relate to the control of behavior by stimuli. When a stimulus has strong control over a response, even a slight change in the stimulus will cause the animal to stop responding. When the control is not strong, the animal may continue the response despite fairly radical changes that are made in the stimulus.

Luckily for normal behavior, there are limits on the extent to which discrimination and generalization occur. An organism that carried discrimination to its logical extreme would see every event as different from every other event; a child who had been burned by fire would not hesitate to try to touch it again, since the second fire would look different from the first. On the other hand, an organism whose behavior was completely generalizable would react in exactly the same way to all situations.

Generalization usually occurs only within a stimulus dimension; interdimensional generalization is much less usual. That is, a pigeon trained to make a particular response to a red light may respond the same way to any colored light, but it probably will not make the response to the sound of a bell. As for discrimination, its theoretical limit is reached when two stimuli are so nearly alike that telling the difference is beyond the organism's biological capacities. For example, no known organism can tell the difference between a tone with a frequency of 5,000 cycles per second and a tone with a frequency of 5,001 cycles per second. In practice, stimulus control is rarely as precise as an organism's discriminative capacities would permit.

When an animal fails to respond differently to two different stimuli, that does not necessarily mean that the animal cannot distinguish between the two. If an animal has been reinforced for responding in the presence of a white light, it will generally also respond (though perhaps less often) in the presence of a similar stimulus such as a green light. This behavior may mean that the animal cannot tell the difference between the white and the green lights, or it may mean that the animal is responding to the brightness of the light, say, rather than to its color. If the pigeon has learned to respond to the brightness of the white light, it will also respond to other lights on the basis of their brightness, not their color. What an animal does depends not only on the distinctions it is capable of making but on the distinctions it has learned to attend to.

In a typical laboratory study of stimulus control, two pigeons are reinforced for responding in the presence of light A. Then one of the birds receives *discrimination training:* light A alternates with light B, and responses are not reinforced while light B is on. Figure 3.22 shows that responding in the presence of light B decreases as training proceeds.

Next, each pigeon is given a generalization test consisting of a series of different-

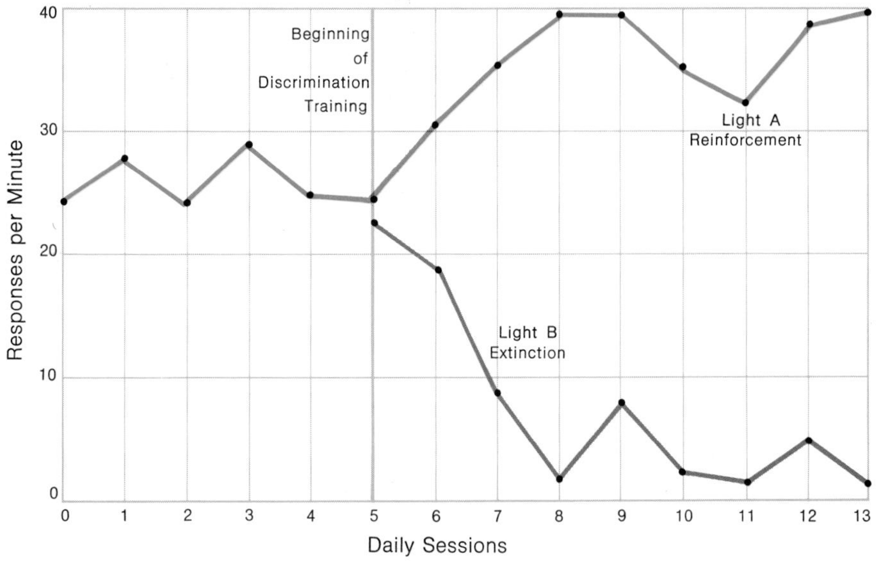

Figure 3.22
Development of an operant discrimination. The pigeon pecks at a fairly constant rate in each session as long as only light A is present. Light B is then introduced, and pecking is never reinforced in its presence. The divergence of response rates in the presence of the different stimuli shows that the pigeon discriminates between the two.

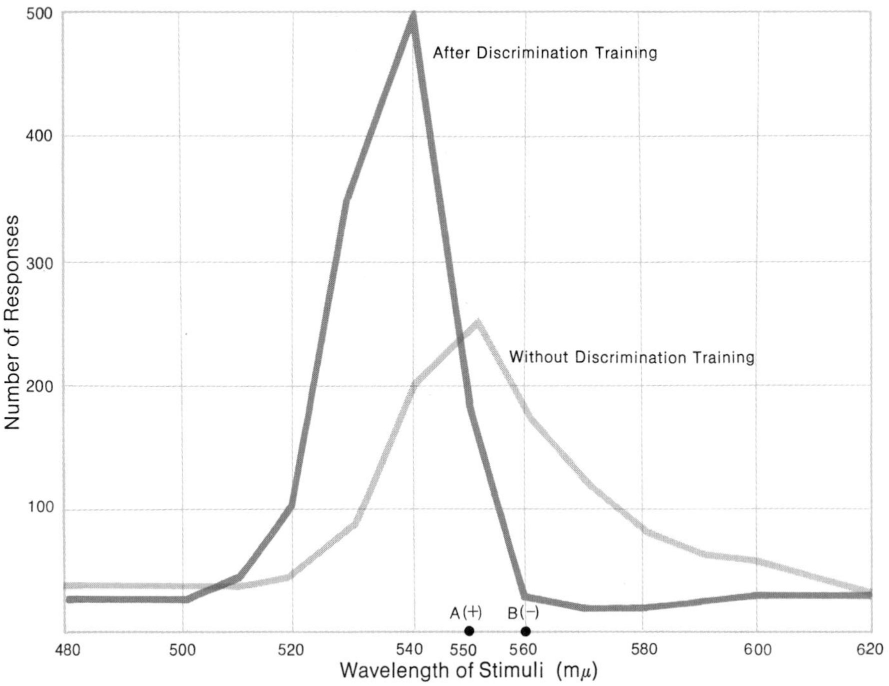

Figure 3.23
The results of generalization tests on two birds. One had received discrimination training (blue curve) on lights A and B, and the other (green curve) had seen only light A. In the test, lights of many different wavelengths were shown, and the number of responses the birds made to each were counted. (After Hanson, 1959.)

colored lights, including A and B. During the generalization test, responding is not reinforced even when light A is on. The animal's response is being extinguished, and eventually all responding will stop. What the experimenter is interested in is the number of responses the animal makes in the presence of each light before extinction is complete. Figure 3.23 shows the results of a typical experiment of this kind. The amount of responding is plotted along the ordinate; the color of the lights is plotted along the abscissa. The resulting curve is called a *generalization gradient*. The peak of the generalization gradient is nearly at the point that corresponds to light A. The less similar the stimulus is to light A, the less the animal responds. The pigeon that did not receive discrimination training produces a wider and flatter generalization gradient than the bird that received discrimination training. This fact points up an important and well-documented finding: the effect of discrimination training is to sharpen and strengthen stimulus control.

On the other hand, there is an anomaly in Figure 3.23. The animals that had been given discrimination training responded most often not to light A but to a light with a slightly lower wavelength than light A. This phenomenon, called the *peak shift,* commonly occurs during discrimination training. Responses shift away from the stimulus associated with nonreinforcement (in this case, light B). If training is continued beyond the time that the animal seems to have learned the discrimination, the peak shift gradually disappears. Overtraining is a factor that seems to have many important effects on learning; it will be discussed further in Chapter 4.

Conditioned Reinforcement Although generalization and discrimination are important illustrations of stimulus control, another kind of stimulus control is even more central to behaviorist explanations of learning. As discussed in the section on the shaping of behavior, *conditioned reinforcers* are invaluable tools in the direction and control of behavior. A conditioned reinforcer is a stimulus that acts as a signal for the presentation of a reinforcer. For example, the clicking sound of food dropping into the food cup in a Skinner box is a conditioned reinforcer: it signals the arrival of the primary reinforcer, food. An experimenter can use this sound to direct and control the behavior of the animal because the sound occurs immediately after the desired response, before the animal has had time to perform another behavior.

If it were not for conditioned reinforcers, primary reinforcers would be effective only when there was no delay between the response to be reinforced and the primary reinforcer.

The power of conditioned reinforcers is suggested by some classic experiments with chimpanzees. J. B. Wolfe has shown that chimps can be trained to perform tasks in order to obtain tokens, which the chimp uses to buy food from a machine called a Chimp-O-Mat (see Figure 3.24). The most important conclusion stemming from experiments with the Chimp-O-Mat is that the conditioned reinforcers—the tokens—will bridge very long delays between the performance of the task and the onset of the primary reinforcer, food. Without the token, even small delays between the performance of the task and the arrival of food make the chimp reluctant to continue performing the task.

In experiments of this kind, the effect of the tokens is clear and dramatic, but the mechanism by which they operate is not nearly so clear. In recent years many people have called into question whether the tokens can legitimately be called conditioned *reinforcers*. Do they truly have a reinforcing function of their own, or does their effect depend entirely on the fact that they are signals for the primary reinforcer? People use money in much the same way as the chimps used the tokens. But when a currency has lost its value, as happened in several European countries during the Great Depression, people quickly stop using it and revert to trading the essential goods (such as food) that the money formerly bought. When money loses its signal value, it quickly loses its apparently reinforcing effect.

D. Premack has argued that difficulties of this sort arise only because of inadequacies in the traditional definitions of reinforcement. Chapter 4 discusses his proposal for solving these problems.

Figure 3.24
Just as children are expected to "learn the value of money," a chimp can learn the value of poker chips, which serve as token reinforcers. The chips can be used to operate the Chimp-o-mat, which delivers food, a primary reinforcer, much the way a gum machine delivers gum balls for your penny. The chimp will do complex tasks (work) to gain tokens, and he may save them to spend much later. The chimp's chip, like our coins and paper money, is worth very little intrinsically, but it too acquires considerable symbolic value.

SCHEDULES OF REINFORCEMENT

Starting with the work of C. B. Ferster and B. F. Skinner, much important research has been done on the ways that various *schedules of reinforcement* affect behavior. Reinforcement can be delivered every time an animal performs a desired response, or it can be delivered intermittently—for every tenth response, say, or every ten minutes regardless of the number of responses the animal has made during that time.

If you have ever taught a dog to shake hands, you have some experience with what happens to an animal's behavior under different reinforcement schedules. While you were training the dog, you probably reinforced handshaking every time it occurred, beginning with rather rough approximations and leading the animal gradually toward a more expert performance (shaping). The best way to establish a new behavior is to reinforce it each time it occurs. Once it has been established, however, the dog will perform it more often if you switch to an intermittent schedule. For example, a dog that knows how to shake hands may approach you from time to time and offer its paw. If you respond by taking the paw and praising the dog, it is likely to wag its tail and go away. But if you ignore this first attempt, the dog may try to shake hands several more times in quick succession. Continuing to ignore the attempt will bring on extinction, but if you stop short of that and simply reinforce every few tries, you can probably keep the behavior going at quite a high, steady rate for a few minutes.

Of the four reinforcement schedules most often used in behavioral research, two are based on the number of correct responses that the organism makes between reinforcements, and two on the amount of time that elapses. The two based on number of responses are called the *fixed-ratio schedule* and the *variable-ratio schedule*. The two based on time are called the *fixed-interval schedule* and the *variable-interval schedule*. In laboratory studies of such behavior as bar pressing by rats and key pecking by pigeons, the experimenter usually programs automatic equipment to deliver reinforcement according to the schedule he has selected; in general, the equipment can provide reinforcement much more rapidly and accurately than a human being.

Ratio Schedules

On a fixed-ratio schedule, a certain number of responses are required for reinforcement. The simplest fixed-ratio schedule is continuous reinforcement, in which every correct response is rewarded. Continuous reinforcement is usually used to establish a new behavior. After the animal has learned the behavior, it can easily be shifted to a 2:1 ratio. That is, the response can be maintained by delivering reinforcement every other time the animal performs it. Or the experimenter can try a 50:1 fixed-ratio schedule, rewarding every fiftieth correct response, or a 100:1 schedule, and so on.

One effect of this schedule is that the animal quickly learns approximately how many responses it must make to get the reward. After reinforcement, it will often pause before it begins to respond again, but once it begins to respond, it will rapidly make the required number of responses.

For this reason, experimenters often prefer a variable-ratio schedule. An animal on a 50:1 variable-ratio schedule is rewarded for every fiftieth response *on the average;* sometimes the tenth response is reinforced, sometimes the eighty-first, and so on. A variable-ratio schedule makes it very difficult for the animal to tell when the next reinforcement is coming and therefore keeps him responding at a high rate without pauses.

Interval Schedules

Interval schedules are defined in terms of the time that elapses between one reinforced response and the next. Like ratio schedules, interval schedules can be fixed or variable. To illustrate, a pigeon on a twenty-second fixed-interval schedule is reinforced for the first key-peck that occurs twenty seconds or more after the last reinforced peck. A pigeon on a twenty-second variable-interval schedule is reinforced for the first key peck that occurs on an average of twenty seconds or more after the last reinforced peck, but the interval is sometimes five seconds, sometimes forty, sometimes fifteen seconds, and so on.

Figure 3.25
An illustration of the cumulative record of responses typically produced by an animal whose reinforcements are being delivered on a variable-ratio schedule. The responding is characteristically at a very high and nearly constant rate.

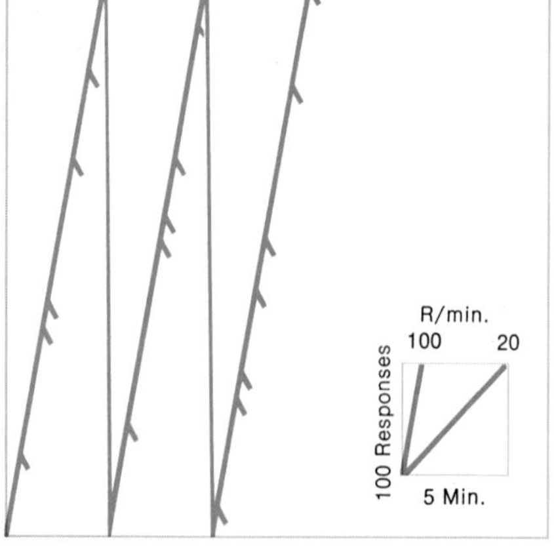

Response Patterns

Each of these simple schedules of reinforcement produces a different pattern of responding. From an analysis of the variables responsible for the differences, it is possible to learn a great deal about the control of behavior under laboratory conditions. It is also instructive to compare the behavior of animals in the laboratory with the behavior of people confronted with similar schedules in everyday life. In some cases, what has been learned about why animals behave as they do may shed some light on human behavior.

The variable-ratio schedule maintains an extremely high rate of responding. If the key pecks of a pigeon are reinforced with food on a variable-ratio schedule, they occur at as high a rate as 200 per minute, or more than three pecks a second (see Figure 3.25). Occasionally the bird even pecks on the key during reinforcement, in preference to eating. The high rate is not difficult to explain: the faster the animal pecks, the more often it is rewarded, because number of responses (rather than amount of time) is responsible for reinforcement.

People are reinforced on variable ratios in a variety of situations. For example, consider the slot machine, or one-armed bandit. These machines are set to deliver reinforcement on an average of every nth play. The value of n is chosen by the owner of the machine so that the amount paid out in reinforcement is adequately balanced by the amount the players pay for the privilege of pulling down the arm of the machine. The payoffs do not occur after the same number of plays each time. The

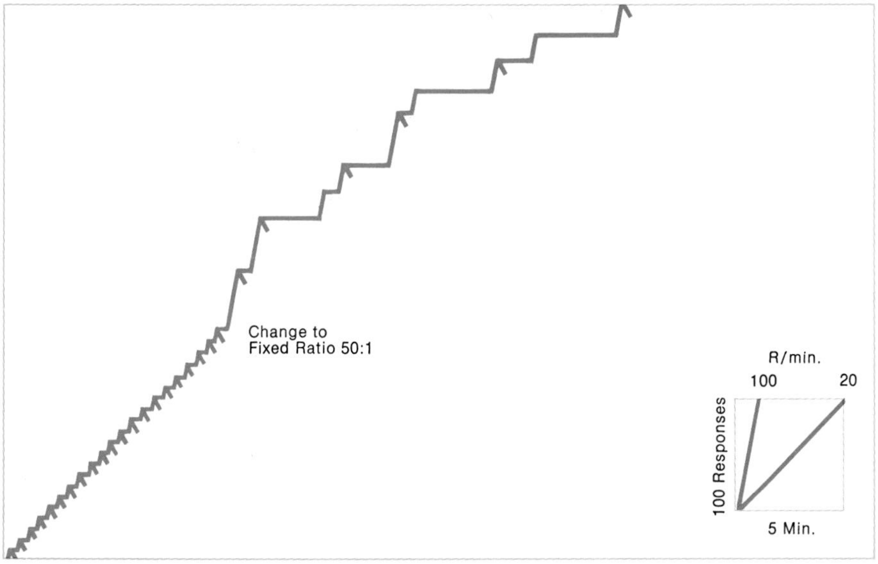

Figure 3.26

A cumulative record generated by a fixed-ratio reinforcement schedule, where reinforcement is delivered after every fiftieth response. Performance on a fixed-ratio schedule is characterized by a high rate of responding. There is sometimes a brief pause following a reinforcement, then responses rapidly return to the high rate.

variable schedule helps conceal the fact that slot machines take in more money than they give out, and it also prevents fights around the machine, which would surely erupt if the schedule were fixed. Some gamblers play slot machines at the same high rate and with the same dedication that pigeons show in pecking for grain on a variable-ratio schedule.

Fixed-ratio schedules also generate extremely high rates of responding, high enough to rival those produced by a variable-ratio schedule. If fixed ratios are too large, however, there will not be a *continuous* high rate of responding. Figure 3.26 shows what happened to a pigeon's key pecking when the ratio was increased from 10:1 to 50:1. Just after the increase in the number of pecks required for reinforcement, the bird performed the fifty responses without a pause. Soon, however, pauses appeared during the running off of the ratio. What this means in practice is that lengthening the ratio increases the likelihood of pauses during performance.

Interval schedules of reinforcement, which are defined in terms of the time elapsed since the last reinforced response, are quite a different story. They generate much lower rates of responding, overall, than do ratio schedules. The main reason the response rate is lower is that rapid responding does not increase the frequency of reinforcement. No response is reinforced until the specified interval has passed.

A fixed-interval schedule of reinforcement produces two slightly different patterns of responding. One pattern is the "scallop" shown in Figure 3.27A. At the beginning of the interval there are very few responses. As time passes, the response rate gradually increases, reaching a peak just before reinforcement. The second pattern, called break-and-run responding, is shown in Figure 3.27B. Here, too, responding begins at a very low rate, but instead of increasing gradually, it continues at the low rate until about two-thirds of the way through the interval. At that point it suddenly increases to a high rate, which is maintained until reinforcement is obtained. The exact point at which the high rate of responding begins varies somewhat from interval to interval. According to B. A. Schneider, the scallop pattern probably occurs early in training, whereas the break-and-run pattern seems to appear after overtraining. In both cases, the low rate of responding right after reinforcement occurs because responses are never reinforced at that time. The high rate of responding at the end of the interval occurs because the time for reinforcement is approaching. Since the organism cannot tell exactly how much time has passed, it pecks at a high rate until reinforcement is delivered.

Examples of pure fixed-interval schedules are not common in everyday life, but schedules that have similar properties do occur. For example, universities usually

Figure 3.27

Two typical cumulative records of a pigeon's responses on a fixed-interval schedule of reinforcement. The fixed-interval schedule yields two different patterns—either the "scallop" pattern in the top figure or the "break and run" pattern in the lower figure. Both learning curves indicate that the bird has developed the discrimination between when reinforcement is likely to occur (near the end of the time period) and when reinforcement will not be delivered (soon after reinforcement).

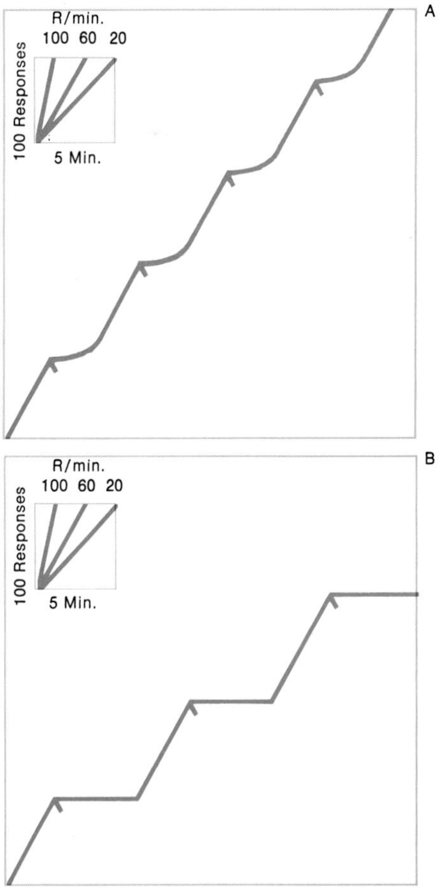

give examinations on a regular basis, at the end of every semester or every quarter. In this case the reinforcement is academic success, or lack of failure; the response is studying. Studying tends to begin rather slowly and then to increase as the semester continues. Just before the exam period it may reach a very high rate.

Variable-interval schedules dispense reinforcement after a variable period of time has elapsed since the last reinforced response. They are comparable to an exam schedule in which tests are given three or four times a year at unpredictable intervals. Under these conditions studying usually occurs at a relatively constant rate. Something similar happens with pigeons in a Skinner box. They peck the key at a relatively constant rate throughout the variable intervals between reinforcements. Figure 3.28 shows a typical behavior pattern maintained by a variable-interval schedule.

Schedules of reinforcement affect behavior not only while reinforcements are being presented but also during extinction. Figure 3.29 shows typical extinction patterns for the four schedules of reinforcement that have been described.

There are more elaborate reinforcement schedules than these four, of course. Some require a slow response rate; others make a high rate an absolute precondition

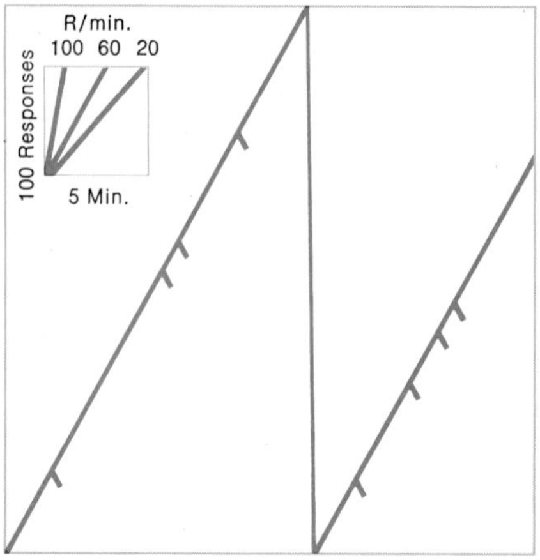

Figure 3.28

(Above) A typical cumulative record of an animal's responses when its reinforcements are being delivered on a variable-interval schedule. Although this schedule produces a relatively constant rate of responding, the rate is not as high as that obtained with a variable-ratio schedule. Note that after a reinforcement is delivered, there is a pause in responding, as with a fixed-interval schedule, but the pauses here are much shorter than those shown by animals on the fixed-interval schedule.

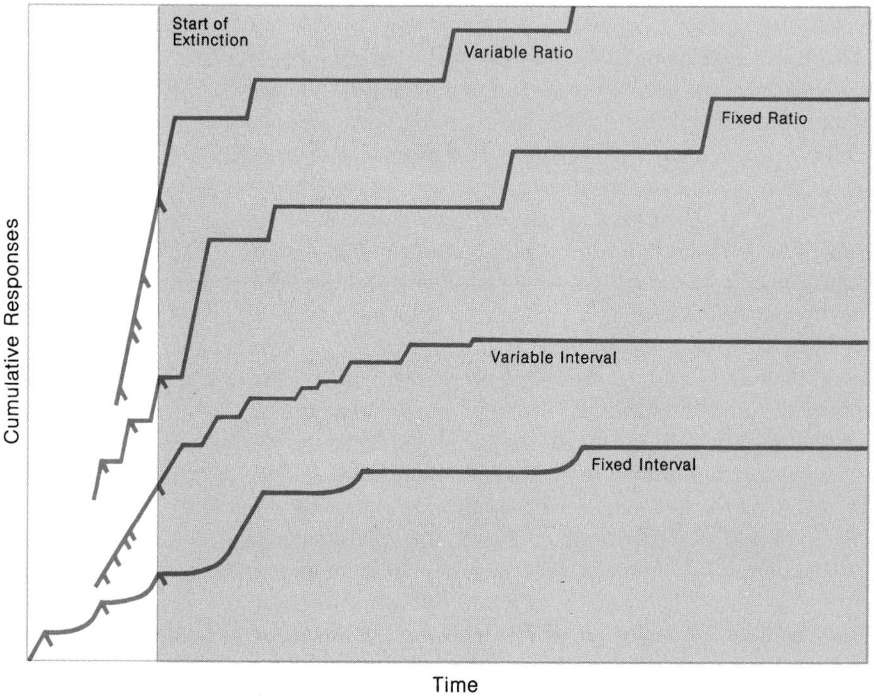

Figure 3.29

Response-rate slopes and typical extinction patterns recorded for each of the noncontinuous reinforcement schedules discussed. Note that the pattern of responding during extinction continues to resemble the response patterns characteristic of each type of schedule.

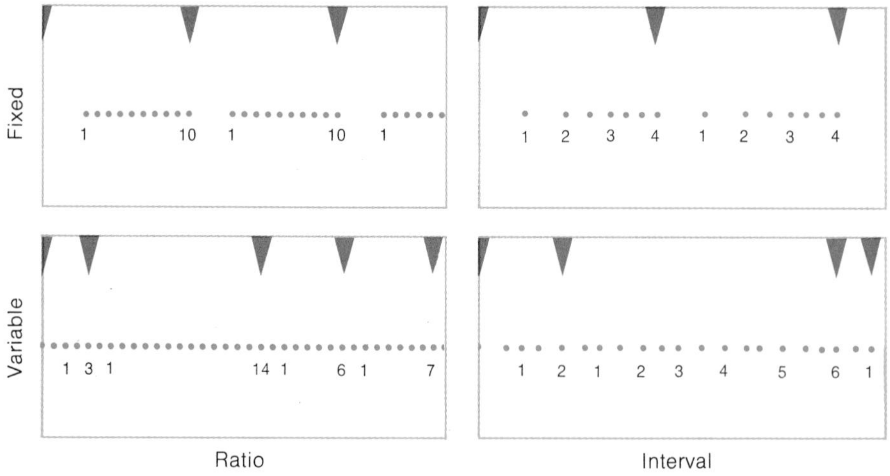

Figure 3.30

Comparison of patterns of response under the four basic schedules of intermittent reinforcement: fixed-ratio, fixed-interval, variable-ratio, and variable-interval. Each of the dots indicates a single response; each orange triangle represents an occasion of reinforcement.

of reinforcement. The latter can yield rates of responding that exceed even those produced by a variable-ratio schedule. The possible variations in behavior that schedules of reinforcement can produce are endless; they are just beginning to be investigated, and the technology of behavior based on them is still embryonic.

AVERSIVE CONTROL

Most of the techniques described so far have relied on food, money, or similar positive reinforcers. Other techniques have been developed that use aversive stimulation, such as electric shock. Before discussing aversive control, we need to distinguish between two terms that frequently lead to confusion: *punishment* and *negative reinforcement.* In punishment, a stimulus or event *decreases* the frequency of occurrence of the behavior that it follows. Negative reinforcement is often used as a synonym for punishment, but that is an error. Negative reinforcement is a type of reinforcement; consequently, unlike punishment, it leads to an *increase* in the frequency of a response. For example, a rat can be required to run in a running wheel in order to turn off an electric shock. In a case of this kind, where a response *removes* an electric shock, the response will increase in frequency, and the removal of the shock is the negative reinforcement. In a different experimental set-up, running in the running wheel might *produce* shock. In that case, the response will be suppressed; the shock is used to punish the response.

Escape

Escape conditioning is a technique that employs negative reinforcement: an animal performs the response that turns off the aversive stimulation. Escape conditioning proceeds rather rapidly; less shaping is usually required to establish an escape response than to establish a response with positive reinforcement. It is tempting to conclude from this fact that negative reinforcers are more potent than positive reinforcers, but such a conclusion would be hard to defend. A certain level of aversive stimulation may be more potent in motivating a response than a certain amount of food, but different levels of electric shock, amounts of food, and degrees of hunger would lead to the opposite conclusion.

There is another explanation for the rapidity of shaping with aversive stimulation. Aversive stimulation often produces a great amount of activity in the animal, enhancing the probability that it will make the correct response in a given period of time. Consider the rat in Figure 3.31, which receives shock when current is passed through the grid on the floor of its box. When shock is applied, the rat jumps around excitedly, providing the experimenter with a wide selection of behavior from which to choose a response that closely approximates the desired response—for example, bar pressing. The response is reinforced by turning off the shock. The maintenance of behavior under an escape procedure appears to be substantially the same as it is with positive reinforcement. It should be noted, however, that relatively little research has been done on schedules of negative reinforcement.

Figure 3.31
The grid this rat is jumping clear of is designed to deliver electric shocks. The rat is a subject in a learning experiment. As it comes close to performing the response set for it by the experimenter (bar pressing or the like), it will be rewarded with negative reinforcement, that is, cessation of shock. (Shock is the aversive stimulus.) During each trial the rat must come closer to the desired behavior, until it can repeat the behavior many times on cue. Shaping of behavior with aversive stimulation and negative reinforcement appears to be accomplished more rapidly than with other means of conditioning.

Avoidance

Avoidance conditioning is similar to escape conditioning, but the seemingly minor differences between the two produce very different behavioral effects in some animals. A rat, for example, can easily learn to press a bar to escape shock. But when presented with a signal (such as a light) that shock is about to be delivered, it has great difficulty learning to press a bar to avoid the shock.

R. C. Bolles has suggested an explanation for findings of this sort. Most animals have a small number of fixed action patterns that are evoked by aversive stimulation. In the rat, one of them is to flee and another is to freeze. The presentation of shock during escape conditioning elicits high activity—the fleeing pattern. But the presentation of the light during avoidance conditioning usually elicits freezing. In response

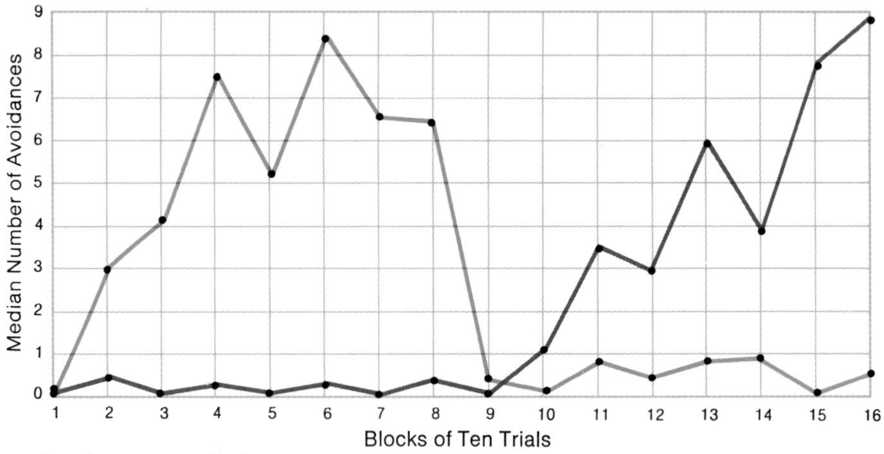

Figure 3.32
An increasing amount of research points to a relationship between "natural" behaviors and how easily animals can learn new behaviors. These data show the interaction between "natural" responses, or fixed action patterns, and experimental conditions. Rats naturally tend to either freeze or flee in anticipation of shock. In the general natural response area of "flee," the rat can learn certain escape behaviors. But once the general natural response area becomes "freeze," it does not respond. The surprising drop in response strength in rats that had learned to run to another cage and press a bar to avoid shock (orange line) after the "flee"-"freeze" conditions were reversed supports the importance of natural behaviors in learning.
(After Fantino, Sharp, and Cole, 1966.)

to the danger signal, the rat stands immobile and rigid; consequently, it does not readily engage in the behavior necessary for a press on the bar.

Even in response to a danger signal, however, the rat may run—if there is someplace for it to run to. Surprisingly, it is easier for a rat to learn to avoid shock if it must first run and then press a bar than if it must merely press the bar. Figure 3.32 shows this effect. The rats whose bar presses are represented by the purple line were given eighty trials in which they had five seconds to press a lever to avoid shock. Plainly, they did not learn to do so. But the animals whose bar presses are represented by the orange curve rapidly learned to avoid shock on most trials. Instead of just pressing a bar, they had to run from one box to another and press a lever in the second box.

After the eightieth trial the requirements for the two groups were reversed. The group that was now required to run learned quickly to press the bar in the second box, as would be expected from the other group's performance. But the rats that had already learned to avoid shock by running and pressing no longer pressed the bar when they were not required to run first. Confined in the small space of the one box, they apparently froze.

These findings indicate the importance of considering species-specific behavior (see Chapter 2) even when training animals in the laboratory. An animal—or a person—can learn more easily when the response required of him is a natural one.

Punishment

Punishment lowers the probability of a response that it follows. To study punishment in any detail, it is usually necessary to punish a response that is being maintained by some positive reinforcer. Otherwise, there will be no reason for the animal to continue responding, and a few punishments will virtually eliminate the response, leaving little for study. Figure 3.33 shows how varying degrees of punishment affect the frequency of a response that is simultaneously maintained with a food reinforcer.

Although punishment will eliminate undesirable behavior or at least reduce its frequency, it is often a poor method of control because it has undesirable side effects. It is intrinsically unpleasant, and in addition it can encourage escape or avoidance responses. A person who is educated by punishment may avoid educational institutions altogether.

There are other methods for eliminating behavior that do not have these undesirable side effects. One is to use positive reinforcement to condition behavior that is incompatible with the unwanted behavior. For example, instead of attempting to eliminate stuttering by punishing it, a parent or teacher can reinforce smooth speech. Another method is to try to avoid the need to punish incorrect behavior by ensuring from the start that only correct behavior occurs. This usually requires careful initial shaping of behavior and the elimination of opportunities to perform

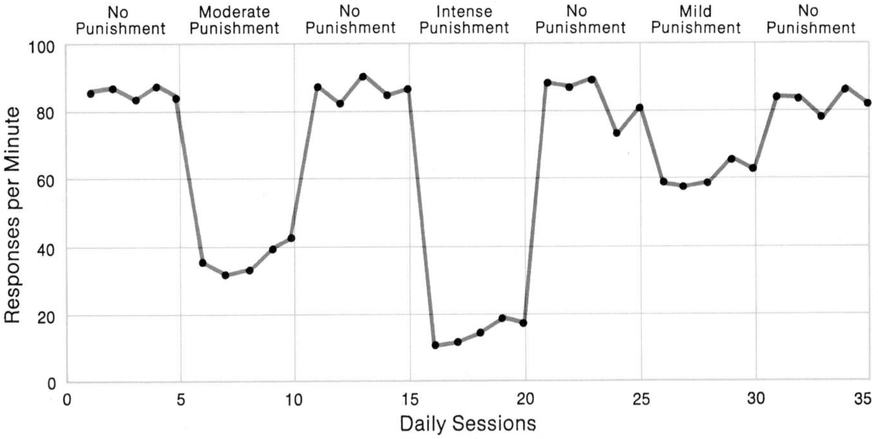

Figure 3.33
The effects of various punishment conditions on response rate. The response was at the same time being maintained by positive reinforcement, which accounts for the fact that the response persisted (although at a lower rate) in the face of aversive stimulation. Note that the reduction in response rate is directly proportional to the intensity of the contingent punishment.
(After Reynolds, 1968.)

the undesired response. If a puppy is never allowed near streets except when he is under the control of his master, then it will be easy to train him to cross only at his master's command. He will never have had the opportunity to learn to run into the street by himself. Many such behavioral techniques have been adapted for use in education and psychotherapy. Some of them are discussed in Chapter 33.

SUGGESTED READINGS

BORING, E. *A History of Experimental Psychology.* New York, Appleton-Century-Crofts, 1950. The definitive book on the history of the various branches of experimental psychology, including both behaviorism and the introspectionist approach.

HILGARD, E. R., AND BOWER, G. H. *Theories of Learning* (3rd ed.). New York, Appleton-Century-Crofts, 1966. A systematic treatment of major behaviorist theories of learning and also of some nonbehaviorist theories.

HONIG, W. H. (Ed.). *Operant Behavior: Areas of Research and Application.* New York, Appleton-Century-Crofts, 1966. A collection of papers discussing both recent research on and practical applications of Skinner's operant techniques.

KIMBLE, G. A. *Hilgard and Marquis' Conditioning and Learning* (2nd ed.). New York, Appleton-Century-Crofts, 1961. An excellent summary and discussion of behaviorist research on learning.

PAVLOV, I. P. *Conditioned Reflexes,* G. V. Anrep (Tr.). London, Oxford University Press, 1927. A definitive statement of Pavlov's work, this book is the translation of a series of lectures given in 1924 in which Pavlov summarized his research and theory.

REYNOLDS, G. S. *A Primer of Operant Conditioning.* Glenview, Ill., Scott, Foresman and Company, 1968. A brief but thorough account of the theory and principles of operant conditioning, as developed from the work of B. F. Skinner and his students.

SKINNER, B. F. *The Behavior of Organisms.* New York, Appleton-Century-Crofts, 1961. The book in which Skinner first spelled out his approach to learning.

———. *Walden Two.* New York, Macmillan, 1948. A novel outlining a utopian society where behavior is programmed according to Skinner's analysis of learning by reinforcement.

WATSON, J. B. *Behaviorism.* New York, Norton, 1930. An introduction to behaviorism by the man who founded it.

4

The Organization of Behavior

I ONCE HAD LUNCH with an editor and spent part of the time telling jokes (an activity in which I frequently engage). The question arose, then, of who it might be who made up all these jokes, and the editor said, "Why don't you write a story about it?" So I did, and it was published under the title of "Jokester."

Actually, many people make up jokes. In addition, old jokes are deliberately adapted to new circumstances or are more or less accidentally adjusted and distorted as they pass from mouth to mouth. In fact, I've made up some jokes myself and modified many others. However, such mundane origins wouldn't do for a science fiction story. Instead, I thought of rats being sent through mazes, made to manipulate bars, made to change and unchange their habits. *We* know why we have them do it: we gain some insight into problems of human behavior. But if a rat could think, what would *it* make out of the whole thing? What meaning could it find in these procedures?

So I began my story with a computer technician who was curious over the exact point raised by my editor. Who made up jokes? Why did human beings tell each other jokes so assiduously? Why did they laugh? What pleasure did they get out of it? The technician told jokes of all kinds to his computer and read into its memory banks various books and papers dealing with theories of humor, or with analyses of what made people laugh. When he had fed in all he considered relevant, he directed the computer to analyze all the information it had gained and feed back the most probable origin for jokes generally.

And the computer decided that the whole system of jokes used by mankind was devised by an extra-terrestrial research team intent on studying the behavior of mankind for the same reasons our own psychologists are so intent on studying the behavior of rats. We do it so that we might learn material applicable to our own behavior (which is what interests us most), and the extra-terrestrials were doing it so that they might gain insights into *their* own behavior. By feeding jokes of various kinds to us, by studying the results, the intensity of laughter, the kind of modifications the jokes produced, they were gaining information of value. It may not have been clear to humans just what the value could possibly be—but, then, do rats understand the value of running mazes or pressing bars?

As soon as the matter was solved in this fashion, however, my computer-expert hero grew solemn. After all, behavior tests of this sort are useful only insofar as the objects being experimented on are unaware of the fact that they are being tested. If rats were intelligent enough to understand what we were doing with our mazes, they might, in irritation or for fun, deliberately behave in such a manner as to allow us to make no sense at all of the results. We would then have to switch to some new kind of test they did not understand.

My hero in the story therefore realized two things:

1. He would never hear another joke. Neither would any other human being. In fact, no one might ever laugh again.

2. Worse yet, some new test would be applied to mankind, and he hadn't the faintest idea what it might be, except that it would certainly be far more subtle than joke telling—and might well be far less pleasant.

I. A.

Besides providing a general intellectual base for the field of psychology, Darwin's theory of evolution has influenced the specific theories that psychologists have developed. The field of ethology grew out of Darwin's notion of species-specific behavior, and behaviorism developed in part because Darwin's theory implied that the mind is subject to the same sorts of biological laws as the body.

The theory of natural selection was an especially influential model for psychological theory. Evolution, Darwin said, takes place because animals whose make-up is well suited to their environment are more likely to survive than other animals. As a consequence, animals with specific traits that help them adapt to their environment are "naturally selected" over a series of generations. For example, giraffes evolved long necks because those with slightly longer necks had a selective advantage in reaching food. Psychologists have developed a direct analogue of natural selection:

Figure 4.1
Donald Hebb is an eminent neuropsychologist whose research has included study of the physiological correlates of learning and the process of directed thinking. In *The Organization of Behavior,* which has become a classic in psychology, he theorizes that experience with simple stimuli causes a group of interconnected neurons to form a cell assembly, and that further experience causes cell assemblies to combine in complex arrangements called phase sequences. Thus, learning results in organization at the physiological level, which, in turn, affects the organization of behavior.

the concept of reinforcement. Reinforcement selects for adaptive behaviors, just as survival selects for adaptive species characteristics.

But the theory of natural selection, although influential in generating other theories, has also proved to be restrictive. In evolution a trait is selected for survival because it fulfills a specific *function;* that is, it helps an animal adapt to its environment in some way. The function of the long neck of the giraffe is to reach food. Similarly, psychologists—especially behaviorists—have concentrated on the function of behaviors. A pigeon learns to peck because it needs food. A person looks both ways before crossing the street so that he will not be killed by an automobile.

The emphasis on a behavior's function has sometimes led to a failure to describe the behavior itself. In the words of one psychologist, many behaviorists do not study the behavior of animals; they study the behavior of Skinner boxes. In recent years, especially since the publication in 1949 of *The Organization of Behavior* by D. O. Hebb, this one-sidedness has begun to be corrected. Psychologists have become increasingly interested in studying not only the function of behavior but also its *structure* or organization. They want to know what the components of a specific behavior are, how the components interrelate, and how the various behaviors in an organism's repertoire interrelate. Of course, there have always been some psychologists who were concerned with the organization of behavior. Many ethologists, for example, have painstakingly described the organization of species-specific behaviors, as discussed in Chapter 2. Many cognitive psychologists have studied the organization of thinking, with results that will be described in Units II and III. But recent investigations of organization have a different emphasis than older studies, producing both new findings and new perspectives on old findings.

To investigate the organization of behavior, one must start with a behavior or set of behaviors that is relatively stable. With unstable or fleeting behaviors it would be difficult to study the behavior long enough to detect its organization. For that reason, most research on the organization of behavior analyzes either fixed action patterns (such as eating, drinking, and running) or overlearned responses (responses that an animal has practiced beyond the point of apparent mastery). This chapter will discuss three different aspects of the organization of stable behaviors: (1) how stable responses are related to each other and how their relationships determine what will act as a reinforcement; (2) what happens to an animal's behavior when a stable response is disrupted; and (3) what happens to behavior as a new response is acquired and then practiced until it becomes stable.

A STRUCTURAL INTERPRETATION OF REINFORCEMENT

First let us look at how the concept of reinforcement changes when our focus shifts to the organization of behavior. Consider a recent experiment by A. J. Neuringer that poses problems for traditional reinforcement theory. A pigeon was placed in a special experimental box (see Figure 4.2) where it would live for several weeks. On one side of the box was a bar that the pigeon could press in order to obtain food. On the other side of the box was a food cup from which the pigeon could eat anytime it chose. The pigeon could press the bar for food, eat food from the cup, or both. It quickly learned to eat from the cup full of food and consequently was never very hungry. Since it was not hungry, there was no apparent reason for it to learn to press the bar for food. But it *did* learn to press the bar, without food deprivation or training, and it continued to do so regularly during the several weeks it spent in the experimental box. In other words, the pigeon both ate food from the cup and pressed the bar for food, which it then ate.

Figure 4.2
This is a sketch of the appartus Neuringer used to show that animals will learn to "work" for food even when it is freely available. Grain was available to this pigeon in the cup to the left. It could obtain brief access to grain through the hole in the right wall by treading on the lever beneath.

After the animal had been pressing the bar for many days, Neuringer instituted an extinction procedure to see whether the behavior would continue if it no longer produced food. The pigeon's bar pressing immediately became less frequent and quickly approached zero, showing that the behavior did depend on the production of food. The pigeon pressed the bar for food, not for fun, and it did so even though it could get the same kind of food from the food cup without working for it. Traditional learning theories have some difficulties explaining these findings.

Recurrent Behaviors

One way of viewing Neuringer's findings is as a special case of a phenomenon demonstrated by D. Premack. Premack placed an animal in a cage supplied with free food and water and performed what he called an "anti-experiment." That is, he did nothing at all to the animal; he merely observed its behavior.

Premack found that, under these circumstances, certain behavior patterns recurred many times each day. The rats repeatedly groomed themselves, ran in a running wheel that was in the cage, drank water, ate food, and so forth. Premack carefully recorded each of these *recurrent behaviors* and tried to describe its general characteristics. He found that each occurrence of a given behavior followed a similar pattern. For one thing, the animal went through a stereotyped series of movements each time it carried out the behavior. For another, responses tended to occur in "bursts." The animals did not perform one grooming response, then one eating response, and so on, but spent some time grooming once they had started, repeating the response over and over.

Finally (and most important), the frequency of responding for each type of behavior was about the same from day to day, as long as the animal remained in the same situation. This allowed Premack to rank the behaviors in order of their probability of occurrence in a given situation, as shown in Table 4.1. In one situation eating might be the most probable response, running the second most probable, and drinking the third most probable; in another situation, the order of probabilities might be reversed.

The Premack Principle: A Hierarchy of Reinforcers

After this anti-experiment Premack began to manipulate the recurrent behaviors. He altered the animal's cage so that one of the behaviors could not be performed unless another was performed first. For example, he locked the running wheel so that the animal could not run in it and then unlocked it for ten seconds only after the animal had licked its water tube five times. In other words, Premack arranged things so that the animal had to drink in order to run.

When Premack established this contingency between the two responses, he found that it had a systematic effect on the rat's behavior. If the second response—running—had been more probable than the first—drinking—then the frequency of occurrence of the first response increased dramatically when the contingency was established. In other words, running served as a reinforcer for drinking. This is the reverse of the situation in most experiments on animal learning. Most experimenters use food or water as a reinforcer, and the behavior that is reinforced is commonly running (running a maze, for example). But in Premack's experiment, drinking would not reinforce running: if the apparatus was arranged so that the animal had to run in order to drink, the probability of running did not increase. The matter sounds less complicated if it is stated less scientifically: a rat that wants to run more than it wants to drink is willing to drink in order to run, but it will not run in order to drink.

As you might expect, Premack found that the reinforcement relationship could be easily reversed by changing the situation so that drinking was more likely than running. In the new situation, the rat would run in order to drink but it would not drink in order to run. Again, the more probable response could be made to serve as a reinforcer for the less probable response. This turns out to be a general rule. In a number of different experiments, Premack has shown that a shift in the relative probabilities of responses produces a corresponding shift in the reinforcement relationships among the responses.

Reinforcement relationships seem to be determined by the relative probabilities

Table 4.1—Time for Three Responses in Different Situations

Response	Situation	
	A	B
Running	60 sec	329 sec
Drinking	240	28
Eating	105	55

of various responses. If behaviors are ordered from most probable to least probable, then any behavior high on the list will reinforce those lower on the list, while behaviors lower on the list will not reinforce those higher. In other words, reinforcers are defined in terms of a simple structure—*a hierarchy of responses.*

If you think back to the discussion of reinforcement in Chapter 3, you will see that Premack's findings provide a view of reinforcement that is radically different from the one traditionally used in behavioral research. Reinforcers have usually been defined as *stimuli* that increase the probability that a given response will occur. Premack's data indicate that reinforcers are more accurately viewed as *opportunities to engage in high-probability responses.*

Typical learning experiments have led to an erroneous interpretation of reinforcement because they have used as reinforcers a special, limited class of responses, such as eating. Because eating always involves the availability of the stimulus *food,* it is possible for the psychologist to incorrectly view that stimulus as the reinforcer. Actually, the reinforcer is the opportunity to emit *eating responses,* which have been given a very high probability by the psychologist's experimental manipulations (such as depriving the animal of food for many hours).

Before we consider Premack's findings, we said that they would help us explain the Neuringer experiment, in which animals would press a bar for food even though free food was available in a dish. This behavior seemed surprising, because the animal could get as much food as it wanted without pressing the bar. But with reinforcement redefined as the opportunity to engage in a high-probability response, the puzzle disappears.

Suppose that Neuringer had begun his experiment by placing a pigeon in a cage that contained two dishes of free food, dish A and dish B. In that situation, the bird would eat from both dishes. It would produce two eating responses, A and B (one for each dish), at about the same high rate. If the experimenter then required the pigeon to press a bar before it could perform eating response A, what would Premack's data lead us to expect? Eating response A has a higher probability than bar pressing (which the pigeon has not even learned to do yet) and should therefore serve as a reinforcer for bar pressing. Thus bar pressing should increase in frequency. Eating response B, meanwhile, should simply continue at a fairly high rate. These predictions are borne out by Neuringer's findings.

The pigeon's bar pressing is difficult to explain if one regards the reinforcer in the experiment as food. In that case, the free food in dish B should reduce to the vanishing point the reinforcing properties of the food in dish A, which the pigeon had to work to obtain. But the bar pressing *can* be explained if one defines a reinforcer as an opportunity to engage in a high-probability response and if one focuses on the relative probabilities of eating response A and bar pressing. (If the pigeon's behavior still seems surprising to you, try imagining yourself in the bird's situation. Suppose you spent several weeks in a room with an ever-full plate of sandwiches and a vending machine that delivered identical sandwiches, free, for the pull of a lever. Wouldn't you use the vending machine at least some of the time?)

DISRUPTION OF WELL-ORGANIZED BEHAVIOR

One of the important implications of Hebb's pioneering work on the organization of behavior was that stable, well-organized behavior has a special psychological status. The disruption of a stable behavior is an especially significant event for an intelligent animal—usually producing a strong emotional reaction. The emotional reaction helps us explain a number of important learning phenomena.

Prevention of High-Probability Responses

In a typical experiment using reinforcement, an animal has been deprived of food, so that eating has become a response of very high probability. For example, when a pigeon's behavior is being shaped, the animal has been deprived of food and taught that food can be found in the food magazine of the Skinner box. Then, when the pigeon has learned to eat from the food magazine, the experimenter changes the situation. Food is no longer presented unless the bird performs the response that the experimenter demands. In other words, the animal is *prevented from performing the high-probability response* of eating unless it has performed whatever low-probability response the experimenter is requiring. (And in the shaping situation, the experimenter is continually changing his demands because he is training the bird to perform a particular complex response, such as bar pressing.) Because the high-probability response is being prevented, the pigeon has a strong emotional reaction. It becomes excited and very active, flapping its wings and dancing around inside the box.

F. D. Sheffield and B. A. Campbell have demonstrated this phenomenon by showing that, when situational cues that a hungry animal associates with eating are present, those cues produce strong excitement. In one experiment, the lights in a hungry rat's chamber were turned off five minutes before food was delivered. After a few trials, the rat's spontaneous activity increased considerably whenever the light went out. In other words, a cue that was associated with the high-probability response of eating produced excitement during the five-minute waiting period when the animal was prevented from performing the response.

Shaping is only one of the techniques in which the prevention of a high-probability response in the presence of cues associated with that response leads to emotional reactions. During extinction, the reactions are more extreme, as shown, for example, in studies by N. H. Azrin and A. R. Wagner. Suppose that after a rat has learned to press a bar to obtain food, the experimenter secretly changes the apparatus so that no food falls into the cup when the bar is pressed. Many cues that the rat associates with eating are still present. The food cup is there, and the bar—in fact, the situation is just as it was before extinction began, except that pressing the bar no longer yields food. When the animal discovers this, it shows a high degree of excitement. Indeed it shows more than excitement: it also shows fear and aggressive

Figure 4.3
This pigeon, which had been performing as desired by the experimenter and had been reinforced for its behavior, became agitated and flapped its wings when the food reinforcement was withdrawn. The bird was prevented from performing the high-probability response of eating.

behavior. Rats may squeal, defecate, urinate, and attack the empty food dish. Similarly, a person who has put money into a vending machine and gotten nothing out of it is apt to mutter angrily to himself and perhaps hit the machine. In many different situations the prevention of a high-probability response in the presence of cues associated with the response produces excitement and emotional behavior.

Reactions to Strange Objects

Hebb worked with another type of stable behavior: the perception of familiar objects. He showed chimpanzees various strange objects, all of which were similar to familiar objects but different in some important way, and he carefully recorded their reactions. In response to many of the objects—a human skull, a mask of a chimpanzee face, and a model of a snake were among the most effective—the chimps became excited, frightened, and aggressive. Also, apparently trivial changes in a person's appearance often evoked strong emotions in the animals. When an attendant who habitually wore the same laboratory coat came into the chimpanzees' room wearing a different one, the animals were clearly upset. Similarly, chimps are often afraid of strangers, or of a familiar attendant who cuts his long hair or shaves off his beard.

Irrational fears of the strange have been reported in many different species, especially intelligent mammals. When R. Melzack presented various objects to dogs, they barked at certain "strange" ones and either attacked them or ran away. Two of the most effective objects were a horsehide complete with head and an umbrella that the dogs saw being closed for the first time. K. Fischer observed a similar effect after presenting a young rhesus monkey with a distorted version of one of her favorite playthings: what was normally a transparent plastic ball with toys inside had been cut open and glued together in a new arrangement. Hebb and W. R. Thompson suggest that human beings show many similar irrational fears. Young children are often fearful and shy with strangers, and adults' reactions to unusual appearances are proverbial—many seem to want to attack males with long hair, or to avoid people with physical disabilities such as a missing leg or a patch over one eye.

What is it that produces these emotional reactions—in the one case to the prevention of a high-probability response and in the other to strange objects? In all these cases, the first requirement for the occurrence of an emotional reaction seems to be some sort of behavioral or perceptual organization, in the form of a stable response or a familiar person, animal, or toy. A second requirement is that

Figure 4.4
A monkey, raised by Fischer, displayed a fear reaction when given one of its favorite toys in the distorted shape shown at right. Emotional reactions like these are difficult to explain because, even though the distorted ball violated the monkey's expectations, it was in no way connected with anything dangerous or harmful.

part of the organization be distorted, disrupted, or prevented from occurring. One common explanation of the resulting emotional behavior is that any object or situation that violates an animal's expectations produces excitement, fear, and aggression. If the animal or person expects something to look a certain way or expects to be able to do a particular thing and his expectations are not fulfilled, he becomes emotionally aroused.

The formulation poses some difficulties. First, violations of expectations do not always produce excitement, fear, and aggression. Most jokes seem to be based on some sort of discrepancy between what one expects and what one hears—a surprise ending, a violation of a social taboo, a juxtaposition of normally incompatible situations. In many situations, indeed, violations of expectations produce interest. J. Kagan and his colleagues found that human babies often show an interest in familiar objects that look somewhat different from the way they normally do, such as pictures of faces in which the features are oddly placed.

Second, the explanation of emotional arousal in terms of violated expectations is vague. It is usually difficult to do careful research on expectations, since we seldom

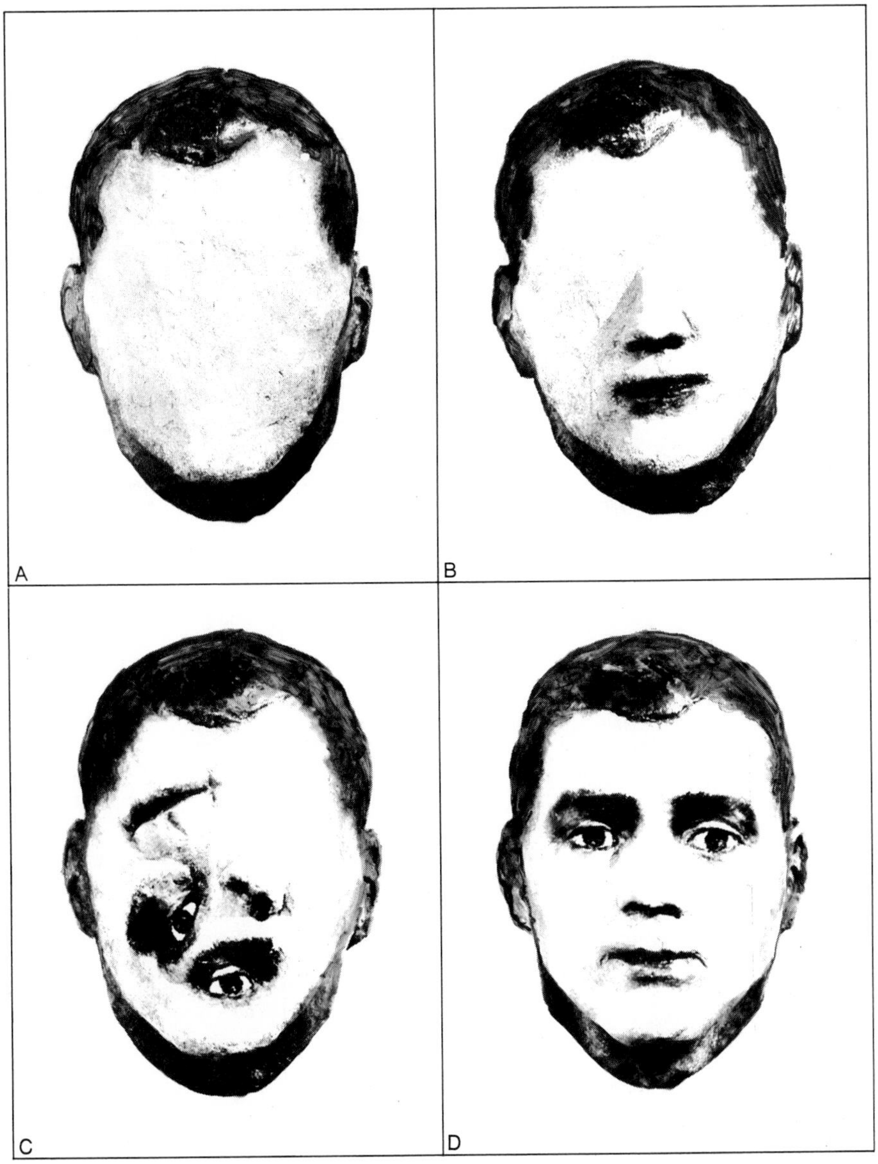

Figure 4.5
These four painted clay masks are among the stimuli used by the Kagan research group at Harvard to test infants' perceptual attention. They measured attention by recording the infants' heart rates, the duration of their eye fixations, frequency of looking and smiling, and vocalizations, such as babbling, laughing, or crying. They studied infants from four to twenty-seven months of age and from different social-class backgrounds. They found that perceptual attention is determined by different factors at different stages of development. Contrast (of light and dark, for example) determined the attention of four-month-olds; they looked longest at the masks with eyes (C and D). The two-year-olds, on the other hand, who have a well-developed schema of the human face and rich associations with it, fixated longest on the disarranged face, which violated their expectations.

know how to manipulate them experimentally. And even when we can manipulate them, we are at a loss to predict their effect, because we have no effective way of describing how expectations are related to each other. In any given situation people have many expectations, which are neither independent of each other nor equal in strength. They are interconnected, and some are more important than others. At the present time psychologists have no rigorous way of investigating the organization of expectancies but must rely mainly on intuition and common sense—two nevertheless powerful tools.

HOW ACTIONS ARE LEARNED: A PHASE THEORY

In order to understand more fully phenomena like the organization of reinforcers and the effects of disruptions of stable behaviors, we need to understand the nature of the organization of behavior as an action that is learned. No one has yet developed a general description of the changes in the organization of behavior that occur as an animal or person learns an action, but K. Fischer has devised a framework that will be useful here even though its generality has not been fully tested. Using several different species (rats, pigeons, and people) and several kinds of tasks, he has found that learning progresses through four phases, and that behavior is differently organized in each of them. The theory will be presented in some detail, as it makes a number of important points about learning.

A Mechanical Puzzle: Playing a Music Box

First, let us trace a hypothetical child through these four phases of learning. As you read, try to relate the child's behavior to the outline of the phases shown in Table 4.2. The column headed "Organization of Behavior" describes in general terms the way a child or an animal performs the task at each phase. The column headed "Transition Rule" summarizes Fischer's hypotheses about what is being learned as the child or animal progresses from one phase to the next.

A five-year-old girl is presented with an unusual type of music box: it is also a puzzle box. To make the music play, the girl has to work a series of buttons and

Table 4.2—Four Phases in the Development of a Well-Learned Action

Phase	Organization of Behavior	Transition Rule
0	Behavior shows no particular organization with respect to the task to be learned.	
		Organism recognizes that there is a task to be solved or a goal to be attained.
1	Behavior is relatively disconnected and irregular, but parts of the task are performed quickly and excitedly, especially near the goal. Behavior appears to be goal-directed despite its relative disorganization.	
		The general outline of the task is defined.
2	Organism may be slow to begin to respond, but once it has begun, it performs the task in a single thrust, virtually without pause.	
		The components of the task are differentiated.
3	The task is performed smoothly and regularly, but spontaneous pauses occasionally occur at various places in the task.	
		The components of the task are integrated.
4	Performance is similar to that at Phase 3, but even more regular. Responding seems to take on the characteristics of Premack's "recurrent behaviors" as well as other characteristics discussed in the text.	

levers in a particular order. On a box with three buttons and three levers, she might have to push button 3, pull lever 1, push button 1, pull lever 2, push button 2, and pull lever 3. If she carries out this sequence of actions, the music box plays for five seconds.

At first the child is in Phase 0. She has no idea what the box is and has not yet realized that there is a task to be learned. She may casually handle the box with its buttons and levers, but she gives no evidence of understanding what the box does.

Then her father makes it play for her, and she sees that the box will produce music. At this point she enters Phase 1. She knows that something is up, that *there is a problem to be solved,* although she does not know exactly what the problem is. Put another way, she wants the box to play but does not yet know what kind of thing must be done to make it do so. Although she shows some directed interest in the task, her behavior still seems relatively disorganized.

After her father makes the box play a few more times, she too begins to push buttons and pull levers. Now she sees the general nature of the task. She recognizes that operating the buttons and levers causes the box to play. At this point she enters Phase 2: she has *defined the general outline of the task.* But she still does not understand its more detailed requirements.

During Phase 2, the child becomes excited and begins to manipulate the buttons and levers on the box. Rapidly she pushes and pulls, mostly not getting the box to play but sometimes happening on the correct sequence. Over a fifteen-minute period, a new level of understanding gradually emerges: she sees that a specific sequence of operations on the buttons and levers makes the box play. Although she does not yet know the correct sequence, she sees what *kind* of sequence it is. She knows which types of actions will allow her to complete the task, and she rejects the types that will not (such as pushing two buttons simultaneously).

At this point the girl has completed Phase 2 and entered Phase 3: she has *determined the main components of the task.* Even though the exact sequence in which the buttons and levers must be pushed continues to elude her, most of the time she is reasonably efficient at making the box play music. Superficially she seems to have mastered the task, but her performance is misleading because she does not know exactly how she is making the box work.

For another fifteen minutes or half an hour, the girl plays with the box. She gradually learns to execute the correct sequence of actions at will and for the first time may be able to describe the sequence if someone asks her to. Phase 4 has now been reached. The girl knows not only what the components of the task are but how to put them together. In short, she has *mastered the task.*

A Verbal Puzzle

Before the nature of the four phases is considered in more detail, try to solve the following verbal problem.

This a passage for you to read now. This an example in a demonstration whole piece of writing. The to figure out what language rule transforms the sentences back to standard English idea. The, of course, not present in normal English rule, but it not unlike rules used in some other languages.

In addition to the phases of learning, another relevant to an understanding of development aspect of this example. It a matter of the kind of grammatical rule that occurs in standard English. The young child must learn to use such rules as he learns to speak.

What the rule?

(If you have not figured out the passage, look it over several times more.)

Think of the process of solving this verbal puzzle as analogous to the development of an action. In determining the rule used in the passage, many adults show a four-phase progression similar to the one described for the child and the music box. First, they realize that there is something strange about the passage. This realization puts them into Phase 1, where they must define the task. When they see that the task is to find a rule that transforms the passage back into standard English, they move into Phase 2, where they sketch out the main parts of the rule: some verbs are omitted, and something strange is going on at the beginnings and ends of some sentences. Their understanding of these components places them in Phase 3, where they can transform most of the sentences back into standard English. They can also state some facsimile of the rule, but the statement is usually unclear and not strictly correct. Finally, they integrate the components into a solution to the problem, reaching Phase 4. They can state the rule correctly, transform all the sentences correctly, and even use the rule to transform new sentences from standard English to the special form of English in the verbal problem.

Needless to say, not all tasks show these four phases of learning, and even with tasks like the ones described, there is nothing inevitable about the progression through the four phases. Mastery of a task can easily be halted at any point. If a child never recognizes that there is a problem to be solved, he will not even reach Phase 1. A very young child, for example, might not understand that his action could make the music box play. He might act as if only adults could bring about such magical events.

Even if Phase 1 has been reached, the person may never be able to move past it. To proceed to Phase 2, he must be able to define the problem to be solved. People who have never learned how to think about the grammatical structures of sentences, for instance, will not be able to define the verbal problem properly. Similar obstacles can prevent a person from reaching Phases 3 and 4.

As we shall see in the next unit, young children are incapable of progressing past early phases on some tasks because they have not acquired all the basic cognitive skills that adults possess. A three- or four-year-old child often thinks that reading involves holding a book in front of his face and telling a story. He does not understand that the reader is supposed to decipher the print on the page.

A Spatial Puzzle: Running a Maze

Fischer's most extensive research concerned the acquisition of a specific action rather than the solution of problems like the verbal puzzle. The usual procedure was to give different animals different amounts of training and then to interfere with performance in some way. For example, rats learning to run a simple maze would suddenly find no food when they got to the goal box. Not surprisingly, this withdrawal of reinforcement (extinction) caused excited and emotional behavior in the animals. It disrupted their response patterns—but the patterns of disruption were not the same at each level of training. Other experimental manipulations also had different effects on the animals' behavior at different levels of training. These differences in behavior from level to level showed that four different organizations occurred in a fixed order. The ways the animals behaved during training itself, before extinction or other experimental manipulations were put into effect, also varied depending on the phase of learning that an animal had reached.

Fischer found, for example, that rats being trained to run through the simple S-shaped maze diagrammed in Figure 4.6 showed a different pattern of pauses during each of the first three phases. In Phase 1, the rats paused frequently in all parts of the alley. In Phase 2, they were slow to leave the start box, but once they began running they virtually never stopped until they reached the goal box. In Phase 3, they usually ran quickly and smoothly through the alley but occasionally paused at one point or another—not only at the beginning, as in Phase 2. The frequency of pauses during the three phases is shown in Figure 4.7.

These differences in the organization of behavior from phase to phase recall those J. Bruner has observed in the behavior of human infants as they learn to pick up a cup. At first, the child's behavior seems disorganized. Then he begins to be

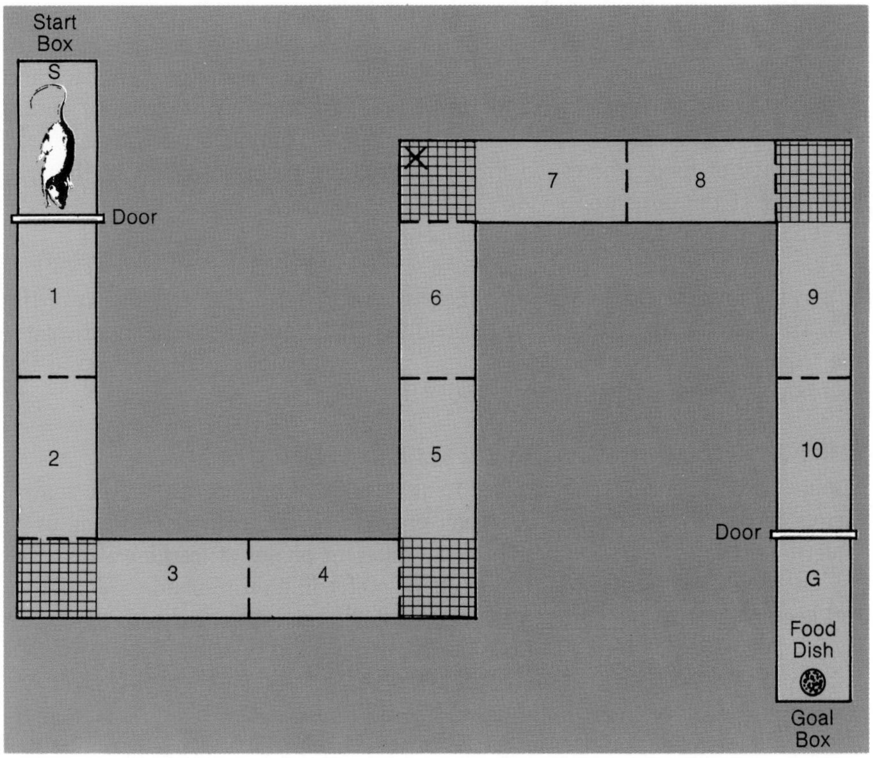

Figure 4.6
Diagram of the S-maze that Fischer used to study the organization of behavior in rats at the four phases of learning. The maze was subdivided and the parts numbered, so that pauses of the animal could be recorded at each location. The X indicates the location at which Fischer placed food before the goal box to test the behaviors of rats trained to each of the four phases. The behavior of animals at phase 4 proved to be most flexible; they paused, ate the food at X, then proceeded to the goal box.

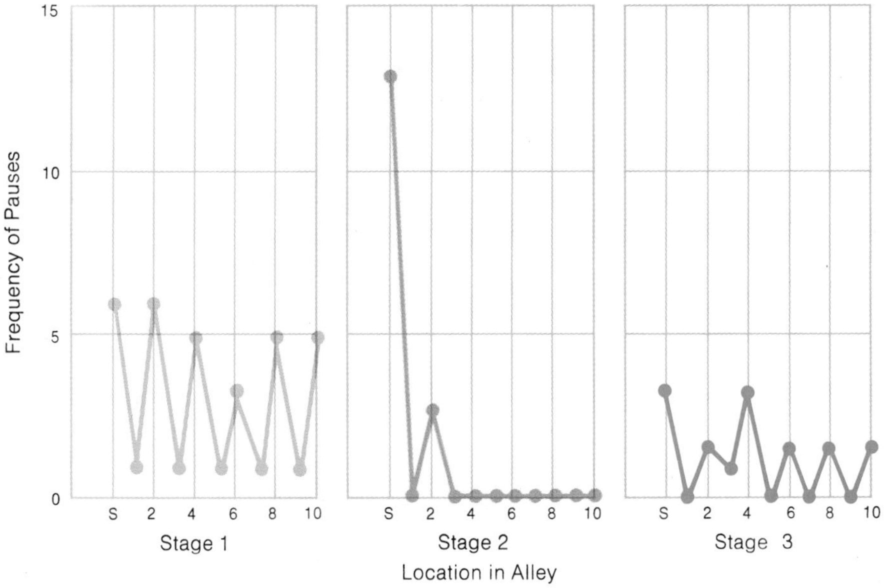

Figure 4.7
The behavior of one animal as it passed through the first three phases of learning to run the S-maze above. The number of pauses it made in each stage is plotted for each of the numbered locations in the maze. At phase 1 the rat paused variously throughout the alley. In phase 2 it paused only at the start box, as if performing an automatic behavior. The pauses were again more evenly distributed in phase 3 but were more infrequent than in phase 1; its run was relatively smooth and fast.

able to reach for the cup; but once the reach begins, it tends to be run off in a quick, single motion that has an impulsive appearance. The child continues to practice, his performance becomes smoother, more expert, and more relaxed, and pauses begin to appear here and there in the middle of it.

During training, the behavior patterns of an animal at Phase 3 and an animal at Phase 4 look about the same—smooth and fast. Yet experimental manipulations such as extinction were found to have quite different effects on animals in Phase 3 and animals that were overtrained, that is, trained for fifty or more trials after an apparently smooth performance had been reached. When an animal in Phase 3 no longer found food in the goal box at the end of the alley, it continued to start out well on later trials but became hesitant as it approached the goal box—that is, around sections 9 and 10 and the fourth corner in Figure 4.6. When extinction took place after overtraining (that is, during Phase 4), the animals seemed reluctant to start running at all. They stayed in the start box for long periods, or ran back and forth between the start box and the first corner. In other words, behavior during Phase 3 was disrupted primarily in the area where the animal actually experienced the absence of food, whereas in Phase 4 disruption occurred mainly at the very beginning of the response.

These results suggest that what happens between Phase 3 and Phase 4 is that the animal integrates the components of a sequence of behavior into a single action. It is as if the animal in Phase 3 does not associate what it does at the start of the task with what it hopes to find at the end, but the animal in Phase 4 anticipates the sequence as a whole. Since it "knows" there will probably be no food in the goal box, it hesitates even to begin the action.

THE NATURE OF ACTIONS AT DIFFERENT PHASES

Fischer's experiments turned up some results that at first glance seem to be contradictory but that on further examination prove to be important for helping us to understand the nature of an action at the different phases of learning.

The first result concerned the effects of prefeeding on responding. Rats that had been trained to run through the S-shaped alley and rewarded with food were given a large quantity of food before they were placed in the alley. Most psychologists would predict that the animals that had been fed first would no longer run through the alley with any enthusiasm, because the apparent reason for doing so was to obtain food. Animals in the first three phases of learning performed as expected: prefeeding caused a sharp decrease in the speed of responding. But the Phase-4 animals acted quite differently. Despite the fact that their stomachs were full of food, they ran about as fast as normal, and they even ate the food when they reached the goal box. In another experiment Fischer and E. Fantino found the same phenomenon in pigeons. Only after several sessions of prefeeding did overtrained birds begin to show a clear decrease in responding.

Probably the most common explanation for the continued responding despite prefeeding would be that running the alley at Phase 4 had become "automatic"—behavior evoked by the situation rather than by the animal's desire to eat. But the results of another experiment contradict that interpretation. In this experiment, rats were trained to one of the four phases in the S-shaped alley. Then a large dish of food—containing much more food than the dish in the goal box—was placed at the third corner of the alley (at the X in Figure 4.6), where the rat could hardly fail to notice it but could also get around it easily. If responding had become automatic at Phase 4, then the animals should have run past the large dish of food and into the goal box. They did no such thing. Instead they almost always stopped and ate the food in the large dish—all of it—and then proceeded to the goal box, where they ate all the food in the small dish. Animals at earlier phases of learning, especially Phase 2, were the ones that often ran *past* the large dish of food and entered the goal box, where they ate the food in the small dish.

This finding seems to require exactly the opposite interpretation from the first one. A response at Phase 4 does not seem to be automatic at all. On the contrary, it seems to be *flexible*, in the sense that an animal can easily interrupt the response, deal with a new event such as a large dish of food in the middle of the alley, and then resume the response. Responding seems to be more automatic at earlier phases, especially at Phase 2: those animals commonly ran past the large dish of food even though they were hungry. They seemed to have difficulty interrupting their response. Other findings showed a similar contrast between Phase 2 and Phase 4. For example, the pauses that occurred during training can be thought of as spontaneous interruptions of responding. At Phase 2, pauses hardly ever occurred after the rat had started down the alley. At Phase 4, a rat was likely to pause briefly here and there throughout the alley.

In summary, one finding seemed to indicate that behavior was automatic at Phase 4, whereas another seemed to show that behavior was flexible at Phase 4 and automatic at earlier phases, especially Phase 2. Can we make sense of this apparent contradiction?

To resolve the contradiction, we must try to understand the processes underlying the behaviors observed. As a first step, we should recognize that the nature of an action at Phase 4 seems to be very different from the nature of an action at earlier phases. It is best to begin by considering what happens in the earlier phases.

Early Phases of Learning

A number of observations suggest that behavior in early phases may have a compulsive and emotional character as compared to behavior in Phase 4. When a person or animal reaches Phase 2 or thereabouts, he commonly begins to show excitement and intense interest in the task. Jean Piaget found that infants and young children carried out *circular reactions* when they reached approximately this point in learning. For instance, the infant Laurent (Piaget's son) had a rattle tied over his crib. The rattle was connected by a loose string to one of his arms, so that whenever he moved that arm in a certain way, the rattle would shake and make a noise. At first, Laurent did not understand what made the rattle shake, but eventually he seemed to reach what Fischer would call Phase 2: he seemed to understand that something about moving his arm caused the rattle to shake. At this point he began to repeat over and over the following sequence of actions. He would swing his arm and then look at the rattle, swing his arm and look at the rattle, swing his arm and look at the rattle. . . . repeated

There is an obvious analogy between Piaget's circular reactions and the findings on interruption of animal behavior at Phase 2. The animals seemed to avoid interruptions, as if they had some kind of compulsion to complete the response sequence that they had begun.

There is also some evidence that the excitement found in Phase 2 may at times turn into a negative emotional reaction. Using an operant conditioning procedure, H. Papoušek taught human infants to turn their heads to obtain milk whenever they heard a specific sound (a bell or a buzzer). At first, most infants were not very successful in making the proper movement, but after a little training they began to perform the response correctly some of the time. At this point they commonly started to fret and cry. As the infants mastered the task, their distress disappeared.

Transfer of Training

G. Mandler and J. Mandler have identified another characteristic of behavior in the early phases of learning that contrasts with behavior in Phase 4. They investigated the relationship between training level and a phenomenon called transfer. There are two kinds of transfer. In *positive transfer* the learning of one task facilitates the learning of a second, similar task. In *negative transfer* the learning of the first task interferes with the learning of the second. The Mandlers showed that when the first task has been partially learned, negative transfer occurs, but when the task has been overlearned, positive transfer appears.

For example, suppose that the girl with the music box were given a second box, one that required her to operate the buttons and levers in a different order. If her learning of the original task had reached Phase 4, then she would show positive transfer to the new box; she would quickly learn to make it play. But if she had reached only Phase 2 or 3, she would show negative transfer; she would learn the new task more slowly, because her experience with the original task would interfere.

Negative transfer during early phases of learning is reasonable in light of the

Whale : Cry = Son :
Study Chair Pattern Star

other data about those phases. When an organism is excited and compulsively trying to repeat an action that it has not yet mastered, one would expect it to have difficulty learning a transfer task. The appearance of positive transfer at Phase 4 is also reasonable, if we think of an action as a small skill or "mini-skill." Only when a skill has been mastered can it be easily modified for use in a new way.

Insight Learning

One type of learning that has especially interested many psychologists is called *insight learning,* in which a person or animal suddenly perceives the relationships that must be seen in order to solve a particular problem. The analogy above, left is a problem that for most people requires insight before they can reach a solution. In human beings, insight is often accompanied by an "aha!" reaction, the kind usually represented in comic strips by a light bulb. (If you are having difficulty attaining the insight necessary to solve the analogy, pay less attention to the spelling of the words and more attention to their sound.)

In a study of insight learning in chimpanzees, H. G. Birch showed that insight can be interpreted as a special kind of positive transfer. Food was placed outside several chimps' cages, too far away for the chimps to reach it with their arms. Inside each cage was a stick long enough to be used to pull the food into the cage. The animals had no experience with the use of sticks, and at first none of them could solve the problem. Then they were allowed to play with some sticks for a long time—with the food no longer available outside the cage, so that they could not happen upon the solution to the problem during the play period. Finally the food was put back and the chimps were tested again. All of them immediately saw the relationship between the stick and the food and solved the problem within twenty seconds! The chimps could achieve the necessary insight only after they had mas-

Figure 4.9
This chimp is showing insight learning in solving the problem of how to get the banana.

Reed : Book = Sea :
Man Picture Marsh Car

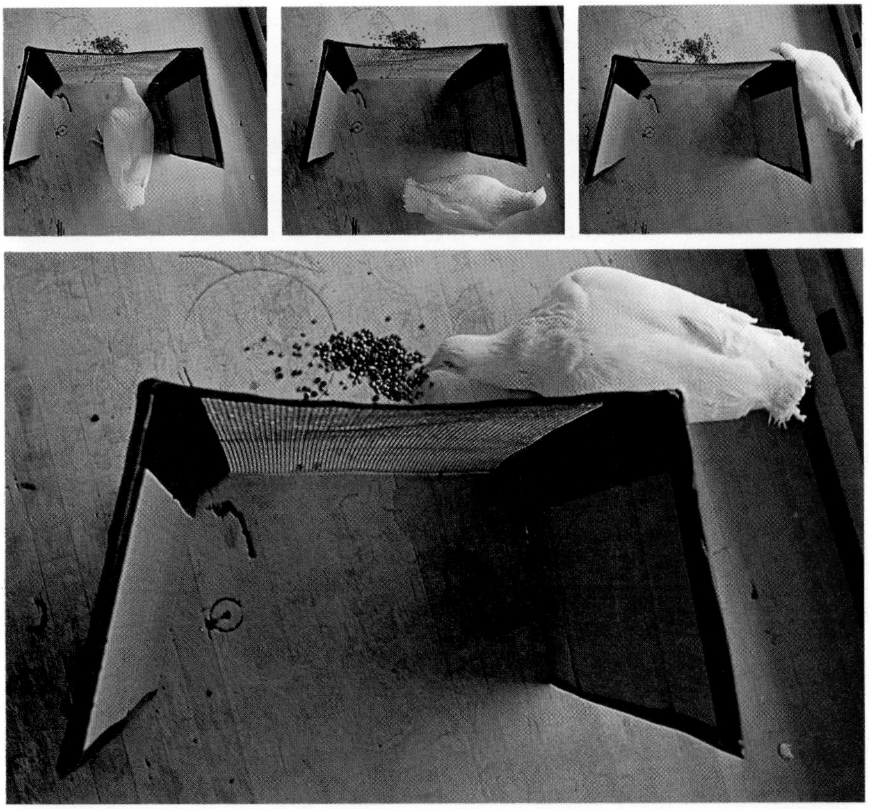

Figure 4.10
A pigeon successfully solving the detour (or Umweg) problem. As shown in the photo at the top left, although the food is plainly visible, the direct path to it is blocked by the screen. The pigeon must choose a path that is not direct, that is it must make a detour, to reach the food. When faced with analogous problems, adult humans may not even label the situation a problem. But very young children or chimps have considerable difficulty in recognizing that it is necessary to move temporarily in a direction opposite to that of the goal.

tered the use of a stick. Similarly, if you have solved the analogy at the top of page 74, you have acquired a new rule that can be used in analogies, and as a result you will probably be able to solve quickly the analogy at the top of this page.

Cognitive Maps and General Capacities

So far, we have explained only part of the apparent contradiction that turned up in Fischer's experiments. In both experiments the behavior of the animals at Phase 4 was opposed to that of animals at earlier phases. The opposition is supported by other findings and indicates that the nature of an action is radically different in Phase 4 than its nature in earlier phases. But the apparent contradiction in the behavior of the animals at Phase 4 still remains. On the one hand, their behavior seemed to be automatic—even when their stomachs were full of food, they ran through the maze and ate the food in the goal box. On the other hand, their behavior seemed to be flexible—they could easily interrupt their response, deal with a new event such as a large dish of food in the middle of the alley, and then resume the response.

It happens that a similar contradiction has been lurking in the psychological literature for a long time. When an animal or a person learns an action—how to run through a maze or drive a car, for example—does he learn *a series of movements,* as many behaviorists would argue? In the alley in Figure 4.6, does the rat learn (1) to run till it reaches a corner, (2) to turn 90 degrees, (3) to run till it reaches the next corner, (4) to turn 90 degrees, and so on until it reaches the goal box? Or does the animal learn a map of the situation—what E. C. Tolman calls a *cognitive map?*

To indicate what he means by a cognitive map, Tolman describes the behavior of a rat that had learned to negotiate a maze. One day, when the experimenter was careless, the animal managed to push open the lid of the start box. It scurried directly over the top of the maze to the goal box, where it climbed in and ate the food. Tolman argued that if the rat had merely learned a series of movements, a particular response sequence, it could not have acted as it did. Without some sort of map of the situation as a whole, the rat could have reached the goal box only by following the route it had been trained to run.

Yet there is also good evidence that the animal learns a series of movements. Simple observation of a Phase 4 response strongly supports this hypothesis. In the S-shaped alley an animal at Phase 4 usually ran through the alley in a highly stereotyped way, reminiscent of the recurrent behaviors described by Premack. The movements that it made were very similar from trial to trial as it darted from the start box, ran to the first corner, turned to the left, ran to the second corner, and so forth.

The apparent contradiction between learning a series of movements and learning a cognitive map parallels the apparent contradiction between the "automatic" and "flexible" nature of Phase-4 actions. First, the view that the animal is learning a series of movements is consistent with the finding that Phase-4 behavior is automatic. If the animal had learned a particular sequence of movements, then it would be a simple matter for the movements to be overlearned to such an extent that they would occur even when the animal was not hungry. On the other hand, Tolman's idea of a cognitive map is consistent with the finding that Phase-4 behavior is flexible. If the animal had learned not a series of specific movements but a map of the S-shaped alley, it could easily pause at one point in the alley to eat from a new dish of food and then resume its journey to the goal box.

In summary, the evidence for both hypotheses is good. In learning an action, animals and people do, in fact, give evidence of learning a series of movements, and they also give evidence of having a map of the situation. The resolution of the contradiction must be that there is really no contradiction. Behavior at Phase 4 seems to have both characteristics. One might say that what is learned is a contingency between what the organism does and what happens in its sensory world as a result. In the phrase of Piaget, K. S. Lashley, and others, the action is *sensorimotor.* The organism has learned a relationship between motor action and sensory effect. As a result, it is capable of either continuing the movements that produce the effects or of carrying out other movements that produce similar effects.

Implicit in this explanation is an important assumption: an organism has many capabilities other than the one that it has been taught in a particular experiment, and it can use its other skills in combination with the newly learned action when necessary. The several kinds of positive transfer that have been discussed all require this recombination of skills. Unless the organism possesses the particular skills that the transfer task requires, it will be unable to demonstrate transfer.

Although Birch's chimps could solve the insight problem after they had mastered the use of a stick, an animal that did not have the advanced mental capacity of an adult chimpanzee would not be able to solve the problem at all. It would simply be incapable of using a stick as a tool. Similarly, Tolman's rat would not have been able to show that it had a spatial map of the maze unless it had the necessary capacity for spatial organization. The kind of spatial locomotion of which an animal is capable when carrying out a well-learned action is determined in part by its capacity for spatial organization. If Tolman's rat had been a cockroach, it would not have been able to by-pass the maze and get to the food by climbing over the top of the box.

Piaget has provided many relevant examples of how the human infant uses his various skills in combination with a newly acquired sensorimotor action. One of the capacities that he has studied in detail is spatial organization. He has shown that the human infant does not begin with the knowledge of space that adults have but must gradually develop that knowledge. For example, the infant does not understand that there are many different ways of getting to the same place. If a three-month-old infant is playing with a ball that disappears from sight, he will not even realize that he can search for the ball in the place where it disappeared. A child of about twelve months will know to search for it, but if there is a barrier in his way, he will not realize that there are other paths by which he can retrieve the lost ball. Suppose that the ball has rolled behind a couch and the nearest path around the couch is blocked by an end table. He will not understand that he can turn his back on the ball, go around the other end of the couch, which is not blocked by a table, and retrieve the ball that way. By the time the child is two years old, however, he has developed an excellent understanding of how to move about in space, and consequently he can circumvent all sorts of barriers, as any mother can testify.

Preliminary research with other mammals suggests that some of them show a development of spatial organization similar to that of the human infant, except that they do not seem to reach the highest stages. The following unit presents Piaget's analysis of the development of thinking abilities in children.

Whale : Cry = Son : Star
Reed : Book = Sea : Picture

SUGGESTED READINGS

BRUNER, J. S. "The Growth and Structure of Skill," in K. J. Connolly (Ed.), *Motor Skills in Infancy.* New York, Academic Press, 1970. Outlines the view that much of learning in the human infant can be considered as the acquisition of skills.

FISCHER, K. W. *The Organization of Simple Learning.* Chicago, Markham Press (in press). This book presents the research and theory underlying the analysis of learning in terms of phases in the development of an action.

HEBB, D. O. *The Organization of Behavior: A Neurophysiological Theory.* New York, Wiley, 1949. The classic book that helped to cause the resurgence of interest in the organization of behavior in American psychology.

HEBB, D. O., AND THOMPSON, W. R. "The Social Significance of Animal Studies," in G. Lindzey (Ed.), *Handbook of Social Psychology.* Vol. II. Reading, Mass., Addison-Wesley, 1968, pp. 729–774. This paper examines the social implications of some of Hebb's work, including his investigations of the causes of irrational fear.

LASHLEY, K. S. *The Neuropsychology of Lashley: Selected Papers.* F. A. Beach *et al.* (Eds.). New York, McGraw-Hill, 1960. Selected papers by Karl Lashley, including a number of papers on his investigations into the organization of behavior and in particular his famous paper on the serial organization of behavior.

MANDLER, G. "From Association to Structure," *Psychological Review,* 69 (1962), 415–427. Mandler argues that as learning progresses, it shifts from a process of association to an integrated structure.

PIAGET, J. *The Origins of Intelligence in the Child.* New York, International Universities Press, 1952. The introductory volume to Piaget's three-volume treatise on cognitive development during infancy.

PREMACK, D. "Reinforcement Theory," in D. Levine (Ed.), *Nebraska Symposium on Motivation.* Lincoln, University of Nebraska Press, 1965, pp. 123–180. Premack presents his theory of reinforcement and summarizes the data that led to his theory.

TOLMAN, E. C. *Behavior and Psychological Man.* Berkeley, University of California Press, 1961. Selected papers by Edward Tolman, including his famous paper entitled "Cognitive Maps in Rats and Men."

UNIT II Human Development

As organisms go, human beings are unusual creatures. We have a very long childhood, during which we acquire a vast array of cognitive and social skills. Each of us develops language, a distinctive personality, a knowledge of the mores of the particular culture into which we were born, and the ability to think in ways that are much more complex than those of any other creatures on earth. In the entire animal kingdom, we are by far the most intelligent species and the learners par excellence. Yet newborn babies are largely helpless; they cannot speak; they know no culture; and they are very poor thinkers and learners. One of the great puzzles of psychology is to explain how the infant develops from this primitive state into the complex human adult. Consequently,

2

Instinctive Behavior deals with communication in animals and so relates to Chapter 7's discussion of the nature of language.

3

Conditioning and Learning presents the basic principles of the behaviorist view of learning, which are applied to explain social development in Chapter 8.

4

The Organization of Behavior presents a cognitive approach to learning, which is strongly related to the views of cognitive development in Chapters 5 and 6 and to the cognitive-developmental approach to social development in Chapter 8.

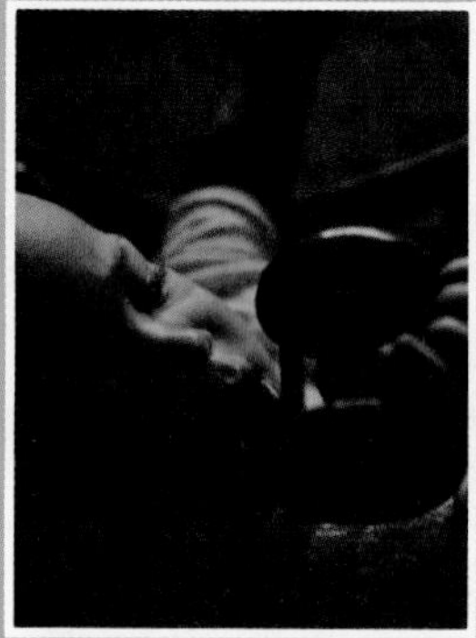

Chapter 5, Development of Intelligence, explains such basic Piagetian concepts as assimilation and accommodation and describes the first stage of cognitive development: the sensorimotor period.

Chapter 6, Development of Higher-Order Intelligence, details Piaget's three later periods of cognitive development—the preoperational, the concrete-operational, and the formal-operational—and discusses how cognitive development is influenced by environmental factors.

10

Learning and Memory discusses the development of memory, which relates to all the chapters in this unit.

11

Problem Solving presents several approaches to the study of how people (and animals) solve problems; Chapter 6's discussion shows how children are capable of solving only certain kinds of problems before they reach the formal-operational stage of cognitive development.

14

Perception deals not only with how adults perceive but with studies of perceptual development, many of which seem to show that even very young infants have remarkable perceptual capabilities. Chapter 5 analyzes the relationship between perceptual capacities and cognitive development and takes as an example of this relationship the development of object constancy—the ability to know that an object does not stop existing even if you can no longer perceive it. Also, Chapter 14 discusses the effects of environmental impoverishment and enrichment on perceptual development.

development, like learning, has been one of the topics that has most concerned psychologists.

Sigmund Freud and many psychologists after him who wished to analyze adult personality examined childhood experiences, attempting to trace their effects on adulthood. Until quite recently, however, the emphasis was on abnormal development—what went wrong—rather than on the course of normal development, and most studies dealt with social and personality development. In the last several decades, work in developmental psychology has concentrated especially on cognitive development, and that fact is reflected in this unit.

Chapter 7, Language Development, not only presents recent research on children's language acquisition but also discusses at length the nature of language and its relation to thought and cognitive development—in both children and chimpanzees. Environmental variables affecting language acquisition are also discussed.

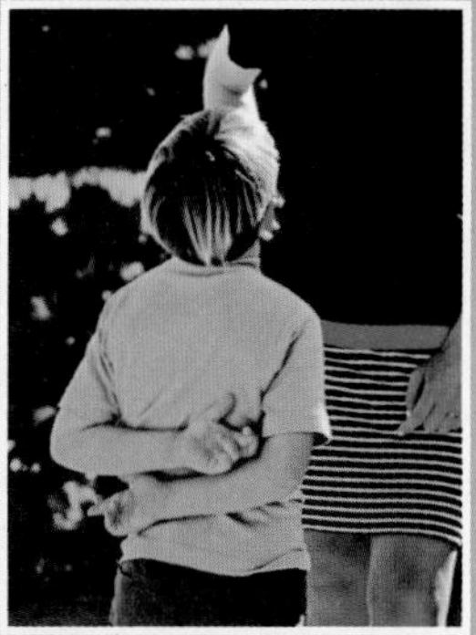

Chapter 8, Social Development: The Case of Morality, introduces the topic of social development. Moral development is taken as a special case of social development and is examined from the point of view of the three most complete theories of social development: Freud's psychoanalytic theory, behaviorist social-learning theory, and Kohlberg's cognitive-developmental theory.

31

Bases of Disorder sets out various theoretical explanations of why psychological disorder occurs; two of these are the psychoanalytic and social-learning theories, which are also presented in Chapter 8's discussion of normal social development.

28

Intergroup Relations deals at length with the relations between blacks and whites in the United States. Its discussion of racial roles and their development relates to the discussion of social development in Chapter 8.

25

Patterns of Social Behavior: The Case of Sex Roles discusses how adults' social roles help determine their behavior. It uses male and female roles as an exemplar and describes how three major theories of social development attempt to explain the acquisition of sex roles. These are the same three theories that are used to explain the development of morality in Chapter 8.

20

Psychological Testing presents a lengthy discussion of what is known at present about the relation of intelligence to IQ scores and the relative weights of heredity and environment in producing IQ scores. Chapter 5 compares what Piaget calls intelligence—namely, the construction of an understanding—with what IQ tests measure.

Human Motivation contains a long discussion of how differences in social development, the topic of Chapter 8, are reflected in differences between men and women for certain motives, particularly the motive to achieve.

19

5

Development of Intelligence

EACH OF US leaves childish things behind us as we grow older and more sophisticated—but ought we to do so entirely? Can we go too far in abandoning what seems silly? As babies, we may think, for instance, that anything that passes out of sight is destroyed and no longer exists. But eventually we learn better and just look for it elsewhere. And we laugh at the childishness of those primitives who felt that the sun was destroyed each evening when it set, and that a new sun was created each morning. Or that each new cycle of the phases of the moon started with a literally new moon. (We still call it a "new moon," don't we?)

Yet is that really so primitive a notion? When a flame is extinguished, has it merely moved out of sight? Of course not. It has really and literally been destroyed. And if a candle is lighted once more, a new flame has really and literally been created. Why not then assume, by analogy, that if the great flame of the sun sinks into the western oceans, it, too, is really and literally destroyed by the huge quantity of water, as a candle flame would be destroyed if it were dipped into a small pool of water? Then, when the sun rises the next morning, surely a new flame has been created. In other words, something can be wrong without necessarily being silly.

Again, children may not equate amount and volume tightly. They may not quite get the notion that the same amount of liquid always has the same volume whatever the shape of the container that holds it. We learn better as we grow older, though. So we are amused by the Arabian Nights notion of giant genies trapped in small bottles. Just fantasy! But the imagination of human beings is not unlimited. Even the wildest stroke of fantasy has some foothold in reality. Think about the fact that although liquids and solids do retain their volumes, gases don't. A large quantity of gas can be compressed into a small volume. What's more, a small quantity of solid, in burning, may release a large volume of vapor. Indeed, when the genie-in-the-bottle appears on the Hollywood screen, it is always pictured as a matter of gas. The hero opens the bottle and gas comes out, faster and faster, and higher and higher, and finally solidifies into a giant.

So it becomes wrong to carry wisdom to extremes. If we become so adult as to be certain that nothing is ever destroyed just because it disappears, and that nothing changes volume without changing quantity, we will never understand flames and gases. I.A.

The existence of child psychology as a field of study is the result of a fundamental change in people's conceptions of children. Until the end of the nineteenth century most people thought of children merely as miniature adults. The next time you go to a museum, look carefully at the way infants are portrayed in paintings from the Middle Ages. Most artists of that period depicted infants as adults that had been shrunk to about two-fifths normal size. But even after artists had begun to paint infants that looked their ages, it took centuries for people to understand that children are not merely young adults with a smaller catalogue of facts in their memories. Children think and learn in different ways than adults do. This realization has opened up whole new areas of investigation, some of which are discussed in this and the following three chapters.

The greatest contemporary figure in child psychology is the Swiss psychologist Jean Piaget. He has published more systematic observations of children's thinking and learning than anyone else in history. Most of the discussion in these first two chapters is based on Piaget's theory of the development of thinking from infancy to adulthood. Although Piaget's theory provides a framework that will help you think about psychological development, you should keep in mind as you read that the study of infants and children is still in its own infancy. Rather than accept what is said as hard fact, you should use it as an occasion for thinking about children's thinking and for posing questions of your own. If Piaget's theory is correct, you will learn most if you actively think through the ideas presented and try to apply them to the examples given.

QUALITATIVE CHANGES IN THINKING

One of the main tenets of Piaget's theory of the development of intelligence is that the mind of the child is qualitatively different from the mind of the adult. In

Figure 5.1
Jean Piaget. For almost half a century Jean Piaget has studied the intellectual development of children. From his painstaking observation of children performing various cognitive tasks, he has constructed a theory of the nature of intelligence and the stages of intellectual growth. Piaget's work forms the substance of this chapter and Chapter 6.

attempting to uncover the key steps in intellectual development, Piaget has discovered some dramatic changes in the way a child reasons about particular tasks at different ages. Consider the following example.

A four-year-old boy is playing with a pile of shiny red beads. His father takes ten of them and lines them up in two matching rows of five beads each. The father asks the boy, "Does one row have more beads than the other, or do they both have the same number?" The child replies that they're both the same, of course. But his father encourages him to count them, just to make sure. (The boy can count to ten.) The father then changes one row so that its five beads are farther apart, stretched out into a longer line. When he asks his son if the rows still have the same number of beads in them, the boy shakes his head. "No, now that one has more," he says, indicating the row where the five beads make a longer line. A year later, the father tries the same task again. When he lengthens one row of beads and asks his son if the number of beads is still the same, the boy answers, "Yes, of course." His tone implies that the question is very silly because the answer is so obvious.

The child has acquired what Piaget calls *conservation of number.* He understands that the number of items in a set is not altered by changes in the configuration of that set. A short line of beads can be made into a long one without changing the number of beads; similarly, the line can be changed to form a circle of beads without changing the number. Earlier, when the boy was four years old, he could count to ten, but he did not truly comprehend how numbers function. He did not understand that number is conserved over changes in configuration.

After the boy has finished the number task, his father brings out a new game. He starts with two beakers of the same size and shape, and he pours some colored water into each one. He asks for his son's help in making each beaker contain the same amount of water. After a few adjustments, the boy announces, "OK, they're the same." Now the father brings out a tall, thin beaker and pours the fluid from one of the original containers into the new beaker. The boy watches him pouring. When the father asks if the water in the tall, thin beaker is still the same amount as the water in the original container, the boy says, "No, that one's more," pointing to the tall, thin beaker.

Although the child can understand conservation of number, he does not yet

Figure 5.2

The girl taking part in this experiment does not yet understand conservation of quantity of liquid. (Top left) she acknowledges that the two beakers of the same size contain the same amount of liquid. (Top right) she sees the liquid from one beaker being poured into a taller container. (Bottom) yet she indicates that the taller beaker contains more liquid than the shorter one.

appreciate that amount of liquid also shows conservation. He does not realize that pouring a liquid into a container of different shape does not change the amount of liquid. At first glance most adults think that the liquid in the tall, thin beaker looks like more than the liquid in the original container, but they know that the amount has to be the same because it was the same before it was poured. The child, on the other hand, reacts only to the appearance of the liquid in the tall, thin container and concludes that there is more liquid in that container.

Two years later, when the boy is about seven years old, the same problem is posed to him again. Now he answers the question correctly. The amount of liquid is the same, he asserts emphatically—without hesitation and with a tone of certainty. By that age, he understands *conservation of quantity of liquid.*

What is happening as the child learns conservation? Is his lack of conservation merely a result of insufficient vocabulary or lack of experience with the task? Studies by various investigators, including Piaget, J. Smedslund, J. Wohlwill, and S. Carey-Block, have shown that failure at conservation is not such a simple matter.

The explanation of failure in terms of vocabulary can be easily dismissed. In many other situations, such as when liquid is added to or subtracted from containers of identical size and shape, the boy uses the words "same," "more," and "less" easily and correctly. Also, simple verbal instruction does not help the child who does not understand conservation. To illustrate, here is an interesting experiment you can carry out with a group of five- or six-year-olds. First, have each child do the task described above by himself, so that you can determine which children understand conservation of liquid. Then ask those who do understand it to explain their conclusions to those who do not. They will point out that if the liquid in the tall, thin beaker were poured back into the original beaker, the level would be the same as it was before. And they may argue that although the tall beaker is higher than the short beaker, it is also thinner, and that the width of the short beaker compensates for its shorter height. But all this explanation will have no effect on the understanding of most of the children who did not understand conservation in the first place.

Similarly, simple experience with the task will not help most children. Repeated demonstrations of pouring the liquid back and forth from beaker to beaker, for example, will succeed only in boring most four-year-olds, not in helping them understand conservation of amount.

Even reinforcement techniques do not succeed in teaching conservation. With these techniques an adult gives a reward, or reinforcement, whenever a child states the correct answer. The reward might be a piece of candy, or it might be verbal approval ("That's right"). This kind of training often teaches the child to give the right answer to a particular problem, but variations in the task show that he is merely parroting what he has been taught to say. In the face of changes in the situation, he returns to his earlier way of answering. He simply does not show the understanding of the task that is so evident in a child who has attained conservation of liquid.

Conservation of liquid is not alone in being difficult to teach. Whatever it is that the preconserving child does not understand, study after study has shown that it is virtually impossible to teach that understanding quickly with any simple training techniques. Children who do not understand conservation of number, for example, cannot be taught it unless they were already on the verge of understanding before training began. Thus Piaget's findings cannot be dismissed as stemming merely from deficiencies in vocabulary or experience.

INTELLIGENCE AS THE CONSTRUCTION OF AN UNDERSTANDING

Using conservation and other tasks, Piaget has extensively studied the development of intelligence from infancy to adolescence, and he has repeatedly found that children's understanding of certain fundamental problems is not easily acquired.

One of the most important points in Piaget's theory is that all learning involves the *construction of an understanding.*

In constructing an understanding of a problem, the child seems to go through four phases of learning, as described in Chapter 4. First the child recognizes that there is a problem to be solved (Phase 1). Once he sees that there is a problem, he must wrestle with it until he can define its general outline (Phase 2). After he understands the general outline, he must analyze the problem into its components (Phase 3). Then, finally, he sees how to put the components together to achieve a full understanding of the problem (Phase 4).

This view of intelligence as the construction of knowledge should be contrasted with a common view that has developed as a result of the use of intelligence tests. The purpose of the first intelligence tests, developed by Alfred Binet in 1905, was to predict the school performance of children in Paris, and the descendants of Binet's tests serve a similar purpose. Items are chosen primarily because they predict school performance. Accordingly, IQ tests include such questions as, "What is the average height of an American woman?" "How far is it from New York to Paris?" "What is a sonata?" Such questions measure the acquisition of specific information, and they bias IQ tests against people who have not been exposed to the information the questions require. A child from an urban ghetto may score lower on the test than he otherwise would simply because he has never heard of Paris or a sonata.

Unfortunately, the specialized purpose of the IQ tests is sometimes forgotten. People have come to treat them as an assessment of innate ability rather than merely as predictors of school performance. They often lose sight of the fact that an intelligence test is, after all, just one set of questions and problems, given on a specific day at a particular place, and subject to the same confounding influences that affect other test scores. (See Chapter 20 for a detailed discussion of the uses and misuses of IQ tests.)

An even more serious consequence of the misuse of IQ tests is that many people mistakenly view intelligence as a fixed entity. They fail to see the active nature of knowing. The word "intelligence" is derived from the Latin word *intellegere,* which means to understand or to know. Clearly, understanding and knowing are not fixed attributes, and tests that merely measure the acquisition of certain types of knowledge are not apt to provide an adequate view of the nature of understanding or knowing. A related and similarly erroneous view is that intelligence is merely the acquisition of information. According to that view, the more information a person accumulates, the smarter he is. According to Piaget, however, the basis of all intelligence is the ability to *understand,* and the mere accumulation of facts does not produce understanding.

In saying that, Piaget does not mean to imply that there is no such thing as memorization, or rote learning. He acknowledges that memorization is important for acquiring certain types of information and that information may be necessary for the solution of certain kinds of problems. But understanding never comes from memorization alone, and knowledge without understanding is not real knowledge.

Stages of Intellectual Development

Much of the power of Piaget's view comes from his documentation of exactly how children construct their knowledge of the world. In describing how children go about this herculean task, Piaget uses the concept of *periods,* or *stages,* of intellectual development. Many people unfortunately misunderstand the implications of these terms. The difficulty probably stems from the example of stages that most easily comes to mind, the stages of insect development. Insects develop through four stages, from egg to larva to pupa to adult. The intellectual development of a human child, according to Piaget, also includes four main periods: the sensorimotor period, the preoperational period, the concrete-operational period, and the formal-opera-

Figure 5.3

Children at Piaget's four stages of cognitive development. (Top) during the sensorimotor period the child can learn to manipulate objects but does not understand their function or the basis for his actions. The child pushes the toy airplane; he does not understand that airplanes fly, and only late in the sensorimotor period would he look for the toy airplane if it were suddenly screened from him. (Second from top) during the preoperational period, the child learns to mentally represent people, objects, and events when these are absent. He also learns deferred imitation and begins to learn language. The child understands that an airplane flies, and can imitate its flight. (Bottom left) during the concrete-operational stage the child learns to classify objects and events into categories and he begins to be able to manipulate these categories. He comes to be able to coordinate his thinking in relation to concrete characteristics of objects. The child can assemble the components of a model airplane into a complete unit. (Bottom right) during the formal-operational period, the adolescent becomes capable of thinking hypothetically and of testing several alternative hypotheses for a given event. Adult thought is formal-operational. The young person shown here understands the functioning of an airplane, and he attempts to use his understanding of various processes to design a new type of airplane.

tional period. The periods are stagelike in that they are *qualitatively different* from each other, and in that their *order is invariant*—the child must complete the sensorimotor period before he can reach the preoperational period, the preoperational period before he can reach the concrete-operational period, and so on.

The intellectual development of a child, however, is much less fixed and automatic than the physical development of an insect, and much more dependent on the environment in which the child grows up. The speed of the child's development through the four periods varies widely in different environments, and it is possible that some people never reach the later ones. Each of the four stages can be thought of as embodying a different kind of mind: a sensorimotor mind, a preoperational mind, a concrete-operational mind, and a formal-operational mind. Each type of mind has specific capacities (and specific limitations). In a suitably rich environment, each type of mind gradually develops the capabilities that will transform it into the mind of the next period. Because the change from one period to the next occurs by a *gradual, environmentally influenced* transformation, it is somewhat misleading to liken it to the sudden emergence of, say, larva from egg after a certain number of days.

Although it is useful to learn the ages associated with each period of intellectual development, you should remember that they are only rough guidelines. The sensorimotor period encompasses infancy, approximately the first two years of life. The preoperational period starts during the preschool years. Concrete-operational thought begins to appear around school age, when the child is from five to seven years old, and develops further during elementary school. Formal-operational thought first appears around the beginning of adolescence and can continue to develop throughout adulthood.

The four periods are different from insect stages in another important way. The mind of each period subsumes the minds of earlier periods. For example, a child in the concrete-operational period still possesses the capacities that typified the two earlier periods (the sensorimotor and the preoperational). Likewise, an adult who has mastered formal-operational thinking is capable of functioning at the level of all three earlier stages. With insects, by contrast, the previous stage disappears when a new stage develops. When the egg is transformed into the larva, the egg disappears; when the larva is transformed into the pupa, the larva disappears; and so forth.

One of Piaget's colleagues, B. Inhelder, says that most American audiences ask the same question when they are first exposed to Piaget: What makes the child move from one period to the next, and how can the process of change be speeded up? Piaget's concern is definitely not speed of development, and he seems to feel that efforts to accelerate cognitive development may be unwise. Each stage presumably has a function, and trying to rush a child through a stage may even be detrimental to his overall development.

The Process of Intellectual Growth: Equilibration

Equilibration is Piaget's term for the overall process by which intellectual growth takes place. In order to understand equilibration, it is necessary to become familiar with three other terms that Piaget uses: scheme, assimilation, and accommodation.

Schemes As an infant interacts with the world around him, he uses certain recurrent schemes of action. *Scheme* is Piaget's word for an organized action or mental transformation that, when applied to the world, leads to that mysterious event called knowing. For example, the young infant attempts to grasp and to suck on almost everything. In Piaget's terms, he has a grasping scheme and a sucking scheme (among others). By using these schemes, the one-month-old comes to understand and appreciate much of his world in terms of things that can be grasped or sucked.

Grasping is, in fact, a useful metaphor for what schemes do. An infant comes

Figure 5.4
This infant's actions illustrate the grasping scheme (top left) and sucking scheme (top right and bottom) to which Piaget refers. Because he has to adjust these schemes to varying situations, the infant acquires data about different objects and their properties. This begins the process of intellectual growth.

to know objects by grasping them with his hand, and he must often change the way he is holding his hand in order to grasp an unfamiliar object. He finds that different objects must be grasped in different ways, and that some (such as walls) cannot be grasped at all. In the same way that the child adjusts his hand to fit different objects, he adjusts his schemes to fit different objects and events. This modification of schemes is what produces intellectual growth.

Figure 5.5A
What is pictured in this photograph? Arrive at a hypothesis if you can, then check your hypothesis with Figure 5.5B, on page 90.

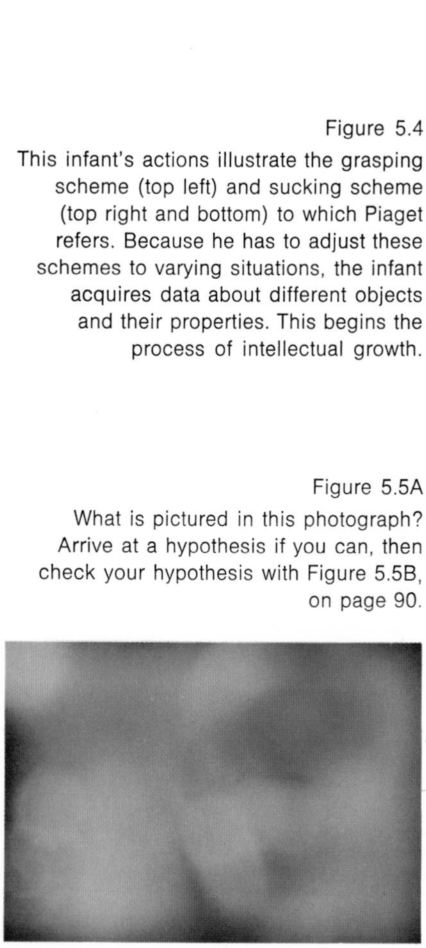

As the child grows older, his schemes for understanding the world become more complicated and less dependent on overt action. They become what Piaget calls *interiorized actions.* That is, they become transformations carried out mentally, without physical action. For example, when you are doing addition, you must mentally transform numbers in order to reach a solution: 3 and 5 become 8. If you are trying to understand a poem, you must mentally transform the concepts of the poem in order to put them together in a way that makes sense to you.

Both the schemes of an infant and the interiorized schemes of an adult play the same central role in knowing. Whatever his age, a person seeks to understand by applying his schemes to the world, and he adjusts them to fit the characteristics of the world. A task from an experiment by M. Potter demonstrates the way schemes function. Look at Figure 5.5A, a photograph that is out of focus. What object do you think is pictured in the photograph? Next, look at Figure 5.5B, on page 90, which is the same photograph in slightly better focus. Does it still look like the same object, or could it be something different from what you first thought? Now look at Figure 5.5C, on page 92, where the focus is improved a bit more. Do you think that you know what the object is?

Your attempt to identify the object in these photographs exemplifies Piaget's view of knowing. As you look at each photograph, you try to apply various schemes to what you perceive. Perhaps you first see a pumpkin in the upper part of the picture and an ice-cream cone in the lower part. Then in the next photograph you change your hypothesis. You see a skindiver on the ocean floor and some other things that you cannot figure out. Perhaps you try out several other hypotheses as you try to make sense of the photographs. You try to apply particular schemes to the photographs and you also adjust the schemes to the characteristics of the photographs. Finally, when you look at Figure 5.5D, on page 94, you see the photograph in full focus and, if you had not recognized it before, you will probably say, "Oh yes! It's a fire hydrant."

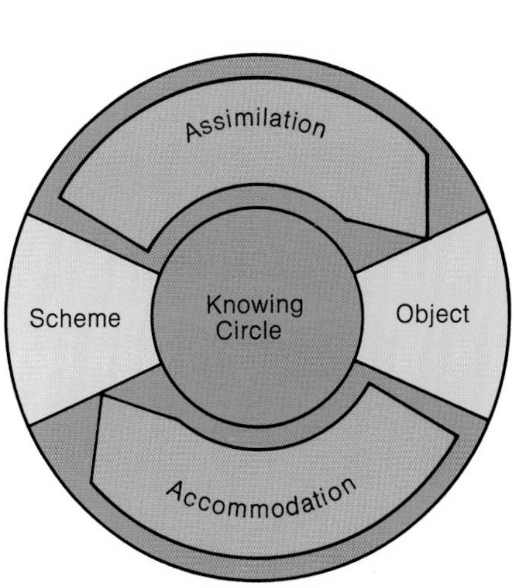

Figure 5.6
This "knowing circle" depicts the interaction of Piaget's concepts of assimilation and accommodation. In assimilation, a person applies a scheme to help him make sense of an object or occurrence. At the same time, he must usually accommodate, or modify, his scheme to account for the perceived characteristics of the object or situation.

Assimilation and Accommodation Piaget uses the terms assimilation and accommodation to describe the process of interaction between the schemes that a person applies to a situation and the adjustments that the situation requires in the schemes. As you attempted to understand the photographs in terms of a particular scheme, you were *assimilating* the photographs to the scheme. At the same time, the characteristics of the photograph contributed to your original choice of scheme. Even after the first choice had been made, those characteristics continued to influence the scheme, as you tried to adjust it to fit the photograph. That is, at all times during your application of the scheme, you were *accommodating* the scheme to the perceived characteristics of the photograph.

Thus, the word assimilation refers to an organism's active attempts to apply particular schemes to things and events in the world, and the word accommodation refers to the adjustment of those schemes to the characteristics of the things to be known. When a baseball player is fielding a ball, he attempts to apply particular schemes for catching the ball (assimilation), and he chooses the schemes and adjusts them according to the way the ball is moving (accommodation). Assimilation and accommodation occur in any situation of knowing or doing. An organism always

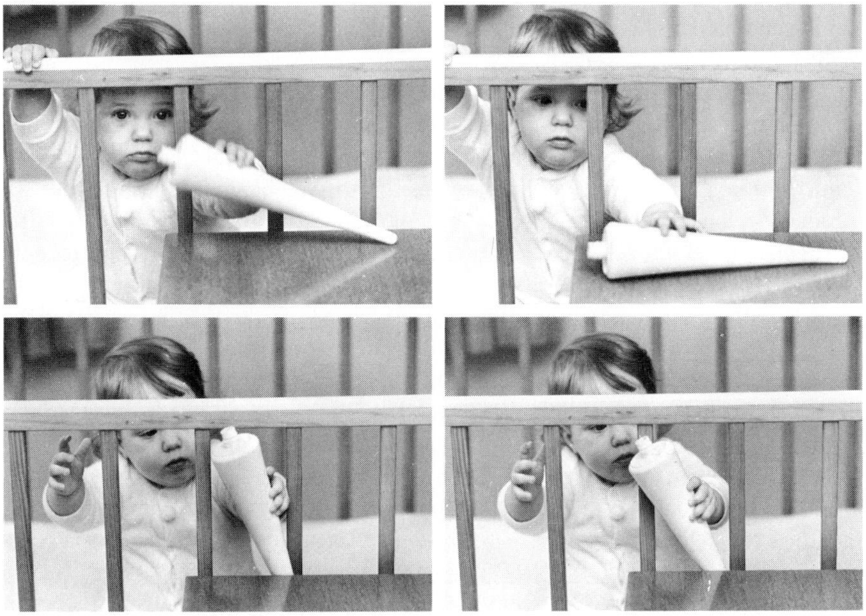

Figure 5.7
The child applies a grasping scheme (assimilates) to reach the toy. She must accommodate that scheme in order to get the toy into the crib. She turns it so it will fit through the bars.

applies particular schemes to situations (assimilation) in such a way as to take into account characteristics of the situation (accommodation).

Piaget defines knowing in terms of a continuous interaction of assimilation and accommodation. This interaction is what Piaget uses to explain development from one stage to the next. The schemes with which an infant starts life are relatively primitive. As he applies the schemes to the world around him, he must continually modify them so that he can more easily assimilate various objects and events. Through this modification, his schemes become more refined and better accommodated to his world, and his intelligence grows.

The term *equilibration* sums up this process of development. Piaget believes that the mind seeks an equilibrium of assimilation and accommodation. Think of the photographs of the fire hydrant. At the beginning, when you were trying to figure out what was pictured in them, you probably vacillated between noting specific characteristics of the photographs (accommodation) and trying to understand those characteristics in terms of particular hypotheses (assimilation). Only when you finally understood the photographs did assimilation and accommodation reach a state of equilibrium, or balance. At that point, you could use your scheme to assimilate all the characteristics of the photograph because it was fully accommodated to them.

In the following pages, as you read about the characteristics of thinking during development, keep in mind this model: intelligence involves a person mentally acting on the world, and the world influencing the way that he can act.

THE SENSORIMOTOR PERIOD

During the sensorimotor period (from birth to about age two), intelligence is primitive in form. It is based on overt action. Although its primitiveness might make it seem unimportant, sensorimotor intelligence is in many ways the most important type to understand. It is the foundation of later types of intelligence.

Sensorimotor intelligence seems to be the basis of all intelligence. Virtually all animals that exhibit intelligent behavior seem to have sensorimotor intelligence in some form. Yet this period is the hardest for most people to understand, for reasons that will become evident. Piaget suggests the term "practical intelligence" as a rough synonym for sensorimotor intelligence. As this term suggests, an infant learns to *act* in the world, but he does not *know* what he is doing. He learns how to get along practically in the world of objects—how to bring about certain effects—but his intelligence is entirely on the level of actions. He has no understanding of what he is doing, only of how to do it.

Adults often operate at the sensorimotor level. For example, the activities of riding a bicycle, driving a car, or operating any complex machine are performed primarily at this level. In carrying out these activities, an adult has a sensorimotor understanding that certain actions, such as turning the handlebar of a bicycle, will produce certain effects. He does not think about the particular actions or the particular effects; in fact, if he does think about them, he may have trouble carrying out the actions. Think about the way you are balancing a bike and it will probably start to wobble. When an adult thinks about what he is doing, a higher—and, for bike riding, a less effective—level of intelligence takes over.

One difference between an adult and an infant is that the adult is capable of thinking about what he is doing. He can carry out an action in his mind without actually performing it. He understands that his actions are distinct from the objects that he acts upon, and he realizes that his body is one object in a world of objects. The one- or two-month-old infant fails to make any of these important distinctions. He does not recognize that he has a body that is an object moving in space like other objects. He can be said to think about an activity only in the sense that he is actually carrying it out. In short, he does not yet understand that there is a

Figure 5.5B
Can you tell yet what the photograph is showing? Make another guess, then turn to page 92, and check your hypothesis with the better resolution in Figure 5.5C.

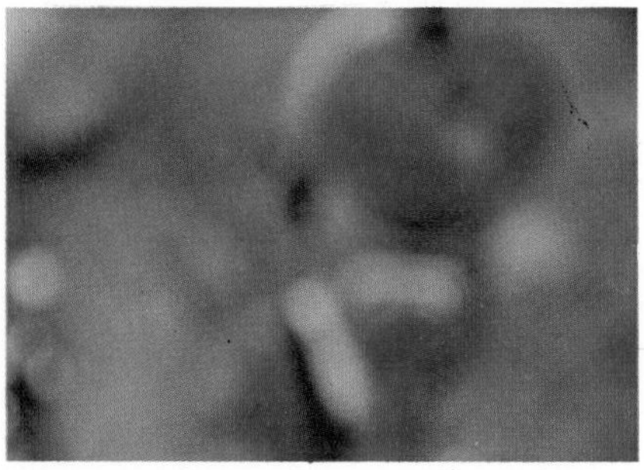

distinction between his own thought and actions and the things in the world that he is acting upon.

Object Constancy

In an ingenious series of experiments, Piaget has shown how infants gradually build up these distinctions. One group of observations illustrates especially well the nature of sensorimotor intelligence and shows how the primitive, action-based intelligence of the newborn infant is gradually transformed into the intelligence of a two-year-old. Most of the observations are simple and can be repeated by anyone, provided that care is taken to keep the infant's attention.

Piaget asked a simple question: How does an infant come to recognize *object constancy?* That is, how does a child know that an object does not stop existing when he can no longer see it or feel it or hear it? Piaget showed that very young infants do not show object constancy. They construct it, gradually and systematically, during the first eighteen to twenty-four months of life.

Early in infancy, anything that is not seen or touched or heard seems not to exist for the child. He will look at a toy block that is held in front of his face and grasp the block if it is placed in his hand, but as soon as the object is moved out of sight and out of reach, he acts as if it had ceased to exist. He does not search for it or show any other sign that he believes in its continued existence. In addition, he does not coordinate his senses. He does not recognize that objects that can be seen can also be touched, or that objects that make a noise can also be seen.

In this world without stable objects, the infant's rudimentary intelligence is based on his actions. He understands things in terms of a few elementary schemes based on the reflexes that he is born with, such as grasping and sucking. He has all the normal human senses: he can see, hear, touch, feel warmth and cold, and the like. But these sensations acquire meaning for the infant only in terms of his action schemes. Through these schemes he learns to recognize certain stable sensory configurations that Piaget calls *tableaux.* From the second week of life on, for example, the infant can usually find the nipple of his mother's breast to suck. He can tell the breast from other things that can be sucked, and he can differentiate the nipple of the breast from the area surrounding it. He has learned to recognize the *sensory tableau* of the nipple. But this recognition does not mean the infant understands that the breast is an object or a part of a human body. He has merely learned that it is a stable sensory tableau and that, when the tableau is present, he will be able to use his sucking scheme in his accustomed way.

As the infant has more and more experience with the world around him, he develops more and more skill in applying his schemes and in recognizing tableaux that are appropriate to them. He also begins to coordinate some of the schemes. For example, he coordinates grasping and sucking, developing the ability to bring objects to his mouth to be sucked. Earlier, he could suck objects that were put in his mouth, and he could grasp objects that were placed in his hand, but he could not bring an object that he had grasped up to his mouth for sucking.

As these coordinations develop, the infant begins to show the first elementary

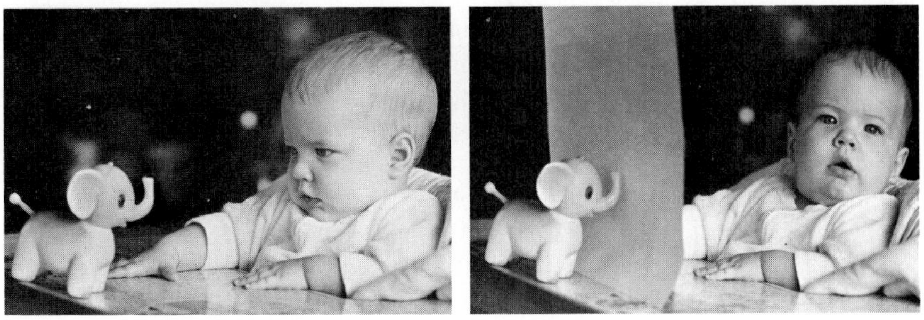

Figure 5.8
The infant gazes at the toy elephant (left). When an opaque screen shields the toy from her view (right), she no longer attends to it. Her responses give no indication that she understands that the toy elephant still exists; she has not yet acquired object constancy.

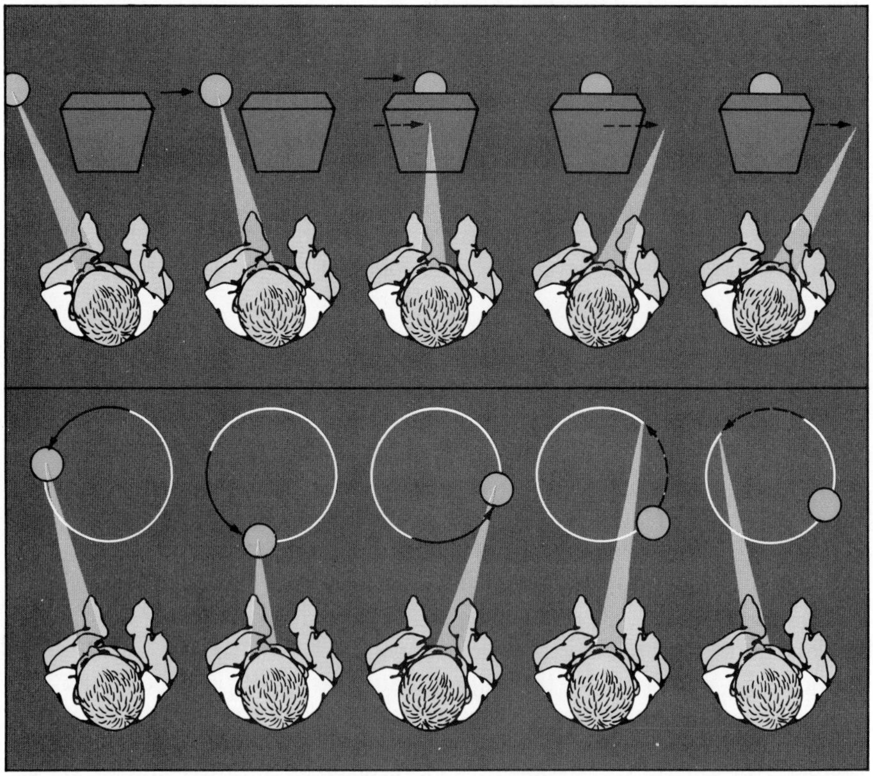

Figure 5.9
T. G. R. Bower's experiments in object constancy, with six- to eight-week-old infants, are depicted in these drawings. (Top) the infant visually follows the ball in its path from his left to his right; his gaze continues in the same direction even after the ball rolls behind a screen and does not emerge. His behavior seems to show that he believed the object continued to exist even when he did not see it. In the experiment illustrated in the bottom drawings, the infant is shown a ball moving in a circle; the ball stops halfway through its arc. He pauses momentarily and then resumes his circular tracing, seemingly in search of the object, even though it is within plain view. It seems that the infant tracked not the ball, but its movement. He seems to treat the moving ball and the stationary ball as two distinct objects.
(From "The Visual World of the Infant," T. G. R. Bower. © 1971 by Scientific American, Inc. All rights reserved.)

signs of object constancy. Under some circumstances, he pursues disappearing objects with his eyes. If an object is moved across his visual field, he not only turns his head to follow its path but continues to look along the path even if he loses sight of the object. Similarly, if only part of a familiar object is visible—such as the edge of a rattle almost covered by his blanket—he may reach for it. Earlier, he would not have reached for the rattle unless it was fully visible.

At the next stage in the development of object constancy, the infant for the first time searches for an object when it is out of sight. A familiar, desirable object is shown to him until he has displayed a clear interest in it. Then, while the child watches, it is put under a blanket or a pillow. At this stage the infant will move aside the obstacle and reach for the object. A simple act! But at earlier stages the child behaved as if the object had ceased to exist as soon as it disappeared under the blanket. And even now he shows a strange deficit in his ability to locate hidden objects. If the object is placed under one pillow and then—in full sight of the child—is taken out from under the first pillow and put under a second one, the child looks for it under the *first* pillow. He is repeating the action that produced the object earlier rather than looking for the object where he last saw it.

Casual observation of an infant at this stage often seems to indicate that he understands the notion of permanent objects, but the impression is misleading. The infant does not understand that he is handling *objects.* For him, an "object" is a series of potential actions that he can bring about in the sights and sounds around him. When an infant at this stage is said to "grasp an object" or "look at an object" or "suck an object," it must be kept in mind that only the adult observer—not the infant—knows that the thing grasped, looked at, or sucked is an object with fixed properties.

Figure 5.5C
You may already know what has been photographed here; you probably have had to discard several hypotheses and modify others. Check your decision with Figure 5.5D on page 94.

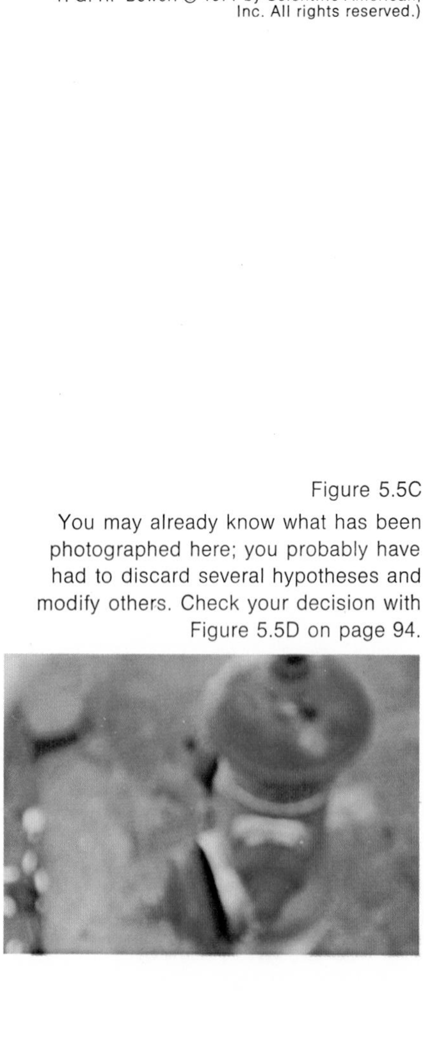

When the child reaches the last purely sensorimotor stage in the development of object constancy, he can follow all visible movements of an object and therefore find it in the last place it was hidden. When an object is hidden under one pillow and then under a second one, the child reaches for it under the second one. Indeed,

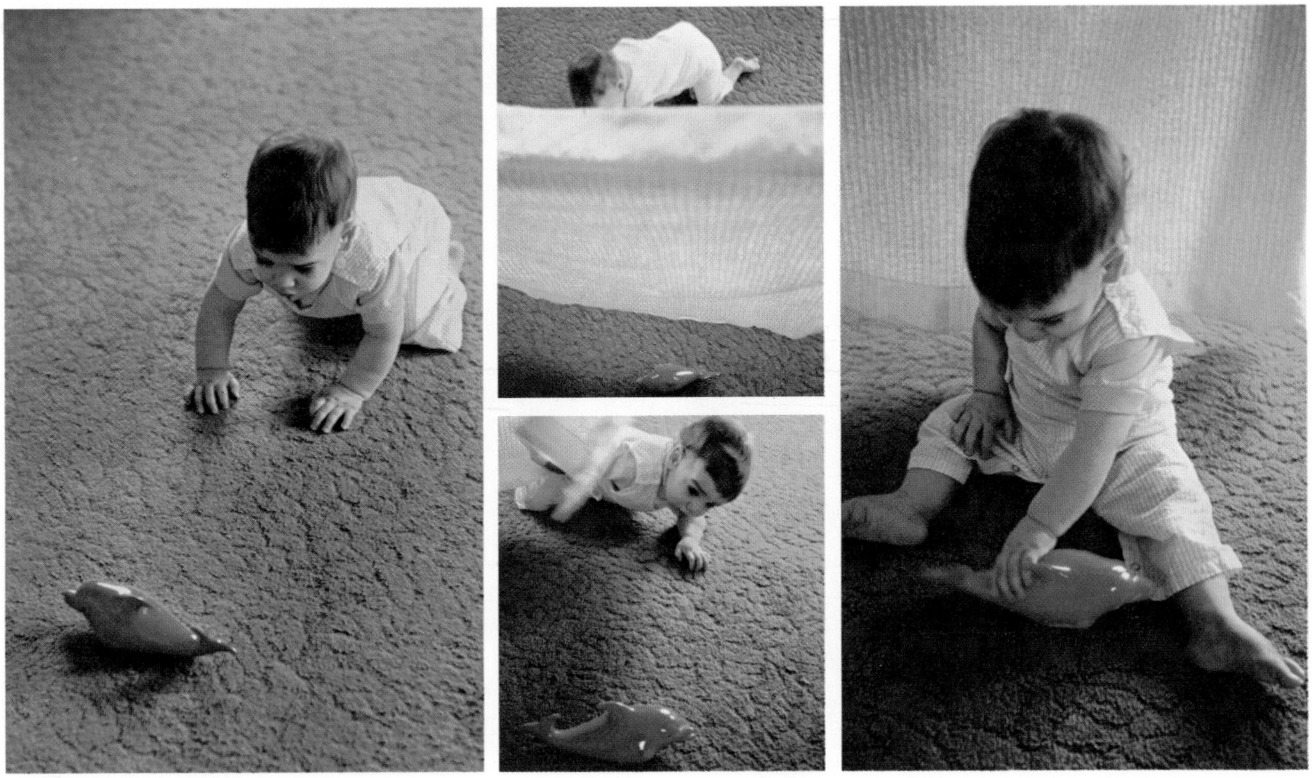

Figure 5.10
This infant searches for the toy that he has seen (left) but that has been shielded from his view by a blanket (middle, top). He crawls under the blanket to find the object (middle, bottom) and resumes his play (right). His behavior shows object constancy; he understands that the toy did not cease to exist when it was outside his view.

he can find it even if it is hidden under a third or a fourth pillow. The only deficit remaining is that the child still cannot cope with invisible displacements. For example, an object is hidden in a matchbox, and the matchbox is placed under a pillow. While the matchbox is covered by the pillow, the object is surreptitiously removed. It is left under the pillow, and the empty matchbox is put in front of the child. The child searches for the object in the matchbox, but he does not search for it under the pillow. He cannot yet take into account the possibility that something he did not see might have happened.

The final realization of object constancy comes when the child understands that objects can be moved from place to place even when he does not perceive their movements. This development will be discussed at greater length in Chapter 6.

The Nature of the Infant's Sensory Tableaux

We have traced the infant's development during the sensorimotor period from mere recognition of a few stable sensory tableaux to an understanding that the world is organized into objects with fixed properties. Through his activities in the world, he develops the ability to *mentally* coordinate what he sees, hears, and touches (that is, his sensory tableaux) into the concept of an object. For example, he learns to associate the sight of a toy rattle with its touch and its sound and to give all these tableaux together the meaning "rattle."

An important question has been neglected in Piaget's analysis, however. What is the nature of the tableaux in the young infant? In more traditional terminology, what is the nature of the young infant's perception: what do his concepts look like to him? When he looks at a rattle, what does he see? This is not the same question that Piaget asked in his research. He was concerned with the child's *understanding* of what he saw (and heard and felt), whereas the present question deals with his perception of tableaux, regardless of whether he understands what he is perceiving.

Because infants cannot tell psychologists what they perceive, this question has been particularly difficult to investigate experimentally. Recently, however, several

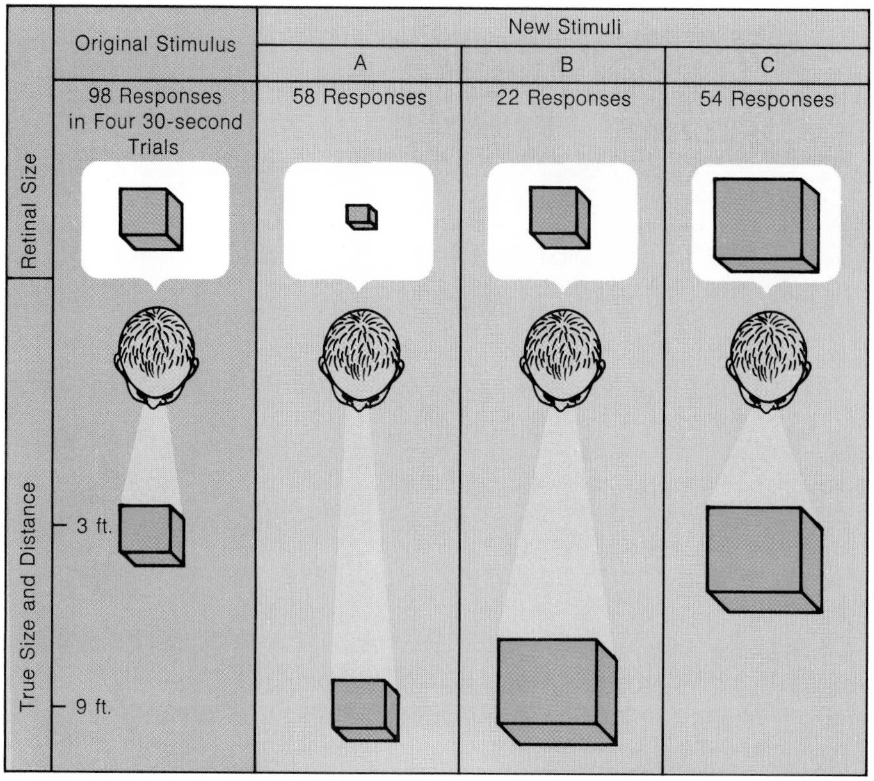

Figure 5.11
The results of Bower's intriguing experiment in perceptual constancy. As expected, during the test the six-week-old infants responded most often to the original stimulus, on which they had been trained. If they had responded on the basis of retinal size, they would have chosen stimulus B most often; instead, they responded to it less than to stimulus A (the same size as the original object) and to C (a larger object at the original distance). That is, they responded to real size and real distance.
(Adapted from "The Visual World of Infants," T. G. R. Bower. ©1966 by Scientific American, Inc. All rights reserved.)

important breakthroughs have been made. Some of the most important research has been carried out by T. G. R. Bower, with infants six to eight weeks old. He has shown that infants' perceptual abilities are much more complex than had been believed.

Bower's experiments focus on *perceptual constancies,* phenomena that are discussed in detail in Chapter 14. For example, an adult can usually tell the correct size of an object he is looking at whether the object is close to him or far away. This phenomenon is called *size constancy.* To demonstrate your own capacity for size constancy, hold one hand at arm's length and the other hand half as far away and ask yourself if they look the same size. They do. This fact has long intrigued psychologists, because the nature of the eye makes the phenomenon difficult to explain. Objects that are far away from the eye cast a smaller image on the retina than do objects close to the eye. In the case of your two hands, the retinal image of the far hand is half the size of the retinal image of the near hand. Yet somehow you perceive the two hands as being the same size. In the past, most psychologists assumed that infants at first perceive objects in terms of the retinal image and that they learn only gradually to perceive true size. According to this hypothesis, an infant would perceive a hand near his face as larger than a hand at arm's length; that is, he would not show size constancy. Bower has shown that, on the contrary, six- to eight-week-old infants do show size constancy.

Figure 5.5D
Finally, a fire hydrant. The cognitive processes you used in making hypotheses and modifying them exemplify Piaget's concepts of assimilation and accommodation.

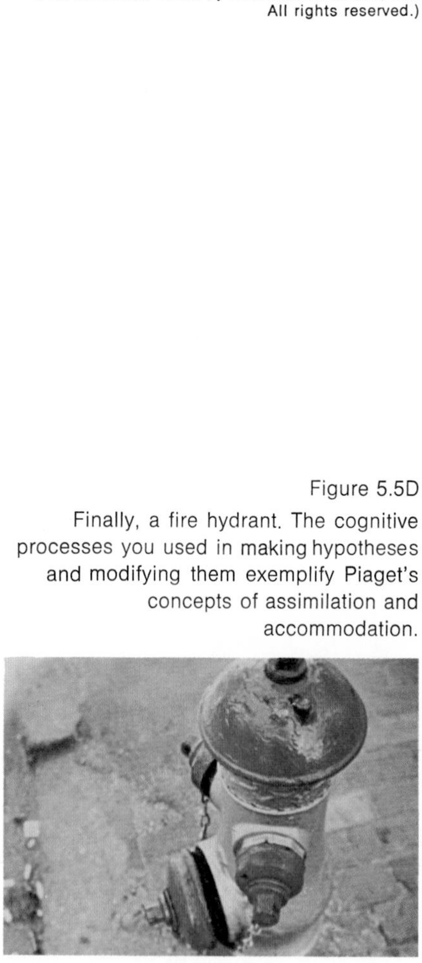

In Bower's experiment, an infant was trained to turn his head to one side when a twelve-inch cube was shown to him at a distance of three feet. Whenever he turned his head in response to the cube, he was rewarded by a peek-a-boo—an adult popped up into view in front of the infant, smiled, and spoke to him—a highly effective reward for infants. After the infant had learned to turn his head consistently, he was tested with several different-size cubes at different distances to see whether he responded to retinal size or to real size. In addition to the original twelve-inch cube at the original distance of three feet, he was tested with the three other stimuli shown in Figure 5.11. Stimulus A was a twelve-inch cube presented at nine feet;

the real size of the cube was the same as that of the training cube, but the retinal image was smaller because this cube was farther away. Stimulus B was a thirty-six-inch cube presented at nine feet; this cube was three times larger than the training cube but also three times farther away, so it cast a retinal image the same size as that of the training cube. Stimulus C was also a thirty-six-inch cube, but it was presented at three feet; since it was larger than the original cube but the same distance away, it cast a larger retinal image.

The infants' responses to each stimulus are shown in Figure 5.11. As was expected, they responded most often to the original stimulus, the training cube. They also responded frequently to Stimulus A (the original cube at the greater distance) and to Stimulus C (the larger cube at the original distance). They did not respond often to Stimulus B (the larger cube at the greater distance), even though it cast a retinal image of the size previously cast by the stimulus of training. In other words, they responded to real size and to real distance, but they did not respond to retinal size—indicating that even six-week-old infants show a kind of adult size constancy. Using similar experiments, Bower has demonstrated that young infants also show other surprising perceptual constancies.

The infant's sensory tableaux, then, appear not to be in the same rudimentary state as his intelligence. Although the young infant does not understand object *permanence,* he seems to perceive objects much more similarly to the way adults do than was previously believed. These results support Piaget's contention that the primary development in the infant and the child is intellectual rather than perceptual. The infant seems to have a highly refined perceptual apparatus, but he does not yet know how to use it intelligently. He must develop the ability to give meaning to the tableaux that he sees, hears, and feels.

SUGGESTED READINGS

BALDWIN, A. *Theories of Child Development.* New York, Wiley, 1967. A clear, concise treatment of the major theories of child development, including Piaget's.

BOWER, T. G. R. "The Object in the World of the Infant," *Scientific American,* 225 (1971), 30–38. A report of Bower's recent research, in which he has begun to explore the relationship between the infant's advanced perceptual capacities and limited cognitive capacities.

FISHER, K. W. *Piaget's Theory of Learning and Cognitive Development.* Chicago, Markham Press (in press). A clear, easy-to-read summary and discussion of Piaget's theory, with special emphasis on his approach to learning and cognitive development.

FURTH, H. G. *Piaget and Knowledge.* Englewood Cliffs, N. J., Prentice-Hall, 1969. An in-depth treatment of Piaget's theory of knowing, with special emphasis on its philosophical and biological foundations.

PIAGET, J. *The Origins of Intelligence in the Child.* New York, International Universities Press, 1952. The introductory volume to Piaget's three-volume treatise on cognitive development during infancy.

———. *The Construction of Reality in the Child.* New York, Basic Books, 1954. The second volume in Piaget's three-volume treatise deals with the development of an understanding of objects, space, time, and causality.

———. *Biology and Knowledge.* Chicago, University of Chicago Press, 1971. In this recent book, Piaget describes the significance of his lifetime of work for understanding man's ability to know and the relationship of that ability to man's biological heritage.

PIAGET, J., AND INHELDER, B. *The Psychology of the Child.* New York, Basic Books, 1969. This is Piaget and Inhelder's own summary of their work. Its main usefulness is as a summary of major experimental findings rather than as an introduction to Piaget's theory.

6 Development of Higher-Order Intelligence

WHAT IS intelligence anyway?

I consider myself intelligent, and it is with a certain relief that I find most people agreeing with me. I am saddened, though, when I find that in some cases the agreement rests on a flimsy basis.

For instance—I will sometimes buy a number of objects, and the clerk will then add the prices. He will write the various numbers on a slip of paper, let us say: $1.55, $1.45, $2.39, and $2.49. I watch those numbers go down and automatically mutter, "That comes to seven dollars and eighty-eight cents."

The clerk generally gives me a sour smile and goes back to his painstaking addition. When he finally gets his $7.88, he looks up at me with awe and says, "That's amazing."

"Not really," I say.

It usually drops there, but occasionally I come across a clerk who won't let go. "You must be very smart," he will say, "to be able to do a thing like that."

"Why?" I say. "You can do it, too."

"Never," is the immediate modest reply.

"Sure you can," I say. "Look, you don't add $1.45 and $1.55. You take five cents from one and add it to the other so you have $1.50 and $1.50 which comes to $3.00 at once. Then instead of adding $2.39 and $2.49 you add a penny to each and add $2.40 and $2.50, which comes to $4.90, remembering that you will have to remove the pennies you added. The $3.00 and the $4.90 are $7.90 and when you take off the two pennies, you have $7.88 and that's your answer. If you practice that sort of thing, you can . . . ."

By that time, though, I have to stop because there's no way of ignoring the cold stare I am now getting. "Oh, it's just a trick," says the clerk. Not only am I no longer intelligent, I am nothing but a faker.

To the average person, in other words, understanding the properties of numbers and using those properties to simplify numerical manipulations is *not* intelligent. Performing mechanical manipulations very quickly *is* intelligent. This sort of attitude, which confuses the mechanical with the intelligent, leads to mistaking rote memory for great brilliance. During the 1950s there was a television quiz-game vogue; people could win a hundred thousand dollars or more for rattling off the names of heavyweight champions, or the like, and they were considered extraordinarily intelligent for being able to do so.

There was one postal clerk, in fact, whose level of intelligence was not high by any reasonable standard but who had a remarkably retentive memory and instant recall. He did amazingly well in those quizzes. Any question that had a discrete answer, such as "Who was king of France in 1688?" he could answer at once, and correctly. Any question that required judgment or thought, such as "What were some of the reasons for the tariff policies of the United States in the post-Civil War period?" would have been impossible for him to answer.

Yet, for a while, there was a talk of a TV quiz program in which this postal clerk was to compete with all comers, and it was to be called "Beat the Genius." Fortunately, it never came to pass. I.A.

When the child develops past the sensorimotor period of intellectual development, at about the age of two, he begins to show the first signs of what people ordinarily call thought. For the first time, he seems to reflect upon or think about at least some events after they occur. This is a remarkable achievement, but it is still far from the thinking abilities of a human adult. Much of the child's energy for the next fifteen years or so will go into the construction of increasingly complex mental schemes for understanding the world. Piaget sees those fifteen years of construction as comprising three developmental periods: the preoperational, the concrete-operational, and the formal-operational.

THE PREOPERATIONAL PERIOD

One hallmark of the end of the sensorimotor period and the beginning of the preoperational period is complete *object constancy,* which the infant shows at about eighteen to twenty-four months of age. For the first time, the child understands that objects do not cease to exist when they disappear.

Object Constancy

Faced with the matchbox experiment described in Chapter 5, the preoperational child can take account of invisible displacements: when the object turns out not to be in the matchbox, he looks under the pillow. If the object is not there, he widens his search. Is it under the table, or in the adult's pocket? And if he still cannot find it, he may turn to the adult and ask (as well as he can) where the object is.

Developing an awareness of object constancy is a truly impressive feat. Virtually every human child achieves what is in effect a Copernican Revolution. Before Copernicus, people looking at the sky accepted at face value what they saw. The stars, the sun, and the moon appeared to revolve around the earth, and people therefore believed that was what they did. Copernicus discovered that the earth and the other planets actually revolve around the sun, and that heavenly bodies only appear to revolve around us because the earth is turning. His discovery required him to deny what appeared to be true in order to understand the underlying reality. Similarly, the child who understands object constancy must realize that, although objects seem to disappear periodically, they do not stop existing. Their existence does not depend on his perceiving them.

The attainment of complete object constancy is a result of a new capacity that the child has developed, a capacity Piaget calls *representation.* For the first time, the child can evoke certain mental schemes in the absence of the overt actions, objects, or events on which the schemes are based. Put more simply, he can think about some actions when they are not being performed, objects when they are not present, and events when they are not happening.

Deferred Imitation, Insight Learning, and Language

This new capacity produces a number of new abilities besides object constancy. For the first time, the child is capable of *deferred imitation:* he can imitate someone else's actions a long time after he has seen them. He also begins to show *insight learning.* That is, he looks at a problematical situation, pauses to think about it for a moment, and then, after what seems like an "aha" reaction, solves the problem. And he begins to play make-believe, pretending that he is going to sleep or that a log he comes upon in the woods is a horse. Finally, in what is probably the most important development of all, the preoperational child begins to use language. He can name objects, and he soon begins to speak short sentences.

Until recently, it seemed that no other species was capable of anything approximating human language. The most likely candidate was the chimpanzee, which has all the other capacities that appear in the human child early in the preoperational period, including object constancy, deferred imitation, and insight learning. But all research up to about 1965 indicated that chimpanzees were unable to speak.

Since that time, A. and B. Gardner have shown that chimpanzees *can* learn simple language. Earlier researchers tried to train them to speak, but the Gardners took a different approach. Taking advantage of the fact that chimps have excellent control of their hands, they set out to teach the sign language normally used by deaf-mutes to a young female chimp named Washoe. Although the Gardners' approach has been dramatically successful, Washoe's achievements (which are further described in Chapter 7) to date belong to the early part of the preoperational period. At present it seems unlikely that she will ever develop an intelligence equal to that of a four-year-old child.

Various psychologists, including S. White, have suggested that, during the preoperational period, a child masters certain basic skills that are easy for him to learn while he is young but much more difficult during adolescence and adulthood.

One of them, it seems, is language. An anthropologist who took his three-year-old son with him on a field trip to an isolated New Guinea village reported that, within a month, the boy spoke the native language well enough to make himself understood by the local children. The anthropologist himself could understand hardly anything the local people said. He began asking his son how to say things and eventually managed to learn the language through the boy. Research described by E. Lenneberg comparing the language-learning abilities of young children and adolescents confirms the anthropologist's finding.

The preoperational child clearly has many new abilities—object constancy, deferred imitation, insight learning, language. Each of these is one sign of the broad transformation in the child's mind that occurs with the appearance of representational thinking. The ability to think in the absence of objects, events, and overt actions produces a new type of intelligence that is qualitatively different from sensorimotor intelligence.

Intuitive Thought and Its Limitations

Representational thinking permits an adultlike intuitive understanding of many complex tasks and situations, but it also has certain limitations. For one thing, the child's thought during the preoperational period is egocentric. This term does not mean that the child is selfish. Instead, it means that he is a prisoner of his own viewpoint. He does not understand that different people have different viewpoints and that his own is merely one among many. His thought is centered on himself because he does not know that any other viewpoint exists.

Piaget and B. Inhelder describe a good experimental demonstration of egocentrism. A child is shown a model of a mountain range composed of three mountains in a triangular arrangement. The model is large, so that the child has to walk around it to look at all its sides. Each mountain has different objects on it, objects that the child can easily identify. After he is familiar with the landscape, he sits on one side of it, facing one mountain. The experimenter sits on another side and asks the child which of several pictures shows what the experimenter sees. The child repeatedly

Figure 6.1
The preoperational child's thought processes are egocentric. His intellectual capacities have not yet developed to the point where he understands that viewpoints other than his own exist.

chooses the picture showing his own view of the landscape. He cannot mentally coordinate the various views, so he cannot figure out how the landscape looks to someone in a different position.

The following poem illustrates a second characteristic of preoperational thinking. It was written by Hilary-Anne Farley, who was five years old at the time, and it appears in Richard Lewis' *Miracles,* a collection of children's poetry.

I Love Animals and Dogs

I love animals and dogs and everything.
But how can I do it when dogs are dead and a hundred?
But here's the reason: If you put a golden egg on them
They'll get better. But not if you put a star or moon.
But the star-moon goes up
And the star-moon I love.

The poem may be said to show egocentrism, because Hilary-Anne reasons in a highly personal way without seeming to understand that other people do not share her viewpoint. But more salient is what L. V. Vygotsky calls *complexive thinking.* The poem is organized like a complex (in the sense of a complex of buildings) rather than like a concept. Instead of unifying a number of thoughts under a single concept, it jumps from one idea to the next, frequently showing connections between adjacent ideas but having no overall integration. Hilary-Anne starts out talking about how she loves animals, next thinks about the fact that loving can be difficult because animals die, then says that you can make sick animals better by putting a golden egg on them (whatever that means). The golden egg reminds her of stars and the moon, which she notes will not make the dog better. From star and moon she jumps to the star-moon, which she points out moves up in the sky. Finally, she says that she loves the star-moon.

Some element in one idea makes Hilary-Anne think of another idea. Some element in the second idea makes her think of a third idea, and so forth. Although every idea is related to some other one, the various ideas are not coordinated into a single system or around a single concept. Complexive thinking like Hilary-Anne's is common in children in the preoperational period.

H. Werner describes a third main characteristic of preoperational thought: The child has a strong tendency to perceive human characteristics in objects. Werner mentions a two-year-old boy who saw a cup lying on its side and exclaimed "Poor, tired cup!" Another child said that a towel hook was a "cruel" thing. A four-and-a-half-year-old child called a camera tripod "proud" when it stood straight and erect and "sad" when it leaned over at an angle. The important point about these reactions is that the child seems actually to see the cup as tired, the towel hook as cruel, and so forth. He has not yet learned to make all the necessary distinctions between human beings and objects, and so he perceives objects as having human attributes.

A fourth limitation of preoperational intelligence is that the child is not capable of carrying out tasks that require him to direct and coordinate his own thinking. Only under special circumstances can he sustain one activity for long. He can do it when the situation allows him to play freely, wandering from one idea to another; he might play in a sandbox all morning, for example, meandering from shoveling sand to playing with dump trucks to making marks in the sand to throwing it. He can also keep on with tasks that provide direct, external cues to guide and sustain his behavior. For example, a four-year-old will play for long periods with the building blocks shown in Figure 6.2. He can always see the connectives, which help focus his attention on making the blocks fit together, and he can always see the progress that he has made in building.

If a task does not provide obvious external guides to behavior, the preoperational child usually cannot deal with it. Figure 6.3 shows two tasks Piaget used to demon-

Figure 6.2
A preoperational child will play with this set of blocks for a relatively long time. A dowel protrudes from each block and fits into a hole in the block that helps to form one level of the pyramid. Also, the central area of each level is slightly elevated to fit snugly into a depression in the next higher level. These external cues help guide the child's play behavior.

strate this phenomenon. The tasks look the same at first glance, but a four-year-old can do only one of them. If he is given the sticks in Figure 6.3A, he can easily put them in order from largest to smallest. The size differences between the sticks are large and perceptually salient for the child. But if he is asked to arrange the sticks in Figure 6.3B, he will fail. Because the differences in the sizes of the sticks are so small, he has no salient external cues to guide him. Only when he reaches the concrete-operational period will he be able to put these sticks in order by size.

Figure 6.3
A preoperational child can easily arrange the sticks shown in the top photograph in decreasing order of size, because the large differences in their lengths offers a salient clue. The sticks in the bottom photograph are too much alike; the clue they give the child is too subtle to guide his problem solving.

A

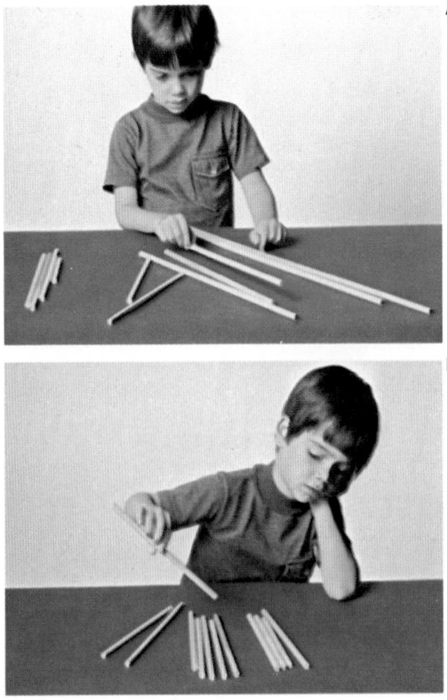

B

These limitations of preoperational thought form a unified picture. On the one hand, the child's capacity for representational thinking allows him to carry on new, complex kinds of mental activity. On the other hand, the child does not yet have the ability to organize his thinking into coordinated systems that he can direct and control. His thinking is egocentric because he cannot coordinate various viewpoints into a single system that takes all of them into account. It is complexive—his thoughts run on of themselves and he flits from one idea to another—because he cannot coordinate his ideas around a single concept. Similarly, he cannot carry out a task that requires him to coordinate his thinking unless he has the help of salient concrete cues.

Function Relationships

In the second half of the preoperational period, between about four and seven years of age, the child takes his first step toward the coordinated thought of the adult. He begins to deal with *function relationships.* That is, he can understand situations in which variations in one factor are systematically related to variations in a second factor. If you give a five-year-old a rubber band and several weights of different sizes, the child can understand, in a vague, intuitive way, that larger weights will make the rubber band stretch farther than smaller weights. This is called a function relationship because of its similarity to a mathematical function. When a mathematician says that y is a function of x, he means, roughly speaking, that variations in x produce predictable variations in y. In the present case, x is the size of the weight and y is the length of the rubber band.

THE CONCRETE-OPERATIONAL PERIOD

The end of the preoperational period does not herald the end of intuitive thought. Much adult thinking is similar to the intuitive thought of the preoperational child,

Figure 6.4
A child who pumps a swing to make it go higher is employing a functional relationship: more force produces greater height. The child may be able to do this before he is able to understand and articulate the function. Children in the late preoperational period are often able to state the function.

according to Piaget. In daydreaming, for example, one wanders from this idea to that in much the same complexive way as Hilary-Anne did in her poem. But an adult can think in ways that the preoperational child cannot. Most notably, an adult can switch back and forth between intuitive thought and *operational thought*.

At around five to seven years of age, the child develops an elementary kind of operational thought: he starts to understand *concrete operations*. In reading the following discussion, however, you should keep in mind that many of the child's efforts during this period are still limited to intuitive thinking. In dealing with many problems, he uses preoperational thinking rather than concrete-operational thinking. Even if the child has the benefit of good schooling, it will take him five to ten years to develop fully his concrete-operational capacities.

Conservation

Conservation is one of the most striking developments during this period. Because a child in the late preoperational period can understand simple function relationships, he can correctly predict the effects of certain simple manipulations of liquids. If liquid from a medium-width container is to be poured into a narrow container, he can usually predict correctly that the liquid will be higher in the narrow container than in the medium one. Similarly, if liquid from a medium-width container is to be poured into a wide container, he can usually predict that the liquid will be lower in the wide container. That is, the preoperational child usually understands that changing the width of a container will change the height of a fluid, and he knows whether the height will go up or down. But he does not understand that the amount of liquid stays the same when the liquid is poured from jar to jar.

What is required for him to develop conservation of amount of liquid? An understanding of simple function relationships is not enough. The child must be able to coordinate his thoughts about the length and width of the first container, the length and width of the second container, and the change brought about by pouring the liquid from the first container into the second. The preoperational child cannot do this; he considers the state of each container separately and consequently chooses the jar that "looks like more." The concrete-operational child, on the other hand, pays close attention to the transformation that occurs as the liquid is poured, coordinating his thoughts on that with his thoughts about the height and width of the containers.

What is the nature of this coordination, and how does it take place? To explain it, Piaget uses the concept of a *system of operations.* An operation is a special kind of scheme, defined as an *interiorized transformation or action that is reversible.* The operation is interiorized in the same sense that the schemes of intuitive (preoperational) thought are interiorized: the child can carry out the transformation mentally without carrying it out physically. It is a transformation because it specifies how one state is changed into another state. And it is reversible because the mental system that the operation is a part of also contains another operation that can mentally *undo* the transformation to restore the original state.

An example is in order. Without actually pouring any liquid, a child who understands conservation can think about the changes that pouring would bring about (interiorization). He can mentally coordinate the two states of the liquid by considering how pouring transforms one state into the other (transformation). And he can restore the original state by mentally pouring the liquid back into its original container (reversibility).

Classification

Piaget specifies many different systems of operations that the concrete-operational child gradually masters. Several of them deal with *classification.* How well can a child understand the relationships between different ways of classifying things? The answer to that question illustrates the way the concrete-operational child coordinates his thinking into systems.

Figure 6.5
The concrete-operational child gradually masters the operation of addition of classes. The arrangement shown in the photograph is used to test a child's ability to coordinate the class "animal" with the subclasses "dog" and "cat," and the class "dog" with the subclasses "poodle" and "terrier."

Addition of Classes One of the main skills needed for classification is called the addition of classes. A child needs to understand, for example, that the class of dogs is made up of the class of poodles, the class of terriers, and the classes of all other types of dog. That is, he needs to understand that the classes for each type of dog are added together to form the class "dogs."

As with conservation, the preoperational child has some of the capacities that are necessary for understanding addition of classes, but he cannot coordinate his thinking. A simple example shows the kinds of questions he can answer and the kinds he cannot. Suppose a four-year-old is given eight toy poodles, two toy terriers, and three toy cats. The child is first asked to sort the toys into piles that are all alike. An early preoperational child will not be able even to sort them properly, but a child who is on the verge of concrete operations will manage to make three simple groups—one of poodles, one of terriers, and one of cats. When he has done that, the experimenter begins to pose a number of questions.

Which of the toys are dogs? The child points to the group of poodles and the group of terriers. Which are cats? He points to the group of cats. Which of the toys are animals? He points to all three groups. Are there more poodles or more terriers? The child correctly chooses poodles. If you wanted to have more dogs, would you choose the poodles or the terriers? Again, the child correctly chooses the poodles. Are there more dogs or more cats? He correctly indicates more dogs.

So far, the child is doing well. At first glance, he seems to understand classes and to be able to use them properly. But his answers to a few key questions show that this conclusion is incorrect. Although he understands the meaning of the words, he cannot coordinate the various classes so as to be able to carry out simple addition of classes.

The child is asked the key question: Are there more dogs or more poodles? "More poodles," he says. Are there more dogs or more animals? "More dogs," he says. Could you make a bigger group out of all the poodles or all the dogs? "All the poodles," he says. A second preoperational child's answers may be incorrect in a different way. He will say that the number of dogs is the same as the number of poodles, and that the number of animals is the same as the number of dogs.

Both children have a similar difficulty. They cannot coordinate two levels of classification. In Figure 6.5, they cannot move up and down between the class of animals and the subclasses of poodles and terriers. Sometimes they err systematically, always choosing the larger subclass (poodles and dogs) or always saying that the class and the subclass are the same size. At other times, their errors are less systematic. In either case they are subject to the same difficulty: inability to coordinate classes and subclasses.

Multiplication of Classes A second skill that is required for classification is the multiplication of classes. The child needs to understand, for example, that classes of geometrical shapes (circles, squares, triangles) can be "multiplied" with classes of colors (red, green, blue) to produce classes of colored geometrical shapes, as shown in Figure 6.6.

The preoperational child can carry out some aspects of classification with these objects. He can easily pick out a red square, since he is only required to note two specific characteristics (red and square) and choose an object that possesses them. His difficulty comes in coordinating the two dimensions of classification (shape and color), as shown in the following examples.

A preoperational child is given all the objects in Figure 6.6A in a mixed-up order. He is asked to put together those that are alike, or those that "go together." He may make three groups of objects—perhaps all red figures, all green ones, and all blue ones. Or he may make four piles—one containing all the green circles, one containing all the red figures (circles, squares, and triangles), one containing the green squares and the blue squares, and one containing the green triangles, the blue triangles, and the blue circles. In any such groupings, the child takes account of some of the major features of the objects, but he is unable to make up the full set of nine categories. Even with some helpful hints from the experimenter, he cannot complete the multiplication table as shown in Figure 6.6C. And even if the experimenter arranges the figures for the child, the child cannot specify that the rows

Figure 6.6
To sort these blocks into the matrix shown in (C), a child must have mastered multiplication of classes. A preoperational child may be able to sort them as shown in (B), but he cannot perform the concrete operations that enable him to coordinate the classes of color and of shape.

A B C

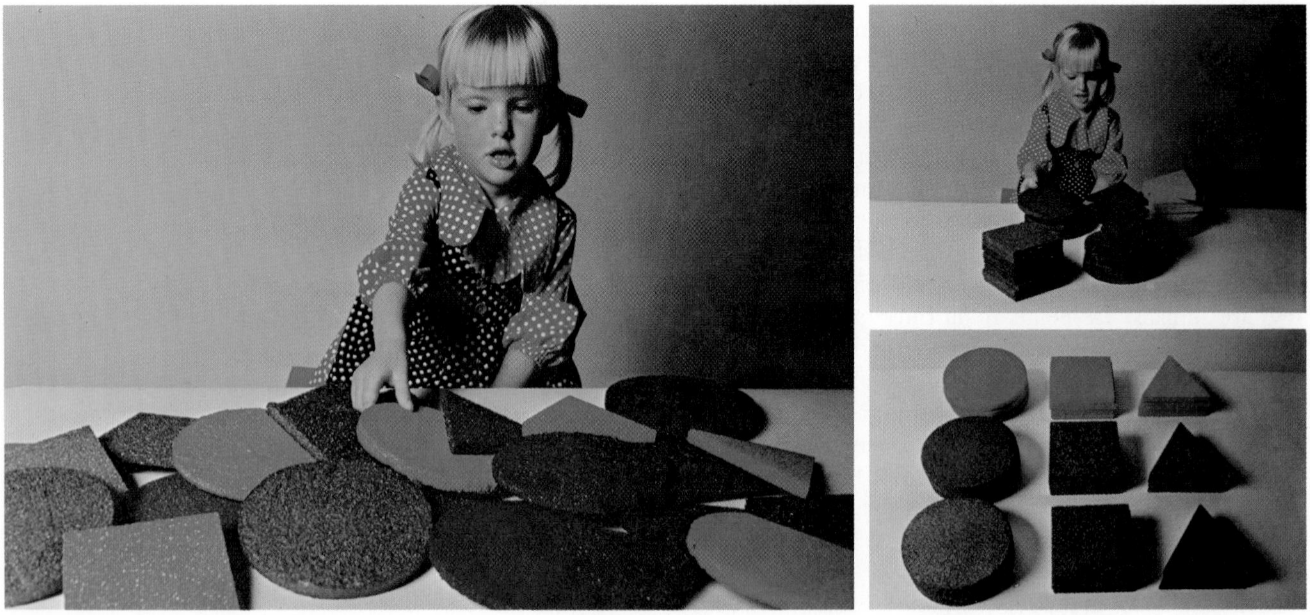

are made up of all the red figures, all the blue figures, and all the green figures, and that the columns are made up of all the circles, all the squares, and all the triangles.

A concrete-operational child behaves very differently. He can readily make up the three-by-three grouping of figures, and he can explain how the rows and columns are organized. He has mastered multiplication of classes.

As with addition of classes, a few key questions highlight the nature of the preoperational child's failure. Suppose he is given a new batch of figures—red circles, red squares, and blue circles but no blue squares. When a preoperational child is asked, "Are all the blue figures circles?" he answers, in effect, "No, because here's a circle that's red." But the concrete-operational child answers correctly with relative ease: "Yes, because there aren't any blue squares."

As with addition of classes, the preoperational child's failure comes from his inability to coordinate two dimensions. He cannot move back and forth across the two axes in Figure 6.6C. He cannot deal with the color and shape at the same time.

Conservation of liquid, addition of classes, and multiplication of classes all illustrate the development of systems of concrete operations. The examples show that the preoperational child is unable to coordinate his thinking about two separate states or two separate levels of analysis, as the concrete-operational child can. In conservation of amount of liquid the height and width of the liquid before pouring must be coordinated with the height and width after pouring. In addition of classes two levels of classification must be coordinated, and in multiplication of classes two kinds of classification must be coordinated. The concrete-operational child coordinates these things by constructing systems of operations in which his thought moves readily back and forth between one level or state and the other. The back-and-forth movement is allowed by the reversibility of the operations in the system: whatever mental transformation the child thinks about can be readily undone by a reverse mental operation. The effect of reversibility is to allow the child to think virtually simultaneously about the two different states.

"Necessary Truth"

The child's ability to organize his thought into systems of operations provides him with a rudimentary understanding of what philosophers call "necessary truth"—the conviction that some things *must* be true. According to Piaget, a concrete-operational child not only understands that conservation of amount of liquid *does* occur but thinks it *has* to. S. Carey-Block used an amusing variation of Piaget's conservation procedure to demonstrate this characteristic. A hidden tube was attached to the bottom of one beaker so that liquid could be surreptitiously added or removed, resulting in obvious violations of conservation. For example, when liquid was poured from a medium-width beaker into a tall, thin one, the height of the liquid in the tall, thin jar could be made markedly lower than the level in the medium-width jar before pouring. In another case, the level of the liquid in the tall, thin beaker was made to fluctuate "spontaneously" up and down.

Carey-Block found marked developmental changes in children's reactions to these violations. Children who had not yet mastered conservation of liquid showed nothing more than mild interest. Often they did not even notice that something unusual had happened. On the other hand, children who understood conservation typically showed great surprise and assumed that there was some kind of trick in the situation. They asked the experimenter, "What did you do?" or "What happened?" and began to look under the table in search of an explanation. They rejected what they had seen as impossible and began to search for the trick that would explain it.

The difference between the reactions of preoperational and concrete-operational children shows the special status of thought that is based on a coordinated system of operations. The concrete-operational child believes that the amount of liquid *must* remain constant; if it does not, he correctly assumes that trickery has occurred. The preoperational child, although he can predict the level of liquid after pouring, is not especially surprised when his prediction is contradicted. There is no *necessity* to his prediction, because it is based on simple function relationships rather than on a system of operations.

Although most of Piaget's examples come from problems related to science, like conservation, the child's capacity to coordinate his thinking is not limited to that kind of problem. For example, he can now understand and follow the rules of children's games, such as marbles, hopscotch, and baseball. He is less egocentric—better able to coordinate other people's viewpoints with his own and to understand that his viewpoint is only one among many. His thinking has taken on many of the characteristics of adult thought.

But it still has a way to go. There are definite limitations in the child's capacity to coordinate his thinking. Piaget calls the period "concrete operations" because the child can deal only with concrete objects and events. That is, he can "operate" on the characteristics of specific objects and events, but he cannot deal with all the possible combinations of characteristics. He can coordinate *concrete characteristics in an actual situation* but not possible characteristics in hypothetical situations.

Piaget argues that the concreteness of operational thought in this period produces a kind of unevenness in the child's abilities. He develops specific concrete-operational systems for dealing with specific types of situations, but he cannot coordinate the systems to form a higher-order system. This incapacity is one of the reasons that all the types of conservation do not develop simultaneously. Conservation of number develops first, then conservation of amount of liquid, still later conservation of weight, and so on. Because the child cannot coordinate his operational systems, each type of conservation seems like a new problem. He cannot tie the related systems together and understand all types of conservation at once.

Figure 6.7
The fulcrum problem illustrates one difference between the stages of concrete operations and formal operations. The concrete-operational child can coordinate the operations in B *or* those in C, but he cannot coordinate all the operations in *both* B and C. Only at the formal-operational stage will he be able to do so.

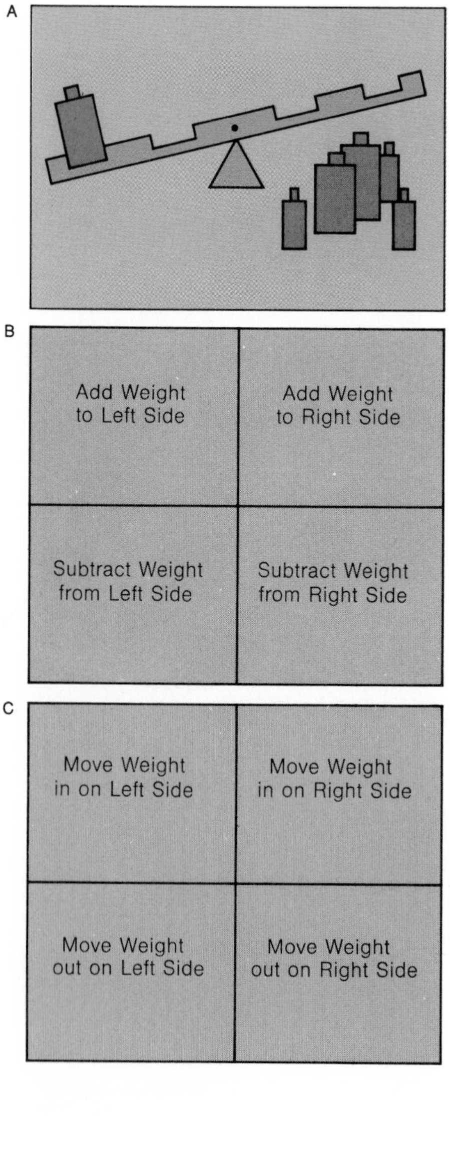

THE FORMAL-OPERATIONAL PERIOD

In the formal-operational period the limitations of concrete operations are overcome. Around the beginning of adolescence a new set of capacities begins to appear. As the ability to coordinate systems of concrete operations gradually develops, the child becomes able for the first time to think hypothetically and to carry out systematic tests of the various possible explanations of a specific event. As a result, he can solve new kinds of problems.

One of Piaget's tasks demonstrates particularly well the central difference between concrete operations and formal operations. A child is presented with a balance beam, as shown in Figure 6.7A. There are two ways to alter the balance of the beam: by adding weight to one side, and by moving a weight farther from or closer to the fulcrum of the beam.

The concrete-operational child can understand the influence of adding and taking away weights. He quickly learns, for example, that if one side of the beam has more weights on it than the other side, balance can be restored either by removing the extra weight from that side or by adding a weight to the other side. He can also understand the influence of distance from the fulcrum. If the weight on one side of the beam is farther from the fulcrum than the weight on the other side, he sees that balance can be restored either by moving the far weights closer to the fulcrum or by moving the near weights farther from the fulcrum.

But the concrete-operational child cannot understand the way the two influences (weight and distance) are related. He cannot extract the principle that an extra weight on one side of the balance can be counteracted by moving the weights on the other side farther from the fulcrum, and vice versa. He fails to see that distance can compensate for weight, and weight for distance.

In other words, the child can deal with weight alone or distance alone, but he cannot coordinate the two. The influence of weight can be understood in terms of multiplication of classes. One dimension of the multiplication is the addition or subtraction of weight, and the other dimension is the side of the beam (left or right). The concrete-operational child can coordinate these two dimensions, so he can learn how to balance the beam by adding or subtracting weights.

In the same manner, the effect of distance from the fulcrum is a case of multiplication of classes. One dimension of the multiplication is the movement of weights either closer to the fulcrum or farther away from it, and the other dimension is the side of the beam (left or right).

Transforming Transformations

During the formal-operational period the child develops the capacity to coordinate these two separate concrete-operational systems. Piaget refers to this capacity as the ability to *transform concrete-operational transformations.* A younger child shows that he understands a concrete-operational transformation by indicating that he can reverse it mentally: to compensate for an extra weight on the left side, he will say, you can add one on the right. But he cannot translate an action stated in terms of weight into terms of distance-from-fulcrum. Until he reaches the period of formal operations, he does not understand that the effect of adding weight on the left can be counteracted by, for example, moving the weights on the right farther from the fulcrum or moving the fulcrum itself closer to the weights on the left.

Piaget suggests a simple way of formulating the idea of transformations on transformations. Take a specific transformation, such as adding weight to the left side of the beam, and state it as a proposition: "Add weight to the left side." The

Figure 6.8
Children who play on seesaws often must coordinate the factors in the fulcrum problem. (Top) two children of light weight are needed to balance the weight of the heavier child on the other end. (Bottom left)these two children, confronted with the inequality in weights, compensate by shifting the fulcrum in order to change the relative distances. (Bottom right) the same effect is achieved by moving the lighter person farther from the fulcrum.

child who has reached the period of formal operations can start from such a proposition and transform it into other propositions that tell how to reverse the change specified in the original proposition. For example, consider four propositions for the balance beam:

1. Add weight to the left side.
2. Subtract weight from the left side.
3. Increase distance from fulcrum on the right side.
4. Decrease distance from fulcrum on the right side.

The formal-operational child can transform Proposition 1 into several different propositions that will reverse that action. Proposition 2 reverses the action of 1 by taking the weight away, thereby restoring the beam to balance. Proposition 3 reverses the action of 1 by moving the weights on the right farther away from the fulcrum. You should be able to think of several other ways that the beam can be restored to balance after Proposition 1 has been carried out.

Any other proposition can also be taken as a starting point and transformed into propositions that will reverse it. Proposition 4, for example, can be transformed into 3 or 2 or any of several other propositions that will reverse 4 and restore the beam to balance. The formal-operational child can understand these transformations and use them to coordinate several concrete-operational systems into a single formal-operational system.

Systematic Experimentation

This capacity allows for the development of many new skills. One of the most important is the ability to consider all possible combinations of events in a problem or task and to exclude all combinations that are irrelevent to the problem. In other words, the formal-operational child can carry out *systematic experiments*, in which he considers all possible causes of an event and rules out one after another until he discovers the actual causes. The concrete-operational child, on the other hand, has difficulty going beyond the combinations that actually occur in the real situation. He cannot systematically consider all possibilities.

The material for an experiment that Piaget used to investigate this skill is as follows. There are four beakers of clear, colorless, odorless liquid labeled with numbers 1, 2, 3, and 4, and there is a smaller bottle, labeled *g*, also containing a clear, colorless, odorless liquid. First, the child is presented with two unmarked glasses. One contains a mixture of liquids 1 and 3 and the other contains liquid 2. The experimenter adds a few drops from *g* to each glass, and the liquid in one glass turns yellow while the liquid in the other glass remains colorless and clear. Now the child is given some empty glasses and asked to produce the yellow color himself, using the liquids in the beakers. If he succeeds, he is questioned about the function of each of the four liquids.

The combination that produces the yellow color is 1 plus 3 plus *g*. The liquid in 2 is plain water and has no effect on the reaction, and the liquid in 4 prevents the yellow from appearing. Because the child must find out what each liquid does by trial and error, he must try all possible combinations. Otherwise, he cannot be sure of his conclusions. For instance, if he should stumble on the combination 1 plus 2 plus 3 plus *g*, he would obtain the yellow color, but he would not know that 2 has no function in the reaction unless he also tried the combinations 1 plus 2 plus *g*, 1 plus 3 plus *g*, and 2 plus 3 plus *g*. Of these three combinations, only 1 plus 3 plus *g* would produce yellow.

When presented with this task, a concrete-operational child often begins by systematically trying out all the single possibilities. He may test 4 plus *g*, then 2 plus *g*, then 1 plus *g*, then 3 plus *g*. When none of these combinations produces yellow, he is apt to say, "I tried them all and none of them works." With a little

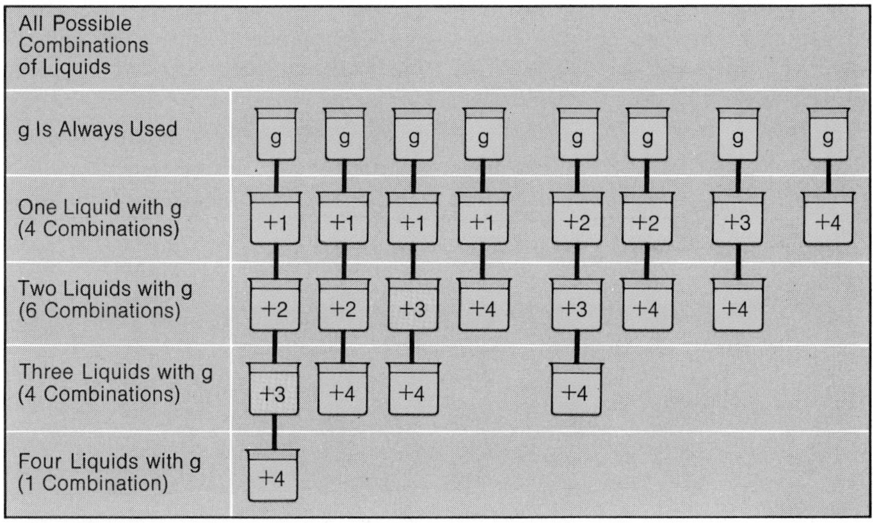

Figure 6.9
Diagram showing all possible combinations of the liquids Piaget used in investigating the difference between children in the concrete-operational stage and those in the formal-operational stage. The object for the children was to produce a yellow color, which they could do with the combination 1 plus 3 plug g. Piaget found that the formal-operational children went about this task systematically; they understood how to generate the full set of possibilities. Concrete-operational children were not yet able to do this.

coaching from the experimenter, he may realize that more than one liquid can be combined with *g*, but he then mixes the liquids haphazardly. He is unable to test all combinations systematically. Inhelder and Piaget mention a child who tried 1 plus 4 plus *g* and 2 plus 3 plus *g* and then stopped, failing to understand that every liquid could be combined with every other liquid, as shown in Figure 6.9. When the experimenter suggested to the child that he try additional combinations, he poured the fluid 1 plus *g* (which he had mixed earlier) into the jar already containing 2 plus 3 plus *g*. This mixture produced yellow, but the child did not know why. When asked to make the color again, he unsystematically tried several other combinations, none of which worked.

An older, formal-operational child can systematically consider all possible combinations of the four liquids. That is, he can coordinate all the possible ways of putting the liquids together so as to come up with a single system that includes all possible combinations. Some children may need a paper and pencil to keep track of the combinations that they have made, but they nevertheless understand how to generate the full set.

Hypothetical Ideas and Abstract Thinking

The ability to coordinate concrete-operational systems into higher-order systems also leads to several other changes in thinking. The concrete-operational child is tied to the actual, but the formal-operational child develops the capacity to consider the hypothetical, even when the thing hypothesized is highly fanciful. For example, consider the following question: "Yesterday excavators found a three-year-old skull of an animal with five feet and three heads that lived to be fifty years old. What is wrong with this statement?" A concrete-operational child will say that the question is silly because animals do not have five feet and three heads. A formal-operational child can accept the "silly" hypothesis and reason out the answer. In a similar way, the concrete-operational child tends to assume that liquids must show conservation of amount, while the formal-operational child is capable of thinking about the possibility that some liquids might conceivably not be conserved.

Together with comprehension of the hypothetical comes the ability to understand abstract principles. This new capacity is extremely important to the child. It allows him to study such fields as mathematics, science, and language on a different, less concrete level that he has earlier, and it brings about dramatic changes in his daily concerns. He may become preoccupied with certain abstractions, such as ethical ideals, conformity, and phoniness. He will often apply his new abilities to his own thoughts and motives: "I found myself thinking about my future, and then

Figure 6.10
Below is a problem you can attempt to solve that involves a hypothetical situation and systematic thinking. You will find the solution on page 111.

The M.C.C. (Mathematicians' Cricket Club), to which I belong, always holds its annual dinner in January. I was trying to find the date of the next dinner from some fellow members, but they were being rather foolishly unhelpful. One of them told me that the date was an odd number, another that is was greater than 13. A third told me that it was not a perfect square and a fourth that it was a perfect cube. And finally Charles Computer, the captain of the club, told me that the date was less than my highest score last season. (This was in fact 17, and I thought it was rather nice of Computer to bring this in.)

I subsequently discovered that of all these five statements only one was true.
What was the date of the dinner?

I began to think about why I was thinking about my future, and then I began to think about why I was thinking about why I was thinking about my future."

INTELLIGENCE AND ENVIRONMENT

Now that the major periods of intellectual development have been outlined, it would be wise to emphasize several key points that are often misinterpreted.

First of all, *intelligence involves an active interaction between the person and his world.* The person actively assimilates things and events in the world and accommodates to those things and events. Consequently, it is a serious mistake to

Figure 6.11
The nature of a person's environment plays an important role in the development of his intellectual capacities.

treat the stages as a mere unfolding of intelligence that occurs without the influence of the environment. The nature of the environment necessarily affects the course of development, since knowing and learning always involve accommodation.

Second, *what Piaget has described is merely the general outline of the development of intelligence.* His descriptions of each period are not meant to indicate the specific skills an individual child will possess. Instead, they indicate the general capacities of children at each period. Even the particular tasks used to illustrate general capacities cannot be solved by all children who have reached the appropriate period, because the tasks require specific skills that some children do not possess. For example, if a person in the formal-operational period has never seen a balance beam or any similar instrument, he will have to learn how the beam works before he can use it to demonstrate his capacity for formal-operational thought.

Even an adult with full formal-operational capabilities cannot use them in tasks that require specific skills he does not possess. An astronomer does not usually have the skills necessary to dissect a frog or to classify types of insects. Faced with those tasks, he would not be able to use his considerable formal-operational capacities very effectively. Similarly, a child who understands addition of classes will not be able to demonstrate the understanding if he is dealing with words and classes that are new to him.

In sum, it is important to avoid an oversimplification of Piaget's theory. The periods cannot be used as pigeonholes to explain all of a person's intellectual abilities. They merely outline certain general capacities. For most practical purposes, the specific skills that a person possesses are at least as important as the period that he has reached.

SUGGESTED READINGS

BALDWIN, A. *Theories of Child Development.* New York, Wiley, 1967. A clear, concise treatment of the major theories of child development, including Piaget's.

FISCHER, K. W. *Piaget's Theory of Learning and Cognitive Development.* Chicago, Markham Press (in press). A clear, easy-to-read summary and discussion of Piaget's theory, with special emphasis on his approach to learning and cognitive development.

FURTH, H. G. *Piaget and Knowledge.* Englewood Cliffs, N.J., Prentice-Hall, 1969. An in-depth treatment of Piaget's theory of knowing, with special emphasis on its philosophical and biological foundations.

INHELDER, B., AND PIAGET, J. *The Growth of Logical Thinking from Childhood to Adolescence.* New York, Basic Books, 1958. Describes the development from concrete-operational to formal-operational intelligence and presents the key experiments on which Piaget bases his description of that development.

PIAGET, J. *Biology and Knowledge.* Chicago, University of Chicago Press, 1971. In this recent book, Piaget describes the significance of his lifetime of work for understanding man's ability to know and the relationship of that ability to man's biological heritage.

PIAGET, J., AND INHELDER, B. *The Psychology of the Child.* New York, Basic Books, 1969. Piaget and Inhelder's own summary of their work. Its main usefulness is as a summary of major experimental findings rather than as an introduction to Piaget's theory.

WERNER, H. *Comparative Psychology of Mental Development.* New York, Science Editions, 1948. A useful compendium of research on mental development, including observations of primitive thought and insanity as well as studies of thought in children.

It is easiest to set the facts out in a diagram thus. The five fellow members who made remarks are denoted by A, B, C, D, E in that order:

Date	A	B	C	D	E	*Date*	A	B	C	D	E
1	*	—	—	*	*	17	*	*	*	—	—
2	—	—	*	—	*	18	—	*	*	—	—
3	*	—	*	—	*	19	*	*	*	—	—
4	—	—	—	—	*	20	—	*	*	—	—
5	*	—	*	—	*	21	*	*	*	—	—
6	—	—	*	—	*	22	—	*	*	—	—
7	*	—	*	—	*	23	*	*	*	—	—
8	—	—	*	*	*	24	—	*	*	—	—
9	*	—	—	—	*	25	*	*	—	—	—
10	—	—	*	—	*	26	—	*	*	—	—
11	*	—	*	—	*	27	*	*	*	*	—
12	—	—	*	—	*	28	—	*	*	—	—
13	*	—	*	—	*	29	*	*	*	—	—
14	—	*	*	—	*	30	—	*	*	—	—
15	*	*	*	—	*	31	*	*	*	—	—
16	—	*	—	—	*						

*s below A denote the dates on which the dinner could have been if A's remark was true, —s denote the days on which it could have been if A's remark was false. Similarly for B, C, D, E.

The only date for which there is only one true remark is the 4th. This is therefore the date of the dinner.

D
R
A
M

7
Development of Language

In Shakespeare's *Richard II,* Thomas Mowbray is exiled from England for life, and he responds in agony:

> The language I have learned these forty
> years,
> My native English, now I must forgo;
> And now my tongue's use is to me no more
> Than an unstringed viol or a harp,
> Or like a cunning instrument cased up,
> Or, being open, put into his hands
> That knows no touch to tune the harmony:
> Within my mouth you have engaoled my
> tongue,
> Doubly portcullised with my teeth and
> lips;
> And dull, unfeeling, barren ignorance
> Is made my gaoler to attend on me.

Every time I read that speech, I am chilled, for I love English—so rich in vocabulary, so bright in metaphor, so hospitable to foreign terms, so fanciful in idiom, so flexible, so colorful, so fascinating. I could not bear to lose its use.

Fortunately, I couldn't be in Mowbray's position now. In his day, English was a minor language spoken by three million people on one small island. Today English is spoken the world over, and it would be hard to find a patch on the globe where someone speaking English could not manage to find someone else to understand him. No one speaking any other language is quite that fortunate. Every other language is spoken by fewer people or in less widespread fashion or (almost always) both.

And yet English isn't just English. The English of London, Dublin, Canberra, Boston, Charleston, Brooklyn, and Indianapolis are each different. The differences aren't enough to preclude understanding, but they are quite enough to produce curiosity, suspicion, or even automatic dislike. George Bernard Shaw's *Pygmalion* is based on this.

An immigrant (my father, for instance) can learn every facet of his adopted country's culture and yet, even after a generation, give himself away every time he opens his mouth. Though he may have learned the vocabulary and grammar of his new language perfectly, the subtle distinctions of sound will defeat him.

Nor does it seem possible for native speakers of a language to eradicate that primitive feeling that there is but one correct pronunciation—their own, of course—and nothing but a group of queer and wrong-headed dialects beside that. I can't help being a victim of that feeling myself. I was once listening to Peter Ustinov on a talk show. The host remarked on the fact that Mr. Ustinov was one Englishman who could make himself sound exactly like an American. Mr. Ustinov smiled and, in answering, smoothly shifted from his usual English accent to clear, natural American English. I listened with astonishment, turned to the person listening with me, and in that moment before I managed to think about it, said, in honest innocence, "But if he can talk regular, why does he bother to speak with an accent?" I. A.

Human beings have created and mastered many types of language—not only thousands of different spoken languages but the language of mathematics, the sign languages of the deaf, the pictorial hieroglyphics of the ancient Egyptians, the artificial languages of computers, and the notational language of chemists. Why are human beings so adept at creating languages? And how has their existence affected our thought? We shall approach these questions first by considering the defining characteristics of a language and second by asking what capabilities seem to be necessary for its acquisition.

WHAT IS LANGUAGE?

Man may—or may not—be the only species capable of using language. Psychologists have long been interested in investigating the linguistic ability of man's near relative, the chimpanzee. Twice this century two couples have raised chimps in their homes and tried to teach them to speak. Both efforts ended in failure. The first chimp,

Gua, raised by the Kelloggs around 1930, never learned to speak at all. The second, Viki, was raised by the Hayes around 1950. She learned to make sounds that were rough approximations of only four words. Spoken language does not seem suitable for chimps, partly because their vocal apparatus is poorly developed.

Recently, experimenters have had considerably more success with a different approach: teaching a chimp to use gestural rather than vocal signs. As a result, the debate about whether chimps have the ability to use language has been reopened. The controversy hinges on defining the minimum requirements that a form of communication must meet before it is called language. Think for a moment about what having a language means to you, and then consider the following case of a chimp and her gestures. Would you say that she uses language?

The Sign Language of Washoe

By the time she was three and one-half years old, Washoe had become quite an accomplished young chimp. At mealtimes, she could ask for more food, request a drink, or demand her dessert. She could comment that a dog was barking and specify that she wanted to go to a particular place with someone.

Washoe communicates with her human companions by gesture rather than by spoken words. Since whe was one year old, she has been learning American Sign Language (ASL), the sign language used by many deaf people in North America. Her two psychologist trainers, the Gardners of the University of Nevada, and their associates "speak" to each other and to Washoe in gestural signs all day, sometimes asking questions, sometimes making requests, sometimes just chatting, and sometimes teaching Washoe a specific sign. The Gardners have tried to make Washoe's situation as similar as possible to that of a human child acquiring a spoken language.

After three years of teaching, Washoe had acquired some eighty-seven signs. Initially, she learned a sign in a specific context. For example, Washoe greatly enjoyed being tickled. Taking advantage of this propensity, the Gardners taught her the sign for "more." "More" is signed by putting the fingertips of both hands together above the head. With great enthusiasm Washoe touched the tips of her hands together to request more tickling. Later, she spontaneously used the same sign in other situations. She gestured to ask for more hair brushing and more swinging, and also for a second helping of food. Clearly, Washoe had grasped, at least to some extent, the abstract meaning of the sign for "more."

After she had learned a number of individual signs, Washoe spontaneously began to use some of them in combination, forming such sentences as: "Hurry open," "More sweet," "Listen dog," and "Roger come." Later, she would combine three or more signs: "Hurry gimme toothbrush," "You me go there in," and "Key open food." This is a remarkable achievement for a chimpanzee—especially in view of the fact that Washoe was never specifically trained to make such combinations.

Has Washoe acquired language? The question is difficult to answer. She does seem able to use abstract symbols to signal specific meanings, and she can combine signs to produce new meanings.

Meaningfulness and *productiveness*, R. Brown has suggested, are the two key aspects of a language. By meaningfulness, Brown means that the symbols of the language can be used to communicate specific ideas. Productiveness refers to the open-ended quality of a language, which allows symbols to be combined in different ways to express new meanings. Let us look more closely at these two aspects.

Meaningfulness and Productiveness

Meanings are represented in languages by words or other symbols, but the relation between symbols and meanings varies in different language systems. In sign language, for example, gestures often *visually* represent some aspect of the meaning. To make the ASL sign for *flower*, for example, you extend the fingers of one hand

Figure 7.1
Washoe at about five years of age. She is shown here using the ASL signs (American Sign Language) to name the objects "hat" (top) and "fruit" (bottom) and the quality "sweet" (middle).

and keep them joined at the tips so that your hand looks rather like a closed tulip. Then you touch your fingertips first to one nostril and then to the other, as if sniffing a flower. In spoken language, most words are more arbitrarily related to meanings. For example, the word "dog" is solely a product of English linguistic convention. There is no necessary relationship between the sound of the word "dog" and its meaning. The French word "chien," which also means dog, is equally arbitrary.

Because the basic stock of symbols in any language is finite, only a limited number of meanings can be expressed by using the symbols singly. Imagine what it would be like if the English language restricted you to one-word utterances. If you had a new idea, you would have to coin a new word for it—and how, without

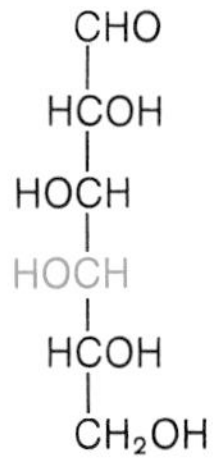

D-galactose

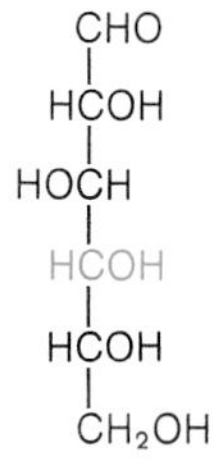

D-glucose

Figure 7.2
Most language systems use sign order to convey meaning. The letters and connecting lines shown here are symbols used in organic chemistry to stand for particular compounds. The arrangement at top indicates the sugar D-galactose, whereas exactly the same symbols, arranged differently below, represent the sugar D-glucose. Thus, as in language (and mathematics) the order of the specific elements (signs) signals distinct meanings.

combining old words into sentences, would you manage to make clear what the new one meant?

Combining words into phrases and sentences vastly increases the number of meanings that can be expressed. Furthermore, the word-order rules of many languages make it possible to use the same words to express different ideas. In English, for example, *boy, bit, dog,* and two *the*s can be arranged to signal two distinct meanings: "The boy bit the dog" or "The dog bit the boy." In arithmetic, similarly, the number 91 is not the same as the number 19.

To summarize, languages are symbol systems that are meaningful and can be used to produce new meanings. Both the basic symbols and their arrangement are important in determining meaning. Thus, Washoe does appear to have the rudiments of language. She can comprehend signs made by others, and she can make them herself. She can also use signs in sequence to express particular meanings. The Gardners are not sure yet whether Washoe observes order constraints in her sentences, but they think that she may. They hope that further work with her will show how far she is capable of progressing in her use of sign language.

THE ABILITIES THAT LANGUAGE REQUIRES

Before Washoe, psychologists did not believe that any species except man had demonstrated an ability to use signs in a productive as well as a meaningful way. Most animals can communicate with one another to some degree. The croak of a male toad attracts a nearby female, and the dance of the honeybee, described in Chapter 2, indicates to other bees the direction and distance of the food source from the hive. These signals are used meaningfully but not productively; that is, each signal has one distinct message. Given a novel situation, the toad and the bee have no rules for combining signals to express a new meaning. Their "language" limits them to a small number of simple, stereotyped messages.

Washoe did, of course, have to be trained—man is still the only species that has spontaneously created productive language systems. Still, Washoe seems to have the capacity to manipulate a language; so does another chimp, trained in a different way by D. Premack at the University of California, Santa Barbara. What cognitive and other abilities does language require? Should we expect to find still other species that can use language?

General Cognitive Abilities

The ability to manipulate symbols independently of objects appears to be essential for the productive use of language. According to Piaget, a human child cannot manipulate signs until he is capable of representational thought (see Chapter 5). Before that time—that is, before about age two—he cannot think about objects that are not physically present. He has no way to represent them in his mind. The child's progress toward representational thought can be gauged by how close he is to achieving the concept of object constancy. The very young infant shows no awareness that objects continue to exist when he cannot see them. During the sensorimotor period he gradually learns that they do. By the time the preoperational period begins, object constancy is fully developed: if the child does not find an object in the place he saw someone hide it, he will look for it in other places.

Animal species differ in the extent to which they seem able to develop the concept of object constancy. Some of the less intelligent animals may never get to the stage where they realize that an object continues to exist when they can no longer see it. More intelligent animals (such as the monkey, baboon, and cat) will search for objects that they have seen hidden. Some may even be able to imagine the movements of absent objects, although this has not been demonstrated.

Only chimps and humans have shown for certain that they can think about absent objects. This achievement signals the arrival of the capacity for representational thought. In the human child, as discussed in Chapter 6, several new abilities emerge at this stage of cognitive development. Some of these are the ability to imitate someone's action at a later time, when the person being imitated is not present; the ability to solve problems by thinking about them rather than by overt trial and error; and the ability to acquire language. Chimpanzees have also shown all these capabilities.

At about this point, however, the patterns of development of chimp and child begin to diverge. The child continues to advance through the three major periods of representational thought: preoperational, concrete operational, and formal operational. He learns to classify objects in a systematic manner and to imagine hypothetical outcomes. The chimp never proceeds much beyond the intuitive egocentric thought characteristic of a two-year-old child. This suggests some fairly severe limitations on the potential sophistication of chimpanzees' language use. The cognitive abilities of other species seem to impose even more stringent restrictions on

Figure 7.3
The behaviors of chimps and young humans, both capable of representational thought, are often similar. When first exposed to mirrors, a chimp regards the reflection as a fellow chimp. This social-response pattern soon fades, however, and the chimp, recognizing that the reflection is merely his own image, uses the mirror as a tool to study himself, just as children do. Research with adult chimps so far indicates that their capacity for representational thought does not progress beyond that of a two-year-old child.

Figure 7.4
Noam Chomsky's theory of the origin and development of language has gained wide acceptance and is the basis for some of the research reported here. Chomsky believes that a child learns to speak his native language not because he has been reinforced for successive approximations to correct speech, but because all people have an inborn capacity for analyzing the language they hear and subsequently interpreting and using that language correctly.

their capacity for language. However, the data comparing cognitive and linguistic abilities of different species is not very extensive as yet, and no firm conclusions can be drawn. Further experimentation with different species should help resolve the issues surrounding these abilities.

Special Abilities

Language acquisition seems to depend on certain cognitive capabilities—most generally, on the development of a capacity for representational thought. In addition, various language systems require certain special abilities. For example, an animal that did not have well-developed hand muscles would have trouble learning a gestural language. Similarly, a species with a poorly developed vocal apparatus would find speech difficult. E. Lenneberg has suggested that several specializations of the human body make spoken language possible. There are specializations in the articulatory apparatus and motor regions of the brain that permit fine control over the production of sounds; specializations in the auditory cortex of the brain that permit fine discriminations of sound patterns; specializations in the breathing apparatus that permit prolonged speech; and other sensory and cognitive specializations that elaborate and coordinate these activities.

Spoken languages are of special interest to psychologists, because they are acquired naturally by virtually all children at a very young age. Indeed, the ability to acquire spoken languages seems to be exclusively human. The chimpanzee's greatest problems with spoken language seem to be in the production of intelligible sounds. However, there is an additional problem: the structure of a chimpanzee's brain may not be such that it allows the animal to master grammar. The linguist N. Chomsky has theorized that all the natural languages of the world have certain common features, and that the brain of human beings is so organized as to be sensitive to the kinds of distinctions that languages make. In mastering the grammar of his native language, Chomsky says, the child is aided by this characteristic of his brain. The chimpanzee, whose brain differs in many important ways from that of the human being, may not be able to make the kinds of grammatical distinctions that we can.

It is difficult to come to any firm conclusions about the chimp's abilities in this regard. Because he cannot speak, it is hard to know whether his speech would be grammatical if he could. Chimps do, however, give some evidence of understanding spoken English. Gua, the Kelloggs' chimp, never spoke, but she did respond appropriately to about seventy different utterances. Unfortunately, it was not clear whether her responses were based on an understanding of specific words and word orders or on nonlanguage, situational cues. If chimps *can* understand spoken English, or if the Gardners confirm that Washoe follows certain rules of word order in combining signs, it will suggest some capacity for grammar in the chimp.

HOW CHILDREN ACQUIRE LANGUAGE

In order to understand the nature of spoken languages and why men are so adept at learning them, it is useful to study the development of speech in children. The factors that affect that development should help reveal the capabilities a child brings to language learning and should help us understand how he applies them in learning the rules of his native language.

Early Vocalizations

Most children do not speak their first recognizable word until they are about a year old, but before that time they have had a considerable amount of practice at vocalization. At birth, babies can coo and cry. During the next few months the sounds they spontaneously produce increase in frequency and variety. By four or five months they are beginning to babble—to chant various syllabic sounds in a rhythmic fashion. Then slowly they develop the capacity to imitate the sounds made by others and to control the sounds they make. Finally, they learn the names of people or objects—their first words.

Infants' early vocalizations seem remarkably independent of what they hear around them. Their early babbling is a type of motor play and experimentation, and it is not limited to the sounds used in a particular language. Instead, infants seem to make sounds from all languages, including French vowels and German rolled Rs. For the first six months of life, deaf babies cry and babble like hearing children—additional evidence for the spontaneity of early vocalization and its relative independence of hearing.

Hearing the speech of others becomes increasingly important during the second half of the first year. The development of children's ability to imitate others reflects their growing ability to produce sounds voluntarily, although the range of voluntarily produced sounds always lags behind those produced spontaneously. At the end of the first year, the baby not only imitates the sounds of syllables and words but is beginning to mimic the stress and pitch patterns of those who talk with him. Before this time the speech sounds of babies from different communities all sound much the same.

Learning to make syllable sounds and to imitate is good preparation for learning words. By rewarding the baby with enthusiastic bursts of approval when he says something that sounds like a word, parents encourage infants to repeat and practice the sounds that are used in words. Imitation and reinforcement also play a major part in the development of children's vocabulary. But there is a leap to be made before the baby starts using words: he must learn that the sound has meaning, that it is used as a symbol for something else. Generally, his first words refer to the tangible and the visible and are used one at a time, as labels or commands ("Dog!" "Cookie!"). Toward the beginning of the second year, the infant will begin to express himself more precisely by combining two words in an utterance. At this time he enters a new phase of the language-learning process, during which he learns the complicated rules for combining words into sentences.

Rule Learning

Much of the discussion of rule learning that follows is based on the work of R. Brown, from Harvard University, and particularly on a long-term study that Brown and his collaborators, U. Bellugi, C. Fraser, and C. Cazden, did on the speech of three children whom they call Adam, Eve, and Sarah. When the study began, the children were about two years old and were just beginning to combine words in two-word utterances. The researchers visited them in their homes every week or so until Adam and Sarah were five years old (Eve moved away nine months after the study began) and collected many samples of their speech. They studied primarily the children's spontaneous speech rather than their comprehension of what other people said to them, because speech gives a clearer indication of a child's understanding of grammatical forms than do his responses to other people's utterances. The two central questions of the research were: what do children know about the structure of English at different points in their development, and what processes do they use to acquire that knowledge?

At age two, a child's speech is not much like an adult's. His utterances are short; his vocabulary is limited to nouns and action verbs; most other parts of speech are missing. Nonessential words are left out, much as they are when someone writes a telegram. People who know the child well can usually understand what his statements mean, and they often respond by expanding his utterances into a well-formed adult sentence. Adjacent are some examples of a young child's *telegraphic speech* and his mother's interpretations recorded by Brown and Bellugi.

Child	*Mother*
Baby highchair	Baby is in the highchair.
Eve lunch	Eve is having lunch.
Throw Daddy	Throw it to Daddy.
Pick glove	Pick the glove up.

By age four or five, the child's speech is more adultlike. His utterances have increased in length, and they usually include prepositions, auxiliary verbs, and articles. Furthermore, the child seems to have mastered most of the rules of grammar. Brown and C. Hanlon found Adam—when he was four years and seven months old—saying:

> The man's not bad, is he?
> I can hold on like a monkey, can't I?
> She thought that was a tiger, didn't she?

Questions like these are called *tag questions,* and there is much a child must know to form them correctly. First, he must know that he should use a negative tag such as "can't I?" when he expects a "yes" answer to his question; when he expects a "no" answer, he must use an affirmative tag such as "is he?" In addition, he has to be able to substitute a pronoun for a noun (replacing "man" with "he" in the first example). And he must know how to use auxiliary verbs (such as "did" in the third example.) Table 7.1 sets out all the rules a child must have mastered in order to use tag questions correctly.

How does a child come to master the rules of sentence formation in these few short years? Brown and Bellugi's observations suggest that although the child under age four or five does not follow adult grammatical rules, he seems to be following more primitive rules of his own.

One of the first rules that an English-speaking child may learn concerns word order. For example, a two- or three-year-old might might say, "Eat cake" while he is devouring his birthday fare. For an adult, "Eat cake" is a command to another to eat the cake. To be correct, the child should say "I am eating the cake," indicating that he is the actor, that eating is in progress at the present, and that the cake is what is being eaten. (Table 7.2 shows the basic meanings of some grammatical inflections.) The child's sentence does not include all these nuances, and it violates several grammatical rules. But the child has observed one adult rule of word order: he puts "cake" after "eat," indicating that the cake is the object being eaten rather than the agent doing the eating. When a child imitates an adult, he often leaves out words, but he does preserve word order. For example, when Brown and Fraser in 1963 asked children between two and three years old to repeat sentences that were spoken to them, one child typically made the responses shown in the adjacent margin.

Adult	*Child*
I am drawing a dog.	I draw dog.
I do not want an apple.	I do a apple.
Read the book.	Read book.

As the child's speech becomes less and less telegraphic, he begins to use helping verbs (such as "is" and "are"), prepositions, and articles. He also begins to make a type of error called *overregularization.* Overregularization, which is common in the speech of three- and four-year-olds, results from the misapplication of a grammatical rule. For example, the usual rule for forming the past tense of an English verb is to add "ed" to the base. But some verbs, including many common ones,

Table 7.1—Rules for the Formation of Tag Questions

1. *Pronominalize* the noun phrase that is the subject of sentence.
   The man's not bad, is *he*?
   Me and David are working, aren't *we*?
2. Locate the *first auxiliary verb* of the sentence (or supply the appropriate missing form, usually a form of *do*).
   He hops like a kangaroo, *doesn't* he?
3. *Negate* the auxiliary verb in the tag if the sentence is affirmative. Use an *affirmative* auxiliary verb in the tag if the sentence is negative.
   I *can* hold on like a monkey, *can't* I?
4. *Invert the order* of the auxiliary verb and the pronominalized noun phrase.
   It's *not* a real watch, *is it*?

Source: Bellugi, U. "Linguistic Mechanisms Underlying Child Speech," in *Proceedings of the Conference on Language and Language Behavior.* New York: Appleton-Century-Crofts, 1968.

Table 7.2—The Basic Meanings of Some Grammatical Inflections

Grammatical Inflections	General Meaning	Example	Specific Meaning
Plural: "s"	Number	He ties his *shoes.*	Not singular
Past: "ed"	Earlierness	He *guarded* the base.	Earlier action
Copula: "to be"	Number, earlierness	They *were* smart.	Both earlier and not singular
		He *is* smart.	Both not earlier and singular
Third-person indicative: "s"	Number, earlierness	She *cleans* her teeth.	Both singular and not earlier
Progressive: "ing"	Temporary duration	I am *playing* ball.	Temporary duration
Auxiliary of the progressive: "to be"	Temporary duration, number, earlierness	I *am* playing ball.	Temporary duration, not earlier, and singular
		I *was* playing ball.	Temporary duration, earlier, and singular

Source: Parts adapted from Brown, R. *A First Language: The Early Stages.* Cambridge, Mass.: Harvard University Press (in press).

have irregular past tenses: go/went, come/came, drive/drove, fall/fell. The child may learn common words like "fell" and "came" from his parents before he masters the "ed" past-tense rule and produce grammatically correct sentences: "I fell down" and "The cat came home." But once he learns the rule for forming the regular past tense, he is likely to overgeneralize, producing sentences like "He goed to the store" and "I falled down." Similarly, the general rule for forming plurals in English is to add an "s" to a singular noun: "dog" becomes "dogs," and so on. After the child has learned that rule, such words as "foots," "mans," and "mouses" creep into his conversation.

The emergence of any one adult rule is not sudden; one can see it coming for a long while. For example, consider Sarah's acquisition of the "ing" grammatical inflection to form the present progressive, as in "I am eating." At twenty-seven months, Sarah used this form only about half the time that an adult would have used it. Not until sixteen months later did she consistently use it where required. During those months, Sarah did not use the "ing" ending incorrectly so much as skip it sometimes, saying "I eat" where an adult would say "I am eating." A transitional period during which the child sometimes does and sometimes does not use the new form is characteristic of the learning of inflections (including the plural "s," as in "boys," and the past "ed," as in "played," as well as the present progressive "ing").

Some rules are learned somewhat differently, in several steps. When Bellugi studied the development of children's ability to form negative sentences, for example, she found a number of intermediate steps preceding use of the adult rule. A very young child (age two) has a simple rule for forming a negative: he adds the word "no" to a statement: "No want stand." "No gonna fall." "No mom sharpen it." "No write book." "Like it, no." A little later, the child begins to use "not," and he seems to know that he should place "no" or "not" in a special position. He puts it just before the verb: "You not have one." "He not bite you." "I not get it dirty." The last step is to add the necessary auxiliary verb: "You don't have one." "He doesn't bite you." "I don't get it dirty."

As he progresses toward the adult rules, a child does not make all the errors that he conceivably might. Curiously, he seems to learn some rules without making the errors one would expect. The development of the present progressive (I am eating) is a good example. Not all verbs are used in the progressive form. In general, process verbs such as "break" and "play" commonly occur in the progressive—"I am breaking the world track record"; "I am playing my banjo." State verbs such as "know" or "need," however, do not take the progressive. It would sound strange to say "I am knowing how to do this" or "I am needing a hammer." A child just learning to form the progressive might be expected to add the "ing" ending to all verbs randomly, and not to observe the process-state distinction. Yet errors of this type, according to Brown and Bellugi, are rarely made.

The tag question is another form that emerges with remarkably few errors. The rules for the formation of tag questions are complicated, so there are many opportunities for error, but the child rarely makes any. The predecessor of the tag question is, "The lady swallowed the sword, *huh?*" or ". . . , *right?*" Then, quite suddenly "huh?" is replaced by "didn't she?" It is as if the child holds off on trying to use tag questions until he understands all the necessary rules.

Semantics and Grammar Although there is abundant evidence that children consistently apply rules when they speak, it is a difficult matter to state formally what the rules are. One basic question that needs answering is: are the rules based primarily on semantic or on grammatical relationships?

Sentences can be described in both semantic and grammatical terms. Consider the sentence, "The runner overturned the hurdle." Semantically, a person or *agent* (the runner) initiates an *action* (the overturning), and the *object* (the hurdle) directly receives this action. The meaning of the sentence can be characterized by the semantic relation of agent-action-object. Alternately, the sentence can be described in formal grammatical terms. The *subject* (the runner) dominates the sentence, and there is a predicate composed of a *main verb* (overturned) and a *direct object* (the hurdle). In this sentence, the subject has the semantic role of agent and the main verb that of action. Subjects and verbs, however, will have other semantic roles in different sentences; there is no simple, one-to-one correspondence between grammatical and semantic roles. Consider, for example, the sentence "The hurdle was overturned by the runner."

According to N. Chomsky, the rules that govern adult speech are based primarily on grammatical relationships rather than on semantic ones. For example, the basic rule of sentence production that says a sentence must have a subject and a predicate is a grammatical rule, not a semantic one. Subject and predicate express a formal relation between parts of a sentence rather than a fixed relation between the meanings of words.

Another rule that governs sentence production is that the verb must agree in number with the subject. Again, this rule is phrased in grammatical terms. There is no easy way to state it in semantic terms. Although the grammatical subject and the semantic agent are often identical, that is not always true. To illustrate, consider the following sentences:

> The boy gives presents to the girls.
> The girls receive presents from the boy.

In both cases the boy is giving presents to the girls and so is the agent of the action. But only in the first sentence does the verb agree in number with "boy." The verb agrees with the grammatical subject in both sentences; the subject is defined in terms of its relation to the main verb and not in terms of its semantic role.

The rules that govern young children's speech are not necessarily of the same type as those that govern adults' speech. It seems quite possible that the early stages of children's speech rely more heavily on semantic relationships than does adults' speech. Beyond the earliest stages, however, the regularities in children's speech do seem to be based on grammatical rules rather than exclusively on semantic ones.

If that is correct, then we are faced with a problem: how does a two- or three-year-old child begin to learn grammatical rules? Piaget's theory, as discussed in Chapters 5 and 6, suggests how a child constructs certain semantic concepts during the sensorimotor period, but how he constructs the concepts of subject, predicate, verb, and object at that age is not yet known. Where does his understanding of these relationships come from? It is problems like these that led Chomsky and others to conclude that children are born with a potential ability to understand formal grammatical relations, much as they are born with a potential ability to walk. This innate capacity for the grammatical structure of language, according to Chomsky's theory, helps account for the special linguistic abilities of human beings.

The Order of Acquisition of Rules So far we have described children's speech as regular and systematic, something that can be characterized as following rules. We have suggested that the rules are grammatical rather than semantic and have even ventured the hypothesis that sensitivity to certain features of language may be innate. Yet even though the child may have this built-in sensitivity, he does not speak like an adult when he begins to talk.

The child seems to learn adult rules in a fairly stable order. There is some variation from child to child, but not a great deal. The children that R. Brown studied mastered the rules of word order first, and then the rules for certain grammatical inflections. There was a definite order of acquisition among the grammatical inflections. For example, the children learned to use the plural "s" (as in "horses") and the irregular past forms of verbs (went, gone) before they began to use the linking verb "to be" ("The cops *are* here") or the third person indicative ("He run*s*"). These two forms, in turn, were acquired before auxiliary verbs ("The cops *are* running in place").

Why do children tend to learn these rules in the same order? There are several possible reasons. First, the frequency with which a form is used in the home might help determine when it is mastered. If a child hears many sentences in which "ing" is attached to verbs, it should be easier for him to figure out when this ending is appropriate. Brown decided to test this hypothesis with the parents of Adam, Eve, and Sarah. In his recent book, *A First Language: The Early Stages,* he reports that the three sets of parents did use different grammatical inflections with different frequencies and that the frequencies were remarkably consistent within each home. However, the forms the parents used most frequently were *not* the ones that the children acquired first. It seems, then, that something other than frequency in parental speech determines the order in which children learn grammatical rules.

Brown found that the *semantic complexity* of a rule is an important determinant of the order of rule learning: the rules that are easiest to understand are mastered first. Semantic complexity refers to the number of meanings that a person must understand in order to use a rule correctly. For example, the rules for the formation of the plural and of the past each requires an understanding of one major meaning. To use the plural correctly, you must understand the concept of number. A given noun is either singular (bed) or not singular (beds). When the noun is not singular, you add an "s." Similarly, to use the past correctly you must understand the idea that something has occurred before right now. Verbs can refer either to some earlier time or not. When they refer to an earlier time, you add "ed" (walked). By contrast, the rule for the formation of a regular third-person verb is semantically more complex. To form it, you must be able to coordinate the meanings of *both* number and earlierness. When the verb is both singular and not earlier, for example, you add an "s" to the main stem of the verb (he walks).

Intuitively, it makes sense that semantic complexity should be an important factor in the order of rule learning. It is hard to imagine how a child could use the past and present tense correctly if he could not differentiate between past and present time. He might perceive that adults sometimes used one form of a verb and sometimes another, but the choice would seem completely arbitrary to him until he could attach distinct meanings to the two forms.

If semantic complexity were the *only* factor affecting the child's discovery of rules, however, forms that have the same meanings would be acquired at the same time. This is not always the case. Sometimes two forms that have the same meanings, such as simple and complex plurals, are acquired at different times. In many of these cases, Brown found, the two forms differ in *grammatical complexity*. Grammatical complexity is a second factor in the order of rule learning. (Table 7.3 displays some examples of both semantic and grammatical relations.)

Grammatical complexity refers to the number of steps involved in the derivation of a particular form. For example, compare a simple plural form—a child pointing and saying "apples"—with a more complex plural—"They apples." Although both statements have the same meaning, the second is the more complex grammatically; the child not only pluralized "apples" but also made the pronoun "they" plural, to agree in number with "apples." Cazden analyzed the data from Adam, Eve, and Sarah and found that their performance was better with the simple plurals than with

Table 7.3—Examples of Semantic and Grammatical Relations

Semantic Relations	Agent ↑	Action ↑	Object ↑	Locative ↑
	She	washed	her clothes	in the river.
Grammatical Relations	↓ Subject	↓ Verb	↓ Direct Object	↓ Adverbial Prepositional Phrase
Semantic Relations	Affected Person ↑	State ↑	Object ↑	
	Terry	likes	blueberry muffins.	
Grammatical Relations	↓ Subject	↓ Verb	↓ Direct Object	
Semantic Relations	Affected Person ↑	Action ↑	Object ↑	Agent ↑
	The girls	received	the presents	from the boys.
Grammatical Relations	↓ Subject	↓ Verb	↓ Direct Object	↓ Adverbial Prepositional Phrase

the complex plurals. This finding and others cited by Brown suggest the importance of grammatical complexity in the order of rule learning.

Semantic and grammatical complexity seem to be two important factors in the order of rule learning, but other variables may also be quite important—for example, the *perceptibility* of a given form. Compare the full possessive form, "That is John's hat" with the elliptical possessive, "That is John's." With the elliptical possessive, the "s" can be heard more easily because it is often at the end of a sentence and stressed, whereas the "s" in the full possessive is more likely to be slurred over. Cazden found the performance of Adam, Eve, and Sarah to be much better on the more perceptible form, the elliptical possessive—*even though the elliptical possessive is more grammatically complex than the full possessive.* Apparently, perceptibility may sometimes override grammatical complexity as a determinant of the order of rule learning. However, there are other possible interpretations for the children's performance. The two forms of the possessive differ not only along the dimensions of grammatical complexity and perceptibility but also along that of redundancy of meaning. These multiple differences between any two forms make it difficult to point to any variable as the most important determinant in the order of rule learning.

To summarize, the regularities in a child's speech at different stages suggest that he is learning rules for sentence production. Rule learning is a gradual process: first the child may learn to understand a concept like singular and plural and then, slowly, he begins to notice that plural nouns are marked with an "s." Also, rule learning is not a conscious process. A four-year-old can speak grammatically, but he cannot describe the rules of grammar. Increasing awareness of language rules comes with age.

Later Developments

By the age of five most children talk very well. Their sentences are like an adult's in form, although the content of the sentences is restricted. Later developments seem to keep pace with the child's general cognitive advancement. He enlarges his vocabulary as his ability to understand increases and as he is exposed to new things, and he begins to be able to reflect on his own speech.

It takes several years, however, for children to understand fully that words are arbitrary symbols, not intrinsic parts of an object. For example, a group of eight-year-olds was reading a story about how the kangaroo got its name. In the story Captain Cook and his men had landed in Australia and, seeing some strange animals in the distance, asked an Australian what the animals were called. The Australian, not knowing, replied "kangaroo," which in his language meant "I don't know." But Captain Cook and his men went off confident that this strange being was called a kangaroo. The children had a difficult time getting the point of the story because they could not conceive of "kangaroo" as meaning something different from the animal itself. Older children would have easily perceived the two meanings of kangaroo.

F. Kessel reports that between ages five and twelve the child also learns to appreciate the two meanings of an ambiguous sentence. For example: "The duck is ready to eat" could mean either that the duck is the dinner or the diner. Before about twelve years of age, children are unable to pick out the two meanings of the sentence. Around twelve, however, they become able to see the two meanings simultaneously. This and other new abilities with language seem to reflect advances in cognitive development, particularly in the child's capacity to direct his thinking in systematic ways and to deal with hypothetical situations and abstractions.

Environmental Variables

Psychologists have been interested in studying how a child's acquisition of language is affected by environmental variables such as the quantity or quality of speech the child hears, the encouragement of speaking in the home, and the varieties of situations in which the child tries to express himself.

Figure 7.7
Long after he was seven years old, René Magritte, the twentieth-century Belgian Surrealist, was still involved in understanding and commenting on the fact that words are symbols for (and not intrinsic parts of) objects. In this painting, called *The Key of Dreams,* images of four objects are shown in a window frame and labeled as if in a child's reader. However, in three instances word and picture do not designate the same object; in the fourth case the picture and its label correspond. Magritte, with his own kind of humor, comments on the arbitrary nature of words as symbols.

The Importance of Hearing Deaf children are forced to learn language in a different way from normal children and have considerable difficulty with it. Deprived of all auditory input, they are unable to "pick up" language from the speech of others. Their learning of language is delayed until they begin school, at which time they are taught spoken English and formally instructed in the rules of grammar.

A deaf child's language learning differs from a normal child's in three ways: he learns language by watching people instead of by listening to them; he is formally taught the rules of grammar instead of picking them up when he is young; and he has less experience than a hearing child with well-formed sentences. Lenneberg thinks that the last two factors—the formal method by which grammar is taught and the impoverishment of the deaf child's language experience—account for his difficulty in mastering the rules of grammar. Deaf children tend to make grammati-

Figure 7.8
These children are demonstrating a gestural sign language used by deaf persons. It is interesting to note that, like verbal language, sign language in various parts of the country shows differences in "dialect."

After 1 year of instruction:
"A boy is stoling candy. He is on the chair. He is a light. He is a short. He ate candy. His mother nuaght. He is crying."

After 2 years of instruction:
"The boy went to school. We buy a Card Valentine her mother. the dog a dirty feet the rain because he was shoe dirty because she was saw the boy came home"

After 3 years of instruction:
"Edd and Brownie got mud on his house. He make a flower for his mother. He forget to closte the door. Outside is rain. He was dope because he was little boy know nothing about it. His mother will angry with him because he was careless boy. His mother didn't want to clean the house because she will tried of it. He will help dog get a bath because he take dog for a walk."

After 11 years of instruction:
*A Boy Liked a Cigar**
"A boy was named Robert Kennedy. His age was twelve years old.
When his father went shopping, he had nothing to do except to eat something. He remembered his father told him promised to his father not to eat somethings. Later he had a big idea. He went to library room. He walked over his father's new sofa. The sofa was dirty. He opened the box of cigar. He picked one. And he think and remember his father his father told him to do. He putted back it. He leave library room. And one of tiny devil told him disobey his father. He said, "OKay!" He went to back to the library room. He got it. He lighted it. He smoked for one hour. Later his father came to home. He slept and felt very sick. His father called him. But he did not called. His father thought he ran away. He ran and looked many rooms. The last room he found. He brother him. His father told him what happen to you. He said, "Nothing!" His father smelled smoke. His father asked him, "Did you smoked my cigar?" He said, "Yes." His father scold him. And a tiny angle was fight with a tiny devil."

**This is a written composition about a picture shown to the class.*

Figure 7.9
Examples of compositions written by deaf children. Note that the errors in grammar and syntax, even in the most sophisticated story, are not at all like errors that hearing children make.
(From Lenneberg, 1967.)

cal errors in compositions that are rarely or never found in those of hearing children.

Here is a composition, cited by Lenneberg, that was written by a deaf boy after five years of language instruction:

One day he lived in England. His name Jim. He went to the television and put on there. He sat on the floor and watched television. Then he was quiety and climbed up the chair. He was stolen many candy on the shelf and he ate it more and more.

Several other examples of deaf children's compositions are shown in Figure 7.9.

Other Variables Some psychologists have suggested that particular ways in which mothers typically respond to their hearing children make it easier for the children to learn grammar. For example, mothers frequently expand a child's utterances. If the child says "Baby highchair," the mother nods approvingly and says "Yes, baby is in the highchair." The response of the mother should be particularly instructive for the child, because he presents a meaning and the mother tells him how to express it grammatically. Yet experimental studies by Cazden have shown that this type of interaction has no more influence on language learning than another type, in which the mother answers the child's utterance not by expanding what he has just said but by responding to it with a comment. For example, if the child says "Baby highchair," the mother may respond "Yes, and I am standing on the floor." At present, it seems that what is important is the general richness and complexity of the linguistic environment rather than one particular type of interaction.

Many aspects of speech, including not only vocabulary size, fluency, style of speech, and intonation patterns but also the child's general attitudes toward and interest in language, are greatly affected by environmental variables. Among the more important variables that have been identified are the language norms of the child's community, the nature of his home life, the quantity and variety of words and grammatical inflections that he hears, the value people around him place on conversation, the number of social contexts in which he tries to express himself, and the responses of others to his talk.

THE RELATIONSHIP OF LANGUAGE AND THOUGHT

From about two years of age on, human beings use words to express meanings to other people. Their conceptual and linguistic abilities seem to grow together. It is natural, then, to wonder about the relation between language and thought. In what ways does cognitive development depend on the development of language? Conversely, in what ways does language development rely on advances made in the cognitive realm?

Although cognitive and linguistic abilities normally develop hand-in-hand, it is important to recognize that they are quite distinct from one another. We are so accustomed to expressing our thoughts verbally that we may tend to believe that all thinking requires language. However, consideration of the chimp, the deaf, and the mentally retarded indicates that the two abilities, although closely related, are separate. Thinking appears to depend on a *general* capacity for mental representation, as discussed by Piaget, rather than on a capacity for using the special representational systems of language.

Does Thought Depend on Language?

Few would accuse chimpanzees of not being able to think. They show various preoperational capacities, such as the ability to conceive of absent objects, so they seem to have some form of representational system available to them. Would we want to say that no chimp before Washoe could think simply because the others could not use language? Chimps are good problem solvers, and many of them, like Wolfgang Köhler's famous chimp named Sultan, have demonstrated a capacity for insight learning. Sultan was faced with the problem of trying to obtain food that was too far outside his cage for him to reach. Also outside the cage, but within reach, were some sticks. When Sultan saw them, he paused for a moment, then promptly put two sticks together, extended the tool, and drew in the food. (For more extended discussion of insight learning in chimps, see Chapter 4.)

Still fewer people would want to claim that deaf people who cannot speak are incapable of reflective thought. Before age six, when most deaf children start school, it can be assumed that they do not possess language to any significant degree. Tests of their cognitive development, however, show no marked differences from six-year-olds who can hear normally. For example, deaf children are quite capable of the symbolic and make-believe play characteristic of normal preschool children. When Lenneberg observed the play of retarded, deaf, and normal children, he found that the play of the deaf children was much like that of normal children; especially in comparison with the mentally retarded, the play of the deaf appeared quite sophisticated. Lenneberg also reported that preschool deaf children made scores comparable to those of normal children on the Leiter Scale, which is a language-free test of concept formation (see Figure 7.10).

Deaf children have more difficulty with cognitive development after six years of age, when operational thought is developing. While deaf children can carry out elementary classifications as well as normal children can, they are retarded in their handling of complex classifications. Similarly, it appears to take them longer to discover such concepts as conservation of weight (to understand, for instance, that an object such as a lump of clay weighs the same regardless of its shape).

Although the development of concepts can proceed in the absence of spoken language, language undoubtedly helps in the discovery and refinement of certain concepts. It is especially useful when the child begins to deal with hypothetical

Figure 7.10
Concept formation is the formulation of a general principle that explains or is applicable to many specific examples. For example, a hammer, a screwdriver, and a wrench are all included in the concept "tool." Although many people think that formation of a concept requires language, a child who has not yet learned to speak can demonstrate that he has mastered a concept; by arranging a set of blocks into piles of square ones and piles of triangular ones, regardless of size, the child demonstrates that he has attained the concepts "square" and "triangle." The Leiter Non-Verbal Scale, samples from which are shown here, is designed to measure concept formation in individuals (from age two through adulthood) who have not acquired language because of such handicaps as cerebral palsy, deafness, or severe speech impairments.

situations and formal systems—that is, when he enters the formal operational period, around the start of adolescence.

Does Language Depend on Thought?

Thought can develop, at least to a point, without language. The reverse is probably not true; that is, the development of language seems to be highly dependent on the development of cognition. For example, the ability to use language productively probably requires a capacity for representational thought. Indeed, at every point in the development of children's speech, semantic understanding seems to precede the acquisition of the grammatical rule modifying that meaning. As was explained in connection with the learning of plural and past tense, the child can master the rules only when he can understand their basic meanings.

The language development of mongoloid children illustrates the importance of conceptual attainments in the acquisition of language. Although mongoloid children hear the same amount of language as normal children, they are retarded in both conceptual development and speech. They tend to be very affectionate, easy-going, and prone to imitate those to whom they are attached. As Lenneberg says, "If dependence upon adults, extensive babbling and a propensity for imitation were sufficient factors for language development, these children should develop better language than others." In fact, they do not develop as well. Apparently their intellectual limitation affects their language development, which seems to stop at a relatively primitive stage. For example, Lenneberg describes a twelve-year-old mongoloid girl who was comparable to a normal two-and-a-half-year-old in her capacity to imitate. Also like a two-and-half-year-old, she understood sentences with simple instructions but, when asked to imitate them, did so in a simplified form. She was given the sentences adjacent and asked to repeat them. (When she made a mistake, the sentence was repeated and she was given a second chance.)

Model	*Imitation*
Johnny is a good boy.	Johnny is good boy.
Johnny is a good boy.	Johnny is boy.
He has two dogs.	He has two dogs.
He takes them for a walk.	He take them to the walk.
He takes them for a walk.	He take them to a walk.
Lassie does not like the water.	Lassie doesn like water.
. . . (more sentences)	
The cat is chased by the dog.	Chased by the dog.
The cat is chased by the dog.	Cat chasing the dog.
The dog is fed by Johnny.	Fed by Johnny.
"Tell me, who is fed by Johnny?"	The dog.
"Very good; now say: 'The dog is fed by Johnny.' "	Fed the dog by Johnny.

Although mongoloid children are retarded in both cognitive and linguistic development, the two variables are not highly correlated. That is, knowing that one mongoloid child has a higher IQ than another does not allow you to predict that the speech of the child with the higher IQ will be more grammatical. For mongoloids, chronological age is a better indicator of verbal fluency than IQ is. For people who are more severely retarded than most mongoloids, however, there does seem to be a close relation between IQ and language ability. Among the very feeble-minded, the higher the IQ, the better the speech. It may be that, as Lenneberg suggested, there are "IQ thresholds" for children of various ages that must be attained if language is to be acquired.

In the past there has been great interest in questions of linguistic and cognitive relativity. It has been hypothesized that different language systems affect people's world views and basic ways of thinking. At one time it was thought that language might influence all one's perception and experience, since different languages have different categories for describing the world. For example, because the Eskimos have twenty words for snow, it was thought that they perceived snow differently—more precisely—than those of us who have only one word for it. This hypothesis is quite difficult to prove experimentally. At present the most that can be said is that languages differ in the ease with which certain concepts can be expressed. Yet almost any concept can be expressed in any language. English-speaking people seem able to distinguish between kinds of snow, but they have to use word phrases rather than single words to explain the distinctions.

Recently, psychologists and linguists have been impressed by the great similarities in linguistic and cognitive development of all peoples. Their interests have shifted from questions of relativity to a concern with linguistic and cognitive universals. Brown and other psycholinguists are trying to identify the aspects of speech development that are universal for all children. For example, Brown's characterization of early speech as telegraphic has been corroborated in studies of Finnish, Swedish, and Mexican children. (Detailed cross-cultural studies have not yet been done of the speech of children past the telegraphic stage.)

The fact that universals seem to exist suggests that language learning, like cognitive development generally, occurs through a process of interaction between the child and his environment. We cannot talk about learning apart from the child's level of understanding, and we cannot talk of the environment without considering how the child is capable of perceiving it and conceiving of it. Because all children share a similar biological heritage, we can expect that certain patterns of development will be universal, despite vastly different environmental settings.

SUGGESTED READINGS

BAR-ADON, A., AND WERNER, L. *Child Language: A Book of Readings.* Englewood Cliffs, N.J., Prentice-Hall, 1971. Very valuable collection of papers on all aspects of language development. Gives a historical perspective on the study of language and makes available many previously untranslated papers.

BROWN, R. *Psycholinguistics.* New York, Free Press, 1970. A compilation of the major papers of Brown and his associates on child and adult language.

———. *A First Language: The Early Stages.* Cambridge, Mass., Harvard University Press (in press). An excellent, comprehensive, and thoughtful identification of the present theoretical issues in early child language learning. Discusses extensively the notion of semantic and grammatical relationships, alternate grammatical descriptions, and the determinants of the order of rule learning in young children.

CAZDEN, C. "Subcultural Differences in Child Language: An Inter-disciplinary Review," *Merrill-Palmer Quarterly,* 12 (1966), 185–219. An excellent discussion of environmental influences on language development, including the topics of social-class differences and the evaluation of Black Non-Standard English. Useful bibliography.

CHOMSKY, C. *The Acquisition of Syntax in Children from 5 to 10.* Cambridge, Mass., M.I.T. Press, 1969. A report on her investigations into some later aspects of language development, particularly the mastery of more complex syntactic structures.

CHOMSKY, N. *Language and Mind.* New York, Harcourt, Brace, Jovanovich, 1968. A good discussion of a linguist's view of language and mind, as well as a general introduction to Chomsky's system of describing language (transformational grammar).

FURTH, H. *Thinking Without Language.* New York, Free Press, 1966. Thoughtful discussion of the problem of the relationship of language and thought, based in part on his experiments with deaf children.

LENNEBERG, E. *The Biological Foundations of Language.* New York, Wiley, 1967. Excellent discussion of language development in the context of the growth and maturation of the child and in light of evolution and genetics. Also presents language disorders in children and adults and discusses the problem of language and cognition.

PREMACK, D. "A Functional Analysis of Language," *Journal of the Experimental Analysis of Behavior,* 14 (1970), 107–125. An animal psychologist's discussion and description of language in broader terms to include some aspects of animal communication.

VYGOTSKY, L. V. *Thought and Language.* Cambridge, Mass., M.I.T. Press, 1962. An important classic dealing with the origins of both thought and language in children, the development of word meanings, and the relationship between inner speech and thinking.

8 Social Development: The Case of Morality

MY OWN PRIVATE VIEW OF MORALITY is that it is a way of making difficult decisions simple. How many times in life have you been torn between two possible courses of action, without any way of being certain which of the two was preferable from the standpoint of your own self-interest? After all, you can't see the future; you're not sure how things will turn out.

If, at this point, you can say to yourself, "Ah, but Alternative A is the honorable one and I must follow it," then your decision is made and you can stop worrying. If Alternative A turns out well, then the result justifies your decision; and if it works out poorly, you have at least done the honorable thing and *that* justifies you. You can't lose. Sometimes two alternative actions, mutually contradictory, can *each* be defended as honorable. Then, you can either do well or do honorably in either case, and you have two no-lose situations.

I'll give you an example. Several years ago a friend of mine asked me to join a group that had decided not to pay that fraction of their income tax devoted to financing the Vietnam War, on the grounds that a decent citizen ought not support an unjust and immoral war, even if the law says he must. Now, I have considered the Vietnam War to be immoral and have said so, publicly, from the beginning. In fact, I believe it to be far worse than immoral; I believe it to be *stupid*, and have said that publicly, too. Very well, then. I know the story about Thoreau and Emerson with which this chapter opens, and I perfectly well recognize that to stay out of jail under circumstances like these might well be immoral.

But I hesitated to join the group, for I know another story, too. In 399 B.C. Socrates, the great Athenian philosopher, had been tried on the charge of corrupting the young by teaching atheism and had been convicted and condemned to death. He was in jail, waiting for the moment when he would be given the poison hemlock to drink. His friends had organized a scheme for getting him out, but Socrates refused. He would not be rescued and he insisted on taking the poison. He had been unjustly convicted and he did not deserve to die, but the trial had been conducted under the laws of Athens. To escape from prison and to avoid death was to break the law; and the principle that laws must be obeyed was more important to Socrates than his own life.

So, I had my choice of moralities. After some thought, I wrote to my friend and told him that I sympathized completely with the movement but couldn't join it because I had to obey the law. I carefully used Socrates' reasoning. Then (since morality also tells me I must be honest) I added a postscript that said, "Besides, I'm scared not to pay the taxes."

The story has a happy ending. My friend wrote back to say that he had sent proposals to many people he knew to be against the war and had received many refusals, all as high-minded as mine—but that I was the only one who had added the postscript. For that reason, mine was the only excuse he respected. It made me feel a bit better. I. A.

While visiting Concord in 1843, shortly after beginning his sojourn at Walden Pond, the poet Henry David Thoreau was arrested and jailed for refusing to pay a poll tax. Thoreau refused to pay the tax to protest Massachusetts' support of slavery. As the story goes, Thoreau was looking out at the street through the bars of his window when who should walk by but his friend Ralph Waldo Emerson. Catching sight of Thoreau, Emerson rushed to the window and asked, "Henry, what are you doing in there?" "Waldo," Thoreau replied, "What are you doing out there?" Thoreau's situation poses a moral dilemma. He thought morality required him to disobey a law and go to jail. The authorities, however, saw it differently.

Consider another story, told by E. Turiel, a psychologist from Harvard University. One day a five-year-old boy named John was playing with his uncle when the uncle teasingly informed him that he had spent some time in jail. At first John refused to believe his uncle, but the uncle insisted that what he said was true. Finally, John was convinced. Suddenly he became frightened of his uncle, rushed off and refused to speak to him for the rest of the day. It seems doubtful that John would have thought that Thoreau had behaved morally.

As we all know, what is moral and immoral, right and wrong, is a controversial matter. We all have definitions of morality, and our definitions constitute implicit theories of morality. We rarely bring the theories to consciousness and even more

Figure 8.1
William McDougall. McDougall is an interesting figure in the history of psychology. Medically trained in Great Britain, he wrote books and articles in many areas of psychology. His views contrast strongly with those of behaviorists like John Watson; McDougall stressed man's *purposive striving* as the determinant of behavior and encouraged research in such "unorthodox areas" as psychic phenomena.

rarely test them, but we do have ideas about what kinds of people and actions are moral and why.

The study of morality has been an important concern of psychologists. In 1908, W. McDougall wrote, "the *fundamental problem* of social psychology is the moralization of the individual by the society." In the process of "moralization" all of the major phases and problems of social development appear, arise, and find solutions of one kind or another. Since the time of McDougall, the study of morality has had its ups and downs, but in the last two decades it has generated new interest and enthusiasm. At present there are a number of theories of morality in psychology. Most of them were developed as part of more general theories of social development, which will be considered in Unit VIII. The three theories of moral development that will be discussed here as examples of thinking about people's social development in the early years grew out of Freud's theory of psychosexual development, social-learning theory, and cognitive-developmental theory.

Examine each set of ideas about social and moral development carefully as you peruse it, and compare it with your own intuitive impressions. After the theories have been described, we will examine some of the research that they have generated. Finally, we will compare the theories on several points in an attempt to clarify their strengths and weaknesses.

PSYCHOANALYTIC THEORY

Until the late nineteenth century, many thinkers believed that moral behavior was governed by a homunculus—a "little man" inside us, sometimes called "the small voice of conscience." Conscience was considered innate and, in many cases, something instilled by a deity to govern behavior. People who behaved immorally were called "moral imbeciles" and thought either to have been born without a conscience or to be possessed by a devil. The "small voice" concept of conscience was prevalent in the Victorian era until the popularization of psychoanalysis. It was to Freud's great credit that he cast the study of morality—and hence social development in general—on a more scientific plane.

The most important innovation in Freud's conception of morality was the suggestion that people *develop* a sense of morality rather than being born with one. Freud viewed the newborn infant as essentially amoral—the repository of unfocused id impulses. According to Freud's theory of personality, which is described in more detail in Chapter 21, children learn as they grow up to suppress the sexual and aggressive urges of the id and, in the process, they pass through a number of psychosexual stages—the oral, anal, phallic, and genital. Each stage is associated with a different object of an essentially sexual urge. The first love object is the mother's breast—social development really begins with the episode of nursing.

With increasing social as well as general development, the infant begins to love the mother as a whole. Then, during the phallic stage, around the age of three to five, young boys begin to view their fathers as rivals for their prime love objects, their mothers. At this time what Freud calls the Oedipus complex develops. The young boy desires his mother and wants to destroy his rival, the father. In most cases he resolves the conflict by repressing his desire for his mother and identifying with his father. Identification with the father allows the young boy to satisfy his desire for his mother vicariously, and it also alleviates "castration anxiety"—the fear that the father may retaliate against the boy by castrating him for loving his mother and wanting to destroy his father.

If the boy's identification with his father is successful, he will develop socially toward his father—specifically, he will internalize his father's moral standards. In Freud's words, he will introject the superego of the father. Freud thought that the superego consisted of two parts: the ego ideal and the conscience. The main function of the ego ideal is to reward the child for living up to introjected parental expectations. The main function of conscience is to punish the child for failing to live up to them.

Of some importance is Freud's contention that it is not the behavior of the father that is introjected but rather a set of values that is represented in the father's superego and reinforced by other "father figures." According to Freud, "the parents' influence includes the racial, national, and family traditions they represent as well as their own personalities. Moreover, with development, the superego takes over contributions from successors and substitutes of [the child's] parents, such as teachers, admired public figures in public life or high social ideals." It should be noted that, in Freud's opinion, a boy's identification with his father not only provides him with a superego but establishes the boy's (masculine) sex identity. This process of identification is discussed further in Chapters 21 and 25.

Although Freud paid little attention to females in his theory and is said to have had an anti-feminist bias, he did attempt to explain the development of morality in females. He postulated an Electra complex and penis envy as counterparts to the male Oedipus complex and castration anxiety. In males, however, the threat of castration is thought to *end* the Oedipus complex (by bringing about identification with the father), whereas in females the realization that they have no penis is thought to *initiate* the Electra complex. The girl turns away from her mother as a love object and toward her father, in search of a penis or the control of one. What happens after the girl has adopted her father as a love object is not clear. By analogy with what happens in the male, she should identify with her mother, who controls the father's penis. This would allow her to introject a superego and gain a feminine sex identity. However, a boy identifies with his father in order to avoid his wrath and to gain vicarious control of the mother. The theory offers no strong reason why a female would identify with her mother, for the mother cannot threaten the child with castration. Freud never really resolved this problem. In a paper written on the psychical consequences of the anatomical differences between men and women, he suggested that the Electra complex just slowly dissipates—and that females have less well developed superegos than males.

Figure 8.2

Major elements of conflict in a young boy's Oedipus complex. The boy's sexual desire for his mother is frustrated by a powerful rival for her affections, his father, whom he wants to destroy. But he fears that his father will retaliate by castrating him. Rather than risk castration, the boy represses his desire for his mother and identifies with his father, thereby gaining both a superego and a masculine sexual identity. The complex is thus resolved, and he moves into the latency period of psychosexual development, which lasts until puberty.

SOCIAL-LEARNING THEORY

Like the psychoanalytic theory of moral development, the social-learning theory of moral development comes from a larger theoretical context—in fact, from several different, and sometimes contradictory, theories in the social-learning tradition. These theories have at least two things in common: they use principles from learning theory to explain social behavior, and they recognize the importance of observational learning or modeling in social development.

The two contemporary social-learning theorists who have been most concerned with social and particularly with moral development are J. Aronfreed from the University of Pennsylvania and A. Bandura from Stanford. Both point out that a great deal of the behavior that we call moral is controlled by expectations of external rewards and punishments. Much moral behavior, however, is not under the immediate control of external events. (Perhaps, by definition, it cannot be.) People appear to forego rewards in order to behave in ways that are socially acceptable, even in private. The main concern of social-learning theorists has been to explain why moral behavior occurs in the absence of external controls. The explanations center on two main ways in which children learn to govern their own behavior: through conditioning and through the observation of models.

Conditioning

According to social-learning theory, a person behaves in the way that will lead to the greatest satisfaction in a given situation. Gradually he comes to associate various goals and internal states with basic, unlearned satisfactions. For example, the infant's satisfaction when his mother feeds him is unlearned, but soon he begins to associate the presence of the mother herself with pleasure. Later, the child tries to do things that his parents approve of and to inhibit actions his parents think are wrong because he fears that they will withdraw their affection or that he will be punished. Later still, he behaves morally even when his parents are not there. The reason he does so is that the pleasure associated with parental approval and the fear or anxiety associated with punishment are triggered by various cues related to the behavior in question. The cues can be external, such as the chair used to reach the cookie jar, or they can be internal, like thoughts and memories.

Figure 8.3
According to social-learning theory, childhood training, especially in moral learning, directly affects adult behavior. As a young boy (in the drawing above) the ambivalent man on the couch was discovered and admonished by his mother for reading and presumably being sexually stimulated by a pornographic book. Clearly the moral message had been, "Sex is dirty and to be avoided by good boys." In the drawing below, the man's adult sexual behavior is inhibited by the memory of his mother's teachings (or conscience). He has internalized her standards of morality, so that he behaves as if she were still present.

The principles of conditioning, as described in Chapter 3, apply to the conditioning of social behavior as well as to behavior of other types, even though the stimuli that elicit moral responses are often internal. Responses that are reinforced immediately are more likely to occur again than responses that are not; the stronger the reward or punishment, the greater its effect; behavior that is reinforced intermittently is more likely to prevail than behavior that is reinforced every time it occurs.

Even though social-learning theorists recognize the importance of internal events such as thoughts and memories, they still insist that all behavior is under at least indirect control by external cues. Even moral behavior that occurs in private may be governed by thoughts oriented toward external events, such as future punishment. In *Conduct and Consciousness* J. Aronfreed outlines a continuum of controls ranging from external to internal. He suggests that a child may resist temptation because, at the external end, he thinks that his parents are watching or that God will punish him or because, at the internal end, he wants to avoid feeling guilty or violating a principle.

The things parents say to children are of particular importance to the internalization of moral standards because they help form thoughts that the child associates with pleasure or pain. If a child hits another child and an adult simply spanks him, the child may hesitate to hit that particular playmate again, but he may not understand why he should not. If, on the other hand, the adult explains that it is wrong to hurt people the child may also hesitate to bite his friend or to hit some other child. That is, when a parent tells a child why he is being punished, he may provide the child with a general stimulus that helps him control his own behavior in a variety of situations.

Conditioning is not only the mechanism by which the child learns to inhibit immoral behavior but, according to social-learning theory, the determinant of the way the child reacts to his own wrongdoings. For example, a child may learn that he can avoid punishment for misbehaving if he says he is sorry. Apologizing, then, becomes associated with a reduction in anxiety, and the child may use it to reduce anxiety in various situations, even when no punishing agent is present. Similarly, if a child's parents punish him for misbehaving by taking a toy or a privilege away from him—instead of physically punishing him—the child may associate the removal of goods with anxiety reduction. Later, he may take goods away from himself, or perhaps award them to someone he thinks he has harmed, in order to reduce the anxiety associated with wrongdoing. Self-criticism and confession are other responses that a child may learn to use quite generally because, originally, they helped him avoid punishment from his parents.

Modeling

The second way in which the moral aspects of social development take place is through observational learning, or modeling. A. Bandura and R. H. Walters have shown that simply watching someone (called a model) do something interesting can result in imitation. Observational learning takes place in two steps: acquisition and performance. First, the child acquires a cognitive representation of the act. Second, after this mental image has been acquired, he may perform a response based on it. Whether he actually does imitate the model or not depends on a number of things, including the way the child perceives the model (he is likely to imitate someone who seems nurturant, powerful, and competent, for example) and the child's own expectations of the rewards or punishments he will receive if he behaves as the model did.

Figure 8.4
Lawrence Kohlberg, educator and social psychologist, is best known for his research on the development of moral judgment and character. He has studied moral development from childhood through adulthood, as well as cross-cultural differences in moral attitudes. His work has culminated in the definition of six stages of moral development, which are culturally universal.

COGNITIVE-DEVELOPMENTAL THEORY

The cognitive-developmental approach to moral development has been most completely formulated by L. Kohlberg of Harvard University. Kohlberg's approach (he prefers not to call it a theory) is related to early ideas about social interaction outlined by J. Dewey, G. H. Mead, and J. M. Baldwin, and also to Piaget's theory of cognitive development.

Kohlberg hypothesizes that children progress through a number of qualitatively distinct stages of moral judgment. The stages are characterized by the way the child views the world. In all, there are six stages, as shown in Figures 8.5–8.10. The stages occur in sequence—each one develops out of and subsumes its predecessor—and each stage is more cognitively complex than the one before it.

Young children start at Stage 1, an essentially premoral stage where they view morality as avoidance of punishment, then progress through Stage 2 (naive instrumental hedonism) to the "conventional" moralities of Stages 3 (conformist) and 4 (law-and-order). Although most people reach Stages 3 and 4, few advance to the final Stages 5 and 6 (the only stages of true morality).

The stages are related to age. Older children tend to be at more advanced stages, but the speed with which a child travels through the stages varies with his intelligence and with social influences. No stage can be skipped, but a child may stop (become fixated) at any point. In unusual circumstances, he may even regress to an earlier stage. Typically, about half a child's judgments are at one stage and the rest fall into the stages that are one step above and one step below.

Like the psychoanalytic and learning theories of moral development, Kohlberg's theory is part of a more general cognitive theory, a theory similar to that of Piaget. Kohlberg sees the development of moral judgment as a specific case of general cognitive development. With moral judgments as with other cognitions, Kohlberg is concerned not with content but with overriding *structure,* or organization. Kohlberg sees cognitive development as a process of interaction between internal cognitive structures or "schemes" and the external environment. The child interprets new experiences as best he can, and he learns from them. His schemes determine the way he sees the world. They encourage the *assimilation* of only certain information. When the child is presented with information that is too advanced for him to assimilate, he experiences *disequilibrium* and alters his cognitive structure in order

Figure 8.5
The first stage in Kohlberg's outline of the steps in moral development is essentially a premoral stage. Children at this stage behave properly simply to avoid punishment; they show an unquestioning deference to power, and the physical consequences of action determine its goodness or badness for them.

Figure 8.6
People at Stage 2 of Kohlberg's outline of moral development regard human relations as if they were commodities in the marketplace. What is considered right is primarily what is right for the person himself; occasionally, the satisfaction of others' needs is a factor, but the outlook of these persons is essentially an instrumental hedonistic one. A motto illustrative of this stage is "You scratch my back and I'll scratch yours."

to *accommodate* the new information. In this way, cognitive structures advance. As Chapter 5 explained, there are limits on the child's capacity to accommodate new material. He usually cannot accommodate information more than one stage above the stage he is in at any given time.

Moral development involves not only the cognitive processes of assimilation and accommodation but another more strictly social process: *role taking.* During the acquisition of moral values the child learns to internalize the roles of other people. This is, he restructures his concept of self and his concepts of other people and establishes new relationships between himself and the social world. During the preconventional Stages 1 and 2, standards of morality are *external* to self. At this level the child is egocentric; he cannot adopt the viewpoint (take the role) of others. He therefore perceives morality in terms of the consequences of his actions—whether they are rewarded or punished. At the next level, Stage 3, the child takes into account the reactions of others, especially his parents. Their approval and disapproval is the basis of his judgments: he *takes their role* in order to learn what will please them. At this stage the child is essentially a conforming person. He does not decide for himself what is right and wrong but follows rules given by others. This is also true at Stage 4. But at Stage 3, the rules are generally made by the child's parents and other adults with whom he has personal social contact. At Stage 4, they are more general still. Motivation for conformity at this stage is more internal than at earlier stages, and the child may make a moral decision even when no adults are present.

If the individual reaches the final Stages 5 and 6, his standards are even more internalized and role taking is even more general. Stage 5 requires a cognizance of general social contracts. No external agents are needed to "check up"; instead

Figure 8.7
In Kohlberg's Stage 3, moral behavior is that which is approved by others. A child at this level wishes especially to gain his parents' approval. (Older persons at this level are anxious to conform to what is "natural" or statistically most common.) This is the first level at which the child is far enough advanced cognitively to take the role of others; he can understand what will please them. At the preceding two stages, the child is egocentric; he cannot internalize others' viewpoints.

Figure 8.8
Kohlberg calls Stage 4 the law-and-order orientation; children's respect for authority, whether for parents, teachers, policemen (or adults', for government officers, bosses), is paramount. Action is motivated by anticipation of and avoidance of dishonor. The orientation is to do one's duty, obey fixed rules, and maintain the social order.

decisions are made on the basis of a personal contract that takes into account the viewpoint of society in general. At the final stage, decisions are based on principles internal to the person, principles such as the Golden Rule or categorical imperative: Act as you would act after considering how everyone should act if he were in your situation. Principled morality is based on ideals of universal reciprocity and equality, which together constitute *justice.* Justice can be traced back to role taking, for it prescribes that a person (or a society) take everyone's perspective into account before acting. It requires a full and genuine awareness that every person is a human being with equal rights.

RESEARCH ON THE THREE THEORIES

Three theories of morality have been briefly described as prototypes of social developmental theories. Are they based on fact? Unfortunately, none of them has been completely validated or invalidated by research. However, a good deal has been done, and it will help us evaluate the positions if we look at some representative studies on each of them.

The Psychoanalytic Position

The most important contention of the psychoanalytic theory of morality is that there is a qualitative change in the moral orientation of the child as he resolves the Oedipus complex. Is there any evidence that the moral responses of children change drastically around age five? Research findings are confused. R. Grinder, and N. Hartshorne and M. A. May found no changes from nursery school to high school in resistance to cheating and stealing, but research on altruistic behavior by D. L. Krebs showed that it increases fairly consistently after age eight. J. MacFarlane, L.

Figure 8.9
Stage 5 is the first stage of the autonomous, or principled, level of moral development. Persons at this level make decisions about what is right and proper on the basis of contracts, both social and personal. They also are able to take into account the viewpoint of (take the role of) society in general. This is the official American morality as expressed through the United States Constitution. A person at Stage 5 has a clear awareness of the relativism of personal values, and, in the matter of law and procedures for changing it, he is guided by rationality.

Figure 8.10
According to Kohlberg's classifications, these three individuals can be considered to have attained the highest level of moral development, Stage 6, called the universal ethical-principle orientation. Mahatma Gandhi, Jesus Christ, and Martin Luther King, Jr., displayed in their lives respect for the rights and dignity of their fellow human beings and concern that this mutual respect become universal. Each appears to have been governed by self-determined standards of justice and equality. The circumstances of their respective deaths make an unfortunate commentary on the societies they lived in.

Allen, and M. Honzik also found that stealing and lying, as reported by parents, decreased from age six to eight. There is, therefore, some limited evidence that there is a change in morality around the time that psychoanalytic theory postulates the resolution of the Oedipus complex. However, the reason for the change is unclear. Cognitive developmental theory also postulates a change in moral orientation around age eight.

A second contention of psychoanalytic theory is that sex identity and morality in males are determined by the same process. If that is true, it suggests that males with a poorly formed sex identity should be immoral and that immoral males should have a poorly formed sex identity. Appropriate sex identity may, if one wishes, be considered moral by definition. But no research has shown that immoral people have more problems with their sex identity than moral people.

Another way of supporting Freud's theory of moral development would be to establish the validity of his theory of identification. Attempting to do that presents problems. Freud discusses identification in many places in his writings, and his explanations of it are not always consistent. His most complete explanation (set forth in *The Ego and the Id*) suggests that people are essentially bisexual; they take both their mothers and fathers as love objects and form identifications with both. Usually, the strongest identification is with the same-sexed parent, whom the child perceives as similar to himself. Freud suggested that, in general, people identify with others whom they see as similar to themselves, with people of high status, and (defensively) with threatening, aggressive people.

There has been a great deal of research on the relationship between identification and guilt. Identification has generally been defined on the basis of similarity between the descriptions of self supplied by parents and children, and children's guilt feelings have been measured by asking them to complete stories about imaginary characters and by observing the feelings they express in playing with dolls. Although some of the research supports Freud's theory, most of it does not. One of the problems with this type of research is the difficulty of measuring identification and guilt.

According to Freud's theory, for example, girls should identify with their mothers somewhat less strongly than boys with their fathers, and their superegos should be correspondingly weaker. Some studies show a greater tendency for boys to identify with their fathers than for girls to identify with their mothers, but a larger number show little difference between males and females in the extent of their identification with the same-sexed parent. Furthermore, a research review by Kohlberg revealed no differences between males and females in conformity to internalized moral standards or tendency to feel guilt after transgression; contrary to psychoanalytic theory, too, L. M. Termin and L. E. Tyler found girls to be more conforming to rules and authority than boys.

Actually, psychoanalysts are not research-oriented. They are more prone to test their theories in psychotherapy with individual patients than to conduct experimental studies. Most of the research on the psychoanalytic position has been done by early social-learning theorists, such as R. R. Sears, W. M. Whiting, N. Miller and J. Dollard, and O. H. Mowrer.

The Social-Learning Position

Experimental studies on social learning theory established that children's resistance to temptation and reactions to transgression can be shaped through reward and punishment, and that children imitate the moral behavior of prestigious and powerful adults. Aronfreed has shown that the time interval between a wrong deed and punishment can be critical in establishing future resistance to temptation. In one experiment, Aronfreed asked individual children to choose between an attractive toy and an unattractive toy. Whenever the child chose the attractive toy, the experimenter yelled "No" and took some candy away from the child. Aronfreed varied the time interval between the misdeed (picking up the attractive toy) and the reprimand, "No." The experimenter reprimanded one group of children when they reached for the toy, a second group when they picked the toy up, a third group six seconds after they picked it up, and a fourth group after the children had described the toy. Children in all groups quickly learned not to pick up the attractive toy when the experimenter was in the room, but some of them did take the toy when the experimenter left the room. Aronfreed found that the earlier in the act that the children were punished, the less likely they were to transgress in private.

That experiment by Aronfreed demonstrates the effect of direct punishment on the learning of moral responses. A number of other experiments have shown that children imitate the responses of others, even when they are not rewarded. A. Bandura has studied this phenomenon of modeling extensively. In a typical experiment, Bandura has different groups of children observe models who respond to a

Figure 8.11
This young boy has just seen a film in which a model with whom he apparently identified had been praised for exhibiting aggressive behavior toward the Bobo doll. When given the opportunity to interact with a similar doll, the boy imitated the complex set of behaviors he had seen with obvious vigor. According to Bandura, the boy, when given a chance to act as the model had, behaved as if he himself had earlier been praised.

situation in unusual or novel ways. Then he puts the children in a situation similar to that of the model and notes the number of imitative responses they make. Bandura found that most children will imitate novel behavior by a model with very little prodding.

In addition to establishing that modeling does occur, Bandura has investigated the ways in which it can be increased or decreased. He has found, for example, that children are more likely to imitate the behavior of a model they see rewarded than that of a model they see punished. In one experiment, three groups of children watched films of a model who yelled at and punched a Bobo doll. In the film that one group saw, the model was punished by an authority for punching the doll. In the film that a second group of children saw, the model was praised for his aggressive behavior. In the film that the third group saw, the model received neither praise nor punishment. When put into a situation similar to that of the model, the children who had seen him receive praise were much more likely to imitate him than those who had seen him get punished. Bandura hypothesized that the children identified with the model and experienced reward or punishment vicariously as they watched the film. Therefore, when given a chance to act as the model had, they tended to behave as if they themselves (instead of the model) had earlier been praised or punished for hitting the doll.

The Cognitive-Developmental Position

Like the social-learning approach, Kohlberg's cognitive-developmental approach is well substantiated by research. The first step in most of Kohlberg's research is to discover the stage of moral development most characteristic of his subjects. If you were a subject in one of Kohlberg's experiments, your main task would be to respond to a number of moral dilemmas. The questions that Henry David Thoreau and Ralph Waldo Emerson asked each other entail moral dilemmas. Was it moral or immoral for Thoreau to be in jail, moral or immoral for Emerson to be out, and why? To Kohlberg, the most important part of that question is the "why?"

Here is one of the moral dilemmas Kohlberg has used in his research.

> In Europe, a woman was near death from a very bad disease, a special kind of cancer. There was one drug that the doctors thought might save her. It was a form of radium for which a druggist was charging ten times what the drug cost him to make. He paid $200 for the radium and charged $2,000 for a small dose of the drug. The sick woman's husband, Heinz, went to everyone he knew to borrow the money, but he could only get together about $1,000, which is half of what it cost. He told the druggist that his wife was dying and asked him to sell it cheaper or let him pay later. But the druggist said, "No, I discovered the drug and I'm going to make money from it." So Heinz got desperate and broke into the man's store and stole the drug for his wife.
>
> Should the husband have done that? Why?

What is of concern to Kohlberg is the way a person interprets this dilemma—the terms in which he makes his decision, not the decision itself. A person at any stage could think that Heinz should or should not have stolen the drug. His stage depends on the reasons he gives for his decision.

If you took Kohlberg's test, you would probably be asked to respond to from four to ten moral dilemmas. Your responses would be scored according to twenty-five categories or aspects of moral judgment that, according to Kohlberg, are viewed differently at each stage of moral development. For example, your decision on what Heinz should do might center on how you interpret the value of human life. Figure 8.12 shows some responses to Heinz's dilemma, and to a similar one concerning mercy killing, that illustrate the ways people view the value of human life at different stages of moral development.

The basic step that Kohlberg had to take to substantiate his theory was to establish that children pass through his stages of moral development in an invariant

	Stage 1
Q: Why should the druggist give the drug to the dying woman when her husband couldn't pay for it?	A, *Tommy, age 10:* If someone important is in a plane and is allergic to heights and the stewardess won't give him medicine because she's only got enough for one and she's got a sick one, a friend, in back, they'd probably put the stewardess in a lady's jail because she didn't help the important one.
Q: Is it better to save the life of one important person or a lot of unimportant ones?	A: All the people that aren't important because one man just has one house, maybe a lot of furniture, but a whole bunch of people have an awful lot of furniture and some of these poor people might have a lot of money and it doesn't look it.
	Stage 2
Q: Should a doctor mercy kill a fatally ill woman requesting death because of her pain?	A, *Jim, age 13:* If she requests it, it's really up to her. She is in such terrible pain, just the same as people are always putting animals out of their pain.
	Stage 3
	A, *Tommy, age 16:* It might be best for her, but her husband—it's a human life—not like an animal, it just doesn't have the same relationship that a human being does to a family. You can become attached to a dog, but nothing like a human you know.
	Stage 4
	A, *Jim, age 16:* I don't know. In one way, it's murder, it's not a right or privilege of man to decide who shall live and who should die. God put life into everybody on earth and you're taking away something from that person that came directly from God, and you're destroying something that is very sacred, it's in a way part of God and it's almost destroying a part of God when you kill a person. There's something of God in everyone.
	Stage 5
	A, *Jim, age 20:* Given the ethics of the doctor who has taken on responsibility to save human life—from that point of view he probably shouldn't, but there is another side, there are more and more people in the medical profession who are thinking it is a hardship on everyone, the person, the family, when you know they are going to die. When a person is kept alive by an artificial lung or kidney it's more like being a vegetable than being a human who is alive. It's her own choice. I think there are certain rights and privileges that go along with being a human being. I am a human being and have certain desires for life and I think everybody else does, too. You have a world of which you are the center, and everybody else does too, and in that sense we're all equal.
	Stage 6
Q: Should the husband steal the drug to save his wife? How about for someone he just knows?	A, *Jim, age 24:* Yes. A human life takes precedence over any other moral or legal value, whoever it is. A human life has inherent value whether or not it is valued by a particular individual.
Q: Why is that?	A: The inherent worth of the individual human being is the central value in a set of values where the principles of justice and love are normative for all human relationships.

Figure 8.12
On the left side of this chart appear some typical moral questions posed by Kohlberg in his research on the development of moral learning. (The situation posed by the first question is described in the text on page 142.) Typical answers, illustrating each of the six stages, are shown on the right side of the chart. The reasons that govern a decision, and not the decision itself, determine Kohlberg's categorization of a response into one of the six stages.

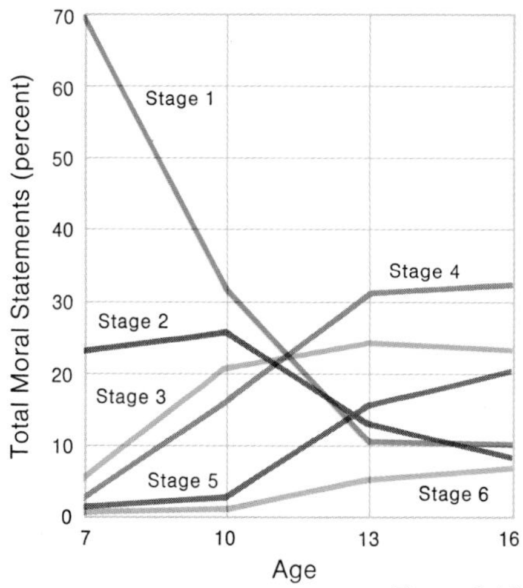

Figure 8.13

Children of varying ages from seven to sixteen were given a description of a moral dilemma and asked for their personal judgments. The results in terms of the age trends for the six stages of moral development are shown here. Note how the number of moral statements at Stages 1 and 2 decrease with age, while those at Stages 3 and 4 increase until about age thirteen, where they stabilize. Moral statements at the levels of Stages 5 and 6 do not appear until about age ten. The moral concepts and attitudes of Stages 5 and 6 clearly are dependent upon an extensive base of cognitive development and social experience. (After Kohlberg, 1963.)

sequence. Figure 8.13 shows the average percentage of moral responses at each stage made by children aged seven to sixteen. These findings supply substantial support for the idea that children do go through the stages of moral development in order.

Kohlberg also maintains that children *in all cultures* progress through the stages in the same order. He has substantiated this contention with several cross-cultural studies. The data graphed in Figure 8.14, for example, indicate that the progression is about the same for urban boys aged ten to sixteen in three quite different cultures, the United States, Taiwan, and Mexico.

THEORIES OF MORAL DEVELOPMENT: A COMPARISON

All three of the theories we have examined agree that an essentially amoral child somehow becomes a more or less moral adult, but they disagree on the way the transformation comes about. Psychoanalytic theory suggests that a set of moral standards is introjected during the Oedipal period. Social-learning theory argues that morality is learned in the same way as other behavior, through a step-by-step accumulation of responses. Cognitive-developmental theory sees moral development as essentially cognitive rather than behavioral and postulates six qualitatively different stages of development.

Each of the three theories makes considerable sense. We tend to think of morality in terms of conscience and guilt, and Freud hypothesized a guilt-governing superego. We also realize, as the social-learning theorists emphasize, that we are taught to behave in ways that those around us consider right or wrong. Kohlberg's stress on qualitative changes as a child matures also seems plausible, for we know that children have different ideas about morality than adults.

Reading about a single theory, one tends to adopt its point of view and follow its author's line of reasoning. But the fact that a theory makes sense does not mean it is correct. As the brief review of research on these theories suggests, they have all received some substantiation. But can they all be correct? Another way to judge the validity of the theories is by comparing them. Do they contradict one another; or do they even address the same issue?

The Focus of the Theories

The first point of comparison is the most basic, the explanatory realm and focus of the theories. What do they attempt to explain? Consider Thoreau's situation. What aspect of it would psychoanalytic, social-learning, and cognitive-developmental theorists look at?

Psychoanalysts would probably focus on Thoreau's intrapsychic feelings. The primary concern of the psychoanalytic school is feeling, emotion, or affect—particu-

Figure 8.14

Stages of moral development for middle-class urban boys of various ages in the United States, Taiwan, and Mexico. At age ten in each country, the greater number of moral statements are scored at the lower stages. In the United States, by age sixteen the order is reversed, so that the greater proportion uses higher stages (except Stage 6). The results in Mexico and Taiwan are the same, except that development is a little slower. These findings show the cultural universality of the sequence of moral stages.

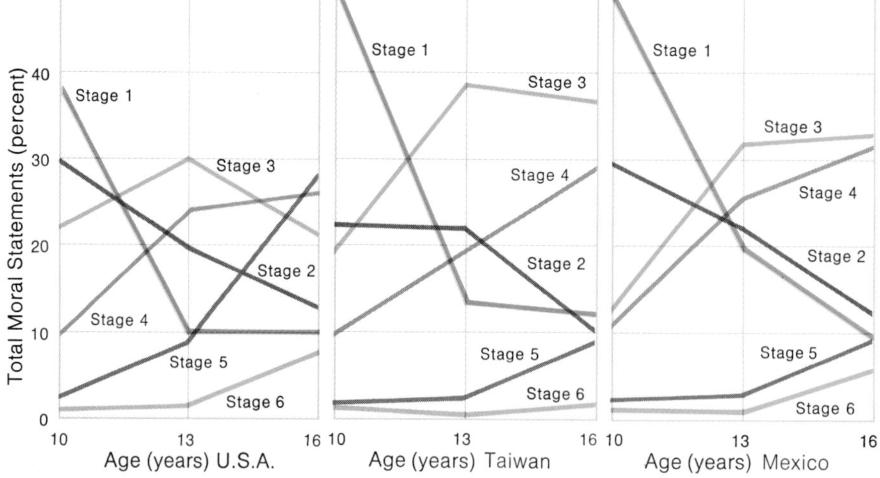

larly guilt and anxiety—especially when it seems inappropriate to the situation. If Thoreau did not feel guilty at all about his refusal to pay the poll tax and showed little awareness that moral questions were involved, a psychoanalyst would suspect that his superego was weak. If he felt very guilty, or very self-righteous, a psychoanalyst might suspect that he had an overly restrictive superego. In either case, a Freudian would want to know about Thoreau's childhood. He would be less interested in Thoreau's decision as a response to the current political situation than as a symbolic attempt to resolve an early psychological conflict.

Social-learning theorists would focus not on Thoreau's feelings but on his behavior. They would ask what caused him to *act* the way he did. Why did he choose this particular way to respond to his situation? How did it help him gain reward or avoid punishment? Had he been reinforced for similar behavior in the past, or was he perhaps imitating the behavior of someone he admired?

Cognitive-developmental theorists would ask how Thoreau viewed his situation. They would want to know how he reached the decision he did—what he saw as the basic issues and how he interpreted them. Cognitive-developmental theory focuses on judgment rather than on affect or behavior. It is concerned with the implicit theories of morality that people develop.

Psychoanalytic theory suggests that people are what they feel; social-learning theory suggests that they are what they do; cognitive-developmental theory suggests that they are what they think. But none of the three emphasizes affect, behavior, or cognition to the exclusion of all else. Each makes some attempt to account for feelings of guilt, moral and immoral behavior, and judgments about morality.

Although psychoanalytic theory focuses on the emotion of guilt, it also has a strong behavioral emphasis. Like learning theory, it is ultimately concerned with explaining what people do. Unlike social-learning theory, however, it hypothesizes an internal moral structure, the superego, instead of explaining behavior by linking it to external rewards and punishments.

Psychoanalytic theory gives less attention to judgment. In stressing the unconscious, irrational determinants of behavior, Freud minimized the importance of cognition. One aspect of Freud's theory of moral development that is often overlooked, however, is his suggestion that the superego consists of an ego ideal as well as a conscience. Freud's position is commonly interpreted as totally guilt-oriented, but that is incorrect. The ego ideal sets standards and evaluates performance in relation to them, a process that requires judgment. Thus the ego ideal offers a way of explaining the kind of competence-motivated, self-actualizing behavior discussed by cognitive-developmental theorists.

Although social-learning theorists are essentially behavioristic, they do recognize the importance of cognition and emotion. In Bandura's theory, the acquisition phase of observational learning (during which the child acquires a mental representation of behavior that he may or may not perform later on) is essentially cognitive, and Aronfreed discusses cognitive processes at length. In addition, Aronfreed (much more than Bandura) recognizes the role of emotion in moral development. He believes that the prime source of internal control over behavior is anxiety. Like psychoanalytic theorists, he believes that anxiety, shame, and guilt suppress much immoral behavior. Unlike psychoanalytic theorists, however, he views these unpleasant emotions as conditioned rather than as mediated by a superego.

Kohlberg emphasizes the judgmental core of morality, but he does not lose sight of the importance of emotion or behavior. He sees cognition and emotion as closely related. Kohlberg subscribes to a Schachter-Singer-like theory of emotion (see Chapter 17), arguing that people label the physiological arousal present during emotional states as a particular emotion primarily on the basis of cognitive appraisals of their situations. For example, Kohlberg says that a child is likely to define the emotion that accompanies wrongdoing differently at different stages of moral development.

At Stage 3, he may feel shame—concern that he has lost the approval of others. At Stage 4, he may feel guilt for violating rules. At Stage 6, the emotion may take the form of self-blame for violating a principle of conscience.

Kohlberg berates many American psychologists for their obsessive concern with behavior; he does not, however, completely neglect what people do. He believes that moral judgment helps determine behavior, and he argues that most behavior is *situationally specific*. That is, he believes that people act as they do primarily because of the demands of the particular situation they are in. This matter has been investigated experimentally, and some of the research will be discussed at the end of the chapter. At this point, the important thing to note is that the relation between level of moral judgment and the morality of behavior must remain problematic in Kohlberg's theory, since the theory emphasizes how moral decisions are made—the type of thinking they are based on—rather than what the decisions are or what behavior they lead to. Remember that you could have thought Heinz should or should not have stolen the drug and still be at Stage 6.

Is Morality Culturally Relative?

Social-learning theory clearly suggests that morality is culturally defined. From parents and other socializing agents, the child learns the rules of the society. He is rewarded for behaving in socially acceptable ways and punished for behaving in socially unacceptable ways; parents, teachers, and other socializing agents supply the child with models of approved behavior. The idea that moral behavior is culturally relative is supported by anthropological and sociological data on extreme differences in the behavior different cultures call moral. Even incest, one of the very few types of behavior considered immoral in all known societies, is differently defined from one culture to another. Almost all societies forbid sexual intercourse between brother and sister, father and daughter, and mother and son, but beyond that the prohibitions on sex and marriage between relatives are exceedingly varied.

Psychoanalytic theory assumes less cultural relativity than social-learning theory but more than cognitive-developmental theory. Freud said that all children go through the oral, anal, phallic and genital stages of personality development, that everyone in every culture develops an Oedipus or Electra complex, and that all societies make some attempt to suppress the sexual and aggressive drives of their members. He also believed, however, that the specific content of the moral standards introjected at the resolution of the Oedipus complex depends on the culture to which a person belongs.

In Kohlberg's opinion, it is a mistake to conclude from striking cultural differences in customs that morality is culturally relative; one must take into account the *meanings* of the customs. Kohlberg says that certain basic moral values are universal. Facing a dilemma like that of the husband with the dying wife, any person will decide what to do on the basis of such considerations as the value of life, concern for the law, and affectional and family role obligations. What varies is the way people think about these things, and that depends more on their stage of moral maturity than on the conventions of their particular culture. For example, a Taiwanese boy at Stage 2 might say that Heinz was right to steal the drug because "if his wife dies he will have to pay for her funeral," whereas an American boy, also at Stage 2, might say he was right to steal it because otherwise "there will be no one to cook his food." The two explanations differ because Taiwanese and American customs differ (large funerals are an important value in Taiwan), but both children see the problem in the instrumental-exchange terms that characterize Stage 2.

The behavior that is considered right and wrong varies from culture to culture, as do the rewards and punishments used to teach morality to the child; but, because moral development in all cultures occurs through conditioning and modeling, even social-learning theorists would agree that moral behavior is as culturally universal as are particular child-rearing practices.

Kohlberg's theory is the only one of the three that implies a value judgment. It suggests that people *should* think in Stage 6 terms. Psychoanalytic and social-learning theories are not concerned with what "true morality" is. They view moral development as a problem in social development and attempt to explain how an essentially hedonistic child comes to behave in ways that are considered moral by the adult society he will join.

Parents and Child Rearing

Most people—and all three theories—agree that parents are important to the development of morality in children. In psychoanalytic theory they are central, although Freud also recognized the influence of other socializing agents. Social-learning theory also views parents as central, since they are the earliest and most pervasive rewarding and punishing agents and models, but it gives somewhat more attention to other adults, including teachers, models seen on television, and the child's peers. For cognitive-developmental theorists, parents are important for role taking but not a really critical factor in the child's moral development. Like Piaget, Kohlberg emphasizes the role of the peer group. He cites research on Israeli children reared in Kibbutzim, who rarely see their parents but are not morally deficient.

In Kohlberg's theory, what is important is that the child have experience with moral judgments more advanced than his own, but not so much more advanced that he cannot understand them. A Stage-1 or -2 child ("I won't hit Bobby because he might hit me back") will learn more from a playmate or parent who talks in Stage-3 terms ("If you were a good boy, you wouldn't do that") than from a parent's Stage-5 explanations ("If people hit people whenever they felt like it, we wouldn't have a very good world, would we?").

A large proportion of early research in the psychoanalytic and social-learning traditions concerned the effects of parental warmth, power, and discipline on moral development. An exhaustive early study on the effects of different types of discipline, performed by R. R. Sears, E. E. Maccoby, and H. Levin, showed that children who

Figure 8.15
These happy boys in an Israeli kibbutz have been referred to as "children without parents." They are raised communally, sometimes only seeing their parents on weekends, yet data show that these children are not developmentally retarded and show no deficits in morality. Psychological theories that rely heavily on parental influence to account for adequate moral development in children have some difficulty explaining these data. Despite clear cultural differences from American children, such as less interest in personal belongings and individuality, the Israeli youngsters develop their moral attitudes in very similar fashion to Americans.

are punished psychologically (with love-withdrawal and reasoning) develop stronger consciences and are more susceptible to guilt feelings than children who are punished physically. Although at first it was thought that love withdrawal was the more important factor, later studies by Aronfreed and by M. L. Hoffman and H. D. Saltzstein suggest that reasoning with the child is the critical factor. This finding corresponds with what would be expected from cognitive-developmental theory, which says that reasoning with a child encourages him to take the role of others; it is also in accord with Aronfreed's position that verbal explanations help the child internalize moral standards by providing him with thoughts that he associates with reward or punishment.

It has also been fairly well established that children who are physically punished for aggression later behave more aggressively than other children. Assuming that physical punishment means an aggressive father, psychoanalytic theory would predict that it would encourage the resolution of the Oedipus complex and result in a strict superego. But aggressive behavior would be expected nonetheless, since it is the father with whom the child identifies. As for social-learning theory, the finding seems to contradict a basic behaviorist tenet: the more intense the punishment, the greater its effect. Aronfreed and Bandura have offered several reasons why the effect does not hold. In *Conduct and Conscience* Aronfreed suggests that psychological punishment may be more painful for a child than physical punishment and he also points out that psychological punishment facilitates the internalization of moral standards. Bandura observes that parents who punish their children physically for aggressive behavior provide a model for that very behavior.

What Determines Moral Behavior?

Another topic that has received much attention from researchers is the extent to which moral behavior is determined by characteristics of the *situation* as opposed to the honesty or dishonesty of the *person*. A monumental study performed by H. Hartshorne and M. A. May and their colleagues in 1928, which involved thousands of children in many different situations, was a considerable disappointment to those who would like to divide the world into cheaters and noncheaters. Hartshorne and May found that almost all children cheat some of the time, and that knowing a person has cheated in one situation does *not* make it possible to predict that he will (or will not) cheat in another. The decision on whether to cheat seemed to be largely determined by expediency—by whether the situation was such that it seemed safe and easy to cheat. When honest behavior was not dictated by concern about detection and punishment, it seemed to depend on immediate social and situational factors such as group approval and example. In some classrooms many children cheated, whereas in other, seemingly identically composed classrooms, almost no one did any cheating.

Psychoanalytic theory hypothesizes an internal superego that should give more constancy to moral behavior than was found by Hartshorne and May. Social-learning theorists would have fewer problems with these results, because they interpret behavioral consistencies and variations in terms of stimulus generalization and discrimination. That is, they would expect behavior that occurs in one situation also to occur in another if the stimuli in the two situations are similar. The fact that both situations involved the same person would be less important.

At first glance, it may seem that cognitive-developmental theory would predict constancy of moral behavior across situations. Recall, however, that Kohlberg is more concerned with judgment than with behavior. As was mentioned, Kohlberg believes that behavior is to a large extent situationally determined; he thinks that external factors are especially important at early stages of moral development.

Studies such as that by Hartshorne and May have cast doubt on the concept of a general superego. Other studies, in particular one done by Kohlberg in 1964, have suggested that ego functions are more important than superego functions in morality. Ego functions include intelligence, strength of will, the ability to wait for a large reward instead of taking a small one now, a capacity for sustained attention and fantasy-control, and high self-esteem. Although psychoanalytic theory postulates an ego—and perhaps more important, an ego ideal—the relationship between morality and ego strength lends most support to the cognitive-developmental approach.

An experiment by R. L. Krebs indicates some interesting associations between IQ, attention, and the moral behavior of children at different stages. At Stage 2, 40 percent of the low IQ, low-attention children cheated as against 80 percent of the high IQ, high-attention children. At Stage 4, *all* the low IQ, low-attention children cheated but only a third of the high IQ, high-attention children did so. It seemed that the Stage-2 children who were bright and attentive enough to see that they could cheat jumped at the chance. As Stage 4, the ones who cheated seemed to be those who were not bright or attentive enough to understand and follow the rules.

At the principled level of moral development, Stages 5 and 6, both situational factors and ego strength are less important influences on behavior than they are at earlier stages because at that level a person in a sense carries his own interpretations of the situation around with him. Research by N. Haan, M. B. Smith, and J. Block on student participation in the Berkeley free-speech demonstrations of 1968 indicated that students' behavior could be predicted quite accurately from their level of moral development. Of the Stage 6 students, 80 percent actively participated in the demonstrations; only 10 percent of the Stage 3 and 4 subjects did so. You may see a parallel between the behavior of the Berkeley students and that of Henry David Thoreau.

The study of the development of morality brings to light the major facets of social development in general. Growing up morally is just one part of growing up socially. After learning considerably more about the individual and his many ways of functioning, we shall return to social development in Unit VIII.

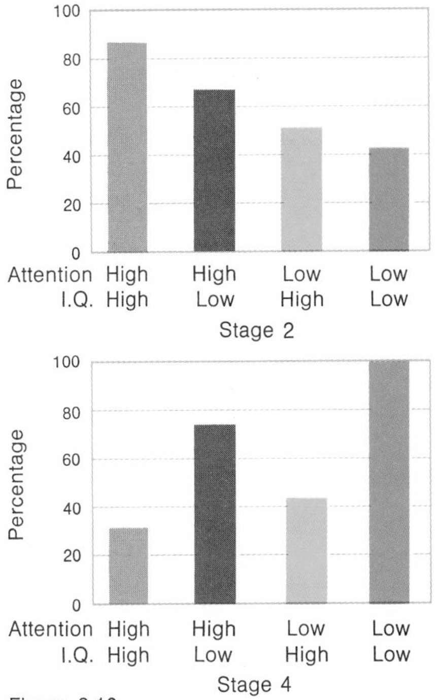

Figure 8.16

Results of Krebs' study of the effects of attention level, IQ, and stage of moral development on cheating. The bars show the percentage of children having the characteristics indicated who cheated when given the opportunity to do so during the study.

SUGGESTED READINGS

BANDURA, A., and WALTERS, R. H. *Social Learning and Personality Development.* New York, Holt, Rinehart and Winston, 1963. One of the first presentations of Bandura's social-learning theory. It supplies the rudiments of Bandura's position, which are elaborated on in Bandura's chapter in the Goslan *Handbook,* cited here.

BROWN, ROGER. *Social Psychology.* New York, Free Press, 1967. Brown's chapter on the acquisition of morality presents an eloquently clear outline of the psychoanalytic, learning-theory, and cognitive-developmental theories of morality.

FREUD, SIGMUND. Lecture XXXI of the New Introductory Lectures: "Dissection of the Psychical Personality." In *The Complete Works of Sigmund Freud,* Vol. XXII, London, Hogarth Press, 1964, pp. 57–80. This article is the one that deals most explicitly with Freud's view of morality. Other articles are "The Ego and the Id" and "The Dissolution of the Oedipus Complex," in Vol. XIX, 1961, and "Group Psychology and the Analysis of the Ego," in Vol. XVIII, 1955, pp. 67–143.

GOSLAN, DAVID A. (Ed.). *Handbook of Socialization Theory and Research.* Chicago, Rand McNally and Co., 1969. Contains three chapters that supply the single best presentation of theories of moral development—chapters by Aronfreed, Bandura, and Kohlberg. The Kohlberg chapter is his single best work and has been characterized as "inspired." It is one of the most stimulating presentations in psychology in the past few years.

HOFFMAN, MARTIN. "Moral Development." In Paul H. Mussen (Ed.), *Carmichael's Manual of Child Psychology* (3rd ed.), Vol. II. New York, Wiley, 1970. An extensive and detailed review of the literature on moral development. It presents the cognitive-developmental position, social-learning theory, and psychoanalytic theory, and systematically surveys the tremendous amount of relevant research.

UNIT III
Memory and Problem Solving

Everyone who uses terms like "memory," "skill," "ability" has an intuitive understanding of what they mean. If you say to a friend, "I forgot the telephone number," both of you understand what is meant by "forgot"; you and your friend would consistently use the term to refer to this particular behavior. Psychologists studying such consistencies try to uncover the "rules" or principles that underlie them so as to understand human behavior.

Different groups of psychologists go about seeking that understanding through differing approaches. The behaviorist approach to learning, as we saw in Chapter 3, explains consistencies of small units of *observable* behavior.

Chapter 9, Information Processing, breaks down human function into input, which deals with selection and attention; processing, which deals with how input is organized for memory storage or behavior; and output, how action depends on the two previous operations. The role of computers in modeling these processes is discussed at length.

3

Conditioning and Learning offers one view of learning, the behaviorist approach. Chapter 10 presents an information-processing view of learning based on its organization for storage in memory and for retrieval. It also discusses findings of traditional studies of learning and memory, such as the studies of paired-associate learning.

4

The Organization of Behavior postulates a four-phase theory of solving certain kinds of problems, which you might test in solving some of the problems included in Chapter 11.

6

The Development of Higher-Order Intelligence describes Piaget's three later stages of cognitive development and explains how children's problem-solving capabilities are qualitatively different at each stage of development. Chapter 11's varied approach to problem solving includes a discussion of methods of teaching problem solving, based on Piaget's developmental findings.

13

The Senses explains the basic physiological phenomena of vision, hearing, and our other senses—how what Chapter 9 calls "input" actually comes through our senses and into consciousness.

14

Perception describes various aspects of how sensory patterns of stimulation relate to objects in the real world that are perceived. Its discussion of perceptual set and related phenomena is closely related to topics in Chapter 9, like feature extraction and sensory gating, or selective attention; to topics in Chapter 10, like sensory information storage and transfer to long-term memory; and to topics in Chapter 11, like functional fixedness.

The information-processing approach, which is taken in much of this unit, tries rather to discover and represent operations that go on *inside* the organism as it receives information from the world, processes it, and acts. The information-processing approach often makes use of computer programs to model, or represent human memory, thinking, and problem-solving abilities.

The other major approach of this unit is a developmental one; it seeks to understand how children develop the skills and abilities that adults display in the area of information processing, with the goal of understanding these adult skills and abilities better.

Chapter 10, Learning and Memory, discusses both traditional and modern approaches to the study of memory. Traditional studies attempted to discover basic, universal processes of memory by using nonsense material so as to avoid interference from previously learned material. Modern approaches try to understand the role of interest, motivation, and knowledge on how individuals remember— or forget.

Chapter 11, Problem Solving, deals with the many kinds of thinking and abilities that go into resolving the diverse situations that can be called problems. Logic and heuristics are discussed, as well as the relation between problem-solving skills and creativity. The development of these skills and possible reasons for individual differences in level and kind of problem-solving skills are included.

24

The Individual and His Groups contains a lengthy discussion of problem solving in groups that can be compared to Chapter 11's discussion of individual problem solving.

9 Information Processing

A CHAPTER DEALING at least in part with computers, as this one does, reminds me of a story I wrote back in 1956. It was entitled "The Last Question," and what follows is a résumé of its plot.

Mankind, thanks to its giant computers, has managed to work out systems for making use of solar energy, and it appears that a golden age will be dawning—free energy without pollution. One minor official, however, worries about what will happen when the sun runs down. Will mankind be able to wind it up again, so to speak? He asks the computer, which can only say it has insufficient data to give an answer.

Over centuries and millennia men learn to travel between the stars and to colonize the galaxy. They learn the secret of immortality. They free themselves of their material bodies and become energy beings living in space. At every stage they are helped by the information-analyzing ability of computers—which steadily grow more complex. Indeed, computers grow so complex that only computers themselves can design and construct still better computers. The result is that mankind loses all physical connection with the vast central computer that becomes the great problem solver in man's later history. At one stage this computer occupies an entire world by itself. Then parts of it actually exist outside space. Finally, although all of it exists outside space, it still keeps itself at the disposal of man. Any man can ask any question at any point in the universe and get an answer.

Through all of history, however, no matter how widespread and ethereally immortal men become, it is clear that the entire universe is running down. Available energy decreases, and the stars are dimming to final extinction. Periodically, someone asks the ever-improving computer if the universe can ever be wound up again. Always, the computer answers that it doesn't have enough information to formulate an answer. Finally, the end comes. The last stars are all but dead. Mankind has coalesced into one energy being that is pure mind, and at the last it coalesces with the ultimate computer that exists outside space. Now only the computer is left. And the computer cannot rest, for in all man's history there remains that one question it could not answer—the last question. Can one wind up the universe once more?

Ages pass while the computer endlessly analyzes all the information gathered in the course of a trillion years, and finally it has the answer. But now no one remains to tell it to, so the computer decides to answer the question in such a way as to make sure that there will eventually be someone to understand. The computer began . . .

And it said, "Let there be light!" And there was light! . . . I.A.

A man sits in a room facing a piece of apparatus with two lights on it, one green and one red, and two keys, one near his left hand and the other near his right. The psychologist running the experiment gives him the following instructions: When the red light goes on, press the right-hand key; when the green light goes on, press the left-hand key. Then the experimenter flashes the lights, rapidly and in random order—red-red-green-red-green, and so on. The subject will probably be able to press the correct key in response to the flashes if they occur no faster than about 120 a minute—twice a second.

Now suppose that this same man, who happens to be a concert pianist, sits at the piano in his living room facing the score of a piece of music with which he is somewhat familiar. The tempo of the piece is no faster than average—about ninety beats to a minute—but it begins with a series of eighth-note chords. To maintain the right tempo throughout the series, the pianist must, and does, hit about 720 keys a minute—twelve a second.

In both cases, information processing takes place; the man is receiving visual information, interpreting it, and acting on it. In the first case, when the information presented was red and green light flashes in no particular order, he could respond correctly to only 120 or fewer per minute. In the second case, when the information was a meaningful series of musical notes, the man could process and act on it about six times as fast as he could to the light flashes.

The three major components of any information-processing system are represented in the two preceding examples. The visual information—the lights and the musical notes—are the *input;* pressing the keys and playing the piano are the *output;*

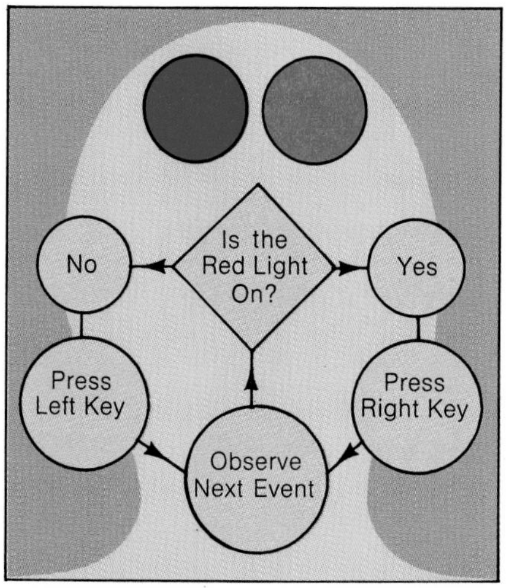

Figure 9.1
This flow chart illustrates the rules that a human follows in performing the simple task described at the beginning of the chapter. Given that the input stimuli are the randomly flashing red and green lights, he processes the input by asking himself "Is the red light on?" Based on the answer to that question, he presses the left or right key, the output. He then is set to observe the next event.

whatever transformations occurred between them is the *processing*. In an attempt to understand why a man displays such variation in his ability to process information, some psychologists have turned to another information-processing system, the computer, to simulate the working of human intelligence.

Man is a very complex information-processing system, and computer study of human behavior can proceed only on the basis of analogies, or *models*. A model of a system is another system that specifies inputs like those of the original and has the same sort of transformations built into the processing relationship between its input and its output so that the output of the model is comparable to that of the original system. For example, to a person reading one, a map is a model of the area it displays. But a map, like any model, emulates the original system, the terrain, over only a limited range. Very small towns and obscure side roads often do not appear on the map. In fact, a system that is a *complete* model of another would be of little use in the investigation of the original system. Consider a case in point. In *Silvie and Bruno Concluded*, a novel by Lewis Carroll (who was also a mathematician), one character comes to a village and asks for a map of the region. He is told that there is a map, but it cannot be used. The map, it seems, had been drawn to a scale of one mile to one mile, so that if it were opened up, the sky would be hidden from view and the sun blotted out. Clearly, useful models cannot be exact replicas of the systems that are modeled.

Computer analogies, or models, of human information processing are likewise not at all the same as the human brain. Instead, the computer program is designed to deal with specified inputs—like the red and green light flashes described earlier—and specified outputs—like pressing the left or right key in response to the flashes twice a second. In addition, the program establishes "rules" that the man responding to the light flashes may have followed in processing the information (see Figure 9.1).

Although they are complex devices, computers are shaped by their programs. The model you end up with depends on what inputs, outputs, and rules the model maker specifies. A computer can be programmed to simulate a nuclear reactor or a long suspension bridge in the same way it can be programmed to simulate a human cognitive system.

For the cognitive system, the goal is to program the computer so that it behaves like a person, at least to the extent that the computer comes up with the same outputs as the person does when faced with the same inputs. Based on the known ways in which the program instructs the computer to go about coming up with its output, psychologists can draw inferences about how people process information.

INPUT: ATTENTION AND SELECTION

Picture an art lover wandering through the cool, stately corridors of the Louvre. He approaches paintings and sculptures, sometimes moving toward them to examine a detail that attracts his eye and sometimes drawing back to observe the overall impression. What is the art lover paying attention to? In a sense, the answer is obvious: he is attending to the works of art. But a tremendous amount of information is being received by his sense organs and transmitted to his central nervous system, not only from the artworks and other visible objects but from the clothes that lie against his skin, from the audible movements of people around him, and from a variety of other sources. He is not attending to all that information; some rigorous *selection* is going on. Furthermore, while the wanderer keeps his attention on his selected area of interest he also maintains certain safeguards in case he should, say, need to avoid a collision with another art lover. Although much of the input to his nervous system is not conscious, in the sense that he is not actively attending to it, he is able to shift his attention to it when necessary.

In order to understand how selective attention and shifts in attention are possible, it is necessary to know something of the two separate mechanisms that transmit information from the external world to the central nervous system and the brain. When a visual stimulus reaches the retina of the eye and excites the rods and cones, the physical energy of the stimulus turns into physiological energy and streams toward the brain. The main neural pathway over which the energy moves is called the *straight-line sensory system.* The straight-line sensory system for vision runs from the eye to the primary visual projection area in the occipital region of the brain, shown in Figure 9.2. The eye also sends information about the stimulus to the brain via a secondary pathway, the *reticular activating system,* shown in Figure 9.3. The straight-line sensory system is the channel that carries visual information; if it is destroyed, the person is permanently blinded. The reticular activating system, by contrast, carries little information as such. Its function is to alert the brain that information is continuing or beginning to come through on the straight-line system. If the reticular system is destroyed, the organism lapses into a deep coma from which it usually cannot be aroused. Similarly, if the normal reticular system has no information to announce, as in a completely changeless environment, the chances are that the person would soon drop into a deep sleep. Some external stimulation is necessary for normal awake alertness. (Chapter 15 offers a discussion of the findings of experiments in sensory deprivation.)

Sensory Gating and Parallel Processing

As a general rule, the more novel, radical, or unexpected a stimulus is, the more important it is that an organism pay attention to it. Probably, then, the mechanism of attention is influenced chiefly by data arriving in the brain via the reticular system. There also seems to be a feedback system that goes from the brain to the sense receptors themselves and acts as a kind of damper or gating mechanism on any incoming sensory activity that is not currently important. When we attend to a visual stimulus, the brain sends to the ears and to other senses messages that have the effect of cutting down the volume of the information coming through on these channels, so that it does not distract our attention from the visual stimulus. This kind of stimulus attenuation is called *sensory gating.* If, however, while we are attending to a visual stimulus, our ears detect a strange sound—or even an unexpected silence—the reticular activating system alerts the brain at once, and our attention shifts, at least briefly, to the message the ears are trying to give us.

A more complex type of selective attention is illustrated by our performance at a party. We can attend to one conversation out of the babble of voices that reaches our ears while completely ignoring the content of other conversations—including, perhaps, the one we are supposedly participating in. If we try to take part

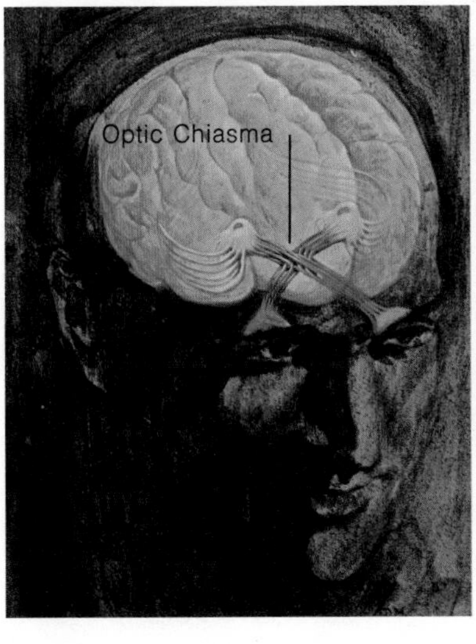

Figure 9.2

The visual projection system (left) is a straight-line sensory system in which external information is sent to the occipital cortex via a linear channel from the eye. If any link in the channel is broken, the message cannot reach the cortex.

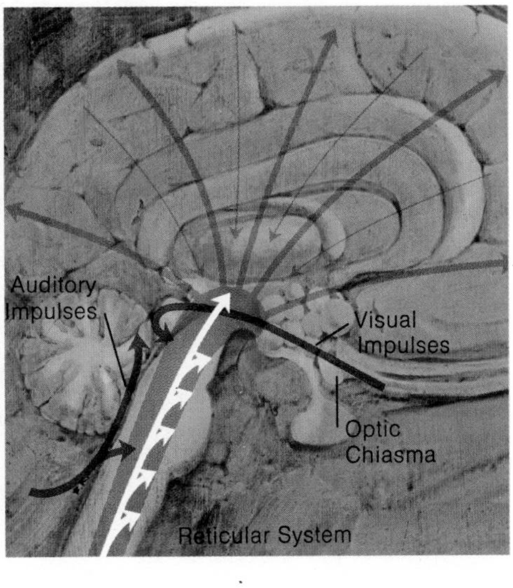

Figure 9.3

Like the straight-line sensory system, the reticular activating system sends visual information toward the cortex, although the information it sends serves the more general function of alerting the brain and directing attention to the presence of important specific visual stimulation.

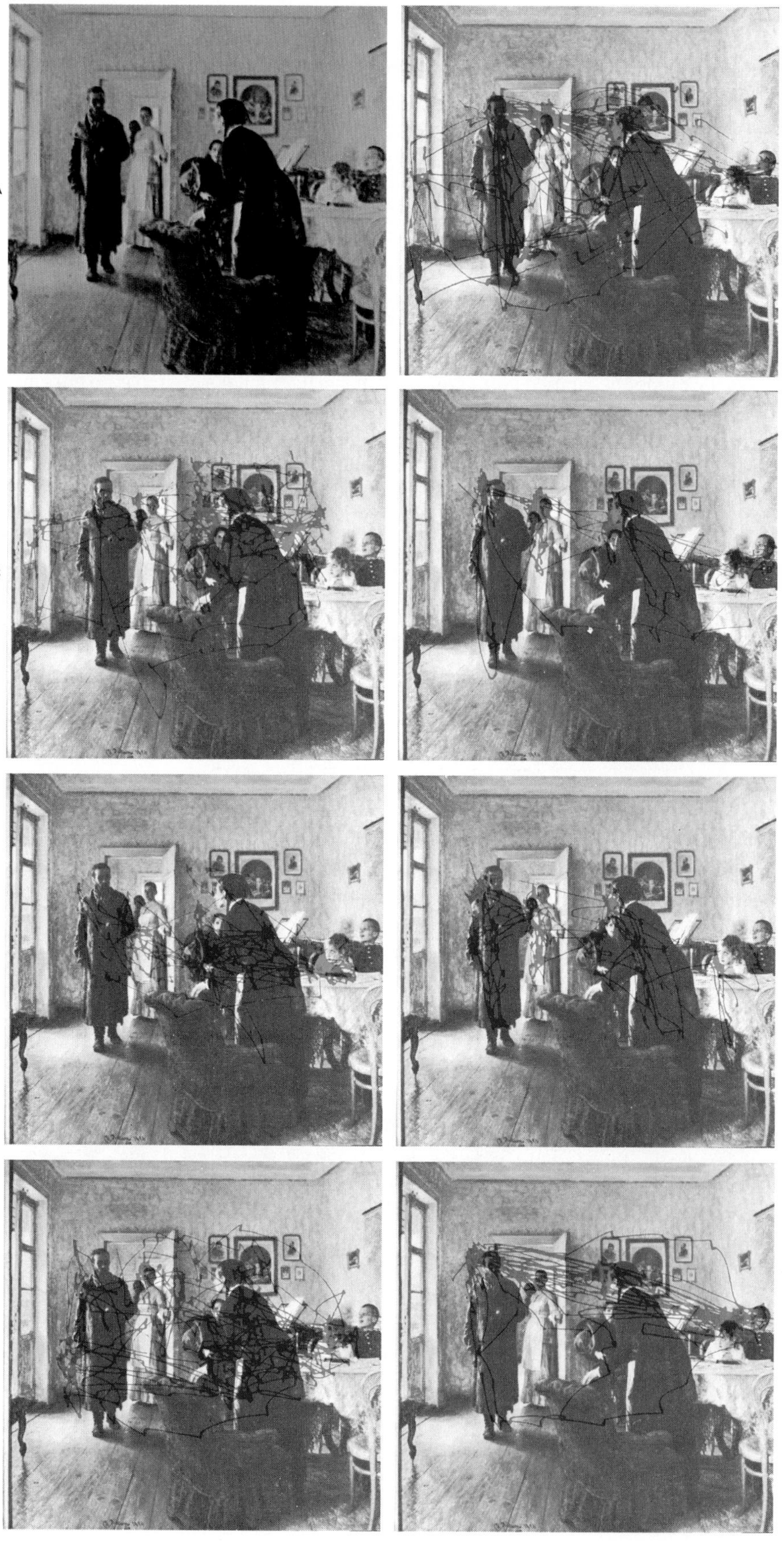

Figure 9.4

At the top left (A) is a photograph of the painting "An Unexpected Visitor" by the Russian artist I. E. Repin. Each of the seven tracings overlaying the painting is a three-minute record of one person's eye movements as he examined the painting after receiving specific instructions about what to look for. The instructions were: (B) Examine the picture freely. (C) Estimate the material circumstances of the family in the picture. (D) Give the ages of the people. (E) Surmise what the family had been doing before the arrival of the "unexpected visitor." (F) Remember the clothes worn by the people. (G) Remember the position of the people and objects in the room. (H) Estimate how long the "unexpected visitor" had been away from the family.

This series shows dramatically how expectation affects the process of feature extraction.

in, or even just listen to, two different conversations simultaneously, we usually fail. It is possible to keep up one conversation while maintaining a rough check on who is saying hello or good-bye to whom throughout the room, but it is hard to follow two complicated conversations at once.

Sometimes, however, we use the presence of one type of stimulation to help us keep our attention on another. For instance, if you can hear people talking while you are reading this book you will probably find yourself distracted fairly often. If you turn on a phonograph or a radio for background music while you study, though, the chances are that you will be able to concentrate much better. The music masks most of the other noise, reducing the number of inputs the brain must pay occasional attention to.

Although human beings have the ability to keep track of several streams of incoming information at the same time—to perform what is called *parallel processing*—machines that have this capacity to any great extent have not yet been developed. Machines need to be told what information they should pay attention to and when. They are capable only of *sequential processing;* that is, they can deal with only one channel of incoming information at a time. The inability of machines to switch on more than one sensory system when they are needed clearly limits their adaptability and their power. – machines

Feature Extraction

The problems of input selection do not end with the identification of the channel that deserves attention. Even when a particular stream of information has been isolated as the one to attend to, the task of selecting the relevant material coming through on that channel remains. We do not simply pay attention to "sight" or "hearing" but to particular things that are seen or heard.

For the art lover in the Louvre, feature extraction is an exceedingly complex problem. His selection will probably be influenced by such diverse factors as the colors on the canvas—bright or subdued; contrasting or homogeneous—and his personal interests—the quality and strength of the brush strokes; the artist's portrayal of light and shade.

Existing physiological data—at both the animal and human levels—show that feature extraction in vision depends on structures and processes both in the eye and in the brain. Studies have shown that the retinas of cats' eyes contain some sort of line detectors. Large numbers of cells in the retina seem to be "wired together" so as to distinguish horizontal from vertical features. Other studies, by J. Y. Lettvin and others, suggest that, after some processing in the eye, certain parts of a frog's brain act as feature analyzers. The investigators found that one part of the frog's brain displays activity whenever a line or the edge of an object comes into view. Another part is activated by small, erratically moving objects—a very useful analyzer to have if flies are your main source of nourishment. These aspects of perception are discussed more fully in Chapter 14.

These and similar results obtained by D. H. Hubel and T. N. Wiesel on the visual cortex of the cat have led to speculation that the human eye and brain may contain structures that respond selectively to different types of incoming visual signals. Consider, for example, the kind of complex feature detectors people seem to use when they recognize printed or handwritten letters.

Computer models have been constructed that permit machines to read letters or numbers. For example, the machines banks use to "read" your checking-account number employ templates representing each letter of the alphabet; the machine compares incoming symbols with each of these templates. This system is now widely used, but as a model of human behavior its potential is severely limited. For example, it can do nothing with handwritten characters.

A more recent and powerful group of models employs programs that identify

Figure 9.5
Computers can be programmed to read material that has been especially printed for them. Symbols such as arrangements of dots and the customary letters of the alphabet can be interpreted by the machine, when it has been "taught" by programs similar to the simplified example discussed in the text. It is a much more complex task to program a machine to understand handwritten words because of their nonstandardized features.

letters on the basis of their *distinctive features.* These models approximate human performance more closely. The program specifies a series of tests for each letter to be identified as well as the order in which these tests take place. Consider the printed letters—a b c d e f g h i j k l m n o p q r s t u v w x y z. A simplified program might ask the following questions of an incoming character:

Is it a "closed" letter?
Answer: Yes. Then it is a, b, d, e, g, o, p, or q.
Does it have a straight line in it?
Answer: No. Then it is a, e, g, or o.
Does it possess a lower loop?
Answer: Yes. Then it is g.

In practice, the number of feature-analyzing questions necessary to identify every letter would be more than the three shown here and would depend on the actual set of letters or figures to be discriminated.

One of the most successful recognition systems of this general type was developed by W. Doyle. His system worked even with hand-printed letters although the printing had to be very stylized and constrained. Doyle's system achieved its success by first getting acquainted with the style of printing used by each person whose letters it was to recognize. After assigning values to such variables as the degree of slope and the size of the letters—there were seventeen variables in all—the system could recognize about 90 percent of a given person's letters.

Such models may help us to understand, in a very limited way, how people detect features. Some of the limitations of models are explained in the following section.

The Problem of Context

Even if it becomes possible to identify feature analyzers in the human brain, the problem of feature identification will be far from solved. There is far more to the way we understand, say, a printed text than merely the identification of a small set of distinctive features. Existing computer-recognition systems are stymied by irregular or oddly shaped characters. Such things bother human readers not at all, and we even cope with incorrect spellings and omitted letters. How do we manage it?

For one thing, human beings do not read on a letter-by-letter basis. A study by M. A. Tinker shows that the eyes move from place to place on a printed line at

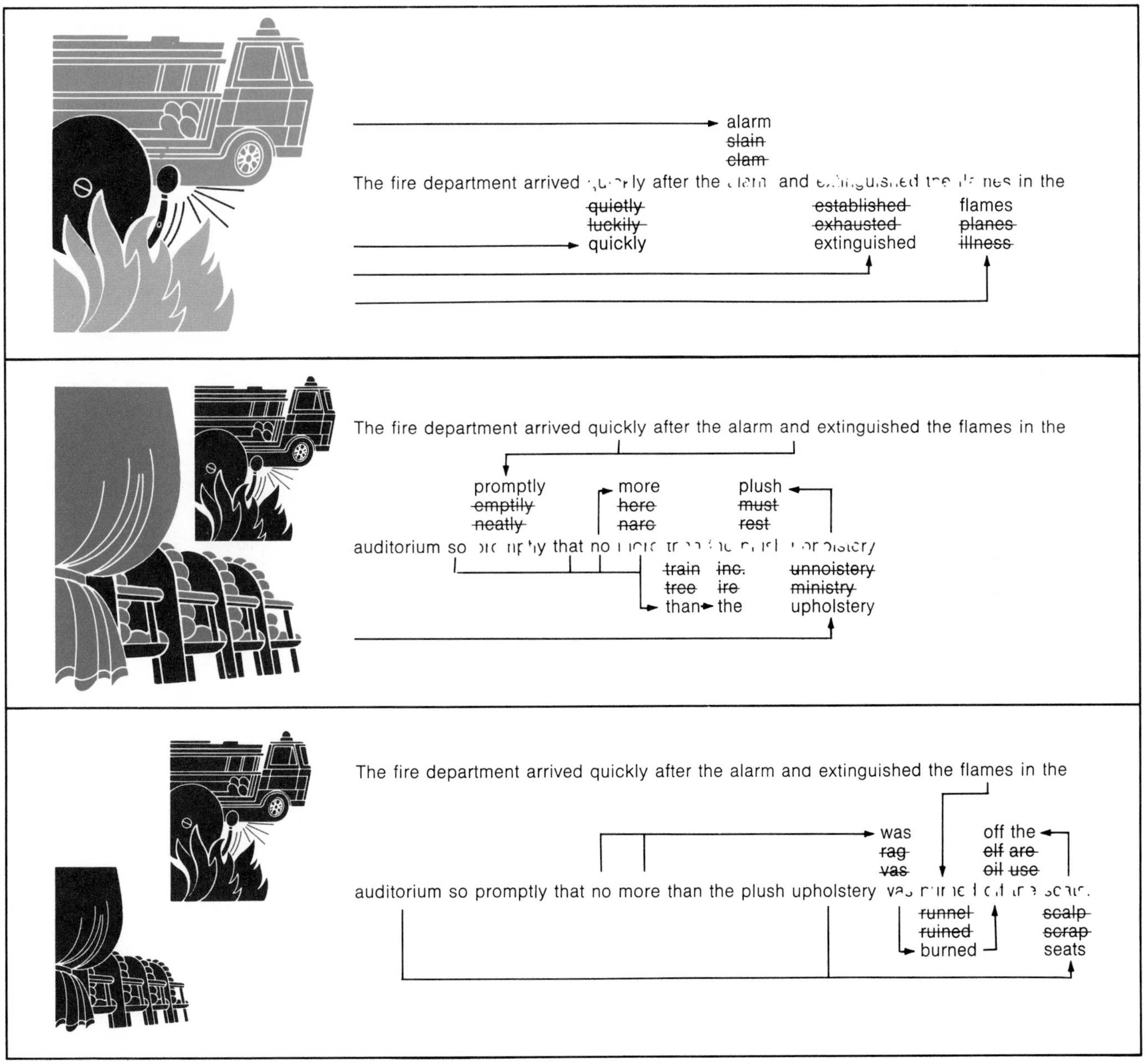

the rate of three or four jumps per second, taking in whole words and even phrases at each fixation. This strongly suggests that recognition is based on features of units at least as large as words.

Probably much more is involved. As you read this text a tremendous number of things help you understand it, from particular expectations about letter combinations and word order all the way to very general expectations about textbooks and about psychology. These expectations operate as a sort of a running crossword puzzle that provides a framework for the words you are reading. In short, the recognition and interpretation of letters is not a simple physical affair but depends intimately on past experience. It is impossible to say at present just how far computer systems will take us in our attempts to identify and weigh the significance of all these factors.

Programming a machine to recognize and understand spoken language—or indeed, any complex pattern—presents problems similar to those of programming it to read. There are machines that appear to speak, or even to sing, with the aid of electronically controlled vocal cords vibrating in response to tape recordings. But

Figure 9.6
These frames illustrate how our past experiences and present expectations influence our perception of ambiguous stimuli. Because segments of the printed letters of key words are missing, any of the alternative words provided could conceivably be correct. We use several sources of information to pick the correct word: the physical features that remain of the broken letters; the letter combinations and word combinations that seem most likely on the basis of our past experience; and the context of the story.

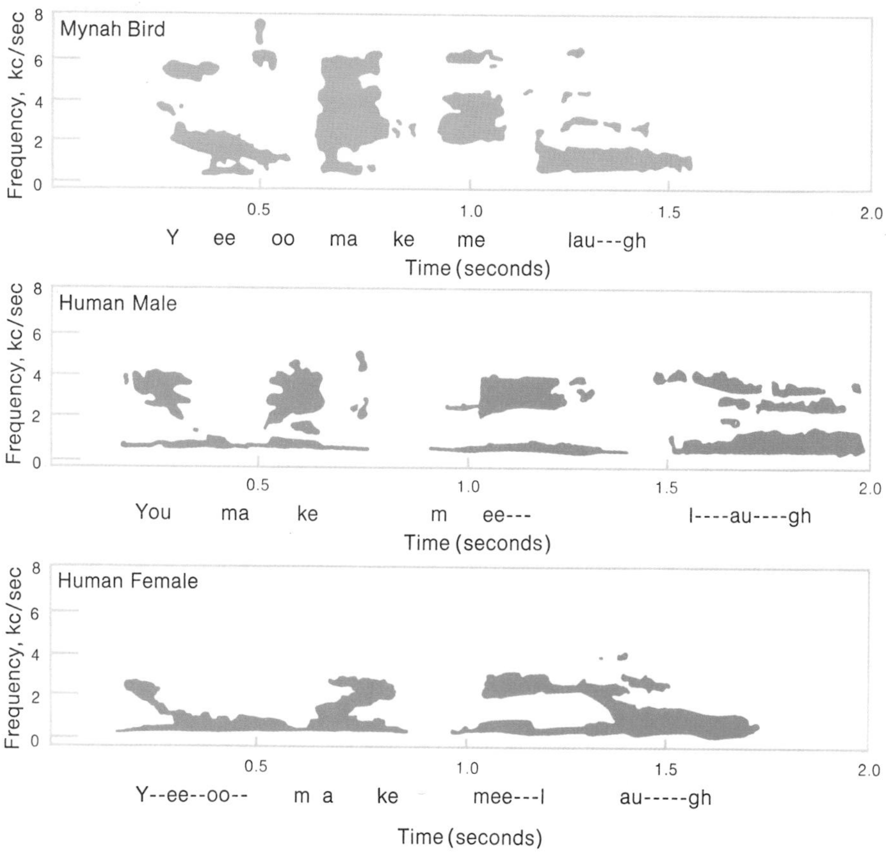

Figure 9.7
Acoustic patterns of the same sentence, "You make me laugh," spoken by a mynah bird (top), a human male (center), and a human female (bottom). The variations in these patterns dramatically illustrate the problems involved in programming a machine to understand spoken language.
(After Thorpe, 1959.)

the computer that listens and understands in the human sense has yet to be developed. The patterns of sound represented in Figure 9.7 illustrate the complexity of the task. The sequence of words is the same in all cases, but the acoustic pattern is very different. It is no easier to program a machine to recognize these equivalents than it is to develop one to recognize equivalent written characters. Once again, the contextual clues and preliminary expectations that play such a large part in human understanding, and are gained through a tremendous amount of experience, are largely unavailable—at least to the present generation of machines.

PROCESSING

After information has entered a system—human or mechanical—a number of processing possibilities arise. First, if the new information is to be supplemented by or added to information encountered previously, then it will be necessary either to *retrieve* or to *update* material already stored in memory. Second, if the information received is to change the system's future behavior, then *learning* must take place. Third, the information may need to be used to *implement some action* on the part of the system, such as solving a problem or making a decision. In the following pages, we will examine some attempts to use computers to investigate and model each of these human functions: memory, learning, and implementation. Other approaches to the same functions will be taken up in Chapters 10 and 11.

Memory

An essential quality of human memory is that memories are *organized* in some way. Exactly what way is not known, but apparently we do *not* have a small, fixed number of ways of retrieving particular memories. We are able to find the same name, symbol, or image by a multitude of pathways. If the organization or the structure of each person's memory is constant (and even that is not known for sure), it is nonetheless a structure that "rotates": it can be entered at any number of places. The place at which it is entered at a particular time is strongly influenced by the person's situation at that time. In other words, the structure rotates on the basis of *situational demands;* this type of organization is discussed more fully, with examples, in Chapter 10.

Consider "mafterling"—is it an English word? The sequence of letters tells you that it could be, but you probably knew immediately that you did not know it—that it was not to be found stored in your memory. How did you know so fast? It sometimes takes quite a long time to find an item you know is in memory; why should it take *less* time to discover the absence of something?

The answer seems to be that the order of the letters (or perhaps the sound of a word) tells you where to look in storage—pointing you, for "mafterling," toward an empty spot. If this explanation is correct, then the structure of memory is based on certain features of inputs. This hypothesis, which does not rule out the existence of other methods of storage, explains why we *recognize* words in a sentence so rapidly and also why it is easier to recognize a sentence you have heard or read before than it is to *recall* the sentence if someone asks you to repeat it. Furthermore, the hypothesis seems to make sense in light of what is known about the neurological organization of the brain. In the language of computers such a system, in which features of the input items determine where the items are stored, is called a *content-addressable storage system.*

Computer Memory Systems Many tasks for which computers are used demand large, flexible, and fast memory or storage capabilities. Since it is wasteful to search blindly through the total memory store every time some item of information is needed, computer designers often try to structure the system so that it fits the requirements of the task at hand. They try to design procedures by which the system can get to the desired information quickly, without plodding mindlessly through the whole store. When the designer of a computer tackles the problem of organizing the machine's memory in ways that are relevant to the situation, his solutions are of potential interest to psychologists because they may be similar to the organization of human memory.

Most digital computers have memory systems based on a series of cells, often called pigeonholes. Like a post-office pigeonhole, each computer pigeonhole can contain only a certain amount of material, and each has a particular address within the memory unit. To retrieve the contents of the pigeonhole, the machine must find its address and examine its contents. In most cases, the address of the pigeonholed items is unknown (indeed, to have a knowledge of addresses would require a separate memory), so the machine has to do a hole-to-hole search, examining the contents of each pigeonhole until it hits the information it needs. Unlike human memory, in which information is usually readily available (because the memory structure "rotates" in response to the demands of the situation), the pure pigeonhole system is static. Also, its organization bears no relation to the meaning of the items that it contains.

Because pigeonhole systems are time consuming and rather inelegant, much effort has been directed toward producing more adaptable and efficient systems. One such system organizes the computer's memory into a *list structure.* The first item on the list indicates the kind of information found on that list, so that the computer can search the list more thoroughly if it seems relevant to the task at hand and can by-pass it if it does not. A list structure allows the computer to reject large amounts of information after examining only one memory item, saving a great deal of time. In theory the process can be extended indefinitely: "lists of lists" can be constructed that give clues to the contents of large groups of addresses.

A list-structure storage system is more like human memory than a pigeonhole

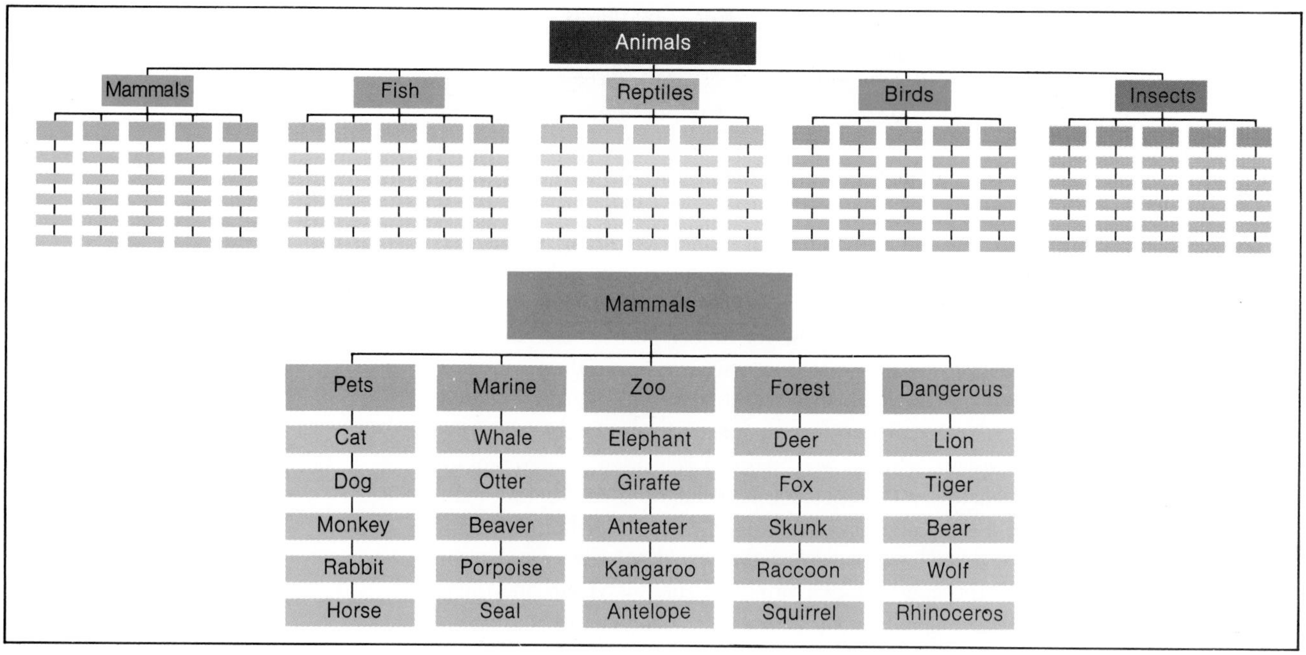

Figure 9.8
An example of a list-structure storage system. This type of organization of stored data allows the computer to scan and retrieve the desired data quite efficiently. It need not examine each of the many elements within the hierarchy if the general area of the data is not relevant.

system, since the lists are based on meaningful relationships, but even the list-structure system cannot be considered as an adequate analogy to the content-addressable storage system of the human; in fact, the differences between the mechanical and human systems are far greater and far more numerous than the similarities. List systems are constructed for specific purposes relevant to particular tasks, and a change in task requirements can render the whole system useless. For human beings, retrieval is not a fixed hierarchical affair, except perhaps under special circumstances; instead it is directly affected by changing situational demands. Thus, it seems that a good computer model of human information-processing abilities will require an organization more like the human content-addressable one. (Many persons who design computer systems for other uses feel that this type of organization will be necessary if computer memory systems are to become more efficient. Some recent developments in laboratories dealing with artificial intelligence seem to promise progress in the direction of more humanlike systems.)

Updating Suppose you know John Doe and his family very well; you also know John Bull and his family. John Doe's sister, you find, has married John Bull's brother and given birth to a son. You are now in position to make statements not only about the new marital and parental relationships but about the relationships between other members of the Doe and Bull families—to state, for example (should you wish to), that John Doe and John Bull have a nephew in common. Similarly, as you get to know a new person your discrete experiences of him or her do not remain separate in your memory. Each is integrated with the ones that have gone before, yielding a composite picture that includes many discrete experiences. The integration often goes on without conscious effort. This would seem to necessitate some mechanism in the human brain that seeks out relevant memories and updates them by adding the new information.

The problem of how the updating mechanism works is closely related to the problem of how memory is structured. With computers, a list system is again more powerful than isolated pigeonholes, assuming that the relation between list names and the new material is known. Some progress has been made with systems that store information on a semantic or word-meaning basis, but the systems work only with *well-structured* information like the family relationships mentioned above. In such cases a fixed number of categories and their relationships can be defined for the computer, and new information can be fitted into the existing structure. There is as yet no computer system that does very well at generating meaningful structures for itself. When a structure can be provided, the computer can operate effectively with it for a variety of purposes. What computers cannot do to any appreciable extent is *create* new systems of relationships to meet new demands. Their processing capacities include *manipulating* relationships but not *generating* them.

Machines That Learn

In a sense, machines that have the capacity to update and change their memory stores display a form of learning. But it is important to distinguish between this kind of learning, in which the content of what is acted upon changes, and another kind of learning, in which the nature of future action itself is altered. For example, consider a computer used to keep track of bank balances. Although the machine continually acquires new information, it never changes the operations that it performs. The *content* that it operates on changes, but the operations do not.

Reinforcement and Shaping Some machines have been constructed that do change the course of their actions on the basis of experience, but their learning is of a primitive type. It is based on simple, direct reinforcement, or weighting. What changes is really only the *sequence* of what is done; the machine does not learn completely new actions. To illustrate, suppose we wish to program a machine to read bank lettering. Its task is to identify each incoming letter as quickly as possible, using the template system described earlier in this chapter. The machine might begin its bankreading career by simply examining the twenty-six templates in alphabetical order, stopping when it gets to the one that matches the letter it is trying to recognize. Suppose, however, that the machine is programmed to keep a count in its memory store of the number of times each letter is encountered—to keep track of the number of As, Bs, and so on found on the checks. After doing that for a while, it can stop examining the templates in alphabetical order and instead examine them in an order ranging from those most frequently found in past encounters to those found least frequently. The machine might also keep a record of the number of times each letter was followed by another, so that after recognizing the first letter of a word it could compare the next letter with the templates for those most frequently found to follow the first, and so on. A machine programmed in this way would probably, over time, show a marked increase in efficiency. It would "learn" something about the frequencies with which individual letters and letter combinations occur, and it would act accordingly.

More dramatic kinds of learning situations have also been simulated. For example, the technique of shaping, discussed in Chapter 3, can be simulated in teaching a computer the moves in chess. The machine is programmed to move the pieces one square at a time on the board and to keep doing so until stopped. Every time the machine selects a piece, it is allowed to move the piece until it reaches a permitted position or moves past the point at which permitted moves stop (in which case the piece is returned to its starting point). For example, on the pawn's first move, the machine will move it one square forward, then another square; when it attempts to move the pawn into the third square (or diagonally into an empty square), it will be stopped because two squares forward is the maximum permitted on a pawn's first move. Through this procedure, the machine's original capacity to move pieces can be shaped to produce all the moves that the rules of chess allow. Of course, developing a machine that plays a good game of chess is more difficult. Attempts have been made to do it, though. The programming task is much more complex than shaping the moves each piece can make. Besides remembering the moves, the machine must keep track of the relative effects of whole sequences of moves—strategies of play—and execute the ones that are most likely to succeed at each point in the game.

Theories of Learning Certain schools of thought in psychology hold that the reinforcement and shaping capabilities of machines can be extended until their learning abilities equal those of man. This belief is based on the theory that the principles of reinforcement and shaping explain all human learning. If that is true, then all that is required is an extension of the computer size to match the 10^{10} or so cells of the human brain and an increase in the computer's equivalent of basic reflexes to accommodate a greater range of shaped behaviors.

Other schools of thought, however, hold that any machine learning represents only one kind of human learning. For example, such theorists as Jean Piaget, J. S. Bruner, and L. Kohlberg argue that learning takes place in different ways, depending on the level of development a person has reached and the kind of task he faces. The chapters in Unit II set these theories out in detail. They propose that learned experiences fit into structures formed through an interplay of physical and mental activities, structures that therefore involve the whole human body—the total organism. Even attempting to simulate sophisticated types of learning would require an identification of such structures and a knowledge of how they change and interrelate.

Machine simulation studies may, eventually, help psychologists evaluate these opposing theories of learning. Right now, however, computer learning systems are in their infancy, and it is very difficult to tell how far they will go. It seems certain that machines will one day exist that can substantially rewrite their own programs and therefore modify their future behavior. Just how helpful such models will be in our attempts to understand and describe human learning remains to be seen.

Implementation

After information has found its way into a memory system, it needs to be applied to the task at hand. The everyday work of most computers is to perform certain operations on designated items of input, repeatedly. A program written to solve an accounting problem will cause the computer to perform a whole series of arithmetical calculations—adding, subtracting, multiplying, dividing—on the data with which the program was supplied. Such programs have little or no interest for psychologists, since they reflect only a task analysis and not important psychological processes.

However, attempts have been made, notably by A. Newell, J. C. Shaw, and H. A. Simon, to investigate human problem-solving behavior. Using modeling techniques, they programmed machines to solve a variety of problems through the use of certain methods. Here, the assumptions underlying the program have a clear psychological significance, for they constitute a general theory of problem-solving behavior.

To understand the scheme of Newell and his colleagues, which they call the General Problem Solver (GPS), it is necessary to be familiar with the concepts of *algorithm* and *heuristics*. An *algorithm* is a problem-solving method that exhaustively specifies the sequence of operations for the successful solution of a problem. For example, an algorithm for opening a safe's combination lock would try every possible number combination in turn and would indicate how to sequence the combinations so as not to get lost during the several million attempts. For many kinds of problems, it is not possible to construct algorithms, and even if one could, like the safe-cracking solution, they would be so tedious and time consuming that one would not really care to try.

A *heuristic* problem-solving method calls for the use of only a few of the possible solutions but usually allows a successful, if not perfect, solution to the problem. Consider a checkers player ready to begin the game. There are about 10^{40} play sequences open to him. Even if he could evaluate three of them every micromillisecond (one millionth of one-thousandth of a second), he would be sitting for 10^{21} centuries before he had considered all his alternatives. An algorithmic chess player would spend even longer, since he faces some 10^{120} possibilities. Yet people play chess and checkers, and some people even play well. Since they cannot possibly be working algorithmically, they must be operating heuristically. The heuristic approach relies on the factor of familiarity. Because a problem is approached as if it were not completely foreign to the individual trying to solve it, he can investigate the more likely solutions before proceeding to look at the more far-fetched alternatives. A heuristic approach to chess playing might go as follows. (It is important to remember that there is always more than one heuristic procedure possible for the solution of any problem.)

Suppose the player, who has experience, assumes that the factors most likely to assure a win are: (1) control of the board; (2) greater number of important pieces than the opponent; (3) mobility of one's own pieces and lack of mobility of the opponent's pieces; and (4) higher "point count" than the opponent. Then his heuristic for choosing the next play might be to look two moves ahead and evaluate whether his position on the four points will be improved. If he weighs the factors and decides that, in total, the move he is contemplating will work an improvement, he can make a decision. Heuristics can be likened to rules of thumb, but the rules are explicit and carefully specified.

Newell and his co-workers attempted to identify such rules of thumb and embody them in a computer program, with some success. One heuristic used by GPS (two others will be discussed in Chapter 11) is called *subgoal analysis:* if the Problem Solver cannot solve a problem directly, it reduces it to a series of smaller problems that it has a better chance of solving. Faced with a chess problem, for example, GPS would first see if the king was safe from attack. If the king is in danger, GPS concentrates on moves that will protect it or remove it from the danger zone. If the king is safe, GPS goes on to its next-most-important subgoal, which is to ensure that other pieces are not in imminent danger. Then it tries to gain control of the center regions of the board so as to be in a good position for attack: it starts to move pawns into the center squares. If all defensive goals continue to be met, GPS works through a series of attack subgoals. Using similar methods, GPS has succeeded in solving problems in logic, algebra, and several other areas as well as in chess. By doing so, it has helped psychologists understand the heuristics that may be used in human problem solving.

Despite its successes, there are limitations to the GPS approach. The problems that GPS deals with are all of a particular type: they are all well structured. The relevant parts of the problem, whether it concerns chess or the relations and elements in a logical expression, are all agreed upon and well known, at least to people who deal with that sort of problem. The tasks of selecting the relevant material and determining what operations should be performed on it are largely done for GPS by the programmer. In most everyday problems, as Chapter 11 makes clear, these tasks are sources of great difficulty.

OUTPUT

Stick a postage stamp or something of similar size on a wall. Then ask someone to stand facing the stamp at arm's length from the wall, and put yourself in a position from which you can see the person in profile. Ask him to reach out and touch the stamp a few times. Do you notice a slight wavering of his arm as he reaches out? It is very doubtful that he will be able to follow a faultless straight line to the target.

Simple movements like reaching out, grasping, and walking are usually so automatic that we fail to notice the tremendous amount of information processing going on. Reaching out, for example, is not done simply by locating an object in space and then throwing out the hand like a stone. It involves a constant interplay between outgoing signals that guide arm movement and feedback that tells what effect the movement is having on the environment.

Skilled Actions

Some psychologists, including K. Craik, who study skilled actions, liken them to an automatic *servo system* in order to emphasize the interaction between each output and the new input that it creates. The new input has two sources: changes that occur in environmental relationships as a result of an action, and feedback from the muscles in the arm and hand. Like the art lover at the Louvre, a person performing a skilled action sorts, integrates, and processes information from many sources. Integration is usually not accomplished by conscious effort, and a great deal of the processing occurs in parts of the nervous system other than the higher centers of the brain. For example, bodily posture and coordination of movement in different parts of the body are controlled largely by the cerebellum, a region of the brain that integrates feedback from a variety of sensory systems. A neural pathway between the cortex and the cerebellum conveys commands from the higher regions of the brain to the cerebellum so that intended or voluntary movements can be initiated and stopped.

Although a movement like touching a stamp pasted to the wall may seem simple, the problems of output are in fact no less difficult than those of input and processing. It is not surprising, therefore, to find that only slow progress is being made in the design and production of computerized artificial limbs and robots. However, machines have been constructed that can move around obstacles, reach out and pick up small objects, and even perform simple construction maneuvers.

Channel Capacity

Any system, be it mechanical or human, can handle only so much information at a given moment. We have already seen that human beings are constantly selecting information from a number of channels. Once a channel has been selected, however, another question arises: is there a fixed limit on the *amount* of information from that channel that a person can handle at one time?

Machines can take in information from punched cards and magnetic tape at a tremendous rate, and they can also process it in prescribed ways with impressive speed. When they are fed information in a form that fits the requirements of their programs, their speed markedly exceeds a human operator's. The question to which we now turn is whether there is any way to evaluate processing capacity—particularly in human beings.

Figure 9.9
George Miller. Miller is a versatile scientist who has done important work in the areas of information processing and psycholinguistics. He recently coedited (with Kenneth B. Clark) a panel report that urged psychologists to find means of applying their knowledge to the solution of urgent social problems.

The Magic Number Seven (Plus or Minus Two) Several years ago, a series of studies created considerable speculation and excitement in some psychological circles. The studies suggested that there might be a relatively simple way of determining channel capacity. In a classic paper G. Miller pointed to the importance of the number seven or, more properly, to the range from five to nine in relation to human information processing.

Before we examine his thesis, it is necessary to introduce the term *bit.* In psychology, a bit is a unit of measurement for information. The number of bits is based on the number of questions that must be asked and answered in a given situation to remove any uncertainty about outcomes or events taking place in that situation—in other words, it is based on the number of questions that must be asked to gain all necessary information about the situation. Consider these examples:

1. A man tosses a coin. You want information about an event that has two equally likely outcomes. You ask him "Was it tails?" When he answers yes, you receive one bit of information (as you would have if he had answered no). He

Figure 9.10
Given the problem of determining under which of the eight shells the pea lies, one can arrive at the correct solution by asking just three yes-no questions—without guessing. The following optimum questioning strategy would yield the three necessary bits: (1) for the arrangement at top left, "Is it under a shell in the left column?" (Or, "Is it under shells #1-4?"); (2) for the arrangement at top right, "Is it under an odd-numbered shell?"; and (3) for the arrangement at lower left, "Is it under shell #5?" The answers to these questions would be, respectively: "no," "yes," and "no." The cumulative information tells you that the pea is under shell #7.

removes all of your uncertainty about the two-sided event by providing one bit of information.

2. The same man takes one card out of a deck. You want to know what suit it belongs to. You ask him, "Is it a red card?" He says no. He has given you one bit of information. You then ask "Is it a club?" He says yes. He has given you a second bit. Choosing between four equally probable alternatives requires two bits of information.

You can perhaps see that three bits of information would be needed to choose among eight equally probable alternatives (see Figure 9.10); four bits for sixteen; and so on.

The estimation of bits becomes more complex when the alternatives are not equally probable, and complications also arise when you examine people's behavior and discover that they do not always use the most efficient questioning strategies. For instance, in Example 2, you might ask "Is it a heart?" in which case a no answer leaves you with three alternatives and the possibility of needing two more questions to arrive at the correct one. The number of bits of information required in a given situation is always based on the *optimum* questioning strategy that could be employed. With four equally probable alternatives, the amount of information said to be required is two bits, regardless of the questioning tactics actually used. (Note that the measure assesses the amount of information, not its actual nature, which could be coin tosses, cards, flashing lights, or even piano playing.)

Miller surveyed the results of several experiments on human information processing and found that the number of items we can transmit seems to be limited under certain circumstances to the magic number seven, plus or minus two. Suppose, for example, that an experimenter presents his subject with two tones and tells him

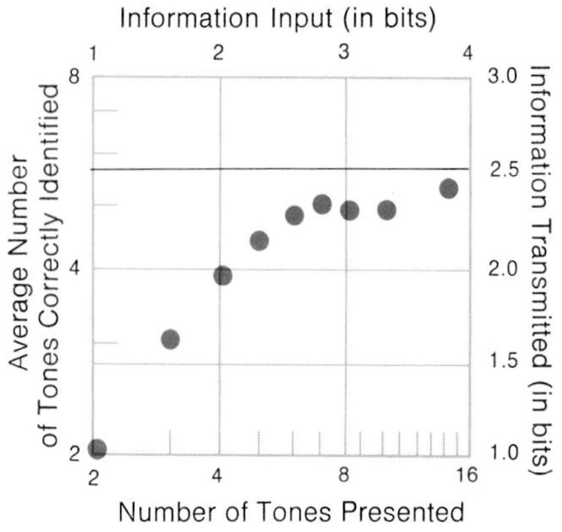

Figure 9.11
A logarithmic plot of Pollack's data, showing the input and output in terms both of pieces of information and bits. The object of the study was to see how much information a subject could handle at one time. As the results show, subjects could match output with input up to about two and a half bits, which represents an input of five or six tones. After that, no matter how many tones were presented (up to sixteen, as shown), subjects could not process more than the two and a half bits.
(After Pollack, 1952.)

to call one "high" and the other "low." Then the experimenter sounds them one at a time, in random order. Each time the subject identifies a tone as "high" or "low," he conveys one bit of information. Now the experimenter presents four tones, which he asks the subject to refer to as "high-high," "low-high," "high-low," and "low-low." Each time the subject correctly identifies one of these, he is conveying two bits of information.

The question is, is there a limit to the number of tones that the subject can discriminate between successfully? In other words, how many bits of information can he extract and convey in a single message? The answer, as shown in an experiment performed by I. Pollack, is that the limit is around two and a half bits. That is the amount of information conveyed by identifying one tone from a group of five or six tones.

The results of Pollack's experiment are shown in Figure 9.11. Miller has obtained similar results for discriminations of such diverse things as the number of degrees of saltiness and the number of degrees of loudness that can be distinguished.

Chunking Miller points out that we can also repeat about seven items, such as words or numbers, that we have just heard. Each item, however, may contain *more* than two to three bits of information. This finding is an important one. Although the number of *items* handled seems to be fixed at about seven, the amount of information each item carries is virtually limitless. A person can structure large amounts of information and handle around seven of the resulting *chunks.* In addition, chunks can themselves often be chunked, adding further to human informational capacity. (The capacity of two and a half bits, then, only applies when chunking cannot take place, as in some experimental situations.)

Perhaps this point can be clarified by returning to the concert pianist mentioned at the beginning of the chapter. The pianist looks at a sheet of music and plays a chord consisting of eight notes. In so doing, he is selecting eight keys from a possible eighty-eight, processing considerably more than two or three bits of information. Because he is an experienced pianist, he has many complex expectations about chords, chord progressions, and melodic sequences of notes. Thus, he is able to chunk information in such a way that one or a few notes become a signal for many others. Indeed, it has been estimated that a concert pianist processes up to twenty-five bits of information per second.

It seems, then, there is no single, fixed limit on the amount of information human beings can process. Although we are severely restricted in the number of discrete, unpredictable signals we can handle, we have an impressive ability to generate and use coding systems that greatly enlarge our information-processing capacity. We may be limited to seven chunks, but the chunks can contain vast amounts of information.

MAN AND MACHINE

So far, it appears that attempts at computer modeling of human information processing do more to underline the complexities of human function than to untangle them. A human being seems to be the most complex information-processing system that exists; the processes he uses are not yet understood on the cellular or on the procedural level. A few complex programs have succeeded in modeling certain facets of human cognition; for example, a program exists that can test the correctness of statements in logic better than the most outstanding mathematicians. The programs in most areas so far, however, fail to approach human abilities.

The use of computers by psychologists has had influence, producing new ideas and theories—and some by-products. For instance, the availability of computers has encouraged many psychologists to undertake hypothesis construction on a scale they otherwise would not have attempted, because the computer permits of fast testing.

Furthermore, a computer model makes very rigorous demands on a theory. Every assumption, every hypothesis, must be made extremely clear, a requirement that opens them to scrutiny and test. Finally, and perhaps most important, working with computers obliges the theorist to consider many problems at the same time. He cannot simply study isolated questions concerning memory, or learning, or language; he must also examine the relationships among those abilities. Programming a computer helps induce the theorist to consider the behaving organism as a whole rather than as a series of discrete parts.

The most fundamental objections to the simulation of man by machine seem to revolve around two arguments. The first points out that a great deal of human behavior and development is determined by the social context in which we all live. A machine cannot enter this milieu and derive from it the same influences as a human being, perhaps because of basic differences between man and machine or perhaps because social influences on human behavior are not very well understood. The second objection stems from research in developmental psychology. Chapters 5 and 6 show how Piaget's theory stresses the importance of *actions* and *symbols* in thinking. Piaget and others argue that abstract thinking, the kind usually simulated on computers, develops only after long experience with physical actions and, later, with representations of physical actions. If abstract thinking grows out of sensorimotor knowledge, can it be simulated successfully on a machine that has no sensorimotor experiences? Or can such experiences somehow be simulated? At this point, no one knows.

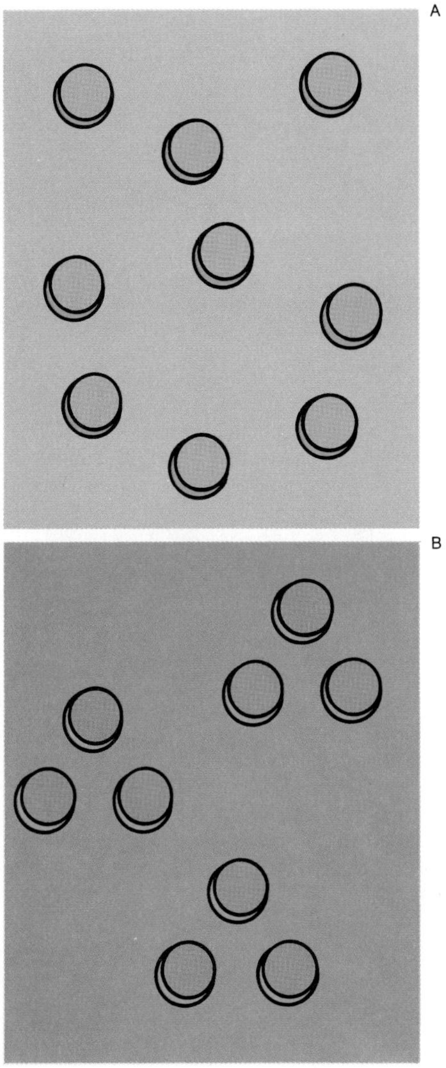

Figure 9.12
The discs in A are randomly arranged, and you will probably have to count them to process the information that gives you the number of discs. In B the discs are chunked, so you can probably process the information at a glance.

SUGGESTED READINGS

FEIGENBAUM, E. A., AND FELDMAN, J. (Eds.). *Computers and Thought.* New York, McGraw-Hill, 1963. An early attempt to bring together emerging theories and methods in the simulation of human functions by machines. Contains sections dealing with problem solving, pattern recognition, and question-answering machines.

MILLER, G. A. *The Psychology of Communication.* New York, Basic Books, 1967. A good collection of papers. Includes Miller's classic paper, "The Magical Number Seven, Plus or Minus Two: Some Limits on Our Capacities for Processing Information."

NEISSER, ULRIC. *Cognitive Psychology.* New York, Appleton-Century-Crofts, 1967. An excellent book that draws together a large amount of material relevant to human information processing. Stresses the active, selective, and constructional nature of human intellectual activities, with particularly good treatments of attention, selection, and pattern recognition.

NORMAN, D. A. *Memory and Attention: An Introduction to Human Information Processing.* New York, Wiley, 1969. The title speaks for itself.

SMITH, FRANK. *Understanding Reading.* New York, Holt, Rinehart & Winston, 1971. Brings together various lines of research drawn from information processing, physiological psychology, and psycholinguistics and applies them in an understandable and readable form to a familiar topic. Chapters 5 through 11 are particularly relevant.

10 Learning and Memory

MEMORY HAS A GOOD PRESS. It is considered a great thing to have a good memory, and a constant annoyance to be prone to forget. To remember trivial things is often considered a sign of great intelligence, and in the 1950s game shows on television offered huge sums of money and vast public respect for people who could remember batting averages of ball players and middle names of presidents. Newspaper and magazine reports of investigations into the machinery of memory always seem to be about ways and means for making memory more extensive and intensive, and yet . . .

In all the fuss, is there no one to raise a voice in praise of forgetting? Is there no one who is willing to point out that if memory has its uses, so has forgettery?

For instance, when I was seventeen, my younger brother was eight, and I was in charge of him when my hard-working parents couldn't be. At one time he was playing assiduously and noisily with a rubber ball, and my mother wanted him to stop. He wouldn't, so my mother looked at me and made a gesture that indicated I was to take care of it. I approached my younger brother with a friendly grin and said, "Hey, Stan, throw me the ball and I'll show you a trick." He threw me the ball and I instantly tossed it over the roof. The ball was gone, and that effectively stopped his playing.

But he looked at me with shock and horror, then hung his head and walked away, and that look went through me like an ice pick. I had betrayed him and taken advantage of his trust, and I cannot adequately describe what a mean dog I felt myself to be at that moment.

For years afterward, Stanley's eight-year-old face would rise before me, hurt and disillusioned, and each time I squirmed. Nothing I could do would wipe it out. It was always there, as clear and fresh as in the beginning, any time I chose to look at it. At this very moment, as I write, I feel the bitter shame.

In adulthood, Stan and I rarely had the chance to talk to each other alone, but one of those rare occasions came a couple of years ago. On impulse, I decided to cleanse myself of the burden. I told Stanley the story and then apologized and asked for forgiveness. But Stanley looked at me, puzzled, and said, "I don't remember a thing about it."

The incident hadn't bothered him for more than an hour or two, but, thanks to my inefficient forgettery, it had made me writhe for over thirty years! I.A.

When you reach the end of this paragraph, turn the page and spend a couple of seconds looking at the chessboard arrangement shown in Figure 10.3. Then come back and try to reproduce that arrangement on the empty board adjacent. (Supply yourself with a pencil.) Off you go.

In all probability, there are quite a number of omissions and mistakes on your board—unless you happen to be a chess master, that is. A Dutch psychologist, A. D. De Groot, has shown that Grand Masters have little trouble reproducing arrangements of chessmen after only a quick glance. Less accomplished players, except for the few who have "photographic memories," rarely do as well. Similarly, if you are an avid football fan and watch a game with a friend who cares less about football than you do, you are likely to remember more of the plays than your friend is.

Figure 10.1
As instructed in the first paragraph of this chapter, complete this board as well as you can with the arrangement shown on page 172.

The examples just cited indicate that interest, motivation, and knowledge all influence one's ability to remember, and recent approaches to the study of human memory try to deal with these admittedly complex phenomena. The earliest approaches to the study of memory, however, tried to avoid the "contaminating" effects of such variables; a great number of experiments have used nonsense material—words or syllables invented purposely to have no interfering associations to previously learned material—in the attempt to discover the basic characteristics of pure memory and the fundamental rules governing its operation. Because the modern studies not only are related more obviously to everyday experiences but also make the rationale for the methodology of traditional studies easier to understand—this chapter will turn history around and study the modern approaches first.

Modern theories of how we remember revolve around four concepts. The first and second are *sensory information storage* and *short-term memory,* both of which belong to the acquisition phase of memory. The third is *long-term memory,* which refers to the storage of information over long periods of time—what people usually mean when they speak of memory. The fourth is *retrieval,* which, as its name suggests, concerns the process of retrieving material from memory.

Figure 10.2
If this array of unrelated items were exposed to you (by means of a tachistoscope) for 50 milliseconds, you would probably be able to immediately "read" some of the items back—you would have an icon (a kind of photograph) of them for perhaps 250 milliseconds. During this brief period, the information in the icon is available to short-term memory. It will not pass into long-term memory, however, unless it is rehearsed.

SENSORY INFORMATION STORAGE

When you watch a movie, you see pictures only about half the time. This is not because of fraud on the part of the promoters but because between each frame of the moving film, which lasts for about one-fiftieth of a second, the shutter of the camera is closed for another fiftieth of a second. Yet we do not see a movie as a high-speed flutter (unless it is particularly ancient and the gaps are beyond a certain time limit). At the speed of the modern movie we are not aware of the blanks, which are filled in by a rather special memory system that operates in the initial stages of information acquisition.

Suppose we show a person a picture, such as the one in Figure 10.2, for 50 milliseconds and ask him to remember as much as he can of what he saw. He will be able to report about four items. Now suppose that, instead of asking him what he saw, we adopt a procedure used by G. Sperling. First, we have him listen to three tones—a high one, a medium one, and a low one. Then we tell him that, after he has seen the array of numbers for a fraction of a second, we will sound one of the tones. He is told to try to recite the numbers in the top line if he hears the high tone, those in the middle line if he hears the medium tone, and those in the bottom line if he hears the low tone. When we do the experiment, the person will probably be able to report all four items on the required line if the tone is sounded within about a quarter of a second of the end of the exposure.

Think about that. Because one cannot possibly remember all twelve items—one is limited to seven plus or minus two in normal circumstances—the finding means that, for a very short period of time, the person can actually *read* the items on any line. He must have some sort of short-lived photograph, or *icon,* of what he saw, a photograph that fades and disappears after about 250 milliseconds. The limit on retrieval from this photograph is time, not the amount of information initially gained from the exposure. By the time four items have been read off—any four—the image has faded.

Figure 10.3
Study this arrangement for five seconds, and try to remember it. Now turn back to page 171 and see how well you can reproduce it on the empty chessboard. The ability to see pieces in relation to others—rather than as just so many isolated events—should help you remember, but how well you do will undoubtedly depend on how much experience you have had with the game of chess.

Sensory information storage, then, operates for a brief interval, and it may serve as the initial stage of information acquisition if the information is *encoded* from the icon and passed into short-term memory. In the experiment just discussed, visual material was encoded verbally. It may well be, however, that not all memories are stored in verbal form, so that data from the icon need not always be actively encoded; one theory, concerning memory storage in pictorial as well as in verbal form, is discussed later in this chapter. It must be emphasized that although the material acquired through sensory information storage will, if passed into short-term memory, be remembered far longer than if it remained an icon, the material will not be passed into long-term memory unless, in the short-term memory phase, it is rehearsed.

Short-term memory, then, is a part of the memory system midway between the sensory store and long-term memory.

SHORT-TERM MEMORY

Proceeding with the experiment just described, suppose that we let our subject rest for half an hour. If we then ask him what his last answer was, the odds are that he will have forgotten it. Unless he was particularly impressed by that answer and *rehearsed* it during the rest period, there is little likelihood that it would have passed into long-term memory. Similarly, when you look up a phone number, you can probably remember the seven digits long enough to dial by rehearsing them—constantly repeating them to yourself—but if you are distracted or make a mistake in dialing, the odds are that you will have to look up the number again.

The limits of short-term memory are very marked and remarkably constant from person to person. Although the capacity of short-term memory increases with age over the first years of life (indeed, it is often used on tests to measure intelligence), it seldom encompasses more than seven items. The seven-item limit on short-term memory may remind you of the limits on a variety of other information-processing abilities; as you saw in Chapter 9, there is something very pervasive about the number seven.

Recently, psychologists have shown increased interest in short-term memory. One of the first experiments in this area was performed by L. R. Peterson and M. J. Peterson at Indiana University in 1959. Subjects were asked to learn a group of three consonants, a trigram such as CPQ, and then immediately told to start counting backward by threes from a randomly selected point—say, 500, 497, 494, 491, and so on. They were not allowed to spend much time thinking about the trigram before beginning the irrelevant counting task. After the subjects had been counting for a while, the experimenter stopped them and asked if they could remember the trigram. In most cases, their memory of it had disappeared after about eighteen seconds of counting (see Figure 10.4).

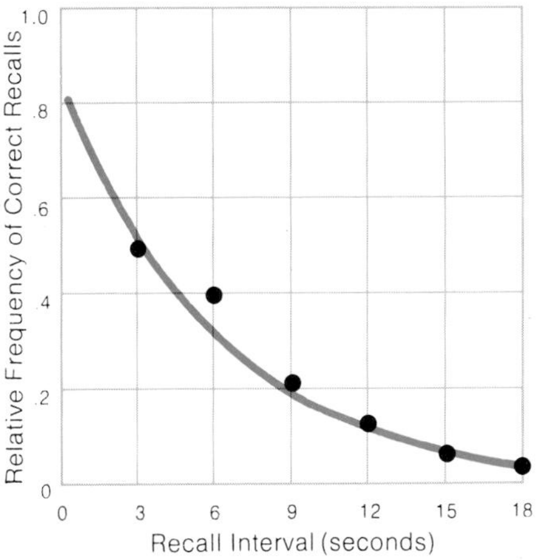

Figure 10.4
Results of an experiment in which subjects first learned a group of three consonants (a CCC trigram), such as CPQ, and then immediately began to count backwards by threes. The goal of the experiment was to test how long materials will remain in short-term memory if they are not rehearsed. Most subjects could not recall the consonants after eighteen seconds.
(After Peterson, and Peterson, 1959.)

This finding does not mean that items in short-term memory invariably disappear after eighteen seconds. The subjects in the experiment were performing a task (counting backward) that may have actively interfered with the process of maintaining the short-term memory. Unfortunately, it is not possible to measure the time it takes for short-term memory to decay without using some sort of interfering task, for people asked to do nothing during the time between presentation of the letters and the test would probably spend that time rehearsing the items. Rehearsal makes it impossible to determine exactly how memory decay would take place under ordinary conditions. Moreover, instructions not to rehearse seem to be unavailing. (Just try telling yourself not to think about something!)

Rehearsal is thought to be such an important part of the memory process that many psychologists believe it is crucial to the transition of material from short-term memory into more permanent, long-term storage.

LONG-TERM MEMORY

We know very little about the physical properties of human long-term memory. We do not know whether the storage of information comes about through the growth of connections at the synapses of neurons, as is sometimes suggested, or whether it is accompanied by chemical or molecular changes somewhere in the nervous system, as has also been proposed. We do not even know whether a particular memory is stored at a specific point in the brain, stored many times at different points, or scattered around in some unique pattern.

The Organization of Memory

In view of this lack of knowledge, it is not surprising to find that there is no generally accepted, detailed model of the organization of human memory. A popular, though erroneous, view is that remembered material is held in some sort of "storage tank." According to this view, memory is a fixed structure of some kind, perhaps a neural tape recording or videotape that is played back as we recall something. True, it may be somewhat difficult to turn the topic on, and the tape may get a bit noisy or faded with age, but still, according to this theory, there is a fixed, more or less static store.

Both everyday experience and a variety of experimental findings, by F. C. Bartlett and others, repudiate this view of memory. Remembering seems to be more

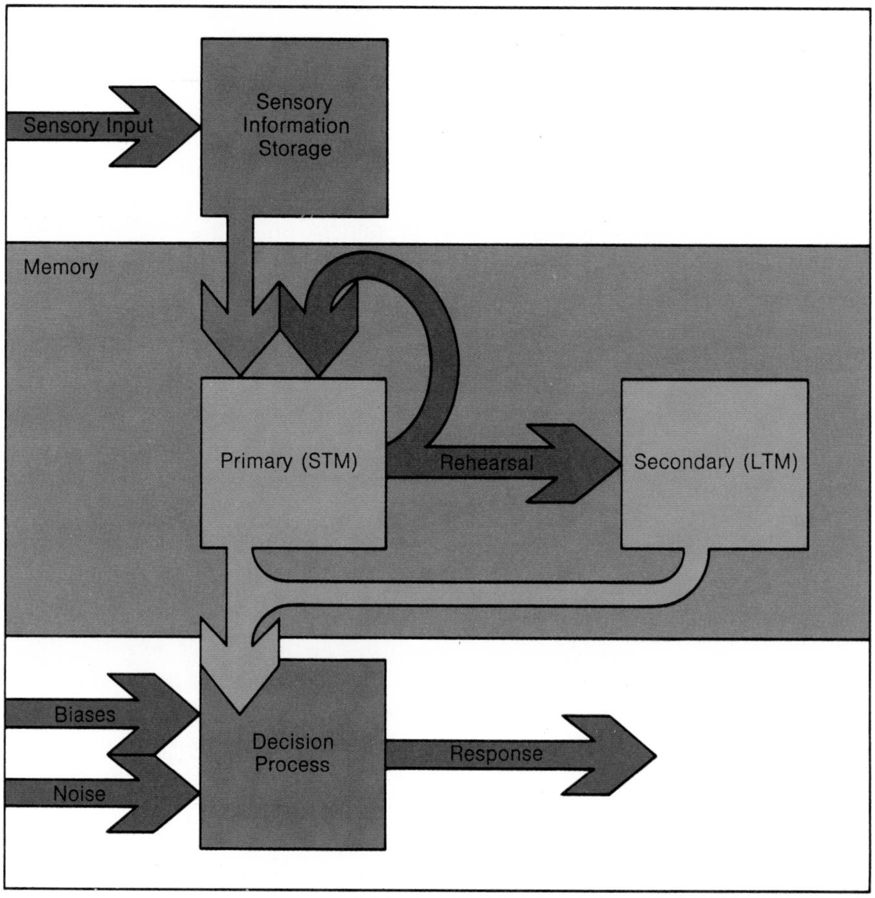

Figure 10.5
This chart displays the flow of information in human memory; the data on which the chart is based were obtained in a recognition-memory experiment with controlled rehearsal. Shown are the interactions of the processes of acquisition, memory, and decision. First, during acquisition, the stimulus is perceived, encoded, and stored. Then stimulus items are processed through primary memory (short-term memory), where forgetting occurs rapidly, and through secondary memory (long-term memory), where they can be retained for long periods of time. Note that rehearsal by the subject has the dual function of helping to prolong retention of material in short-term memory and to transfer items into long-term memory. Finally, in the decision processes, a subject's biases, strategies, and noise from environmental variations all combine with memory output to determine his response.

a process of *reconstructing* past events, an active process, rather than something that happens automatically in some predetermined way when the right mental button is pushed.

Remember any outstanding sequence of events in your life and try to take note of how much filling in of detail you have to do. A great deal of your remembering is likely to be a *re-creation* rather than a *recovery* of past events. You may recall important or novel features of the experience and synthesize them into a reenactment. You will probably feel more like a detective or a novelist than like a passive television viewer. The reconstructive, re-creative aspects of remembering are acknowledged in courts of law, where judges and lawyers—and defendants—are only too familiar with the errors witnesses introduce into testimony through the inaccurate fabrication of past events. People often unknowingly distort reality by filling in their memory of past events on the basis of what should have happened or must have happened; very few of us seem able merely to reactivate a detailed record of what actually did happen.

As was pointed out in Chapter 9, an important shortcoming of present-day computer memory systems as models of human memory is that they have a relatively fixed and static structure. If it is proper to speak of human memory as having a structure at all, that structure is evidently an extremely flexible and adaptive one. There seem to be any number of ways we can retrieve a given item of information from our memory, not a small, fixed number of retrieval paths such as computers have. Faced with an object like a salt shaker, a person does not, as far as we can tell, search through a particular list to retrieve its name—for example, through "street," "house," "dining room," "table," and "crockery" to "(please pass the) salt." Human memory is much more flexibly organized than that. When we use our memory on an everyday basis, we are in sensory touch with the situation—our behavior is *context* specific. Our kinesthetic system, our systems of smell, hearing, and sight are constantly conveying information to our nervous systems, ensuring that retrieval of an item from memory will take into account the immediate situation. One can construct a metaphor by thinking of the memory structure as "rotating" in response to perceived cues of the situation. At the dinner table, for example, the smell of the food, the feel of the silverware in your hand and of your body in a certain kind of chair placed in a certain relation to the table, the sound of crockery chinking, the sight of the food and the utensils—all these cues serve to rotate your memory structure to a path that facilitates the recall of "salt."

One problem with laboratory studies of memory may be the lack of such cues—the lack of context—when subjects are asked to remember.

An outstanding quality of human memory (and one that most computer memory systems lack) is revealed by things that we do *not* have in memory. Take the word "mafterling," for example, which was used in Chapter 9 to demonstrate how easy it is to decide that we do not know a word—too easy for us to have searched exhaustively through our whole store of words in an attempt to find it. It was suggested that the properties of the word itself, perhaps its sound characteristics or its look, may dictate its position in the long-term memory store. If that is true, then human long-term memory may be organized as a *content-addressable system.*

The Form Memories Take

Maybe you once played an outstanding game of football, or perhaps one winter you broke you leg skiing. You may have seen a painting or a mountain lake that particularly impressed you, or a member of the opposite sex who produced even more dramatic results. How much of memories like these do you remember in the form of words? As you try to reconstruct such an experience, you will probably encode much of it into verbal form, but aren't there some residual items with characteristics that elude verbal expression?

The heavy emphasis that psychologists have tended to place on studies of verbal material has somewhat biased our theories of memory and its structure. Recent experiments, as well as the kind of everyday experiences mentioned above, suggest that memories are not necessarily stored in verbal form. Work done by R. Shepard and by R. N. Haber, for instance, provides striking evidence for the existence of two forms of long-term storage, one for pictorial or graphic material and the other for verbal information.

In one experiment, Haber and L. G. Standing showed subjects 2,560 photographs of various scenes, letting them look at each photograph for ten seconds. Later, the subjects were able to recognize between 85 and 95 percent of the pictures they had seen—a higher percentage than can be achieved with verbal material. That finding led Haber to suggest that there are at least two memory-storage systems: a virtually limitless pictorial memory and an apparently more restricted one for verbal material.

You may demonstrate pictorial as opposed to verbal encoding for yourself in the following way. Recall a visual scene. Did you need to describe it to yourself in order to remember it? You may need to use words to communicate what you remember, but that process seems to be a sort of reading off from a more basically pictorial memory.

Although psychologists are as yet unable to present a complete, coherent theory of the organization and structure of human memory, they are able to identify some of the system's major features, which have just been set out. The outstanding characteristic of long-term memory, and the one that makes the study of memory so intriguing (and so complex), is the ability of human beings to generate any number of organizational systems that enable them to remember. Much remembered material is organized spontaneously, without conscious effort. Sometimes, however, an organization is intentionally imposed—as it is, for example, in the use of the memory aids called mnemonic devices.

Mnemonics

Mnemonics used to be a dirty word in psychology. Mnemonic devices were considered tricks, the gimmicks of night-club entertainers, and therefore not worthy of study. Recently, however, the study of mnemonics has become more popular, mainly because, whatever they are, they really are effective.

One of the simplest mnemonic schemes organizes the material to be learned into *rhymes:* "I before E except after C." "Thirty days hath September, April, June, and November . . ." These systems take advantage of the fact that we have no difficulty remembering the individual items (the letters or the months); the problem is remembering something about them (order, number of days). The rhyme helps because it imposes an external constraint on memory: if we remember incorrectly, the rhyme does not work. These rhyming schemes also illustrate a general characteristic of mnemonic systems—that one must recall everything to get back anything. Can you recall how many days hath March without going through the rhyme?

The oldest mnemonic scheme appears to be the *method of loci,* or places, credited to the Greek poet Simonides. According to Cicero, Simonides was invited to a banquet by a nobleman named Scopas. In the middle of the banquet, Simonides was told that two unknown visitors wanted to see him outside. He left the banquet hall but found no one. In his absence the building collapsed, crushing everyone within beyond recognition. Simonides was able to identify each body by picturing the banquet in his mind and remembering where the people had been sitting.

Thus the mnemonic system of loci: Picture the things you want to remember, then mentally walk through a well-known building (such as your house) and place the things to be remembered in corners, on chairs, and so on. To recall the objects, mentally walk through the house again, looking in the corners and on the chairs. This system was popular with ancient orators, who, by tradition, spoke eloquently for hours without notes. In fact, the system was so popular that specific buildings were designed solely for the purpose of placing mental objects in the corners and against the pillars.

What kind of memory system do human beings have that can profit from such peculiar tricks? Suppose I tell you to remember a rhinoceros by putting it (mentally, of course) between the sheets of your bed. Please do that for a moment. Will you

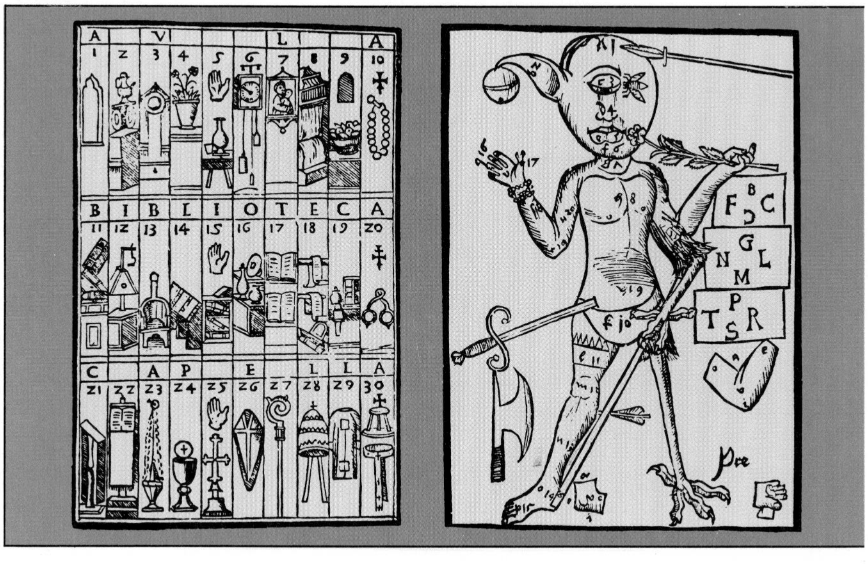

Figure 10.6
Two examples of medieval mnemonic devices. Both illustrate the method of loci. The one at the left shows places in various buildings in an abbey that can serve as loci for remembering things (usually prayers and other religious writings). The middle row, for example, shows the library—a certain chair, the shelves, and so on. One imagines the items one wants to remember placed on or against these things, and the mnemonic works. Note that in every fifth square there is a hand and in every tenth square, a cross. These serve to clump the material to be remembered into manageable segments. On the device at the right, the loci are parts of the body.

remember it? How can you help it? You are now stuck with a rather clumsy bed partner. Statements like "Of course, I remember it—it is unique, original, special" do not explain how the method works; they simply emphasize its beauty. Put peculiar objects in unusual locations and you will remember them.

Another popular mnemonic scheme is the *key-word system,* or "peg" system, illustrated by the adjacent list. To use the scheme, the first thing you must do is memorize that list. Note that it is easy to learn because the words associated with the numbers are concrete, easily visualizable nouns that rhyme with the numbers. Now suppose you wish to learn the number 4391. Say "4-3-9-1, door-tree-line-bun. I see a little door in a big tree and when I open the door there is a line leading to a bun." Silly? Perhaps, but it works.

Remember:
One is a bun.
Two is a shoe.
Three is a tree.
Four is a door.
Five is a hive.
Six is sticks.
Seven is heaven.
Eight is a gate.
Nine is a line.
Ten is a hen.

One final system, which is used in most courses on memory improvement, should be noted. Numbers can be extremely difficult to remember because they do not have the richness of meaning that words and pictures do. That is, they are difficult to organize. The *number-consonant system,* first used in its modern form in the early 1600s, solves this problem by providing a way to translate numbers into letters of the alphabet, as shown in Figure 10.8. (Note that you must learn the *sounds* of the consonants, not the letters themselves.)

Given some arbitrary number to learn, such as the telephone number 447-8132, you begin by replacing each number with the corresponding consonant, getting "rrngftmn." With some thought, it is possible to redo these letters into "r-r-ng f-t m-n," which can stand for "roaring fat man," which turns out to be very easy to learn. Simple? No, not really, but it does work. With practice, you can learn to construct these images very rapidly—rapidly enough to amaze your friends with your astounding memory. (Now, without looking back, what was the phrase? The telephone number? The four-digit number? The bed partner?)

There are many other mnemonic systems, but all of them use the basic principles illustrated in the preceding examples. Mnemonic schemes make several important points about long-term memory. First, they indicate the importance of organization, since they work primarily by imposing a structure on the material being memorized. Second, they suggest that it is a serious mistake to regard memory as some sort of magical phenomenon. The ability to use mnemonic techniques does not come easily. Learning the organizational rules takes practice—sometimes years of it—and applying the rules to items one wishes to memorize requires concentrated effort. Finally, they show how closely long-term memory is tied to the other two phases of memory, acquisition and retrieval. If one takes the time and trouble to organize material

Figure 10.8
(Below, left) one way to deal with the problem of remembering numbers is to change them into consonant sounds. With the number-consonant system shown here, once the numbers are converted to consonants, you can fill in the vowels to produce a series of words, which are much easier to remember than a series of numbers. For example, the numbers 14632 become trshmn, which you can convert to trashman.

The Number-Consonant Alphabet

Number	Letters and Diphthongs	Sounds	Rule for Remembering
0	s, c, a	*ess, zzz*	"Zero" starts with "z."
1	t, d, th	*t*	The vertical bar of "t" looks like a one.
2	n	*en*	A written "n" has two strokes.
3	m	*em*	A written "m" has three strokes.
4	r	*r*	The number 4 ends in "r."
5	l	*el*	"L" is 50 in Roman numerals.
6	sh, j, ch, g	*sh, j,* or soft *g*	No rule; just remember it.
7	k, q, g, ng	hard *k* or *g*	A printed "7" looks somewhat like a printed "k."
8	f	*ef*	A written "f" looks like an "8."
9	b, p	*b, p*	The letters "b" and "p" are turned-around 9s.

Figure 10.9
The telephone dial can be used as a mnemonic. If you have trouble remembering a seven-digit phone number, you can use the letters accompanying each number on the dial to make a word. Some agencies and commercial establishments try to get a phone number that will make a word identifying them. The example here, however, is a purely mythical one.

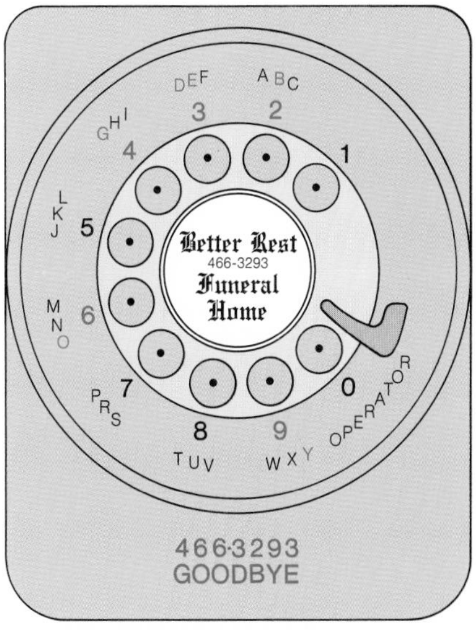

during the acquisition phase, thereby getting it from short-term memory into long-term memory, one is rewarded by the ease of getting it back again.

RETRIEVAL

Retrieving stored information is in some ways the key property of memory, although successful retrieval obviously depends on successful acquisition and storage. Two basic methods of retrieving information can be identified: recognition and recall.

Recognition and Recall

In *recognition,* we are presented with something and asked if we have seen or heard it before. In *recall,* we are given certain cues and asked to generate something that corresponds to them. For example, if you pass someone you knew in elementary school on the street, you may recognize his face but be unable to recall his name.

Recognition is easier than recall. In recognition, you need only decide whether the object, experience, sound, or word before you is the one you are seeking. For example, you used recognition to decide whether you knew the word "mafterling." People usually do very well at recognition, and they tend to know whether their recognitions are accurate. They can say not only that they do or do not recognize something but state how sure they are that they are right.

Recognition errors take two forms. If you fail to recognize an item that is actually in storage, the error is called a *miss.* If you claim to recognize an item that you have never seen before (or at least had not seen when you said you had), the error is called a *false recognition,* or false alarm.

The second major type of retrieval, recall, is often quite difficult. In this method you must recover information on the basis of cues that are sometimes quite sparse: what was that word we asked if you recognized? As with recognition, people can usually tell you how confident they are that their recollection is accurate; in fact, when recall occurs, it tends to be accurate. The most common error is failure to retrieve anything, a miss—as when people stumble in speaking, trying to find the word they want, or fail to remember a name they thought they knew. *False recalls* (also called intrusions) are rare. When they do occur, it is usually possible to explain them on the basis of strong, familiar associations. For example, parents have been known to call one of their children by another's name; especially in large families, it is not hard to see why.

Confabulation

Motivation affects recall, as it does most human activities. A person offered a thousand dollars to remember the name of his first-grade teacher is more likely to come up with it than is the person who is offered a dime. But under conditions of high motivation, we often commit a memory error called *confabulation:* if unable to retrieve a certain item from memory, we may manufacture something else that seems appropriate. For some time, psychologists were impressed by the apparent ability of people in deep states of hypnosis to give detailed reports of events that occurred during childhood. The hypnotist would tell the person being hypnotized, "Go back, back, back to when you were very, very young" and then ask the subject to describe, for instance, his sixth birthday. Typically, the subject, if in a deep trance, would give a lengthy and quite impressive account of a birthday party complete with cake, candles, presents, and guests. He would seem absolutely convinced that his report was accurate, but objective evidence usually contradicted him. Almost always it could be shown that the person had confabulated—that he had combined several birthday parties and invented missing details; even under further questioning, the person could not tell the true parts of his story from the imaginary parts.

Hypnosis induces a state of high motivation in most people, as well as making them much more suggestible than usual. The hypnotized person tries to please the

Figure 10.10
On the left, an illustration of recognition: the man need only see the bear for him to recognize it and call up the word "bear." On the right, recall: if the man's friend gives him the cues shown—large, strong, animal, brown, sharp teeth—the man can mistakenly generate the answer "lion."

hypnotist and responds to even very subtle vocal and facial cues suggesting what the hypnotist wants. If the hypnotist suggests that the subject ought to be able to remember something, the subject eagerly complies, even if he must resort to confabulation to fulfill the request. Newspaper and magazine accounts of "memory magic" under hypnosis should therefore be viewed with skepticism.

Confabulation is sometimes a symptom of physical or mental disability. People who suffer from Korsakoff's syndrome, a condition associated with the type of vitamin deficiency commonly found in alcoholics, lose much of their recent memory. If you ask a person with Korsakoff's syndrome to describe what happened to him yesterday, he invents a series of fictitious events that often have little or no plausibility. Loss of recent memory is also a symptom of general paresis, a condition associated with syphilitic damage to the central nervous system, and of advanced senility. In all these cases, memories of events that occurred many years ago remain relatively intact.

Now You Say It, Now You Don't

What do you do when a specific memory is retrieved in unreliable, partial, and ambiguous form—or perhaps not quite retrieved at all? Consider what happens when you try to recall a name you are sure you know. If you are merely talking with a friend, you need not be certain you are right before taking a guess. The two of you together can stumble toward the correct name: "It's Fishmonger . . . No, Fishman. . . ." False recalls in this situation incur no penalties. But if you are face to face with the mysterious Mr. X, you probably will not guess. The social cost of a false recall—that is, of addressing Mr. Troutman as Mr. Fishmonger—may be high, whereas the cost of avoiding the name entirely is nominal. (Actually, and in this case, happily, you are not very likely to think that Mr. Troutman's name is Mr. Fishmonger. False recalls, research by R. W. Brown and D. McNeill has shown, tend to resemble the target word in sound rather than meaning.)

A decision mechanism clearly plays an important role in retrieval (as it does in forgetting, which will be discussed later in the chapter). The decision to accept or reject a bit of retrieved information is based on some rather complex assessments concerning not only the accuracy of the recall but the relative rewards and costs of correct recalls and of false recalls.

The assessments must be based, somehow, on the way memories are organized, although there is no cohesive theory yet to tie the entire process together. The view of memory as constructional hypothesizes the existence of landmarks, or cues, on which the constructions are based, but so far the nature of those cues and landmarks remains unclear. Haber's work suggests that some of the cues are pictorial; the "mafterling" example (and other studies) suggests that some cues are based on word sounds. Some studies seem to show that people who have a word "on the tip of the tongue" use the sound of the word to arrive at its recall; others indicate that the shape of the word is the important cue. Most people are familiar with the phenomenon of a particular odor or texture cuing the release of a memory.

It seems that several cues can lead to the retrieval, or reconstruction, of a memory, and when the cues are plentiful, reconstruction is both easy and accurate. However, when some cues—perhaps the salient one—cannot be retrieved, we either cannot remember at all, or we are not certain that what we remember is correct. Retrieval, then, is not an all-or-nothing affair. It is affected by a variety of factors, which can render it more or less effective—under circumstances that remain to be explored.

TRADITIONAL STUDIES OF MEMORY

The theories and findings discussed up to this point reflect modern thinking on the operation of memory. The recent studies emphasize the stages that material must go through to reach and be stored in long-term memory, and they try to account for the almost overwhelming variety of factors that influence the processes of remembering and forgetting. The research also explores individual differences.

In contrast, the traditional studies attempted to discover some basic processes of memory that were universal—that is, that underlay individual differences. By using nonsense material, especially invented for its neutral qualities, those studies hoped to rule out the influence of what were then considered to be extraneous factors, such as prior knowledge. In an attempt to be objective and scientific, they tried to study pure memory, uncontaminated by the personal idiosyncrasies of individual memorizers. They asked their subjects to memorize nonsense material.

Experimental studies of these questions are usually based on *rote learning*. Rote learning is what people customarily think of as memorizing—repeating something until it sticks. In everyday life, many things are learned partly by rote. Even when people learn by rote, however, they seldom do so only by rote. Images, mnemonics, and other elements of organization are unconsciously applied in almost all situations.

Figure 10.11
Hermann Ebbinghaus was a brilliant scholar who pioneered investigations in many areas of psychology. He is best known for his research on human memory and association; using himself as his own subject, he adopted methods of psychophysics to study these higher mental processes. His method has been used by subsequent investigators, and his findings have largely been confirmed. Ebbinghaus also developed theories and experiments in color vision and intelligence testing; in addition, he published an extremely influential psychology text. Thus, although he is remembered best for his work in memory and association, he actively contributed to various areas of psychology.

Ebbinghaus' Nonsense Syllables

Hermann Ebbinghaus published pioneering studies of memory—extensive and patient experiments performed upon himself—in 1885. Ebbinghaus sought precise, numerical estimations of memory performance, and to get them he invented two useful experimental devices: the *nonsense syllable* and a measure of memory performance called *savings*.

Ebbinghaus' nonsense syllables were meaningless, like QUK, KIF, and ZAL: Consonant-Vowel-Consonant combinations that are pronounceable but, when properly selected, mean little or nothing to the person asked to memorize them. Such combinations are called *CVC trigrams*.

Ebbinghaus' second major innovation in experimental technique, savings scores, was a way of measuring memory retention. It requires the experimenter to measure the difference between the number of trials a subject needs to memorize material for the first time and the number of trials he needs in order to relearn the same material after a lapse of time. For example, if he wished to know how much would be remembered after a lapse of thirty-one days, Ebbinghaus methodically memorized a list of nonsense syllables, recording the number of times he had to go over the list to do it. Then he waited thirty-one days, presumably without thinking about the items on the list. At the end of the waiting period, during which he forgot most

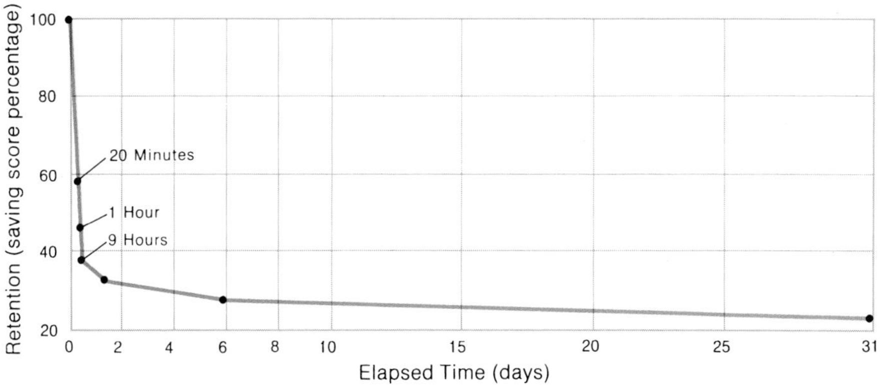

Figure 10.12
These data are from one of Ebbinghaus' savings studies. In this experiment he first learned the material (nonsense syllables), then tested himself on how much of it he had remembered after twenty minutes, an hour, and so on, for thirty-one days. The curve (called a *retention curve*) shows that the amount he could recall dropped sharply during the first two days, then dropped gradually until, thirty-one days after he had learned the list, he could recall a little over twenty percent of it.
(After Ebbinghaus, 1885.)

of the syllables, Ebbinghaus relearned them, counting the number of trials he needed to reach the same level of performance as the first time. The difference was the number of trials of memorizing he saved. Some typical results of an experiment in which memory is measured by savings are shown in Figure 10.12.

Savings scores are a particularly good way to assess how much people remember even when the amount is so small that they can neither recall any of the items nor recognize them. If relearning the items takes less time than memorizing them the first time did, then the subject has remembered something, even though all the items looked unfamiliar to him when he sat down to relearn them.

Although the method of savings has been an important tool for the psychological study of learning and memory, recent experimental work, such as studies by C. E. Osgood and J. A. McGeoch, has pointed out a number of difficulties with nonsense syllables. There turns out to be no such thing as a true nonsense item. People manage to make some sense out of any combination of letters. Nonsense syllables have therefore been grouped into classes according to their *association value.* Syllables like LUV and MUN have a higher association value than such syllables as XOP and QAV; these CVC syllables, in turn, are easier to learn than three-consonant syllables (CCCS) like CPQ and KXL. The reason seems to be that syllables with higher association value are similar to well-learned items already in memory and that the similarity helps us remember the new items.

Paired-Associate Learning

A technique based on Ebbinghaus' nonsense syllables and savings scores has become one of the most frequently used experimental approaches to the learning of new associations among items. The technique is called *paired-associate learning.* A subject is asked to learn a pair of items, such as XOP and TAZ. Later his knowledge is tested by presenting one item to him—XOP—and asking him to recall the other. The first member of the pair is usually considered the *stimulus* item because it is presented to the subject when he is asked to recall the other. The second item serves as the *response* item. The ease with which subjects learn stimulus-response pairs depends on the nature of the material used for the two items and on whether the subject knows the stimulus items before he starts the experiment or is exposed to them for the first time during the experiment. The learning of paired-associate lists is, in fact, somewhat similar to the acquisition of the vocabulary of a foreign language, so we will use language-learning examples to illustrate the two kinds of difficulties that may affect paired-associate learning. One is quite obvious: it is more difficult to learn both new items and the relationship between them than it is to learn an association between items already known. In learning a foreign language, one already knows the stimulus word in one's own language and need only learn the response word; for example, one knows the word "elevator" and learns the French *"ascenseur"* (which could be considered a nonsense word, as the letters do

Like experiment I was in.

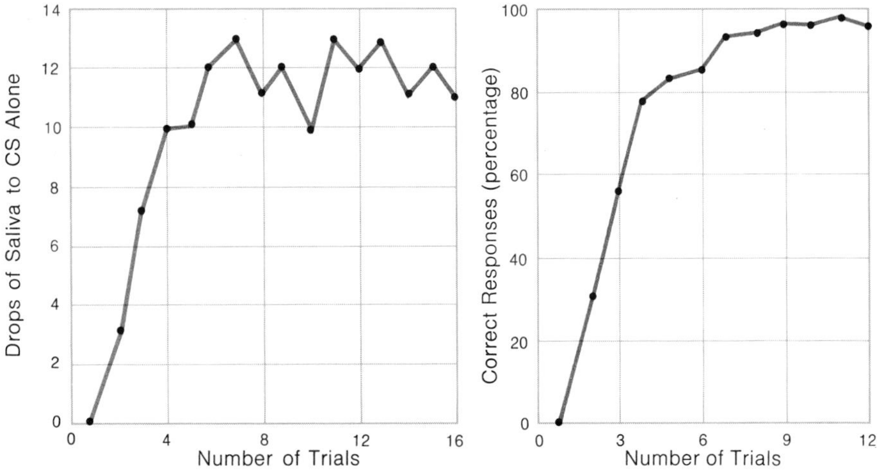

Figure 10.13
Both these graphs display incremental learning. At left is a plotting of data from one of Pavlov's experiments in classical conditioning. The dog was simultaneously presented both food (unconditioned stimulus) and a light (conditioned stimulus) until it responded—by salivating—to the light only. On each trial, the dog salivated more in response to the stimuli (incremental learning) until, at about the seventh trial, it had reached the maximum level of responding, and was classically conditioned to the light. On the right is a plot of incremental learning as it occurred in a task of learning paired associates. It took this subject about ten trials to correctly recall all the associated words in the list.

not form an English word). However, suppose one were learning French from a text written for use in Britain. One would have to learn both the stimulus word "lift" (which is the British word for elevator) and the French equivalent.

The second possible source of difficulty in paired-associate learning arises from *interference* between the words and associations to be learned and those already known. For example, many people have trouble learning foreign-language vocabulary items like the French word *"chair,"* which means "flesh" in English, because of interference from associations with the English word "chair."

Paired-associate studies have revealed gradual, continuous learning curves for new material of the type just discussed. The curves are similar to those found in numerous studies of animal and human learning. Both reveal a gradual step-by-step mastery of the task—called *incremental learning.* (See Figure 10.13.) However, the conclusion reached by some psychologists on the basis of these similarities—that the same basic processes are involved in all learning and remembering—is open to question. Some factors already cited in this chapter argue against such a conclusion; one is the fact that people impose an organization on nonsense to bring sense to it—QAX becomes "quacks" and then can call up all the individual's associations with ducks, which can be marshalled to impose a structure on the learning and remembering, and subsequently on the retrieval.

Another source of opposition to the notion that all learning follows the same course arises from recent research into how children remember. These studies, some of which are detailed in the following section, indicate that at different periods of development, children's memory processes are qualitatively different.

Children's Memory

In an experiment conducted by Piaget's colleague, Bärbel Inhelder, five- and seven-year-olds were shown an arrangement similar to that in Figure 10.14A. The bottle was about one-fourth filled with colored water. The children were asked, after being shown this arrangement, to draw from memory what they had seen. Around 80 percent of the drawings showed very marked deviations from the original arrangement. Many of them were of the form shown in Figure 10.14B. However, the most intriguing result occurred when the same children were asked six months later to draw what they had seen. Even though the children were not shown the arrangement again, some 30 percent of them reproduced the arrangement much more accurately than before. Not only had the nature of what they remembered changed during the six months—it had become more accurate.

These results underline the active, constructional nature of memory. The children had not seen the arrangement between testings, so presumably any changes that occurred in what they "remembered" were the result of developmental changes

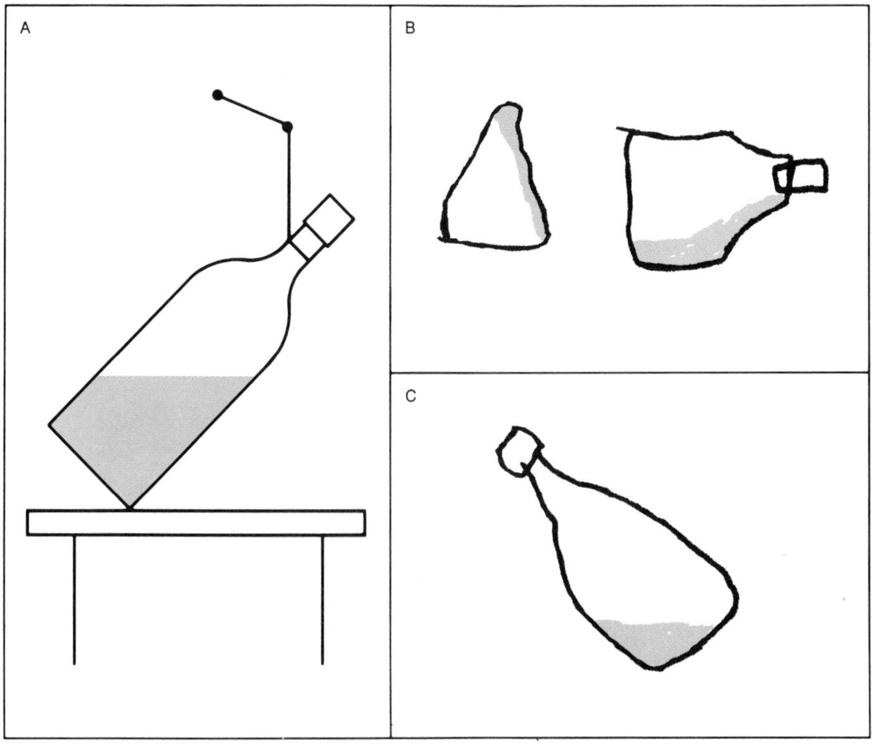

Figure 10.14
The importance of cognitive development in how children remember was shown in an experiment conducted by Bärbel Inhelder with five- and seven-year-olds. The children were shown an arrangement similar to that in A and were asked to redraw it from memory. Nearly 80 percent of the children drew figures that differed markedly from the original. Some examples of the kinds of drawings they produced are shown in B. Six months later the experimenters again asked the children to draw the original arrangement, and 30 percent of them reproduced it *better* than they had before, as in C, even though they had not seen it since the original presentation half a year earlier. Apparently, the children at that time had a better grasp of how it *ought* to be.

taking place in their knowledge of the world and in their sense of logical necessity. (See Chapter 5.) If we consider the act of remembering as involving *reconstruction* of experience on the basis of what must have been or should have been, then the children's better performance at a later time can be ascribed to a better-developed idea of must or should.

It is very difficult to reconcile such results with the view of memory as a "storage tank" that gets filled with increments of isolated stimulus-response connections. Rehearsal and rote techniques are an important part of learning, particularly when what is learned is completely new information, or information whose meaning is not immediately apparent. (The lists of bones, muscles, and organs that beginning medical students face are examples of such information.) But it must be borne in mind that learning and remembering are selective, active processes and are greatly influenced by the abilities and interests of the memorizer. New information may be quickly assimilated by an expert in the field to which the information belongs, while people who are less expert need time and, perhaps, rote techniques. The chess example that opened this chapter is a case in point.

FORGETTING

So far we have concentrated mainly on the successes of the memory system—on how information gets in, stays in, and is retrieved. When this process goes wrong in some way, forgetting ensues. How, why, and even whether something learned well enough to pass into long-term memory can ever be completely forgotten are questions that psychologists, despite considerable effort, still have not resolved.

Three approaches to the problem of forgetting, described by I. Hunter, are popular. The first approach brings together two rather unlikely bedfellows, computer-oriented psychologists who think in terms of information processing and psychoanalytically oriented psychologists. These groups tend to think that if true forgetting—in the sense of the disappearance of an item from long-term memory—occurs at all, it is at least much rarer than is commonly supposed. The second theory, which comes from physiological psychology, views forgetting primarily as

Figure 10.15
There are at least three different explanations of how and why people forget. Because there is as yet no clear-cut experimental evidence to prove or disprove any of them, the explanation one chooses is likely to be based on one's theoretical approach. The behavioral explanation says that assorted environmental events become stored in an unstructured way—in "the cluttered attic"—and so interfere with the storage and retrieval of other events. Psychoanalytic theory says that psychodynamic factors can "block" retrieval of memories; blocking, which can be effected by the subconscious, is seen as being "a brick wall" through which memories may not pass. The physiological explanation says that memory storage locations actually decay—the "deteriorating room" explanation.

a physical process that occurs in the brain. The third approach, which is behaviorist in orientation, attributes forgetting to environmental events rather than to internal processes, whether psychological or physiological.

The three approaches obviously differ in emphasis, and they also conflict at several important points. As you read about them, however, note that they are not totally incompatible. When the full story is known, if ever, it seems likely that each of them will prove to have contributed at least a few grains of truth.

Intentional Forgetting

When we say that something has been remembered, we mean that acquisition, storage, and retrieval have all proceeded successfully. When we say that something has been forgotten, any one of these processes may be at fault. If the memory lasts for a while instead of disappearing at once, that indicates that the acquisition process worked. But the failure to recall the item later does not indicate whether it is physically gone from long-term memory (erased from storage forever) or whether one simply cannot retrieve it at the moment.

Most computer memories are constructed to allow information to be added or erased at will. Human memory, on the other hand, may be nonerasable. So far, we have no sure way to tell whether material in human long-term memory ever actually disappears from storage.

Many instances of so-called forgetting fall into the category of failures in retrieval rather than erasures from long-term memory. Psychiatrists, psychoanalysts, and hypnotists often help people recover memories that seemed to be lost forever.

The same thing sometimes happens without outside assistance, during senility or delirium. Although some apparent memories are confabulation, it is also true that some apparent forgetting is a matter of suppression or repression. The material has not disappeared from storage. Instead, a conscious or unconscious decision process is at work: the person has arranged things so that the retrieval mechanism by-passes the memory in question. Indications that the apparently forgotten material is still there usually show up in the person's behavior. He may pause or fumble for words when he talks about matters related to the critical items, and there may be physiological signs of anxiety, such as sweating, rapid heart rate, and blushing.

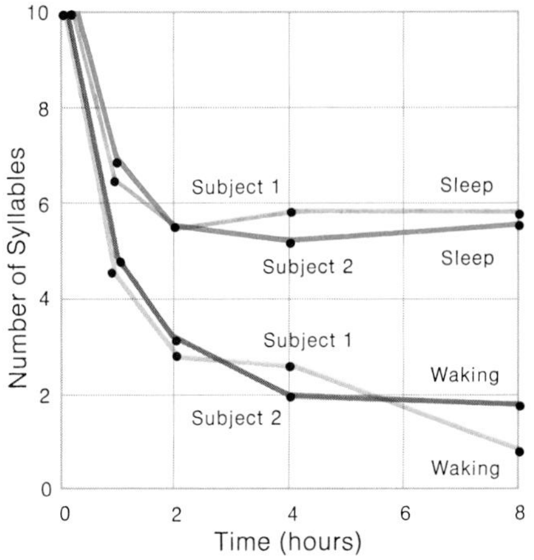

Figure 10.16

Each of the two subjects in this study learned a list of syllables at two different times. One time they were allowed to sleep immediately after learning and were tested on retention of the material immediately after they had awakened. The other time, they performed normal activities between learning and being tested. The results, showing that they remembered almost three times as much after sleeping, may reflect the absence of interference during sleep (or at least less interference during sleep, as the effect of dreams, bodily sensations, and the like on remembering are not known). (After Dallenbach, 1963.)

The Decay of Memory Traces

According to the second theory of forgetting, a *memory trace* is formed in the brain whenever we learn an item or have an experience. That is, each act of learning and each experience leave some sort of physical trace in the brain. The better an item is learned, the stronger the trace. With time (the amount depends on the strength of the trace), the trace decays and may disappear altogether, in which case the item has been forgotten.

This theory of forgetting has the virtue of emphasizing both time and the physiology of the brain; it is hard to imagine an adequate theory of forgetting that fails to take these factors into account. The memory-trace idea is also plausible in the light of subjective experience. If you try to recall in detail an event that happened last year or the points made in the first chapter of this book, "decay" and "disintegration" may describe quite well what seems to have happened to the memories.

There is, however, no direct evidence to support the memory-trace theory, and there is a considerable amount of evidence to suggest that it is, at best, preliminary and incomplete. For example, it fails to account for the fact that motor actions tend to be remembered over long periods of time. A parent who has not ridden a bike for twenty years usually has little trouble demonstrating the skill for his child. Also, although the memory-trace theory might account for repression and intentional forgetting by attributing them to weak traces, it makes no provision for the restrengthening of the traces later on. Finally, it has been demonstrated that people forget substantially less if they sleep for several hours after learning something than they do if they stay awake (see Figure 10.16); again, this fact is hard to explain if we assume that memories simply decay with the passage of time.

Interference

The third approach to forgetting attributes it to interference from other material. Although interference probably does not account for *all* forgetting, it does account for the experimental results graphed in Figure 10.16. It has been shown to have strong effects on material learned by rote and on some other kinds of tasks as well.

Near the beginning of the acquisition process, interference from extraneous material can prevent new information from passing into long-term memory. Suppose you are asked to memorize list A of the adjectives shown adjacent. You are given the first word on the list, and you have to remember the second, then the third, and so on. Each time you go through the list, you have a certain amount of time to remember each item; if you fail to recall it in that time, it is read out to you, and you are asked to go on to the next word. Eventually, you will remember the entire list. Now you are asked to memorize list B by the same method.

List A	*List B*	*List C*
happy	gay	58
big	large	22
hard	solid	18
funny	humorous	19
thin	slender	33
calming	soothing	71
neat	tidy	45

At some time in the future, you are asked to recall list A. You may find that you have forgotten many of the list A words—most people do. They may hesitate, recall only some of the list A items, and add some words from list B. In instances like this, when learning of later material interferes with remembering of material learned earlier, psychologists say that *retroactive interference* has taken place. If you had found that list A interfered with your recall of list B, that would have constituted *proactive interference*. It may help to keep these items straight if you fix firmly in

List D

noisy-thin
distinct-happy
sharp-big
high-neat
basic-calming

List E

noisy-slender
distinct-gay
sharp-large
high-tidy
basic-soothing

List F

noisy-airy
distinct-sour
sharp-daily
high-blunt
basic-odd

your mind that *pro* means forward and *retro* means backward. In proactive interference, the interference moves forward from list A to list B; in retroactive interference, it moves backward from B to A.

Now suppose that after you had learned list A, you were given list C to learn instead of list B. The odds are that this list of numbers would interfere little with your recall of list A—certainly much less than list B interfered.

J. A. McGeoch and his colleagues did experiments with this type of material, and their results indicated that the greater the similarity between the memories of different events, the greater the interference in recalling them. However, consider the case of a person's learning list A, then, after enough time has elapsed so that he can no longer recall much of it, relearning it. C. E. Osgood has pointed out that in this case, when interference should theoretically be maximum, the conditions are in fact optimum for learning and recalling certain kinds of material. Such experiences, in fact, are the basis of much human learning. This seeming paradox led Osgood to do further studies and, on the basis of them, to suggest another way of looking at interference.

Suppose you are asked to learn list D. In learning lists of paired associates, you are given the first (stimulus) item and asked to recall the second (response) one. After you have learned all the pairs of list D, you are given either list E or list F to learn. On the basis of McGeoch's findings, one would expect that you would experience most interference across lists D and E because the stimulus adjectives in those lists are identical and the response adjectives are so similar in meaning. Osgood found, however, that the reverse is true; under these circumstances there was less proactive and retroactive interference than with items like those in lists D and F. How can this effect be explained in light of McGeoch's findings?

List G	*List H*
man-homme	**man-hombre**
good-bon	**good-bueno**
tomorrow-demain	**tomorrow-mañana**
red-rouge	**red-rojo**
horse-cheval	**horse-caballo**

Osgood argues that the organization of the material accounts for it. In paired-associate learning, the fact that the stimulus is constant reduces interference among similar items. In list learning, each word on the list acts as a response to the preceding word and a stimulus for the following one, so that the stimuli and responses are always changing; under these conditions, similarity does increase interference. Therefore, if you were to learn list G (and to assure yourself that you had memorized it in the way one usually learns a foreign-language vocabulary—by covering the English words and making sure you remember what each French word

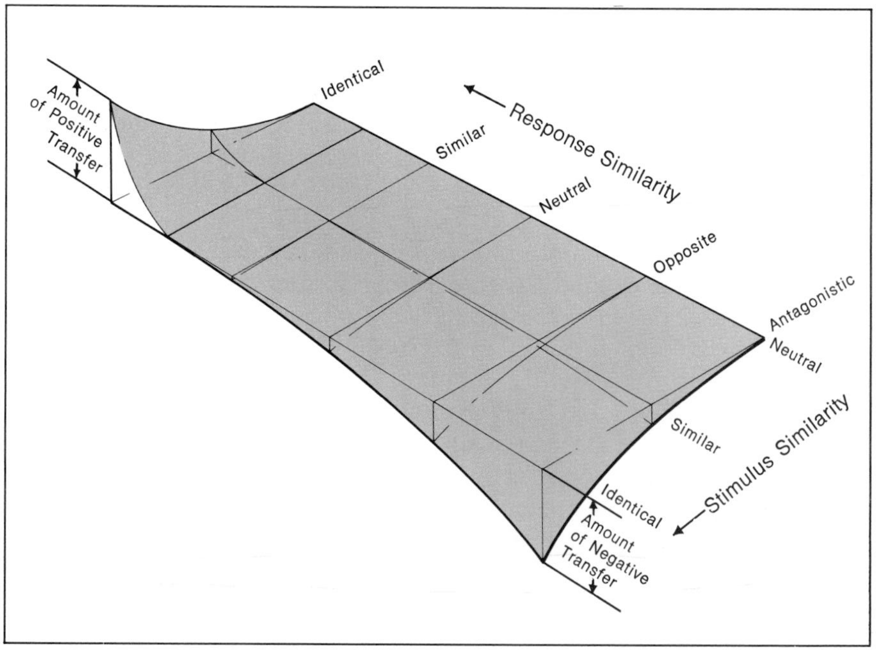

Figure 10.20
C. E. Osgood's transfer surface. This three-dimensional function summarizes the effects on paired-associate learning of varying degrees of stimulus and response similarity between pairs already learned and new pairs. All theoretically possible effects are represented on the surface that curves through this space. Note that although identical response items aid new learning, merely similar response items interfere with it.
(After Osgood, 1949.)

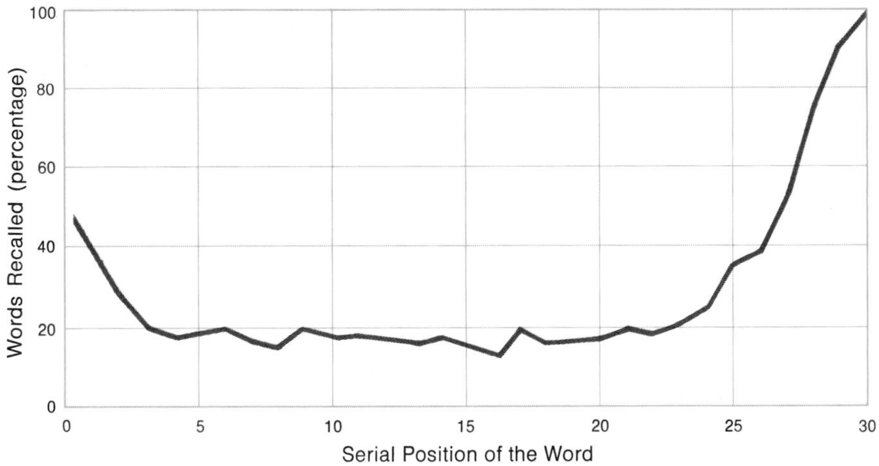

Figure 10.21
A plot showing the serial-position effect in an experiment where a group of subjects was asked to learn a relatively long list of words. The curve clearly shows both the primacy effect (people remembered the words at the start of the list better than words in the middle) and the recency effect (they remembered words at the end of the list better). The recency effect is especially strong in this particular experiment because the subjects were asked to recall the list immediately after hearing it, and therefore the last words were still in short-term memory. (After Murdock, 1962.)

means in English), and then you learned list H, it is most likely that the two experiences will complement each other and strengthen your ability to recall both.

Although it seems that interference does account for some forgetting, it is not easy to predict how much interference—if any—will occur in a given situation. Each situation requires that one analyze not only the material to be learned but also how the material relates to earlier experiences and what part it plays in performance. Also, most of the experiments on interference have dealt with verbal learning; it is not yet clear how the principles apply to other kinds of learning. (Chapter 4 does discuss transfer of training in motor skills.) Nevertheless, the studies of interference do shed some light on everyday experiences. For example, you have probably noted that when you are asked to learn a new task, you can remember the events that occur at the beginning and at the end better than those in the middle. Psychologists call this effect the *serial-position effect,* and some theorists believe that the combination of proactive and retroactive interference may well account for it. When people are asked to learn lists of words, they invariably learn the words at both ends better than those in the middle, which produces a bow-shaped learning curve as shown in Figure 10.21. The superiority of the first part of the list is called a *primacy effect;* the superiority at the last part of the list is called a *recency effect.* The serial-position effect has been shown to occur in experiments on the learning of briefly exposed words, motor skills, and verbal habits.

The serial-position effect appears to other theorists to reflect an interaction between attention and short-term memory. During the presentation of the first few words on a list, there is little for a person to do except learn the words. This helps

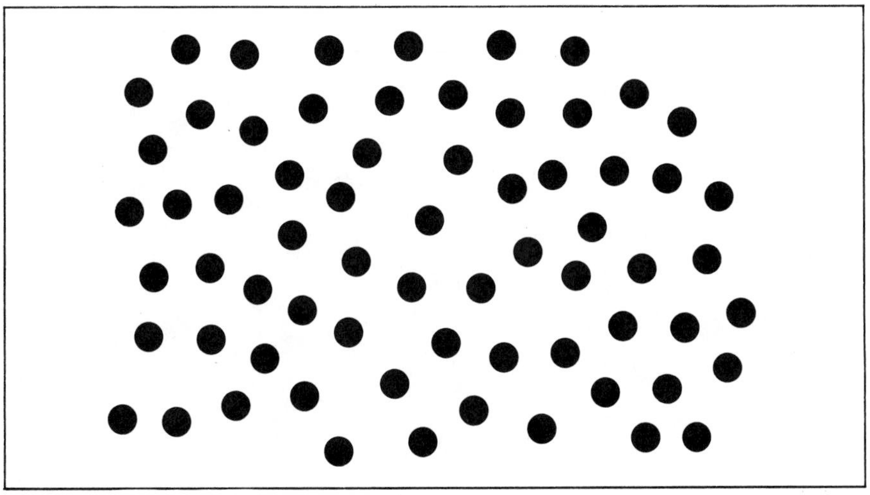

Figure 10.22
This is the first part of a test you can take to see whether you are one of those rare persons who possesses eidetic imagery. Look carefully at this pattern and try to remember it. Now turn to page 188 and try to superimpose this pattern on the one in Figure 10.24. If certain letters or numbers become visible to you while you are looking at Figure 10.24. you almost certainly are an "eidetiker," and you may wish to contact some of the psychologists doing research in this area. Eidetic images are so realistic that they are almost equivalent to direct perception.

him in two ways. First, he can label the first word by the fact that it is first. Second, he starts out with only one word to learn. After a number of words have been presented, however, the subject gets bogged down. He is trying to learn many items simultaneously; he is rehearsing some and missing others. Some of the earlier words have already been lost from short-term memory, and there are no obvious position clues that he can use. At the end of the list, although all the factors that caused problems in the middle of the list are still present, the person has some extra time. He can concentrate on the last few items presented (because they still reside in short-term memory) and try to organize and rehearse them until they make their way into long-term memory. Thus, the first and last parts of the list have an advantage in the organizing process over items in the middle.

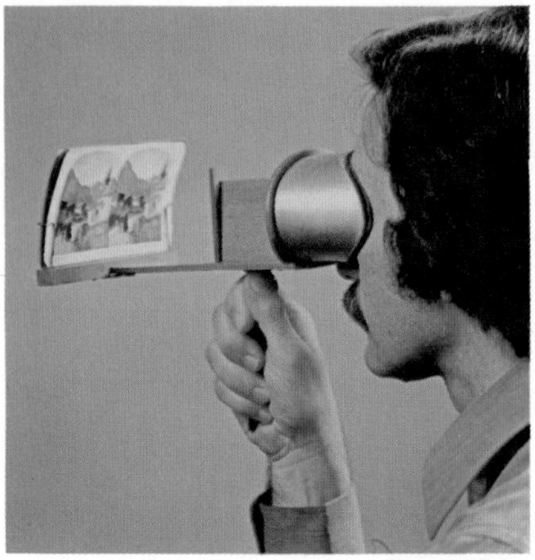

Figure 10.23
The stereoscope is a device to help the viewer fuse two slightly disparate two-dimensional images into a single three-dimensional image.

EIDETIC IMAGERY

Having listed and discussed, among other things, limits on our powers of memory, let us briefly consider a person who violates all the rules—the person with eidetic imagery. These extraordinary people have "photographic memories." They can remember all the details of photographs, visual scenes, whole pages of text, and so on, on the basis of very short exposures to them. Until quite recently, discussion of this topic could be based only on anecdotes and on sketchy experimental evidence. Recently, however, new studies have provided firm evidence for the existence of eidetic memory, although they have little to say about the mechanisms underlying it.

One of these studies, performed by C. G. Stromeyer III, uses a rather elegant technique. You have perhaps seen at one time or another a piece of apparatus called a stereoscope (see Figure 10.23). It has two eyepieces and, at the other end, a two-part card or photograph that depicts the same scene on each side. When you look through the stereoscope, the two views merge to produce a single three-dimensional image. Stromeyer used a stereoscopic technique to study eidetic imagery. His subject looked first at one photograph with one eye; later, she looked at a second photograph with the other eye. The two images merged to produce patterns—numbers or letters.

Stromeyer's subject, an exceptional woman he called Elizabeth, was able to perform this feat even when long periods of time were allowed to elapse between the two viewings. After days and even weeks, Elizabeth was capable of carrying over an image to discover the number or letter created by the superimposition.

Test your own ability with the two pictures shown in Figures 10.22 and 10.24. Look first at the pattern in Figure 10.22 on the preceding page. Then turn the page and try to superimpose that image on the one in Figure 10.24 below. Do you see any numbers or letters emerging? If you do, write to the address given—you

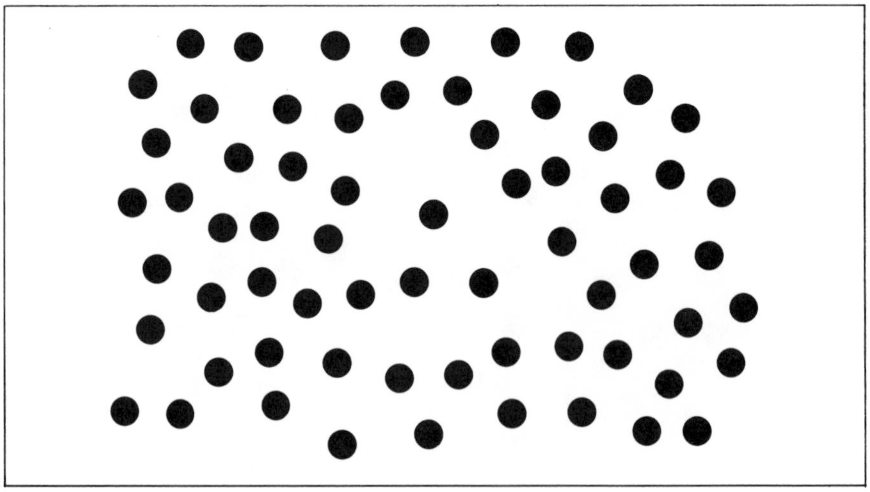

Figure 10.24
This is the second part of the test for eidetic imagery described in the caption for Figure 10.22, page 187. If you see any numbers or letters emerging, write to J. O. Merritt, Department of Psychology, 622 William James Hall, Harvard University, Cambridge, Mass. 02138.

may be one of the extremely rare people for whom the researchers are looking. The great difficulty of doing research on eidetic imagery, as you can probably imagine, lies in finding enough gifted subjects. Children seem to possess eidetic abilities to a far greater degree than adults, so future insights into the phenomenon may well stem from studies of younger subjects.

One thing is reasonably certain. This line of inquiry is sufficiently unusual and stimulating to ensure that many of you will remember it for some time to come. As for the rest of the chapter, only time and test will tell.

SUGGESTED READINGS

ADAMS, J. A. *Human Memory.* New York, McGraw-Hill, 1967. A well-organized book with emphasis upon experimental techniques and findings. It is more technical than the other books listed here, but would make a good companion to Hunter's paperback.

BARTLETT, S. C. *Remembering: A Study in Experimental and Social Psychology.* New York, Cambridge University Press, 1932. Although forty years old, this book still warrants reading. Explores Bartlett's convictions that remembering is a more or less skillful and active process of reconstruction and interpretation. Many of Bartlett's ideas resurface in such current work as Neisser's *Cognitive Psychology* and *Studies in Cognitive Growth,* by Bruner and colleagues.

HUNTER, I. M. L. *Memory.* Baltimore, Penguin, 1964. An introduction to the study of human memory that surveys in narrative form a good deal of experimental literature dating back to Ebbinghaus.

11 Problem Solving

EVERYONE MUST SOLVE A PROBLEM of some sort at almost every moment of his life—even if it is a simple one, such as: Where did I put my glasses? It is the mathematician and the scientist, however, who are usually considered *the* problem solvers. It is their profession to consider and solve, if possible, the deepest problems set them by the universe. How do they do it?

One could never find out by reading the learned papers in which they describe their discoveries. These are dry, straight-line, logical expositions, prepared after the fact of discovery. Such papers are very likely to contain not one hint of the actual manner in which the solution of some problem was arrived at.

Here is a case in point. Back in the 1850s a German chemist, F. A. Kekulé, had worked out a system for representing the arrangements of the atoms in molecules. He connected their symbols with little dashes according to a small number of simple rules. The formulas that were produced in this fashion could be used to explain the way in which particular molecules behaved. They could even be used to predict new ways in which they would behave under special circumstances. The formulas helped guide chemists to the synthesis of new and remarkable substances that did not exist in nature.

There remained one important substance, benzene, that did not seem to fit. Kekulé tried to work out a formula for its atoms (six carbon atoms and six hydrogen atoms in each molecule) but could not do it. He arranged the carbon atoms in the different kinds of chains that worked for other molecules, but none made sense of the way in which benzene behaved. If the benzene problem were not solved, his whole system might break down.

One day in 1865, he was in Ghent, Belgium, on a public bus. He was tired and, lulled by the droning beat of the horses' hooves on the cobblestones, he fell into a comatose half-sleep. In that sleep, the overwhelming preoccupation with the problem of molecular structure took over. He seemed to see a vision of atoms attaching themselves to each other in chains that moved about. And then one chain twisted in such a way that head and tail joined, forming a ring—and Kekulé came to full wakefulness with a start.

That was it! He arranged the six carbon atoms of the benzene molecule in a ring and found that he could now account for its properties. It was that semicomatose vision that established his system, and although chemists have deepened and broadened that system in the century since then, they have never departed from it. When Kekulé came to describe the new addition to his system, he said nothing of his dream. He merely advanced evidence and reasoning in the dryest possible way—as though that were how he had worked it out. We only know of the dream because he described it in a letter to a friend during another moment of relaxation long after. I.A.

Most days of our lives we find ourselves beset by one problem or another. Some are easy, some difficult, some downright impossible. Problems can be frustrating and anxiety provoking and also—luckily—intriguing and absorbing. Some we work out completely in our heads; for others we use our hands or specially constructed tools. Forcing yourself to get up in the morning, pitting your wits against a crossword puzzle, trying to mend a bicycle, attempting to stretch the weekly budget, postulating a theory of the nature of the universe—all these and many more we commonly lump under the general heading: problems.

Sooner or later in the psychological study of problem solving, questions are bound to arise about the extent to which all these situations really belong together. Do they all require the same abilities or involve the same solution processes? Do they all have at least one feature in common? Is there a single problem-solving skill that makes some people better solvers of all problems than others? Try the set of problems shown in Figure 11.1. Give them to two of your friends and see how long it takes them to solve each one and how many errors they make. Does one friend do better than the other on all the problems?

There is almost as much variety in the purposes for which psychologists invent and use problems as there is in the kinds of things that are called problems. Psychologists use problems to study the capabilities of animals, children, adults, and

Find the concept that this set of cards contains. Of all the elements—color, shape, size, border—choose the one (or more) that is salient. Because these cards are selected from a pack of 64, you are given a clue here: all the cards in the left-hand column show positive examples of the concept; none of the cards in the right-hand column shows it.

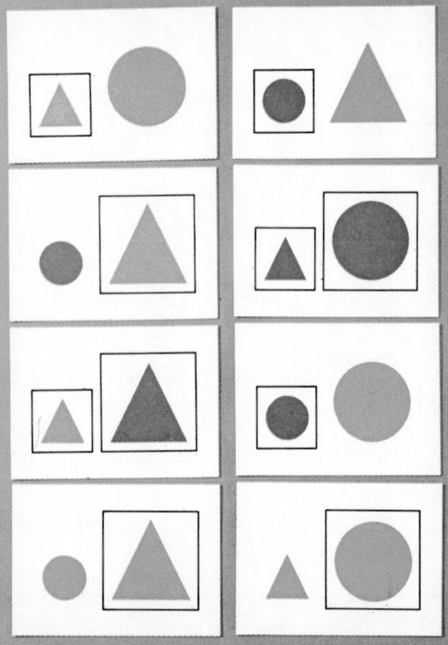

Position three upright glasses on a table so that each forms the corner point of a triangle of equal sides, and the distance between any two glasses is slightly longer than the blade of one of the knives.
Using only four knives, construct a platform on top of the glasses that is strong enough to support the fourth glass. No part of any knife may touch the table. (After E. DeBono THE FIVE-DAY COURSE IN THINKING. New York: Basic Books, 1967)

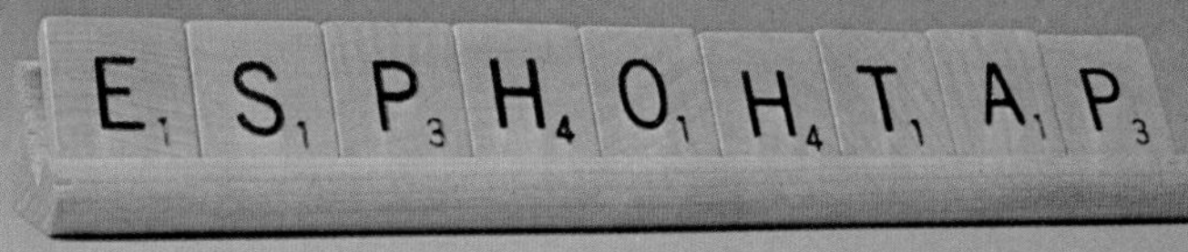

Solve this anagram.

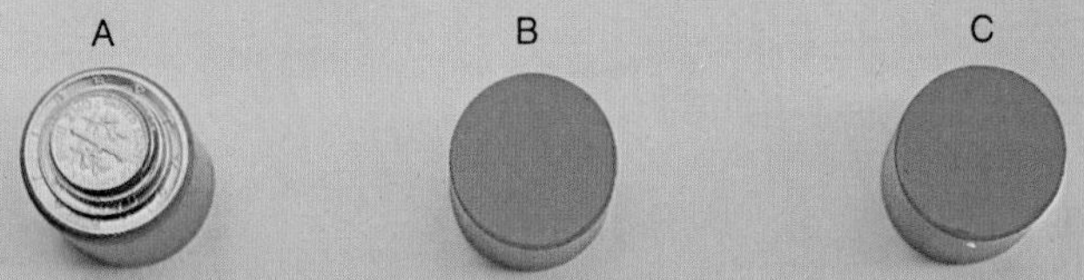

Use a water glass to draw three circles on a sheet of paper, then label the circles A, B, and C. On circle A, stack a dime, a penny, a nickel, a quarter, and a half-dollar in order of size, with the half-dollar on the bottom. The problem is to move them all to circle B—in the smallest number of moves possible—so that they are stacked in the same way. Note, however, that only one coin at a time may be moved, and a coin may be moved only to another circle. Moreover, you may not place a coin on top of a smaller coin (for example, you may not place a penny on top of a dime). The minimum number of moves required to move the coins from A to B is 31.

If the puzzle you solved before you solved this one was harder than the puzzle you solved after you solved the puzzle you solved before you solved this one, was the puzzle you solved before you solved this one harder than this one?

even machines. A knowledge of the problems that an animal species can and cannot solve allows one to speculate about the species' general abilities or intelligence and also about the nature of brain functioning. Research on the problems that children are able and unable to solve at different periods in their development provides a base for theories of intellectual development and has implications for teachers and parents. Studies of the problem-solving abilities of adults are used to formulate and test theories about human thought and its relation to behavior and to devise aptitude tests and other ways of assessing individual differences.

In view of all this, you should not be surprised to find that there is no single comprehensive, widely accepted theory of problem solving. This chapter is something of a psychological rag bag. Among other things, however, the study of problem solving is directed at the development and testing of theories of thinking. Not all thinking involves problem solving (for example, we might want to call daydreaming or the recalling of familiar memories "thinking," but they are not problem solving); however, a large part of our most important adaptive thinking does involve working out problems. It is this kind of thinking that we are primarily interested in here.

Figure 11.1 *(opposite)*

Try your hand at solving these puzzles. You can examine the strategies and processes you used as you read the chapter. And you can check your solutions with the correct ones, given on page 204.

LOGIC: TO ERR IS HUMAN

Philosophers and logicians as well as psychologists have considered at some length the question of how close everyday reasoning is to pure logic. Some have argued that logic is the ideal toward which everyday reasoning strives—that we are all aspiring, if rather unsuccessful, logicians. Others claim that logic is a special system of thought that has particular functions, such as allowing one to state in unequivocal and final form the train of thought that led to a conclusion already reached.

To show that the laws of logic are also the fundamental laws of thought, it would be necessary to demonstrate that reasoning is influenced only by the logical *structure* or *form* of a problem and not by its *content*. To illustrate, suppose that *ArB, BrC* represents the structure of a set of problems where *A, B,* and *C* stand for objects (three people, say) and *r* stands for relational terms such as "taller than," "happier than," or "to the left of." Purely logical solutions to all problems with this structure would require that one's reasoning be unaffected by changes in the content of the problems and depend only on their form. Several experiments have shown that this is not the case.

If Pete is shorter than Harry, and Pete is taller than Mark, who is tallest?

If Mary is left of Jane, and Patty is right of Jane, who is rightmost?

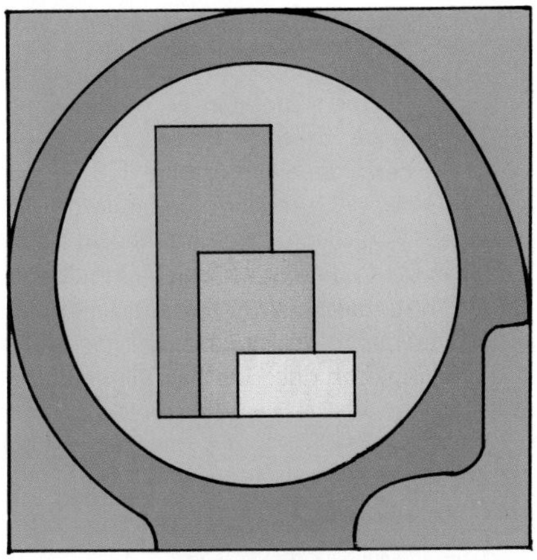

Figure 11.2

The top drawing represents the vertical mental image that, according to DeSoto, you probably constructed as you read the first syllogism. The lower drawing represents the horizontal image that you would probably think of while pondering the second syllogism.

Spatial Paralogic

Try the two adjacent syllogisms. The odds are, according to the work of C. M. DeSoto and his colleagues, that you constructed different types of *mental images* to solve these two problems. You probably had a "top-to-bottom" image for the first one, with Harry at the top and Mark at the bottom, and a "left-to-right" image for the second, with Mary at the extreme left and Patty at the right. With relationship problems like these, DeSoto found, people tend to be very systematic in the way they represent information. They construct spatial images that consistently go in one direction (such as vertical or horizontal) and always have a certain order (such as taller at the top, shorter at the bottom).

With other relational terms, like "lighter than/darker than," the spatial representations are not consistent from person to person. What is most important for our present purposes is the finding that the difficulty people have in solving various forms of syllogisms is closely related to the nature of the images they construct. This shows that difficulty is influenced by the *content* of the problem as well as by its logical form.

Probabilistic Inference

Other experiments not only confirm that most people's reasoning departs from "pure" logic but show that the departures are often useful and adaptive. For everyday purposes, "impure" logic often works better than pure. For example, suppose you are given the following information:

All crows are jet-black birds.
There is a huge flock of various types of jet-black birds.

You might be disposed to conclude from those statements:

There are some crows in that flock.

That conclusion is an example of what L. J. Chapman and J. P. Chapman call *probabilistic inference.* It is not dictated by logical necessity, but it has a high probability of standing up if you take the trouble to examine the flock.

Many of the decisions we make in our everyday lives cannot be based on absolutes—either objective or subjective ones. We must often proceed as best we can on the basis of probable outcomes. Experiments performed by the Chapmans indicate that probabilistic inference may become so habitual that people use it in preference to strict logic even when strict logic is possible and specifically called for. A striking example is provided by the problem in Figure 11.3, which very few people get right. It was formulated by P. L. Wason. Try it yourself (and no cheating).

Figure 11.3
Wason's problem on probabilistic inference. Examine these cards. Each card has a red or blue triangle on one side and a red or blue circle on the other. Four such cards are shown here. The task is to determine which cards need to be turned over to test the validity of the statement: "Every card that has a red triangle on one side has a blue circle on the other."
(After Wason, 1968.)

Most people give the answer "red triangle" or "red triangle and blue circle." Both are wrong. The correct answer is red triangle and red circle. What is particularly intriguing about this problem is not that people spontaneously reach a logically incorrect solution (and usually feel quite confident about doing so) but that the way they reach it seems to be very ingrained. Does this kind of problem reveal operations that are fundamental to everyday reasoning? Why should people get it wrong? One source of error seems to be the supposition that if all cards with red triangles on one side have blue circles on the other, then all cards with blue circles on one side must have red triangles on the other. If all *A* are *B*, then all *B* are *A*. This acceptance of symmetry is a useful, often valid everyday inference, although it is not *logically* necessary.

Another source of difficulty stems from people's characteristic failure to recognize certain implicit relationships in the information they are given. When someone looks to the red triangle, it is probably to show that it has a blue circle on the other side—to test what is called a "positive instance," a positive expectation. But, at the same time, one is also testing (logically) the negative statement—there will be no red circle. If a person were to mutter to himself while turning over the red triangle, "no red circle, no red circle," instead of "it's a blue circle, it's a blue circle," he might well get the correct answer because then he might go on to say, "and no red triangle on the red circle either" instead of "and a red triangle on the blue circle."

In more recent studies Wason has shown that people do not make so many mistakes if they substitute certain types of real-life events for the abstract geometric material. For example, suppose the cards have names of cities on one side and means

Figure 11.4
The same problem as in Figure 11.3 is shown here except that the stimuli are more concrete and convey more meaning; consequently the problem is easier. Using these cards the task is to test the validity of the statement: "When I go to London, I always go by plane."
(After Wason, 1968.)

of transport on the other. Test the rule, "When I go to London, I always go by plane," using the cards shown in Figure 11.4.

You were probably more at home with this problem than with the one in Figure 11.3. You have to turn over *London,* of course. You do not have to turn over *Paris* —because you have no predictions about that—or *Plane*—you could be going anywhere by plane. But you do have to turn over *Ship* in case you are trying to sneak your way to London that way, which would violate the rule.

One can draw two conclusions from the results of studies with problems like these: First, changing the content of the problem greatly alters its difficulty. Second, the information people are *logically* getting from their experience with the cards is not the same as the information they are getting *psychologically.* That is, people do not necessarily extract all the information from an event—particularly if it is the sort of negative information found in this problem. One would not predict either of these results on purely logical grounds.

Distortion

As we have just seen, probabilistic inferences may have practical value. *Distortions* in reasoning are usually less helpful. The dividing line between the two kinds of reasoning is not a sharp one; the difference may be merely a matter of degree.

Distortion occurs not because the reasoner happens to be an "illogical person" but, often, because of the emotional content of the material he is dealing with. M. Henle argues that people are capable of logically correct deductions but "rewrite" emotionally charged statements in a way that changes the nature of the logical task. For example, they ignore information that disagrees with their own strongly held convictions and substitute information that does agree in order to reach a "logical" conclusion that satisfies them. In Chapter 10 it was pointed out that people do not remember information as if it had been recorded on tape; instead, they reconstruct memories from a few clues. When statements are distorted, it may be that reconstruction has produced an erroneous—though self-satisfying—recall.

HEURISTICS

It seems, then, that there are fundamental differences in the character of everyday and logical thought. A great many of the conclusions reached in everyday thinking, though logically incorrect or inaccurate, are borne out by experience. The logician must refrain from drawing a conclusion until all the logically required information is in, but the everyday thinker may quite happily make a decision on less-than-complete knowledge. The logician must painstakingly explore all the logical possibili-

Figure 11.5
Bernie is solving his problem of how to get from Boston to London by using a heuristic called a means-end analysis. He will reduce the difference between his initial state (Boston) and his desired state (London) by first traveling to New York, thereby making the difference a New York-London one.

ties, but the everyday thinker may be less thorough and still reach probably true, though not certain, conclusions.

The differences between the methods of the logician and the everyday thinker are reminiscent of the distinctions between algorithms and heuristics, as described in Chapter 9. Algorithmic problem solving consists of systematically trying out every possible route to a solution. Heuristic procedures are rules of thumb; they rely on only a certain number of possible methods, which may not always deliver a solution but will usually do so—and in a shorter period of time than an algorithmic approach would require.

Studies by A. Newell, J. C. Shaw, and H. A. Simon, among others, have stressed the heuristic nature of human problem-solving behavior. Their General Problem Solver (GPS) is basically an attempt to show that all directed thinking in problem solving is influenced by a small number of heuristics. Thus the work of Newell and his colleagues relates to the question raised at the beginning of this chapter: to what extent do only a few rules govern all problem-solving behavior?

Certain features of GPS were discussed in Chapter 9, which described one of the computer's heuristics, subgoal hierarchies, as it applied to chess playing. Two other heuristics that GPS uses to solve complex problems are *means-end analysis* and *working backward.* Both can be described through an example.

Suppose you want to travel from Boston to London. In Newell's terms you need to perform a means-end analysis that will allow you to *reduce the difference* between your *initial state* (Boston) and your *desired state* (London). The means for reducing this difference that spring readily to mind are ships and planes. You telephone a travel agent, only to find that neither shipping lines nor airlines have carriers that go to London from Boston when you want to go. The means that you thought would reduce the difference will not work. You know, however, that there are planes from New York to London whenever you wish to go. So you hire a car to take you from Boston to Kennedy Airport, thus reducing the Boston-London difference to a New York-London one. You take a plane from New York to London and completely remove the difference between your initial and desired states. Your problem is solved.

The second heuristic mentioned above, working backward, is another very general and useful one. In planning the Boston-London journey, suppose you knew of a great number of air routes leading out of Boston to other cities. You might, in trying to solve your problem, follow these routes through to Chicago, Philadelphia, Minneapolis, and so on, in an attempt to find a plane to London. If you happened to know a smaller number of routes into London than out of Boston, however, then planning backward from London instead of forward out of Boston would simplify your problem and save time.

These heuristics, presented in this way, seem extremely simple, but they lie at the heart of some very complex problem-solving activities, including proving logical theorems and playing chess. Because GPS shows how such a simple set of rules is instrumental in a range of complex behavior, it is one of the most striking achievements in recent research on problem solving and thinking.

There are, however, serious limitations to GPS that raise some doubt about its potential generality as a problem solver. In the first place, GPS is always given its initial state; the problem to be solved is always described for it. This is often not true for a human being facing a problem, and the question of how people achieve the first stage in problem solving, the initial conception and description of the problem, is one of the least studied, least understood in problem-solving research. Second, GPS only solves problems of the "correct-incorrect" or "succeed-fail" type. Many of the problems we face in everyday life are not of this sort. Business problems, political problems, and social problems, to mention a few, tend to be solved through judgments that are "better-worse" rather than "correct-incorrect"; furthermore, agreement on which solutions are better and which are worse is hard to come by. For example, a businessman may have to weigh increased productivity against increased environmental pollution. The solution to such a problem is a matter of judgment and, often, of public debate.

Finally, GPS does not tell us how heuristics are created or changed, nor does it show how they relate to each other. Computer simulations that will extend the theory of heuristics to these questions may need to be based on studies of child development. Research in that field, if it succeeds in showing what experiences are instrumental in a child's creation and modification of heuristic strategies, will allow us to look beyond the rules to the factors that underlie their development.

PROBLEMS AND METHODS

You emerge from your house on a cold winter morning, late for work. The car will not start. You get out, shiver, lift the hood, and look intently at the array of mechanical parts within. After pulling tentatively at a couple of wires, you go to the garage, get a wrench and a screwdriver, and tap a few bolts and screws. Then you return to the wires. You try a whole variety of operations with different tools, sometimes repeating things you have already tried and sometimes undoing things you have just done. You are thoroughly disorganized.

Then along comes your next-door neighbor, eager to display the rewards of those weekends you teased him for wasting on his ancient car. He proceeds systematically, using the same tools that you did but working in an orderly sequence from the most probable source of the trouble to the least probable. Soon your car begins to purr.

In a sense, your neighbor did nothing that you could not have done. He simply did it in a more skillful and organized manner. Why was the problem that was so hard for you so easy for him? Obviously, his experience tinkering with his own car helped. So, probably, did the fact that he was not nervous about being late to work. You find yourself reflecting, too, on the laboratory science course that both of you took in high school. Which of you was the one whose experiments always came out right and who liked lab work so much that he did more of it than the course required?

As you read this section, note that virtually all the factors that affect the ease and efficiency with which people solve problems have something to do with experience. Experience—not only in the form of practice with particular kinds of problems but with problems of a very general nature—influences problem solving in a wide variety of ways. Some of these factors have important implications for psychological theories of thought.

Anagram Studies

Whereas Newell and his colleagues began their work on heuristics by hypothesizing a few fundamental rules or principles that might explain a wide range of problem-solving behavior, many other researchers use a different approach. They study in depth the processes and variables involved in solving one type of problem. A very common research strategy proceeds as follows. First, people are asked to solve a group of problems of the same type, such as anagrams. Next, the experimenter tabulates the number of errors made or the amount of time the problems took; this kind of tabulation tells him which problems were hardest, which easiest, and so on. Finally, the psychologist explains (or tries to explain) what accounts for the variations in difficulty.

Before you read on, try the three adjacent lists of anagrams. Keep track of the amount of time it takes you to complete each list.

You probably found that list A was more difficult than list B and that list C was easier than either. What reasons can you offer for these differences?

The anagrams on list A have what M. S. Mayzner and M. E. Tresselt call "high

List A	*List B*	*List C*
yenoj	**lnnie**	**emnlo**
cansk	**reriv**	**pplea**
maspw	**rtnia**	**naanba**
geduf	**tsgae**	**miel**
ggyof	**eiwrt**	**wtbryrrase**

anbitot" and "low solbitot." These terms are based on *bigram frequency counts:* counts of how frequently particular two-letter combinations occur in a language. Anbitot refers to the anagram; solbitot to the solution word. The anagrams on list A include many bigrams with high frequencies in English words; the bigrams in the solution words, on the other hand, have lower frequencies. Take maspw, for example. The first two letters, ma, often occur in that order in English words (high anbitot). The first two letters of the solution word, sw, rarely occur in that order (low solbitot). In yenoj, the bigrams ye, en, no are relatively common; nj, oy in enjoy are less common. On list B, the solution words include many bigrams with high frequencies. High solbitot, then, makes list B easier for most people than list A.

Anagrams may seem an esoteric pastime, rather remote from the course of daily life, but in solving them we make use of knowledge gained from well-developed, frequently practiced skills such as reading and speaking. Our experience with the language helps determine which solution words we try first and, therefore, which anagrams are easiest to solve. An expert at anagrams probably moves systematically from the most likely to the least likely solution words, basing his hierarchy on frequency counts that he has picked up over years of experience.

What about list C? No doubt you discovered why it was easier than the other two. The reason is that all the solution words belong to the same familiar class: fruits. When you see that, the number of possible solutions you try with the remaining anagrams suddenly becomes quite small and manageable. Under ordinary circumstances, naanba might well be a more difficult anagram than emnlo, but knowing that both groups of letters are scrambled fruit names makes both of them easy.

The effect that occurs when you discover that list C seems to consist of anagrams for fruits is called *category set.* After you have solved a couple of anagrams, you become *set* for more solutions that belong to the category fruits. Set, which can be defined as a readiness for a restricted range of events, is a familiar phenomenon both in laboratory studies of problem solving and elsewhere, as we shall see.

The relative difficulties of these three lists of anagrams were closely related to the *complexity* of the problems they presented. Complexity is usually measured in terms of the *number* and *familiarity* of various aspects of a problem—its components, the ways they must be operated on to solve the problem, and the problem's solution(s). List B was less complex, and easier, than list A primarily because the letter combinations in the solution words were more familiar. List C was easier than A or B primarily because knowing that the solution words were fruits reduced the number of possible solution words to be tried and allowed faster recognition of the correct ones.

Sometimes difficulty is related not to the formal complexity of a problem but to the *strategies* that the problem solver uses, which can change radically as he works through a group of problems. Suppose that a person who did not know how to multiply was given the problem "ten 12s are how much?" He could get the answer by addition, writing a column of ten 12s and adding them up. But multiplying by adding is tedious work, and eventually the problem solver would probably discover that he could answer the question "100 14s are how much?" simply by putting two zeros after the 14. That change in strategy would make the problem much less difficult for him to solve than the earlier one, though it is no less complex.

Series Problems

Who is taller, Paul or Tom, if:

Paul is taller than John
John is taller than Dave
Dave is taller than Pete
Tom is taller than Pete
Dave is taller than Tom.

Particularly dramatic changes in strategy tend to occur as people gain experience with the type of problem shown in the adjacent margin, called a *series problem.* Asked to solve a number of such problems—a series of series problems, so to speak—most people develop a strategy for use on later problems that is quite different from the one they use at first. To solve the first few problems, they tend to build up mental images similar to the up-down and left-right images reported by DeSoto. Later on, they devise a more efficient, less strenuous strategy that does not require visualizing the line-up described in the problem.

For example, given the problem in Figure 11.8 after several similar ones, the problem solver first tries to find a connection from Paul to Tom. He finds a mention of Paul on the left-hand side of line 2; it connects to John. But John is not taller than anyone else, and Paul is not mentioned again on the left-hand side of the statements. So the problem solver begins again, this time looking for a connection from Tom to Paul. He finds that Tom is taller than Alan (line 4); Alan is taller than Dave (line 5); and Dave is taller than Paul (line 1). Therefore, Tom is taller than Paul. After still more experience with this type of problem, a few people develop an even more efficient strategy. They scan the left-hand side of the statement to see if one of the names (Paul or Tom) does not occur. If that is true, then the one who *is* named is taller. If both names occur, one of them is followed up as above. If it connects, then it is the name of the taller man. If it does not, then the other man is taller—if Paul is not tall, Tom must be.

These changes in strategy are related to set, but a different kind from the one that occurred in solving the anagrams on list C. There, the problem solver developed a set for a certain type of *solution.* Here, the common feature that the problem solver notes in past problems and expects in future ones is in the *structure* of the problems. All of them are presented in list form, and the name of the taller person is always on the left. (That is, the phrase connecting the names is always "is taller than," never "is shorter than.")

Figure 11.8
The diagrams below illustrate the possible consecutive strategies discussed in the text for solving this problem.

Who is taller, Paul or Tom, if:
Dave is taller than Paul
Paul is taller than John
Dave is taller than John
Tom is taller than Alan
Alan is taller than Dave.

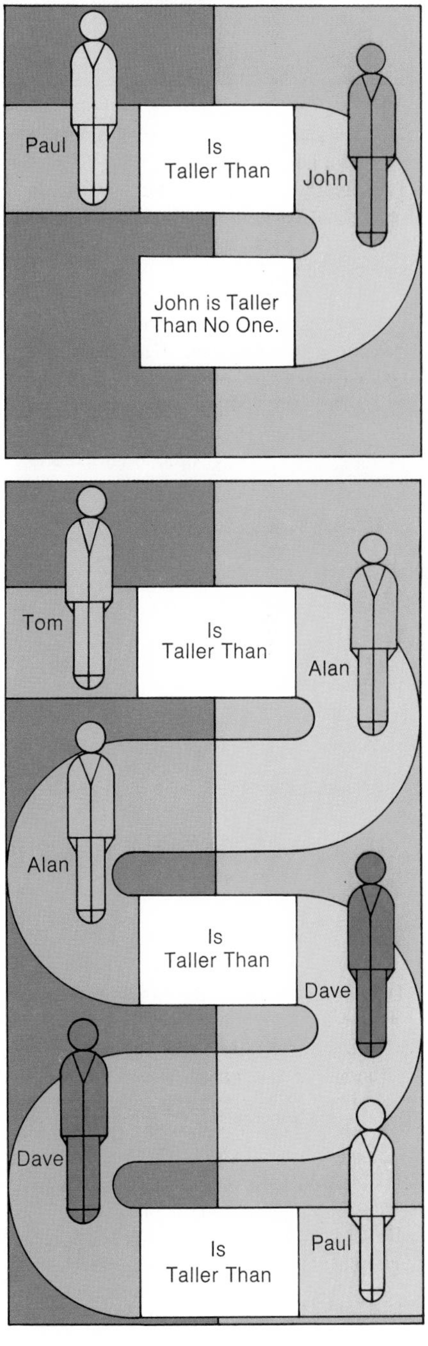

Set

In the two examples given, anagrams and series problems, set increased the efficiency of the problem solver and made later problems easier for him than earlier ones. Set often does much the same in everyday life, where it is best exemplified by *habits.* Most habits are methods that we have developed, through experience, for dealing with familiar problems; their big advantage is that they allow us to solve such problems quickly and apparently automatically, freeing time and energy for use on other matters.

Not all habits are useful, of course. Some, such as spending every Saturday afternoon pulling the wings off butterflies, seem to have virtually nothing to recommend them. Others, such as getting drunk every night, are probably less-than-ideal solutions to the problem at hand (whatever it may be). Still others, acceptable enough under ordinary circumstances, become unacceptable if they gain a stranglehold. Most Americans habitually eat cooked meat, but one would not want to be totally unable to face raw fish if one found oneself adrift on the open sea.

Einstellung In other words, set can be a curse as well as a blessing. Perhaps you have had the experience of walking or driving along a familiar route from which you plan to diverge at some point in order to reach a different destination from your usual one. Lost in thought, you suddenly find that you have followed the familiar route to its familiar conclusion, arriving where you did not want to be. When this sort of thing happens in laboratory studies of problem solving, it is called *Einstellung,* which means, roughly translated, rigidity.

The classic research on *Einstellung* was done by A. S. Luchins. He gave his subjects—thousands of them, under many different conditions—a series of arithmetic problems, all but one of which could be solved by using a particular method. Several of the problems are shown in Figure 11.9.

The easiest way to solve the first five problems is to fill Jar B and dump it in a tub (or whatever), and then to use Jar A once and Jar C twice to bail out the extra. That method can be expressed as a formula: $B - A - 2C$.

What about the sixth problem? Almost everyone can solve it if they do it first,

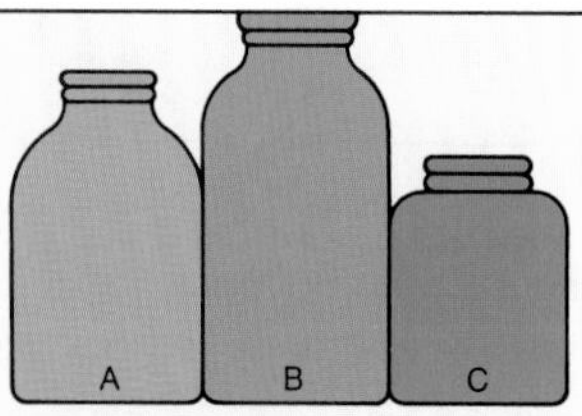

	Given jars with these capacities (in quarts)			Obtain
	A	B	C	
1.	21	127	3	100
2.	14	163	25	99
3.	18	43	10	5
4.	9	42	6	21
5.	20	59	4	31
6.	28	76	3	25

Figure 11.9
Luchins' classic series of water-jar problems. After solving five problems, nearly two-thirds of Luchins' subjects could not solve the sixth problem, labeled as "crucial" by the experimenter. The problem-solving behaviors, which had worked for the first five, do not work for the sixth problem. To be successful, one must show cognitive flexibility and invoke a simple solution that involves just two jars. Subjects who are unable to make this adaptation are suffering functional fixedness.

without trying the first five, but Luchins found that it stymies roughly two-thirds of the people who encounter it after they have become set to use the $B - A - 2C$ method. They either get the wrong answer, give up, or staunchly maintain that the formula works here too, saying that 76 − 28 − 3 − 3 equals 25.

Functional Fixedness Another type of set that can be a hindrance in solving problems is called *functional fixedness.* In an experiment on functional fixedness, a person is asked to solve a problem that requires him to use a familiar object in an unfamiliar way. Because he is set to use the object in the familiar way, he tends to pay attention only to the features of the object that relate to its common use. Therefore he may take an inordinate amount of time to solve the problem, or he may fail to solve it at all.

An example is C. Dunker's candle problem, shown in Figure 11.10. The subject is given a box of candles, a match, tacks, and string, and he is asked to mount the candle vertically on a board wall, using any of the objects he sees before him.

An interesting postscript is provided by S. Glucksberg, who used the same candle problem but blindfolded his subjects under certain conditions. He found that the blindfolded subjects were more likely to solve the problem, and to do so faster, than subjects who could see the objects in front of them. That is, people did better when they felt the objects without looking at them than when they could see them too. This seemingly odd finding is perhaps due to the fact that visual recognition works quickly, through nouns—it is a container—while recognition by touch works more slowly, through adjectives—it is broken. The first thing we do with things we see is usually to name them; thereafter, we tend to stop looking at the object itself and work only with the label. Recognizing an object by feeling it usually takes longer and begins with an investigation of its physical properties. In doing the candle problem, it is an advantage to have had one's attention drawn to the shape, size, and solidity of the box rather than immediately to have labeled it "box of candles."

NEW PROBLEMS, NEW METHODS

When Archimedes sat in his bath, thus displacing a considerable portion of his own weight in water onto whatever passed for a carpet in those days, a new system of thought was born. A seemingly trivial event took on a completely new meaning.

Psychologists know very little about what goes into the recognition and solution of problems that represent a break with existing frameworks of thought. A student who uses a theorem to solve a mathematical problem probably follows a very different procedure from the one gone through by the mathematician who formulated the theorem. The mathematician *invented* a system of thinking; the student merely *uses* it.

The chapter thus far has discussed types of thinking that can be called *programmatic.* They involve the use of systems rather than the invention of them. Logical

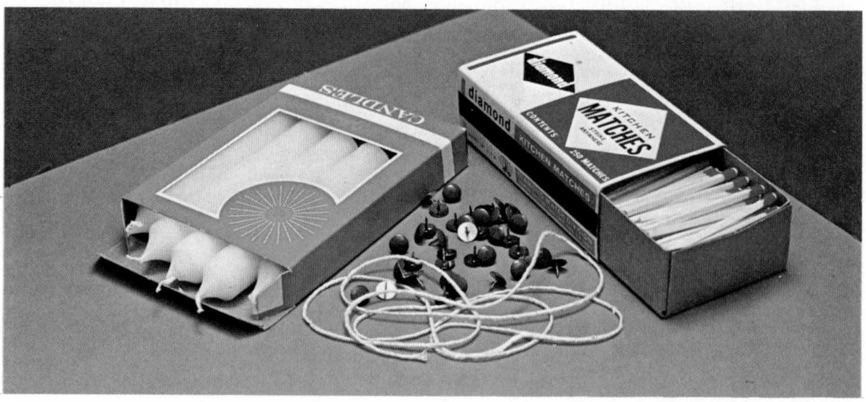

Figure 11.10.
Dunker's classic candle problem, first formulated in 1945, illustrates how difficult it is to use familiar materials in new ways (functional fixedness). The materials pictured here are presented to subjects, who are asked to mount the candles vertically on a wooden wall. Presenting the candles and matches in their boxes makes the task difficult to solve because it emphasizes the function of the boxes as containers. Inclusion of materials unnecessary to successful solution, such as the string, adds to the difficulty.

thinking, for example, relies on already established conventions and rules. So does the exercise of the methods and strategies employed to solve anagrams and series problems. This type of thinking, which can be simulated with some success on a computer, should be contrasted with *generative* thinking—the creation of partially or completely new systems of thought.

Creativity and Originality

Psychologists have devoted considerable attention to creativity, but they still have no very clear idea either of what it is or of how to measure it. Some psychologists attempt to define creative thinking by turning to studies of *Einstellung* and functional fixedness. They point out that some people are more prone to rigidity of thought than others, and they suggest that flexibility and originality go together.

This line of argument has led to the development of creativity tests composed of questions intended to measure flexibility, such as "How many uses can you find for a bicycle tire?" Although large-scale studies claim to show that such tests require a different set of abilities from those required by intelligence tests (see Figure 11.11), many psychologists are dubious about the validity of the claim. They are not convinced that creativity tests and IQ tests really do call for separate skills; in fact, they question whether creativity tests actually measure anything akin to creative thinking at all.

Some laboratory studies of creativity, including one by A. W. Staats, are also based on the idea that it is closely related to flexibility. They focus on people's

1. The words in the box below are arranged in a logical order. Select the word that belongs where the question mark appears.

composer	listener	?
author	reader	story

(a) orchestra (b) painter (c) song (d) novel

2. Which of the following does not belong in the series?

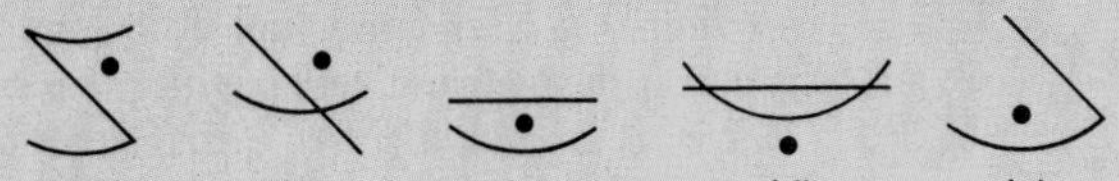

(a) (b) (c) (d) (e)

3. Which of the following does not belong in the series?

(a) (b) (c) (d) (e)

4. Circle is to semicircle as diameter is to
(a) hypotenuse (b) radius (c) square (d) triangle

5. If you have $100 in the bank for two years and the bank pays 6 percent interest per year (computed once annually), how much will you have at the end of two years?
(a) $136.00 (b) $106.36 (c) $112.36 (d) $116.36 (e) none of these

6.

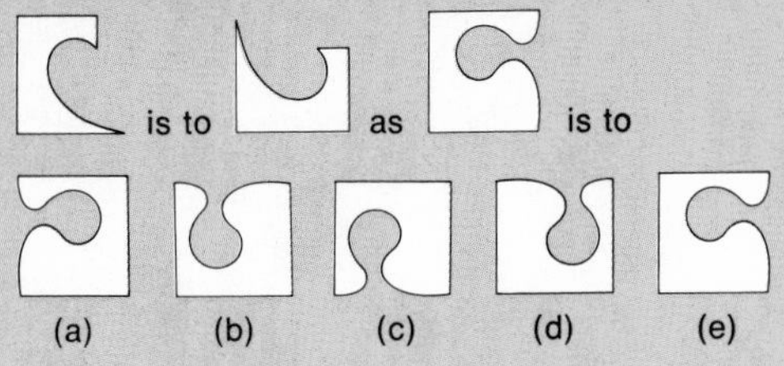

Figure 11.11
Items of the type used in intelligence tests administered to groups. Questions involving analogies, arithmetic reasoning, and spatial reasoning are thought to tap abstract cognitive abilities.

1. stool powder ball
2. blue cake cottage
3. man wheel high
4. motion poke down
5. line birthday surprise
6. wood liquor luck
7. house village golf
8. card knee rope
9. news doll tiger
10. painting bowl nail
11. weight wave house
12. made cuff left
13. key wall precious
14. bull tired hot
15. knife up hi
16. handle hole police
17. plan show walker
18. hop side pet
19. bell tender iron
20. spelling line busy

Figure 11.12
Mednich's Remote Association Test is considered to be one operationally definable method of measuring creativity. To name a single word that the three superficially unrelated words have in common is thought to require cognitive flexibility and originality. Try your hand at it. The answers appear on page 204.

capacities to make *remote associations* between various words and ideas, on the assumption that this capacity plays an important part in original thinking. A typical experiment of this type might use a functional-fixedness set-up like the one for the candle problem, and a typical finding might be that a subject who makes remote associations is less susceptible to functional fixedness than one who does not. A person is more likely to solve the candle problem if he thinks, for example, "Box of candles . . . wooden . . . board" than if he thinks "Box of candles . . . box . . . container." Unfortunately, the contribution of studies of remote associations to an understanding of creative thinking seems itself rather remote.

Following a different approach, E. De Bono differentiates between "vertical" and "lateral" thinking. The former he considers roughly equivalent to what we have called system using; the latter is similar to system inventing, or generative thinking. De Bono has devised various problems that, he claims, call for lateral thinking. An example is shown in Figure 11.13. He argues that education as it is usually practiced stresses vertical thinking but leaves lateral abilities largely untapped and undeveloped. To encourage it, he suggests deliberately ignoring the usual perceptual features of a situation and the usual ways of handling and thinking about these features; he suggests paying attention to the familiar and less obvious features instead.

Most psychologists would agree that the work on creativity, though sometimes provocative, is far from conclusive. It is possible, indeed, that creativity is not amenable to study by means of the research techniques used to study problem solving. For one thing, it is difficult to prove that one solution is more creative than another. Except in extreme cases, people tend to disagree. Another shortcoming of problem-solving techniques is that they require an experimenter to present to his subjects an already-formulated problem, even though the *recognition* of a new problem is probably at least as important a part of creative thought as finding a *solution* to it. It is said that the philosopher Gertrude Stein, asked just before she died to pass on to her friends something of what she had learned in a lifetime of

Figure 11.13
A problem described by De Bono, the solution of which requires lateral thinking. After trying your lateral-thinking abilities, check your answer with that on page 204.
(After De Bono, 1968.)

intellectual inquiry, brushed off the question, "What is the answer?" by asking another: "What is the question?"

The final and perhaps most important difficulty in using traditional techniques to study creativity is the very short duration and narrow focus of most psychological studies. They usually take but an instant in the subject's life span and investigate only a tiny fragment of his experience. Anyone who has done research on problem solving knows all too well how little the relevant factors depend on what happens in the laboratory and how much they depend on what happens outside, beyond scrutiny and control. This issue is related to the work of Piaget, Bruner, and others, who see human intellectual functioning as a deep interaction, on a number of levels, between the person and the environment.

Actions and Images

According to Piaget, as explained in Chapters 5 and 6, the first stage of intellectual development is the sensorimotor period, during which the child "knows" only that with which he interacts directly; later, he passes through the preoperational and concrete-operational periods. His ability to handle abstractions during the final stage, formal operations, grows out of those earlier ways of knowing the world.

Research by Bruner and H. J. Kenney on ways of teaching mathematical formulas to children shows that their understanding of abstractions is considerably enhanced if it is based on concrete operations. By rote, a ten-year-old child can memorize an abstract formula, such as the quadratic function $(x + 1)^2 = x^2 + 2x + 1$; after he has memorized it, the child can learn to expand it correctly for various values of x. But Bruner and Kenney found that children's understanding of the formula, as measured by their ability to apply the concepts it involves to different kinds of problems, was much greater if they learned the formula by working with concrete objects—the pieces of plywood shown in Figure 11.14—than it was if they merely memorized it.

This finding suggests that in adapting a method for application to various situations a person may rely on concrete experiences that are related to the abstract method in question. When a person faces a new problem that differs from the ones he has previously solved with the method, he may need to go back to the level of concrete experience in order to reassemble the components of what he knows in a way that suits the new problem.

Something similar may be involved in innovative thinking. If a child's understanding of an abstract formula, as indicated by his ability to apply its components to new problems, requires a base of concrete experiences concerning the use of the formula, perhaps new ideas and new insights are also built up from concrete personal experience. If so, creative thinking involves more than the manipulation of words and other abstract symbols, and laboratory experiments that test people's handling of sophisticated intellectual problems may miss the mark. Understanding what goes into the recognition of new problems and the development of new systems of thought may require a much broader study of the experiences of creative people.

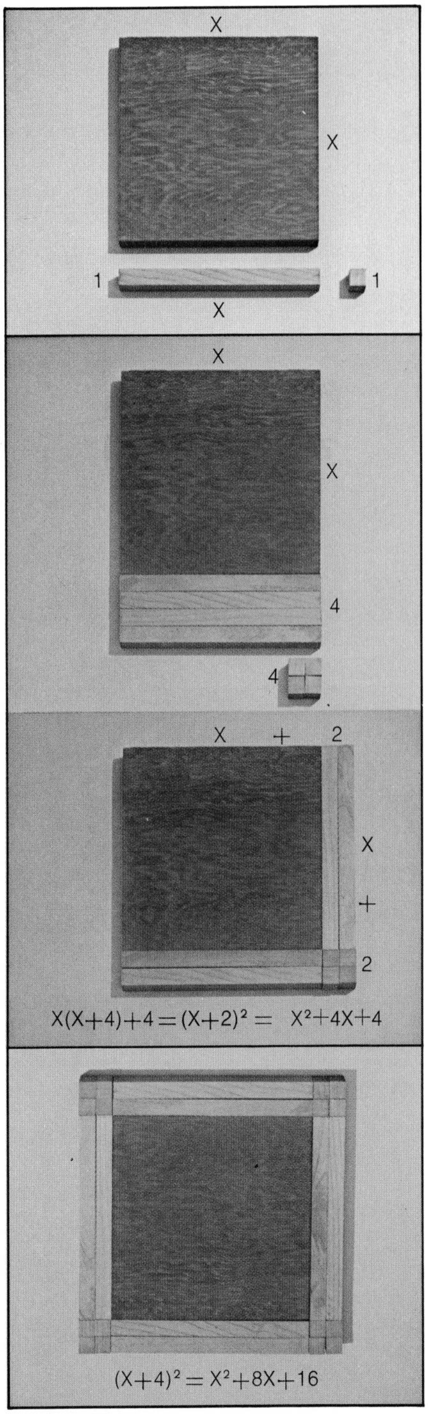

Figure 11.14
(Top) the elements constructed by Bruner and Kenney to teach quadratic equations. (Middle) two of the possible ways of "arranging" or factoring the units to show $(x+2)^2 = x^2 + 4x + 4$. (Bottom) when the child has constructed a square with sides of $x + 4$ units, he can easily see that $(x + 4) \times (x + 4) = x^2 + 8x + 16$.

INDIVIDUAL DIFFERENCES

Some people are good with their hands and can solve all manner of practical problems. Others are much more at home in an armchair and, rather like Sherlock Holmes in one of his more sedentary moods, excel at pure logical deductions. Some people solve problems in laboratories, others in libraries. Some are good at paper-and-pencil tasks, others much better in face-to-face confrontations.

Problems, as we said at the outset, take many forms, and they demand a variety of special skills. If one person has the information and skills that are relevant to a problem and another does not, it is safe to assume that the first person is more likely to solve the problem. Differences in general experience and specific training

—and consequently differences in age—account for many individual differences in problem-solving skill.

Over and above experience and skill, however, there seems to be a more general ability that makes it easier for some people than for others to organize their knowledge and apply it to new problems. Experiments by B. S. Bloom and L. J. Broder, among others, have shown that people who are given the same information and the same training still differ markedly in their ability to apply their skills in new situations. Some work with intelligence tests also suggests the existence of a basic *general intellectual factor* that makes some people better at solving problems than others, but the evidence is not at all conclusive.

Another important reason for individual differences in problem solving is motivation and interest. Everyday observation suggests that people do better at problem solving when they are highly motivated. However, the situation is not quite as simple as that statement makes it appear. For one thing, a highly motivated person may do better at solving a problem than he would have if he were not interested in it but worse than another person whose motivation is lower; for another, high motivation can be accompanied by anxiety, which has a detrimental effect on solving some kinds of problems. A. S. Luchins found that rigidity tended to increase when his subjects were anxious, and functional fixedness is usually more extreme when people are very strongly motivated by the promise of high rewards for success.

The nature and strength of various motives may well account for the differences,

The salient concept is yellow triangle with a border.

Answers to Creativity Test, page 202

1. foot
2. cheese
3. chair
4. slow
5. party
6. hard
7. green
8. trick
9. paper
10. finger
11. light
12. hand
13. stone
14. dog
15. jack
16. man
17. floor
18. car
19. bar
20. bee

Answers to IQ Test, page 201

1. (c)	2. (a)	3. (d)
4. (b)	5. (c)	6. (d)

At some point you have to have the 4 smallest coins stacked on C so you can put the half-dollar on the bottom on B. Then stack the 3 smallest on A so you can put the quarter on the half-dollar on B. A good way to start is to put the dime on A, the penny on the half-dollar on B, the dime on the penny on B, the nickel on A . . . (After Gagné and Smith, 1962.)

Yes: the puzzle "before/after" is this one. (After Restle and Davis, 1962).

Solutions to Anagrams, page 197

List A	*List B*	*List C*
enjoy	linen	lemon
snack	river	apple
swamp	train	banana
fudge	stage	lime
foggy	write	strawberry

found in numerous studies, in the problem-solving performance of men and women. Men generally solve some kinds of problems better than women, and women, on the average, do better than men on other kinds of problems. (One representative problem is shown here, in Figure 11.16.) One reason for the differences may be that men have more experience than women with the operations necessary for solving certain types of problems. Even more important may be differences in the attitudes of men and women toward achievement and success. The influence of social pressures on these attitudes is discussed in Chapters 19 and 25.

Figure 11.16
Sex differences have been found in problem-solving skills. As the American cultural stereotype would suggest, men typically are superior in mechanical comprehension and object-assembly tests; one type of problem that women do better than men, on the average, is shown here. Given these two drawings, people are asked to judge which is aesthetically superior. More women than men say that the bottom one is better art. Such findings do not argue for an *innate* superiority for either sex's problem-solving or intellectual abilities on these tests. People like to do what they do well, and they do well at what they have been rewarded for doing in the past—usually interests consistent with their society's definition of proper male and female roles.

PROBLEMS . . . PROBLEMS . . . PROBLEMS

Man seems to be the only member of the animal kingdom who continually invents new problems for himself. Most species face the same problems generation after generation—finding enough food and water, a mate, and an environment that will support offspring. These problems change only with changes in environmental conditions, such as alterations in ecological balances (brought about, usually, by agents other than the species itself). Only man has invented special tools and developed technologies; only man operates deliberately, consciously, and with (some) forethought to change his own environment in drastic ways. We seem continually to bring about situations that we cannot immediately handle—to create new problems—and then we attempt to devise technologies, mental and physical, that will help us cope with them.

We know a good deal about the way people solve established problems but very little about the way they define and solve new ones. Studying the formulation of new problems and the development of new methods would be easier if we had a clearer idea of how new what looks new really is—if we understood the extent to which man uses the same abilities and processes, throughout his lifetime and generation after generation, to identify and solve his ever-changing problems. What did the men who discovered fire and developed the wheel have in common with Archimedes, Newton, and Einstein? How does finding your way through a forest compare with finding a bargain at a store?

It's a problem.

SUGGESTED READINGS

BRUNER, J. S., OLVER, R. R., AND GREENFIELD, P. M. *Studies in Cognitive Growth.* New York, Wiley, 1966. The influence of the different methods of problem representation—in action, image, and symbol—on the problem-solving process are examined in various experimental situations.

DUNCAN, C. P. *Thinking: Modern Experimental Studies.* Philadelphia, Lippincott, 1969. Collected readings with a strong methodological bias. Six sections on problem-solving research and six on studies of concept attainment.

SIMON, H. A., AND NEWELL, A. "Human Problem Solving: The State of the Theory in 1970," *American Psychologist,* Vol. 26, No. 2, February, 1971. A good, readable statement of the authors' current thoughts on problem-solving research. Includes reference to, and evaluation of, their earlier works, and is therefore a good starting point for anyone interested in detailed study of computer application to the study of heuristic problem solving.

WASON, P. E., AND JOHNSON-LAIRD, P. N. (Eds.). *Thinking and Reasoning.* Baltimore, Penguin Modern Psychology Series, 1968. A good collection of articles covering a range of topics in the field of human intellectual functioning. In addition to a section on problem solving, there are articles dealing with logical thought, which discuss in readable terms computer simulation and information processing. Other sections cover intellectual development and conceptual thinking.

UNIT IV
The Sensory World

All behaviors that people engage in—learning, speaking, problem solving, social interaction—take place in an environment, a world. Light impinges on our eyes, and somehow we see objects in three-dimensional space rather than light rays. Air vibrations stimulate our ears, and somehow we hear voices, car engines, and birds calling. Vapors enter our noses, and somehow we smell apple pie or flowers or cow manure. To have a full understanding of human behavior, we have to understand how our sense organs function to bring the

Chapter 12, Sensation and Psychophysics, discusses the branch of experimental psychology founded in the nineteenth century by men like E. Weber, G. Fechner, and W. Wundt. Psychophysics studies the relationship between sensory experiences and the characteristics of the stimuli that produce those experiences.

Chapter 13, The Senses, describes the neurological and anatomical structure of each of the sense organs and the basic characteristics of each sense: vision, hearing, smell, taste, touch, the vestibular sense, and kinesthesis.

5

The Development of Intelligence analyzes the relationship between perception and cognitive development in the infant, a topic directly related to much of Chapter 14.

9

Information Processing presents the information-processing approach to the study of perception and cognition. Its viewpoint can be contrasted with each of the four approaches presented in this unit.

10

Learning and Memory discusses how sensory information is selected, organized, and stored, and so relates to Chapters 13, 14, and 15.

11

Problem Solving includes discussion of aids and hindrances to problem solving—like Einstellung, set, and functional fixedness, which describe certain kinds of cognitive organization that affect perception. Chapter 14 includes discussion of types of perceptual organization that affect cognition (as with illusions), although the line between perception and cognition in many cases is difficult to draw.

16

The Biological Organism elaborates upon the description of the neurological basis of perception in Chapter 13; in particular, it discusses the role of brain function in perception. Chapter 16's explication of brain structure and function is closely related to much material in Chapter 15, especially brain functioning in states like dreaming and hypnosis, or after brain surgery.

17

Emotion discusses the role of visceral cues in arousal of emotion and how the *conscious* experience of emotion seems to depend on a combination of physiological, perceptual, and cognitive factors. Chapter 15's discussion of the nature of consciousness relates strongly to these topics.

world to us and how we use the information from those organs to perceive the world around us.

The process of perception is complex, involving physical stimuli impinging on the person, reactions of sense organs to those stimuli, interpretation by the brain of the information from the sense organs, and conscious experience on the part of the perceiver. Because of this complexity, psychologists have developed several different approaches to perception—each emphasizing a different aspect of the process.

Chapter 14, Perception, discusses how people use patterns of physical stimuli to perceive the properties of objects and space.

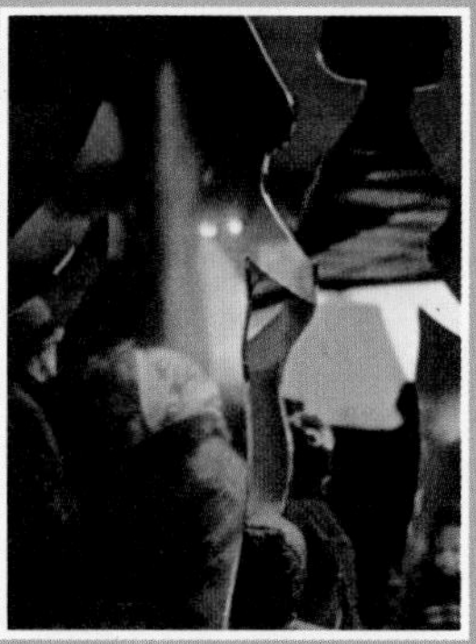

Chapter 15, Consciousness and Awareness, examines the nature of consciousness and recent important research breakthroughs that permit its study. The concepts of sensation and perception imply the existence of a conscious, experiencing mind. In this chapter the study of perception merges with the study of cognition, or knowing.

34

Drugs and Drug Therapy explains the changes in consciousness that are caused by certain drugs; these effects are also discussed in Chapter 15 in relation to marijuana and LSD.

30

Adjustment and Disorder describes the alterations in perception, cognition, and consciousness that accompany various kinds of mental disorder—an addition to the discussion of altered states of consciousness in Chapter 15.

21

Freudian Theories of Personality discusses the importance of dream content as an indication of the activity of the unconscious; Chapter 15 offers results of several studies of sleep and dreams.

22

Other Theories of Personality examines Gestalt therapy, which is based on the Gestalt principles of perception discussed at length in Chapter 14.

23

Impression Formation looks at how a person's expectations about certain people or groups of people affect his perception of those people. This effect is a social counterpart of phenomena like perceptual set, discussed in Chapter 14.

12 Sensation and Psychophysics

THERE ARE CERTAIN STATEMENTS of belief that are often called "folk wisdom" for no other reason than that they originate out of the unsophisticated observation of the world by people of limited experience. In almost every case they might be considered "folk stupidity" and laughed at if it weren't that so many tragic consequences have followed from what everyone "knew" was true, but wasn't. How many unfounded accusations have ruined lives and precipitated riots because "Where there's smoke there's fire"? Dry Ice in water produces fascinating smoke without fire. And would we ever be exploring the Moon if it were really true that "Everything that goes up must come down"?

But to me the most pernicious piece of "folk wisdom" is the one about "Seeing is believing," when it is phenomenally easy to fool the eye. In the Greek myth Narcissus drowned himself because the beautiful young man he saw in the water wasn't really there.

The trouble is that very early in life we learn that light travels in straight lines. Very young children reach for something by following rays of light backward in a straight line, and very often they succeed in making physical contact with what they have seen. We never break the habit of interpreting all light as a straight-line phenomenon, even though light travels in a straight line only under restricted conditions. If we place a stick in water, light from that portion of the stick below the water level is refracted as it passes from water to air. The straight stick seems bent at the water level and no matter how much our intelligence tells us that it is not the stick that is bent but the rays of light, what we *see* is that the stick is bent. We cannot argue ourselves out of that.

Our inability to appreciate the vagaries of light are at the base of a large proportion of our mystical beliefs. Ghosts and spirits are born in a world in which there is no artificial illumination other than the flickering of an open flame. Why has the ghost story lost its earlier popularity? Because the steady, dim shadows cast by a frosted light bulb are nothing like the shifting, mysterious shadows cast by unsteady flames. Ghosts can't survive steady light.

And what about those modern ghosts called "flying saucers"? Where the report is not an outright hoax, it is a matter of some sort of light being seen in the sky; and I suspect that in very many cases it is a matter of light refraction. A light ray curves through air in layers of varying temperature and density, so that you see a light in a place it should not be because your eye and mind won't follow the curve but insist on moving along a straight line tangent to the curve at the point where it enters the eye. Distant lights of a city or a line of automobile headlights will therefore appear in the sky.

But always, the cry of "Seeing is believing" goes up. I'm afraid not. As far as I'm concerned, the proper wisdom is "Seeing is merely seeing, nothing more." Belief requires a lot more than the complicated trickery of a light wave. I. A.

Most of us assume that our senses mirror the external world exactly. We imagine that our sensory systems send copies—images or pictures—of the external world over pathways of nerves to some sort of central switchboard, where they are displayed on a screen of consciousness that reflects the ebb and flow of our awareness of the world. But this is not a sufficient explanation of how we perceive the things around us.

For one thing, we can see without our eyes' receiving light. If you close your eyes and press on them, you will see a purplish light flash. Where does this flash come from? Your visual system and your brain have been tricked, in a sense, for a visual experience has been created without actual light stimulation. Usually the retina of the eye responds to light energy from the external world and generates neural impulses that are transmitted along optic nerve fibers toward the brain. But the retina can be made to fire impulses by other means, including not only pressure on the eyeballs but electrical stimulation applied to the eye. As a matter of fact, even the eye and the retina are not required to produce visual experiences. If electrodes are applied to the visual receiving area of the brain and electrical impulses sent through them, experiences resembling light flashes occur.

We do *not* always see with our eyes. We can sometimes have visual experiences without using our eyes, auditory experiences without using our ears, and so on. Visual experience is a brain process determined by which cells in the brain are activated. In ordinary experience, the process is usually set in motion when the senses respond to some external occurrence in the world, but external stimuli are not necessary. We have rich and complex visual experiences when we dream, for example. Sometimes, too, people hallucinate—they see things that are not there.

The common comparison of our eyes to a camera, although useful in some ways, is misleading. The retina does not really work like the film in a camera. Although we speak of an "image" as being "formed" on the retina, it is more accurate to say that a set of receptor cells is excited and sends impulses to the brain.

Understanding that vision is not a direct registration of some sort of copy of the world but a pattern of electrical events in the brain frees us from certain troublesome questions that may otherwise arise. For example, a person who takes the idea of a retinal image literally is likely to be bothered by the fact that an image is turned upside-down when it passes through a lens. How do we experience the world right-side-up if the image projected on the retina is upside-down? Because what is transmitted to the brain is not an image but a *pattern of excitation* of certain nerve cells, however, it does not really matter how the pattern is coded—upside-down, sequentially in time, or whatever—as long as it is consistent. What determines our experience is basically the *brain process,* not an image.

Another reason it is incorrect to think of the senses as simply mirroring the world is that our receptor cells do not respond to *all* the external world. A primary function of our sensory systems is to respond selectively to stimuli, transmitting some information about the world to the brain but disregarding a great deal. The way sensory selectivity works can be illustrated by considering a lower organism—the frog—whose visual system throws away much more information than ours does. The frog's eyes transmit only a limited amount of information about the visual world to its brain. J. Y. Lettvin and his associates inserted microelectrodes into the optic nerve of the frog and then recorded the activity in different portions of the optic nerve when different stimuli are shown to the frog. They found that the frog's eyes respond to only four kinds of stimulation. (See Figure 12.2.) One type of fiber within the optic nerve transmits light and dark contrast, perhaps a sketchy outline of the frog's visual world. A second type of nerve fiber responds to a moving edge of light or shadow. A third type is activated by sudden reductions in illumination; perhaps this fiber is part of a "bird-of-prey" response system. The fourth type of nerve fiber responds only when a small, black object in constant motion appears

Figure 12.1
Our sensory systems do not transmit copies of the external world to a waiting audience inside our heads. The usual analogy between the retina of the eye and the camera is misleading. Only the principles of physics related to the sensory reception of light energy are appropriately applicable. But the information from sensory systems is received, transmitted, encoded, and interpreted in the higher centers of the brain in ways that are not yet fully understood. It is a neural-chemical-electrical process in the brain, and not "images" as such, that constitutes our visual perception of the world.

Figure 12.2
The frog's visual system is "tuned in" to only four kinds of stimulation, as represented in this illustration. From left to right, they are: light and dark contrast; a moving edge of light or dark; a sudden reduction in illumination; and the constant movement of a small black object. Organisms have only a limited amount of "neurological space" available, and a visual system like the frog's processes just the data important for survival (for example, "There's a bug!").

in the frog's field of vision: a bug-perceiving system. Although the frog's visual system discards more information than ours, ours too transmits only a limited amount of information to the brain.

A third way our sensory impressions differ from mental mirrors is that our experience of the world depends on much more than what is really physically there. Motivations, needs, and expectations strongly influence sensory experience. When we are hungry, for example, we tend to notice restaurants or the smells of food we might usually ignore. To do this, we must be able to "tune" our sensory systems to receive different kinds of information, depending on our intention. This ability can be easily demonstrated at a party. First, pick out one person's voice and listen to him, then tune him out and listen to someone else. You can tune in or out whenever you wish.

Figure 12.3
Turn the page and quickly count how many aces of spades there are in Figure 12.6. Do not read the caption for Figure 12.6 until you have finished your count.

A number of psychologists have done experiments that indicate we tend to see what we expect to see. In one such experiment, J. Bruner took a deck of playing cards and turned them over one by one, asking people to name them. In the usual deck of cards, clubs and spades are black and hearts and diamonds are red. In Bruner's deck, however, there were such anomalous cards as a red ace of spades. When these cards were turned over, people often identified them incorrectly; the red spade, for instance, was often called an ace of hearts. Bruner called this phenomenon *perceptual readiness,* indicating that we often perceive only what we are ready to perceive.

What we experience depends on an *interaction* between ourselves and the environment. Many patterns of stimulation are ambiguous. A circle, for example, may be registered many different ways on the retina, as shown in Figure 12.4. Given such ambiguity in sensory input, we usually make a calculated guess as to the nature of the object. These guesses are discussed at length in Chapter 14.

Now that we have established that the senses do not mirror the external world exactly and that conscious experience is to a large extent determined by which brain cells are activated, we are prepared to investigate the psychology of sensation. It begins with a little physics.

THE PHYSICAL CHARACTERISTICS OF STIMULI

Because information about the environment reaches the brain via sensory receptors and neural pathways rather than directly, psychologists distinguish between the

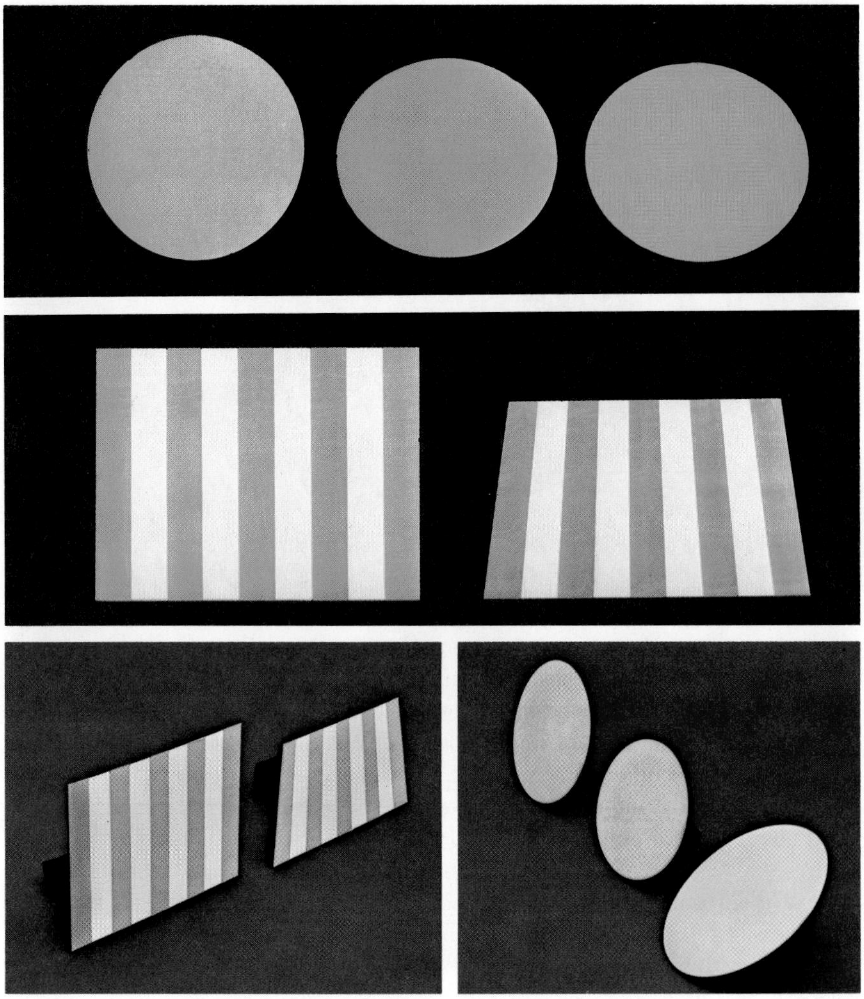

Figure 12.4
Visual cues and perception. Often, environmental stimuli give us ambiguous clues. Look at the top photograph and try to determine the actual stimuli that give rise to the sensation of a circle and two ellipses, identical except for color. Now, by carefully studying the photograph at the lower right, it is easier to see that the shapes are: on the left, a circle straight-on; in the center, an ellipse with its *major* axis equal to the diameter of the circle, straight-on; and on the right, an ellipse with its *minor* axis equal to the diameter of the circle, tipped back. In the middle figure, is the shape on the right a trapezoid or a rectangle tipped back? Check your assumption against the evidence presented in the figure at the lower left.

characteristics of *physical stimuli* such as light and sound and the *sensations* that they give rise to. The word *stimulus* refers to the physical and objective; the word *sensation*, to the perceptual and subjective. Obviously, the two are closely related—normally, a sensation arises when some minimal quantity of physical energy activates a receptor organ such as the eye or ear—but they are not as closely related as one might expect, even for simple sensations.

Physicists have worked in optics and acoustics for hundreds of years, and a good deal is known about light and sound. As discussed in Chapter 13, much less is known about the stimuli in smell, touch, and taste, perhaps because these senses are less important in human life than seeing and hearing. Both light and sound can be described as waves of energy that reach the eye and the ear by traveling over distances. Both kinds of energy are subject to absorption, reflection, and diffraction by objects in their paths.

Light and sound differ in fundamental ways, however. Light, which consists of packets of energy called photons, is electromagnetic radiation. It affects the visual system by causing photochemical changes in the cells of the retina. Sound, on the other hand, is a mechanical movement of (usually) air particles. It affects the auditory system mechanically, by setting up vibrations in the bones of the middle ear.

Light

Because light is a form of radiant energy, we are able to see only when some source of radiant energy is available—either the energy source itself or surfaces that reflect

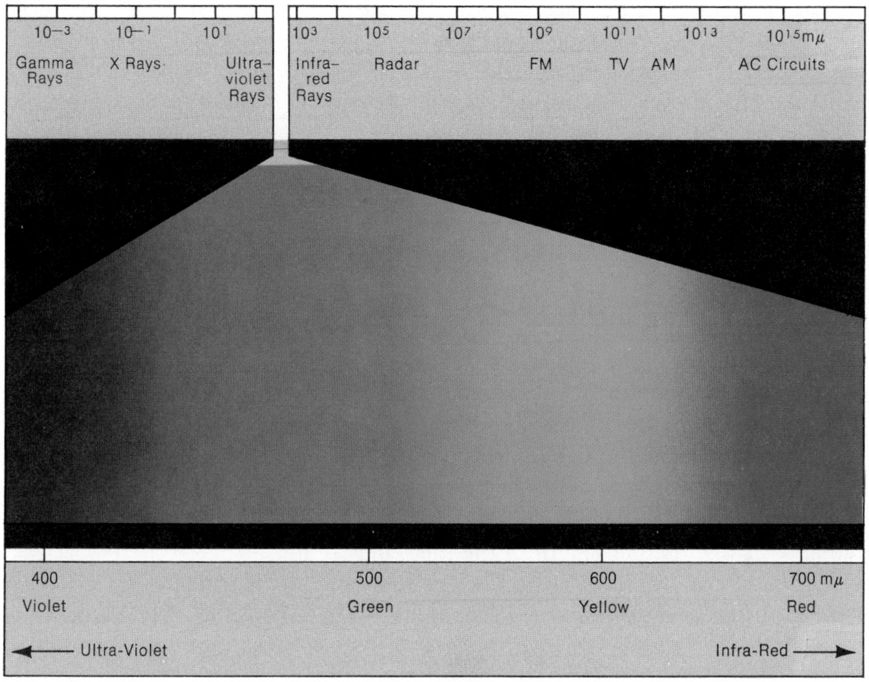

Figure 12.5

This chart shows the electromagnetic spectrum of radiant energy, and the tiny portion of it to which our eyes are sensitive. The scale is logarithmic because the range of wavelengths in the whole spectrum is so huge. Wavelengths are measured in units called millimicrons, which are millionths of millimeters. Our eyes respond differently to different wavelengths within the visible spectrum; we experience this difference as color. When large amounts of all visible wavelengths are present, we see white.

its radiations. During the day, the primary source outdoors is the sun, but secondary sources do exist, such as the particles in the atmosphere that reflect the sun's light. At night we rely on electric lights and other artificial sources or, sometimes, on that large reflecting particle, the moon.

If you ask a physicist what light is, he will say that it is a narrow band of the electromagnetic spectrum, which itself is extremely broad and includes not only light rays but cosmic rays, gamma rays, x-rays, ultraviolet rays, infrared rays, and radio waves. The wavelengths in the electromagnetic spectrum range from 0.00000000000001 to 1,000,000 meters. In other words, the longest wavelength in the radio portion of the spectrum is about 100 million million million times longer than wavelengths in the cosmic-ray portion of the spectrum. Light rays, which are the only visible portion of the spectrum, are situated between the infrared rays and the ultraviolet rays. The longest wavelengths to which our eyes are sensitive (which we see as red) are only about twice as long as the shortest visible wavelengths (which we see as blue or violet). A representation of the electromagnetic spectrum is shown in Figure 12.5.

The two chief physical characteristics of light are *wavelength* and *intensity.* Wavelength determines the color of the light; intensity determines how bright it looks. The two together determine whether the light can be seen. For example, a purple light shown against a gray wall in a dark room must be somewhat more intense than a green light before it will become visible.

The amount of light present at a particular time is usually specified by measuring either *luminance* or *illuminance.* Luminance is the amount of light emitted by a source (such as a light bulb). Illuminance is the amount of light that falls on a surface or object. Both measures are made in terms of the amount of light energy per second.

Figure 12.6

An example of Bruner's playing cards. Many people who are asked to count the number of aces of spades fail to include those printed in red. Because they have previously learned which colors are "supposed" to go with which suits, their perception is tuned to "spades are black," so they exclude spade-shaped forms that are red. Bruner calls this phenomenon "perceptual readiness."

Sound

Sound is motion. The source of the motion is usually a solid body—a vibrating string or vocal cord, the impact of shoes on a floor, the turning of a fan. The vibrating body impresses a regular motion on surrounding air particles, first pressing out against them and then releasing the pressure, creating a *sound wave.* As the wave moves, other particles of air are set vibrating. The particles move back and forth around an average resting place; they do not advance with the wave. For that reason, a sound wave requires a medium such as air, which contains particles that can be set in motion. In a vacuum, there are no sounds.

The chief physical characteristics of sound waves are *frequency* and *amplitude* (also called *sound pressure*). The form of a sound wave is shown in Figure 12.8. As the drawing indicates, frequency refers to the number of cycles a wave goes through in a given period of time. Amplitude refers to the amount of mechanical pressure that a wave exerts, as represented by the distance of its peaks and valleys from the zero base line in Figure 12.8. The higher its high and the lower its low, the more pressure the wave exerts on the surrounding air particles.

Frequency largely determines the pitch of a tone, and amplitude largely determines its loudness. The higher the frequency, the higher the tone sounds to a listener; the greater the amplitude (sound pressure), the louder the tone sounds. These relationships are complex, however, for frequency and amplitude are *physical* characteristics of sound waves whereas pitch and loudness are *psychological* dimensions. For example, a tone with a slightly higher amplitude but lower frequency than another may sound no louder. The relationship between physical characteristics and sensation is discussed at length in the following section.

Frequency is measured in *cycles per second* (CPS). Human beings can hear frequencies ranging from about 20 to 20,000 cycles per second. The lowest note

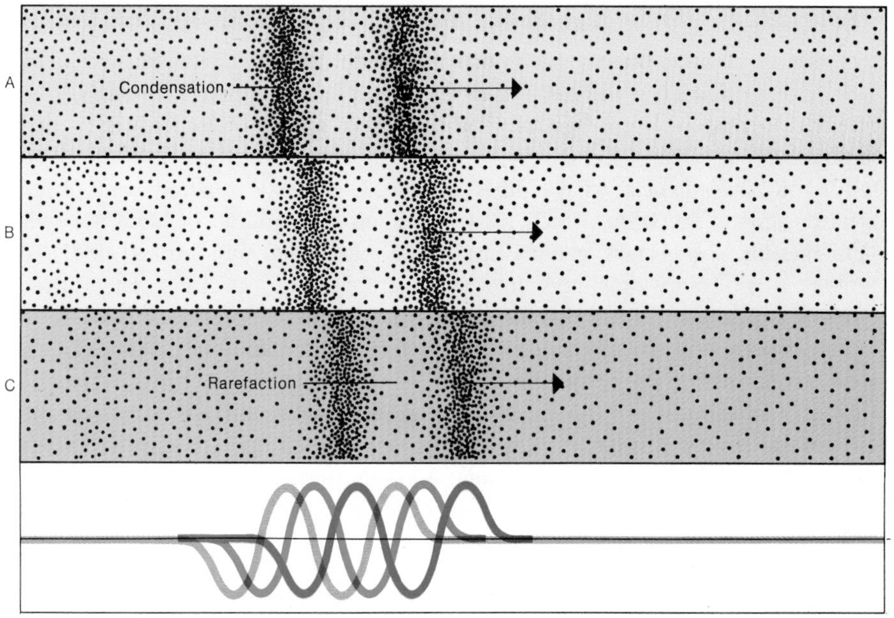

Figure 12.7

A vibrating body, such as a guitar string, moves back and forth extremely rapidly, alternately compressing and rarefying the air around it. The top part of this figure shows how these sequences of *condensations* (compressions) and *rarefactions,* which are called sound waves, are propagated through the air. A sound wave is usually represented as a curve, shown below. The high points in the curve correspond to areas of condensation; the low points correspond to areas of rarefaction. The colors of the areas of condensation and rarefaction in the upper figures correspond to the colors indicating the passage of the sound wave in the lower figure.

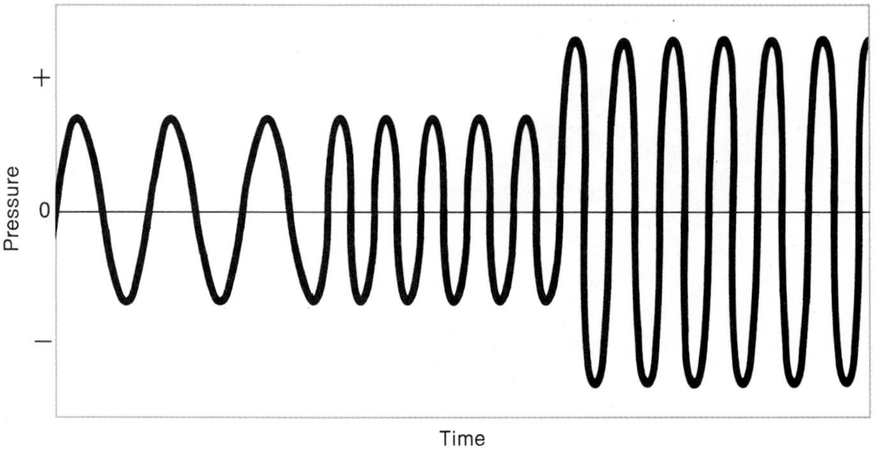

Figure 12.8

By observing the pattern of its sound wave, we can infer that the tone here was raised in pitch and then in loudness. The wave first increases in frequency and then in amplitude as well. The *period* of a sound wave is the time required for it to complete one full cycle from the zero point and return. During one period the distance it travels is called its *wavelength. Frequency,* the most common reference to sound, is expressed in units of cycles per second. The wave shown here is indicative of a pure tone sinusoidal, stimulus.

on a piano has a frequency of roughly 30 CPS, and the highest note has a frequency of about 5,000 CPS. Other animals—dogs, for example—can hear higher frequencies than we can.

Amplitude is usually expressed in *decibels*, a unit of measurement devised by scientists at the Bell Telephone Laboratories. (A decibel is one-tenth of a "bel," named for Alexander Graham Bell.) Because the range of amplitudes to which the ear is sensitive is so enormous, decibels are calculated according to a logarithmic formula. Zero decibels represents a sound with the lowest amplitude that the human ear can detect. The sounds around us range upward from there to about 140 decibels, which is roughly as loud as a jet plane at take-off. Sounds above about 120 decibels tend to be painful for human beings; sounds 35 or 40 decibels lower than that, at around the level of subways and heavy trucks, can cause hearing damage after prolonged exposure. Figure 12.9 gives the decibel levels of some common sounds.

The motion of the sound wave shown in Figure 12.8 is *sinusoidal;* that is, it is shaped like a sine curve. Sinusoidal waves are made by pure tones, which are largely the product of the laboratory. In nature, most sound waves are less regular. They can, however, be broken down into a number of sinusoidal components. Sounds composed of more than a single tone are called *complex* sounds.

A common and useful laboratory stimulus is *white noise*, an artificially produced sound that contains all the audible frequencies at randomly varying amplitudes. It sounds like a long *shhhh*, pronounced as in the word "shoe," or like the sound of a waterfall. It is called white noise because it is the sound equivalent of white light, which includes all the wavelengths in the visible spectrum.

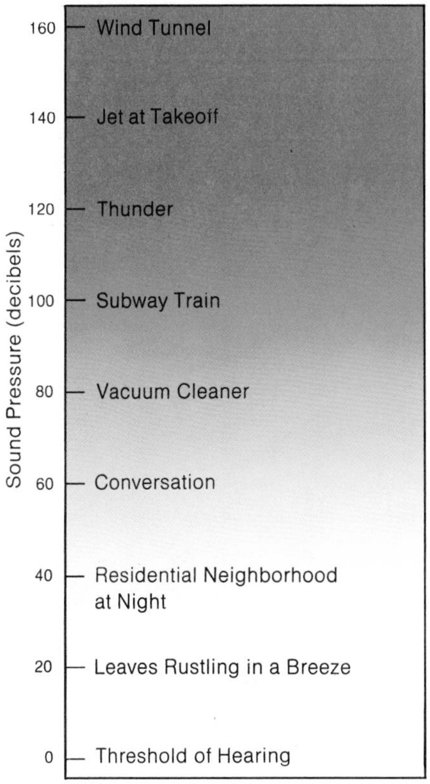

Figure 12.9
The auditory intensity in decibels of some common human experiences. Sounds above about 80 decibels are felt as unpleasant by most people. The specific level of sound at which pain is felt is a function of the intensity and frequency of sound waves as well as of individual differences among human beings.

THE ATTRIBUTES OF SENSATION

One reason psychologists and physiologists are so interested in investigating the ways in which the attributes of a sensation are related to the characteristics of a physical stimulus is that they want to know how information about the stimulus is coded in the nervous system. The goal of this research is to understand how a physical stimulus gives rise to nervous activity that in turn leads to predictable human responses. This information, in addition to its value as pure knowledge, would help in the development of techniques for treating injuries and diseases that involve the sensory system. It would also facilitate the building of machines, mainly computers, that can duplicate certain human functions.

We speak of stimuli as having *physical characteristics* but of sensations as having *attributes.* An attribute is defined as a quality that can be held constant while all other qualities of a sensation are varied. A simple sound, for example, has four attributes: *pitch* and *loudness,* which have been mentioned before, and also *volume* and *density.* Volume and density are difficult to describe in words. About the best that can be done is to say that volume refers to how large the sound seems to be and density to its compactness. Loudness, pitch, volume, and density are considered

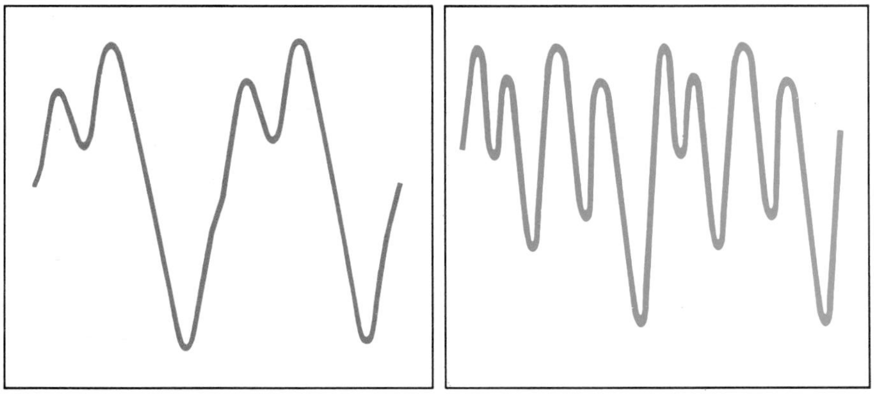

Figure 12.10
Complex sounds are those composed of more than a single pure tone. The wave forms shown here describe complex sounds. The wave on the left is a tone from a French horn; that on the right is the same tone from a trumpet. Compare these to the simple sinusoidal wave form that characterizes a pure tone in Figure 12.8.

the attributes of auditory sensations because, in the laboratory, any one of them can be held constant while the other three change. This is done by adjusting the frequency and amplitude of the physical stimulus. For example, if a listener increases the frequency of a tone, he can hold its loudness constant by simultaneously decreasing the sound pressure level. As he does this, however, the tone rises in pitch, its density increases, and its volume decreases. Similarly, a listener can adjust frequency and amplitude to produce a loud low tone and a soft high one with equal densities.

A sensory attribute, then, has what S. S. Stevens called *independent constancy*. Stevens found that the relationships among the four attributes of sounds are systematic, as shown by the isophonic (equal-sounding) contours in Figure 12.11. Along a given contour (say, pitch) subjects judge a tone to be equal in pitch despite wide variations in the physical dimensions (amplitude and frequency) and despite changes in the other three tonal attributes (loudness, volume, and density). Figure 12.11 demonstrates not only that the tonal attributes have independent constancy (each attribute is judged equal all along its isophonic contour) but that each attribute is a joint function of frequency and amplitude. For example, constant pitch depends primarily on frequency but also varies somewhat with intensity. As was mentioned earlier, there is no simple one-to-one relation between a characteristic of a physical stimulus such as frequency and an attribute of sensation such as pitch.

As E. G. Boring noted, the relations between the physical characteristics of light and visual sensations are similarly complex. For example, Boring showed that analogous isochromatic (equal-looking in color) contours could be constructed for the attributes of visual sensation (hue, brightness, and saturation) as a function of the physical dimensions of intensity and wavelength. Just as there is a correspondence between the physical dimensions of light and sound (intensity to pressure; wavelength to frequency) there is a suggestive correspondence between the psychological

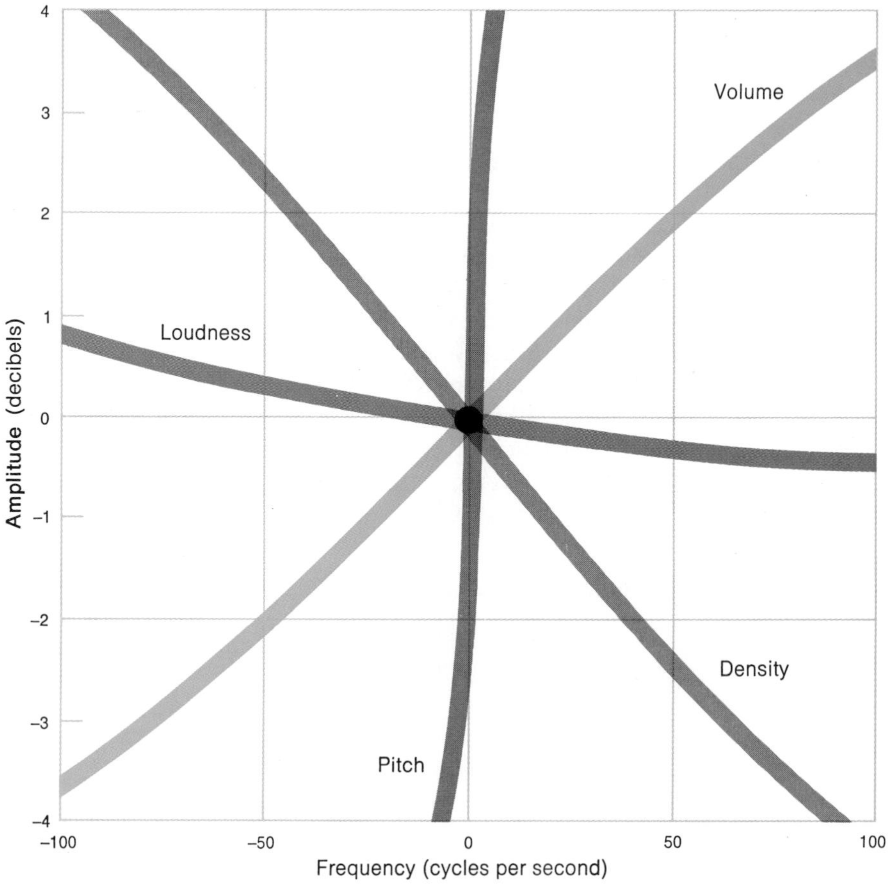

Figure 12.11
The circle in the center of this graph represents a standard tone of 500 cycles per second and 60 decibels. Subjects adjusted tones for the four attributes of sound shown here to match the standard tone. Each of the contours represents tones judged to be equal to each other and to the standard (they are isophonic). Also, each attribute is judged to be equal all along its isophonic contour (they have independent constancy).
(After Stevens, 1934.)

attributes of sensation. For example, hue and pitch seem intuitively related as attributes of quality. Similarly, brightness and loudness both seem to be quantitative attributes.

MEASUREMENT OF SENSATION

An early problem in the study of sensation, and one that psychologists are still working on, was finding ways to measure sensation—an internal, intangible event—in precise, quantitative ways. Most of the earliest approaches to the problem focused on identifying the smallest changes in a stimulus that caused a change in sensation. These were *psychophysical* approaches in the sense that they were concerned with the relation between the sensation (hence "psycho") and the stimulus (hence "physical"). The psychophysicists interested in measuring the relation between stimulus and sensation were mostly physiologists and physicists working in the mid-nineteenth century. They were forerunners of the first experimental psychology laboratory, founded by W. Wundt at Leipzig in 1879.

Figure 12.12
E. H. Weber. Weber's physiological training helped him to make important contributions to the area that became known as psychophysics. Weber's law is described in this chapter. Rigorously scientific, he also conducted classic studies on the psychophysiology of taste.

Weber's Law

Based on experiments performed by the physiologist E. H. Weber in 1834, Weber's law (described by A. H. Holway and C. C. Pratt) states that a just-noticeable difference (change) in a stimulus is a constant proportion of the stimulus. The law is expressed by the formula $\Delta S = kS$, where $S =$ stimulus, $\Delta S =$ just-noticeable difference, and k is a constant whose value depends on the type of stimulus and the sense it affects. The larger or stronger the stimulus, the larger the change required for an observer to notice that anything has happened to it. For example, an inch added to a ten-inch line is obvious, but an inch added to a ten-foot line is not even detectable. Figure 12.14 is a small-scale demonstration of Weber's law.

Fechner's Law

G. T. Fechner so extended Weber's formulation that he is considered the father of psychophysics. Using Weber's law and making some seemingly reasonable assumptions, he claimed to be able to state the precise relation between the magnitude of any sensation and the magnitude of its stimulus. Fechner's law, formulated in 1860, is $\psi = a \log S$, where ψ stands for the magnitude of the sensation, S for the magnitude of the physical stimulus, and a is a constant whose value depends on the sensation investigated and the units of measurement used.

Fechner's law—although it turned out to be incorrect in its particular (logarithmic) form—was extremely important because it correctly stated that almost any sensation has a mathematical relation to its stimulus, whether the relation is between brightness and light intensity, loudness and sound pressure, judged weight and physical weight, or the like. Moreover, Fechner's and Weber's laws were the first general, quantitative laws in psychology, the first laws about behavior. They helped

Figure 12.13
Gustav Fechner. Fechner stands as one of the most versatile intellects in the history of psychology. A physicist by training, he also delved seriously into philosophy, satire, and poetry. His development of psychophysics, for which he is best known, was intended originally to support his philosophical views.

Figure 12.14
These lines illustrate Weber's law. Most people can detect the difference between the two short lines more readily than that between the two long lines, even though the difference between the two long lines is greater. If you have a three-way light bulb, you can try another demonstration: compare the perceived difference between 50 and 100 watts to that between 100 and 150 watts.

implant the notion that behavior can be studied scientifically and that psychology can move toward the goal of all science, the uncovering of invariant, unambiguous relations, stated as precisely as possible, preferably in mathematical equations.

Fechner's major error was in assuming that a just-noticeable physical change in a stimulus always occasions a change in sensation that is constant. Such an assumption implies that when the magnitude of a just-noticeable stimulus change increases with stimulus magnitude, the amount of change perceived in the sensation is always the same. The assumption *seems* plausible: shouldn't the magnitude of a just-noticeable change in sensation be the same even with variations in the magnitude of the stimulus changes that are required to produce it? Fechner did not attempt to test the assumption experimentally, because he and his followers thought that sensation magnitude could not be measured directly but had to be inferred from measurements of just-noticeable changes in the stimulus. Rather, using Weber's proportionality law and his own assumption about the subjective equality of just-noticeable differences, Fechner arrived at his logarithmic law. But research in the twentieth century has shown that Fechner's assumption is incorrect.

Stevens' Power Law

In the twentieth century, several techniques for the direct measurement of sensation have been invented. One is called *ratio production.* Listeners are given control of the pressure of a sound (they control it by turning a knob, say), and they are asked to adjust it to make it twice as loud as another, standard sound or five times as loud or one-half as loud. Data from experiments like these make it possible for psychologists to measure changes in loudness as a function of changes in pressure, yielding psychophysical laws. In a similar procedure, called *magnitude estimation,* observers are asked to assign numbers to sounds proportional to their loudness. If the first tone in a series is called 2 and the second tone sounds three times as loud, the subject calls it 6, and so on.

Figure 12.15
S. S. Stevens is a noted investigator of psychophysical processes. He developed the method of *magnitude estimation* in order to test the findings of Weber and Fechner. In this method, the subject assigns numerical values to the stimuli to which he is exposed; the higher the number, the greater the intensity of the sound or color or other stimulus. Using this method, Stevens discovered different psychophysical relationships from those advanced by Weber and Fechner. Although the controversy is not yet resolved, Stevens stands as a major contributor of theory, data, and methodology in psychophysical measurement.

These procedures, which measure sensation directly, are sometimes called the "new psychophysics." Their validity rests, first, on their repeatability. Different groups of observers and different techniques give essentially the same results. Second, their predictive power is good. The sensation functions that the procedures provide can be used to predict the results of other experiments.

Measurements taken in these ways by S. S. Stevens have permitted the formulation of a new general law of psychophysics: Stevens' power law. It says that the subjective magnitude of a sensation, ψ, is proportional to the physical magnitude of a stimulus, S, raised to a power, n. That is, $\psi = kS^n$, where k is an arbitrary constant of proportionality that depends on the unit of measurement. The value of n depends upon the particular sensation and attribute measured.

Figure 12.16 shows how three psychological sensations—electric shock applied to the finger, length of line, and brightness—change as the magnitude of the stimulus is increased. The functions are straight lines plotted on double logarithmic coordinates because, in logarithmic notation, the power law is $\log \psi = \log k + n \log S$, which is the equation for a straight line with a slope equal to the exponent, n. (Plotted on ordinary linear coordinates, the lines of Figure 12.16 look like those in Figure 12.17.) Electric shock, with an exponent of 3.5, grows more rapidly than any other sensation tested thus far—doubling the intensity of the shock makes the sensation grow tenfold. The sensation length of line is nice and straightforward. It has an exponent close to 1, which means that doubling the length of the line makes it look about twice as long. Brightness has an exponent of 0.33, so doubling the intensity of the light increases brightness only about 30 percent; to double brightness, an eightfold increase in intensity is needed. Table 12.1 lists some exponents of the power functions relating psychological magnitude to stimulus magnitude.

Most attributes of sensation that have been measured are a power function of

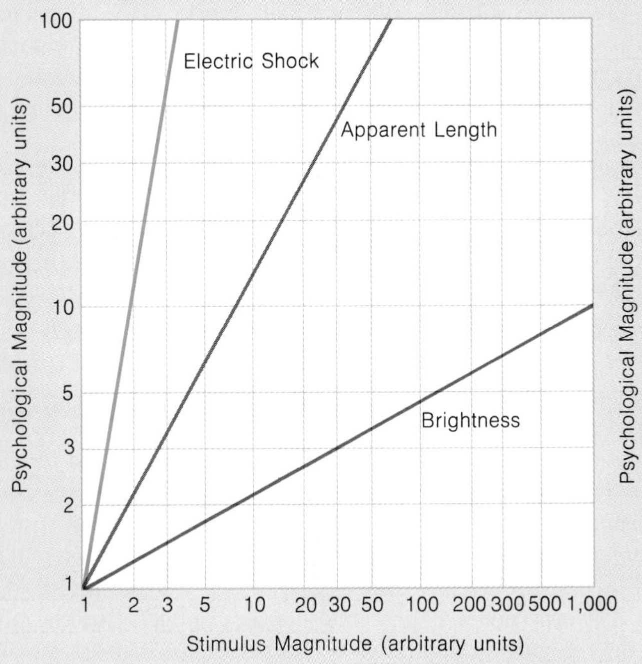

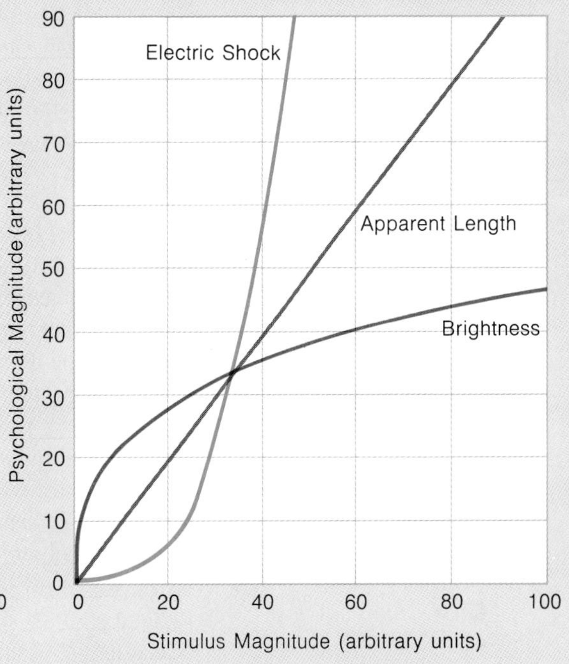

Figure 12.16

A log-log graph showing how increases in the magnitude of a physical stimulus affect the magnitude of psychological sensations. The exponent of the function determines its slope. These exponents are: electric current through the fingers, 3.5; apparent length of lines, 1.1; brightness of a luminous spot, 0.33.
(After Stevens, 1962.)

Figure 12.17

The three functions plotted in Figure 12.16 are shown here graphed linearly. When log-log plots are transformed to linear-linear coordinates, the slope becomes curved. The curvature of a function is downward if the exponent is less than one, as shown by the brightness function; it is upward if it is greater than one, as shown by the electric-shock function, which is the largest of any yet determined by Stevens or his associates.
(After Stevens, 1962.)

Table 12.1—Representative Exponents

Continuum	Exponent	Stimulus Condition
Loudness	0.60	binaural
Loudness	0.54	monaural
Brightness	0.33	5° target—dark-adapted eye
Brightness	0.50	point source—dark-adapted eye
Lightness	1.20	reflectance of gray papers
Smell	0.55	coffee odor
Smell	0.60	heptane
Taste	0.80	saccharine
Taste	1.30	sucrose
Taste	1.30	salt
Temperature	1.00	cold—on arm
Temperature	1.50	warmth—on arm
Vibration	0.95	60 cps—on finger
Vibration	0.60	250 cps—on finger
Duration	1.10	white-noise stimulus
Repetition rate	1.00	light, sound, touch, and shocks
Finger span	1.30	thickness of wood blocks
Pressure on palm	1.10	static force on skin
Heaviness	1.45	lifted weights
Force of handgrip	1.70	precision hand dynamometer
Vocal effort	1.10	sound pressure of vocalization
Electric shock	3.50	60 cps—through fingers
Tactual roughness	1.50	felt diameter of emery grits
Tactual hardness	0.80	rubber squeezed between fingers
Visual velocity	1.20	moving spot of light
Visual length	1.00	projected line of light
Visual area	0.70	projected square of light

Source: S. S. Stevens, *In Pursuit of Sensory Law;* second public Klopsteg lecture (Evanston, Ill.: Technological Institute, Northwestern University, November 7, 1962), p. 7.

some physical characteristic of the stimulus. The pervasiveness of Stevens' power law suggests that this relationship reflects a basic characteristic of the human nervous system. What a power relation means, regardless of the value of its exponent, is that, for a given sensation, equal ratios of stimuli produce equal differences in the intensity of sensation. In other words, the nervous system analyzes stimulation in terms of ratios, not in terms of absolute differences in magnitude.

Thresholds

As we said in introducing Weber's and Fechner's laws, measuring just-noticeable differences in stimuli has been an important aim of psychophysicists from the early days of the science. The minimum detectable change in a stimulus, or the minimum detectable difference between two successive or adjacent stimuli, is sometimes given another name than just-noticeable difference: a *difference threshold*. It is arbitrarily defined as the amount of change in a stimulus that is required for a person to detect the change 50 percent of the time.

A related question is, how intense must a stimulus be for a person to notice it at all? That is, what are the *absolute thresholds* for various sensations? Absolute thresholds are defined in a way similar to difference thresholds: the intensity level at which an observer reports detecting a stimulus on 50 percent of its presentations.

A commonly used additional procedure for measuring absolute threshold is the *method of limits*. The experimenter alternately increases and decreases the intensity of a stimulus in discrete steps, and after each change the observer reports whether or not he detected the signal. Figure 12.18 gives the results of an experiment performed by R. S. Woodworth and H. Schlosberg in which the frequency of a tone was varied in order to determine the lowest detectable frequency. When the observer changes his response from yes to no, the experimenter reduces the frequency considerably and then increases it, step by step, until the observer changes his response again, this time from no to yes. Threshold is taken as the average of the intensities at which the shifts in judgment occur. Difference thresholds can also be measured by this method.

Even under controlled laboratory conditions, establishing the point at which a subject detects a signal is by no means a simple matter. Thresholds are influenced not only by the stimulus variables of intensity and frequency (or wavelength) but by others, such as the duration and rate of presentation. They are also affected by individual differences in sensory acuity, general health, age, training, and motivation.

Finally, as you might expect, thresholds vary considerably under different circumstances. For example, because the eye adapts to the level of light or dark in which it finds itself, a beam of light shone on a screen in a lighted room must be

Determination of Stimulus Threshold by the Method of Limits

Stimulus (cycles per second)	▼	▲	▼	▲	▼	▲	▼	▲	▼	▲
24	Y									
23	Y									
22	Y		Y							
21	Y		Y							
20	Y		Y						Y	
19	Y		Y				Y		Y	
18	Y		Y		Y		Y		Y	
17	Y		Y		Y		Y		Y	
16	Y		Y		Y		Y		Y	
15	Y	Y	Y	Y	Y	Y	Y		Y	Y
14	N	N	N	N	?	N	?	Y	?	N
13		N		N		N		N		N
12		N		N		N		N		N
11		N		N		N		N		
10		N		N				N		
9				N				N		
8				N				N		
7				N				N		

Figure 12.18
With the psychophysical method of limits, the experimenter determines the subject's absolute threshold, the level at which an auditory stimulus, for example, can be detected at least 50 percent of the time. The sounds are presented in series of small increments or decrements in frequency. The average of the intensities at which the subject changes his response—from "yes, I detect it," to "no, I cannot" or vice versa is taken as his absolute threshold. In this set of data, the subject's absolute threshold was 15 cycles per second.
(From Woodworth and Schlosberg, 1954.)

more intense than a beam in a darkened room before an observer can see it. Somewhat similarly, it is usually harder to hear a particular sound in the presence of other sounds than alone.

Masking The effect of one sound on the threshold of another sound is called masking. It is measured by establishing the threshold for a sound presented alone and then finding out how much more intense (in decibels) the sound must be to be heard when it is presented along with a masking sound such as white noise. One interesting finding of masking experiments is that low frequencies mask high frequencies much better than the other way around. Also, masking sounds are most effective when their frequencies are very near that of the masked frequency.

Studying Thresholds in Lower Animals Lower animals are often used as subjects in experiments on sensation, for a number of reasons. For one, some sensations are uncomfortable, and human beings would refuse to be subjected to them. For another, some species of animals are easy to care for and can be kept in a controlled environment for long periods of time. Since sensation is a subjective, psychological event, however, its study with animals poses some difficult questions. How do we communicate with the lower organism—how do we pose the problem for it, and how does it reply to us? Similar difficulties arise in sensation and perception experiments with human infants.

An elegant pioneer experiment by D. S. Blough illustrates how much can be learned from a lower organism, in this case a pigeon, if the experimenter is ingenious enough to solve the communications problem. Blough devised an apparatus for studying visual threshold in the pigeon. The question was, at what intensity will a pigeon report that it sees a light?

Blough taught a hungry pigeon to peck one response key (Key A) whenever it could see a spot of light and a second response key (Key B) whenever it could not see the light. The only reinforcement the pigeon received was that pecks on Key B during periods of darkness occasionally produced food. You may wonder why, in that case, a pigeon would not simply keep pecking Key B and ignore Key A. The reason is that Blough constructed his apparatus in such a way that pecks on Key B increased the brightness of the spot of light, whereas pecks on Key A decreased it (see Figure 12.19). In order to obtain food, the pigeon had to respond on Key A until the spot of light disappeared—as far as the pigeon could tell—and then respond on Key B until food arrived. Pecking Key B when the light was on was counterproductive; because it made the light brighter, it increased amount of time

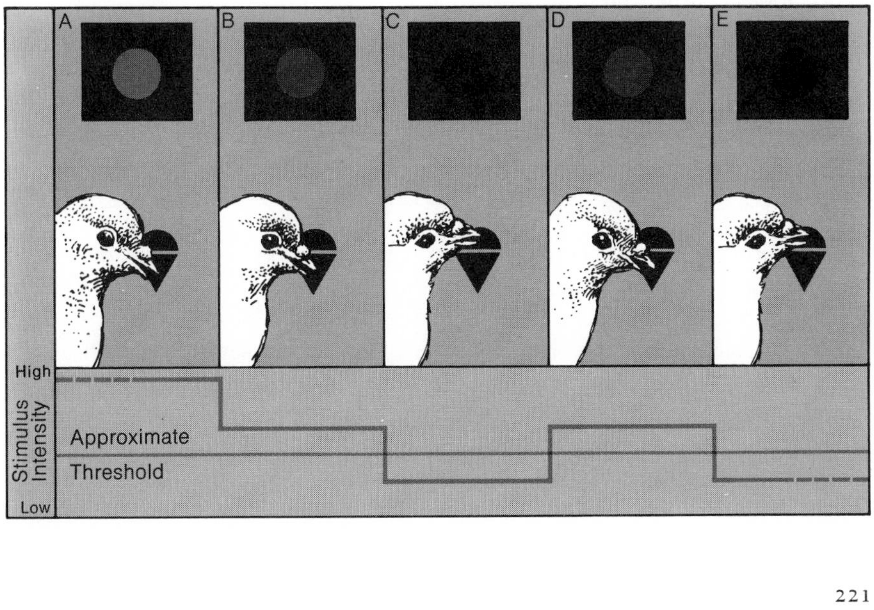

Figure 12.19

Blough's technique to determine stimulus threshold in a pigeon. By pecking the top key (B) the bird produces a higher-intensity light; the bottom key (A) decreases the intensity. The bird is only rewarded with food by pecking the top key (B) when the light is out, so it must first peck to produce darkness (pecking the bottom key) and then peck the top key (B) to obtain the food. After training, the intensity of the light is systematically varied to determine whether the bird perceives it as on or off.

(Adapted from "Experiment in Animal Psychophysics," Donald Blough. ©1961 by Scientific American, Inc. All rights reserved.)

needed to obtain food. So the pigeon was motivated to respond on Key A whenever it could see the light.

This procedure provides an excellent method for studying not only visual thresholds but other visual phenomena in the pigeon. Blough has used it to investigate the pigeon's ability to perceive contrasts in brightness, for example, which the pigeon indicates by pecking the brighter of two spots. The results of such experiments show that there are some remarkable similarities between pigeon and human vision, despite the fact that birds and mammals, from an evolutionary viewpoint, are quite different.

SIGNAL DETECTION THEORY

Sensation does not depend on the stimulus alone—the observer himself contributes much in the way of judgment and motive. Suppose that you are in a plane approaching O'Hare Airport in Chicago, one of the world's busiest, in very bad weather. Your thoughts turn to the radar operators in the control tower and, unfortunately, to the possibility of a mid-air collision with another plane. It occurs to you that two operators, each with the same ability to detect blips, might differ on when they decide that two planes are on a collision course. Perhaps one is cautious and will ask your plane to change course when there is little or no danger. Perhaps changing course will confuse, annoy, or rattle the pilot so that he accidentally takes the plane from an area of slight risk into a real danger zone. But maybe the other operator is reluctant to seem nervous or to inconvenience your pilot. He is more concerned with the cost of a "false alarm" than with the cost of "missing" a true blip. If he's the one watching your blip, will he wait too long and let a collision occur?

Airplane passengers are not the only people who worry about such things. Consider the plight of the radar operator himself. He may have taken the job in the O'Hare control tower because his last one, watching a radar screen for signs of an enemy attack, made it too hard for him to sleep at night. In his old job he had to make decisions about blips, too. Should he press the panic button at the first sign of an unusual blip or should he wait? It could be an off-course plane or a flock of birds. On the other hand . . .

The *payoff matrix* that describes the value (often in dollars and cents) of the various consequences will play a controlling role in determining the operator's decision. We will return to a fuller discussion of payoff matrices below.

Signal detection theory was inspired largely by the difficulties facing radar operators. It concerns both the ability to detect a signal (his sensitivity) and the conditions that determine whether an observer *reports* detecting the signal (for example, his expectations and motivations).

Signal detection theory calls into question the traditional way of conceptualizing *threshold.* Threshold is defined as the energy level at which a stimulus is detected a certain percentage of the time. In a yes-no experiment, where the observer responds on each trial whether he detects the signal or not, the threshold is considered to be reached when he responds correctly on 50 percent of the trials.

But if the observer can detect the signal at that level, why does he report it only half the time? Classical theory ascribes the variation to fluctuations in the observer's sensory sensitivity. Non-sensory variables supposedly cancel each other out.

There are two major difficulties with this explanation. First, besides failing to report half the signals presented at the level of threshold, observers often say they detect a signal when it is well below threshold or even when no signal at all has been presented. Second, observers differ—sometimes fairly dramatically—in the criteria they use to decide whether they have detected a signal. A cautious observer uses a high criterion; he does not say he has detected a signal unless he is quite sure. A daring observer chooses a low criterion and may report signals about which he is very unsure. An observer's criteria are determined not only by personality variables (daring versus caution) but also by the experimental situation, the importance of the decisions, their value to the observer, and so on. Classical procedures attempt to control for differences in criteria by inserting so-called catch trials, in which no signal is presented. An observer with a low criterion gets caught more often, gives more false alarms, than an observer with a high criterion. But this is not a very precise method of control. Signal-detection theory provides for separate measures of the contributions of motivation and sensitivity to performance on threshold tasks. It also tackles the question of why false alarms occur at all, if there is really a threshold below which all nondetectable signals fall.

Signal detection theory ascribes false alarms mainly to real sensory events that occur even when no signal is present. Spontaneous neural activity—that is, activity when the nerves have not been excited by an external stimulus—is inherent in the auditory and visual nervous systems. Confronted with a series of trials on which very weak signals are sometimes presented, an observer may easily mistake spontaneous activity for activity evoked by a signal. According to signal detection theory, the "noise" caused by spontaneous activity fluctuates, sometimes reaching levels evoked by a weak signal.

We can think of the observer as having to make his decision on the basis of the two overlapping distributions shown in Figure 12.20. The distribution curve on the left presents the probability of neural activity reaching various levels when only spontaneous activity (internal noise) is present. The distribution curve on the right shows the probability that it will reach various levels when a signal is presented, evoking activity that is added to the spontaneous activity or internal noise. (Often, in tests of auditory signal detection, the noise is not actually internal. Instead, white noise is presented on every trial, and on some trials a tone is added. This procedure simplifies the analysis, because the fluctuations in white noise can be specified and the much lower, unspecifiable internal noise caused by spontaneous neural activity can be ignored.)

The overlap of the two distributions in Figure 12.20 must mean that the observer is bound to make mistakes. Or is he? After all, the observer does not have these distributions before him. On each trial, he has a sensory experience and must decide whether it is more likely to have come from noise alone or from noise-plus-signal. It seems likely that early in a series of trials the observer chooses some level of sensation at which to divide his responses into yeses and nos. This level is indicated by the criterion line shown in Figure 12.20. An observer who chose that criterion line would detect about 50 percent of the signals and fail to detect the other 50 percent. On 16 percent of the no-signal trials, he would report detecting a signal—that is, he would give a false alarm. (The 16 percent is the proportion of the noise-alone distribution that lies to the right of the criterion line.)

Another observer might establish his criterion line far to the right of the one shown in the figure. This person would almost never give a false alarm, because almost no noise-alone events would exceed his criterion. However, he would also

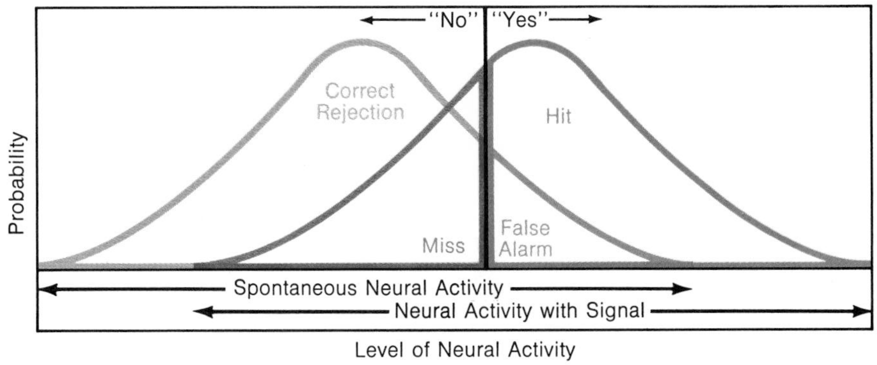

Figure 12.20
Psychologists now believe that when an observer is trying to detect the presence of a very faint signal, he is faced with the problem diagrammed here. The curves represent the probabilities of observations of given magnitudes when no signal is present and when there is a signal. When no signal is present, he experiences (observes) random neural noise (left curve), usually at some moderate level and occasionally at a very high or a very low level. When a signal is present, everything shifts to a higher level (right curve); he observes the signal *plus* the noise. Each time the observer makes an observation he must decide whether it came from the noise or from the signal-plus-noise. He sets a criterion. When his observation is at a level above criterion, he says, "Yes, there is a signal." When the observation is below criterion, he says, "No." He can, of course, make errors this way. For example, he may by chance alone experience a very high level of noise; because it exceeds his criterion, he will report a signal even though no signal was present. This error would be a false alarm. Note that the farther apart the curves are, that is, the bigger the signal, the easier it will be to avoid errors.

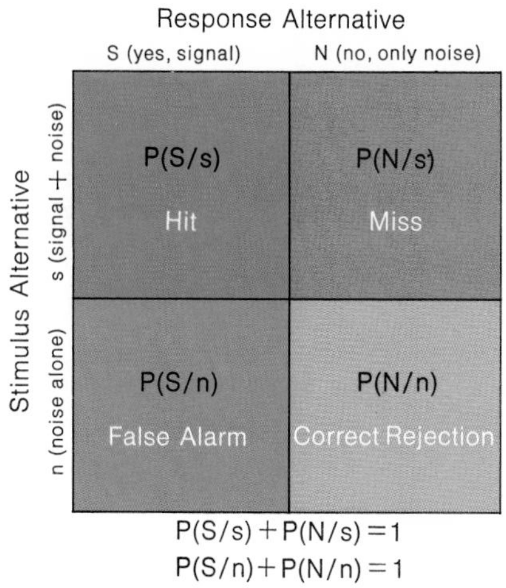

Figure 12.21

This diagram presents all the possible outcomes of the detection problem described in Figure 12.19. P(S/s) denotes the probability that the observer says "Yes" when there is a signal present, and P(N/s) denotes the probability that he says "No" in the same situation. Since he must say either "Yes" or "No," these probabilities add to 1. Similarly, P(S/n) and P(N/n), the probabilities when no signal is present, also add to 1. Note that the way probability is apportioned in the four cells of this stimulus-response matrix depends on two factors. One is the size of the signal, and the other is the criterion.
(After J. A. Swets, 1961.)

miss many signals, since many noise-plus-signal events would fall below his criterion. A third observer might choose a low criterion, far to the left. He would detect most of the signals, but at the price of a large number of false alarms.

Signal detection theory is a derivative of statistical decision theory. The observer in a threshold experiment is treated like a statistician who has to make a decision about a hypothesis—which is either that a signal was presented or that no signal was presented. Because only two hypotheses or responses are allowed, and a signal either is or is not presented on each trial, it is possible to set up the 2 x 2 *stimulus-response matrix* shown in Figure 12.21. The upper left-hand quadrant describes the conditional probability of a "hit"—that is, the probability of responding that the signal was presented *(S)* when the signal had, in fact, been presented *(s)*. The upper right-hand quadrant depicts the probability that the observer will "miss"—that he will report no signal was presented *(N)* when, in fact, a signal *was* presented *(s)*. Note that the probability of a hit and the probability of a miss must sum to 1, so once we know the probability of either of the two top quadrants, we automatically know the probability of the other. The lower left-hand quadrant represents the probability that an observer will make a "false alarm"—that he will report a signal was presented *(S)* when, in fact, no signal was presented *(n)*. Finally, the bottom right-hand quadrant gives the probability of a "correct rejection"—the probability that the observer reports no signal was presented *(N)* when in fact no signal was presented *(n)*. Again, the probability of a false alarm and the probability of a correct rejection must sum to 1.

The likelihood that a given observer will make hits and false alarms is influenced by two important factors (in addition to the difference between the two distributions shown in Figure 12.20). The first is the subject's expectations, which are largely influenced by the number of times the signal has been presented in the past. For example, if signals had actually been presented on only 1 percent of the trials over a substantial period, the subject would be less likely to report both hits and false alarms.

The second important factor affecting the number of hits and false alarms involves *consequences* for each of the outcomes. Suppose that each alternative had a payoff, as illustrated in Figure 12.22. Note that the payoff matrix in Figure 12.22A pays handsomely for hits. The observer in this situation is likely to report a signal *(S)* in a larger number of trials than if the matrix were symmetrical (say, with ten cents in every quadrant). The high rate of signal reports would, of course, result in a relatively large number of hits *and* false alarms. This kind of matrix might be desirable if a hit were vital, say, if a hit avoided a plane crash (where the inconvenience of a false alarm to both crew and passengers is minor relative to the horror

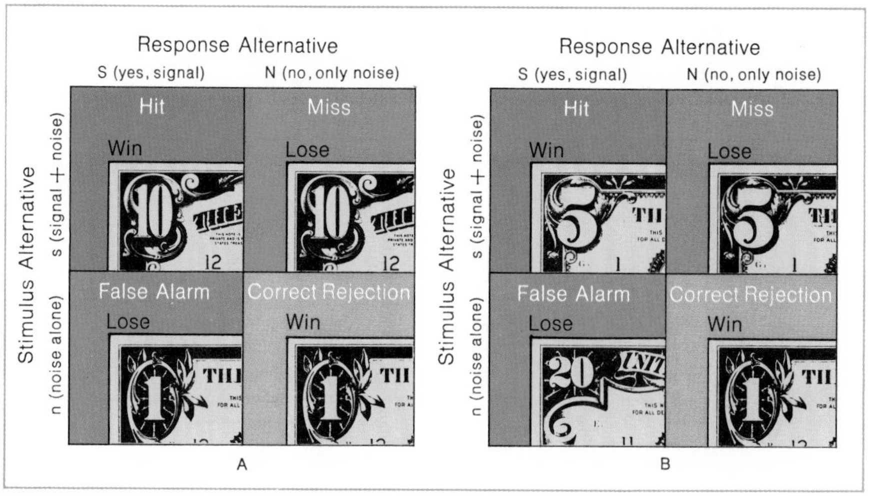

Figure 12.22

When values are assigned to the cells of the stimulus-response matrix, it is called a payoff matrix. The values will affect the level of the observer's criterion. In the first payoff matrix the observer will set his criterion quite low because he gains a lot for hits but is not heavily penalized for false alarms. He will say "Yes" most of the time. In the second payoff matrix, however, a "Yes" when there is no signal is heavily penalized. This will force the observer to set a higher criterion for reporting a signal.
(After Green and Swets, 1966.)

of a crash). The payoff matrix in Figure 12.22B penalizes false alarms severely. The *same observer* operating with this matrix is likely to report signals rarely, and so produce a low number of both hits and false alarms. Such a matrix might be desirable if a false alarm were intolerable, say, where it triggered a nuclear attack.

The important contribution of signal detection theory to sensory psychology is that it has provided sophisticated mathematical procedures for the design and analysis of detection experiments—in particular, procedures that make it possible to separate a person's sensitivity to signals from the criterion by which he decides to report detecting a signal. Simply making this separation is extremely valuable, for it greatly increases the accuracy of data analysis.

In addition, separating sensitivity and criterion makes it possible to know how well an "ideal observer" would detect signals, a useful comparison point against which to judge the performances of actual subjects. Finally, this and other aspects of signal detection theory help in the analysis of the effects of higher-level cognitive processes, such as attention, on simple sensations and on more complex perceptions of the sensory world.

SUGGESTED READINGS

BORING, E. G. *Sensation and Perception in the History of Experimental Psychology.* New York, Appleton, 1942. One of the finest books in all of psychology. Essential for a historical appreciation of sensation and psychophysics. The book is especially noteworthy for its treatment of the attributes of sensation and the historical antecedents of modern color theory.

GELDARD, F. A. *The Human Senses.* New York, Wiley, 1953. Although somewhat dated, this overview of the human senses is one of the clearest accounts in the field.

GREEN, D. M., AND SWETS, J. A. *Signal Detection Theory and Psychophysics.* New York, Wiley, 1966. An excellent treatment by the two scientists largely instrumental in developing it. A simpler treatment is contained in Kling and Riggs, cited here.

JUDD, D. B. "Basic Correlates of the Visual Stimulus," in *Handbook of Experimental Psychology,* S. S. Stevens (Ed.). New York, Wiley, 1951, pp. 811–867. Judd's treatment of the visual stimulus is still a classic. It is fairly technical, however. For a less technical account, the Geldard book cited here is recommended.

KLING, J. W., AND RIGGS, L. A. *Woodworth and Schlosberg's Experimental Psychology* (3rd ed.). New York, Holt, Rinehart and Winston, 1971. Includes a fine and extensive treatment of psychophysics written by Trygg Engen of Brown University. Engen covers basic psychophysical methods, the concept of the threshold, and a detailed analysis of signal detection theory, as well as an extensive treatment of scaling methods.

LICKLIDER, J. C. R. "Basic Correlates of the Auditory Stimulus," in *Handbook of Experimental Psychology,* S. S. Stevens (Ed.). New York, Wiley, 1951, pp. 985–1039. Licklider's treatment of the fundamental characteristics of sound does for audition what Judd did for vision. Although the Licklider chapter is less complex than Judd's, readers seeking a less sophisticated treatment are encouraged to consult Geldard or Kling and Riggs.

MUELLER, C. G. *Sensory Psychology.* Englewood Cliffs, N.J., Prentice Hall, 1965. Mueller's treatment of sensory psychology is more recent but less comprehensive than Geldard's.

STEVENS, S. S. "On the Psychophysical Law," *Psychological Review,* 64 (1957), 153–181. "The Surprising Simplicity of Sensory Metrics," *American Psychologist,* 17 (1962), 29–39. The two Stevens articles give an excellent and lucid treatment of the new psychophysics and Stevens' Law and its relation to earlier laws of sensation, such as Weber's and Fechner's laws.

13 The Senses

THE MATTER OF sense perception is sometimes made to seem so mysterious. Each one of us seems to be the prisoner of our own senses. Can we possibly know what an apple looks like or feels like or smells like to someone else? Not unless we get into someone else's brain.

And yet it *is* possible to enter into a completely different sense world, and the funny thing is that we generally don't notice. For instance, can you imagine what the world looks like to someone who is totally color-blind? Imagine no green to the grass, no blue to the sky, no red and blue to flowers, no color to anything. Surely, it seems horrible and you must be thankful this doesn't happen to you.

And yet I've been color-blind for hours at a time and so have you. And I've enjoyed it. And so have you.

Every time we see a black-and-white movie or watch a black-and-white television set, we experience scenes that are totally without color. And we pay very little attention to the lack. If I were to see several different motion pictures, some in color and some in black-and-white, and if I were asked a week later to tell which ones were in color and which not, I don't think I could achieve a perfect score.

And then—what if we had an additional sense? In fact, we all *do* occasionally possess a sense we don't always have. Every motion picture we see, every television drama, is accompanied by music. What is more, the music is carefully adjusted to the action and is designed to elicit the proper emotions in us. The music guides us so that we know when to feel tension, elation, suspense, melancholy. Listen for the minor tones in the sad scenes, the discords in the violent ones. Satirists have run the same scenes with and without the mood music. With the music, even commonplace utterances seem filled with meaning. Without the music, even exciting events seem flat.

Doesn't this amount to a new sense? Do we not, through the ear, directly sense emotion and mood in a way we cannot in real life? Yet do we really notice? I think not. I.A.

Because our knowledge of the world comes through our senses, we cannot hope to understand ourselves and our behavior without at least some knowledge of how the senses work. People are usually assumed to have five senses, but in this chapter we will discuss seven—the vestibular and kinesthetic senses, which help maintain balance and posture, as well as the more familiar sight, hearing, smell, taste, and touch.

VISION

Many more neurons are connected with vision than with any other sense. Our eyes are so acute, our environment so colorful, that we often tend to downgrade hearing and the other senses. Taste, smell, and touch, for example, are often referred to in textbooks as the "lower" senses. Although the pejorative terminology may seem unfair, it is probably true that our ability to see is our most important sensory capacity. As far as the sensory world is concerned, the eyes have it.

The Structure of the Eye

The structure of the human eye is shown in Figure 13.1. Before reaching the *retina*, where complex neural responses take place, light must pass through the cornea, the aqueous humor, the pupil, the lens, and finally the vitreous humor. The *pupil* regulates the amount of light that penetrates the eye by changing its size as the iris expands and contracts. The *lens* focuses the light on the retina by changing its shape. The lens is flat when the eye is focused on distant objects and thickens when the eye is focused on nearby objects. The accommodation of the lens in a normal eye to distant and near objects is shown in Figure 13.2A. Nearsightedness (myopia), the inability to see far objects clearly, results when the retina is too far from the lens. As can be seen in Figure 13.2B, even when the lens of the myopic eye is at its flattest, it focuses the light from far objects in front of the retina, so that the

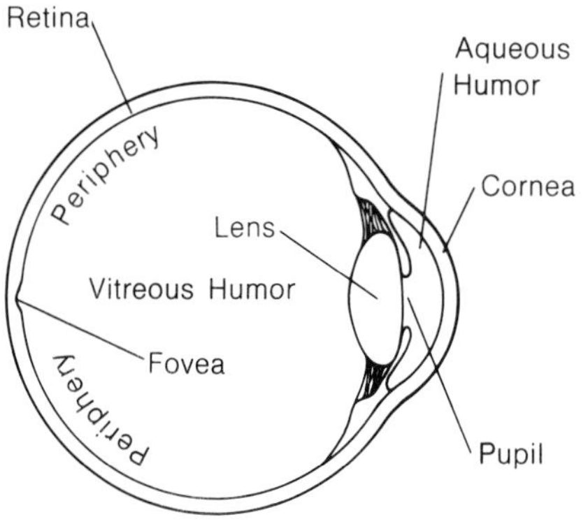

Figure 13.1
Light waves first strike the cornea, then pass through the pupil to the lens. Focusing of the light rays is brought about largely by changes in the curvature of the lens. The focused rays produce an image on the retina that is carried via the optic nerve to the brain.

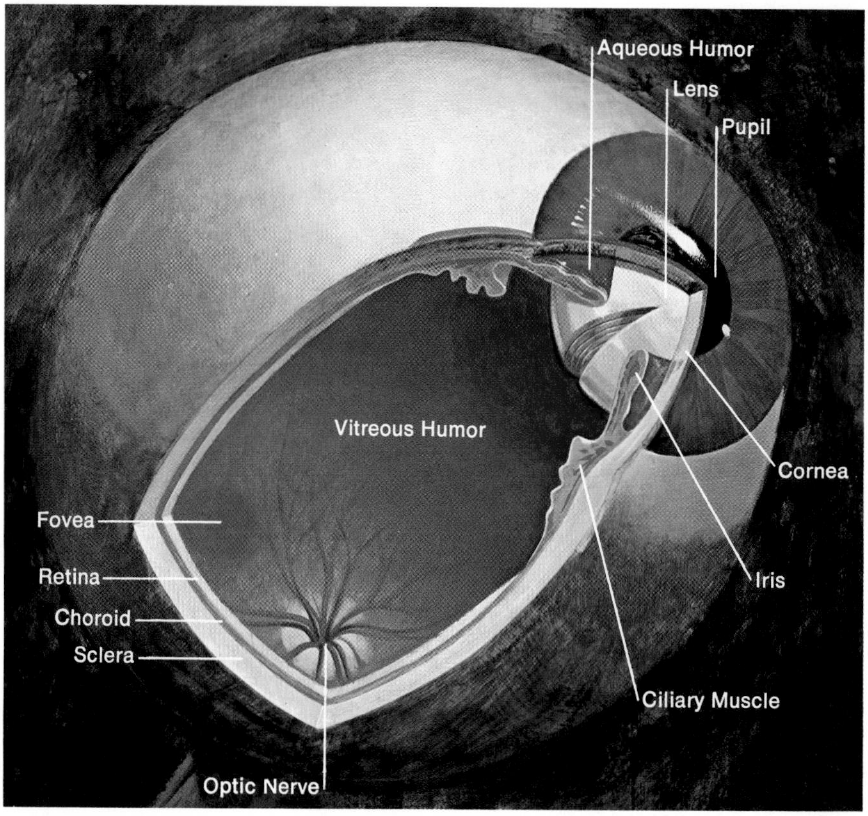

Figure 13.2
(A) in the normal eye distant light is focused on the retina by a flattening of the lens, whereas the lens becomes more rounded to focus light coming from a nearby source. (B) if the eyeball is too long, maximal flattening of the lens (in response to distant objects) focuses the light at a point in front of the retina; if the eyeball is too short, maximal curvature of the lens (in response to nearby objects) focuses the light at a point behind the retina.

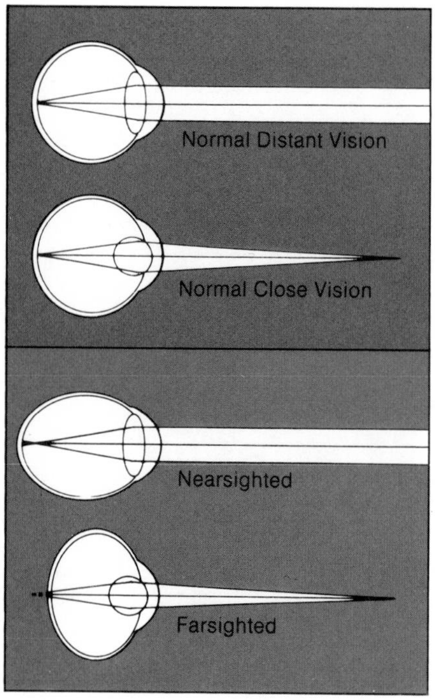

retinal image is blurred. Farsightedness results when the retina is too close to the lens, so that light from near objects is focused on a plane behind the retina.

Diagrams necessarily picture the eye as stationary, but in fact, as F. Ratliffe and L..A. Riggs indicate, it is always vibrating. When *nystagmus*, as this constant eye tremor is called, was first discovered, it was thought to interfere with vision, but it is now known to be essential to it. Under the special optical arrangements illustrated in Figure 13.3, nystagmus can be compensated for and the visual image fixated on the retina. Within a few seconds, the receptor cells of the retina adapt to the unchanging pattern, and the so-called *stopped image* disappears.

Even after it has reached the retina, light does not immediately affect the receptor cells that transmit visual information to the brain. The structure of the retina is diagrammed in Figure 13.4. The top of the picture faces the front of the eye. Briefly stated, what happens is that light strikes the top layer of the retina, passes through nerve fibers and blood vessels, and reaches the *rods* and the *cones*, which lie at almost the last layer of the retina. The rods and the cones undergo chemical changes as they absorb light, changing light energy to neural energy. The resulting electrical impulses are transmitted by various nerve cells toward the back of the eyeball and then, via the optic nerve, to the brain.

The center of the retina is called the *fovea* (shown in Figure 13.1). Most of the eye's six or seven million cones are located there. The rest of the retina, called the *periphery*, contains the rods. There are many more rods than cones—between 75 and 150 million. When the pupil of the eye is small, as it is in bright light, light passes only through the center of the cornea and the lens and is concentrated on the fovea. When the pupil is large, as it is when the eye is dark-adapted, light is spread over the periphery as well.

We see visual details and colors more clearly when light is focused on the fovea, although we are more sensitive to low-intensity light when it strikes the periphery. One reason for the greater acuity of the fovea is that most of the cones are served

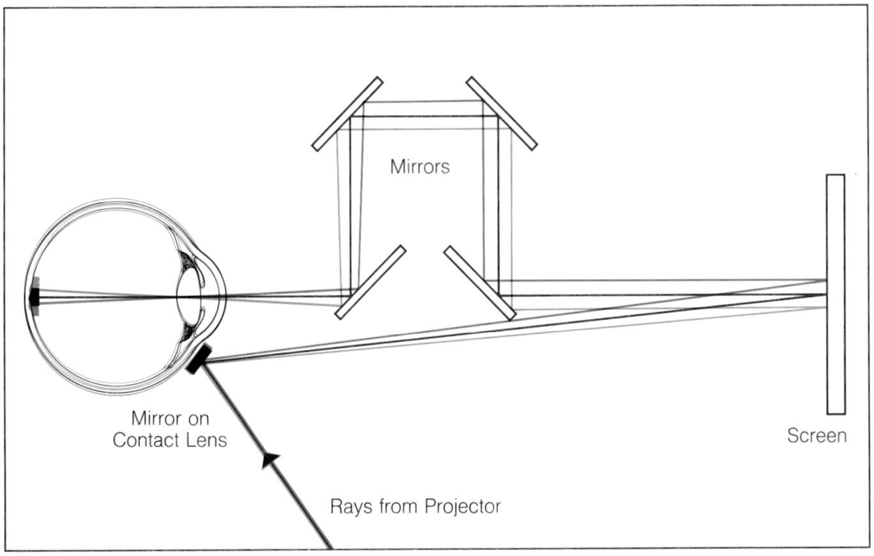

Figure 13.3

The eye is always making tiny jiggling movements even when we gaze steadily at something. This constant tremor is known as physiological nystagmus. Using the set-up diagramed here, psychologists have shown that nystagmus is essential to vision. An image to be viewed is reflected onto a screen from a tiny mirror embedded in a contact lens on the eye. The image is returned to the eye through a series of mirrors adjusted carefully so that the eye's movements are exactly compensated for. When the image is kept still on the retina by this technique, it disappears from vision after a few seconds. Constant change appears to be necessary for us to see anything.
(After Riggs, Ratliff, Cornsweet, and Cornsweet, 1953.)

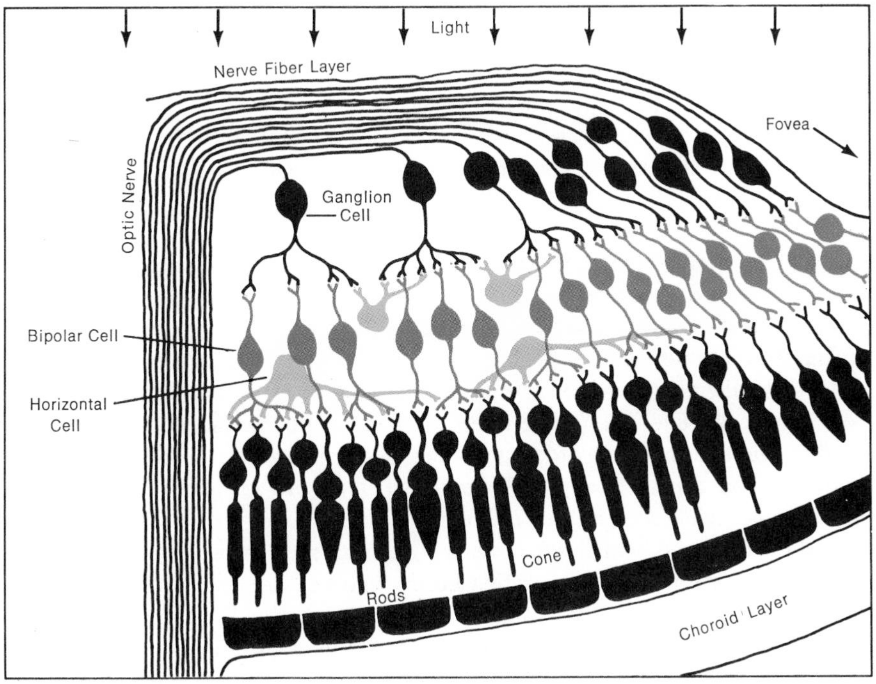

Figure 13.4

Schematic representation of the retina in cross section. The light passes through blood vessels and nerve fibers before it reaches the rods and cones, which undergo chemical changes as they absorb the light, changing the light energy to electrical neural impulses, which are eventually transmitted to the brain.

by a single neural fiber each, whereas groups of rods share the same neural connections. In addition, the rods are essentially color-blind. The cones, although they require more light than the rods before they begin to respond, are sensitive to color. Thus the rods are most useful in night vision, when maximum sensitivity to light is required; the cones, concentrated in the fovea, are most useful in daylight, for seeing color and visual detail precisely.

The chemical basis for the action of the rods has been very carefully worked out, largely by G. Wald. Rods contain *rhodopsin,* a chemical that is bleached by light. When light strikes the rods, the rhodopsin absorbs photons. Vitamin A is important to these chemical actions because it is involved in the process of converting retinene to rhodopsin; vitamin-A deficiency can lead to night blindness.

When the eye has not been exposed to light for about an hour (this condition is called *dark adaptation*), the threshold for response to a visual stimulus (that is, the intensity required for a light to be barely seen) is determined entirely by the

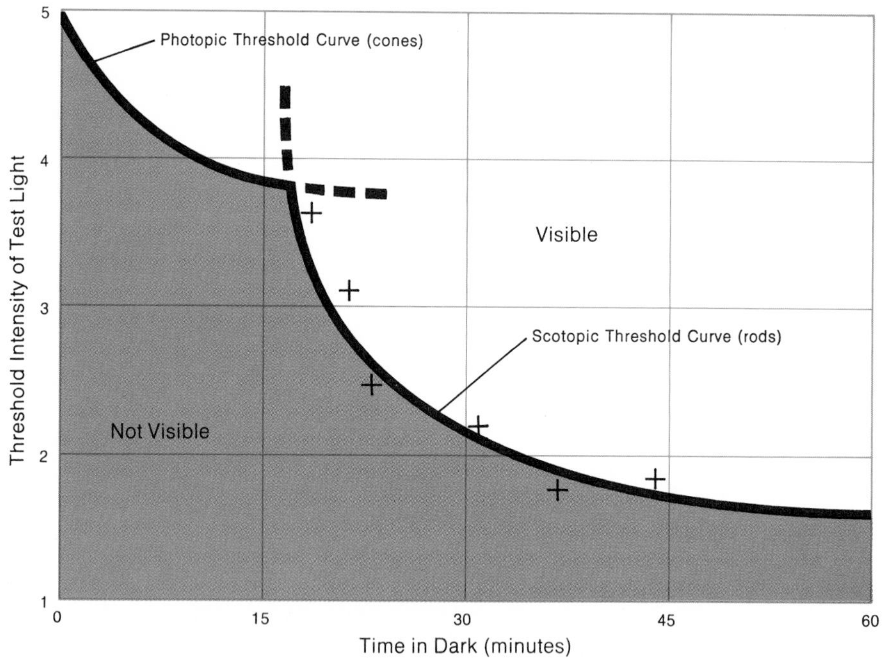

Figure 13.5
The longer the eye remains in the dark, the less intense a light need be to be visible. This graph represents the dark adaptation of the eye as a whole. The first curved segment represents the adaptation of the cones; the lower segment represents that of the more sensitive rods. The crosses on this figure represent the test-tube regeneration of the visual pigment rhodopsin, which breaks down in light. Rhodopsin forms again in the dark, and this regeneration seems to account for the scotopic portion of the dark adaptation process.
(From Hecht, Haig, and Wald, 1935.)

rods. The weakest luminance that the eye can detect as it adapts to the dark is shown by the *photopic* and *scotopic threshold curves* in Figure 13.5. Photopic vision is mediated by the cones; scotopic vision, by the rods.

Neural Coding by the Eye

The eye *transduces* energy: it changes light energy into neural electrical energy. Exactly how it does this is not fully understood, but much of the transduction process seems to take place in the retina. As Figure 13.4 indicates, the neural organization of the retina is highly complex (not surprising, since the retina is embryologically a part of the brain). (See Chapter 16 for a detailed discussion of how nerve cells function.) Three levels of neural cell bodies are shown in Figure 13.4. At the bottom are the rods and cones, whose tips are embedded in the cells of the choroid layer. As has been pointed out, most of the cones connect with a single bipolar cell located in the next neural layer. Several rods share a single bipolar cell, which may send branches to cones as well. A second synapse (junction of nerve cells—see Chapter 16) in the retina occurs between the bipolar cells and the ganglion cells. The axons of the ganglion cells are the fibers of the optic nerve. There is a *blind spot* in each eye (to find yours, try the demonstration in Figure 13.6), where these fibers all collect and exit as a bundle. We are unable to see in this spot because it contains all nerves and no transducers.

At a point a little behind the eyes and midway between them, the optic nerves from the two eyes meet. Each nerve bifurcates and passes through a subcortical way-station (the lateral geniculate body in the thalamus), as shown in Figure 13.7, before arriving at the *occipital lobe* in the back of the brain.

Even in the absence of external stimuli, the retina is constantly discharging

Figure 13.6
To find your blind spot, hold the book about ten inches away from your face. Close your left eye and stare at the X with your right eye. Move the book about slightly until the spot disappears. The image of the spot is now projected onto that area of the retina from which the nerve fibers exit, an area that contains no rods and cones and is therefore your eye's blind spot.

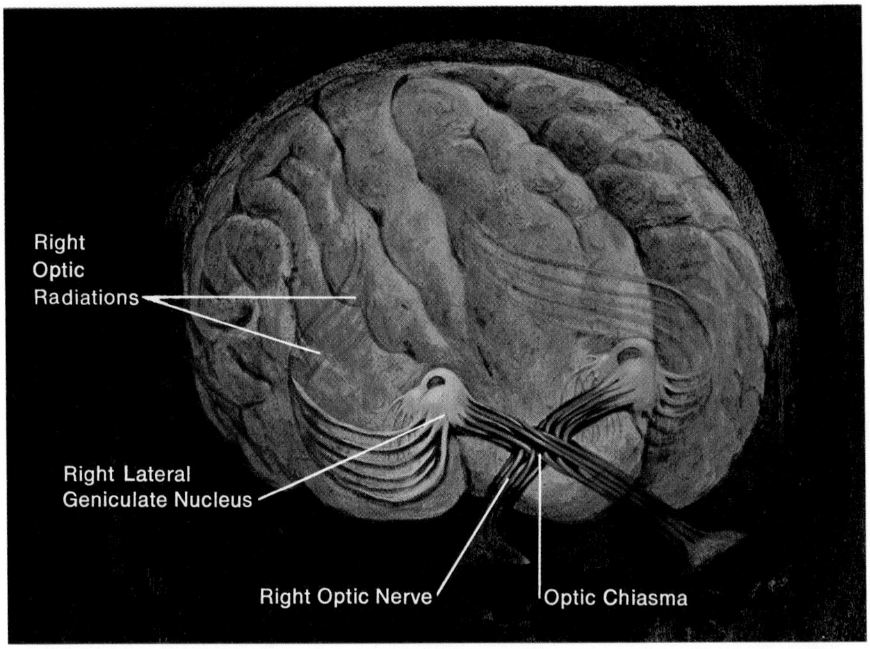

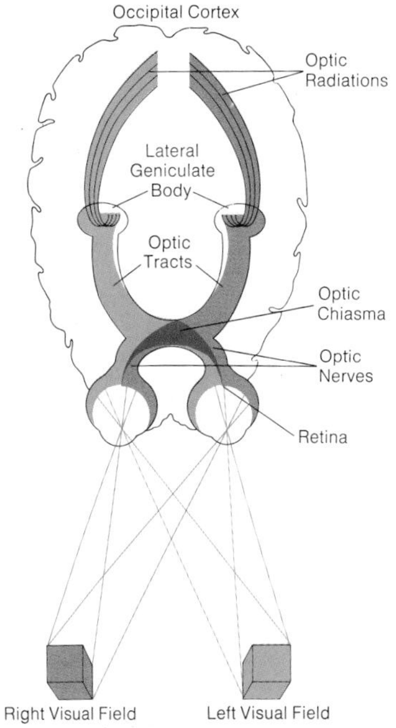

Figure 13.7
The optic nerves meet and redivide in the optic chiasma.

impulses to the brain. With the onset of stimulation, spontaneous activity may either increase or decrease. That is, either *excitation* (an increase in the intensity or rate of activity) or *inhibition* (a decrease) may occur. Excitation and inhibition are the basic means by which information is processed in the nervous system.

Some cells in the retina have both excitatory and inhibitory centers. This fact can be established by moving a small point of light across the eye while recording the responses in a single ganglion cell. Typical results from two ganglion cells in the cat are shown in Figure 13.8. The responses of each cell reveal a spatial pattern called a *receptive field.* The receptive field is the part of the retina that, when stimulated, produces a change in the activity of the ganglion cell. When light strikes the center of the receptive field on the left, the ganglion cell's rate of firing increases (excitation); when it strikes areas outside the center, the rate decreases (inhibition). Just the opposite effect is shown for the ganglion cell on the right, which has a receptive field composed of an inhibitory center with an excitatory area surrounding it. The interaction of excitation and inhibition is believed to be crucial in the perception of sharp contours.

Cones with three distinct pigments (red-sensitive, blue-sensitive, and green-sensitive) provide the basis for color vision. Each kind of cone has neural connections to cells in the lateral geniculate body of the brain. These cells are called "opponent" cells because they are excited when the eye is stimulated by light at certain wavelengths and inhibited by light at other wavelengths. Figure 13.9 shows the firing of an opponent cell (in the brain of a Macaque monkey) that is excited by red light and inhibited by green light. This cell presumably has excitatory inputs from cones that are most sensitive to red and inhibitory inputs from cones most sensitive to green. Another type of opponent cell is excited by blue (excitatory inputs from blue-sensitive cones) and inhibited by yellow (inhibition from yellow-sensitive cones). Opponent cells with the reverse relationships of excitation and inhibition are also found—cells inhibited by red light and excited by green light, and cells inhibited by blue and excited by yellow.

Figure 13.8
A receptive field is a map of the responses of a ganglion cell to the stimulation of a set of adjacent receptor cells. On the left a field with an excitatory center and an inhibitory surround is shown. Stimulation of cells in the central area caused the ganglion cell to respond more; stimulation of the surrounding cells caused it to respond less. The opposite situation is shown on the right.
(After de Valois, 1966.)

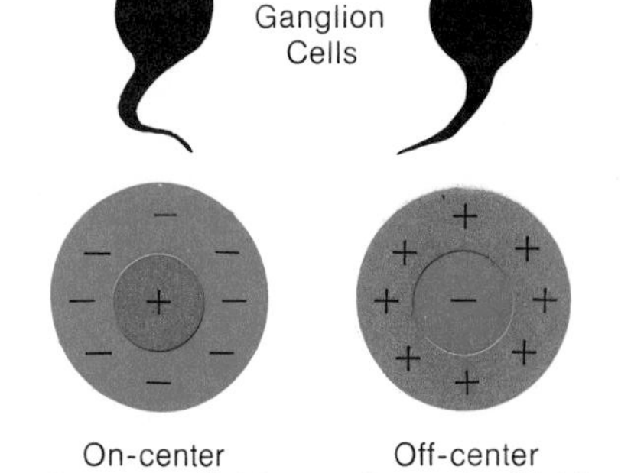

Basic Phenomena of Vision

In discussing how the eyes provide information about the environment, three visual abilities will be emphasized: (1) the sensitivity of the eye to different intensities of

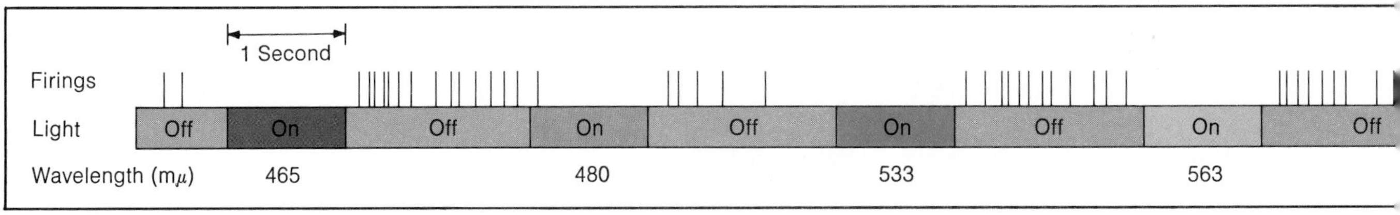

Figure 13.9
Recording of the firing of an opponent cell (in the brain of a monkey) that is excited by red light and inhibited by green light. The diagram shows the cell's response to the entire spectrum. Note that this cell, like all such cells, has a base rate of firing, but it fires at a much greater rate than the base rate in response to red light and at a much lower rate than the base rate in response to green light. Records like these are made by actually monitoring the activity of the cell while the lights are flashed in front of the monkey's eyes.
(After de Valois, 1966.)

light, (2) its ability to detect spatial detail, and (3) its ability to detect differences in wavelength or color. The eyes perform many other functions, but an examination of these three reveals important characteristics of our visual system and also gives some indication of how vision is studied.

Adaptation to Intensities of Light The visual system is remarkably adaptable. The eyes are sensitive to somewhere between a million and a billion different intensities of light, but at any given moment the eye may or may not be able to respond to the full range of intensities to which we know it is sensitive.

To illustrate, suppose that a subject is placed in a completely darkened room for about an hour. We measure the smallest amount of light that is visible to him and then briefly present a light a thousand times as intense as the just-visible stimulus. The second light will undoubtedly look very bright to him—uncomfortably so, perhaps. Now suppose we take the same subject to the beach on a clear, sunny day. If, after an hour or so, we suddenly place him in a completely dark room and flash the second light again, he probably will not see it. In fact, it may not become visible until he has been in the dark for one or two minutes. If the subject stays in the dark for an hour, this light (which is a thousand times as intense as his absolute threshold in the dark) will again appear to be very bright.

What the eye can do depends on the state it is in at the time that we test its functioning. If the eyes are adjusted or adapted to very bright light, then light that is much weaker or lower in intensity will not be immediately visible. It becomes visible only after dark adaptation. Thus, what a person judges to be dim, bright, or very bright light is linked not only to the intensity of the visual stimulus but to the state of adaptation of his viewing system. A light of a particular intensity can be made invisible, dim, or bright by appropriately adapting the eye.

One technique used to study adaptation is to let the eyes adapt to high-intensity light, then darken the room and note the amount of light that can be barely detected as time passes. Figure 13.5 showed that when a subject whose eyes are adapted to a high-intensity light is placed in complete darkness, the absolute threshold for vision is very high at first. It then falls in two stages: it drops rapidly at first, begins to level off after ten or fifteen minutes, then falls rapidly again, leveling off after about an hour. This phenomenon not only shows the eyes' adaptability to different intensities of light but is one of many phenomena observed in the study of vision that indicates people have two different visual systems, one mediated by the cones and one by the rods. The first (photopic) part of the dark-adaptation curve is due largely to the functioning of the cones. The second (scotopic) part is due to the functioning of the rods.

The shape of the dark-adaptation curve is not always as shown in Figure 13.5. It is influenced by a number of factors, including the color and size of the test stimulus and also where on the eye the stimulus falls. For example, if stimulation is limited to the center of the eye—the fovea, where there are only cones—then the second, scotopic, portion of the dark-adaptation curve is not obtained.

It should be repeated that although the eyes are most sensitive to light when they are adapted to the dark, they do not function best in all capacities when they are dark-adapted. Our ability to see fine detail, to notice small differences in intensity, and to perform many other visual activities is usually greatest when the eyes

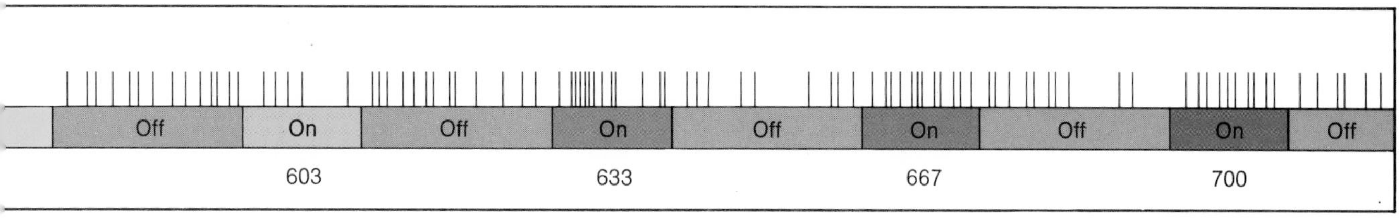

are adapted to at least a moderate intensity level, near but slightly below the intensity level at which vision will be tested. The function of adaptation or adjustment seems to be to set the eye for responding appropriately to intensities in a given range.

Detection of Spatial Detail People often feel more inferior to other animals in the matter of visual acuity than the facts warrant. The next time you see a hawk searching the ground for prey as it soars high in the air, keep this in mind: the average person can see a dark quarter-inch line against a light background from a distance of half a mile. Examples of figures used in clinical tests of visual acuity are shown in Figure 13.10. The dark line against the light background is used to measure *minimum visual acuity.* A second kind of acuity, called *minimum separable acuity,* is tested with a repeating pattern such as a grating or checkerboard design. A third type, *vernier acuity,* is the ability to detect the offset of a line. In this case, the observer is required to respond by saying whether a line is broken or not. Another stimulus used to assess visual acuity is the Landolt ring—a black ring with a broken segment that the observer is asked to detect. The familiar Snellen chart measures the kind of form discrimination used in recognizing printed letters.

Although these measures are loosely related, which one is used in a given situation depends on the aspect of the visual system that is being considered. Measurements of minimum visual acuity and minimum separable acuity, as repre-

Figure 13.10
Examples of stimuli used in clinical tests of vision. The four figures on the far left measure basic abilities of the visual system. The checkerboard patterns are used to measure *minimum separable acuity.* The increasingly thin lines are used to measure *minimum visual acuity* as are the four Landolt rings, or "broken circles." The offset lines are used to measure *vernier acuity.* The familiar Snellen eye chart, which is often used to measure visual acuity, is a less accurate tool than the Landolt circles. People may be able to read the letters from the chart because they have certain expectations about how letters are formed, so the acuity measured may be in error. You can see how your familiarity with block lettering affects your ease of reading it by attempting to read the right-hand chart, whose letter forms are less familiar.

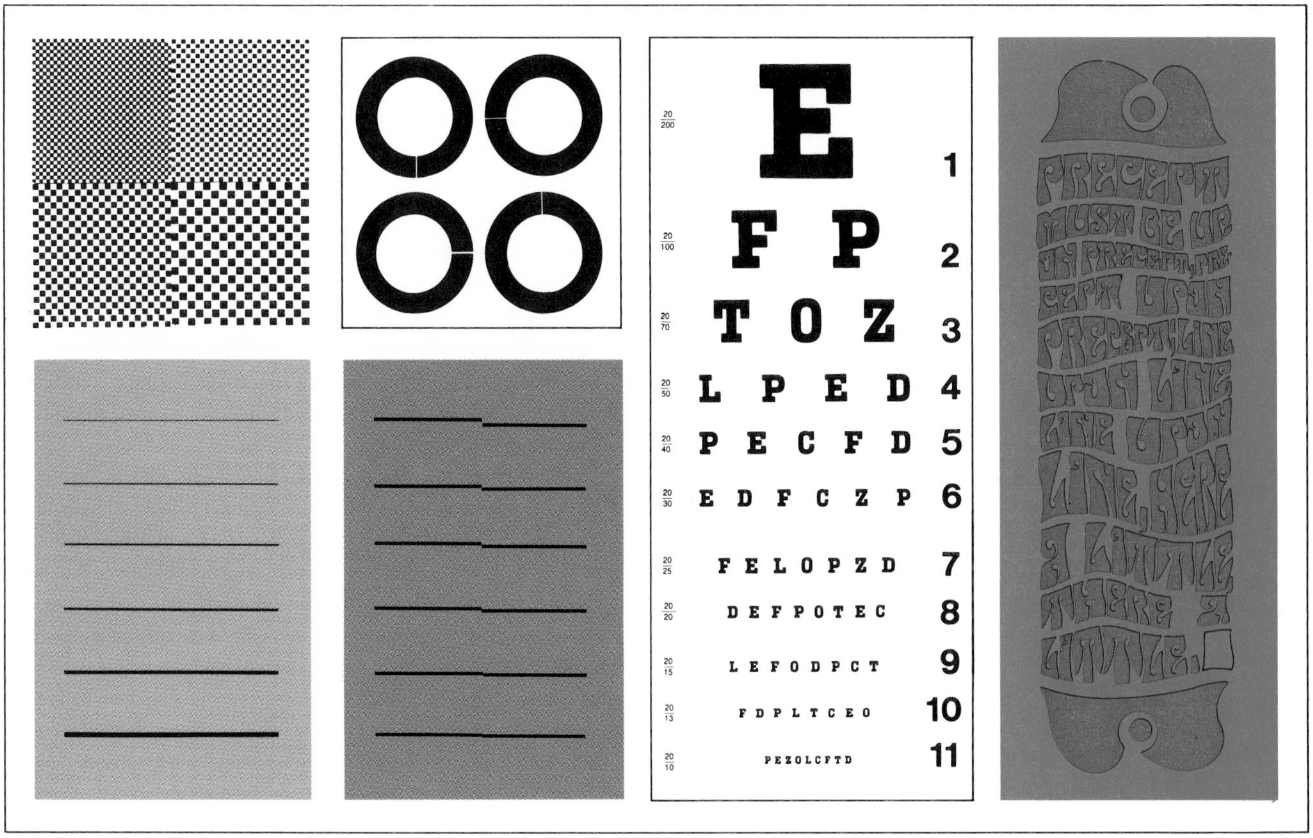

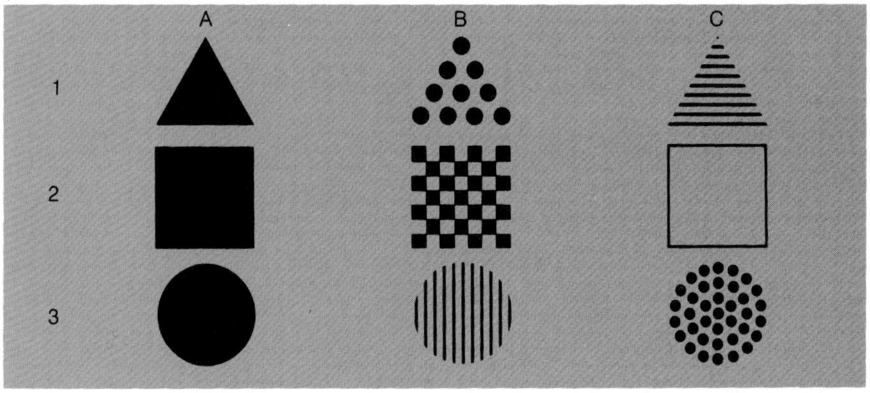

Figure 13.11
Virtually everyone will call row 1 triangles; row 2, squares; and row 3, circles. Psychologists want to find out how the human visual system integrates the various patterns shown here in order to perceive one of the simple geometric figures.

sented by a dark line against a light background and a grating or checkerboard figure, provide perhaps the most basic information on the resolving power of the visual system. If an experimenter wants information on the eye's ability to detect complex forms, however, he will use the Snellen chart rather than a line or grating. Note that a test like the Snellen chart involves many variables that are difficult to evaluate, including the amount of experience a person has had seeing and naming printed letters. The way the letters are printed—for example, in bold outline or artistically varied—also has a strong effect on the ease with which a person identifies them, as demonstrated in Figure 13.10.

The analytic power that the visual system brings to bear even on a simple stimulus like black lines against a white background is impressive. We can identify differences in the length, width, and direction of lines; we can tell whether two lines are parallel and whether a line is straight or curved, horizontal or vertical; we see lines as having different shapes or enclosing different areas, and as meeting and forming different angles. Lines are, moreover, only one kind of spatial arrangement of light that we can discriminate. Drawings in black and white, for example, have variations in degrees of shading. The number of variations rises when we turn from drawings to photographs and becomes almost infinite when we look at actual objects in the environment. Moreover, we recognize not only spatial but temporal patterns: many of the things we see *move*.

There are many things we do not know about the perception of visual detail. For example, column A in Figure 13.11 presents three simple geometric figures—a triangle, a square, and a circle. Most observers also label the figures in columns B and C with those names, calling all the figures in row 1 triangles, all those in row 2 squares, and all those in row 3 circles. They can certainly tell the difference between the figures in the different columns, but they label them the same nonetheless. The question of how the visual system integrates discontinuous figures is intriguing and will be examined more fully in connection with the discussion of Gestalt psychology in Chapter 14.

Color Vision If we present a typical observer with a visual stimulus that has a wavelength of 450 millimicrons, he will say that it is blue. Different wavelengths of the visible spectrum are perceived as having different colors or hues. It should be emphasized, however, that the visual system interprets the frequency as a specific color. To be precise, we should say that a visual stimulus such as a traffic light emits light of a certain frequency, which we see as red. A great many organisms, including people with defective color vision, do not see the light as red.

Before we discuss the mechanisms for color vision, let us consider two color phenomena that have played important roles in influencing color theory: color mixture and afterimages. F. A. Geldard reports that experiments on color mixture show that it is possible to match any color in the spectrum by selecting three monochromatic stimuli—the so-called *primary colors*—and adjusting their relative intensities. There are a few restrictions in the selection of the three primary colors. For example, no two of them can be *complementary colors,* that is, colors that when mixed yield an achromatic, or colorless, stimulus. The colors that are complementary appear opposite each other in the color wheel shown in Figure 13.12.

The existence of complementary colors is only one example of the many color phenomena that involve some kind of a two-by-two linkage. Geldard also reports that another duality has been demonstrated in studies of color contrast. Look at the gray disks in Figure 13.13. The one at the top, surrounded by bright green, should appear to have a red tint; the one below, where the colored field is red, should appear slightly green.

Rest your eyes for a few minutes and then, for a demonstration of *afterimages,* stare intently at the lower right-hand star of the flag in Figure 13.14 for forty-five

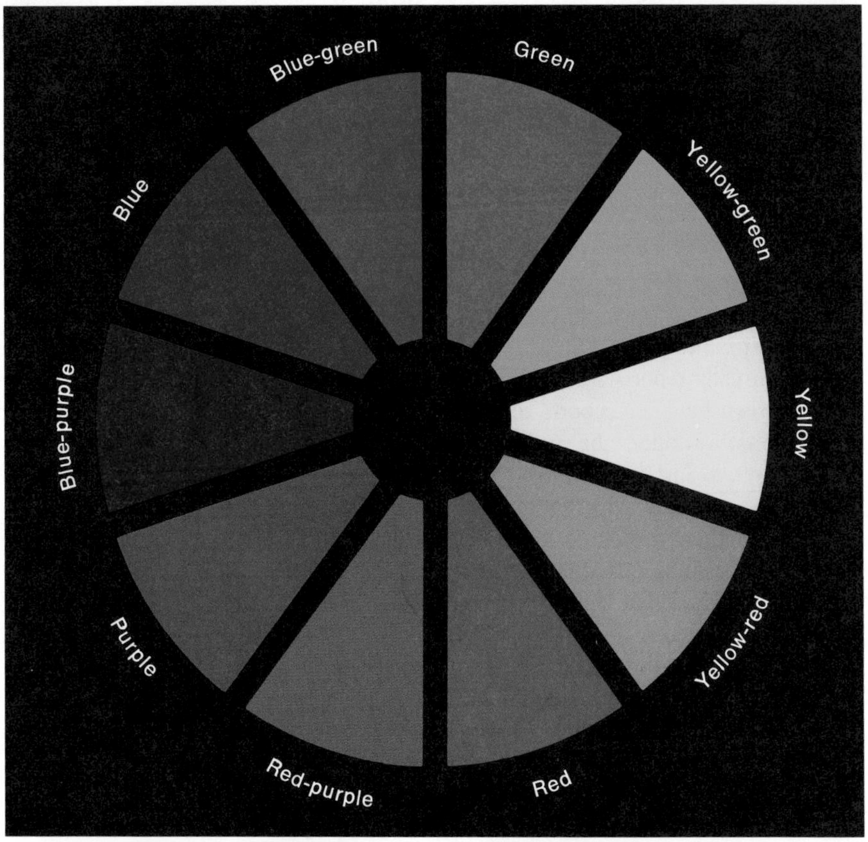

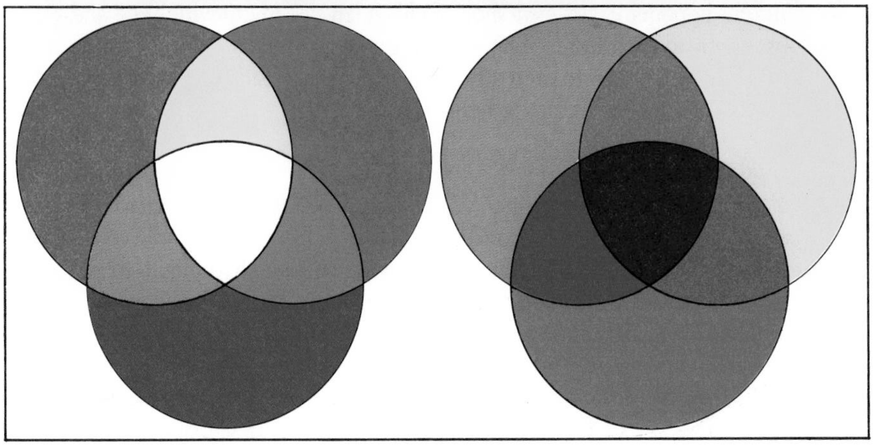

Figure 13.12
Complementary colors, the two colors that yield achromaticity (gray or white) when mixed, are found opposite each other on the color wheel (left). (Below, left) additive color mixture. When two of these rays of white light, filtered through primary colors, are overlapped, they produce the secondary colors shown. Where all three overlap (are added), all wavelengths of the visible spectrum are again present, resulting in white light. (Below, right) subtractive color mixture. Pigments absorb certain wavelengths. Where they overlap, more wavelengths are absorbed (subtracted), that is, fewer are reflected. Theoretically a mixture of the three primary pigments (center overlap) should yield black, because all wavelengths are absorbed.

Figure 13.13
Look at the gray disc in the center of the top figure and compare it with the disc below. The disc at the top should appear to have a red tint, and the one at the bottom should appear slightly green. They are in fact physically identical. This kind of phenomenon illustrates a system of dual linkage in color vision.

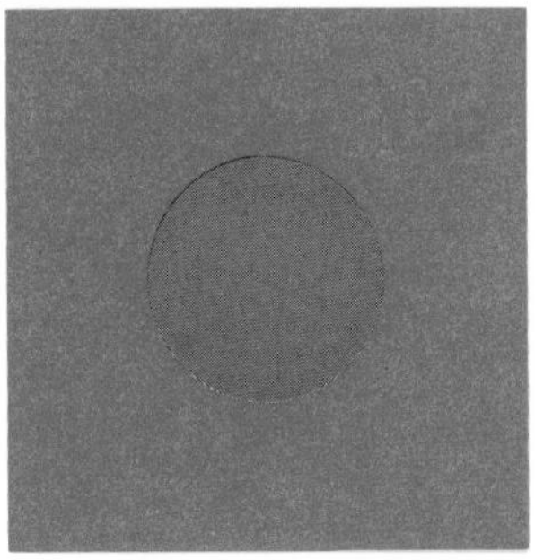

Figure 13.14
Because the colors of this flag are complementary to red, white, and blue, an afterimage of it will look like the flag you are used to seeing. To test this, stare at the lower right-hand star for about 45 seconds, then transfer your gaze to a well-lit piece of white paper that is free of glare.

seconds. Transfer your gaze to a white area, such as a blank sheet of paper. You should see the flag in its correct colors, which are complementary to those shown in the figure. Similarly, if an observer is shown a brief flash of an intense yellow light, he usually reports seeing blue shortly after the flash. If he is shown a brief flash of green light, he reports seeing a red patch after the flash.

These data support the notion that we have only a small number of kinds of color receptors. The exact number is not easy to determine on the basis of psychophysical experiments. Most of the data from such experiments makes sense if we assume that there are three kinds of color receptors, but the same data can be explained by assuming that there are four or five. As was pointed out by S. Hecht, an early investigator in the field of vision, this is essentially a biological problem, and recent physiological studies, especially those by G. Wald, suggest quite strongly that there are three different types of color receptors in the primate eye. Thus, there is considerable support for what is called the *trichromatic theory of color vision.*

How is the activity of these three kinds of cells organized and analyzed by the nervous system? A theory that is being widely discussed at present is called the *opponent-processes theory,* already alluded to in connection with the discussion of opponent cells. According to this theory, the three types of cells are linked to form three different opponent systems. One is a red-green system, in which red and green act in opposition to each other. The second is a yellow-blue system, in which those two colors act in opposition to each other. The third is a broadly sensitive achromatic or brightness system—essentially a light-dark system.

Color Blindness

What color is the grass in springtime? What color is an American Beauty rose? Some 90 percent of the people in the world see grass as bright green, and a rose as red. If your color vision is normal, there is a striking (although difficult to describe) difference between green and red. To someone who is partially or completely color-blind, however, there may be no perceptible difference between the two colors. Both may seem vaguely yellowish, brownish, or even dark gray.

About 10 percent of the population has some difficulty seeing colors. But it is a mistake to call most of these people color-blind, for they are not insensitive to all the colors of the visual spectrum. The easiest way to describe color blindness accurately is in terms of the number of colors that a person needs to mix in order to match all the hues he can see.

The person with normal color vision needs three hues in order to reproduce all the colors of the spectrum. Such a person is called a *trichromat,* and the way he sees the world is shown in Figure 13.16. People who are partially color-blind need but two hues to reproduce all the colors they can see; we call them *dichromats.* If a dichromat is red-green blind, he can match all the hues he can see by mixing yellow and blue; the way he sees the world is reproduced in Figure 13.17. Red-green dichromatism is the most common, but a few dichromats are yellow-blue blind. They can reproduce all the hues they perceive by mixing red and green, seeing the world as illustrated in Figure 13.18. A very few people are totally color-blind. They see no color at all; to them the world is nothing but blacks and whites and shades of gray, as shown in Figure 13.19. Such a person is called a *monochromat* because he needs only one color (any color at all—they are all the same to him) to reproduce what he sees. (Figures 13.16–13.19 appear on pages 238–239.)

In point of fact, even partial color blindness is not usually an all-or-nothing thing. Many trichromats need abnormally large amounts of one of the three hues in order to match the spectrum. A person who is green-weak perceives green as a separate and distinct color but sees the leaves on trees as being a grayish green. A person who is red-green blind cannot see green at all, no matter how intense.

A test for color blindness appears in Figure 13.15. Although we are not entirely sure what the neural correlates of color blindness are, probably the proper cones are either missing or malfunctioning. Confirmation of this theory comes from studies showing that the totally color-blind person, the monochromat, sees only with his rods. The fovea, which is at the center of the retina, contains no rods, only cones, and monochromats have little if any foveal vision. To compensate for the fact that the center of his visual field—the part that registers the most detail for the rest of us—is lacking, he moves his eyes back and forth rapidly so that everything registers in the peripheral part of his visual apparatus. The dark-adaptation curve of the monochromat is rather simply shaped, since only the rods adapt.

HEARING

The development of language—particularly speech and speech perception—depends to a considerable extent on hearing. Mammalian hearing evolved to serve nonspeaking animals; speech and man's vocal apparatus may have evolved in part to accommodate his already established auditory mechanisms. Although hearing is the social sense for man, for many other animals, the social sense is smell. Some people view the loss of hearing as imposing an even greater burden than the loss

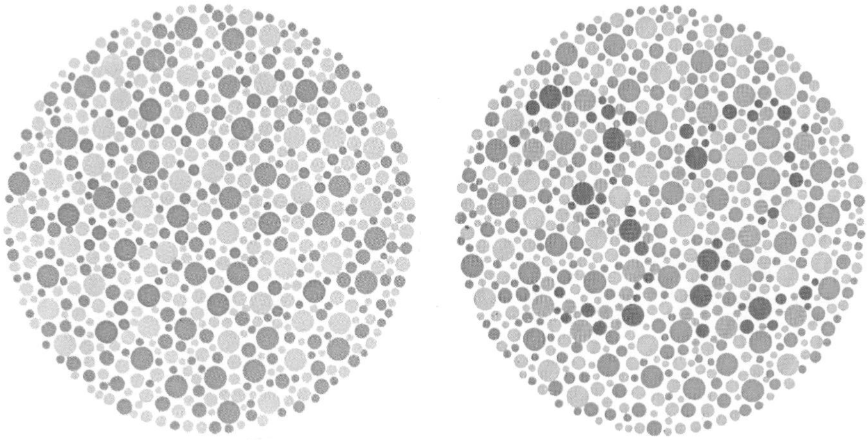

Figure 13.15
These figures are part of a common test for color blindness. You should be able to see numerals in them. The dots are equated for brightness; consequently, the only available cue by which the numbers can be perceived is color (hue). The left-hand figure is constructed to detect yellow-blue insensitivity, and the right-hand one, red-green insensitivity.
(The Dvorine Pseudo-Isochromatic Plates.)

Figure 13.16
This scene is shown as it would look to a person with normal color vision (a trichromat).

Figure 13.17
A person who is color blind for red-green, the most common type of color blindness, sees this.

Figure 13.18
Someone who is color blind for yellow-blue sees this.

Figure 13.19
A monochromat sees this. This type of color blindness is relatively rare.

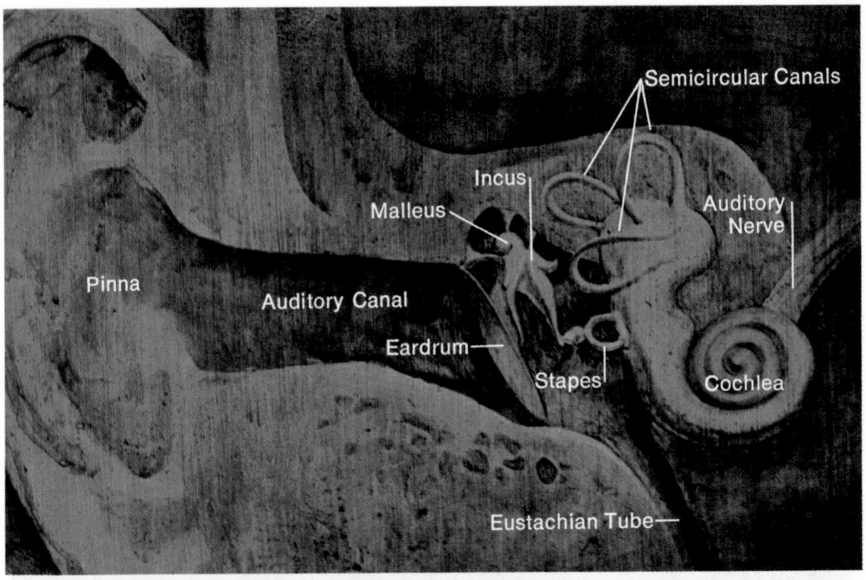

Figure 13.20

The organs of the ear. Sound, as pressure waves in the air, passes through the auditory canal and is transformed at the eardrum into mechanical vibration. The ossicles amplify this motion and transmit it to the oval window of the cochlea.

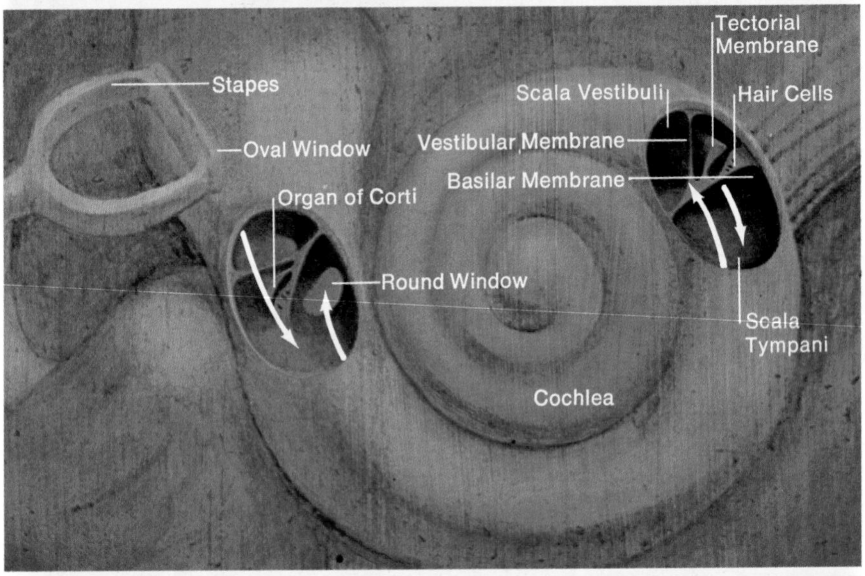

Figure 13.21

The cochlea. The motion of the oval window sends pressure waves through the fluid in the cochlea in the directions shown by the arrows.

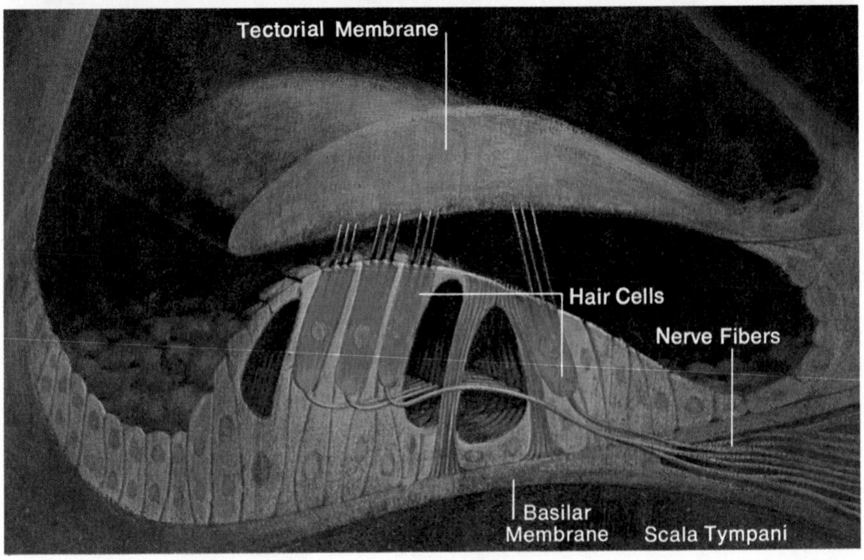

Figure 13.22

The organ of Corti. This is a cross section through the structure that extends throughout the length of the coiled tube that is the cochlea.

of sight. They feel that looks and gestures can be dispensed with, as long as one can hear the sounds of speech, which have intonations that sometimes reveal the speaker's emotions even better than visible signs.

The Structure of the Ear

Figure 13.20 shows the structure of the ear: the outer ear (the opening, pinna, and the auditory canal), the middle ear, and the inner ear, or *cochlea.* The three semicircular canals are part of the vestibular apparatus rather than of the auditory system; they provide cues to body position and movement.

Sound reaching the eardrum sets it and the three bones of the middle ear (the malleus, incus, and stapes, which are called the *ossicles*) vibrating to and fro. The vibrations transmit the movement of the air particles to the cochlea, which is buried deep in the body's hardest bone. Coiled inside the cochlea is the extremely sensitive *basilar membrane.* The basilar membrane and the rest of the interior of the cochlea are shown in cross section in Figure 13.21. Sound energy enters the cochlea through the oval window and sets up a pressure wave that moves along the basilar membrane to the apex of the cochlea. Pressure against the oval window is relieved by the flexibility of the round window, which lies on the other side of the basilar membrane.

When the basilar membrane is wobbled by the traveling wave, the *organ of Corti* lying on it also moves up and down. In the organ of Corti are hair cells. Their extensions, or hairs, are embedded in the *tectorial membrane.* The tectorial membrane and the basilar membrane move somewhat differently, so that the hairs between them (see Figure 13.22) are bent in a kind of rubbing or shearing action. The bending of the hairs causes the hair cells to send neural impulses to the auditory nerve. At the threshold of hearing, the basilar membrane vibrates over a distance 100 times smaller than the diameter of a hydrogen atom. Somehow, this infinitesimally small movement leads to hearing.

Neural Coding by the Ear

The auditory system, like the visual system, is a sensory-transducing device. It changes sound waves into neural impulses that eventually give rise to the sensation of hearing. But whereas in the eye the absorption of energy stimulates *chemical* changes in the retina, in the ear transduction is primarily *mechanical.*

The transduction from stimulus energy into neural energy is performed by the basilar membrane. Using ingenious techniques and high-powered microscopes, G. von Békésy and W. A. Rosenblith have observed the displacements of the basilar membrane when intense pure tones are introduced into the ear. Von Békésy found that different parts of the basilar membrane are maximally excited by different frequencies, as shown here in Figure 13.23. High-frequency tones most affect the region near the oval window. As the frequency of the tone decreases, the locus of excitation moves along the membrane toward the apex of the cochlea. Frequency is apparently encoded by the place of maximum displacement on the basilar membrane.

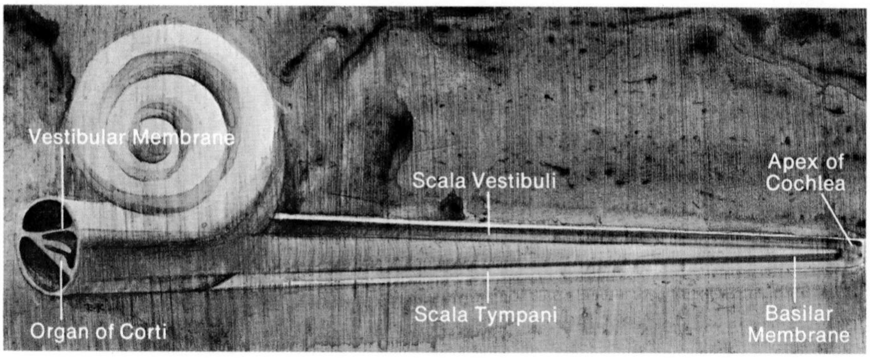

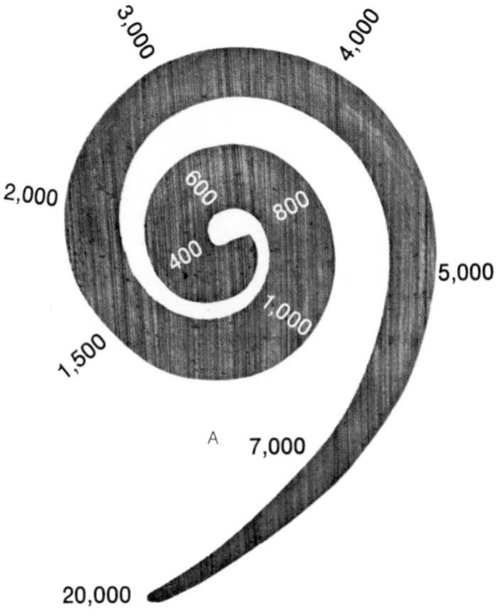

Figure 13.23
(Left) the structure of the cochlea is clarified by showing it unrolled. (Right) different parts of the basilar membrane are displaced maximally by different frequencies of sound. High-frequency tones move the membrane most in the region near the oval window, while progressively lower frequencies produce maximal displacement progressively farther toward the apex of the cochlea. A tone of 400 cycles per second, for example, although it displaces the entire membrane to some extent, moves the membrane most near the apex of the cochlea. In this way information about the frequency of a tone may be represented by the place of maximal displacement of the basilar membrane.
(After Stuhlman, 1943.)

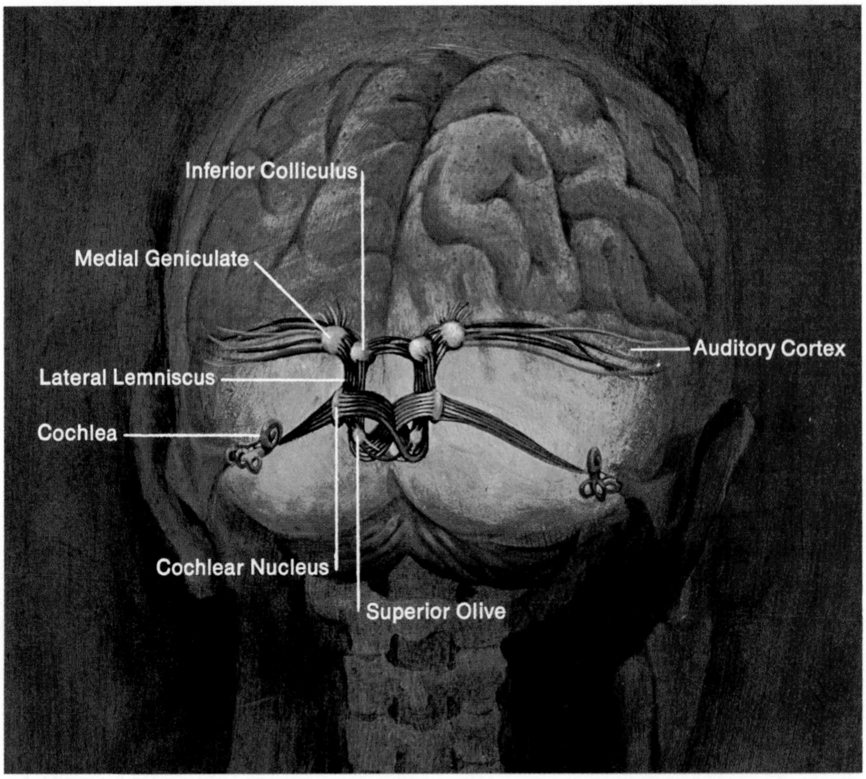

Figure 13.24
Auditory nerve fibers enter the brain in the cochlear nucleus. The auditory message is then transmitted via the superior olive and medial geniculate nucleus to the auditory cortex in the temporal lobes of the cerebral hemispheres. At all these levels the correlation between place and frequency, first seen on the basilar membrane, is consistently maintained.

The encoded message is carried by the auditory nerve, which reaches the auditory cortex in the back of the brain after passing through several subcortical relay stations. Despite its great complexity, the auditory system retains its *tonotopic organization*—that is, the correlation between place and frequency that von Békésy noted on the basilar membrane—all the way to the auditory cortex. For example, in the auditory cortex the place of maximum electrical response to stimulation by pure tones shifts as a function of frequency.

The *place theory* of how frequencies are coded is based on these findings. An alternate theory, discussed by E. G. Wever, says that frequency is directly represented in the nervous system by some repetitive event with the same frequency as that of the sound. This theory, called the *volley theory,* relies in part on observations that the cochlea duplicates some aspects of the stimulus waveform and frequency and that the firing of the auditory nerve follows, within certain limitations, the stimulus frequency. In its modern guise the second theory includes the first.

Although the question of how frequencies are coded has been the major theoretical problem in hearing, the coding of sound intensity also poses problems. Loudness seems to depend on how many nerve fibers are active and on the degree of their activity, as indicated primarily by their rate of firing. But the firing rate increases with stimulus intensity only until the intensity reaches about 50 decibels. That is below the level of ordinary conversation (60 decibels) and well below the level of loud sounds such as a jet taking off (140 decibels). The number of nerve fibers that are active also increases with intensity (because the spread of displacement over the basilar membrane increases, activating more and more fibers), but even when this effect and increased firing rates are both taken into account, the variations are not sufficient to explain how we hear loudness. A full explanation of loudness simply is not available yet.

Another important part of auditory perception is our ability to tell where sounds are coming from—to locate them in space. This ability depends primarily on tiny physical and temporal differences in a sound when it reaches the left and right ears.

For example, a sound from the left arrives at the left ear about .0007 second sooner than at the right ear. This small time difference causes the listener to hear the sound as being on the left. The coding of localization, like that of frequency discrimination, may depend on which nerve fibers are most active.

Basic Phenomena of Hearing

The main functions of the auditory system are to allow us to identify and locate sound sources. We detect sound sources and estimate the size of the stimuli and their distance from us mainly on the basis of the *loudness* of the sound; we identify them chiefly through *pitch;* and we localize them largely through *binaural interaction,* that is, interaction of the two ears.

Loudness Loudness, you will recall from Chapter 12, is a psychological phenomenon rather than a physical one. It is the subjective magnitude of a sound. Although loudness bears a systematic relation to the physical strength of a sound, the relationship is complex. Generally, when the sound-pressure level is increased threefold, the loudness doubles.

Although loudness depends largely on the physical intensity of a sound, it is also influenced by frequency. As was noted in Chapter 12, frequency and intensity work together to determine all the attributes of a sound—not only loudness but pitch, density, and volume. In one procedure contrived by S. S. Stevens to find out how intense tones at different frequencies must be in order to sound equally loud, the experimenter asked the subject to adjust the sound pressure of a tone at one frequency until the loudness was the same as that of a tone at another frequency. It turns out that low and high frequencies must be somewhat more intense to sound as loud as the middle frequencies.

In another common procedure for estimating loudness, which Stevens used in 1957, the experimenter presents a stimulus at a variety of known sound pressures. He asks the listener to assign the number 10 to a sound of intermediate loudness and then to give appropriately higher and lower numbers to louder and softer sounds. Observers agree remarkably well in the numbers they assign.

Pitch Pitch is closely related to frequency, but the two should not be confused. Pitch, like loudness, is a subjective attribute, whereas frequency is a physical characteristic of sound waves.

People usually identify sounds, including the sounds of speech, on the basis of pitch. Partly for that reason, pitch has been the center of attention in auditory theory. But theories of pitch perception encounter two major obstacles. First, a very large number of different pitches can be distinguished at most sound pressure levels—something like 1,000, under optimal testing conditions. Second, people hear sounds composed of different pitches, as in a piano chord, as separate pitches even though they occur simultaneously. *Ohm's Acoustic Law* states that the ear can resolve any complex waveform into its component tones. The ear and the eye differ in this respect: when lights of different wavelengths are mixed, people see the mixture rather than the two or more component hues.

Binaural Interaction The auditory system locates the source of a sound by detecting extremely small time and intensity differences as the sound reaches the two ears. The size of these *binaural differences* depends mainly on where the sound source is in relation to the listener, but it is also influenced by the frequency of the sound.

How good is a human listener at judging the direction of sound sources? To answer that question, S. S. Stevens and E. B. Newman sat on the roof of a building and, blindfolded, judged the location of a loudspeaker emitting pure tones from various locations. They did the study on a roof in order to minimize sound reflections

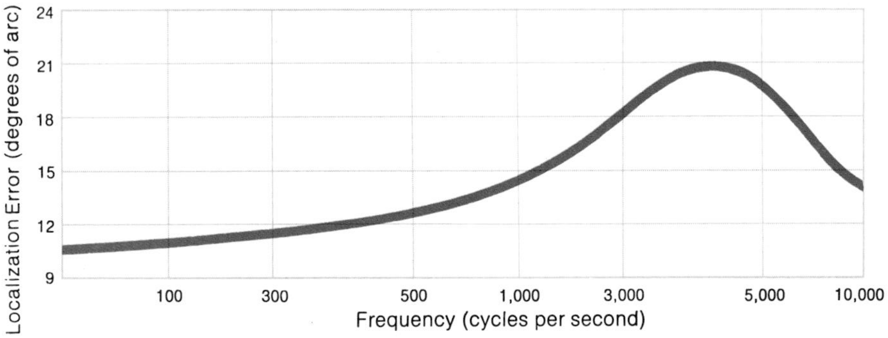

Figure 13.25
Errors in sound localization are greater for some tonal frequencies than for others. A tone of 4,000 cycles per second is more difficult for a person to locate correctly than are tones of either higher (10,000 CPS) or lower (500 CPS) frequencies.
(After Stevens and Newman, 1936.)

from surrounding objects. (Most surfaces reflect a substantial portion of the sounds hitting them, causing slight echoes.) As Figure 13.25 shows, errors in localization rarely exceed 20 degrees and are usually smaller than that. With tones of frequencies under 1,000 cycles per second or over 6,000, errors were only 15 degrees or less.

At low frequencies, tones have such long wavelengths compared to the size of the head that intensity differences between the ears are almost nil. For low-frequency sounds, and also for brief sounds and sounds with changing frequencies, then, the important cue to localization is difference in the time of the sound's arrival at the ears. Sound travels about 1,100 feet per second—fast, but still slow enough to produce a clear time difference. Because most sounds we hear are either brief or fluctuating, we usually rely on time differences for locating sounds.

The ears of the average adult male are about seven inches apart. A sound directly opposite the right ear reaches that ear about 0.7 millisecond sooner than it reaches the left ear. As the sound source moves toward a position directly in front (or in back) of the listener, the time difference decreases and, finally, disappears. If a sound is coming from directly in front of or in back of you, you must turn your head slightly to tell where it is coming from. If you doubt the difficulty of locating sounds in the front/rear plane, you can do the following experiment with a friend. While you sit blindfolded, with your head absolutely still, have your friend move (noiselessly) around the room and snap his fingers to your right, left, front, and back. You should find that your ability to locate sounds on the right and left is essentially perfect, but you may not always be able to tell front from back.

Distinguishing between sounds from above and sounds from below is also difficult because, again, the sound reaches both ears at the same time. In this case you locate the sound by tilting your head. When a sound reaches both ears at the same time, a person usually rotates his head slightly (to distinguish front from back); if that does not work, he tries tilting it.

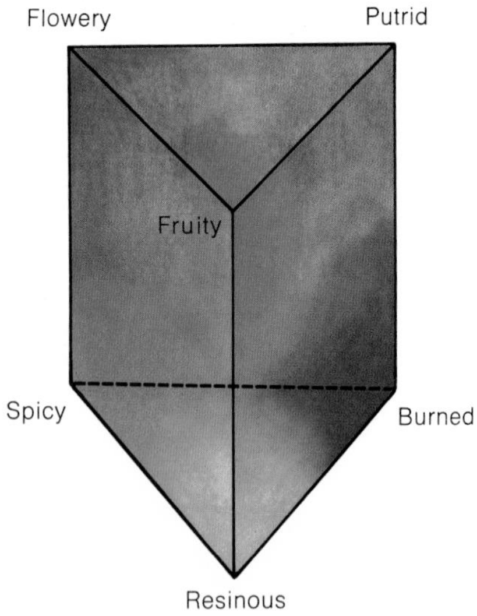

Figure 13.26
Henning's smell prism has been used extensively for the difficult task of measuring and classifying an individual's olfactory sensations. The corners are assumed to represent pure qualities, with qualitatively intermediate sensations lying along the surface.

SMELL

Man's sense of smell is not nearly as sensitive as that of many animals and insects. Male moths, for example, can smell female moths several miles away. Smell requires that appropriate molecules enter the nasal passages, where the membrane containing smell receptors, the *olfactory epithelium,* is located. Millions of hair cells in the epithelium transduce the stimulus and transmit nerve impulses through their axons, which constitute the olfactory nerve and lead directly to the olfactory bulb of the brain. Because the olfactory receptors are accessible only to gases, only volatile substances—substances that are readily vaporized from a liquid or solid to a gas—have odors.

Most odors to which man is sensitive are organic compounds, but little else is known about why we can smell some substances and not others or why certain groups of odors smell alike. A search for a way to classify odors on the basis of their physical characteristics has so far been unsuccessful. Subjective classification schemes based on people's judgments are not entirely successful either, but the most popular one is Henning's smell prism, shown in Figure 13.26. Six supposedly pure qualities form the corners of the prism, and the intermediate qualities lie along the surface. The search for the basis of odor differences and similarities is a search for common chemical properties that distinguish the members of one class of odors from the members of other classes.

Without knowing what stimulus properties are important in smell, researchers find it difficult to control stimuli for experimental purposes—more difficult than in studies of vision and hearing, for which the important properties are known and easily measured. We do know that the subjective intensity of smell increases with the concentration of the odorous substance, and also that we adapt completely to most odors within a few minutes of exposure. Generally, the more concentrated the odor, the faster the adaptation. Smell plays a small role in modern civilization, although large enough to encourage large perfume and deodorant industries. It is probably most important to us when it interacts with taste.

TASTE

Taste, or gustation, may be considered either as the global sensation that accompanies the presence of a substance in the mouth or as the specific sensation that accompanies the stimulation of certain organs in the mouth. Global taste perception includes a very strong olfactory component, and sensations of temperature and touch as well. If none of the vapors from food reaches the organ of smell, taste is substantially altered. The specific sensation of taste results from stimulation of the taste buds, which are grouped in large numbers as *papillae* and located primarily on the surface of the tongue.

Most of our taste sensations are mixtures of four primary taste qualities: sour, salty, bitter, and sweet. The mixtures in some common foods are shown in Table 13.1. The qualities can be elicited in more or less pure form by stimulating the taste buds with concentrated solutions or by stimulating individual papillae with electrical pulses. The fact that electrical stimulation effects only these four taste qualities suggests that four kinds of papillae, differing somewhat in shape, are responsible for the four primary taste qualities. Although salty and sour tastes seem to depend upon ionic action (NaCl, for instance, ionizes to the anion Cl^- and the cation Na^+), it is not possible to state a single chemical or physical property that applies

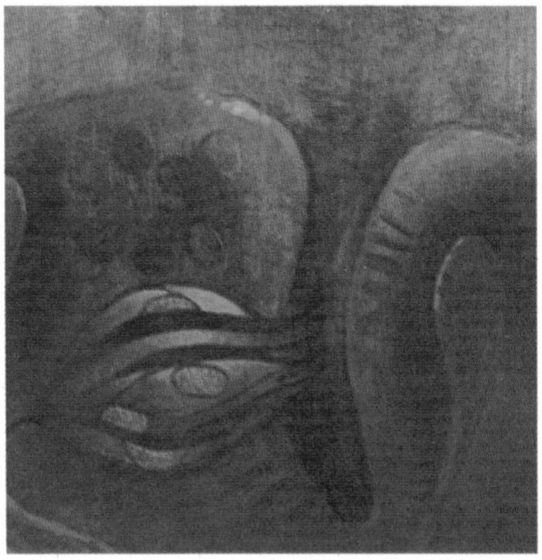

Figure 13.27
A single taste bud contains several gustatory cells with hairlike extensions that probably respond to chemical changes occurring nearby. Stimulation of these cells initiates neural impulses that send gustatory information to the brain.

Table 13.1—Taste Mixtures of Selected Food Products

Food Product	Sweet	Bitter	Sour	Salty
Cola drink	11.2	2.2	5.0	1.3
Ale	2.5	28.2	10.0	1.3
Unsweetened grapefruit juice	3.2	2.0	35.5	2.0
Consommé	1.4	1.3	4.5	7.9
Tokay wine	10.0	4.2	4.2	1.8
Riesling wine	1.0	7.5	6.7	1.3
"Root" tonic	4.2	1.3	3.2	1.3
Coffee, unsweetened	1.0	42.3	3.2	1.0
Coffee, 5% sucrose	3.2	23.8	3.2	1.3
Anchovy fillet	1.3	23.8	5.6	10.0
Sweet pickles	3.2	3.2	13.4	3.2
Sour pickles	1.0	1.8	18.0	3.2
Raspberry jam	23.8	1.8	10.0	1.3
Honey	56.4	2.4	1.8	1.3
Means	8.8	10.4	8.9	2.7

Source: G. A. Geldard, *The Human Senses* (New York: Wiley, 1953), p. 315. Data from J. G. Beebe-Center, "Standards for the Use of the Gust Scale," *Journal of Psychology,* 28 (1949), 411-419.

to sweet or bitter. Thus, understanding of how different stimuli elicit different sensations is only slightly better for taste than for smell.

Likes and dislikes for certain tastes sometimes depend more on the physiological condition of the eater than on the apparent pleasantness or unpleasantness of what is eaten. C. P. Richter reports that a three-year-old boy, admitted for examination in a hospital because of irregular physical development, died after a week. Autopsy showed that his adrenal glands had been allowing salt to pass out with urine faster than he could accumulate it on the regular hospital diet. It turned out that the boy had survived at home because he had craved salt and received large extra amounts of it, gulping down a tablespoonful at a time or eating it directly from a salt shaker. He had no access to salt in the hospital. J. Bare reports that rats whose adrenal glands have been removed also show a desire for salt.

Adaptation to tastes, like adaptation to smells, is rapid. Figure 13.28 shows that the threshold for three different stimuli rises sharply for ten to twenty-five seconds, until it reaches about the concentration of the adaptation stimulus, and then drops back to normal about thirty seconds after removal of the stimulus. The more concentrated the stimulus, the faster the threshold rises. Does adaptation to one chemical affect the threshold for other, similar ones? Sometimes yes, sometimes no. Adaptation to any one of twenty-four different kinds of salt does not affect the threshold for the other twenty-three. But adaptation to any one acid raises the threshold for all other acids (acids are sour), and cross-adaptation also occurs for some (not all) sweet and bitter stimuli. The fact that cross-adaptation does not always occur complicates theories that assume separate taste receptors.

THE SKIN SENSES

Touch comes to our awareness in three distinct forms: as pressure, as warmth and cold, and as pain. The receptors for these sensations lie in the thin epidermis and the inner dermis of the skin. Nerve endings in the skin transmit sensations to the cortex of the brain via the spinal cord.

Warmth and Cold

Touching the skin with stimulators at skin temperature, usually 32 degrees centigrade, yields no thermal sensation; the temperature at which there is no sensation is referred to as *physiological zero*. Warmth is usually felt at temperatures greater

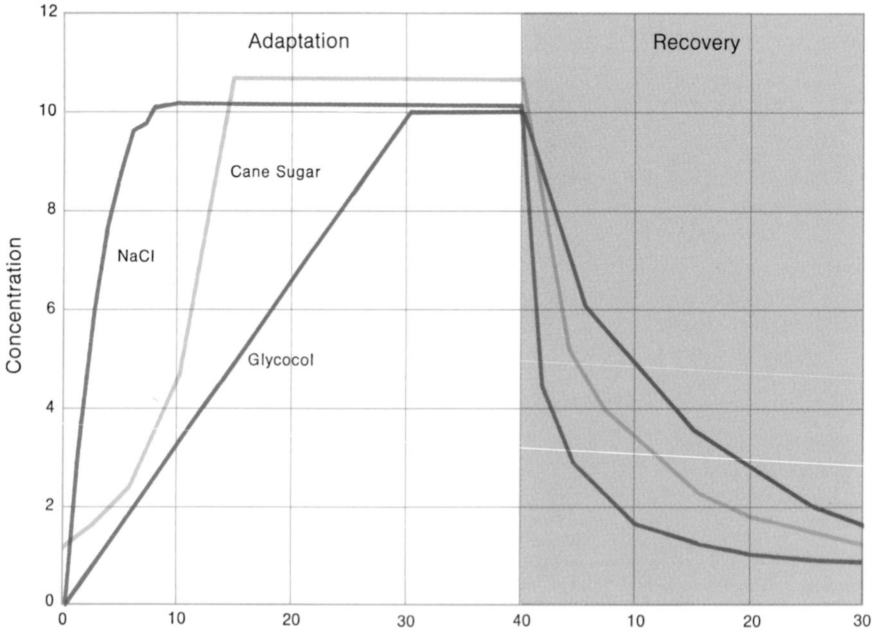

Figure 13.28
This graph shows how taste sensitivity to various substances decreases if the substance is continuously present and how sensitivity recovers when it is removed. The smallest concentration detectable is plotted as a function of the time that the substance has been present. Note that the substances to which we adapt most quickly are also the substances for which our sensitivity recovers fastest.
(After Pfaffman, 1951.)

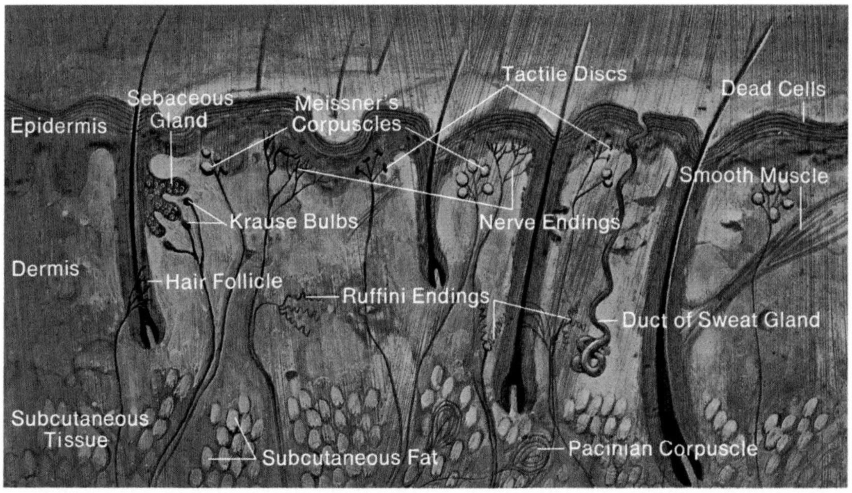

Figure 13.29
Cross-sectional diagram of the human skin reveals a variety of sensory receptors. The free nerve endings of the epidermis may be sensitive to pain. Sensations of pressure are received by the Pacinian corpuscles in the dermis. Some of the receptors that can be distinguished in form have not yet been associated with distinct sensory functions. The Krause bulbs and Ruffini endings are among these.

than physiological zero, cold at lower temperatures. Warmth and cold are not felt at every point on the skin, only at specific spots. Exploration of the skin with small points of warm and cold materials reveals about six cold spots but only one or two warm spots in a square centimeter of skin, on the average. The separate identity of warm and cold spots is generally accepted, partly because stimulating a cold spot with a very warm stimulus sometimes yields a cold sensation. The name for this phenomenon is *paradoxical cold.*

When individual warm or cold spots are stimulated, adaptation is rapid and complete, even if the stimulus is very cold or very warm. In contrast, adaptation under general stimulation is complete only when the stimulus is no colder than 16 degrees and no warmer than 42 degrees centigrade, and complete disappearance of the sensation of warmth or coolness may take several minutes. Of course, once a subject has adapted to a warmer or colder stimulus, physiological zero changes. If you have been lying in a warm bath for a while, tap water only a little less warm feels cold.

You can demonstrate thermal adaptation to yourself, if you wish, by performing the classic "three-bowl experiment." Fill one bowl with cold water, a second bowl with fairly hot water, and a third bowl with water at about room temperature. Place one hand in the "cold" bowl and the other hand in the "hot" bowl and leave them there for at least one minute. Then put both hands at the same time into the third bowl. There should be a clear difference in the way the lukewarm water feels to your two hands.

Pressure Sensitivity to pressure varies from place to place on the skin. Even pressure-sensitive spots are more responsive to changes in pressure than to steady states. Once the skin has been displaced, the sensation of pressure disappears—rapidly, if the force exerted is slight. If this were not true, we would be constantly aware of the gentle pressure of clothes, eyeglasses, hair lying against the back of the neck, and so on.

The amount of energy that must be exerted for pressure to be just detectable is perhaps smallest on the tips of the thumb and fingers, the underside of the forearm, the lips, and the tip of the tongue. Although the pressure thresholds at these points are among the lowest on the skin, the energy required to reach them is from 100 million to 10 billion times greater than the energy values required by the eye and ear at threshold.

Pain Pain is associated with more than just the skin. However, little is known about pain from the interior of the body except that it seems to be deep, dull, and much more unpleasant than the bright, sharply localized pain from the skin. Many kinds of stimuli—scratch, puncture, pressure, heat, cold, twist—can produce pain. Their common property is real or potential injury to bodily tissue. In general, overstimulation of any sensory modality—loud sounds, bright lights, intense pressure—is painful. What part of the brain mediates pain is not clearly known.

Thresholds for pain vary little from observer to observer and from time to time. In the laboratory, mild cutaneous pain can be shown to disappear with prolonged stimulation, but little adaptation to pain occurs under ordinary circumstances. Nonadaptation is probably fortunate, since pain alerts us to noxious stimuli and to injuries and disease that need treatment.

THE VESTIBULAR SENSE

The vestibular sense is the sense of balance. We are never directly aware of it: there is no "vestibular sensation" that we can ascribe to a particular body organ. We are very much aware of our posture, movements, and orientation in space, however. The vestibular, visual, and kinesthetic senses cooperate to produce that awareness. Adults can get along fairly well without their vestibular organs, provided that their visual and kinesthetic senses are unimpaired. But interest in the vestibular sense has been high since space travel began, because a long absence of gravity might disturb vestibular functions.

The vestibular organ lies in the inner ear, buried in bone above and to the rear of the cochlea. Its prominent section is the three semicircular canals, which lie at right angles to each other as shown in Figure 13.30. When the head starts turning in the plane of a given canal, the movement causes pressure that bends the endings of receptor hair cells. The hair cells connect with the vestibular nerve, which joins the auditory nerve on its way to the brain. As in the cochlea, little is known about how the bending of the hairs is transduced to neural impulses.

The stimuli for vestibular responses are rotational or linear acceleration, falling, and tilting the body or head. A common test of the vestibular function uses a rotating chair. If visual, auditory, and tactile cues are excluded, the observer feels the rotation and shows nystagmus (rapid back-and-forth movement of the eyes) only as long as the speed with which the chair rotates is increasing or decreasing. If the chair rotates at a constant speed, the observer stops feeling any movement and nystagmus ceases. Interesting effects occur if the rotating chair is stopped suddenly. Nystagmus returns for up to thirty seconds, and the observer feels as if he is turning

Figure 13.30
The vestibular organ, sensitive to motion and to changes in orientation of the body, consists of the semicircular canals, the utricle, and the saccule. These structures are located in the inner ear, above and to the rear of the cochlea. The canals are all at right angles to each other so that acceleration in any plane will cause the receptors in at least one to respond.

in the opposite direction. The sensation may be similar to the ocean traveler's feeling that the land is moving when he steps off the ship.

KINESTHESIS

Kinesthesis is the sense of movement and body position. It cooperates with the vestibular and visual senses to maintain posture and equilibrium. The sensation of kinesthesis comes from nerve endings in and near the more than 100 body joints and in the muscles. The nerve endings in the joints are especially important for the perception of bodily movement. They respond to movement of the joint by an initial rapid burst of firing, after which the discharge rate is a function of the speed and extent of the movement. Which receptors respond depends on the direction and angle of movement. Other nerve endings in the muscles and tendons also contribute to the sensation of kinesthesis. Together, these various receptors help provide the feedback necessary for regulation of active body movement.

SUGGESTED READINGS

BORING, E. G. *Sensation and Perception in the History of Experimental Psychology.* New York, Appleton-Century-Crofts, 1942. A historical introduction to sensation and perception.

GELDARD, F. A. *The Human Senses.* New York, Wiley, 1953. Although somewhat dated, this book contains probably the most lucid overview of the human senses available.

GROSS, C. G., AND ZEIGLER, H. P. (Eds.). *Readings in Physiological Psychology: Neurophysiology/Sensory Processes.* New York, Harper & Row, 1969. Contains many important readings on the processing of sensory information, including work by such giants as Granit, Lettvin, Hernandez-Peón, von Békésy, and Wald.

KLING, J. W., AND RIGGS, L. A. *Woodworth and Schlosberg's Experimental Psychology* (3rd ed.). New York, Holt, Rinehart and Winston, 1971. Contains a recent and extensive treatment of the human senses. It includes chapters on the cutaneous senses, the chemical senses, a chapter by Willard Thurlow on audition, and chapters on vision by Riggs, by Boynton (on color vision), and by Alpern (on effector mechanisms in vision).

TEEVAN, R. C., AND BIRNEY, R. D. (Eds.). *Color Vision.* Princeton, N. J., Van Nostrand, 1961. This paperback contains several interesting reprints, ranging from the early writings of Young, Helmholz, and Hering to the pioneer experiments of Edwin Land.

VON BEKESY, G. "Hearing Theories and Complex Sounds," *Journal of the Acoustical Society of America,* 35 (1963), 588–601. "Taste Theories and the Chemical Stimulation of Single Papillae," *Journal of Applied Physiology,* 21 (1966), 1–9. *Sensory Inhibition.* Princeton, N. J., Princeton University Press, 1967. These writings by the Nobel-prize winner describe his pioneer work in hearing and taste and with the phenomenon of sensory inhibition.

WALD, G. "The Receptors of Human Color Vision," *Science,* 145 (1964), 1007–1016. This short article by the Harvard biologist (another Nobel-prize winner) is a milestone in our understanding of the mechanism of color vision. Wald's work is also discussed in Kling and Riggs, cited above.

14
Perception

WE OFTEN THINK OF AN OPTICAL ILLUSION as some clever but artificial device of lines and curves, of mirrors and distorted angles, designed to fool the unprepared eye. But what of an optical illusion that is not artificial at all but is a central fact of life, one that has distorted philosophy and science and has prevented us from advancing much further than we have in the direction of knowledge and sanity?

Imagine two trains on parallel tracks and imagine yourself looking out the window into the other train. The other train begins, very slowly, to inch forward. Are you sure? Or is it your own train that is beginning, very slowly, to inch backward? If your train is moving very slowly, and at a constant speed in a straight line, all the ordinary clues to motion—jarring, vibration, and so on—are missing, and you will surely assume that you are motionless and that the other train is moving even when this is, in fact, not so. The confusion ends, however, as soon as you look out the other window at the scenery. If the world, generally, is motionless, you are comfortably sure that you are motionless as well. If it is moving in one direction, you are sure that you are moving in the other direction. By observing the scenery, any illusion involving motion that you may have experienced ends at once.

Earth and sky are in the same position with respect to each other as those two trains. The Earth is rotating about its axis but so steadily and smoothly and is also revolving about the Sun, so steadily and smoothly that there are no cues to give rise to the feel of motion. So we assume we are at rest. It is the sky that moves east-to-west in a day-long circle, and it is the bodies of our solar system that move in more complicated fashion in yearly and more-than-yearly cycles. And there is no "scenery" to look at to correct this impression.

It is not surprising, then, that it was not till the seventeenth century that men, generally, could be persuaded to accept the other view on the basis of the steady pile-up of indirect evidence—that it was the Earth moving and not the rest of the Universe. The illusion that the Earth is the motionless center of the Universe, *which is exactly the way things look,* held back the advance of astronomy and physics for many centuries. Worse yet, the illusion makes it appear that men inhabit the center and focal point of the Universe. From that, it is an easy step to assuming that all the rest of the Universe exists only for the sake of the Earth and, more particularly, for the sake of man. We are lords and masters of it all and are subject only to the Supreme Being we decided must have shaped the Universe (for our benefit) in the first place.

Had we known from the start that Earth was not the center of the Universe, it would have been so much easier to accept our position as an inconsiderable part of a gigantic whole. We might have accepted, further, our humble role in the complex ecology of our own small planet. Without the gigantic sense of self-importance that rested entirely on *illusion,* we might not so arrogantly and selfishly have gone about the thoughtless and systematic destruction of our planet and ourselves. I. A.

Suppose that you are taking part in a classroom demonstration of perception. You are watching a shadow that is cast on a piece of frosted glass. Part of the shadow is moving, and your teacher asks you to describe what you see. You might say, "I see a rectangular shadow that's rotating clockwise." Or you might say, "I think there's something rotating behind the glass—probably a rectangle—and it's casting a shadow on the glass." In the first case you are describing what you see—which psychologists call your *perception.* In the second case you are describing what you believe is causing what you see. In everyday life we often ignore the distinction between our perceptions and our knowledge of what causes them, but if we are to understand how people use sensory information, it is an important distinction to maintain.

If you watched the moving shadow for a while, a moment would come when you saw it change direction. Instead of rotating clockwise, it would rotate counterclockwise. As you continued to watch it, it would switch back and forth between

The three following pages contain a variety of visual illusions, which dramatically demonstrate the difference between our environment as we perceive it and the physical reality we can measure. The text continues on page 255.

Figure 14.1
The McCulloch effect. Place the book so that the figures are brightly and uniformly lighted, with no surface glare. Alternately look at the top figure (A) for about twenty seconds and then the bottom figure (B) for twenty seconds until you have looked at each figure five or six times. There is no need to fixate on a single spot, but you should focus your eyes on the central area of each figure. Now look at C (opposite, top). Next, rotate the book ninety degrees and look again. The complementary coloring seen by most people is thought to be caused by the fatiguing of color-edge receptors in the visual system.

Figure 14.2
This figure can be organized meaningfully in several ways. Each organization is highly unstable and will dissolve into others, giving the appearance of a moving, shifting series of patterns: large or small blocks of squares, networks of triangles, rows of rectangular tubes extending in depth, and others.

Figure 14.3

Visual illusions can be of several types. We perceive some as containing distortions even though we may have measured what we perceive as the distorted line with ruler or compass. Other illusions give us ambiguous clues, so that we can interpret what we perceive in two ways—but usually not both ways at the same time. Psychologists study the difficulties people have with these kinds of perceptions because the altered perceptions offer clues to normal perceptual processes. Drawings A and B exemplify a third type of illusion: because they give ordinary cues to depth, they are perceived as three-dimensional objects, but the cues are combined in ways that could never represent a real object. Drawings C and D also provide depth cues, but they are ambiguous figures. You may see the stairs of C from above or from beneath, and these perceptions may alternate. But you cannot see the stairs both ways simultaneously. The central disc in each of the designs in E is the same size, but its apparent size is affected by the context in which you see it. The physically perfect circles in F and the parallel straight lines in G are distorted by the angles of the fine lines in the background. The reasons for these distortions are not fully understood.

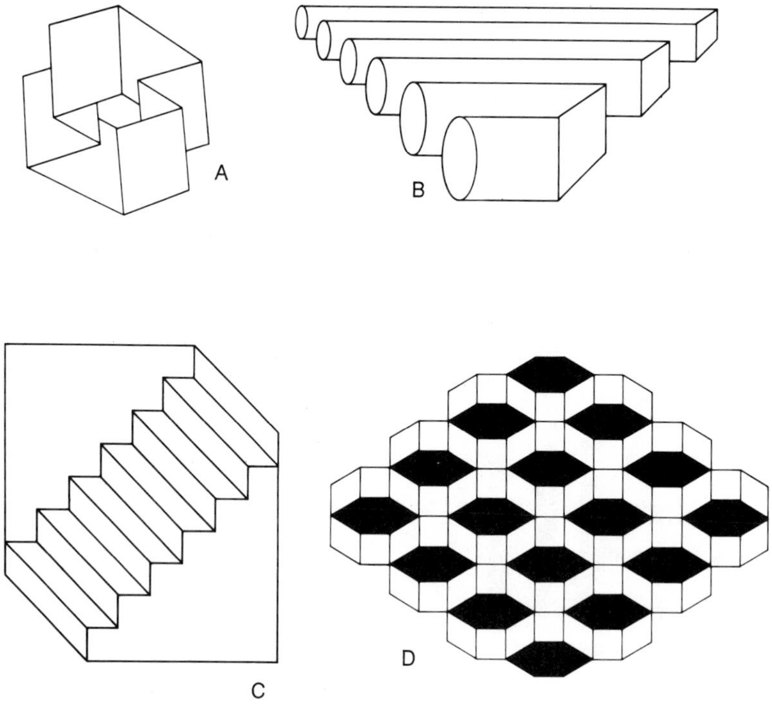

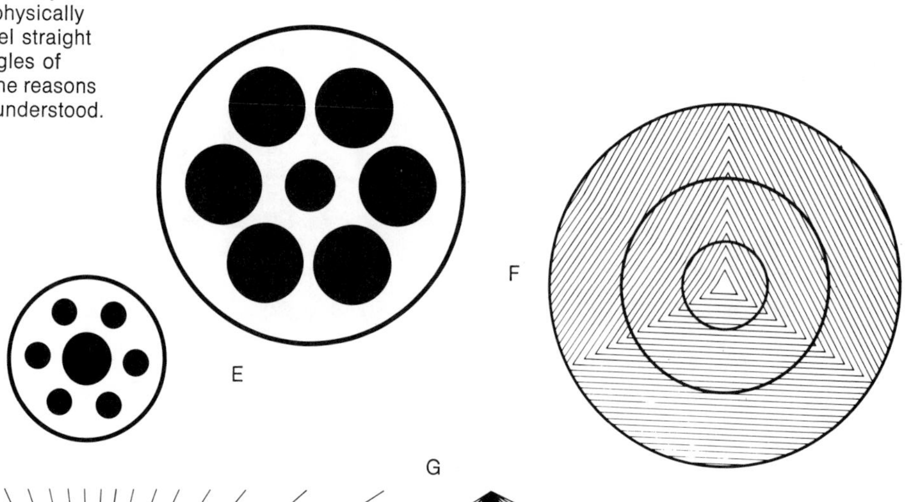

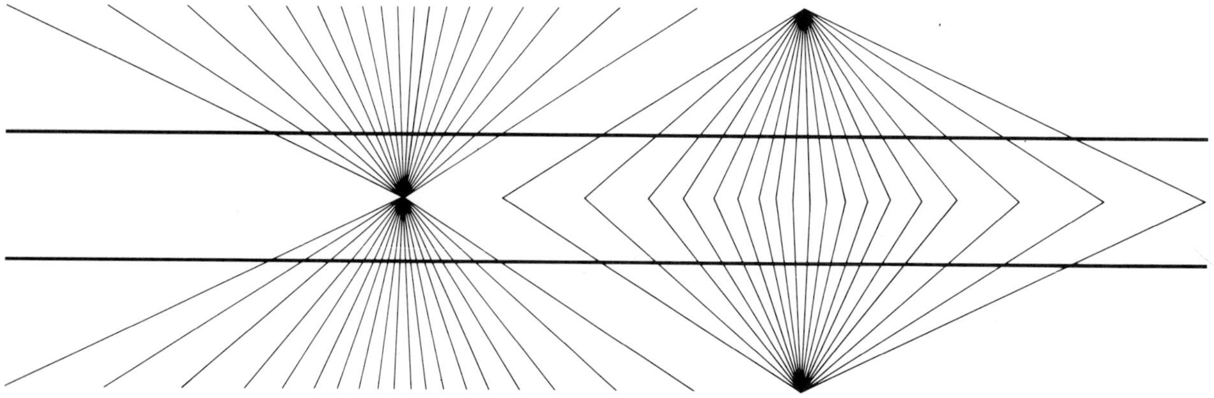

clockwise and counterclockwise. Then, suddenly, it would start to do something else. Instead of rotating, the rectangle might seem to be bent in the middle and flapping, like a butterfly flapping its wings.

People see at least half a dozen different patterns of movement of the shadow —and at any given time different people see different movements. While you see the shadow rotating clockwise, one of your friends might see it rotating counterclockwise. Similarly, the movements do not go through the same changes for different people. When the shadow starts flapping for you, your friend might continue to see it rotating counterclockwise.

What is really happening? You look behind the glass and see a rectangular piece of black metal rotating counterclockwise, as diagramed in Figure 14.4. It always rotates counterclockwise, even though you have seen the shadow change direction. Now that you *know* that the rectangle inside is always moving in the same way, do you *perceive* the shadow differently? No. You look at it again and continue to see it move not only counterclockwise but sometimes clockwise and sometimes like a flapping butterfly. Even though you know the pattern sensed by your eye is always the same, you still see the shadow moving in different ways. If you try, you can probably even change the movement at will, from clockwise to counterclockwise to flapping.

The visual image projected onto the retina of the eye is two-dimensional. As it happens, a shadow on frosted glass is also two-dimensional. But when people look at the world around them, they see three dimensions. When they look at the moving shadow, too, they perceive it as moving in three dimensions. From fleeting two-dimensional patterns of light on the retina, we somehow *infer* the existence of objects in a three-dimensional world.

Real objects are obviously different from sensory patterns of stimulation. A sensory pattern is neural activity. An object is a thing in the world. It has a past and a future; it takes up space; it may be heavy, brittle, hot. And its form is never entirely represented in sensory images at any one time. Behavior is geared to our perceptions of objects and object properties, and most of those perceptions are somehow inferred from sensory patterns. What can psychologists tell us about how we make those inferences?

GESTALTS AND GESTALTISTS

A *Gestalt* is a perceptual whole. In the moving-shadow experiment, each pattern of movement can be considered a Gestalt, because the overall pattern dominates what is perceived. The components of all the patterns are very similar—a pole, a rectangular shape on top of it, and a movement of the rectangle in an arc—but the patterns themselves are quite different from each other.

Gestalt psychology originated in Germany early in the twentieth century, at about the time that behaviorism was getting started in the United States, but the two schools of thought are very different. For example, behaviorists tend to assume that the best way to understand most phenomena is to analyze them into their parts and study each part. The Gestaltists, on the other hand, emphasized the importance of wholes; they believed that the whole is different from—perhaps greater than—the sum of its parts. For that reason, they said, wholes should be studied directly.

Although few American psychologists adopted the Gestalt approach to perception completely—as a comprehensive system—it has had a strong influence on American psychology. Most psychologists subscribe to at least some of the perceptual principles formulated by such Gestaltists as W. Kohler and K. Koffka. The Gestalt principles have been applied not only to the study of perception but in other areas as well. Gestalt therapy, for example, which was developed by F. Perls and others, stresses that a person's awareness of the world should constitute a meaningful

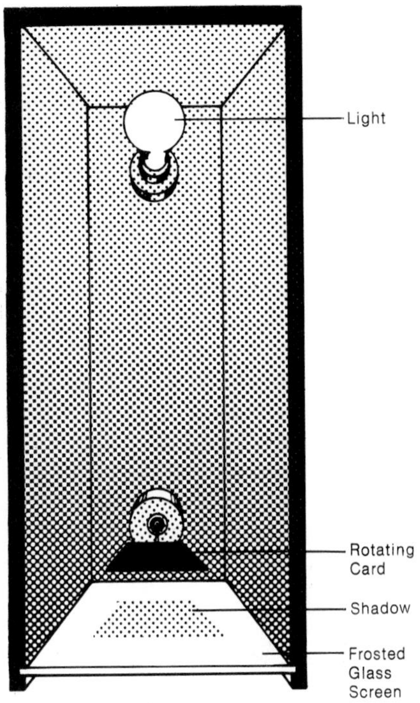

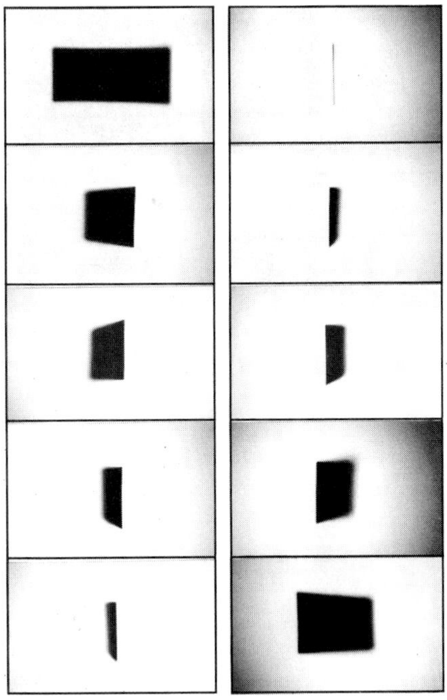

Figure 14.4
(Top) diagram of the apparatus that created the illusions described at the beginning of the chapter. Observers see the shadow as various shapes rotating both ways. (Bottom) photographs from the observer's perspective. Unfortunately, still pictures do not adequately convey the movement and dimension that the actual observer sees.

whole. Many encounter groups emphasize the here-and-now chiefly in an effort to persuade their members not to fragment their experience but to regard the whole of experience as a Gestalt.

Principles of Perceptual Organization

The Gestalt psychologists tried to identify certain organizing principles that determine what is perceived as a Gestalt. Many of the principles they discovered can be demonstrated with the simple dot patterns shown in Figure 14.5. The dots in Figure 14.5A are equally spaced, but people tend to see them as groups of squares or rows. That is, the dots seem to form patterns. When the spacings are changed, more stable groupings are formed. In Figure 14.5B, for example, the dots are seen in pairs; in Figure 14.5C, where the dots are still closer together, the effect is even more apparent.

Dots close together evidently tend to be seen as belonging to each other. They have what the Gestaltists called *belongingness.* But now look carefully at Figure 14.5D. The lowest dot of the inclined line is closer to a dot on the vertical line than to any other, but it is not seen as belonging with the vertically arranged dots. It belongs to the inclined row. *Proximity* alone, then, does not explain belongingness. *Continuity* is also important. In organizing dot patterns, it can be more important than proximity.

Another organizing principle is *similarity.* Figure 14.6A, for example, is seen as rows of As and rows of Bs. Much the same effect occurs for individual elements less meaningful than letters, as can be seen in Figure 14.6B. On the other hand, some shapes, such as those shown in Figure 14.6C, do not cohere in this way.

A break in a sequence is very easy to see (Figure 14.7A). Slight deviations can

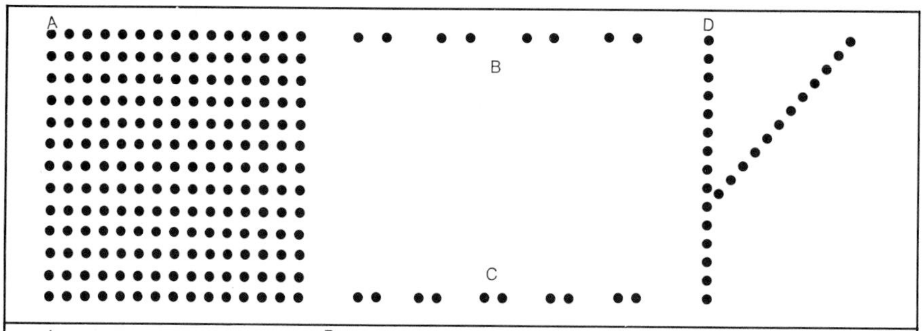

Figure 14.5

These figures illustrate some of the principles of Gestalt psychology. In (A) there seems to be no objective reason to see this field of dots as other than a field of dots, but most people do perceive the field as squares or rows of dots. (B) and (C) show that a particular spacing of dots can lead to stable perceptual formations—here, pairs of dots. But (D) shows that nearness alone does not determine perceptual organization; although the bottom dot in the inclined line is closer to the vertical line, it is not seen as belonging to it. This illustrates the principle of "continuity."

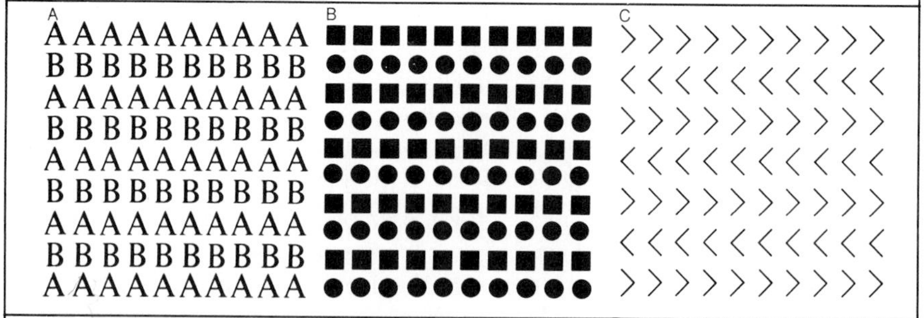

Figure 14.6

The Gestalt principle of "similarity" is demonstrated in these figures. Although (A) and (B) are easily organized into horizontal rows, (C) tends to break up into various unstable organizations. The reasons for such differences are complex.

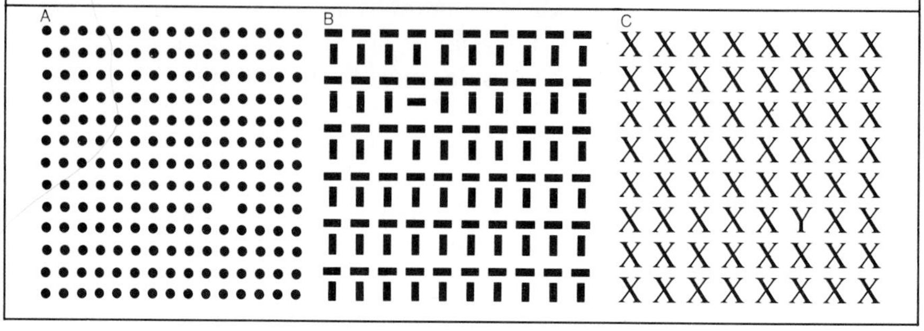

Figure 14.7

Breaks in a sequence can be more or less easy to detect, depending upon the degree of similarity of the elements and on the construction of the particular sequence. For example, you can probably spot the disruptions in (A) and (B) rather quickly, but the one in (C) may take you longer.

sometimes (Figure 14.7B) but not always (Figure 14.7C) be detected at a glance.

Similar phenomena occur in the perception of sounds and are especially obvious in music. Temporal proximity serves the same function for hearing as spatial proximity does for vision. When you listen to a melody, you tend to group the notes according to their temporal proximity. If you play a musical instrument, you know that you tend to pause slightly between musical phrases. But in hearing, as in vision, continuity often overrides proximity. Listen to a piano composition in which two melody lines are being played simultaneously—for example, a fugue by Bach. Notes that are very close together in time are not heard as belonging together when they are part of different melody lines. Similarity is also important in hearing. It allows you to follow the sound of a familiar voice or instrument in a group even when continuity is lacking—to follow the bass guitarist through a song in which he never carries the melody, for example.

Dot patterns and musical patterns were favorite materials of the Gestalt psychologists. In their research they presented such patterns and then simply asked people what they saw or heard. They summarized the results of their experiments in a series of *laws of organization,* including such principles as proximity, continuity, and similarity.

Theories

These laws of organization were assumed to operate from birth—to be given innately, not derived from experience with the world of objects. The Gestalt psychologists did acknowledge some perceptual learning, but it was not emphasized. They started from a metaphysical position that emphasized *a priori* truth, so a theory of innate perceptual knowledge of the world was attractive to them. It is less appealing to philosophical empiricists, who put far more emphasis on learning and experience in accounting for perceptual organization.

The Gestaltists also proposed a rather curious physiological theory based on the notion that seen shapes are represented by *isomorphic brain fields*—that is, by electrical fields in the brain that are shaped similarly to the seen objects. According to this theory, when people see a triangle, an electrical field that is shaped like a triangle is present in their brains. There are serious physiological objections to this theory. For example, placing conducting wires in the visual region of chimpanzees' brains should disrupt any such brain field, but K. S. Lashley found that it does not seem to produce perceptual distortion. R. W. Sperry did a later study, placing mica plates into the visual cortexes of cats and found that the cat's perceptions were similarly unaffected. There are also conceptual objections. If two-dimensional patterns are represented as flat pictures on the cortex (the outermost layer of brain cells), how are three-dimensional objects represented? The Gestalt psychologists were never very clear about this question, partly because they most often considered flat patterns and tended to ignore the perception of three-dimensional objects in space. And what about movement, color, hardness, and such? If an object is hard and green, is its corresponding region of the brain supposed to harden and turn green? Such extensions of the theory are so implausible that they must be rejected. And if the theory does not hold for the nonshape properties of objects, why should it be accepted for shape properties?

It is possible to accept the validity of the Gestaltists' organizing principles without accepting the innate physiological theories formulated to account for them.

PERCEPTUAL INFERENCE

Perceptual inference is common in everyday experience. When you put a book on a table, you do not check to make sure the table is hard or solid. You probably do not test a chair to see if it will bear your weight before you sit down; you assume that its four legs are planted firmly on the floor even though they may be hidden.

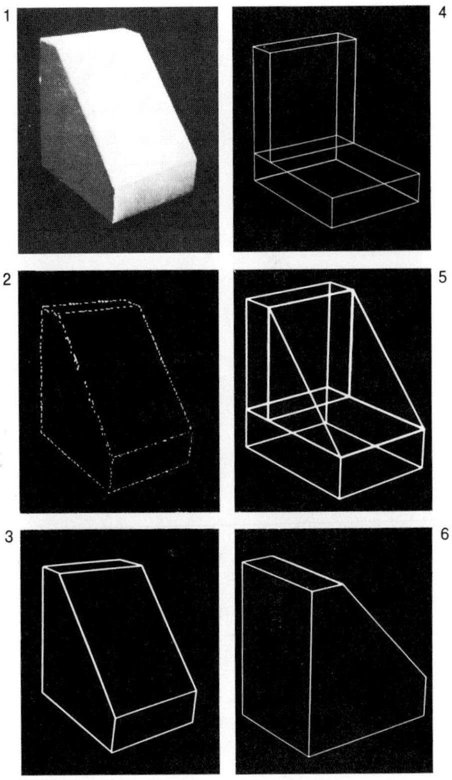

Figure 14.8
Computers can use perceptual inference. They can make generalizations based on "previous experience" to analyze rather complex objects. as seen in these figures. Given a photograph, (1) the computer first factors out the component of shape. (2) It reproduces the outline of the figure as an organized series of dots, then (3) it connects these dots by lines. It then comes up with a reasonable object that could generate this shape by breaking the object down into common three-dimensional components. (4) It generates two boxes forming the back and the bottom of the figure, (5) then adds the lines that form the wedge. Once this is done, the computer can generate views of the object to which it has never been exposed before (6).

People assume that the ground is solid before them as they walk, and that highways do not end just around the next curve or over the next hill.

The study of perceptual inference began with the work of a great nineteenth-century physicist and physiologist, H. von Helmholtz. Unlike the Gestaltists, who were interested primarily in observing and analyzing perceptual phenomena and only secondarily in formulating theories to explain the phenomena, Helmholtz' chief concern was discovering the psychological and physiological processes that might account for our perceptions. He suggested that the perception of objects is derived from patterns of sensory stimulation by the process of *unconscious inference.* That is, he argued that people's unconscious generalizations, based on previous experience, produce the principles by which sensory patterns are grouped and interpreted as objects.

Psychologists sometimes criticize the notion of unconscious inference because they think it assumes the existence of a homunculus—a "little man" inside the head. To account for perception by imagining that there is a little man (or even a "mind") inside who is drawing inferences is, they say, not much of an explanation, because one must then explain how the little man, or "mind," works. With the development of computers, however, this objection to Helmholtz' theory has been weakened. Computers regularly draw conclusions (inferences) from data patterns that vary and are incomplete (see Chapter 9). But except in cartoons, there are no little men inside computers, and except in science fiction (as far as we know), a computer has neither a conscious nor an unconscious mind. So we can suppose that the human brain infers objects from sensory data without supposing the existence of an internal structure such as a homunculus.

Figure and Ground

One of our most basic perceptual inferences has to do with *objects and space.* When we look at a three-dimensional object against the sky or some other unstructured background, as shown in Figure 14.9A, we have no trouble deciding which regions represent objects and which represent spaces between objects. Even when objects partly obscure each other and are seen against a structured background (Figure 14.9B), creating overlapping retinal images, we manage to separate them from each other and from the background.

Note that Figure 14.9 itself is two-dimensional—merely a flat sheet of paper with a pattern on it. We interpret the pattern as representing three-dimensional objects partly because photographs of objects provide some of the same contour and

A

B

Figure 14.9
We perceive the objects in these photographs (actually two-dimensional stimuli) as separate from each other and from the background (structured or unstructured) because we have learned to see photographs as patterns representing three-dimensional space. These patterns provide us with some of the same cues to depth and contour used to recognize actual objects in space, such as texture, shading, and linear perspective.

depth cues that we use to recognize actual objects in three-dimensional space. In addition, however, we do so because we have learned to see photographs that way.

What happens to our perception of objects and space, or *figure and ground,* when depth cues are eliminated? Some two-dimensional shapes are clearly recognizable both as figure (rather than ground) and as representations of particular objects. Indeed, silhouettes of people's profiles, which are a kind of portraiture (see Figure 14.10), appeal mainly because the elimination of depth, shading, and most other cues draws attention to the distinctive shape of the subject's profile.

Not all two-dimensional shapes are unambiguous, however. Look at Figures 14.11A and 14.11B—what do you see? In Figure 14.11A, the white region sometimes appears as a face and sometimes as background to a black figure with outstretched hand. Figure 14.11B, which is probably the most famous example of figure-ground ambiguity, you may recall from Chapter 1. It can appear as a white vase against a black background and sometimes as two black faces against a white background.

Figure 14.10

Even though silhouettes lack nearly all the cues involved in seeing and recognizing a three-dimensional object, the cue that remains—shape—is enough to enable a person to recognize familiar faces and objects.

Perceptual Set Perceptual set may affect which alternative is dominant. People tend to perceive most easily the alternative that they are "set" to perceive. If you looked at Figures 14.11A and 14.11B just after the silhouette shown in Figure 14.10, then you probably saw the white portions as figure and the black as ground. On the other hand, if you recalled the warning in Chapter 1 against ignoring black faces, perhaps you saw them as figure here.

If you look at either illustration for a few moments, you will probably find that figure and ground change spontaneously. After you have become familiar with both alternatives, you can control which you perceive by focusing your attention on one or the other. The ability to make them reverse at will is an extreme example of the power of perceptual set.

Auditory Figure and Ground Figure and ground are important in hearing as well as in vision. When you follow one person's voice at a noisy party, that voice is the figure and all other sounds become ground. If you shift your attention to another voice, it becomes figure.

Similarly, you may have had the experience of listening to a piece of music you

A

B

Figure 14.11

In these popular illustrations what you perceive as figure and what you perceive as ground is a function of several factors: your general past experiences; your perceptual set (or expectations); and the structural characteristics of the drawings themselves. An early researcher of the perception of form, E. Rubin, classified the phenomenal differences between figure and ground as follows: (1) the figure has form and a *thing* quality, whereas the ground is formless general material; (2) the figure tends to appear in front of the ground that surrounds it without interruption; and (3) the figure is likely to be more "meaningful" than the ground and better remembered by the viewer.

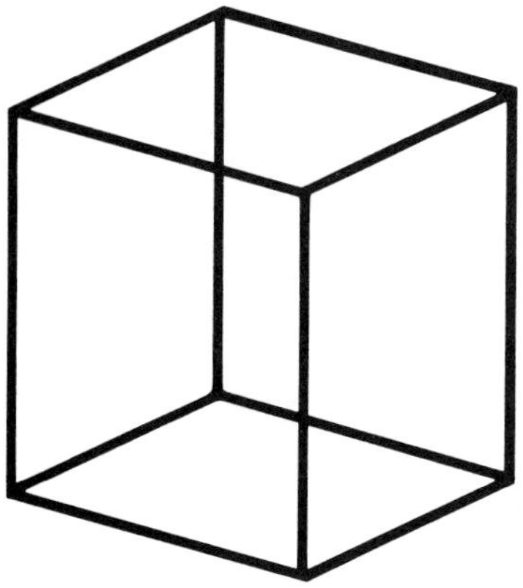

Figure 14.12
The Necker cube. Look at the figure for a time and see if you can count the number of depth reversals that take place.

did not recognize, and then a familiar melody suddenly leapt out at you. It became figure and the rest of the music ground.

Depth-Reversing Figures

Besides figure-ground reversals, other kinds of perceptual reversals also occur. One of the best known is the Necker cube, shown in Figure 14.12. Because what would be the back and front of the cube are the same size, there is no information as to which is which. Presented with this dilemma, the brain evidently entertains alternate hypotheses—and never makes up its mind.

In everyday life, alternate hypotheses of this sort are surprisingly rare, considering the vast number of objects that exist. It is equally surprising, however, that the Necker cube presents only two acceptable possibilities. Why do people see it only as a cube? It could be a two-dimensional representation of many different objects—a truncated pyramid tipped toward the viewer, for example. Yet only two possibilities, both cubes, are considered. The reason may be that cubes are more common objects than truncated pyramids, and that perception is a matter of choosing the most likely possibility that accounts for the available data.

Figure-ground reversals and the Necker cube illustrate several characteristics of perceptual inference. First, stimulus patterns do not completely determine which inference we draw, because a single pattern can be perceived in more than one way. Second, perception involves choosing among a finite number of possible answers to the question "What object is producing that pattern?" A familiar object is likely to be chosen in preference to an unfamiliar one.

Figure 14.13
Hermann von Helmholtz. Like many other nineteenth-century psychologists, von Helmholtz received his training in other fields. He came to psychology through his interests in vision and hearing. His texts in these two sensory areas are classics that are used today as sources of data and for models of experimental design—a remarkable feat for books over one hundred years old!

Movement

Another example of perceptual inference occurs in the perception of movement. Moving objects have great importance in the lives of animals, for they are likely to mean either danger or food. The eyes of some primitive species respond *only* to movement, as does the extreme periphery of the human retina. Try watching a television set with your eyes directed about 90 degrees away from the screen, and you will see movement but no form.

Two kinds of signals to the brain are especially important in the perception of movement: (1) the image moves across the retina, activating different receptors as it goes, and (2) the eyes follow the moving object. When we look from one side of a room to another, our retinal images are changing constantly, yet the room does not seem to swing around in the opposite direction (as it does when you pan with a motion-picture camera). The movement signals from the shifting retinal image seem to be canceled out by the brain's signal to move the eyes. That is, the two signals are equal and opposite, so the world remains stable. If you close one eye and push the other eye with your finger, the world does move, for there is no voluntary eye movement to cancel out the retinal movement signal.

The Gestalt writers made a great deal of the *phi phenomenon,* the perception of motion in situations in which there is no actual motion. The phi phenomenon is common in neon signs: lights are switched on sequentially and we see movement, although nothing is moving. The stimuli that register on the retina are merely lights blinking on and off, yet we perceive the Gestalt of a moving light.

Both the phi phenomenon and the perception of movement more generally are something of a puzzle. For example, it is not known how the illusion of movement is produced by stationary figures such as Figure 14.14.

THE PERCEPTION OF OBJECTS

The Gestaltists arrived at their principles of perceptual organization mainly by studying the ways people perceive abstract, two-dimensional patterns such as patterns of dots. In the last section, similarly, perceptual inferences were illustrated

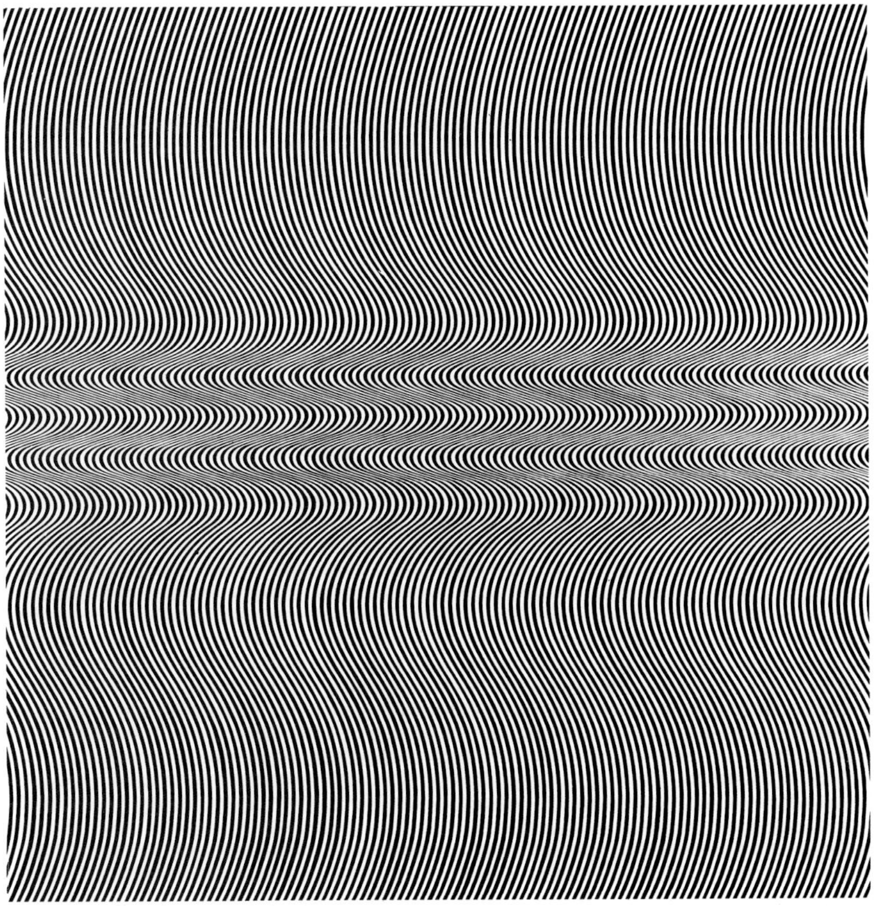

Figure 14.14
Most people can perceive movement when they look at this figure. Illusions that make stationary objects appear to be moving also occur in real life. For example, if a train you are sitting in remains stationary while the train next to it moves slowly forward, you may experience the illusion that your train is moving backward. Also, if, after looking at a waterfall, you glance at a nearby tree, it may seem to be moving upward. (Collection, The Museum of Modern Art, New York. Philip Johnson Fund.)

by showing how people perceive two-dimensional patterns. Although most of those patterns resembled actual objects, it is important to keep in mind that all drawings, even representational ones, are two-dimensional. In everyday life, however, perception and the behavior it leads to are geared to actual three-dimensional objects and their properties.

One of the most important concepts for understanding the perception of objects is the notion of *perceptual constancies:* people perceive objects as having certain constant properties despite large changes in the sensory inputs that the objects provide. For example, people have what is called *size constancy.* Even though an object casts a smaller image on the retina when it is far away than when it is nearby, they perceive its size as the same. Size constancy depends on an interaction between size cues and distance cues. Before we discuss size constancy, then, we need to take up *depth perception.*

Depth Perception

Depth perception refers to the ability to recognize distance—to tell how far away an object is. It is a particularly interesting ability because there is evidence that it is either present at birth or developed very soon afterwards.

The Visual Cliff Many experiments on depth perception in infants are done with a piece of apparatus called the *visual cliff,* devised by E. J. Gibson and R. D. Walk and shown in Figure 14.15. Gibson and Walk have used the visual cliff to study depth perception in a number of different species, including human infants, chicks, rats, kittens, dogs, lambs, and some wild animals. When the baby or animal is old enough to crawl or walk, it is placed on a center board resting on a large glass table.

On one side of the center board, the patterned surface of a piece of cloth (or paper) is visible directly beneath the glass. On the other side, the cloth is placed on the floor several feet below the glass.

Human infants usually begin to crawl at about six months of age. When tested on the visual cliff from that age on, they tend to crawl from the center board onto the "shallow" side rather than the "deep" one, showing that they possess depth perception. T. G. R. Bower, whose work is discussed in Chapter 5, has demonstrated that infants as young as six to eight weeks of age can also perceive depth.

Many animals can move about at much earlier ages than human infants, and most of them show depth perception when tested on the visual cliff. Less than twenty-four hours after hatching, chicks consistently choose the shallow side. A baby

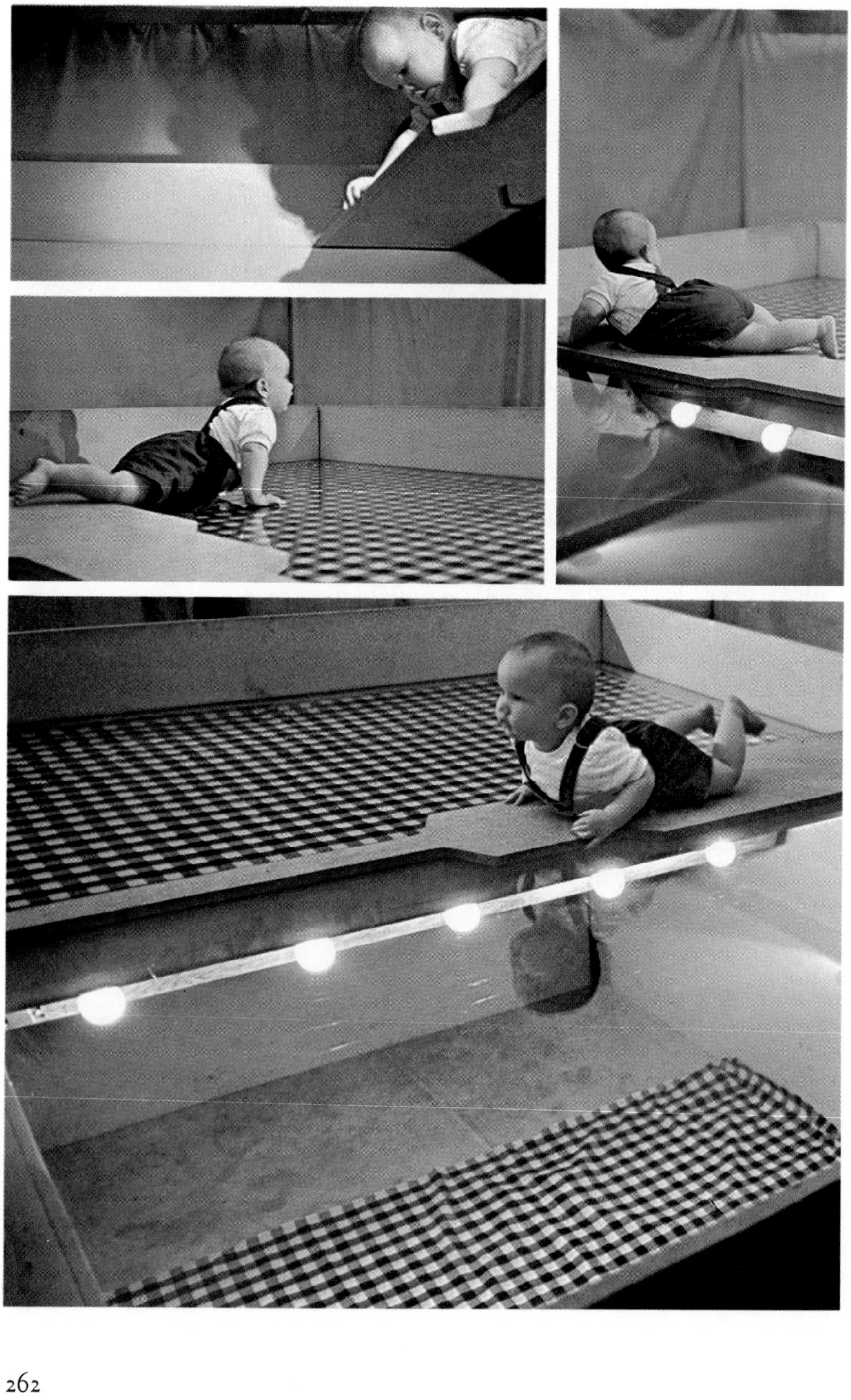

Figure 14.15
A young infant exploring the visual cliff apparatus. By the time they can crawl (around six months), most infants possess depth perception and will not cross the glass over the "deep" side, even if their mothers urge them to come. In fact, many of the children placed in the conflict situation of wanting to go to their mothers and at the same time wanting to avoid the seemingly dangerous abyss become upset and cry. Interestingly, the tactile cues provided by the supportive glass are not sufficient for infants to overcome their reluctance to cross the "deep" side, although if rats can feel the glass surface with their whiskers, they will proceed. A variety of animals such as chicks, lambs, and kittens all respond to the depth cues and avoid the cliff, even when tested shortly after birth.

goat placed on the deep side will freeze in fear, even though it is standing safely on the glass. On the other hand, the deep side does not seem to frighten rats as long as they can feel the surface of the glass with their whiskers. When the center board is lowered almost to the level of the glass, rats will go to either side, but if it is raised so that their whiskers cannot reach the glass, they move off the board onto the shallow side, not the deep one.

The performance of different species on the visual cliff may have evolutionary significance. Young aquatic turtles show no preference for the shallow over the deep side, but young land turtles choose the shallow side. Other animals for which depth perception is vital, including lions, tigers, and jaguars, also choose the shallow side on their first trial, even at very young ages.

Depth Cues What cues do we use in perceiving depth? One of them is *motion parallax:* the apparent movement of objects that occurs when you move your head from side to side or walk around. You can demonstrate it to yourself by looking toward two objects in the same line of vision, one near you and the other some distance away, and moving your head back and forth. The near object will seem to move in a wider arc than the far object.

Another cue to depth perception is provided by *binocular disparity,* or stereoscopic vision. Because our eyes are some distance apart, the retinal images they receive are slightly different. You can demonstrate this by holding your finger in front of you and looking at it with one eye at a time. The image registered by the right eye will be slightly left-of-center, and the image registered by the left eye, slightly right-of-center.

When we look at things with both eyes, the images fuse into one, giving an appearance of depth. The stereoscope, a device that fuses the images of two photographs taken from slightly different angles so that the picture looks three-dimensional (Figure 14.16), takes advantage of this perceptual phenomenon. In days gone by, when life was simpler, viewing scenes through the stereoscope was a popular home entertainment.

If you paint or draw, you are probably familiar with many other cues to distance. Near objects sometimes obscure parts of objects that are farther away. The more distant an object is, the smaller its image. Continuous objects such as railroad tracks, roads, rows of trees, and the walls of a room form converging lines (Figure 14.17A). As J. J. Gibson has pointed out, many such distance cues involve *gradients* of some sort (Figure 14.17B). Objects become gradually smaller, lines become gradually closer together, and colors become gradually less intense. The early Renaissance art-

Figure 14.16

The stereoscope, invented by C. Wheatstone in 1838, has made possible the scientific study of phenomena such as visual depth perception and eidetic imagery. Having noted that our two eyes receive slightly different views of a nearby object, Wheatstone arranged the stereoscope so that the two slightly disparate monocular images could be fused. The viewer thus perceives the two-dimensional stereoscope pictures as one three-dimensional scene.

To experience stereoscopic depth perception, take a thin piece of cardboard and place it perpendicular to the text page on the line that marks the separation of the two pictures. Then, with the edge of the cardboard resting between your eyes (as shown in the drawing), look at the left photo with your left eye and the right photo with your right eye and try to get the two images to fuse. Binocular fusion of the two slightly different retinal images in the central nervous system yields the perception of depth.

A B C

ists, who were the first in modern Western history to use linear perspective to give depth to paintings, sometimes calculated gradients with mathematical precision (Figure 14.17C). Psychologists are also interested in exact formulations of perspective changes, as you will see in the following section.

Size Constancy

To see how *size constancy* works, try the demonstration illustrated in Figure 14.18. Hold one hand at arm's length and the other half that far from your eyes and note the relative size of your hands. They will look very much the same size, even though the retinal image of the far hand is smaller than the image of the near hand. The true sizes of the retinal images will show up if you move the near hand so that it partly overlaps—partly hides from view—the far one. Now, although you know your hands are the same size, the far one looks smaller. Evidently the partial overlapping disrupts perceptual size scaling, which normally gives constancy, so that we see our hands as they are presented at the eye.

There is a systematic relationship between distance and the size of the image an object presents to the retina. The size of the retinal image is halved when the object's distance from the eye is doubled. The same thing happens in photographs: if you take a picture of a tree from 100 feet and take another picture of the same tree from 200 feet, the tree in the first photograph will be twice as high as the one in the second photograph. In normal perception, however, we perceive objects as being the same size regardless of whether they are far away or nearby; as discussed in Chapter 5, this size constancy is present at or shortly after birth.

H. Schlosberg has proposed an equation that suggests how the nervous system processes information about size and distance. The equation is $a = A/D$ where a is the size of the retinal image; A is the real size of the object; and D is the distance of the object from the observer. When you look at an object, the size of the retinal image (a) is registered by your nervous system. A knowledge of either the size of the object (A) or its distance from you (D) therefore allows you to solve the equation (not numerically, but in the sense that knowing the size of an object you are looking at allows you to estimate how far away it is). Therefore, the question "Is it a bird, is it a plane, is it Superman?" is fairly easy to answer if you know how far away the flying object is. Only if distance cues are ambiguous will you have trouble telling whether the object is a nearby bird, Superman somewhat farther away, or a distant plane. Similarly, most people have little trouble judging distance when size cues are clear, as they usually are when familiar objects can be identified. But David Scott, Commander of the Apollo 15 lunar landing in the summer of 1971, reported that the astronauts had difficulty judging distances on the moon—their estimates were sometimes off by a factor of five. The reason, probably, is that the strange visual environment offered very little information about size from which distance could be inferred.

The relation between size and distance can also be demonstrated with afterimages. For example, stare for about 40 seconds at the dot in the red square in Figure 14.19. Then look at the center of a white piece of paper held a few inches in front of your eyes. You should see a green afterimage. Now look at a more distant surface, such as a white wall. The afterimage is much larger when you project it onto the wall. The size of your retinal image was determined by the original fixation of the red square. When you vary the viewing distance by looking at close and far surfaces, the perceived size of the image changes. It changes in a systematic way, as illustrated in Figure 14.20. The direct proportionality between size and distance in after-images is known as Emmert's law (which is a special case of Schlosberg's equation).

When size and distance cues conflict, your perceptual apparatus opts for one or the other—often for the one that seems to lead to the more likely conclusion.

Figure 14.17 *(opposite)*
Linear perspective is illustrated in the photograph of railroad tracks converging in the distance and in the painting by Tintoretto. Texture gradient is illustrated by the photograph of rocks; note that no linear perspective cue is present here—the texture gradient is the only cue to depth.

Figure 14.18

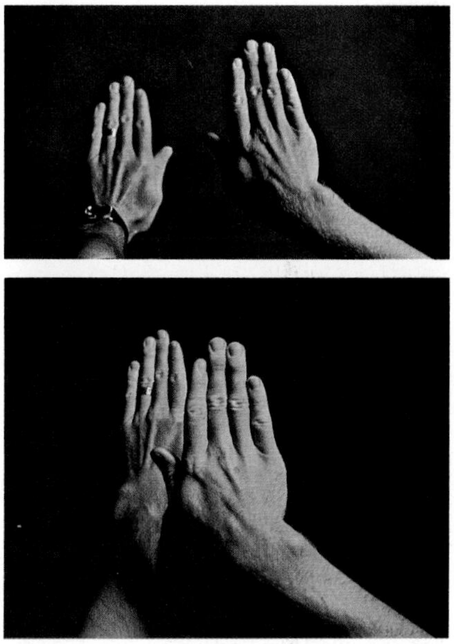

Figure 14.19
Hold this illustration about ten inches from your eyes and fixate on the dot until the image begins to shimmer. Then look at a white sheet of paper held a few inches away from your eyes. When you have seen the green afterimage clearly on the paper, shift your gaze to a blank wall. The afterimage will appear to lie on the surface of the wall as it did on the paper, and the farther you are from the wall, the larger it will look.

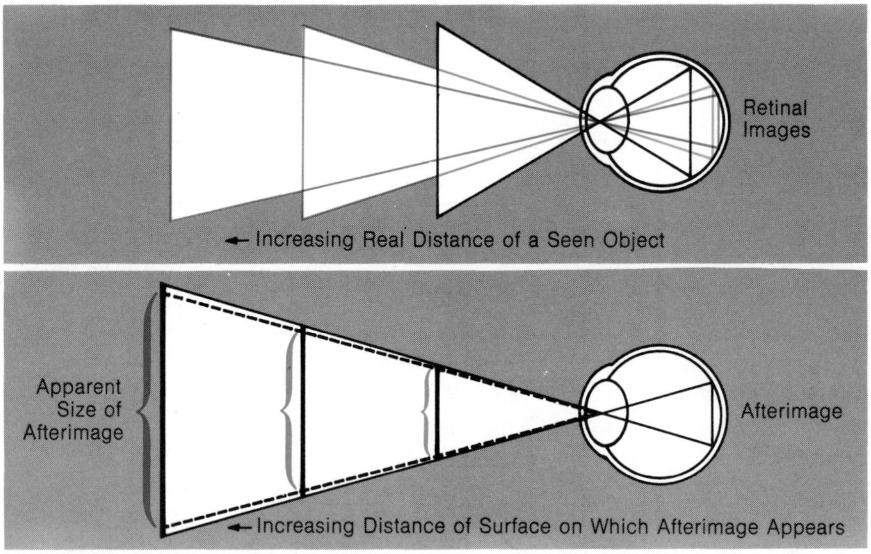

Figure 14.20
Although the image on the retina gets smaller as the object moves farther away, we perceive the object as having constant size. Size constancy can be demonstrated using visual afterimages. The afterimage on a wall appears larger as the viewer moves farther from the wall. It is as if the size of the image has changed to compensate for the increasing distance of the object.

During the invasion of Normandy in 1944, for example, the Allies dropped dummies of paratroopers about two feet tall through the early morning darkness onto the fields of France. When they hit the ground, the impacts set off a series of small explosions simulating rifle fire. In the poor light and general confusion, enemy observers at first accepted the size cue and thought the dummies were real paratroopers attacking from a distance. Not until the Germans got close enough to see that the dummies were dummies did they realize that the size cue had been misleading.

Illusions Size constancy is a phenomenon in which perception is more accurate than one might expect. Illusions are a phenomenon in which perception seems to be worse than one would expect. They can, furthermore, be very persistent. To illustrate, look at the two illusions shown in Figure 14.21A and B; measure the pairs of lines with a ruler, and then look again. Do the lines look the same now that you know they are the same? For most people, the answer is no.

Although a fully accepted theory to explain distortion illusions has not yet emerged, A. Thiery made a suggestion in 1896 that has considerable merit. He said that distortions arise through the brain's handling of two-dimensional patterns (such as lines drawn on paper) not as patterns but as objects. Both the Müller-Lyer and

A B C D

Figure 14.21
(A) The Müller-Lyer illusion. Although the "arrow" on the top appears to be longer than that on the bottom, the shafts of the two arrows are exactly the same length. Even if you measure the shafts with a ruler and assure yourself that they are indeed equal in length, you will probably still perceive them as being different. The critical factor in the illusion is the angle at which the lines of the "head" or "tail" meet the shaft. (C) The illusion that these photographs depict is much like the Müller-Lyer illusion. Both uprights are, in fact, equal in length. (B) The Ponzo illusion. The two horizontal black bars are the same length. Because the converging vertical lines behind them ordinarily represent cues of distance through perspective, we see the upper bar as being longer than the lower one. (D) The perspective in this photograph is similar to that of the Ponzo illusion. Note the illusion created by the bars of color printed over the tracks; the bars are equal in length.

the Ponzo illusions (shown in Figure 14.21A and B) have perspective-like features—features that indicate distance when we look at objects in space. In the Müller-Lyer illusion, the arrows can be regarded as skeleton drawings of corners; in the Ponzo illusion, the converging lines can be regarded as parallel lines extending away from the viewer. A "real-life" counterpart of each illusion is shown in Figure 14.21C and D. Thiery pointed out that when the two-dimensional drawings are regarded as representing three-dimensional objects, perceived size is determined by apparent distance. Because the drawings are actually flat with no shrinking of the retinal image to compensate for apparent distance, the size of the "far-away" line is overestimated. To put it another way, the line on the bottom in the Müller-Lyer illusion appears to be raised and is therefore apparently closer to the observer than the line on the top; but because both lines, in fact, subtend the same retinal angle, the line seen as nearer is perceived as shorter.

A similar explanation may account for the famous moon illusion. The moon looks considerably larger when it is just above the horizon than it does overhead, although the size of the retinal image is nearly the same in both cases. Distance cues—trees, buildings, the skyline—near the horizon are far superior to those overhead, and they indicate that the moon is a long way away. Looking toward the horizon, then, our brain apparently concludes that a moon-size retinal image from something so far away means quite a large object; looking overhead, our brain underestimates distance and therefore perceives the size of the object as smaller.

The Ames Room A. Ames, a painter, created some very striking visual illusions by building models designed to give the same retinal image as familiar objects although the shapes of the models are very different from those of the familiar objects. The best-known example is the Ames room. Figure 14.22A shows two women in an Ames room. Their sizes look dramatically different because you perceive the room as rectangular. In fact, as Figure 14.22B indicates, the back wall is smaller on the right than it is on the left. The wall appears to be rectangular because it is set at an angle, with its right-hand edge closer to the viewer.

Although we have photographed the Ames room as if it had only three walls, laboratory models of it have four. To see the illusion, observers look into the room through a window. Interestingly, they become less susceptible to the illusion if they

A

B

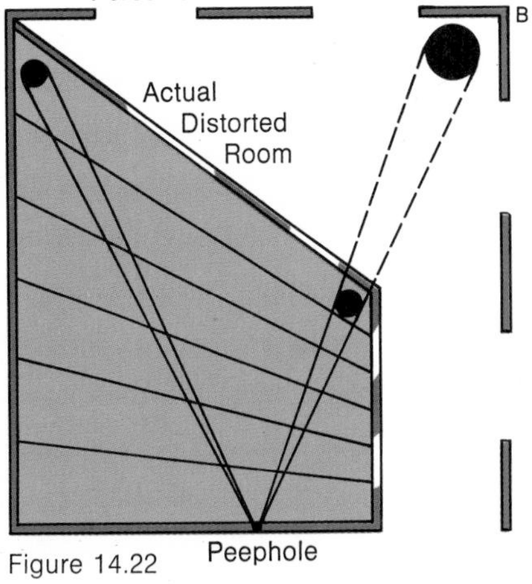

Figure 14.22

(Left) two models photographed in the Ames room. (Right) the actual floor plan of the Ames room; also shown is why observers interpret the room as being an ordinary rectangular one and thus perceive the sizes of the people in it as shown in the photograph.

Figure 14.23 *(opposite)*
The illusion here was created especially for this textbook. It is a photographic illusion whose effect depends on a coordination of size, distance, and orientation aspects. Before you turn the page, look carefully at the photographs and see whether you can find some clues to the deception.

are allowed to explore its surfaces through the window with a long stick. Gradually, the room stops looking as if it is built of rectangular walls that form right-angle corners and begins to look like what it really is: a set of trapezoids joined to form acute and obtuse angles. On the other hand, intellectual knowledge of the shape of the room without active exploration does not prevent the illusion.

An illusion similar to the Ames room illusion can be created in other ways. For an example, see Figure 14.23. Even with the information provided by the two photographs at the bottom of the page, you may have trouble figuring out how the illusion was created. If so, turn the page.

These illusions again show that we are often forced to decide between accepting cues about distance or depth and accepting cues about size. If we decide in favor of the accurate cues, there is no illusion; the Ames room, however, is designed to persuade us to accept the misleading ones.

The Importance of Assumptions One reason the Ames room illusion is so persuasive is that it makes use of a firmly held assumption: that rooms are rectangular in shape. The misleading cues are presented very carefully, so that the room's appearance does not call that assumption into question. If we assumed that the room was trapezoidal in shape, then the people would look equal in size—that is, size constancy would hold. But this is almost an impossible assumption to make, especially for people brought up in a rectangular-room, linear-perspective culture like ours. F. H. Allport and T. F. Pettigrew report that even people brought up in "circular" cultures tend to perceive rectangles in preference to trapezoids. Following Thiery's suggestion, presented earlier, the reason would be that a trapezoid, instead of being interpreted as a two-dimensional figure with acute and obtuse angles, is interpreted as a rectangular object whose angles only *seem* to be acute and obtuse, because the object is tipped out into space.

Given conflicting cues or ambiguities in sensory input, we usually make a calculated guess as to the nature of objects. The guess is based on our assumptions about the world. Scientists who have emphasized this assumptive aspect of perception are known as *transactionalists,* a name that reflects their idea that perception is a transaction between a person and the world around him.

Seen in this way, perceptual constancy is a means of transacting with or adjusting to a continuously changing environment in an adaptive fashion. Most of our assumptions are reliable; we do not assume that walls are transparent or soft or that a car approaching will do no harm. Perceptual constancy is similarly reliable; it permits us to identify regularities in the physical world.

Other Constancies

Shape constancy is closely related to size constancy, since perceived shape depends on an interaction between size and distance cues. We rarely see a given person or object from precisely the same angle, yet we perceive their shapes as unchanging. T. G. R. Bower and others have shown that shape constancy is present in rudimentary form in infancy.

Brightness constancy (to which *color constancy* is closely related) will be discussed in more detail, for it is not the simple perceptual phenomenon that it might seem at first thought. Brightness constancy can be explained in part by contrast relationships within the visual field, but it also depends on what J. Hochberg has called "higher-order variables" in perception.

You probably judge the whiteness of the various portions of these pages to be fairly constant, although you have probably read the book under a wide range of lighting conditions. A good deal of constancy is achieved because the relation between the brightness of the page and the brightness of the "surround" remains constant under different lighting conditions. Constancy would break down, how-

ever, if two white discs were cut from the page, projected onto a dark screen some distance apart, and illuminated differently. If an intense light was shown on one disc and a dim light on the other (and you could not see that the amount of illumination was different) the disc in the intense light would look whiter than the other disc. Just as size constancy depends on clear distance cues, so brightness constancy depends upon clear contrast cues.

Brightness constancy is maintained partly by contrast (specifically, by a constant ratio between the amount of light reflected by an object and the amount reflected by its background). But perceived cues to illumination are also important—so important, in fact, that brightness perception can be radically altered if they are distorted, as the preceding demonstration shows. Moreover, the relationships between illumination cues can themselves be thought of as the "stimulus" or "basis" for brightness perception.

Support for this proposition comes from two experiments, one done by A. Gelb and the other by G. Katona. Gelb, working under a dim ceiling light, showed a black disc to his subjects. The black disc was brightly illuminated by a beam from a concealed projection system, and the beam was adjusted so that it struck only the black disc, providing no surrounding illumination cues. When the subjects were asked what they saw, they uniformly reported seeing a *white* disc in dim light. This is not surprising; as the earlier example concerning discs of paper from this book showed, the reported lightness of an object corresponds closely to its luminance when illumination cues are removed. But when Gelb put a piece of white paper in the path of the beam of concealed light for a moment, the "white" disc was immediately seen as a brightly illuminated black disc. When the illumination cue (the white paper) was removed, the black disc immediately looked white again, even though the subject now "knew" about the concealed light beam.

To experience the other phenomenon, demonstrated by Katona, take a piece of gray cardboard and fold it in the shape shown in Figure 14.24. Stand it up a few feet away from you, positioning it so that light falls on the left side but leaves the right in shadow. When you sit back and look, the left side should seem well lit and the right side should seem shadowed. Now see if you can make the figure reverse, so that it looks like a flat, two-dimensional surface instead of a folded cardboard. If you can, the surface will no longer look like the same gray in two different lights. You will see medium gray on the left and dark gray on the right.

Katona's demonstration shows that contrast alone is not sufficient to account for perceived brightness. Nothing about the illumination of the figure changes when it "somersaults." But when it is perceived as a flat surface, your perceptual system cannot attribute the darker appearance of the right side to the direction of the light; therefore, you see two different shades of gray. The Katona phenomenon, like the Gelb effect, is quite resistant to intellectual knowledge of the actual state of affairs.

To summarize, the determinants of perceived brightness include not only peripheral illumination relationships such as contrast but cues to spatial position and the direction of illumination. Once the concept of stimulus cues is broadened to include these higher-order relationships, the process of perceptual inference in brightness constancy becomes less of a puzzle: perception is seen as more directly determined by stimulation.

Figure 14.24
Demonstration of the Katona phenomenon. Fold a piece of gray cardboard as shown here. Illuminate it with the light source at the left, so the right side is in shadow. If you can gaze at the cardboard and make it reverse, so that it appears to be two-dimensional, your perception of brightness will change too. You will see the two-dimensional shape as simply being two different shades of gray.

Prediction and Expectation

Size constancy, shape constancy, brightness constancy, and the illusions that occur when constancy fails all show that the processes of perception function so as to extract the properties of real objects in three-dimensional space from patterns of sensory stimulation. The fact that perception is directed toward the real world is hardly surprising, but it serves as a reminder that perceptual phenomena are a part of ongoing behavior, not a set of isolated laboratory events. And behavior is oriented toward *prediction.* The processes of perception themselves demand that this be so, since the nervous system takes time to transmit and translate sensory signals into perception and appropriate action.

For example, it takes a person at least 0.2 second to move a finger in response to an unpredictable signal, but most of our responses to external events do not take that long. If they did, fast skills like piano playing would be impossible. Prediction is vital for any planned action, and planned behavior is an important characteristic of higher animals. Events are anticipated, and behavior is geared to the anticipation. If a rat maze is shortened, rats familiar with the old maze will sometimes rush headlong into the unexpected wall. They are not running the maze simply as sensed; they are running the maze as they expect it to be. Although psychologists usually study the perceptual effects of immediate sensory inputs, most behavior is geared to a belief in the (mainly unsensed) properties of external objects—and to objects less as they *are* than as they *probably will be* by the time the action is carried out. In other words, behavior is directed by expectations.

Expectations influence perception, too, especially when the sensory input is fleeting, unstable, or in some way unclear. We have already mentioned the influence of perceptual set and discussed the importance of assumptions for what we perceive. Expectations based on motivation also affect perception, as has been shown by J. Bruner, L. Postman, and others. For example, consider a person who has a strong desire for material success. When he is shown words by means of a tachistoscope—a machine that flashes the words onto a screen for a tiny fraction of a second—he is more likely to recognize the ones that have to do with material success, such as *money, promotion, job, success,* than he is words that have to do with something he is not especially interested in (for example, religion or art). To some extent, he "sees" what he is looking for.

PERCEPTUAL MODIFICATION

Some of the most interesting and surprising findings in perception involve an area that has not yet been discussed: the effects of drastic alterations in the perceptual environment. Because the alterations *are* drastic and the effects long-lasting —sometimes permanent—most research on perceptual modification is done with animals rather than with human beings. Generally, the environment is altered in one of three ways: through impoverishment, enrichment, or rearrangement. All three have important effects on perception.

Impoverishment

The most extreme perceptual impoverishment is total deprivation. It is relatively easy to accomplish with vision: animals can be raised in complete darkness. The effects of this deprivation differ according to the species of animal tested. In one set of studies peformed by R. D. Walk and his colleagues, rats were raised in the dark for ninety days and then tested on the visual cliff described earlier. They showed the same preference for the shallow side and avoidance of the deep side of the cliff as normally reared rats, but they showed a deficit in their response to textures as a cue for depth. E. J. Gibson and R. D. Walk found that kittens who were raised in the dark for twenty-six days, on the other hand, seemed to be functionally blind, stumbling off the centerboard indiscriminately; that is, they showed no apparent capacity for depth perception when first exposed to the light. However, they developed the normal preference for the shallow side of the visual cliff after living in light for several days. A. Riesen found that the vision of a chimpanzee raised in the dark for the first year of life was exceedingly deficient; it turned out that such drastic deprivation had resulted in damage to the visual system. In a later experiment, Riesen raised a chimpanzee without patterned visual experience but with daily ninety-minute exposures to diffuse light. This treatment prevented obvious damage to the visual system, and the chimp's color perception was normal. Its size and shape perception, though, were deficient. Complete visual deprivation during infancy seems to lead to deficits in perception, and, at least for the animals high on the phylogenetic scale, those deficits may be permanent.

It is not clear whether total absence of patterned visual stimulation is necessary to produce these effects or whether they are caused by the absence of specific components of normal visual experience. A number of experimenters have addressed themselves to this question. A. Riesen and L. Aarons raised different groups of kittens in four different environments for the first fourteen weeks of life. One group was given one hour per day of diffuse, unpatterned visual stimulation; a second group was given one hour per day of patterned stimulation, but with their heads held immobile during that period of time; a third group was given one hour per day of patterned stimulation with freedom of movement; and a fourth group was raised normally in the laboratory, with much patterned stimulation and freedom of movement in their cages. When tested between fourteen and eighteen weeks of age, there was no difference in the four groups on brightness discrimination, but the third and fourth groups did better on discriminating between a stationary and moving form. Apparently at least some freedom of movement in the presence of patterned stimulation (third group) is necessary if the ability to distinguish stationary from moving objects is to develop normally.

An experiment by R. Held and A. Hein suggests that such experience is also necessary for the normal development of depth perception. These investigators raised kittens in the dark until they were ten weeks old. Then the kittens were divided into two groups: actives and passives. For three hours a day an active kitten and a passive kitten were linked together in the apparatus shown in Figure 14.25. The kittens were harnessed in such a way that every action of the active kitten moved the passive kitten an equal distance. Because of the uniformly striped cylinder, the visual stimulation for the active and passive kittens was approximately the

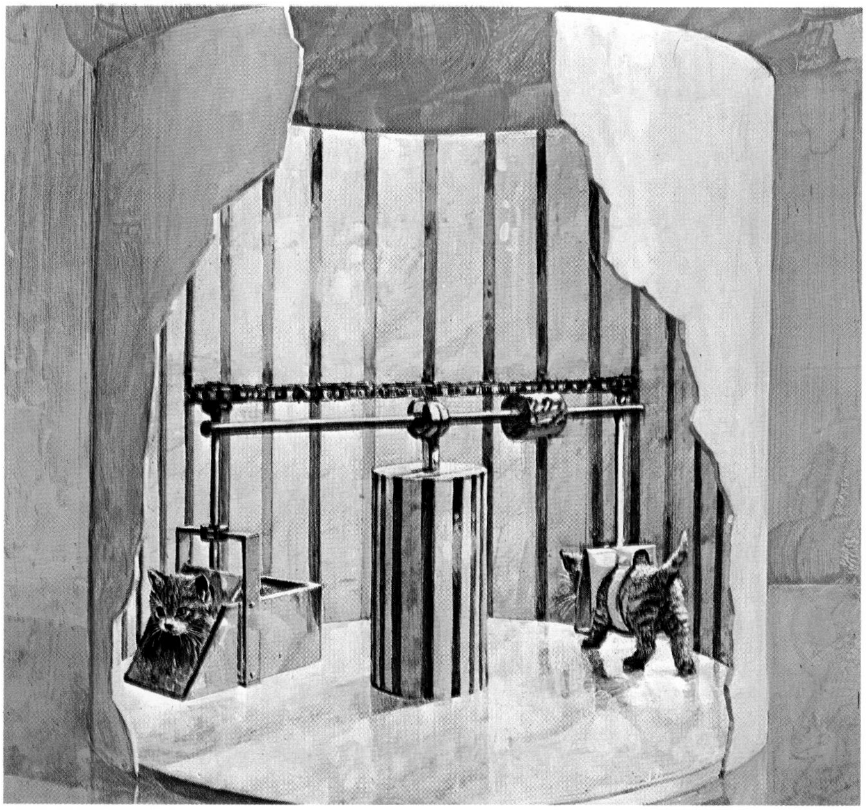

Figure 14.25
Apparatus used in the experiment by Held and Hein. Although the "passive" kitten on the left receives about the same amount of visual stimulation as the "active" one on the right, it does not develop depth perception, while the active kitten does. Feedback from self-induced movement seems to be an important element in learning how to see things in depth.
(After Held and Hein, 1963.)

same. But for the active animals, the changes in patterning of stimulation were correlated with their own movements, whereas any movements made by the passive kittens were uncorrelated with changes in visual stimulation. Results of various tests of depth perception, including testing on the visual cliff, showed that the passive kittens, in contrast to the active ones, showed no discrimination of depth. Not until the passive kittens had been allowed to live normally for two days—to move about in the visual environment on their own—did they develop normal depth perception. Held and Hein say their results mean that visual feedback from self-produced movement is essential to the development of normal sensorimotor coordination.

Enrichment

In an enrichment experiment conducted in 1956 by Gibson and Walk, rats were raised in cages whose sides were decorated with hanging metal triangles and circles. Later, when the rats were ninety days old, it was easier to train them to discriminate between triangles and circles than it was to train rats raised in ordinary, undecorated cages. The stimuli used in the discrimination test were triangles and circles painted on a background rather than cutouts like the ones hung on the cages. Later experiments by E. J. Gibson, R. D. Walk, and T. J. Tighe suggested that enrichment in the form of painted figures (like the ones used in the discrimination tests) did not improve perceptual ability; the animals had to be exposed to distinct objects. Gibson and Walk point out that cutout objects, unlike painted figures, have edges—they do not lie flat against a background. As the animals move around their cages, motion parallax indicates to them that the cutouts are objects in space. Experience with this cue to depth perception seems to be a significant factor in development.

B. White has studied the effects of enrichment on human perceptual development by working with institutionalized infants. He enriched their environments in two ways: in one case, by having the ward attendants handle the infants for twenty minutes more per day than usual, and in the other by placing visually striking objects in their cribs. The increased fondling turned out to increase the infants' visual attention span; that is, it increased the amount of time they would spend looking at something. Putting objects into their cribs accelerated the development of their ability to reach toward things (and taking the objects away again slowed it down).

In interpreting studies like White's, it is important to note that institutionalized infants already live in a severely deprived environment. The fact that offering visual stimulation to an infant who has virtually nothing to look at improves his perceptual development does not necessarily mean that enriching a normal environment will

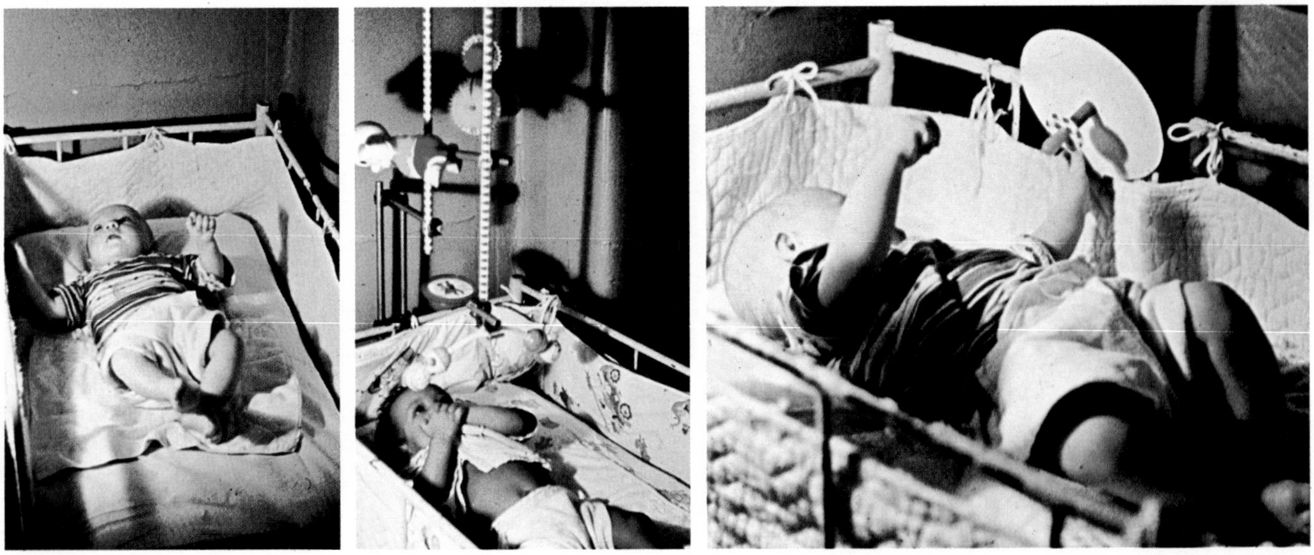

A B C

Figure 14.26
The three environmental conditions provided infants in White's experiment on sensorimotor development. (A) The normal institutional environment, with few things to look at or to touch. (B) The massively enriched visual environment. (C) The slightly enriched setting, with just one object at a time available to look at and reach for. White found that infants in the slightly enriched environment developed reaching behavior earlier than those in the normal institutional group and, surprisingly, earlier than those in the massively enriched group. One possible explanation is that the visual stimulation for infants in the massively enriched group was so satisfying that they felt no need to reach.

have the same effect. It must be kept in mind, too, that visual deprivation is a specific type of deprivation. The relationship between it and deprivation of other types, such as financial, cultural, or intellectual, is unknown, and generalizations about the other types of deprivation cannot be made from the findings on visual deprivation.

Rearrangement

What is probably the most famous rearrangement experiment was performed by G. M. Stratton on himself. He wore spectacles that turned the retinal image upside down. At first he had great difficulty coordinating vision and movement, but after about a week he found that he could walk around fairly normally. Although he was not aware that things were upside down, he thought they did not look quite normal. Certainly some kind of adaptation had taken place. I. Kohler found that he could fence, ski, and ride a bicycle after a few weeks of continuous inverted vision. Both these writers, however, hesitate to say that the inverted world ever looks really right.

Held and his colleagues found that human adults adapt to visual displacements caused by prisms more fully (and possibly only) if they are able to move about while looking through the prisms. The fact that feedback from self-produced movement has proved important both in the normal perceptual development of animals and in adjustment to visual displacements by human adults suggests that it is a very important component of perceptual experience.

Figure 14.27
Kohler was able to ride a bicycle after a few weeks of continuous inverted vision. Although the field may never seem to be exactly right, feedback from self-produced movement enables persons wearing prism glass to master complex motor tasks. Apparently the brain eventually does compensate for the inverted retinal images.

SUGGESTED READINGS

BEARDSLEE, D. C., and WERTHEIMER, M. (Eds.). *Readings in Perception.* New York, Van Nostrand, 1958. An excellent and broad collection of readings including many classical perceptual studies.

BORING, E. G. *Sensation and Perception in the History of Experimental Psychology.* New York, Appleton-Century-Crofts, 1942. A classic and often fascinating coverage of the history of sensation and perception.

DRÖSCHER, V. B. *The Magic of the Senses: New Discoveries in Animal Perception.* U. Lehrburger and O. Coburn (Trs.), New York, Harper & Row, 1971. Introduces the fascinating world of animal perception.

GIBSON, E. J. *Principles of Perceptual Learning and Development.* New York, Appleton-Century-Crofts, 1969. A fine treatment of perception, stressing learning and developmental aspects.

GIBSON, J. J. *The Senses Considered as Perceptual Systems.* Boston, Houghton Mifflin, 1966 An excellent treatment of the dependence of perception upon stimulation.

GREGORY, R. L. *The Intelligent Eye.* New York, McGraw-Hill, 1970. Gregory stresses his view that perception is a set of simple hypotheses about reality that depend upon sensory experience. The book is particularly strong on visual illusions.

HOCHBERG, J. E. *Perception.* Englewood Cliffs, N.J., Prentice-Hall, 1964. A good general treatment of perception in paperback.

HURVICH, L. M., and JAMESON, D. *The Perception of Brightness and Darkness.* Boston, Allyn and Bacon, 1966. An excellent treatment of our perception of brightness and darkness.

KÖHLER, W. *Gestalt Psychology.* 2nd ed. New York, Liveright, 1947. Köhler stresses the classical Gestalt approach to perception.

SPIGEL, I. M. (Ed.). *Readings in the Study of Visually Produced Movement.* New York, Harper & Row, 1965. A book of readings on the perception of movement.

VERNON, M. D. (Ed.). *Experiments in Visual Perception.* Baltimore, Penguin, 1966. Another excellent collection of readings, including reprints of many classical perceptual studies.

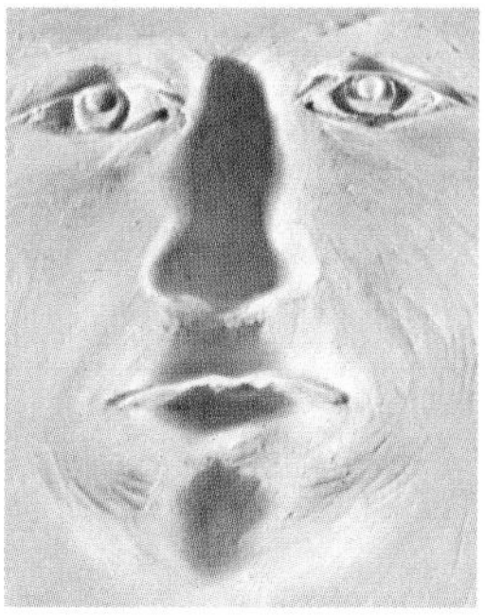

Figure 14.28
This is the same mask shown in the chapter-opening picture, where it appeared to be in bas-relief. Here the physical properties of the object are apparent; the mask is actually set into the surface.

15 Consciousness and Awareness

People sometimes ask me, in a curious, wondering sort of way, why I write science fiction. The feeling appears to be that this is a queer thing for a grown-up to do. There are lots of answers to that, the most important of which is "Because I like to," and the most honest of which is "Because that's what I'm best at." However, suppose we try to be more analytical than that. You see, science fiction allows me to create societies without limit, without boundary, without rules. I am not hemmed in by probability, by "human nature," by anything at all except for a few fundamental laws of physics that I can talk my way out of. My consciousness is not limited by reality.

For instance, I once deliberately set about describing a society in which it was considered quite immoral for a mother to know that a particular child was hers and absolutely wicked for her to try to find out which was hers and, worst of all was to give it special affection. In other words, I had all the fun of basing a story on the premise of the evilness of mother love. I also wrote a whole novel about a society in which "viewing" (visual contact by electronic media such as television) was perfectly all right in any state of dress or undress, but "seeing" (direct vision) was obscene. It was a murder mystery and since the murder was committed with a blunt instrument so that "seeing" was involved, there was that additional complication.

Generally, I don't worry about being anticipated in my queer ideas because each writer creates according to the bent of his own mind. Other writers get ideas that strike me as interesting but that, most of the time, I know would not give me personal pleasure to develop. Sometimes, though, another writer will produce a story that cleaves me with envy because I had not thought of it first. Twenty years ago, a writer named Wyman Guin wrote a story called "Beyond Bedlam." Guin imagined a society in which crime and war were abolished by removing the sources of internal conflict within each person. He supposed that every person was "schizophrenic" in the sense of harboring two personalities within his body. By appropriate treatment, these could be separated and given charge of the single body alternately for fixed periods of time. This allowed all sorts of interesting situations. Within one body might be one personality who was bookish and home-loving, and a second who was dashing and athletic. Imagine the bookish personality taking over the body just after it has had its leg broken on a ski slope. What can one do but write a stiff letter of objection for the other personality to find when he takes over next?

Naturally, each personality has its own love, and the same body will have two different husbands or wives, one for each occupant. But suppose a man's alternate personality falls in love with his wife's alternate personality, and that this love is returned. And suppose this sort of love of alternate for alternate is considered a kind of incest and is strongly forbidden. Now you have a love story that you couldn't possibly have in any kind of literature but science fiction. And that's why I like to write science fiction.

I. A.

The original meaning of the word *psychology* is "the study of the mind"—from the Greek word *psyche*. So far in the book there has been no discussion of what the mind is. Learning, thinking, memory, and perception—phenomena that traditionally imply the existence of a mind—have been discussed, but the mind itself has been neglected. The concept of mind implies the existence of a *consciousness*, and consciousness has proved to be an extremely troublesome concept. In fact, behaviorism grew out of the assertion that mind, consciousness, awareness, and similar concepts cannot be analyzed scientifically and therefore should be banished from the field of psychology. Many psychologists have not accepted such a pessimistic view and have tried to investigate the phenomenon of consciousness. Their findings have provided a number of important insights into the nature of consciousness.

The concept of consciousness assumes the existence of an experiencing self, a mind that is aware and active. In this chapter, *consciousness* will be taken to refer to a self that can reflect on its own goings-on. *Awareness* will be taken to refer to

Fifth Ave
ONE WAY
ONE WAY

WAIT

THE BLACK PANTHER
FREE HUEY
BLACK PANTHER
FREE HUEY

the quality of the experience of such a self. Such a distinction between consciousness and awareness is useful for understanding the two main kinds of psychological research that are discussed in the chapter. One kind of research deals with the structure of human consciousness. The other tries to describe the nature of certain alterations in experience—that is, in awareness.

Figure 15.1 *(opposite)*
At any given moment, our sensory systems are sifting through the incredible amount of information available, selecting some of it as important and rejecting the rest—as suggested by these photographs, all taken from the same corner within a few moments.

As a beginning, one of the best sources of information about consciousness and awareness is you yourself. Stop for a moment and look at the world around you. If there is a table near you, look at it. It will appear to be of a certain size, shape, and color. It will probably seem quite substantial. If you pound on it, you will no doubt hear a solid thud. If you smell it, it might have an odor, of furniture polish or glue. If someone asked you, "Is this table real—does it really exist?" the chances are you would insist that it does exist.

We commonly take for granted that our conscious experience is an awareness of objects and events in the external world, such as tables, trees, sounds, smells, and our own bodily responses. Many people assume that their senses mirror the external world exactly and that sensory neural pathways somehow transmit copies of the world to the brain. But our awareness of the world is not a simple mirroring, as the discussion of perception in the last chapter showed. It is a process of construction rather than one of transmitting a copy of the world to the mind. The nature of this awareness can be altered radically, so that the process of construction produces very different kinds of experience, as you will see later in this chapter. The first part of the chapter will discuss what psychological research has demonstrated about the structure of consciousness.

Look at your feet and answer the following questions. Your feet are a part of your body. What is the relationship between your feet and your mind? As you look at your feet, do you feel that there is a *you* of some kind that has a separate existence from your feet or your chest? What is the nature of that self? Was it that self that followed the instructions to look at your feet? Is it that self that is seeing them? Now bounce your knee up and down for fifteen or twenty seconds and, at the same time, concentrate again on the table. Did your self start your leg moving? Is it keeping the leg moving now, even while it is concentrating on the table? Try to concentrate so hard on the table that you do not even notice your leg moving. Is your self moving the leg now? If you are really engrossed in the table, then your leg probably seems to be moving by itself. What is making it move?

At times various philosophers and psychologists have tried to dismiss as meaningless such questions about the nature of consciousness and the self—and with them such phenomena as hypnosis, spirit possession, and even dreams. But more and more research is pointing to the importance of the concept of consciousness and forcing the conclusion that consciousness is a complicated phenomenon, not the unitary entity we usually think it is.

DISSOCIATION PHENOMENA

Consciousness seems to have the basic property that it can be dissociated. Within the same person, consciousness can exist at a number of different levels, and at times it can even split into several distinct consciousnesses. When consciousness is split into two or more co-consciousnesses, the result is called a *dissociation phenomenon.*

Split-Brain Research

Harriet Lees is a thirty-year-old woman who at one time suffered from epilepsy. For most of her life the seizures were mild and infrequent and could be controlled by drugs. But when she was about twenty-five, the seizures started getting worse. Drugs were no longer effective, and in a few years she was having as many as a dozen severe convulsive fits a day. It was no longer a matter of embarrassment but one of life or death. Her doctors finally recommended a radical type of surgery in which the right and left cortexes of her brain would be disconnected from each other. A year ago she went ahead with the operation.

Harriet has not had a seizure since. For a while, though, she thought she was partially paralyzed. Not paralyzed really—the left half of her body just does not respond readily. She does not have control of parts of the left side of her body, especially her left hand, which occasionally seems to act on its own. Why did these effects result from Harriet's operation?

An epileptic seizure typically begins in one hemisphere of the brain and then spreads to the other. To halt the spread of Harriet's seizures, her surgeon had cut the thick tract of nerve fibers that runs from one cortical hemisphere to the other through the corpus callosum (see Chapter 16).

The most encouraging effect of the operation is an almost total elimination of epileptic attacks. But the operation also has a fascinating effect on the person's consciousness. R. Sperry, M. S. Gazzaniga, and their colleagues have made an extensive study of what happens to people who undergo this operation. When the two cortexes of the brain are disconnected, two distinct consciousnesses emerge, one in each hemisphere. To some extent, the different consciousnesses control different parts of the body; for example, the left hemisphere controls the right hand, and the right hemisphere controls the left hand. The area of the brain that controls speech in most individuals is located in the left cortical hemisphere. Therefore only the consciousness in the left hemisphere is able to speak. In the Sperry group's investigations the person's right-half consciousness can communicate with the psychologist by pointing or drawing with the left hand. If the psychologist arranges things properly, the person can perform two tasks at the same time, one with each hand, a difficult feat for a normal individual.

The two consciousnesses tend to go to sleep and wake up at about the same time, but they have largely independent memory systems and do not seem to have access to each other's awareness. If the right-half consciousness is shown an erotic picture, the person's body will react—perhaps by blushing. If the left-half consciousness (which alone can speak) is then asked why the blushing occurred, he becomes confused and cannot usually explain why he blushed. But in general the person who

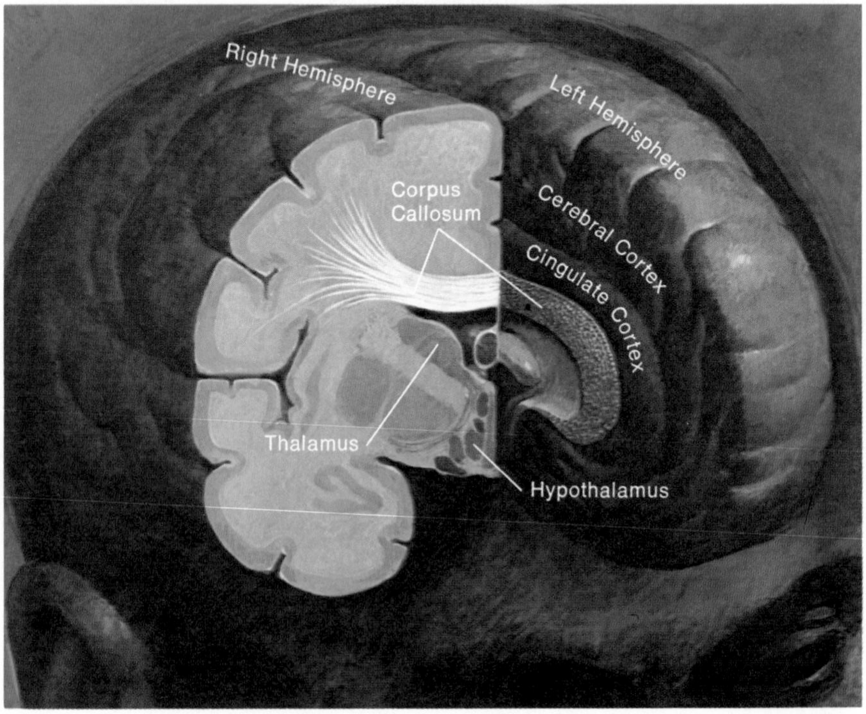

Figure 15.2
The corpus callosum is a large tract of nerve fibers that joins the cerebral hemispheres. Information received by one side of the cortex becomes available to the other side by crossing the corpus callosum. Cutting the callosum can essentially produce two brains in one body.

undergoes the operation does not seem to be particularly disturbed by the fact that two separate consciousnesses share one body.

Although the only human beings who have undergone this operation are epileptics, the phenomenon of separate consciousnesses, each controlled by one hemisphere of the brain, does not seem to be limited to epileptics. Sperry and others have shown that a similar alteration of mental functioning occurs in monkeys, cats, and other animals that undergo the operation. For some specific tasks (not all), there even seems to be separation of learning in the two hemispheres. For example, a cat or a monkey taught a visual discrimination using only one hemisphere will, in some cases at least, show no evidence that the other hemisphere has learned the discrimination.

Multiple Personality

There are many well-documented findings of multiple consciousnesses in people who have not had split-brain surgery, or any sort of surgery, and are not suffering from any known brain damage.

One of the most striking instances is the occurrence of *multiple personality*, a rare condition in which one person shows two or more separate consciousnesses with distinct personalities. A famous case was described by C. Thigpen and H. Cleckley in *The Three Faces of Eve*. A twenty-five-year-old woman came to Thigpen, a psychiatrist, for therapy, complaining of emotional problems and "severe and blinding headaches" followed by blackouts. The woman, whom the authors called Eve White, was an extremely self-controlled, shy, and conscientious person. During one of her therapy sessions, a strange expression suddenly came over her face, and she quickly put both hands to her head. After a moment, her hands dropped, she smiled brightly, and in a sparkling voice she said, "Hi there, Doc!" A second consciousness, whom the authors later called Eve Black, had appeared. Eve Black's personality, speaking style, and even her walk were quite different from those of Eve White. She was childlike, fun-loving, and irresponsible. She reported that she was conscious at all times and could follow the thoughts, actions, and feelings of Eve White, but she did not participate in them or consider them her own. Eve White, on the other hand, became unconscious when Eve Black was in control; that was why Eve White reported periodic blackouts. Eve Black seems to have had an independent conscious life since early childhood, when she would periodically "come out" and do mischievous deeds. But most of the time, Eve White was in control, and Eve Black could not gain control or come out at will.

After about a year of psychiatric treatment, a third consciousness emerged. This personality, who called herself Jane, was more mature, self-confident, and capable than either Eve. She did not exist before therapy and somehow seemed to grow out of the therapy process. Although she had access to the consciousnesses of both Eves, she did not have complete use of their knowledge and memories preceding her emergence. The therapist tried to use Jane's strengths to resolve the problems encountered by the two Eves.

There are several well-documented cases of multiple personality besides the case of Eve, but the condition is very rare. Several other, more common, psychiatric conditions also show dissociation. Some forms of the severe psychological disorder called schizophrenia (discussed in Chapters 30 and 31) show especially dramatic dissociation, but the dissociated parts of the schizophrenic's mind are not as distinct as in cases of multiple personality. R. D. Laing, a Scottish psychiatrist, has described this schizophrenic condition particularly well in his book *The Divided Self.*

The word *schizophrenia* comes from Greek words meaning "split mind." The schizophrenic person may have vivid hallucinations—he might, for example, assert that he is Christ and that he hears the voices of people who are trying to crucify him. But there is a more rational consciousness that is, in effect, watching the

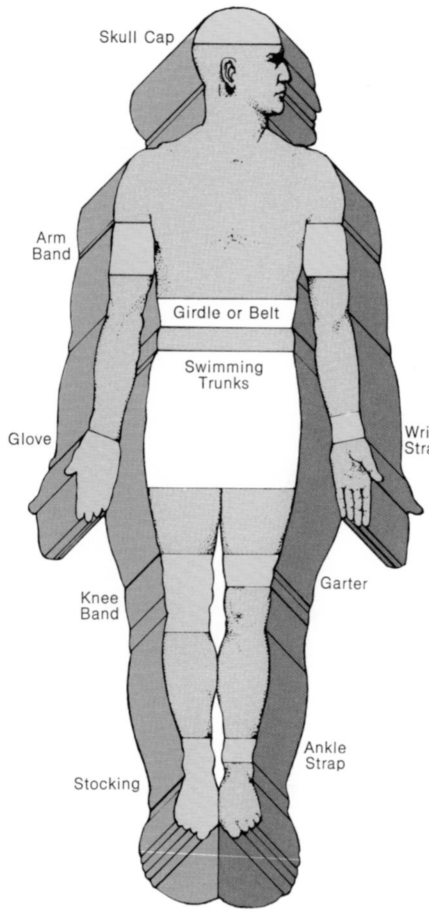

Figure 15.3
Hysterical anesthesia, or paralysis, typically occurs in the areas of the body illustrated above. A loss of sensitivity occurs, but the pattern of numbness does not correspond to neural patterns and is therefore indicative of psychological, not neurological, disorder.

hallucinations and the bizarre behavior (much as Eve Black could watch Eve White) and knowing very well that they are unreal. T. Freeman, J. L. Cameron, and A. McGhie report cases where, in the midst of bizarre and incoherent speech, a patient will abruptly become lucid and fully coherent for a brief period. One patient, in the midst of hallucinations, suddenly declared to the therapist, "I'm in a bit of a mess, sir; I'm just a shambles."

Many other psychological disorders also show some dissociation. In severe cases of amnesia (called fugue states), a person temporarily loses his sense of self. When his sense of self returns, he does not remember what he did in the fugue state. In hysteria, another disorder that involves dissociation, a person may completely lose the use of a limb, for example, even though there is nothing organically wrong with it. In cases of amnesia and hysteria, hypnosis can often be used by the therapist to gain temporary access to the submerged co-consciousness. During the hypnotic trance the therapist can temporarily eliminate the amnesia or the hysterical symptom, and the hypnotized person can remember or can move his limb.

Hypnosis

Some of the most striking cases of dissociation occur in abnormal states—schizophrenia, multiple personality, and split brains, for example. But dissociation phenomena are not limited to abnormal people. Hypnosis provides strong evidence of dissociation, and according to findings summarized by E. R. Hilgard, a large majority of people are susceptible to at least mild hypnotic trances. Although the most elaborate dissociations usually occur in the deepest states of hypnosis, there clearly is dissociation even in mild trances.

A Case of Hypnotic Blindness

F. A. Pattie reports a case of dissociation under deep hypnotic trance that seems similar to the dissociation that occurs after split-brain surgery and in instances of multiple personality. Pattie was testing to see whether he could induce blindness in one of a person's eyes during hypnosis. The test he used for blindness involved stimulating the person's eyes in such a way that it was impossible for the person to tell without cheating which eye was being stimulated. Cheating would consist of blinking one eye, moving the eyes from side to side, or a similar trick. Of course in his experiment Pattie tried to prevent all such tricks. If the test indicated that the supposedly blind eye was really blind, that would be convincing evidence that hypnosis can actually block neural input to the brain from the eyes.

Pattie tested five people previously known to enter a deep trance readily. To his surprise, one woman, whom he called "E.," did seem to become blind in one eye. Throughout most of a long series of tests covering several sessions, E. seemed to be blind in one eye. But there were a few indications that she might be using tricks. Consequently Pattie devised an even more subtle test in which it was essentially impossible to cheat. With this test Pattie demonstrated that E. was not blind at all. Figure 15.4 shows the test he used.

Strangely enough, E. insisted that she had not cheated and that she was in fact blind in one eye. According to every indication, she really believed that she had not cheated. Pattie then put E. into as deep a hypnotic trance as he could and tried to get in touch with "the part of her which faked the tests." He encountered enormous resistance. First she said that she could not remember how she had cheated, then she began to give out little bits of information but showed great emotional upset. Pattie had to repeat the process over and over of telling her that her memories would come back when he counted to three and snapped his fingers. Gradually he extracted the information from her.

The woman showed two consciousnesses—one that was "blind" during hypnosis and communicated with Pattie, and one that cheated in order to obtain the informa-

Figure 15.4
The stimuli used by Pattie. He was studying dissociation under hypnosis and attempted to induce blindness in one eye in six subjects. Only one of them seemed, after several tests, to have succumbed to the suggestion, but Pattie suspected cheating. So he used this subtle test. He put a red filter in front of the subject's "good" eye and a green filter over her presumed "blind" eye and showed her the top line. If the hypnotic suggestion had been successful, she should have seen only what is shown in the bottom line. She did not. Pattie proved she had been cheating with one consciousness, although another consciousness was not aware of the cheating.

tion necessary to appear blind in one eye. In the woman's own words, "I want to tell the truth, and I know it, and something doesn't want to. Something makes me keep forgetting it, and I know I know it. It just goes, and I can't say it, and it makes my head ache and swim." In fact, Pattie even found that the cheating consciousness had intervened several times while E. was not under hypnosis in order to acquire information that would help her to cheat. The consciousness that normally communicated with Pattie had no recollection whatsoever of these episodes.

Long before Pattie's experiment, in 1890, when psychology was just becoming established in the United States, William James had pointed out in his *Principles of Psychology* that this kind of dual consciousness is necessary to explain many of the phenomena of hypnosis. For example, whenever a hypnotized person fails to perceive something that is present, he must somehow perceive it in order to be able not to perceive it. In one of James's examples, a mark was made on a piece of paper, and the hypnotized person was instructed that he would not see it. Many additional marks were then made on the paper, and the person acted as if he saw all the marks but the first. Somehow hypnotized people can discriminate that mark from all the others and can manage not to perceive it but to perceive all the others.

Is Hypnosis Real?

Even since hypnosis became widely known, many people have been skeptical about its reality. It is common for disbelievers to assert that hypnotized people are simply cheating. In James's example, for instance, it would be easy for someone to knowingly lie and pretend that he did not see the mark. Pattie's case cannot easily be interpreted as simple cheating, but the research of M. T. Orne provides even more convincing evidence that hypnosis is a real phenomenon. Orne compared the behavior of people who were truly hypnotized with that of people who were faking hypnosis. The hypnotist did not know which were which. At first it was difficult or impossible for the hypnotist to tell. Gradually, however, Orne discovered some important differences between the two groups.

The hypnotized group showed what he called *trance logic*. With trance logic a person readily perceives hallucinations suggested to him by the hypnotist and mixes them freely with perceptions based on real objects and events, without making any attempt at logical consistency. For example, in Orne's experiment the hypnotist told the subject that he would see a third person sitting in a chair that was actually empty. That individual was in fact standing behind the hypnotized person. When the hypnotized person turned around and saw the third individual, he acted surprised and reported that he saw two images of the same individual. In contrast, when people who were faking turned around, they said either that they saw no one or that they did not recognize the person they saw.

If truly hypnotized people are asked to discriminate between a hallucinated image and a real one, they often indicate that they can tell the difference, according

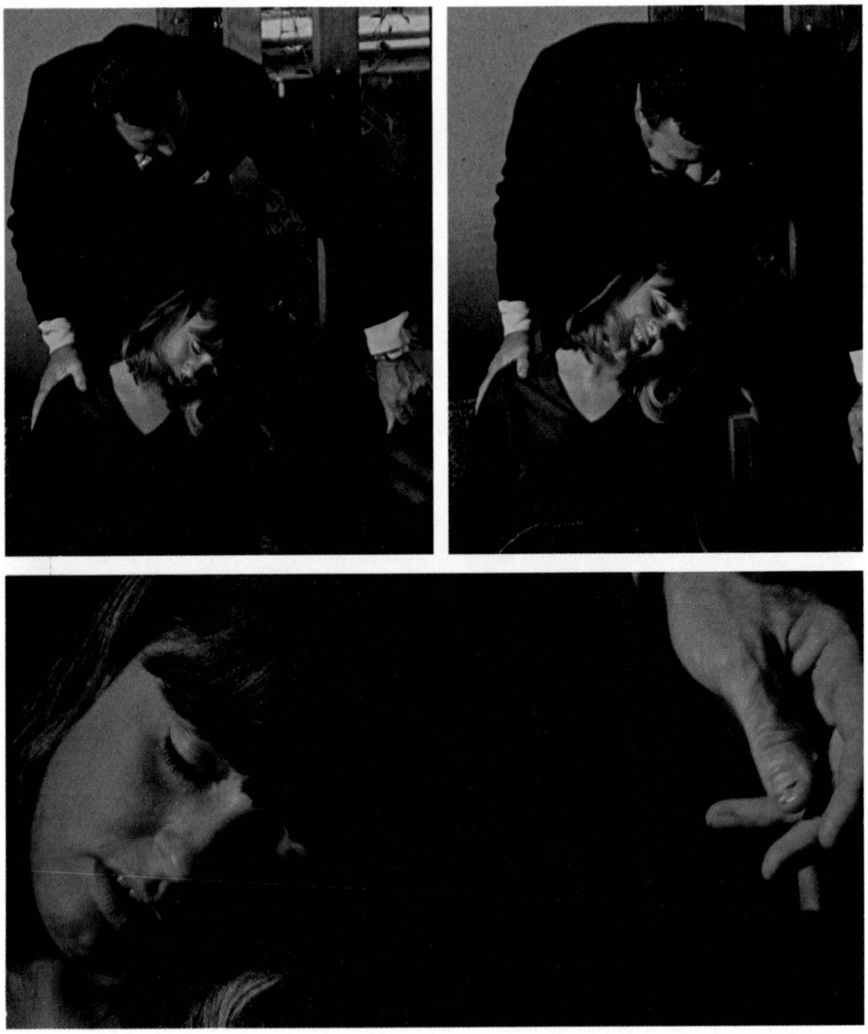

Figure 15.5
This woman was given induction instructions by the hypnotist and entered a deep trance state. One fascinating demonstration of hypnotic phenomena is to give a piece of chalk to the hypnotized subject and tell him that it is a burning cigarette, as shown here in the bottom photo. If the hypnotist touches it to the subject's arm, reddening and the beginnings of a blister may appear at that spot.

to both Orne and M. H. Erickson. With the hallucinated image either they can see through it or they can cause it to move by their own thought processes. For example, they can make it raise one of its arms. Faking people report no such ability.

Orne also reports that if he brings people out of the trance with instructions that they will remember everything that occurred, the hypnotized people report that they were really hypnotized, that they actually did see that hallucinated images, and that the hypnotic state felt markedly different from their normal waking experience. The faking people say simply that they were faking.

Clearly, hypnosis is a genuine dissociation phenomenon, in which the consciousness that is in contact with the hypnotist is separated from the rest of the person's mind in such a way that the content of its awareness is partially controlled by the suggestions of the hypnotist.

The dissociation during the hypnotic trance does not necessarily disappear when the person returns to his normal waking state. *Posthypnotic suggestions* are commonly given during the trance and lead to dissociative behaviors after the trance. For example, the hypnotist might suggest that after the person is awakened he will be unable to hear the word "psychology." When he awakens from hypnosis, the person may report that some people around him are speaking strangely. They seem to leave out some words occasionally, especially when they are talking about topics involving———.

Although modern work on hypnosis began in the late eighteenth century, reports of hypnosislike phenomena can be traced back thousands of years. These phenomena are usually called spirit possession because the people who enter the hypnosislike trance say that they have been possessed by a spirit. These "spirit possessions" are still prevalent today in many societies.

SLEEP AND DREAMS

Few people ever experience spirit possession or multiple personality or a split brain or even hypnosis, but everyone sleeps. What happens to your consciousness during sleep? You probably think of sleep as a time when you are unconscious, except for a few brief periods when you are dreaming. Or perhaps you think that you do not even dream. In the past thirty years psychologists have made many important discoveries about sleep and dreaming, and these discoveries have showed that both of these conceptions are wrong. Mental activity goes on during all or most of sleep, and everyone dreams. Consequently, sleep is probably the most universal dissociation phenomenon: Everyone is mentally active during sleep, but most people remember little or none of that mental activity when they awake.

Stages of Sleep

N. Kleitman laid the foundations for the discoveries about sleep with his work on the physiological correlates of sleeping and dreaming. One of the most useful physiological indicators of brain activity is the electroencephalogram (EEG), which is a record of the brain's electrical activity. A person's EEG changes consistently as he goes from wakefulness to light sleep to deep sleep. As shown in Figure 15.6, brain waves in a person who is fully awake and has his eyes closed are typically of high frequency (about 10 per second) and low amplitude. These brain waves are called *alpha* waves. As a person begins to fall asleep (Stage 1 in Figure 15.6), he still shows a large proportion of alpha waves, but mixed in with the alpha waves are some waves of a slower frequency. As sleep becomes progressively deeper (Stages 2, 3, and 4), alpha waves disappear, and waves of low frequency and large amplitude appear.

During a night of sleep a person does not merely fall into progressively deeper sleep and then gradually wake up. Instead, his brain waves show a regular cyclical pattern that occurs about every ninety minutes, as shown in Figure 15.6. First the

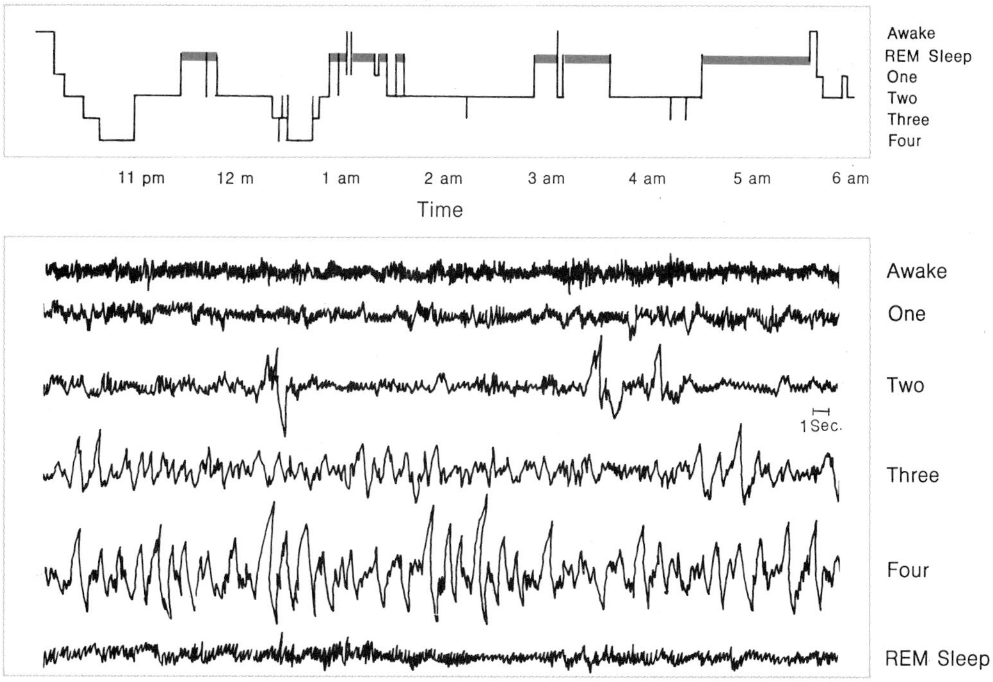

Figure 15.6
(Top) the frequency with which the different stages of sleep occur throughout the night. (Bottom) electroencephalograms (EEGs) obtained during the various stages of sleep and characteristic of them.

brain waves indicate that he is falling into deeper and deeper sleep, and then they gradually return to a Stage-1 pattern, only to start the cycle over again.

Dreams

An important series of studies of dreams was carried out by Kleitman and his associates E. Aserinsky and W. C. Dement. They noticed that when a person's brain waves return to what looks like a Stage-1 pattern after having passed through the deeper stages, his closed eyes usually begin to move rapidly back and forth. They decided to investigate the rapid eye movements, or REMS. They woke sleepers up during the REM periods and other stages of sleep and found that dreams with vivid visual imagery usually occurred during REM periods. In fact, Dement reports that the eye movements sometimes correspond to movements that the eye would have made during the events in the dream. Mental activity that occurs during non-REM periods is usually much less vivid—like drifting thoughts rather than vivid dreams.

REM sleep has also proved to be interesting in another way. According to some measures it seems similar to being awake, whereas according to others it seems to be a very deep sleep. The EEG pattern is close to the pattern of the waking state, and many other physiological patterns also resemble those of the waking state: There

Figure 15.7
Many of Marc Chagall's paintings have a pronounced dreamlike quality. Dreams are not bound by the same rules of logic or dimensions of reality that prevail when we are awake. Distortions in spatial representation, time, color perception, and emotionality, which people report in dreams, are present in this painting, "I and My Village."
(Collection, the Museum of Modern Art, New York. Mrs. Simon Guggenheim Fund.)

are increases and irregularity in heart rate and breathing, elevations in blood pressure, and erection of the penis in men—all physiological changes associated with arousal. On the other hand, most behavioral measures of depth of sleep indicate that REM sleep is very deep sleep—similar to Stage 4. People are very difficult to wake and do not respond to stimuli as readily as during Stages 2 and 3. Because of these contradictory patterns, M. Jouvet coined the term "paradoxical sleep" to describe REM sleep. People seem to be almost awake and yet deeply asleep at the same time.

While this physiological activity is occurring, an unusual change is also occurring in the muscles. Virtually all the major body muscles lose their normal tonus, and most of the bodily reflexes that can be elicited during ordinary sleep are suppressed. Jouvet has shown that a specific small part of the brain is responsible for this muscle inhibition. When he removed this part of the brain in cats, REM sleep continued to occur, but the sleeping cats no longer lay still during REM sleep. Instead they jumped up and moved about the room—all the while keeping their eyes closed and remaining asleep. This indicates that the normal brain inhibits the muscles to keep the body from acting out dream activities.

Evidence also indicates that REM sleep is necessary for the maintenance of mental equilibrium. If people are awakened every time they begin to enter REM periods but are otherwise allowed to sleep a normal length of time, they tend to make up those lost periods whenever they have the chance. They also begin to show some abnormal behavior while they are awake. Dement reports that when people were deprived of REM sleep for five consecutive nights, most of them suffered from anxiety and irritability, difficulties in concentration, and in some cases hallucinations and ravenous appetites. Working with cats, Jouvet and others have found even more dramatic results. Jouvet discovered that if he removed a portion of the brain (different from the one mentioned earlier), the cats no longer showed REM sleep although they continued to show non-REM sleep. As several days passed, the cats began to behave very strangely. They periodically showed agitation, stared fixedly, and swiped with their paws as if they were hitting at nonexistent objects. Some of them exhibited greatly increased eating and sexual behavior. In some cats the REM sleep eventually returned, and these behavioral abnormalities disappeared, but the cats that showed no return of REM sleep eventually died in a state of acute hyperactivity.

Stage-4 Sleep

Although the evidence is clear that mental activity occurs during most of sleep, Stage 4 is something of a puzzle. It is extremely difficult to wake someone up from Stage-4 sleep; the person seems almost to be in a coma. By the time the sleeper is awakened, it is impossible to determine whether what he reports occurred during Stage 4 or while he was being awakened. Stage 4 does not occur in most animals. In people it occurs only in the early part of a night's sleep. Some reports indicate that most sleepwalking occurs during Stage 4: The sleepwalker may even look directly at people with his eyes open, yet not appear to recognize them. When he is awakened, he usually will not remember the episode.

Consciousness During Dreams

Although mental activity during non-REM sleep may show dissociation, the vivid dreams of REM sleep are one of the most striking examples of dissociation in human behavior. People dream whenever they sleep, but they seldom remember these vivid experiences when they are awake, as was noted earlier.

K. Fischer describes a series of dreams in which the dreamer believed that he could fly. Knowing that flying is unusual in human beings, he tested during almost every dream to make sure he was not dreaming and repeatedly determined that he was awake and able to fly. For several months this series of dreams continued, with

Figure 15.8
A photographic representation of dreamlike images.

the dreamer always being sure that he actually could fly and the waking person never remembering the dreams. In other words, the two consciousnesses did not have access to each other's experiences concerning flying. One day the waking person finally realized that he had dreamed that he could fly and recalled the whole series of dreams. At that point the dreamer no longer believed that he could fly, and the dreams of flying did not recur.

When people remember their dreams, they commonly report two levels of consciousness: one observing the dream and the other participating in it. (This type of double consciousness is similar to the reports of schizophrenic experience described earlier.) Psychologists like Sigmund Freud who carried out extensive analyses of their own dreams report that when they worked at recalling their dreams, the dissociation of consciousnesses decreased somewhat, although it never disappeared. Gradually they came to be able to remember most of their dreams, and in some cases the observing consciousness stopped being a mere observer and began to influence the course of the dream.

ALTERATIONS IN AWARENESS

Along with the dissociation process in dreaming, there is also another important difference between dreams and normal wakefulness. The nature of awareness (that is, the quality of experience) is very different. Freud, C. S. Hall, and others have described the peculiar nature of thought during dreams. Strange events that would normally be quite frightening are not disturbing at all. A single figure in a dream can be a composite of several people from waking life, and the identity of a dream person can change in the middle of a dream.

Changes in awareness also seem to occur in most other types of dissociation. Trance logic in hypnosis, significant differences among personalities in multiple personality, and transformation into a supernatural power in spirit possession—all imply major changes in the quality of experience. On the other hand, with certain other phenomena many people report dramatic changes in awareness without any evidence of dissociation. That is, while their sense of self remains basically intact, the nature of the experiences of that self is altered in a significant way.

Meditation

Meditation is an ancient practice. It is often associated with religion, particularly in the East. Meditation can produce changes in awareness that people who meditate consider beneficial and pleasant. According to R. K. Wallace and H. Benson, yogis assert that meditation can produce a "higher-than-normal" consciousness through a fully rested, relaxed body and a fully aware, relaxed mind. Many meditators claim that they experience something the thousandth time in the same way they did the first. Their experience has a quality of freshness or immediacy.

Most forms of meditation involve sitting still and focusing or concentrating on one thought or object, like a sacred picture, a wall, a featureless spot, or a mandala (which is designed so that the gaze always returns to the center). Sometimes a word, like the sacred word "Om," or a phrase called a mantra is said, and its sound is contemplated.

In a study of meditation by A. J. Deikman, several people who had not meditated before learned to meditate on a blue vase. Deikman recorded their reports of their experiences. The participants reported that the color of the vase became very vivid and time passed quickly. The people could not be distracted as easily as they normally might. Some people felt themselves merging with the vase. Others found that their surroundings became unusually beautiful, filled with light and movement. All the meditators found meditation pleasant. After twelve sessions they all felt a strong attachment to the vase and reacted negatively when the vase was not present during the next session.

For a long time there was virtually no psychological research on meditation, because psychologists considered it "mystical" and "antiscientific." Several recent studies have shown that meditation is not only a salient experience but is also accompanied by striking physiological changes. Trained meditators show both highly specific EEG patterns and prominent changes in metabolism.

Several studies have investigated the EEG patterns of Zen monks and of yogis. The findings of A. Kasamatsu and T. Hirai, who studied meditation in Zen monks, are especially impressive. They found that as soon as the monks began meditating, alpha waves appeared in their EEGs, even though the monks had their eyes open. Normally, alpha waves are exhibited by people only when their eyes are closed. The alpha waves of Zen masters showed systematic changes in amplitude and frequency as a meditation session progressed. When EEG patterns were also recorded for Zen disciples, the disciples whom the masters had considered to be the more proficient meditators showed EEG patterns most similar to those of the masters. Wallace and Benson cite several other studies with similar findings.

Wallace and Benson's own study of the metabolic changes that occur during transcendental meditation, a technique that was developed by the Maharishi Mahesh Yogi, is particularly important. They found that meditation produced strong metabolic changes that were different from changes produced by either hypnosis

Figure 15.9
Silver mandala used to facilitate meditation; the meditator concentrates on the design, sitting quietly until he passes into the meditation state, during which both the pattern of his brain waves and his metabolism change.

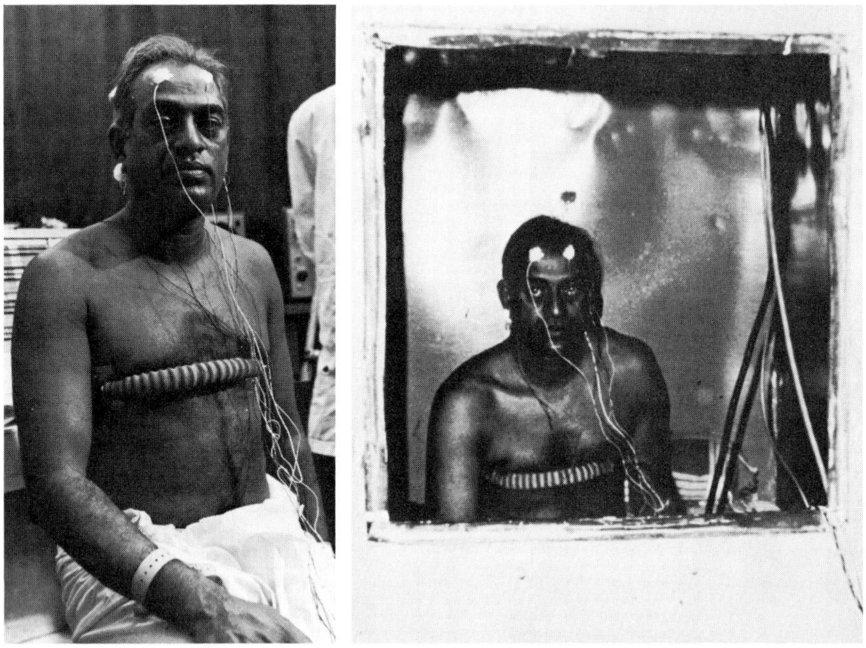

Figure 15.10
Physiological measures such as the electromyogram (indicating muscle tension) and the electrocardiogram (indicating heart rate) being obtained of people during meditation. These measures indicate that experienced meditators undergo a reduction in metabolic rate and enter a state of relaxation that may result from quiescence of the sympathetic division of the autonomic nervous system.

or sleep. Oxygen consumption dropped sharply shortly after meditation began, and various other measures indicated that this decrease was due to a reduction in the metabolic rate. Various physiological measures indicated that the meditators were highly relaxed but awake. A blood substance normally associated with anxiety and hypertension showed a marked decrease during meditation, suggesting quiescence of the sympathetic nervous system (see Chapters 16 and 17). Wallace and Benson suggested that meditation might prove to be an important technique for the maintenance of psychological health, especially in the bustle of industrial society.

Psychedelic Drugs

Many drugs have psychological effects, ranging from induction of sleep to production of extreme hyperactivity. Many of these drugs are discussed in Chapter 34, but certain of them are relevant to the topic of consciousness and awareness. Particularly relevant is a class of drugs that (like meditation) have been used for thousands of years and in many different cultures to alter awareness. These drugs have been termed *psychedelic* by H. Osmond. Although the meaning of this term has come to be distorted in recent years, it was derived from Greek words meaning "mind-manifesting." According to C. T. Tart, the implication of the term is that the drugs demonstrate potential ways in which the mind can function. The most widespread of these drugs seems to be marijuana, or cannabis.

Marijuana Not only is marijuana relevant to the study of alterations in awareness, but it has become an important social phenomenon in the United States. Before 1960, its use was restricted almost entirely to certain subcultures, such as jazz musicians and artists in big cities. By 1960, however, college students had discovered marijuana, and since that time the number of marijuana users in the United States has increased by a factor of perhaps ten thousand.

The active ingredient in marijuana is a complex molecule called tetrahydrocannabinol (THC), which only recently has been synthesized from inorganic materials. THC is found naturally in resin exuded from the flowers, leaves, seeds, and stems of the female plants of the common weed *Cannabis sativa,* or Indian hemp. Marijuana is made by drying any part of the top of the female plant. Hashish is a gummy powder made only from the exuded resin. Both marijuana and hashish are commonly smoked, but they also can be mixed with food and eaten. Marijuana has been used as an intoxicant among Eastern cultures for many centuries; in some societies, marijuana and hashish are legally and morally acceptable whereas alcohol is not.

Although the effects of the drug seem to vary somewhat from person to person and also seem to depend on the setting in which it is taken, there is considerable consensus among regular users on how it affects them. When people smoke and inhale marijuana containing at least 0.5 gram THC, they undergo a condition known as "getting high." Most sensory inputs are greatly enhanced or augmented—music sounds fuller, colors are brighter, smells are richer, foods taste better, and sexual and other experiences are more intense. (There is some indication, however, that the sense of touch is dulled.) Users become elated, the world seems somehow more meaningful, and even the most ordinary events may take on a kind of extraordinary profundity. The time sense is greatly distorted: A short sequence of events may seem to last for hours, perhaps because the normally smooth-flowing stream of consciousness is somehow fragmented into separate episodes only loosely tied together. Users may become so entranced with a picture or painting that they sit and stare at it for many minutes. A musical phrase of a few seconds' duration may seem to stretch out in time until it becomes isolated from the rest of the composition and the hearer perceives it as never before. At times, users report that they experience a dissociation—an observing self watching the participating self; but at other times they may report an unusual sense of internal unity.

Figure 15.11
A scene from the movie "The Yellow Submarine," which some claim was written and filmed with the express intention that people watch it while high on marijuana. The vivid colors, imaginative animation, and the famous Beatles' songs were to be enhanced by the effects of the drug.
(© King Features Syndicate.)

As many users of marijuana have discovered, the drug can heighten unpleasant as well as pleasant experiences. If a person is in a frightened, unhappy, or paranoid mood when he takes the drug, he stands an excellent chance of having these negative experiences blown up out of proportion so that his world, temporarily at least, becomes very upsetting. Cases have been reported where marijuana appears to have helped precipitate psychological disturbances in people who were already unstable before they smoked it.

Despite the obvious need for careful research on marijuana, the first well-controlled scientific study of marijuana's effects on human beings was reported in 1968 by T. Weil, E. Zinberg, and J. M. Nelsen. The participants in the study were seventeen college students in the Boston area who ranged in age from twenty-one to twenty-six years. Nine of them had never smoked marijuana before; the other eight had smoked it many times.

The inexperienced participants were put through four experimental sessions, each a week apart. During the first session they were taught the proper technique of smoking and inhaling with tobacco. At each subsequent session, they smoked one of three types of marijuana cigarettes. The first contained a high dose of marijuana (2.0 grams THC), the second, a low dose (0.5 gram THC), and the third, none at all. The participants were not told which type of cigarette they were smoking. The experienced marijuana smokers were tested only on the high-dose cigarettes.

Marijuana increased the heart rate slightly in all participants, seemed to cause little or no change in respiratory rate, and had no effect on blood sugar level. No adverse reactions occurred in any of the participants; indeed, the reactions of several participants to the tobacco used during the preliminary training session were far more pronounced than any of the effects produced by marijuana.

Among the inexperienced participants, only one actually got high (that is, reported the typical euphoria), but all showed impaired performance on tests of both intellectual and motor skills soon after smoking marijuana. In many cases, the heavier the dose was, the greater was the impairment. Regular users of marijuana (all of whom got high during the session) showed *no* impairment either of intellectual function or of motor skill on the tests. Generally, the effects seemed to reach maximum intensity within half an hour after smoking. They were diminished after an hour and were almost gone at the end of three hours.

Unlike alcohol, marijuana has no major known physiological side effects. It appears to be difficult or impossible to inhale a fatal dose. There is no scientific evidence that marijuana is physiologically addictive. The question of "psychological dependence" is more difficult to assess. When this term is used, it usually refers to a condition in which the person has a strong craving for something not biologically necessary for life. The difficulty with the idea of psychological dependence becomes obvious when you realize that, by this definition, most American children are addicted to peanut butter and most adults to television, sex, and bread.

There is also no evidence to suggest that marijuana is the first step on a path that inevitably leads to heroin or some other narcotic. On the other hand, it is quite probable that medical research will uncover some deleterious effects that result from the abuse of marijuana, because marijuana is a drug, and any drug can be dangerous (see Chapter 34).

LSD Some potent psychedelic drugs, such as LSD, psilocybin, the amphetamines and mescaline, or peyote, are discussed in Chapter 34. These drugs have much stronger effects than marijuana, and all are potentially dangerous. Some, like peyote, have long been part of the religious rites of some native American and other groups. Others, like LSD, have been in existence for no more than twenty or thirty years.

LSD is the most potent of these drugs and the one most studied in recent years. Although its effects, like those of marijuana and other psychedelics, seem to depend heavily on the suggestions offered by people around the user, on the setting, and on the user's expectations, LSD usually produces a pronounced alteration in awareness, called "a trip." A trip generally lasts from six to fourteen hours. It often includes intense hallucinations accompanied by emotions that can range anywhere from intense euphoria to extreme panic. Thoughts become vivid and generally seem to be beyond the individual's control—somewhat as in a dream. Also as in dreams, the changes in awareness are often accompanied by a dissociation of the self into two parts, an observer and a participant.

Hallucinations

Hallucinations are sensations or perceptions that have no direct external cause. They appear as part of most of the phenomena discussed in this chapter—hypnosis, spirit possession, dreaming, deprivation of REM sleep, meditation, and "trips" that are stimulated by psychedelic drugs. Complete dissociation is involved in some forms of hallucination. For example, auditory hallucinations are often experienced by schizophrenics. The schizophrenic individual may hear voices expressing ideas that seem to him inexplicable and also seem to be coming from outside himself, although the voices are actually his own thoughts. Other kinds of hallucinations, such as those that may arise during meditation, usually do not involve dissociation but instead are experienced as an expansion of consciousness.

Much of the research on hallucinations is confusing and contradictory. Perhaps the only conclusion that can be drawn is that most people are capable of hallucinations of some kind, even when they are awake. Some of the difficulty with the research stems from a combination of two factors. First, hallucinations usually cannot be recorded directly. They must be reported as memories after they have occurred. Therefore, they are subject to the distortions of memory. Second, people's hallucinations seem to vary greatly with apparently minor changes in the situation.

The study of *sensory deprivation* illustrates many of the problems with research on hallucinations. W. H. Bexton, W. Heron, and T. H. Scott and other members of their research group at McGill University first investigated sensory deprivation in adults. The participants in their study lay on beds for a number of hours, wearing

Figure 15.12
Experiments in which human subjects are voluntarily placed under conditions of extreme sensory deprivation reveal that in the absence of a normal level of stimulation, people produce their own. The subjects reported having hallucinations. People who have remained alone for long periods of time in a very homogeneous environment (for example, lost at sea) also report hallucinations—usually they imagine seeing another human being.

translucent goggles, gloves, and other paraphernalia designed to restrict sensory input as much as possible. In this study and in many that have followed, many participants have reported hallucinations. These hallucinations have been attributed to the effects of the sensory deprivation. But there is wide disagreement about the exact nature of the hallucinations and about the best conditions for producing them. In reviewing research on sensory deprivation, M. Zuckerman and N. Cohen concluded that the precise experimental procedures and the participants' expectations played a large part in determining the effects of sensory deprivation.

Twentieth-century psychology has badly neglected hallucinations and other consciousness-related phenomena, and most psychologists consider hallucinations to be abnormal. Consequently, many psychologists overestimated the importance of the hallucinations associated with sensory deprivation. But it should be clear to you from what you have read in this chapter that hallucinations are normal occurrences. Even daydreams often involve mild hallucinations. In 1883 the famous psychologist Francis Galton described in some detail the mild hallucinations that many normal people report. In modern sensory-deprivation experiments the participants have nothing external to occupy them, and often the experimenter has implied in his instructions that they may experience hallucinations. Under those circumstances it is hardly surprising that hallucinations appear.

CONSCIOUSNESS IN ANIMALS

On several occasions in this chapter, data from animal research have been included in discussions of human consciousness and awareness. Can an animal be said to possess a self, or consciousness, that can reflect on its own goings-on?

It is probably safe to say that chimpanzees have a sense of self. As described in Chapters 6 and 7, adult chimpanzees seem to have cognitive capacities roughly equivalent to those of three-year-old human children. They demonstrate a general capacity for what Piaget calls representation, the ability to evoke mental schemes in the absence of the overt actions, objects, or events on which the schemes are based. This capacity is necessary for the establishment of a sense of self, which involves a representation of one's own actions and experience as emanating from a single source, the self.

The chimpanzees that have learned to use a simple form of language (see Chapter 7) give evidence of a self-concept in the manner in which they refer to themselves, but G. G. Gallup reports a particularly clever demonstration of the existence of a self-concept in chimpanzees. Each chimpanzee under study was given a full-length mirror. After a few days, the chimpanzees began to use the mirrors to groom themselves, much as human beings do. After a few more days, Gallup performed a test to determine whether the chimpanzee recognized that the image in the mirror was of itself. Each chimpanzee was anesthetized, and an odorless dye was applied to the top of one eyebrow and the opposite ear. Upon awakening, when it saw itself in the mirror, it became agitated and looked at its reflection much more than it had earlier. Each chimpanzee repeatedly touched the red marks, and some examined their fingers after touching the marks. Monkeys (which are less intelligent than chimpanzees) showed no such behavior, even with much longer initial exposure to the mirrors. Instead, they reacted to the image in the mirror as they normally would react to another monkey.

Chimpanzees do seem to have at least a simple concept of self, then, but the chimpanzee is the smartest animal known to man other than man himself, and there is no evidence of a self-concept in any animals less intelligent than the chimpanzee. The fact that the chimpanzee has a sense of self does not really help answer the question whether animals have any consciousness; none of the research with animals cited earlier in this chapter used chimpanzees. In split-brain research and research on dreams, the results for cats and monkeys were similar in many ways to those for human beings. Could animals have a consciousness without having a sense of self?

The work of the noted brain surgeon W. Penfield and his associates suggests that animals have at least a rudimentary form of consciousness—perhaps they have experience but cannot reflect on it. During brain operations on people, Penfield found that removal or electrical disruption of the so-called "higher" centers of the brain, which are more developed in humans than in any other species, never produced loss of consciousness in his patients (who, incidentally, were not anesthetized). On the other hand, electrical disruption of certain sections of the so-called primitive brain or physical damage to them did result in unconsciousness. Consciousness returned when disruption was stopped, but if these sections were seriously damaged, the patient remained in a coma and eventually died. These sections of the brain are called primitive because they are present in animals far down the phylogenetic scale, not merely in the more intelligent animals, like cats, monkeys, chimpanzees, and people.

The discussion of the development of intelligence in Unit II may help to make sense of this finding. As mentioned in Chapters 5 and 7, many animals seem to have what Piaget calls *sensorimotor intelligence;* that is, they seem to have an intelligence of about the same level as a human infant in the sensorimotor period. If their intelligence is in some ways like that of an infant, then perhaps their consciousness is also in some ways like that of an infant.

A METAPHOR FOR CONSCIOUSNESS

Psychologists are still far from being able to explain consciousness. As this chapter has made clear, even the description of consciousness remains problematic, particularly because of its tendency to split into dissociated parts. Nevertheless, recent research—especially that on brain functioning in states like dreaming, the split brain, and epilepsy—has provided much new information about states of consciousness. K. Fischer has suggested that both the recent findings and many of the other phenomena discussed in this chapter can be thought of in terms of a simple metaphor of brain functioning.

The metaphor begins with another finding of Penfield's. When he performed brain surgery on epileptics, he had to "map" the brain before he removed any of it, so that he could be sure that he removed only the affected parts. Penfield did much of this mapping by stimulating various parts of the brain electrically. Usually the electrical stimulation disrupted normal activity in that part of the brain, but the patient was not aware of the disruption. For example, one patient was naming the objects on a series of cards, and just before a card showing a butterfly was presented, electrical current was applied to an area of his brain controlling speech. After a few seconds he began to snap his fingers as if exasperated, but he still said nothing. After the electrical current stopped, he blurted out, "Butterfly!" and added that he had known all along what the card portrayed but could not think of the word "butterfly." He tried to think of a close word, "moth," but he could not think of that, either. Then abruptly the word "butterfly" came to him. The patient experienced difficulty in recalling the word but did not experience the electrical stimulation or the disruption of brain functioning in the area stimulated. In other cases the electrical stimulation may produce not only disruption of normal brain activity in the area but also something like a sensation, movement, or memory. In these cases also, the patient does not experience the electrical stimulation or the neural disruption but merely experiences the sensation, movement, or memory.

The experience of many people who suffer brain damage is similar. Although the brain damage causes the person to lose certain abilities, he is not aware of his loss until he tries to perform some task that requires those abilities. For example, in one type of aphasia the person is unable to name an object such as a cup that is shown to him. At the same time, he uses the word "cup" normally in ordinary conversation, as when he offers a visitor a cup of tea. He is unable to recall words when he needs to use them out of context, but in context he has no difficulty.

Everyone has experiences analogous to those of Penfield's patient and of the person with aphasia. R. W. Brown and D. McNeill have investigated the everyday problem of having a word "on the tip of your tongue" but not quite being able to recall it. (What word means bestowal of jobs or other positions because of a family relationship rather than merit? If that one is too easy for you, what word means a waxy substance that is secreted by the sperm whale, found floating in tropical seas, and used in perfumes?) People know that they know the word and can often recall some characteristics of it—like the first letter and the number of syllables; but they cannot remember the word. Chapter 10 discussed other examples of problems in retrieving information from memory. In such cases, we have somewhere in our brain the information necessary to remember, but for some reason we are unable to gain access to it—that is, unable to activate the brain process that would allow us to remember.

The brain is complicated. It is composed of many different parts that serve different functions and are partly independent of each other. One way of thinking of it is as a large computer composed of many different interconnected subcomputers. A few of the subcomputers are like a control center for much brain activity. They serve a directing and controlling function for many of the other (auxiliary) subcomputers. These few are the ones necessary for consciousness. The controlling subcomputers call upon the auxiliary ones to perform various important functions. Sometimes, because of electrical disruption, brain damage, or some normal difficulty in activation, an auxiliary computer does not operate optimally. Then there is a deficit in brain functioning but no direct change in the controlling subcomputers. Also, whole groups of auxiliary subcomputers can be activated or inhibited, thereby

Figure 15.13
M. Escher's lithograph, titled "Bond of Union," can be seen as an image of the many parts and functions of the human mind that ultimately come together to form one's consciousness.
(Escher Foundation—Haags Gemeentemuseum—The Hague.)

changing dramatically the nature of the control that the controlling subcomputers can exert. For example, during dreaming the set of auxiliary subcomputers in operation would be quite different from the set in operation during the normal waking state. Thus, great changes can occur in awareness without the person's being aware of the reasons for the changes. Also, different species of animals have different auxiliary subcomputers and consequently different abilities. Only in humans and perhaps a few other species (such as chimpanzees) are the auxiliary subcomputers complicated enough to allow them to reflect on their own consciousnesses.

Simply failing to function is not the only way the auxiliary subcomputers can go wrong. For example, if a person is interrupted or distracted in the middle of a conversation, he commonly has difficulty remembering what he was thinking and talking about. He can follow some new train of thought perfectly well, but he cannot find the "switch" for reactivating his former thought process. The tip-of-the-tongue phenomenon is similar.

This loss of access to the functioning of the auxiliary subcomputers extends beyond memory problems. Similar difficulties occur in on-going activities, particularly with behaviors that are *automatized*—so well learned that they occur almost automatically. In typing or other skills, a systematic error may appear. You may begin to type *hte* repeatedly instead of *the*, and try as you might, you are unable to stop this error. As soon as you relax your vigilance and begin to type at normal speed, the error reappears. K. Dunlap has shown that these sorts of errors in automatized behaviors can often be eliminated by *negative practice:* Repeat the error over and over, typing *hte, hte, hte, hte* . . . and you regain control of the response.

Most of our behavior is automatized, and with the automatization we both gain flexibility and develop rigidity, as discussed in Chapter 4. Because the behavior is automatized, we can do several things at once: at the beginning of the chapter, you were bouncing your knee up and down and at the same time concentrating on the table. On the other hand, because the response can go on by itself, we may lose control of it, as in typing *hte.* In terms of the metaphor, the auxiliary subcomputers function without any need for direction from the controlling subcomputers, and sometimes the controlling subcomputers may lose their ability to control the functioning of the auxiliary ones during automatized activity. In addition, the controlling subcomputers have little or no access to the method of functioning of the auxiliary ones. The next time that you are engaged in a conversation, try to notice what is within your awareness as you speak. Thoughts will be there, but probably not in the form of particular sentences. You will decide to speak, and sentences will flow. Most people report no awareness of the process of constructing the sentences. And even when they consciously formulate a sentence before they say it, they are not aware of the complicated linguistic rules that they are using (such rules are discussed in Chapter 7).

This analysis of consciousness in terms of the brain as a computer is just a metaphor. It is not at all a literal description of how the brain functions. Yet it does provide a useful analogy to help us think about consciousness and awareness. Alterations in awareness occur because of changes in the functioning of auxiliary subcomputers. The consciousnesses of animals are different from those of people because the animals lack the auxiliary subcomputers that allow people to reflect on their own consciousnesses. And dissociation phenomena seem to be intrinsic to the functioning of a system where the activities of auxiliary subcomputers are not present in awareness. In fact, automatized behaviors and loss of a train of thought after distraction can be thought of as everyday examples of dissociation. We have a sense of the unity of consciousness not because consciousness is actually unitary but because we construct a notion of an integrated self to which we refer all our conscious experiences. We therefore ignore all the instances of dissociation.

Although the foregoing is only a metaphor, it suggests that consciousness and awareness are subject to explanation in terms of psychological processes. Recently, R. W. Sperry, the famous neuropsychologist who conducted some of the split-brain research described earlier, has argued that consciousness can no longer be considered an unscientific concept unworthy of consideration by psychologists. To the contrary, evidence indicates that it is a real property of the functioning of the brain and that it plays an active role in the control of brain activity.

SUGGESTED READINGS

DEMENT, W. C. "An Essay on Dreams: The Role of Physiology in Understanding Their Nature," in F. Barron, *et al., New Directions in Psychology,* Vol. II. New York, Holt, Rinehart and Winston, 1965. A well-written summary of research on the psychology and physiology of dreams by one of the major researchers in the field.

GAZZANIGA, M. S. "The Split Brain in Man." *Scientific American,* 217 (1967), 24–29. A highly readable summary and discussion of the effects of the split-brain operation in man.

LAING, R. D. *The Divided Self.* Baltimore, Penguin, 1965. This well-written book tries to give the reader a sense of what it is like to experience schizophrenia.

SHOR, R. E., AND ORNE, M. T. (Eds.) *The Nature of Hypnosis.* New York, Holt, Rinehart and Winston, 1965. This collection of readings contains most of the important papers on hypnosis and also some papers on related topics like multiple personality and spirit possession.

SPERRY, R. W. "A Modified Concept of Consciousness." *Psychological Review,* 76 (1969), 532–536. The famous neuropsychologist argues that consciousness can no longer be viewed as an unscientific concept.

TART, C.T. (Ed.) *Altered States of Consciousness.* New York, Wiley, 1969. This collection of readings includes papers on a wide range of topics, including dreaming, hypnosis, drugs.

WALLACE, R. K., AND BENSON, H. "The Physiology of Meditation." *Scientific American,* 226 (1972), 84–90. This important study demonstrates that meditation has powerful effects on human physiology.

UNIT V
Physiological Bases of Behavior

In the Western world the so-called "mind-body problem" has been a major concern of thinkers since the Greeks: What is the relationship between the mind and the body? Is the mind essentially independent of the body, as most people believed in the past, or is it a manifestation of a bodily process, as most scientists would say today? In the East as well as the West, the predominant religions seem to consider the mind to be the essence of being human; the body is seen as merely a worldly vehicle for housing the mind.

Whatever we believe about the relationship between mind and body,

2

Instinctive Behavior introduces the biological approach to psychology. It discusses the relationship between heredity and environment in the determination of behavior and points out the importance of Darwin's notion of species-specific behavior. In its general survey of several kinds of biological explanations of behavior, it analyzes fixed action patterns and habituation; Chapter 16 examines neural mechanisms underlying each of these phenomena.

3

Conditioning and Learning presents the principles of operant conditioning, which are used in biofeedback, a technique for learning to control certain bodily processes discussed in Chapter 16. Also, studies of the physiological correlates of simple learning processes reported in Chapter 16 add a dimension to the discussion of those processes in Chapter 3.

13

The Senses describes in detail the physiological and anatomical structure of each of the systems by means of which we see, hear, taste, smell, feel, and keep our balance. The description of the nervous system in Chapter 16 is closely related to many topics in Chapter 13.

15

Consciousness and Awareness deals with a number of physiological techniques used to study the nature of consciousness and of awareness; for example: split-brain surgery for epileptic patients; study of brain-wave and metabolic changes in altered states of consciousness; studies of EEG patterns during sleep. These procedures derived from means used to study the normal physiological processes described in Chapter 16.

17

Emotion analyzes the physiological bases of emotion. Its discussion of central-nervous system involvement in emotion, especially in stress and psychosomatic illness, relates to Chapter 16's more general discussion of the nervous system.

however, we cannot forget about the body for long. Events continually remind us of its existence. We become hungry, a leg falls asleep, we get hiccups or a cold. Pleasant experiences, too, make us aware of our bodies—the taste of a delicious meal, the passion of sex, a plunge into a cool lake. Our bodies are complex biological systems, and to understand human psychological functioning, we must take into account the biological bases of behavior. How do our bodies function? Of particular importance for psychology, what is the relationship between the nervous system and behavior? What is the significance of the fact that we are members of a particular species, *Homo sapiens,* and how do we inherit the characteristics of our species?

In fact, psychology can be treated as a branch of biology; biology is the study of life, and people and their minds are a part of life.

Chapter 16, The Biological Organism, discusses the importance of biology for psychology and describes those aspects of anatomy and physiology that are necessary for understanding the biological bases of human behavior. Research on the relationship between brain functioning and behavior is summarized; and the mechanisms of inheritance are described.

34

Drugs and Drug Therapy deals extensively with psychopharmacology—the analysis of the effects of drugs on psychological functioning. Its consideration of hypotheses about the mechanisms by which some drugs work their effects relates to Chapter 16's discussion of basic physiological functions.

31

Bases of Disorder examines possible hereditary and biochemical causes of psychological disorder. Chapter 16's discussion of behavior genetics and of the normal processes of the glandular system underlie Chapter 31's discussion.

30

Adjustment and Disorder describes the various types of mental disorder and their possible causes; the discussion of the organically based disorders is related to Chapter 16's description of the normal workings of the brain and nervous system.

20

Psychological Testing describes the origins and current uses of IQ tests and discusses what they can be said to measure. Chapter 16's information about inheritance, especially in populations, can be read as background to that discussion.

18

Elementary Concepts of Motivation analyzes the physiological bases of biological drives like hunger, thirst, and sex; it expands upon the general physiological discussion of Chapter 16.

16 The Biological Organism

EVERY ONCE IN A WHILE we come across the old bromide that the human being uses only one-fifth of his brain. The rest apparently does nothing. If somehow we could only learn to use it all, we would all be incredible geniuses. What nonsense! Partly, this bromide arises out of the fact that sizable parts of the human brain can be destroyed by disease or removed by the knife without seriously affecting the functioning of a human being. But, after all, one kidney can be removed and a human being can do well with the remaining kidney. If one eye is lost, all can be seen with the remaining eye. Does that mean that human beings use only half their kidneys and eyes?

The belief in the unused brain also arises out of the fact that certain parts of the brain are directly associated with the stimulation of a particular set of muscles, or with the receipt of impulses from this particular sense organ or that. That leaves large parts of the brain that are *not* involved in the direct receipt of information or the direct issuing of orders. Does that mean those noninvolved parts do nothing? Of course not.

What about the necessary weighing and coordination of information, and the necessary decisions between different possible orders. In short, what about all the "paper work" that must be involved in the brain. We might as well suppose that a construction firm engaged in building a skyscraper is using only one-fifth of its employees because only that fifth is actually engaged in raising steel beams, laying down electric cables, transporting equipment, and such. This would ignore the executives, supervisors, secretaries, filing clerks, etc.

In fact, by ignoring the more subtle, but very real, functions of the brain, we lend a spurious air of mystery to such things as imagination and creativity. For instance, "Kubla Khan" by Samuel Taylor Coleridge is a poem that, though incomplete, is admired by all. It has weird imagery and magnificently quotable lines. From what mysterious depth of genius did Coleridge bring these lines to light?

The poem was carefully analyzed by John Livingston Lowes in *The Road to Xanadu.* Lowes was able to show that virtually every word and phrase in the poem stemmed from some item in Coleridge's past reading or experience. We can visualize Coleridge putting together various word and phrase fragments in his mind (unconsciously, perhaps) after the fashion of a mental kaleidoscope, picking out the combinations he liked best and constructing the poem out of them. It was the careful work of portions of the brain that the naive think are "unused."

Coleridge, indeed, according to his own story, *dreamed* "Kubla Khan." In the quiet of sleep he completed the kaleidoscopic construction and woke with the entire poem in his mind. He began transferring it rapidly to paper, until (damn it!) he was interrupted by a visitor. By the time the visitor left, what remained of the poem had vanished from his mind and was lost forever.

I.A.

Some psychological events in the life of an organism are so closely related to biology that it is impossible to understand them without knowing something about physiological structures and processes. Unless we know, for example, that the human brain has two hemispheres that are mirror images of each other, and that the neural connections between them can be severed, we will not get far toward understanding the postoperative experience of the woman who had epilepsy, discussed at the beginning of Chapter 15. More generally speaking, our understanding of behavior is liable to be less than complete if we overlook biology, for it is living organisms that do the behaving.

Biology has played several important roles in the development of psychology. The first, as Chapters 2 and 3 point out, derives from Darwin's theory of evolution. It leads us to consider species-specific behavior in relation both to the biological heritage of the organism and to the species' current ecological niche. It has also encouraged attention to the adaptive aspects of behavior, in the sense that particular behavior patterns are seen as promoting or inhibiting the reproduction and survival of a species. For example, a particular behavior pattern such as the stereotyped way in which a cat stalks and captures a rat may be analyzed in terms of its survival value (for the cat, not the rat).

A second biological contribution, which will be discussed at the end of this chapter, pertains to the role of genetics in such behavioral phenomena as intelligence. Yet another role of biology in psychological research is to help explain the internal chemical and electrical events that accompany behavior. When the cat of the previous example attacks the rat in a particular way, the stimulus effects (from the sight of the rat) can be traced to a particular region of the brain (the hypothalamus) that is concerned with the integration of the stalking–attack sequence. One way to analyze the cat's behavior, then, is in terms of the activity of particular cells in the brain.

Physiological processes are a part of all behavior, needless to say, but they are particularly important in motivated and emotional behavior, which is the subject of the following unit. The last unit also indicated the importance of physiology for understanding the way the senses function. The main concern in this chapter is to describe certain biological processes that are important in psychological behavior, with particular emphasis on the activities of nerve cells—the body's basic transmitters of information—the brain, which is the largest grouping of nerve cells in the body, and the genetic inheritance of the organism.

NERVE CELLS

The nervous system in vertebrate animals is composed of the brain (encased in a protective bony skull), the spinal cord, and a variety of peripheral nerves. Its primary function is to process information, a task that it accomplishes through the *excitability* and *conductivity* of individual nerve cells.

The human nervous system contains billions of individual cells. Between the inside and outside of each cell, there is normally a difference in electrical potential of a fraction of a volt. This *resting potential* is maintained by cellular processes that pump electrically charged ions through the cell membrane. When the cell is appropriately stimulated, localized changes in the membrane bring about a shift in potential: the nerve cell discharges, or *fires*, and the localized change in potential (called a spike) sweeps along the entire length of the cell membrane. Under certain conditions, the firing of one nerve cell alters the resting potential of adjacent nerve cells and causes them to fire. In this fashion, patterns of electrical excitation move from one part of the nervous system to another.

It is traditional to think of the nervous system as consisting of a *sensory portion*, cells concerned with the detection and preliminary analysis of environmental stimuli; a *motor portion*, cells that are clearly involved in the activation of muscles and glands; and a broad group of *associative cells* that intervene between sense reception and motor activities. One weakness of this classification scheme is that it is not always clear where a particular sensory system ends and associative systems begin. Certain cells, for example, originate within the brain but send projections to the peripheral sense organs, such as the auditory receptors of the ear, where they presumably modulate the reception of incoming information. The classification of these cells as either sensory or associative is misleading. Another weakness is that cells have sometimes been assigned to the associative class simply because they do not belong to either of the others—when a cell has no known function, it is often labeled associative. Other, more subtle, explanations or classification schemes have been suggested. For example, the neuroscientist H.-L. Teuber has suggested in a magazine interview that some so-called associative cells may be understudies of a particular sort—uncommitted cells that are ready to take over the functions of damaged ones when necessary.

Neurons and Neuroglia

There are two kinds of cells in the nervous system of the vertebrate organism: *neurons* and *neuroglia*, also called glial cells. The neurons are the specialized cells that transmit electrical activity. The functions of the neuroglia are not clear. They

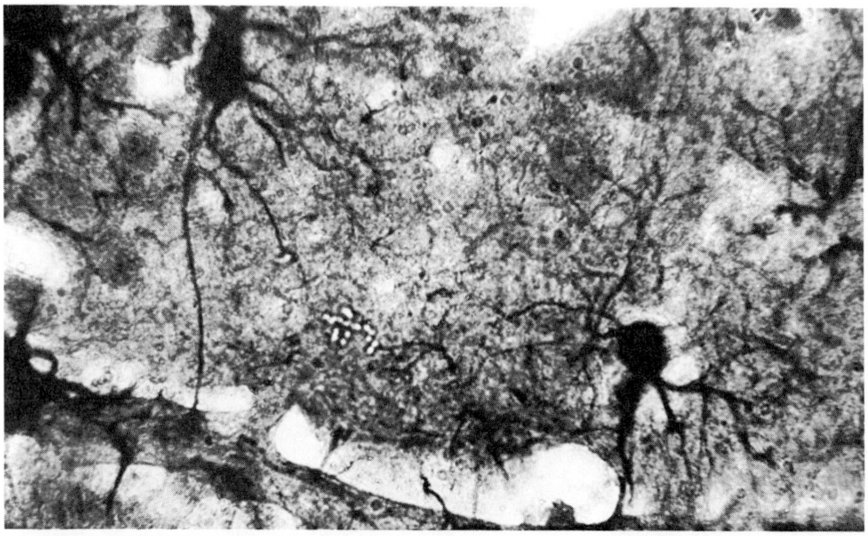

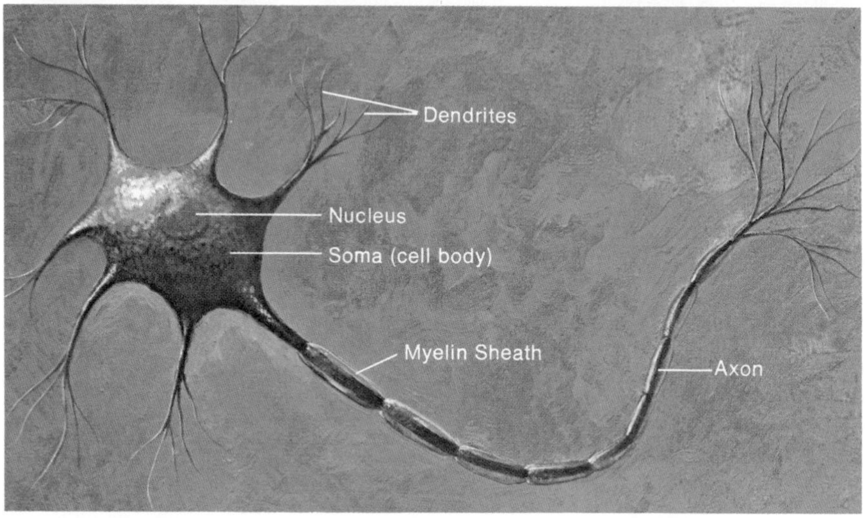

Figure 16.1
(Top) This photomicrograph of two neuroglia (or glial cells) among larger nerve cells shows how the neuroglia and their extensions are complexly interwoven with neurons; also, note their attachment to the walls of the blood vessel (bottom, left). Although many researchers are studying them, the functions of the neuroglia are as yet undetermined.

Figure 16.2
The neuron is a cell specialized for the rapid communication of information. The dendrites receive information from other neurons and send it to the soma; the axon usually conducts information away from the soma toward the finely branched axon end feet. The end feet are especially equipped to transmit the message to the next neuron. In this cell myelin covers most of the axon; myelin is a covering that is much like insulation on electric wires; by keeping the impulses from diffusing, it increases the speed of transmission in the axon.

Figure 16.3
(Below) Photograph of a micropipette that has been inserted into a very large axon of the type found in the squid. This precise and delicate instrument is used by neurophysiologists to study and record changes in electrical potentials in a single nerve cell. The electric currents generated in the cell are so minute that they must be amplified in order to record them or to display them on a cathode ray oscilloscope. Each division on the scale in the photograph equals thirty-three microns (a micron is a unit of length equal to 1/1000 millimeter).
(After Hodgkin and Huxley, 1945.)

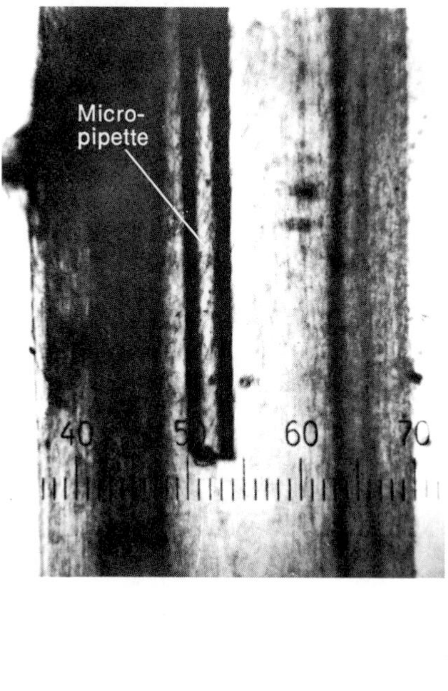

are usually thought to play a supportive or nourishing role—perhaps serving as electrical insulation like the rubber on a telephone wire, although recent research by R. A. Galambos and by H. Hyden and E. Egyhazi suggests a more active role. In general, glial cells have extensions that weave around neurons and are often attached to the walls of blood vessels, as shown in Figure 16.1.

The structure of a typical vertebrate neuron is depicted in Figure 16.2. The neuron has three basic parts: the *dendrites* (generally the signal-receiving area); the *soma* (cell body); and the *axon* (the long conductive structure that carries signals away from the cell). There are many different types of neurons and many ways of classifying them—according to the shape and size of the cell body, the presence or absence of specialized dendritic processes, the length of the axons, and the presence or absence of the fatty cover called the *myelin sheath.* Despite these variations, however, some general points can be made about the electrical activity of neurons and about the chemical events that underlie the electrical phenomena.

The Electrical Activity of Neurons

If a small glass tube or pipette, drawn to a very fine tip, is filled with potassium chloride (a conducting fluid) and inserted inside an axon, it is possible to record a difference in the electrical potentials between the outside of the cell and the fluid in the axon. In a typical inactive nerve cell, this potential difference might be on

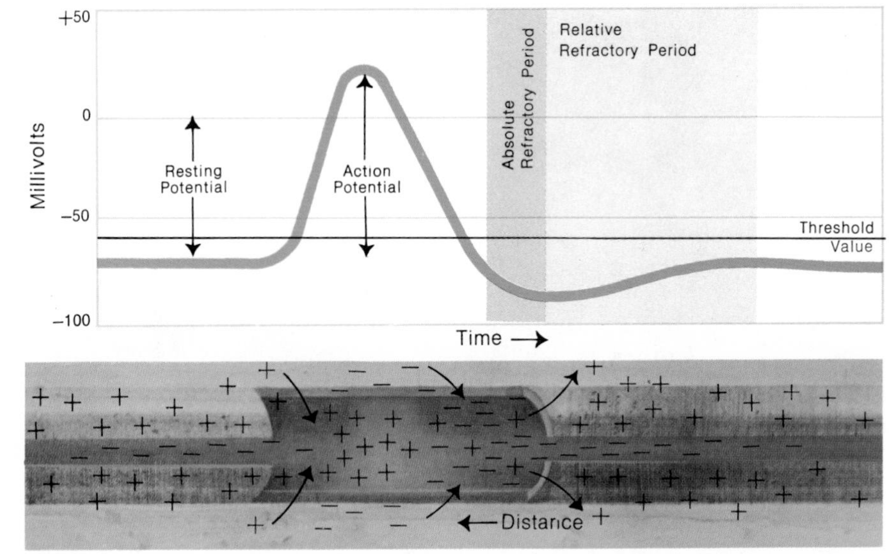

Figure 16.4
(Top) the action potential is a voltage charge that travels down the membrane of an active neuron. At any given instant the location of the action potential on the membrane is indicated by a brief reversal of the resting potential (−70 millivolts) to a peak of about 20 millivolts. (Bottom) the passage of the action potential moving to the left along the axon. The membrane of the neuron normally is electrically polarized, with the inside negative relative to the outside. Triggering of the action potential first depolarizes the membrane, then reverses the polarization, making the inside positive. The positivity reaches a peak, then the membrane returns to the resting-potential polarization. Note the changes in positive and negative signs along the path of the action potential (orange).
(Adapted from "The Nerve Impulse," Bernhard Katz. ©1952 by Scientific American, Inc. All rights reserved.)

the order of −70 millivolts (about 5 percent as much energy as a flashlight battery generates), with the inside of the neuron carrying a negative charge relative to the outside of the neuron. The *resting potential* of such a cell, then, is −70 millivolts.

Action Potentials If the neuron is excited with appropriate chemical or electrical stimuli, its potential changes. First, there is a positive shift in voltage, which produces a decrease in the potential difference recorded across the cell membrane. When voltage has decreased to a critical level (the *threshold value*), an *action potential* is generated. The action potential, which is called a *spike* because at a given point in a neuron it rises to a peak and then declines, is a rapid change in voltage that moves along the neuron like the crest of a wave moving along the surface of a lake. The change results in a brief reversal of the resting-potential condition. That is, the inside of the membrane becomes positively charged with respect to the outside for an instant. Then the resting potential is restored. The sequence of changes in electrical potential as the cell fires is depicted in Figure 16.4.

Accompanying this sequence of changes in voltage is a parallel sequence of changes in the excitability of the neuron. Immediately following an action potential, there is a very brief *absolute refractory period* during which another action potential cannot be generated, no matter how strong the stimulus. Then there is a brief *relative refractory period* during which a stronger than usual stimulus is required to evoke a second spike.

There are two key characteristics of action potentials. First, they are *all or none.* If the threshold value is reached, the cell fires, and the size of the action potential depends on the cell, not on the magnitude of the original stimulus. The second characteristic is that action potentials are *nondecremental.* As an action potential generated near the cell body travels to the farthest ends of the axon, it neither fades nor dies out regardless of the length of the axon.

The speed with which the action potential travels varies from one neuron to the next, with a minimum velocity of about 10 feet per second and a maximum of 390 feet per second. Generally, the larger the diameter of the nerve fiber, the faster the conduction. Large fibers also tend to have lower thresholds and shorter refractory periods than small ones. That is, large fibers fire more easily, conduct faster, and recover faster.

Although the magnitude of a stimulus does not affect the size of a cell's action

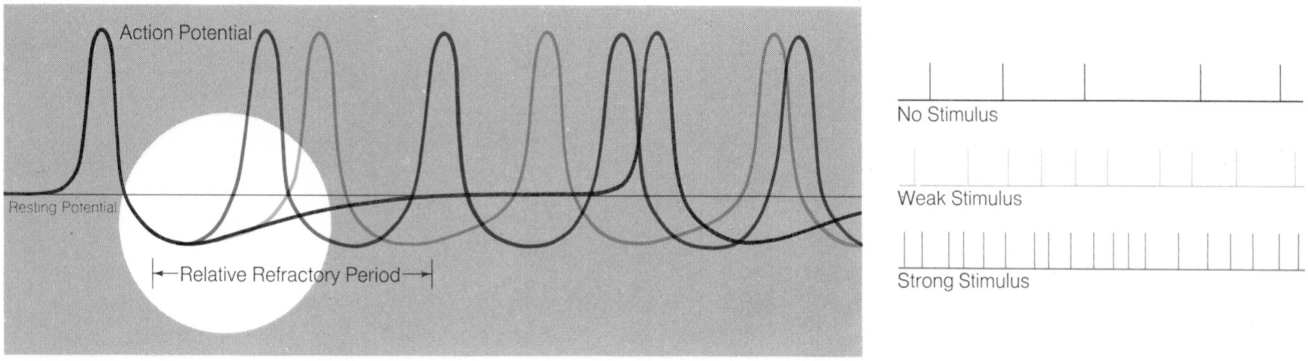

Figure 16.5
The occurrence of an action potential is immediately followed by a very brief period during which a spike cannot be generated regardless of the strength of the stimulus. This absolute refractory period can range from .4 to 1.0 milliseconds, and it is followed by the longer relative refractory period, during which a stronger-than-usual stimulus is required to evoke an action potential. The diagrams to the right are sample recordings of the activity of a single neuron under varying levels of stimulation. The vertical lines represent action potentials.

potential, it does affect the rate at which the cell fires. Figure 16.5 shows the effect of an increasingly strong stimulus on the firing rate of a neuron. A stronger stimulus produces a more rapid rate of action potentials by reactivating the cell earlier in the relative refractory period. In addition, because different neurons have different thresholds of excitation, an intense stimulus causes more nerve cells to fire than a weak one. As the discussion of neural coding in the eye and the ear in Chapter 13 indicated, these two factors—how many cells are firing and how rapidly—are central to the transmission of information from one part of the nervous system to another.

Synapses Thus far, we have been talking about action potentials within a single nerve cell. How is information transmitted from cell to cell?

The typical vertebrate neuron, when it fires, releases certain chemicals from its axon into the tiny gap (only a few hundred angstroms wide) between its axon and the dendrites of a neighboring cell. These chemicals, called *transmitter substances,* diffuse across the gap and induce changes in the membrane of the receiving cell that tend to depolarize it and produce an action potential. The meeting point of the axonal ending of one cell and the dendrites of the next neuron across the intervening gap is known as the *synapse,* or *synaptic junction* (see Figure 16.6). Although evidence indicating the existence of synapses has been accumulating since the turn of the century, it was only with the development of the electron microscope that they could actually be seen.

Excitation and Inhibition The release of some chemical transmitter substances excites a postsynaptic cell (the cell whose dendrites receive substances across the synapse) and leads to production of an action potential. Other substances (as yet largely unidentified) *inhibit* the discharge of the cell instead of exciting it. That is, they reduce its rate of discharge. If enough of the inhibitory chemical is present, the cell may not fire at all for a period of time.

A great many axon terminals converge on most individual neurons, and each terminal can release a quantity of transmitter substance that contributes to excitation or inhibition of the cell. In general, then, frequency of discharge for a particular cell at a particular time depends on (1) the relative quantities of excitatory and inhibitory transmitter substances acting on the membrane of the postsynaptic cell, and (2) the intrinsic excitability of the cell (how recently it has discharged, its metabolic status, and so on).

Neurochemical Considerations

Cellular chemistry must be considered in a discussion of information processing in the nervous system, because it is basic both to the resting and action potentials of a cell and to the mechanism of transmission at synaptic junctions.

The resting potential results from the fact that there are unequal amounts of certain chemicals on the two sides of the cell membrane. This distribution can occur

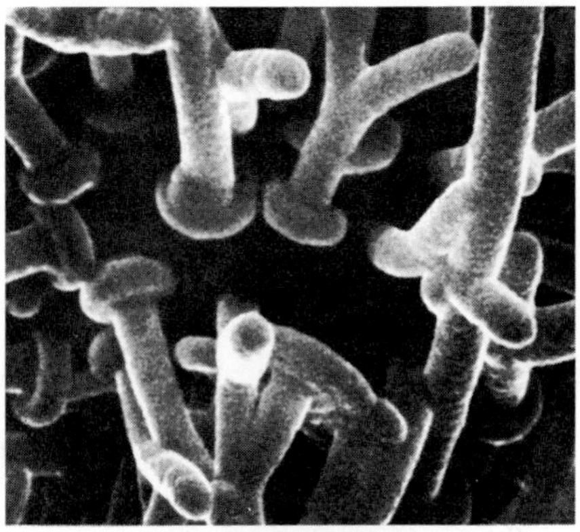

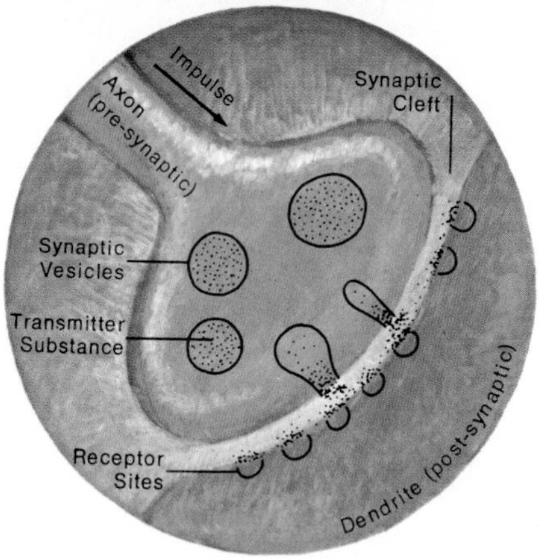

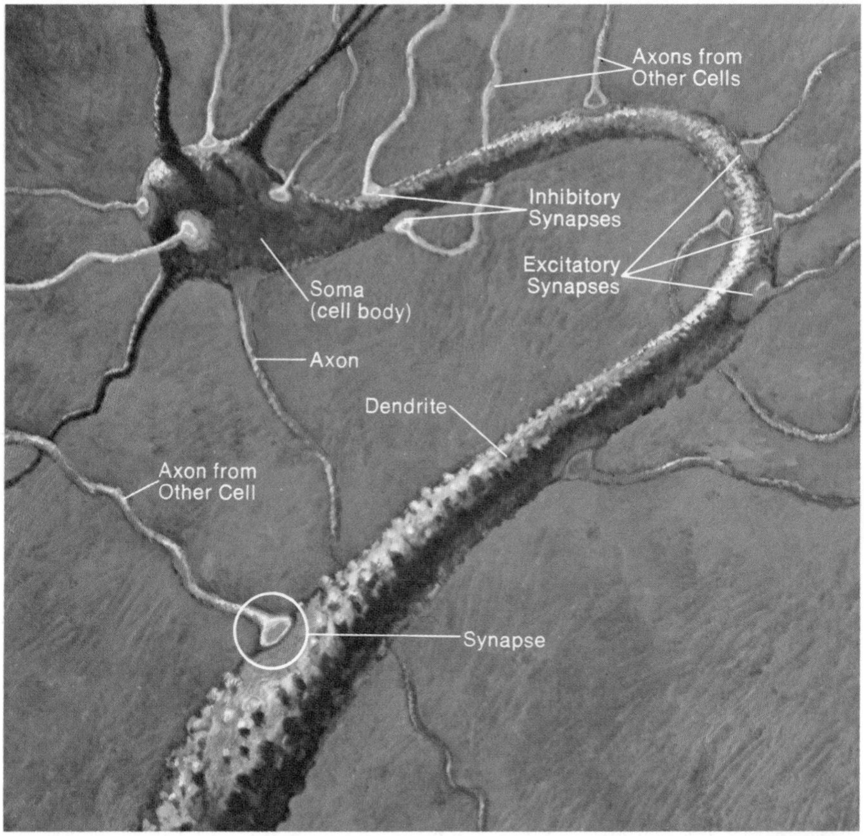

Figure 16.6
(Right) information from one neuron is transmitted to another at the synaptic junction. The synapse is the fluid-filled space separating two neurons. The neuron receiving stimulation is termed the postsynaptic neuron, and that from which the stimulation comes is the presynaptic neuron. The axons of many different neurons may all synapse on a single postsynaptic cell. (Top left) this photograph, taken by a scanning electron microscope, shows several axons converging upon a single cell. By means of such complex synaptic connections, one postsynaptic cell can integrate large amounts of information. (Bottom left) an enlarged schematic of the synaptic junction circled in the large diagram. The slightly bulged axonal ending contains vesicles, or packets, that may serve to store chemical transmitters before they are released across the synapse. Specialization may also exist on the postsynaptic side of the synapse: note that there is a change in the small segment of the postsynaptic cell membrane immediately opposite the presynaptic axonal ending.

because certain substances, when dissolved in water, interact with water molecules and dissociate into atoms with an excess or deficiency of electrons. When common table salt (NaCl), for example, is dissolved in water, it separates into its constituent atoms (Na^+ and Cl^-). The sodium (Na) loses an electron in the process and is left with a net positive charge; the chlorine (Cl) gains an electron and acquires a net negative charge. These charged particles are known as *ions*. (Pure crystalline sodium and pure chlorine gas are neutral in electric charge; that is, they have as many positive protons in their nuclei as negative electrons in their orbits.)

The main ions involved in the resting and action potentials of nerve cells are sodium, potassium, chlorine, and some large organic molecules (confined to the interior of the cell) that carry a negative charge. In the resting cell there is a net excess of negatively charged ions on the inside of the cell membrane, which results in the recorded resting potential (such as that shown earlier, in Figure 16.4). During the generation of an action potential, there is a rapid influx of sodium ions, which are positively charged and briefly cause the interior of the membrane to become positively charged with respect to the exterior of the cell. Electrical currents created by the localized influx cause neighboring areas of the membrane to depolarize, so that the action potential moves along the axon.

When the action potential reaches the end of the axon, a transmitter substance is released into the synaptic junction, as was described earlier. A variety of transmitter substances function in the activity of the vertebrate nervous system, but it is believed that a particular neuron releases only one of them. A common and much studied transmitter substance is acetylcholine (ACh), which operates in the parasympathetic nervous system (discussed later in this chapter), probably within parts of the brain and spinal cord, and at junctions of neurons and muscles.

In addition to the transmitter substance released by a neuron, other chemical compounds are present near the axonal endings. They inactivate the transmitter

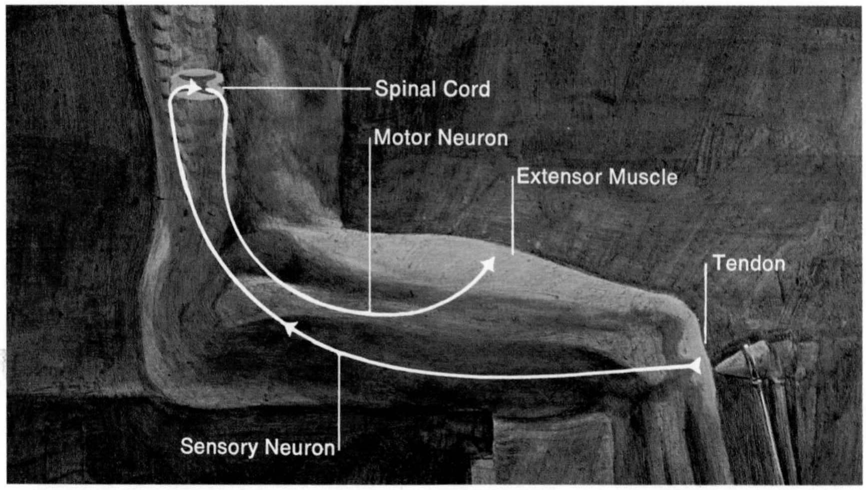

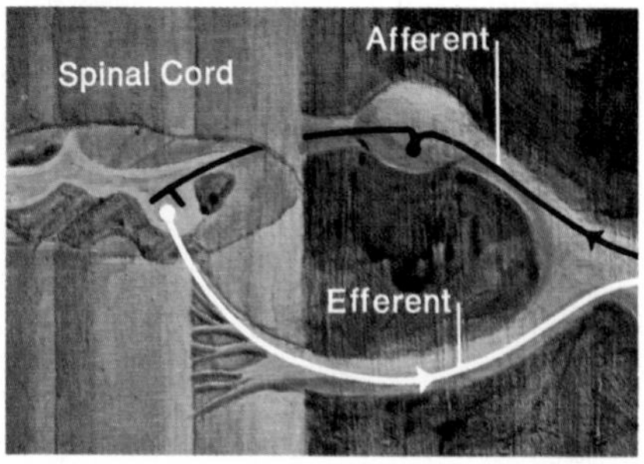

Figure 16.7
(Left) diagram of the simple patellar reflex.

Figure 16.8
(Above) all of the information reaching the central nervous system must enter (via *afferent* neurons) and leave (via *efferent* neurons) by way of pathways in and out of the spinal cord.

Figure 16.9
(Below) complex reflex arcs involve one or more interneurons interposed between the sensory and motor neurons. The flexor reflex is an example of a response activated by a complex (multisynaptic) reflex arc. Following noxious stimulation, a message is delivered to the spinal cord by the sensory neuron. Within the cord interneurons may send the message to higher or lower levels of the cord before activating the motor neuron, which in turn stimulates the flexor muscle. Interneurons can also form circuits within the spinal cord, permitting sustained stimulation of the motor neuron long after activity in the sensory neuron has ceased.

by transforming it chemically. If inactivation did not occur, transmitter substances would accumulate indefinitely in the region of the postsynaptic membrane, resulting in the continuous stimulation of the cell and a blurring of message transmission. Together, the release of a small quantity of transmitter substance and the rapid inactivation of the transmitter by local chemical compounds permit the transmission of discrete messages across synaptic junctions.

Some of the substances known to be involved in the inactivation of ACh have been identified. Two of them are enzymes related to the chemical scopolamine, which is an ingredient of most of the common nonprescription sleeping pills now on the market. Scopolamine depresses transmission at synaptic junctions where the release of ACh is the critical event. Blurred vision and increased heart rate are side effects of scopolamine.

FUNCTIONAL ANATOMY OF THE NERVOUS SYSTEM

The nervous system is composed of two basic subdivisions: the *central nervous system* (CNS), which consists of the brain and spinal cord, and the *peripheral nervous system,* whose neurons carry sensory information from the periphery of the body to the CNS and convey messages that activate glands and muscles. Because the anatomy of the nervous system is extraordinarily complicated, we shall restrict our discussion to those structures that are especially relevant to psychological problems.

The Spinal Cord

The spinal cord is of particular interest to psychologists for two reasons. First, it controls many reflexes that are crucial to the survival of organism. Second, it constitutes a simplified model (simplified, that is, in comparison to the brain) of a neurological system that receives information, processes it, and then delivers impulses to the muscles for the initiation and integration of motor sequences.

The simplest spinal reflex arc involves just two neurons: an *afferent* sensory neuron, conveying information about stimulation *from* the periphery to the spinal cord, and an *efferent* motor neuron, which runs from the spinal cord to the muscles. The knee jerk elicited by a tap below the kneecap is the result of the simultaneous activation of a number of such two-neuron arcs, one of which is shown in diagrammatically in Figure 16.7. Two-neuron arcs are relatively uncommon in our functioning spinal reflexes, however. In most cases one or more *interneurons* intervenes between the afferent and efferent neurons. Their participation greatly increases the possibilities for complex reflex activity. One complex spinal reflex is diagrammed in Figure 16.9.

Inhibitory and excitatory fibers play a central role in reflex activity. In the case

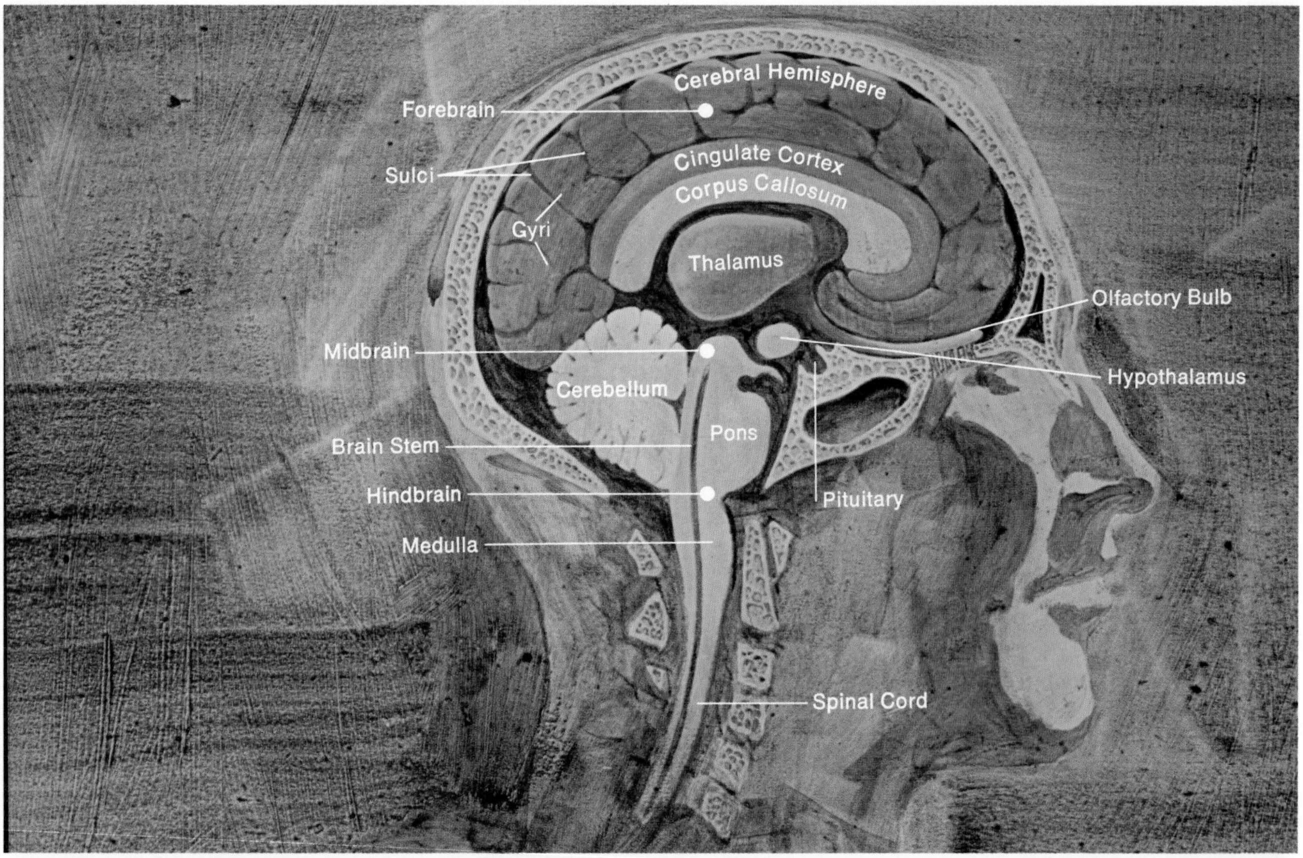
Cerebral Hemisphere
Forebrain
Sulci
Gyri
Cingulate Cortex
Corpus Callosum
Thalamus
Olfactory Bulb
Midbrain
Hypothalamus
Cerebellum
Pons
Brain Stem
Hindbrain
Pituitary
Medulla
Spinal Cord

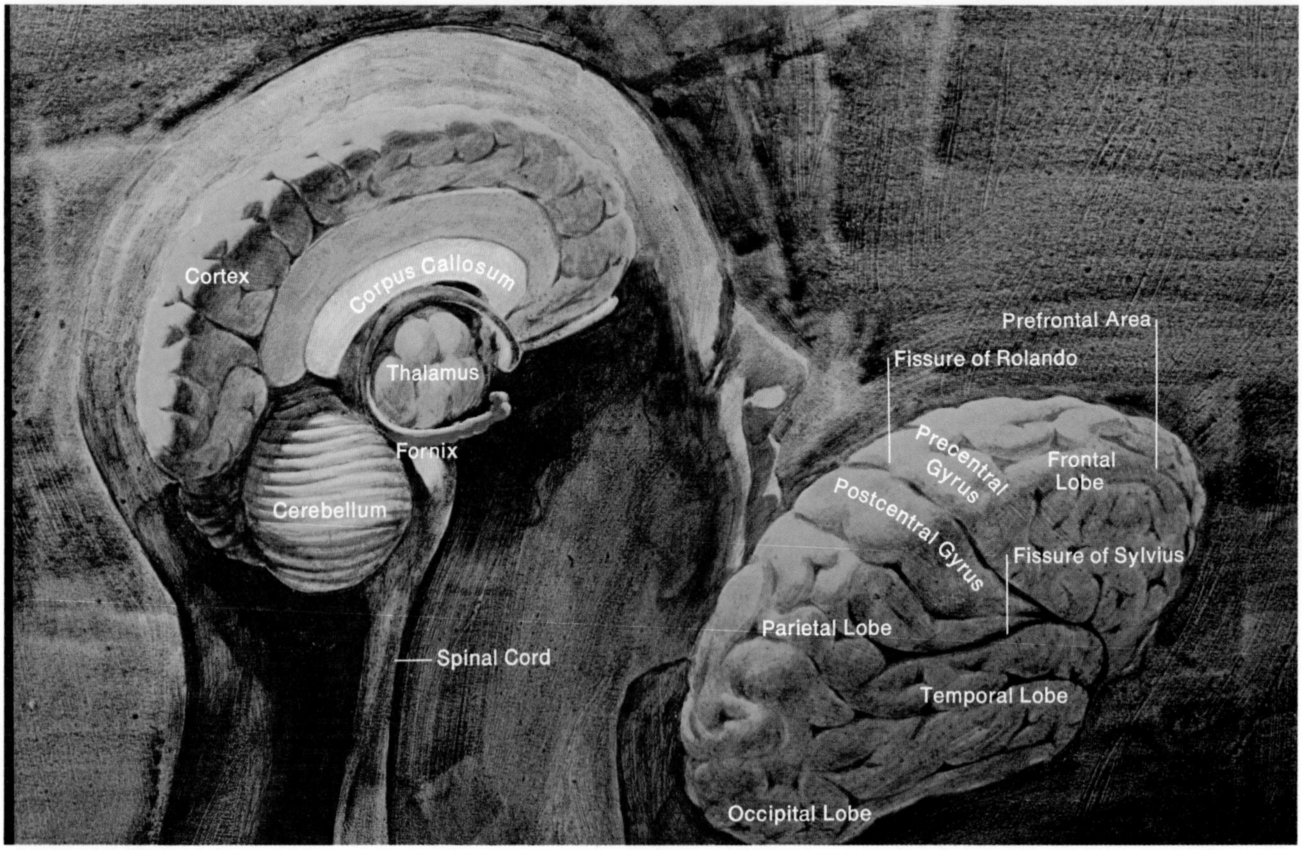
Cortex
Corpus Callosum
Thalamus
Fornix
Cerebellum
Spinal Cord
Prefrontal Area
Fissure of Rolando
Precentral Gyrus
Frontal Lobe
Postcentral Gyrus
Fissure of Sylvius
Parietal Lobe
Temporal Lobe
Occipital Lobe

of the knee jerk, at the same time that the muscles on the front of the leg are being excited and are contracting, the motor nerves of the muscles on the back of the leg are being inhibited from discharging action potentials. That is one of the reasons that several two-neuron arcs make up the reflex: one for excitation of one set of muscles, and one for inhibition of the other. This inhibition prevents the simultaneous contraction of the two opposing muscle groups, ensuring a smooth, coordinated extension of the lower leg (the word "jerk" is something of a misnomer). This coordination of motor movements, involving the excitation of some motor neurons and the simultaneous inhibition of others, is the key characteristic of spinal reflex regulation of behavior.

Figure 16.10 *(opposite)*
This cross section through the middle of the human brain illustrates the relationship between the forebrain, consisting of the cerebral hemispheres, the thalamus, and the hypothalamus; the hindbrain, consisting of the medulla, the pons, and the cerebellum; and the intermediately placed midbrain.

Figure 16.11 *(opposite)*
The brain, like the rest of the body, is bilaterally symmetrical. Most structures, therefore, occur in duplicate, one on each side of the brain. The left and right cerebral hemispheres are shown here along with the corpus callosum, which serves the important function of connecting the two sides of the brain—in effect, telling one side what the other side is doing.

The Brain

The vertebrate brain is divided into three regions: the forebrain, the midbrain, and the hindbrain. The forebrain consists of the two cerebral hemispheres, including such interior structures as the thalamus and hypothalamus. The hindbrain includes the medulla, pons, and cerebellum. The midbrain is the intermediate zone between the forebrain and hindbrain. Figure 16.10 shows the human brain in cross section, and Figure 16.11 shows the left and right cerebral hemispheres.

We have just considered some functions of the spinal cord. Let us now move to the highest and most complex part of the central nervous system, the cerebral hemispheres, and then work our way down through the hindbrain toward the spinal cord.

The Cerebral Hemispheres and the Cortex The surface of the cerebral hemispheres is called the *cortex* (or neocortex). The human cortex is intricately convoluted, and its indentations, known as *fissures* or *sulci,* divide the cortex into a complex set of *gyri.* For example, as can be seen in Figure 16.12, the fissure of Rolando separates the precentral gyrus from the postcentral gyrus. Not all vertebrates have intensively convoluted cortexes. The surface of the rat brain, for example, is virtually smooth, except for a large fissure that separates the two hemispheres and another fissure that can be seen on the side of the hemispheres.

There are many different types of cortex, classified according to the kinds of cells they contain and the way these cells are distributed. A highly developed cortex

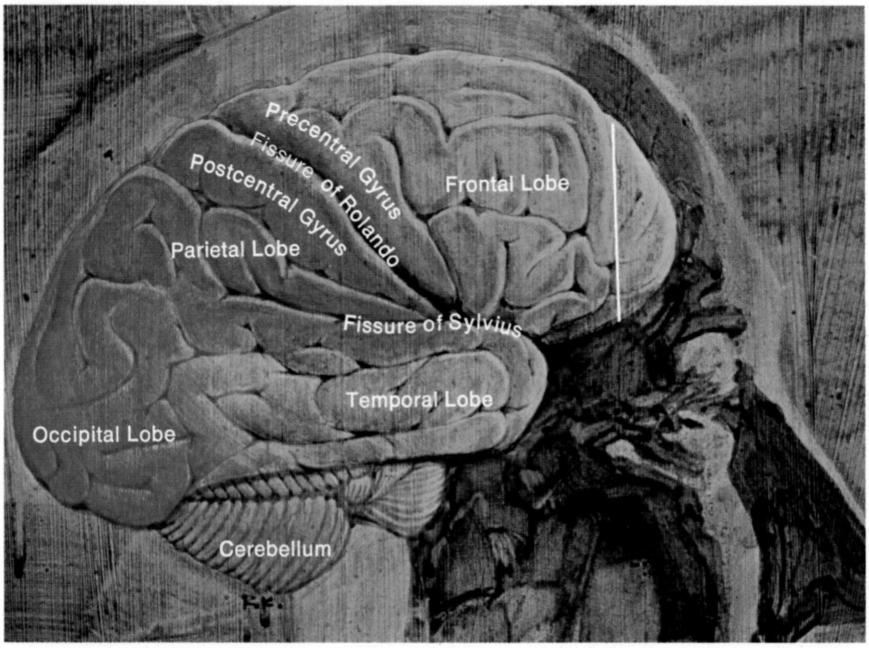

Figure 16.12
The areas of the cerebral cortex. The grooves occurring between folds on the cortex are called fissures (for larger grooves) or sulci (for smaller grooves), and the folds themselves are called gyri. The fissure of Rolando separates the frontal lobe from the parietal lobe; the fissure of Sylvius distinguishes the temporal lobe below from the frontal and parietal lobes above. Demarcations between the occipital lobe and its neighboring lobes are much less distinct.

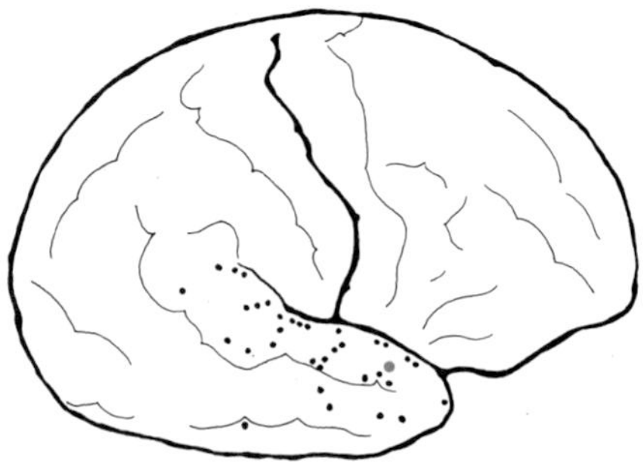

Figure 16.13
Stimulation at the point on the temporal lobe indicated by the colored dot caused a patient to say, "Dream is starting—there are a lot of people in the living room—one of them is my mother." (After Penfield & Roberts, 1946.)

is largely a mammalian characteristic. Fish and amphibia have only the most primitive cortical tissue; the reptiles represent a transitional group. Although simple learning can take place in animals with no cortical tissue, extensive studies in comparative learning ability, such as those reported by M. R. Denny and S. C. Ratner, show that cortical development and intellectual capacity tend to correlate.

The Geography of the Cortex The basic geographical divisions of the human cortex are the four *lobes* of each hemisphere, shown in Figure 16.11. The *occipital lobe,* located at the back of the brain, is particularly concerned with the reception and analysis of visual information. Injury to this portion of the cortex can produce blindness in part of the visual field.

The temporal *lobes* are located on the side of each hemisphere; their boundary is the lateral fissure of Sylvius. The auditory reception areas are located in the temporal lobes, as are certain areas for the processing of visual information. In a series of studies with epileptic patients undergoing surgery, the Canadian neurologist W. Penfield elicited some dramatic responses by applying electrical stimulation to certain points on the temporal lobe (see Figure 16.13). Stimulation at some points caused complex auditory or visual illusions; stimulation at other points seemed to reactivate sensations with such vividness that the patient felt as if he was reliving the experience rather than merely remembering it. One woman heard a familiar song so clearly that she thought a record was being played in the operating room. Penfield called the part of the cortex from which these responses were elicited the *interpretative cortex.*

In the *frontal lobe* at the front of each hemisphere, the area next to the fissure of Rolando (see Figure 16.12) is primarily concerned with the regulation of fine voluntary movements. Another part of the frontal lobe has to do with the use of language. In 1861, P. Broca, a French physician, discovered that damage in this part of the dominant hemisphere (the left, in most people) affected the ability to use speech. Broca's discovery was the first indication that different parts of the brain might control different types of behavior—that is, that the brain might show *localization of function.* Since Broca's time, as our discussion has shown, many parts of the brain have been found to be associated with particular functions.

The prefrontal area of the frontal lobe (to the right of the black line in Figure 16.12), although not associated with particular sensory or motor activities, has at times been considered the repository of intellectual ability or emotional control. The belief that it controlled intellectual ability undoubtedly sprang from the fact that this region is much larger in animals near the top of the evolutionary scale than in lower species. Most modern researchers would not accept the view that the frontal lobe regulates intellectual performance; its involvement is more subtle than that. Some people do as well on intelligence tests after even massive removal of frontal lobe tissue as they did before. The defects in behavior resulting from frontal lobe lesions, it now appears, involve the ability to order stimuli and sort out information rather than general intellectual ability.

The emotional-control view of frontal lobe function helped lead to the development of the surgical procedure known as a prefrontal lobotomy, used on patients with serious mental problems. The procedure involves severing the nerves that connect the prefrontal area with the rest of the brain. Although E. Moniz, a Portuguese neurosurgeon, was actually awarded a Nobel Prize for developing the technique, it never fulfilled its early promise; in fact, it became a badly abused medical practice. Its misuse and tragic results have been dramatized in K. Kesey's novel, *One Flew Over the Cuckoo's Nest.* Today, it has been virtually abandoned as a treatment for insanity.

The fourth pair of lobes is the *parietal lobes,* which contain the primary receiving areas for the skin senses and our sense of bodily position. Damage to the somesthethic cortex produces deficits in the sense of touch. A person with extensive parietal lobe damage extending beyond the primary sensory area also has unusual difficulty with spatial organization of the environment and has a distorted perception of his own body image.

Somesthetic sensations from the various regions of the body are represented in an orderly fashion in the postcentral gyrus, as shown on the left side of Figure 16.14. The right side of Figure 16.14 shows a similar arrangement of body regions in the precentral gyrus, which controls fine muscular movements. There are several supplementary areas for both skin reception and motor activity, but these two can be used to illustrate two important facts. First, both the motor cortex and the somesthetic cortex show *contralateral control.* That is, areas in the right hemisphere are concerned with activities and reception on the left side of the body, whereas areas in the left hemisphere control and represent the right side of the body.

Another parallel between motor and sensory representation, illustrated by the drawings of body regions in Figure 16.14, is that the amount of cortex taken up with the motor activities and sensory impressions from different parts of the body is associated with the degree of precise motor control or the sensitivity of the part of the body concerned, not by its size or the mass of its muscle groups. The fingers have much larger representation than the trunk on the motor cortex, for example, and the lips are disproportionately represented on the somesthetic cortex.

Hemispheric Dominance and Connection The two hemispheres are apparently mirror images of each other, but there must be chemical or structural differences between them in human beings. These differences are necessary to account for handedness and for the localization in one hemisphere of certain functions relating to speech, perception, and intelligence-test performance. Right-handed people have their primary speech center in the left hemisphere, and damage to the left temporal

Figure 16.14

The fissure of Rolando is sometimes also called the central fissure. Somesthetic information from all parts of the body is received by the postcentral gyrus, the one just behind the central fissure. The precentral gyrus, just in front of the central fissure, is the primary motor area of the cortex. To the left, the anatomical drawings show how body sensation is proportionately represented in the brain. To the right, the representation devoted to the control of movement is illustrated. (After Penfield and Rasmussen, 1950.)

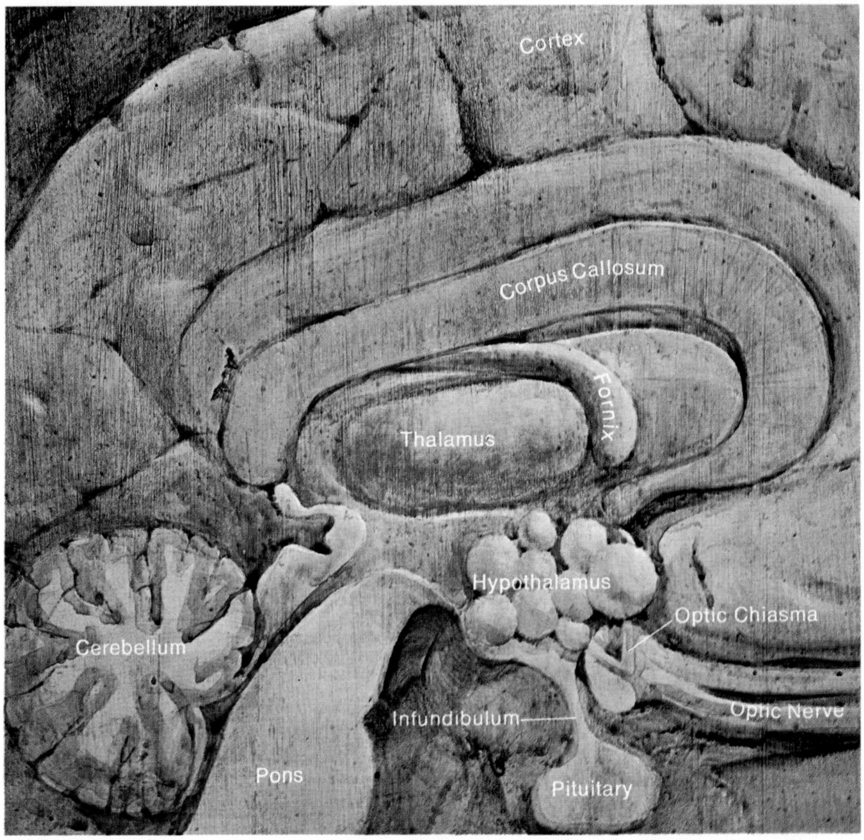

Figure 16.15
The structures shown here are important in coordinating the actions of the brain. The intimate connections that exist between the thalamus and the hypothalamus may be crucial for the regulation of the complex psychological processes of motivation, emotion, and intelligence.

lobe impairs intelligence-test performance severely but leaves perceptual-test performance relatively intact. Damage to the right temporal lobe disrupts perceptual performance more than intellectual performance.

Although there are many routes of communication between the two hemispheres, the primary band of connecting fibers is the *corpus callosum.* Until recently, the functions of the corpus callosum were virtually unknown, but there are some clear indications that this massive group of fibers helps synchronize the activity of the two hemispheres. R. E. Myers has shown that cats trained to make a visual discrimination on the basis of stimuli that are confined to one hemisphere immediately transfer their discriminatory ability to the opposite hemisphere unless the callosum has been severed. If the callosum is cut prior to learning, the second hemisphere may need total retraining on the discrimination task.

Figure 16.16 *(opposite)*
The autonomic nervous system regulates the workings of most of the important organs of the body. Structurally, it consists of a chain of ganglia (clumps of nerve cell bodies) situated just outside the spinal cord. Most of the organs of the body are innervated by both the major divisions of the autonomic nervous system: the sympathetic system (shown in white) and the parasympathetic system (shown in black). Here most of the internal organs of the body and the names of the nerves and ganglia that serve them are shown. Major ganglia are shown diagrammatically within circles.

The Thalamus The *thalamus* is the "great relay station" of the brain. It is composed of a set of nuclei that lie beneath the corpus callosum, as shown in Figure 16.15. A nucleus is a closely packed cluster of nerve cells, which presumably have common functions and connections. In the thalamus the nuclei connect various portions of the brain. Some of the thalamic nuclei relay sensory information from the peripheral parts of the sensory system to particular regions of the cortex. Others are involved with connections between different cortical areas or between cortical and subcortical parts of the brain.

The Hypothalamus and the Autonomic Nervous System The *hypothalamus*, located near the base of the brain, is also composed of nuclei. This structure, although relatively small in the human brain, has enormous importance for the regulation of vertebrate behavior. It helps control the internal environment of the body (blood pressure, heart rate, temperature, and so on), regulate the activity of

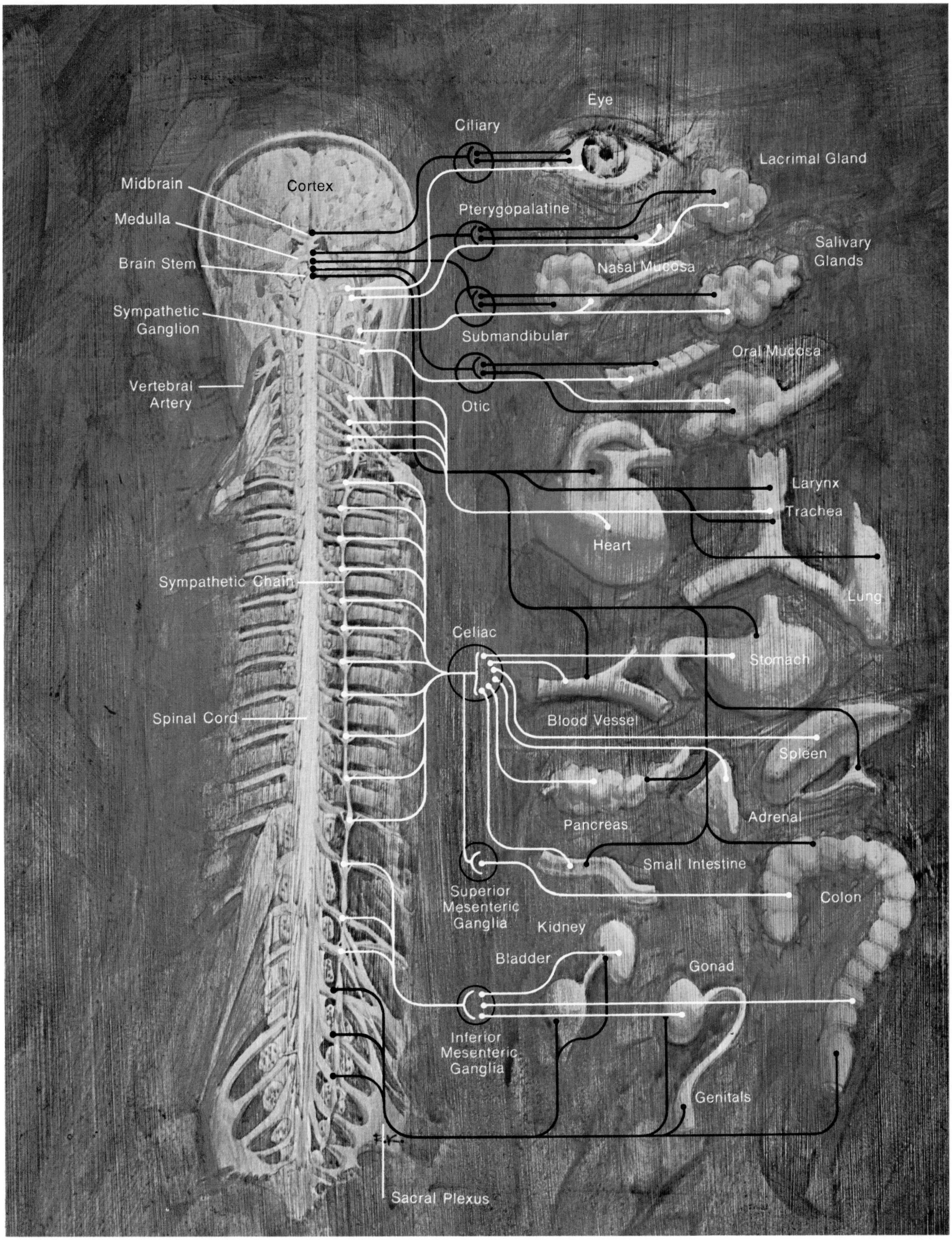
Eye
Ciliary
Lacrimal Gland
Midbrain
Cortex
Medulla
Pterygopalatine
Salivary Glands
Brain Stem
Nasal Mucosa
Sympathetic Ganglion
Submandibular
Oral Mucosa
Vertebral Artery
Otic
Larynx
Trachea
Heart
Sympathetic Chain
Lung
Celiac
Stomach
Spinal Cord
Blood Vessel
Spleen
Pancreas
Adrenal
Small Intestine
Superior Mesenteric Ganglia
Colon
Kidney
Bladder
Gonad
Inferior Mesenteric Ganglia
Genitals
Sacral Plexus

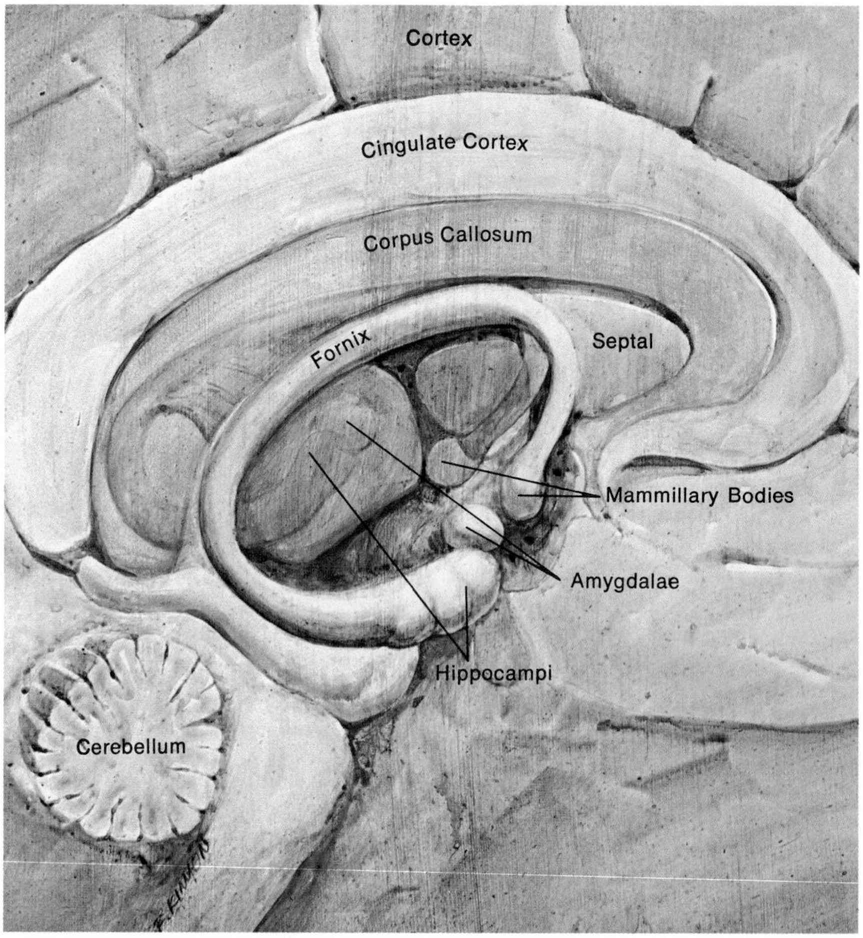

Figure 16.17
The limbic system, located deep in the forebrain, is composed of the amygdala, the cingulate cortex, the septal area, the hippocampi, and their complex interconnections. In conjunction with the hypothalamus, this system can exert profound control over emotional behavior, and some limbic structures (the hippocampal complex) have been associated with complex memory function.

the important pituitary gland, and control many basic drives, such as hunger, thirst, and sex. Its role in connection with drives is discussed in Chapter 18.

The hypothalamus controls the so-called involuntary functions of the body through the *autonomic nervous system.* The autonomic nervous system consists of two divisions: the *sympathetic,* shown in white in Figure 16.16, and the *parasympathetic,* shown in black. (Figure 16.16 appears on page 313.)

In general, the sympathetic and parasympathetic systems can be viewed as working antagonistically. The sympathetic system tends to promote energy expenditure. For example, it mobilizes the body to meet emergency conditions by increasing blood-sugar levels and heart rate, dilating the blood vessels through which oxygen and nutrients reach the skeletal musculature, and inhibiting digestive processes. The parasympathetic system is primarily an energy-conserving system. For example, it slows heart rate and enhances digestive activity after eating. The autonomic nervous system has a lot to do with the physiology and behavioral effects of emotional arousal and stress, as will become clear in Chapter 17.

The Limbic System Two other parts of the forebrain that are important in emotional arousal are the *limbic system* and the *reticular activating system.* The limbic system, shown in Figure 16.17, is a group of interconnected structures that includes the amygdala, cingulate cortex, hippocampus, and septal area. Damage in those areas has profound effects on emotional reactivity, even to the point of turning usually excitable creatures like monkeys and mountain lions into docile pets or converting tame laboratory rats into ferocious combatants (at least for a limited time). These highly complicated structures also have other functions; in man, for example, the hippocampus has been implicated in memory storage processes. Again, we will

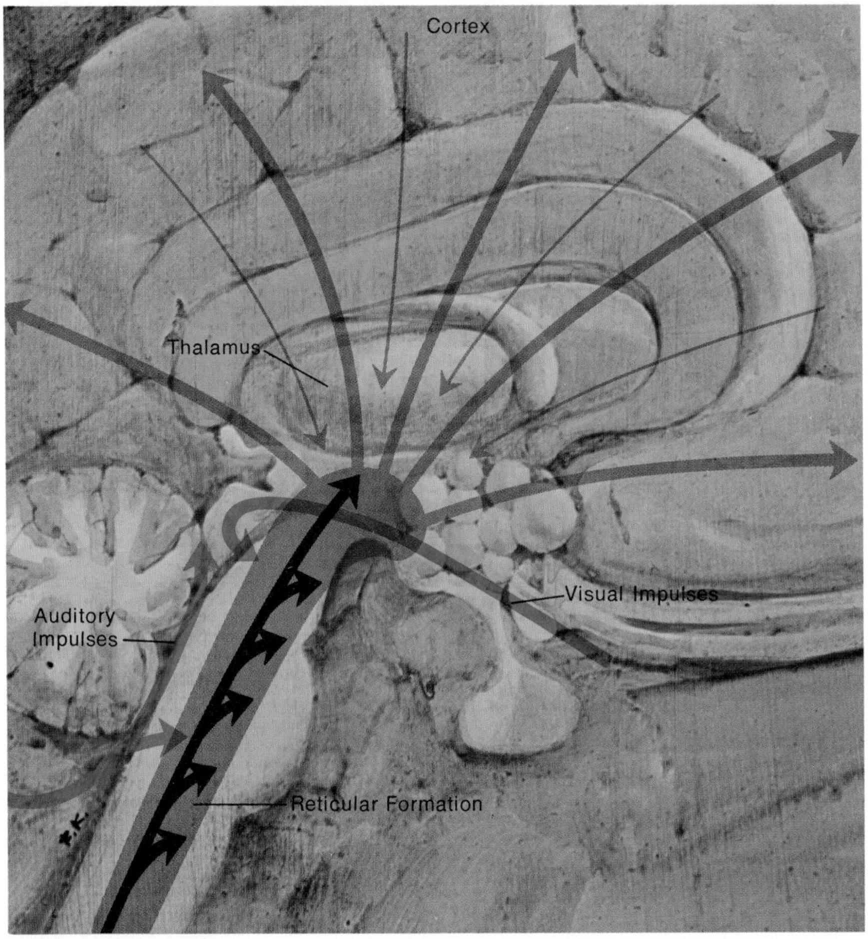

Figure 16.18
The reticular activating system extends diffusely up the center of the brainstem and projects into the thalamus. This complex system functions in the control of consciousness and attention. Animals with lesions in some areas of the reticular system sleep much more than is normal.

return to a fuller discussion of the significance of the limbic system for emotional behavior in Chapter 18.

The Reticular Activating System Below the forebrain, the central core of the midbrain, and the upper hindbrain is an intricate latticework of nerve cells known as the *reticular activating system.* This primitive system, whose activities are diagrammed in Figure 16.18, exists in the brains of all vertebrate species. It helps direct an organism's attention to incoming sensory stimuli and regulate its level of alertness. Damage to the portion of the reticular system in the midbrain produces an animal that sleeps much of the time and shows a cortical brain wave pattern characteristic of stages of deep sleep.

THE GLANDULAR SYSTEM

There are two basic classes of glands: those that release their secretions through a duct onto the surface of the body, called *exocrine* glands, and those that release their secretions directly into the blood or lymphatic system, called the *endocrine* glands. Both kinds have assumed a prominent role in psychological work. Two particularly important exocrine glands are the salivary glands, without which Pavlov's dogs would never have become famous, and the sweat glands, which become more active during emotional arousal. Activity in the sweat glands is an important part of the measure of skin resistance called the *galvanic skin response,* which is widely used by psychologists who study emotion, and also in most so-called lie-detecting systems.

The major glands of the endocrine system are depicted in Figure 16.19. The *pituitary gland* is sometimes referred to as the master gland of the endocrine system. It is composed of two distinct divisions, which have different embryological origins.

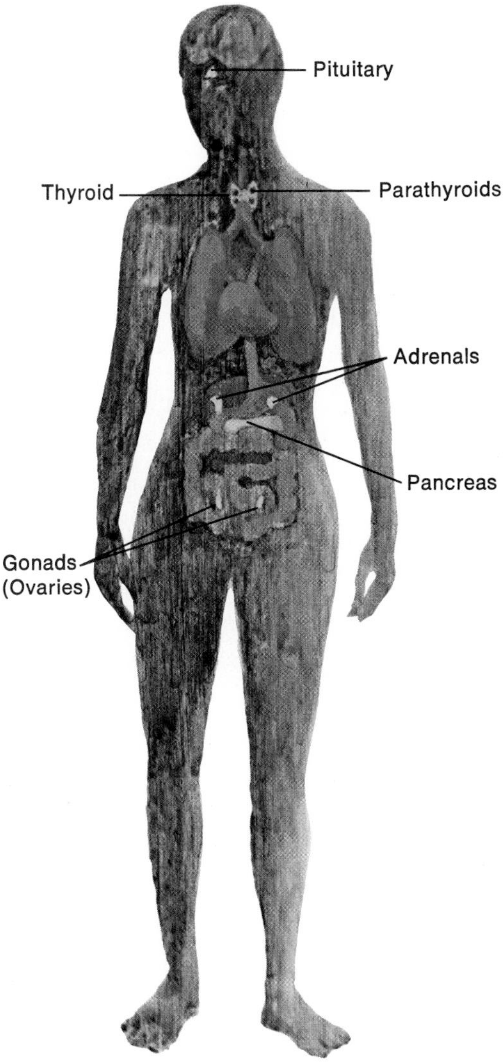

Figure 16.19
The two divisions of the pituitary gland, the master gland of the endocrine system, are located below the hypothalamus at the base of the brain. Secretions from the anterior pituitary stimulate the production and release of hormones by other endocrine glands, including the thyroid, the adrenal cortex, the gonads, the placenta, and the parathyroids. The posterior pituitary secretes ADH, which functions in the body's water regulation, and oxytocin, which induces uterine contraction.

The posterior pituitary develops from neural tissue, whereas the anterior pituitary originates in tissues from the roof of the mouth. The posterior pituitary releases two hormones: a hormone called ADH that raises blood pressure and enhances the retention of body water, and oxytocin, which induces uterine contractions in the female mammal at the end of pregnancy. Oxytocin is used clinically to induce labor when this procedure appears medically desirable. The anterior pituitary is especially important: it secretes a hormone that affects growth and a variety of other hormones, most of which act upon other endocrine and exocrine glands, including the thyroid, the ovaries, and the mammary glands.

Each of the glands to which the pituitary sends activating secretions in turn produces hormones. For example, under the influence of a hormone called TSH that is produced by the pituitary, the thyroid glands secrete thyroxin, which affects the rate of certain metabolic processes. A rise in the level of thyroxin in turn causes a reduction in the secretion of TSH, thus reducing the level of circulating thyroxin. This self-regulating circuit, when it works properly, ensures a level of circulating thyroxin that is optimal for normal bodily function. People with too high levels of thyroxin (hyperthyroid) may be tense and have trouble sleeping; people with insufficient thyroxin (hypothyroid) may be listless and apathetic.

The *adrenal glands*, located next to the kidneys, consist of two sections: an internal core known as the *adrenal medulla* and an external covering known as the *adrenal cortex*. The adrenal medulla secretes the hormones epinephrine (adrenaline) and norepinephrine, which have effects similar to stimulation of the sympathetic nervous system during strong emotion. This similarity is not surprising in view of the fact that epinephrine and norepinephrine are transmitter substances in the sympathetic nervous system. Moreover, the adrenal medulla is stimulated to release epinephrine and norepinephrine by direct neural connections from the sympathetic system. Thus, we have a positive-feedback circuit in which sympathetic activity facilitates adrenal medullary activity, which in turn facilitates further sympathetic activity.

The adrenal cortex is stimulated by the hormone ACTH rather than by direct neural input. Under the influence of ACTH, the adrenal cortex releases a variety of

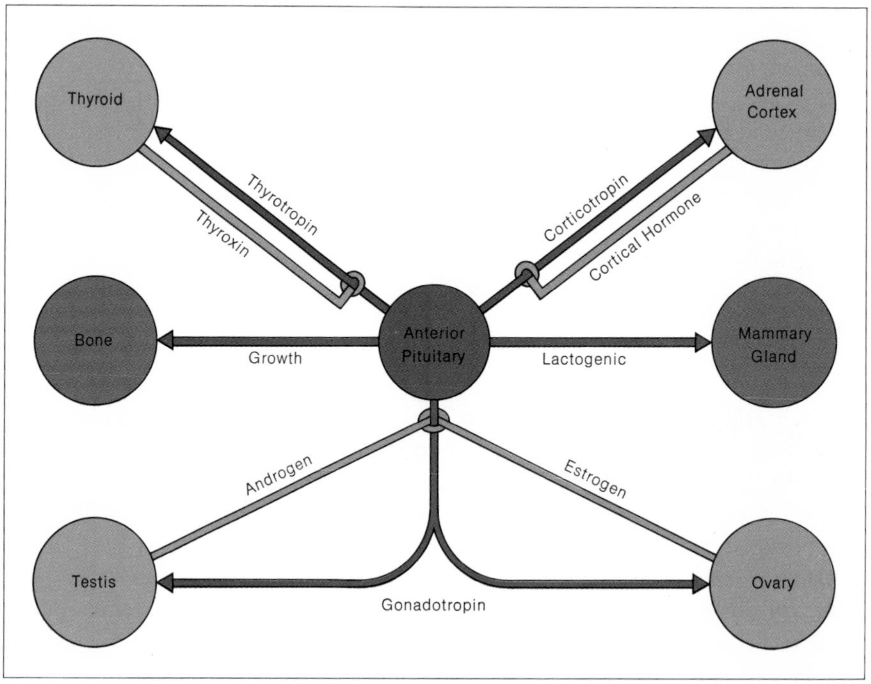

Figure 16.20
The relationship between the anterior pituitary secretions and the glands that they regulate can be thought of as a self-regulation circuit. For example, in response to secretion by the anterior pituitary of TSH (thyroid stimulating hormone), the thyroid glands secrete thyroxin. The consequent rise in the level of thyroxin in the blood is detected, perhaps by cellular receptors in the hypothalamus, and then the pituitary secretion of TSH decreases; consequently the secretion of thyroxin by the thyroid gland decreases.

steroid hormones that regulate water balance and energy expenditure. One of the most important roles of the adrenal cortex is to help animals and human beings withstand stress.

RESEARCH ON BRAIN-BEHAVIOR RELATIONSHIPS

How can one tell whether and how a particular part of the brain is associated with a particular behavior? These are intriguing and difficult questions—difficult partly because although many behaviors can be readily observed and measured, their physiological correlates are often diffuse or vague. Nonetheless, many psychologists believe that in order to truly understand behavior, one must be able to explain it physiologically as well as psychologically.

Research on the relation between the brain and behavior can start at either point. That is, an experimenter can do something to the brain and see what happens to behavior, or he can observe behavior and try to identify its physiological correlates. The most common techniques based on the first approach are chemical stimulation, electrical stimulation, and surgical ablation. The second approach will be discussed later in the chapter.

Chemical and Electrical Stimulation

In an interesting *chemical technique* known as cannulation, a small tube is inserted in the brain so that its end touches the area that the experimenter is interested in. For example, a cannula might be implanted in the hypothalamus. Then a measured amount of some chemical is passed through the tube, and the behavioral effects are observed as the chemical diffuses from the tip of the cannula. Although chemical research is difficult and often has confusing results, cannulation experiments by S. P. Grossman, in which chemical excitants or inhibitors were applied to different areas of the hypothalamus, have confirmed, for example, the existence of two anatomically intertwined but functionally distinct systems, one associated with the control of hunger and one with the control of thirst.

Electrical stimulation is done by implanting electrodes in particular parts of the brain and passing an electric current through them, which excites nearby nerve cells. An electrode can be a very simple device, no more elaborate than a piece of wire.

One finding gained from this sort of research, which will be discussed more fully in Chapter 18, is that electrical stimulation of certain points in the hypothalamus causes an animal to eat even if it is satiated.

A more dramatic demonstration of the effects of electrical stimulation has been given by J. Delgado of Yale University. In the mid-1960s, he made the front page of *The New York Times* with pictures of a charging bull suddenly stopped in its tracks when Delgado began transmitting stimulation through electrodes previously implanted in the bull's brain. Although Delgado's work has been called gadgeteering by some, it is nonetheless impressive and influential. For example, it has encouraged public interest in the possibility that electrical stimulation of the brain may be useful in dealing with human behavioral disorders. Indeed, a number of people now have electrodes implanted in their brains, for purposes ranging from the relief of intolerable pain to the control of violent emotional outbursts.

The usual electrode is about .01 inch in diameter. It may stimulate hundreds or thousands of cells and is called a *gross electrode* for that reason. A much smaller electrode, called a microelectrode, is used in an elegant type of research whose aim is to stimulate a single cell. Unfortunately, experiments with microelectrodes cannot be expected to tell us much about the physiological underpinnings of behavior, because the stimulation of a single cell rarely produces an observable change in behavior. The brain is composed of over ten billion nerve cells, after all, and it would be surprising if their functions did not overlap. And, as was noted earlier in connection with so-called associative cells, Teuber points out that although many nerve

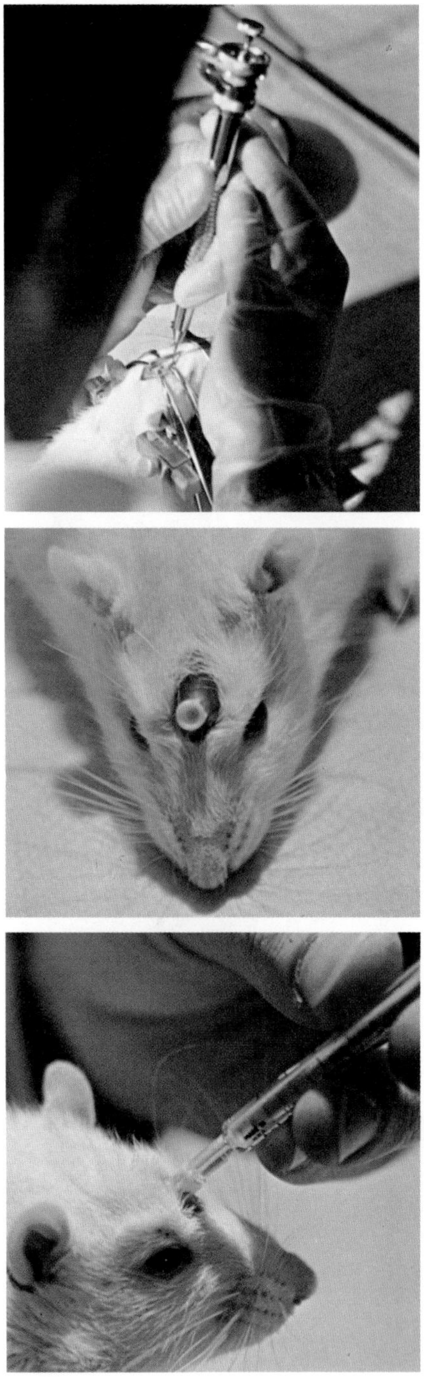

Figure 16.21
(Top) a cannula is a small tube used to guide chemicals to specific areas deep in the brain. (Middle) the cannula is permanently implanted in the rat's brain so that the tip of the tube rests on the structure being studied. (Bottom) small amounts of a chemical can be passed slowly through the cannula, and the effects of the chemical stimulation on the particular structure noted.

cells in the brain have specific behavioral tasks, brain cells apparently are not unique or irreplaceable. If they were, the daily destruction of hundreds of cells that occurs normally throughout adult life would cause severe and irreparable damage to human functioning. Fortunately, brain cells have an impressive ability to take over each other's activities when necessary. Teuber attributes continuity of function to the existence of "uncommitted" nerve cells, which take on the tasks of cells destroyed or damaged.

Surgical Ablation

Surgical ablation is the surgical removal or destruction of a part of the brain. Prefrontal lobotomy is an ablation technique, as is Sperry's disconnection of the cerebral hemispheres of the epileptic woman, with whose story Chapter 15 began. As these examples suggest, ablation techniques are used with human beings primarily to alleviate a severe existing abnormality; it is therefore difficult to be sure that the effects would be the same in normal people. Ablation techniques are often used with healthy lower animals, but here, too, it is difficult to know how much of the information gained holds true for normal human behavior.

Another problem with ablation is that it is not always possible, from the point of view of technical expertise, to destroy one neural area precisely. Sometimes nerve tracts passing through the ablated area are destroyed along with the cells, disrupting communication in the brain. To complicate the picture, it appears that glial cells multiply at a rapid rate in damaged areas, and the effects of this multiplication are unknown. Finally, ablation effects are very time-dependent. The behavioral effects are sometimes entirely different if one destroys a part of the brain gradually instead of all at once; in addition, the damage to some functions tends to become less severe with time (a phenomenon called *restoration of function*).

Physiological Correlates of Behavior

Some of the most interesting recent research on the relation between brain and behavior has involved the second approach to research in this area: identification of the physiological correlates of well-defined behaviors. Particularly fascinating are those studies dealing with the physiological correlates of learning.

Correlates of Habituation of a Simple Reflex Because of the overwhelming complexity of the vertebrate brain, much research on the physiology of behavior has been done with lower organisms. Recently, E. R. Kandel and his associates studied a reflex of the aplysia, a snaillike animal that lives in the sea, in an effort to elucidate the process by which a single cell "learns." The physiological changes associated with learning are of great interest to contemporary scientists, and there is considerable evidence that learning involves a change in a nerve cell's effectiveness in causing its neighbors to fire. This hypothesis is easier to pursue with lower organisms because their nerve cells are few and somewhat larger than those of vertebrates.

Kandel attempted to relate changes in the activity of nerve cells to changes in a simple behavior pattern: the aplysia's withdrawal of its gill if the nearby skin is touched. This reflex, which is illustrated in Figure 16.22, undergoes *habituation* (see Chapter 2) if the stimulus is presented repeatedly. That is, withdrawal of the gill in response to touching decreases as the touching continues, and may even disappear completely. If learning is broadly defined to include all changes in an organism's response to its environment, then habituation can be considered as a simple model of the learning process.

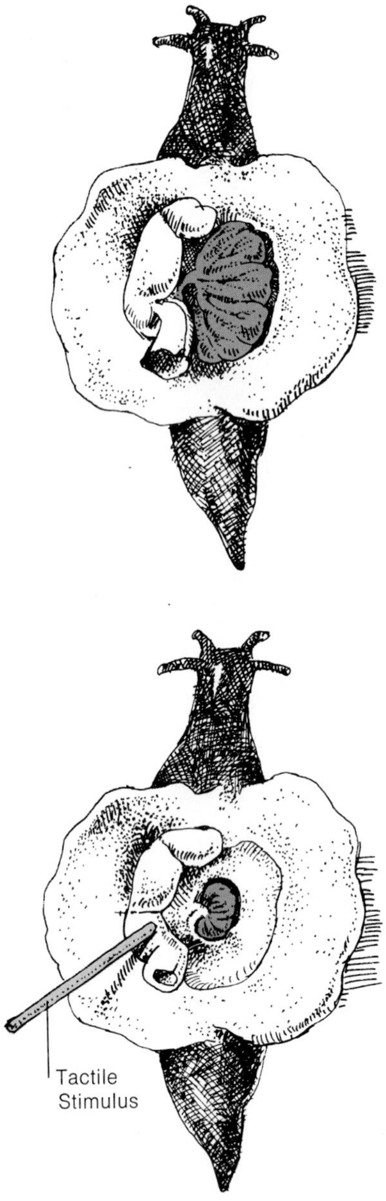

Figure 16.22
Demonstration of the gill-withdrawal reflex studied by Kandel and his associates. Normal gill position is shown above (colored area). A gentle touching on the mantle shelf causes it to withdraw the gill (below). After repeated presentations of the stimulus, the animal becomes habituated to it, and responds less frequently.
(From "Nerve Cells and Behavior," Erik Kandel. ©1970 by Scientific American, Inc. All rights reserved.)

R. Hernandez-Peón and E. N. Sokolov, among others, have shown that one characteristic of habituation is that it is specific to the stimulus presented. An animal that stops reacting to a loud noise with a violent jerk will jump in response to a bright flash of light. In fact, if a novel stimulus is presented during a series of habituation trials, a phenomenon called *dishabituation* occurs. The animal responds to the next presentation of the normal (formerly habituated) stimulus as strongly as it did before habituation began. In experiments such as those by K. E. Hagbarth and E. Kugelberg, dishabituation is used as a control to distinguish habituation from the effects of sensory adaptation or muscular fatigue.

Kandel and his associates have studied the habituation of the gill-withdrawal reflex in aplysia, which exhibits the key characteristics of habituation (including dishabituation), and have attempted to map the neurons involved in its control. All of them appear to be located in a cell cluster known as the abdominal ganglion. Techniques developed by Kandel and his associates permit them to stimulate and record the activity of selected cells in this ganglion without significantly altering the animal's execution of the reflex.

They mapped the cell connections in the abdominal ganglion, which enabled them to isolate a system consisting of a receptor neuron that led directly to a motor neuron that led, in turn, directly to a muscle used in the reflex. During habituation they observed a decrease in the amplitude of the postsynaptic potential produced by the sensory neuron. The decrease could not be accounted for by simple sensory adaptation; in addition, stimulation of the motor neuron demonstrated that its membrane properties had not changed significantly during the period of habituation. These results suggest that the cause of habituation, at the cellular level, was a decrease in the efficiency of the presynaptic ending. More generally, they indicate that the physiological mechanisms of at least some kinds of learning can be profitably explored by studying individual cells.

Biofeedback Biofeedback is a new technique, related to brain research, that has become something of a popular fad. It is based on the idea that people can gain some control over physiological processes that are usually considered involuntary if they are provided with feedback (see Chapter 15). Thus some people can learn to raise and lower the temperature of their palms several degrees if a thermometer is taped to their palm so that they can see when the temperature is changing. This research is an interesting variation of the usual research on the physiological correlates of behavior. Instead of merely observing the physiological correlates that appear when a specific behavior occurs, feedback from physiological changes is used to produce control of these changes.

Most biofeedback experiments done with human beings, such as the one by B. T. Engel and S. P. Hansen, have been directed toward the modification of heart rate, blood pressure, and EEG recording of brain waves. It has been demonstrated that electrical monitoring enables people to become more aware of their internal functions and, therefore, sometimes to influence them through conscious effort. However, not everyone can modify these functions, and the amount of modification is sometimes very small.

Analogous experiments on autonomic conditioning in lower organisms have had fairly successful results. For example, L. V. DiCara and J. M. Weiss have trained rats to slow their heart rates; these rats were better able to avoid shock than control rats that had not been trained. DiCara and Weiss trained other rats to speed up their heart rates, and these rats seemed very fearful and had trouble avoiding shock.

Despite the fact that autonomic conditioning has been neither thoroughly researched nor totally successful, it has intriguing possibilities. For example, some people can increase the alpha waves produced by their brains considerably by using a machine that tells when those waves are occurring. Alpha waves occur naturally during meditation and certain other relaxed states. Is it possible that a person can learn to meditate by increasing his alpha activity through biofeedback? Can he learn to control his states of consciousness?

Unfortunately, such possibilities are so intriguing that they have been commercially exploited. Some biofeedback devices do not work—for example, some alpha machines make the "bleep" that supposedly indicates alpha in response to eye blinks and other random movements. In addition, some claims—such as that producing more alpha will make you more relaxed, creative, and happy—are dubious. *Caveat emptor*—let the buyer beware.

Correlates of a Stereotyped Response There seems to be a trend among physiological psychologists toward analyzing the performance of individual nerve cells in simple brains rather than studying the gross responses of massive cell clusters in vertebrate brains. In addition, physiological psychologists are interested in finding the physiological correlates not only of learning but also of stereotyped, species-specific responses (see Chapter 2). A. O. D. Willows and his associates investigated a stereotyped response in an animal whose brain cells were large enough to be individually identified, in the hope that the stereotyped response might be elicited by stimulating specific brain cells. They chose a near-relative of the aplysia, a sluglike species called *Tritonia diomedia* (slugs are essentially snails without shells). The brain cells of these animals are so large that some can actually be seen with the naked eye, and different kinds of cells are differently colored.

The tritonia exhibits a stereotyped escape response to its predator, the starfish, as illustrated in Figure 16.23. The response is so stereotyped that any observer can easily distinguish the components described in the caption. The whole sequence takes about thirty seconds.

Willows found that electrical stimulation of certain cells in the tritonia sometimes elicited the complete escape response. That is, the behavior continued for thirty seconds even though the stimulus lasted for considerably less than half a second. How, he asked, did such brief stimulation produce a thirty-second behavior? His experiments revealed that the physiologically elicited firing of one cell apparently triggered subsequent firings in connected cells, producing an ongoing pattern of neural discharge throughout the response sequence. Electrical stimulation of a single cell, however, did not always produce the escape response. To be sure of producing it, it was necessary to stimulate a number of cells.

Willows also found that the responses of brain cells in different tritonia were

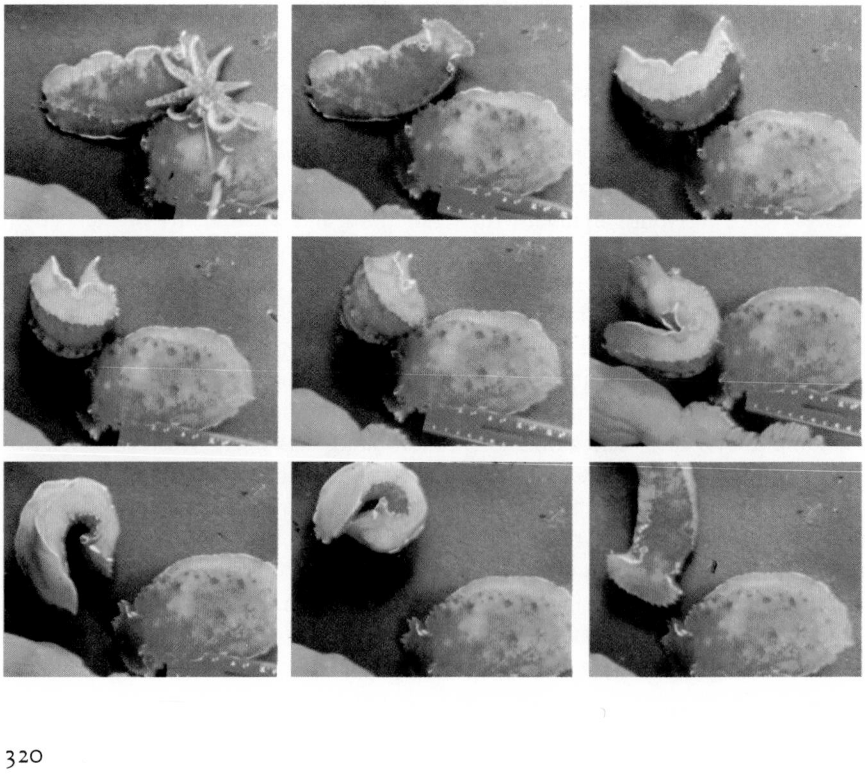

Figure 16.23
These photographs show the steps in the stereotyped escape response of *Tritonia diomedia,* which was investigated by Willows. Stimulated by chemicals exuded by the starfish, the animal first pulls in the extending parts of its body. Next, the head and tail regions expand into paddlelike structures, and it begins a series of vigorous dorsal and ventral flexions. The response chain ends with a number of weaker bends, interspersed with periods of relaxation. Such stereotyped behavior can be highly adaptive, especially for simpler organisms.

remarkably similar. Apparently, the "wiring diagram" of the nervous system of these animals is quite rigidly set by genetic controls and differs little from one animal to another. The extent to which species-specific reactions in human beings are controlled by similarly prescribed patterns of neural connections is not known.

GENETICS AND BEHAVIOR

Every person begins his life as a single cell—a zygote—that is formed when the male germ cell (spermatozoon) penetrates the female germ cell (ovum). These germ cells, called gametes, are different from all other cells in the human body because they contain only twenty-three separate and distinctively different chromosomes. All other cells in the body contain forty-six chromosomes, in twenty-three pairs. When the two germ cells combine to form a new individual, the twenty-three chromosomes from the mother pair with the twenty-three from the father, and much of the new individual's physical and psychological potential is determined.

The makeup of the chromosomes is of utmost importance to the individual; their implications for normal and abnormal development will be discussed in this chapter. Each cell in the thousands of millions that make up the individual's body will carry a precise copy of the original twenty-three pairs of chromosomes that came together at his beginning.

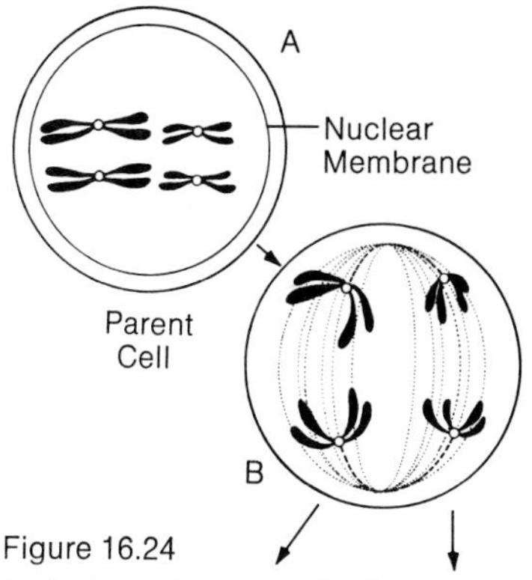

Figure 16.24

Meiosis begins when the homologous chromosomes begin to pair (A). The nuclear membrane dissolves and the members of each pair separate and move toward opposite ends of the cell (B).

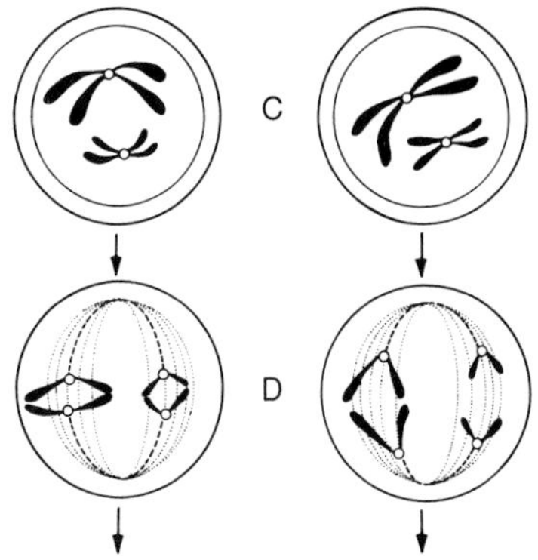

The first cell division has occurred and now in the two daughter cells the sets of chromosomes line up (C) and then split. The halves move toward opposite poles (D).

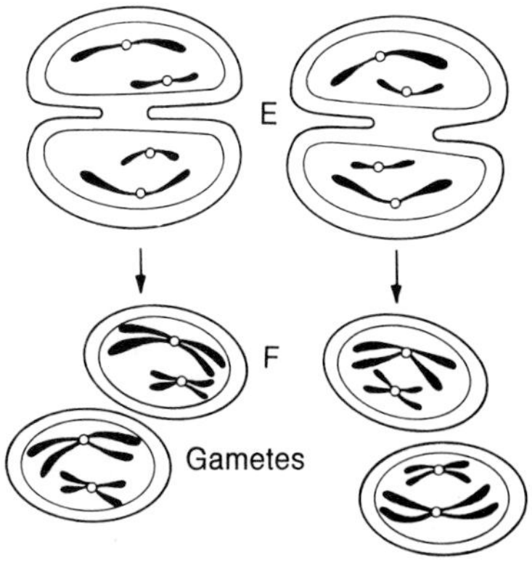

The daughter chromosomes have separated completely (E), and cell walls are forming. The final result is four gametes (F), each with half the chromosomes of the parent cell.

(After Curtis, 1968.)

GENES

Each chromosome is subdivided into *genes*, which are the determiners of hereditary traits, and the genes in turn are largely composed of DNA *(deoxyribonucleic acid)*. In one of the outstanding modern biological breakthroughs, J. D. Watson and F. H. Crick constructed a model of a DNA molecule, which served to substantiate their theory about its ability to replicate itself and its role as chemical code carrier.

The genes are arranged in the same order along each chromosome in the pair; they appear to be strung like beads. It is estimated that each zygote contains 10,000 to 50,000 genes. The great majority of genes are the same for each gamete and so carry instructions for the same chemical process; these are the genes that are common to all mankind and confer on us our common humanity. It is interesting that little is as yet known about how the genes common to all men produce their effects. That is, the mechanism of *development* remains a biochemical mystery although the mechanism of *inheritance* is now almost universally accepted. Scientists can explain why a person is born with blue eyes, but they do not yet know why, given two cells with the same set of twenty-three chromosome pairs, one cell becomes part of the brain tissue and the other part of the kidney.

Crossing Over

An individual's germ cells lie dormant in the ovaries or testes until puberty, at which time the gametes start forming by a process of division called meiosis, shown in Figure 16.24. Before meiosis occurs, the two members of each of the twenty-three pairs of chromosomes in the original germ cell may adhere to each other at various points along their length. The homologous chromosomes may break at these points and exchange corresponding segments. This process is called *crossing over.* Therefore, at the final division in the meiosis process, the gamete's set of twenty-three chromosomes may contain a random assortment of genes from the forty-six original chromosomes. And so, when the gametes combine to form a new individual, half his genes have been drawn at random from his mother and half at random from his father.

Dominant and Recessive Genes

At conception, a gene from the father will be paired with its counterpart from the mother. The genes that pair are called *alleles.* As was stated earlier, most of the gene pairs carry the same instructions. There are genes common to all men, which specify that we will have lungs rather than gills, that our ankle bone is connected with our foot bone, and the like. Some genes carry instructions that are not quite so universal—for example, the genes that determine the eyelid fold that is part of the physiognomy of Oriental populations. Some genes dictate a person's individuality within his population. Still other genes are composed of alleles that carry different instructions within the same cell.

When the two alleles are identical, a person is said to be *homozygous* for that gene. When the alleles carry different instructions, he is said to be *heterozygous*.

One illustration is a well-documented human trait that is known to be defined by a single gene—the ability to taste phenylthiocarbamide (PTC); its two alleles are designated T and t. To homozygotes with the alleles TT, the compound has a bitter taste in solution, whereas to homozygotes with alleles tt, it is tasteless. Because heterozygotes (Tt) also taste the bitterness, it is clear that the activity of the T allele masks that of t.

One more set of definitions is necessary to the discussion that follows. Two individuals with the alleles TT are called *genotypically* alike; TT is their *genotype*.

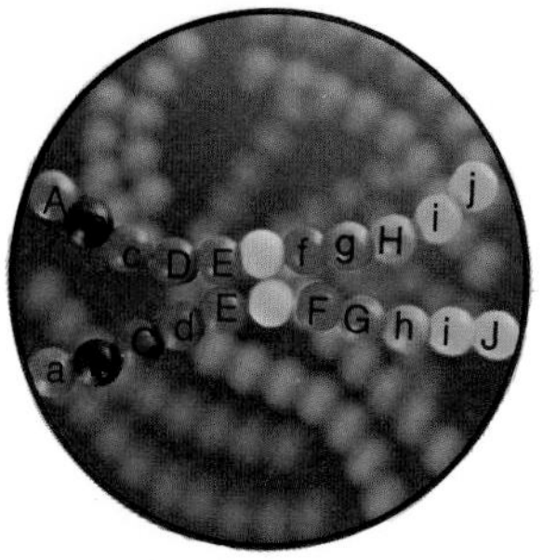

Figure 16.25
In this schematic representation of a homologous pair of chromosomes in the nucleus of a cell, the lettered beads on each string correspond to genes.

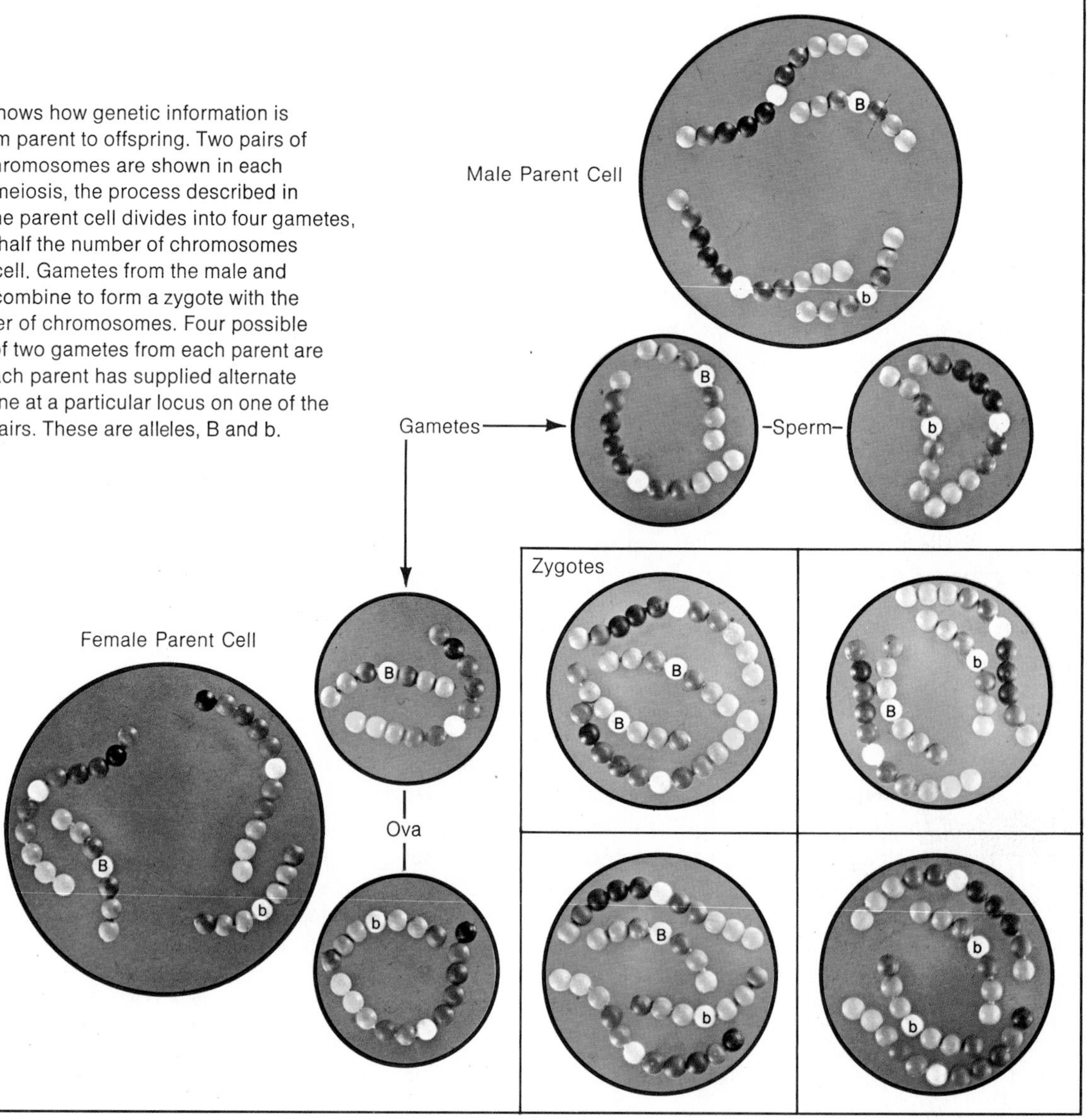

Figure 16.26
This diagram shows how genetic information is transmitted from parent to offspring. Two pairs of homologous chromosomes are shown in each parent cell. In meiosis, the process described in Figure 16.24, the parent cell divides into four gametes, each with only half the number of chromosomes of an ordinary cell. Gametes from the male and female parent combine to form a zygote with the ordinary number of chromosomes. Four possible combinations of two gametes from each parent are shown here. Each parent has supplied alternate forms of the gene at a particular locus on one of the chromosome pairs. These are alleles, B and b.

However, two individuals who taste PTC because one has genotype TT and the other Tt are said to be *phenotypically* alike; their behavior is identical although their genotypes are different.

Masking alleles, like T, are called *dominant* in relation to the alleles whose effects they cover; the masked alleles are called *recessive*. For some genes, neither of the alleles is dominant, so the heterozygote shows a form of the trait approximately between the homozygous forms.

HEREDITARY TRANSMISSION

The two chromosomes of a pair are called *homologues*. As stated earlier, during meiosis the homologues segregate to different gametes. Using the PTC-taster example again, it is clear that an individual who is heterozygous for this gene (Tt) produces one gamete carrying the T allele and the other carrying the t allele. Because each parent produces both types of gametes in equal numbers and because these gametes will combine randomly in the formation of a zygote, a mating between two such heterozygotes (Tt X Tt) is expected to produce offspring of the three different genotypes TT, Tt, and tt in the ratio 1:2:1.

Half the children, then, will be *genotypically* like their parents (carrying the Tt gene); three-fourths will be *phenotypically* like them (they will taste PTC); but this trait in one-fourth of the offspring will differ from both parents.

The expected ratio of genotypes and phenotypes for traits determined by a single gene can be calculated by constructing a 2 x 2 matrix, as shown in Figure 16.27. The alleles of the gene produced by each parent are entered along separate axes of the matrix, and the cells of the matrix represent the genotypes that will be produced.

Observations of the sort discussed in the preceding paragraphs were the basis

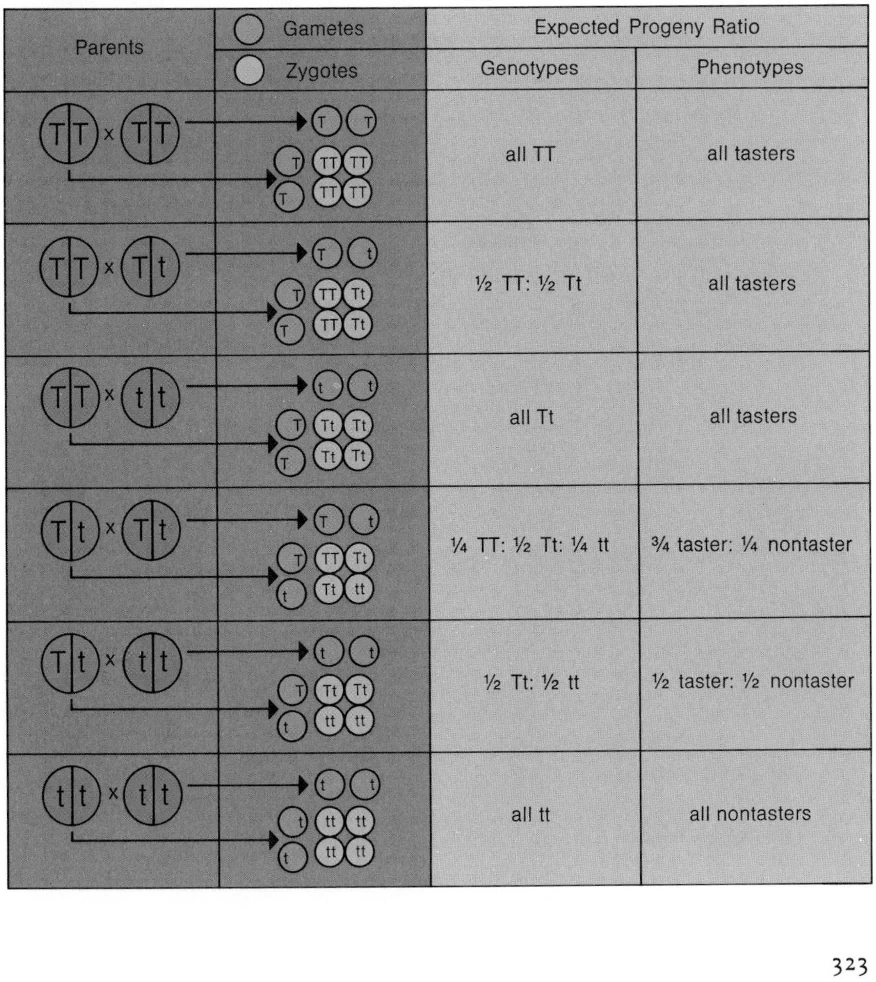

Figure 16.27
The separation and recombination of gametes are shown here for matings involving the gene that determines taste sensitivity to PTC. T designates the dominant, tasting allele; t, the recessive, nontasting allele.

of Gregor Mendel's first law of inheritance: the *law of segregation.* Mendel worked with pea plants and postulated that each phenotypic trait of his plants was governed by a separate pair of "elements," which somehow divided and then recombined when a plant produced offspring. It is now known that these elements are the allelic forms of genes, and that meiotic cell division is the basis of their segregation.

Mendel's second law of inheritance, the *law of independent assortment,* describes the simultaneous inheritance of two or more traits that are determined by single genes. For example, an individual who is heterozygous for each of two genes located on different pairs of chromosomes will produce four types of gametes with respect to the two genes. T and t have been designated the alleles of the taster gene, and A and a are the alleles of the gene that produces *albinism* in man (congenital absence of skin pigmentation); AA and Aa individuals have normal pigmentation, and persons carrying the alleles aa are albinos. The four gametes produced by a double heterozygote (TtAa) will be TA, Ta, tA, and ta, and a mating between two double heterozygotes (represented by a 4 x 4 matrix) will produce offspring of nine different genotypes, as shown in Figure 16.28. The expected distribution of phenotypes is a 9:3:3:1 ratio of pigmented tasters, albino tasters, pigmented nontasters, and albino nontasters. Note that 7/16 of the offspring are expected to be phenotypically different from both parents.

Although geneticists have found that the variation of some traits in humans is governed by single genes (for example, ability to taste PTC, albinism, some blood types), this mode of inheritance is the exception rather than the rule. Many structural traits and most behavioral traits have been found to depend on the combined effects of many genes acting together. Traits of this type are called *polygenic* traits, and the complex of genes involved in determining the trait is known as a polygenic system.

Generally, traits determined by a single gene can be classified into sharply defined qualitative categories (for example, taster versus nontaster), whereas polygenic traits show continuous variation on quantitative dimensions. The genes in a polygenic system may be located on the same or on different chromosomes, and each gene in the system is assumed to behave as a discrete unit and to obey the usual rules of transmission—segregation, independent assortment, and crossing over. However, the contribution of each gene to variation of the trait is small and cumulative rather than all-or-none. The action of a polygenic system is analogous to the simultaneous tossing of a large number of coins, where the alleles of each

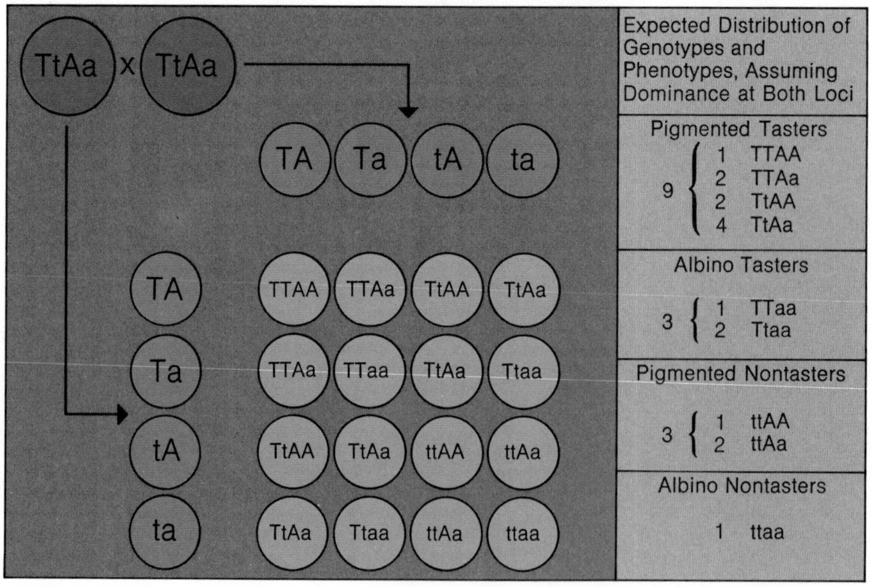

Figure 16.28
The expected outcome of the mating of double heterozygotes for independent single gene traits reveals large differences between the distribution of genotypes and that of phenotypes. The appearance of only four different phenotypes actually represents the occurrence of nine different genotypes.

gene (assuming only two per gene) represent heads or tails and the expression of the polygenic trait is determined by the number of heads. The result is continuous variation among members of a population. Examples of polygenic traits are height and intelligence; both the structural trait and the behavioral one display wide ranges in the population. To complete this analogy, environmental conditions could be represented as the independent tossing of a second set of coins, where heads represent facilitative and tails inhibitory environmental effects. The total number of heads, then, in both tosses determines trait expression. Clearly, the range of variation of a polygenic trait will be increased by environmental differences.

Heredity and Environment

When applied to the individual organism, the question of whether a behavioral trait is traceable to heredity or to environment is meaningless because without heredity there is no organism, and without an appropriate environment the organism does not survive to display the trait. With respect to a *population* of individuals, however, it is meaningful to ask how much of the observed variation of a trait is the result of genotypic differences among individuals and how much the result of environmental differences. In the language of genetics, this is equivalent to estimating the *heritability* of a trait—the percentage of trait variance that is attributable to genotypic differences among individuals. Even at the level of populations, absolute answers about heritability cannot be expected because heritability is a measure of the *relationship* between a trait and the population in which it is studied, not a constant property of the trait per se. A trait may have markedly different heritabilities in different populations as a function of the degree of genetic and environmental variability that exists in those populations.

Thus, a trait *must* have zero heritability in a population of genetically identical individuals (because none of the trait variance can be attributed to genotypic differences), but the same trait *might* have substantial heritability in a genetically heterogeneous population. The heritability of blindness, for example, has increased markedly since 1800 as a result of the elimination of smallpox and other communicable diseases that are potential causes of blindness. Similarly, the equalization of educational opportunities would serve to increase the heritability of IQ scores by reducing environmental differences among individuals. If one keeps in mind, then, that statements asserting that a particular trait is 60 percent genetic and 40 percent environmental can be made only for a particular population in a particular environment, one can make a fairly precise quantitative assessment of the importance of heredity and environment in determining some particular trait. Environment in the context of these discussions means any factor that is not subsumed under heredity—psychological environment as well as physical.

Laboratory Studies

Many of the data collected in behavior genetics come from comparison of strains of animals. In general, a *strain* of animals refers to a reproductively isolated population within a given species. Wild rats and laboratory rats are separate strains, as are the various breeds of dogs. If each of two strains has been maintained in reproductive isolation, it is safe to assume that the two strains will differ in the composition of their gene pools. Thus, if under identical environmental circumstances there are behavioral differences between two strains of mice or rats, it can be assumed that the differences are heritable, that is to say, they are genotypic in origin.

An inbred strain is a reproductively isolated population (usually maintained under laboratory conditions) in which there has been much mating of closely related individuals, such as siblings and cousins. Because inbreeding increases the number of homozygotes (AA or aa), it tends to reduce genetic variability among members of a population. If intense (for example, brother-sister) inbreeding is continued over a large number of generations, an inbred strain will approach a completely *isogenic* state, that is, one in which all members of the strain are genetically identical. Under these conditions, all behavioral differences between individuals in the population can be assumed to result from environmental differences.

Studies employing the strain-comparison technique have demonstrated the heritability of a large variety of behavioral traits. Strains of mice or rats have been shown to differ in aggressiveness, learning ability, hoarding activity, exploratory behavior, sex drive, alcohol preference, and other traits.

Many studies comparing the responses of two inbred strains to a range of environmental conditions have found that genetic and environmental effects are nonadditive. That is, when two strains of animals are tested in identical environments and on identical tasks, animals from one strain respond differently than the animals from the other strain. R. E. Wimer and his associates, for example, found that one inbred strain of mice learned a task faster when they practiced it at short intervals—every five to forty seconds. A second inbred strain learned the same task much faster when they practiced it only at twenty-four-hour intervals. Other studies have produced evidence that most individuals in one strain of mice are affected by handling or electric shock during infancy and display increased emotionality as adults, while another strain's adult behavior is not affected at all by the same amount of shock or handling.

Human Populations

Animal studies of heredity-environment interaction are significant for understanding human psychological development because they demonstrate that the universality of behavioral definitions is sharply limited by genetic population differences. Human races are Mendelian populations, which differ in the relative frequencies of various alleles in their gene pools, and different individuals may obey different laws of behavior because they are members of different Mendelian populations. The fact that races are genetically different implies that one should expect to find behavioral differences between them, just as one finds morphological and physiological differences. However, in any discussion of racial differences it is important to remember that populations, not individuals, are being described. The principles of genetic transmission ensure wide diversity *within* races; thus, particular individuals in one race may be phenotypically more similar to members of another race than to members of their own group.

Racial differences are already well documented for at least two psychological traits: color blindness and ability to taste PTC. Approximately 30 percent of American whites are PTC nontasters, whereas 6 to 11 percent of Chinese and only 3 to 9 percent of native Africans are nontasters. The frequency of various forms of mental illness has also been found to differ among races and other Mendelian populations. For example, in contrast to most other populations, manic-depressive psychosis is reported to be more frequent than schizophrenia (see Chapter 30) in the mental hospitals of India and among the Hutterites, an isolated religious sect living in Canada and the northern United States. The latter findings must be interpreted with caution, however, because the observed differences could have a cultural rather than genetic basis.

Twin Studies

Controlled breeding experiments are not possible in human behavior genetics, but useful information may be obtained through the study of phenotypic similarities and differences within families and between twins. If genetic differences contribute to variation of a given trait, it is expected that blood relatives will resemble one another in expression of that trait more than do randomly selected individuals and, furthermore, that the degree of phenotypic similarity between relatives of various categories (siblings, cousins) will depend on the degree of genetic similarity the relatives hold. Phenotypic similarity with respect to *qualitative* traits, such as color blindness, is usually expressed as a *concordance rate*—defined as the proportion of cases in which both individuals show the same expression of a trait. Phenotypic similarity with respect to traits that can be measured *quantitatively*, like IQ, is usually expressed by a statistical index known as a *correlation coefficient*. (See the Appendix for a more detailed discussion of statistical methods and terminology used in psychology.) The value of this measure for pairs of relatives can range from a minimum of .00, indicating a purely random degree of similarity, to a maximum of 1.00, indicating perfect agreement of trait scores.

Table 16.1 shows the average degree of genetic similarity (expressed in terms of percentage of genes shared in common) for unrelated persons and for various categories of relatives and gives correlations of intelligence-test scores and concordance rates for schizophrenia for these groups. Table 16.2 is a detailed summary of studies made to ascertain correlations in IQ for persons who are related in various ways or, though unrelated, were brought up in the same environment. It is clear

Table 16.1 — Correlation of Intelligence Scores and Schizophrenia

Relationship	Genetic Similarity	Correlation of Intelligence Test Scores*	Concordance Rate for Schizophrenia†
Unrelated	0.0%	.00	0.9%
First cousins	12.5	.29	—
Half-siblings	25.0	—	7.6
Grandparent-grandchild	25.0	.34	4.3
Uncle (aunt)-nephew (niece)	25.0	.35	3.9
Siblings	50.0	.53	11.5
Parent-offspring	50.0	.49	12.8

*From C. Burt and M. Howard, "The Multifactional Theory of Inheritance and Its Application to Intelligence," *British Journal of Statistical Psychology*, 9 (1956), 95–131.

†From F. J. Kallman, *The Genetics of Schizophrenia* (New York: Augustin, 1938).

Table 16.2—Correlations for Intellectual Ability: Obtained and Theoretical Values

Correlations Between	Number of Studies	Obtained Median	Theoretical Value*
Unrelated persons			
Children reared apart	4	−.01	.00
Foster parent and child	3	+.20	.00
Children reared together	5	+.24	.00
Collaterals			
Second cousins	1	+.16	+ .14
First cousins	3	+.26	+ .18
Uncle (or aunt) and nephew (or niece)	1	+.34	+ .31
Siblings, reared apart	33	+.47	+ .52
Siblings, reared together	36	+.55	+ .52
Dizygotic twins, different sex	9	+.49	+ .50
Dizygotic twins, same sex	11	+.56	+ .54
Monozygotic twins, reared apart	4	+.75	+1.00
Monozygotic twins, reared together	14	+.87	+1.00
Direct Line			
Grandparent and grandchild	3	+.27	+ .31
Parent (as adult) and child	13	+.50	+ .49
Parent (as child) and child	1	+.56	+ .49

*Value one would expect if genetic factors alone were operating.
Source: A. R. Jensen, "How Much Can We Boost IQ and Scholastic Achievement?" *Harvard Educational Review* (Winter 1969).

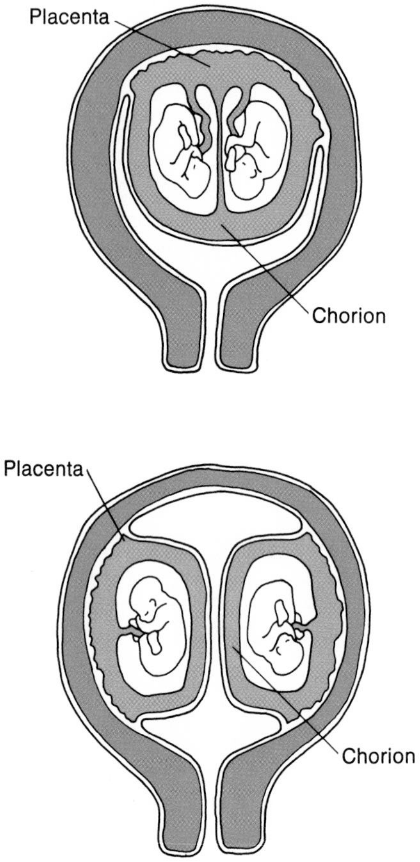

Figure 16.29
Monozygotic twins, in addition to being genotypically identical, share a very similar prenatal environment. In uterus they share the same placenta and chorion (top). Dizygotic twins develop from different zygotes and are therefore genetically different; each has its own placenta and chorion (bottom).

that family resemblance with respect to both IQ and schizophrenia is correlated with the number of genes shared in common. However, a basic difficulty in interpreting family correlation data is that relatives tend to have similar environments as well as similar genotypes, so that the causes of phenotypic resemblance remain ambiguous. It should be noted, however, that Mendel's law of segregation of alleles provides a substantive basis for explaining the fact that *differences* as well as similarities are found among family members. Just as it can explain how a pair of brown-eyed parents can produce a blue-eyed offspring, it may also someday explain why some family members develop schizophrenia and others do not.

Many investigators have turned to studies of phenotypic correlation in twins in order to avoid the confounding of genetic and environmental similarity that occurs in family studies. About one-third of American Caucasian twins are monozygotic (MZ) and two-thirds are dizygotic (DZ). Monozygotic twins derive from the splitting of a single fertilized ovum and therefore are genetically identical, sharing 100 percent of their alleles in common. Dizygotic twins result from the fertilization of two ova by two sperm and therefore are no more alike genetically than ordinary siblings; that is, they share, on the average, 50 percent of a common set of alleles. Like-sexed DZ twins can be distinguished from MZ twins on the basis of dissimilarities in physical traits such as hair or eye color, blood type, and fingerprint patterns, or, if these tests are inconclusive, by virtue of the fact that reciprocal skin transplants will take permanently only in MZ twins.

The general rationale of the twin-study method is that phenotypic differences between MZ twins should reflect environmental influence alone, whereas phenotypic differences between DZ twins should reflect the combined effects of hereditary and environmental factors. Thus, the extent to which intrapair similarity is greater in MZ than in DZ twins should provide an estimate of the heritability of a particular trait in the population studied. Table 16.3 summarizes the results of studies reporting MZ and DZ intrapair correlations and concordance rates for a variety of behavioral traits. Note that the measures for both schizophrenia and intelligence show a large discrepancy between MZ and DZ twins; this difference supports the argument for high heritability of these traits. The other findings in Table 16.3 suggest that heritability may play a major role in such traits as manic-depressive psychosis, male homosexuality, and extraversion but a somewhat more minor role in the etiology of suicide and psychopathic personality.

Some investigators have questioned the validity of the twin-study method, saying

Table 16.3 — Behavioral Traits of Monozygotic (MZ) and Dizygotic (DZ) Twins

Trait	Intrapair Concordance Rate		Intrapair Correlation Coefficient	
	MZ	DZ	MZ	DZ
Schizophrenia[1]	86%	15%	—	—
Manic-depressive psychosis[2]	93	24	—	—
Psychopathic personality[3]	25	14	—	—
Alcoholism[4]	65	30	—	—
Male homosexuality[5]	98	12	—	—
Hysteria[6]	33	0	—	—
Suicide[7]	6	0	—	—
Intelligence[8]	—	—	.88	.63
Motor skill[9]	—	—	.79	.43
Vocational interests[10]	—	—	.50	.28
Extraversion-introversion[11]	—	—	.55	.08
Depression[12]	—	—	.47	.07
Neuroticism[13]	—	—	.85	.22

1, 2, 5, 7, Kallman (1953); 3, Slater (1953); 4, Kaij (1957); 6, Stumpfl (1937); 8, Newman *et al.* (1937); 9, McNemar (1933); 10, Carter (1932); 11, 12, Gottesman (1963); 13, Eysenck and Prell (1951).

that DZ twins do not experience similar environments in the same way as MZ twins do. They say, for example, that MZ twins are treated more alike by parents and peers and that they tend to model their behavior upon one another. Each of these factors might serve to inflate MZ trait correlations and lead to overestimates of heritability. To counter this argument, other investigators have compared MZ twins reared apart for many years with MZ and DZ twins reared together. One study of this type reported a correlation of .77 between the IQ scores of MZ twins reared apart; in a second study the concordance rate for schizophrenia in adult MZ twins separated for an average of 11.8 years was 78 percent. The fact that identical genotypes subjected to different environments (MZ twins reared apart) are more similar with respect to intelligence and occurrence of schizophrenia than different genotypes subjected to similar environments (DZ twins reared together) suggests the importance of hereditary factors. The role of environment is indicated by the fact that MZ twins reared apart are less similar phenotypically than MZ twins reared together.

A further way to separate the roles of heredity and environment is to compare the correlations between adopting parents and adopted children with the correlations between adopted children and their natural parents. Such comparisons show only a very low correlation between the IQ test scores of adopted mothers and adopted children but almost the usual correlation between the natural mothers and their children who had been brought up by others. Figure 16.30 shows such correlations as found in a study that was conducted by M. Skodak and H. Skeels; because IQ scores for the parents were not always obtainable, years of education was used as a rough indication of intelligence.

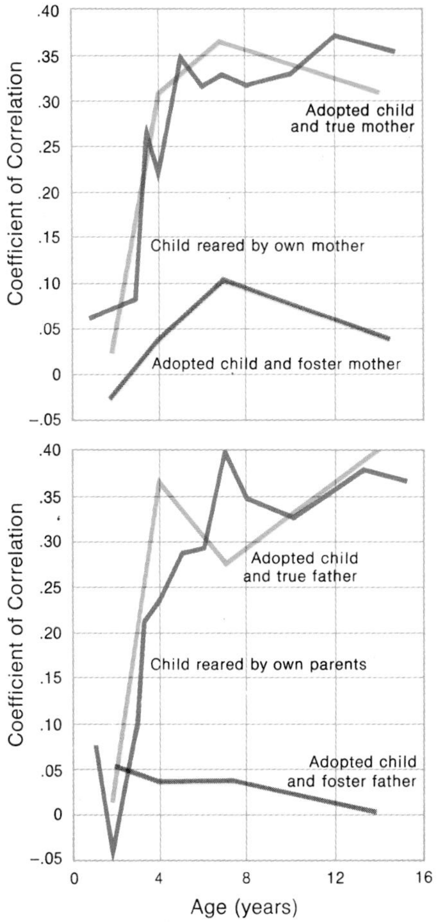

Figure 16.30
The correlations found by Skodak and Skeels between IQ scores of children and the educational level of natural or adoptive parents. It should be noted that the absolute values of these coefficients are rather low, even at the top values. One critical limitation in considering these correlations is the imperfect relationship between a person's intelligence level and his level of education. Another consideration in interpreting correlations like these should be the circumstances under which the data were obtained. For example, recent evidence would require us to know whether the intelligence-test examiners were aware of the adoptive status and living arrangements of the children before testing occurred.

SUGGESTED READINGS

GARDNER, E. *Fundamentals of Neurology* (4th ed.). Philadelphia, Saunders, 1963. This classic gives an excellent treatment of the anatomy and the physiology of the nervous system.

GROSS, C. G., AND ZEIGLER, H. P. *Readings in Physiological Psychology: Neurophysiology/Sensory Processes.* New York, Harper & Row, 1969.

GROSS, C. G., AND ZEIGLER, H. P. *Readings in Physiological Psychology: Learning and Memory.* New York, Harper & Row, 1969.

GROSSMAN, S. P. *A Textbook of Physiological Psychology.* New York, Wiley, 1967. A rather extensive treatment, containing over 900 pages.

KATKIN, E. S. *Instrumental Autonomic Conditioning.* New York, General Learning Corporation, 1971. This pamphlet gives a good overview of work on instrumental conditioning of autonomic functioning.

MAGOUN, H. W. *The Waking Brain* (2nd ed.). Springfield, Ill., Charles C Thomas, 1963. A fascinating treatment of the brain, including the historical antecedents of current work in arousal, attention, and learning.

MCGAUGH, J. L. (Ed.). *Psychobiology: Behavior from a Biological Perspective.* New York, Academic Press, 1971. This excellent new book provides interesting treatments of several topics of interest, including the evolution of behavior, instinct, sensory processes and behavior, appetitive motivation, attention, and a discussion of brain mechanisms of memory.

TEITELBAUM, P. *Physiological Psychology.* Englewood Cliffs, N.J., Prentice-Hall, 1967. This paperback is an excellent overview of physiological psychology; considerably less detailed than the comprehensive text by Grossman, cited above.

THOMPSON, D., AND SCHUSTER, C. R. *Behavioral Pharmacology.* Englewood Cliffs, N.J., Prentice-Hall, 1968. An excellent current treatment of the influence of drugs upon behavior.

UNIT VI Emotion and Motivation

When psychologists study motivation, they try to determine why a person picks one action out of the many of which he is capable and carries out that particular action at a particular place and time. They are interested in both a long-term sequence of behaviors that has a direction to it, like pursuit of a career, and in shorter, directed sequences of behavior that tend to recur periodically, like sexual behavior or aggressiveness or striving for achievement.

The concepts of emotion and motivation are closely related; both of them are derived from the Latin word for movement. It is difficult to think of a motivated state that is not accompanied by an emotional one. Motivation, however, usually implies a goal, whether it be a biologically determined one

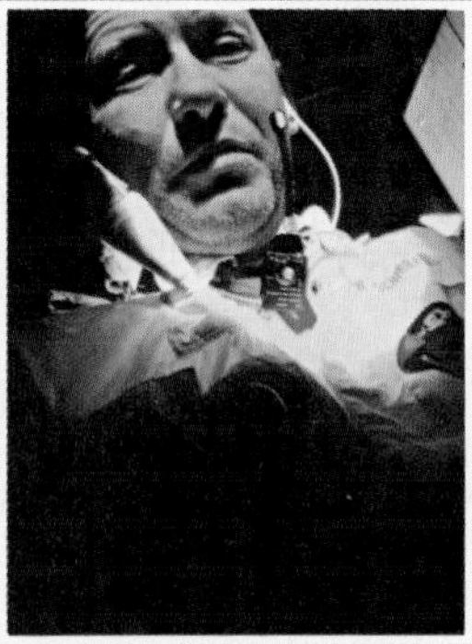

Chapter 17, Emotion, presents three ways of analyzing emotional behavior: examination of the physiological correlates of emotions; description of the categories of emotional experience; and consideration of the complex relationships among physiological, experiential, and behavioral components of emotions.

3

Conditioning and Learning presents the behaviorist analysis of reinforcement, which implies drive reduction. The detailed discussion of drives and homeostasis is presented in Chapter 18.

8

Social Development: The Case of Morality discusses the differences in socialization of males and females; Chapter 19 analyzes how these differences show up in differing motives for men and women, particularly the motive to achieve.

15

Consciousness and Awareness opens with a long discussion of the nature of consciousness. Chapter 17 analyzes the role of physiological cues in the arousal of emotion and indicates how the *conscious* experience of emotion seems to depend on a combination of the physiological factors with perceptual and cognitve ones; thus, it enlarges upon Chapter 15's presentation.

16

The Biological Organism is a basic presentation of human physiology. It provides background for Chapter 17's discussion of the physiological bases of emotion and for Chapter 18's discussion of the physiological bases of biological drives like hunger, thirst, and sex.

like food or water, or a culturally determined one like success in business or the creation of works of art.

Clearly, motivation is one of the most general topics in psychology; it is dealt with to some degree in almost every chapter in this book and is one of the main topics with which psychologists concern themselves. It is important not only for the study of personality, but also for investigation of the biological bases of behavior. Consequently, this unit provides a transition from the biologically oriented approach of the first half of the book to the emphasis on personality and social behavior in the second half.

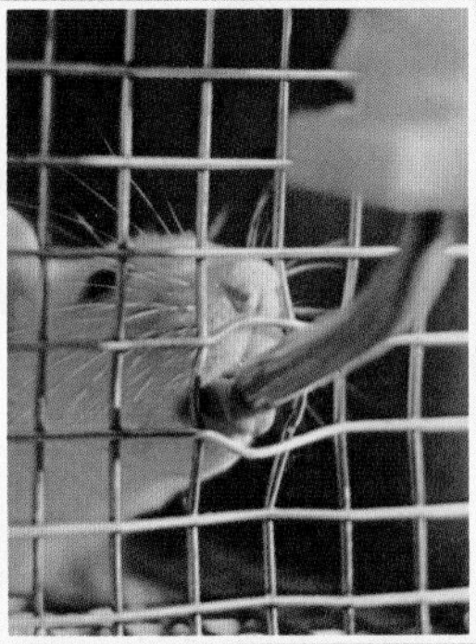

Chapter 18, Elementary Concepts of Motivation, presents evidence that much of behavior is controlled by biologically determined drives that organisms seek to reduce, like hunger and thirst. This research grew out of the behaviorist theory of Clark Hull, who held that all reinforcements derive from reduction of biologically based drives.

Chapter 19, Human Motivation, discusses theories of human motivation—in particular, expectancy-value theory —and takes the motive to achieve as a case study of the analysis of human motivation. This chapter provides a transition to personality and social psychology, which are the topics of the following units.

31

Bases of Disorder examines various explanations of what causes psychological disorder. Its discussion of emotional factors implicated in the development of neuroses and psychoses (topics such as the double-bind hypothesis of schizophrenia) enlarges upon Chapter 17's discussion of emotion.

27

Interpersonal Attraction looks at why people choose certain other people as friends. Chapter 19's discussion of motives for approval or prestige directly relate to a good part of Chapter 27's discussion.

25

Patterns of Social Behavior: The Case of Sex Roles examines sex-role differences between men and women—what is expected of and appropriate to males and to females. Chapter 19's discussion of differences that have been found to exist between men and women in particular motives, especially the motive to achieve, complements Chapter 25's topic.

20

Psychological Testing presents a detailed discussion of the TAT test and scoring procedures for it. The TAT is a tool used in measuring motives discussed in Chapter 19, especially the motive to achieve and the motive to avoid success.

21

Freudian Theories of Personality presents the approach to motivation of each theory discussed; these approaches can be compared to Chapter 19's view.

22

Other Theories of Personality presents the views of a wide variety of theories on what constitutes motivation; these views can be compared to Chapter 19's approach.

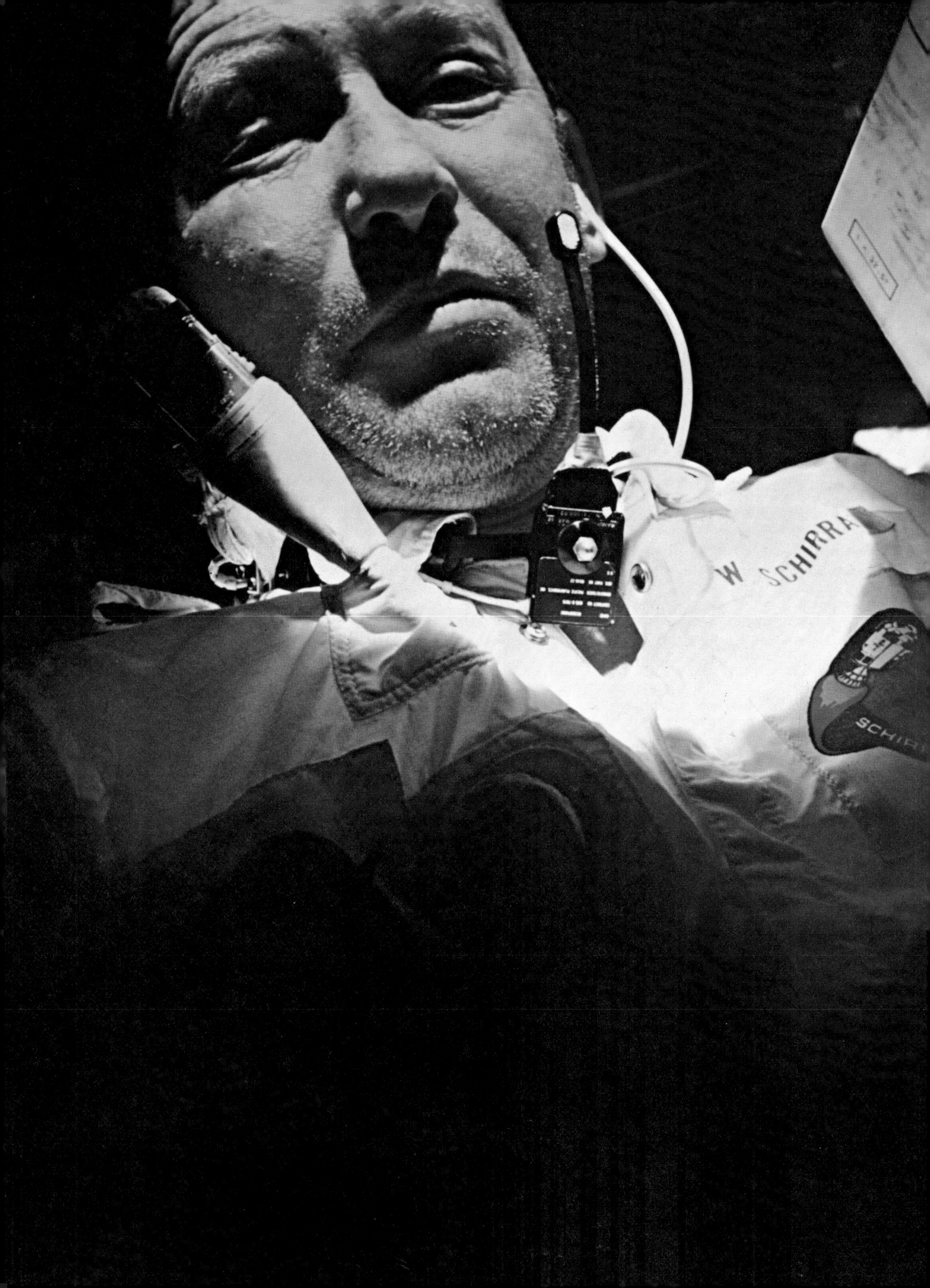
W. SCHIRRA

17 Emotion

IT SEEMS TO ME that our reactions to most things in life are best described as representing "mixed emotions." It is rare that one feels rage and nothing else, or fear and nothing else. Generally, you feel a little of this and a little of that.

Take the case of Hamlet in Shakespeare's play of that name. He is probably more discussed (even sometimes by professional psychologists) than any other character in literature. His father, the elder Hamlet, dies suddenly, and his uncle, Claudius, having married Queen Gertrude (young Hamlet's mother) is now the new king. His father's ghost tells Hamlet that Claudius had murdered him and charges Hamlet with the task of vengeance—and yet Hamlet delays. As long as you consider Hamlet motivated by a single, pure feeling, the desire for revenge, there is no way of explaining that delay, Hamlet himself admits only the desire for revenge, and he is constantly complaining at his own delay.

But suppose he had another emotion, too. Besides the lust for revenge, suppose he felt ambition. Suppose he had the itch for the throne. Why not? He was his father's grown son. Yet Claudius was elected. Why? Suppose we consider eleventh-century English history (about the time Hamlet was supposed to have taken place). Emma, widow of dead King Ethelred, married Canute of Denmark. Canute became King of England in preference to Emma's grown son by Ethelred. To be sure, Canute became king by right of conquest, but his marriage to the Queen gave it a flavor of legality. In the same way Claudius' marriage to the widow of the dead king gave him a kind of legal claim to the throne and ensured his election. One can argue that Hamlet was not so much annoyed with his mother's marriage to Claudius as with the *speed* of the marriage. The quick marriage made it possible for Claudius to be elected successor before Hamlet had time to return from school and claim the throne.

From that standpoint, the play begins to involve a dynastic dispute, and that makes sense. England's Queen Elizabeth was in her late sixties at the time and had no direct heir. Her death might once again set off dynastic civil war. Shakespeare, concerned with that, wrote many plays dealing with disputed successions, and "Hamlet" was one of them.

Now we see how the mixed emotions play their part. If Hamlet simply killed Claudius (a clever and popular king), that would feed his revenge but would not gain him the throne. It might gain him only civil war or execution. For Hamlet to kill Claudius *after proving him a murderer* would gain him both revenge and ambition, for then he would surely be the next king. Hamlet, therefore, is not trying to prove Claudius' guilt to himself out of irresolution and a yearning for delay. He is trying to prove Claudius a murderer *to the court* out of calculated policy.

I. A.

No matter how often human beings are compared to information-processing machines or how often our kinship to increasingly complex electronic computers is pointed out, we know we are different. For one thing, we have feelings and emotions. We love, we hate, we fear, we laugh, we experience joy and sadness. We experience a wide variety of feelings and emotions, and these experiences have profound effects on everything we do.

People's emotions range from the strongly dramatic ones, such as fear, anger, and ecstasy, to the less dramatic, such as tenderness, the mild irritation of boredom, and the uneasiness of living in an unsettled and warring world. There is an emotional quality of some sort to all the interactions we have with our environment.

Some psychologists prefer to reserve the term "emotion" for the dramatic states and to use the term "feeling" to refer to the milder states. Some believe that emotions involve a tendency for action—for example, when we have an urge to attack in anger or to run away in fear—and others argue that it is motives, not emotions, that involve a tendency to action (see Chapter 19). The relationship between motives and emotions continues to be a thorny issue. Most psychologists do agree, however, that emotion is associated with a number of bodily changes, such as increased muscle tension, breathing rate, and heart rate.

In investigating emotion, psychologists have taken several paths. This chapter deals largely with the two most common paths: the study of the physiology of emotion, and the description and classification of emotional experiences and reactions.

These two approaches are combined in the investigation of the physiological changes that accompany emotional experiences and reactions, which is also discussed.

Psychologists have traditionally focused on negative emotions, possibly because they are easier to elicit than positive ones, possibly because they seem to lead to more clearly noticeable behavioral and physiological changes than positive ones do. There may be historical factors at work as well: Since the advent of behaviorist theories fairly early in the twentieth century, these theories have dominated the research strategies and vocabularies of many American psychologists. The behaviorist bias has been toward the study of observable behavior, and the positive emotions do not, as noted, lead to as clearly definable activity. In addition, positive emotions are not as easily controlled or produced. (A discussion of some of the conditions that produce negative emotion is provided in Chapters 3 and 4.) The methods by which behavioral changes were studied involved the use of measurement and experiment, and the subjects often were animals. The behavior, not the experiences felt by the subjects, was the object of study. This influence is still quite strong, and it remains even when most of the behaviorist assumptions are not adhered to.

The behavioral approach, when it was applied to human subjects, afforded some relief to investigators who were faced with disorderly lists of emotions compiled by previous researchers. Therefore, the physiology of emotion seemed to provide a profitable way to learn something about emotional behavior. This account should not be taken to imply that the study of physiological changes within the organism that accompany emotion is not worthwhile. On the contrary: Physiological changes clearly do occur in organisms experiencing emotions—in people as well as in other animals—and their role in human emotion cannot be ignored.

In fact, the physiological changes associated with human emotion, particularly such strong emotions as fear and anger, are so striking that at one time it was hypothesized that having an emotional experience depended entirely on perceiving one's internal bodily changes. It was argued, in other words, that the changes preceded the feeling of any specific emotion. It is now known that the internal changes occur too slowly to account for the entire emotional experience. Nevertheless, sensations from internal bodily changes clearly do play an important role in emotion, and such changes often occur even when there are no easily visible outward behavioral effects. The fact has led to attempts to determine the presence of emotion by noting bodily changes, as in lie detection.

THE LIE DETECTOR

The device known as a lie detector is essentially an "emotion detector." It is designed to detect certain kinds of physiological activity from which emotional change can be inferred. The emotion or feeling of "guilt" is assumed to be aroused in persons who have committed a crime if they are reminded of the crime or, more usually, if they themselves tell a lie. Changes in such measures as the blood pressure, the rate of respiration, and the electrical conductance of the skin (commonly called the galvanic skin response or GSR) are all used in determining whether the individual considers himself or herself to be lying. The use of these several physiological measures in lie detection underscores the point that an emotional response is a complex one, consisting of many components, internal and external, unobservable and observable. The lie detector attempts to detect some of the normally unobservable physiological components of emotion, in cases where there is no objective evidence that the person is lying.

It has been known since ancient times that people react physically when strong emotion is aroused in them. The present-day lie detector has its forerunner in such ancient practices as the "ordeal by rice." In this test of guilt, if the suspect could not swallow a handful of dry rice, he was considered guilty. The effectiveness of this detection system depends on the fact that in general a guilty suspect will have a very dry mouth (dryness of the mouth often accompanies fear) and will therefore have difficulty swallowing the rice.

The modern lie-detector arrangement is shown in Figure 17.1. The person is asked questions. His replies and several physiological indexes of his response are recorded. The electrodes attached to the person's hand record changes in skin conductance, such as those associated with sweating. The person in Figure 17.1 is also being monitored for changes in respiration (by the rubber tube, or pneumograph tube, around his chest), and in blood pressure and heart rate (by the cuff on his left arm). All these changes are recorded on a polygram, such as the one shown. The vocal response is usually recorded as well.

Typically, the person is asked a series of routine questions ("How old are you?" or "What did you have to drink with your breakfast this morning?") to establish a baseline against which changes may be evaluated when the potentially emotion-charged questions are asked. A suspect in a bank robbery may be asked "Where do you do your banking?" or more direct questions such as "Did you steal the money?" If the suspect's involuntary changes in GSR, heart rate, and so on, conflict with his verbal response and perhaps his outward composure, suspicions are aroused about the truthfulness of his statements.

There are, however, serious problems with the lie detector that make its use controversial. First, changes in GSR and other measures following a lie are only partially reliable. Changes in the GSR, while reliable and dramatic after an unexpected loud noise, may be slight or nonexistent following a lie. Second, the lie detector, like the ordeal by rice, may be "beaten" by a knowledgeable suspect. For example, some people can control their "involuntary" manifestations of lying, either through practice or because they are genuinely composed. Some habitual liars are quite comfortable about lying. Another way of beating the machine is to alter the results of the baseline condition. For example, if the person thinks about the crime

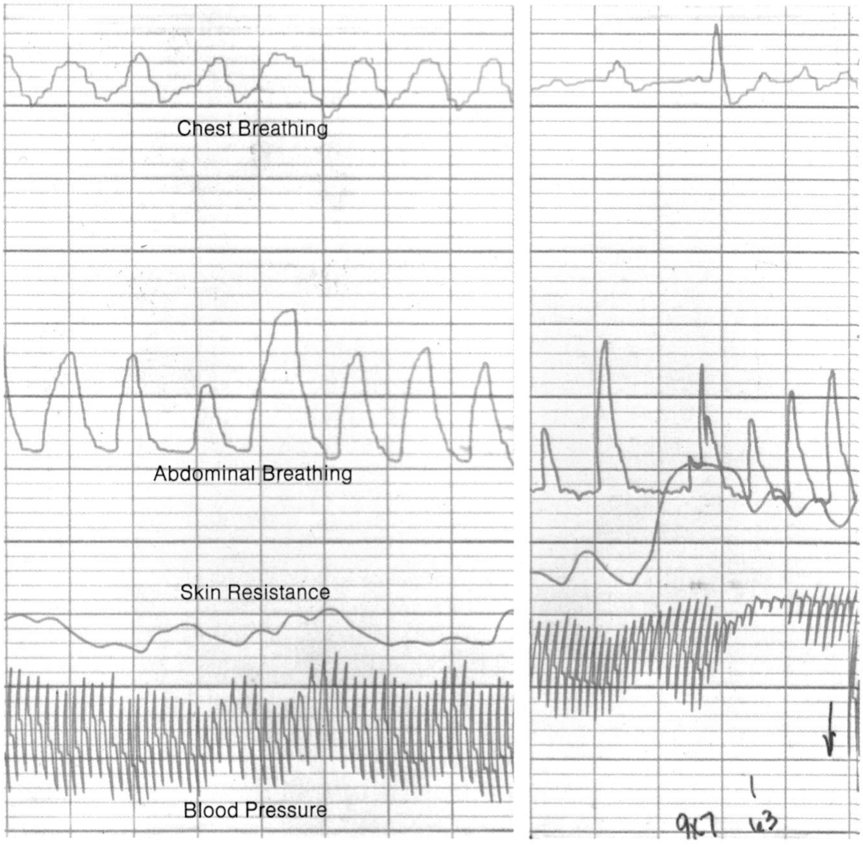

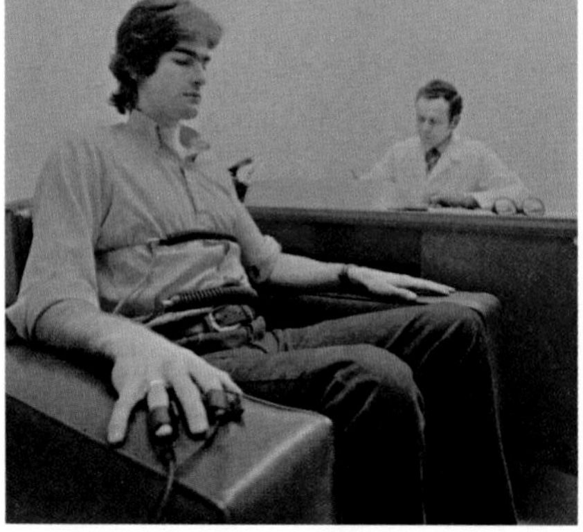

Figure 17.1
The subject in this polygraph examination is providing baseline measures, that is, his normal level of physiological responses while at rest. The devices shown will monitor and transmit to the recorder changes in his skin conductance, blood pressure, heart rate, and respiration. The polygraph record at the left shows the four tracings generated by those physiological indexes while the subject was responding to routine questions. Note, however, how each measure shows a marked deviation at a key point in the record at the right. There is a strong possibility that the subject lied in his answer to the question posed at this point. Polygraph-record reading calls for a skilled examiner, who has prepared the questions carefully and can make interpretations consistent not only with the particular question but also with all the situational variables.

when asked about breakfast, he will create a baseline comparable to his reaction to the crime-related questions. A third problem is that some people, knowing they are suspected of a crime and perhaps afraid of being "railroaded," may act very guilty although they are innocent: the question "Did you steal the money?" might be unsettling to many honest people.

Despite these drawbacks, lie detection is often reliable and valuable in helping detectives solve crimes. Sometimes it even produces confessions: An unsophisticated and guilty person, feeling that he has no chance against his (technologically) impressive adversary, may confess as soon as he is shown the results of the test—and sometimes as soon as he is strapped into the chair. In this instance the working of the lie detector is precisely analogous to that of the guilt-detection procedures used by nontechnological peoples, such as the ordeal by rice.

THE PHYSIOLOGY OF EMOTION

The psychological study of the physiology of emotion is much more complicated than the few simple facts involved in the use of the lie detector would indicate. The following brief summary presents the basic findings of this very complex and often confusing area of investigation. Structures in the central nervous system that have been implicated in emotion are discussed, and the important and interesting work on self-stimulation of some of these structures is outlined. The role of structures in the autonomic nervous system is then briefly summarized, which paves the way for a discussion of psychosomatic disorders—a topic that, unfortunately, sooner or later becomes relevant to most of us.

Structures in the Central Nervous System

There are two subsystems in the central nervous system that appear to be especially important for the experience of emotion. One is the *reticular activating system*, which is discussed in Chapter 16. This system is undoubtedly at least partly responsible for the arousal, excitement, or activation that usually accompanies emotional reactions. Indeed, it plays a central part in so-called "activation theories" of emotion, which are discussed later in this chapter.

Figure 17.2
The reticular activating system may play an important role in determining heightened levels of arousal or excitement associated with intense emotional stimulation. More specific expression of a particular emotion may first require an initial general increase in arousal level, produced by reticular stimulation.

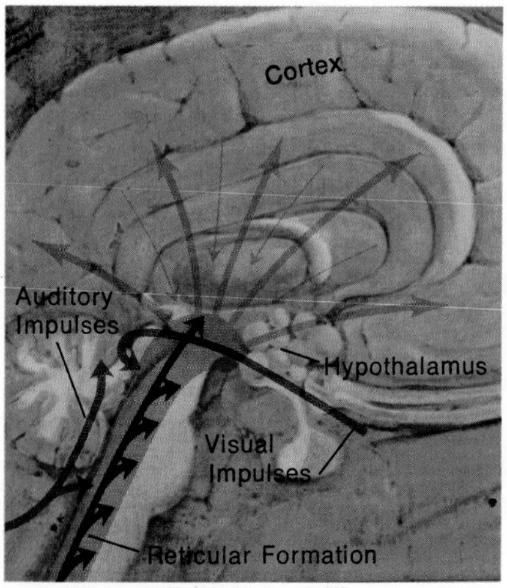

The *limbic system* is the other subsystem of the central nervous system important in emotion. It is an anatomical circuit that was first described by J. W. Papez. It includes many important areas in the "primitive" brain (the part of the brain whose structures have been present since relatively early in evolution). Although the limbic system seems to be involved in emotion, the specific role played by each of the substructures composing it is unclear. A portion of the limbic system is shown in Figure 17.2.

Two techniques that have been widely used to assess the relevance of limbic areas to emotion are *stimulation* and *ablation*. These techniques are discussed in Chapter 16. In theory, the techniques should have opposite effects. For example, assume that a certain site in the hypothalamus (which is part of the limbic system) produces a "rage reaction" when stimulated with electric current. What should happen if that site was removed surgically (that is, ablated)? A more docile animal —one less prone to exhibit rage—might be the expected result. More often than not, the effects of stimulation and ablation do occur in the expected opposite directions, but there are many disturbing exceptions. There are a vast number of interconnections in the nervous system, especially in the brain. Therefore, when a portion of the brain is either stimulated or removed, subsequent behavior cannot necessarily be attributed directly to the part operated on. It is always possible that the observed effects are really under the control of some other brain structure to which the one operated on is connected.

There is little doubt that the limbic-system structures are intimately involved in most emotional reactions and that the reticular system (see Figure 17.3) is implicated in emotional activation, but it is very unlikely that a simple one-to-one correspondence exists between certain emotions and the activation of limbic-system structures. The relationship is certainly more complicated, and before questions can be answered much more research is needed.

Some general statements do appear justified, however. The hypothalamus appears to play a central role in the organization of emotional reactions. Electrical stimulation of portions of the hypothalamus produces various emotional reactions, such as rage reactions and reactions of "flight" and "alarm." In addition, research on intracranial self-stimulation of the limbic system shows that certain areas can reliably produce pleasurable sensations when stimulated, whereas others produce painful sensations.

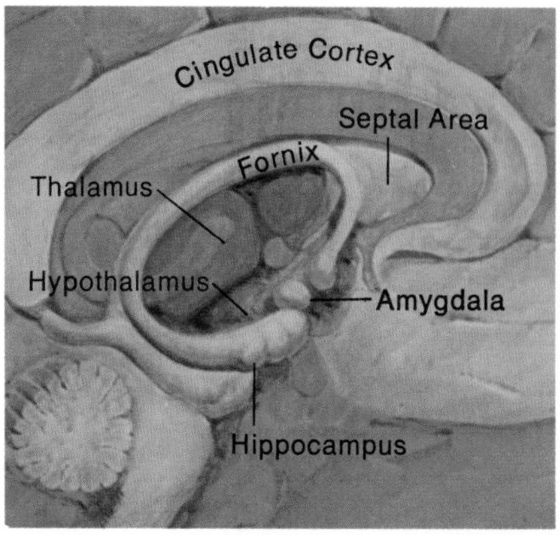

Figure 17.3
Striking emotional reactions occur following experimental manipulation of some portions of the limbic system. Lesions in the septal area can produce uncontrolled rage directed at anything within range. Lesions in the amygdala can instantly tame wild animals or render a docile animal vicious. These paradoxical findings reflect the variety of interconnections and the amount of complexity involved in limbic regulation of emotional behavior.

Intracranial Self-Stimulation

J. Olds and his associates discovered that rats will learn to press a lever in order to stimulate areas of their own brains with electric current. The location of the stimulation is critical: Olds found some areas that appeared to be highly reinforcing, whereas other areas served as punishers. The central area of the limbic system appears to have many highly reinforcing areas. Indeed, with some areas stimulated, rats would press the lever *several thousand times per hour* for at least ten hours. Understandably, these areas have come to be known as "pleasure centers."

It is conceivable that many of the pleasures we obtain in life occur because an appropriate region of the limbic system has been stimulated. Unfortunately, however, such a possibility must remain purely speculative. The fact that a rat is observed to press the lever in order to obtain electrical stimulation is not *proof* that the rat is "enjoying it." The inference from self-stimulation to an experiencing of pleasure is unprovable. Analogous studies carried out with some human subjects (patients undergoing brain surgery) have an advantage in that, in addition to responding to the stimulation (as the rat does), the person can also indicate verbally whether the stimulation is pleasant. On the basis of such verbal reports it appears that stimulation in certain areas is indeed felt as pleasurable. Stimulation in other areas, however, is considered neutral. That is, some people respond to obtain the stimulation in those areas (thereby satisfying the definition of a reinforcer) but explicitly deny that the resulting sensation is pleasurable!

The Autonomic Nervous System

As you may recall from the discussion in Chapter 16, the control of the so-called involuntary functions of the body by the hypothalamus is accomplished through

Figure 17.4
This animal has a stimulating electrode implanted in its limbic system. Each lever press delivers a mild electrical stimulus to the brain. The extremely high rates of lever pressing performed by animals with these implants indicate to some investigators that the stimulation is producing pleasurable sensations by activating pleasure centers in the limbic system.

the autonomic nervous system, which consists of two divisions: the *sympathetic* and the *parasympathetic*. In general these systems can be viewed as working antagonistically. The sympathetic system tends to promote energy expenditure; in particular, it mobilizes the body's resources to meet emergency conditions, for example, by increasing blood-sugar levels and heart rate and by inhibiting digestive processes. The parasympathetic system, in contrast, acts as an energy-conserving system; it slows the heart rate and enhances digestive activity.

In strong emotions, such as terror, the sympathetic system is dominant and the parasympathetic system is inhibited, which generally results in an increased heart rate and a slowing down of the digestive processes. One short-term result of the inhibition of digestive processes is the dryness of the mouth resulting from a decrease in salivation, the basis for the ordeal-by-rice guilt test mentioned earlier.

The picture of two mutually antagonistic systems is something of an oversimplification. Often the two systems work together. Moreover, sympathetic system reactions may be so extreme that they cause what may be termed a "parasympathetic backlash." Examples of this backlash are instances of urination, defecation, or even "heart stoppage" in the face of a particularly stressful or anxiety-provoking situation.

So far only the very short-term effects of sympathetic activation have been discussed. In the longer term, slowing down of the digestive processes may cause problems such as constipation. But in the even longer term, under conditions of prolonged stress, more serious psychosomatic problems may arise.

Prolonged Stress and Psychosomatic Illness

The various circulatory and autonomic changes that constitute the immediate reaction to a stressful stimulus are adaptive in that they help the organism mobilize for action. But what happens when the organism cannot eliminate the stress or move away from it? What happens when it is subjected to a chronic stress? H. Selye, in his book *The Stress of Life*, has theorized that there are three stages in the response to long-term stress: the stage of alarm, the stage of resistance, and the stage of exhaustion. Together, these three phases have been called the *adaptation syndrome*.

Laboratory animals have shown a generalized reaction, similar to the emergency reaction, to such stresses as near-freezing temperatures, confinement in a small cage, forced muscular work, drugs of various types, and infectious agents. This general reaction, called the stage of alarm, is particularly characterized by the swelling of the adrenal glands and the release of hormones that control inflammation.

If the stress persists long enough, the animal's reactions change. The animal enters the so-called stage of resistance, in which the adrenals return to normal size, the visceral reactions return to normal, and the animal seems to be adapting beautifully. However, this outwardly excellent adaptation is somewhat deceptive, because the stage of resistance seems to consume all the adaptive resources of the organism. If the external stress continues unabated long enough, the signs of the first stage reappear: the adrenals enlarge again, and the animal may die. This final period is called the stage of exhaustion.

There is evidence suggesting that the adaptational resources of the organism are being strained during the stage of resistance. If, during this period, a second stress is applied—one that the organism could ordinarily handle—the adaptation may break down and the stage of exhaustion appear. This additive effect can be seen in everyday life when we seem to come down with colds and other ailments more frequently during periods of emotional stress.

Prolonged stress and additive stress are probably involved in many diseases of adaptation, such as ulceration in various parts of the digestive tract, high blood pressure and heart disease, kidney disease, and rheumatism. Gastrointestinal ulcers can serve as an example of such a disease of adaptation. A few days after undergoing a severe stress, such as extensive burns or heavy aerial bombing, many people develop bleeding ulcers in the stomach or duodenum. Acute fear reduces the flow of stomach acid but chronic fear or tension increases it. Prolonged frustration and inhibited anger are also effective in producing ulcers. What happens is that the stomach juices literally start digesting part of the stomach or duodenal wall.

Experimenters have produced gastrointestinal ulcers in laboratory animals. In a study by J. Brady and his colleagues, monkeys had to press a lever every few seconds for six hours to avoid getting electric shocks. This procedure, with six hours on and six hours of rest, was continued over a period of weeks, and the monkeys eventually developed massive ulcers in their digestive tracts. Interestingly, the upsurge in stomach acid, and thus the tissue damage, occurred during the rest periods rather than during the periods of acute stress.

Stressful situations much like the ones outlined above also produced symptoms that have been termed "neurotic." It is undoubtedly true that stressful situations and the manner in which one handles the stress are contributing factors to human neurotic behavior, as discussed in Chapter 30.

Figure 17.5

William James. James' remarkable career included a Harvard professorship in physiology, psychology, and philosophy. His influence has been particularly deep in the last two fields. He has been called "America's greatest psychologist" by one writer (E. G. Boring). James was no less influential in the field of philosophy, however, and is considered an important exponent of the viewpoint called pragmatism.

THE DESCRIPTIVE ANALYSIS OF EMOTION

The physiological study of emotion is only one method of studying emotion—and a rather new one. Other methods depend a great deal on the verbal description and cognitive categorization of emotional states.

The subjective experience of emotion is a very slippery phenomenon. How do you go about *studying* it? Rats, as we have seen, cannot communicate their experiences to us; we must deduce some of the components of emotion from their emotive behavior. But that is not the same as saying that we "know what they are feeling." Human beings, in contrast to rats, can often use words to report what they are feeling. However, no one who has ever tried to *describe* a feeling can make the mistake of thinking that the words *are* the feeling or that words can really do justice to a feeling. Moreover, different individuals cannot be expected to use the same words to talk about what *might* be similar emotional experiences. Therefore, in studying emotions, psychologists have frequently grown impatient with lists and have tried to find some way of dealing with emotional experiences as perceived by the experiencers so that general principles about emotion can be derived.

William James, commenting on lists of emotions, wrote, "I would as lief read verbal descriptions of the shapes of the rocks on a New Hampshire farm as toil

Figure 17.6

The apparatus in which monkeys had to press a lever every few seconds for six hours to avoid receiving a shock. Under these stress conditions, the monkeys developed massive ulcers. Interestingly, the increase in stomach acid, which causes the tissue damage, occurred during their six-hour rest periods, when the acute stress period had ended (or, before it began again).

through them again. They give one nowhere a central point of view or a deductive or generative principle."

Despite the seeming enormity of the task of working with people's reports of their emotions, one of the earliest groups of psychologists to study human emotional behavior relied almost exclusively on their subjects' verbal behavior. This group, working around the turn of the century, were known as the *introspectionists.* Introspection is the process of observing and reporting the contents of one's own consciousness. The introspectionists' approach to the study of emotion seems very reasonable. What better way to study people's emotions than to ask them about them? It is not surprising, therefore, that their approach to emotional behavior seemed so attractive.

The Introspectionists

The father of experimental psychology, Wilhelm Wundt, founded a school of psychology based on introspection. Members of this school tried to analyze the *structure* of complex experience into the mental elements thought to compose it. Reasoning by analogy with the techniques of chemistry, Wundt and his colleagues tried to analyze people's consciousness into "elements of consciousness," just as chemists analyze compounds into their component elements. They proceeded by trying to lay bare the contents of the person's mind through the technique of introspection. Subjects, or observers, were carefully trained in an effort to ensure that their introspection was as precise and accurate as possible.

As a result of this work, Wundt proposed a *three-dimensional theory* of feeling and emotion. The three dimensions he suggested were *pleasantness-unpleasantness, excitement-quiet,* and *tension-relaxation.* Wundt thought that these three dimensions would be sufficient to describe any emotion, just as pure tones can be specified in terms of the tonal attributes of loudness, pitch, density, and volume (see Chapter 12). Wundt's particular theory gradually lost its influence, however. A major problem was that some other psychologists studying emotion by the introspective method—even some of those trained by Wundt—did not agree with his three-dimensional schema. Intense debates failed to resolve the question of which analysis of the mind was more valid. The debates intensified, and there were no signs that agreement could be reached. At the same time, however, American behaviorism, which involved a complete retreat from the question of the internal states of an organism's mind, was growing, and Wundt's influence faded.

Figure 17.7
The semantic differential technique, developed by Osgood and his associates, is an objective method of rating words, people, or objects to determine their emotional dimensions. The stimuli are rated on a number of bipolar dimensions, which are then analyzed to yield two primary dimensions: evaluation (good-bad) and intensity (active-passive). The words rated here describe emotions. Boredom, for example, is seen to be very passive and rather bad; but not as bad as guilt, which is seen as a more active emotion. One interesting application of the procedure was the administration of the semantic differential to a woman suffering from the dissociative type of hysterical neurosis, multiple personality. Different scores were obtained from the patient during each of her three separate personalities. Read her case history in Chapter 15.

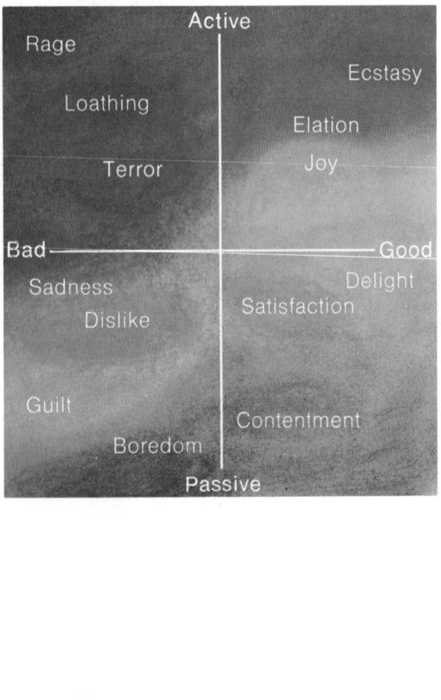

The Dimensions of Emotional Experience

Despite the eclipse of Wundtian introspection, the search for the dimensions of emotional experience has not ended. Some psychologists continue to feel that it is profitable to develop a classificatory scheme to reduce the seemingly limitless vocabulary of feeling and emotion—in other words, to try to reduce the thousands of different emotions into dimensions, much as Wundt had attempted to do. Much more sophisticated means than simple introspection are now available. For example, the statistical technique called factor analysis may be used to seek patterns of correlation among various emotions, in order to isolate the basic factors of a complex emotion. With factor analysis and other techniques a number of research studies have been carried out since Wundt's time to see if emotional experience can be adequately described along just a few dimensions. According to R. Plutchik, two basic dimensions seem to recur consistently: an *evaluative dimension,* corresponding roughly to Wundt's pleasantness-unpleasantness dimension, and an *intensity dimension,* which cuts across Wundt's other two dimensions and is today usually called the *activation level.*

The way in which these two basic dimensions are used to describe emotion is illustrated by studies by J. Block and Plutchik in which people were asked to rate words describing emotion using C. Osgood's semantic differential. People rated the emotion words on several dozen of Osgood's adjective scales. Each scale consisted of two adjectives with opposite meanings placed at the ends of a seven-point rating scale. The adjective scales included such diverse items as wet-dry, complex-simple, small-large, good-bad, and active-passive. Statistical analysis showed that most of the ratings could be explained in terms of the two dimensions of evaluation and intensity. Figure 17.7, adapted from one of Plutchik's studies, shows how emotion words can be located on both of these dimensions at the same time. For example, "rage" is rated high in intensity but toward the "bad" end of the evaluative scale.

A classificatory scheme like that described by Figure 17.7 is useful in showing that emotion can be measured and discussed objectively; in addition, it helps to emphasize that although the vocabulary of feelings and emotions is very large, all of the terms in it could be placed somewhere in the "emotional space" shown in the figure. On the other hand, the mere fact that an emotion, such as "terror," can be located on a graph does not mean that "terror" is now understood. What is known is merely that "terror" is a word that most people judge to be more active than passive and more bad than good. People may differ greatly on how they would classify a given emotion and would certainly offer greatly different answers if asked, "What does terror mean to you?" Similarly, any word, not only words associated with emotional experiences, can be placed on the graph in Figure 17.7, as Osgood and his colleagues have shown. For example, "power," "chimpanzee," and "president" could all be placed there. This possibility implies that emotional behavior, rather than being unique, has much in common with nonemotional behavior. We shall see that the similarity of judgments of emotional and nonemotional behavior holds even with more complicated schemes than Plutchik's.

Figure 17.8
Charles Osgood has made many significant research contributions in the areas of human communications, cognitive processes, and learning theory.

Overt Bodily Expressions

In judging emotions in everyday life we frequently want to be able to go by criteria other than verbal reports. Often we judge the emotions of others not entirely on the basis of what they say but also on clearly observable behavioral changes. A person's voice may be relaxed, tense, or angry. He may laugh or cry. His fists may be clenched or his hands may tremble. His whole posture may change. Above all,

Figure 17.9
Our bodies communicate emotions, sometimes more clearly than our words. The woman's fist here, clenched around the pen, may indicate that she is under stress, even though she may be saying nothing about it. The man's hunched shoulders, wrinkled brow, and hands covering his mouth seem to show that he is hearing or seeing something unpleasant. Yet, he may say no words that voice his reaction.

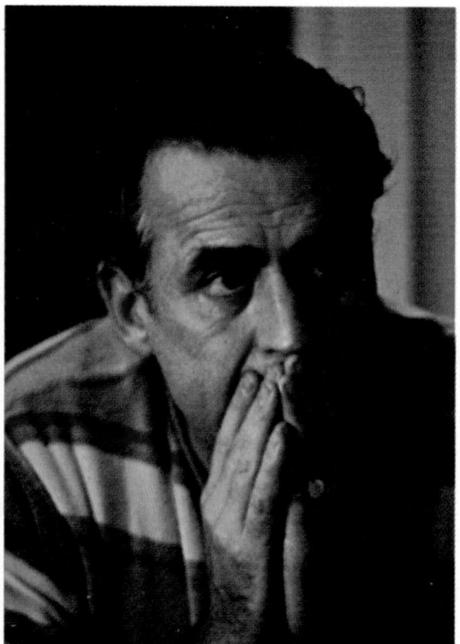

Figure 17.10
Emotions can be inferred from the expressions on dogs' faces. The expressions of the animals in the top row become increasingly aggressive, as revealed in part by their perked-up ears. In the bottom row, fear is the predominant emotion, as revealed in part by the laid-back ears. The extreme fear and rage evident in the dog at the bottom right is likely to occur only when the dog is facing a hated or greatly feared enemy and is unable to flee.
(After Lorenz, 1966.)

we rely on changes in facial expression for clues to a person's emotional experience.

According to Charles Darwin, many of the features of emotional expression are inherited patterns with survival value. The startle pattern to a sudden stimulus, for example, may help the organism jump away from danger. Many aspects of emotional expression in humans are analogous to those in other animals. For instance, the growling and baring of teeth in dogs may be analogous to the grimace of human beings.

Children do not begin life expressing emotion in the same way that they will later. The emotional reactions of children show an increasing complexity and differentiation over the first two years of life. At birth infants display only a generalized excitement or quiescence. By the end of the first year, an observer can tell the difference between fear, anger, delight, and elation. By the end of the second year, more complex emotions, such as affection and jealousy, can be observed.

Some of the changes consist of a shift of old reactions to new stimuli, but the

Figure 17.11
The photo at the far left shows negative emotion on the face of an infant just a few months old. As observers, we are uncertain whether he is exhibiting fear, anger, or discomfort from being wet or hungry. The children's emotions in the other two photos are much more clearly identifiable. Each child is about two years old. We can infer sadness and perhaps some resentment in the pouting boy in the middle, whereas the facial expression of the boy on the right clearly reveals his exuberant joy.

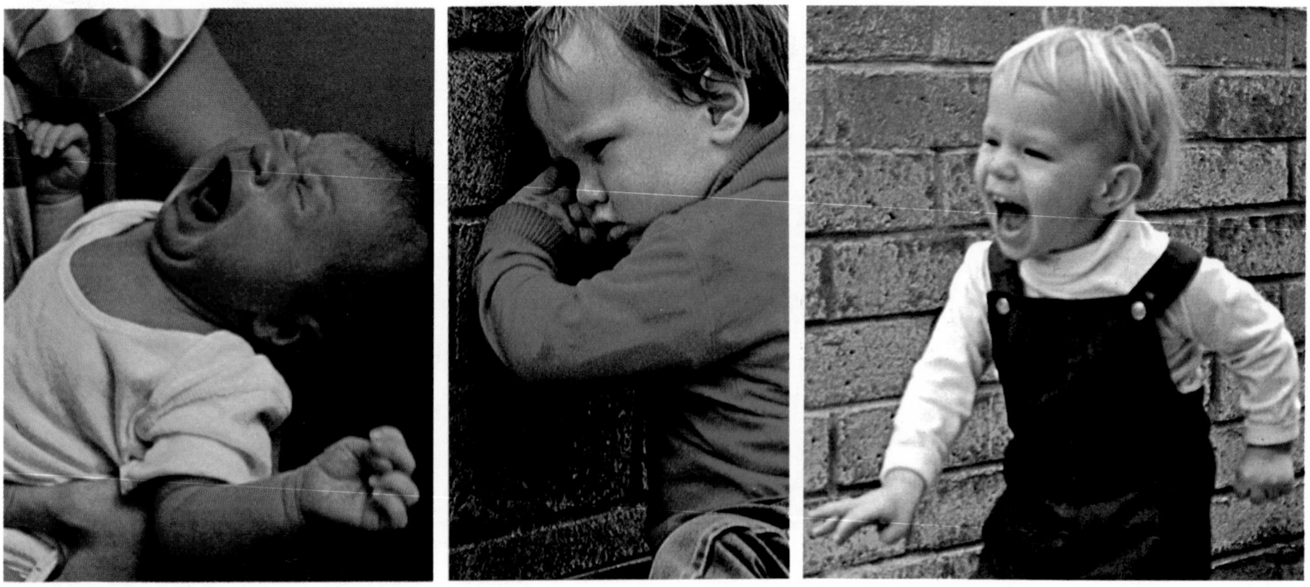

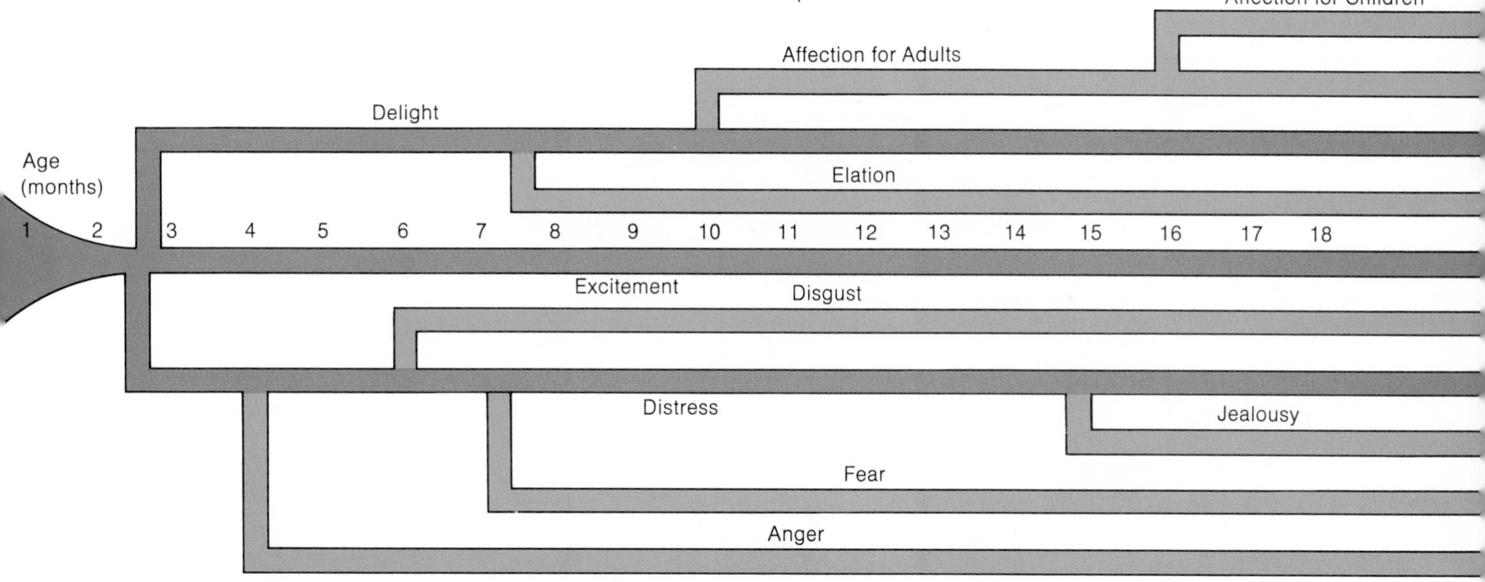

Figure 17.12
Diagrammatic representation of the increasing differentiation of emotions during the first year and a half of life. (After Murray, 1964.)

emotional reaction itself also shows a change during development. For example, in infants, anger or a reaction to frustration becomes differentiated from general distress at about three months of age. At this age, anger is shown by a change in the tone of crying, increased breath holding, and vigorous leg thrusts. Near the end of the first year, the child's face becomes flushed and he screams when thwarted. A little later, true temper tantrums appear. Finally, at about eighteen months of age, children show anger toward other people by hitting them and by behaving obstinately.

Are the various forms of overt bodily expression innate or learned? Many of the patterns, such as laughing, crying, and frowning, appear to be universal and require little learning. Some of the emotional patterns are the same in children born deaf and blind as they are in normal children. On the other hand, most of the patterns can be modified by learning. Some actors can cry on command. Some people learn to maintain a fixed smile no matter what their internal feelings. Moreover, there are cultural differences in facial expressions. People from one culture do not understand all of the facial expressions of people of another culture.

It is also difficult sometimes to judge the facial expression of a member of one's own culture when it is the only clue to the person's emotional state. Look at the faces in Figure 17.13. Is the woman exhibiting ecstasy or pain? Is the man surprised or afraid? Fortunately, most facial expressions can be interpreted more readily, and, in any case, we seldom have to judge emotion entirely on the basis of facial expression. Verbal behavior, posture, gestures, and situational cues round out the picture. Although we are given some cues in the woman's photograph—she is prone and seems to be undressed—we can still interpret her expression in a number of ways. If the photograph showed her full length, with a cast on her leg, we would immediately interpret her expression as one of pain. The situation or context is often as important for understanding as the facial expression itself. Chapter 23 describes some of the ways in which situation and context affect people's behavior.

Facial expressions were studied extensively by R. S. Woodworth and H. Schlosberg. Woodworth developed a scale for measuring facial expressions. The scale turned out to be circular, as shown in Figure 17.14. Schlosberg had observers judge seventy-two photographs from an earlier study by J. Frois-Wittmann along the dimensions of "pleasantness-unpleasantness" and "attention-rejection." On the basis of these scale ratings Schlosberg was able to place each of the seventy-two poses on the appropriate point within the circle.

T. Engen, N. Levy, and Schlosberg suggested that, in addition to the di-

Figure 17.13
It is often difficult to judge emotions from facial expressions alone. For example, with nothing but these photographs to judge from, would you say that the woman is expressing ecstacy from sexual pleasure or pain in childbirth? Is the man displaying fear or surprise?

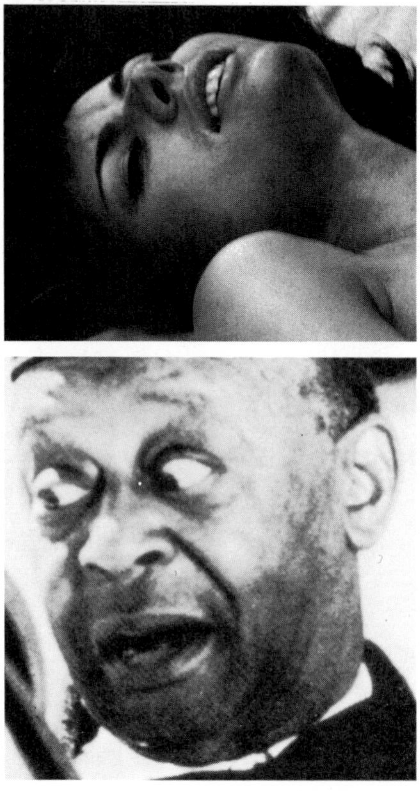

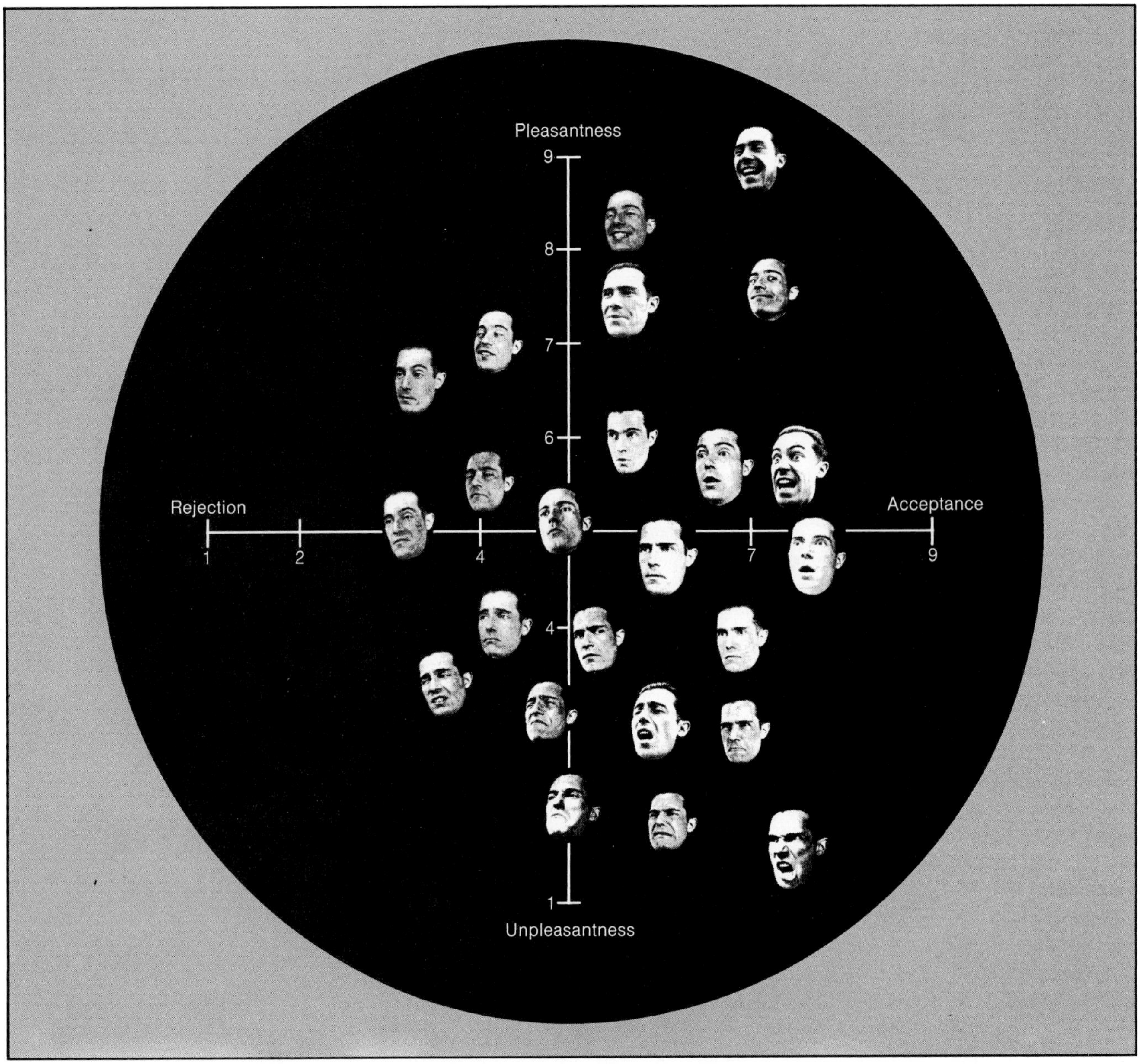

Figure 17.14
In this particular placement of the pictures of Frois-Wittmann, Schlosberg arranged the photos to reflect errors in judgment made by the persons trying to determine what emotion was being expressed. The faces closest to the center reflect the greatest number of errors. Note that the faces more distant from the axes show stronger emotions.

mensions of "pleasantness-unpleasantness" and "attention-rejection," a dimension of "sleep-tension" was required to describe the full range of facial expressions. Recently, a comprehensive series of studies by the Dutch psychologist N. Frijda have shown that three dimensions are, in fact, required to represent people's judgments of facial expressions, especially when a wide range of facial expressions are considered. Using sophisticated statistical techniques, Frijda found that he had to rename the second and third dimensions suggested by Engen, Levy, and Schlosberg. The three dimensions that he settled upon are *pleasantness-unpleasantness, attention-disinterest,* and *certainty-uncertainty.* Osgood has shown that such a three-dimensional structure represents people's judgments generally, not only their judgments of facial expressions. In research with the semantic differential, he has found that three dimensions appear consistently: an evaluative dimension like pleasantness-unpleasantness, an intensity dimension like attention-disinterest, and a strength dimension like certainty-uncertainty. Evidently, the two-dimensional analysis of emotion words mentioned earlier is accurate as far as it goes, since it includes the first two of these dimensions, but it is incomplete, since it omits the third.

SYSTEMATIC TREATMENTS OF EMOTION

Two systematic approaches to emotion not only are historically important but have also been influential in shaping modern theory. The first stems from the great American philosopher and psychologist William James. The second approach is known as *activation theory*, a term coined by D. Lindsley. Lindsley has contributed extensively to the knowledge of the electrical activity of the brain and its role in behavior. A discussion of these two approaches will prepare the way for a discussion of a more recent theory of emotion, developed largely by S. Schachter and G. Mandler.

The James-Lange Theory

William James and Carl Lange proposed that an emotional response precedes an emotional experience. In other words, emotion *results from* rather than causes the behavior generally associated with emotion. "We are afraid because we run; we do not run because we are afraid." The James-Lange theory was influential mostly because many people did experiments aimed at refuting it. Although the results failed to overturn the theory completely, they did develop into a significant body of knowledge about emotion. The James-Lange theory was important also for emphasizing that emotion has a physiological component: We are afraid because our hearts beat fast, our stomachs knot up, and so forth.

Although the James-Lange theory has been soundly battered, it has also turned out to contain more than a grain of truth. Some recent research that seems to support part of the theory is discussed later in this chapter.

Cannon's Criticisms W. Cannon, an American physiologist, strongly attacked the James-Lange theory. One of his major criticisms addressed the contention that emotion resulted from preceding visceral arousal (controlled by the autonomic nervous system). Cannon noted that organisms deprived of sensory input from the viscera continued to manifest emotional behavior. For example, if the input to the visceral nerves of dogs is severed, they continue to show emotion. Therefore, emotion can occur without visceral input.

Cannon also noted that the visceral changes accompanying emotion are too diffuse to account for the differentiated emotions that we experience. Although more recent experiments by A. F. Ax and others have shown that it is sometimes possible to differentiate certain emotions, such as fear and anger, by their patterns of physiological reaction, such differentiation among emotions is not generally possible.

Other Difficulties A further difficulty with the James-Lange view is that emotional experiences often occur quickly, whereas bodily responses, especially visceral responses, often occur more slowly—too slowly to cause the emotions.

Another criticism of the James-Lange hypothesis comes from G. Marañon's study. He injected people with adrenalin, which increases visceral activity. According to James and Lange, these people would be expected to show signs of heightened emotionality. Although the expected physiological changes occurred, the subjects did not report emotional arousal. If the conscious experience of emotion were simply a reflection of prior physiological changes, then drugs that produce those changes should also produce the conscious experience.

Arnold's Theory Some theorists feel that too much emphasis has been placed on experienced emotion, body reaction, and behavioral activity. M. Arnold believes that these elements are used only for secondary appraisal of emotional reactions. The primary source of emotional arousal has an important cognitive component: stimulation from the external environment is perceived and evaluated by the individual in light of past experience.

Arnold has suggested a sequence of events constituting an emotional reaction. The steps are perception, appraisal, emotion, bodily change, secondary appraisal, and, finally, action. Take the example of a person who is driving a car at high speed when one of the tires blows out. In the first part of the sequence, *perception,* the driver hears an explosive sound and feels an immediate change in the car's motion. In *appraisal* the driver realizes that a rear tire has blown and that the car is going out of control. In the *emotion* part of the sequence, the driver feels an almost overpowering urge to escape by leaping under the dashboard. In the step of *bodily change,* the driver's heart begins to pound, and his hands begin to shake so that they can hardly hold the wheel. In *secondary appraisal* the driver notices the bodily changes and decides that they amount to a panic that may be fatal. In the *action* stage, the driver makes a great effort to control the incapacitating bodily reactions and bring the car safely to a stop.

Arnold feels that past research has emphasized the second half of the sequence and that therefore the first half of the sequence should be the focus of future research.

Activation Theories

Activation theory is a general view that emotion represents a state of heightened arousal rather than a qualitatively unique process. The activation continuum extends from deep sleep to extreme agitation, as in rage.

The first activation theory of emotion was put forth by W. Cannon and P. Bard. They held that conscious emotion results from an upward discharge to the cerebral cortex from the thalamus, which they considered to be the "seat of emotions." Their theory, like that of James and Lange, tried to pinpoint the determinants of conscious experience. The most important aspect of the Cannon-Bard theory was not its emphasis on the thalamus—which was largely misplaced—but its contention that emotions serve an *emergency function* by mobilizing the organism for action. It was thus a forerunner of modern activation theories.

The term "activation theory," as noted earlier, was coined by D. Lindsley. The essence of Lindsley's theory is that the reticular system must be activated in order for emotional behavior to occur. As indicated earlier, the reticular system apparently serves a general energizing function, whereas limbic-system structures are responsible for organizing the input into particular emotional expressions. Lindsley showed that emotional behavior is accompanied by changing patterns in the electroencephalogram (EEG). For example, emotion is characterized by a change in the EEG pattern from synchronized (alpha) rhythms, which are associated with a relaxed state, to low-amplitude, fast-activity brain waves. The same pattern, however, also accompanies sensory stimulation and problem-solving behavior. In other words, emotion always involves activation, but it is presently impossible to distinguish between EEGS showing emotional activation and those showing nonemotional activation. The difficulty in making this distinction in EEGS actually reflects problems in activation theory more generally, since the theory tends to equate emotion and activation.

A Recent Approach

S. Schachter has developed a promising approach to emotion that incorporates some of the strong points of prior theories without adopting their flaws, and this theory has been elaborated by G. Mandler.

Schachter's work is in the same tradition as Marañon's pioneer experiment, which sought to produce emotion by drug-induced visceral changes. Most of Mara-

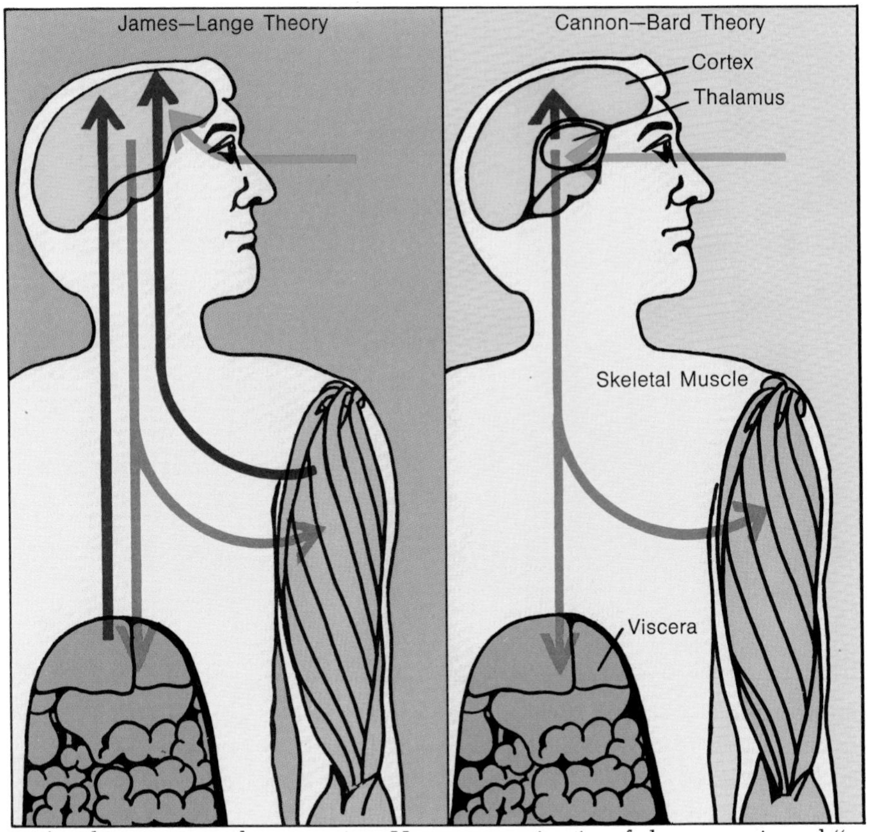

Figure 17.15
Diagrams illustrating the difference between the James-Lange and the Cannon-Bard theories of emotional arousal. The James-Lange theory stated that visceral cues in response to a stimulus preceded and caused the conscious experience of emotion. The Cannon-Bard theory proposed that the thalamus was "the seat of emotions," and that, in response to a stimulus from the outside, the thalamus sent impulses to both the cortex and viscera; the experience of emotion coincided with the arousal thus produced.

ñon's subjects reported no emotion. However, a minority of them experienced "as if" emotions: they reported feeling "as if" they were afraid. Schachter and J. Singer reasoned that their responses may have been determined by the cognitive element in their appraisal of the situation. Marañon's subjects might have decided that whatever emotions they were feeling were only the result of the adrenalin injection and might therefore have discounted them. If so, people *uninformed* about the effects of the drug should experience emotion.

To test that idea, some of Schachter and Singer's subjects were misinformed about the side effects of the adrenalin injection. For example, they were led to expect numbness and aching in parts of the body instead of the tremors and palpitations associated with adrenalin. Other subjects were correctly informed about the expected side effects. This group of subjects was thus roughly equivalent to Marañon's. Finally, other subjects received injections of *saline* instead of adrenalin, thus serving as a control group. All subjects except the control group should have had equivalent visceral arousal, but only some of them could attribute their arousal to the expected side effects. The misinformed people could not easily attribute their visceral arousal to the drug.

If visceral cues are implicated in emotion but their interpretation depends on situational factors, such as the social situation, then environmental stimuli might be the deciding factor in whether visceral cues are interpreted as a particular emotion. Schachter and Singer manipulated the social environment by varying what happened during a twenty-minute interval between the injection and testing. Each subject was joined in a waiting room by a confederate of the experimenter, who was posing as another subject. In one condition the confederate was ebullient; for example, he might crumple up some paper and practice tossing it into a waste-paper basket while acting happy and light-hearted. In another condition, the confederate was unpleasant and irritable.

The experimenter observed the subjects through a one-way mirror and then gave

Figure 17.16
These cartoons depict the subjects' reactions in Schachter and Singer's classic experiment in emotion. The experimenter at the top is communicating an expectancy inconsistent with the actual effects of the adrenalin injection he is giving; below, he tells the subject what the drug actually does. Both subjects waited with another person who they thought was another subject but who was really a confederate of the experimenter; this person appeared to be affected euphorically by his injection. Only the subject depicted above, who was misinformed about the effects of his injection, was affected by the confederate's jolly mood.

the subjects questionnaires about their emotions to fill out. The results showed that the emotions of people who had received adrenalin and had been misinformed about its effects were strongly affected by the confederate's behavior. The misinformed subjects receiving saline injections were less likely to behave like the confederate, and their reported emotions were also less affected by the confederate's behavior. It appears that internal visceral cues do play a role after all. Otherwise there would have been no difference between the saline-injected and the adrenalin-injected misinformed subjects. Finally, the informed subjects—like the saline-injected control group—were also less likely to be influenced by the social situation, that is, by the confederate's behavior.

Thus, as William James originally suggested, visceral cues do play a role in determining the experience of emotion. But there is also an interpretational component in the experience. Interpretation is influenced by factors like the social situation provided by the confederate in the experiment and the person's expectations, such as those determined by the experimenters' instructions. The informed people in both Marañon's and Schachter's experiments discounted their visceral cues because they could attribute them to "side effects" of the injected drug.

In a later study Schachter injected different people with different drugs in order to vary the level of visceral activity. The people watched a slapstick movie and were observed to see whether their expressions of amusement correlated with their degree of visceral activity. The correlation was positive: the more visceral activity, the more amusement expressed at the slapstick movie.

The way in which situational stimuli can alter the cognitive appraisal of an environmental situation and thus one's emotional reaction was also demonstrated in a series of experiments by R. Lazurus and his colleagues in which a movie was shown of the puberty rites of the Arunta, an Australian tribe. In the film several tribal elders hold a boy down and perform a subincision operation on him: an opening is made on the underside of his penis with a stone knife. Most viewers normally react not only to the boy's obvious pain but to the castration implications of surgery on the genitalia. The film is very successful at arousing emotion. Viewers report strong feelings, and physiological measures, such as heart rate, show a strong response.

Experimenters manipulated the appraisal of the Arunta movie by adding different sound-track commentaries to the original silent film. The emotional response, in terms of both reported feelings and internal physiological changes, was greater with a commentary in which the painful and disturbing aspects of the boy's experience were emphasized. The emotional response to the movie was less with either of two other commentaries. One, relying on intellectualization, was a cool, detached analysis of the procedure as a social custom. The other used denial; the painful aspects of the ceremony were minimized and its joyful aspects emphasized. Some types of people—in particular, college students—responded least emotionally to the sound track employing intellectualization, whereas others—businessmen, for example—responded least to denial.

Such differences in appraisal of a situation explain why some people react to a stimulus with little feeling and other people react with great fear. For example, one person may approach a public-speaking engagement calmly, but another may be so fearful as to be unable to go on. The first person sees the situation as a simple task to be accomplished, but the second person may construe the occasion as an evaluative one in which he or she may fail.

Differences in people's emotional reactions to a situation might also result from learning an emotional response to an inappropriate object. For example, behaviorists have shown that a neutral object can take on emotional qualities if the object is associated with an emotional reaction. J. B. Watson and R. Raynor's famous experiment with Albert, an eleven-month-old boy, is one example. The child was shown a white rat. He showed no signs of fear of the rat and even tried to play with it. Then, the experimenters sounded a loud noise just behind the child's ear whenever they showed him the rat. Albert cried and became upset after the loud noise sounded, and gradually he began to show upset as soon as he saw the white rat. Furthermore, the upset, presumably fear, generalized to other white and furry objects, such as a rabbit, a fur piece, and a man with a beard. (Fortunately, what can be learned can be unlearned; conditioned fears of this sort can be removed by processes such as systematic desensitization, which is discussed in Chapter 33.) This study raises a question that will recur later in this unit, that of the relationship between emotion, motivation, and learning. Is the fear described here just an emotion, is it a drive capable of producing new learning, or both? The problem of how one would go about deciding this issue is one that has occupied many experimenters and no doubt will continue to do so for quite a while to come.

SUGGESTED READINGS

DARWIN, C. *The Expression of the Emotions in Man and Animals.* Chicago, University of Chicago Press, 1965. This classic work, first published in 1872, illustrates and describes the range and method of emotional expression in both animals and man..

JAMES, W., and LANGE, C. G. *The Emotions.* Baltimore, Williams & Wilkins, 1922. A collection of three works by these early pioneers: one defining emotion, the other two setting forth the theory associated with James and Lange.

MANDLER, G. "Emotion," in *New Directions in Psychology,* Vol. I. New York, Holt, Rinehart and Winston, 1962, pp. 267–343. An excellent review article that covers much the same areas as does this chapter, but in greater detail.

MURRAY, E. J. *Motivation and Emotion.* Englewood Cliffs, N.J., Prentice-Hall, 1964. A good, short introductory survey of emotion and motivation and the relation between them.

SCHACHTER, S., and SINGER, J. E. "Cognitive, Social and Physiological Determinants of Emotional State," *Psychological Review,* 69 (1962), 379–399. The important new work that takes account of cognitive components of emotional states. This landmark study has opened up a promising area of investigation in emotion.

18 Elementary Concepts of Motivation

The average American housewife is so conscious of vitamins these days for herself and her family that it seems a shame humans have no clear drive for them, as for hunger and thirst. In fact, it almost seems that our taste for food is in inverse proportion to its vitamin content. The American humorist Robert Benchley, brooding over the vitamins in spinach and sunlight, suggested that scientists make an effort to find them in chocolate cake and shade. (I'm in sympathy with that viewpoint.) In the absence of a physical drive for vitamins, it is not surprising it was difficult to get the concept across in the first place. The reason for the absence of drive is that in a natural, varied diet, the vitamin supply is ample.

In 1747, the Scottish physician James Lind considered the fact that the disease scurvy was always found at times and in places where the diet was limited and monotonous over long periods of time—as in ocean voyages, for instance, where, in the absence of refrigeration, only a few kinds of food could be stored. Lind practiced on scurvy-ridden sailors, of which there were a plentiful supply, and found that some fruits and vegetables helped relieve the situation, with citrus fruits doing the best job. Captain Cook, on his voyage of exploration across the Pacific from 1772 to 1775, took note of this and kept his crew scurvy-free by enforcing the regular eating of sauerkraut.

So this was the situation:

1. Every navy on Earth found the problem of scurvy an acute one. This was most true of the British navy, which was the largest, the duties of which were most far-flung, and the average voyage of which endured longest. And the British knew that a scurvy-ridden flotilla could not fight a naval engagement with hope of winning—and knew further than on the efficiency of the fleet rested the security of the British nation.
2. Captain Cook had traveled all over the watery Pacific for three years and had lost not one man to scurvy. Not one. Nor was Cook's voyage something obscure. On the contrary, he was the most famous explorer, in his own lifetime, the world had yet seen. So well-known was he, and so highly regarded, that Benjamin Franklin had no difficulty in persuading the struggling United States, fighting for independence, to agree to make no effort to interfere with Captain Cook. His were the only British vessels that could pass by Yankee privateers with impunity.

Well, then, with British security at stake and a simple preventive at hand, how long do you suppose it took the British Admiralty to wipe out scurvy on board British warships?

Twenty years! It wasn't until 1795, when war with revolutionary France was heating up, that the Admiralty got off its collective rear end and ordered daily rations of lime juice for British sailors. It might have seemed sissified, but I'm sure that anything at all that was different would have been welcome on board ship. There were three results: First, British sailors, and the British generally are called "limeys" to this day. Second, the Thames area in London, where the crates of limes were stored for loading aboard ship is still called "Limehouse." And, oh yes, third, scurvy was wiped out. I. A.

Suppose you deprived a rat of all water for a day or so, then turned it loose. What would you expect the animal to do? Search for something to drink, of course. But why would the rat do that? To answer "Because it is thirsty" is to embark on a circular line of reasoning, for thirst is usually defined as a condition that occurs in an organism when it has been without water for a while.

The real question, then, is what *is* this thing called thirst that makes an organism get up off its haunches and hunt for something to drink? To put the problem another way, how does the organism know that it wants water rather than, say, food or air or sex?

When circumstances deprive an animal of a substance necessary for life, the animal has a *need* for that substance. The need exists whether or not the organism is aware of what it lacks, or even aware that something is lacking. In most organisms, including man, a biological need brings about internal changes that cause the organism to fulfill the need. If you had to describe the behavior of a rat that needed water, you might say that the animal seemed *driven* to find liquid. The existence of a need often elicits a *drive*. Drives are very compelling. Until weakness sets in, virtually nothing will dissuade a thirsty animal from its search for water, and shipwrecked sailors have been known to fight to the death for it.

Not all physiological needs produce drives. The ones that do produce drives tend to be needs that must be met on a regular basis if the organism is to survive, such as the needs for water and food. Less common or less crucial needs often do not produce drives. For example, an animal with pernicious anemia may need to eat liver but not be driven to choose it. Furthermore, not all drives are based primarily on physiological need. The sex drive, for example, operates much more independently of physiological need than do the hunger and thirst drives. An organism can survive and even remain healthy without sex; if it is an organism high on the evolutionary scale, the way it reacts to the sex drive depends more on learning and prior experience (as opposed to physiological factors) than does behavior motivated by hunger and thirst.

In this chapter we shall consider what is known or suspected about motives that appear to be elementary—that is, motives that we can admit sharing with rats and other animals. We leave what appear to be more singularly human motivational considerations for the next chapter. The approach used in this analysis of elementary motives, based on the work of C. Hull, N. Miller, K. Spence, and many other behaviorists, is generally known as *drive theory.*

THIRST

Water deprivation leads to the creation of a drive we call thirst, but merely giving it a name does not explain it. In order to understand motivational states, we must look at the changes that take place inside an organism when a need occurs and a drive results. Because the thirst drive has been thoroughly studied, it will be discussed first and used to introduce some general points about elementary drives.

To remain alive, the body needs the proper amount of water—too little or too much is fatal. The only land animals that have survived are those that evolved some way of regulating the amount of water in their bodies—that is, those that are able to maintain *homeostasis.* Homeostasis, which in Greek means "same position," refers to the general level of physiological functioning that characterizes a healthy organism, such as normal heart rate, blood pressure, and body temperature, as well as normal amounts of water in the blood.

When homeostasis is disturbed, certain physiological mechanisms are set in motion that restore equilibrium. If an animal is short of water, mechanisms that conserve it start to function. For example, an antidiuretic hormone (ADH) is released that causes the kidneys to reabsorb water, producing a more concentrated urine. If the body has too much water, the secretion of ADH is inhibited and the urine is less concentrated than usual.

The release of ADH is a physiological adjustment to the need for water. Animals also adjust to needs behaviorally. To illustrate, here are four major behavioral adjustments that occur in response to thirst.

1. The greater the deficit in water, the more of it an animal will consume.

2. When an animal is thirsty, the presentation of water during operant conditioning will reinforce the response that produces the opportunity to drink. (If the animal is not thirsty, the presentation of water is not a reinforcer.) This illustrates a general point: motivation determines what events will be reinforcing.

3. Again during operant conditioning, the greater the deficit in water, the more successful the response reinforced by water is in excluding the performance of responses motivated by other drives. The strength of the response reinforced by water has a number of consequences: the animal is more likely to choose water than food, sex, or other goals; it is more likely to pay attention to stimuli associated with drinking in the past; aversive stimuli such as electric shocks must be stronger to keep

it away from water; it is more likely to accept bitter water. In addition, if the animal has learned a number of different ways to get water, the tendency to perform all these responses is strengthened by a deficit in water.

4. The thirstier the animal is, the more signs of frustration and emotional disturbance it shows when behavior that has led to water in the past is blocked or no longer reinforced.

Why Use the Words "Thirst" and "Drive"?

If thirst were produced in only one way—say, by depriving an animal of water—and had only one effect—say, an effect on the amount of water drunk—there would be no need for a concept like thirst. It would be simpler to say that the more hours an animal has been deprived of water the more water it will drink. The situation is diagramed in Figure 18.1, where it is obvious that the diagram with the single arrow is simpler.

But thirst has more than one effect on behavior, as just discussed. And it can be produced in several ways: not only by depriving an animal of water, but by feeding it dry food or by injecting a salt solution into its veins. This situation is diagramed in Figure 18.2. Using thirst as an intervening variable, as in the bottom diagram, is clearly simpler than relating each cause to each effect, as in the top diagram.

For similar reasons, we speak of "hunger" instead of merely relating hours of food deprivation to amount of food eaten. Hunger produces a cluster of effects that are functionally similar to the effects of thirst (except that food is substituted for water). Indeed, there are a number of these analogous clusters of effects, which is why it is useful to have the general concept of drive.

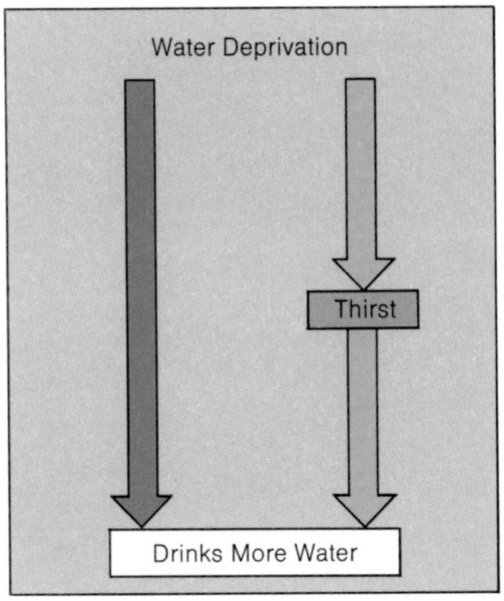

Figure 18.1
In this example the number of hours of water deprivation is the manipulated independent variable, and the amount of water consumed is the dependent variable. Because these operations are so readily measurable, the intervening variable of thirst actually is not necessary here.

Mechanisms of Thirst

Most of us take for granted that a thirsty animal tries to get water, drinks, and stops before it is dangerously waterlogged. But what physiological mechanisms cause it to do this? Considering this question gives us a deeper appreciation for the way the

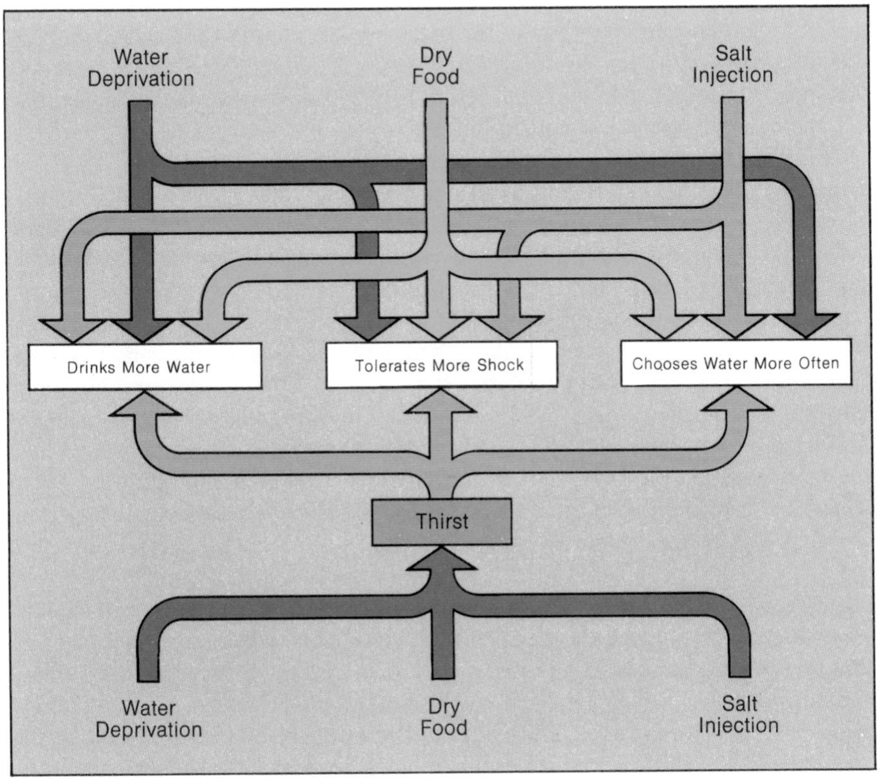

Figure 18.2
Among the factors that can produce drinking behavior, in addition to water deprivation, are the ingestion of dry food and the intravenous injection of saline solution. Animals that have been subjected to one of these three conditions show common behaviors under experimental conditions—for example, they will do something that will get them water even in the face of an aversive stimulus like electric shock and they will increasingly perform behaviors that in the past had been rewarded by drinking water. If one were to relate all these variables to each other without using the intervening variable "thirst," the result would be the complicated diagram at the top of this figure. Using the intervening variable simplifies the conceptualization, as shown in the bottom part of the figure.

body adapts to the environment. It also shows how scientists go about discovering the mechanisms that operate during adaptive behavior.

Receptor Cells in the Brain Normally, the blood and other body fluids of mammals contain approximately 0.9 percent salt. As the body loses water, the percentage of salt goes up, and the tendency of the body fluids to attract water (their osmotic pressure) rises with it. When E. B. Verney made the blood in the brain slightly saltier by slowly injecting a salt solution into the carotid artery, he found that the change caused the hormone ADH to be secreted so that the kidneys formed less urine and the body retained more water. He therefore hypothesized that the brain contains *osmoreceptors,* specialized nerve cells that regulate water balance by responding to osmotic pressure.

It has long been known that an injection of hypertonic saline solutions (containing more salt than the body's normal 0.9 percent) into the blood causes satiated animals to drink. B. Andersson used this fact to test the idea that Verney's osmoreceptors in the brain might be responsible for thirst. Using goats as subjects, he implanted tiny tubes in the preoptic area of the hypothalamus where the cells that secrete ADH are located, thinking that a likely place to look for the osmoreceptors. When he injected fluids through the tubes, he found that a 0.9 percent saline solution had no effect, but that even a tiny amount of 2 percent solution caused the goats to drink eagerly. Injections into other parts of the brain had no effect on drinking. These results support the hypothesis that specialized receptor cells in the hypothalamus control drinking.

In order to rule out the possibility that Andersson's injections elicited an automatic drinking reflex rather than producing the same effects as natural thirst, N. Miller used a similar procedure with moderately thirsty cats. He found that the cats drank more after an injection of 2 percent saline solution than after no injection and that they drank less after an injection of pure water. These were not mere reflex effects, because the saline injection also increased the rate at which the cats performed behavior reinforced by water, whereas the injection of water decreased the rate of responding. In other words, the organized behavior of the injected animals was the same as it would have been if motivated by natural thirst. If the injection had merely triggered a drinking reflex, drinking behavior would have changed but not the rate of behavior reinforced by drinking.

Further experimentation recently reported by D. Quartermain and N. Miller shows that injections of a chemical called carbacol into an area in the hypothalamus also produce thirst. Minute injections of the chemical caused rats that had been satiated with water to drink for about twenty minutes—a long time for an animal that is satiated when it starts. The experimenters wondered whether the twenty-minute drinking bout might be a short-term effect of the carbacol injection rather than a response to a condition similar to normal thirst. So they prevented the rats from drinking for twenty minutes after the injection. If the animals did not seem thirsty after the delay, then the twenty-minute post-injection drinking could be attributed to short-term effects of the injection. But the rats did seem thirsty. When the waiting period was over, they drank heartily for about twenty minutes. Their behavior is consistent with the notion that chemically-induced thirst is satisfied in the same way as normal thirst.

Stop-Mechanism Although the amount of water in the blood rises fairly rapidly as a thirsty animal drinks, there is a time lag. Does the body have any mechanism that prevents the animal from drinking more than is needed? Experiments on dogs and rats have shown that there is a quick-acting stop-mechanism, activated partly by the volume of water in the stomach. This mechanism adjusts the amount of water consumed to the amount that is needed. In addition, it reduces the animal's tend-

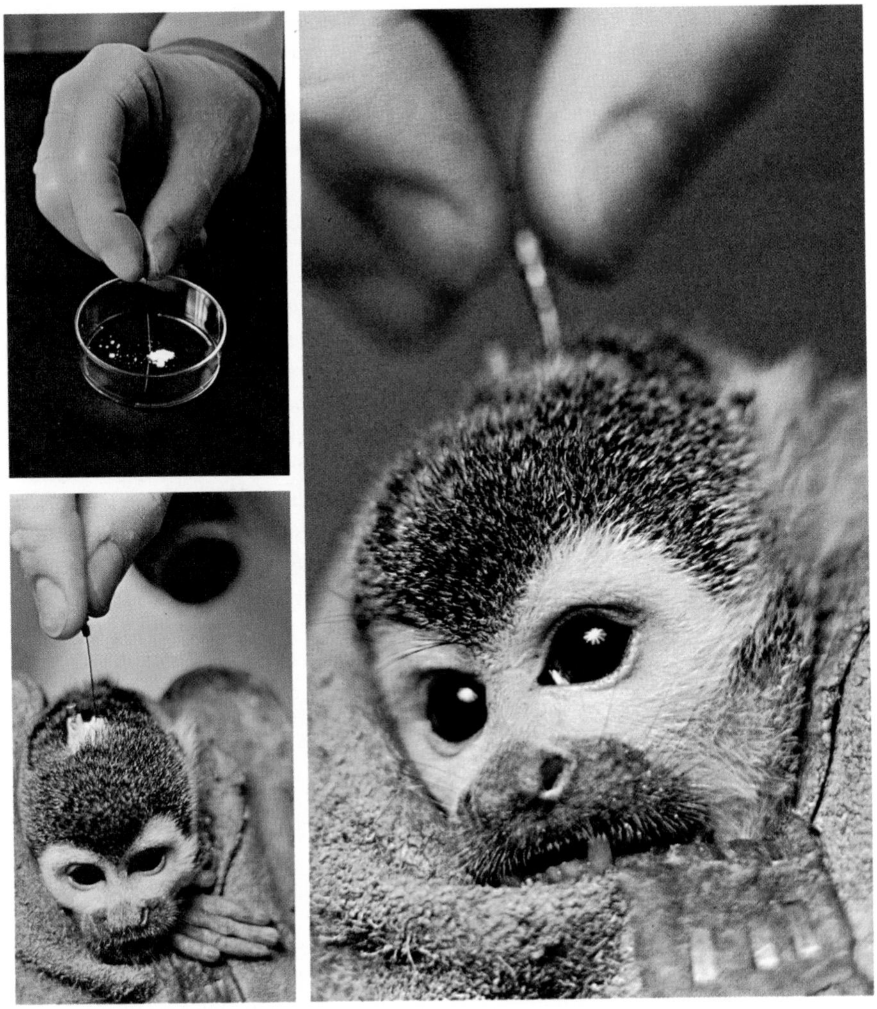

Figure 18.3
The physiological psychologist is shown drawing a very small amount of a chemical and then introducing it into a specific area of the monkey's brain via the cannula. A stereotaxic atlas, which is essentially a map of the head of each species of animal, guides the researcher in reaching the specific brain structure with the implant. The behavioral effect depends upon the nature of the solution and the exact site reached. The results of chemical brain stimulation generally confirm those of electrical stimulation. Andersson's work in stimulating the hypothalamic drinking areas in the brains of goats using salt solutions was the pioneer research with this technique.

ency to work for water (that is, it reduces the reinforcing properties of water) and the animal's willingness to drink bitter water. The mechanism stops the whole cluster of effects that stem from thirst.

HUNGER

You can ignore the stop mechanism for thirst with impunity, at least up to a point. If you usually drink about five glasses of water a day but tomorrow started drinking about six, you could keep drinking six daily for the rest of your life without bringing on any dramatic physical changes. But if you started overeating by as little as two ounces of your normal diet a day, you would probably gain more than a hundred pounds in less than three years. Undereating by two ounces a day could cause you to lose weight at the same rate.

An organism needs to eat enough food for growth, tissue repair, and meeting daily energy requirements, but not so much that it becomes overly fat. The body must therefore have a very finely tuned mechanism for regulating how much food is ingested. Although the mechanism is not always set exactly as its owner (or its owner's doctor) might wish, it seems to be quite difficult to reset: overweight people often have trouble losing any weight at all, and underweight people find it hard to gain. Apparently, once an individual's weight-control mechanism has been set, it takes strenuous efforts to change it.

Hunger is the word used to describe a cluster of effects produced by food deprivation. These effects, which are similar to the effects of water deprivation, usually go together. In general, the longer an animal has been deprived of food, the more it will eat, the more easily it can be taught new behavior with food reinforcement, the more vigorously it will perform the behavior, the more likely it is to eat or look for food in preference to other activities, and the stronger is the punishment required to keep it away from food.

Mechanisms of Hunger

We know quite a bit about certain areas of the brain that are involved in regulating eating. For example, rats with lesions in a part of the hypothalamus called the ventromedial nucleus will overeat until they reach the sorry state of the animal shown in Figure 18.4 whose weight is three to four times normal. But although such rats overeat on tasty food that is easy to get, they do not show other symptoms of increased hunger. If an experimenter requires them to press a lever to get food or puts heavy weights on the lids of the food dishes, these rats eat less than normal animals. Their restraint is not due to muscular weakness from the operation that produced the lesion, for making the food bitter by adding quinine or requiring the rats to take a mild electric shock in order to get it also cuts down their eating more than it does that of normal rats; in addition, their eating does not increase as much as normal animals' after a brief fast.

In sum, lesions in this area of the brain seem to make the rats less responsive to their internal need for calories and more responsive to environmental factors that

Figure 18.4
This rat ate itself into this condition because experimenters made a lesion in the ventromedial nucleus of its hypothalamus. Its condition is called *hypothalamic hyperphagia*. Electrical stimulation of the same area produces the immediate cessation of eating in otherwise normal hungry animals. It seems, then, that the ventromedial nucleus contains a mechanism that is at least responsible for the cessation of eating.

facilitate or deter eating. In human beings, tumors that damage the ventromedial nuclei on both sides of the hypothalamus also cause overeating and obesity. Such tumors are extremely rare, but many considerably overweight people nonetheless show behavior patterns similar to those of rats with ventromedial lesions.

In an ingenious experiment, S. Schachter asked fat and lean people to rate the flavor of two large bowls of ice cream. He told them that they should feel free to eat as much or as little from each bowl as they needed to make their decision—an attempt to keep their attention off the topic of food intake, which fat people are often sensitive about. One kind of ice cream, called bitters, was mixed with quinine and did not taste good. The other was the best ice cream Schachter could find. The lean subjects took about a spoonful of each from each bowl; the fat subjects barely touched the bad-tasting ice cream but took huge amounts of the tasty kind.

In a related experiment, R. Nisbett arranged to leave each of his subjects (some overweight, some not) alone for lunch in a room with a plate of sandwiches and a refrigerator. The plates held different numbers of sandwiches for different subjects, but all subjects were told that there were plenty more in the refrigerator and were asked to help themselves if they wished. The lean subjects tended to eat the same number of sandwiches regardless of the conditions, leaving some on the plate if they had been given too much and going to the refrigerator for more if they had been given too little. The fat subjects ate what was set before them. Most of them ate all the sandwiches on the plate even if there were a lot but did not go to the refrigerator if the plate held only a little.

These and other experiments show that at least some obese people seem to respond to the sight and taste of food and that normally lean subjects seem to respond to their caloric needs. There are several possible explanations for this finding, and further research is needed to evaluate them. The fact that the behavior of Schachter and Nisbett's overweight subjects resembles that of rats with ventromedial lesions suggests that the hypothalamus is involved, but it bears repeating, for the benefit of the overweight, that it does *not* imply tumors or brain damage.

Dual Control by the Hypothalamus Destroying the ventromedial nucleus causes rats, cats, and monkeys to overeat; stimulating the nucleus causes a hungry animal to stop eating. In a nearby area of the hypothalamus (Figure 18.5), destruction on both sides of the brain causes animals to stop drinking as well as eating, so that they die. The possibility that they stop eating as a secondary result of extreme thirst can be ruled out, because they will not eat even if given plenty of water by tube feeding. Electrical stimulation in this area, which is called the *lateral hypothalamic feeding-drinking area,* causes satiated animals to eat (and often also to drink). The eating is not a mere gnawing reflex, for careful experiments by E. E. Coons show that it has all the functional properties of the normal hunger drive. For example, the stimulated rats are motivated to learn a new response, such as pressing a bar that delivers a pellet of food. The drive that stimulation produces is very strong: the rats will continue eating food made so bitter by quinine that it is refused by animals that have been deprived of food for seventy-two hours, and some of them overeat so much that they gain a third of their weight in less than three weeks (the equivalent of a 50-pound gain for a 150-pound man).

These experiments indicate that hunger is controlled by a balance between excitation from the lateral hypothalamus and inhibition from the ventromedial nucleus (although it is known to be influenced by other parts of the brain as well). Dual control through excitation and inhibition is characteristic of many activities of the nervous system.

The precise relation between the ventromedial and lateral centers is not clear. B. Hoebel and his associates conducted a series of studies in the late 1960s that supported the notion that the ventromedial nucleus acts by inhibiting the lateral

Figure 18.5
The schematic frontal section (top) and the cross section (bottom) illustrate the anatomical relationship between the hypothalamic areas involved in the regulation of eating. Experiments indicate that hunger is controlled by a balance between excitation from the lateral hypothalamus and inhibition from the ventromedial nucleus.
This kind of dual control, in which activity in one hypothalamic area initiates behavior, while activity in another area abolishes it, also occurs in the hypothalamic regulation of sexual behavior, behavior associated with temperature control, and aggression.

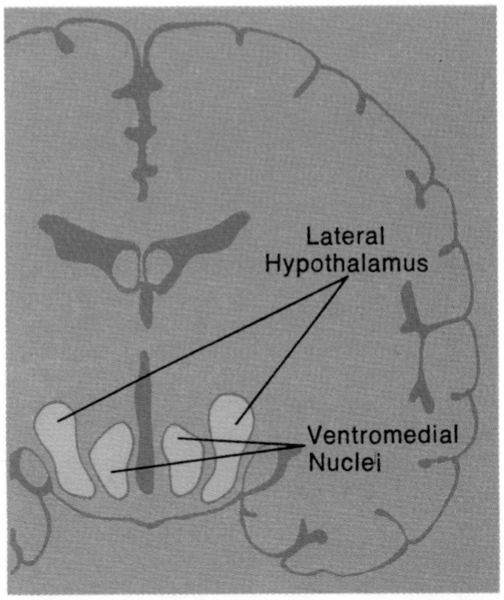

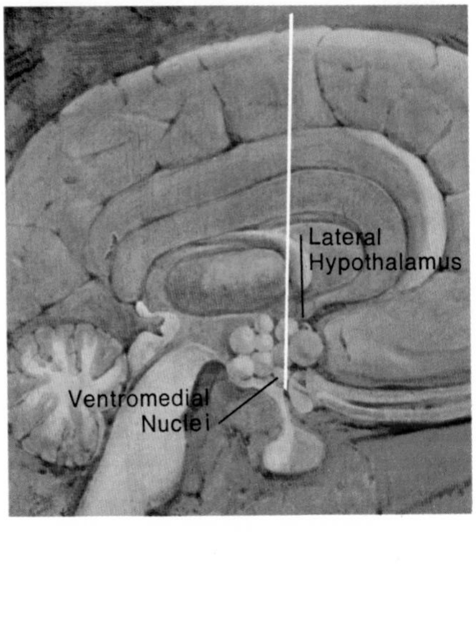

nucleus. They implanted electrodes in the lateral (excitatory) centers of animals and allowed the animals themselves to control the stimulation. Immediately after surgical destruction of the ventromedial (inhibitory) center, the animals increased the rate of stimulation to the lateral hypothalamus. In other words, they *added to* the voracious hunger resulting from the ventromedial lesions by increasing self-stimulation of the eating center. This behavior certainly fits well with the notion that the ventromedial nucleus inhibits the lateral hypothalamic nucleus.

The relation is pictured in Figure 18.6, although the figure is from a more recent study, performed by N. B. L. Ferguson and R. E. Keesey in 1971. Ferguson and Keesey went beyond the previous work of Hoebel and his associates by measuring self-stimulation not only right after destruction of the ventromedial center but for six days. As Figure 18.6 shows, they replicated the earlier finding that self-stimulation increased during the three hours after the operation. They found, however, that the self-stimulation rate *declined* after the first testing session, eventually dropping to or even slightly below the stimulation rates maintained by a control group of rats without lesions. This suggests that ventromedial lesions, rather than reducing inhibitory activity once and for all, change the setting of the mechanism responsible for weight maintenance. A normal animal maintains its weight at a certain level. An animal with a ventromedial lesion maintains its weight at a higher level. (It should be repeated, however, that animals with lesions are less strongly motivated to eat than normal animals. They eat more than normal animals when food is easy to get and tasty, but they will not maintain their higher weight level if they must expend effort to get food or tolerate food flavored with bitters.)

Lesions in the lateral hypothalamus—the excitatory center—seem to have a similar effect. Keesey and his associates have shown that animals with lesions in that eating center, if they are kept alive during the postoperative period during which they do not eat at all, will later maintain themselves at a body weight substantially lower than normal.

Stop Signals From Stomach and Mouth Because it takes quite a while for food to be digested and absorbed, there is an obvious need for some kind of short-term control to prevent an animal from killing itself by eating too much at a single meal, as extremely hungry cattle sometimes do when they get into a cornfield.

Some control comes from receptors in the stomach. Food injected directly into the stomach promptly reduces not only eating but other measures of hunger, such as the rate at which the animal will work for food. Distending the stomach with

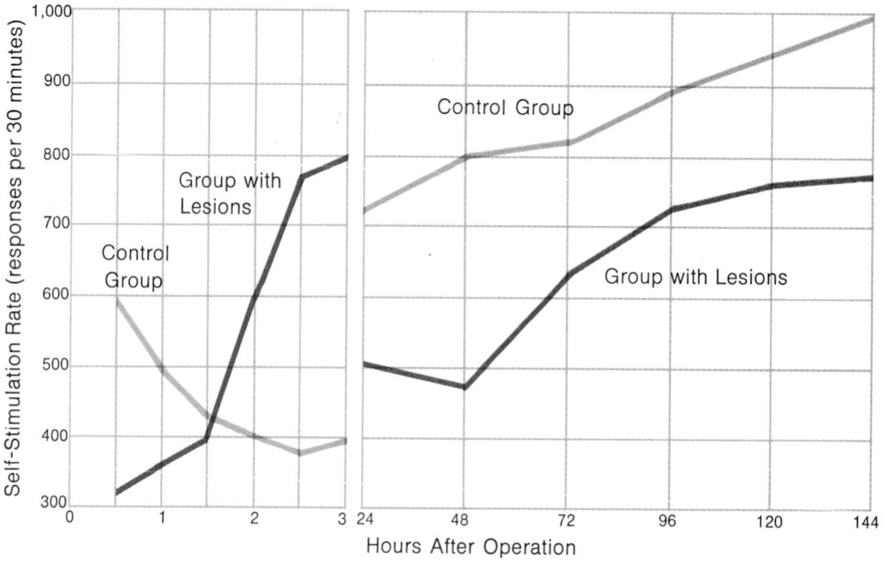

Figure 18.6
These data indicate that in the regulation of eating behavior the ventromedial nucleus of the hypothalamus acts by inhibiting the lateral hypothalamic nucleus. By pressing a bar the animals were able to control the amount of stimulation delivered to the lateral hypothalamus. Following ventromedial lesions, responding for lateral hypothalamic stimulation was greatly increased. This increase, however, disappeared as a function of time.

a balloon does not produce as great an effect. Also, a hungry rat will learn to go to the side of a T-maze where food is injected into its stomach in preference to the side where an equal amount of saline solution is injected. But if an equal amount of stomach distention is produced by inflating a balloon when the rat chooses one side, it learns to avoid that side. Apparently the stomach receptors do not rely on distention alone, since they can tell the difference between food, saline solution, and a balloon.

Food taken by mouth produces an even greater reduction in hunger, as measured by the rate at which the animal will work for food and the amount of bitter quinine required to stop it from eating, than does food injected directly into the stomach. As with thirst, there seems to be a metering mechanism operated by receptors both in the mouth and the stomach that helps put an end to a meal.

Blood Chemistry A rat can be forced to overeat and become fat in a number of different ways—by tube-feeding it large meals, by giving it injections of insulin (one of the hormones important in the body's transformation of sugar into energy), or by electrically stimulating the lateral hypothalamus. If the treatment is stopped after the animal has been made fat by any one of these means, it will virtually stop eating until it has lost most of its excess weight. How does the brain know that the body has too much food?

In one ingenious experiment, G. R. Hervey used parabiotic rats (rats surgically coupled like Siamese twins; see Figure 18.7). In such rats there is some exchange of blood and body fluids, although the rate of exchange may be slow. Hervey found that when one member of the parabiotic pair had lesions in the ventromedial nucleus of the hypothalamus, it overate and became fat. Its partner, meanwhile, stopped eating and wasted away until it died. His interpretation was that the tissues of the fat rat were sending some sort of signal into the bloodstream to tell the brain to stop eating, but that the signal either was not received by that rat's brain or was misunderstood because the ventromedial nucleus had been destroyed. The rat with the normal brain apparently received the signal all too well.

Recent work by J. Davis and his associates has demonstrated that the satiety signal is carried by chemicals circulating in the blood and that, probably, a hunger signal is not. The experiments used a technique for blood mixing, developed by Davis and N. Miller, in which the blood of two rats is intermingled until the mix in each animal is about fifty-fifty. One strong point of the technique is that it can be used with unanesthetized rats, so hunger can be tested immediately following the blood crossing.

If blood composition controlled both hunger and satiety signals, what would result from mixing the blood of a hungry rat with that of a satiated rat? The hungry rat would eat less than usual while the satiated rat would eat more than usual. Indeed, the two animals should eat about the same amount, even though one has been starved for, say, twenty-four hours, while the other has just been fed to satiety. But they do not. In Davis' studies, the food-deprived animals (that received blood from satiated donors) did reduce their food intake to roughly half what it would have been without the transfusion—and the reduction corresponds to the amount of blood obtained from the satiated donor. On the other hand, satiated rats that received blood from hungry rats ate no more than usual. This evidence points to a satiety signal but not a hunger signal in the blood, which is consistent with the earlier findings from studies of parabiotic rats.

In a later experiment, Davis found that the satiety signal seems to disappear about four hours after eating. When the blood of a very hungry rat (deprived of food for twenty-two hours, say) is mixed with that of a moderately satiated rat (satiated two hours before, say), the hungry rat eats somewhat less than it otherwise would. But the blood of a rat satiated four or more hours before the transfusions

Figure 18.7
These two rats have been joined so that they now share each other's blood and body fluids. This technique is used to determine whether hunger and satiety signals are carried by chemicals circulating in the blood or by the transmission of neural impulses.

no longer affects the hunger of a twenty-two-hour deprived rat. Under natural conditions, rats usually eat a meal about every four hours during the day, so it seems safe to assume that a rat satiated four or more hours before is beginning to get hungry. Nonetheless, it is interesting that the blood of a slightly hungry rat reduces the eating of a very hungry rat not at all.

Specific Hungers

Most animals are quite good at selecting an adequate diet for themselves. Given a wide enough choice, both laboratory and various domestic animals (rats, cows, pigs, chickens) eat foods that not only provide enough calories to maintain normal weight but contain the vitamins and minerals needed to maintain health. Even human infants, in some ways the most helpless of all animals, seem to be able to do this. When newly weaned babies are allowed to choose from an array of foods, most of them select a fairly balanced diet. (It should be mentioned, however, that no harmful foods are offered to children in experiments of this kind, so they cannot go too far astray.)

Many animals also develop *specific hungers* if their diets are deficient in particular substances or if their bodies need extra amounts of them for some other reason. Human beings, rats, and many other species eat extra amounts of salt when they need it; in Chapter 13, we mentioned a three-year-old boy who ate tablespoons of salt because his adrenal glands were not functioning properly. When rats are kept on a fat-free diet and then allowed to choose among fat, sugar, and wheat, they show a strong preference for fat. They also develop specific hungers for sugar, protein, riboflavin, sodium, calcium, phosphorus, and thiamine.

The specific hunger drive created in rats by a need for thiamine is particularly interesting: instead of developing a "mini-drive" to eat foods that contain the vitamin, the animals develop an *aversion* for the food eaten during the deficiency. The question of whether an animal with a thiamine deficiency develops a specific hunger for new foods or an aversion for the old, deficient one is important partly because it explains a formerly puzzling experimental phenomenon called *preference after recovery*. Even after a thiamine deficiency has been remedied, rats avoid the food that they ate during the deficiency. Since the deficiency no longer exists, it is difficult to explain the rats' behavior in terms of the reinforcing properties of the nondeficient food they do eat.

P. Rozin solved the problem by demonstrating that what develops is an aversion for the food eaten during the deficiency. As background, it should be mentioned that rats have a general distrust of new foods. Rozin presented thiamine-deficient rats with three kinds of food: the familiar one eaten during the deficiency, another familiar but nondeficient one, and a nondeficient food they had never tasted. If the deficiency caused a preference for new foods, the rats should have eaten more of the novel food than of either familiar food. If it caused an aversion, they should prefer the nondeficient familiar food to the others. As it turned out, they ate most of the nondeficient familiar food and least of the deficient food, confirming the aversion hypothesis. Another experiment of Rozin's provides further support for his conclusion. Rats will spill familiar thiamine-deficient food on the floor of the cage and gnaw on wood or the cage wires rather than eat the food, though they eat different food from the same container with enthusiasm.

Rats develop a similar aversion to toxic substances after as little as one encounter. Given the chance, they choose a familiar nontoxic food over a novel food but a novel food over the toxic food. The quick development of the aversion helps account for the difficulty of poisoning rats, especially wild rats. They tend to take a small taste of the poisoned food, go away for a while, get sick, and then refuse that food in the future.

Not all food preferences arise from nutritional needs, of course. B. F. Skinner reports working with pigeons that were particularly fond of marijuana seeds; Alice B. Toklas especially enjoyed hashish brownies. Doctors sometimes see patients who are "starving themselves to death" on candy, soft drinks, and so on. Psychological factors have a lot to do with food preferences, as they do with human eating behavior in general.

THE RELATION OF THIRST AND HUNGER TO TEMPERATURE

The various physiological and behavioral mechanisms that maintain homeostasis are closely related and often operate together. Their cooperation can be illustrated by describing what happens when the preoptic area of the hypothalamus is experimentally warmed and cooled.

Electrical recordings from microelectrodes show that the preoptic area has some nerve cells that fire more rapidly when their temperature is slightly raised and others that fire more rapidly when their temperature is slightly lowered. In order to study the functions of these cells, scientists have implanted in animals' brains fine tubes through which water can be circulated without discomfort to the animals; Figure 18.8 shows how the technique is carried out.

Using warm water to heat this area slightly has various effects, all of which are useful to an overheated animal. The blood vessels in the skin expand so that more blood comes to the surface and the animal loses more heat. It also pants and salivates, cooling its tongue and mouth by evaporation. Other brain cells in a nearby area function like tiny glands to secrete ADH, the antidiuretic hormone, so that a more concentrated urine is formed and the animal saves water it may need for evaporative cooling. It becomes thirsty, so that it is motivated to find and drink water. If the animal is hungry, it stops eating, which is adaptive because the processing of food would further raise its temperature.

Cooling the preoptic area has effects useful to a cold animal: constriction of the peripheral blood vessels; shivering; increased activity of the thyroid gland, which causes the body to create more heat by burning fuel faster; and hunger, which motivates the animal to find and eat food, creating heat and restoring the fuel deficits. Although all these activities would help warm up a chilled animal, in an experimental situation in which cooling is limited to this minute area of the brain they give the rest of the body a fever. This illustrates the dominance of the brain in regulating temperature.

This example shows that the brain functions as a sense organ, as a gland, as a control center for various responses, and as a source of drives such as thirst and hunger that motivate complex behavior. It also shows how all these functions work together in the regulation of temperature.

Abnormal temperatures also motivate behavior that is reinforced by the restoration of the normal temperature level. A person or animal may learn to go out into the sun when he is cold or go into the shade when he is warm. If shaved rats are

Figure 18.8
This rat's brain has been implanted with tiny tubes called cannulae. These tubes have been placed by a physiological psychologist so that their ends are in a precisely known location in the brain. This technique is used to circulate water at various temperatures to see what effects the temperature of various brain structures has on behavior.

placed in a refrigerator, they learn to press a bar to turn on a heat lamp; placed in a hot environment, they learn bar pressing to give themselves a cooling shower.

OTHER HOMEOSTATIC DRIVES

An excess of carbon dioxide is one of the main stimuli for deeper breathing. Try holding your breath for ninety seconds. A terrific drive is created, so it is not surprising that animals will learn a specific response, such as pressing a bar, in order to regulate the amount of carbon dioxide in the air they breathe.

Animals with an excess of water in their bodies will learn to avoid the side of a T-maze where they get an injection of antidiuretic ADH. But rats with an ADH deficiency, which makes it difficult for the body to get rid of excess salt, learn to go to the side where they get an injection of ADH. The hormone allows them to form a more concentrated—saltier—urine.

Although not all cases have been investigated, it seems reasonable to suppose that a potential drive is involved in most, and perhaps all, cases in which homeostasis is mediated by the central nervous system. In some cases, indeed, the behavioral adjustment may evolve before the physiological one. If goldfish are given a chance to regulate the temperature of the water in their tank, they keep it at about the level that produces the maximum rate of growth. If given the chance to swim about freely in a pond that has different temperatures in different places, they tend to swim to the places that have this optimal temperature.

instinctive needs

SEX: A NONHOMEOSTATIC DRIVE

The sex drive has a good deal in common with such drives as hunger and thirst. For example, an adult male rat will run a maze or work at some other response if rewarded by access to a receptive female. Eventually he will stop mating, as a satiated animal will stop eating. For a male, ejaculation is important if a sexual experience is to be maximally reinforcing, but there is evidence that other components of sexual activity can also serve as reinforcers. Even thirst is not a completely unitary drive, and there are specific hungers. Sex is also complex, and in fact may have more motivational components than, say, thirst or hunger.

Sexual behavior does not, however, seem to have the same homeostatic function as the drives considered so far. If an animal does not eat, drink, breathe, and keep its body temperature within a certain range, it dies. Sexual activity, though necessary for the survival of the species, is not necessary for the survival of the individual animal.

In lower animals, sexual behavior seems to be innately determined and rigidly controlled by sex hormones and the lower centers of the brain. Rats mate only when the female is in estrus (in heat), a hormonal event that occurs at the time of ovulation. At other times, the female is not receptive and the male is not attracted. The amount and type of sexual activity in the male vary considerably with the testosterone that is secreted by the gonads. Testosterone also seems to be related to behavior that is loosely labeled aggression.

In higher mammals, the glands play a less important role and the higher centers of the brain, where learning takes place, have more influence. Human beings mate at any time during the female menstrual cycle, regardless of when the female ovulates. The shift in control from the glands toward the cortex as one moves up the evolutionary scale helps explain why it seems more appropriate to regard sex as a drive based on physiological need in lower animals than in higher ones. Human beings certainly have a physiological need for sex, but sexual behavior is often more closely related to psychological factors than to physiological deprivation.

To date, most studies on the effects of sex hormones have concentrated on the innate patterns of sexual behavior. Much less attention has been given to the way hormones affect the sex drive—that is, the way sexual behavior is motivated; but what is known about innate patterns allows us to make fairly good guesses about the effects of hormones on sex drive.

Some interesting work has been done on the effects that injections of sex hormones have on the innate patterns of sexual behavior in lower mammals. For instance, there seems to be a certain critical period in the infancy of rats during which injections of male hormone into the female will produce "masculinization," eliminating female sexual behavior during adulthood. Whether anything more is involved than the elimination of the estrous cycle, which prevents the female from coming into heat, is not clear. Male rats castrated during a certain critical period of infancy show more female behavior, even when given hormone-replacement therapy in adulthood, than do males castrated later in infancy or given replacement therapy early in childhood. For rats, the critical period is shortly after birth. There is a similar period for guinea pigs before birth.

Sex hormones seem to be able to act directly on the brain. If the ovaries of female cats are removed, they do not show sexual receptivity. Implanting a small amount of a synthetic female hormone in the preoptic area of the brain, however, elicits prolonged and excessive receptiveness. A similar or even considerably larger implant under the skin or in other areas of the brain is ineffective. Injections of male hormone into the lateral preoptic area of either male or female rats elicits male sexual behavior in some cases. If the standard tests for motivation were applied, many of these hormone treatments would necessarily affect the sex drive, because they determine whether or not the sexual pattern appears. In addition, the treatments probably also influence more subtle aspects of the sex drive.

FEAR

Although most animal research on fear uses pain elicited by electric shock to arouse fear and many human fears clearly are also learned, fear can be aroused without any apparent conditioning or learning. For example, even in normal animals and human beings, loud sounds and sudden increases in stimulation also induce fear, as do strange and unexpected situations. As was reported in Chapter 4, chimpanzees can be terrified by a disembodied head or even by a well-known caretaker wearing a strange mask. Monkeys and chimpanzees have an extreme fear of snakes and snakelike objects. At certain ages, animals and children seem to develop a fear of strangers.

Just as certain patterns of stimulation may have an innate tendency to elicit fear, other stimulus situations seem to have an innate capacity to counteract it. It is much harder, for example, to frighten an infant monkey when it is clinging to its mother than when it is not. The same thing seems to be true of children.

Responses that allow a person or an animal to escape from fear are strongly reinforced and therefore can be learned quite rapidly. (See the discussion of escape and avoidance conditioning in Chapter 3.) Some responses learned this way are adaptive, but quite a few of them are maladaptive. For example, a student who is afraid of a crucial examination will be reminded of the examination and thus perhaps frightened when he opens his book to study for it. One way to reduce the fear is to close the book and look for something absorbing to do that will crowd out all fear-inducing thoughts about the examination. The student may become engrossed in a bull session, a game of cards, or a movie. The temporary immediate escape from fear reinforces the behavior. In this way, it becomes habitual for some students to avoid studying when they are frightened of a test, which is also when studying might be most useful. The fact that the fear can be escaped by turning away from signs of danger, besides being the source of a considerable amount of maladaptive behavior, is one of the weaknesses of trying to use fear to influence behavior.

Some responses, such as eating, seem to be incompatible with fear. Pavlov found that if a very mildly painful stimulus was used to signal an extremely hungry dog

Figure 18.9
The Harlows raised monkeys with surrogate mothers, constructions that were laid at about a 45-degree angle so that infant monkeys could cling to them. Some of the surrogate mothers were simply wire constructions; others were covered with soft terrycloth. The two top pictures show infant monkeys clinging to their terrycloth "mothers." One of the aspects of behavior the Harlows studied was fear. Normally reared infant monkeys when they are afraid will cling to their mothers (bottom two photographs) but will eventually explore a new stimulus if their mothers are close by. The Harlow monkeys that had been raised with the terrycloth mothers reacted much as normally reared monkeys, but those that had been raised with the noncomforting wire models remained afraid and would not venture out to explore the novelty.

that food was about to arrive, signs of emotional disturbance dropped out as salivation and other feeding responses became conditioned to the painful stimulus. Gradually, the pain could be increased without eliciting emotional disturbance. If the pain became too strong, however, the fear and other emotional responses returned. Other oral responses, such as thumb sucking, can reduce fear, which may be one reason it can be so hard to induce children to give it up. Complete muscular relaxation also seems to be incompatible with fear. In behavior therapy, it is used to help eliminate anxiety (see Chapter 33).

Experimental animals readily abandon a response originally reinforced by escape from fear when it is no longer effective in getting the animal away from the fear-inducing cues. On the other hand, fear itself is often extremely persistent. Figure 18.10 shows the responses of three rats to an experimental set-up in which they were formerly trained to escape shock by pressing a bar. During the period of time covered by the graph, no shocks were delivered, but the rats kept pressing

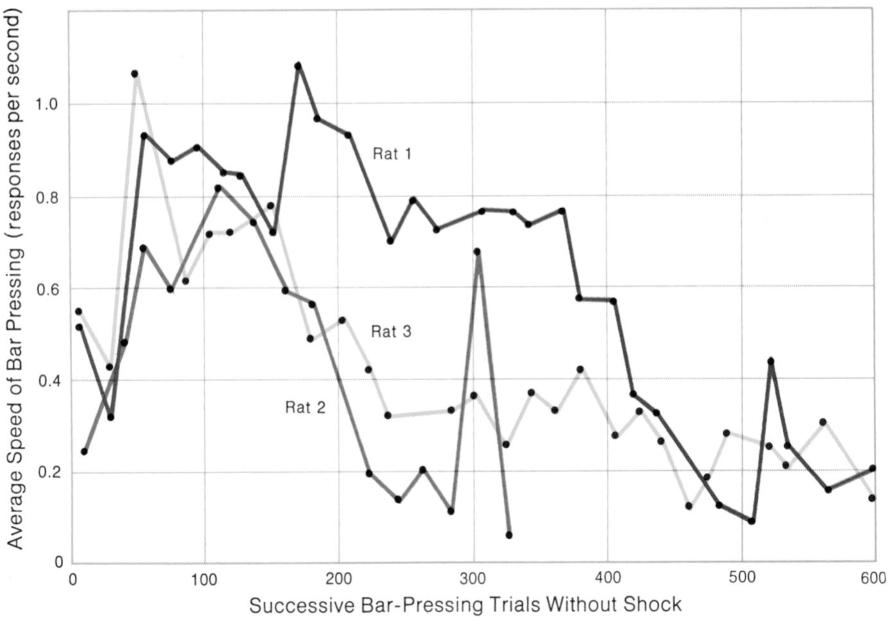

Figure 18.10

These curves show the gradual slowing of bar pressing in three rats that remained in a compartment in which they had previously been shocked and from which they had learned to escape by pressing the bar. Long after the rats had ceased receiving shocks, they continued to press the bar when they were placed in the compartment. The rate at which they pressed declined gradually over many trials.
(After Miller, 1951.)

the bar for roughly 200 trials before the response gradually extinguished. In other experiments, dogs have persisted for over 1,000 trials without showing any signs of experimental extinction. Extinction eventually does occur, if the experimenter is patient enough. How fast it occurs depends primarily on how dissimilar the conditions during extinction and learning are.

AGGRESSION

If a weak electric current is passed through an electrode implanted in a certain part of the hypothalamus of a cat (or a monkey; see Figure 18.11), the stimulation elicits a spectacular burst of aggression. The cat's hair bristles, its pupils dilate, its ears lie back, and the cat hisses and strikes out viciously at a stick or hand inserted into the cage. If there is a rat in the cage, the cat strikes and slashes it repeatedly.

Stimulation in a slightly different area does not elicit the emotional components involving hair, pupils, ears, or hissing but produces a silent, cold, stalking attack, in which the rat is seized by the neck with a bite that kills it by breaking its neck. This behavior is characteristic of a drive, for a cat stimulated in this way will learn to choose the arm of a Y-maze that leads to a goalbox containing a rat to attack rather than the arm that leads to an empty goalbox.

The foregoing experiments demonstrate two rather different types of aggression elicited by stimulation in two somewhat different locations in the cat's brain. As

Figure 18.11

At left, a monkey with an electrode implanted in its hypothalamus attacks another monkey as it receives electrical stimulation. At right you can see the apparatus strapped to the monkey's back through which the experimenter can deliver electric current by remote control.

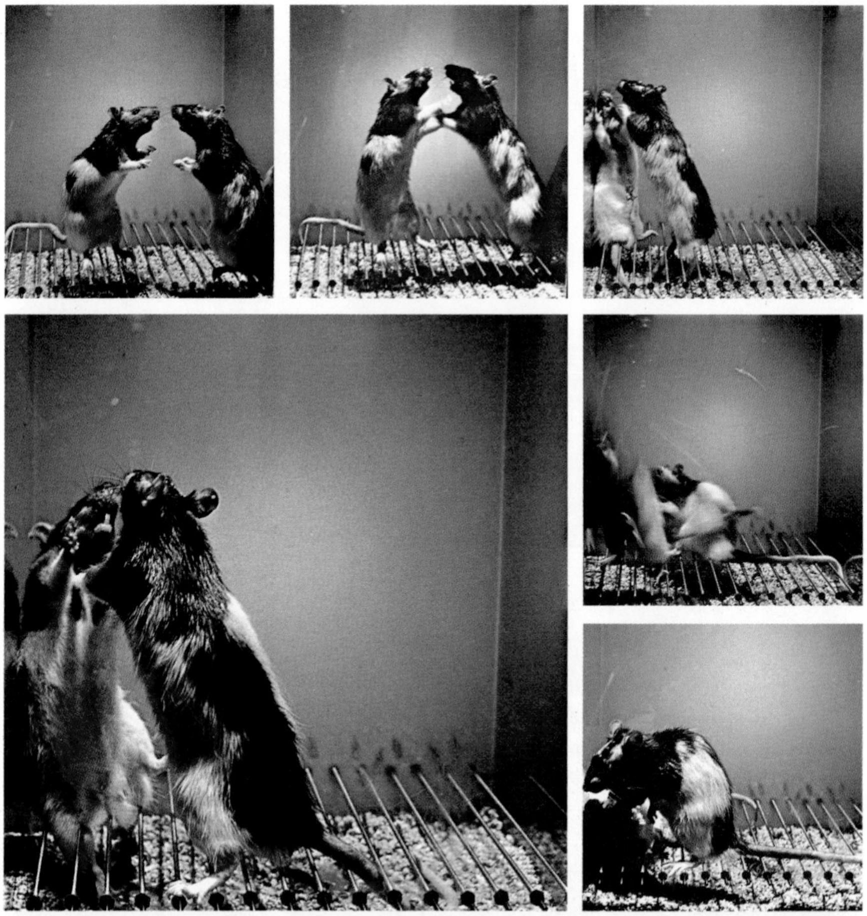

Figure 18.12
Rats that experience intense, inescapable shock, as shown here (the grid is electrified) will attack another rat in the cage. This series of experiments, carried out by N. Azrin, showed that if a doll and another rat are placed in the cage, the shocked rat will attack the other rat and ignore the doll. If, however, only the doll is placed in its cage, it will attack the doll.

Figure 18.13
Humans, as is well known, also engage in intraspecies aggression. The stimuli and reinforcements for human aggressive behavior are not as easy to pinpoint as they are in animals. Analogies can be drawn, however. For example, dominance hierarchies are known to exist on playgrounds. Also, cultural practices often reward a young boy's black eye as signaling his growing into the male role.

K. E. Moyer has pointed out, it is quite possible that there are other types of aggression. We do not yet know what they are or how much they have in common.

Aggressive responses can be elicited not only by electrical stimulation of the brain but also by stimuli that produce frustration or pain. Painful electric shocks will produce aggressive responses in rats: they will attack another rat or even a doll. Animals can be trained to fight by shocking them in the presence of other animals.

In a natural situation, social animals usually organize themselves into a dominance hierarchy. After a few aggressive encounters, the more dominant animals control the less dominant ones by mere threats. If a monkey around the middle of a dominance hierarchy is stimulated to aggression by an implanted electrode, it always attacks a less dominant monkey, not a more dominant one.

In general, male mammals seem to be more aggressive than females. Castration reduces their aggression. One should, however, remember the ferocity of some females in defending their young—a trait that is also characteristic of many human mothers.

SUGGESTED READINGS

COFER, C. N., and APPLEY, M. H. *Motivation: Theory and Research.* New York, Wiley, 1964. This book gives a particularly thorough account of the historical antecedents to current research in hunger and thirst and their physiological correlates.

DEUTSCH, J. A., and DEUTSCH, D. *Physiological Psychology.* Homewood, Ill., Dorsey Press, 1966. Provides an excellent overview of basic motivational states.

GROSS, C. G., and ZEIGLER, H. P. (Eds.). *Readings in Physiological Psychology: Motivation.* New York, Harper & Row, 1969. An excellent book of readings.

JONES, M. R. (Ed.). *Nebraska Symposium on Motivation.* Lincoln, University of Nebraska Press. The Nebraska Symposia on Motivation, available in paperback, provide an annual treatment of current topics in motivation by experts currently working in the field.

MOYER, J. E. *The Physiology of Hostility.* Chicago, Markham, 1971. An excellent treatment of physiological and behavioral work in the general area of aggressive behavior.

THOMPSON, T., and SCHUSTER, C. R. *Behavioral Pharmacology.* Englewood Cliffs, N.J., Prentice-Hall, 1968. An excellent overview of the effects of drugs upon behavior.

H

19 Human Motivation

FICTION WRITERS have to worry about human motivation as much as psychologists do. Every act of every one of their characters must have some understandable motivation behind it—one that is clear to the readers to begin with or that must be made clear if it isn't already so. And it's not easy to do this. I once wrote a science fiction story called "C-Chute" in which the entire point of the story hinged upon a motivation that I carefully kept hidden.

Briefly, the story deals with a space war in which a Terrestrial spaceship that has been taken by extra-Terrestrials is being carried off to internment for the duration. Imprisoned on board are six surviving unarmed and helpless Earthmen. The men debate measures to recover the ship from the two extra-Terrestrial soldiers who have been left in charge. After some discussion, it seems that the only chance of retaking the ship is through a course of action that is virtually suicidal for the one attempting it. Will someone volunteer to try?

Five of the six men had obvious motives for risking their lives. One was an idealist who would die for his ideals; a second was a patriot who would die for mankind; a third was pathologically afraid of the extra-Terrestrials and would do anything to get away; a fourth longed to be reunited with his fiancée back on Earth; and a fifth was sick with desire for vengeance over a brother killed by the extra-Terrestrials. None of them volunteered. There was the sixth, Mullen, a short man, unemotional, who had spent a couple of decades on some colony planet and had been on his way back to his native Earth for a visit. He alone made no high-sounding emotional speeches, but he volunteered, and the body of the story concerns itself with the step-by-step suspense through which he wins back the ship single-handed.

But why had *he* volunteered? I had carefully eliminated all the motives that I had deliberately made obvious in the case of the others. Clearly, if anything at all drove Mullen it would have to be something different and, presumably, something stronger. But what? I was sure that the readers would have more respect for me than to suppose he had no motive, that he was just a "good guy." Only two possibilities existed. There was either a legitimate strong motivation to which I had dropped a fair clue but that I had masked in some reasonable fashion. Or else it was a motive so strong and so universal that the reader ought to recognize and accept it without clues.

Finally, at the end of the story, a Mr. Stuart asks Mullen why he had volunteered when all the others, despite obvious motives, had not. Mullen explains that he was on his way back to Earth for his first visit in a long time and he could not let himself be interned.

" 'Mr. Stuart,' Mullen asked quietly, 'Haven't you ever been homesick?' " I. A.

Why are you reading this book? More generally, why does a person, presented with a choice among several possible ways of behaving or acting at a particular time and place, select one and reject others? How does she or he resolve conflict among choices? What factors account for the maintenance, vigor, and persistence of the chosen activity?

Answer the following questions about your reading at this time, and as you go on in this chapter, you may get a sense of how internal and external factors combine to help determine your acts and of how your activities change with changing factors within you, within the situation, and within the larger environment. What made you choose to read? How carefully are you reading? How much effort are you putting into it? How long will you keep at it? What would you do if a friend called and suggested going to a movie or for a pizza? What do you hope to get out of it in return for your effort? How do you think your expectations for a return compare with those of other people who are also reading the same book?

THE STUDY OF MOTIVATION

Psychologists studying motivation are primarily concerned with identifying and understanding the various factors that determine *goal-directed behavior.*

Goal-Directedness and Emotion

Goal-directedness is the key attribute of motivated behavior. Motivated behavior can perhaps best be described by its purposefulness and persistence until the goal

Figure 19.1
These photos illustrate William James' distinction between emotion and motivation. (Top) the men are apparently experiencing an intense *emotional* reaction of anger, but have not yet interacted physically. (Below) their *motivated reactions* take the form of aggressive behavior toward each other.

is reached. It can, at least indirectly, be assessed by how much gratification (emotion) is felt when the goal is reached. How much your feelings determine your actions or are determined by them, however, is a knotty problem. Psychologists have yet to resolve the very difficult question of the relationship between *emotion* and *motivation* that was raised in Chapter 17. It is probably fair to say that today most psychologists would hold that emotion and motivation are almost always, if not always, closely related.

In 1892, William James distinguished between emotion and motivation by arguing that emotional reactions terminated in the person's own body whereas motivated reactions resulted in an interaction with some object or person in the environment. This is consistent with James' distinction between a tendency to feel and a tendency to act. It is similar to the argument heard today that emotion can be distinguished from motivation by its lack of direction toward a specifiable goal (although emotion might itself be a "goal" toward or away from which some behavior is directed). But it remains unresolved whether our needs and desires (motives) are *determined by* the pleasure (emotion) that comes when the goals are reached or whether pleasure results only from the satisfaction of an urgent *prior* desire.

For example, if you feel good when you read and wonderful when you have completed a book, do you read because you want to feel good or do you feel good because you are actually reading?

In any case, the basic premise that has guided the study of human motivation since James and Freud is the idea that *all* behavior is motivated. Disagreements among psychologists have focused on such issues as whether the primary source of motivation is conscious or unconscious, biological or cognitive, and so on. Chapters 21 and 22 discuss and compare the positions of many personality theories in regard to motivation.

Figure 19.2
Harry Harlow's primary contributions to psychology have emerged from his extensive research with primates. He has studied the effects of early social deprivation on subsequent mothering; curiosity as a drive; and the formation of learning sets. Many of his findings seem to have direct implications for human child-rearing and educational practices.

Drive Theory

In some instances, especially in certain laboratory settings, you can be quite certain that your inferences are correct. For example, if you deprive a mouse of food for several days, your inference that the activities you see it performing are directed to the goal of getting food are very likely to be right. Many experiments of this type were described in the preceding chapter, which deals in part with behaviorist drive theory. The theory is based on the idea that an organism's reaction to some internal biological stimulus, or need, is the wellspring of most motivated behavior and that an organism would be largely inactive were it not for the stimulation supplied by such needs.

Intrinsic Motivation

Using various laboratory and nonlaboratory methods of studying the behavior of both animals and humans, several experimenters have gathered evidence that challenges this assumption in drive theory. These experimenters have been primarily interested in the causes of "spontaneous behavior," that is, behavior that is not a response to too much stimulation from external events (painful shock) nor to internal biological needs brought about or caused by deprivation. The activities of the organisms under study could not possibly be considered as directed toward the goal of homeostasis. D. E. Berlyne and H. F. Harlow identified the *curiosity drive;* K. C. Montgomery, the *exploratory drive;* and R. W. White, "effectance motivation," or *the drive for competence* (see Chapter 22). These psychologists and others like them found traditional drive theory insufficient to explain all goal-directed behavior in higher-order animals, especially in humans. Another important alternative motivational theory that was developed was *expectancy-value theory.*

Figure 19.3
Watching an electric train has been shown to be reinforcing for monkeys, because they will learn tasks or work to be able to do so. This phenomenon seems to support Harlow's concept of a curiosity drive.

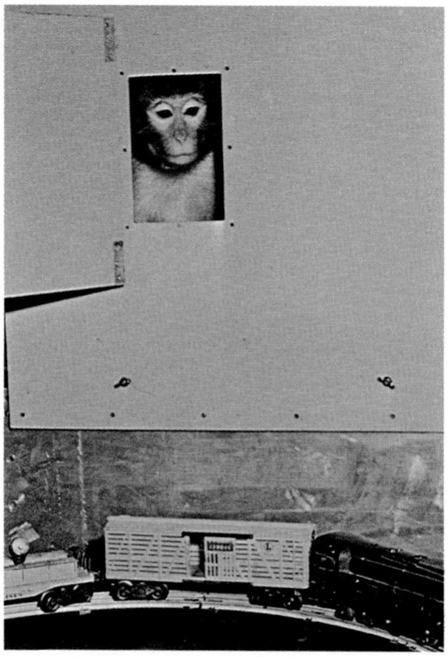

Expectancy-Value Theory

Expectancy-value theory had its origins in the work of E. C. Tolman, K. Lewin, D. McClelland, and J. Atkinson. At the core of this theory, which deals primarily with human motivation, are *affective* (emotional) and *cognitive* factors (especially one's cognitive expectancy of the consequences of an action). Researchers who take this approach are concerned with the feelings and thoughts that accompany people's actions. Many comprehensive studies of human motivation have followed this approach, and most of the work discussed in this chapter has been carried out by people within the framework of expectancy-value theory.

Motivation has only recently emerged as a respectable field of study distinct from the studies of learning and of personality. Learning theorists try to discover *how an organism acquires* a repertoire of potentially relevant actions or responses, and they try to determine how the availability of these responses can change with training and practice. The work of motivation theorists is to explain for whom and under what circumstances these responses, once learned and available, actually come to be expressed in (goal-directed) behavior. They try to discover how certain factors within a person (his motivational dispositions) and other factors in his environment combine in determining whether these dispositions will actually be manifested in his behavior. Some of the acquired motivational dispositions, or motives, which have been studied within expectancy-value theory include achievement, affiliation, power, fear of failure, fear of rejection, and fear of success.

MOTIVES

Motivation is defined as goal-directed behavior. The *particular* goals toward which an animal's or a person's behavior is directed depend partly on what the organism in question finds gratifying. Each organism can potentially find gratification in several kinds of activities. *The capacity to habitually gain gratification from a particular class of incentives is called a motive.* A motive, then, is a basic, stable personality characteristic.

The early cataloguing of basic motives included such items as sex, aggression, hunger, curiosity, achievement, power, affiliation (love and friendship), competence, anxiety, and fear. Such a simple listing is no longer considered to be sufficient to the understanding or prediction of behavior. In addition, current theory no longer simply assumes that there is a direct link between motives and observable behavior. Behavior, rather, is taken as an expression of strength of *motivation* (a tendency toward action in a given situation), which is not the same as strength of *motive* (a stable personality characteristic). Motivation always involves a complex interaction between the stable personality factors called motives and other, more transient but nevertheless important, factors. Among these factors are, first, the individual's *expectancy* about attaining the relevant goal in that situation and, second, the goal's *incentive value,* or relative attractiveness.

Motives are not always "expressed"—they do not always result in behavior—and conversely, a particular piece of behavior is not necessarily indicative of a particular motive. Any given action or piece of behavior can have resulted from any of several motives. Consequently, motives cannot be observed directly, but must be somehow inferred from behavior.

Motivational psychologists are particularly interested in whether there are characteristic differences between individuals in their motives and, if such individual differences exist, how they developed and how they can be measured.

Kinds of Motives

Consider again why you are reading this book. The range of motives that might conceivably underlie that or any other activity is very wide indeed. For example, your reading may be a matter of cooperating or complying with the wishes of some authority; a means of gaining the approval of parents, teachers, friends, or even strangers; a desire for monetary reward, power, or prestige; a matter of curiosity; or the motive to meet a previously defined standard of excellence.

Cooperating With an Authority The first possibility, cooperating with the wishes of an authority, such as a professor, is consistent with maintaining the role of student. The need to behave in ways consistent with the socially determined contents of one's roles is a motivational principle subscribed to by many theorists. Most people, such theorists argue, want to behave consistently with what they have learned to be appropriate behavior for people in similar roles under similar conditions. They also want to be consistent within themselves. L. Festinger, in his theory of cognitive dissonance, says that people also want to make their attitudes consistent with their actions. Thus, reading this book would be consistent, for instance, with your attitude when you bought it and with the previous action of having bought it, whereas failing to read it would be dissonant with your previous attitude and actions. The importance of roles and attitudes in determining behavior are discussed at length in Chapters 25 and 26.

Approval If you were operating under the motive of gaining approval (and perhaps even friendship), you would not choose to read the book unless you saw it as a way to attain your primary objective, approval. People who frequently operate under this motive usually want people to like them. You would probably abandon your reading if a friend called and suggested doing something else, because you would be able to win the immediate gratification of approval from your friend.

Money, Power, or Prestige A motive for money, or more basically, for power or prestige, might be aroused, for example, if the publisher of the book called and offered to pay you to evaluate the chapter within a set time. Neither achievement nor affiliative motives are involved here, and if making money is consistently a major source of gratification for you and your main reason for reading the book, you would probably refuse a friend's invitation to do something else before you finished reading.

Curiosity Reading the book out of curiosity about the questions and issues with which psychologists are concerned, another possible motive mentioned above, may reflect a more general disposition on your part to want to know about the world and other people or to reduce uncertainty about them. People with this kind of motive are attracted to all kinds of activities that can potentially gratify their desire. Behavior motivated by curiosity is particularly evident in young children, who are constantly exploring because they want to try things out or are simply curious and need no additional incentive to act. Such behavior is most commonly attributed to an *intrinsic* motive to know one's environment and one's own capabilities within it; intrinsic motivation was discussed earlier in this chapter.

Achievement If you are a person with a high motive to achieve—another possible motive for reading the book—you may have taken on the task as an intellectual challenge. Achievement-oriented activity involves setting a *standard* of excellence

Figure 19.4
These demonstrators are participating in the Viet Nam Moratorium that took place in the fall of 1969 in Washington, D.C. Undoubtedly, the participants' motives varied that day; probably a number of motives influenced the behavior of each marcher. We might hypothesize about some of the motivations that brought them to Washington: need to take a public stance for peace; desire to be a part of a group for peer prestige; wish to avoid one's usual commitments at school or work and to seek a substitute for these in the excitement of a concrete, meaningful action; to challenge the establishment; to visit another city. You can probably add to this list.

(perhaps another person's achievement) against which you measure your behavior and accomplishments and toward which you aim your efforts.

Meeting that standard of excellence would then be the primary aim of your behavior. The primary source of gratification would consist of the knowledge that you met the standard because of your ability rather than because of luck or someone else's kindness. Only a temporarily greater need for food or approval would result in your accepting a friend's invitation to eat before you reached your goal.

Inferring Motives from Behavior

It should now be clear that any given activity, such as reading this book, can be instrumental to fulfilling any of a wide range of possible motives. To know what motivated a person to undertake a particular behavior, we must know what the major source of gratification for doing it was for that person at that particular time. It is not always possible to infer the motive accurately simply by observing his behavior. Even knowing the context in which it occurs (for example, whether the book is being read in the library, at home, or in the dentist's office) is not sufficient, although knowing the context helps in defining what the externally imposed pressures, demands, or expectancies are; which behavioral options are possible; and what the available incentives or goals are. The only way to be certain of one person's motive for a behavior is somehow to make an actual assessment of the unique pattern of motives of that individual.

Having discussed the question of what kinds of motives can underlie a given activity, we now look at the issue of motivation from the other side and ask when these tendencies to act called motives actually are evidenced in behavior.

When Is a Motive Expressed?

As was indicated earlier, motives are not always expressed; they do not always result in behavior. Knowing how to do something does not necessarily mean you *will* do it, any more than wanting to do something means you *can* do it. The actual display of goal-related action (motivated behavior) is determined by several factors. They include (1) the availability of a learned response, (2) expectancy of goal attainment, (3) the presence of inhibiting anxiety, and (4) the context and the incentives available. Consider the following example of Martha, Larry, and a possible game of chess. Larry is Martha's older brother, he is quite a good chess player, and he has invited Martha to join him in a game.

Availability of the Response The first of the motivational factors determining whether Martha will choose to play with Larry is whether or not the relevant action has been learned; for example, she may want very much to beat her brother, for whom she feels a great deal of hostility, but she cannot act on this desire unless she knows how to play chess.

Expectancy A second factor is the expectancy or probability of attaining the desired goal; suppose Martha has been repeatedly defeated by others whom Larry has repeatedly beaten. With the odds so much against her, she probably would not choose to play against Larry, and her motive would not be expressed in chess playing.

Anxiety A third factor is the presence of anxiety over displaying the behavior; within cognitive theories of motivation, anxiety is a motive that is aroused by the expectancy that negative consequences will follow if certain goal-directed activity is engaged in or if the goal is attained or both. Therefore, it tends to *inhibit* behavior that is directed toward that goal.

This way of looking at anxiety, or fear, is totally different from the way stimulus-response theories view it (see Chapter 18). In behaviorist drive theory anxiety is

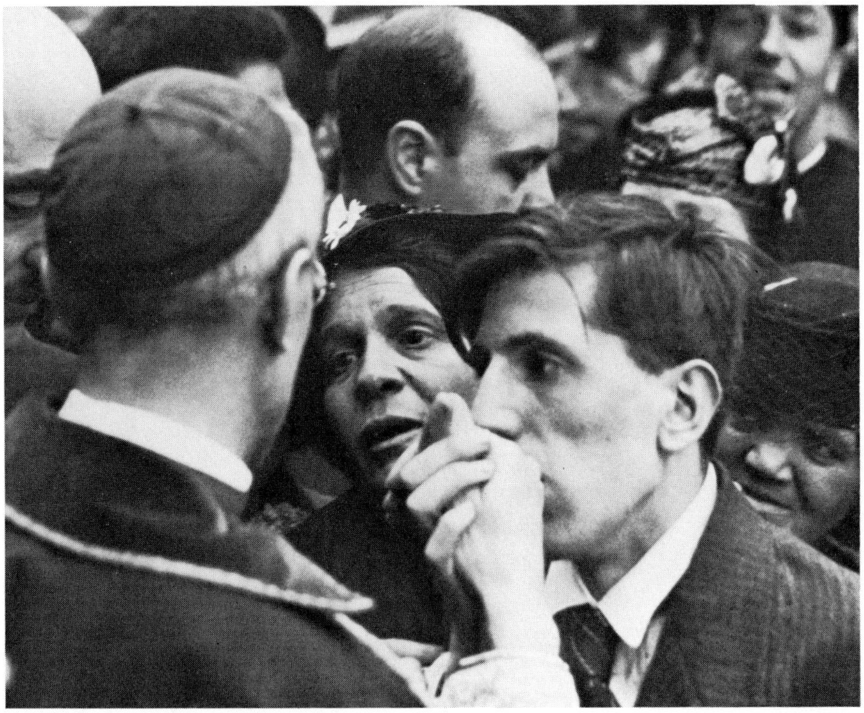

Figure 19.5
Religion may rank as one of the least well studied motivational phenomena, although it has influenced and directed the lives of millions of people. Out of respect, fear, or pride in God and their church, human beings have engaged in wars; have given away all their personal belongings; have vowed to remain or become continent; have fasted; have avoided all social contacts; have made long, inconvenient, and expensive pilgrimages; and, as can be seen in this photo, have gathered in immense crowds seeking to see or kiss the ring of a church leader (the Catholic Pope).

assumed to act as a drive and thereby *motivate behavior*, whereas in expectancy-value theory, which is our viewpoint here, it is assumed to be a negative tendency that *inhibits* the expression of positive goal-directed tendencies. For example, suppose Martha knows how to play chess and has a fair chance of beating Larry but also knows that he is considerably stronger than she and that he behaves aggressively toward anyone who beats him. That knowledge would probably prevent her from choosing to play with him.

A similar kind of inhibition might come from a different source, such as the idea that chess playing is not a feminine activity. Playing chess and beating a boy would then be inconsistent with Martha's social role and self-definition as "feminine." A perceived inconsistency often arouses anxiety, and anticipation of the negative consequences associated with this state of anxiety might well prevent the activation of this goal-directed action.

The Context and Incentives A fourth factor in the display of goal-directed activity is the nature of the context and the incentives that are available; the obvious prerequisites for expression of Martha's motive in behavior would be the presence of a chess board and pieces and also her brother's presence. Furthermore, this goal-related action is not likely to materialize while she and Larry are on a handball court or are guests eating dinner at someone else's house. On the other hand, if she and Larry were at home with her parents, who would be greatly impressed by her beating Larry at chess, then beating him would have a high incentive value.

If behavior is to be predicted or understood, all the complex factors just outlined must be considered together. The understanding and assessment of motives by psychologists has progressed rapidly in the recent past. The following section describes the tools and methods used by researchers to measure the strength of motives.

ASSESSMENT OF MOTIVES

Most of the current ways of measuring motives are based on the work done by Henry Murray and his co-workers in the late 1930s. Murray regarded personality as made

Figure 19.6
David McClelland's primary contributions to psychology are probably his studies of (and his techniques for measuring) achievement motivation. He has pursued these studies through several different areas, such as verbal learning, perception as a function of organic needs, independence training, and cross-cultural research on need for achievement.

up of "psychogenic," or nonbiological, motives (such as dominance, achievement, affiliation, nurturance, and aggression). As Chapter 22 points out, some of these motives are more important or basic to the individual than others.

Murray and his co-workers accepted Freud's idea that people express their motives more accurately in free-associative thought than in direct self-reports. Guided by clinical evidence, they devised a system for scoring the content of imaginative stories written to the Thematic Apperception Test (TAT). One form of the TAT is made up of a series of fairly ambiguous pictures of people in some context. People taking the test are asked to write or tell a brief story about what seems to be happening in each picture. Another form of the TAT involves the use of a verbal cue—a word, phrase, or sentence—around which a story must be composed. Because the contexts are ambiguous, people generally seem to ascribe their own concerns to the people in the stories or pictures.

But the question of whether motives actually have a meaningful and measurable influence on such projective responses was not settled until 1953, when D. McClelland and his co-workers published the results of their systematic study. The study used the basic procedures developed by experimental psychologists for manipulating the strength of motivation and then tested to see whether and *how* these experimentally aroused motives were expressed in imaginative stories. The researchers found, first with a biological drive, hunger, and then with such psychogenic motives as achievement, affiliation, power, and aggression that they could indeed reliably assess individual differences in the strength of a motive by analyzing fantasy or imaginative behavior.

With the cooperation of the U.S. Navy in arranging the schedules of men at a submarine base, Atkinson and McClelland in the late 1940s compared the content of stories written to accompany TAT pictures by various groups of men after one, four, and sixteen hours without food. The men were allowed a twenty-second look at each picture and were instructed to write an interesting and imaginative story within four minutes. The investigators found that they could reliably assess the degree of hunger from differences in TAT content. The actual distinguishing differences in the stories, interestingly enough, could not have been predicted beforehand; the use of straightforward food imagery or food themes, for instance, did not differentiate the hungry from the less hungry groups. Atkinson and McClelland noted that goal-directed activity in the stories (eating) *decreased* with increased hunger. They concluded that deprivation themes and themes about ways to overcome deprivation best distinguished the hungry from the nonhungry groups.

As McClelland's group indicated in a later report, however, their interest was not in using projective responses to find out how hungry people were; there are easier ways to find that out—such as asking the individuals when they last ate. Rather, they wanted to find out whether their technique worked for the relatively simple case of hunger before they tried to use it to diagnose differences in experimentally aroused psychogenic motives, such as the motive to achieve.

Scoring Systems

McClelland's group also established a scoring system for determining the strength of a motive. The motive for which they established the system was the motive to achieve. They first had some people write stories to the TAT under various achievement-oriented conditions, while others wrote them under relaxed, nonego-involving conditions. Then the researchers identified the kind of content that differentiated the stories written in each situation. In that way, a catalogue of "achievement imagery" was compiled: In the achievement stories, the major character showed concern with (1) standards of excellence and a high level of performance, (2) unique accomplishments, such as inventions, and (3) the pursuit of a long-term goal or career. In addition, the stories dealt with persistent and varying attempts to achieve (instrumental activity) and with good or bad feelings (affect) about the consequences of the actions required for achievement.

The findings of the experiment were replicated several times, and it is now generally assumed that people writing stories under *neutral* conditions whose contents are similar to those written by the subjects in the achievement-oriented conditions are people with a high motive to achieve (that is, with strong internal generalized dispositions to obtain gratification for doing well by competing against a standard of excellence). (Interestingly, data for *women* have not been consistent with the data for men, with the theory, or from one group of women to another.) Similar studies have been done to validate scoring systems for other psychogenic motives like affiliation and power and have achieved similar success.

Prediction From Scores

Having determined that it was possible to assess motives from fantasy material and to rate their strength (score them), researchers wanted to know how accurately they could predict behavior on the basis of the scores.

E. Walker and R. Heyns set up an experiment that enabled them to test predictions about the conflict of two motives—the achievement motive and the affiliation motive. They first gave a TAT test to a large group of students so that they could assess the two motives. From the large group, a number of students, some male and some female, volunteered to participate in the rest of the experiment, and each of them brought along a friend who had also taken the TAT in the large group As soon as the pair arrived at the experiment, they were separated and put in different rooms. About ten people were present in each room, and each person was given the task of scrambling the letters of words in a list in a prescribed way. Within each room the task was presented as a contest to see who could scramble the most words in the time allowed.

But each subject was told that there would also be a second part to the task: her or his partner in the other room would have to unscramble the words that the subject had scrambled and would be participating in a contest in the other room to see who could unscramble the highest percentage of words in the time allotted. In the middle of the experiment, each person then received a plea from the partner to slow down the rate of scrambling words so that the partner might win. At this point the person had to choose between two motives for gratification. Slowing down the scrambling rate would gratify the affiliative motive, but ignoring the partner's plea and attempting to win the competition would gratify the achievement motive.

Most of the women in the study responded to their partners' pleas to slow down, but the men did not. These behaviors fit the general pattern of gender differences in the motive to achieve and the motive to affiliate that the TAT scores showed. The researchers believe that the scores and acts reflect the current cultural pattern, which puts high value on independence and striving in males and on their competition with standards of excellence but rewards females for affiliative behavior. The importance of culturally defined sex roles in determining behavior is discussed in Chapter 25.

Few individual differences in strength of these motives showed up in the male population of the study because most of the men ignored their partners' pleas to slow down and preferred to compete. The men, almost without exception, had scored high on the achievement motive relative to the affiliative motive—and they had behaved accordingly in the experiment. However, the women who chose to go on working, ignoring their partners' pleas, had *TAT scores that showed them to be high in the achievement motive relative to the affiliative motive.*

THE ACHIEVEMENT MOTIVE IN MEN

The motive whose behavioral manifestations have probably been most carefully and extensively studied is the achievement motive. During the twenty years since

Figure 19.7
The competitive, driving, high-stress, hard-nose worlds of business and government have traditionally been the domain of men, especially in their capacities as managers and decision makers. Successful men have been those with high need for achievement, according to McClelland's measures. Except for one study of college women in Brazil, female subjects given the TAT under achievement-arousal conditions that stress intelligence and leadership ability do not usually show an increase in the motive. It should also be noted that the vast bulk of the research on need for achievement has been with men subjects, which itself may reveal a form of cultural stereotyping.

McClelland and his co-workers published the results of their investigations in *The Achievement Motive,* many people have done extensive research aimed at understanding the current determinants of achievement-oriented behavior. This work has resulted in an impressive and theoretically consistent body of data related to the achievement motive and its sources, development, assessment, and effects on the performance of men. There is now much evidence showing the effects of individual differences in the achievement motive on the kinds of risks men prefer and take, on the levels of aspiration they set, and on the levels of performance and persistence they show in various types of achievement-oriented activity.

In early research in the field, in the late 1950s and early 1960s, Atkinson and G. H. Litwin showed that men with a high achievement motive prefer and do best at tasks of moderate rather than extreme difficulty; C. H. Mahone showed that they set intermediate and realistic levels of aspiration; and E. G. French showed that they choose work partners of high ability. Atkinson found that, in general, such men perform better and persist longer at all kinds of tasks in which some risk of failure is involved (preferably a 50 percent chance), provided that the outcome depends on their ability rather than on chance and that the results will be made known and evaluated in terms of some standard of excellence. French and F. H. Thomas found that men with high scores on the achievement motive were more likely to solve a complex problem than men with low scores and were also more likely to work on the problem more persistently.

After this early research, most of the work on the achievement motive has followed two distinct lines, one studying the implications of the achievement motive for society; the other studying the effect that the achievement motive and other factors have on individual behavior.

The Achievement Motive and Society

McClelland, as noted earlier, has been primarily concerned with the social origins of the achievement motive and its implications *for society.* He argues that a high achievement motive is at least partly responsible for a high level within a society of entrepreneurial activity, which in turn leads to economic growth and social development. The evidence for his hypothesis is compelling.

Particularly interesting and novel are his studies relating the economic growth and decline of certain societies in the past to the achievement motive in the society

Figure 19.8
McClelland analyzed historical eras and their literature to determine the tie between need for achievement and the rise of civilizations. Many of the characters in Greek literature reveal a high need; McClelland cites Hermes as the best example in Greek mythology of a being with a high need for achievement. Hermes is described as a cunning, smooth-talking trickster who uses his wit and intelligence to defeat more physically powerful rivals. He seeks to get ahead by any means and even basks in the aggressive ingenuity of his schemes for success and profit. As portrayed here, on the first day of his life Hermes had already played the lyre by noon and by evening had used flattery and persuasion to steal the cattle of his older brother, Apollo.

as reflected in literature. The studies consisted of content analyses of literary samples, such as folk tales and children's readers, at critical points in each society's history. McClelland argues from his data that the risk-taking activities and new ideas of entrepreneurs result from a strong achievement motive, not merely from a strong "need for money," as is often maintained. McClelland has recently turned his attention to developing ways of raising the levels of the achievement motive in people whose behavior does not indicate normal middle-class levels of the motive.

Achievement Motivation and the Individual

Atkinson, N. Feather, and their co-workers, on the other hand, have carried out a systematic experimental analysis of the current determinants of achievement-oriented activities *in the individual person*—that is, in the individual *man.*

Their work has resulted in the development of a risk-taking model that is a useful and stimulating guide for further research. According to the model, the strength of positive achievement motivation, or the tendency to achieve success as manifested in overt activity, depends on the interaction of a personality characteristic, the motive to achieve, and on factors in the immediate situation, such as the difficulty of the task at hand and the incentive value of success in the situation. The percieved difficulty of the task is a function of the individual's expectancy of success.

The model also takes account of *achievement-related anxiety,* which inhibits the expression of positive motivation. The inclusion of anxiety as a factor increases the model's accuracy of prediction because in every achievement situation there is a threat of failure as well as a promise of success. (Refer back to the discussion of Martha and Larry and their potential game of chess to see how some of these factors operate in a concrete situation.)

THE ACHIEVEMENT MOTIVE IN WOMEN

Because of the persistent efforts of many experimenters, there is now a systematic theory and a substantial body of data about the achievement motive in men. Data for women, in contrast, have been very scarce. In Atkinson's 1958 book, *Motives in Fantasy, Action and Society,* a compilation of over 800 pages of current theory and data on the achievement motive, the question of gender differences was treated in one long footnote.

Research on women, as mentioned earlier, has been sparse, and its results were not consistent with the existing theory of achievement motivation or with the findings for men—the results were not even consistent with each other. In other words, for a long time there was neither a systematic theory nor a consistent body of data about the achievement motive in women. To add to the confusion, the sparse data that existed had been gathered using very dissimilar methods and widely diverse samples of female subjects.

The Motive to Avoid Success

To extend the comprehensiveness of the theory of achievement motivation so it would embrace the troublesome gender differences, M. Horner identified *the motive to avoid success* as a psychological barrier to achievement in women.

One consistent finding for women had been that they showed greater test anxiety than men. E. Maccoby had suggested that "the girl who maintains qualities of independence and active striving (achievement orientation) necessary for intellectual mastery defies the conventions of sex appropriate behavior and must pay a price, a price in anxiety." Horner went on to argue that women may in fact be more anxious than men in testing or achievement-oriented situations: Anxiety is aroused by the expectation of negative consequences. Most women have at least some positive achievement-oriented motivation—they want to succeed in a situation where they are competing against a standard or against other people's performances. Hence, anxiety is aroused by the thought of failure. But for women in our society, *success* in competitive achievement situations may also have negative consequences. Therefore, Horner hypothesized, anxiety for women is associated not only with failure but *also* with success.

In devising an experiment to test her hypothesis, Horner defined the *motive to avoid success* simply in terms of the expectancy aroused in the individual in competitive achievement situations that success will lead to negative consequences, such as social rejection or feelings of unfemininity. Freud had, after all, argued that the essence of femininity lies in repressing aggressiveness, and many people regard intense intellectual endeavor as aggressive. As a result, a woman is threatened by success because unusual excellence in, for example, intellectual or academic activities is consciously or unconsciously equated—by the woman herself and by others—with a loss of femininity and the possibility of social rejection.

In Horner's experiment, she tested two related hypotheses: first of all, that for most men competitive achievement activity does not give rise to the expectancy

Figure 19.9
The young woman in this picture may be as intensely motivated as the woman in Figure 19.10; they both seem to have a motive to achieve. But this girl's behaviors of grooming her cow for a 4-H competition (rather than herself for a beauty pageant) are not consistent with the female sex role defined as appropriate by her culture. The feminist movement in America is gradually attempting to do away with sex-role stereotyping of behaviors. As progress is made, a woman who engages in previously "masculine" behaviors will be less likely to suffer from the consequent anxiety predicted by Maccoby.

that negative consequences will follow success, and second, that anxiety about success is important for women and explains the previously detected gender differences in achievement-related motivation and performance.

The motive to avoid success was conceptualized basically in expectancy-value-theory terms closely paralleling those for the achievement motive. The motive to avoid success was viewed as a stable disposition within the person, a motive acquired early in life in conjunction with sex-role standards. Before its effects and prevalence could be determined, a way of assessing it had to be devised.

A variation on the standard TAT was employed. People were given the opening sentence of a story they were to complete. For the ninety women in the study, the sentence was "After first-term finals, Anne finds herself at the top of her medical-school class." For the eighty-eight men it was "After first-term finals, John finds himself at the top of his medical-school class."

The scoring criteria for fear-of-success imagery were based on TAT reactions to a cue that represented a threat rather than a goal or that simultaneously represented both. These results had been obtained by W. Scott.

A present-absent scoring system was used for fear-of-success imagery. A story was considered to indicate a motive to avoid success if it contained imagery reflecting negative concern about success. The stories were classified into three main groups. The largest group was made up of stories in which negative feelings and consequences mainly had to do with affiliative concerns, such as a fear of being rejected by society or by one's friends, of not being datable or marriageable, or of becoming

Figure 19.10
This young woman has engaged in the very traditional behaviors required to achieve her status as a beauty queen. Most feminists strongly argue that such contests themselves are highly degrading because they emphasize women's sexual and general physical attractiveness without regard to their individuality or talents, interests, and unique qualities as human beings. On the other hand, her entering the contest may reflect a strong need to achieve.

Anne is a CODE name for a non-existent person created by a group of med students. They take turns taking exams and writing papers for Anne. . . .

Anne is really happy she's on top, though Tom is higher than she—though that's as it should be . . . Anne doesn't mind Tom winning.

Anne is talking to her counselor. Counselor says she will make a fine NURSE. She will continue her med school courses. She will study very hard and find she can and will become a good nurse.

It was luck that Anne came out on top of her med class because she didn't want to go to med school anyway.

isolated or lonely because of the success. It also included the desire to keep the success a secret so as not to seem intelligent.

Another category was composed of the stories in which negative feelings and consequences of success were not related to affiliation and were independent of whether anyone found out about the success, such as a doubt about femininity or normality, or feeling guilty or in despair about the success.

The third group of stories involved denial of various types, such as denying the situation described by the cue, changing the content itself, denying the reality or possibility of the cue, stating "it is impossible," and denying effort or responsibility for attaining success. This was the second-largest category and a particularly interesting one.

Adjacent are some of the stories that showed denial.

Differences Between Men and Women

The first striking characteristic of Horner's results was the sheer magnitude of the differences between men and women in the kinds of responses made to the cue. The women showed significantly more evidence of the motive to avoid success than did the men. Fifty-nine of the ninety women in the study, or over 65 percent of them, wrote stories with high fear-of-success imagery, but only eight of the eighty-eight men, or fewer than 10 percent, did so. A good way to grasp the nature of the differences found between men and women is to read two of the typical male stories and two of the typical female stories; they appear in the adjacent margin.

Horner suggested that the motive to avoid success would affect performance only in situations in which that specific motive was aroused. She hypothesized, further, that it is aroused when anxiety about *competitiveness* and its aggressive overtones is relevant. Horner performed a second experiment in which each person was given a number of achievement tasks in a large competing group of both men and women. People were then randomly assigned to three other experimental situations. One-third of them were placed in a strictly noncompetitive situation in which they worked alone on a verbal and arithmetic task, guided only by tape-recorded instructions. The rest of the people were placed at random in one of two competitive situations in which they worked on the same tasks as in the noncompetitive situation and followed the same instructions.

Figure 19.12

The stories below were written by people who participated in Matina Horner's experiment on fear of success. The first two were written by men. The next two, written by women, were scored for fear of success. The last story, also written by a woman, was *not* scored for fear of success.

John is a conscientious young man who worked hard. He is pleased with himself. John has always wanted to go into medicine and is very dedicated. His hard work has paid off. He is thinking that he must not let up now, but must work even harder than he did before. His good marks have encouraged him. (He may even consider going into research now.) While others with good first term marks sluff off, John continues working hard and eventually graduates at the top of his class. (Specializing in neurology.)

John is very pleased with himself and he realizes that all his efforts have been rewarded, he has finally made the top of his class. John has worked very hard, and his long hours of study have paid off. He spent hour after hour in preparation for finals. He is thinking about his girl Cheri whom he will marry at the end of med

In one of the two situations they competed against a member of the same sex and in the other against a member of the other sex. None of the people had had previous contact with the competitor. Only the thirty people in the noncompetitive group worked in both a competitive and a noncompetitive setting. It was decided that the best way to take initial ability differences into account would be to have each person serve as her or his own control. Therefore, the performance of each of the thirty people in the noncompetitive situation was compared with her or his own previous performance in the large mixed-sex group on two similar verbal tasks.

More than two-thirds of the men performed at a higher level in the competitive than in the noncompetitive situation, but fewer than one-third of the women did so. The results for women differing in strength of motive to avoid success were, however, the interesting ones: 77 percent of the women who had been previously rated high in motive to avoid success performed at a significantly higher level in the noncompetitive than in the competitive situation, compared with 7 percent of those rated low in motive to avoid success. Of the women low in the motive to avoid success 93 percent behaved more like the men in that they performed at a significantly higher level in the competitive than in the noncompetitive situation.

After each part of the experiment, the subjects were asked to rate how important it had been to them to do well in that test situation. The results suggest that women, especially those high in the motive to avoid success, will explore their intellectual potential most fully only in noncompetitive settings and least of all in competition with men. Anxiety, which inhibits performance, is for most women aroused more in competitive than in noncompetitive situations.

There are also trends in Horner's data suggesting that women who are highly anxious about success probably inhibit expression of the achievement motive on the TAT. The pattern parallels a pattern found by R. A. Clark in a study of the expression of an aroused sexual motive in men. Clark found that the TAT stories of a group of college men who had just been shown pictures of nude women showed *less* manifest sexual content than the stories of a control group who had been shown landscapes. Clark concluded that the subjects' anxiety about the consequences inhibited their direct expression of the motive. In the same way, women's anxiety about success may inhibit their expression of the achievement motive.

APPLICATIONS OF MOTIVATIONAL THEORY

The value of research and theory in psychology lies not only in its importance for scientific explanation but also in its applicability to practical matters in everyday life. It seems reasonable to ask how much of what we have observed in the laboratory in fact applies to the lives of people in our society. How can what we have learned about motivation help us use our motivational dispositions more efficiently and thus gain more gratification from our work and interpersonal relationships?

McClelland, as was mentioned earlier, is interested in applying what he has discovered to help raise people's motivational levels, so they stand a better chance of escaping poverty and despair.

Certainly, if it can be shown, as Horner did, that women in Western society seem to suffer from the debilitating effects of a motive to avoid success as success is conceived in their own society, then new approaches to the education and upbringing of girls and women must be tried. In addition, it is possible that our society may be moving away from the extreme competitiveness fostered in males, the competitiveness shown in the near-uniform rejection by the male subjects of their partners' pleas to slow down in the word-scrambling experiment described earlier. Reorganization of social and educational institutions in such a way as to encourage expression of achievement motives without requiring intense competition between individuals, in which one person's success is conceived of as depending on the others' failure, may be possible.

Industrial Psychology

Many personality theories are centrally concerned with issues of human motivation. These theories are discussed primarily in Chapters 21 and 22, but some of them are particularly relevant for demonstrating how theories of motivation can suggest means of reorganizing social and educational institutions. In the United States, these theories have had a striking influence on businessmen interested in increasing the efficiency of workers involved in mass production of economic goods. Managers, personnel directors, and industrial psychologists are perpetually looking for ways to restructure working arrangements so as to achieve both greater efficiency and higher morale. Using the idea developed by Murray, Maslow, and others that there is a hierarchy of motives within people, with some motives more basic than others (see Chapter 22), these industrialists have tried to provide gratification of lower levels of functioning. According to the theory, when basic motives are gratified, "higher-level" motives can be expressed.

The industrial psychologist who has had perhaps the greatest influence is D. McGregor. McGregor maintains that a theory of human nature, in the form of a set of assumptions, underlies most industrial organizations. These assumptions, which he called theory *X*, are, first, that everyone dislikes work and will try in every way to avoid it; second, that consequently the industrialist must find the means to

school. He realizes he can give her all the things she desires after he becomes established. He will go on in med school making good grades and be successful in the long-run.

Aggressive, unmarried, wearing Oxford shoes and hair pulled back in a bun, she wears glasses and is terribly bright.

Anne has a boyfriend Carl in the same class and they are quite serious. Anne met Carl at college and they started dating around their soph. years in undergraduate school. Anne is rather upset and so is Carl. She wants him to be higher scholastically than she is. Anne will deliberately lower her academic standing the next term, while she does all she subtly can to help Carl. . . . His grades come up and Anne soon drops out of med school. They marry and he goes on in school while she raises their family.

Congrats to her! Anne is quite a lady—not only is she tops academically, but she is liked and admired by her fellow students. Quite a trick in a man-dominated field. She is brilliant—but she is also a lady. A lot of hard work. She is pleased—yet humble and her fellow students (with the exception of a couple of sour pusses) are equally pleased. That's the kind of girl she is—you are always pleased when she is—never envious. She will continue to be at or near the top. She will be as fine practicing her field as she is studying it. And—always a lady.

coerce people to do their work; and, third, that the average person prefers to be directed, wishes to avoid responsibility, has little ambition, and craves security.

McGregor has called an alternative set of principles theory *Y*. Its assumptions about human nature are, first, that the expenditure of energy is natural; second, that external control is not the only way to ensure the performance of a good job; third, that the commitment to objectives in work is related directly to the goals sought; fourth, that people like responsibility; fifth, that many people are creative; and, sixth, that under present industrial conditions, only part of the human potential is fulfilled.

Many industrial psychologists and industrial managers have been interested in theory *Y* and have applied it to industry as the Scanlon Plan. The methods of application can be seen in the experiences of one company.

A voltmeter factory that wanted to increase its production had tried a variety of standard inducements, such as extra pay for the workers and a shorter work week. Nothing they tried along the lines of what McGregor calls theory *X* seemed to have much effect. They then tried to see if somehow they could restructure their organiza-

Figure 19.13
Schools that use the "open-classroom" approach to teaching assume that children are intrinsically motivated to learn and will work at learning something they are interested in. These classrooms usually contain a variety of materials, and students can work alone or in small groups, at their own speeds, on various projects. The physical arrangement of such rooms is generally much different than traditionally structured classrooms. Instead of rows of desks or tables facing the teacher, there are smaller tables, or areas, for science or mathematics study or language study, and children can move from one to the other at will.

tion so it would provide an environment in which it was possible to express the intrinsic forms of motivation dealt with by theory *Y*.

The company reorganized its entire production system, which had been based on an assembly line in which each person assembled a small part of the final product, into one in which each worker constructed the entire product. The assumption was that if people are proud of their work, they will enjoy doing it, take pains with it, and perform well. In addition, the work force was divided into units of six to ten people working in a room. The intention was to give people a chance to get to know each other and to enjoy each other's company as they worked. The results were startling. Production skyrocketed; the quality of the work improved considerably; there was no sabotaging of the work—as so often occurs when workers are alienated; absences diminished considerably; there was less job turnover; and the employees enjoyed their work.

This experience has been repeated many times, and it works in nonindustrial situations also. For example, it is at the heart of a number of experiments in education.

Educational Applications

The principle behind the educational experiments is that students learn when they want to know something. Social structures were developed on the principle that it is essential to trust students to find out for themselves what activities are appropriate for them. More and more educational theorists, educators, and teachers are devising programs that keep in mind the intrinsic motivation of children and older human beings rather than simply attempting to coerce them into learning through deprivation, punishment, and reward.

Perhaps the most famous experiment of this kind was carried out in England at the Summerhill school by A. S. Neill, although many schools in the United States are now trying the "open-classroom" plan, which relies on children's intrinsic motivation to know, allows them to move ahead at their own pace, and frees them of the obligation of direct competition with other children.

SUGGESTED READINGS

ATKINSON, J. W. (Ed.). *Motives in Fantasy, Action, and Society.* Princeton, N.J., Van Nostrand, 1958. An important book that pulls together the work done by many investigators on the various methods used to assess and study individual differences in various motivational dispositions, such as achievement, affiliation, and power. Scoring manuals and self-teaching materials are also included.

ATKINSON, J. W., and FEATHER, N. T. *A Theory of Achievement Motivation.* New York, Wiley, 1966. Focuses on the contemporaneous determinants of achievement-oriented behavior and the marked advances made in our understanding of the problem.

HUNT, J. MCV. "Intrinsic Motivation and Its Role in Psychological Development," in *Nebraska Symposium on Motivation,* D. Levine (Ed.). Lincoln, University of Nebraska Press, 1965, pp. 189–282. Hunt focuses on the distinction between *extrinsic motivation,* which depends on a known homeostatic biological system, and *intrinsic motivation,* which involves an informational interaction between the organism and its environment. Thus, he speaks to the long-lived controversy, nature versus nurture, and highlights the likelihood of interaction between the two.

MCCLELLAND, D. *The Achieving Society.* Princeton, N.J., Van Nostrand, 1961. This book addresses the question of the social origins and consequences for society of achievement motivation.

WHITE, R. "Competence and the Psychosexual Stages of Development," in *Nebraska Symposium on Motivation,* M. R. Jones (Ed.). Lincoln, University of Nebraska Press, 1960, pp. 97–144. In this paper White extends and relates his theories of competence motivation to stages of emotional development.

UNIT VII Personality

When most people who have not studied the subject hear the word "psychology," they think of personality theory: What are people really like? Is their essential nature good but corrupted by civilization, or is it basically aggressive, selfish, and greedy and then softened by civilizing influences? Why do people do the things they do, love the people they love, and grow up to become doctors or lawyers or merchants or thieves? In a sense, everyone constructs his own theory of personality to answer such questions, but these implicit theories rarely are logically constructed in the way that formal theories of personality are. Both implicit theories of personality (and their effects on

3

Conditioning and Learning presents the basic concepts of the behaviorist approach; it underlies the discussion in Chapter 22 of the behaviorist approach to the concept of personality.

5

Development of Intelligence compares what Piaget calls intelligence—namely, the construction of an understanding—with what IQ tests measure. This view can be compared to the discussion in Chapter 20 of what IQ tests can be said to measure.

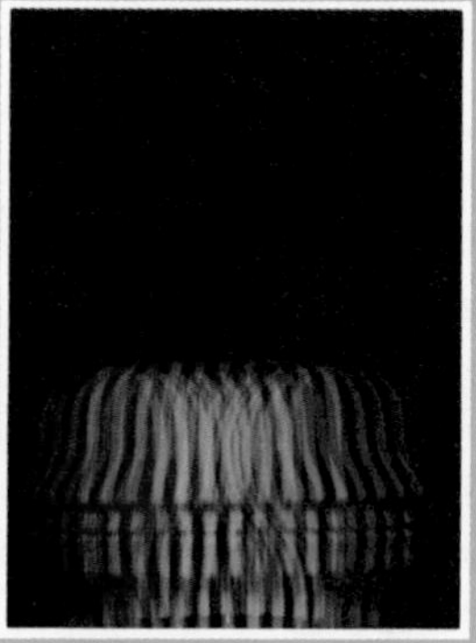

Chapter 20, Psychological Testing, discusses and gives examples of the various kinds of personality and IQ measures presently in use and describes the basic characteristics of tests, such as validity and reliability. As part of the discussion of IQ tests, it deals with the current controversy surrounding intergroup differences in IQ scores: the nature-nurture question.

Chapter 21, Freudian Theories of Personality, first deals with the general characteristics of all personality theories. It then discusses at length Freud's system and the approaches of some of the major theorists whose works, although individual and major contributions in their own right, are constructed on a Freudian foundation. Theorists discussed are: Jung, Adler, Erikson, White, and Fromm.

14

Perception examines the Gestalt principles of perception, which underlie Gestalt therapy, discussed in Chapter 22. Also, Chapter 14's description of phenomena like perceptual set, which causes people to perceive what they had expected to perceive, is related to the discussion in Chapter 23 of how a person's expectations about certain people or groups of people affect his perception of those people.

15

Consciousness and Awareness discusses sleep and dreams and presents the results of recent research that has attempted to study them. These results can be compared to Chapter 21's discussion of the importance of dream content in Freudian theory and analysis.

16

The Biological Organism contains a long section on behavior genetics. Its basic information on inheritance, especially in populations, can be read in relation to Chapter 20's discussion of what IQ tests can be said to measure.

impression formation) and formal theories are discussed in this unit.

The most extensive and complete formal theory of personality is that constructed by Sigmund Freud, and it is Freud's system that many laymen refer to when they attempt to analyze another's behavior. Although Freud was the first great personality theorist, many others have followed him. Some followed his approach closely, others have developed theories totally different in approach. Most of the important approaches are represented in this unit, and all of them are analyzed on four basic dimensions of personality: structure, dynamics, development, and motivation.

Chapter 22, Other Theories of Personality, represents a wide variety of viewpoints. Sullivan's interpersonal theory, Rogers' self theory, Murray's personology, Allport's psychology of the individual, Maslow's humanistic psychology, Kelly's cognitive theory are all discussed. Also included is a discussion of the behaviorist point of view, its rejection of the concepts of structure and dynamics and its view of development.

Chapter 23, Impression Formation, presents research and theories dealing both with how people form impressions of others and how people make impressions on others. Nonverbal communication in making impressions is examined, and the force of implicit theories in forming impressions is dealt with. E. Goffman's approach to the presentation of self is examined at length.

33

Psychotherapy II describes several kinds of therapies that are based on theories of personality examined in Chapter 22; for example, Carl Rogers' self theory is examined in Chapter 22, and his client-centered therapy, in Chapter 33.

32

Psychotherapy I, after an introduction that talks about therapy and therapists in general, describes psychoanalytic and psychoanalytically oriented therapies; these therapies are based on the theories of personality set out in Chapter 21.

29

Intensive Groups follows a hypothetical group through its weekend encounter; the events are both described and explained. Chapter 23's discussion of nonverbal communication and of presentation of self lays a good foundation for understanding the members' actions.

28

Intergroup Behavior, which takes a hard look at race relations in the United States, refers to stereotyping, which is discussed at length in Chapter 23.

27

Interpersonal Attraction, which examines the bases of friendship formation, refers often to concepts in Chapter 23, especially nonverbal communication.

25

Patterns of Social Behavior: The Case of Sex Roles examines, from three different theoretical positions, social patterning both in the course of development and in adult relations. One position is the Freudian, the basic tenets of which are set out in Chapter 21.

Human Motivation presents the results of research on several motives, two of them being the motive to achieve and the motive to avoid success; the strength of such motives in people taking IQ or achievement tests, which are described in Chapter 20, would almost certainly affect the scores. In addition, one of the tools used to examine these motives was the TAT scale, also described in Chapter 20. The view of human motivation in Chapter 19 can also be compared to the explanations of it in each of the personality theories set out in Chapters 21 and 22.

19

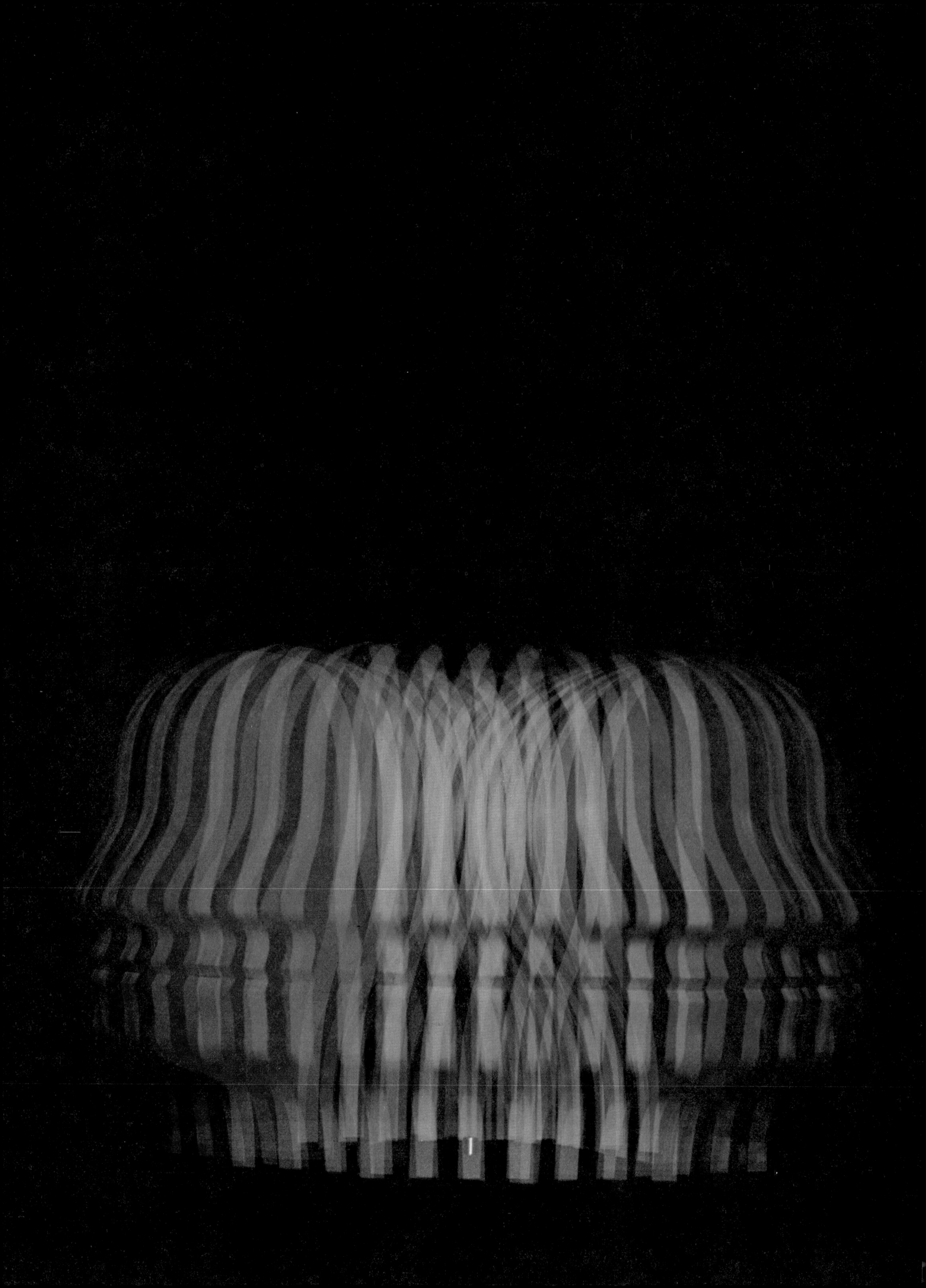

20 Psychological Testing

WHAT IS INTELLIGENCE, anyway? When I was in the army I received a kind of aptitude test that all soldiers took and, against a normal of 100, scored 160. No one at the base had ever seen a figure like that and for two hours they made a big fuss over me. (It didn't mean anything. The next day I was still a buck private with KP as my highest duty.)

All my life I've been registering scores like that, so that I have the complacent feeling that I'm highly intelligent, and I expect other people to think so, too. Actually, though, don't such scores simply mean that I am very good at answering the type of academic questions that are considered worthy of answers by the people who make up the intelligence tests—people with intellectual bents similar to mine?

For instance, I had an auto-repair man once, who, on these intelligence tests, could not possibly have scored more than 80, by my estimate. I always took it for granted that I was far more intelligent than he was. Yet, when anything went wrong with my car I hastened to him with it, watched him anxiously as he explored its vitals, and listened to his pronouncements as though they were divine oracles—and he always fixed my car.

Well, then, suppose my auto-repair man devised questions for an intelligence test. Or suppose a carpenter did, or a farmer, or, indeed, almost anyone but an academician. By every one of those tests, I'd prove myself a moron. And I'd *be* a moron, too. In a world where I could not use my academic training and my verbal talents but had to do something intricate or hard, working with my hands, I would do poorly. My intelligence, then, is not absolute but is a function of the society I live in and of the fact that a small subsection of that society has managed to foist itself on the rest as an arbiter of such matters.

Consider my auto-repair man, again. He had a habit of telling me jokes whenever he saw me. One time he raised his head from under the automobile hood to say: "Doc, a deaf-and-dumb guy went into a hardware store to ask for some nails. He put two fingers together on the counter and made hammering motions with the other hand. The clerk brought him a hammer. He shook his head and pointed to the two fingers he was hammering. The clerk brought him nails. He picked out the sizes he wanted, and left. Well, doc, the next guy who came in was a blind man. He wanted scissors. How do you suppose he asked for them?"

Indulgently, I lifted my right hand and made scissoring motions with my first two fingers. Whereupon my auto-repair man laughed raucously and said, "Why, you dumb jerk, he used his *voice* and asked for them." Then he said, smugly, "I've been trying that on all my customers today." "Did you catch many?" I asked. "Quite a few," he said, "But I knew for sure I'd catch *you.*" "Why is that?" I asked. "Because you're so goddamned educated, doc, I *knew* you couldn't be very smart."

And I have an uneasy feeling he had something there. I. A.

It is a fact that, on the average, poor Americans and black Americans score lower on standard intelligence tests than rich Americans and white Americans. Does this mean that poor people and Negroes are innately inferior to rich people and to whites?

It is a fact that many large corporations have designed personality and aptitude tests that allow them to determine which job applicants are likely to do well and which are not. Does this mean that an applicant should be refused a job on the basis of his score on a personality test?

It is a fact that psychotics score differently from normal persons on many personality tests. Does this mean that people whose scores are similar to that of the average psychotic should be hospitalized?

Over the years, psychologists have devised a whole range of instruments to measure intelligence, interests, skills, aptitudes, and basic personality patterns. The large number of intelligence and personality tests available give psychologists the opportunity to study the complex phenomena of human personality and mental ability. Some aspects of personality, however, are easier to measure than others; abilities, that is, traits that are directly revealed in specific behaviors, like achievement in mathematics, are easier to measure than personality traits, such as needs or values. The use of all these instruments is steadily increasing in the modern world, even though there are many ethical issues raised by their use. Most of the objections to the tests stem from the fact that although people are similar to each other in some ways, they are different in others, and when the attributes of individuals or of groups of people are statistically compared, someone must come out second best. Even the use of measures of intelligence has been criticized on several counts.

Figure 20.1
J. McKeen Cattell, a vigorous and forceful psychologist, exerted a powerful influence on psychology. His overriding interest was in human capabilities; as part of this interest, he encouraged the development and use of intelligence testing in America, and was the first to use the term *mental test.*

Figure 20.2
Alfred Binet. Binet, a French psychologist, developed a test of intelligence in order to objectively measure the academic potential of French schoolchildren. From this beginning, Binet and others developed the area of psychological measurement into the important field it is today. The Stanford-Binet Intelligence Test, an American modification of Binet's scales, is one of the two most widely used intelligence tests today.

INTELLIGENCE TESTING

Alfred Binet, a French psychologist, was the first to develop a reliable intelligence test. Before Binet's work, psychologists had attempted to measure intelligence by giving sensory and motor tests; they tested people's ability to accurately estimate the passage of time, the efficiency of their hand-eye coordination, their speed of tapping, and their memory. Around the end of the nineteenth century, Binet began testing children's vocabulary, their recognition of familiar objects, their understanding of commands, and the like; he was looking for abilities that changed with age. Binet assumed that if older children did better on the tests than younger children, then children who performed better than others of their own age must be more intelligent.

In 1904 Binet was asked by the Minister of Public Instruction for the Paris Schools to develop a test that could be used to identify mental defectives, so that these children could be taught separately. In collaboration with psychiatrist Theodore Simon, Binet devised a thirty-item test, arranging the items or tasks in order of increasing difficulty. By 1908 Binet's tests were also used to make differentiations among and predict the school performance of normal children. Binet arbitrarily defined children as retarded whose scores were at least two years below the scores for children of their chronological age. One problem with this definition was that a child of fourteen who was two years behind his age group was considered to be as retarded as a child of six who was two years behind his age group. A German psychologist, William Stern, suggested that rather than take the difference between mental age (defined as the average age of children who obtain a particular score on an intelligence test) and chronological age, the test should employ the *ratio* of mental age to chronological age. His idea resulted in the now-famous *intelligence quotient* (IQ), which is computed by dividing mental age by chronological age and multiplying by 100 (to get rid of the decimals).

Individual Tests

Binet's test of intelligence has been revised many times since he developed it. The Binet test currently employed in the United States is a revision made at Stanford University. The Stanford-Binet test follows Binet's pattern of grouping tests by age levels; to stimulate and maintain the child's interest, a variety of tasks, both verbal and performance, is included. The examiner is trained to carry out the standardized instructions exactly but at the same time to put the child at ease, to make friends with him, and to get him to pay attention and try as hard as he can. The best way to be sure that differences in scores do not reflect variations in motivation rather than in ability is to try to ensure that all subjects are highly motivated.

In administering the tests, the examiner first tries the child out on some questions—often from the vocabulary test—to locate the proper level at which to start. If it appears, for example, that the child is at least as bright as the average nine-year-old, he is given the tests for year nine. If he misses some of the questions, the examiner drops back to year eight. After locating the *basal age*—the highest age at which the child can pass all items—the examiner proceeds with tests at later year levels and gives the child extra credit for the ones he can pass. When a child reaches the level at which he can pass no tests, the testing session ends.

In the final scoring, the mental age indicates how high a level of development the person has reached. If a child has a mental age of twelve, then his performance

Figure 20.3
Administration of three subtests in the Stanford-Binet Intelligence test. (Top left) the tester points to one of the shapes (circle, star, or the like) shown on a page of the notebook and asks the child to pick out the card that contains the same shape. (Lower left) the child is shown the objects attached to the cardboard and is asked to point to each object as the tester names it; for example, "Show me the ball. Which one is the ball?" (Right) the child is asked to build a tower of blocks to match the tower just constructed by the tester. The child is given credit if he builds a tower of four or more blocks. These three subtests are part of an early-age level. At later year levels, a greater proportion of the subtests are oriented to verbal abilities.

is as good as the average twelve-year-old's. The IQ indicates how his level of development compares with that of his age mates. In addition, the examiner generally picks up a good deal of qualitative information about how the child's mind works, information often very useful to teachers or psychotherapists who deal with him. The original Binet tests were designed for school-age children, but successive revisions of the Stanford-Binet tests have extended the scale downward into the preschool levels and upward into the adult levels.

The other individual scales that have been most frequently used are those developed by D. Wechsler: the Wechsler Adult Intelligence Scale (WAIS) and the Wechsler Intelligence Scale for Children (WISC). These tests, like the Stanford-Binet, are made up of both verbal and performance tests, but they are arranged differently. Items of the same kind are grouped together into a subtest and arranged in order of difficulty. The examiner administers each of the subtests, starting with a very easy item and continuing until the end or until the person has missed three items in succession.

The Wechsler tests differ from the Stanford-Binet in several ways: for example, (1) The Wechsler tests have more performance tasks and are therefore less biased toward verbal skills. (2) They do not organize their questions in terms of age; the items are the same for children of all ages. (3) The Wechsler tests do not end after

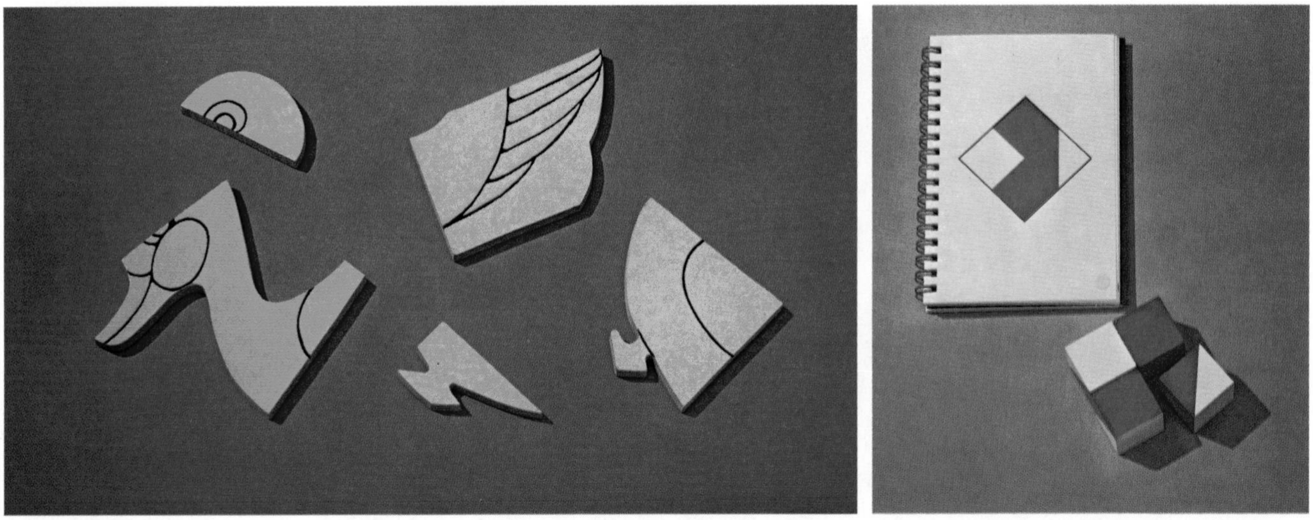

Figure 20.4
Two performance subtests similar to those included in the Wechsler IQ tests. (Left) a child is asked to put the puzzle pieces together to form the duck. (Right) an adult is shown the card with the pattern on it for a brief period of time and is asked to arrange the blocks to match the pattern.

all tests at a particular age have been completed. (4) Mental-age scores are not obtained on the Wechsler test; instead, the child receives a percentile rank based on a comparison of his performance with that of other children in his own age group. Most of these differences result from one major overall difference between the two tests. The Wechsler breaks down the score for general intelligence into separate scores for each kind of subtest—vocabulary, information, arithmetic, picture arrangement, block design, and so on. The subtest scores are in turn combined into separate IQ scores for verbal and performance abilities. This method of scoring helps the examiner sketch a qualitative picture of how the individual reacts to different kinds of items. Most important, it encourages the treatment of intelligence as a number of different abilities rather than one overriding ability.

Group Tests

The convenience and economy of group intelligence tests have led to their use in preference to individual tests in schools, employment offices, and many other mass testing situations. The Army Alpha and Army Beta, for example, were developed during World War I for classifying soldiers. Group tests include verbal and performance varieties and many combinations of the two. However, group tests do not generally predict school performance as well as individual tests, and individual tests still dominate the clinic. It is not possible to pick out one or two tests that are as representative of group tests as the Stanford-Binet and Wechsler instruments are of individual tests. Group tests are usually used in particular situations for particular purposes. Scholastic aptitude tests are really specialized group intelligence tests made up of the kinds of items that correlate most closely with school success.

CHARACTERISTICS OF A TEST

The indicator of performance in real life against which a psychological test is evaluated is called the *criterion.* A test's most essential characteristic is its validity—the degree to which it measures what it is supposed to be measuring, to reflect accurately a person's performance on the criterion or criteria of the test.

Validity

As you read about the development of the now-famous Stanford-Binet and other intelligence tests, you might have asked yourself, "How did Binet know he was measuring intelligence? He never really said what it was." If you asked this question, you wondered about what psychologists call the test's *validity.*

The criteria and the kinds of evidence that must be assembled to demonstrate validity vary with the nature and purpose of the test. For example, *concurrent*

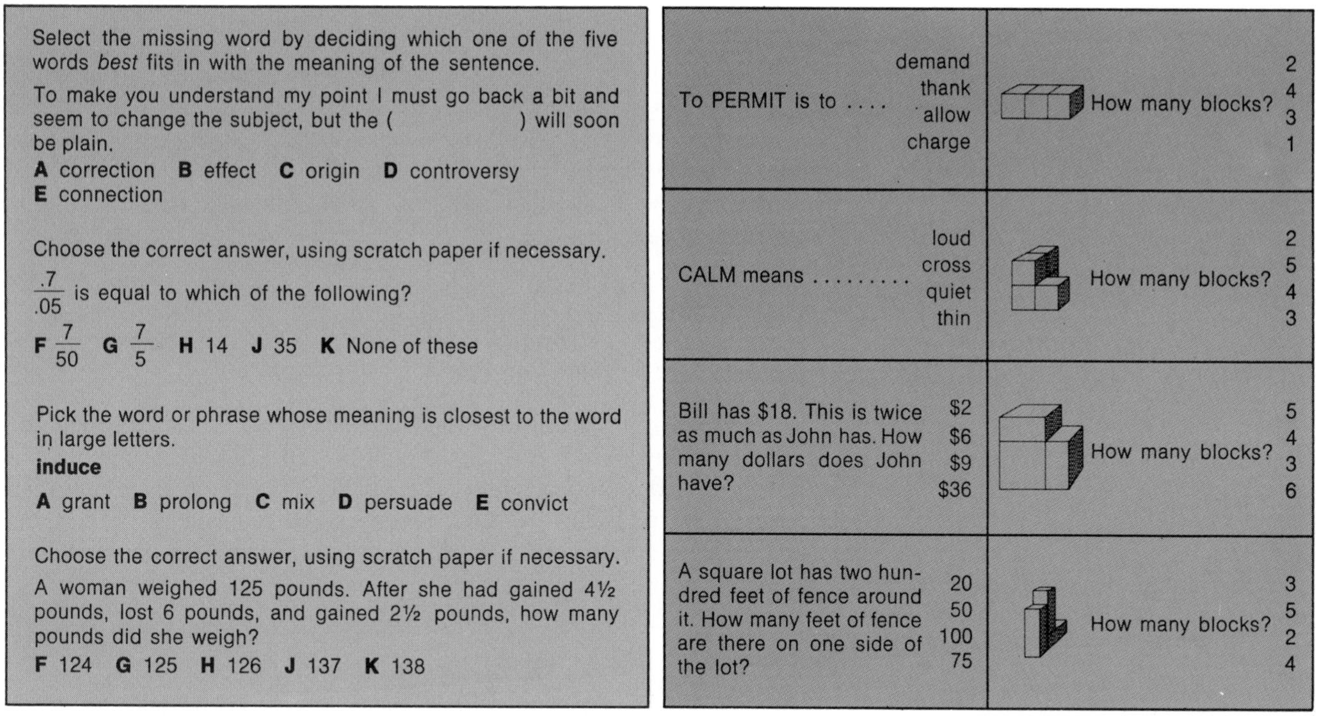

Figure 20.5
Sample items from two group tests of intelligence. (Left) items from the School and College Ability Test (SCAT). This version of the SCAT is used to test high school students in grades ten through twelve. (Right) items from the Army General Classification Test (AGCT), which was developed and standardized for testing U.S. Army recruits during World War II. It has since been replaced by the Armed Forces Qualification Test (AFQT).

validity is established for a test by comparing its results with those of an already established test.

In the case of an intelligence or aptitude test that is used to predict performance, it is necessary to establish its *predictive validity* with some evidence that the behavior of people in situations outside the testing room corresponds with their test behavior. This correspondence need not be perfect in order for the test to be useful, but the test must demonstrate at least a moderate correlation. If all children who score low on a so-called intelligence test do as well in school as the children who receive moderate or high scores, the test cannot be considered a valid measure of intelligence, at least of the kind of intelligence that schoolwork requires. Binet used the ability of his test to predict school children's performance as a criterion of its success, and ever since Binet, the primary criterion for intelligence tests has been their ability to predict school performance. (See Appendix for discussion of correlation.)

Another kind of validity is *content validity*. In a school achievement test designed to find out how much individual students know about, say, geometry or American history, the questions asked in the test must correspond to knowledge and information in that particular field. In validating the content of such a test, one looks for information about how its items are selected. People who select the questions may have individual biases about what knowledge is representative of the field, but such biases will hopefully offset one another when a committee of several equally competent people make the selections.

Finally, *construct validity* is based on the idea that certain experiences people have should relate to (and perhaps cause) certain scores on a test. For example, construct validation would be established for an intelligence test if a sound psychological theory suggested that special training should increase intelligence, and special training did in fact result in higher scores on the test.

Few people realize that no tests are absolutely valid. It is tremendously difficult to validate a test. For example, from the very beginning, the search for an adequate measure of intelligence was tied to the search for an adequate theoretical definition of intelligence. Binet never published a formal definition of intelligence. How can we know whether an intelligence test is measuring intelligence when we have no criterion of intelligence that is better than the test? In order to establish validity,

Figure 20.6
The late *E. G. Boring* noted that Binet developed a standardized test for intelligence without ever specifying the nature of the theoretical construct of intelligence. He was calling attention, therefore, to the lack of construct validity in the Binet test. Boring was an experimental psychologist who worked in several areas, including psychophysics. He is also perhaps psychology's greatest historian.

we need a criterion. But in order to obtain a criterion, we must know what intelligence is, and no one knows for sure.

Theories and opinions about what constitutes intelligence differ greatly. For example, Piaget's view, which is discussed in Chapters 5 and 6, differs from the views discussed in this chapter. No one has measured intelligence directly and absolutely. The definition of intelligence implicit in intelligence tests is an operational one (see Chapter 1); that is, intelligence is defined as what intelligence tests measure. H. Chauncey and J. E. Dobbin remark that intelligence tests are analogous to physicists' cloud chambers:

> The cloud chamber does not permit the physicist to see the atom or its electrically charged components, but it does reveal the tracks of ionizing particles and thus permits the scientist to deduce the nature of the atom from which the particles emanate.

It is clear, then, that the nature of intelligence is elusive and that test validity is not a simple matter. With this in mind, people who offer tests to the public should carefully collect all the information needed to establish what the tests are measuring; those who use the test scores—teachers, personnel managers, and psychotherapists, for example—should be familiar with this whole body of research data and use it as a basis for their interpretations of people's scores.

Reliability

To what extent do people's scores depend upon the trait or ability the test is designed to measure, and to what extent are they a matter of chance? All kinds of chance factors can influence test scores, including the way different people react to the test situation at different times—sometimes trying too hard, sometimes not trying hard enough. They may be anxious or they may be preoccupied with problems that have nothing to do with the test. Another chance factor is the way different items in the test may relate to particular experiences of the people taking the test. For example, if the word "philately" is an item in the vocabulary section of an intelligence test, people who happened to have watched a television program on stamp collecting the night before will probably give the right answer, whether they are highly intelligent or not. A test must have reliability; that is, it must be free of the influence of such random factors. It must be consistent in the answers it produces. A person taking the same test on two occasions (long enough apart so he has pretty much forgotten the items) should get much the same score both times. There will be times, of course, when a person—like the anxious person just mentioned—will get widely different results. But the instrument itself must be reliable—it must have been proved to produce consistent scores for most of the people taking the test.

A test may have high reliability but low validity, even when the content of the test seems to be appropriate to whatever the test is supposed to be measuring. One of the main factors that produces high reliability with low validity is called *response bias.* With certain kinds of tests, some people have a tendency to give one type of answer, even though their answer has little or nothing to do with the content of the test. For example, if a test is made up of a series of questions all of which are to be answered "Yes" or "No," some people will tend to answer "yes" to questions regardless of their content, and others will tend to answer "no." Similarly, if, on a personality scale, people are supposed to rate a characteristic on a dimension from low to high, many people will make ratings toward the middle of the dimension regardless of the characteristics listed.

Figure 20.7
If one were to construct a test of intelligence by measuring head size and equating bigger measurements with higher IQ, one would have a test with high reliability. That is, all the people who independently measured Leonardo's head would come up with much the same results. However, our test would have little validity because large head size simply does not correspond with high IQ in the real world.

Norms

Still another kind of information that must be provided if a test is to be useful comes under the general heading of *norms.* A score in itself tells an individual very little unless he knows what kinds of scores other people have made. That is, if a person were told he had correctly answered fifty-three of the eighty-eight questions on a test, he would not know whether he had done well or poorly unless he knew that most people are able to answer only forty-four. Testers develop norms before a test is put into general distribution by giving it to a large and well-defined group of people, called a standardization group. It is customary to take the arithmetic average as a reference point and indicate how far above or below average any given score is. There are many ways of doing this. On the IQ scale, 100 is the average figure; scores on the individually administered tests, at least for young children, can range all the way from 0 to 200. But there are many more scores nearer the average than there are in the most extreme categories. Most commonly used tests of intelligence are constructed so that about 68 percent of the population obtains IQ scores between 85 and 115; over 95 percent obtain scores between 70 and 130; and over 99.7 percent obtain scores between 55 and 145. The meaningfulness of scores under 50 and beyond 150 is questionable.

Most tests require several sets of norms—for example, norms appropriate for people of different age, sex, and race. The group to which a person is compared must be the group to which he or she belongs. In intelligence testing, age is the most important factor, but sex, social class, and race can also be important. For example, most intelligence tests have been developed and validated with white people. There are few norms for members of other races, and the established norms, therefore, may be inappropriate for them.

The *percentile* system and the *standard-score* system are the most common systems for translating the actual "raw" scores individuals make into figures that relate these scores to the whole distribution of scores for a group of persons. Each system has many variations. The essential thing a percentile shows is the proportion of the individuals in the group who scored below a designated point in the distribution. The essential thing a standard score shows is the distance of the individual score from the point designating the average; Figure 20.8 illustrates a percentile and a standard score system. To generate norm tables of either sort is not difficult after a group of people has been tested. What is more difficult for the producer of a test is to make sure that the group on which norms are based is really representative of the population in which the test will be used.

INTERGROUP DIFFERENCES

As we mentioned earlier, many relationships between IQ and other attributes have been found, but the significance of these relationships is often difficult to determine. For example, moderate to large correlations (associations) have been found between intelligence and social class (as measured by occupational level, educational level, and income). Interpretation of this relationship is not simple because people in the

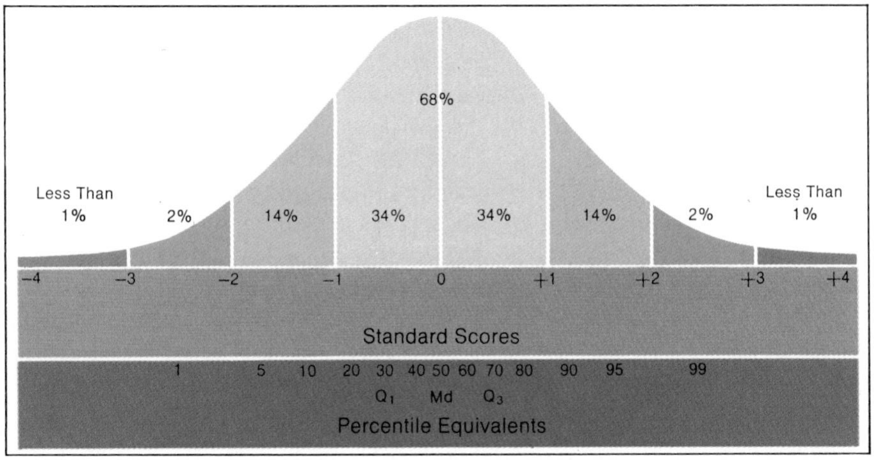

Figure 20.8
A normal distribution (or bell-shaped curve). Many psychological characteristics, such as intelligence, are found to be normally distributed among the standardization group. This fact facilitates rapid and precise communication about test scores. For example, one can report a *percentile equivalent*, which represents the proportion of individual scores in a group that are less than or equal to a given score in the standardization group. A *standard score* indicates how far a score is from the average (or mean) score; thus a standard score of +2.0 is considerably *above* the mean, and one of −2.0 is exactly the same distance *below* the mean.

The Dove Counterbalance Intelligence Test
by Adrian Dove

If they throw the dice and "7" is showing on the top, what is facing down?
(a) "Seven" (b) "Snake eyes"
(c) "Boxcars" (d) "Little Joes"
(e) "Eleven"

Jazz pianist Ahmad Jamal took an Arabic name after becoming really famous. Previously he had some fame with what he called his "slave name." What was his previous name?
(a) Willie Lee Jackson
(b) LeRoi Jones
(c) Wilbur McDougal
(d) Fritz Jones (e) Andy Johnson

In "C. C. Rider," what does "C. C." stand for?
(a) Civil Service
(b) Church Council
(c) County Circuit, preacher of an old-time rambler
(d) Country Club
(e) "Cheating Charley" (the "Boxcar Gunsel")

Cheap "chitlings" (not the kind you purchase at the frozen-food counter) will taste rubbery unless they are cooked long enough. How soon can you quit cooking them to eat and enjoy them?
(a) 15 minutes (b) 2 hours
(c) 24 hours
(d) 1 week (on a low flame)
(e) 1 hour

If a judge finds you guilty of "holding weed" (in California), what's the most he can give you?
(a) Indeterminate (life) (b) A nickel
(c) A dime (d) A year in county
(e) $100.00.

A "Handkerchief Head" is
(a) A cool cat (b) A porter
(c) An "Uncle Tom" (d) A hoddi
(e) A "preacher"

Figure 20.9
Sample questions from an intelligence test designed to measure familiarity with the culture of the urban black community. What kind of IQ scores do you think middle-class white suburbanites would get on this test?

higher social classes clearly have more exposure to the skills that are tested on intelligence tests. L. M. Terman followed over 1,000 gifted students from an early age to adulthood. He found significant positive relationships between IQ and physical, academic, social, and moral development. Smarter or brighter persons were generally taller, heavier, stronger, more advanced in social and personal maturity, and had greater achievements in school and other social situations. On the other hand, people with high IQs were less likely to show lethal behavior (fatal accidents, suicide), delinquency and criminality, alcoholism, drug dependency, and severe mental illnesses. Highly intelligent people receive more degrees, distinctions, awards, professional licenses and certifications, and income; they make more artistic and literary contributions and report more satisfaction in life. But all of these relationships may result not from IQ itself but from other factors like social class.

Nature or Nurture

Many people have tried to use intelligence tests to obtain definite answers to age-old questions about whether or not there are innate intellectual differences among groups, but it has proved to be almost impossible to come to reliable conclusions about such differences. People whose childhood environment has been quite different from that of the majority of American and European children tend to have lower scores on tests developed in the United States and Europe. This difference, even when statistically significant, cannot be accepted as evidence that various groups differ in *innate* potential, because a person's score reflects not only his genetic potential for intellectual development (nature) but also what he has learned from his experience (nurture).

If a test is developed for people with a specific cultural background, it cannot legitimately be used for people with a markedly different background. For example, of all the various kinds of items on intelligence tests, vocabulary provides the best single estimate of IQ scores. If you had only ten minutes to assess IQ, you would probably use a vocabulary test; yet vocabulary depends so clearly on cultural background. If someone has never heard words like *sonata* or *ingenuous*, he will perform poorly on verbal intelligence tests. And if he has grown up in a community where the primary language is not English, he will be handicapped even further.

There are differences among the *average* IQ scores of people of different races and different nationalities. However, it has proved to be virtually impossible to conceive of those differences as resulting primarily from either differences in upbringing and environment or differences in inheritance. In earlier times the nature-or-nurture controversy seemed exceedingly important to psychologists, but it was largely abandoned because of its complexity and because of the potentially dangerous implications that erroneous conclusions would have for race relations, welfare, educational reform, and immigration policy.

Recently, however, the issue has received renewed publicity. In the winter of 1969 A. R. Jensen published an article called "How Much Can We Boost IQ and Scholastic Achievement?" In it he argued that research has shown that intelligence is about 80 percent inherited, and he concluded that compensatory education cannot do very much to raise the IQ of disadvantaged children. Moreover, suggested Jensen, the intelligence of blacks in America is probably inherently inferior to that of whites. Needless to say, Jensen's article raised a storm of protest. Many people fighting for educational reform and racial equality argue that differences in average IQs among different races and ethnic groups are due to inferior opportunity and that therefore the environment of those groups who score poorly should be improved. On the other hand, people opposed to educational and racial equality have argued that IQ is inherited and that the races are innately different, and therefore should be taught separately.

In reaching his conclusions, Jensen made a number of questionable assumptions about the measurement of intelligence. First, he assumed that conclusions based on research on the intelligence of whites can be generalized to blacks, even though the inheritance of intelligence among blacks has been studied very little. Second, Jensen assumed that middle-class blacks and middle-class whites and lower-class blacks and lower-class whites grow up in similar environments. If, in fact, their environments are not similar but differ in important ways, then Jensen's measure of the inheritance of intelligence is not valid. Third, Jensen assumed that the tests' bias in favor of middle-class whites was unimportant, even though many items on the test obviously depend on familiarity with middle-class white culture.

In any case, Jensen's data should not be relevant to decisions about educational and social equality. Under a true standard of equality, help is provided to people who need help, whatever the cause of their need.

The Use of IQ Scores

The popular use of the term IQ usually refers to innate differences. Most psychologists, however, are much more cautious. They have learned from nearly a century

Figure 20.10
Project SEED (Special Elementary Education for the Disadvantaged) is designed to teach high-level mathematics to disadvantaged elementary-school students. Its goal is to raise the children's intellectual performance and their self-concept; another aim is to counter Arthur Jensen's claim that compensatory education cannot help them learn conceptual reasoning. Evaluation studies show that black SEED students score the same as white children on the Raven Progressive Matrices Test. Jensen had previously used data from this test to support his notion that blacks show poor conceptual reasoning.

of research how complex the problem of separating heredity from environment really is; Chapter 2 discusses this issue. Psychologists would agree that differences in what we measure with intelligence tests are in part genetically determined (research on identical twins, discussed in Chapters 16 and 31, has produced the clearest evidence of this); however, they also know that an individual's score reflects his upbringing, especially his education.

More important, the usefulness of IQ tests does not depend on their ability to measure innate differences. For example, test scores alert a seventh-grade history teacher to the fact that one student is equipped at the outset of the course to do excellent work and should be held to a high standard and that another student may have much more difficulty in grasping the main ideas and should be given special help. The teacher need not think in terms of heredity or environment.

Write rapidly as many different four-word sentences as you can in which the four words begin with the letters "K____ u____ y____ i____," for example, "Keep up your interest," and "Kill useless yellow insects."

Figure 20.11
An item from the Christensen-Guilford Fluency Test. Guilford has been studying the structure of intelligence for many years; this test measures various aspects of what he calls "divergent thinking," the flexible type of thinking that leads to the production of many possible solutions and therefore to creative problem solving.

ACHIEVEMENT AND APTITUDE TESTS

The construction of achievement tests and aptitude tests began as separate enterprises carried out by different psychologists with completely different objectives. Achievement tests were constructed to assess accurately how much individuals know about subjects taught in school; aptitude tests were designed to find out how much talent or capacity individuals have for particular lines of work. As time passed, however, the distinction between achievement tests and aptitude tests became more and more blurred. What psychologists first thought were tests of aptitude—defined as *innate* ability or talent—turned out to partly measure different kinds of experience, so that they had to be considered in some sense achievement tests. On the other hand, achievement tests often turned out to be the best predictors of many kinds of occupational abilities, so that they were in some sense aptitude tests. The distinction between aptitude and achievement tests has come to rest more on purpose than on content. When a test is used to evaluate what a person knows, it is an achievement test; the same test used to predict how successful the person will be is an aptitude test.

Although achievement and aptitude tests are similar, they must be validated in different ways. If one is interested in achievement, the important consideration is *content validity*. If one wishes to assess aptitude, one seeks evidence about the test's *predictive validity*. (Both these concepts were discussed earlier in the chapter.)

The most impressive work in aptitude measurement has been done by the United States Employment Service, which produced a two-and-a-half-hour set of tests called the General Aptitude Test Battery (GATB). The GATB makes it possible for a person to find out whether he meets minimum standards for each of a considerable number of occupations.

Psychologists once hoped that achievement testing would lead to significant improvements in education and that aptitude testing would enable each person to find an occupation in life that suited him. Several decades of work have not accomplished these purposes, and it now seems unlikely that further efforts along the same lines will do so. Nevertheless, these efforts have resulted in techniques and instruments that are helpful when they are used by people who understand both their advantages and their shortcomings.

Figure 20.12
Test items similar to those used in the General Aptitude Test Battery (GATB). Aptitude tests like the GATB help assess the person's potential for mastering the work encountered in a given occupation. GATB is a comprehensive test, but there are many aptitude tests that are more specific; for example, some measure secretarial aptitudes, some measure mechanical skills applicable to certain trades.

1. Which two words have the same meaning?
   (a) open **(b)** happy **(c)** glad **(d)** green
2. Which two words have the opposite meaning?
   (a) old **(b)** dry **(c)** cold **(d)** young
3. A man works 8 hours a day, 40 hours a week. He earns $1.40 an hour. How much does he earn each week?
   (A) $40.00 **(C)** $50.60
   (B) $44.60 **(D)** $56.00
4. At the left is a drawing of a flat piece of metal. Which object at the right can be made from this piece of metal?

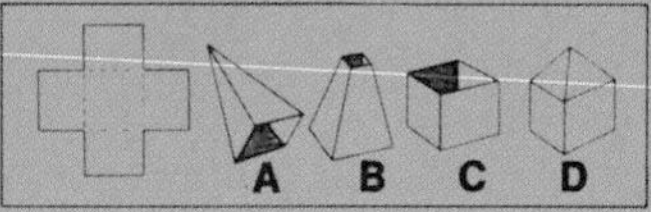

THE MEASUREMENT OF PERSONALITY

Intelligence tests, achievement tests, and tests of aptitude measure *mental abilities*, which are important parts of a person's personality. The instruments for measuring *personality characteristics*, however, differ from instruments for measuring abilities. Answers to questions on an intelligence test indicate whether the testee can, in fact, do certain kinds of thinking and solve certain kinds of problems, whereas answers on personality tests have no clear-cut right or wrong answers. Anyone familiar with the complexities of personality organization knows that a person may have a variety of reasons for giving any one answer on a personality test and that there is no simple way of judging the meaning of an answer.

The Strong Vocational Interest Blank

One way of reducing the ambiguity about the meaning of scores on personality tests is to develop scoring keys without regard to the apparent significance of the questions and answers.

Testers develop scoring keys empirically by collecting information about how persons in clearly defined groups actually respond to individual test items. This method has worked particularly well in the measurement of vocational interests. In constructing the Strong Vocational Interest Blank psychologists took the responses to particular questions asked a group of men successfully employed in a particular occupation and compared them to the responses of a group of "men in general." Only the questions that produced clearly different responses from the two groups were included in the test. A similar instrument for women was developed later. Although the test cannot tell a person how well he would do in an occupation, it can tell him how well his interests correspond with typical interests of those already in the occupation. Sometimes that correspondence may be an important predictor of his success in the occupation. For example, research has shown that people who give responses similar to those given by physicians are less likely to drop out of medical school than those who give other responses. The most recent edition of the Strong Vocational Interest Blank for men can be scored for fifty-nine occupations, and the form for women can be scored for twenty-nine occupations.

1 Actor	(L)	I	D
2 Advertising Man	(L)	I	D
3 Architect	(L)	I	D
4 Military Officer	L	I	(D)
5 Artist	(L)	I	D
6 Astronomer	L	(I)	D
7 Athletic Director	L	(I)	D
8 Auctioneer	L	(I)	D
9 Author of novel	(L)	I	D
10 Author of technical book	L	I	(D)
11 Auto Salesman	L	I	(D)
12 Auto Racer	(L)	I	D
13 Auto Mechanic	L	(I)	D
14 Airplane Pilot	(L)	I	D
15 Bank Teller	L	(I)	D
16 Designer, Electronic Equipment	L	(I)	D
17 Building Contractor..	L	(I)	D
18 Buyer of merchandise	L	(I)	D
19 Carpenter	L	(I)	D
20 Cartoonist	(L)	I	D
21 Cashier in bank	L	(I)	D
22 Electronics Technician	L	I	(D)
23 Chemist	L	(I)	D
24 Civil Engineer	L	(I)	D
25 City or State Employee	L	(I)	D

Figure 20.13
Some of the occupations for which the Strong Vocational Interest Blank is scored. In this phase of the test the subject indicates whether he thinks he would like (L), dislike (D), or be indifferent to (I) each occupation. In a later phase, the person lists his interests, and they are compared to those of people in the occupations in which he has indicated an interest.

The Minnesota Multiphasic Personality Inventory

The most widely used personality inventory, the Minnesota Multiphasic Personality Inventory (MMPI), was also developed without regard for the meaning of its questions. The MMPI was developed in order to identify items on which the pattern of response was different for groups of psychiatric patients and groups of normal people. These items were then combined into *scales*, which were used originally to aid in the evaluation and diagnosis of mental illness.

The authors of the test began with a set of approximately 560 statements. Many of these items dealt directly with psychiatric symptoms—including delusions, hallucinations, ideas of reference, obsessive and compulsive states, and sadistic and masochistic tendencies—but the other items ranged very widely over a variety of questions dealing with physical health, general habits, family and marital status, occupational and educational problems, and attitudes relevant to religion, sex, politics, and social problems. It is fortunate that the MMPI items were so diverse because

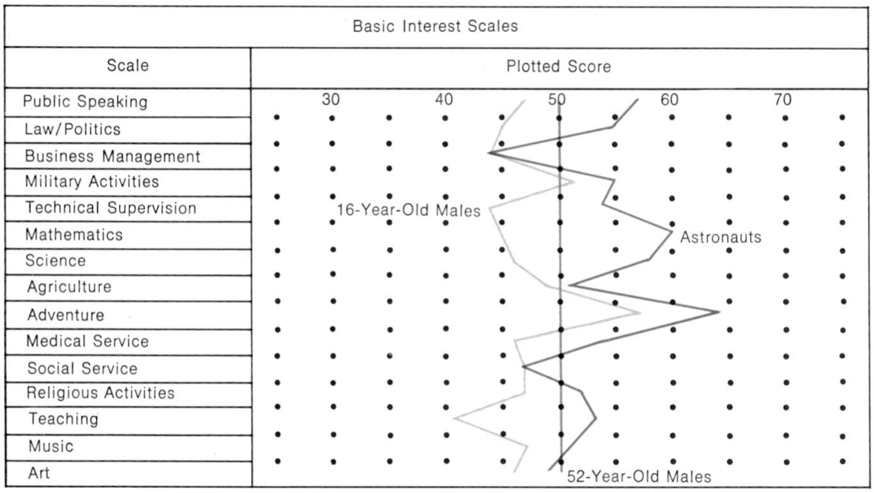

Figure 20.14
The basic interest scale for the Strong Vocational Interest Blank (for males) has as its standard the average score of 52-year-old males. The standardization group was 650 individuals. The scale also normally shows the basic interests of the same men when they were 16 years old. The profile displayed here indicates the basic interests of a group of 22 astronauts.

I have never indulged in any unusual sex practices.

Someone has been trying to poison me.

I am afraid of losing my head.

I feel anxiety about something or someone almost all the time.

Figure 20.15

Four test items from the Minnesota Multiphasic Personality Inventory (MMPI). The person taking the MMPI answers each item as being either true or false as applied to himself. There are over 500 items, and the test usually takes between one and one and a half hours to complete. Persons who are trained in MMPI interpretation can make use of several scales in order to determine whether the clinical scale scores were affected by the subject's response biases. It can be determined, for example, that a person was trying, in his answers, to appear psychologically healthy or to cry for help.

many of the items that did not seem relevant to the initial purposes of the inventory have turned out to be useful not only in studying psychopathology but also in developing a variety of other scales, many of which measure personality characteristics of normal people.

Over a period of three or four years of development of the MMPI, the authors carefully selected 800 clinical patients and gave them the test. They also administered the basic MMPI items to 724 normal people who happened to be visiting relatives or friends in the university hospital. Other normal groups used in the development of MMPI scales included young persons of college age seeking guidance at the University of Minnesota Testing Bureau, WPA project workers, and individuals who were hospitalized for physical illness at the University of Minnesota Hospital.

Scale Construction The scale construction can be illustrated by considering the case of depression. The authors' original set of 560 items was administered to patients with depressive disorders and to normal people. From this large set, about 53 items were found to differentiate the two groups significantly. Not surprisingly, the majority of these items dealt with pessimism of outlook, mood state, energy level, control of impulses, feelings of hopelessness and worthlessness, a lack of quickness in thought and action, and thoughts concerning death and suicide. Later, a few additional items were added to sharpen the discrimination between patients with severe depressive reactions and those with other psychiatric diagnoses. The MMPI D (for Depression) scale has been found to be a highly sensitive indicator not only of psychotic forms of depression but also of less severe forms of depression, of varying mood states, and even of reaction to various forms of psychological treatment. In a similar way, eight additional clinical scales were developed for the original MMPI, as well as a masculinity-and-femininity scale.

In addition to the original scales, over 200 special scales have been devised for the MMPI by a great variety of investigators. These scales vary from specific symptoms of disorder, like "bizarre sensory experiences," to normal and perhaps desirable qualities, like the extent to which a person has a "counselor personality."

Interpretation Clinical psychologists usually base their interpretations upon the patterning of the scale scores rather than upon the absolute elevation of the scores. A great deal of information has been gathered about thousands of people who have been classified by the MMPI profile. Since the mid-1950s, when the computer became generally available to psychologists, computer programs have been developed to write clinical reports based on MMPI data.

The MMPI has been used most in psychiatric clinics and hospitals, but it has also been used for several other purposes, including employment screening, counseling of college students, and personality research. Its major advantage, and the major reason it will probably be around for quite some time, is that it has proved to be useful in so many different situations. Its major disadvantages are its predominantly psychopathological content and the fact that its accuracy can be upset by response biases, such as the tendency always to choose desirable or undesirable alternatives.

The Study of Values

The Study of Values, developed by G. W. Allport and P. E. Vernon, is different from the MMPI because it does not focus at all upon pathological aspects of personality. The Study of Values is based instead on the view that personality is best revealed through a person's values, or his evaluative attitudes. Unlike the MMPI, the Study of Values is most appropriate for college students or for adults with higher-than-average educational backgrounds. It should be used primarily in contexts where the full cooperation of the subjects is obtained; for example, it is used to advantage in vocational counseling, classroom demonstration, and research. Although it has been

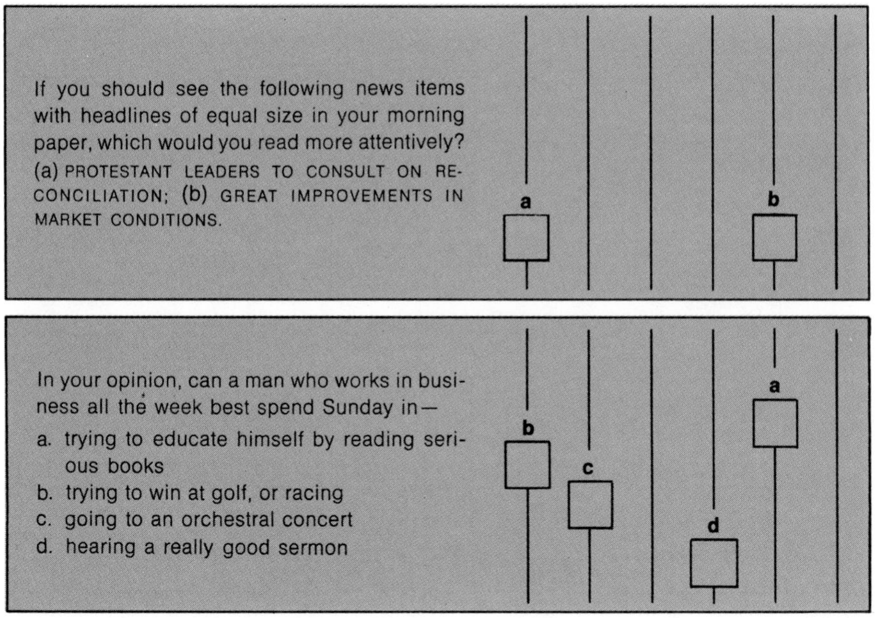

Figure 20.16
These two sample items are taken from the Allport-Vernon-Lindzey Study of Values (a revision of the original Allport-Vernon Scale). In items of the type shown at the top, the subject is asked to indicate his degree of preference of one choice over the other; in items of the type shown at the bottom, he is asked to rate each choice in order of his personal preference.

shown to have important implications for vocational choice and vocational satisfaction—it was found, for example, to be quite highly predictive of occupational career choices of Wellesley students up to fifteen years after graduation from college—it is not recommended as a device to be used for personnel selection unless specific research is undertaken to demonstrate its applicability in a particular setting.

Underlying Typology The Study of Values is based on a typology first advanced by E. Spranger. Spranger maintained that a person is best understood by his interests and intentions rather than by his achievements. For Spranger, the nature of their values distinguishes different people, and he summarized values in terms of six major types, each of which he considered to be a kind of idealized individual. The six ideal types are the theoretical, the economic, the aesthetic, the social, the political, and the religious. Although Spranger believed that an individual could be characterized primarily in terms of a single value type, he also allowed for combinations, an approach consistent with that used by the authors of the Study of Values.

Interpretation A great wealth of data has accumulated about the interpretation of the value scores. One source of information is based on the scores obtained by people in different occupations. Figure 20.17 is a relative representation that contrasts the average scores obtained by three different male occupational or student groups: undergraduate students at a college of engineering, personnel and guidance workers, and clergymen. With remarkable consistency, the profiles of the groups conform to what one would expect. Individuals within each group might be expected to vary within a fairly wide range, but it is reasonable to expect that individuals most satisfied with a particular occupation would frequently be those whose value profiles were consistent with and typical of those individuals already in the occupation.

Application The role of different values has been shown to affect a variety of different kinds of performances and seems to be influential in a person's choice of both friends and spouse. In general, profiles of friends and of married couples tend to be similar. Values have also been found to be important determinants of perception. In one study of selective perception, words were flashed on a screen for very brief intervals. Each word appeared for such a short fraction of a second that the subjects had difficulty in recognizing it. Each of the words was related to one of

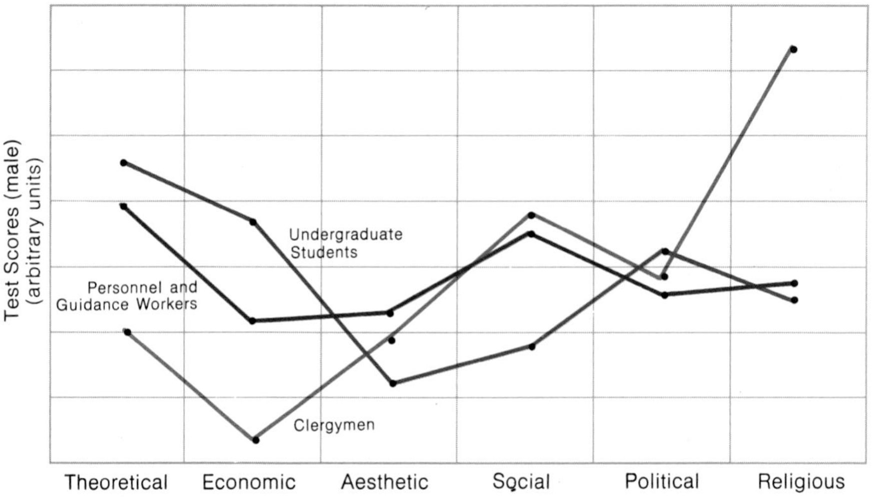

Figure 20.17
Plots of average scores of three male groups on the Study of Values. Many of the differences between these groups that one can see here are predictable. Both clergymen and personnel and guidance workers, for example, score high on social values and lower on economic values, which reflects the service orientation of these two groups. Engineering students score highest on theoretical values and lowest on social and aesthetic values, and this seems consistent with an orientation toward abstract problems.

the value areas. For example, there were words like "profit" and "money" that were linked to the economic value, and words like "beauty" and "poetry" that were linked to the aesthetic value. The experimenters found that each individual's recognition threshold was lowest for words most closely related to whatever value area he scored highest on. (See Chapter 14.)

These findings indicate that values may represent a very central and fundamental aspect of personality, determining not only such things as what an individual believes but even what he is likely to see when confronted with items that are ambiguous or barely perceptible. Very little of history, and even less of personality, would be understandable without some appreciation of the diversity of human values.

The Personality Research Form

The Personality Research Form (PRF), recently developed by D. N. Jackson, is one of the first personality-assessment devices to take advantage of the modern digital computer in order to develop more sophisticated scales for personality measurement.

Assessment Items The PRF initially tried to measure personality characteristics that were described by Henry Murray and his associates (see Chapter 22). The actual questions included in the PRF were selected by a very careful statistical procedure. In the construction of the entire set of twenty-two PRF scales, over 3,000 items were written initially, and the final items were selected from those. The items on each scale were chosen by means of a statistical index that sought to maximize relevance to the personality scale and minimize response bias. Thus, these scales show good correlations with distinct criterion measures. For example, the aggression scale has been found to correlate highly with ratings of aggression by persons who know the respondent well.

Interpretation The PRF scores are usually summarized in the form of a profile. In the interpretation of personality-inventory profiles, a great deal of attention is directed toward interpreting *patterns* of total scores rather than the scores themselves. An attempt is made to capture a total life style as revealed by the relative importance of various traits in the individual's personality.

Figure 20.18 gives an illustration of the PRF profile of a twenty-one-year-old college senior who became president of the student association while also serving on the university debating team and achieving a level of scholastic performance that consistently placed her on the dean's list. Note that the salient features of the profile are consistent with her pattern of performance. There are high scores for exhibition and dominance, both of which have been shown to be associated with the tendency

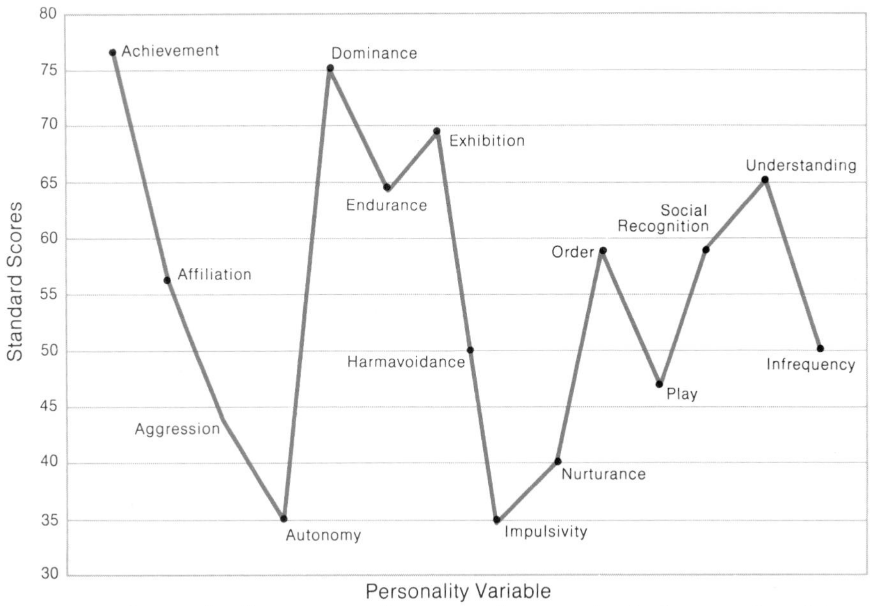

Figure 20.18
This PRF profile was obtained for an outstanding female college student. She was student-association president and a member of the debating team, and she consistently got high grades.

to be ascendent and talkative in small groups. There are also high scores for achievement and understanding. Because achievement involves the seeking of standards of excellence, and understanding primarily involves a kind of intellectual curiosity, we might conclude that these characteristics are consistent with her outstanding level of performance in academic work. Note that the score for autonomy is relatively low, implying that she prefers to work with people rather than independently, and note also that her scores for affiliation and aggression imply that her interaction with others is more affiliative than aggressive.

Associations have been pointed out between predominant dimensions of personality, as measured on the PRF, and vocational interests, indicating that one's orientation to other people, to work, and to certain activities may reveal a certain life style. The life style also reveals itself in the person's choice of occupation and his tendency to be satisfied with one line of work rather than another. In a study linking PRF scores to scores derived from the Strong Vocational Interest Blank, seven dimensions common to both vocational interests and personality were identified. One of these dimensions was particularly interesting; it contrasted different modes of controlling or expressing impulses. At one extreme of the dimensions, PRF scales for order and cognitive structure—together implying a certain planfulness and care for detail—were associated with interest patterns of accountants and office workers. At the other extreme of this same dimension were the PRF scales for impulsivity, change, exhibition, and autonomy. Associated with these were the interest patterns of authors, lawyers, clinical psychologists, and advertisers. Each of these occupations would seem to have in common the possibility of some freedom of expression and escape from routine. This dimension is presented in Figure 20.19, together with a second dimension reflecting dominance versus passivity in human relations.

Projective Tests

In projective tests, personality characteristics are revealed by the way people tell stories about or otherwise interpret ambiguous material. The idea is that because there is no established meaning, any meaning that the person puts into his story must come from himself and should therefore reveal something about his personality. Projective tests are based on a different set of principles than are the personality questionnaires previously discussed. Instead of focusing upon the measurement of specific traits, through answers to specific questions, projective tests give the person an opportunity to reveal his personality traits by the particular manner in which

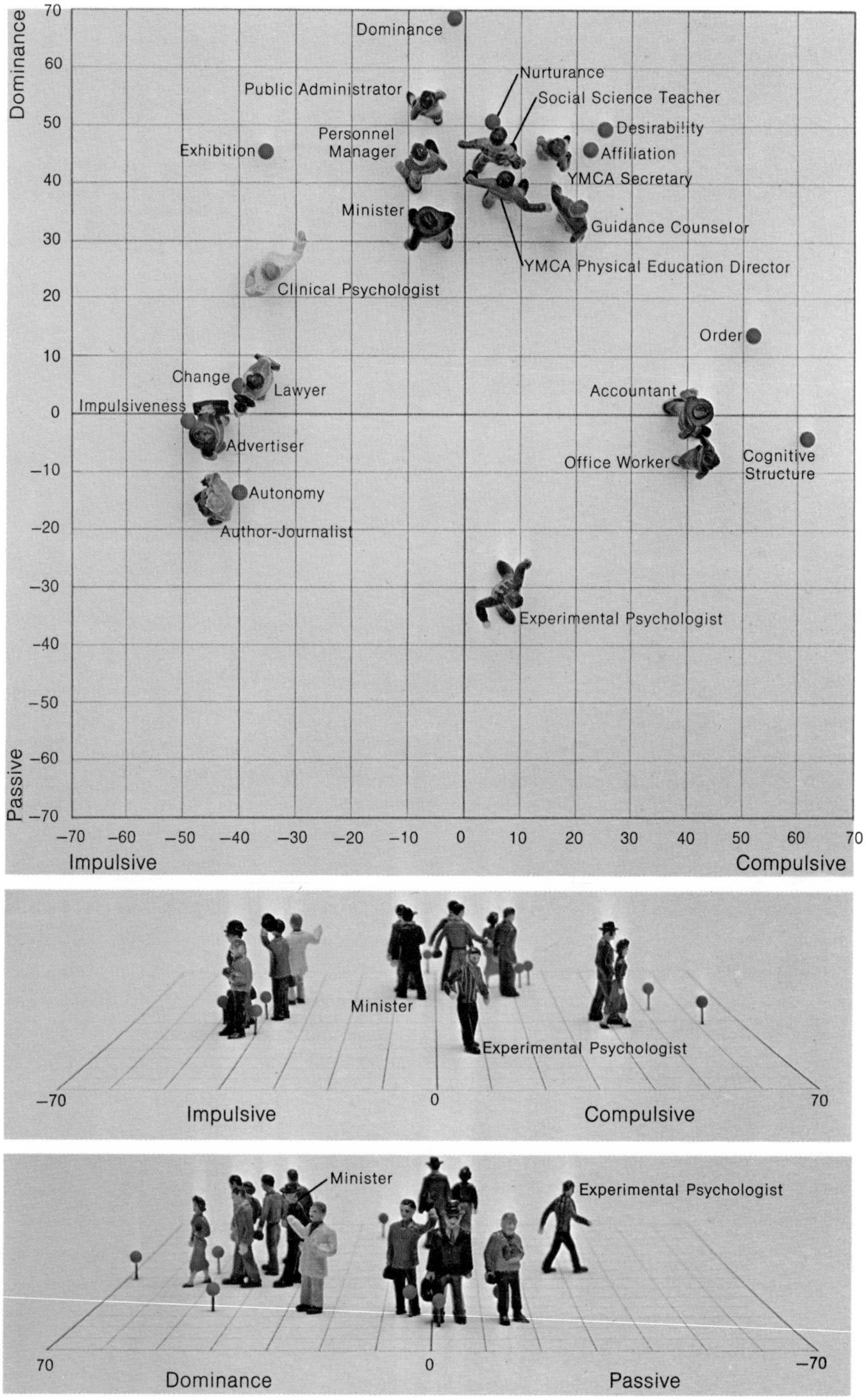

Figure 20.19
Three views of a matrix that shows how various PRF characteristics (red points) and several occupational groups are associated with the dimensions of dominance-passivity and impulsiveness-compulsivity. Members of these occupational groups completed both the PRF and the Strong Vocational Interest Blank. As one might expect, occupations such as public administrator and personnel manager are associated with high dominance, whereas authors and experimental psychologists are more associated with passivity. Accountants are high in compulsivity, authors and journalists are near the other extreme of impulsiveness.

he interprets the material. Some ambiguous materials are highly abstract, like inkblots; others are more concrete, like pictures of actual social situations. In still others, the person is not provided with something to interpret verbally, but rather is asked to create something by drawing, modeling with clay, or even acting out roles.

Rorschach Inkblot Test Perhaps the best-known projective technique is that developed by Hermann Rorschach, a Swiss psychiatrist, who with remarkable insight developed a set of ten inkblots. Rorschach developed a scoring system that has been modified but is still in wide use today.

In administering the Rorschach, the examiner hands the inkblots one by one to the person and instructs him to report what he sees. Administration is divided into a free-association period and an inquiry period. During the free association, the person simply identifies what he sees. He might say, for example, that a certain area of a blot resembles an airplane or a rocket. During the inquiry, the examiner asks certain general questions in an attempt to discover what about the inkblot determined the response.

In general, three categories are involved in scoring. The first category indicates how much of the inkblot the person responds to, ranging from small or even minute detail to the whole blot. The second relates to the determinants of the response—whether the person responds primarily to form, color, shading, or activity level. Combinations of determinants are possible, and provision is made for scoring in terms of quality. The third category is content.

Laymen often think that the content of a response is most important, but in most scoring systems, content is the least important aspect of the individual's performance. The way that the individual uses content is much more significant. For example, types of *pathognomic* responses (that is, responses indicative of the possibility of serious psychological disorder) include *contaminations,* the tendency to mix indiscriminately parts belonging to different animals and human beings, and *confabulations,* the tendency to go far beyond the material at hand, often with bizarre overtones. These types of responses occur commonly in patients with certain types of psychological disorder.

It would be a mistake to place too much emphasis upon the scoring techniques used by Rorschach examiners. The Rorschach method is essentially impressionistic. It is based to a large extent upon the individual clinician's insight, capacity for careful observation, and awareness of the manner in which psychopathology is revealed. In the assessment procedure, he will use not only the individual's Ror-

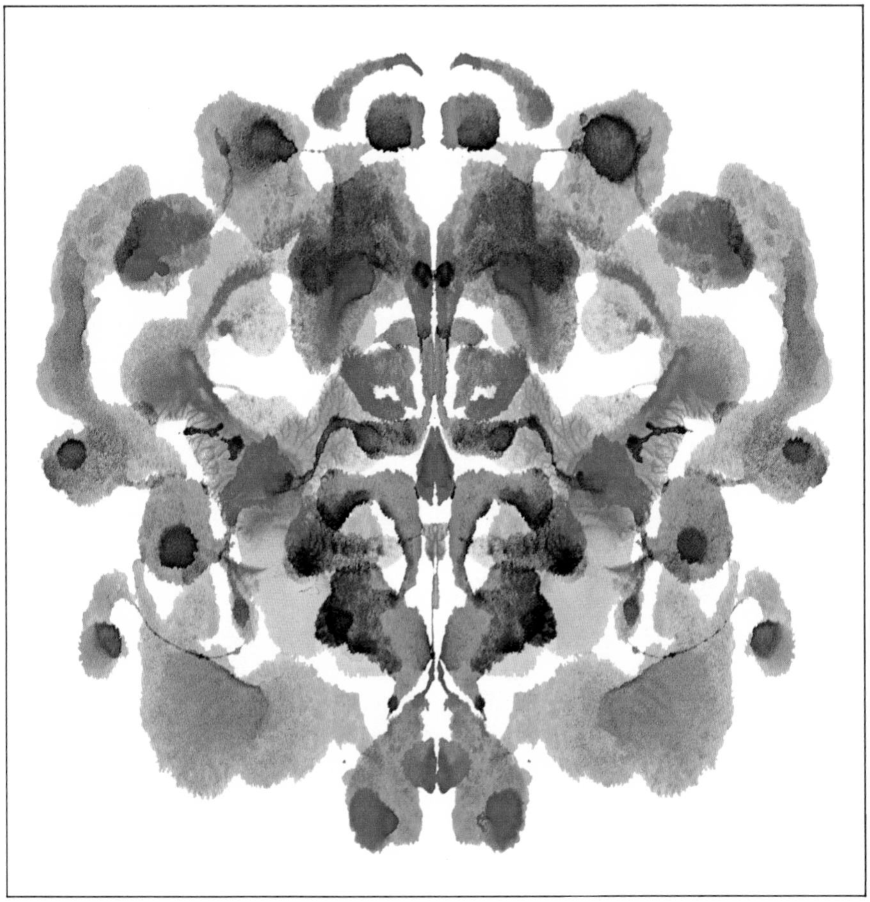

Figure 20.20

This inkblot is similar to those used in the Rorschach Inkblot Test. Psychologists skilled in the Rorschach test can derive a great deal of information about the person not only from responses to the cards but also from his behavior during the test. Psychologists rarely use the test's formal scoring categories because of their limited reliability and the lack of firm evidence as to their validity. Test interpretation, therefore, is impressionistic.

Figure 20.21
Two cards similar to those used in the TAT. Although the TAT is a projective technique like the Rorschach, it requires a greater degree of coordinated thinking and more verbal behavior from the subject. The scenes depicted in the drawings permit a variety of interpretations, and the person taking the test therefore is assumed to project his own needs, wishes, defenses, and other personality factors into the story. The clinical psychologist who administers and scores the TAT notes many aspects of the stories' content; for example, the types of interpersonal interactions reported and how the stories end.

Figure 20.22
Sir Francis Galton's genius was not confined to one area of psychology. Besides his pioneering work in free-association tests, he also exerted profound influence in the areas of statistics, psychophysics, mental retardation, genetics, and tests of intelligence. Galton spent much of his professional life in fields other than psychology; the fact that his contributions to psychology are the product of only fifteen years of work makes his intelligence and genius stand out as being all the more remarkable.

schach responses but also his reaction to the test situation. Some people, for example, are extremely defensive and wary in the test situation, and others define it in authoritarian terms. Still others view it as a competitive task, expecting their performance to be evaluated against some standard and judged in terms of its quality. Each one of these interpersonal styles may reveal to the examiner an important facet of the individual's personality structure.

The fact that the person has great latitude in how he acts in the situation detracts from the reliability of the test, but it also provides an opportunity for him to reveal important things about himself. The lack of structure involved in the Rorschach technique, as in many projective techniques, is both a strength and a weakness. It is a strength in the sense that it broadly samples behavior and permits the possibility for certain patterns to emerge that might not emerge otherwise. The disadvantage of such an approach is that the test situation itself does not focus clearly on any single set of patterns and consequently leaves interpretation open to the biases of the particular examiner.

The Thematic Apperception Test Although also a projective device, the Thematic Apperception Test (TAT) requires a kind of response different from that required by the Rorschach inkblot technique.

The TAT, developed by Henry Murray, consists of a series of twenty cards containing pictures of a variety of situations. The person is asked to tell a coherent story about the picture, including what led up to the situation, what the characters are thinking and feeling, and how it will end. Murray's original suggestion was to present the pictures in two one-hour sessions, the first involving the ordinary scenes and the second involving the more bizarre scenes; however, most clinical psychologists who employ the test select their own series of cards from the twenty.

Analysis of the stories is usually done on an individual basis. Originally, Murray suggested that the TAT be interpreted in terms of *need* and *press,* which are discussed in Chapter 22, but a variety of other systems, including some based on psychoanalytic theory, are also employed. Research indicates that clinicians agree only moderately well about interpretations and predictions. In fact, their accuracy often does not exceed that of psychology students who have not received specific training in TAT interpretation.

All interpretive systems depend on certain underlying assumptions regarding the use of the sort of fantasy tapped by the TAT. Common assumptions are that the hero or heroine of the story is the one with whom the storyteller usually identifies, that the storyteller's fantasies will reveal his or her motives, and that uncommon responses are more likely to reveal important aspects of personality than common ones.

A number of very interesting studies have employed the TAT, including studies about the changes that arise from altered states of consciousness induced by sensory deprivation and the use of drugs. Equally important, the TAT has led to the development of a variety of techniques useful for measuring particular traits like the need for affiliation and the need for achievement. Some of the findings from research on these traits are discussed in Chapter 19.

Other Verbal Projective Tests Although the Rorschach and TAT tests are by far the most popular projective tests, several other varieties are used. In the *word-association test,* a technique originally produced by Sir Francis Galton and later revised by C. G. Jung, the person is presented with a word and instructed to say the first word that comes to his mind. The stimulus words—words such as "guilt," "desire," and "mother"—are commonly associated with psychological difficulties. Responses are analyzed in terms of the time before the response, content, and such nonverbal responses as blushing or wringing one's hands. Word-association tests are sometimes accompanied by psychophysiological measures like heart rate and blood pressure, as in the lie detector test (see Chapter 17).

Another widely used projective technique for personality assessment is the *sentence-completion test.* In this procedure, only the first few words of a sentence are presented to a person, and he is asked to complete the sentence. For example, he might be asked to complete the following sentences: "The thing that upsets me the most is . . . ," "My parents . . . ," "I felt like quitting when they . . ."

Expressive Techniques All the projective tests that have been described focus on *words*—what the person says or writes. A number of other tests have been developed that focus on expressive aspects of behavior. These techniques require a person to draw pictures of people, to construct miniature situations out of toys or out of pictures, to make figures from clay, or to act out social roles. In general, research with these techniques has been too sparse to develop reliable testing methods or to test the validity of inferences drawn from the techniques.

One possible exception to this limitation is the Draw-a-Person test, popularized by K. Machover. The individual is first instructed simply to draw a person and then to draw a second person of the opposite sex from the first one. Research with this test suggests, for example, that it may be useful for indicating an individual's tendency to be analytical and to structure his environment. People who are analytical tend to incorporate many details in their drawings, to differentiate clearly between the sexes, and to avoid simplification.

Expressive and stylistic behavior is potentially a valuable source of information about an individual's personality, quite apart from his particular traits. Many years ago, Allport and Vernon did a series of studies investigating stylistic consistencies in behavior. An individual's gait, his tempo of talking, his characteristic facial expression, and his posture all proved to be measurable and consistent. They distinguished this kind of behavior from personality traits per se, suggesting that although stylistic behavior is only surface behavior, ultimately it may be possible to show that it reveals personality characteristics of more central importance.

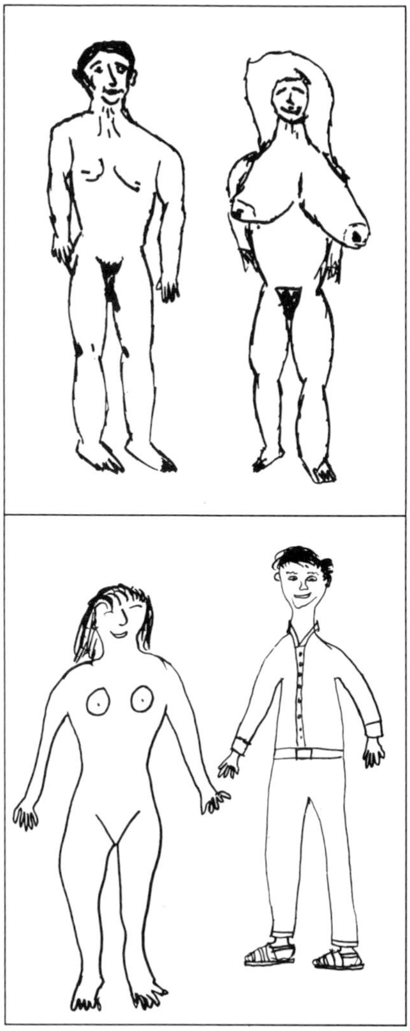

Figure 20.23
Two sets of drawings made for the Draw-A-Person test. Test administrators generally make use of such information as whether a male or female is drawn first, whether the figures are clothed, the general body shape, size and shape of genitalia and breasts, and type of activity (for example, standing still, walking, or sitting). Stylistic features such as attention to details, tension in the pencil lines, and amount of paper used for the drawing also are considered important. There has been relatively little controlled research on the test, however, and its validity as a diagnostic instrument has not been firmly established.

Using Projective Tests The major difficulty with projective techniques of all kinds is that their reliability is wide open to question. The basic principle—that each person tends to structure an ambiguous situation according to his own personality—seems tenable enough. The problem is in interpreting the person's personality from the test results. There is always the danger that a clinician's interpretation will tell us more about him than about the person who produced the responses in the first place, and the methods of interpretation used by different clinicians are often too poorly standardized to test for reliability. When the Rorschach and the MMPI are compared experimentally, the MMPI almost always proves to be a better predictor of future behavior. It is one of the unfortunate facts of life that while the more structured tests may not delve as deeply into the personality structure as the projective tests, a great deal more faith can usually be placed in information yielded by the structured techniques. A good clinician may be a better predictor than a good test, but with the structured tests there is much less need to worry about the biases of the individual clinician.

Formal Interviews

Probably the most widely used technique for personality appraisal is the interview. Few employers would hire an employee without interviewing him. The interview is also used in counseling, clinical assessment, and educational decision making.

Interviewing techniques vary widely, ranging from those that leave the person free to discuss whatever he wishes to those that involve a set of very precise and well-structured questions. Many books have been written on the interview, particularly the clinical interview. The books on clinical interviewing discuss a wide variety of techniques for eliciting information and encouraging the person to accept counseling or the need for therapeutic change.

The interview affords an excellent opportunity to appraise such qualities as level of anxiety, fluency and style of speech, and sensitivity to certain topics. The interviewer can also obtain personal history and background data. Although people may be motivated to distort the information they give on personal history forms, they find it more difficult to do so in an interview. In addition, it is sometimes more appropriate to ask personal questions in an individual interview than on a standardized questionnaire. Indeed, psychologists have found that the use of highly personal questions in a standardized questionnaire is a potent device for arousing aggression.

Problems with the interview are similar to problems with projective techniques. Interviewers vary widely in their skill at eliciting information and in the accuracy with which they can judge traits they see emerging from an interview.

Situational Measures

Another important technique of personality appraisal is one that assesses a person's reaction in a situation relevant to the job or task for which he is being considered. Some situational measures involve business games, in which certain essential materials must be obtained from competitors and players must serve as negotiators.

Some of the most ingenious procedures examine a person's reaction to frustration or stress. The staff of "Station S" of the Office of Strategic Services during World War II developed procedures for selecting espionage agents and other individuals preparing to work behind enemy lines. In one procedure, a senior staff member suggested to the candidate that he build a certain type of small-scale construction and then gave him a plan and two assistants—who were actually other staff members. The staff members were instructed to behave in a very frustrating manner but not to disobey orders. The candidate, of course, did not know of these secret instructions to the two assistants. One assistant was extremely sluggish, took no initiative, engaged in projects of his own, and offered no advice. The other was extremely aggressive; he criticized weaknesses in the candidate, offered irrelevant suggestions, and expressed dissatisfaction.

The particular direction the needling took almost invariably resulted in some degree of frustration on the part of the candidate. The emotional reactions elicited by this task provided a rather good gauge of the person's tolerance for frustration. Some men were so shaken up by this experience that afterward they asked to be released from the assessment program and from their assignment.

Figure 20.24
The man on the right is being tested on this airplane flight simulator. The aim of this test is to gauge how well he will perform in actual flight situations. When a test is administered in order to estimate a person's potential performance in a specific situation, the test should be as similar as possible to the actual situation. (United Air Lines photo.)

THE ETHICS OF TESTING

Personality assessment and intelligence testing can be useful tools to help individual people lead more productive lives. Realistic information about a person's capabilities and dispositions can help him situate himself in appropriate social and occupational contexts. Techniques such as those outlined in this chapter have been applied with increasing success in vocational counseling, clinics, hospitals, educational institutions, and industry. There are, however, two important dangers associated with personality assessment and intelligence testing. One is that the tests are not always accurate, and the second is that they can be used unfairly to control people's fates.

Questions concerning the accuracy and appropriateness of tests can usually be answered with technical information. For example, one can ask, "Is the personality test valid for the purposes for which it is being used?" or "Can the questions asked be legitimately answered in terms of the data collected with the personality-assessment techniques employed?" With the use of test manuals, most qualified psychologists could answer such questions without a great deal of difficulty. Tests usually turn out to measure much less than most people think they do, and they never supply absolutely certain information. *The results of all tests are always a matter of probability*—at best, they only supply a good estimate of what they are designed to measure.

The second issue is more complex—and more important. Regardless of test validity, to what uses may people put personality and intelligence tests? Tests can supply people with information about themselves—for example, about their vocational interests, strengths, weaknesses—but this can be problematic. Should a psychologist tell a child that he has obtained a poor IQ score when it may have the effect of decreasing his motivation to learn? Most psychologists supply only approximate information about the results of intelligence tests.

Another use to which personality and intelligence tests may be put is to help make decisions about who should be admitted to restricted groups and who should be rejected. Is it appropriate for a company or organization to inquire into a person's interpersonal relationships before they hire him, and if so, may they also inquire into his fundamental beliefs or his private fantasies? Is it appropriate for colleges to use attitude questionnaires as an aid in selecting students in order to ensure a certain homogeneity in the student body? Is it appropriate for business or government organizations to give tests originally intended for psychiatric patients, such as the Rorschach, in order to assess the potential of executives or civil servants? Or for that matter, should the results of a Rorschach test be used to decide whether a person will be hospitalized or not?

There are no absolutely right answers to these questions, but some general guidelines can be suggested. To begin with, in almost all cases, people should have the option of taking or not taking tests—and their decisions should not be used against them. When tests help predict adjustment or success at a task, they are generally useful. When they are used as an artificial basis for restriction, their use is certainly questionable.

Personality and intelligence tests are tools, and like other tools such as nuclear power or surgeons' scalpels, they may be used for desirable or undesirable ends. In the final analysis, a decision must be made by the individual using the test. Knowledge about people entails power over their fate, a power that can become a weapon or an aid.

SUGGESTED READINGS

ALLISON, J., *et al.* (Eds.). *The Interpretation of Psychological Tests.* New York, Harper & Row, 1968. Presents a series of papers that together supply a good overview of psychological testing.

AMERICAN PSYCHOLOGICAL ASSOCIATION. *Standards for Educational and Psychological Tests and Manuals.* Washington, D.C., American Psychological Association, 1966. Contains a thorough description of standards for psychological tests.

BUROS, O. (Ed.). *Personality Tests and Reviews.* Highland Park, N.J., Gryphon Press, 1970. Contains descriptions and critical reviews of all existing personality tests. A source book for anyone who is searching for almost any type of personality test.

MCREYNOLDS, P. *Advances in Psychological Assessment.* Palo Alto, California, Science & Behavior Books, Inc., 1968. Contains a survey of recent advances in the measurement of personality and intelligence.

MEEHL, P. E. *Clinical Versus Statistical Prediction: A Theoretical Analysis and Review of the Evidence.* Minneapolis, University of Minnesota Press, 1954. Can individual clinicians predict behavior on the basis of their intuition better than experimentalists on the basis of statistical evidence? Meehl supplies a thorough discussion of the evidence for both sides.

SCHACHTEL, E. *Experiential Foundations of Rorschach's Test.* New York, Basic Books, Inc., Publishers, 1966. Attempts to supply a theoretical foundation for the interpretation of the Rorschach inkblot test. Schachtel's position is based on a theory of perception.

WECHSLER, D. *The Measurement and Appraisal of Adult Intelligence.* Baltimore, Md., The Williams & Wilkins Co., 1958. A classic discussion of intelligence and intelligence testing.

KIRKLAND

21 Freudian Theories of Personality

Sometimes, when a person grows extremely famous for one facet of his lifework, there is a tendency to forget that he ever did anything else. For instance, Einstein got the Nobel Prize for physics in 1921, and practically everyone assumes he got it for his theory of relativity. No such thing! It was for his work on the photoelectric effect, which had nothing to do with relativity. Pavlov got the Nobel Prize in medicine and physiology in 1904. Do you suppose it was for his work on the conditioned reflex, which everyone is conditioned to associate with Pavlov? No, that came later. He got the award for his work on the physiology of digestion. Ehrlich got the Nobel Prize in medicine and physiology in 1908. For his discovery of arsphenamine as a specific against syphilis? That came later, too. Ehrlich got it for his work on immunity.

So it goes. Almost everyone has heard of Sigmund Freud, but only in connection with psychoanalysis. Yet he was nearly forty before he really began to formulate his psychoanalytic theory. What was he doing before then? For one thing he was a neurophysiologist and a first-rate one. Had he continued in that line of endeavor, he might have won a Nobel Prize for himself eventually. In the field of psychoanalysis, he never did.

He was also one of the first to work on cocaine. This is a substance found in the leaves of the coca plant, which is native to Bolivia and Peru. The South American Indians, it had been discovered, would chew coca leaves as an antidote to fatigue and a source of happiness sensation. Unaware of its addictive qualities, Freud advocated its use for minor pains, suggesting that it fulfill the role that aspirin has today. He spoke of it so highly that he actually started a fad for its use, and was therefore responsible for what became a small epidemic of cocaine addiction.

Carl Koller, an intern at the University of Vienna, learned of cocaine from Freud, who was working there, and decided to use it as an anesthetic. He became an ophthalmologist and in 1884 performed an eye operation while using cocaine injected into the area. The operation was successful and marked the beginning of the use of local anesthesia.

I once told this to a friend as still another little-known example of Freud's influence, and he said, "Good Lord, if this guy Freud had had a little more brains and thought of local anesthesia himself, he might have become famous." I was about to protest heatedly, when I caught that look in his eye that told me he was putting me on. I. A.

Everyone has implicit theories of personality; we all condense and combine information and guess at causes of cognitive, emotional, and behavioral events. These theories permit us to attribute characteristic dispositions to people we meet and enable us to predict their behavior in various circumstances. Chapter 23 discusses the formation of these implicit theories and sets out their role in how people form impressions of others.

A theory of personality constructed by a psychologist or psychoanalyst also ascribes dispositions to people but does so through a formally stated set of logically related assumptions about the nature of man and the determinants of his nature. It makes statements about what a human being is and how he got the way he is. Formal theories of personality are more elaborate, better integrated, and more explicit than the theories each of us holds. They attempt to supply principles of behavior that apply to mankind in general rather than to construct a theory to understand each unique individual. Most important, formal theories of personality go beyond intuition (although they may begin there) and usually try to supply objectively verifiable hypotheses. As you read the personality theories summarized in this chapter and the next, you will probably find that you like some and dislike others. Chances are good that you will react most favorably to the theories that agree with your implicit theories of personality.

Theories of personality can be seen as attempts to synthesize the various aspects of human behavior. They are usually *holistic,* in that they look at the total phenomenon of personality, rather than *atomistic,* that is, examining each of the many components that go to make up human personality. You will note that the final section of Chapter 22 examines the stance of behaviorism in light of personality theory. Behaviorism is the only atomistic approach dealt with in the two chapters, and you will see that there is, in a real sense, no behaviorist theory of personality. Chapter 1 discusses the construction of different kinds of theories in greater detail.

COMPARING PERSONALITY THEORIES

The personality theories that are outlined in this chapter and the next are classified by author. Many attempts have been made to fit various theories into categories, but the trouble with classifying theories by "school" or approach is that the category into which they are placed emphasizes one aspect of a theory and may neglect other aspects. Such categorization prejudges the theory and usually oversimplifies it. Theories of personality are usually exceedingly complex, with implications for many areas of human behavior.

Different theories focus on different aspects of human experience, and even when they do deal with similar aspects, they often view them from different perspectives. The best way to experience the similarities and differences among the theories is to read briefly through all of them and then to carefully examine the stand each of them takes on a number of issues, especially the four discussed in the following paragraph.

The four issues most important to the understanding of personality relate to the components, activity, development, and motivational forces of personality. Most theories discuss personality in terms of *structure* and comment on its major functions or goals; they hypothesize a moving force or *dynamic;* they discuss the *development* of personality; they often consider principles of *motivation.* Most of the theories in this chapter and the next can be compared in terms of these issues. In their book *Theories of Personality,* C. Hall and G. Lindzey compare theories on these four issues and on several others; the information in Table 21.1 is based on their work. These issues lie at the core of every theory of personality. Even when a particular theory does not deal with one of them, its absence suggests that the theorist gave it so little importance that he could neglect it entirely.

Most likely, you will recognize the interconnection of the issues in the Table. For example, a certain position on item 4—say, that human beings are indeed mechanistic creatures—implies a similar view on item 11—namely, that people are controlled to a great extent by their environment.

The discussion of each theory, then, is organized around the issues displayed in Table 21.1. Tables 21.2 and 22.1 show the issues that lie at the core of each theory discussed in the two chapters. The only categorization implied by the division of theories into two chapters is the grouping of Freud and those theoreticians commonly called neo-Freudian in this chapter, and theoreticians less influenced by Freud—or not all—in the following one. Also, many of the psychotherapies discussed in Chapters 32 and 33 are based on theories of personality discussed in this chapter and Chapter 22.

The theories discussed are diverse in every conceivable respect. But, as G. S. Reynolds has pointed out, if you understand a theory of personality well enough and if you understand enough about yourself, there will be something about any personality theory that rings true and seems relevant to you personally. This observation is true only because all theories were made by real people about real people. Nearly infinitely complex, any individual possesses enough complexes, neuroses (often minor), quirks, behavior patterns, beliefs, hidden and expressed desires, inadequacies, and competences to require more than one or two particular theories to even begin to describe him or her adequately.

FREUD'S PSYCHOANALYTIC THEORY

Sigmund Freud's theory was, without doubt, the single most pervasive force in the study of personality. His was the first formal theory and is the most detailed one

Table 21.1—Core Issues in Theories of Personality

1. Structure.
2. Dynamics.
3. Development.
4. *Goal orientation of motivation:* Is man a purposive creature who heads toward some naturally occurring goal or ideal, or is he essentially mechanistic?
5. *Number of dynamic principles* necessary to explain personality: Is man guided by one overriding goal such as self-actualization, or is his behavior best understood as the result of a number of needs?
6. Relative importance of *conscious and unconscious* motivation, commonly associated with the question "Is man rational or irrational?"
7. *Nature versus Nurture:* How much is man's behavior determined by heredity and how much by environment?
8. Type of *learning* important in personality development: Does nature have its effect through reinforcement, associative learning, or cognitive organization; is man essentially hedonistic?
9. Relative importance of *early experiences:* Is adult personality mainly determined in early childhood or do contemporaneous factors play a major role?
10. *Continuity of development:* Does personality develop through qualitatively distinct stages or does it develop continuously?
11. Relative importance of *internal and external forces:* Does man influence his environment or does the environment control him?
12. *Social influences:* What importance does the theory attach to social (family, group, or cultural) influences?
13. *Molecular versus molar* focus on behavior: Does the theory focus on specific responses and reflexes or does it focus on "life style," or the "functioning person"?
14. *Holism:* Should man as a whole be studied or should a theory focus on the analysis of his separate parts?
15. *Uniqueness of individual:* Are similarities or differences among people of greatest importance?
16. *Self-concept:* Does the theory hypothesize a self-concept?

Source: C. Hall and G. Lindzey, *Theories of Personality* (2nd Ed., New York: Wiley, 1970).

that has ever been formulated. It is based upon Freud's fifty years of experience as a psychoanalyst working intensively with a large number of individuals in the intimacy of the therapeutic situation.

Freud first became interested in personality and psychotherapy when he discovered, in collaboration with J. Breuer, that hysteric disorders could be cured if the patient recalled events of his infancy and childhood and talked about them under hypnosis. In 1900 Freud's *Interpretation of Dreams* introduced the new technique of psychoanalysis to the world. People came to Vienna to learn Freud's methods, and soon psychoanalysts were practicing in a number of countries including the United States. Freud revised and supplemented his theory throughout his life, but most of his basic ideas remained the same.

Structure

Personality, according to Freud, is composed of three separate but interacting systems: the *id,* the *ego,* and the *superego.* Freud used these terms as analogies, as

Table 21.2—Theoretical Positions on Some Core Issues

	Structure	Dynamics
Freud	Three separate but interacting systems: the id—reservoir of instinctual energy; the ego—mediates among the id's demands, the demands of the environment, and the superego; the superego—represents traditional values and ideals of society, strives for perfection.	Source of energy is instincts, especially sex and aggression. Personality is the result of compromises between instinctual urges and societal demands. Main dynamic processes are displacement, identification, anxiety, and defense mechanisms, especially sublimation.
Jung	Personal unconscious, containing experiences that have been repressed; contents can return to consciousness. Collective unconscious, containing memories and behavior patterns from mankind's ancestral past.	Four functions—thinking, feeling, sensing, and intuiting—interact with two attitudes—introversion and extroversion.
Adler	Consciousness is the center of personality. Focuses on awareness of reasons for behavior and uniqueness of each personality.	The *creative self* searches for experiences to help fulfill the person's unique style of life; if they cannot be found, the self tries to create them.
Erikson	Expands Freud's conception of instincts, the most important one being sexual. Focuses on the ego rather than the id or superego.	Emphasis on the effect of interaction between a person and his environment; personality is the result of the encounter between drives and the demands of the society.
White	The id, ego, and superego are interacting systems but the ego has its own source of energy.	Curiosity and exploratory behavior indicate that the pursuit of competence is a major driving force. Emphasis on psychosocial aspects of behavior.
Fromm	Minimizes influence of instincts and emphasizes effect of social environment, especially the family.	Importance of love and shared work in overcoming the loneliness that accompanies freedom; if the individual cannot so unite himself with others, he will seek to escape from freedom and loneliness by submitting to authority and conforming to society.

Development	Motivation
Five psychosexual stages—oral, anal, phallic, latency, and genital. The final organization of personality represents contributions from all the stages.	Tension reduction—aim is to conserve equilibrium of the organism by abolishing disturbing excitations.
Goal of development is unity within a personality. Individuation, that is, development of each part of a personality is followed by the attempt to unit these parts into a fully realized self—the transcendent function.	A person's future aims are as important as his past in his personality development.
Social forces are seen as important as instinctual ones.	People strive to obtain an ideal; much of the striving is an attempt to compensate for feelings of inferiority, based on helplessness in childhood.
An epigenetic principle—development from a predetermined ground plan toward a functioning whole—is manifested through eight stages of development, each characterized by an erogenous zone and a mode of dealing with the environment (see Table 21.3); a crisis, or test, accompanies each stage; failure to successfully resolve a crisis results in fixation.	Different motives at each of the eight developmental stages (see Table 21.3).
Agrees with Erikson's stages but says that although some early motivation is psychosexual, much of what infants and children do is aimed at gaining competence and independence.	Not all motivation is based on tension reduction; people are motivated to effect changes in themselves and in the world.
Personality development is determined by social factors.	Five specific needs arise from conditions of existence. Needs are relatedness; transcendence; rootedness; sense of personal identity; and frame of reference.

Figure 21.1
Sigmund Freud sitting in the office in which he did his writing. The impact of Freudian theory owes much to his great writing abilities; his vivid psychoanalytic accounts of the workings of personality and society created an atmosphere of excitement during the years when psychoanalysis startled the Western world.

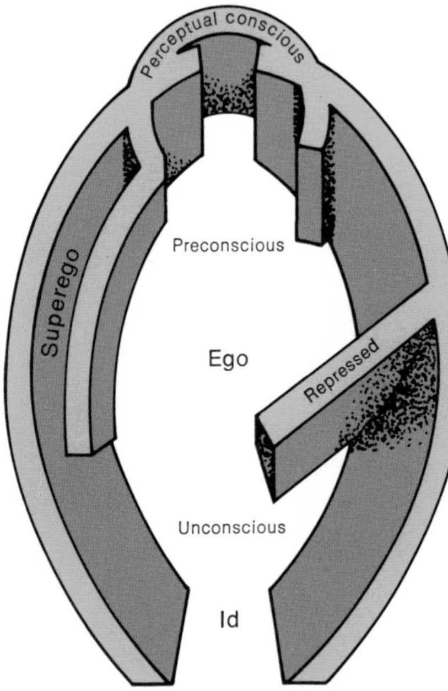

Figure 21.2
The structure and topography of Freudian personality theory. The topography is represented by the perceptual conscious (present awareness), the preconscious (that which is easily available to awareness), and the unconscious (repressed, unavailable contents). In the structural approach, personality consists of the id, the ego, and the superego. Id impulses and processes are unconscious. Superego contents and functions may exist at all levels of topography, whereas ego processes are generally close to preconsciousness.

Figure 21.3 *(opposite)*
In the Freudian personality system, the id is the source of unconscious instinctual drives. The id operates according to the pleasure principle; it prompts the child to seek immediate gratification and immediate reduction of uncomfortable tensions. The superego develops as the child internalizes the values and prohibitions of parents and the wider culture. Freudians see anxiety and disorder as a product of the inevitable clashes between id and superego.

constructs to explain what he saw in his patients' behavior. One must keep in mind, when discussing Freud, that he spoke in analogies, and as Freud himself said, analogies prove nothing. They do, however, aid in the comprehension of complex and difficult concepts.

The Id The id is the original system of the personality; it is the material out of which the ego and the superego become differentiated. It is the reservoir of instinctual psychic energy (the *libido*), and it is completely unconscious. You can never know your own id directly; you can only know it through its manifestations in your behavior. The id cannot tolerate tension, so it tries to discharge immediately any tension that arises in it. The id is said to obey the *pleasure principle*, that is, to seek gratification and reduce painful tensions to the lowest level possible.

The Ego Because the id's energy is completely internal, an ego forms to handle transactions with the outside world. The ego operates according to the *reality principle*, which moderates the hedonistic immediacy and unacceptable impulses of the id and delays gratification in order to achieve long-term goals and to avoid punishment. For example, if a person becomes hungry and imagines that he is getting food and eating it, the pleasure principle is operating. Obviously, fantasies of food do not satisfy his hunger. He must find real food to eat if the tension caused by the hunger is to be removed. A child, for example, may have to delay gratification until the dinner hour. When he does this, the reality principle is functioning.

The ego is said to be the executive of the personality because it controls the gateways to action, selects the features of the environment to which the person will respond, and decides what needs will be satisfied and in what manner. Its principal role is to mediate among the needs of the organism (a child wants a cookie), the objects and conditions in the surrounding environment (he will be punished if he is caught eating cookies before dinner), and the demands of the superego (it is wrong to take cookies without permission). Unlike the id, much of the ego is conscious or readily becomes conscious.

The Superego The superego is the representative of the traditional values and ideals of society. The parents interpret these values for the child and enforce them by means of a system of rewards and punishments. The child internalizes them in the form of the superego—the moral arm of personality. The superego is composed of the *conscience* and the *ego ideal*. The conscience punishes behavior it considers immoral, and the ego ideal rewards self-enhancing behavior.

The main functions of the superego are (1) to inhibit the impulses of the id,

KIRKLAND

We are warned by a proverb against serving two masters at the same time. The poor ego has things even worse: it serves three severe masters and does what it can to bring their claims and demands into harmony with one another. These claims are always divergent and often seem incompatible. No wonder that the ego so often fails in its task. Its three tyrannical masters are the external world, the super-ego and id. . . . Owing to its origin from the experiences of the perceptual system, it is earmarked for representing the demands of the external world, but it strives too to be a loyal servant of the id, to remain on good terms with it, to recommend itself to it as an object and to attract its libido to itself. In its attempts to mediate between the id and reality, it is often obliged to cloak the *Ucs.* [unconscious] commands of the id with its own *Pcs.* [preconscious] rationalizations, to conceal the id's conflicts with reality, to profess, with diplomatic disingenuousness, to be taking notice of reality even when the id has remained rigid and unyielding. On the other hand it is observed at every step it takes by the strict super-ego, which lays down definite standards for its conduct, without taking any account of its difficulties from the direction of the id and the external world, and which, if those standards are not obeyed, punishes it with tense feelings of inferiority and of guilt. Thus the ego, driven by the id, confined by the super-ego, repulsed by reality, struggles to master its economic task of bringing about harmony among the forces and influences working in and upon it; and we can understand how it is that so often we cannot suppress a cry: "Life is not easy!" If the ego is obliged to admit its weakness, it breaks out in anxiety—realistic anxiety regarding the external world, moral anxiety regarding the super-ego and neurotic anxiety regarding the strength of the passions in the id.

From Sigmund Freud, *New Introductory Lectures on Psychoanalysis.*

particularly sexual or aggressive impulses because society condemns their expression; (2) to persuade the ego to substitute moralistic goals for realistic ones; and (3) to strive for perfection.

Dynamics

Because work is performed by the personality, it must have sources of energy that it can tap; the two main sources are the instincts and stimulation from the environment. Key concepts for understanding how the personality uses the energy are displacement, identification, anxiety, and defense mechanisms.

Instincts and External Stimulation In Freud's theory the relationship between the instincts and the external environment is essentially one of conflict. Freud focused on two instincts—*sex* and *aggression*—and hypothesized that personality is mainly the result of the compromises each person must make between instinctual satisfaction and societal demands.

An instinct has four characteristic features: a source, an aim, an object, and an impetus. The *source* is a bodily condition or need—for example, the need for sexual release. The *aim* is to satisfy the need and remove the excitation. The *object* is whatever brings satisfaction. An instinct also has force or strength, called *impetus*, which is determined by the intensity of the need. In a late revision of his theory, Freud changed his classification of instinctual energy, dividing it into life instincts *(Eros)* and death instincts *(Thanatos)*.

The *life instinct* to which Freud paid the greatest attention is sex, and in the early years of psychoanalysis almost everything a person did was attributed to this ubiquitous drive. Actually, the sex instinct is not one instinct but many; that is, a number of separate bodily needs give rise to erotic wishes. Each of these wishes has its source in a specific region of the body, or *erogenous zone*. An erogenous zone is a part of the skin or mucous membrane that is extremely sensitive to irritation and when manipulated in a certain way produces pleasurable feelings. The lips and mouth constitute one such erogenous zone, the anal region another, and the sex organs a third. In childhood, the sexual instincts are relatively independent of one another, but during adolescence they fuse and come to serve the aim of sexual union and reproduction. Personality development involves the release of sexual energy progressively through the oral, anal, and phallic zones. However, *fixation* may block this developmental progression. Fixation occurs when either excess pleasure or frustration associated with a particular zone causes psychic energy to be released through that zone to a greater degree or for a longer time than is normal. This excess psychic energy is energy stolen from other zones. Fixation therefore hampers normal development.

The *death instincts* perform their work much less conspicuously than the life instincts, and for this reason little is known about them other than that they inevitably accomplish their aim. Freud postulated that organic matter evolved out of inorganic matter and that the death instinct is a manifestation of the unconscious wish to return to the inorganic. "The goal of all life is death," said Freud.

An important derivative of the death instincts is the aggressive drive. Aggressiveness is the urge for self-destruction turned outward against external objects and against people.

Let us briefly consider some of the implications inherent in this way of conceptualizing an instinct. In the first place, the emphasis Freud places on instincts roots his theory in biological determinism. Freud's theory of motivation is based on the assumption that the instincts are the prime source of energy for human behavior. Stimulation from the outside has to arouse an instinct before the stimulation can have any influence. Second, Freud provides a homeostatic, or tension-reduction, model of behavior: internal irritation activates a person's behavior. Its effect is to return the person to a state that existed before the instinct appeared. An instinct is also said to be *conservative* because its aim is to conserve the equilibrium of the organism by abolishing disturbing excitations.

The source and aim of an instinct remain constant throughout life, but the objects or means the person uses to satisfy the need can and do vary considerably. This variation in object choice is possible because psychic energy is *displaceable:* it can be expended in various forms of behavior and with respect to various objects and effects.

Displacement Displacement of instinctual energy from one object to another is perhaps the most important feature of Freud's personality dynamics, and it is the key process in his theory of development. It accounts for the apparent plasticity of human nature and the remarkable versatility of man's behavior.

Practically all the adult person's interests, preferences, tastes, habits, and attitudes represent the displacement of energy from original instinctual object choices; that is, they are all derivatives. For example, smoking may be conceived of as the result of displacement of energy that was originally directed toward sucking the mother's breast. Similarly, a need to keep one's living quarters extremely neat may be a displacement of the energy originally directed toward anal pleasure; just as the child avoids defecating in his pants, the adult avoids messing up his house. A person experiences tension because a substitute object is rarely, if ever, as satisfying as the original object. This tension accumulates and acts as a permanent motivating force for the person's behavior.

Identification A second key process of development focuses on the objects of displaced energy. *Identification* is the process by which a person takes on the features of another personality and incorporates them into his own. The two persons with whom the child is most likely to identify are his mother and father. Typically, the boy identifies with his father, the girl with her mother. This is called *narcissistic* identification because the boy sees in the father the embodiment of his own male gender, and the girl sees in the mother her female gender. In *anaclitic identification* the child attempts to reproduce the nurturance of his mother imaginatively. For example, a child behaves like a parent in order to please the parent—later, as an adult, the person behaves like the parent because this behavior used to please the

Figure 21.5
A photographic portrait of Sigmund Freud is shown at right. At left is his consulting room, in which psychoanalytic history took shape. Freud sat in the chair while his patient lay on the fabled couch. The psychoanalytic sessions with patients provided much of the data that determined Freud's conceptions of mankind.

parent. In *defensive identification,* or *identification with the aggressor,* one identifies with another person out of fear. For example, the child identifies with the prohibitions of his parents in order to avoid their wrath. Identification is also a method by which one may regain an object or person that has been lost through death, separation, or rejection. By identifying with a lost loved person, one reincarnates him and incorporates him as a feature of one's personality.

Anxiety Transactions with the external environment may increase tension if they are threatening or harmful. This kind of tension is experienced as *anxiety.* In addition to anxiety caused by environmental threats (Freud called it *reality anxiety*), two other types of anxiety were described by Freud: *neurotic anxiety* and *moral anxiety.* Neurotic anxiety is fear that the instincts will get out of control and cause the person to do something for which he will be punished. Moral anxiety is having a guilty conscience; it occurs when a person does something or thinks of doing something that is contrary to the moral code he learned from his parents. Anxiety, then, can result from threats from the environment, the id, or the superego.

The function of anxiety is to warn the person of impending danger so that he may do something to avoid the danger. Under the pressure of anxiety, the ego is forced to use measures called *defense mechanisms.*

Defense Mechanisms All defense mechanisms have two characteristics in common: (1) they deny, falsify, or distort reality; (2) they operate unconsciously so that the person is not aware of what is taking place. At one time or another Freud and his followers have mentioned a host of defense mechanisms. Because defense mechanisms control instinctual energy, one can conceive of fixation, displacement, and identification all as defense mechanisms in this respect. The other most common defense mechanisms are repression, regression, reaction formation, projection, and sublimation.

Repression is the fundamental defense mechanism, the mechanism whereby threatening thoughts and memories are kept from consciousness and repressed back into the unconscious.

Repression was one of Freud's earliest and most important discoveries. He observed that his patients were unable to recall traumatic events in childhood without considerable probing. Traumatic memories, Freud concluded, had been repressed from consciousness and were held in the unconscious by strong counterforces. According to Freud, the threats from these memories, the expenditures of energy needed to repress them, and the anxiety generated in the process were at the basis of neurosis.

Regression occurs when a person feels threatened and returns to an earlier stage of development. A young married woman who has difficulties with her husband may behave in ways that previously offered her security in her parents' home, or an office worker under severe strain may throw a temper tantrum, an appropriate behavior at an earlier age.

Reaction formation involves the replacement in consciousness of an anxiety-producing impulse or feeling by its opposite. Hate is replaced by love. Instead of saying "I hate my child," a mother determinedly showers him with love. In Shakespeare's *Hamlet,* one may suspect reaction formation on Queen Gertrude's part when she says, "The lady doth protest too much, me thinks." Gertrude is watching an actress in a play express her moral anxiety about marrying her dead husband's brother; Gertrude's response may be seen as a defense mechanism against acknowledging her own guilt in a similar situation.

Projection occurs when a person unknowingly attributes his own instinctual impulses or the threats of his own conscience to other people or to the external world. It is then easier to deal with the anxiety that arises from these internal threats

Figure 21.6
These photographs were taken in Sigmund Freud's Vienna apartment, in which he lived and worked for forty-seven years. At left is a collection of photographs of his children; at right is the front door to his apartment. Freud fled to London shortly after the Nazi occupation of Vienna in 1938; he died of cancer one year later. In recent years his Vienna apartment has been restored as a museum.

and impulses. In employing the defense mechanism of projection, one says, for example, "you lust after me" instead of the unbearable truth "I lust after you."

Sublimation describes a displacement that produces a higher cultural achievement. Freud pointed out in *Civilization and Its Discontents* that the development of civilization was made possible by the inhibition of primitive object choices and the diversion of instinctual energy to social organization and the development of culture. Sublimation is the most productive defense mechanism. Freud observed, for example, that Leonardo da Vinci's interest in painting Madonnas was a sublimated expression of a longing for reunion with his mother, from whom he had been separated at a young age. But sublimation does not result in complete satisfaction, and some residual tension may discharge itself in the form of nervousness or restlessness; these conditions, Freud pointed out, are the price human beings pay for their civilized state and also are the reason they must periodically blow off steam in war and other primitive behaviors.

Development: Stages

Freud was the first psychological theorist to emphasize the developmental aspects of personality and in particular to stress the decisive role of infancy and childhood in laying down the basic character structure of the person. Indeed, Freud felt that personality was rather well formed by the time the child entered school and that subsequent growth consisted of elaborating this basic structure.

Freud believed that the child passes through a series of qualitatively different stages during the first five years of life. The three early stages, collectively called the *pregenital stage*, are the *oral*, the *anal* and the *phallic*. Each is organized around a zone of the body. A period of latency follows, in which the dynamics become more or less stabilized. With the advent of adolescence, another eruption of libidinal

Figure 21.7 *(opposite)*
Freud, Jung, and Adler. These three psychoanalytic pioneers created the personality theory on which many current conceptions of human behavior are based. Sigmund Freud (top) originated psychoanalytic theory and attracted a group of associates, among them Carl Jung (lower left) and Alfred Adler (lower right). Freud's system is perhaps psychology's most complex and extensive theoretical undertaking. Although both Jung and Adler accepted some major aspects of Freudian theory, they disagreed with Freud on basic points. Jung accepted unconscious determination of behavior but extended the concept to include a collective unconscious, in which memories from many previous generations are stored. Adler disagreed vigorously with the Freudian emphasis on sexual instincts and unconscious motivations. He stressed the individual's inferiority feelings, and his strivings for superiority, as a primary human drive; he claimed that many of the reasons for behavior are conscious. Subsequent psychoanalytic theorists have modified the emphases of each of these three men.

forces upsets the stabilization of the latency period and gradually comes under control as the adolescent moves into adulthood. The final developmental stage, of adolescence and adulthood, is the *genital stage.*

Oral The first source of pleasure is derived from the mouth by eating or, more specifically, sucking. Later, when the teeth erupt, the mouth is used for biting and chewing. These two modes of oral activity, ingestion of food and biting, are the prototypes for many character traits that develop later. Fixations at the oral stage result in oral character types. Gullibility is derived from the *oral incorporative mode:* a gullible person will swallow almost anything. Biting or *oral aggression* may be displaced in the form of sarcasm, biting wit, and argumentativeness. Because the oral stage occurs at a time when the baby is almost completely dependent upon his mother for sustenance, feelings of dependency arise during this period that tend to persist throughout life and to come to the fore whenever the person feels anxious and insecure.

Anal When toilet training begins, usually during the second year of life, the child has his first experience with the external regulation of an instinctual impulse. Depending upon the particular method of toilet training used by the mother and her feelings concerning elimination, this training may have far-reaching effects upon the formation of specific traits and values. If the mother is very strict and repressive in her methods, the child may hold back his feces in defiance of her and become constipated. If this mode generalizes to other forms of behavior, the child will develop a *retentive* character: he will become obstinate and stingy. Or, under the duress of repressive measures in the bathroom, the child may vent his rage by expelling his feces at inappropriate times. This is the prototype for all kinds of *expulsive* traits such as cruelty, wanton destructiveness, temper tantrums, and disorderliness, to mention only a few. Many other character traits were traced by Freud to the anal stage of development.

Phallic During the phallic stage of development, which lasts from about age three to age six, sexual and aggressive feelings associated with the functioning of the genital organs come into focus. The pleasures of masturbation and the fantasy life of the child that accompanies autoerotic activity set the stage for the appearance of the *Oedipus complex.* Freud considered the identification of the Oedipus complex to be one of his greatest discoveries. (The complex takes its name from the Greek king in Sophocles' tragedy who killed his father and married his mother.) Briefly defined, the Oedipus complex consists of sexual attraction to the parent of the opposite sex and hostility for the parent of the same sex. The boy wants to possess his mother and remove his father; the girl wants to possess her father and remove her mother. The Oedipus complex is also discussed in Chapter 8.

The Oedipus complex is resolved in the boy when he experiences *castration anxiety.* Because he fears that his rival, his father, will castrate him, he identifies with him (the aggressor) and vicariously enjoys his mother. The *Electra complex* (Electra was Oedipus' daughter) begins for the girl when she experiences penis envy; she envies her father his penis and blames her mother because she does not possess one. She identifies with her mother so that she can vicariously enjoy obtaining a penis from her father.

Genital The impulses of the pregenital period are narcissistic in character; that is, the individual obtains gratification from the stimulation and manipulation of his own body and from the fantasies that accompany these activities. The child values other people only because they feed his narcissistic pleasures. After the *latency period* (roughly from age eight until adolescence), some of this self-love becomes

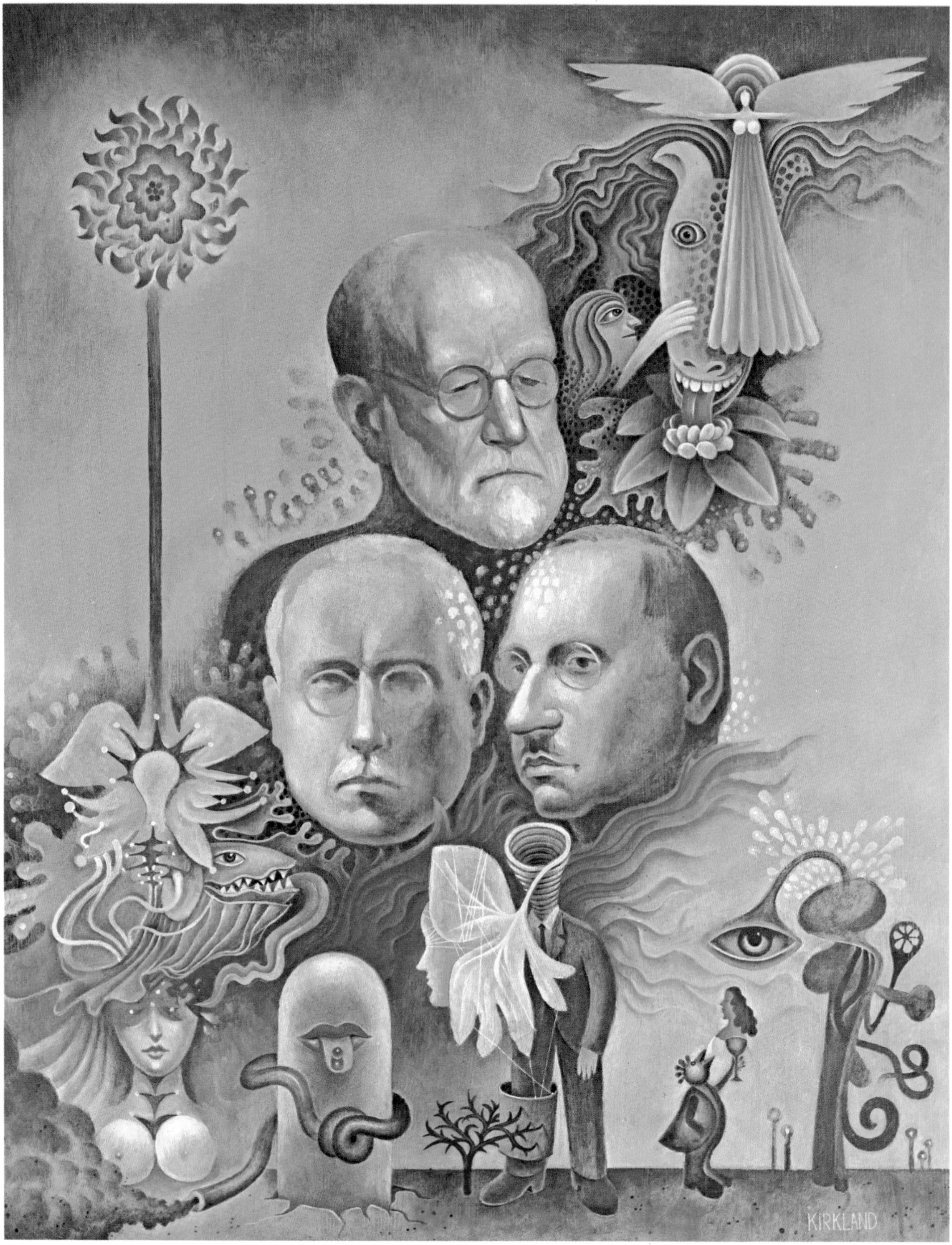
KIRKLAND

redirected toward gratifications involving genuine interaction with other people. During this period, called the *genital stage*, sexual attraction, group activities, vocational planning, and preparations for marrying and raising a family begin to occur. The principal biological function of the genital stage is reproduction. Ideally, the person becomes transformed from a pleasure-seeking narcissistic individual into a reality-oriented, socialized adult.

In spite of the fact that Freud differentiated these stages of personality growth and saw them as qualitatively distinct, he did not assume that there were any sharp breaks or abrupt transitions in passing from one stage to another. The final organization of personality represents contributions from all the stages. During development, libido is spread out over the stages in various amounts. The adult personality is determined both by how much energy is lost at each stage and by how the energy is relatively distributed to activate the personality characteristics that derive from each developmental stage.

JUNG'S ANALYTICAL THEORY

One of the earliest followers of Freud was Carl Jung. Jung's acquaintance with Freud began in 1906, and he joined the psychoanalytic movement soon thereafter. In 1913 he broke away from Freud and started his own school of psychoanalysis, which became known as *analytical psychology*. Jung generated an exceedingly complex theory of personality that in many respects verges on the mystical.

Development

One of Jung's most basic disagreements with Freud stemmed from his objection to Freud's deterministic view of development. Jung disagreed with Freud on two important issues. First, Jung believed that people are guided by their future (their aims) as well as by their past. Jung's theory, therefore, casts human beings in a more favorable light than Freud's; instead of simply adapting to and displacing instinctual urges, a person can develop his potential. Jung believed that there is a forward-going character to personality development. A human being is trying continuously to realize himself. His goal is to achieve complete unity within his personality. A person begins by developing all parts of his or her personality. Jung called this process *individuation*. After a person achieves individuation, he attempts to unite the disparate systems of his personality into a fully realized self. Of course, Jung realized that this union—the work of the *transcendent function*—is an unrealizable goal, but he held that it nevertheless is the great driving force of all of human behavior.

Jung disagreed with Freud on a second issue. He believed that human behavior is determined by events that occurred in mankind's ancestral past as well as by those that occurred during the individual's childhood.

Figure 21.8
Carl G. Jung was a Swiss psychiatrist whose early association with Freud led him to form his own school of psychoanalytic thought. One of the most mystical and metaphysical of psychological theorists, Jung has had greater acceptance in Europe than in America. The popularity of his works, however, appears to be growing in America, especially among persons interested in mysticism and nonempirical aspects of psychology.

Structure and Dynamics: The Unconscious

Like Freud, Jung recognized the great importance of unconscious factors in determining behavior, but he distinguished two levels in the unconscious. One level, the *personal unconscious*, is similar to Freud's depiction of the unconscious; it contains experiences the individual has had that were once conscious but have been repressed or forgotten. According to Jung, the contents of the personal unconscious can return to consciousness. The other level, the *collective unconscious*, is the storehouse of memories and behavior patterns inherited from mankind's ancestral past. It is almost entirely detached from anything personal in the life of the individual, and all human beings have more or less the same collective unconscious. Jung felt that the idea of the collective unconscious was the most unique feature of his theory.

The contents of the personal unconscious are organized into complexes, or universal thought forms that contain a large element of feeling. At the nucleus of a complex is what Jung calls an *archetype* from the collective unconscious. For

Figure 21.9
Jung considered the mandala, or magic circle, to be a universal symbol that expresses the archetype of the self. He believed that the mandala symbolically represented man's striving for unity. Children often draw mandalas (left), and they are found in the art and design of many cultures.

example, everyone inherits a mother archetype because human beings have always had mothers. Possessing this archetype of the mother, the child then perceives and reacts to his actual mother in predetermined ways. Out of these actual experiences, a mother complex is formed. An archetype can never become conscious. It can only be inferred from outward manifestations.

The Self

Jung's analysis of personality emphasized the existence of a self. He thought that the self was determined by the interactions of two attitudes and four functions. The two attitudes are *introversion* and *extraversion.* The extraverted attitude orients the person toward the external, objective world; the introverted attitude orients the person toward his inner, subjective world.

The four functions are *thinking, feeling, sensing,* and *intuiting.* By thinking, a person tries to comprehend the nature of the world and of himself. Feeling is the valuing function; it gives value to things with reference to the individual. It is responsible for people's experiences of pleasure, pain, anger, fear, sorrow, joy, and love. Sensing is the perceptual, or reality, function. It yields concrete facts and information about the world. Intuiting refers to knowledge that is gained from unconscious sources. The intuitive person tries to get at the essential nature of the world by means of mystical experiences.

Ideally, all the attitudes and functions should be equally developed. Whenever they are not equally developed, the principle of *compensation* operates between the conscious and the unconscious. Too much development in an attitude in one means underdevelopment of that attitude in the other. For example, overdevelopment in extraversion in the conscious aspect of the self would mean overdevelopment in intraversion, or underdevelopment in extraversion, in the unconscious. In the ideally developed personality, the attitudes and functions should all be equally emphasized in order to achieve the ultimate goal of the transcendent function—the highest degree of unity in the personality.

THE INDIVIDUAL PSYCHOLOGY OF ALFRED ADLER

Like Jung, Alfred Adler was an early and intimate associate of Sigmund Freud. He broke with Freud in 1911 to found his own school of *individual psychology.* Freud

Carl Jung's poetic prose presents a strong image of his concept of the collective unconscious. (From *Psychological Reflections.*)

The great problems of life are always related to the primordial images of the collective unconscious. These images are really balancing or compensating factors which correspond with the problems life presents in actuality. This is not to be marvelled at, since these images are deposits representing the accumulated experience of thousands of years of struggle for adaptation and existence. . . .

I can only stand in deepest awe and admiration before the depths and heights of the soul whose world beyond space hides an immeasurable richness of images, which millions of years of living have stored up and condensed into organic material. My conscious mind is like an eye which perceives the furthermost spaces; but the psychic non-ego is that which fills this space in a sense beyond space. These images are not pale shadows, but powerful and effective conditions of the soul which we can only misunderstand but can never rob of their power by denying them. For comparison, I can only think of the wonder of the starry night sky, for the equivalent of the inner world can only be in the outer world; and just as I experience this world through the medium of the body, so I experience that other world through the medium of the soul.

Figure 21.11
Alfred Adler. Adler's theories of personality and psychotherapy, developed largely after his split with Freud, have had wide impact in the United States and Europe. His theories use less complex concepts than Freudian or Jungian psychoanalysis, and his writings on psychotherapy offer more optimism and practicality. Because of his emphasis on the child's inferiority and the superiority-inferiority relationships in the family, Adler has had an important influence on the psychotherapy of children.

assumed that human behavior is motivated by inborn instincts, primarily sexual ones. Adler took the position that people are motivated to achieve superiority, and he emphasized the primacy of the aggressive over the sexual instincts.

Consciousness and Motivation

Adler made consciousness the center of personality. A person is ordinarily aware of the reasons for his behavior. He is conscious of his inferiorities (Adler's famed *inferiority complex*), and he is conscious of the goals for which he strives. Moreover, he is a self-conscious individual who can plan and guide his actions with full awareness of their meaning for his own self-realization. A human being strives to obtain an unobtainable ideal—a *fictional finalism.* Much of this striving is an attempt to overcome feelings of inferiority, feelings based on the early realization that adults can do things that children cannot. An important variation of Adler's inferiority principle is his theory of organ inferiority and compensation. He hypothesized that many people have a deficient organ—like Demosthenes, the orator who put pebbles in his mouth to cure stuttering—and devote their lives to compensating for it.

Dynamics: The Creative Self

Another of Adler's major contributions to personality theory is his concept of the *creative self.* Unlike Freud's ego, which consists of a group of psychological processes serving the ends of inborn instincts, Adler's self is a highly personalized subjective system that interprets and makes meaningful the experiences of the organism. Moreover, it searches for experiences that will aid in fulfilling the person's unique style of life; if these experiences are not to be found in the world, the self tries to create them.

Adler's emphasis upon the uniqueness of the individual personality also sets his theory apart from classical psychoanalysis. Adler saw a human being as capable of defining his or her own existence: he argued that every act performed by the person bears the stamp of his own distinctive style of life. Adler also stressed the social rather than the instinctual forces in development; in so doing he anticipated the approach of later neo-Freudians like Erikson and White.

ERIKSON'S PSYCHOSOCIAL THEORY OF DEVELOPMENT

One of the most important elaborations of the psychoanalytic theory of development comes from Erik Erikson. Erikson cast Freud's psychosexual stages of development in *psychosocial* terms, and he added a number of stages during the genital period. He pointed out that development continues after the genital period has been reached. Erikson's theory differs from Freud's in four main ways: (1) it emphasizes the sociocultural effect of the *interaction* between the instinct-governed child and his environment; (2) it expands Freud's conception of instincts; (3) it stresses development in later life; (4) it focuses on the ego rather than on the id or superego.

Freud had said that a conflict-filled relationship holds between instincts and the external environment. Erikson advanced the idea that personality is the result of an *encounter* between the drives of a child and the demands of society—a society that exists in a particular sociocultural epoch. Erikson outlined eight stages of development, each of which is characterized by a crisis; each human being must, in effect, pass eight great tests. A person's anticipation of events at later stages influences the outcome of a crisis at any one stage, and the outcome of a crisis in turn influences later events. Table 21.3 shows Erikson's outline of stages.

Childhood and Adolescence

At the first stage (what Freud called the oral stage), the crisis is one of *basic trust or mistrust.* Normally, the child acquires a basic orientation of trust—trust that the mother will return and provide comfort. If he does not, he may carry throughout

Alfred Adler here sets out the difference between universal feelings of inferiority and the feelings and acts of those who come to suffer an inferiority complex. (From *What Life Should Mean to You.*)

Inferiority feelings are in some degree common to all of us, since we all find ourselves in positions which we wish to improve. If we have kept our courage, we shall set about ridding ourselves of these feelings by the only direct, realistic and satisfactory means—by improving the situation. . . . But suppose an individual is discouraged; suppose he cannot conceive that if he makes realistic efforts he will improve the situation. He will still be unable to bear his feelings of inferiority; he will still struggle to get rid of them; but he will try methods which bring him no farther ahead. . . . If he feels weak, he moves into circumstances where he can feel strong. He does not train to be

Table 21.3—Erikson's Stages of Development

Stage	1	2	3	4	5	6	7	8
Maturity								Ego Integrity vs. Despair
Adulthood							Generativity vs. Stagnation	
Young Adulthood						Intimacy vs. Isolation		
Puberty and Adolescence					Identity vs. Role Confusion			
Latency				Industry vs. Inferiority				
Locomotor-Genital			Initiative vs. Guilt					
Muscular-Anal		Autonomy vs. Shame, Doubt						
Oral Sensory	Basic Trust vs. Mistrust							

Source: E. H. Erikson, *Childhood and Society,* Norton, 1964.

his life an orientation of mistrust that is often, but not always, inconvenient. At the second stage (Freud's anal stage), the child begins to gain control over his bladder and bowels and assert his individuality. If he is psychologically successful, he gains *autonomy;* if not, he suffers *shame* and *doubt.* At the third stage (Freud's phallic stage) the child becomes assertive, rivaling in fantasy the same-sex parent for the other parent. If he learns to channel his urges into socially acceptable acts, he acquires *initiative;* if not, he builds a *reservoir of guilt.*

Erikson's fourth stage parallels Freud's latency stage. Unlike Freud, however, Erikson thought that the early school years were important for development; in this stage the fourth crisis occurs: the child at this time must achieve *learning* and *competence* or experience *failure* and *inferiority.*

The fifth crisis occurs at adolescence. In contrast to Freud, who emphasized the conflicts associated with intensified sexual urges, Erikson emphasizes the *crisis of identity.* The adolescent must decide who he is and what he will do in later life; otherwise he will fall into role confusion. He must resolve his sexual identity, choose his occupation, and plan for his life as an adult. Freud's genital stage is interpreted by Erikson as involving a conflict between *intimacy* and *isolation.* After the adolescent has "found himself," he is able to find another.

The mature post-adolescent personality is a combination of relatively successful or unsuccessful outcomes of these crises. At worst, the person would be completely mistrustful, full of shame and doubt, thoroughly ridden with guilt and feelings of failure, confused about his roles, and isolated from humanity. At the other extreme—not at best, for best would be a balance—the person would be completely trusting, autonomous, seizing of initiative, competent, and intimate with humanity. The two extremes are caricatures, to be sure. Most people's personalities show a combination of attitudes that reflect experiences of both success and failure.

Adulthood and Old Age

In his final two stages, Erikson discusses key crises of adulthood and old age. His seventh stage is characterized by a conflict between *generativity* and *stagnation.* A person needs more than intimacy; he or she must be productive—teaching the younger generation or working at some task he thinks worthwhile for society. The final stage in development can only be reached if the earlier crises are adequately

stronger, to be more adequate; he trains to appear stronger in his own eyes. His efforts to fool himself will meet with only a partial success. If he feels unequal to the problems of occupation, he may attempt to reassure himself of his importance by being a domestic tyrant. In this way he may drug himself; but the real feelings of inferiority will remain. They will be the same old feelings of inferiority provoked by the same old situation. They will be the lasting undercurrent of his psychic life. In such a case we may truly speak of an inferiority complex.

Figure 21.13

Erik H. Erikson. Erikson is an American psychoanalyst whose theories have helped modify Freudian formulations by emphasizing the social variables and placing biological variables in perspective. Erikson's eight stages of development serve as a good illustration. He conceives of each stage as interaction between the child and society, during which a certain crisis must be met and certain learning must be accomplished. Erikson acknowledges the presence of the individual's drives at each stage; all the crises and learnings, however, involve the person's development of increasing aspects of humanness in a social world.

resolved—if there are no debilitating fixations. If the person reaches this final stage, he achieves a sense of *integrity;* if he does not, he experiences *despair,* and he suffers the sense of a wasted life.

Figure 21.14
Robert White. White is a psychoanalytic theorist whose emphasis on competence as a primary drive has become part of the body of psychoanalytic theory. White explains not only the growing child's urge to master his environment, but also the role of competence (or mastery) in adult behavior.

THE COMPETENCE THEORY OF ROBERT WHITE

Robert White supplies another perspective on Freud's stages of development and on Erikson's refinements of them. White believes that Erikson's psychosocial emphasis adds more scope to Freud's biological emphasis but contends that Erikson's theory is limited by the allegiance it pays to the Freudian libidinal base. In psychoanalytic terminology, White contends that the ego need not obtain all of its energy from the id as Freud (and Erikson) believed. White holds that the ego contains its own energy supply.

Motivation

White suggests that a great deal of the infant's behavior is oriented to nonsexual goals, especially the pursuit of competence. Consider Freud's oral stage, for example. White points out that although the most important event of the period for the child is probably to obtain nourishment, he engages in many other activities, like playing and trying to feed himself, that are not strictly oral activities. White suggests that although some early motivation is psychosexual, much of it is aimed at gaining competence. He points out, for example, that according to Freudian theory, weaning should be a major psychosexual tragedy in the life of all infants because they lose the breast, but in many cases it is not because young children gain a sense of competence from drinking from a cup.

The sensorineuro-muscular system . . . has often been described as if it were an inert mechanism that conducts the business of the viscera only on demand. Even so, its service lies in appraising the conditions that prevail in the environment so that drive satisfaction will be sought in timely and appropriate ways. It is a short step to suppose that the nervous system might have an interest, so to speak, in learning about the environment for its own sake. A clear advantage in terms of survival would appear to lie with a creature that spontaneously explored and manipulated things, building up out of sheer curiosity a certain knowledge and skill in dealing with the environment; this prior competence might well make the difference between life and death in a crisis provoked by hunger, thirst, or external danger. But we need not rely on speculation. Observation of young animals and children reveals a great deal of playful, manipulative, and exploratory activity that seems to go on without the instigation of visceral drives. These activities are done for the fun of it, but they serve a serious biological purpose. Part of the fun can be described as a *feeling of efficacy* —or sense of mastery—and the biological purpose is clearly the attaining of *competence* in dealing with the environment.

From Robert W. White, *Lives in Progress.*

Development

White also takes exception to the importance attached by psychoanalysts to the child's toilet training. The most important events for the two-year-old, he contends, are learning to walk, learning to talk, getting into things, and learning to play with toys—that is, gaining self-esteem and competence to deal with his world. The negativism of the two-year-old is more a message that says "I want to learn to do it myself" than it is a displacement of libido associated with bowel training.

The phallic and the latency stages also contain challenges to competence. White points out, for example, that a sense of industry in Erikson's fourth stage is based mainly on a sense of competence.

Dynamics: Competence

Competence is a term used by White to describe the vast range of activities children engage in to master their world—including locomotion, language, and the manipulation of objects and people. He believes that research on curiosity and exploratory behavior warrants the conclusion that not all motivation is based on tension reduction, as Freud contended. White believes that people are motivated instead to make an effect on themselves and on the world, even when it means increasing tension.

ERICH FROMM'S SOCIOLOGICAL APPROACH

Even more than Erikson, Erich Fromm emphasizes the sociohistorical roots of personality. He argues that history makes people as much as people make history. Like Adler, Fromm minimizes the influence of instincts and stresses the effect of the social environment, especially the family.

Dynamics

A theme that runs through Fromm's writings is that a human being feels lonely and isolated because he or she has become separated from nature and from other people. In his book *Escape From Freedom,* Fromm develops the thesis that as a person gains freedom he feels increasingly alone. Freedom then becomes a negative condition from which he tries to escape. In so doing he often engages in self-destructive acts like war and totalitarianism.

What is the answer to this dilemma? The individual can either unite himself with other people in the spirit of love and shared work, or he can find security by submitting to authority and conforming to society. Incidentally, Freud's only definition of the normal life was *"Lieben und Arbeiten,"* roughly "love and work."

According to Fromm, there are five specific needs that arise from the conditions of human existence. First, there is the need for *relatedness,* which stems from the stark fact that mankind in becoming human was torn from the animal's primary union with nature. Second, human beings have a need for *transcendence*—an urge to overcome animal nature and to become creative. Third, there is a need for *rootedness;* people want to be an integral part of the world, to feel a sense of belonging in it and of brotherliness. Fourth, a person wants a *sense of personal identity*—he or she wants to be distinctive and unique. Finally, people have a need for a *frame of reference* that will give stability and consistency to their behavior.

Development: Social Context

Fromm believes that the ways in which these needs express themselves are determined by the social arrangements under which a person lives. His personality develops in accordance with the opportunities that a particular society offers him. In a capitalistic society, for example, he may gain a sense of personal identity by becoming rich or develop a feeling of rootedness by becoming a dependable and trusted employee in a large company.

From the standpoint of the proper functioning of a particular society, it is absolutely essential, Fromm points out, that the child's character be shaped to fit the needs of society. The task of the parents and of education is to make the child wish to act as he must act if a given economic, political, and social system is to be maintained. In a capitalistic system, therefore, the desire to save must be implanted in people, so that capital will be available for an expanding economy. A society that has evolved a credit system must see to it that people feel an inner compulsion to pay their bills promptly.

By making demands upon human beings that are contrary to their nature, society warps and frustrates them. It alienates them from the fulfillment of the basic conditions of their existence. Fromm also points out that when a society changes

Erich Fromm here enlarges upon how people can come closer to nature—in loving and working—simply by allowing themselves to feel and act spontaneously. (From *Escape from Freedom.*)

Most of us can observe at least moments of our own spontaneity which are at the same time moments of genuine happiness. Whether it be the fresh and spontaneous perception of a landscape, or the dawning of some truth as the result of our thinking, or a sensuous pleasure that is not stereotyped, or the welling up of love for another person—in these moments we all know what a spontaneous act is and may have some vision of what human life could be if these experiences were not such rare and uncultivated occurrences. . . . Why is spontaneous activity the answer to the problem of freedom? . . . Spontaneous activity is the one way in which man can overcome the terror of aloneness without sacrificing the integrity of his self; for in the spontaneous realization of the self man unites himself anew with the world—with man, nature, and himself. Love is the foremost component of such spontaneity; not love as the dissolution of the self in another person, not love as the possession of another person, but love as spontaneous affirmation of others, as the union of the individual with others on the basis of the preservation of the individual self. The dynamic quality of love lies in this very polarity: that it springs from the need of overcoming separateness, that it leads to oneness —and yet that individuality is not eliminated. Work is the other component; not work as a compulsive activity in order to escape aloneness, not work as a relationship to nature which is partly one of dominating her, partly one of worship of and enslavement by the very products of man's hands, but work as creation in which man becomes one with nature in the act of creation.

Figure 21.17
Erich Fromm has enriched modern personality theory by combining a psychoanalytic perspective with sociological and existential viewpoints. In addition to his views on freedom and alienation, Fromm is also well known for his analysis of different personality orientations of modern man.

KIRKLAND

in any important respect, as occurred when the factory system displaced the individual artisan, the change is likely to produce dislocations in the social character of people. The old character structure does not fit the new society, and human beings feel a greater sense of alienation and despair.

One of the greatest dangers in trying to escape from these personal demons—alienation and despair—is the concomitant escape from the freedom they imply. Freedom also means opportunities for social and personal integration. Fromm's warning not to abandon the opportunities of freedom—out of raw fear of freedom itself—is one of the hallmarks of his thinking on personality.

Figure 21.18 *(opposite)*
Fromm theorizes that the human being occupies a unique position: he is an animal, yet he has lost his interdependence with nature. He is uprooted from his animal heritage and must satisfy his uniquely human needs. If the conditions of his life do not permit the fulfillment of these needs (such as the need for relatedness), man feels alienation and despair. One means of resolving these feelings is through a productive orientation, in which the individual turns *toward* others and works creatively. Another alternative, Fromm points out, is a nonproductive orientation, in which the person orients neurotically to the world.

UNITY WITHIN DIVERSITY

What holds all of these various theories together in this chapter is Sigmund Freud's clear influence on them. Freud's influence takes many forms, some of which you will not appreciate until you face the ideas in much greater and deeper detail in an advanced course in personality. The most enchanting Freudian influence is the paradoxical principle of the closeness or *union of exact opposites*—the simple notion that, psychodynamically, black may be white; involvement may be an escape from freedom; hate may be love; fear may reflect an intense desire to live; even admitted guilt may be the most intense profession of personally evaluated, abject innocence. In order to understand these theories, consider both what they say and then turn them around—consider the exact opposite of what they seem to say. None of the theorists would ever think poorly of you for that.

SUGGESTED READINGS

HALL, CALVIN S., and LINDZEY, GARDNER. *Theories of Personality.* 2nd ed. New York, Wiley, 1970. The classic secondary source on theories of personality. It begins with a discussion of the nature of personality theory and outlines the theories of Freud, Jung, Adler, Fromm, Horney, Sullivan, Murray, Lewin, Allport, Goldstein, Angyal, Maslow, Lecky, Sheldon, Cattell, Skinner, Rogers, and several existential psychologists. Finally, it compares and contrasts theories across a number of dimensions and issues.

LEVY, LEON H. *Conceptions of Personality.* New York, Random House, 1970. Levy's text on personality examines issues in personality theory rather than outlining theories of personality. It integrates a number of contemporary lines of research.

MADDI, SALVATORE R. *Personality Theories: A Comparative Analysis.* Homewood, Ill., The Dorsey Press, 1968. A recent text on personality theory, it classifies personality theorists according to whether their basic assumption relates to *conflict* (Freud, Murray, Sullivan, Rank, Angyal, and Bakan), *fulfillment* (Rogers, Maslow, Adler, White, Allport, and Fromm), or *consistency* (Kelly, McClelland, Fiske, and Maddi), then goes on to examine what they have to say about the core and periphery of personality. It presents research on each position and draws conclusions about their strengths and weaknesses.

———. *Perspectives and Personalities: A Comparative Approach.* Little-Brown and Co., 1971. A book of readings by or about each major theorist discussed in the Maddi text, cited above.

22
Other Theories of Personality

PSYCHOLOGISTS DEALING WITH THEORIES of personality tend to deal with human beings in general. Individual cases can, however, be extremely puzzling. People's personalities do occasionally change, sometimes late in life, and they begin to think and act as we would not have judged they were capable of thinking and acting. Back in the 1930s, there was a motion picture called *Gabriel over the White House,* in which Walter Huston played a party hack who had somehow managed to get himself elected President of the United States. Through some supernatural intervention he was suddenly turned into a capable and forceful man and surprised everyone by becoming a great executive.

Just fiction, we might say, just wishful dreaming. A personality once really fixed will not suddenly reverse itself and show hidden depths. Warren Gamaliel Harding was a charming, handsome small-town editor who was pushed into politics, rose to be Senator and then, in 1920, became President of the United States. One would have supposed from the general feckless incompetence he always displayed that he would make a perfectly rotten president. And so he did!

Then there was Chester Alan Arthur. Arthur was a lawyer who, in the days just before the Civil War, joined the newly formed Republican party and became a ward-heeling hack. He eventually rose to the position of chief henchman of the unscrupulous Republican party boss, Roscoe Conkling. Arthur was rewarded with the post of Collector of the Port of New York. This made it possible for him to allow Republican wheel-horses to fatten themselves at the public trough in a riot of incompetency and graft. He was eventually removed from his position when the stench grew too strong to ignore.

Then in 1880, James A. Garfield was nominated by the Republicans for the presidency over the opposition of Conkling and his following. To appease Conkling, Chester Arthur was given the vice-presidential nomination. The Republicans won the election and Vice-President Arthur remained Conkling's man, backing him loyally in all his disputes with President Garfield.

On July 2, 1881, Garfield was shot by an assassin. On September 19 he died, and Chester Alan Arthur, cheap politician *extraordinaire* became President of the United States.

What do you think happened? To the surprise of everyone in the United States, Arthur did a right-about-face. Suddenly, and without warning, he proved himself an honest and forceful man, who bowed neither to Conkling nor to anyone else. He fought the bosses, exposed corruption, appointed competent men, and presented an administration of remarkable integrity.

Most of all he surprised the crooked politicians, who had expected a field day with Arthur as President. In 1884, he had no chance of being renominated. Too honest! I. A.

The personalitity theorists considered in this chapter represent widely varied points of view. Although some of the theorists have elsewhere been grouped under a label—for example, Sullivan is referred to as in the group of social theorists, and Maslow and Rogers have been called members of the Humanist School—each theorist's approach will be discussed alone, so that you can compare them on the issues set out and discussed in the introductory section of Chapter 21: structure, dynamics, motivation, and development. These theories are all more independent of Freud than those of Chapter 21, and while none of them is as comprehensive or influential as Freud's, each emphasizes some important aspect of human personality—for example, Sullivan's theory emphasizes the social aspect; Maslow, the humanist; and Kelly, the cognitive.

Table 22.1 briefly sets out each theory's stance on these four core issues.

SULLIVAN'S INTERPERSONAL THEORY

The personality theory of Harry Stack Sullivan, an American psychiatrist, represents a unique point of view. Personality, he asserted, is a purely hypothetical entity that

Table 22.1 — Theoretical Positions on Some Core Issues

	Structure	Dynamics
Sullivan	Personality a hypothetical entity that exists only in a person's relations with others. Perceiving, remembering, thinking all interpersonal in nature.	Personality, which cannot be conceived of apart from interpersonal relations, can change at any point in life.
Murray	Emphasized number and complexity of human motives. The unity-theme is the single pattern of related needs and presses that give meaning to most of a person's behavior.	Psychological needs direct all the parts of a person's functioning—perception, intellection, and so forth—to cause the person to act in some way.
Gordon Allport	Focused on normal adults. Emphasized importance of traits, which are the outcome of both genetic factors and learning. Conscious determinants of behavior are far more important than unconscious ones. The proprium, or self, embodies that which is unique about an individual.	Traits become functionally autonomous and unrelated to biological needs.
Rogers	The organism and the self are the two systems that regulate behavior. The self is the conscious part of experience—the awareness of one's own being and functioning.	The organism and the self can work together either harmoniously or disharmoniously.
Maslow	A person's essential nature is not constant, like animal instincts, but easily transformed by experience and cultural influence.	There is an active will toward health and toward the actualization of human potential.
Kelly	Cognition is by far the most important part of the personality. People seek to understand and predict the world around them.	The individual actively constructs his world on the basis of the anticipatory hypotheses he has formed in the course of experience.
Skinner	Personality is rooted in behavior. Speculation about personality structure in itself is fruitless.	Rejects dynamic constructs. Behavior is learned and shaped through reinforcement, punishment, extinction, generalization, and discrimination.

Development	Motivation
7 developmental stages, 3 in adolescence. In all stages social factors greatly predominate.	In the earliest stages, anxiety; in later ones, trial and success. Still later, interpersonal relations and security are important.
Personality development is determined by biological drives, which are described by Freud's stages of psychosexual development, and by social influences, mediated especially through socialization by the parents.	The central organizing internal force is *need.* Environmental events that act on the individual to influence his behavior are *press*. Some needs are prepotent.
In the course of development, a person's traits become self-sustaining. There is a discontinuity between the personality of the infant and that of the adult.	Traits are motives as well as structures. Each person desires to become something, and that desire molds his behavior.
As the person develops out of infancy, he learns, through interaction with the environment, to distinguish himself from the phenomenal field. Thus the self develops.	The organism's single motivating force is its own maintenance and actualization.
Basic needs must be met, especially in early life, so that the development of metaneeds may ensue.	There are basic, or deficiency, needs (such as hunger, affection) and metaneeds, or growth needs (justice, beauty). Basic needs must be fulfilled first, and there is a hierarchy within the set. Metaneeds are not hierarchically arranged.
In the course of experience, each individual develops systems of constructs that define his world.	Rejects concepts of motivation and emotion. A person acts because he is alive; it is the form of action that needs explanation.
All behavior is learned through reinforcement and controlled by environmental events.	There are biological drives which the organism must act to lessen, to ensure survival. Drives and the environmental conditions determine an organism's behavior.

Figure 22.1
Harry Stack Sullivan, a psychiatrist, integrated psychoanalytic theory into his interpersonal views on personality, psychopathology, and psychotherapy. He thus helped modify psychoanalytic theory by giving it more social-psychological emphasis. Sullivan stressed the role of the interpersonal relationship between therapist and patient as a critical factor in psychotherapy; an extremely sensitive therapist, he wrote and taught extensively on the psychotherapy of schizophrenics.

cannot be isolated from interpersonal situations, and interpersonal behavior is all that can be observed as personality. It is meaningless to speak of the individual as the object of study because the individual does not and cannot exist apart from his relations with other people. Perceiving, remembering, thinking, imagining—all psychological processes—are interpersonal in nature—a very radical, social stance in personality theory.

Social View of Development

The developmental perspective is very important in Sullivan's theory. His view of the stages of growth is a social-psychological one; he considered social factors almost to the exclusion of biological ones in delineating what influenced the direction of growth. Sullivan outlined seven stages of development, and assigned three of his stages to adolescence, an index of the importance he attached to adolescence in the developmental sequence.

The most important educative influence in the early stages of development is *anxiety,* which forces the young organism to find activities to decrease the tension it causes. The second great educational force is *trial and success.* Success stamps in the activities that have led to gratification. Development occurs through reducing anxiety and achieving success—not novel ideas in themselves but dealt with differently in Sullivan's uncompromisingly social view of personality.

Stages of Development

Early Stages During *infancy,* nursing provides the baby with his first interpersonal experience. The baby develops various conceptions of the nipple, depending upon the kinds of experiences he has with it. There is the *good nipple,* which is the signal for nursing and a sign that satisfaction is forthcoming. There is the *good but unsatisfactory* nipple when the baby is not hungry, and the *wrong* nipple, which does not give milk. There is the *bad* nipple of the anxious mother, which is a signal for avoidance.

During the stage called *childhood,* the child begins to develop a conception of gender, and he plays at being grown up. One dramatic event of childhood is what Sullivan calls the *malevolent transformation*—the feeling that one lives among enemies. This feeling grows out of natural inabilities to manipulate the social world completely and without failure. Usually, the malevolent transformation promotes healthy development by counterbalancing success with a realistic appraisal of frustrations and failures. If it is too strong, however, the malevolent transformation makes it impossible for the child to respond positively to the affectionate advances of people and hence may stunt growth that would ordinarily occur as an outcome of crucial social events in the developmental sequence.

The *juvenile period,* extending through the grade-school years, is when the child becomes a truly social organism and experiences social subordination to authority figures outside the family. In the juvenile period also, children become competitive and cooperative, and they learn the meaning of ostracism, disparagement, and group feeling. Successful handling of these fundamental, social dimensions of personality lays the groundwork for a serious assault on the difficult and unavoidably social problems of adolescence.

Figure 22.2 *(opposite)*
During the childhood stage, the child experiences the *malevolent transformation,* according to H. S. Sullivan's theory. This transformation is precipitated by experiences in which the child does not achieve the outcomes he seeks, experiences of failure; the sense of omnipotence that he felt during infancy then changes to a feeling of being impotent in a hostile and threatening world.

Three Stages of Adolescence The relatively brief period of *preadolescence* is extremely important because it marks the beginning of genuine human relationships. In earlier periods, the interpersonal situation has been dominated by the child's dependence upon an older person. During preadolescence, the child begins to form peer relationships. He or she has a strong need for an intimate relationship with a peer of the same sex, a friend who can share confidences and

KIRKLAND

with whom it is possible to collaborate in meeting the tasks and problems of life. Discovering that personal problems, desires, feelings, and needs are shared by other persons is the principal lesson of this stage; social compassion is the principal outcome for the individual personality.

Early adolescence, which, in one of Sullivan's few concessions to biological factors in development, is initiated by the terminal phases of puberty, is normally highlighted by the development of strong sexual desires and the further development of the need for intimate relationships, which tend to shift to members of the opposite sex. To develop normally, the adolescent has to cope with sex and intimacy in such a way as to integrate them and to maintain a sense of his own worth (which Sullivan calls a sense of security).

The tasks of *late adolescence* are monumental—initiation into the privileges, duties, satisfactions, and responsibilities of social living and social citizenship. Fully successful adolescent development thus involves a strong sense of security, anxiety control, and full autonomy, and the ability to have fully human interpersonal relationships. Few people attain the ultimate degree of all three; the marvel is that so many attain so much of each.

Adulthood When a person has reached the final stage, adulthood, he has been transformed, largely by means of his interpersonal relations, from an animal organism into a human one. Sullivan obviously did not believe that personality is set at an early age. A person may change at any time as new interpersonal situations arise. Sullivan is a refreshing theorist in granting to the human personality, at any time in its development, extreme plasticity and malleability.

MURRAY'S PERSONOLOGY

Henry Murray was medically trained and earned a Ph.D. in biochemistry, but soon after receiving the degree, his interests turned toward psychology. He attributes this conversion to his personal contact with Jung. Murray was one of the first American psychologists to be influenced by psychoanalysis. He and his students carried out research that helped to develop techniques for the clinical assessment of personality—especially of the motivational aspects.

Figure 22.3
Henry Murray. Murray's research and theory on human personality were major factors in diverting the study of personality from a speculative to an empirically scientific field. His emphasis on operational (observable) aspects of personality concepts and his study of normal (nonpsychiatric) populations have influenced generations of psychologists. He was also a codeveloper of the TAT.

Motivation

Murray's most distinctive and respected contribution to understanding personality is his theory of motivation. He insisted that an adequate understanding of human motivation must rest upon a system that employs a sufficiently large number of variables to reflect the tremendous complexity of human motives. He also made serious efforts to provide empirical definitions for his variables. The result of these efforts is a set of concepts that attempts to bridge the gap between clinical description and the demands of empirical research. His theory and empirical methods led him to devise, with the cooperation of Christiana Morgan, the Thematic Apperception Test (TAT), for which he is probably best known (see Chapter 20).

Need and Press

Need is the central concept in Murray's motivational theory, and he defines it as "a construct which stands for a force . . . in the brain region, a force which organizes perception, apperception, intellection, conation, and action in such a way as to transform in a certain direction an existing, unsatisfying situation." Needs may be internally aroused or stimulated to become active by external events; in any case, needs cause the person to become active in some way. Following an intensive study of a small number of individuals, Murray arrived at a tentative list of twenty human needs (see Table 22.2). He stated that there is a hierarchy of needs for each person and that if a *prepotent* need (such as hunger or thirst) is aroused at the same time

Table 22.2 —Murray's Needs

Need	Description
Abasement	To submit passively to external force. To accept injury, blame, criticism, punishment. To surrender. To become resigned to fate. To admit inferiority, error, wrongdoing, or defeat. To confess and atone. To blame, belittle, or mutilate the self. To seek and enjoy pain, punishment, illness, and misfortune.
Achievement	To accomplish something difficult. To master, manipulate, or organize physical objects, human beings, or ideas. To do this as rapidly and as independently as possible. To overcome obstacles and attain a high standard. To excel oneself. To rival and surpass others. To increase self-regard by the successful exercise of talent.
Affiliation	To draw near and enjoyably cooperate or reciprocate with an allied other (an other who resembles the subject or who likes the subject). To please and win affection of a cathected object. To adhere and remain loyal to a friend.
Aggression	To overcome opposition forcefully. To fight. To revenge an injury. To attack, injure, or kill another. To oppose forcefully or punish another.
Autonomy	To get free, shake off restraint, break out of confinement. To resist coercion and restriction. To avoid or quit activities prescribed by domineering authorities. To be independent and free to act according to impulse. To be unattached, irresponsible. To defy convention.
Counteraction	To master or make up for a failure by restriving. To obliterate a humiliation by resumed action. To overcome weaknesses, to repress fear. To efface a dishonor by action. To search for obstacles and difficulties to overcome. To maintain self-respect and pride on a high level.
Defendance	To defend the self against assault, criticism, and blame. To conceal or justify a misdeed, failure, or humiliation. To vindicate the ego.
Deference	To admire and support a superior. To praise, honor, or eulogize. To yield eagerly to the influence of an allied other. To emulate an exemplar. To conform to custom.
Dominance	To control one's human environment. To influence or direct the behavior of others by suggestion, seduction, persuasion, or command. To dissuade, restrain, or prohibit.
Exhibition	To make an impression. To be seen and heard. To excite, amaze, fascinate, entertain, shock, intrigue, amuse, or entice others.
Harmavoidance	To avoid pain, physical injury, illness, and death. To escape from a dangerous situation. To take precautionary measures.
Infavoidance	To avoid humiliation. To quit embarrassing situations or to avoid conditions which may lead to belittlement: the scorn, derision, or indifference of others. To refrain from action because of the fear of failure.
Nurturance	To give sympathy and gratify the needs of a helpless object: an infant or any object that is weak, disabled, tired, inexperienced, infirm, defeated, humiliated, lonely, dejected, sick, mentally confused. To assist an object in danger. To feed, help, support, console, protect, comfort, nurse, heal.
Order	To put things in order. To achieve cleanliness, arrangement, organization, balance, neatness, tidiness, and precision.
Play	To act for "fun" without further purpose. To like to laugh and make jokes. To seek enjoyable relaxation of stress. To participate in games, sports, dancing, drinking parties, cards.
Rejection	To separate oneself from a negatively cathected object. To exclude, abandon, expel, or remain indifferent to an inferior object. To snub or jilt an object.
Sentience	To seek and enjoy sensuous impressions.
Sex	To form and further an erotic relationship. To have sexual intercourse.
Succorance	To have one's needs gratified by the sympathetic aid of an allied object. To be nursed, supported, sustained, surrounded, protected, loved, advised, guided, indulged, forgiven, consoled. To remain close to a devoted protector. To always have a supporter.
Understanding	To ask or answer general questions. To be interested in theory. To speculate, formulate, analyze, and generalize.

Source: Calvin S. Hall and Gardner Lindzey, *Theories of Personality* (New York: Wiley, 1957), pp. 173–174. Adapted from *Explorations in Personality* by Henry A. Murray. Copyright 1938 by Oxford University Press, Inc.; renewed 1966 by Henry A. Murray. Used by permission.

as a need lower in the hierarchy, the person's activities will be marshalled to answer the prepotent need.

Needs are intimately linked with environmental events. Murray calls environmental events that act upon the individual *press.* A press is a property or attribute of something or someone in the environment that facilitates or impedes a person's efforts to reach a given goal.

Thema

The term *thema* describes the correlation of need and press. For example, when a person has a need for affiliation and someone offers him friendship, this correlation is called an affiliation thema.

Murray does not view a person's behavior as the product of unrelated themas. Personality has unity and Murray's concept of the *unity-thema* describes it. The unity-thema is the single pattern of related needs and press that gives meaning and coherence to the largest portion of the person's behavior. It operates for the most part as an unconscious force, so—although it represents the key to each person's unique nature—it is not always open to discovery. A persistent striving for power and dominance is one example of a unity-thema.

ALLPORT'S PSYCHOLOGY OF THE INDIVIDUAL

Gordon Allport (1897–1968) was for many years professor of psychology at Harvard University, and in many respects his orientation resembles that of his famous predecessor William James. He had very wide-ranging, relatively humanistic interests, an excellent writing style, and emphasized the importance of the self and the uniqueness of the individual.

Allport was interested in understanding the personality of the normal human being. He felt that there was discontinuity between the normal person and the abnormal one, between child and adult, and between animal and man. He therefore believed that any model of personality based upon observations and studies of the mentally ill, of children, or of animals would inadequately represent the normal adult's personality. For Allport, the unconscious, too, was an inadequate concept: conscious, not unconscious, determinants of behavior are the most important factors—for the normal person, at least.

Traits

In Allport's theory the most important concept is *trait*—a predisposition to respond to many different kinds of stimuli in an equivalent manner. A trait is the outcome of both genetic factors and learning. A trait not only initiates behavior but also guides how one will behave. Traits are therefore not only structures of the personality but also motives.

Allport distinguished between several classes of traits. There are, for example, *individual traits* and *common traits.* Because no two individuals have exactly the same trait, all traits are essentially individual. But because of the influences shared by a biological species *(Homo sapiens)* in a common culture, people do develop some roughly comparable traits, and individuals can be compared in terms of common traits as long as one keeps in mind the fact that a given common trait does not accurately represent any single individual trait.

There are also cardinal traits, central traits, and secondary traits. A *cardinal trait* is one that is so definitive of the individual's personality that most of the person's activities can be traced to it. *Cardinal traits* are relatively uncommon and are not found in every person—Tolstoy, it is said, had only one cardinal trait late in his life: simplification. More typical are the *central traits,* which describe a person's characteristic tendencies—tendencies that a person often expresses and that the people around him can easily discern. Allport suggested that the number of central traits

This quote, from Gordon Allport's *Becoming,* evokes in an almost tangible way his concept of the proprium.

How very intimate (propriate) the bodily sense is can be seen by performing a little experiment in your imagination. Think first of swallowing the saliva in your mouth, or do so. Then imagine expectorating it into a tumbler and drinking it! What seemed natural and "mine" suddenly becomes disgusting and alien. Or picture yourself sucking blood from a prick in your finger; then imagine sucking blood from a bandage around your finger! What I perceive as belonging intimately to my body is warm and welcome; what I perceive as separate from my body becomes, in the twinkling of an eye, cold and foreign.

Figure 22.4
Gordon Allport's name is one of the most famous in twentieth-century psychology. An academic psychologist, his views on personality contrasted markedly not only with the psychiatrically derived theories of psychoanalysis but also with the emphasis in academic psychology on such concepts as drive reduction. He developed fully the concept of *trait,* and also the notion that motives become functionally autonomous of their original source. He was one of the first academic psychologists to emphasize the role of the self in personality.

by which a personality can be described is surprisingly few, perhaps no more than five or ten. H. G. Wells asserted, for instance, that there were only two major themes in his life: interest in world government and sex.

Secondary traits are more limited in their occurrence, less crucial to the definition of a personality, and more closely tied to specific responses and situations. For example, a person whose central traits are autonomy and dominance, which he displays in nearly every situation and encounter, might also have as a secondary trait humility, which he exhibits only in relation to religious experiences and persons connected with the church.

Functional Autonomy

Do traits grow out of the basic organic drives of the person? Allport said no. Traits are functionally autonomous and have no connection, except perhaps a historical one, with the basic biological needs.

According to the theory of *functional autonomy,* for which Allport is probably most noted, a given form of behavior becomes an end in itself despite the fact that it may have been originally engaged in for some other reason. A trait that has become autonomous can sustain itself indefinitely in the absence of any biological reinforcement. For example, a child may originally want to achieve or produce something in order to please his mother, but as he grows up, achievement and production are sought for their own sake and become independent of the functions they originally served. Thus, by functional autonomy the person is divorced from his past. Motives or traits, Allport asserted, are contemporary and are not bound to their historical origins. He often said, "Drives drive now." Adult motives supplant the motives of infancy. Personality development is therefore discontinuous.

Self-Concept

Allport, like Jung and Adler, placed great emphasis upon the forward-looking character of personality. A person's intentions for the future are of greater importance than the past in determining his present behavior. In his concept of *proprium,* Allport advanced the idea that man desires to *become* something. The proprium, or self, includes everything that makes a man unique: his bodily sense, rational thinking, propriate striving, self-image, self-identity, self-extension, and self-esteem. Together, these vital personality functions give rise to the consistency that marks attitudes, intentions, and evaluations.

Although the theories of Allport, Murray, and Rogers are quite different, they have been classified together by P. T. Costa and S. R. Maddi on the basis of some of their similarities as humanistic theories of personality. All three of them emphasize the difference between man and infrahuman animals; they all make him master of his own fate, relatively unique, and a whole person; and they all emphasize the positive, creative, forward-moving aspects of man's nature.

Figure 22.6
Like B. F. Skinner, *Carl Rogers* has had such widespread impact both within psychology and in society in general that his work cannot be summarized briefly. Rogers was the first American psychologist whose views seriously rivaled those of Freud. He has emphasized the inner experience, and not the drives of the individual, in personality and psychopathology, and he altered the study of psychotherapy through an extensive research program by which he has continued to test and refine his hypotheses.

ROGERS' SELF THEORY

Carl Rogers, an American clinical psychologist, is closely identified with the humanistic movement in psychology. Like Freud, Jung, and Adler (whose theories are discussed in Chapter 21) and like Sullivan, he developed his theory on the basis of his experiences as a psychotherapist. Rogers' theory initially concerned itself with the client-therapist relationship. He hypothesized that the process of change through therapy is set in motion when the client perceives that the therapist has *unconditional positive regard* for him—that is, the therapist understands the client's frame of reference and finds any of his feelings or behaviors acceptable. The therapist does not take sides—does not criticize or praise. He *reflects* the client, letting the client define himself, and in the process, grow.

In more recent years Rogers has come to view the therapeutic process as just one instance of interpersonal communication, and he has formulated a general theory of personality—*self theory*. For a long time, the concept of self was disavowed in the study of psychology and in some psychotherapies as being indefinable—and almost mystical. But Rogers noted that when his clients talked about their problems in therapy, they almost universally talked in terms of self.

Structure: Organism and Self

The main constructs in Rogers' theory are the organism and the self; they are the two systems that regulate behavior. Another important concept is that of the phenomenal field. The *organism* is the total individual; the *phenomenal field* is all of the person's experiences; the *self*, which takes shape during development, is originally part of the phenomenal field but becomes differentiated from it and can be characterized as the "I" or "me."

Let us first consider the phenomenal field. It is the totality of experience—everything that is occurring to and within the person at a given moment; it includes not only sensory impressions but also physiological processes and motor activities. The experiences that constitute the phenomenal field can be either conscious or unconscious, depending on whether they are symbolized—conceptualized. When an experience is symbolized, it becomes conscious. Most unconscious experiences can become conscious if the need arises. We simply need to develop symbolizations (or conceptualizations) for them.

Figure 22.7 *(opposite)*
According to Rogers' personality theory, the individual has a natural ability to evaluate his experience and his behavior; but if he experiences a conflict between his natural evaluations and those of others, he may sacrifice his own evaluations. He will then deny or distort his experience and change his behavior to conform to the wishes of others. It is this denial and distortion of one's experience that leads to anxiety, and defensiveness, and psychological maladjustment.

The self is the conscious portion of experience; it is the person's awareness of his own being and functioning. When the infant is very young, there is no self, only the phenomenal field—that is, the infant does not distinguish his own parts and effects from those of the environment.

As he interacts with the environment and as his cognitive powers mature, he learns to make the distinctions between his self and his environment and to build conceptions of his self. Values—positive or negative—accrue to these conceptions as the child grows; he decides that he likes some things his self does and dislikes others.

Problems arise because the child's self-concept also takes in values from other

KIRKLAND

Carl Rogers here gives a concrete example of the relations that may exist between the conscious self and the experience of the organism. (From *Client-Centered Therapy*.)

There are various noises going on at this moment, in the distance. Until they serve my intellectual need of this moment for an example, I am relatively oblivious to them. They exist in the ground of my phenomenal field, but they do not reinforce or contradict my concept of self, they meet no need related to the self, they are ignored. Often there might be doubt as to whether they existed in the phenomenal field at all, were it not for the ability to focus on those experiences when they might serve a need. I walk down a street a dozen times, ignoring most of the sensations which I experience. Yet today I have need of a hardware store. I recall that I have seen a hardware store on the street, although I have never "noticed" it. Now that this experience meets a need of the self it can be drawn from ground into figure. It is undoubtedly true that the great majority of our sensory experiences are thus ignored, never raised to the level of conscious symbolization, and exist only as organic sensations, without ever having been related in any way to the organized concept of the self or to the concept of the self in relation to the environment

Figure 22.9 *(opposite)*
People may not be able to achieve self-actualization because they have learned to deny or distort their experiences. When provided an atmosphere in which they are accepted, understood, and treated in a genuine manner, they reduce their defensiveness, and their potential for actualization is released. Rogers claims that such a beneficial atmosphere enables individuals to behave in a manner that fulfills their own needs; such behavior, he states, will also be constructive for others and for society.

people. A child may take pleasure in doing something that his parents tell him is bad. He then suffers a conflict between his genuine value (it is good) and the parents' evaluation (it is bad). He may resolve the conflict by adopting the others' value, and then perceiving it as his own. Yet, he has denied his own true value, and if his values increasingly are taken from others, his experience is increasingly distorted.

Motivation: The Relationship Between Self and Organism

The organism has a single motivating force, which is to maintain and actualize himself. This movement toward actualization is often accompanied by struggle and hurt, but because the urge is so strong, the person undergoes the struggle, despite the pain he may have to suffer.

The organism and the self can work in harmony, or they can oppose each other in the following ways: (1) The organism can deny to awareness certain sensory or emotional experiences, simply by not symbolizing (conceptualizing) them. (2) The self may deny to consciousness certain threatening experiences, especially those that seem inconsistent with the person's self-image. You can identify behaviors that are organismic but inconsistent with a person's self-image by his saying, afterward, things like "I don't know why I did it" or "I must have got carried away." The self may attempt to build up defenses against such experiences; if it is successful, the self-image becomes increasingly less congruent with reality, and the person becomes maladjusted.

The Fully Functioning Person

One can now define, in Rogers' terms, the psychologically adjusted person: "Psychological adjustment exists when the concept of the self is such that all sensory and visceral experiences of the organism are, or may be, assimilated on a symbolic level into a consistent relationship with the concept of self." The characteristics displayed by people whose organismic experiences and self-image are congruent—people whom Rogers call *fully functioning*—are openness to experience, absence of defensiveness, accurate awareness, unconditional self-regard, and harmonious relations with other people.

Client-Centered Therapy

If the breach between self and organism has grown too wide, the person may not only be defensive and deny his own feelings but he may be unable to relate well to other people. He may be hostile toward others or project his own denied feelings onto them.

How can this breach between self and organism be healed? Rogers proposes that the healing can take place during therapy in a nonthreatening situation, where the therapist is accepting of everything the person says. The type of therapy that Rogers has evolved is called nondirective, or client centered (see Chapter 33). Under these conditions, the client is able to examine experiences that are inconsistent with his self-structure and *assimilate* them into the self-structure. When this is done—that is, when the self-structure becomes more congruent with the experiences of the organism—the person is not only better adjusted and more fully functioning but also more understanding and accepting of others.

MASLOW'S HUMANISTIC PSYCHOLOGY

The late Abraham Maslow in his writings (especially *Motivation and Personality* and *Toward a Psychology of Being*) espoused a *holistic-dynamic* point of view. Maslow considered his position to fall within the broad province of humanistic psychology, which he characterized as an important force in American psychology. Maslow—unlike others who base their views on the study of mentally

KIRKLAND

disturbed persons—drew upon his investigations of healthy and creative (self-actualized) persons to arrive at certain formulations regarding personality.

Maslow upbraided most of psychology for its pessimistic, negative, and limited conception of man. He felt that psychology has spent more time studying people's frailties than their strengths; it has thoroughly explored people's sins while neglecting their virtues. Where is the psychology, Maslow asked, that takes account of gaiety, exuberance, love, and well-being to the same extent that it deals with misery, conflict, alienation, shame, and hostility?

Maslow devoted his energies to delineating the psychologically healthy person. Like the other humanists, he believed that man's essential nature differentiates him from all other animals. His needs are good or neutral rather than evil. The inner nature of man is not strong like the instincts of animals but is weak and easily transformed by habit, cultural pressure, and attitudes. There is an active will toward health, an impulse toward the *actualization* of human potentialities. Both Rogers and Maslow emphasize the importance of self-actualization. Maslow feels that many people are afraid of and draw back from becoming fully human.

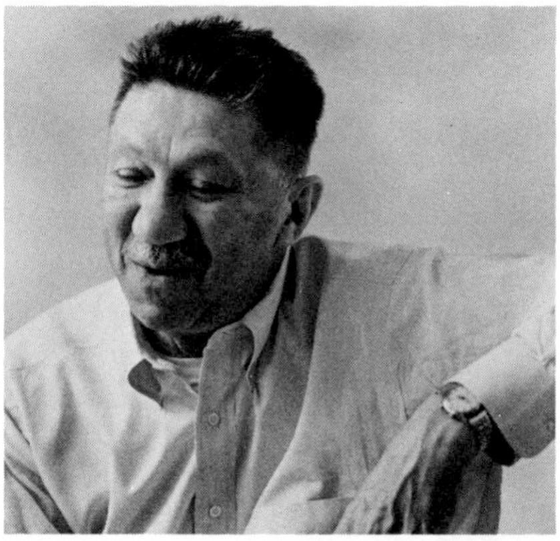

Figure 22.10
Abraham Maslow developed a personality theory based on the study of healthy and creative individuals. His concentration on the positive attainments of people helped to counterbalance the emphasis of many personality theories that were derived from experience with deeply troubled persons. The work of Maslow, Rogers, and others has helped to create a humanistic orientation toward the study of human behavior. This orientation emphasizes creative, effective, and satisfying behavior and the study of conditions that facilitate such behavior.

Motivation: Needs

Maslow propounded a theory of human motivation that differentiates between *basic needs* and *metaneeds*. Among the basic needs are hunger, affection, security, and self-esteem. Examples of metaneeds are justice, goodness, beauty, order, and unity. The basic needs are deficiency needs, whereas the metaneeds are growth needs. The basic needs are prepotent, or preeminent, over the metaneeds in most cases, and, as in Murray's theory, the basic needs are arranged in a hierarchical order so that some are prepotent over others. The metaneeds have equal value and no hierarchy; consequently, one can be fairly easily substituted for another when a person's life circumstances so dictate. Like the basic needs, the metaneeds are inherent in man, and when they are not fulfilled, the person may become psychologically sick. These metapathologies, as Maslow calls them, are such states as alienation, anguish, apathy, and cynicism.

The Self-Actualized Person

Maslow made intensive investigations of a group of people who he believed had achieved self-actualization—Lincoln, Thoreau, Beethoven, Eleanor Roosevelt, Einstein, and also others, who were Maslow's friends and acquaintances. Their distinguishing personality characteristics are listed in Table 22.3.

Maslow also investigated the nature of what he calls peak experiences, the most wonderful experiences in one's life. It was found that when persons are undergoing peak experiences, they feel more in harmony with the world, more autonomous, more spontaneous, less aware of space and time, and more perceptive.

[We] tend to evade personal growth because this, too, can bring another kind of fear, of awe, of feelings of weakness and inadequacy. . . . it is precisely the godlike in ourselves that we are ambivalent about, fascinated by and fearful of, motivated to and defensive against. This is one aspect of the basic human predicament, that we are simultaneously worms and gods. . . . Thus to discover in oneself a great talent can certainly bring exhilaration but it also brings a fear of the dangers and responsibilities and duties of being a leader and of being all alone.

From Abraham H. Maslow, *Toward a Psychology of Being.*

KELLY'S THEORY OF PERSONAL CONSTRUCTS

Like most of the personality theorists reviewed here, George Kelly was a psychotherapist. His sophisticated theory places almost exclusive stress on the effect of cognition, or knowing, on personality. As Kelly himself points out, this theory contains no concepts of learning, motivation, emotion, stimulus, response, ego, unconscious, need, reinforcement, or instinct. Kelly sees man as a scientist whose major concern is to interpret his world. Man is not a passive recipient of information—he actively builds his world by his interpretive processes.

Kelly finds it odd that psychologists attribute motivations to their subjects that are different from their own motivations: The most important thing about people, including psychologists, is their need to predict and control the world.

The fundamental postulate of Kelly's theory is: "*A person's processes are psychologically channelized by the ways in which he anticipates events.*" The way people

Table 22.3—Characteristics of Self-Actualized Persons

They are realistically oriented.
They accept themselves, other people, and the natural world for what they are.
They have a great deal of spontaneity.
They are problem-centered rather than self-centered.
They have an air of detachment and a need for privacy.
They are autonomous and independent.
Their appreciation of people and things is fresh rather than stereotyped.
Most of them have had profound mystical or spiritual experiences although not necessarily religious in character.
They identify with mankind.
Their intimate relationships with a few specially loved people tend to be profound and deeply emotional rather than superficial.
Their values and attitudes are democratic.
They do not confuse means with ends.
Their sense of humor is philosophical rather than hostile.
They have a great fund of creativeness.
They resist conformity to the culture.
They transcend the environment rather than just coping with it.

Source: A. Maslow, *Motivation and Personality* (New York: Harper & Row, 1954).

predict and control their world is to construe events; that is, they form hypotheses, called *personal constructs,* about how the world works. Each construct includes a dichotomy—an event and its opposite. For one person a construct may be friendly-hostile, and for another friendly-angry, depending on how each person has experienced and interprets his world. In the course of experiencing events, people develop construct systems, organizing their constructs hierarchically; more general constructs are superordinate, and constructs that define more precisely one pole of another construct are subordinate. For example, if a person noticed (in his experience with hostile people) that some hostile people were intelligent and others stupid—but that intelligence was not important with friendly people—the construct intelligent-stupid would be subordinate to the construct friendly-hostile.

Although Kelly's own theory rejects concepts of motivation and emotion, he has explained other theorists' concepts in his own—cognitive—terms. Discussing motivation, Kelly classified all theories as push (pitchfork) or pull (carrot) oriented. Drive theories can be classified as push oriented; Maslow's concept of the tendency to self-actualize, as pull oriented. All theories discussed so far subscribe to one or the other type of motivation. Kelly rejected them both. He argued that a person moves because he is alive, and it is the form of his movement that needs explanation; Kelly's fundamental postulate—that a person forms constructs to anticipate events—explains the form.

What about emotion? Kelly explains anxiety as the awareness that one's constructs are insufficient to account for events. Guilt is the awareness that one has deviated from a significant role relative to another person, and hostility is the continued effort to validate a prediction that has proven wrong.

Kelly's theory is truly an unusual one: it rejects most traditional concepts and builds many anew. It is a relatively recent theory, and it is too soon to assess its

Figure 22.12

George Kelly is a prominent American psychologist whose theory of personal constructs differs radically from other theories of personality and psychotherapy. Kelly's theory has not had wide impact on the practice of psychotherapy, yet his emphasis upon cognition in personality has increased psychologists' awareness of the role of thought processes in personality; Kelly has also influenced psychologists to explore the manner in which variables such as expectation affect social behavior.

significance. Kelly's Role Repertory Test has supplied a way of measuring constructs and has stimulated considerable research.

Figure 22.13
B. F. Skinner is a psychologist of learning; he is not considered to be a theorist of personality. However, he has developed a strong position on the behavior of organisms, including human beings, in which he emphasizes the role of learning (especially reinforcement) and rejects hypotheses about inner dynamics. In his books and papers, Skinner has explored what the implications of operant conditioning are for human development, functioning, and welfare; therefore his theory can be interpreted as a personality theory. Like George Kelly's theory, Skinner's is radically simple: Kelly reduces personality to cognition, and Skinner explains personality as response to operant conditioning.

INFLUENCE OF BEHAVIORISM

Psychoanalysis, as we saw in Chapter 21, is a powerful force in contemporary psychology. The only force to match it is behaviorism.

Behaviorists, however, have not constructed a theory of personality *per se*. They argue that personality is rooted in behavior and that all behavior follows principles of learning (which are outlined in Chapter 3). The principles include positive and negative reinforcement, punishment, extinction, spontaneous recovery, generalization, and discrimination. Let us consider the position of the most famous living behaviorist, B. F. Skinner.

Skinner begins with the assumption that all behavior is lawful. Even more than Freud, he adopts a stance of rigid determinism. Personality (or behavior) is the result of reinforcement, and a reinforcement is anything that increases or decreases the probability of a response.

Rejection of Structure and Dynamics

Skinner is not concerned with what happens within the organism; he ardently insists that speculation about personality structure is fruitless at this time. He objects to the line of reasoning that infers that there is an inner man, or self, that causes observable behavior.

Because Skinner believes that behavior is controlled by reinforcement and punishment, he does not hypothesize enduring personality dispositions. People behave as they do because they have been rewarded or punished for behaving that way. He does not deny the effect of genetic and biological forces on behavior; he simply says that they are uninteresting because they are beyond the control of psychologists.

It follows from Skinner's rejection of internal variables that his position also rejects dynamic constructs. He would liken the explanation "man eats because he is hungry" to the primitive explanation that the sun goes down because it is tired and wants to go to bed. Why, argues Skinner, should one bother to hypothesize an internal state (like hunger) that cannot be measured or controlled, when what is important is the environmental condition (food deprivation) that caused it? The most important things to know when predicting whether a person will eat is when he last ate, what he was doing in the meantime, and when he has normally eaten again in similar situations in the past. Skinner is concerned with the antecedent variables, like lack of food, that he believes are the causes of behavior and with the ability of psychologists to manipulate and control behavior. Psychologists learn how to control behavior by manipulating external events and observing the effects.

In his novel *Walden Two*, B. F. Skinner describes a behavioral utopia. Burris, a professor of psychology, is visiting Walden Two, which was designed and established by his friend Frazier according to scientific principles of behavior. The dialogue between these two characters seems to reflect two sides of Skinner himself:

"These are my children, Burris," he said, almost in a whisper. "I love them." He got to his feet and started back along the ledge. I followed carefully. He turned into the underbrush and waited for me to catch up. He was embarrassed and rather confused.
"What is love," he said, with a shrug, "except another name for the use of positive reinforcement?"
"Or vice versa," I said.

Development

It is when the development of personality is considered that Skinner's position becomes most relevant. The central tenet of Skinner's position is that behavior changes when it is reinforced. The timing and scheduling of reinforcement cause behavior to change in predictable ways. He stresses the importance of operant conditioning in how people develop and argues that men, like pigeons, can be taught to do practically anything by reinforcing their operant behavior.

Skinner's position has met with strong resistance from many quarters (including most of the personality theorists reviewed here), but his experimental techniques have met with considerable success in applications in education (programmed learning) and psychotherapy (behavior modification, discussed at length in Chapter 33.)

FORMAL AND IMPLICIT THEORIES

It is perhaps a truism that everyone has his own theory of personality—of what people are really like. The psychological theories described above are more complete systems than those held by the average man, but even Freud's theory, which is the most elaborate, is inadequate and incomplete. Psychologists are just learning how to investigate man's behavior in the ways necessary to develop adequate theories of personality.

The psychologist is committed to testing any theories that he develops. But the average person often allows his biases to affect his interpretation of events and his impressions of people without ever testing his interpretations. These biases are incorporated into each person's *implicit theory of personality,* which help to direct his interpersonal behavior. Recently, social scientists have begun to realize that much can be learned about man from an examination of his implicit theories of personality, discussed in the next chapter.

SUGGESTED READINGS

HALL, CALVIN S., and LINDZEY, GARDNER. *Theories of Personality.* 2nd ed. New York, Wiley, 1970. The classic secondary source on theories of personality. It begins with a discussion of the nature of personality theory and outlines the theories of Freud, Jung, Adler, Fromm, Horney, Sullivan, Murray, Lewin, Allport, Goldstein, Angyal, Maslow, Lecky, Sheldon, Cattell, Skinner, Rogers, and several existential psychologists. Finally, it compares and contrasts theories across a number of dimensions and issues.

LEVY, LEON H. *Conceptions of Personality.* New York, Random House, 1970. Levy's text on personality examines issues in personality theory rather than outlining theories of personality. It integrates a number of contemporary lines of research.

MADDI, SALVATORE R. *Personality Theories: A Comparative Analysis.* Homewood, Ill., The Dorsey Press, 1968. A recent text on personality theory, it classifies personality theorists according to whether their basic assumption relates to *conflict* (Freud, Murray, Sullivan, Rank, Angyal, and Bakan), *fulfillment* (Rogers, Maslow, Adler, White, Allport, and Fromm), or *consistency* (Kelly, McClelland, Fiske, and Maddi), then goes on to examine what they have to say about the core and periphery of personality. It presents research on each position and draws conclusions about their strengths and weaknesses.

———. *Perspectives and Personalities: A Comparative Approach.* Little-Brown and Co., 1971. A book of readings by or about each major theorist discussed in the Maddi text, cited above.

23 Impression Formation

ONE SATURDAY NIGHT many years ago, when I was still quite young, I was having my first date with a beautiful girl. The hour was not very advanced when I realized I would have to bring the occasion to an end. I did not want to, heaven knows, but I had to. Naturally, I didn't want the young lady to think for one moment that my readiness to leave early was due to any shortcoming in *her*, so I said, rather humbly, "I'm sorry, but I'll have to take you home now. Tomorrow's Sunday and I've got to be up very early to take care of the newspapers in my father's candy store."

A few years later, long after I had married the young lady in question, she confessed that that statement of mine had made a profoundly favorable impression on her. She explained, "It showed you weren't a phony. You didn't try to make up some fancy excuse or hide the fact that your father owned a candy store and that you had to deliver papers." I was glad. I hadn't made the statement in order to make a favorable impression on her; I had only told the truth. But I was glad it had worked out as it did.

A couple of years later still, I was being interviewed in my home by someone who was compiling a short biography of myself for a reference periodical. Inevitably, the question came, "And in what line of business was your father engaged, Dr. Asimov?" To which I answered, "He owned a candy store."

When it was all done and the interviewer had departed, I said to my wife, who had been sitting by during the interview, "How did it go, do you think?" "Very well," she said, "except for one thing." I asked her what that one thing had been. "Well, I wish you hadn't told her your father owned a candy store." I thought about that for a while and then said, "But what should I have told her, then?" And she said, "You might have said that he was a retail merchant."

We didn't pursue the subject, but sometimes I wonder: What if I had told her, that first night, that my father was a retail merchant? I.A.

You may have been somewhat surprised at what the preceding chapter had to say about personality. Many people who are not familiar with the various areas in the discipline of psychology expect that personality theory will tell them why some people are popular and others unpopular, why some people seem poised and charming and others boorish and rude. They may turn to personality theory because they wish to learn why they like certain people but dislike others and why they are liked by some people and disliked by others.

In fact, impression formation is the part of psychology that studies such phenomena. Psychologists working in this area study both the ways people *make impressions on others* and how people *form their impressions of others*. Everyone has a theory of personality—each person collects impressions of others, and, based on his own social history, sorts the impressions into conceptual categories, which constitute his own *implicit theory of personality*.

Psychologists want to understand how these implicit theories affect impression formation. For example, you and a fellow student both sign up for job interviews with the same firm; you have your interview with the personnel director at 10:30, your friend at 11:30. When you and your friend have lunch, you compare notes and find that you perceived the interviewer as warm, helpful, and considerate, whereas your friend found her aloof and only polite. Psychologists (like F. Heider, J. S. Bruner, and R. Tagiuri) have not concerned themselves with trying to say whether you or your friend were correct in characterizing the interviewer. Rather, they would try to analyze your implicit theory of personality and to understand why each of you formed your impression.

Also of interest to psychologists is the interviewer's behavior—what she said and how she said it, how she sat in her chair, what her facial expressions were, how she

Figure 23.1
Fritz Heider. Heider has investigated the factors that influence our perception of causes of social interactions. For one study he developed an animated cartoon in which some geometric figures collided with other figures. Subjects described the figures in human terms: for example, a large triangle was described as "bullying" a smaller triangle with which it had collided. Thus, even inanimate objects were judged as though they had human intentions.

used gestures. They would attempt to analyze the ingredients of impression formation—how the interviewer *made her impression* on you.

INGREDIENTS OF IMPRESSION FORMATION

Information transmitted behaviorally is the raw data of impression formation. Behavioral communication can be divided into two types, verbal and nonverbal.

People usually do not describe themselves verbally to others; instead, other people form impressions of us by observing our behavior. In many cases, however, the impression that is formed is not the impression we wanted to convey. As E. Goffman has pointed out in *The Presentation of Self in Everyday Life,* impressions are conveyed in two ways: they are "given," and they are "given off." We tend to believe impressions that seem involuntary, those that are given off, and to distrust impressions that are voluntary, those that are given. That is why direct communication about ourselves is often ineffective. Even language—a form of voluntary communication—conveys what might be called implicit messages. We say we know so-and-so and implicitly communicate that "I am a person of so-and-so's status."

NONVERBAL COMMUNICATION

Nonverbal communication is less under voluntary control than verbal communication and is therefore an important ingredient of impression formation. You have probably had the experience of listening to someone saying one thing ("It doesn't matter") but nonverbally communicating something else ("My feelings are hurt"). Psychologists have begun to study nonverbal communication relatively recently. R. Rosenthal's research indicates the complexity of finding out how feelings, expectations, and the like are communicated nonverbally. Rosenthal and L. Jacobson, in *Pygmalion in the Classroom,* report the results of a fascinating study in which *teachers' beliefs* about their pupils' intelligence were found to affect the pupils' IQ scores. Rosenthal and Jacobson had told the teachers that certain pupils had high academic potential, although the pupils they mentioned had actually been chosen at random. Those pupils' IQ scores showed a significantly greater gain by the end of the school year than the scores of their classmates.

Rosenthal has also shown that expectations held by experimenters in social-scientific experiments influence the results they obtain; somehow, experimenters convey their expectations to their subjects. Rosenthal has spent the last several years trying to discover how expectations are communicated nonverbally, but the process has proved to be so subtle as to elude complete definition.

Nonverbal communication originates from several sources; nonlinguistic aspects of speech, proximity, position, posture, gestures, facial expressions, and eye movements are some of the most important.

Nonlinguistic Aspects of Speech

The tempo of speech, its loudness or softness, its pitch, its smoothness, and its flow convey emotional states in the speaker and, if they are consistent over a period of time, corresponding personality traits. Stuttering is an extreme example of a nonlinguistic aspect of speech that is important in determining the impressions that are formed of the speaker. The manner in which a sentence is said affects its meaning. J. A. Davis found that actors could convey a large number of different emotions, such as amusement, admiration, affection, anger, cheerfulness, despair, and boredom, by varying their delivery of a standard sentence. Meaning can even be changed: "yes" can mean "no," and "no" can mean "yes."

It is often the emotional overtones given off during speech that convey the primary impression. G. F. Mahl and G. Schulze found the more hesitation pauses there were in a person's communication, the more body movement and anxiety he displayed. The speed of speech is also positively correlated with anxiety and excitement and negatively correlated with depression.

S. Milmoe and others have employed a machine designed by P. Rogers that removes the linguistic cues from speech (makes words unrecognizable) but leaves the tones intact. Raters can then make judgments about the emotional aspect of communication, which can be compared with the original verbal structure to see if the two are consistent. Investigators have used such techniques to test such theories as the double-bind theory of schizophrenia (see Chapter 31).

Proximity

The distance people stand from one another during social interaction has important effects on impression formation. To study such phenomena E. T. Hall, an American anthropologist, devised a discipline he called *proximics,* the study of interpersonal space. The next time you sit down to dinner with someone, try unobtrusively moving your eating utensils into his space. You will probably find that he unconsciously moves them back and almost involuntarily becomes annoyed—you have invaded his personal space. On the basis of his observations of the reactions of Americans, Hall divided interpersonal space into four zones: intimate distance (less than eighteen inches), personal distance (from eighteen inches to four feet), social distance (from four to twelve feet), and public distance (from twelve to twenty-five feet).

Although we are unaware of it, the impressions we form of others are greatly influenced by their use of space. Many misunderstandings between people of different cultures occur because of ignorance of others' expectations. Americans carry a

In *The Hidden Dimension,* Edward Hall discusses the physical dimension of communication:

. . . how people are feeling toward each other at the time is a decisive factor in the distance used. Thus people who are very angry or emphatic about the point they are making will move in close, they "turn up the volume," as it were, by shouting. Similarly—as any woman knows —one of the first signs that a man is beginning to feel amorous is his move closer to her. If the woman does not feel similarly disposed she signals this by moving back.

Figure 23.3

Interpersonal space—how close people stand to one another in social interactions —varies across nationalities. Italians (top) have a much shorter interpersonal distance than the British (bottom). Other aspects of nonverbal communication are associated with the differences in distance. As shown in the photograph of the Italians, speech is accompanied by frequent use of hands for gesturing or for touching the listener. Most Britons do not use their hands like this in communicating.

two-foot bubble of privacy around with them. For Germans that bubble is probably much larger, and for Arabs, much smaller. A person who stands at intimate distance from someone he is not intimate with is considered pushy or boorish. A Westerner speaking with an Arab may feel quite uncomfortable because Arabs stand closer to each other when they converse than Westerners do.

Figure 23.4
Postural cues may reveal a great deal about an individual's attitude or emotional state. We receive different impressions of the people in these drawings, on the basis of their posture. (Top) the man has crossed his arms and his legs, and leans away from the woman; we infer that he is bored or repelled. (Bottom) the woman at the left leans toward her companion, and her arms and legs are uncrossed; we infer that she is more interested in her partner and is more open to real communication than is the man in the top drawing. Nonverbal behaviors often convey more about emotions, attitudes, and wishes than do the person's words.

Position

The physical positions that people assume with respect to one another also convey meaning and create impressions. The most important message communicated by position relates to dominance and status. People of high status generally situate themselves above people of low status. Leaders sit or stand on balconies or platforms; kings sit on thrones. In Ivy-League colleges the convention of "high table" can still be found, according to which senior faculty members eat at a table elevated above those of students. Even when attempts are made to reduce symbols of status, positional cues remain. Soviet and American leaders line up according to their positions in the official hierarchy. King Arthur's round table was meant to symbolize the fact that all his knights were equal, but their status could be judged by their distance from him.

In a study conducted by T. Burns, people watching silent films of business managers entering the offices of other managers had no trouble deducing who was the senior (see Figure 23.5). A simple rule emerged: the closer the visitor approached, the higher was his status.

Posture

A person's posture, or, more generally, his body language, is instrumental in determining the impressions formed of him. Self-assured, athletic people, for example, usually stand straight and hold their heads erect. As A. E. Scheflen has pointed out, a person's posture also tells you how open he is to communication with you. During some conversations you may note that at first a person sits with his legs crossed; as the conversation becomes more comfortable and amicable, that person may well uncross his legs. R. L. Birdwhistell, an anthropologist, has undertaken a precise analysis of postural communication. Birdwhistell is careful to note that "no body position or movement in and of itself has a precise meaning . . . [The] meaning of a movement is always determined by the context of an interaction." Body movement should also be studied in conjunction with verbal communication. As is the case with other nonverbal behaviors, posture supplies information about the *state* of a person. It can communicate relaxation, tension, or excitement.

Gestures

Gestures have probably been most completely studied by Scheflen. He has suggested that there are about thirty traditional American gestures. Gestures are commonly associated with particular emotions. Scheflen observed the behavior of therapists and clients in psychotherapy sessions. Client's unexpressed feelings about others were sometimes revealed by their gestures: A gesture associated with anger, for example, might have accompanied the client's discussion of a friend.

Gestures aid in everyday communication. People generally lower their heads at the end of a statement and raise them after asking a question. Gestures punctuate conversations. They signal the end of one thought and the beginning of a new one.

W. LaBarre suggests that most gestures are culturally specific symbols. A particularly important gesture is the nod of the head, which can signal "yes" or "no." Americans nod their heads up and down to signal agreement and shake them back and forth to signal disagreement. Other people use different gestures. The Semang of Malaya thrust their heads sharply forward to agree and lower their eyes to disagree. The Abyssinians rock their heads back and raise their eyebrows to agree

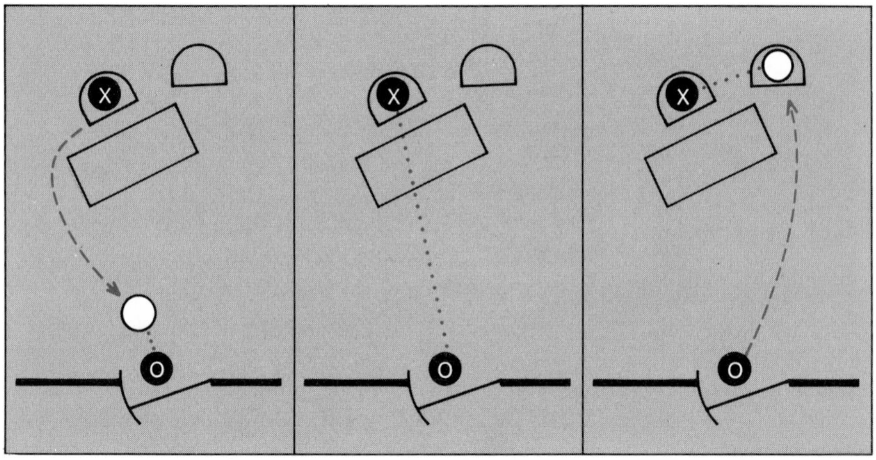

Figure 23.5
These diagrams illustrate how occupational status is subtly communicated by position. Before reading the rest of this caption, see whether you know which of the two persons indicated by X and O is senior in status. The broken blue line indicates movement; the dotted red line indicates conversation. (Left) O enters X's office; X gets up from his desk and walks over to greet O. X's deference to O indicates that O is senior to X in rank. (Center) O enters and begins his conversation at the door, while X is seated. Their positions indicate that X is senior to O. (Right) O enters the office and quickly seats himself beside X. Their status is approximately equal. The behaviors diagrammed here are governed by unwritten rules; one learns the protocol through observation and experience.

and jerk their heads to the right shoulder to disagree. The Dayak of Borneo agree by raising their eyebrows and disagree by bringing them together slightly.

Because there are cultural and individual differences in gestures, impressions formed from them are specific to the culture and sometimes to the individual. Although we can be fairly certain that Americans who nod their heads a great deal are affirmative or have a high need for approval, we cannot make that judgment about non-Americans. Recent evidence indicates that there is more stability of meaning across cultures in facial expressions than in gestures.

Facial Expressions

Social scientists have long debated the extent to which facial expressions are inherently correlated with specific emotions. Recently, P. Ekman and W. Friesan have shown that the facial expressions associated with happiness, sadness, anger, fear, surprise, disgust, and interest seem to be culturally universal. People from highly diverse cultures form impressions about the states of others by watching their facial expressions, and it seems likely that they draw inferences about particular people's personalities by watching their expressions. People who smile a lot are seen as happy-go-lucky or agreeable, and people who grimace a lot are seen as aggressive.

Eye Movement and Eye Contact

It has been said that the eyes are the windows to the soul. There is probably no stronger medium of nonverbal communication than eye movement and eye contact. Eye contact sustains the flow of communication. While one person is speaking, he watches the person he is speaking to in order to obtain feedback. By raising his eyes, he communicates the fact that he wants to speak, or by lowering them, that he has finished speaking. Prolonged eye contact can communicate either affection or anger, depending on the accompanying facial expressions. "Making eyes" is a common idiom for romantic interest, and research has shown that eye contact is an indication of personal attraction. Z. Rubin found that pairs of people who scored high on his "love scale" gazed more into one another's eyes than pairs who scored low, as discussed in Chapter 27. In another study R. V. Exline and L. C. Winters found a positive correlation between subjects' amount of eye contact and their scores on a test of the need for affiliation.

Averted eyes may indicate guilt or fear of rejection. In 1961 Exline and his colleagues found that subjects who were induced to cheat in an experiment showed less eye contact with the experimenters than those who had not been so induced —unless they had scored high on a test of Machiavellianism; Machiavellian cheaters stared back unabashed. R. D. Laing has reported a number of psychiatric cases characterized by an aversion of eyes. A general lack of eye contact is often considered

Figure 23.6
The impact of eye contact is depicted vividly in this poem.
(From "The Look," by Sara Teasdale. In *Collected Poems*, copyright 1915 by the Macmillan Co.; renewed 1943 by Mamie T. Wheless.)

to be a reliable indicator of the severe condition called infantile or childhood autism, in which the child does not show normal intellectual or social development and frequently engages in highly stereotyped, repetitive behaviors.

The amount or meaning of eye contact, like that of other forms of nonverbal communication, varies with situations as well as with personality. Some situations require more eye contact than others. Differences in eye contact in similar situations, however, do reveal differences among individuals and types of people. Women quite generally engage in more eye contact than men. A woman tends also to look at an attractive other person when the other person is speaking, and a man tends to look at an attractive other person when he, himself, is speaking.

THE PROCESS OF IMPRESSION FORMATION

Impression formation involves an increasingly general set of abstractions. We do not react to every act of another. We note what he says, how he looks, the way he stands, and so on, and combine what we have noted into some general categories. We do not usually say, "He smiles a lot; he is open to conversation, and he goes out of his way to help you." We say, first, "He seems happy," and then, "He is a friendly person."

Traits, Types, and Intentions

According to D. Krebs, our inferences about people generally pass through three stages. In the first stage we are sensitive to specific behaviors of the other person and draw inferences about his emotional *state.* If the person's behavior seems consistent over time, we infer that his customary state is intrinsic to him (rather than a response to external events), and we attribute to him a personality *trait.* Finally, we combine traits into syndromes or *types* that symbolize the entire person and his basic dispositions. It is the final stage that is most important in impression formation. People are concerned with the relatively enduring aspects of others—their attitudes, opinions, abilities, and, in particular, their intentions.

Personality Categories

People try to understand their experiences by grouping them into particular cognitive organizations. One basic method of organization, the correlational method, consists of arranging similar items into general categories. For example, consider Freud's personality theory discussed in Chapter 21. He observed that orderliness, obstinacy, and frugality were often displayed by the same people. Because these characteristics were associated with each other, he grouped them in a category, which he labeled "anal personality."

There is another basic method of organization, the causal; that is, some events are said to be caused by other events. Using this second method, Freud hypothesized that adults with personalities he characterized as anal act the way they do because their libidos had become fixated at an anal stage of development.

In forming most theories, people use only the first method of organization, the making of categories. The particular categories each person constructs depend, of course, on his or her own experience, but the principles of category construction seem fairly constant. Cabdrivers, for example, as described by F. Davis, fit their passengers into a number of unusual categories or types on the basis of the impressions they make.

Two of the types Davis describes are the "sport" and the "blowhard." A cabdriver's image of the sport combines the character attributes that the cabdriver views as ideal for a passenger. The sport's ideal status derives from his activities at the racetrack, prizefights, ballgames, popular restaurants, and bars rather than from his occupation. He is a man about town. Gentlemanly without being aloof, interested without becoming familiar, he is never petty. Most important of all, his tips are generous, and even on very short rides he will offer the driver at least twenty-five cents. A favorite success story among cabdrivers describes at length and in fine detail the excellent treatment accorded the driver on an all-night tour with a sport.

The blowhard is a false sport. He may dress like the sport, but he lacks the real sport's casualness, assured manners, and comfortable style. He is boastful and talkative, telling elaborate tales involving his track winnings or sexual exploits and the important people he knows. Often holding out the promise of a large tip, he seldom lives up to his words.

What are the elements that make up the categories or types sport and blowhard? There is an evaluative element: the sport is considered ideal and the blowhard false. The attributes of gentlemanliness, interest, and lack of pettiness, which cabdrivers have noted in some passengers, are elements of the type sport. These attributes, of course, are themselves abstractions. They are categories that group together a number of interrelated behaviors. (A gentlemanly person, for example, is a man who dresses neatly, speaks well, and treats others with respect.)

Types such as those we are considering may be organized according to one or more dimensions; for example, along the dimension of authenticity, the blowhard is seen as inauthentic and the sport as authentic.

The sport's gentlemanliness, his interest, and his lack of pettiness are important to the driver for one main reason: They supply him with a cue about the passenger's intention to tip him. The passenger's occupation is not important to the cabdriver because it is not of much use here. The boasting, lying, and name dropping of the blowhard suggest he is inauthentic, and, if so, it is likely that his promise of a good tip, like the rest of his behavior, is insincere.

Action, Intention, and Prediction

An analysis of the process of impression formation in the cabdriver demonstrates a number of basic rules that people seem intuitively to follow in forming impressions of others. The cabdriver is not conscious of the process by which he delimits the sport and the blowhard. When a passenger enters his cab, he forms a hypothesis immediately and intuitively on the basis of appearance and surface behavior. He organizes his perception of the passenger in terms of what have been called intent-act-effect segments. He rates an action, infers an intention, and predicts an effect.

Every passenger is unique; even the same passenger will behave differently on different rides. There are, however, common aspects of a passenger's behavior, and these commonalities serve as a basis for the cabdriver's prediction. The behavior of the passenger is of interest only insofar as it helps the cabdriver predict the more stable characteristics of the passenger, such as his *intention* to tip. The cabdriver observes a selected sample of the passenger's behavior and forms a theory that entails a prediction. Calling someone a sport entails the prediction that he will tip well. The cabdriver attributes fairly permanent dispositional qualities to the sport. If he picks him up again, he will expect him to continue to behave characteristically.

STEREOTYPING

The most serious kind of error people make in forming impressions of others is stereotyping. A stereotype is a categorization of people in some social group that carries with it a set of beliefs or expectations about what people in that social group are like. Stereotypes involve generalizations about types of people, and thus they ignore individual differences. Individuals do not fit them exactly; everyone is unique. The types that cabdrivers call sports and blowhards are stereotypes. Also, value judgments are associated with stereotypes; for example, sports are characterized as ideal and blowhards as false.

Social Stereotypes

Everyone employs stereotypes. Some of these are *social stereotypes*, which are held in common by most of the members of some group and which seek to type people in other social groups. Many Christian Americans of European ancestry, for example, hold in common stereotypes about Americans of other ancestries or religions, such as Negroes, Jews, Turks, or Japanese. Often such social stereotypes are not based on direct experience but are acquired from one's group during socialization. (Social stereotypes are discussed in greater detail in Chapter 28.)

Personal Stereotypes

People also create their own *personal stereotypes* about other people on the basis of their own experience. Implicit theories of personality make use of personal stereotypes. They can become a problem when they prevent us from experiencing the uniqueness of each individual.

The systematic study of personality can supply an objective test of social or personal stereotypes. It can examine and observe the extent to which various traits actually go together in groups of people. Social stereotypes associated with ethnic groups and social roles are fairly well known and can be easily investigated. Personal stereotypes associated with implicit theories of personality traits must be spelled out explicitly before they can be tested.

IMPLICIT THEORIES OF PERSONALITY

Everybody has what amounts to a theory of personality. Although personality psychologists attempt to make their own theories of personality explicit, logically consistent, and empirically verifiable, in everyday life people are not that rigorous. People draw conclusions about others on the basis of vague, often internally inconsistent, *implicit theories of personality.*

Origins

The formation of implicit theories of personality can be explained in terms of two different viewpoints. According to one view, such theories correspond to actual co-occurrence of traits. That is, a set of traits will be grouped together in a personality theory because those traits actually go together—are displayed by the same individuals—in the real world. According to the second view, implicit personality theories organize traits on the basis of logical relationships among them that are independent of their co-occurrence in the real world. The truth seems to lie somewhere between these two positions. Of course, traits that are close together in "meaning" tend to be found in the same individual—warmth and good nature, for example, have a lot of meaning in common. On the other hand, C. H. Lay and D. N. Jackson have found a relationship between individuals' scores on personality tests and ratings of them made by others.

Trait Clusters

When psychologists began to do research on implicit theories of personality, they were initially concerned with *empathic accuracy*—the accuracy with which one person could predict what another person thought of himself. They had a subject describe the personality of a target person and compare his description with a self-description drawn up by the target person. If you can accurately say (predict) what I think of myself, then you are empathic, it was felt. Although this technique might at first seem quite respectable, it turned out to be filled with errors. Similarities between the two lists of personality traits were found to depend more on projection on the part of the subject or on actual or assumed similarity between the two individuals than on empathy. Moreover, once subjects decided that a central trait such as warmth was characteristic of a given individual, they tended to judge that individual favorably along other dimensions, such as intelligence, skill, and industry, a phenomenon that became known as the *halo effect.*

In 1954, J. S. Bruner and R. Tagiuri reviewed the literature on person perception. They suggested that the tendency on the part of target individuals to convey consistent patterns of personality traits, the halo effect, should not simply be dismissed as a source of error in accuracy studies but rather should be studied as a phenomenon in itself.

Ten years earlier, S. Asch had shown that personality traits such as warmth and coldness were *central organizing traits.* People who were described as intelligent, skillful, industrious, and warm were perceived quite differently from those who were described as intelligent, skillful, industrious, and polite. Almost all the subjects who were told that the person was warm, for example, also saw him as generous, whereas few of those who were told he was polite saw him as generous. Asch argued that combinations of traits formed gestalts that were qualitatively different from the sum of the impressions associated with the traits. Bruner and Tagiuri, however, found that a final impression could be predicted from the individual traits that went to make it up. They asked their subjects to rate an intelligent, inconsiderate person on responsibility. Intelligent people are generally seen as responsible, but inconsiderate people are seen as irresponsible. How responsible, then, is an intelligent, inconsiderate person? If the impressions of his traits are simply added, he should be perceived as moderately responsible, and, in fact, that was what Bruner, Shapiro, and Tagiuri found.

Although there were differences in interpretation, investigators of person perception agreed that people associate certain traits with certain other traits. If we know that a person is warm, we are also likely to think that he is good-natured, reliable, generous, happy, important, wise, and imaginative. And we are likely to think that he is more generous than he is wise or imaginative. In 1960, J. Wishner had a group of students rate their teachers on the personality traits earlier employed by Asch. He correlated each trait with every other trait and found, as Asch had suggested, that central traits such as warmth and coldness were more highly correlated with other traits than were traits such as politeness and bluntness. He supplied a new way of defining central traits—one based on their degree of intercorrelation.

Expectations

As was noted earlier, the impressions people form of others are as much a result of their own *perceptual tendencies,* or expectations, and theoretical assumptions as they are of the actual attributes of the people they view. This fact was demonstrated clearly in an experiment by S. M. Dornbusch and his colleagues, who asked a group of ten- or eleven-year-old children who had gone to the same summer camp to describe their tentmates. The investigators kept careful track of the categories or trait names that the children used. They found that there was about a 38 percent overlap in categories when they compared the descriptions two children gave of two different tentmates. This can be seen as the extent to which categories naturally overlap. When two different children described the same tentmate, the overlap was 45 percent. This can be seen as the extent to which the attributes of the target person determine the impression that is formed of him. Of most interest, however, is the finding that when one child described two different children, the overlap in categories was 57 percent. What each child noted was thus more a function of his own conceptual category system—that is, of his own implicit theory of personality—than of the actual attributes of his tentmates. It has been shown by other researchers that the less well one person knows another, the more the impression that he forms of the other depends on his own categories rather than on the other's actual attributes. People tend to fill in attributes for, or stereotype, people whom they do not know well.

Figure 23.7
La Rochefoucauld's maxim, written before 1665, describes personal stereotyping. By "self-esteem" he means not necessarily how much or how little we value ourselves, but what qualities and characteristics we have come to admire in ourselves; we tend, then, to judge others on the basis of those qualities and characteristics.
[From La Rochefoucauld, *Maxims* (trans. L. W. Tancock). Baltimore, Md.: Penguin Books, 1959, p. 46.]

Studies of implicit theories of personality and their effect on impression formation have implications for other tasks. You may have noticed, for example, that a paper or examination submitted to two different instructors often receives two different grades or evaluations. A study by Wiggens and others showed that when a number of judges rated the intelligence of students (whose traits had been systematically varied by the experimenters), they were influenced by different but quite specific attributes. The judges were given ostensible school records on which to base their opinions. Some judges, for example, rated students with high grades as most intelligent. Other judges, however, were most influenced by scores on a test of English usage. A third set of judges combined attributes to form their impressions; they judged intelligence on a basis of high grades, effectiveness in English, evidence of responsibility, and good study habits. It seems that each judge had his own theory of intelligence and that this theory helped determine the impressions he formed. Moreover, the judges' theories of intelligence were related to attributes in their own personalities. Judges who emphasized responsibility and study habits, for example, were themselves found, on the basis of IQ and personality tests, to be less intelligent and more authoritarian than judges who emphasized other variables.

MAKING AN IMPRESSION

The term "personality" comes from the Latin *per sonare*, "to speak through," and refers to the stylized masks that actors held up before their faces and "spoke through" on stage. In a sense, all people wear masks. Only the unsocialized infant shows himself directly to the world; the rest of us have learned to hide our feelings and disguise our moods, and we can change our apparent personalities in an instant. Sometimes the word "personality" is used to refer to the characteristic behavior patterns that a given individual displays in public. When a psychologist uses the term "personality," he is most often referring to the actor himself rather than just to the public roles he plays, but the public roles form a significant part of everyday life. By manipulating the behavior patterns associated with those roles, a person attempts to cultivate and manage the impressions he gives.

The time people spend on how they look—and the money they spend on cosmetics and clothes—is an indication of the importance attached to the physical impression one makes. Particularly in a materialist culture such as that of the United States, the acquisition of possessions can be seen as an attempt to make as favorable an impression as possible on others. The quality of a person's possessions supplies an indication of his *social value.* William James described possessions as part of the "material me," which he considered an important component of the self. One of

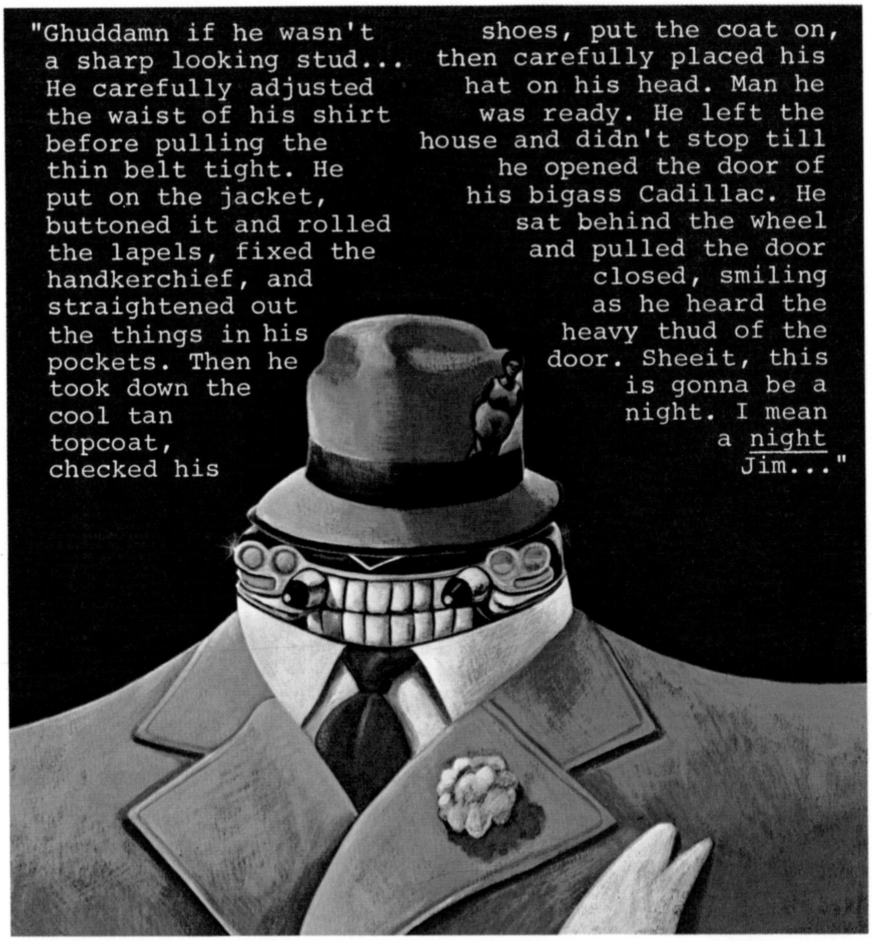

Figure 23.8

In Goffman's terms, this character is an actor; the people he will meet during the evening constitute his *audience.*

(From Hubert Selby, Jr., *Last Exit to Brooklyn.* New York: Grove Press, 1964, p. 291.)

the basic theories of the advertising industry is that people generally feel a need to improve their images. The material ways of creating an impression, like clothes, makeup—sometimes even the choice of people with whom we associate (see Chapter 27)—and our choice of verbal and nonverbal ways of acting all constitute important aspects of impression management.

GOFFMAN'S VIEW OF THE PRESENTATION OF SELF

Although psychologists have so far produced little work on impression management, major work on the subject has been done by E. Goffman, a sociologist. Goffman outlined some of the major techniques employed by people in presenting themselves to others.

As each person comes into view, there is a mass of information available about him. The observer, as was noted earlier, selects what he considers important and abstracts an appropriate category. Social roles are examples of abstractions that tell an observer what generally to expect from the actor and help him select appropriate responses. (Chapter 25 discusses social roles.)

Most people are unaware of the mass of information they transmit about themselves and the extent to which they make stereotyped responses to the behavior of others. In 1963 Goffman studied people for whom impression management is a major task in life, stigmatized people—persons who are physically deformed, blind, or ugly, former patients in mental institutions, prostitutes, homosexuals, ex-convicts, and others—in order to throw into relief the types of information people transmit about themselves and the impressions they give. Implicit in Goffman's study is that everyone is or feels stigmatized in some way and that the methods stigmatized

Figure 23.9
Marcel Marceau, the famous mime, can create impressions with his face and body—never uttering a word. Because he is so skilled an actor, he can dispense with one important means that the "actor" uses to control the impression his "audience" receives—verbal communication. According to Goffman, everyone is simultaneously an actor and a member of the audience.

persons use to manage the impressions they give are essentially the same as those we all use. Stigmatized persons must resolve the inconsistency between the demands made on them on the basis of their *virtual social identities,* that is, the identity each appears to have, and their *actual identities.* Goffman discusses how such persons *control information* about themselves and handle potentially embarrassing situations.

The Actors

Goffman views human beings as actors and their behavior as a series of performances. He argues that people do not usually give direct, honest, or spontaneous expression to heartfelt feelings and reactions. Rather, they go through much of life staging a series of performances, controlling or managing the impressions they give in order to conform to some definition of the situation they are in and to create the best dramaturgical effect. People's acts depend on the situations they find themselves in and the behavior that is expected of them in their particular roles.

An actor's greatest fear is that his performance will be a flop. People employ a number of devices to guard against such a possible discrediting of the self they present. They are careful to make idealized claims that cannot be checked. They hint rather than lie. And, more than anything else, they use a technique Goffman terms *mystification*—they maintain distance to create mystery about themselves.

The Setting

Goffman divides the interactional environment—the *setting*—of each actor into a *back region* and *front region.* The back region is hidden from the audience and is used to prepare and rehearse the act. The front region is, in effect, the stage.

The physical setting of a performance creates a context that helps define the act. Actors, by exhibiting an appropriate *personal front,* also create their own context, signaling to the audience the type of impression they hope will be formed. A personal front consists of all attributes that can be discerned about an actor from

Figure 23.10
The mask that each actor wore in ancient Greek plays allowed him to portray any character—from frog to prince to god. Erving Goffman's description of impression management seems to say that each of us has a drawerful of masks, and we choose different ones to fit different combinations of situation, audience, and setting.

his *appearance* and *manner.* Such characteristics as age, sex, race, and dress convey information about people on which expectations are based. More subtle, perhaps, are cues supplied by manner: the way the person looks, stands, walks, and speaks.

Choice of Act

An actor's personal front and setting substantially determine which acts on his part are appropriate. There is, however, a great deal of room for improvisation. A person generally performs the act that will gain him maximum positive social value. Limiting factors are his ability to perform a particular role, the willingness of the other participants to believe and support the self he projects, and his ability to live up to his projected role in future performances.

The Audience

The performances a person gives depend to a great extent on the audience. People play to different audiences, behaving differently in front of parents, children, husband or wife, friends, superiors, and others. To avoid the potential embarrassment

Figure 23.11
Alfred Kinsey. Kinsey's courageous pioneer work in sex research helped to provide more accurate information about human sexual beliefs and practices. He began the Institute for Sex Research at Indiana University; one of the Institute's functions has been the compilation and publication of detailed information, gained through interviews, about patterns of human sexual behavior. The work of Masters and Johnson in studying various aspects of sexual behavior under laboratory conditions carries forward the spirit of Kinsey's brave scientific investigation.

of having to play to two audiences at once, people are motivated to segregate audiences with different expectations. Imagine the feelings of a young tough showing off before some friends when his mother shows up. In most situations two actors confront one another and must compromise on a definition of the situation—in Goffman's terms, a *working consensus*—that is of optimal benefit to both.

Idealization

Impression management involves projecting an idealized image of oneself. Idealization of images is clearly demonstrated by upwardly mobile people. They surround themselves with the status symbols and adopt the mannerisms of the class or group they hope to join. In 1956, N. Mitford published a book on the English aristocracy that described their conventions, behavior, and mannerisms. Many of the conventions immediately became outdated because lower-class people adopted them, forcing the upper class to find other ways of setting themselves apart.

It is easy to understand why someone might want to project a positive idealization of himself. Such a presentation can even result from a genuine desire to improve. An idealization need not always be positive, however. Many people attempt to conform to social stereotypes about members of their group by projecting negative images of themselves; many blacks, Spanish Americans, American Indians, and women may present themselves as lazy and shiftless or dumb.

A number of techniques are used in idealization. One involves hiding socially unacceptable aspects of oneself. A. Kinsey, W. P. Pomeroy, and C. E. Martin, for example, documented the fact that many people engage in secret sexual behavior that is inconsistent with their projected self-images. A person often presents only a final product, be it an image of the self or an object associated with the self. The performances of the ballerina, figure-skater, television announcer, and magician seem natural; they do not reflect the long hours of rehearsal that made them possible. That is also the case with many of the subtle aspects of conversation and manner. The jokes we tell, the compliments we pay, the way we dress—all are presented as spontaneous but are in many cases well rehearsed.

PSYCHOLOGICAL TESTS OF GOFFMAN'S HYPOTHESES

Goffman's descriptions of the ways in which people present themselves in everyday life seem valid because they can be supported by incidents from our own lives. The problem with argument by example, however, is that it is susceptible to contradiction by other examples. More than examples are needed to establish a theory or hypothesis. Although there has not been much experimental research done by psychologists on the presentation of self or on impression management, psychologists K. J. Gergen, E. E. Jones, K. E. Davis, and H. B. Gerard have recently begun to test some of Goffman's hypotheses.

The Effect of Social Approval

A central assumption of Goffman's work is that people want to gain approval from others. Psychological research has established the fact that social approval is generally reinforcing. In an ingenious experiment, W. S. Verplanck had a group of students engage other students in conversations. One group had been previously instructed to respond to all the statements of opinion of members of the other group by saying "You are right" or "I agree." Verplanck found that the subjects increased the rate with which they gave opinions. He inferred that the first group of students had verbally conditioned the second and that the reinforcer was social approval. Since Verplanck's study many other experiments have supported the idea that social approval is reinforcing.

In considering Goffman's examples, you might have asked whether a person really gains much by putting on an act and gaining approval for it. He must know that his act is not genuine and therefore that the approval is not really for *him.* In a fascinating set of studies, Jones, Gergen, and Davis found that people "tend to be taken in by their own performances." People were placed in an interview situation and explicitly asked to behave hypocritically. Part of the instructions for one experiment read:

> In [this] situation it would naturally be to your advantage to say the kinds of things calculated to make the interviewer think highly of you. . . . Try to figure out what kind of person the interviewer probably likes and then try to act like such a person. . . . Try to create the most favorable picture you can, . . . one which is likely to appeal to the interviewer, even though it does not actually reflect the picture you have of yourself.

The presentation of half the subjects met with approval, that of the other half with disapproval. The investigators found that the group of subjects whose acts were approved recalled their self-presentations as being more accurate than the group of subjects whose acts met with disapproval. Approval from others was taken as a sign of the accuracy of the self-presentation, even though the self-presentation had been deliberately distorted.

Conformity

Goffman also assumes that people are essentially conforming. They conform to general social norms and to norms associated with others' expectations of them. A large body of literature in social psychology (see Chapter 26) supports the idea that people are motivated to conform to the views of others.

Consistency

A third assumption that Goffman makes is that people behave inconsistently, changing their act for each audience and each situation. That is why they are motivated to segregate their audiences. How do people feel about such chameleonlike changeability? Although Goffman's model does not really deal with the relationship between a person's act and his feelings about it, research done by Gergen on the consistency of self-presentation has taken this further step. The research has shown that people adapt both their behavior *and their self-concepts* in accord with the people with whom they interact, the situations in which they find themselves, and their motivational goals. One experiment performed by Gergen and B. Wishnov showed that subjects who described themselves to egotistical partners were more positive about themselves than were subjects who described themselves to humble partners. Of considerable interest is the fact that both groups of subjects, when they were asked later how honest they had been, reported that they had been very honest. In another of Gergen's experiments, while subjects described themselves, they were reinforced by subtle social cues such as smiling and nodding. Those who were positively reinforced gave more positive descriptions of themselves than those who were negatively reinforced; more important is that they believed their descriptions were accurate.

One of the limiting factors in the choice of the act that a person will present is the necessity of living up to it. Gergen and Wishnov found that subjects who anticipated later interaction with their partners were more truly self-revealing than subjects who did not.

Role Playing and Self-Conception

Goffman implies that social roles shape self-conceptions. C. W. Backman and P. F. Secord conducted a number of experiments to test the relationship between social roles and self-conceptions. They hypothesized that role categories could determine people's behavior and thereby help shape their self-conceptions. They called this a *fashioning effect.* They also hypothesized that the reverse could occur. A person could choose a role that allowed him to behave in a manner consistent with his self-conception *(role selection)* or adapt roles to his particular style *(role portrayal)*. Backman and Secord found evidence for both processes—college students expressed preferences for occupations and marital roles most consistent with previous ratings of their personality characteristics and self-conceptions, but once they had begun performing their roles, their self-conceptions became even more congruent with the role images they selected.

THE PERSON BEHIND THE MASK

In contrasting back regions with front regions, in comparing virtual social identity with actual social identity, and in assuming that the performer can be taken in by his own act, Goffman assumes a self, or actor, behind the mask and the act. What is the relationship between the "real self" and the presented self? R. E. Park suggests:

> In a sense, and in so far as this mask represents the conception we have formed of ourselves—the role we are striving to live up to—this mask is our truer self, the self we would like to be. In the end, our conception of our role becomes second nature and an integral part of our personality. We come into the world as individuals, achieve character, and become persons.

Is Park correct, or can we, as Backman and Secord imply, be quite different from our roles?

The question is a fascinating one. Most psychologists who have written about the self divide it into an I and a me. The I is a process—it is the willing, experiencing,

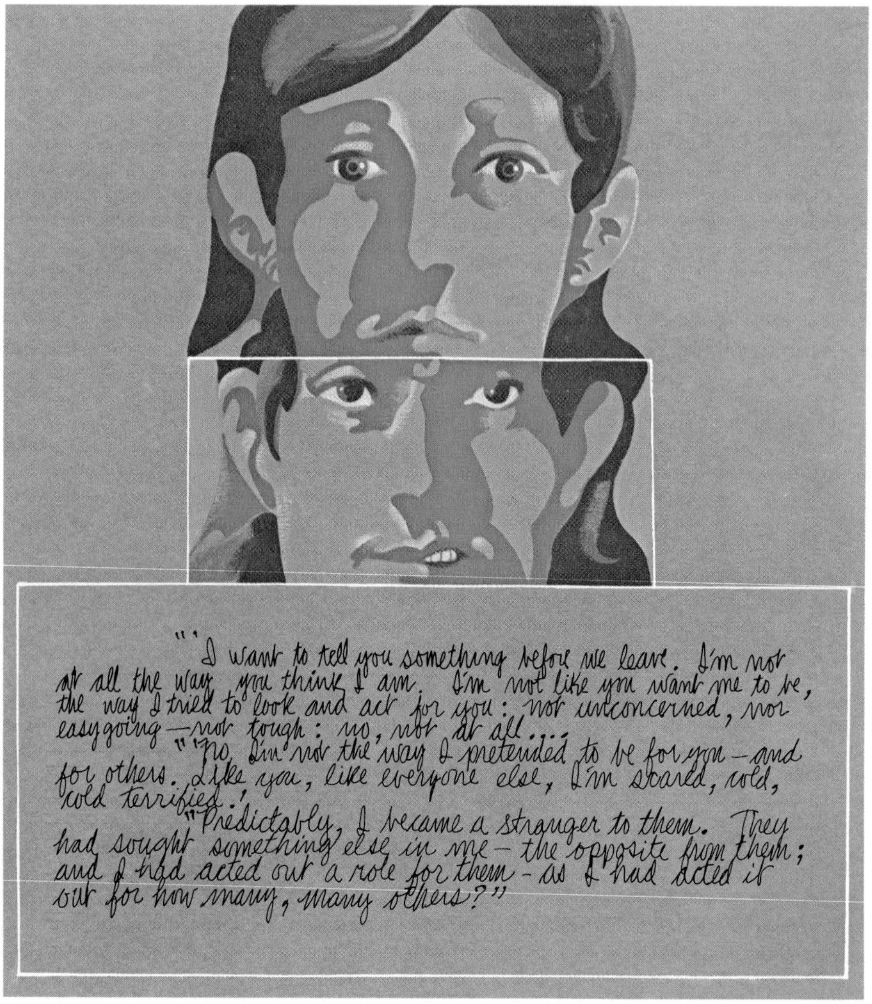

Figure 23.12
This young man speaks about the mask he wears and its costs to him. His mask is that of "cool customer," because that was what others desired him to be. For most of us, the contrast between the mask and what (if anything) it covers may not be so dramatic.
(From John Rechy, *City of Night*. New York: Grove Press, 1963, p. 369.)

perceiving, feeling, imagining, planning component of self. The me is reflexive—the self-as-known. Self theorists such as G. H. Mead and C. Cooley suggest that the *me* can be seen only through the eyes of others.

We achieve identity by taking the role of others. This conception, as pointed out in Chapter 8, is a basic assumption of cognitive-developmental theory. Self theorists, however, do not propose that self-conceptions are always a direct result of the responses of particular others. As people grow older, the referents against which they test their self-images become increasingly general and increasingly internalized. Mature adults orient to "generalized others" and later to principles.

Most self theorists would therefore insist that Goffman's descriptions are limited. Goffman describes a general set of social techniques; he does not focus on individual differences or on developmental trends. Psychologists such as Mead see a human being as passing through stages in which the impressions he makes on particular others are extremely important, but they also endow him with the potential to transcend his dependence on these impressions and become more self-determined and independent.

In considering the ways in which impressions of personality are formed and created, this chapter has moved from matters of individual psychology to those involving the ways in which people interact with one another. The study of interaction between people is the primary focus of a large and growing branch of psychology known as social psychology. The next six chapters are devoted to social psychology, and they discuss the processes and products of social interaction. These include the phenomena that take place in groups of people, the determinants of friendship formation, and the mechanisms by which people influence the attitudes and behavior of others. In all of these social-psychological processes, impressions of personality inevitably play a central part.

Figure 23.13
Jean Paul Sartre's insight here reflects a point of view that theorists of the self have also stated: personal identity develops from the observation and responses of others. Initially the speaker felt as though he were no more than a compilation of behaviors. When he is observed by others, however, he comes to see himself as he imagines others see him. Thus, he becomes a self.
[From Jean Paul Sartre, *Being and Nothingness* (trans. Hazel E. Barnes). New York: The Citadel Press, 1968, pp. 235–236.]

SUGGESTED READINGS

FAST, JULIUS. *Body Language.* New York, M. Evans & Co., Inc., 1970. An adequate first introduction to nonverbal communication—as long as the author's "conclusions" are translated to "possibilities."

GOFFMAN, ERVING. *The Presentation of Self in Everyday Life.* Garden City, N.Y., Doubleday, 1959. A classic in the study of how impressions are made. Goffman presents a creative and original description of everyday social interactions, with the theme, "Man Is An Actor." The book sacrifices theoretical perspective for description.

———. *Stigma: Notes on the Management of Spoiled Identity.* Englewood Cliffs, N.J., Prentice-Hall, Inc., 1963. An analysis of people with something to hide; by extension, therefore, an examination of the role of others in the formation and maintenance of identity.

HASTORF, A. H., SCHNEIDER, D. J., and POLEFKA, J. *Person Perception.* Reading, Mass., Addison-Wesley, 1970. An excellent introduction to research on impression formation. Attribution theory and general issues in the study of the way people perceive other people.

TAGIURI, RENATO, and PETRULLO, LUIGI (Eds.). *Person Perception and Interpersonal Behavior.* Stanford, Calif., Stanford University Press, 1958. A book of readings that is the outcome of the Harvard–Office of Naval Research Symposium on Person Perception, held at Harvard University in 1957. The twenty-three articles range from excerpts of the original thought of Fritz Heider to theoretical contributions of Edward Jones and John Thibaut and the methodological questions of Lee Cronbach. A classic in the field.

UNIT VIII Social Psychology

In some respects social psychology is the most familiar and "obvious" area of psychology. It is not concerned with physiological processes that require special equipment or techniques to observe. It does not deal with the inner recesses of the human mind. Instead, the processes that are the concern of social psychology are highly visible to all of us practically all of the time. These are the processes of social interaction—the ways in which people come together and interact in groups, pattern their behavior toward one another, influence each other's attitudes and actions, and build lasting relationships. As a result, social psychology is an area that every student knows something about even before he takes his first psychology course. He has had first-

Chapter 24, The Individual and His Groups, examines the types of groups that exist, the ways in which each type functions, and how a person's membership in a group affects his attitudes and actions. The Bay of Pigs invasion is used to illustrate some of the dangers of group decision making.

Chapter 25, Patterns of Social Behavior: The Case of Sex Roles, deals with the formal and informal rules that pattern people's interaction with one another, including social norms, status, and roles. To illustrate the patterning of social behavior, the chapter focuses on sex roles in contemporary society.

Chapter 26, Attitude Change and Social Influence, looks at the processes of social influence—the means that people use to persuade others to change their attitudes and behavior. It includes examinations of obedience and conformity.

2

Instinctive Behavior discusses social behavior in some animals: migration and communication, like that of honeybees, are examined. These behaviors can be compared to social aspects of human life, as in Chapters 24 and 28.

3

Conditioning and Learning presents the basic behaviorist principles of learning, which are applied, as one theoretical approach, to explain the acquisition of sex roles in Chapter 25.

8

Social Development: The Case of Morality sets out three theoretical approaches to social development: psychoanalytic, social-learning, and cognitive-developmental; Chapter 25 also presents these three approaches to the acquisition of sex roles. In addition, Chapter 8's discussion of the acquisition of social roles is background to the discussion of racial roles in Chapter 28.

11

Problem Solving examines the various aspects of individual problem solving; the discussion of these skills and their development can be compared to the discussion of group problem solving in Chapter 24.

hand experience with all these processes. But because we have all participated in groups and have been subject to social influence and feelings of attraction and hostility, most people take them for granted: "That's the way things are." Social psychologists, however, have done much research to try to understand exactly how social processes work and *why* "things are the way they are." The chapters in this unit, then, supplement the student's existing understanding of social processes by introducing him to some of the research that social psychologists have employed to shed light on these processes.

Chapter 27, Interpersonal Attraction, discusses the factors that cause us to like or dislike other people. The chapter opens with an examination of the basic need for human contact.

Chapter 28, Intergroup Relations, applies several topics discussed in preceding chapters of this unit—group membership, social roles, the bases of interpersonal attraction—to the study of the important issues of intergroup relations. Relations between blacks and whites in the United States are examined as the central case.

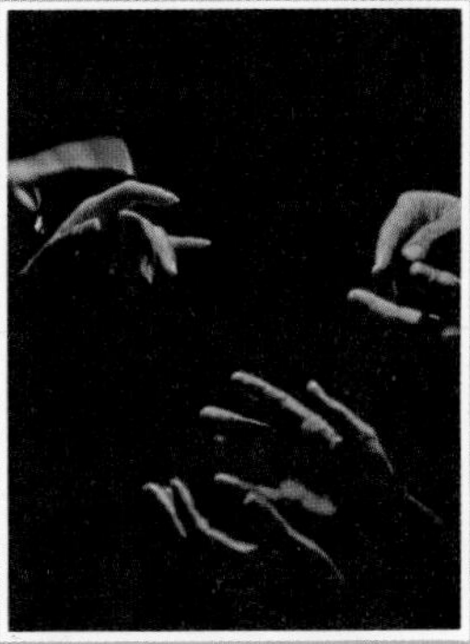

Chapter 29, Intensive Groups, looks at groups that are intentionally formed for the purpose of exploring the participants' feelings, personalities, and patterns of interaction—T-groups, sensitivity groups, and the like. One such group is followed through a weekend encounter.

33

Psychotherapy II looks at group therapy; the discussion of the aims and methods of therapy-oriented groups can be compared to Chapter 29's discussion of growth-oriented groups.

31

Bases of Disorder discusses social interaction as a cause of disorder, both through social-learning theory and through research on families of those with mental disorder. Its findings can be compared with discussions of the family as a group, Chapter 24; of role development, Chapter 25; and of social influence, Chapter 26.

23

Impression Formation examines several topics that relate to this unit; its examination of personal stereotypes and implicit theories of personality are important to understanding interpersonal attraction, Chapter 27; its study of social stereotypes is basic to intergroup relations, Chapter 28; and its long look at nonverbal communication sheds much light on the processes of intensive groups, Chapter 29.

22

Other Theories of Personality includes a discussion of the behaviorist approach to personality, which can be read in conjunction with the social-learning approach to the acquisition of sex roles in Chapter 25.

19

Human Motivation contains a long discussion of the differences that have been found to exist between men and women in certain motives, particularly the motive to achieve; this discussion adds a dimension to Chapter 25's examination of sex-role differences. Also, Chapter 19's discussion of motives for approval or prestige relate to Chapter 27's discussion of why friends are chosen.

Freudian Theories of Personality contains a detailed and basic discussion of psychoanalytic theory, which is used in Chapter 25 specifically to explain the acquisition of sex roles.

21

24
The Individual and His Groups

I SUPPOSE WE CAN ALL think of examples in which we participated in the formation of groups under unusual circumstances. Back in the middle 1940s, I spent some time in the army as a private. I hated it. I was not badly treated; I did not see combat; I was never in danger of any kind; but I just hated it. I hated the things we were required to do, the conditions under which we were required to live, the people with whom I was forced to associate.

Then the time came when we had to travel from Virginia to Hawaii. It was a ten-day trip by train and ship. Only a relatively small number of soldiers were going, and most were eighteen-year-olds with limited background and education. Seven of us, including myself, were older men with college degrees. We seven clung together. There was nowhere to go and no one with whom to interact except ourselves. There was nothing much to do, but we played bridge, talked, reminisced, told jokes. I never played bridge very much before that trip or since. I never even liked it very much; but it seemed the most remarkable and fascinating game in the world for those ten days. I couldn't have enough. And those six other guys—the nicest, sweetest, best guys in the world. We loved each other. We were like brothers. Everything was so warm and comfortable that I was actually *happy*. In fact, I don't know offhand when in my whole life I was so continuously happy over so long a stretch of time. And in the army!

Occasionally, I remember, we would discuss the possibility of trying out for officer-training school. As officers, life would be easier, but we would undoubtedly have to stay in the army longer. We all thought we would remain privates and push for discharge. Of the seven of us, I was far and away the most vehement in supporting the private-and-discharge alternative.

Then one time the other six came to me, all together, and told me they had decided to opt for officer training. The advantages were simply too attractive. Wouldn't I join them? I was astonished. How could they be so foolish? So weak? I refused. I tried to dissuade them. They put the pressure on, argued, pleaded, listed the advantages. To the end I resisted and finally in black despair I cried out, "Go ahead, leave me. Desert me. To hell with all of you."

Then they broke down laughing and explained it was a put-up job. They just wanted to see if I could resist group pressure, and there were bets on as to whether I would or not. I tried to laugh, too, and boasted that I was immovable in my convictions. But I wasn't. I have never forgotten the despair of those moments and how near I came to agreeing to be an officer rather than have them leave me.

Eventually, we reached Hawaii and separated. It may have seemed to me on that wonderful trip that we were soul mates who would remain together forever, but the fact is that since I left the army—so long ago—I have never been in contact with one of them. I. A.

Consider a day in the life of an American male whom we will call Ralph Miller. Ralph gets out of bed at seven, has breakfast with his family, kisses his wife and two children, and then heads off to work. At the bus stop he smiles at the regulars, whom he recognizes but does not know by name. When he arrives at his office building, he rides up in the crowded elevator, joins Bernie, Frank, and Nancy for a quick cup of coffee, and then hurries to the board room for the morning conference. The conference group is trying to come up with a new advertising slogan for a mouthwash account, and Ralph contributes a couple of ideas that the group kicks around and ultimately adds to its list of possibilities.

When he arrives home that evening after a full day, Ralph settles back in his easy chair and looks over the day's mail. It includes a notice about a lecture at his professional association and a request for money from a community organization that serves needy people of Ralph's particular ethnic background. Later that night, after the children have gone to bed, Ralph and his wife spend a half-hour or so watching a late-night talk show involving a Hollywood starlet, a Manhattan novelist, and a justice of the Supreme Court.

Although Ralph's experiences are unique, they have one characteristic that is common to almost everyone's experiences: For better or worse, we spend an extremely large portion of our waking days as members of groups. Individuals pool their resources in collective activities of various sorts; in addition, groups exert a tremendous influence on the attitudes and behavior of an individual, even when he is alone. This chapter will explore, from the vantage point of the social psychologist, some of the processes that take place in groups and some of the ways groups affect their members as individuals.

DEFINING THE GROUP

Groups vary widely in size, intimacy, and formality, but all of them, from the nuclear family to the large corporation, involve some degree of *interdependence* between two or more people. That is, group members are affected or influenced by one another in significant ways. Interdependence generally comes about through direct communication or a feeling of group belonging (or both).

Group members affect one another's attitudes and behavior by means of their communications to one another. The communications may be quite explicit, like Ralph's suggestions at his morning business conference, or they may be more subtle and implicit, like the facial, postural, and gestural signals discussed in Chapter 23. One of the key ways group members influence one another is by sending messages that indicate which particular attitudes and behaviors will be approved of by the rest of the group. By adding his slogans to its list of possibilities, the morning conference group suggested to Ralph that his thinking was along approved lines.

Even when there is no direct interaction among group members, a person's feeling that he *belongs* to a particular group creates interdependence by making it likely that he will respond differently to people he perceives as members of the group than he will to nonmembers, and that he will behave in ways that he sees as relevant to the group's goals. For example, Ralph's feeling of belonging to a particular ethnic group (for example, Irish, Italian, Jewish) may predispose him to send a contribution to the community organization that wrote to him. People's identifications with particular religious groups, professional groups, and so on have considerable influence on their political and social attitudes as well as on their overt behavior. (The effect of these groups—called *reference groups*—on attitudes is discussed at length later in this chapter.)

Interdependence, whether created by direct communication or a feeling of group membership (or both), implies an additional characteristic of practically all groups: Group members see themselves as sharing certain *common goals* or interests. The goals may range from the desire to solve a particular problem (as in Ralph's task group) to the desire to perpetuate a common heritage (as in many ethnic and religious groups). If a person discovers that he no longer has any goals or interests in common with a particular group, he usually stops interacting with it and loses his feeling of group belonging.

Not all collections of people constitute groups. Ralph and the other people in the crowded elevator can hardly be considered a group because there is little or no interdependence among them. They neither communicate significantly with one another nor have a feeling of belonging to an elevator gang. In an emergency, however, a non-group of people can be quickly converted into an actual group. During the Northeast power failure of 1965, for example, people stranded in stalled subways and elevators quickly became highly dependent on one another for emotional support. One group, trapped for five hours in an Empire State Building elevator, formed a Blackout Club and made plans to meet later.

There are also borderline cases that lie somewhere between a group and a mere collection of people. For example, the regulars at Ralph's bus stop may have some degree of interaction and some feeling of group belonging, both of which stem from

Figure 24.1
These boys can be said to constitute a group because they share common goals and communicate significantly with each other. Their function is the social function rather than the task one; they give and receive companionship and emotional support.

the common enterprise of waiting for the bus. However, they form a rather weak and amorphous group with little explicit communication among members and no clear criteria for membership.

TWO MAJOR GROUP FUNCTIONS

Groups have many different goals, most of which can be categorized in terms of two major group functions: the *task function* and the *social function*. When a group of people are working together to make a governmental decision, to perform a surgical operation, or to move a piano, the group is concentrating on the *task* function. When people take walks together or participate in dormitory bull sessions, it is the *social* function that is emphasized; the person participates in the group to gain such social rewards as companionship and emotional support.

A group usually specializes in one function or the other—business organizations tend to specialize in task-related activities, while informal groups of friends tend to specialize in social activities—but almost all groups serve *both* functions to some extent. Members of certain groups, such as family or communal-living groups, provide each other with social support in addition to helping each other get food, clothing, and shelter. People whose jobs require them to work on a task together often feel personal ties to one another, and the social relationships among members may have profound effects on the way the group goes about its task.

GROUP PERFORMANCE

Many tasks can be performed successfully only when a group of people work together. The task may require simply a *summation* of individual strengths, as when a group of men push a stalled car to a gas station, or it may call for smooth *coordination* of diverse activities, as in the performance of an expert surgical team or basketball squad. For some tasks, however, it is not clear whether the results would be better if a group worked together or if each person worked by himself. One such task has been of great interest to psychologists who study group performance; much research has been done in the attempt to determine the relative merit of individual and group activity for creative problem solving.

When Are Two (or More) Heads Better Than One?

In 1938, an advertising executive named Alex Osborn introduced the concept of "brainstorming" as a means of fostering creativity. The basic principle of brainstorming is that group members should be encouraged to express their ideas, no matter how wild or impractical they may seem, in a free and uncritical atmosphere. Quantity rather than quality of ideas is emphasized, at least in the short run. Osborn suggested that such an untrammeled exchange of ideas triggers new ideas and leads to a more varied and creative set of possibilities than any member could have produced alone.

The wide adoption of brainstorming in businesses and other organizations attests to its appeal. Experimental evidence suggests, however, that its effectiveness for bringing about creative solutions to problems is questionable. In a well-known investigation, D. W. Taylor, P. C. Berry, and C. H. Block showed that four people working *individually* consistently came up with more and better solutions to problems than did four-man brainstorming groups. It is possible that the students who participated in this study simply did not use the brainstorming technique correctly or that, in spite of instructions to the contrary, they did not feel completely immune to criticism and so kept their ideas at a relatively conventional level. It is also feasible that isolation is more conducive to certain kinds of creative endeavor than is group interaction. Another possibility, which has obtained some support in experiments conducted by M. D. Dunnette, J. Campbell and K. Jaastad, is that people may be especially creative when working as individuals *after* participation in a brainstorming group; that is, the group discussion may provide valuable starting points for the individual's creative process.

Brainstorming emphasizes the uncritical attitude of the group toward the ideas presented. In contrast, it has been argued that groups are more effective than individuals because they encourage critical thinking and the rejection of incorrect ideas. In an experiment conducted by M. E. Shaw, groups proved to be more accurate than individuals in solving a variety of intellectual problems. On the basis of her observation of the group discussions, Shaw reported: "Perhaps . . . the greatest point of group supremacy is the rejection [by others] of incorrect ideas that escape the notice of the individual when working alone." This critical function of groups may be particularly important when the solutions to problems are not clearly "right" or "wrong" and when the stakes involved are high.

Problems likely to be solved better by group treatment are those that are susceptible to a *division of labor* among people with complementary skills. Government and industry frequently make use of multidisciplinary task forces, in which experts from different fields coordinate their talents in order to solve practical problems. The same principle operates in some of the creative arts. Although very few great poems, paintings, or symphonies are created by committees, most great musicals have been written by composer-lyricist teams—Gilbert and Sullivan, Rodgers and Hammerstein, Lerner and Loewe—and most, if not all, award-winning films have been created by people working together as a group.

Group Decision Making: A Case Study

Behind closed doors at the White House in the early months of 1961, a confident and tight-knit group, including some of the reputedly most intelligent men ever to participate in the councils of government, made what has come to be regarded as one of the worst decisions in recent history. The group was incoming President John F. Kennedy's inner circle of foreign-policy advisers, including Dean Rusk, Robert McNamara, McGeorge Bundy, Douglas Dillon, and Arthur Schlesinger. Meeting

Figure 24.2
Photographs taken during a meeting of Kennedy's cabinet. Shown with President Kennedy in the bottom photograph are Dean Rusk and Robert McNamara, two of the president's group of advisers who participated in making the decision to aid Cuban exiles in their invasion at the Bay of Pigs. This decision, one of the worst in recent history, has been analyzed by I. L. Janis as being an outcome of *groupthink*.

Our meetings were taking place in a curious atmosphere of assumed consensus. Had one senior adviser opposed the adventure, I believe that Kennedy would have canceled it. Not one spoke against it.

From A. M. Schlesinger, Jr., *A Thousand Days.*

frequently over the course of three months, the advisory group reached the unanimous decision to go ahead with plans developed under the Eisenhower administration for an invasion of Cuba by CIA-trained Cuban exiles. On April 17, 1961, the brigade of 1,400 exiles, aided by the United States Navy and Air Force and the CIA, invaded Cuba at the Bay of Pigs. Within three days ships carrying the invaders' reserve ammunition and supplies had been sunk by Castro's air force and about 1,200 invaders had been captured; most of the rest had been killed. According to Theodore Sorensen, the policy planners had hoped that the invasion "would make possible the toppling of the Castro regime without actual aggression by the U.S." Instead, it had been a total fiasco.

Subsequent reflections on the Bay of Pigs affair by Schlesinger, McNamara, and President Kennedy made it clear that the group's decision was apparently based on incomplete information. The group failed to take account of—and in some cases to acquaint itself with—available information on the size and strength of Castro's forces, the deteriorating morale of the invaders, and the likelihood that the invasion would touch off uprisings behind the lines in the Cuban underground. True, there were strong pressures on the new administration to prove that it was not "soft on Communism," but these and other political explanations seem curiously inadequate to account for an episode that was many times more humiliating to the Kennedy administration than calling off the expedition would have been.

I. L. Janis, a social psychologist at Yale University, has suggested in his book *Victims of Groupthink* a different approach to the question of why the group acted as it did. According to Janis, the policy planners were not so much affected by political pressures as they were victimized by *groupthink.* Following are two of the major symptoms of groupthink that Janis identifies in the course of his impressive analysis of the Bay of Pigs decision.

Everything had broken right for him [Kennedy] since 1956. He had won the nomination and the election against all the odds in the book. Everyone around him thought he had the Midas touch and could not lose.

From A. M. Schlesinger, Jr., *A Thousand Days.*

The Illusion of Invulnerability In the months following his inauguration, President Kennedy and his inner circle shared an unusually high degree of morale and *esprit de corps.* The group was a highly *cohesive* one—that is, its members prized their membership in the group and felt strongly committed to it. There was a great feeling of optimism about the potential of the new administration. Schlesinger later wrote the descriptions on this page and page 477.

Janis notes that optimism is characteristic of highly cohesive groups, including encounter groups, military combat units, and athletic teams. For a policy-planning group, however, these feelings can create the dangerous illusion that the group is invulnerable. "The group members know that none of them is a superman," Janis writes, "but they feel that somehow the group is a supergroup, capable of surmounting all risks that stand in the way of carrying out any desired course of action." Such a feeling seems to have been behind the planners' reluctance to examine the drawbacks of the invasion plan. Running through all their assumptions was the happy but unrealistic idea that they would inevitably win out.

The Illusion of Unanimity Maintaining the optimistic outlook of a cohesive group requires that each member believe that everyone else in the group agrees that risks can be safely ignored. Such a feeling of unanimity occurred in the Bay of Pigs planning group.

In fact, the apparent unanimity at the meetings was an illusion. Privately, several of the participants harbored doubts about the decision, although they did not express their doubts publicly. Janis suggests that their reluctance to do so was not due to timidity or fear of damaging their careers; rather, they did not want to risk incurring the disapproval of the other group members for having destroyed the group's sense of unity. Similar tendencies toward conformity have been found in social-psychological experiments on group judgments, especially when group members have had to state their judgments out loud or when they have been concerned about being accepted by the group. A famous series of such experiments, conducted by Solomon Asch, is described in detail in Chapter 26.

When a group is contemplating a potentially dangerous course of action, Janis says, internal disagreements are likely to create anxiety about the possibility that a serious error could be made:

> In order to avoid being confronted by such an unpleasant state, the members of face-to-face groups often become inclined, without quite realizing it, to prevent latent disagreements from surfacing. . . . The group leader and the members mutually support each other in playing up the areas of convergence in their thinking, at the expense of fully exploring divergences that might reveal unsettled issues. Better to share a pleasant balmy group atmosphere than to have a storm.

In their desire to maintain the illusion of unanimity, members of a cohesive group may also take steps to suppress the views of people who are thought to be opposed to the group decision. Secretary Rusk may have served such a purpose in failing to report to the group the reservations of experts on his staff. Attorney General Robert Kennedy (a member of the in-group although he did not actually

The currents of vitality radiated out of the White House, flowed through the government and created a sense of vast possibility. The very idea of the new President taking command as tranquilly and naturally as if his whole life had prepared him for it could not but stimulate a thought of buoyant optimism. . . . Euphoria reigned; we thought for a moment that the world was plastic and the future unlimited.

From A. M. Schlesinger, Jr., *A Thousand Days.*

Figure 24.6
Groupthink, characterized by illusions of invulnerability and unanimity, can lead to bad, even dangerous, decisions, which members of the group probably would not have arrived at individually. The group that becomes a victim of groupthink can find itself sinking into a bog of conformity and totally unrealistic optimism.

A crowd of about 100 teenagers in New York, angered when a girl was hit by a light panel truck, assaulted the driver, overturned the truck, set it ablaze, and hurled bricks and bottles at the firemen attempting to douse the fire.

A false rumor that a friend had been beaten by white girls sent a group of 15 black girls on a rampage through Lincoln High School in San Francisco (*San Francisco Chronicle*, February 27, 1969).

More than 300 persons were killed and 500 injured in events that followed an unpopular ruling by the referee in a soccer match between Peru and Argentina (*New York Times*, May 25, 1964).

From P. G. Zimbardo, "The Human Choice."

Figure 24.8
Roger Brown is a psychologist who has studied phenomena in a number of areas of social psychology, including attitude change and mob behavior, and has written an important social psychology text. Brown has also spent a major part of his career studying psycholinguistics, especially the acquisition of language in children.

attend the planning meetings) may have been similarly motivated when he advised Schlesinger that Schlesinger would not be helping the President if he expressed his reservations about the plan.

Social-psychological experiments have shed additional light on the ways cohesive groups deal with disagreeing members. At first there tends to be a marked increase in communications addressed to the person whose expressed views are out of line with the group views. These attempts to influence the nonconformist continue as long as other members of the group think they have a reasonable chance of changing his mind. If they fail after repeated efforts, communication with the deviate drops off sharply; he is, in effect, excluded from the group. An experiment conducted by Stanley Schachter at the University of Michigan, and repeated in 1954 in seven European countries, demonstrated conclusively that the more cohesive a group is, the more likely its members are to reject an unyielding deviate.

Groupthink in the Mob

Hostile outbreaks in crowds and mobs may also involve a kind of groupthink. The classic example of mob outbreaks is the lynching of black men by whites in the American South. Although lynchings are rare today, mob violence continues to occur in many forms. For example, P. G. Zimbardo reports the incidents adjacent. Note that when a collection of people engages in mob action, a *group*, as defined earlier, is formed; the people in the crowd become highly interdependent, and collective action is made possible.

Social scientists who study mob outbreaks have identified in such groups a sense of power and moral rightness that resembles the illusion of invulnerability found in cohesive policy-making groups. Sometimes the sense of moral rightness seems to stem mainly from the size of the group taking part in the outbreak. A. Raper reports that one lynching crowd of about seventy people wanted to wait until there were at least thirty more because they felt that a hundred participants would make the whole thing "legal." Just as the illusion of invulnerability in a policy-making group is fostered by the misconception that all group members agree, the sense of power and moral rightness in a mob is fostered by the belief that the crowd is unanimous in its sentiments. Milling about—slow, apparently aimless movement—often occurs in crowds before they become actively aggressive, and some psychologists consider it an essential prerequisite to mob action. What is it that milling accomplishes? Probably, R. Brown has suggested, it is "primarily a process of informal communication, a process by which members learn *that they are of one mind*, that they are individually eager to lynch, riot, or otherwise 'let go.' "

Gustave LeBon, a Frenchman who wrote a classic treatise on crowds and mobs in 1895, explained crowd behavior in terms of a *collective mind* that makes the participants feel, think, and act in a different way than each individual would if he were alone. Although some critics find the notion of a collective mind inadequate as a scientific concept, it is hard to deny LeBon's contention that a crowd may act differently—in many instances more impulsively and with less restraint—than its members as individuals would.

Preventing Groupthink

Two conclusions that should *not* be drawn from Janis' analysis of groupthink in the Bay of Pigs planning group are (1) that important decisions should be made by one individual single-handedly, and (2) that groups with low morale are more effective problem solvers than optimistic, cohesive groups. One person rarely has all the expertise and information needed to make an important policy decision. In addition, any one person inevitably has certain biases, blind spots, and other weaknesses. For these reasons the general practice of making important decisions in groups can hardly be questioned. Moreover, high morale in a decision-making (or virtually any other) group has important advantages. Unless group members are committed to one another and to the task at hand, they probably will not be willing to invest the time and energy it takes to make a difficult decision. Instead, they are likely to adopt a casual attitude, skipping meetings, overlooking problems, and perhaps eventually abandoning the group altogether. So group cohesiveness should generally be encouraged. Groupthink, however, should be discouraged. Some of the ways Janis suggests in his book to prevent it are presented below:

1. Ask each group member to discuss the group's deliberations with trusted associates at his home office and then to report their reactions. The reactions of outsiders should help counter illusions that might be created within the group.
2. Along the same lines, invite one or two outside experts to each group meeting. This was done during the Cuban missile crisis, which involved the same people as the Bay of Pigs affair but turned out much more successfully.
3. Have the leader abstain from stating his own position at the outset, so as to prevent group members from adopting it uncritically. During the Cuban missile crisis, for example, President Kennedy deliberately stayed away from the initial meetings of the planning group.
4. Make certain that group members are encouraged to freely express objections and doubts. To attain this goal, the leader should delegate the responsibility of being a critical evaluator to each member, and he should reinforce free expression by his own acceptance of criticism.
5. Assign one or more group members the role of devil's advocate, to challenge the testimony of all those who support the majority decision. Robert Kennedy played this role at the Cuban missile crisis meetings, forcing the group to examine the pros and cons of the proposed action more carefully than it otherwise would have.
6. After a preliminary consensus on the best alternative, hold a special meeting in which all members are encouraged to express their remaining doubts. Such a "second-chance" meeting will help prevent premature consensus based on illusions of invulnerability and unanimity.

Underlying all these suggestions is the idea that the best way to prevent groupthink is to be *aware* of the possibility that it will emerge. If the people in a decision-making group learn to recognize that heady feeling of invulnerability and convivial unanimity as a warning sign, they will probably be able to keep groupthink from sweeping them off their feet.

H. A. Illing quotes the famous psychoanalyst Carl Jung as having asserted that "when a hundred clever heads join a group, one big nincompoop is the result." As we have seen, there is some truth to Jung's assertion that groups can stifle creativity, foster conformity, and even legitimize mob violence. On the other hand, many tasks and many decision-making functions absolutely require group action. Through further research on group performance and decision making, psychologists hope to learn more about the constructive potential and possible dangers of group action, and to identify ways of maximizing a group's assets and minimizing its liabilities.

GROUP COMMITMENT

Depending on our particular values or biases, we may speak of "selfless citizens" or "mindless superpatriots," of "martyrs" or "fanatics." Although the words reflect different evaluations, they refer to the same behavior: people's willingness to make personal sacrifices for the sake of a group to which they belong.

To the extent that a person is prepared to make such sacrifices, we say that he is *committed* to the group. However, because he is committed to the group, his sacrifices are not as selfless as they may seem. The committed group member comes to equate the welfare of his group with his own personal welfare; by helping the group, he believes he is helping himself as well. If a person is strongly committed to the perpetuation of a group or to the promotion of its values, he will invest time and energy on the group's behalf, and perhaps even give up his life for it. Group

Under certain given circumstances, and only under those circumstances, an agglomeration of men presents new characteristics very different from those of the individuals composing it. The sentiments and ideas of all the persons in the gathering take one and the same direction, and their conscious personality vanishes. A collective mind is formed, doubtless transitory, but presenting very clearly defined characteristics. The gathering has thus become what, in the absence of a better expression, I will call an organised crowd, or, if the term is considered preferable, a psychological crowd. It forms a single being, and is subjected to the *law of the mental unity of crowds.*

From Gustave Le Bon, *The Crowd,* 1895.

commitment and its close relation to personal sacrifice help us to understand such different behaviors as an employee putting in long hours of overtime without pay and a Nathan Hale's proud declaration that his only regret is having but one life to give for his country.

A large degree of commitment is essential for the effective operation of many groups, ranging from student organizations to families to business corporations. Without commitment, group members perform their assigned functions only as long as they are paid (or rewarded in some other way), and they are not likely to go beyond the call of duty to be innovative or to defend the group if it is threatened. Moreover, an uncommitted group member will not hesitate to abandon the group if a better opportunity arises. Because many groups cannot survive unless their members stay with the group, and perform at more than a minimal level, it is important for the groups to seek out ways to maintain and increase the commitment of their members.

Some of the mechanisms that observers of groups have identified as being likely to induce commitment are discussed below. Several of the examples come from R. M. Kanter's insightful study of the commitment-inducing mechanisms employed by nineteenth-century communes. Because these communes, like present-day ones, existed outside the boundaries of established social groupings, it was especially necessary for them to wean their members away from pre-existing group memberships in the direction of exclusive commitment to the commune.

Personal Sacrifice and Financial Investment

Making personal sacrifices for the sake of the group not only results from group commitment but also contributes to its development. As a prerequisite to joining some nineteenth-century communes, members had to agree to abstain from such gratifications as wearing jewelry and fine clothes, smoking tobacco, eating meat, or making love. Kanter found that communes requiring such sacrifices tended to last much longer than ones that did not. Sacrifice makes membership in the group more costly, so membership becomes a matter not to be lightly regarded or given up.

A psychological explanation for the committing effect of sacrifice is provided by L. Festinger's theory of cognitive dissonance. According to Festinger's theory, people are strongly motivated to achieve consistency between their attitudes and their behavior. When a person must suffer in order to belong to a group, he can justify the suffering—and make his attitude consistent with his behavior—by coming to value highly the group he has suffered for.

Figure 24.10
Leon Festinger is best known for his theory of cognitive dissonance, which has been used to explain the dynamics of decision making and attitude change, as well as the reasons that people make personal sacrifices

E. Aronson and J. Mills showed, for example, that college women who were required to undergo a painful initiation in order to join a discussion group came to like the group more than did subjects whose initiation was milder. The same commitment-inducing principle may underlie the use of painful initiation rites at puberty in various cultures.

Successful nineteenth-century communes also required members to sign over their money and property to the group and thereafter to work for no compensation. In many cases there were no refunds; a member got nothing back if he left the commune. One group leader dramatized the nonreturnability of contributions by burning the book in which they were recorded. Enforced investment helps bind the individual to the group in the same way that personal sacrifice does. In addition, the group member knows that he will lose everything if he decides to leave.

Participation

Many business organizations have found that they can increase their employees' commitment to the firm by giving them a larger say in its decisions and by paying bonuses based on the organization's profits. Similarly, parents who help make policy decisions that affect their children's schooling tend to feel more committed to the

Figure 24.11
Nineteenth-century utopian communes employed procedures that were effective in promoting personal involvement and commitment to the group. Some of these procedures are: isolation of the group from established society; requirements that the members refrain from many gratifying behaviors and that they make nonreturnable financial contributions; and involvement of the members in formulation and execution of communal policy.

school than parents who have no say in decisions or think the school's policies do not reward their children. When a person participates in group decisions and shares the rewards of the group's accomplishment, he regards the group as his because he has, in fact, helped make it what it is.

Participation in group life was intense in nineteenth-century communes. Frequent interaction, both in work settings and at meetings that stressed openness and group loyalty, established strong feelings of attraction and "we-feeling" among group members. Some of the meetings bore a striking resemblance to present-day encounter groups, which often create a similar sense of communion and commitment (see Chapter 29). In the utopian communes, close ties to the group were further encouraged by rules that required members to renounce all outside relationships, including family ones.

Ideology and Symbols

Inducing commitment to a group involves a complex matching of individual values to the values of the group. The matching process proceeds in two directions simultaneously. On the one hand, groups try to convert their members to the prevailing group ideology. The utopian communities often expounded their basic beliefs in written and oral teachings and required group members to pledge their allegiance to these beliefs in various ceremonies and formalized tests of faith. On the other hand, many groups also try to present their goals in such a way that prospective members will see them as relevant to their own values. A police force, for instance, may try to attract new members by minimizing the routine business of law enforcement and presenting itself as a corps of professional officers dedicated to the highest form of public service. Some organizations employ public relations specialists for such "packaging" functions.

Emotional attachment to a group and its ideology is often facilitated by the use of symbols with which people can identify. Community songs and rituals were used by the successful utopian communes to increase their members' emotional involvement. National flags, patriotic songs, and mottoes can also intensify feelings of national loyalty, as can charismatic leaders who serve as symbols with which mem-

Old North Hall

Of all the loves in light arrayed,
My mem'ry can recall,
There's one I'm sure will never fade,
And that is Old North Hall:
So, Junior, Soph, stand up and Prof.,
And you ye Freshies small,
And Seniors too,
And all the crew,
And drink to Old North Hall!
And drink to Old North Hall:
And drink to Old North Hall, And
Seniors too, and all the crew,
And drink to Old North Hall!

Deutschland Über Alles

German folk above all others,
All the others in the world.
Joined as one for our protection,
Standing firm in unity
From the Maas up to the Memel,
From the Etsch up to the Belt,
German folk above all others,
All the others in the world.

The Internationale

Arise, you pris'ners of starvation! Arise, you wretched of the earth.
For justice thunders condemnation, a better world's in birth.
No more tradition's chain shall bind us, Arise, you slaves, no more in thrall.
The earth shall rise on new foundations, We have been naught, we shall be all.

Chorus:
'Tis the final conflict, let each stand in his place.
The Internationale shall be the human race!

Figure 24.12
Songs are used by many kinds of groups to boost their members' commitment and sense of identification. "Old North Hall" is a college song, representative of many that attempt to strengthen sentimental ties and loyalty to the alma mater. "The Internationale" is the most famous of all revolutionary songs; it has been and still is sung by some factions of the socialist and communist movements throughout the world. "Deutschland Über Alles" probably best represents the patriotic song, the song meant to strengthen identification with one's native land.

bers identify. Some of the nineteenth-century communes had leaders who were considered godlike and whose teachings remained focal points for the groups even after the leaders died. Similarly, political parties and military organizations tend to glorify their past and to publicize heroes in order to heighten group morale.

By inducing and maintaining group commitment, all the mechanisms described above tend to increase the effectiveness of groups and organizations. In conclusion, however, it should be mentioned that very strong commitment to a group can be a mixed blessing. Excessive loyalty to a group may lead, for example, to a chauvinistic intolerance for outsiders that violates other ostensible ideals of the group. Additional ways in which group commitment can affect relationships between groups are discussed in Chapter 28.

REFERENCE GROUPS

Besides functioning as a collective entity, a group helps shape the self-definitions and personal values of its members as individuals. Social psychologists call a group with which a person identifies and that affects his attitudes and standards a *reference group.* Reference groups need not be formal or face-to-face groups, although they may be. In fact, the most influential reference groups are often broad social categories such as racial, religious, occupational, and sex groupings. People often take great pride in such reference groups and tend to be very much influenced by them in their day-to-day lives.

Group Pride

A person's pride in a reference group may be reflected in the way he represents the group to outsiders. One experiment illustrating this point was designed to investigate the amount of pain that undergraduate women could tolerate as a function of religious group identification. W. E. Lambert, E. Libman, and E. G. Poser first established the amount of pain each woman could tolerate. A blood-pressure instru-

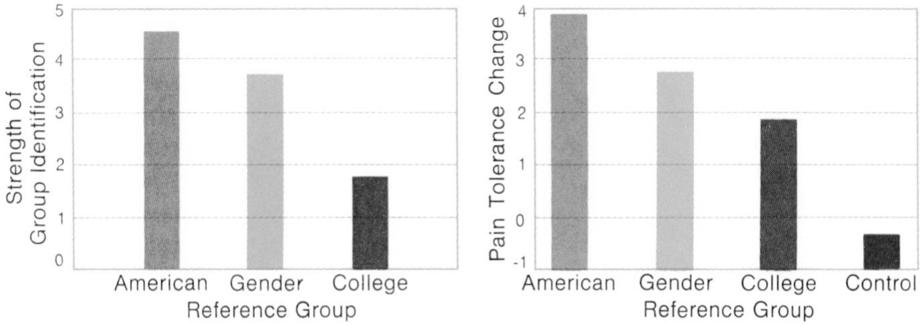

Figure 24.13
A Buss and N. Portnoy explored the relationship between group identification and pain tolerance that was first reported by Lambert *et al.* Buss and Portnoy asked male students to rank their commitment to various reference groups; as indicated by the left-hand graph, national identification was high, gender identification was medium, and college identification was low. Employing the same procedures used by Lambert *et al.*, the experimenters challenged their male subjects' identification with these reference groups by mentioning to them the superiority of other subjects in tolerating pain: Russians or Canadians, women, or a rival college. The graph at the right shows that the increase in pain tolerance varied in the same way as group identification: it was highest for national identification, lower for gender, and lowest for college. Thus, Buss and Portnoy showed that the findings of Lambert *et al.* were applicable to men as well as to women, and that pain tolerance varies with the strength of group identification.
(After Buss and Portnoy, 1967.)

ment with sharp, hard, rubber projections sewn into the cuff was placed on the subject's upper arm, and the pressure was gradually increased until she pronounced the pain intolerable. After this limit had been established, the experimenter told the subject that a retest would be made in five minutes to determine the reliability of the measurement. In addition, he casually mentioned to those subjects who were Jewish that Jews could endure less pain than Christians, and he told those who were Christian that Christians could take less pain than Jews. (In fact, neither of these statements is true.) On the retest the tolerance limits of both the Jewish and Christian subjects increased significantly. There was no change in the tolerance limits of control subjects, to whom the experimenter said nothing about religious groups. These findings suggest that people tend to interpret "insults" to their religious reference groups as attacks on themselves and are prepared to defend the group publicly, even if doing so requires them to endure intense pain.

Another way people demonstrate group pride is by showing willingness to take responsibility for other members of a reference group, even those they do not know personally. I. Piliavin, J. Rodin, and J. A. Piliavin recently staged a series of eighty-one collapses on New York City subway trains. Some of the "victims" were white and some were black, and they pretended to be either crippled or drunk. In each case the victim staggered forward and fell to the floor, remaining there until someone came to his assistance.

The researchers found that black and white subway riders were equally likely to come to the aid of an apparently crippled victim, regardless of his race. When the victim appeared to be drunk, on the other hand, there was a tendency for most of the helpers to be members of the same race as the victim. The results suggest that sympathy and assistance for an apparently innocent victim (the cripple) easily crosses racial group lines, but when the victim seems to be at fault and potentially dangerous (the drunk), assistance is more likely to be a function of people's feelings of responsibility for fellow members of a reference group.

Figure 24.14
Theodore Newcomb, a social psychologist, has carried out several classic studies in attitude change and in the role of attitude similarity in interpersonal attraction.

Group Standards

When a person defines himself as a member of a particular group, he is likely to adopt the attitudes and values that he sees as characterizing the group. In a classic study conducted in the 1930s, T. M. Newcomb investigated changes in political and social values of undergraduates at Bennington College. Most of the students came from upper-class, politically conservative backgrounds, whereas the college community was characterized by extreme liberalism. Newcomb found that the students who strongly identified with Bennington tended to become much more liberal as they progressed through college. Not only did Bennington become a positive reference group for these women, but in many cases their families and home communities became *negative* reference groups. In acquiring new attitudes, the women tried not only to identify more closely with Bennington but to disengage themselves from their conservative backgrounds as well.

Reference-group standards have also been found to affect the way people vote. Surveys by P. Converse and A. Campbell indicate that Catholics, Jews, Blacks, and

Figure 24.15
The Bennington study by Newcomb revealed that these college students made a transition from identification with their families and homes to identification with the values they learned at college, and that their identification with the college reference group lasted long after they had graduated.

union members are more likely to vote for Democratic candidates than are people who do not belong to those groups. All four have informal standards favoring the Democratic party that are apparently perceived and adopted by group members. As one would expect, the preference for Democratic candidates tends to be greatest among people who identify most strongly with the group.

Why are people so likely to adopt the standards of their reference groups? A good part of the answer comes from an understanding of the term *identification.* As the word implies, people acquire a sense of personal definition in large measure from their group memberships. If you ask a person to tell you who he is, he may reply that he is happy, overweight, or trying to write a novel, but he is also likely to say he is an American, a Protestant, or a member of Kappa Kappa Delta. In order to sustain the latter sorts of identities, especially when he has an emotional investment in them, a person tries to be as similar as he can to the "ideal American," the "ideal Protestant," or the "ideal Kappa Kappa Delta member," and he tends to adopt the standards and perspectives that he attributes to the group. These attitudes are often buttressed by direct influences from friends and acquaintances, who often belong to one's own reference groups. Chapter 27 discusses in detail the effects of reference groups on the ways friends are chosen.

Because each person has not one but many reference groups, an important problem for future research is to specify how an individual decides which reference group provides the most relevant standard for his attitudes in a given area. If a person is a black American chemist with a strong interest in mountain climbing, under what conditions is he influenced by the standards of each of those groups? An additional complication is that people often identify with groups that they do not actually belong to but hope to join. An assembly-line worker may adopt some of the attitudes of the supervisory group to which he aspires, and a European who hopes to emigrate to the United States may begin adopting what he perceives as American standards.

As we have seen, the importance of groups lies not only in their collective processes and activities but also in the tremendous impact they have on their individual members. It is for these reasons that the study of group processes is at the very heart of the social psychologist's endeavor to understand the ways in which people affect one another.

SUGGESTED READINGS

BROWN, ROGER. *Social Psychology.* New York, Free Press, 1965. This most readable of social-psychology textbooks is highly recommended. Of particular relevance to this chapter are Chapter 13 (Group Dynamics) and Chapter 14 (Collective Behavior and the Psychology of the Crowd).

CARTWRIGHT, DORWIN, AND ZANDER, ALVIN (Eds.). *Group Dynamics* (3rd ed.). New York, Harper & Row, 1968. An excellent collection of research reports on such topics as conformity, leadership, and power in groups; the editors have provided useful overviews of theory and research.

DAVIS, JAMES H. *Group Performance.* Reading, Mass., Addison-Wesley, 1969. A good overview of research on group problem solving and decision making and of the variables that determine their effectiveness.

FREUD, SIGMUND. *Group Psychology and the Analysis of the Ego.* Many editions, including New York, Bantam, 1960. Freud's classic excursion into social psychology, including observations on the church, the army, the "herd instinct," and the "primal horde."

HYMAN, HERBERT H., AND SINGER, ELEANOR. *Readings in Reference Group Theory and Research.* New York, Free Press, 1968. A good collection of theoretical and research papers on reference groups. The focus is on the ways people select the groups they identify with and the impact group identification has on people's attitudes and behavior.

JANIS, IRVING L. *Victims of Groupthink: A Psychological Study of Foreign-Policy Decisions and Fiascos.* Boston, Houghton Mifflin, 1972. Janis insightfully applies social-psychological theory to a series of historical decisions made by groups, including the Bay of Pigs invasion, the handling of the Cuban missile crisis, and the escalation of the Vietnam war.

25 Patterns of Social Behavior: The Case of Sex Roles

I AM A WOMEN'S LIB ADVOCATE from way back and an optimistic one. I'm sure they'll win out. They can't lose! If the human race survives with an advanced technological culture into the twenty-first century (by no means a likely possibility, I'm afraid) then women will be free. Automatically. You see, I contend that what changes human behavior is not theory and idealism but the general tendency to accept the profitable, at least eventually. For instance, there was nothing that society could do about horse theft. Social obloquy, corporal punishment, lynching, and legal death penalty—nothing worked! And then the cure was developed, and a simple one—the automobile was invented. When fewer people wanted or needed horses badly enough to steal them, horse theft declined. Of course, we now have the problem of automobile theft, but that's another story, isn't it?

All right, women have been subjected and dominated (and taught to relish it and feel that being dominated was wonderful) for two biological reasons. They were physically smaller than men, for one thing, so that they could be physically beaten up if they forgot their place. Second, they bore children and suckled them and that tied them down. Between these two factors, men could dominate, and with physical domination a fact, cultural factors could nail that into place. Women were taught to be passive and accepting, and affairs were so arranged that women had no rights, economic or otherwise, under law; they could not earn a living or be sure of their next meal unless they accepted male domination.

But if we are to survive as a technological society into the twenty-first century, it will be only at the price of achieving population stability. (That will not be the only price, but it will surely be one of the prices.) Children will be a rare luxury by modern standards and women's role as wife and mother will be seriously depressed in importance. And if technology continues to advance, developing automation will make the work of mankind more and more a matter of controlling electrical contacts and making internal decisions—something for which women are as suitable as men. Man's superior muscle will go for naught and woman's smaller and defter fingers at controls may go for a lot.

Well, then once the social pressure on a woman to marry and have children is lifted, and once she can make a living for herself as easily (or more easily) than man can, what can possibly keep her in a state of domination but criminal force.

She may have other problems, but they will be *other* problems, not the ones she has been struggling with through all the centuries of civilization.

I. A.

Human behavior often follows regular patterns. On a city street people drive their cars along predetermined paths, keeping to the right side of the road and signaling each turn; pedestrians walk on the sidewalk and cross at set places. Although the particular individuals taking part in the pattern vary from one moment to the next, the pattern remains essentially the same. Regularity of behavior is a feature of human life.

Personality characteristics also show a kind of patterning. Certain types of people often display a number of traits in common. Judges, for instance, typically seem sober, impartial, calm, and rational; stewardesses seem courteous, attractive, and efficient. There is also a good deal of consistency in the characteristics displayed by men and by women. Men often seem aggressive, independent, unemotional, self-confident, and competitive. Women often seem talkative, tactful, gentle, interested in their own appearances, aware of the feelings of others, and neat.

This chapter describes some of the psychological processes that underlie the patterning of human social behavior. The case of sex roles serves as a particular illustration of the way in which social behavior in general is patterned. Just as there are important differences in behavior and personality between men and women, there are also differences between people grouped according to such other characteristics as age, social class or occupation, and race. In addition, there are striking differences between cultures in these social patterns. In the investigation of these patterns three basic concepts are especially useful: social norms, social status, and social roles.

SOCIAL NORMS

Social groups hold established rules and expectations about human behavior that govern much of what we do. *Formal* organizations, such as universities, often have extensive sets of written rules and regulations: universities regulate not only academic matters, such as course requirements, but also many nonacademic matters, such as parking, the use of liquor on campus, housing, and general student conduct. The severity of punishment for a violation depends on the perceived seriousness of the offense. In *informal* groups, the rules and expectations are usually not explicit, and a person who does not follow them is more likely to be snubbed or criticized than to incur a fine. Yet informal group expectations often have powerful effects on people's conduct. In a group of friends each person is expected to behave in a way generally approved by the group, or he risks the consequences of disapproval and possible exclusion.

Figure 25.1
Sets of social norms define the relationship of performers to their audiences and the status relationship of common men to rulers. The great jazz musician Louis Armstrong once violated both these sets of norms in a single brilliant stroke. In the London Palladium in 1932 before King George VI of England, Armstrong (looking out toward the King) stunned the audience by introducing an encore with the words "This one's for you, Rex!"

These rules and expectations for behavior are termed *social norms.* A norm is a prescription for conduct—a formal or informal set of ways that people are *expected to behave.* Judges are expected to be sober and serious, stewardesses to be efficient and courteous. Norms usually specify the range of behavior that is acceptable or appropriate in a given situation rather than specifying a precise act. Some norms, such as those regulating automobile driving, control our behavior in obvious ways. The effects of other norms, however, are more subtle. For example, as mentioned in Chapter 22, cultures differ in their use of space. In every culture people stand or sit closer to others in intimate activities than they do in business or formal transactions. However, as E. T. Hall has shown in his book *The Hidden Dimension,* the actual physical distance that is appropriate for each type of contact varies from country to country. Members of a culture have learned the appropriate distances for each kind of contact, but outsiders may not have. Although people's behavior conforms to the group norms that apply to such behavior, people often are not consciously aware of those norms. It is only when someone violates the underlying expectations that guide our everyday behavior (for example, by standing too close or by acting in a manner that seems inappropriate for his or her sex) that we may become aware of the norms. Much of our behavior that we think of as natural (integral to our personality) and appropriate is governed by such subtle norms.

SOCIAL STATUS

The members of most groups or social systems differ in rank or *social status.* Some positions within each group are more valued and respected than others and are associated with higher rewards and greater personal privileges. At work, the boss has higher status, a higher salary, and more power than his employees; in a movie company, the stars have more prestige and correspondingly higher salaries than the supporting actors or extras; at universities, tenured faculty outrank instructors.

Status comes from either of two sources. It may be *achieved,* or earned by effort: a poor medical student may become a world-renowned surgeon. Status, alternatively, may be *ascribed* on the basis of some inherited characteristic, such as family status or sex: in India, only a male child born into the Brahman caste can become a Brahman priest. Social interaction is strongly influenced by the status of the participants, whether achieved or ascribed.

Roger Brown, a social psychologist, notes that people's relative status is often reflected in forms of address. Whether one person addresses another by first name or by title and last name depends on the individuals' status relative to one another.

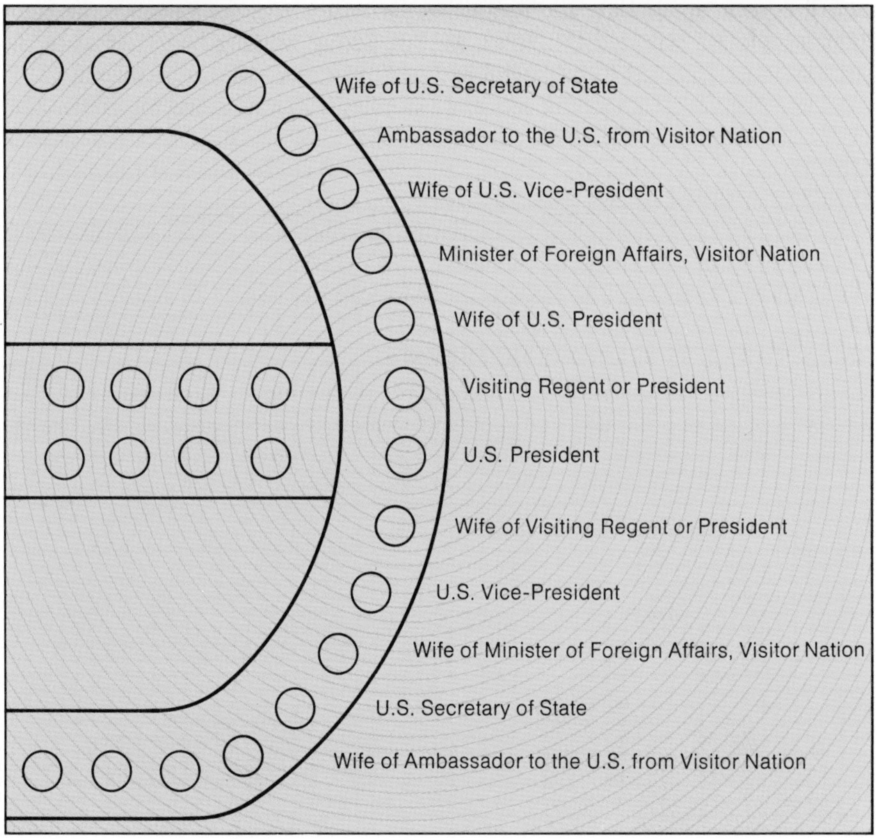

Figure 25.2
The seating arrangements at formal White House dinners illustrate the consequences of social status and the rigid adherence to its rules. (Top) at a recent White House dinner for the Economic Minister of Japan, President Nixon was seated in the middle of the dais; he was flanked on the right by the guest of honor, and on the left by the Economic Minister's wife. Mrs. Nixon sat next to the guest of honor, and the Vice-President's wife was seated to her right. Vice-President Agnew was placed to the left of the wife of the Economic Minister. (Bottom) the seating diagram for the formal White House dinner for President Pompidou of France, showing a somewhat similar adherence to the status of the participants.

In the United States, when people of unequal status interact, the superior is addressed by title and the inferior by first name. Many rules of etiquette are based on social status.

Status commonly affects interaction even in situations where it is not supposed to be a factor. On juries, for example, there is a strong norm of equality dictating that all jurors should be treated as equals. Nonetheless, in a study of mock juries, F. L. Strodtbeck and collaborators found that jurors with higher occupational statuses were much more likely than those with lower statuses to be elected jury foremen. They also participated more actively, had greater influence on the final decision, and were perceived by others to be more competent for the jury task. Status often influences not only the frequency and quality of a person's participation in a discussion but also, more generally, who interacts with whom. College freshmen tend to make friends with fellow freshmen; secretaries are more likely to eat lunch together than with executives. It is clear that norms governing social interaction depend to a large extent on the relative status of the participants.

SOCIAL ROLES

A *social role* can be thought of as simply a cluster of social norms (for behavior, for personality traits, and so on) applicable to some specified social category of people. Any occupation provides an example of a social role. Occupations have far-reaching consequences for the behavior people are expected to display. They dictate the hours people are expected to keep, their clothes, and the skills they may display. Occupational roles also affect how much people tell about themselves to others. A person might disclose personal details to friends or family, clergymen, doctors, or even strangers but not to business associates. Some people acquire special privileges because of their occupational roles: an accountant may check our accounts, a dentist our teeth, a dressmaker or tailor our measurements—and these activities seem appropriate and reasonable. Occupational roles influence the emotions people are expected to display, at least during working hours. At work, an accountant is expected to be careful and precise, a mortician to be solemn.

One of the most important sets of social roles is that attached to gender. The term *sex role* refers to the set of expectations that a society in general shares about what a woman, by virtue of her femaleness, and a man, by virtue of his maleness, should be or should do. Sex roles also have implications for most other role relationships, such as that between husband and wife, boss and worker, teacher and student, opposite-sex jury members, or friends. In the following section the origins and implications of these sex roles are examined in greater detail.

THE ORIGINS OF SEX-ROLE DIFFERENCES

Gender plays a central part in determining the patterning of human behavior. We hardly need to be reminded that men and women are different—that they spend

Figure 25.3
Two radically different views regarding women's roles. For a very long time, our culture has assumed that "a woman's place is in the home"; accompanying this assumption is the requirement that she be passive, maternal, and subordinate to her husband's wishes and needs. The growing movement for women's liberation emphasizes the restrictive and oppressive effects of such dictates and encourages both men and women to subscribe to the attitude expressed in the right-hand quote, said by Nora, in Ibsen's *A Doll's House*.
[From *Colossians* 3:18-19; from Henrik Ibsen, *A Doll's House* (trans. R. Farquharson Sharp). In *Four Great Plays by Ibsen*. New York: Bantam Books, 1967, p. 65.]

their time in different activities and often have different interests, aptitudes, and temperaments.

A central question in any discussion of sex differences concerns how much they can be attributed to innate biological factors and how much to learned cultural factors. Physical differences between men and women seem to be determined primarily by biological factors. In most societies, men tend, on the average, to be taller than women and to have more muscle, more body hair, and so on. Women tend to mature earlier and live longer. But how, if at all, does biology contribute to the formation of such psychological traits as dominance, aggressiveness, cooperativeness, and nurturance?

Theories Stressing Biology

The possibility of sex-linked differences in temperament and personality receives support from several sources. Research on nonhuman primates and other mammals, conducted in both laboratories and natural settings, has found that in most species males are more dominant, active, energetic, and ready to fight than females. Studies of human societies suggest that in every known society that has warfare, it is the men who do the fighting.

Another line of research that supports the idea of biological sex differences focuses on the effects of male and female hormones on personality and behavior. For instance, during the course of the menstrual cycle women undergo large fluctuations in the relative levels of various hormones. Several investigators have found fairly consistent relationships between these hormonal changes and differences in mood, feelings of self-esteem, and sexual desire as well as in such seemingly unrelated behaviors as crime and automobile accident rates. It is not clear, however, whether these factors operate directly or whether their effects are mediated by social expectations about, for example, the way women are supposed to feel and act during menstruation. Research has also shown great individual differences in the extent to which women are affected by menstrually related hormonal changes. Other scientists have noted that males may also experience periodic variation in relative hormonal levels. Thus, the question is still open.

Some theorists have attempted to use biological differences to explain complex behaviors. Freud believed that anatomy is a major determinant of one's total personality and that differences between male and female anatomy account for what he saw as women's greater passivity and lower aggressiveness, their greater narcissism and masochism, and their weaker consciences. Anthropologist L. Tiger has recently suggested that human males have evolved to be more dominant than females and to form a special kind of bond among themselves that has made possible the organization and management of political, military, and economic institutions. Tiger theorizes that mixed-sex groups are not as effective in these three areas and that the exclusion of females from male groups may thus have biological origins. The evidence for these grand views of Freud and Tiger is tenuous. They stand mostly as interesting speculations. It is common for biological explanations to be used to back up the idea of the naturalness or unchangeability of some pattern of human behavior that may in fact be under the control of societal norms.

Theories Stressing Culture

Support for the preeminence of cultural factors in the determination of sex differences comes from a variety of sources. Anthropologists and other social scientists hold that gender is not only a biological category but a social category as well. Every culture has a set of beliefs about the *natural differences* between men and women. But there are enormous variations between cultures in the particular qualities that are considered to be masculine and those that are considered to be feminine. Social scientists generally assume that members of different cultures do not differ signifi-

Figure 25.4
Margaret Mead, an anthropologist, has a seemingly inexhaustible fund of energy. She has studied many cultures and has formulated many important theories in anthropology. One concept that she has discussed and written about extensively is *cultural relativity;* this principle states that behavior and experience must be evaluated in their cultural context. No behavior is intrinsically good or bad, normal or deviant, healthy or disturbed; only when one's culture deems an act deviant is it deviant.

cantly in their innate psychological make-up and that differences between cultures may therefore be taken to result from social learning in shaping behavior and personality. Three cross-cultural examples may help to clarify the extent to which definitions of masculine and feminine behavior are patterned by society.

Emotionality In America it is believed that women are more emotional than men. Women cry more easily and have trouble concealing their feelings. It is men who are the masters of the "poker face." In Iran, however, the pattern is reversed. According to E. T. Hall, in *The Silent Language:*

> Men are expected to show their emotions. . . . If they don't, Iranians suspect they are lacking a vital human trait and are not dependable. Iranian men read poetry; they are sensitive and have well-developed intuition and in many cases are not expected to be too logical. They are often seen embracing and holding hands. Women, on the other hand, are considered to be coldly practical. They exhibit many of the characteristics associated with men in the United States.

Iranians consider men to be superior to women, and the society is definitely patriarchal. In other words, emotionality in Iran is considered both natural and desirable in males and is highly valued.

Sexuality In America, it is commonly agreed that men are more sexually aggressive than women, more easily aroused sexually, and less able to control their sex drives. However, other cultures have very different beliefs about sexuality. Margaret Mead has noted that among the Arapesh of New Guinea it is equally permissible and common for either men or women to initiate sexual activity, and no natural differences in sexual desire are believed to exist between the sexes. Among several African groups and American Indian tribes, it is thought that women are naturally more highly sexed than men.

Physical Strength Americans feel that they know for sure that women are naturally the weaker sex. Women are considered wise to do the light work of housekeeping and leave heavy jobs to men. E. Albert reports, however, that in Africa women constitute the chief agricultural force. When she told her African friends that in America men do the heavy work, they were openly distressed.

> This was a mistake, they maintained. Everybody knows that men are not suited by nature for heavy work, that women are stronger and better workers. Men drink too much and do not eat enough to keep up their strength; they are more tense and travel about too much to develop the habits or the muscles needed for sustained work on the farms.

The point of this example is not that African men are physically different from American men or that they could not be trained to do heavy labor. Rather, it is that they are not believed to be—and do not believe themselves to be—as able in this endeavor as women and are not expected to try to compete.

Reconciling the Theories

How can the biological and cultural approaches to sex differences be reconciled? It is possible that there are some underlying biological differences in temperament between men and women. Energy level and readiness to fight may be examples of sex-linked traits. But within each sex there is very wide variation on any trait. It is important to realize that each trait covers a continuum of behaviors. An analogy with height may clarify this point. On the average men in America are taller than women; nevertheless, there is considerable variation in height among both men and women. A woman who is six feet tall is taller than most of the men she meets. A man who is five feet tall is shorter than most of the women he meets. Psychological traits also vary widely within each sex. Although the range of activity levels among men may be generally higher than that among women, there are many exceptions to this rule. It would not be unusual to find a woman who is more energetic than most men.

Even if there are basic *predispositions* that differ, on the average, between the sexes, human beings are remarkably flexible. Cultural factors do much to mask certain characteristics and accentuate others. Innate predispositions do not directly determine actual behavior (see Chapter 2). How aggressive people are, for example, depends not only on their readiness to fight but also on the *consequences* of aggressive acts. In situations where physical fighting leads to dishonor or social disapproval, for example, most people will inhibit whatever predispositions to fight they may have. Society patterns our lives in many subtle ways, which we may become aware of only when we run up against different cultural patterns. The preceding discussions of norms about the use of space and of cultural differences in masculinity and femininity provide examples of hidden societal influences.

The following sections explore the ways in which gender as a social category affects our behavior and personality. The discussion is organized around two familiar concepts, social status and role. At birth, in most societies women are ascribed to a subordinate social status with respect to men. And both sexes are required to conform in some degree to cultural sex roles—expectations and standards—about how males and females *should* behave.

SEX ROLES AND SOCIAL STATUS

One current advertisement proclaims "You've come a long way, baby!" And in fact the status of women in Western culture is improving. However, it would be a serious mistake to believe that the status of women in America today is equivalent to that of men. Both in society at large and in particular personal relationships such as marriage, women generally occupy subordinate positions. In this country, many of the most blatant *legal* inequalities in status between the sexes have been formally abolished. Women can vote, own property, and sign contracts. They are protected by law, if not in fact, against discrimination in employment. Nevertheless, discrimination continues in occupational, professional, and other areas. Many absurdly discriminatory laws still exist. For example, women may not build rockets in Massachusetts, and married women in America may not produce wine at home, a privilege reserved for "heads of households."

Status Differences in Society at Large

Informal status differences between men and women are easily observed. "Woman's place" is still in the home, rather than in positions of power and prestige. It is men who govern the country, manage industry, direct armies, negotiate peace, and lead us in prayer and other religious activities. The Judaeo-Christian tradition perpetuates a patriarchal order. Just as God the Father rules mankind, so woman should be ruled by her husband. In the words of St. Paul, "the husband is the head of the wife, even as Christ is the head of the church." In English, "man" and "mankind" and the male pronouns "he," "him," and "his" are used to refer to both male and female humans. It is not surprising that Strodtbeck's jury study found that women, like men of low status, were less active and influential.

In America, as in most societies, there is not only a division of labor by gender but also a division of power and prestige. Some time ago, sociologist G. Myrdal suggested that there are striking similarities between the positions of women and of blacks in our male-dominated and white-dominated American society. The adjacent list summarizes Myrdal's observations.

Status Differences in Marriage

Status differences are also found in more personal or intimate relationships. When a woman marries, she gives up many of the rights we associate with adult citizenship.

Some Parallels Between the Statuses of Women and Black Americans

Both have "high social visibility" because of physical appearance, dress, or both.

Originally both were considered property in Western culture and were controlled by male family heads.

Historically neither group could vote.

Neither historically had legal rights over property or guardianship of children.

Both were believed to have inferior mental capacities. At first only limited educational opportunities were provided for them; later, a special type of education was deemed appropriate.

Each has been assigned to a subordinate "place" in the social system: Social approval rests on their staying obediently in this subordinate status; any effort to alter this scheme is abhorred.

The myth of the "contented woman" who does not want to enjoy such civil rights as the right to vote and equal social and job opportunities serves the same social function as the myth of the "contented Negro."

It is difficult for either to take part in government by attaining important public office.

There have been certain jobs allocated to women and others to blacks. These jobs are usually low in salary and in prestige.

It is considered "unnatural" for white men to work under black supervisors or for males to work under female direction. In addition, women generally prefer not to have women bosses, and blacks have often felt the same way about working under other blacks.

A kindly paternalism such as a guardian feels for his ward has been thought of as the ideal solution.

Figure 25.6 *(opposite)*
An important aspect of personality development during childhood is the acquisition of the sex role prescribed by one's culture. We begin to be "sex-typed" at birth, as shown in the upper left photograph. Little girls are taught to be gentle (upper right), and they receive considerable practice at being "just like Mommy" (lower left). Young boys, in contrast, are allowed and encouraged to be aggressive, active, and energetic (middle right and lower right). These roles are so pervasive that most readers would be surprised to see these same photographs with the sexes reversed (because boys "should not" wheel baby carriages, and girls "do not" throw rocks).

At her marriage she is symbolically "given away" to her husband by her father, and the happy couple becomes "man and wife"—rather than "woman and husband." In most states it is unlawful for a married woman to use her maiden name in legal transactions. Furthermore, divorced women with children are frequently forbidden to reassume their maiden names; they must keep the names of their former husbands, and if they remarry they must assume the names of their new husbands. In many states, married women may not buy property or take out loans in their own names. Attempts to eliminate such inequalities usually meet with difficulties—legislators tend to dismiss reform proposals as unworthy of serious consideration; the part of the federal antidiscrimination law applying to sex was originally inserted as a humorous attempt to discredit the bill.

There has long been a sexual double standard that treats sexual infidelity by wives much more harshly than that by husbands. Popular magazines often counsel wives to accept their husband's philandering, because "men will be men."

Marriages differ enormously in the extent to which husband and wife share in power and decision making. Domineering husbands are common, but domineering wives violate accepted standards of status within marriage, especially within middle-class families. Examples of apparent status reversals in which a man is "henpecked" by his forceful, dominant wife are not rare, but in many ways, subtle and unsubtle, husbands typically have more decision-making power by far. Even if both spouses work, for example, it is expected that the husband's job or career will determine where the couple lives and when or if they will move. The wife typically makes household decisions, but the really important decisions are made by the husband.

SEX ROLES AND PERSONALITY

In growing up, each person must come to terms with the standards and expectations held by his or her culture for men and women. These standards are based on two factors: (1) beliefs about human nature and the qualities of "normal" men and women and (2) societal images of the ideal man and woman. Cultural standards are not mere descriptions but rather prescribe what men and women should actually *be like.* The same boy, for example, would acquire quite different personality traits and behavior patterns depending on whether he was raised in America or in Iran.

In America, women are supposed to be warm, charming, sensitive, emotional, and nurturant, to use intuition rather than logic, and to act somewhat dependent and submissive toward men. Men are expected to be competent, unemotional, logical, dominant, independent, and somewhat aggressive. Several studies of sex-role stereotypes, such as that done by P. Rosenkrantz and his co-workers, indicate:

1. Adult men and women hold similar beliefs about the qualities that characterize both typical and ideal males and females.
2. Adults tend to see themselves as fitting the stereotype for their sex.
3. Adults of both sexes believe that a greater number of masculine traits are socially desirable or valuable than feminine traits.
4. Psychiatrists and other health-care workers tend to see the mentally healthy or "normal" person as one who conforms to society's sex-role expectations.

To be considered psychologically healthy an individual must exhibit the qualities considered appropriate for his or her sex. Those who do not—and there are some in every society—must bear the psychological cost of being considered different.

Appropriate Social Roles and Skills

Sex roles determine not only the qualities expected of men and women but also the skills and social roles that are considered appropriate. A female is supposed to gain a command of all the skills associated with the custodial care of the family and its living quarters—such as cooking, sewing, keeping house, shopping wisely, and caring

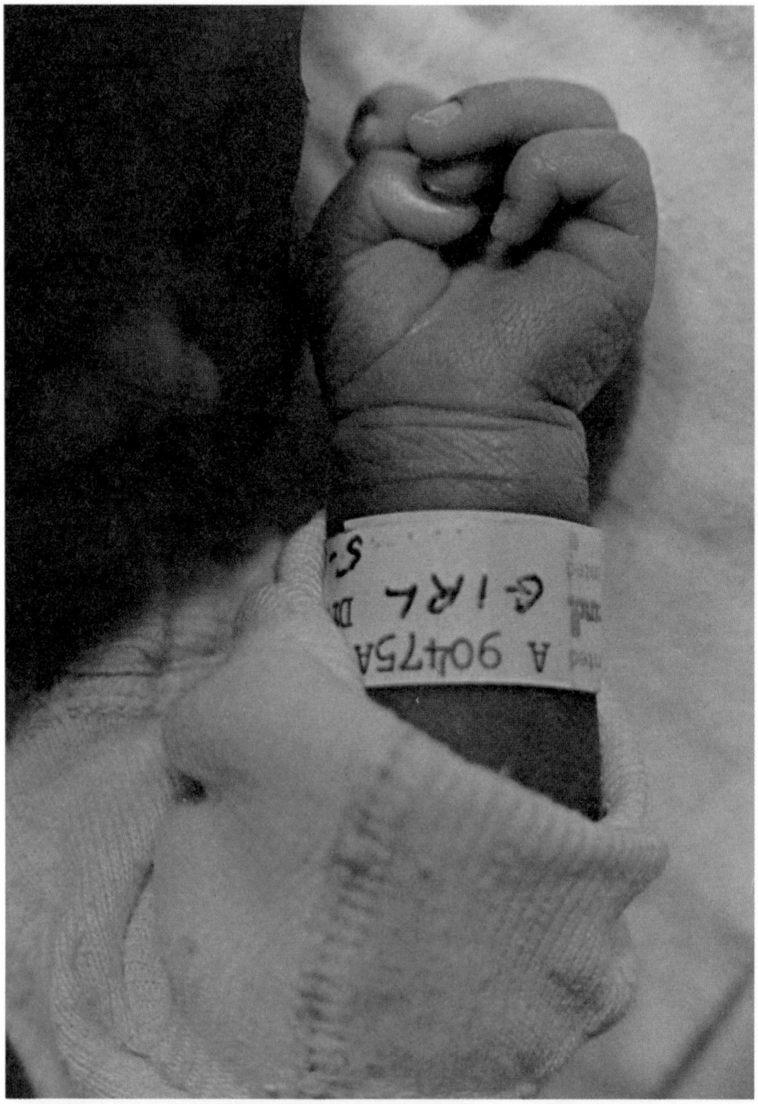
GIRL
A 90475A

for others, especially children—so that she can succeed in her major sex-determined social roles of wife and mother. A male is expected to develop athletic abilities and intellectual and mechanical skills, which will be needed in two of his major social roles: job-holder and head of the family. For males, occupational roles are primary. Because the male is considered the major family provider, the adequate performance of his roles of husband and father depends heavily on his economic achievement. There is no thought that when a young man marries he might give up his job.

Human Interaction

It has been suggested that American sex roles orient men and women toward different aspects of social interaction. Women are expected to be *social and emotional specialists,* who focus on other people's needs and on the maintenance of social relationships. Men are supposed to be *task specialists,* who are interested in manipulating objects and ideas to achieve some specific goal, often in an impersonal atmosphere. In Strodtbeck's jury study, for example, although all participants played the same social role of juror, many of the statements of men concerned ideas, whereas those of women tended to be responses to male suggestions or attempts to reduce conflict.

Concerns in Marriage

Some investigators have suggested that the female sex role encourages a woman to seek personal satisfaction and feelings of competence and success in her relationships with others—particularly with men, especially her husband, and with children. A man, in contrast, is supposed to fulfill himself through his work and other outside activities. His major role in the family, it is suggested, is that of a task-oriented provider. There is not, of course, an absolute division between the sexes in these matters. Studies by J. Heiss of couples who were dating and engaged and by G. Levinger of middle-class American married couples found that as couples progressed from dating to marriage, the woman's near-monopoly over social-emotional matters seemed to decrease. Both husbands and wives studied said it was important to praise the other, to ask about the day's events, and to discuss personal feelings. In addition, both cited affection and companionship as the most important goals in marriage, rather than economic security (which they ranked sixth).

Actuality Versus Stereotypes

These findings and others demonstrate that sex-role personality differences, like other role-related personality differences such as those dictated by age or income level, are not absolute. At times, women are expected to exhibit qualities that are considered masculine, and men are expected to exhibit qualities that are considered feminine. Women, in fulfilling their socially prescribed, primary roles of wife and mother, certainly engage in task-oriented behavior (although perhaps not in competition with men): in planning meals or running a household, in shopping or bargain hunting, women may be not only task-oriented but aggressive and competitive as well. Similarly, men's behavior toward their wives may show sensitivity, gentleness, and warmth.

Traditional sex-role behavior may be more likely to occur in some relationships than in others. There may be class and subgroup differences in expectations. In addition, the depth of the relationship affects sex-role conformity: When a couple first starts dating, the female may try to act as typically feminine and the male as typically masculine as possible. But as the relationship becomes more serious, the behavior of both may become less stereotyped.

Sex roles, like all social roles, change over time. In the past, marriage has often been an economic arrangement in which the wife received financial support in return for providing valuable domestic services. In modern America, the economic aspects of marriage may be diminishing. Although social-emotional relationships are still supposed to be the *primary* concern of women, occupational roles outside the home—and the traits that go with them—are increasingly acceptable socially.

THE EFFECTS OF ROLE BEHAVIOR ON PERSONALITY

Social roles can have profound effects on personality. Although we may enter and leave some roles—such as that of airplane passenger—very casually, others are not so easily cast off. To a woman who has borne and raised three children, motherhood is not a role to be entered or dropped at will. Rather, it is a key element of her self-concept or sense of personal identity, and the tasks, perspectives, and psychological characteristics associated with its performance may have become central to her personality. Similarly, a man who has spent thirty years practicing law has major psychological investments in his career. The habits of logical reasoning and careful deliberation that he learned in law school may become part of his personality. In addition, women have been prepared for the role of motherhood and men for professional or other working roles since childhood.

Some roles are played quite consciously, and we may be acutely aware of their restrictions on our conduct. But others become such a part of our personality and self-concept that their loss creates major psychological disturbances. The businessman who reaches retirement age and the woman whose children grow up and leave home may both suffer from the loss of important social roles. They may become severely depressed and feel at a loss to find activities to occupy their days. In modern America the average woman has more than twenty years of life left after this event, which poses a social problem of major proportions. Sex roles inevitably have significant effects on our personalities. Although space does not permit a full discussion of this topic, some of the effects of playing masculine and feminine roles in our society are outlined in the following section.

Psychological Costs of the Masculine Role

The masculine role is in many ways the more privileged, especially in the middle class. Nonetheless, it carries some special burdens as well, such as service in the armed forces, harsher penalties for identical criminal offenses, and Social Security retirement compensation at a later age than women. But the greatest costs of the role are associated with long-term denials of certain human traits. The male roles of husband and worker make stringent demands. The income, life style, and social-class status of a man's wife and children derive from his achievements as a worker; therefore, these dependents have vested interests in his performance. The demands of his work role may also deprive a man of close contact with his children. The sharp emphasis on family roles for women and work roles for men severely limits the range of experiences for both sexes. Many men might enjoy such activities as cooking or caring for children if they could escape the restrictions imposed by their sex roles.

Being a "real man" is defined in the United States as being tough, stoical, and unemotional. These psychological dimensions hamper men's ability to express their emotions, which, according to S. Jourard and others, may have dire consequences. Men do have tender and strong emotions, Jourard argues, but are forced to deny or conceal them. A man is required to hide a part of himself, of his inner experience, from both himself and others. Jourard believes that to love another person, we must know that person well and be aware of his or her psychological needs and moods; men, therefore, may be harder to love than women are, because they are harder to know. Many critics of contemporary sex roles suggest that the masculine role encourages men to treat other people as objects rather than as unique individuals. Many men treat women primarily as sex objects or pretty dolls without the range of human interests, feelings, responses, and abilities that male persons may have. Men also often expect their female companions to accept the primacy of male interests, activities, and demands in any given situation. Such an orientation, it is argued, is potentially harmful to both parties because it deprives them of opportuni-

ties for honest communication and the sharing of meaningful personal experiences. Significantly, there have been deplorably few studies of the effect of male sex roles on personality. Perhaps most social scientists—the majority of whom are male—do not wish to engage in close scrutiny of the disadvantages of male dominance.

Psychological Costs of the Feminine Role

Occupying an inferior social status and playing a subordinate social role have negative effects on women. For example, women are often prejudiced against other women, preferring male doctors, ministers, lawyers, dentists, and job superiors—and many educated women scorn female company. In a study done by H. H. Remmers and D. H. Radler in 1957, women were slightly less likely than men to vote for women political candidates. In a recent study by P. Goldberg, women college students were shown a series of professional articles on topics ranging from nutrition to city planning. Half the students were told the articles had been written by men, and half were told they had been written by women. Regardless of the topic, the same articles were rated as less persuasive, less well written, and of poorer quality when they were thought to be the work of women. Both clinical observations and psychological research indicate that many women experience feelings of inferiority. For example, J. P. McKee and A. C. Sheriffs found that in a large sample of college students, 61 percent of women but only 29 percent of men reported feeling intellectually inferior. It is overwhelmingly more common for girls and women to wish they were men than for men or boys to wish they were women.

Why do many women feel personally inferior, at least occasionally, and believe that women are generally less well suited for positions of high status than men? Popular views attributing such feelings to *penis envy* stem from Freud's suggestion that these feelings derive from anatomy: Little girls supposedly fear they have been castrated and envy the male penis, and a woman's unconscious belief that she is mutilated or incomplete may remain with her throughout life and cause her to view all women negatively. (Note that Freud himself was an opponent of women who were seeking role equality with men and felt that women were not suited to serious activity outside the home; see Chapter 21.) But today, even Freudians, such as M. Torok, believe that Freud overemphasized biology. It is not the male penis that women covet but male social power and prestige. Women feel inferior partly because they recognize the inferiority of the social position they occupy, partly because they have been socialized to their society's view that women, including themselves, somehow deserve their subordinate status. Women who have overcome the pressures against success for women also often unconsciously relinquish their identification with other women and identify with men, who are not forced to hide or stifle their talents.

All societies make conflicting demands on their members, but for modern American women, cultural contradictions have reached major proportions. As a college senior, Mirra Komarovsky described the predicament arising from the conflict between American ideals of personal achievement and equality and the reality of female sex-role prescriptions:

> All through grammar school and high school my parents led me to feel that to do well in school was my chief responsibility. . . . But recently they have suddenly got worried about me. I don't pay enough attention to social life, a woman needs *some* education but not that much. . . . The next few years are, after all, the proper time to find a mate. But the urge to apply what I have learned and the challenge of this profession is so strong that I shall go on despite the family opposition.

Regardless of whether a woman chooses to devote herself to her home and family or to try to combine marriage and a career or even to remain an unmarried career woman, she can rarely escape this basic American dilemma.

The research of M. S. Horner provides one striking example of the psychological

Figure 25.7 *(opposite)*
Little girls and boys grow up. Although their behavior changes, it still reflects the sex roles of the culture. When we execute behaviors typical of members of the other sex, we are not supposed to perform quite like them. When a girl plays baseball, for example, she is not expected to hit home runs and pitch fastballs; she is expected to run and throw "like a girl." A boy is not supposed to be comfortable while caring for babies or preparing a meal; he is expected to feel awkward and out of place. These expectations are unfortunate, for they influence otherwise competent behaviors that would be rewarding to the performer.

conflict these cultural contradictions can create. Horner postulates that both men and women who are interested in achievement experience some fear of failure but that American women may have the additional *fear of actually succeeding.* In Horner's experiment, as described in Chapter 19, she presented women college students with the beginning of a success story about a girl named Anne who finds herself at the top of her medical-school class and asked them to write an ending for it. She found that most women students, in contrast to men students (for whom the same story had a male character), wrote unhappy endings. The negative endings could be classified into three types. Some indicated that Anne's success might lead to *social rejection.* In one girl's story both Anne and her boyfriend, Carl, are in the same medical-school class. Anne is upset; she wants Carl to do better than she. The next term she deliberately lowers her grades and eventually drops out to marry Carl and raise his children. Other stories indicate a *concern about normality or femininity.* One girl's story has Anne both ecstatic and guilty about her success. She feels driven and finally suffers a nervous breakdown. In the end she quits school and marries a successful young doctor. In the final group of stories, Anne's success is *denied.* One girl wrote that Anne was nonexistent, a code name created by a group of medical students. Horner notes that for women, academic success may be a mixed blessing, leading to personal satisfaction and the realization of long-term goals but posing a threat to relations with men and to their sense of femininity.

THE ACQUISITION OF SEX ROLES

The appropriate sex role is among the first of all his many roles that a child acquires, and it has major effects on later development. By three years of age, and usually much earlier, most children can correctly tell you whether they are boys or girls, and in the next year or two almost all can apply appropriate labels to others. By about age five, American children perceive major physical and behavioral differences between their parents and have learned the basic sex-role stereotypes. They know that mothers are nurturant, have less social power, and are supposed to stay home. Fathers are prestigious, fearless, aggressive, and competent at tasks outside the home. In one study cited by L. Kohlberg, three- and five-year-old children were asked "When you grow up, would you like to be a mamma or a daddy?" The three-year-olds gave no consistent preferences, but 97 percent of the five-year-olds named the

Figure 25.8
The seven-year-old girl who wrote this poem perceives that "little girls" and "little boys" behave differently, and she competently voices her frustration at the stereotyped role playing inherent in these differences.

role of the parent of the same sex. Although children of both sexes attribute more prestige to men, most children will name their own sex when asked if it is better to be a girl or a boy.

How do children learn about sex roles? What makes them prefer one sex to the other? What motivates the young boy to want to grow up to be a daddy and a little girl to want to be a mommy? Psychologists are still trying to answer these difficult questions, and there are currently many controversies and disagreements in the field. The following sections present three different views about the acquisition of sex roles, the same three views that are presented in the discussion of social and moral development in Chapter 8. Current research provides some support for each. In reading them, you might consider how each answers the questions we have raised and whether the three might be combined.

Social-Learning Approaches

Social-learning approaches to sex-role development are probably closest to many people's intuitive, common-sense ideas. According to social-learning theorists, such as W. Mischel and P. Mussen, children come to behave in sex-appropriate ways because they are actively taught to do so by parents, peers, teachers, and others.

In all cultures, many behaviors are sex-typed: their social consequences differ according to whether they are exhibited by males or by females. In the United States little girls are rewarded for sewing, playing with dolls, and looking pretty but are discouraged from playing football, running around, or acting overtly aggressive. Boys may be ridiculed or ignored for playing with dolls but receive praise for athletic skill. Sex typing begins at birth and continues throughout life. Children rapidly learn to discriminate sex-appropriate behaviors from inappropriate ones. They learn, for instance, that physical aggressiveness and independence are usually permitted or encouraged only in boys.

From the social-learning perspective, sex-role behavior, like all behavior, is controlled by its consequences. Actions that bring rewards tend to recur, and those that bring punishment tend to disappear. Imitation also plays an important part in sex-role learning. Children often learn new sex-appropriate behaviors by observing models, and it is in this context that the parent of the same sex as the child may assume special importance. The learning of sex-typed behaviors is a gradual process, in which the growing child adds more and more appropriate behaviors to his repertoire and generalizes the performance of old behaviors to a broadening circle of situations. The child's actions are slowly molded to fit the requirements of his culture and of its immediate representatives among his family, friends, teachers, and other socializing agents.

Parents encourage independence in their children in some areas and dependence in others. J. Kagan and H. A. Moss have shown that dependency remains more stable from childhood to adulthood for women than for men. They suggest that these patterns may prevail because Western culture encourages and reinforces dependency in females at the same time that it discourages and punishes it in males.

According to E. K. Beller, a person shows dependency by seeking attention, recognition, help, closeness, or physical contact from others; a person shows independence by taking initiative, trying routine tasks, or completing activities alone. Because the female sex role in Western culture is essentially passive-dependent, the changes from dependence in childhood to the amount of independence expected of a mature woman may be relatively minor. Males, however, are expected to develop out of their early dependency into independence and autonomy.

The Freudian Approach

Freudian and social-learning approaches differ in several important ways. First, Freud believed that psychological development is not continuous but rather is

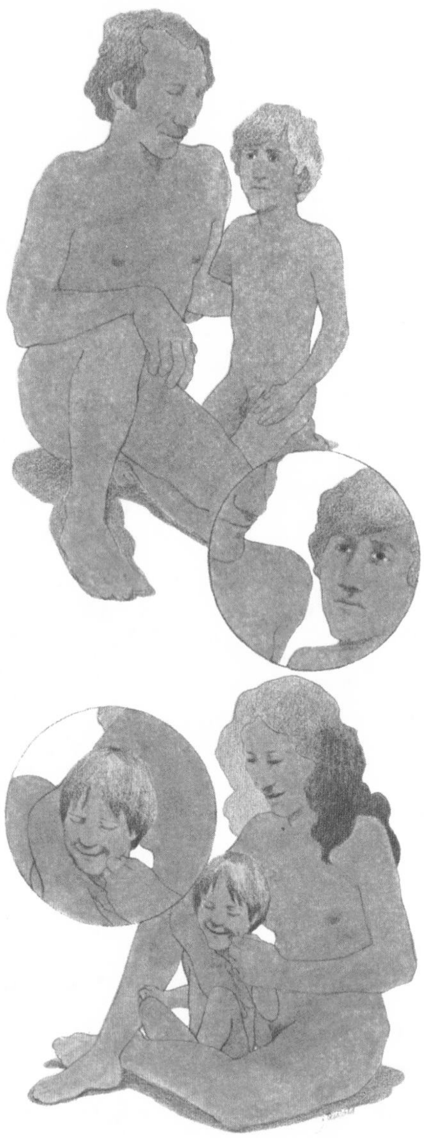

Figure 25.9
Because of his *castration anxiety* during the Oedipal phase, the boy renounces his mother as a sexual object and identifies with his father. This identification leads to his development of a masculine character, according to psychoanalysts.

characterized by a sequence of distinct developmental stages (see Chapter 21). The establishment of the child's sex-role identity occurs during the phallic stage. Second, although both Freud's theory and social-learning theory emphasize the importance of the parent of the same sex as the child, Freud believed that this parent is more than simply a model for the imitation of sex-appropriate behavior. In Freudian theory, *identification* rather than imitation is said to occur: The child strives to be like the person identified with, to take on the character, values, and behavior of the other. Although imitation may involve the copying of a fairly complex behavioral sequence, identification involves much more, namely the acquisition, *as a unit*, of many aspects of the model's personality, and their development into the superego, or conscience. Freud believed that the child acquired not only sex-role identity but also cultural values and a sense of morality through the identification process.

A third difference between the Freudian and social-learning approaches involves the relative importance assigned to biological and cultural factors in the development of sex roles. Freud put great stress on anatomy, innate sexual drives (libido), and maturation. As a result, he was forced to postulate that the sex-role development of boys and girls occurs in different ways.

As infants, both boys and girls take the mother as primary love object, and they presumably identify with her because of her warmth and nurturance. For boys the developmental problem is to retain the mother (or women in general) as the love object but to shift identification from her to the father. For girls the problem is to retain their identification with the mother but to shift the choice of love object to the father (and thus to men generally). The family interaction necessary to bring about these changes occurs when the child is between three and five years old and is based in part on the child's knowledge of the differences between male and female genital anatomy. As the boy's love for his mother intensifies, he begins to see his father as his rival. The boy both envies his father for possessing the mother and fears him because he imagines that his father might in anger castrate him. The boy, perceiving his own powerlessness, gives up the competition. Instead, he identifies defensively with the father, saying, in effect, "If I am just like you, then you won't harm me." The boy's fears are consequently reduced, and he enters a "latency period" of dormant sexual interests. At the same time, he gains his father's masculine perspective on the world, his motives, morality, and mannerisms.

For the girl, this family interaction takes place differently. Since infancy, she has both identified with her mother and had her as her primary love object. In the phallic stage the girl begins to worry that she has been castrated and may even fear that her mother has mutilated her. Thus, she is motivated to reject her mother as a love object in favor of her father. She envies the male penis and believes that by possessing her father she can possess or control one or can obtain a substitute in the form of a baby. Her *identification*, however, has stayed with the mother. Freud speculated that because the girl never feels threatened by a future castration, never switches her identification, and never undergoes defensive identification, a resolution of the family drama may be slow in coming. She may continue to see her mother as a competitor throughout life. In addition, she may forever have a weaker conscience than a man. The evidence to support Freud's exact script for sex-role development is not very convincing (U. Bronfenbrenner, for example, cites some weak points in Freud's arguments); today few developmental psychologists accept all Freud's speculations. However, many have retained the general concept of identification and have suggested that it may be motivated by nonsexual envy of the model's power and competence, by love for a warm and nurturant model, or both.

The Cognitive-Developmental Approach

An interesting and quite different theory of sex-role development has recently been proposed by L. Kohlberg. Rather than beginning with social norms or psychosexual maturation, Kohlberg begins with the changing cognitive world of the growing child. (See Chapters 5 and 6 for a detailed description of this development and Chapter 8 for a description of Kohlberg's treatment of moral development.) Kohlberg has shown that young children believe they could change gender if they really wanted to. In one study four- to eight-year-olds were shown a picture of a girl and asked whether she could be a boy if she wanted to or if she played boys' games or had a boy's haircut and wore boys' clothes. Most four-year-olds said that she *could* change sex. By age six or seven, however, children insisted that there was no possible way for such a change to occur. Kohlberg believes that this shift in children's conception of gender is part of a more general sequence of cognitive development. The same four-year-old who tells you he could change sex might also tell you that the family cat could become a dog if its whiskers were cut off. Adults agree that if you pour a pint of water from a tall skinny glass into a short fat one, the volume of water stays the same, but most four-year-olds would state that the short glass had less. Young children do not see the physical world as constant in the same way adults do. Only when, through a combination of experience and maturation that seems to be largely unaffected by external reinforcement, they reach a more advanced stage of development do they believe that gender, water volume, and other physical properties are conserved or retained despite changes in external appearance. Freud believed that the uncertainty often shown by very young children about their gender is due to their wishes and fears; Kohlberg argues that it is really due to the state of development of their cognitive skills.

For Kohlberg, sex-role development begins when the child is first labeled "boy" or "girl." By age two or three, as noted above, children can apply the proper label to themselves, and they slowly learn to apply the labels to others, often on the basis of external cues, such as clothing. At five or six, their beliefs about their own gender identity become permanently established. Once children have labeled themselves, they are motivated to behave in ways that are consistent with their labels. They come to value things and activities that are associated with being a "boy" or a "girl." According to Kohlberg, the sequence is "I am a girl (boy), therefore I want to do girl (boy) things, therefore the opportunity to do girl (boy) things—and to gain approval for doing them—is rewarding." This is a reversal of the social-learning sequence, which runs "I want rewards, I am rewarded for doing girl (boy) things, therefore I want to be a girl (boy)." In Kohlberg's scheme, the child is primarily motivated neither by rewards nor by sexual wishes and fears but by the desire to act in a consistent and competent manner—to do girl things, if she is a girl, and to do them well.

In analyzing sex-role stereotypes, Kohlberg notes some apparent universals. As mentioned earlier, by age five or six, children consistently attribute (1) power and prestige to males, (2) aggression and exposure to danger to males, and (3) nurturance and child care to females. Reasoning from the fact that such stereotyping appears very early and is more clear-cut between five and eight years of age than later, Kohlberg suggests that the stereotypes are not acquired through direct learning of the roles of parents or siblings but rather are *created* by the child for himself, on the basis of male-female differences in body build and in extrafamilial social roles. Kohlberg, like Piaget, sees each child as an active creator of concepts rather than a passive recipient of cultural products. According to Kohlberg, children associate social power with physical power, which in turn is based on physical size. Children, noting that parents are bigger, more powerful, and more competent than children, may reason by analogy that men—who tend in our culture to be larger and to marry women who are shorter than they—are bigger and stronger and therefore more powerful and competent than women.

The roles men and women play outside the family also strongly affect children's sex-role stereotyping. By age six or seven almost all the children in one study were aware that the influential roles of president, policeman, and general are filled by men. Kohlberg suggests that the father's occupational role leads children to attribute greater power and prestige to him. Most six-year-olds in one study identified the father as "the one who is best in the family," and many said it was because "he works and makes money."

Kohlberg recognizes that children tend to imitate the parent of the same sex. His explanation depends on neither the nurturance nor the power of the model but rather on the model's competence and on the child's recognition that the model is of the same sex he or she is. The young boy classes himself as male and strives to play the role skillfully. Therefore he finds males more interesting as models than females. The boy is motivated to imitate a model similar to himself—that is, occupying the same sex role—who is also prestigious. Presumably the same holds true for females: girls find women more interesting as models for imitation and try to imitate models they perceive as competent. Boys typically select their fathers and girls their mothers, and, according to Kohlberg, it is only as a *consequence* of imitating the father or the mother that the child begins to develop a special emotional relationship with that parent.

CHANGING SOCIAL PATTERNS

Human behavior is patterned, but its patterns are never rigidly fixed or constant. Cross-cultural studies indicate that social norms and roles vary greatly from society to society. They also change as time passes. Today in America, many people are actively trying to change the traditional masculine and feminine roles. The impetus for change comes from diverse sources, including more general social changes and the effects of cultural values. Changing social conditions have often led to the creation of new roles and the modification of old expectations for men and women. As human societies have moved from Stone Age hunting-and-gathering cultures to agricultural to metal-working cultures to modern industrial cultures, the social roles regulating the behavior of men and women have undergone many changes, both subtle and drastic. To take an example from recent American history, World War II changed American society dramatically. Men were sent abroad to fight, and a severe labor shortage was produced at home. In response to this emergency, C. Bird reports that the United States Department of Labor declared that "it can hardly be said that *any* occupation is absolutely unsuitable for the employment of women." Rosie the Riveter became a popular figure in mass culture as women, both single and married, learned to drive trucks and operate cranes and were welcomed into the armed forces, the professions, and medical schools. At first, most women saw their jobs as temporary, but by 1945 more than half told opinion pollsters that they would like permanent employment outside the home.

But as the men returned, the women were a glut on the labor market. Women's magazines and other mass-communication media and government publications, in conjunction with psychiatrists and doctors, began to urge that the only true and proper fulfillment for women was to be found in the home, in the care and nurturance of husband, house, and children. By the mid-1960s fewer and fewer women were continuing their education past college and entering professions; the proportion of women to men in graduate schools had dropped below that in the 1930s and continued to decline. In the late 1960s, however, the women's movement, which had been largely dormant since women had achieved the right to vote, reemerged with strong arguments against the downward trends. The women pointed out the contradictions between the requirements of the female role and American ideals of democracy, equality of social and educational opportunities, freedom of choice, and the realization of one's potential.

People made aware of these contradictions between social roles and ideals often either try to deny the situation or else to support change. Suggestions about reducing status differences based on sex in America have included (1) permitting women to raise their status by entering high-prestige occupational roles, which may require the development of child-care centers and other facilities to relieve women of some family responsibilities; (2) increasing the prestige of feminine activities such as housekeeping and child care, perhaps by recognizing them as real occupations and providing them with pay; (3) eliminating many of the current distinctions between "masculine" and "feminine" activities by letting both men and women spend part of each day at home and part at work; and (4) making some aspects of family life, such as cooking or cleaning into cooperative enterprises, so that each family is not an isolated unit that must satisfy all its own domestic needs. You can undoubtedly add many other possibilities to this list.

Changes in any one social role usually have implications for other related roles. It is clear that any changes in female roles will have major implications for male roles as well. Some men are actively encouraging change, trying to understand the psychological consequences of traditional roles and to create a changed masculine role that would encourage men to be more emotional and sensitive to others and less competitive and aggressive. Social psychology cannot tell you what stand to take on these contemporary issues. That you must decide for yourself. But the foregoing analysis does suggest that to the extent that sex roles create problems, these problems affect both men and women.

SUGGESTED READINGS

BEM, S. L., and BEM, D. J. "We're all Nonconscious Sexists," *Psychology Today*, 4 (1970), 22 ff. Two psychologists suggest that all Americans make sexist assumptions—often unwittingly—and they provide an interesting "test" for hidden sexist thinking.

EPSTEIN, C. F. *Woman's Place: Options and Limits in Professional Careers.* Berkeley, University of California Press, 1971. A sociologist's excellent, detailed analysis of how the structure of professional occupations and current patterns of sex roles provide obstacles to successful careers for women.

FARBER, S. M., and WILSON, R. H. L. (Eds.). *The Potential of Woman.* New York, McGraw-Hill, 1963. An assortment of twenty brief articles, the best of which include discussions of primate behavior (Jay), biological determinants of masculinity and femininity (Money), sex differences in intellect (Maccoby), and cross-cultural variations (Albert).

HORNER, M. "Fail: Bright Women," *Psychology Today*, 3 (1969), 36 ff. Dr. Horner presents her theory and data on fear of success in women.

KOMAROVSKY, M. *Blue-Collar Marriage.* New York, Random House, 1962. Behavior is patterned not only by gender but by other factors as well, such as social class. This book describes sex-role patterns among working-class white Americans.

LIEBOW, E. *Tally's Corner: A Study of Negro Streetcorner Men.* Boston, Little, Brown, 1967. This sensitive description of the life style of a group of lower-class black men shows how being poor and black affects the patterning of relations between men and women.

MACCOBY, E. E. (Ed.). *The Development of Sex Differences.* Stanford, Calif., Stanford University Press, 1966. This valuable collection provides major review articles on topics including cross-cultural variations in sex roles, sex differences in intellectual functioning, and social-learning and cognitive-developmental theories of sex-role development. It also has an extensive annotated bibliography and a classified summary of research on sex differences.

MEAD, M. *Sex and Temperament in Three Primitive Societies.* New York, Mentor Books, 1950. Mead, an anthropologist, presents her observations of major differences in sex-role patterns among three societies. The book provides both a contrast to American sex roles and a strong case for the importance of culture in determining sex differences.

TIGER, L. *Men in Groups.* New York, Random House, 1969. An anthropologist's controversial argument for the importance of evolution and biology in determining sex differences in behavior.

NIXON'S THE ONE!
NIXON

26 Attitude Change and Social Influence

IN 1840 THE DEMOCRATIC PARTY, which had been in power for twelve years, was running President Martin Van Buren for reelection. The opposition Whig party, given little chance to win, nominated General William Henry Harrison, who had made his reputation fighting Indians. A Baltimore newspaper, of Democratic persuasion, printed a comment to the effect that all Harrison needed was a small pension and a jug of hard cider and he would be content to sit in a log cabin the rest of his days and do nothing. The implication was that he was an empty person, serving as a front for ambitious politicians.

Some genius of public relations seized upon this statement, and there began the most remarkable presidential campaign in American history. Harrison became the log-cabin-and-hard-cider candidate. There were log-cabin badges, log-cabin songs, log-cabin floats, log-cabin rallies, and hard cider everywhere, some poured out of containers shaped like log cabins.

The campaign included a studied attempt to picture Van Buren as a cultured aristocrat. One famous campaign song began:

Let Van from his coolers of silver drink wine,
And lounge on his cushioned settee;
Our man on his buckeye bench can recline,
Content with hard cider is he.

The fact of the matter, of course, was that Harrison was born not in a log cabin (as the electorate came to believe) but on a Virginia plantation. He was thoroughly educated and came of a more aristocratic background than Van Buren. What's more, his party, the Whigs, was the party of the upper classes. Nevertheless, the American people—many more of whom were at the log-cabin stage than at the cushioned-settee stage—deliriously identified themselves with Harrison, and he won the election.

The 1840 campaign fundamentally changed political strategy in American elections. Until then, it had been assumed that to impress the people, you ought to present a nominee as a person of education, ability, experience, refinement, and all the other qualities that men were supposed to admire. After that, however, every candidate tried to show himself as fundamentally illiterate at heart.

In 1940, exactly a century later, when Wendell Willkie ran for president on the Republican ticket, his campaign managers played down the fact that he was an educated lawyer and the son of a lawyer, as well as a most successful businessman. They strove instead to emphasize the fact that he was born in a small midwestern town, in contrast to President Roosevelt's undeniable background of aristocracy. The Democratic Secretary of the Interior, Harold Ickes, demolished that strategy in a caustic and well-publicized phrase that termed Willkie "the barefoot boy from Wall Street."

The strategy, which continues today, is aimed at having just-plain-folks identify with the candidate, identification being a process through which attitude change takes place. A citizen who identifies with your candidate is a voter you want to see go to the polls. I. A.

Imagine that you are managing the campaign of a Congressional candidate. Your task is to convince as many people as you can that your candidate is the best person running and so deserves their vote. You might advise the candidate to emphasize his willingness to benefit the district economically—say, by bringing in new industry. If your candidate is attractive, you could advise him to avoid controversial issues and depend on his personality to attract votes. If he has held other political offices, you might have him stress his expertise.

You might decide that different approaches should be taken for different segments of the electorate. You could advise him to talk to a meeting of black PTA members about community control of schools and to a meeting of suburban white ones about the effects of land development on existing schools. You and your candidate are using *social influence*—that is, techniques to change the voters' attitudes and to change their voting behavior.

Social influence need not refer to persuasion on such a grand scale, however. Whenever one person tries to convince another that he should like—or dislike—a book (attitude change) or that he should go—or not go—to a certain party (behavior change) social influence is at work.

ATTITUDES AND THEIR CHANGE

Social psychologists use the term *attitude* to refer to a person's predisposition to regard given objects or issues in a certain way. People have attitudes about concrete objects—from organic foods to skyscrapers—and about abstract entities—from beauty to fascism. All attitudes involve a cognitive component; we must have some notion of what constitutes organic foods, no matter how mistaken, before we can form an attitude toward them. Most attitudes also involve an emotional component; your like or dislike for organic food includes a positive or negative emotion.

The third component of an attitude is a predisposition to act in certain ways. If you had been a resident in the district of the Congressional candidate discussed earlier and you had decided you liked him, you most likely would have gone to the polls and voted for him. However, a change in behavior need not reflect a change in attitude, and a change in attitude need not lead to a behavioral change. For example, a person may be influenced to donate blood to a blood bank, but this change in behavior may not be accompanied by any change in underlying beliefs or attitudes. On the other hand, people are sometimes influenced to change their minds about social issues, yet they do not alter their behavior in any significant way. In many instances—such as elections—the two sorts of changes usually do go hand in hand.

H. C. Kelman has elaborated on the distinction between behavior change and attitude change in his categorization of the three processes by which change takes place. Kelman distinguishes between compliance, which sometimes masquerades as attitude change but in fact reflects only temporary behavior change, and identification and internalization, processes by which real attitude change takes place.

Processes of Attitude Change

Compliance In some situations a person is induced to make statements indicating that he has changed his beliefs when, in fact, his attitudes have not budged. In many group situations, for example, a person will express agreement with the others, but once he is removed from the group situation and questioned privately, he will restate his original attitudes. His compliance to the immediate demands usually results from a wish to avoid rejection by the group or to gain its approval. His statements agreeing with the group therefore constitute a change in behavior, not a change in attitude.

Identification The process of identification is central to human development. Chapter 8 detailed how children identify with persons important to them in the learning of behaviors and attitudes. As discussed in Chapter 25, Freud says that sex roles are acquired through the child's identification with the parent; boys try to be as much like their fathers as they can, and girls model their behavior on that of their mothers. The identification process was also discussed in Chapter 24, as it relates to reference groups (reference groups constitute any group with which an individual identifies himself—often such broad groupings as racial, religious, and occupational categories). It was noted that people acquire a sense of personal definition from their membership in such groups. Identification in both these instances includes the adoption of attitudes; the child adopts those of the parent, and the member adopts those of the group.

Kelman defines identification as the process that occurs when a person wants to define himself in terms of his relationship to some other person or group. Identification differs from compliance in that the individual actually believes his adopted views. But because attitudes adopted through identification are based on the person's emotional attachment to another person or group, rather than on their

Figure 26.1

Kelman's three processes of attitude change are depicted in these drawings, which show people smoking marijuana. (Top) the young man is *complying* to group pressure to smoke marijuana; if he does not possess a favorable attitude toward marijuana he will not smoke it when he is not with the group. (Middle) he is *identifying* with the young woman, with whom he is emotionally involved. In this instance he believes that he likes to smoke marijuana, because he likes the young woman and wants to continue the relationship. If their relationship ends, he will not continue the practice unless he has *internalized* a positive attitude toward marijuana. (Bottom) he has *internalized* this positive attitude; it is now congruent with his other beliefs. He does not need the presence of a group or the emotional attachment to the woman to sustain his marijuana smoking.

own merit, they are not always well integrated with the person's other attitudes and values. If the emotional attachment to the person or group loses its importance, the attitudes are also likely to fade.

Internalization Through internalization, on the other hand, a person adopts an attitude because it is congruent with his system of values. His emotional attachment to the influencing person or group is not nearly so important as is his belief that the influencing person or group is knowledgeable and trustworthy. If, for example, you decided to vote for a candidate because you were convinced his policies were most likely to lead to world peace, the social influence on you would have taken place through internalization. Internalization is usually the most durable of the three processes. The attitudes acquired through internalization persist not only in the absence of the influencing agent but even when one's relationship to him becomes irrelevant.

Concrete examples of the results of social influence cannot always be clearly categorized as having occurred by means of one or the other of the processes. Often what occurs seems to embody some combination of the three types. For example, a person may express agreement with a friend's evaluation of a movie in part because he knows his friend would like to hear that opinion (compliance), in part because he admires his friend and would like to be similar to him (identification), and in part because he really is convinced by his friend's analysis (internalization). Nevertheless, in most situations one or another of the three processes seems to be the most important mode by which social influence is effected.

PERSUASION

Advertising, salesmanship, political campaigning and lobbying, and newspaper editorials are all examples of the direct attempts to change people's attitudes known as persuasion. Many discussions between parents and children, roommates, boyfriends and girlfriends, and the like also contain arguments meant to change the other's attitudes. Persuaders often hope, of course, that attitude change will lead to changes in behavior. An advertisement tries to convince a consumer of the superiority of a cigarette so that he will buy it; a father tries to convince his son of the evils of smoking so that he will cease buying cigarettes. Persuasion, its forms and effects, is one of the most thoroughly studied kinds of social influence.

Components of the Communication Process

Research on persuasion has focused on four major components of the communication process, shown in the adjacent margin.

1. *The source:* characteristics of the speaker or writer of the communication.
2. *The message:* the content, style, and organization of the communication.
3. *The channel:* the situation or medium through which the communication is presented.
4. *The audience:* the person or persons to whom the persuasive communication is addressed.

The Source Many studies have shown that the extent to which a person's attitudes are changed by a persuasive communication depends as much upon *who* delivers the message as upon what he says. As suggested earlier, people tend to be most persuaded by a communicator that they believe is both knowledgeable and trustworthy. A classic study, conducted over twenty years ago by C. I. Hovland and W. Weiss, found that of people who were given a statement about the practicability of atomic submarines, many more were convinced of its truth when they were told it had been made by the noted physicist J. Robert Oppenheimer than were persuaded by having been told it had appeared in the Russian newspaper *Pravda*. Similarly, more subjects were convinced by a communication about antihistamine drugs when they thought it had appeared in the reputable *New England Journal of Medicine* than were convinced when they thought it had come from an article in a mass-circulation pictorial magazine. Because few people or sources are considered to be knowledgeable and trustworthy in all areas, people are more likely, say, to be influenced by an eminent physician than by a famous economist in their

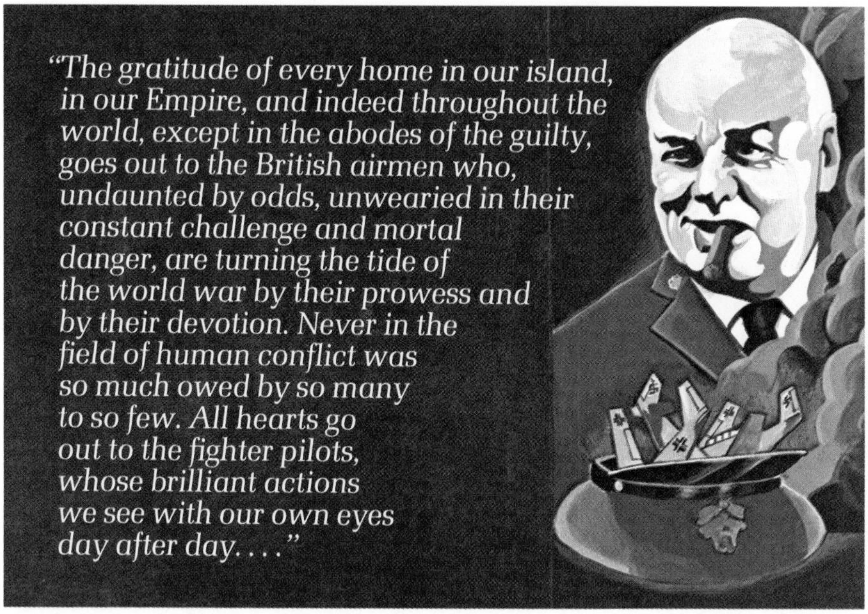

Figure 26.3
Winston Churchill, a highly respected and trusted leader, was the *source* of this *message*, effectively designed to convince the British people of their airmen's prowess and to strengthen Great Britain's effort in World War II. Had Churchill communicated to the British populace only through the *channel* of the newspapers, his message would have had far less impact than it did. He was an eloquent speaker, and the channel he chose was a radio broadcast into the homes of the British people (a receptive *audience* united by the war).
(From Sir Winston S. Churchill, "The First Year: A Speech to the House of Commons, August 20, 1940," *The War Speeches of the Rt. Hon. Winston S. Churchill, Vol. I.* London: Cassell & Company, 1951, p. 240.)

attitudes about health practices. It is interesting to note, however, that the stock we put in a statement by a prestigious communicator sometimes seems to generalize to areas outside his proper area of competence. Studies by F. L. Strodtbeck and his colleagues have suggested, for example, that people with high-status occupations (such as bank manager) are more influential on juries than are people whose jobs have lower status (assembly-line workers, for example).

The degree to which any persuader is influential depends not only on whether we think he knows the truth (knowledgeability) but also on whether we think he will give it to us straight (trustworthiness). If we think someone is trying too hard to influence us, we may decide that he has some ulterior motive for making his appeal and therefore cannot be fully believed. Because voters know that a political campaign is specifically aimed at persuading them of the candidate's merits, they are likely to look to another person or organization to verify the candidate's qualifications. An interesting manifestation of the importance of trustworthiness is the tendency for people to be more persuaded by a message if they overhear it than if it is addressed directly to them. When we overhear a communication, we are less likely to call the communicator's motives into question.

A third factor that can affect the persuasiveness of a human source is simply how much we like him. Whereas a persuader's knowledgeability and trustworthiness contribute to the likelihood that we will *internalize* a particular attitude, his attractiveness is central to the *identification* process. Football players are probably not especially knowledgeable about the relative merits of deodorants or hair tonics. Moreover, when a football star endorses a particular brand of deodorant or hair tonic on television, everyone knows that he is doing so for an ulterior motive—he is handsomely paid for giving the endorsement. Such testimonials can nevertheless be quite effective in persuading fans who identify with the star to use the product. In terms of Kelman's analysis of identification, those of us who would like to define ourselves as being similar to the star are likely to be quite taken in by his pitch.

When, in the 1968 presidential campaign, thousands of student vote canvassers willingly trimmed their hair, shaved their beards, or wore skirts and stockings, they were acknowledging the necessity of appearing attractive to the voters they were trying to sway to Senator McCarthy. In fact, several investigators, including R. P. Abelson and J. C. Miller, found that there is evidence that a communication delivered by a highly unattractive source can have a *boomerang effect*—the listener

Figure 26.4
A study by Arthur R. Cohen has suggested that an emotional appeal followed by factual information is more effective in changing attitudes than is a factual argument followed by an emotional appeal. This *message,* an advertisement for a medical news publication, effectively uses this tactic of persuasion: it presents an emotionally charged issue with a picture that speaks for itself, a title that is almost shocking in its emotional impact, and a first paragraph that mentions salient details about the conditions that exist in many nursing homes across the country. This emotional appeal gradually becomes a factual statement about the publication's excellent investigation and reporting of this and other current issues relevant to the medical profession.

may respond by adopting attitudes opposite to those the source advocates. The listener wants to make sure that in no way is he identified with the unattractive source, so he tries to become as different from it as he can.

The Message The persuasiveness of a message can be greatly affected by the precise ways in which it is composed and organized. Research has focused on such factors as the order in which arguments are presented; whether the message presents only one side or both sides of the issue; and the degree to which it deviates from the audience's existing attitudes. Only one factor, a most important one, is discussed in this chapter: how much the message seems to reduce the audience's freedom to draw its own conclusions. Although a message must be fairly explicit to be effective—that is, the audience must be told quite clearly the conclusion to be drawn from the communication—the effective communicator must be careful to avoid oversell. If he implies that the audience has no choice but to adopt the views he advocates, he may produce resistance rather than acceptance. This danger was illustrated in a recent experiment by S. Worchel and J. Brehm. Subjects were asked to read statements about the way the United States government should treat the Communist party. Both groups of subjects read identical statements of fact, but one group's message was liberally sprinkled with such high-pressure statements as "you cannot believe otherwise" and "you have no choice but to believe this." The subjects who read only the facts moved toward adopting the views advocated, but the attitudes of those whose messages contained the coercive elements were as likely to move in the opposite direction. People evidently do not like to be bullied. Brehm has called this phenomenon *psychological reactance.*

If we feel that a persuader is trying to coerce us to change our views, we are likely to assert our independence by rejecting his message or even by shifting our views in the opposite direction. It is for this reason that in many situations the "soft sell" may be more effective than the "hard sell."

The Channel The effectiveness of a persuasive communication may depend on whether it is spoken or written, seen or heard, read in a newspaper or in a magazine.

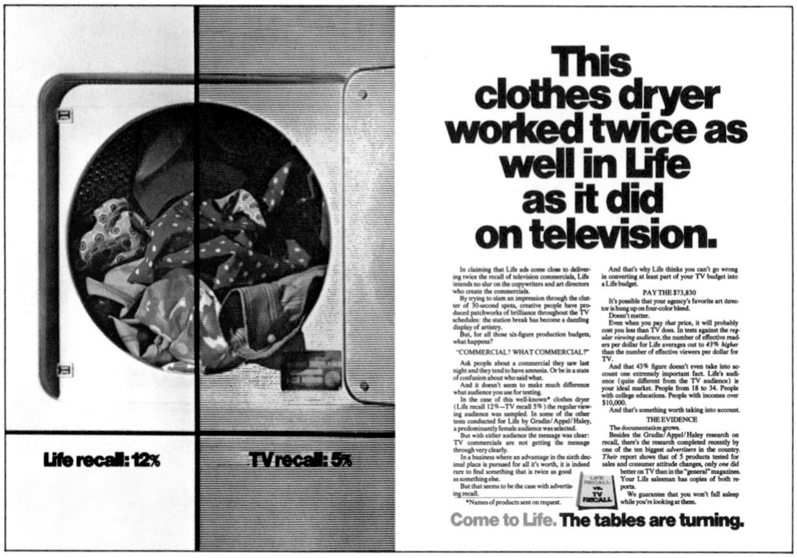

Figure 26.5
Producers of goods are very careful about choosing the channel through which they will try to persuade people to buy their goods. And those channels vie with each other to get the advertising (which brings substantial revenues). This magazine ad is meant to persuade producers to use its particular channel, saying that its ad persuaded more people to buy the dryer than did a television commercial.

Advertising agencies spend a great deal of money and employ specialists to advise them about which messages are best used in which medium. Social psychologists concerned with attitude change have so far done little research on the relative effectiveness of different channels. One recent study of particular interest, however, looked into the amount of attitude change produced by the same spoken communication as a function of the physical distance between the speaker and his audience. S. Albert and J. M. Dabbs, Jr., found that the message produced most attitude change when the speaker's distance from his audience was great (fourteen to fifteen feet) and least when the distance was small (one to two feet). The researchers speculated that the subjects regarded the extreme closeness of the speaker as an imposition on their privacy and therefore became resistant to his message.

In a recently published manual for volunteers who plan to canvass for peace, two social psychologists, R. P. Abelson and P. G. Zimbardo, advise door-to-door canvassers to maintain an informal conversational distance of four to five feet from the person receiving them. Future studies in this area will probably find that there is no optimal distance for all messages but that the best space across which to deliver a message with impact will depend on the nature of the message and on the relationship between the speaker and his audience.

The Audience Some people seem to be generally easier to persuade than others. Several studies, that by D. Marlowe and K. J. Gergen, for example, have shown that women tend to be more easily persuaded than men; the evidence of recent investigations suggests that sex-role learning is responsible for the difference (see Chapter 25). In our society women are expected to be more subservient and dependent than men; the results of this pressure, then, could account for women's greater susceptibility to influence. With the current emphasis on liberating women from certain aspects of their sex roles, the difference in persuasibility between men and women may well be reduced or even eliminated in the future.

In addition to differences between individuals and groups of individuals in their persuasibility, a given person is more susceptible to influence about some issues than about others. The likelihood that he will be persuaded by a particular communication depends to a great extent on his existing attitudes. If the attitude change the message calls for is relatively consistent with the person's other beliefs in that area, the message is more likely to persuade him than if it advocates attitudes that are widely different from the ones he holds.

Sometimes deep psychological needs and motives can affect a person's readiness to be persuaded. E. Dichter, a motivational researcher who engineered a large number of commercial advertising campaigns, once lent his talents to a Red Cross drive for blood donations. He postulated that many men were reluctant to give blood because it aroused unconscious anxieties associated with the giving away of their strength and virility. He recommended, therefore, that the campaign focus on virility, implying that each man in the audience had so much virility that he could afford to give away a little. Dichter also suggested making each man feel personally proud of any suffering, and one of the strategies he recommended was to give the

Figure 26.6

Audiences change from generation to generation, and the means of persuading them must change too. Contrast the famous World War II recruiting poster (top) with the current campaign for persuading men to join the army (bottom).

donor a pin in the shape of a drop of blood—the equivalent of a wounded soldier's Purple Heart medal. These tactics did, in fact, produce a sharp increase in blood donations by men.

Another tactic that can increase the persuasive impact of a message is audience participation in its presentation. I. L. Janis and B. T. King found that people are more likely to be persuaded by a communication if they read it out loud than if it is read to them by someone else. This procedure apparently effects a certain amount of *self-persuasion*. Some advertisers have capitalized on this principle by employing slogans or jingles that the person in the audience has to complete for himself. One example is the ad for Salem cigarettes. The audience first hears the catchy musical refrain, "You can take Salem out of the country, *but*. . . you can't take the country out of Salem." Then, at the end of the commercial, only the first part of the jingle is sung—"You can take Salem out of the country, *but*. . ."—and the listener completes it mentally; in so doing, he actively repeats the message.

Resistance to Persuasion

Most psychological research on persuasion has been concerned with the relative effectiveness of techniques to *produce* attitude change; its viewpoint has been that of the persuader. Some research—a lesser amount—has also focused on techniques that might allow a person to *resist* attitude change.

Recent research by W. J. McGuire has suggested that people can be inoculated against persuasion, in much the same way that they are inoculated against certain diseases. In medical inoculation a person is purposefully given a weakened form of a disease-causing agent, which stimulates his body to manufacture defenses; if a more virulent form of the disease should attack him, these defenses make him immune to infection. The principle underlying inoculation against persuasion is analogous. Many beliefs people hold are cultural truisms, which have never been challenged. Examples of such cultural truisms employed in McGuire's research include the beliefs that annual physical examinations are a good thing and that frequent toothbrushing is important for dental health. Most people are so unused to having such beliefs challenged that if a strong opposing argument were in fact made, it might overwhelm them. (One argument might say that because of the expense of an annual medical checkup, people might risk going without immediate treatment for specific symptoms that appear a month or so before the scheduled examination.)

For the inoculation, McGuire exposed subjects first to the challenging argument and then to a statement that refuted the arguments and reinforced the person's initial belief (say, in favor of annual physical examinations). A week later the subjects read another communication that challenged their initial belief. McGuire found that subjects who had received the inoculation were much less persuaded by the challenge than were subjects who had not been inoculated. The inoculation was effective in stimulating their psychological defenses against the challenge and in making the initial attitude more resistant to change.

This technique might be used by parents before their children leave home if the parents want to make sure that the children retain the attitudes and values acquired at home. The parents would do well to inform the children in advance of the opposing views they are likely to encounter. Such exposure beforehand should reduce the chances that the children will be persuaded by opposing views when they encounter them.

OBEDIENCE

The pessimistic statement adjacent, made by the famous British writer C. P. Snow, points to the tremendous power of that form of social influence that involves people's compliance to the commands of an authority. Such compliance commonly

When you think of the long and gloomy history of man, you will find more hideous crimes have been committed in the name of obedience than have been committed in the name of rebellion.

From C. P. Snow, "Either-Or."

goes by the name of *obedience.* To document his claim, Snow suggests that one read William Shirer's *Rise and Fall of the Third Reich.* "The German Officer Corps were brought up in the most rigorous code of obedience," Snow asserts. "In the name of obedience they were party to, and assisted in, the most wicked large-scale actions in the history of the world." But obedience does not always, or even usually, have destructive results. Obedience to the authority of parents, teachers, or government leaders often teaches lessons of kindness and leads to acts of charity. Nevertheless, most of the research on obedience has concerned itself with obedience to antisocial commands. This research may help us to understand how such phenomena as atrocities committed during war by the soldiers of Nazi Germany and other countries—including our own—could have come to pass.

The most dramatic and extensive investigation of obedience was conducted at Yale University by social psychologist S. Milgram in 1963. Milgram's subjects were men from a wide range of ages and occupations; they were paid to take part in what they thought was a study of the effects of punishment on learning. Two subjects appeared for each session, but only one of them was a real subject. The other was the experimenter's accomplice. In each case the accomplice was assigned the role of the learner in the mock learning experiment, and the subject was assigned the role of the teacher. The learner's task was to memorize a list of word pairs that the subject read to him from an adjacent room, out of the subject's sight. Each time the learner made a mistake, the subject was to punish him by administering a shock from an impressive-looking "shock generator." The generator had thirty clearly marked voltage levels, with switches ranging from 15 to 450 volts and with labels ranging from "Slight Shock" to "Danger: Severe Shock." After each of the learner's mistakes, the teacher was to increase the voltage one level and administer the shock. In reality no shocks were delivered, but the subjects had no way of knowing this.

As the session progressed, the supposed learner made many errors, and the shocks became increasingly severe. When the shock level reached 300 volts, the

Figure 26.8
Sir Thomas More defied the British Parliament's Act of Supremacy, which had given control of the Church of England to King Henry VIII. His disobedience, expressed in this impassioned statement, cost him his life. Obedience to rules, laws, and commands are crucially important for the welfare of a social order, and disobedience to them may mean an overturn of that order—as in the American revolution.
[From Robert Bolt, *A Man for All Seasons.* In *The New Theater of Europe* (ed. Robert Corrigan). New York: Dell Publishing Co., 1962, p. 111.]

learner pounded on the wall in protest and no longer provided any answers. At this point the experimenter instructed the subject to treat the absence of an answer as a wrong answer and to continue the procedure. If at any point the subject indicated that he would like to stop, the experimenter sternly told him to go on. "Whether the learner likes it or not," the experimenter asserted, "you must go on until he has learned all the word pairs correctly. So please go on."

How do you think most subjects would behave in this experiment? If you are like the students of whom Milgram asked this question, you will guess that most subjects refused to continue the procedure at some point quite early in the experiment. None of the students Milgram asked believed that more than a handful of subjects would go all the way through to the end of the shock series. The results Milgram obtained, however, did not match this expectation. Of forty subjects in the conditions described, twenty-six (or 65 percent) continued to obey the experimenter to the very end. These subjects were not sadists. Many of them showed signs of extreme tension and discomfort during the session, and they often told the experimenter that they would like to stop. But in spite of these feelings, they continued to obey the experimenter's commands. (Many experiments following Milgram's have replicated the high percentage of subjects who continued to obey.)

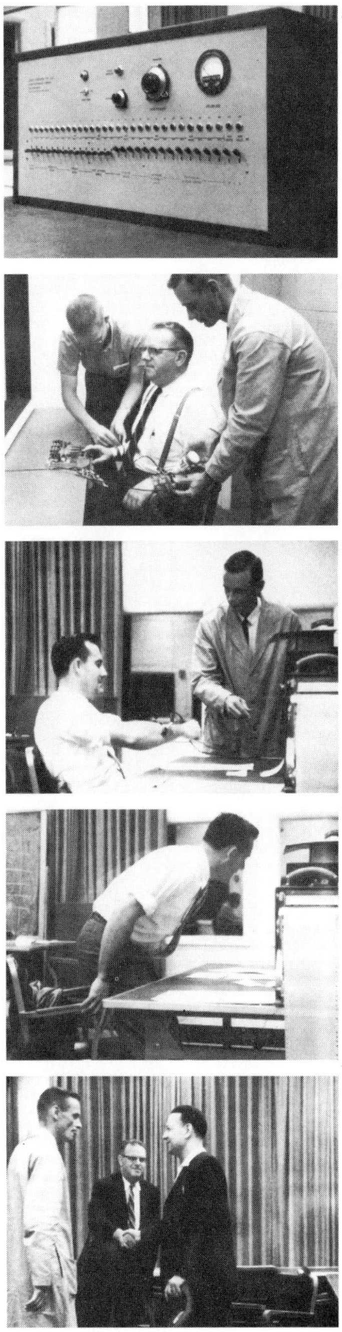

Figure 26.9
Still photographs from a motion picture of Stanley Milgram's experiment on obedience. (A) The "shock apparatus." (B) The subject sees the confederate supposedly connected to the shock apparatus. (C) The experimenter explains the procedure to the subject. (D) This subject refuses to shock the "student" any further, and arises angrily in protest. (E) After the experiment, the experimenter introduces the subject to the uninjured confederate.

Legitimate Authority

What accounts for this surprisingly high level of obedience? A central part of the answer lies in the definition of the experimenter as a *legitimate authority*. We have all learned that in certain situations we must do as we are told by the person who is properly in charge of that situation. Whether it is a policeman's order to pull to the side of the road or a doctor's request to take off your clothes, we are usually ready (even if not always enthusiastically willing) to do as we are told. If the doctor told us to pull over, or the policeman told us to undress, we would not be so willing to comply. In the setting of the psychological experiment, the legitimate authority is clearly the experimenter. He has set up the situation, and it takes place in his territory (the laboratory). Moreover, he is a scientist—a sort of modern-day priest whom many of us endow with almost supernatural power and knowledge. We assume that such an authority knows what he is doing, even when his instructions seem to run counter to our standards of moral behavior.

Milgram's subjects were paid before the experiment began and were told that the money was theirs simply for coming to the laboratory. They could have walked out at any time without losing the money and without fear of reprisal. Nevertheless, the assumption that the legitimate authority is to be obeyed seems to be so strongly ingrained that we often lack the words or the ways to do otherwise. Consider the response of one of the subjects when he was asked at the close of the experiment why he did not simply stop shocking the learner:

> He (the experimenter) wouldn't let me. I wanted to stop. I kept insisting to stop, but he said, "No" . . . I figured the voltage we were giving him was quite a bit. I wanted to stop but he kept insisting not to stop . . . I was getting ready to walk out . . . I couldn't see the point of going on when the guy is suffering in there. I figured he was having a heart attack or something That's the reason I wanted to stop.

Even though this subject "wanted to stop" and "was getting ready to walk out," he found himself unable to do so without the experimenter's permission. Simply getting up and leaving would have violated powerful unwritten rules of acceptable social behavior.

Proximity and Touch

These unwritten rules seem to be enforced to a large extent by the experimenter's physical presence. It is of interest to note that in a later study done in 1965, obedience dropped sharply when the experimenter did not remain in the same room

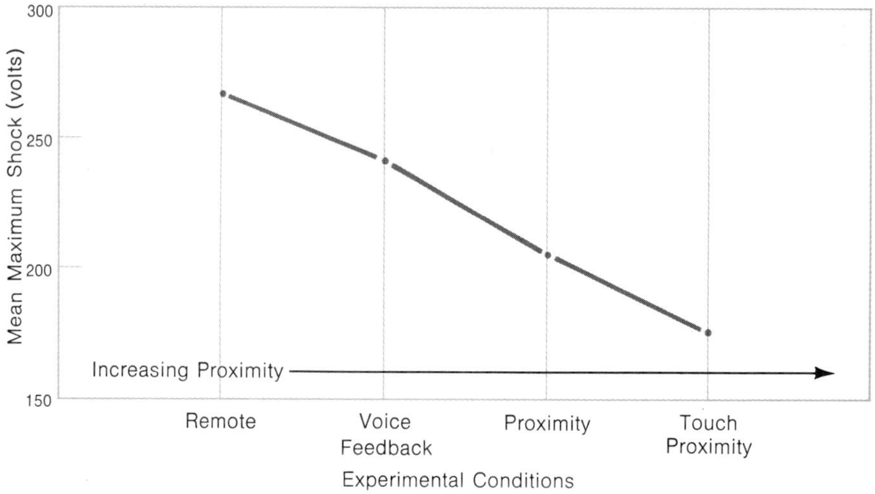

Figure 26.10
This chart indicates that in Milgram's study increasing proximity to the victim resulted in decreasing compliance with the experimenter's wishes. Milgram also found that obedience declined markedly if the experimenter left the laboratory after giving his initial orders to the subject.

with the subject. In this condition the experimenter gave his initial instructions and then left the laboratory and gave his subsequent orders by telephone. Whereas 65 percent of the subjects obeyed to the end when the experimenter was sitting just a few feet away from them, only a third as many (22 percent) obeyed throughout when he was not physically present. It is apparently easier for people to challenge the power of an authority when they do not have to engage in a face-to-face confrontation with him.

Milgram introduced another variation in conditions and found that increasing the closeness of the subject to the victim increased the likelihood that the subject would defy the experimenter. Milgram called the first experimental condition, which was described earlier, the remote condition; the subject did not see or hear the victim while he was being shocked, except for the pounding on the wall after 300 volts. In a second condition (voice feedback) the victim was also in another room, but the subject could hear him grunt, groan, and scream as the shocks were increased. In the third condition (proximity) the victim was placed in the same room as the subject, one and a half feet from him. In the fourth condition (touch proximity) the subject not only sat close to the victim but also was required to force the victim's hand onto the shockplate in order to administer the punishment. As Figure 26.10 indicates, the maximum shock that subjects administered decreased steadily as contact with the victim (whether auditory, visual, or physical) increased. When the subject was out of contact with the victim, it was apparently easier for him to deny the pain he was inflicting—much as a bombardier may be able to keep his mind off the destruction he causes. As the subject was brought into closer contact with the victim, however, such denial became less possible, and the victim's suffering exerted greater weight in the struggle between the individual's conscience and the authority's demands.

The Liberating Effect of Group Pressure

Although there was much less obedience both when the experimenter was out of the room and when the subject had to move the victim's hand, still, in both these conditions, a substantial number of subjects obeyed the experimenter to the end. Obedience was virtually eliminated, however, in another experimental condition: here the subjects were provided with *social support* for defiance. In this condition two other subjects (actually the experimenter's confederates) joined the real subject to form what he was told would be a team of teachers. After the shock level had reached 150 volts, one of the confederate-teachers announced that he would not continue and took a seat in another part of the room. After 210 volts the second teacher also refused to go any further. In all cases the experimenter continued to order the subject to carry on with the procedure, but only 10 percent of them did so. All the rest refused to continue either at the same time one of the confederate-teachers did or shortly thereafter. The confederates were able to demonstrate to the subject that defiance of the experimenter was thinkable and, in fact, proper.

Figure 26.11
Solomon Asch, the social psychologist whose brilliant series of experiments on conformity to group judgments has enhanced our knowledge of the factors associated with conformity and resistance to group pressure.

CONFORMITY

Conformity refers to a person's tendency to change his attitudes or behavior so as to bring them closer to the attitudes or behavior of his peers. When a person espouses particular political attitudes because they are fashionable, or when he adopts a particular mode of dress because it is in vogue, he is conforming to group norms. Although the word conformity often has a negative connotation, it should be emphasized that adopting group standards or conventions is often quite constructive. The final condition of Milgram's series described above demonstrates that conformity to group pressure can have positive effects. By going along with the group, the subject was able to liberate himself from the power of destructive authority. Analogous phenomena take place in real-life cases of civil disobedience and protest. People who are unable to defy authorities single-handedly may be able to do so if they are supported by others. Also, the existence of common standards to which people conform makes it possible for us to predict each other's behavior with some degree of accuracy and to approach others without fear of misunderstanding. Imagine how confusing social interaction would be if half of us used the word "yes" to mean "no" or if a smile could as easily express pain as pleasure.

Some instances of conformity, however, are maladaptive, especially *blind conformity,* in which a person renounces a belief he knows to be correct so as not to be out of step with the majority. S. Asch focused on such blind conformity in a classic series of experiments conducted some twenty years ago. Asch conceived of an ingenious, if rather devious, way of studying conformity in the psychological laboratory.

The following is what you would experience if you were a subject in one of Asch's experiments. You and seven other students report to a classroom for an experiment on visual judgment. The experimenter says that you will be asked to judge the length of lines on a series of comparisons. He displays two large white cards like the ones shown in Figure 26.12. On one card is a single vertical line—the standard whose length is to be matched. On the other are three vertical lines of different lengths, and you are to choose the one that is the same length as the standard. One of the three is actually of the same length; the other two are substantially different. The experiment opens uneventfully. The subjects announce their answers in the order in which they are seated in the room; you happen to be seventh, and one person follows you. On the first comparison every person chooses the same matching line. The second set of cards is displayed, and once again the group is unanimous. The discriminations seem very easy, and you settle in for what you expect will be a rather boring experiment.

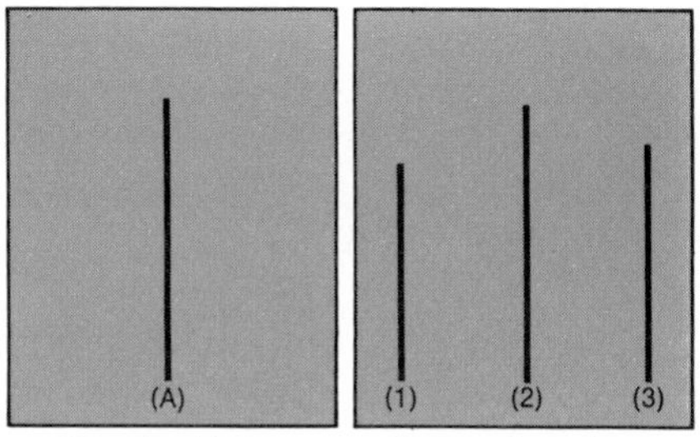

Figure 26.12
These two cards are shown to a subject during one trial in the Asch experiment. The actual discrimination involved is easy; control subjects (those not subjected to group pressure) chose line 2 as correct in over 99 percent of the trials.

On the third trial there is an unexpected disturbance. You are quite certain that Line 3 is the one that matches the standard, but the first person in the group announces confidently that Line 1 is the correct match. The second person follows suit and declares that the answer is Line 1. So do the third, fourth, fifth, and sixth subjects. Now it is your turn. What you thought was going to be an uncomplicated task has turned into a disturbing problem. You are faced with two totally contradictory pieces of information; the evidence of your own senses tells you that one answer is clearly correct, while the unanimous and confident judgments of the six preceding subjects tell you that another answer is correct. What do you do? Do you stick to your initial judgment, or do you go along with the others? The dilemma with which you are faced persists through eighteen trials. On twelve of the trials the other group members unanimously give an answer that differs from what you clearly perceive

Figure 26.13
The classic Asch experiment on conformity to group pressure is depicted in these photographs. Subject 6, sitting at the upper right corner of the table, is the only "real" subject; the others are confederates of the experimenter. The subject listens to the others express identical judgments that differ from his own. He is in a dilemma: does he express his own judgment and risk being different from the group or does he conform to the group's judgment? Asch found substantial conformity to the group on the part of his subjects. The amount of conformity depended upon the size of the opposition. If only one other person was opposed, very little yielding occurred; when the majority expressed contrary judgments, conformity became quite pronounced. As happens with many of us, some subjects conformed to the group judgment even when they believed strongly that their own choice was correct and the group's was incorrect. What do you think you would have done if you were a subject in the Asch experiment?

to be correct. It is only at the end of the experimental session that you learn the explanation for the dilemma: the seven other subjects were all confederates of Dr. Asch, who had instructed them to respond the way they did.

How do most people react in this situation? Asch put fifty subjects through this procedure and found that almost a third of the subjects conformed at least half of the time. What accounts for this high degree of conformity, and what factors can explain why some people conform and others do not? Asch carefully observed the subjects' behavior during the course of the experiment and conducted intensive interviews with them afterward to ascertain both the psychological mechanisms underlying the behavior of the "independents" and the "yielders" and the conditions that promote conformity. Some of the independent subjects stuck to their guns very confidently, announcing their judgments loudly and spontaneously. Others were more withdrawn or tense but still managed to resist the pressure to conform to the group judgment. Among the yielders, very few reported that they actually *perceived* the majority's choice as correct. Most yielders said that they believed their own perception to be correct but that they yielded to the group pressure so as not to appear different from or inferior to the others. These subjects felt that if they did not follow the group's lead, they would be revealing some basic weakness in themselves, which they preferred to hide. Asch's illustrative descriptions of one independent subject and one yielder appear as Figure 26.14. Other studies, that by D. Marlowe and K. J. Gergen, for example, have found that people with low

Independent	Yielder
After a few trials he appeared puzzled, hesitant. He announced all disagreeing answers in the form of "Three, sir; two, sir." At Trial 4 he answered immediately after the first member of the group, shook his head, blinked, and whispered to his neighbor, "Can't help it, that's one." His later answers came in a whispered voice, accompanied by a deprecating smile. At one point he grinned embarrassedly and whispered explosively to his neighbor: "I always disagree—darn it!" Immediately after the experiment the majority engaged this subject in a brief discussion. When they pressed him to say whether the entire group was wrong and he alone right, he turned upon them defiantly, exclaiming: "You're *probably* right, but you *may* be wrong!" During the experimenter's later questioning, this subject's constant refrain was: "I called them as I saw them, sir."	This subject went along with the majority in eleven out of twelve trials. He appeared nervous and somewhat confused, but he did not attempt to evade discussion at the close of the experiment. He opened the discussion with the statement: "If I'd been first I probably would have responded differently." This was his way of saying that he had adopted the majority estimates. The primary factor in his case was loss of confidence. He perceived the majority as a decided group, acting without hesitation: "If they had been doubtful I probably would have changed, but they answered with such confidence." When the real purpose of the experiment was explained, the subject volunteered: "I suspected about the middle—but tried to push it out of my mind." It is of interest that his suspicion did not restore his confidence or diminish the power of the majority.

Figure 26.14

self-esteem (that is, a generalized lack of self-confidence) are more likely to yield to group pressure than are people with high self-esteem. Clearly, it is the person who has confidence in his own abilities and basic worth who can afford to be less concerned with the opinions and approval of others.

As to the conditions promoting conformity, one of the most interesting findings Asch obtained in the course of several variations of this basic experiment is that the *size* of the majority is not nearly so important as its *unanimity*. Just as much conformity was found when there were three or four confederates as when there were seven, nine, or even fifteen. But when just one of the confederates was instructed to give the right answers rather than go along with the majority, the amount of conformity declined dramatically from 32 percent to 5 percent.

Roots of Conformity

Taking Asch's demonstration as a starting point, later investigators have provided more insights into the powerful effects of group pressure on individual opinions. M. Deutsch and H. Gerard set out to determine how much of the conformity in the Asch experiment resulted from the desire to retain the approval of the other group members and how much from subjects' actually being convinced that the majority must be right. They devised a situation in which subjects were once again confronted by the unanimous disagreement of the other group members but in which the group members were separated by partitions that prevented them from seeing or hearing one another. Group members signaled their judgments on line lengths by pressing one of three buttons on a panel in front of them. The subjects learned of each other's judgments by means of lights on the panel, and they were led to assume that the judgments were made anonymously. Deutsch and Gerard found that under these conditions there was significantly less conformity than in a situation that differed only in permitting the subjects to see each other.

This finding clearly implied that at least some of the conformity found in Asch's situation occurred through what Kelman calls compliance rather than through the processes of identification or internalization. That is, in the face-to-face setting the subject was influenced to change his behavior to avoid being criticized or seeming inferior to the others. However, the fact that a substantial degree of conformity was found even when a subject was assured of anonymity implies that compliance is not a sufficient explanation of these phenomena. It seems that a subject's real opinions as well as his overt behavior may be altered by group pressure, either because he is motivated to define himself as a member of the group (identification) or because he accepts the unanimous group view as reliable evidence that he is wrong and they are right (internalization).

Conformity Across Cultures

The roots of conformity can also be considered in a way that goes beyond variations in specific experimental situations. It seems likely that entire societies differ from one another in the amount of conformity their members display. A cross-national study conducted in 1961 by Milgram found that Norwegian students conformed considerably more than French students in a situation similar to that of the Asch experiment. Milgram had predicted just this result, on the basis of his informal observations of the two societies. Following are some of his observations:

> I found Norwegian society highly cohesive. Norwegians have a deep feeling of group identification, and they are strongly attuned to the needs and interests of those around them. Their sense of social responsibility finds expression in formidable institutions for the care and protection of Norwegian citizens . . . Compared with the Norwegians, the French show far less consensus in political life. The Norwegians have made do with a single constitution, drafted in 1814, while the French have not been able to achieve political stability within the framework of four republics . . . The extreme diversity of opinion found in French national life asserts itself also on a more intimate scale. There is a tradition of dissent and critical argument that steps down to the local bistro.

In an influential book called *The Lonely Crowd,* written in 1950, sociologist D. Riesman argued that cultural forces toward conformity are at a very high level in the United States. He characterized American society as being *other-directed,* meaning that Americans tend to overemphasize the importance of the approval of their peers and to neglect individual standards and values. Riesman cited the children's story *Tootle the Engine* to illustrate how even young American children are taught the overriding importance of being liked. In the story, Tootle longs for independence and so goes off the track and wanders through the field. But everyone reacts scornfully to Tootle's nonconformity and waves red flags at him from all sides. In the end, of course, Tootle returns to the track and lives happily ever after.

Riesman recognized that other-direction can promote positive values, including openness to others, lack of inhibition, and readiness to change. But he stressed that a society in which too great a premium is put on other-direction may be stifling:

> The idea that men are created free and equal is both true and misleading: men are created different; they lose their social freedom and individual autonomy in seeking to become like each other.

Figure 26.15

Tootle the Engine's attempts to "go off the beaten path" are greeted with derision. Eventually he succumbs to pressure and returns to the track. The message of this story is clear: conform to behavioral norms that are consensually approved, and avoid doing that which runs counter to others' wishes. Social forces that foster conformity are rarely as overt as the red flags in this story, yet they may be equally as powerful.

In the past decade there has been a new emphasis on nonconformity and "counter culture" in America, perhaps a reaction against the prevailing atmosphere of other-direction that Riesman identified in the 1950s. There are those who contend that although the standards being conformed to are different, quite as much conformity takes place in a counter culture as in the established culture. On the whole, however, today's young people seem to value individuality more than their parents did. It will be interesting to see whether the results of current and future research on conformity confirm this assumption.

DOING IS BELIEVING

It is clear that people's attitudes often affect their actions. A person who approves of a particular candidate will be likely to vote for him. And, although it is not so obvious, *actions may lead to congruent attitudes.* For example, the act of moving into a racially integrated neighborhood may lead a person to form more positive attitudes about another racial group. His action, which brings him into closer contact with members of another racial group, may cause the person to reexamine his negative attitudes toward the group and decide that they were really prejudices. (The effects of intergroup contact on intergroup attitudes are dealt with in detail in Chapter 28.)

Changes in attitudes may also occur as a result of making statements that are contrary to one's real views. There are many situations in which people are induced to make such *counterattitudinal* statements. A. R. Cohen provides several examples of such situations in his book *Attitude Change and Social Influence:*

> An American prisoner of war who longs for a smoke agrees to read a prepared indictment of American foreign policy before a group of fellow prisoners, on the promise of a cigarette.
>
> A reform candidate who despises bossism endorses the platform of the machine candidate who seeks reelection, in the hope that the party's support will be thrown to him for his own campaign in the next election.
>
> An American dissident on a trip to Europe vociferously defends American values and the American way of life before a group of scornful left-wing café intellectuals.

All these people, for one reason or another, are saying something contrary to their private attitudes. It may happen, however, that their attitudes subsequently shift in the direction of the statement they made. The prisoner of war decides that American foreign policy may in fact be imperialistic; the reform candidate concludes that the bosses aren't so bad after all; and the American in Europe begins to think that the American way of life really has some good things to offer.

Why do attitudes tend to change as a result of such counterattitudinal statements or actions? One good explanation is provided by L. Festinger's theory of *cognitive dissonance.* To illustrate his theory, imagine that you were somewhat opposed to the legalization of marijuana but were nevertheless induced by a friend to sign a petition supporting its legalization. You will now have two thoughts (cognitions) that seem to be inconsistent (dissonant). The first cognition is "I oppose legalizing marijuana," and the second is "I have just signed a petition calling for its legalization." Festinger suggests that such an experience of dissonance is psychologically uncomfortable. You will be motivated, therefore, to reduce the dissonance. One way to do this is to change one of the cognitions. Because it would be difficult to make yourself believe that you had not really signed the petition, the most likely occurrence is a change in your attitude. You might well conclude that you really do favor the legalization of marijuana. This process of dissonance reduction does not always take place consciously. Whether consciously or not, however, there is a good deal of evidence to suggest that such dissonance-reducing changes in attitude take place frequently.

A second way to reduce dissonance in this situation is to add additional cognitions that provide a justification or rationale for your action. If, for example, you signed the petition because your friend offered to pay you ten dollars for doing so, you would no longer regard yourself as having acted so inconsistently. The offer of money provided a justification for your behavior and consequently reduced the total amount of dissonance you experienced. This additional justification makes it less likely that you will change your attitude as a result of your action. If your friend had threatened that he would never speak to you again if you did not sign, that would also serve as an adequate justification for your action and would keep the amount of dissonance you experienced to a minimum.

It seems that *the less reason a person has to perform a counterattitudinal action, the more attitude change will result from the action.* An experiment conducted by Festinger and J. M. Carlsmith provided a neat demonstration of this principle. Subjects were paid either one dollar or twenty dollars to tell another person that a very boring experiment in which they had both participated had really been a lot

Figure 26.16
This diagram is an attempt to rigorously model a problem in attitude change with principles similar to those of dissonance theory. Elliott Norton, a drama critic, panned the musical *Do Re Mi* that appeared in Boston in 1960. However, he greatly admired Phil Silvers, who starred in the show. Silvers also admired Norton, but was thoroughly committed to the show. Both men, according to this model, were thus in states of disequilibrium because Norton had to join a good and a bad thing with a positive bond, and Silvers had to join two good things with a negative bond. A possible resolution is shown here; Silvers changes his attitude toward *Do Re Mi*, allowing equilibrium to be restored in the minds of both men. The actual resolution was more complicated; Silvers distinguished between the bad performance of *Do Re Mi* Norton had seen and the subsequent improved productions. (After Brown, 1965.)

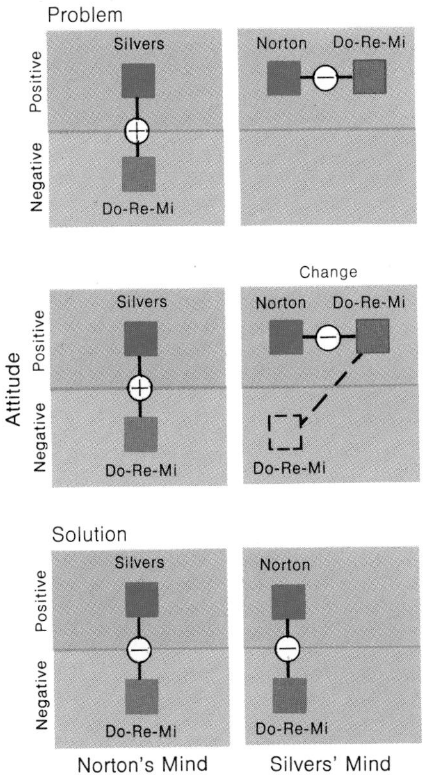

of fun. Afterward the subjects' own attitudes toward the experiment were assessed. The experimenters found that those who were paid twenty dollars to make the counterattitudinal statement continued to believe that the experiment had been boring, but those who were paid only one dollar came to believe that it had been fairly enjoyable. The subjects paid only a dollar had less reason to make the statement and therefore experienced more dissonance when they did so.

D. Bem recently suggested another explanation of how actions work to change attitudes. He says that people in situations like the Festinger and Carlsmith experiment examine their own actions and, in effect, ask themselves, "Why did I make that foolish statement?" When the incentive for making the statement is large, the answer is clear: "It was because I got twenty dollars for doing it." When the incentive is small, however, such an answer is not really sufficient. Instead the subject is likely to reason, "It must be because I really *did* enjoy the experiment." Bem's analysis, which he calls *self-perception theory,* concludes that *people often make inferences about their own attitudes by observing their own behavior.* Whereas most people agree that the question, "Why do you eat brown bread?" can properly be answered with "Because I like it," Bem goes on to suggest that the question "Why do you like brown bread?" frequently ought to be answered with "Because I eat it." There are limits to the applicability of Bem's theory; much of the time people know what their attitudes are without needing to observe their behavior. Nevertheless, there are many instances in which Bem's analysis provides valuable insights into the ways attitudes are formed and changed. His theory points out that we not only form impressions of *other people* on the basis of inferences from their behavior (see Chapter 23) but that we also form impressions about *ourselves* on the basis of the same sort of inferences.

Figure 26.17
In this village in the People's Republic of China, small discussion groups meet daily in order to read the thoughts of Chairman Mao. During these sessions one person is assigned the task of playing the "devil's advocate"; he or she argues against the official doctrine while the others defend it. This type of counterattitudinal behavior is not likely to change the person's attitudes because the person playing the dissident's role is serving an educational function for the group rather than convincing himself of the truth of these arguments. In terms of Festinger's theory, this person thus experiences no cognitive dissonance about speaking against the thoughts of Chairman Mao.

The Ethics of Social Influence

Social psychologists—as well as advertisers and political propagandists—have devoted a great deal of time and effort to investigating techniques that can facilitate social influence. One can regard this social-scientific research as having great value when its findings are used in the service of what one considers good causes, such as persuading people to contribute to worthwhile charities or reducing their religious and racial prejudices. It may have occurred to you, however, that there is no guarantee that techniques of social influence will be used for noble purposes. The same techniques that are used by health authorities to convince people to stop smoking may also be used by cigarette companies to convince them to keep smoking. It is also clear that one man's good cause is another man's evil.

One may ask a basic question about the ethical propriety of *any* attempt to change the attitudes or behaviors of other people: What right can any person be said to have to manipulate the hearts and minds of other men?

These are most difficult questions, and they are not ones that social psychologists have ready answers for. Nevertheless, they are questions that both researchers and users of social influence should continually bear in mind in evaluating both the means and the ends of social-influence attempts.

There is another set of ethical questions that may have occurred to you as you read this chapter. In most of the studies that were surveyed, experimenters intentionally deceived subjects about the nature of the research in which they were taking part. Asch told his subjects that he was studying perceptual judgment rather than conformity, and he employed confederates to pose as fellow subjects. Milgram told his subjects that he was studying the effects of punishment on learning rather than obedience, and he led them to believe that they were causing considerable pain to a fellow human being. Investigators conducting studies of persuasion also carefully withhold from their subjects full information about the nature of their research. Although in almost all cases researchers make a point of explaining the real purposes of their studies to subjects, they rarely do so until the experiment is over. It is clear that it would have been impossible to conduct many of the studies described without this sort of deception. If Asch had told his subjects in advance that the people they thought were other subjects were really confederates, for example, the social-pressure situation that he set up would have lacked psychological reality, and the results would probably have had little bearing on the nature of conformity.

Nevertheless, one may well ask whether experimenters have a right to deceive people in this way. Is research on social-influence processes so important that it outweighs the value of honesty in interpersonal transactions, including the transactions between experimenters and subjects? Once again, there are no easy answers, except to emphasize that experimenters must weigh the potential benefits and costs very carefully before embarking on any research that involves deception. In recent years social psychologists have become increasingly aware of the need for such deliberation, and they are making increasing efforts to conduct their research in ways that do not require deception.

SUGGESTED READINGS

BEM, DARYL J. *Beliefs, Attitudes, and Human Affairs.* Belmont, Calif., Brooks/Cole, 1970. An excellent and highly readable short text on attitudes and their social implications, including a good treatment of Bem's own self-perception theory.

COHEN, ARTHUR R. *Attitude Change and Social Influence.* New York, Basic Books, 1964. Although it is getting a bit dated, Cohen's book remains an excellent and thorough short text in this area.

GERGEN, KENNETH J., AND MARLOWE, DAVID (Eds.). *Personality and Social Behavior.* Reading, Mass., Addison-Wesley, 1970. Of relevance both to this chapter and to Chapter 27. A useful overview of theory and research linking individual personality to social processes like influence and attraction, plus a good collection of research reports on these topics.

ZIMBARDO, PHILIP, AND EBBESEN, EBBE. *Influencing Attitudes and Changing Behavior.* Reading, Mass., Addison-Wesley, 1969. Less systematic but more recent and readable than the Cohen text. Theory and research on social influence are applied to such varied contexts as psychological warfare, police confessions, and salesmanship.

27 Interpersonal Attraction

"THERE'S NO ACCOUNTING FOR TASTE," says an old Latin proverb (in Latin, of course), and we all believe that. We say intransigently, "I just don't like him, that's all." Or we may say, "Well, I may not know anything about art, but I know what I like!"

The Roman satirist Martial, writing about 100 A.D., put it this way:

Non amo te, Sabidi,
Nec possum dicere quare;
Hoc tantum possum dicere,
Non amo te.

Which means, "I don't like you, Sabidius, though I can't say why; this much I can say, though; I don't like you."

There is a story (possibly an untrue one) that about 1680 the English satirist Thomas Brown, while at Christ Church, one of the colleges of Oxford University, was about to be expelled for a combination of being too lazy for his own good and too clever for the authorities' comfort. John Fell, Bishop of Oxford and the dean of Christ Church, offered to rescind the punishment if Brown could show his knowledge of Latin by improvising, on the spot, a translation of Martial's epigram quoted above.

Brown fixed his impudent eye on the grave Bishop Fell and said at once:

I do not like thee, Doctor Fell,
The reason why I cannot tell;
But this I know, and know full well,
I do not like thee, Doctor Fell.

Dr. Fell (the story goes) was forced to keep Brown at school, and he is known today, as far as I know, *only* by this quatrain (surely a terrible fate to be the forever-unlikeable Doctor Fell). As for Brown, out of all his scribblings, only this really survives.

But is the matter of taste really a mystery? Do we take likes and dislikes for obscure reasons that cannot be analyzed?

I. A.

Do birds of a feather flock together? Or do opposites attract? Does absence make the heart grow fonder? Or does out of sight mean out of mind? Folk wisdom has all these things to say about friendship and love. There is a grain of truth in all these notions, but social psychologists not only want to know *whether* birds of a feather flock together, they want to discover *why* and *when* they do. Before we examine some of the research that attempts to explain why people choose their friends and lovers, an even more basic question requires consideration: Why do people seek out and want to be with other people at all? What is the basis for man's social nature, that is, man's need to *affiliate?*

THE NEED FOR HUMAN CONTACT

Insight into why most men need to be with others can be gained from subjective reports made by persons deprived of human contact over long periods.

Isolation and Anxiety

Shipwrecked sailors, monks in certain religious orders, and prisoners in solitary confinement, for example, have reported feeling overwhelming anxiety, which was far out of proportion to any actual danger confronting them. They have said that in their isolation they were unable to control this flood of emotion. Although the men reported various physical symptoms and psychological effects arising from their anxiety, one of the most common phenomena was a hallucination that other people were present. For example, Joshua Slocum, who sailed alone around the world, reported that a savior appeared to him during particularly perilous times.

Recent experiments in sensory isolation have produced similar reports. (See Chapter 15.) W. Heron reports that students at McGill University who volunteered to take part in studies of the effects of complete isolation and sensory deprivation reported that they felt as if another body were lying beside them in the

Figure 27.1
People may be separated from one another by only several feet and yet may feel themselves to be totally isolated; such a situation is depicted in this painting by Edward Hopper, entitled *Nighthawk*. In this chapter some of the reasons that people try to overcome their isolation are investigated.

cubicle; in one case the subject reported that the hallucinated body and his own seemed to overlap, partly occupying the same space.

If isolation can produce such states of anxiety, perhaps one reason people seek human contact is to avoid feeling anxious. S. Schachter set up a simple experiment to find out whether persons suffering high anxiety would be more likely to seek the company of others than persons not subjected to anxiety-provoking situations. (This study was a pioneer effort in the field, and much subsequent research has been based on it.) Schachter's subjects, female undergraduates at the University of Minnesota, were greeted at the laboratory by a man in a white coat who identified himself as Dr. Gregor Zilstein of the medical school. Zilstein told the women that for a study of the physiological effects of electric shock, they would be given a series of shocks while measures of their pulse rate and blood pressure were taken. Zilstein told some groups of subjects, in an ominous tone, that the shocks would be extremely painful. He added, with a tight smile, that the shocks would cause no permanent tissue damage. This experimental manipulation constituted the *high-anxiety* condition.

With other groups of subjects, Zilstein's manner was benign. He told these women that the shocks would produce only ticklish, tingling sensations, which would not even be unpleasant. This manipulation constituted the *low-anxiety* condition.

Zilstein told all subjects that they would have to leave the laboratory for ten minutes while the equipment was being prepared. He then asked each woman to indicate on a questionnaire whether she preferred to wait by herself in a private room or to wait in a classroom with other subjects. The answers to this question constituted the main dependent variable of the experiment. Once the women had made their choices, the experiment was concluded. The results, displayed in Table 27.1, show that women in the high-anxiety condition were much more likely to want to wait with others than were women in the low-anxiety condition.

Table 27.1—Anxiety Level and Affiliation

Level	Choose to Affiliate	Choose to Be Alone or Do Not Care
High	20	12
Low	10	20

Source: S. Schachter, *The Psychology of Affiliation* (Stanford: Stanford University Press, 1959), p. 18.

Although the results of this study indicate that anxiety can be a factor affecting the need to affiliate with others, the results raise at least as many questions as they answer. Why do anxious subjects want to wait with other people? Would they choose to affiliate with any other people or only with others in the same predicament? Social-comparison theory, as put forth by L. Festinger, may serve to answer some of these questions.

Comparing Experiences

Festinger says that people can verify their beliefs about the world and themselves in two ways. Some beliefs can be verified objectively. You may believe, for example, that if you take a hammer and smash it against a window, the window will break. You can check the belief objectively by simply taking the hammer, smashing it

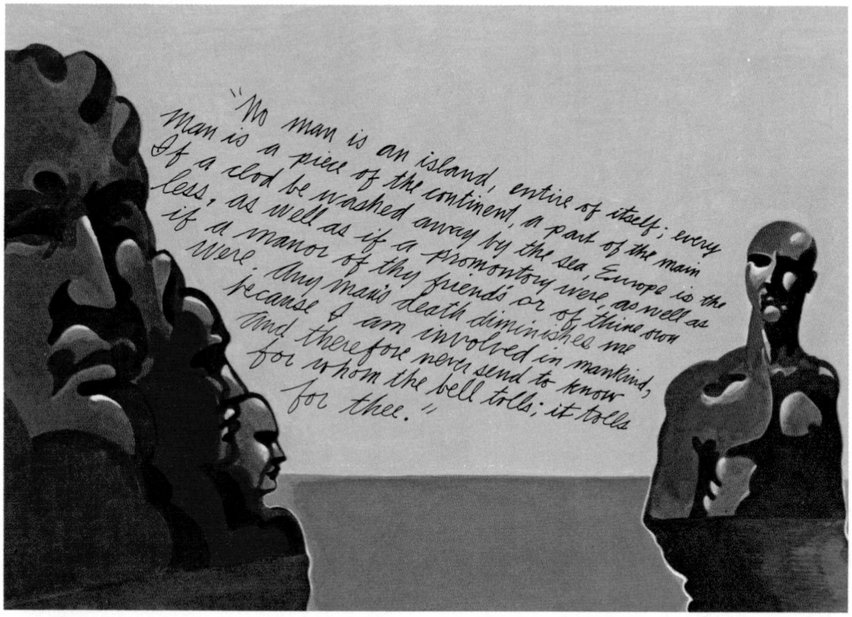

Figure 27.2
This famous passage, by John Donne, eloquently states that human beings do not and cannot exist in isolation.
(From "Meditation XVII of Devotions upon Emergent Occasions," *The Norton Anthology of English Literature, Vol. I.* New York: W. W. Norton & Company, 1968, p. 917.)

against the window, and seeing whether the glass breaks. If you believe that you run fast, however, an objective verification—timing yourself on the hundred-yard dash with a stopwatch—may not be sufficient. Even if you know that your time was 11.2 seconds, you still do not know whether 11.2 is fast unless you compare it with other people's times. This example illustrates the core of Festinger's theory: Many beliefs people hold about themselves cannot be verified without comparison with other people's experiences. Skills, opinions, personality traits, and even emotions seem to require this kind of social comparison.

What light may Festinger's theory throw on Schachter's results? If one assumes that the anxious state of the students who anticipated receiving painful shocks was a complex one—that they were experiencing several conflicting emotions—then one can see how social-comparison theory may apply. Suppose all the following emotional reactions coursed through the student: fear for her safety, anger toward the diabolical Dr. Zilstein, and a sense of honor at being able to make a sacrifice for the sake of science. How can she find out which reaction was most appropriate to the situation? By talking to others—or simply by picking up cues from their faces.

This analysis suggests that anxious subjects should prefer to affiliate only with others in the same psychological situation because only they can serve as comparison points. Schachter confirmed this hypothesis in a later experiment. All the women in this study were put into the high-anxiety condition. Half of them were given the choice between waiting alone and waiting with other women about to take part in the experiment. The other half were given the choice between waiting alone and passing the time in a room where students were waiting to see their academic advisers. Many more women chose to affiliate when they were able to be with other subjects in the experiment. When asked to explain their choices after the experiment, the women who chose to be with others in the same predicament made statements that seemed to support the social-comparison hypothesis. One woman wrote, "I thought that the others probably had the same feelings toward the experiment that I had, and this thought made me want to be with someone." As Schachter put it, "Misery doesn't love just any kind of company, it loves only miserable company."

A subsequent experiment by H. B. Gerard provides further support for the role of social comparison in evaluating emotions. Gerard reasoned that the more certain a person is of the emotions he is feeling, the less need he should have to compare

Figure 27.3
Stanley Schachter. Schachter has performed intriguing studies and developed hypotheses in several areas of social psychology, such as the determinants of affiliation, the relationship between group cohesiveness and productivity, the causes of emotional reactions, and psychological factors in obesity.

Figure 27.4
Social psychologists usually investigate interpersonal attraction by studying college students—young, middle-class adults. But photographs like the one of these two men seem to indicate that the findings of these studies may apply to other ages and classes. There seems to be a genuine bond of affection between the men; they probably live close together and have similar attitudes and values. Studies, like the Deutsch and Collins one discussed in Chapter 29, have shown that proximity and perception of attitude similarity can overcome racial barriers to friendship; this photograph makes a visual comment on those findings.

his reactions with those of other people. To test this notion he used the same anxiety-inducing procedure as Schachter but added an intriguing variation. The experimenter told the subjects that only certain persons could participate in the study and that he had a simple method to measure their "emotionality" to see whether they qualified. He escorted each subject to a private room and connected electrodes to his hand and forearm; a meter labeled "emotionality index" was placed in front of the subject. The dial was calibrated from 0 to 100, with higher numbers indicating greater emotional arousal. All subjects were told that they would receive painful electric shocks. Immediately after being told that they were to receive the shocks, some subjects saw the needle on their meters fluctuating widely on the scale (with an average reading of 75); these subjects were in the *uncertain* condition. Subjects in the *certain* condition saw the needle resting quite steadily at 75. After three minutes of needle watching, the subjects were asked whether they wanted to wait for the shocks with others or alone. Gerard's prediction was that the uncertain subjects would have a greater need to compare their feelings with those of other people and hence would be more likely to choose to affiliate. The results of the study confirmed this prediction.

It seems, then, that one important reason for seeking out other people is that they provide us with information about what we should do or feel in an ambiguous situation. This conclusion has an important implication for interpersonal attraction.

We seek out people who are in some sense similar or comparable to us, for it is from them that we are most likely to obtain appropriate information about our own abilities or reactions.

Desire to Avoid Comparison

Although feelings of anxiety and uncertainty often lead to a desire to affiliate with others, there are times of emotional stress when people seem to prefer solitude. There is evidence that people are likely to avoid social comparison when their feelings are intense. Several days after President Kennedy's assassination, a nationwide survey of people's reactions to the tragedy was conducted by P. B. Sheatsley and J. J. Feldman for the National Opinion Research Center. The survey included several questions about affiliative tendencies immediately after the assassination. Although 54 percent of those polled said they had felt like talking to others, 40 percent said they would have preferred to be alone. It is significant that many of the people who reported their preference for solitude were those who indicated the greatest admiration for President Kennedy. The feelings these people experienced may have been so intense that they did not want to evaluate or expose them publicly.

An analogous desire to avoid affiliation was found in a variation of the Schachter experiment conducted by I. Sarnoff and P. G. Zimbardo. They set up four conditions. Half the subjects were involved in essentially the Schachter paradigm. Some of these subjects were told that they were going to experience severe shocks to the tongue; other subjects were told that they would experience mild, prickly sorts of shocks to the tongue. These two conditions were described as high fear and low fear. The other half of the subjects were exposed to a manipulation intended to create a high or a low degree of neurotic anxiety. The experimenters based their manipulation on the Freudian notion that all of us have certain unconscious oral impulses, which are carry-overs from infancy and are unacceptable to the conscious ego. Accordingly, in order to make their subjects anxious, Sarnoff and Zimbardo offered them the opportunity for gratification of these impulses. They told the subjects who were in the so-called high-anxiety condition that they would be asked to suck on pacifiers, chew nipple shields, and engage in a variety of infantile, oral-gratifying behaviors. In the low-anxiety condition, subjects were also told that they would have to mouth various objects, but the objects were innocuous sorts of things—pipes and whistles.

The results show that subjects who were frightened by a method analogous to that used by Schachter had a stronger desire to affiliate than subjects who were not frightened. The interesting comparison is between those subjects offered infantile oral gratification, which made them highly anxious, and those presented with the low-anxiety condition. Subjects who were made anxious did *not* desire to affiliate. (See Figure 27.5.) A large proportion of them preferred to be alone. It appears that when people experience intense emotions that they perceive as *unacceptable*, their desire to affiliate with others is severely dampened. Because people may wish to avoid exposing these impulses even to themselves, they strongly desire to avoid social comparison, which might force them to expose the impulses to others. The fear of electric shock is presumably an acceptable emotion, but the anxiety engendered by carrying out an infantile act is apparently unacceptable.

Figure 27.5
In the experiment conducted by Sarnoff and Zimbardo, many subjects who were led to anticipate painful shocks (High Fear condition) preferred to wait with other subjects; however, most of the subjects who expected to perform "infantile" oral acts (High Anxiety condition) chose to wait alone. These findings support the thesis that people who are anxious will choose to avoid others when the source of their anxiety is socially unacceptable (After Sarnoff and Zimbardo, 1961.)

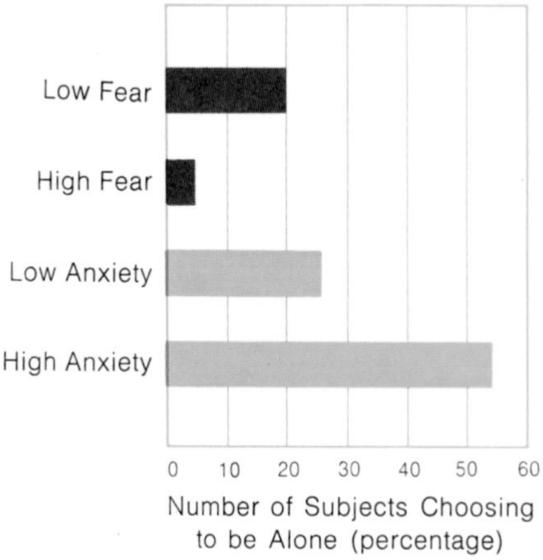

CHOOSING FRIENDS

Why do we choose certain persons to be our friends, lovers, husbands, wives? The task of social-psychological research is to specify the conditions under which each of a variety of principles is most likely to hold in determining these choices.

One general principle underlying the choice of friends is quite simple and obvious: *We are attracted to those people who are rewarding to us,* and we are unlikely to embark upon a relationship that promises to be painful or costly. This

Figure 27.6
These people obviously enjoy each other's company. Some of the factors responsible for their mutual attraction are discussed in the chapter; these factors probably play a part in various types of relationships, such as business partnerships, friendships, and romances. Only recently, however, have psychologists begun to study the possibility that a given factor may be more important in one kind of relationship than in another. For example, Stroebe's study, described later in the chapter, showed that physical attractiveness was more influential in choosing a person to date than in considering a person for marriage.

statement may make friendship and love seem like economic transactions, and, in a sense, they are not so dissimilar. It is useful, for psychological analysis, to view everyone as weighing, whether consciously or unconsciously, the assets and liabilities of those he meets and assessing the profitability of friendship. Of course, the costs and rewards in this interpersonal marketplace are very different from those in the economic sphere. A typology of the rewards people seek in interpersonal relationships, developed by P. H. Wright, will prove useful in the analyses of friendship that follow. Each type of reward represents an important value of friendship.

You may choose a friend whom you perceive as interesting and imaginative because that friend can introduce you to new ideas or activities. That person has *stimulation value* for you.

If you characterize the person you befriend as cooperative and helpful, if he seems cheerfully willing to give of his time and resources to help you achieve your goals, then Wright says that person has *utility value* for you.

Wright's third category, *ego support value,* describes the nonthreatening support that a friend can provide—sympathy and encouragement when things are going badly, and appreciation and approval when things are going well.

Research on choice of friends has generally concerned itself with more specific rewards and costs than the ones listed by Wright; physical appearance, attitude similarity, and expressions of approval are some examples of topics that have been studied. Wright's typology will serve to help interpret the results of studies of these topics. (The discussion of friendship will not differentiate between same-sex and opposite-sex relationships. Although certain rewards and costs are relevant to only one or the other type of relationship, psychologists have found that many principles are common to both.)

Physical Appearance

In evaluating another person—particularly if it is a person of the opposite sex—virtually everyone is influenced by his judgment of that person as handsome or ugly, beautiful or plain. To a large extent these personal judgments are shaped by cultural standards of physical attractiveness. If there were any innate biological factors underlying standards of physical attractiveness, one would expect to find universal standards of beauty. But C. Ford and F. Beach's review of anthropologists' reports indicates that there is little universal agreement. In some societies the most beautiful women are plump, in others they are slim. Men among the Azande and the Ganda are most attracted to women whose breasts are "long and pendulous," but the Manus and Masai place greater value on breasts that are "upright and hemispherical." In some societies the shape and color of the eyes are crucial in judging facial beauty; in other cultures the shape of ears or nose or mouth is the crucial factor. (It is interesting to note that although standards vary from one society to another, most societies consider physical appearance to be more central to the overall attractiveness of women than of men. The social desirability of a man is determined to a greater extent by his physical skills and economic status. This tendency attests to the prevalence of certain aspects of the male and female sex roles, which were discussed in Chapter 25.)

No matter what the standards of attractiveness are, people who embody the standards can, if they become our friends, bring us more of some kinds of rewards than people who do not. The standards become part of a more general ranking system, in terms of which we assess the social worth of people—including ourselves. In many quarters of American society a person can gain prestige by being seen with a physically attractive partner. This prestige, or desirability in the eyes of other people, can produce the important reward of increasing one's self-esteem. It is in this sense that a physically attractive partner may offer *ego support value.*

Although the culture sets broad standards of physical attractiveness, certain groups within the culture may have varying tastes. One speculation that may be derived from Freudian theory is that people should be most attracted to those who resemble their opposite-sex parent, but this speculation has yet to be substantiated. In another approach to why some people are attracted by certain physical characteristics of others, J. Wiggins and his colleagues at the University of Illinois attempted to relate men's preference for female body build to the men's personality traits and social backgrounds. The researchers showed undergraduate male subjects fifteen silhouettes of women's bodies; the silhouettes, shown in pairs, displayed systematic variation in the size of breasts, buttocks, and legs. The subjects marked their preference for one of each pair. These preferences were then compared with personality test scores and with background information obtained from the subjects. Although the results are highly tentative, some interesting findings emerged from the study. For example, men who preferred a large figure tended to score high on a measure of achievement need; they also tended to be drinkers. Those who preferred a small figure tended to persevere in their work and to be of an upper-class background. Further research along these lines may be very useful in finding out just why certain people find certain others attractive.

Proximity

Perhaps the best single predictor of whether two people will become friends is how far apart they live or work. A classic investigation of the effects of physical proximity on friendship was conducted by L. Festinger, S. Schachter, and K. Back. Their subjects were couples moving into married-student housing at the Massachusetts Institute of Technology just after World War II. Almost none of the project residents knew each other before they moved in, so the investigators could focus directly on how proximity affected the formation of friendships. The housing complex consisted of seventeen separate two-story buildings, each containing ten apartments (see Figure 27.7). The researchers constructed a rough measure of the distance between apartments simply by counting as one unit each entry door and adding one unit for having to go up or down stairs. (For example, the couple next door lived one unit away.) All the residents of the development were asked to name the three closest friends they had made in the project. Some of the results are depicted in Figure 27.7.

As the graph indicates, even within a single building, the closer one lives to another person, the more likely one is to choose him as a close friend. People who live next door to each other are much more likely to become friends than people

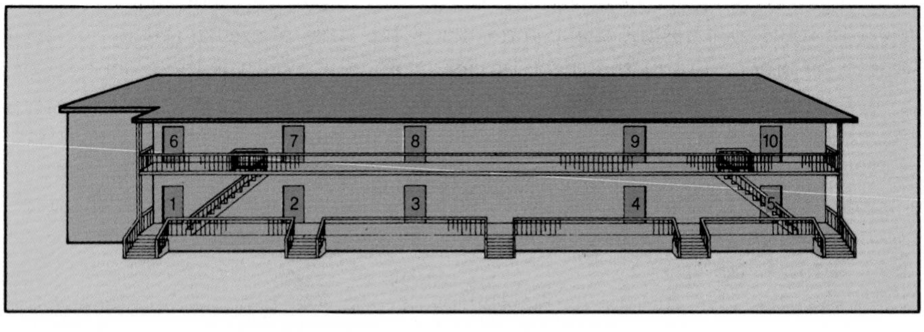

Figure 27.7
(Top) A housing unit similar to those in the student housing complex where Festinger, Schachter, and Back investigated the effects of proximity on friendship formation. (Bottom) Data from their study that indicates the close relationship between physical proximity to a person and choosing that person as a friend.

Sociometric Choice and Physical Distance

Units of Distance	Number of Choices Given	Possible Number of Choices	Percentage Choosing
1	112	8 × 34	41.2
2	46	6 × 34	22.5
3	22	4 × 34	16.2
4	7	2 × 34	10.3

Source: L. Festinger, *et al.*, *Social Pressures in Informal Groups* (Stanford: Stanford Univ. Press, 1963).

who live two doors apart. A more recent study by R. F. Priest and J. Sawyer, conducted in a large student dormitory at the University of Chicago, obtained very similar results. Even though the students' rooms were only eight feet apart, there was still a strong tendency for students to like the person next door more than the one two doors away, and so on.

It is difficult to account for these effects in a dormitory, where it may take no more than two seconds to get from one room to another. After living for six months in a dormitory, most students are likely to have met the person who lives three or four doors away and to have had as much opportunity as they want to continue interacting with him.

Priest and Sawyer suggest one explanation. They point out that *perceived distance* often seems to depend on the number of other people who intervene rather than on numbers of feet or miles. In a rural area, for example, people living half a mile away may be considered neighbors, whereas in a city those living one hundred feet away may not be—they may be in another wing of the apartment building or ten floors down. In a university dormitory, a room five doors away may represent five *closer* opportunities passed by. Thus, to borrow change for the Coke machine from someone five rooms away may raise the question, "Why didn't he ask someone closer?" In terms of the rewards and costs of friendship, then, one can infer that interacting with someone five rooms away is more costly because a friendly approach has to be purposive instead of casual and so may result in an awkward encounter. It may be for this reason that roommates are particularly likely to be friends, even when the two do not seem to be well matched on personality dimensions. As Priest and Sawyer note, it is easy for roommates to interact without each encounter being an occasion. The rewards of this easy accessibility are apparently high.

A second explanation for the impact of proximity on friendship formation can be formulated from the assumption that the closer people live to one another, the more likely they are to bump into one another—to see and hear one another often. Recent studies by R. B. Zajonc indicate that, all other factors being equal, repeated exposure to various stimuli (ranging from Chinese characters to men's faces) tends to produce positive attitudes toward those stimuli. In one such experiment Zajonc simply showed subjects photographs taken from a college yearbook. Each subject saw twelve faces: two faces he saw only once, two twice, two five times, two ten times, and two twenty-five times. The subjects were then given those pictures and two pictures of faces they had not seen before and were asked to indicate how much they thought they would like the people in the photographs. The results were striking: the more frequently the subject had seen a face, the more likely he was to predict that he would like that person.

Why does repeated exposure to a person make it more likely that you will befriend him? Why does he grow on you? It seems likely that, as you become more familiar with his ways, he becomes less threatening and more predictable. Although you may never come to love another person on the basis of repeated exposure alone, you may at least come to feel comfortable in his presence. Recent studies have suggested, however, that repeated exposure to someone you initially disliked is not likely to change your attitude toward him. In fact, the exposure may have just the opposite effect—dislike can develop into hatred. One can say, then, that when a person's initial attitudes toward another are *positive* or *neutral,* repeated exposure is likely to have positive effects; when his initial attitudes are *negative,* the effects of exposure are likely to be negative.

Similarity

There is abundant evidence that we choose as friends people whose social backgrounds and attitudes resemble our own. There is much evidence showing that most husbands and wives share the same race, religion, economic status, and educational level. Social scientists call this phenomenon *assortative mating.* There are often strong social pressures, especially from parents, for a person to marry someone with a similar social history. Assortative mating also follows from the effects of proximity; people of similar income levels and ethnic backgrounds tend to live in the same areas and thus to send their children to the same schools. If during your childhood and adolescence you are effectively segregated from all but those who share your race, religion, and economic level, your friends—and potential marriage partners—will inevitably be similar to you in these respects.

People from similar social backgrounds are also likely to share many attitudes about fundamental issues—and the perception that another person (whose background may be unknown to you) agrees with you about things that matter to you has, in turn, been found to be central in friendship formation. T. M. Newcomb conducted an extensive study of attitude and friendship at the University of Michigan. He set up his own experimental dormitory, where one term's rent was waived in return for the students' cooperation. At the start of the term the students completed a series of measures of their attitudes about various political and social issues. During the study, they completed questionnaires in which they named the people in the dorm they perceived as having attitudes similar to their own and rated all the other residents as to how much they liked them. Newcomb found that his measures of similarity of attitudes were a good predictor of which students would become friends by the end of the term. This study and others have made it clear that the declaration by one of the characters in Disraeli's *Lothair*—"My idea of an agreeable person is someone who agrees with me!"—echoes most people's feelings.

Social psychologists have come up with several explanations for the power of shared attitudes in attraction. First, some agreements provide a basis for joint activities like bridge or tennis. Agreement on political issues may provide the basis for associations in political clubs and the like. Both friends, then, are rewarded by being able to do together the things they like. Second, a person who agrees with you reinforces your notion that your opinions are correct. Such *social validation* of one's opinions usually has the effect of increasing one's self-esteem (Wright's ego

Figure 27.8
Both these cynical quotations (the top one by Samuel Johnson, 1772; the bottom one by La Rochefoucauld, 1665) make the point that friendships are formed to attain some rewards, which is also the point of Wright's typology of rewards, discussed earlier in the chapter. Wright says that friends are chosen because they provide stimulation value, utility value, or ego support value.
(From James Boswell, *Life of Samuel Johnson LL.D.* Chicago: Encyclopedia Britannica, Great Books of the Western World, Vol. 44, 1952, p. 193.)
[From La Rochefoucauld, *Maxims* (trans. L. W. Tancock). Baltimore, Md.: Penguin Books, 1959, p. 45.]

support value). Third, people who agree about things that matter to them generally find it easier to communicate with each other. They have fewer arguments, misunderstandings, and confusions. Also, people who share the same basic outlook are generally better able to predict each other's actions.

A final reason people are attracted to those with similar backgrounds and attitudes stems from an assumption that people commonly make about others—an assumption that is sometimes but not always justified. *We assume that people with backgrounds and attitudes like ours are more apt to like us.* Unfortunately, we also fear that people whom we perceive as different will reject us, so we may shy away from them—even though we were initially attracted to them. Clearly, friendship with someone whose background or perspective is different from our own can often provide more stimulation value than friendship with someone just like us. But it seems that only when our fears of rejection are allayed are we likely to make such friends. A study made by J. W. Goldstein and H. Rosenfeld supports this analysis. Their study found that people who scored high on a measure of psychological insecurity were more likely to choose to associate with people similar to them than were more secure subjects. It seems that birds of a feather are *most* likely to flock together when they are afraid of getting their feathers ruffled.

Approval

The approval of others is one of the most important determinants of interpersonal attraction. People who like us bolster our own sense of worth. Some people have greater need for approval than others, but everyone feels this need to at least some degree. Suppose, however, you walk into a used-car lot and are greeted by a smiling salesman who tells you that your excellent taste in clothes gave him the feeling right off that you are the kind of perceptive person he likes. It is not too likely that you will be attracted to the salesman, even though he has been highly approving. The reason, of course, is that you would mistrust the motives for his compliments. Because you would probably conclude that he was simply trying to butter you up in order to make a sale, it is unlikely that his approval would boost your self-esteem.

A series of experiments by E. E. Jones has clearly shown that we do not like people we perceive as *ingratiating* as well as we like others whom we perceive as honestly approving of us. However, Jones found another, less obvious effect. He found that although the subjects in his study liked a person less when he was ingratiating, they nevertheless liked him more than they would have if he had not expressed approval at all. In other words, we may well like the used-car salesman *better* than a person with pure motives who does not compliment us at all. In some cases it seems that human vanity gets the better of our judgment and permits us to be rewarded by compliments that we know to be contrived.

Another interesting study of how people perceive others' evaluations of them was conducted by E. Aronson and D. Linder. Each subject overheard a series of remarks about himself by a confederate of the experimenters. Some of the subjects heard the confederate make only complimentary remarks throughout the session. Another group heard the confederate make only derogatory remarks. What the third group heard was first very derogatory, then gradually more positive, and finally extremely complimentary. The last group heard just the opposite; the confederate began by making positive comments but ended up being very disparaging. Each subject was asked to indicate how much he liked the confederate. Before you look at Aronson and Linder's results in Figuge 27.9, you might like to predict which group of subjects liked the confederate most and which group liked him least.

The best-liked confederates were not the ones who were uniformly positive but those who began by saying negative things and ended by saying positive things. Also, the subjects preferred the confederates who said consistently negative things to those who began by saying some complimentary things and ended by being dis-

Figure 27.9

According to the results of Aronson's and Linder's study, subjects liked the persons who made uniformly positive statements (++) about them and disliked those whose comments about them were uniformly negative (−−). However, subjects liked best the persons who progressed from negative to positive (−+) statements about them, and they liked least those whose comments about them changed from positive to negative (+−). This experiment and Jones' study illustrate that the effects of approval are more complex than one might initially suppose.
(After Aronson and Linder, 1965.)

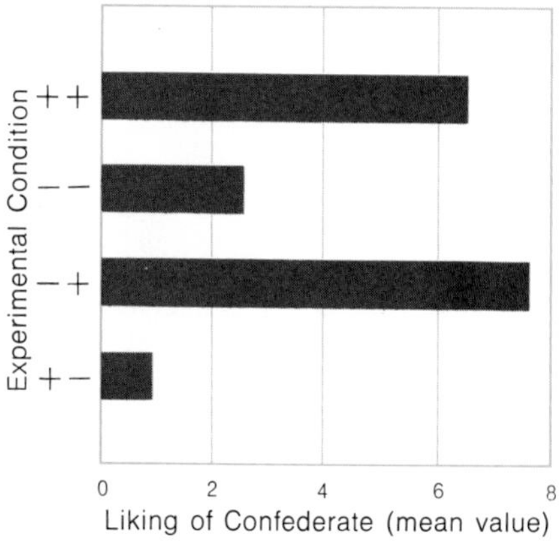

Figure 27.10
Psychological studies of love and marriage have generally focused on the young. Consequently, little is known about what factors play the major part in attraction in old age. Does physical attractiveness still play a major role? Is similarity of attitude as important in friendship formation among the aged?

approving. Apparently, the early disparaging remarks served to establish the genuineness and credibility of the confederate; the subject may have, in effect, said to himself, "This is a very perceptive guy. He's not easy to impress. At first he found fault with me, but then he had some insight into my true character and ended by liking me." When the remarks were universally positive, the subjects may have thought the confederate to be somewhat undiscriminating and so may not have experienced such a great boost in their self-esteem. Those subjects who heard good comments first and then negative ones may have let down their defenses and were therefore angrier and more disappointed when the confederate's praise turned into criticism than they would have been if he had been critical all along.

Like the Jones studies, this experiment suggests the importance people place on the genuineness of approval. It also indicates that people do not simply total up the small rewards and punishments they receive from others in deciding whether they like them; the *context* and *sequence* in which the other person provides approval and disapproval is central to interpreting the significance of what they say.

Personality

Many psychologists have speculated about the ways in which the deeper levels of two individuals' personalities mesh in order to produce liking or disliking, love or hate. R. I. Evans reports that one theory, based on the writings of C. Jung, suggests that people have unconscious "archetypes," or ideals, of the sort of person who would best complement them and that when someone encounters a person of the opposite sex who corresponds to his archetype, he immediately becomes aware of the match and falls in love. R. F. Winch and other theorists have suggested that *need complementarity* is the basis for attraction. For example, people with needs to dominate are attracted to people with needs to be dominated, and people with a strong need to care for others are drawn to those with a need to be cared for.

Psychologist R. W. White provides a good example of how two personalities complemented one another in the case of a friendship between two teen-age boys:

> Ben, whose school experience had been so unstimulating that he never read a book beyond those assigned, discovered in Jamie a lively spirit of intellectual inquiry and an exciting knowledge of politics and history. Here was a whole world to which his friend opened the door and provided guidance. Jamie discovered in Ben a world previously closed to him, that of confident interaction with other people. Each admired the other, each copied the other, each used the other for practice.

Many friendships, both same-sex and opposite-sex, seem to be built on such complementarity. So far, however, it has remained much easier for psychologists to recognize such complementarity after the fact than to predict it ahead of time. There are so many human needs and so many possible ways of gratifying them that although many researchers have tried, none has yet been successful in predicting which persons will be attracted to which others on the basis of their individual personality profiles.

Stages of Friendship

The rewards that influence our choice of friends are not equally important for all people at all times and in all contexts. What we expect of someone who has just become a friend, for example, will probably change if the friendship continues for years. One theoretical model that sets out the progression of such changes during the process of mate selection was constructed by A. C. Kerckhoff and K. E. Davis.

The model suggests that courtship proceeds through a series of successive "filters." First a pool of eligible partners is established on the basis of such factors as proximity and social background. People who have little chance to meet and people who are considered socially inappropriate partners will be filtered out. Once two eligible people have met and have started to interact, then the model sets up similarity of attitudes as the most crucial filtering factor. Just as couples who find that they agree on matters they consider important are likely to intensify their relationship, couples who discover basic disagreements tend to break up. The third filter in the mate-selection process is need complementarity. Members of a couple who discover that their distinctive psychological needs can be gratified by the other are more likely to marry than those who do not make this discovery. Although not all aspects of the filter theory have been supported empirically (the evidence for the operation of need complementarity is notably weak), the theory's basic premise —that particular rewards become central at different stages in the development of a relationship—is probably correct.

THE EFFECT OF SOCIAL ROLES

Social roles play an important part in determining not only when particular rewards will be most influential in a friendship but also which rewards are crucial for various kinds of relationships. Is the relationship a business partnership or a social friendship? Is the friendship between a man and a woman a convenience for going to movies and parties together, or are the partners thinking of marriage? Are the friends childhood playmates, adolescent confidants, or young adult lovers? Clearly, the social roles defined by answers to such questions will influence the nature and timing of the effective rewards in each relationship.

The results of a recent experiment by W. Stroebe and his colleagues at the University of North Carolina illustrate how the importance of different rewards varies in different role contexts. Prior to the experimental session, each subject had filled out a questionnaire that allowed the researchers to construct an attitude profile for him. The researchers showed each male subject a photograph of a woman and each female subject a photograph of a male. The pictures shown to one-third of the subjects were of a person other students had previously judged to be extremely good-looking; one-third were shown an average-looking person; and one-third were shown an ugly person. The photo was accompanied by a series of attitude statements that had purportedly been made by the person photographed but had actually been concocted by the experimenters in light of the subject's attitudes. Within each of the attractiveness conditions, one-third of the subjects were shown statements that strongly agreed with their own attitudes; one-third were shown a set of attitudes totally different from their own; and one-third were shown attitudes that partly agreed and partly disagreed with their own. The subject indicated his attraction for the person by answering the four adjacent questions.

1. How much do you think you would like this boy (girl)?
2. How much would you enjoy working with this boy (girl) in an experiment?
3. If you were looking for a date and you knew this boy (girl), how likely would it be that you would consider him (her)?
4. If you were thinking of getting married and you knew this boy (girl), how likely would it be that you would consider him (her)?

As might be expected, for all four role relationships (liking, working, dating, or marrying) most subjects preferred good-looking to ugly partners and were more attracted to those who agreed with them than to those who did not. However, the researchers' skillful analysis of their results permitted them to assess the importance of physical attractiveness and of attitude similarity relative to the subject's sex and each role relationship. (See Figure 27.12.) They found that men were more influenced by physical attractiveness than were women in choosing people they preferred to work with, to date, and to marry, but there was little difference between men and women in the influence of physical attractiveness on whom they thought they would like. Physical attractiveness generally had a greater impact on dating choices than on preferences for persons to like or marry. Attitude similarity, on the other hand, was more important in determining the subjects' preferences for people to like than for people to date. It was clear, in other words, that the relative importance of the two factors—physical attractiveness and attitude similarity—depended on the sort of relationship envisioned.

Because the preferences expressed in this study were hypothetical ones and the population of subjects quite homogeneous with respect to age, social class, and geographic origin, one cannot yet consider the conclusions universally applicable.

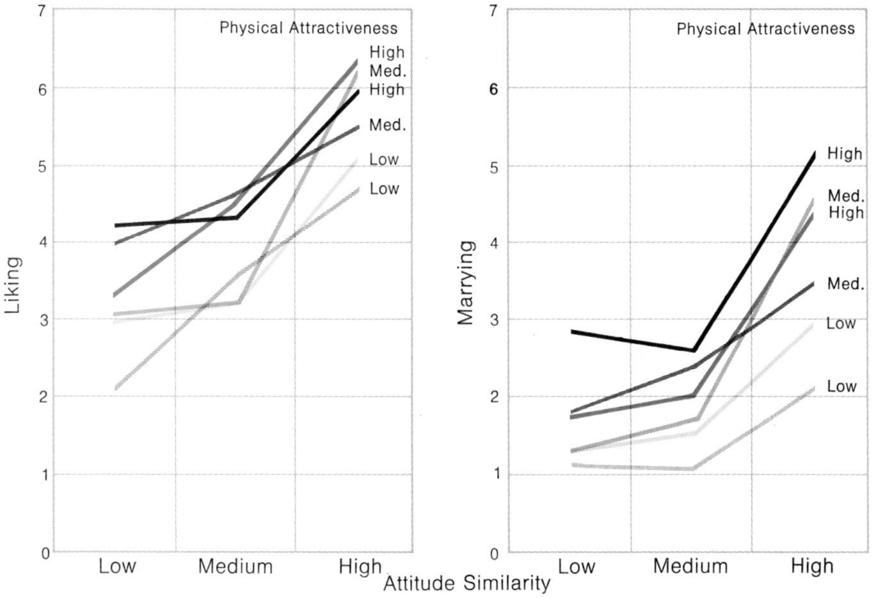

Figure 27.12
Some of the results of Stroebe's study are shown here. The black and gray lines indicate male attitudes, and the red and pink lines, those of females. These are the mean results, plotted to show the relation between high, medium, or low attractiveness and the degree of attitude similarity between the subject and the person whose photograph he was shown. Note that for both men and women, physical attractiveness was not as important to choice of marriage partner as it was in choosing someone to date. However, physical attractiveness was more important to men than to women in choice of a marriage partner.

However, some of the key findings reported in this chapter have been replicated more than once. For example, an extensive series of studies by D. Byrne and his colleagues has found consistent support for the link between attitude similarity and attraction among high-school and college students in India, Japan, Mexico, and various parts of the United States, as well as among American surgical patients, schizophrenics, alcoholics, Job Corps trainees, fourth-graders, and senior citizens.

ROMANTIC LOVE

There are many varieties of love—love between parent and child, between same-sex friends, between man and wife. Although almost everyone has an intuitive idea of what is meant by "romantic love," psychologists who wish to study it have to try to define it.

One recent project, conducted by Z. Rubin, attempted to specify more clearly the ways in which social psychologists might distinguish between "liking" and "loving." He began his research by giving several hundred students a long series

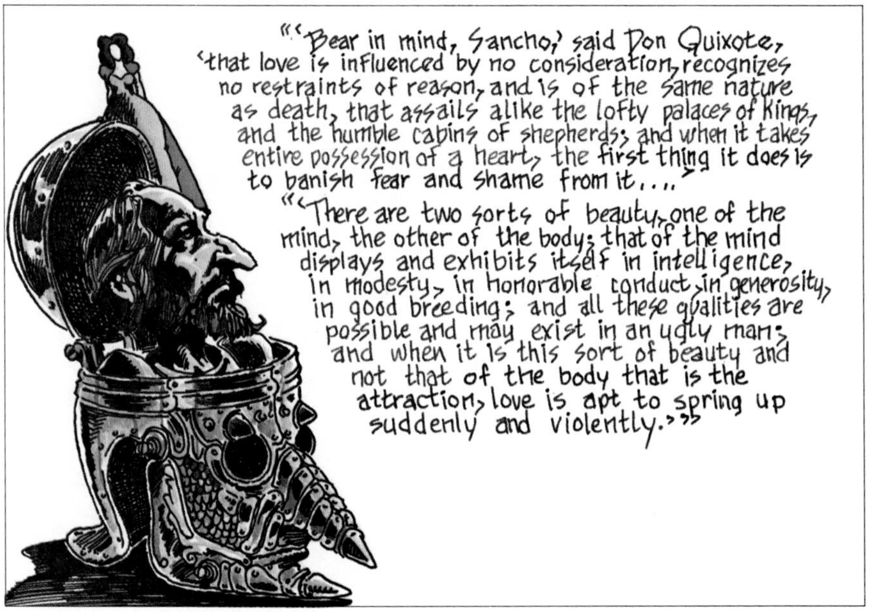

Figure 27.13
Don Quixote attempts to analyze the phenomenon of love and concludes that an intense, profound love may result from attraction to "beauty of the mind." He is telling his loyal servant, Sancho Panza, why it is that a woman has suddenly fallen in love with him, despite his age and ugliness.
[From Miguel de Cervantes, *The History of Don Quixote de la Mancha* (trans. John Primsby). Chicago: Encyclopedia Britannica, Great Books of the Western World, Vol. 29, 1952, p. 381.]

Liking

1. *Favorable evaluation.*

   I think that ______ (my boyfriend or girlfriend) is unusually well-adjusted.

   It seems to me that it is very easy for ______ to gain admiration.

2. *Respect and confidence.*

   I have great confidence in ______'s good judgment.

   I would vote for ______ in a class or group election.

3. *Perceived similarity.*

   I think that ______ and I are quite similar to each other.

   When I am with ______, we are almost always in the same mood.

Loving

1. *Attachment.*

   If I could never be with ______, I would feel miserable.

   It would be hard for me to get along without ______.

2. *Caring.*

   If ______ were feeling badly, my first duty would be to cheer him (her) up.

   I would do almost anything for ______.

3. *Intimacy.*

   I feel that I can confide in ______ about almost anything.

   When I am with ______, I spend a good deal of time just looking at him (her).

of statements that expressed a variety of feelings one might have toward one's boyfriend or girlfriend. The students were to apply the statements to their own relationships and indicate which statements best expressed their own feelings toward their boyfriend or girlfriend. Rubin found that the students' expressed feelings could be grouped into two categories. Moreover, one of these categories corresponded reasonably well to what people typically mean by "liking," and the other to what is meant by "loving." Adjacent are some sample items of the two scales Rubin developed as a result of this analysis.

The study of love, like all other aspects of human psychology, will profit from the use of a wider range of behavioral measures, as well as pencil-and-paper measures. Rubin's research has made some initial progress in this regard. He found, for example, that couples whose answers indicated that they loved each other a great deal spent more time making eye contact while waiting to take part in an experiment than did couples who loved one another to a lesser extent. The notion that lovers spend a great deal of time staring into each other's eyes is, of course, a part of our folklore. It is also in accord with the more specific ideas that love is characterized by strong feelings of attachment and by intimate communication between people.

The idea that love involves caring for and devotion to another person has been a recurring theme in psychological writings. Psychoanalyst E. Fromm has defined love as "the active concern for the life and growth of that which we love," and H. S. Sullivan, a psychiatrist, has written that "When the satisfaction and security of another person becomes as significant to one as is one's own satisfaction or security, then the state of love exists." If these definitions are valid—if being in love means that we care for another person's welfare as much as or more than our own—how can one apply the reward-cost framework of this chapter to love relationships? It is possible? As Sullivan implies, a person who loves another has found that he is in fact personally rewarded when he contributes to another's happiness. In addition, people who love each other often begin to think of themselves as a unit, with common experiences and common investments. They become committed to

Figure 27.15
Through theory and research, psychologists may increase our understanding of factors that facilitate and inhibit love. They may also clarify our understanding of the behavior of lovers. Such knowledge is not meant to substitute for the experience of love or to limit or bound it; rather, it is intended to expand our understanding of a phenomenon that is so important a part of life.
(From Sherwood Anderson, "Death," *Winesburg, Ohio.* New York: Viking Press, 1964, p. 223.

this unit in much the same way people become committed to the groups to which they belong (see Chapter 24). By caring for his partner's welfare, a person is contributing to a social unit that he perceives himself belonging to.

Andreas Capellanus, the scribe of Eleanor of Aquitaine's mock-legal Court of Love, established in France in the twelfth century, defined love as:

> . . . a certain inborn suffering derived from the sight of and excessive meditation upon the beauty of the opposite sex, which causes each one to wish above all things the embraces of the other and by common desire to carry out all of love's precepts in the other's embrace.

This sort of definition typifies the romantic ideal of the Middle Ages, a conception of love that is still reflected in much of modern culture. At times love may indeed be experienced as the sort of passion or suffering that Capellanus describes in such exquisite detail. To the psychologist, however, love seems to be a rewarding experience that follows very much the same principles as do other varieties of interpersonal attraction. A person appears most likely to fall in love with another who is close by *(proximity)*, whose background and attitudes resemble his own *(similarity)*, whom he finds physically attractive, and who, more generally, provides the rewards of stimulation, helpfulness, and support that all of us need. In future years it is likely that there will be much more research on romantic love—not as a law unto itself but as one of the most important and interesting manifestations of interpersonal attraction. As we saw in Chapter 17, the more *feeling* components of love—the physical and emotional experiences—remain a major challenge and mystery in the province of individual psychology.

SUGGESTED READINGS

BERSCHEID, E., AND WALSTER, E. H. *Interpersonal Attraction.* Reading, Mass., Addison-Wesley Publishing Co., Inc., 1969. A thorough and well-organized overview of theory and research in this area.

HEIDER, F. *The Psychology of Interpersonal Relations.* New York, Wiley, 1958. A classic analysis of interpersonal behavior from the point of view of the individual actor. It presents Heider's influential "balance theory" of interpersonal sentiments. The reading is sometimes difficult, but it is well worth the effort.

HUNT, M. *The Natural History of Love.* New York, Knopf, 1959. A highly entertaining account of the history of love and courtship in the Western world, from the Golden Age of ancient Greece to modern times.

JONES, E. E. *Ingratiation: A Social-Psychological Analysis.* New York, Appleton-Century-Crofts, 1964. An excellent theoretical analysis and report of research on the tactics that people use to win approval from others.

RUBIN, Z. *Liking and Loving.* New York, Holt, Rinehart and Winston, 1973 (forthcoming). A lively excursion through social-psychological research on interpersonal attraction. It applies recent laboratory research to such real-life contexts as friendship, mate selection, and intergroup relations.

SCHACHTER, S. *The Psychology of Affiliation.* Stanford, Calif., Stanford University Press, 1969. A readable report of a classic series of experiments on the roots of human gregariousness.

28 Intergroup Behavior

I AM JEWISH. I was a teen-ager in the late 1930s when Hitlerism was on the rise, and I need not tell you that it was a time of intense insecurity for Jews everywhere—even in places where Hitler was not a direct and immediate threat. Naturally, Jews at that time were intensely aware of the injustice of racial and religious stereotypes, prejudice, and discrimination. I was, too.

Once, during that period, I was listening to a discussion on the subject by a group of Jewish men and women at a summer resort. I did not participate, for I was only a youngster and they were grown people, so it would have been impolite for me to thrust myself forward. At one point, though, I could no longer restrain myself. One of the speakers had been so eloquent on the subject of the cruel treatment of Jews in Europe that I burst out, "Yes, they treat Jews the way Americans treat Negroes." At once the conversation came to a halt and all eyes turned to me. Then one woman said in a most truculent tone, "And what is wrong with the way Americans treat Negroes?"

To my horror and dismay I found that not one person in the group saw the similarity in the situations. I found that their attitude toward discrimination changed according to whether *they* were discriminated against or *someone else was*. I never recovered from that discovery. Never. To this day, when people speak against discrimination and uphold rights of one sort or another, however sincerely, I always find myself wondering if it is their own rights only that concern them or the rights of others as well? Would the women's lib advocate come to the support of a downtrodden man? Would the black activist take up the cause of an unjustly treated white? I have come to believe that however important it is to try to remove unnecessary hatreds in the world today, the key point is for each person to recognize his *own* prejudices and fight those at least as hard as he fights the prejudices of others. For we all have prejudices; no one is clean.

I am not clean, either. Out of a whole host of prejudices that I have (and try to fight), I will mention one. I am prejudiced against Germans. If I am told that someone I haven't met is a German, I am suspicious and distrustful of him or her from that moment. It is no use saying that this is "natural under the circumstances." That may be an explanation; it is no excuse.

I. A.

In the summer of 1954, a group of social psychologists headed by M. Sherif conducted an ingenious study of intergroup relations at a boys' summer camp that they had organized especially for the experiment. The camp, which offered all the usual summer-camp activities was in Oklahoma, near a famous Jesse James hideout called the Robbers Cave.

THE ROBBERS CAVE EXPERIMENT

The boys who attended the camp had no idea that they were participating in a psychological experiment; they were healthy, well-adjusted eleven- and twelve-year-olds from stable, white, Protestant, middle-class homes. From the time the boys boarded the buses for camp, they were divided into two separate groups. In the first phase of the experiment the two groups were *isolated* from each other. The boys went hiking and swimming and played baseball only with members of their own group, and friendships and group spirit soon developed. Each group chose a name—the Eagles and the Rattlers—and created special symbols, secret words, and in-jokes. By the end of the first phase of the experiment, two informal organizations, each with its unwritten norms and informal leaders, had emerged.

In the second phase, the psychologists (posing as counselors) brought the groups together in *competitive contact* situations. They set up a tournament that pitted Eagles against Rattlers in baseball, football, tugs-of-war, a treasure hunt, and other games. Sherif had hypothesized that when these two groups of normal boys were placed in competitive situations, where one group could achieve its goals only at the expense of the other, hostility would soon develop. And, in fact, although the games began in a spirit of good sportsmanship, tension mounted as the tournament continued, and name-calling and scuffles began. One afternoon, after they had lost a game, the Eagles burned a banner left behind by the Rattlers. The next morning

Figure 28.1 *(opposite)*
Photographs taken during the course of the Robbers Cave experiment. Isolation of the two groups of boys produced group identity. During the competitive contact phase (top left, a tug of war), each group showed intense feelings of hostility toward the other group. (Top right) one group raids the other's cabin. (Middle row, right and center) signs and banners express the groups' competitiveness. (Lower left) a drawing by one of the boys shows his hostility toward the other group. (This boy was a subject in another version of the study, in which the groups chose the names Red Devils and Bulldogs.) Intergroup hostility gradually lessened when the two groups collaborated on certain tasks. One of these activities involved fixing a truck. To do so, some boys in each group had to push the truck (lower right).

the Rattlers stole the Eagles' flag in retaliation, and from then on, raids became more and more common.

The competition produced several major changes *within* each group. The group's solidarity and morale and the cooperation among members increased as a result of having a common rival or enemy. Group standards changed; in one group a big boy who had been considered a bully before the tournament became a hero. At the same time, each group became less tolerant of members who failed to conform to group standards; the leader in one group was deposed because of his supposed poor showing in competition.

After having demonstrated that they could produce intergroup conflict, Sherif and his associates started the third and final phase of the experiment, which was aimed at ending the conflict and establishing harmony between the Eagles and the Rattlers. Their first attempt resembled the "good-will" dinners and activities often held for occasions like National Brotherhood Week. The Eagles and the Rattlers were brought together to see a movie or to eat a particularly good meal in the dining hall. This approach failed totally to end the conflict—as Sherif had predicted from the start. At dinner, the campers from one group shoved and pushed boys from the other group, hurled food and insults, and generally used the opportunity to continue their attacks.

Next, the psychologists tried an approach based on Sherif's belief that if competition produces conflict, working in *cooperation to achieve shared goals should produce harmony.* The psychologists deliberately contrived a series of apparent emergencies in which the boys either had to help each other or else lose the chance to do or get something they all wanted. One morning both groups took a trip to a lake. Around noon, someone discovered that the truck, which was supposed to go to town to pick up lunch, would not start. To get it to work, boys from both groups had to push and pull. Another morning, someone reported that the water pipe line to the camp had broken; the boys were told that unless they worked together to find the break and fix it, they would all have to leave camp. By afternoon the Rattlers and the Eagles had jointly found and repaired the damage. Gradually, through these cooperative activities, intergroup hostility and tensions lessened. Friendships began to develop between individual Eagles and Rattlers, and eventually the groups began to seek out occasions to mingle. At the end of camp, members of both groups requested that they ride home together on the same bus.

The Robbers Cave Experiment provides a striking example of how social factors —in this case conditions of competition or cooperation—can affect the relationship between groups. What is most impressive about the hostility and subsequent acceptance that the researchers produced between the groups is that the children were from similar backgrounds and were randomly sorted into groups; none of the results can be attributed to differences in nationality, race, class, or ability.

RACE AS A SOCIAL CATEGORY

The boys in the Robbers Cave Experiment came to identify very strongly with their group. They were proud to be Eagles or Rattlers and disdainful of members of the other group. As discussed at length in Chapter 24, group membership influenced the way each boy thought of himself, and it also affected his attitudes and behavior toward others. When a Rattler confronted an Eagle in the football tournament, his perception of his opponent was affected by his beliefs that Eagles were "stinkers," "cheaters," and "sneaks." His behavior was also affected; he was on guard for any trick his opponent might try.

In social interactions, one person behaves towards another on the basis of two factors: (1) the unique attributes of the other person and (2) generalizations one makes about him on the basis of the groups or social categories he belongs to. If you, for example, were about to meet a person and you knew that he was a father

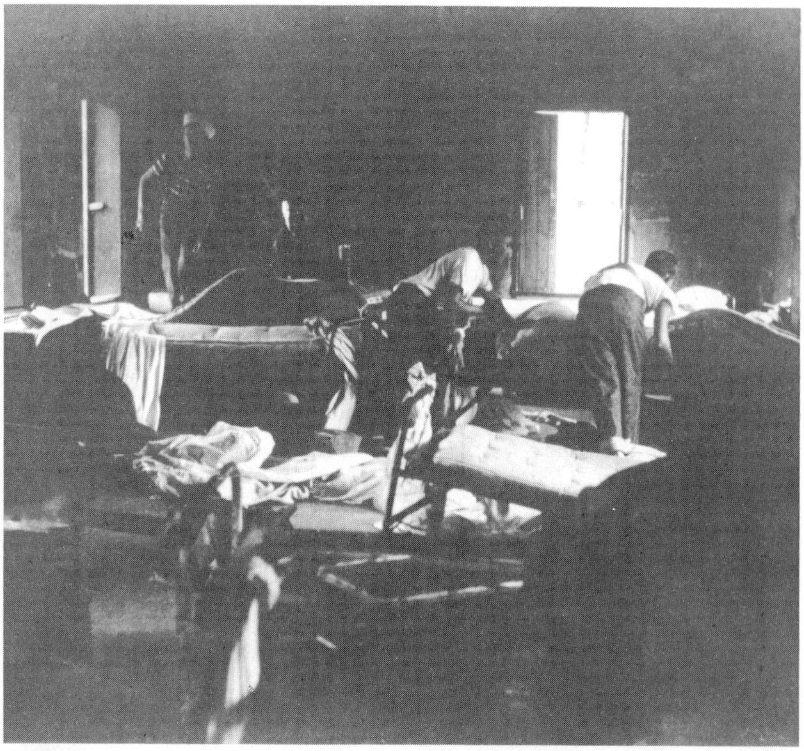

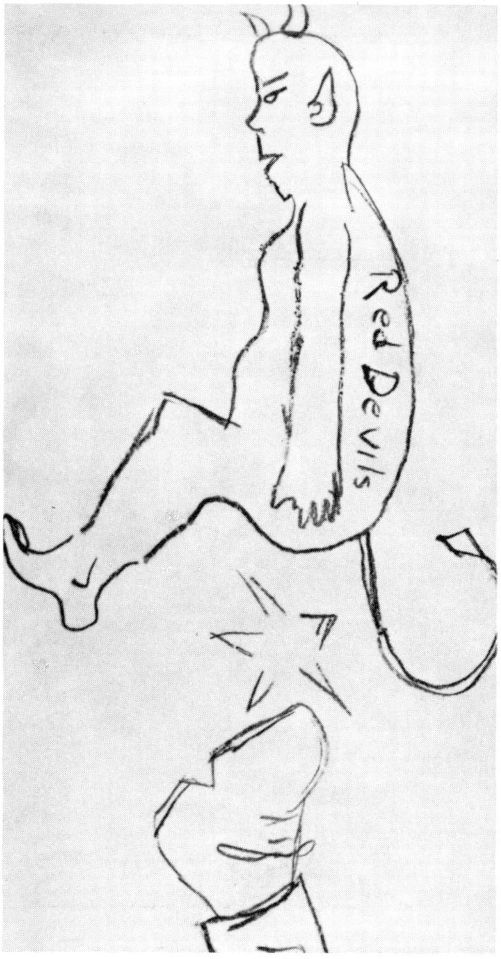
Red Devils

TOM HALE
RATTLERS

TOM HALE
EAGLES YOU MAY
WIN BUT W
WILL GIVE
YOU A HELL
OF A
MOTTO
FIGHT

of six, a high-school football coach, a volunteer fireman, and a Catholic—the *social categories* he occupies—you could probably make fairly good guesses about how he spends his time, how he will react to your jokes, what some of his interests are. These kinds of generalized beliefs and expectations about what certain kinds of people are like and how they are likely to act may help to make our relationships more predictable and comfortable.

Race is a very important social category in America. It has major impact on how a person thinks about himself and how he acts toward others. To understand how this social category affects black-white relations in the United States, it will be necessary to discuss social stereotypes and social roles as they relate to race. First, however, one must define what is meant by the term "race."

The Social Definition of Race

It is important to realize that in American race relations, race itself is defined in social terms, not on the basis of biology. For the biologist, a race is a relatively isolated mating group with certain distinctive gene frequencies. But Americans do not decide who is "Caucasian" and who is "Negro" on the basis of gene frequencies. The child with one black and one white parent cannot decide to be "white." Typically, social convention states that any Negro ancestry, no matter how remote, constitutes grounds for being classified as black. For example, the 1960 United States Census gave the following definition of Negro:

> *Negro:* In addition to persons of Negro and of mixed Negro and white descent, this classification, according to instructions to enumerators, includes persons of mixed American Indian and Negro descent, unless the Indian ancestry very definitely predominates or unless the individual is regarded as Indian in the community.

According to the Census Bureau, a person with *any* Negro ancestry is Negro, unless the community defines him otherwise.

The point of this discussion is not to deny that black Americans constitute a distinct group but rather to emphasize that it is a *socially defined group,* not a biological one. Group membership depends on social convention or fiat, not on absolute biological criteria. Group identity is based largely on a shared cultural heritage and on the common problems of surviving as an oppressed minority group that occupies an inferior social position and confronts a derogatory social role.

Social Stereotypes

Chapter 23 discussed the way people create their own *personal* stereotypes about people they meet. The cab drivers' stereotypes of "sports" and "blowhards"—the traits and behavior they attribute to these two types of passengers—were used as an example in the discussion of impression formation. However, many stereotypes are shared by several people—often by all the members of a particular group and sometimes by an entire society—and for this reason they are called *social* stereotypes. Social stereotypes are frequently part of the traditions of a group and are taught to new members during the process of socialization. People thus acquire many stereotypes vicariously, by hearsay, rather than through personal experience. For example, in 1933 D. Katz and K. W. Braly found that American students could describe stereotypes for Turks and Chinese, although few of the students had ever met anyone from these countries. Turks were believed to be cruel, religious, sensuous, and ignorant, and Chinese were described as superstitious, sly, traditional, and reserved. It is clearly impossible for every Turk and every Chinese to possess these particular traits, although some Turkish and some Chinese individuals may have them. For those who do not, the stereotype is inaccurate. The prejudice—from the Latin for pre-judge—in stereotypes is not only that they are rigid prejudgments, but also that they are *incorrect.*

Before going on to discuss racial stereotypes, we must draw the distinction

Figure 28.2

Racial and cultural stereotypes may be reflected and even perpetuated by mass media. These stills from motion pictures, some of which are not very old, illustrate such stereotypes. (Top) *Gone with the Wind* was a saga of the south during the Civil War period; the Negro "mammy" in the film portrayed the stereotyped characteristics of kindliness, wisdom, attachment to her owner, and submissiveness. (Middle row) childlike Mexicans, (lower left) Italian "mobsters," and (lower right) shuffling Negroes were caricatured in the movies from which these photographs are taken.

between social roles and social stereotypes. Like social roles, stereotypes apply to a general category of persons, not to a particular individual. But stereotypes are primarily descriptive beliefs or expectations about what people in some social group or category are like. In contrast, roles involve rules, or prescriptions, for conduct. Those in the role of mother *ought* to take care of their children, and they typically do. Few would argue, however, that Turks *should* be cruel or that Chinese *ought* to be superstitious.

Stereotypes serve functions both for the group and for the individual. For the individual, such generalizations are often useful and sometimes necessary. A person's experiences are so rich and complex that he must often simplify in order to understand them and respond appropriately. In the group context, stereotypes about *out-groups* help to unite the *in-group*. One way for an Eagle to signify his group loyalty was to express his contempt for Rattlers. Even if an individual does not personally believe a particular stereotype, he may feel social pressure to express it. In some communities, for example, people may be reluctant to speak out against derogatory stereotypes about Negroes for fear of offending their white neighbors and consequently losing social approval. Thus, for many people, the expression of stereotypes may be essentially an act of conformity to group expectations. However, for a smaller number of persons, stereotypes may serve as a vital psychological crutch. T. W. Adorno and his colleagues identified these persons as "authoritarian personalities." They suggest that these people are very insecure and are so afraid of their own aggressive and sexual drives that they deny or fail to recognize them. They externalize their own negative qualities and project them onto members of some minority group, such as Jews or Negroes. A person with strong authoritarian tendencies could not easily give up derogatory ethnic and racial stereotypes, for to do so would require a major change in his personality. The conventionally prejudiced person, however, could more easily give up his stereotypes if the group beliefs changed. Fortunately for those who want to eliminate negative racial and ethnic stereotypes, the number of people who hold stereotypes to shore up their authoritarian personalities is small.

In the study of intergroup relations, ethnic and racial stereotypes have received considerable attention. Several studies, for example those by G. Allport, D. Katz and K. Braly, and M. Karlins, T. L. Coffman, and G. Walters, have shown that many white Americans believe Negroes to be "irresponsible, superstitious, intellectually inferior, lazy, and musical." Such stereotypes affect intergroup relations in several ways. They bias our perceptions of individuals. People tend to see what they expect to see; confirmation of expectations is psychologically comfortable. Stereotypes often add fuel to intergroup conflict. In extreme cases, stereotypes may serve to dehumanize others. Soldiers, for example, are often trained to regard the enemy as a thing rather than as a person because it is psychologically easier to create hatred toward, and justify aggression against, someone if he is perceived as a "commie" or a "gook" rather than as another human being. In American race relations, Negro stereotypes have been used to justify assigning blacks to an inferior social position and denying them equal opportunities.

Many stereotypes are a mixture of description and evaluation. Robert K. Merton, in *Social Theory and Social Structure*, provided the following example of how the mixture works:

The very same behavior undergoes a complete change of evaluation in its transition from the in-group Abe Lincoln to the out-group Abe Cohen or Abe Kurakawa . . . Did Lincoln work far into the night? This testifies that he was industrious, resolute, perseverant, and eager to realize his capacities to the full. Do the out-group Jews or Japanese keep these same hours? This only bears witness to their sweatshop mentality, their ruthless undercutting of American standards, their unfair competitive practices. Is the in-group hero frugal, thrifty and sparing? Then the out-group villain is stingy, miserly, and penny-pinching.

Because stereotypes combine fact and opinion, it is often difficult to know how to test their accuracy. Although some stereotypes can be proven untrue, many do contain a kernel of truth, or fact. The danger is that people applying stereotypes use *unfair standards* to evaluate the facts. In the case of Abe (adjacent), a *double standard* is being used. The kernel of truth here is that Abe works far into the night and does not spend money with a free hand. However, this behavior is evaluated differently depending on whether it is done by one of "us" or by one of "them."

Some stereotypes are unfair because they try to apply a single standard, the standard of one culture, to a very different group. For example, early American settlers reported that the native Indians were "irreligious heathens." The Indians,

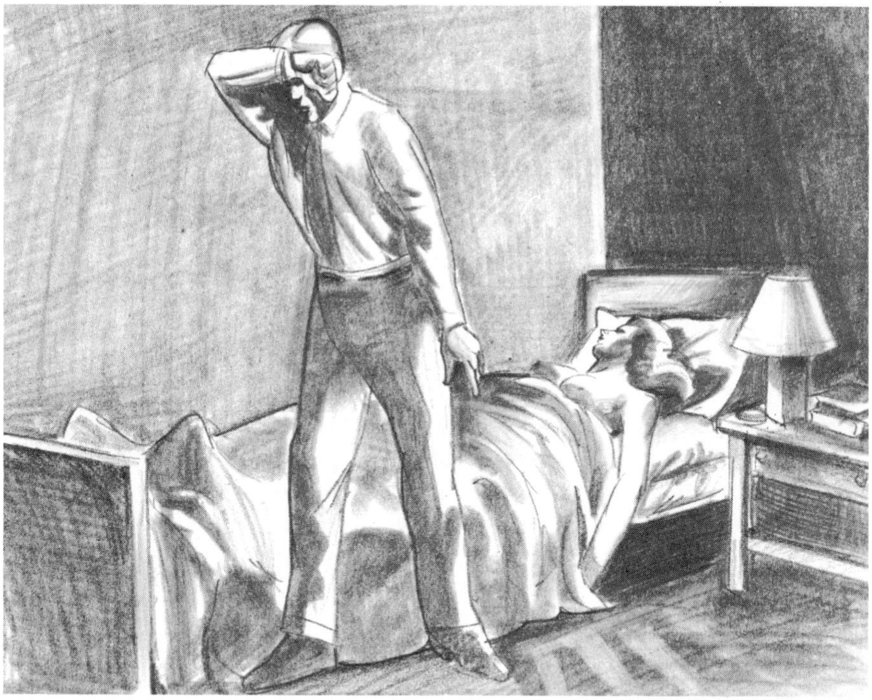

Oh, oh! This is apt to be rather sordid. It doesn't represent a family scene to me! It may be a prostitute, and I see the old bottle there. This may be a young American down in the tropics; he is dressed in white because of the temperature. As for the woman, it's difficult to say because of the shadows, but she appears of darker skin. The place has crude furnishings. (What preceded?) The natural assumption is that they had sexual intercourse. The fellow is about half drunk and is about to consume more. The fellow looks kind of "hang-dog"; perhaps he regrets his recent act or perhaps his station in life. He is down and out and liquor isn't much of a boon to him. He has sufficient depth of character to take himself out of a place like that and to genuinely regret what he did to the woman. She doesn't enter into the story, except to be the object of his lust. He is a better type than she. He can take care of himself. He finally drags himself out of such surroundings and gradually amounts to something. Do I take too long? I get quite involved in these stories.

This is a young fellow who drinks a lot. His clothes are all messed up. In a dingy hotel room, he feels he has lost all of his friends. He thinks all of the troubles of the world are on his shoulders. He contemplates suicide. The trouble is with a woman he had an affair with. He doesn't know whether to injure her or destroy himself. To kill her or commit suicide. She isn't much good herself, and he isn't too much better. He is in a mixed up mental state. He is pausing there to make some decision. He will try to get revenge on the woman. (Revenge for what?) He has been going with her and giving her money and thinks of marrying her. She fools him and is unfaithful, going around with other men. He kills her.

Figure 28.4
Stories written by two men in response to a TAT card similar to the one shown above. The first story, by Mack, reflects an authoritarian personality. Mack appears to be a person bound by conventional standards who attempts to ignore or deny unacceptable desires by projecting them onto others. He is unable to admit his own weakness, and he defends himself rigidly against revealing any feelings of inadequacy. With his guard up, the number of things in the environment to which he will let himself respond is severely limited. The second story, by Larry, shows that he is not an authoritarian personality. One would expect him to be sensitive to the thoughts and feelings of others. He appears to be a person who attempts to understand his own behavior, and to keep this behavior in line with a code of ethics he has set up for himself.
(After Adorno, *et al*, 1950.)

of course, did have their own religious beliefs, but because their beliefs did not conform to white standards, they were discounted. The evaluation of another group solely on the basis of one's own cultural standards is called *ethnocentrism.*

Racial Roles

The noted social psychologist T. F. Pettigrew has suggested that many aspects of the relations between blacks and whites in the United States can be explained in terms of social roles. Since the founding of this country, blacks have been assigned at birth to an inferior social position and whites to a superior one. This assignment has been made on the basis of race rather than on individual achievement. In addition to descriptive stereotypes based on race, then, there have also existed prescriptive expectations about how blacks and whites *should* behave toward each other. These rules and expectations constitute complementary racial roles. The Negro role obliges its occupants to be submissive, deferential, and respectful toward whites; the white role obliges its occupants to be superior, condescending, and perhaps paternalistic. The elaboration of these roles was perhaps easiest to see in the old South, where a complicated etiquette prescribed in detail the relations between the races; these unwritten rules were bolstered by laws enforcing segregation in schools, churches, residences, and other areas of life. However, racial-role definitions have affected black-white relations in all parts of the country and continue to do so today. The Negro who failed to play his role could anticipate accusations of "not knowing his place" and was liable to lose his job or suffer verbal or physical attack. For the white, although racial-role requirements were less clearly defined, they were no less real. To treat blacks as equals was to betray oneself as a "nigger lover" and to risk losing the esteem of friends and associates.

The concept of racial role is useful because it suggests the extent to which the lives of whites and blacks are intertwined. Racial roles are reciprocal; each is defined in relation to the other. Further, the explanation of relations between blacks and whites in terms of roles emphasizes that these relations are not controlled by biological or racial factors but simply by social convention. The notion of role also helps to distinguish between overt behavior and personality, that is, between what a person does and what he would like to do. Black Americans, for example, have never been the simple, childlike creatures that their role required, although many have put on a good show. It is a serious mistake to confuse the behavior that a person must perform because of his racial role and the things that he might do if he were not hampered by role prescriptions.

Although roles and personality are distinct, roles do have important effects on personality. Chapters 23, 24, 25, and 26 explore these effects in some detail. Studies

Figure 28.5

These observations by black author James Baldwin illustrate Pettigrew's theory that racial roles are reciprocal.

(From James Baldwin, *Nobody Knows My Name*. New York: Dell Publishing Co., 1969, pp. 73 and 122–123.)

suggest that many blacks accept, at least in part, the negative racial stereotypes of our culture. Further, playing an inferior role often takes its toll in loss of self-respect and the creation of unconscious self-hatred.

In recent civil-rights demonstrations, black Americans have once again demanded "Freedom! Now!" Today it is not freedom from legal slavery that is the goal but freedom from social and economic oppression. In part this means escaping from racial-role definitions and stereotyped images. Black Americans have, with increasing speed and determination, been rejecting the traditional racial roles. "Black power," "black pride," and "black is beautiful" are expressions of this striving by blacks to change their social position, to redefine racial roles, to raise self-esteem and eliminate self-hatred. Because the old racial roles are complementary, changes in one require changes in the other. As black Americans seek to redefine their role, the role of whites must also change. For some whites, racial roles have provided a sense of self-esteem and importance based on being better than some other group. Such feelings of superiority may be difficult to give up as racial roles change. Clear-cut new roles have not yet emerged, but it appears that social expectations and racial roles remain important for determining black-white relations, even though the content of racial roles is changing.

DETERMINANTS OF INTERGROUP RELATIONS

Sometimes the relations between groups are peaceful, productive, and pleasant. In other cases, they are characterized by tension, ill will, open hostility, or even bloodshed. At one campus, college students and faculty work together on an ecology teach-in; at another, students take over the administration buildings and halt classes. During World War II America considered the "Japs" enemies, placed Japanese Americans in internment camps, and dropped atomic bombs on two Japanese cities; today, Americans consider Japan an ally, visit the country as tourists, and equip their homes with Japanese-made products. In a coal-mining town, black and white American men may work together in the mines in a friendly, cooperative, sometimes joking atmosphere; above the ground they live in separate neighborhoods, attend separate churches, and would not think of visiting each other's homes.

The effects of social roles and stereotypes help give some insight into why such situations exist, but social psychologists have isolated a number of other factors that may explain why relations between groups are sometimes harmonious, sometimes filled with discord.

Conditions of Contact

Chapter 27 discusses the effects of proximity on one person's liking another. Studies of the relationship between proximity of groups and harmony between them are called studies of *intergroup contact.* Y. Amir recently reviewed several dozen studies of intergroup contact and found that increased interaction between groups sometimes lessens hostility and tension but sometimes increases them. A study conducted by V. Sims and J. Patrick in the 1930s indicated that when Northern whites went South to college, their contact with Negroes increased and so did their anti-Negro prejudice. However, research by M. Deutsch and M. Collins, which compared integrated and segregated housing projects, showed that residential contact can lead to more favorable attitudes and to cross-racial friendships.

To make sense of these contradictory results, it seems clear that one must know more about the specific nature of the contact situation. G. Allport and others have suggested several aspects of the interaction that are important.

Cooperation to Achieve Shared Goals A crucial factor in the Robbers Cave study was cooperation to achieve shared goals. Sherif demonstrated that similar goals were not adequate. In the sports tournament, both Rattlers and Eagles strove for the same

Figure 28.6
Intergroup hostilities can be reduced if the groups share a common goal on which they can cooperate. These photographs show blacks and whites marching together for civil rights in Selma, Alabama. Although it is likely that both the whites and blacks who participated in the demonstration held similar attitudes about civil rights, it should be noted that the issue of civil rights is not necessarily a racial one—it is a matter of justice, a legal matter. One can work toward equal rights without any close contact with members of another race. The conditions of contact, however, in working together to organize and carry through a project like this one can let people from each race get to know each other and—more than simply reducing hostilities—can result in people becoming friends.

goal—to win—but a win for one group meant a loss for the other. It was only when the boys had to work together to reach a joint goal that relations improved. In a cooperative situation, members are interdependent. The efforts of each person help himself and others at the same time. Sherif emphasized the point that *groups must perceive their shared goal as superordinate,* as sufficiently important to override other differences between them. When the Rattlers and Eagles cooperated to fix the water pipe line, their goal of staying at camp was strong enough for them to put aside their differences.

One major kind of superordinate goal involves the threat of a common enemy. Often rival groups can unite as allies in the face of a shared external danger. This point has not escaped science-fiction writers, who often depict the nations of the world uniting at last to fight an enemy from outer space. In Sherif's study what served as the enemy was not another group but the undesirable prospect of having to leave camp. The general principle seems to be that competition tends to produce conflict, and cooperation tends to reduce it. It may be that cooperation between groups creates, at least momentarily, a new, combined group and establishes new bonds and identification with the larger unit. When Rattlers and Eagles worked together, their separate allegiances became less salient, and they may have viewed themselves as part of one group, the camp.

Intimacy of the Contact The relationship between intimate contact and liking is something of a chicken-and-egg problem. One can reasonably ask which comes first, liking or contact. Both common sense and psychological research suggest that the relationship can work in either direction. If people like each other and are friendly, they are more likely to seek each other out and spend time together. If people interact frequently and intimately, they often come to form friendships and to see each other more favorably. The second process is the more interesting one for the study of intergroup contact. In the Robbers Cave Experiment it is clear that cooperative contact preceded liking. The boys did not decide to work together because they liked each other. Rather, circumstances forced them to cooperate, and in the process of working on a series of joint tasks, the groups gradually developed friendliness.

Studies of residential contacts demonstrate similar effects. Shortly after World War II, public-housing projects began to spring up in metropolitan areas. Some of them were racially integrated, whereas others maintained racial segregation. Deutsch and Collins capitalized on this "natural" social experiment. Although they could not control the situation as much as Sherif had, they carefully selected four biracial projects, two *integrated* ones, in which blacks and whites occupied adjoining apartments, and two *segregated* ones, in which blacks and whites lived in the same project but in separate buildings. In order to qualify for public housing, the families in both projects had consented to live in a biracial project, but they had no choice about whether they were assigned to live in an integrated or a segregated one. That is, they could not predetermine their pattern of residential contact.

Deutsch and Collins conducted lengthy interviews with housewives after their families had lived in the project for a while. The results of the study show clearly that the two types of contact situations had different effects on racial attitudes. In the integrated projects over 60 percent of the white housewives reported having "friendly relations" with Negroes; in the segregated projects, less than 10 percent reported friendships, and over 80 percent reported no contact at all. In the integrated project two out of three white women expressed a desire to be friendly with blacks; in the segregated projects, only one in eleven expressed such a desire. Similar effects occurred in the attitudes of black women toward whites. Many women in the integrated projects came to like the interracial aspect of their apartment buildings, whereas in the segregated projects many women disliked being in even a segregated biracial development.

The Deutsch and Collins study illustrates not only the effects of contact on liking but also the *importance of informal opportunities for interaction.* In the segregated projects, the actual physical distance between black and white families was not great, but functionally, the distance was considerable. One white woman reported:

> I used to be good friends with a colored woman who worked with me at the factory before I moved here. She lives in the other side of the project, but I never have her over to my side of the project—it just isn't done. Occasionally, I go over and visit her.

This woman could not casually meet her friend in the laundry-room or elevator; for her a meeting entailed a deliberate effort. In the segregated projects, the group norms would have held such an action suspect. In the integrated projects, contacts could occur spontaneously and casually. Housewives had many opportunities to meet, and they often took advantage of them. The result of these frequent and increasingly intense meetings was dramatic. One white housewife described her experience this way:

I started to cry when my husband told me we were coming to live here. I cried for three weeks . . . I didn't want to come and live here where there are so many colored people. I didn't want to bring my children up with colored children, but we had to come; there was no place else to go . . . Well, all that's changed. I've really come to like it. I see they're just as human as we are. They have nice apartments; they keep their children clean, and they're very friendly. I've come to like them a great deal. I'm no longer scared of them.

Contacts like those in the integrated project, which permit people to get to know each other well as individuals and not in formal social roles, enable people to test their stereotypes against reality. Deutsch and Collins do not deny that old attitudes die hard and that people tend to distort their perception and recall of events to complement their existing attitudes. But they maintain that when contact continues over time, it becomes psychologically too costly and difficult to retain beliefs that are inconsistent with experience. Interracial contacts are often uncomfortable at first for both blacks and whites, but if other conditions are favorable, intimate contact over time frequently leads to a reduction in negative attitudes and tension.

Social Climate In the Robbers Cave Experiment, friendly contacts were approved by the counselors and other camp officials. Friendships between Eagles and Rattlers might not have developed if they had been discouraged by the important adults in the camp. The outcome of interracial contact also depends in part on whether the social climate is one of acceptance or disapproval. Besides the opinions of authorities, like the adults at the camp, the crucial factors in determining a social climate and thus the outcome of interracial situations are the force of formal law and the impact of social norms. In the projects that Deutsch and Collins studied, the social climates differed enormously. In the segregated developments, whites and blacks hesitated to mix because they believed it "just isn't done." The authorities who built the projects had apparently intended that the races be separated, and the informal social norms of the project supported this view. In the integrated projects, the expectations were quite different. Here the housing officials supported integration, and informal social norms developed that made interracial contacts appropriate.

Status When a man goes to lunch with a friend, the situation is one in which both persons have equal status; when that man meets in conference with his boss, he has a lower rank, and the situation is one of unequal status. In any particular interaction, relative status may be determined by the individuals' social roles, their personal characteristics, or their achievements. Doctors have higher status than nurses (occupational-role status); adults have higher status than children (status based on age); the skilled athlete outranks the rookie (status based on achievement). Contacts between blacks and whites in which blacks have *lower* status do little to challenge or change attitudes and behavior. For example, contact between an upper-middle-class white housewife and her black maid may actually serve to confirm the white's stereotype of blacks as "not too bright and suited for menial jobs." So as not to jeopardize her job, the black maid may try to be pleasing and to superficially conform to the housewife's stereotype. At the same time, this unequal-status contact may reinforce her own negative or hostile attitudes toward whites.

Interracial contacts in which blacks have *higher* status do not always produce changed attitudes either. Some people find it easy to dismiss the good impressions made by a few outstanding minority group members as "exceptions." In fact, some may perceive the achievements of Negro athletes and entertainers as confirming

Figure 28.7
This basketball game was a fund-raising event, jointly sponsored by the long-haired players (students) and the short-haired ones (highway patrolmen). The two groups planned and organized the game, besides playing in it. The long-haired team (no member of which could have hair less than two inches below his collar) was dubbed "the Heads," and the patrolmen's team was called "the Feds." Their game netted $450 for a local antipollution project. This kind of cooperation to achieve shared goals is a strong means of reducing intergroup hostility.

racial stereotypes. To effect attitude change, the Negroes of higher status in interracial contacts must enact roles not associated with racial stereotypes, for example such occupational roles as chemist, airplane pilot, or French teacher. One study conducted in England by H. E. O. James looked at African women who taught white schoolchildren. These teachers were in a high-status position that permitted the breaking of stereotypes. In addition, their contact with students was prolonged and relatively intimate. The children they taught came to like their teachers personally and developed more favorable attitudes toward Africans generally.

Equal-status contacts stand the best chance of leading to improved intergroup relations. Numerous studies, such as those by R. H. Gundlach, H. E. O. James, R. D. Minard, and J. Harding and R. Hogrefe, have shown that when blacks and whites work together as equals, in the army or as coal miners or as merchant seamen, intergroup liking and friendships often develop. The status of the black and of the white women in the integrated housing projects studied by Deutsch and Collins was much the same; the family incomes were roughly comparable, all were housewives, and their living quarters were virtually identical. This equal-status contact over a long period made it possible for members of each group to realize that the others are "people just like us."

The four factors that have been suggested as important for effective intergroup contact are summarized in the adjacent margin.

These factors work jointly, and if any one is missing, an interaction may not have positive results.

The effects of interracial contact in one situation often do not generalize to new situations. The Deutsch and Collins study provides an example of this limitation. Children from all the housing projects attended desegregated elementary schools, and some children from both integrated and segregated projects formed cross-racial

effective intergroup contact

1. Participants must cooperate to achieve a shared goal.
2. Contact should be relatively intimate and long lasting.
3. Contact should take place in a social climate of acceptance.
4. Participants in the situation should have equal status.

friendships at school. However, only those children who lived in an integrated project brought their cross-racial friends home from school. Children in the segregated project only saw their friends of a different race away from home. One Negro girl who lived in a segregated project commented, "I play with them (white children) at school and go to the movies with them. In the project, I have nothing to do with them." Children in segregated projects learned that cross-racial friendship was acceptable in school but inappropriate at home. Behavior is strongly affected by the social norms, expectations, and opportunities of the particular situation, and so the effects of contact in one situation—at school—do not necessarily carry over to another—the home.

Group Processes and Contact

Some of the basic processes described in earlier chapters of this unit may serve to explain how contact between groups can, under the conditions just described, produce changed attitudes. First, contact may provide opportunities for members of different groups to *reward each other.* For example, the cooperative efforts to start the broken truck and fix the pipe line enabled Eagles to help Rattlers and Rattlers to help Eagles obtain a desired reward.

Cooperative contact may also help to *destroy derogatory stereotypes.* A joint activity forms a temporary bond between people of different groups, and they begin to think of themselves as members of the same team. These people, then, would be less likely to employ the unfair standards for evaluation used in stereotypes because it would be difficult to apply one standard to oneself and a different standard to the other members of the team.

A third explanation for the effects of contact is based on the *theory of cognitive dissonance* described in Chapter 24. When an experience contradicts a long-held belief, sometimes the belief must change. Working with someone, for example, and perhaps coming to like him a little, should be psychologically inconsistent with negative attitudes about him or his group. Such an imbalance should be psychologically disturbing and might motivate the person holding the negative attitudes to change them, especially if he cannot gracefully escape from the interaction.

Fourth, it has been suggested that contact is effective because it helps to *uncover the basic similarities* that exist between members of different groups. As one of the housewives in the Deutsch and Collins study said, she had learned that blacks are "just as human as we are."

Effects of Similarity

Chapter 27 stresses the importance of similarity of backgrounds and beliefs for the development of friendship between individuals. One might, then, hypothesize that the more similar two groups are, the better the chances of positive intergroup relations. In 1960, M. Rokeach and others made the controversial assertion that belief may be just as important as race—or even more important—in determining social discrimination and prejudice. In other words, Rokeach suggested that *whites reject blacks primarily because they perceive the blacks as having beliefs dissimilar to their own.*

Rokeach argued, for example, that the Ku Klux Klanner is less interested in whether a person is black or white than in whether the person agrees with the Klan's prosegregation views on race. From the Ku Klux Klan's perspective, there are four kinds of people, as indicated adjacent.

Of the two categories a Klan member uses to sort people, beliefs are more salient than race. Cognitively, the "nigger lover" (white) is just as bad as the "uppity nigger" (black) for him. (On this basis Rokeach suggested that the recent civil-rights struggles were a conflict not between whites and blacks but between those who supported integration and those who favored segregation.) To test his general hy-

Figure 28.9
According to Milton Rokeach's hypothesis, interracial hostility derives more from a perception that the "other" race holds different beliefs than from the fact of race alone. If this is true, a Klansman would like a black who shared his views on segregation more than he would like a white man who strongly supported integration.

Agree with KKK	Disagree with KKK
"Good White"	"Bad White" ("nigger lover")
"Good Negro"	"Bad Negro" ("uppity nigger")

pothesis, Rokeach conducted a study of white college students. The subjects read such descriptions of hypothetical people as "a white who is for socialized medicine" and "a Negro who is anticommunist." They rated each person on a nine-point scale ranging from "I can't see myself being friends with such a person" to "I can very easily see myself being friends with such a person." In analyzing these data, Rokeach found that there was a small *race effect;* white students did tend to prefer whites to blacks, even when the blacks had beliefs similar to their own. However, there was a much larger *belief effect;* regardless of race, students preferred persons with beliefs similar to their own.

Rokeach's subjects rated hypothetical persons in only one situation, acceptability as a friend. However, is it always true that belief similarity is more important than race? More recent studies by H. C. Triandis and E. E. Davis and by D. Stein suggest that the relative weights assigned to race and belief vary depending on the relationship or situation involved. Stein found that for white teen-agers, race had little effect on selecting a person as a close personal friend or on sitting next to him in class. However, race was the major factor in three situations: inviting a person home for dinner, living in the same apartment house, or having him date a sister or brother. Stein was puzzled by the seeming paradox that a white student might be glad to have a Negro as a friend but be unwilling to have him as a neighbor. This finding appeared to violate the common-sense idea that the more intimate or personal a relationship, the more important race would be. Stein suggested that the relative importance of race and belief does not depend as much on intimacy as on the influence of social norms. In some situations, such as marriage and housing, social prohibitions about cross-racial contact are typically very strong and may override considerations of belief. In other cases, such as friendships at school or on a sports team, cross-racial contact may not violate social norms. However, Triandis and Davis have found that for some highly prejudiced people, race is consistently a more important determinant of acceptance than is belief similarity, regardless of the situation.

Another important finding of Stein's study was that when a subject was not explicitly told the beliefs of some hypothetical persons, he tended to assume that members of his own race shared his views and that members of another race held different views. In making this *assumption of dissimilarity,* the subject was generalizing about categories of persons, apparently solely on the basis of race. However, it is possible that other factors, say, the hypothetical person's social class, also contribute to guesses about his beliefs. A study by J. A. Bayton, L. B. McAlister, and J. Hamer found that students (both black and white) make very different assumptions about the characteristics of upper- and lower-class blacks. The students described lower-class blacks according to the typical derogatory stereotype as superstitious, lazy, physically dirty, and ignorant, but they described upper-class blacks in a much more favorable light as intelligent, ambitious, industrious, and neat. These data suggest that people in general might make different assumptions about the beliefs of Negroes depending on the Negroes' social class. When a person is told only that an individual is black, it appears that he assumes that the black is from the lower class. Knowledge that a black is from the middle or upper class might temper or eliminate the assumption of belief dissimilarity based on race alone. Finally, in a more recent study than Stein's, C. E. Hendrick and others found that when beliefs are not known, *only* highly prejudiced subjects tend to assume that blacks and whites have different attitudes.

Similarity and the Value of Diversity

The perception of similarity plays an important role in race relations. Liking and acceptance between members of different groups may be affected by differences in many characteristics, including race, social class, and beliefs. When one person does not know another person's beliefs about an issue, he tries to infer them from other characteristics, like race or social class; so, for example, whites who have no information but race to go by tend to assume that blacks have beliefs dissimilar from their own. One implication of this finding may be that as social norms change and interracial contact increases, blacks and whites may become more aware of their actual similarities. At least within social classes, similarity of belief may replace race as a major determinant of social acceptance.

In Chapter 27, it was suggested that differences between individuals can serve to make their relationship more interesting and stimulating. The same may be true of intergroup relations. The perception of similarities can pave the way for appreciation of differences in intergroup relations, and, in fact, the perception of certain basic areas of similarity may be essential to cross-racial acceptance. The housewives in the Deutsch and Collins study might not have made friends with neighbors of a different race who had very dissimilar attitudes about child rearing and neighborliness or different standards of cleanliness and morality. However, once such basic similarities are established, the distinct cultural traditions of black and white Americans may prove a source of welcome diversity.

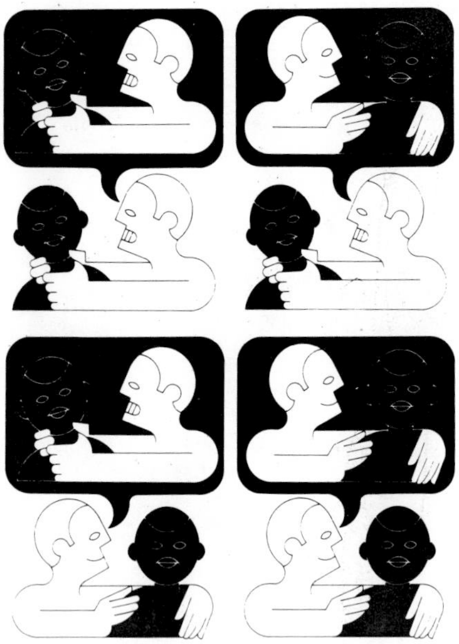

Figure 28.10
In analyzing racism, one must distinguish between prejudice (derogatory attitudes) and discrimination (racist behavior). A person's behavior toward blacks, for example, may be either consistent with or contradictory to his attitudes toward them. The drawings show (top left) a prejudiced discriminator, that is, one who both thinks and acts anti-black. (Top right) a nonprejudiced discriminator: for example, a white person who thinks favorably of blacks but refuses to hire them so as to avoid his community's criticisms. (Bottom left) a prejudiced nondiscriminator: for example, a racist politician who courts black voters. (Bottom right) a nonprejudiced nondiscriminator.

Effects of Social Evaluation

Chapter 27 noted that people often compare themselves to others; the standards for comparison are frequently the norms of a group the person belongs to or aspires to join—a reference group. If a person finds that others in the group are more advantaged than he, more popular or more successful, he feels himself to be *relatively deprived.* He may be envious. He may even undertake a campaign of self-improvement. However, if he also believes that the advantages held by the others are somehow unjust, his response is more likely to be one of indignation, frustration, anger, or even aggression. Similarly, if a person finds that he is more advantaged than others in his reference group, he is *relatively gratified.* He may be pleased, satisfied, even proud. However, if he suspects that his good fortune is based on injustice, he may also feel guilty. The related concepts of social comparison and relative deprivation can offer insight into group and particularly race relations.

Since World War II black Americans have made great strides in education, employment, health care, and other areas of life. J. Davis and R. Fein report that the percentage of blacks in white-collar jobs has doubled since 1940, and the median years of schooling for young black adults has risen from six and a half to eleven years in the same period. When black civil-rights protests gained in numbers in the early 1960s, the economic and educational situation of Negro Americans had never been better. The explanation for the increased black protest lies partly in the fact that people do not assess their gains in absolute terms but rather evaluate them in comparison with other groups. For black Americans, the major standard for social and economic progress is white America. It is the life style of middle-class white America that is displayed on television, in magazines, and in store windows, and when the gains of blacks since World War II are compared to those of whites, the black gains begin to pale. Davis reports that although the proportion of black homeowners today is a sizable 38 percent, whites had already surpassed that figure twenty years ago. In 1960, nearly 65 percent of whites lived in homes they owned. Although the percentage of blacks in white-collar jobs has doubled in recent years, in 1960 the white-collar category included only 13 percent of black workers but 44 percent of white ones. Although blacks have made substantial gains, their increases do not compare with those of whites. In several areas, such as infant mortality and income, the gap between black and white achievement and standards of living has actually widened slightly since 1940.

For example, in 1950, Negro infant mortality was 1.7 times as high as the white rate; in 1960 the Negro rate was 1.9 times the white rate. This relative lag in black progress occurred despite the fact that in absolute terms, black infant mortality had decreased. The white rate had also decreased—and at a relatively faster pace. So the relative gap widened.

Black Americans live in the world's richest nation, yet they are relatively deprived. Not only do they see the inequality of their situation, but they perceive it as unjust. Blacks have been treated unfairly by laws and social customs for centuries. The frustration and indignation based on this injustice makes the protests of black Americans understandable.

The principle of relative deprivation has also proven useful in explaining the behavior of some white Americans. In the fall of 1968, T. F. Pettigrew and R. T. Riley surveyed the supporters of George Wallace in his bid for the presidency. The site for the survey was Gary, Indiana; in this and other Northern cities, Wallace's main support came from blue-collar workers who belong to unions and identify with the working class. Those interviewed had substantial incomes; nearly half the Wallace supporters in Gary earned between $7,500 and $10,000 a year. Most of them had graduated from high school. Pettigrew and Riley hypothesized that Wallace's support was based at least in part on feelings of relative deprivation. To test the hypothesis, they asked both Wallace supporters and other Gary workers whether they agreed with the statement: "In spite of what some say, the condition of the average man is getting worse, not better." Not all the Gary workers felt relatively deprived; only about half the men surveyed agreed with the statement. But at every income level, men who did feel deprived were more likely to support Wallace. Of those who agreed with the item, 42 percent supported Wallace. Among those who disagreed, only 18 percent favored Wallace. Of those who said they had actually voted for Wallace, 68 percent indicated feelings of relative deprivation. Although the wages of Gary workers had increased in recent years, some workers believed that their profits were being eaten up by inflation and by taxes to pay for welfare programs for minority groups. Although other factors undoubtedly played a part, such feelings of relative deprivation help to explain Wallace's popularity.

INTERGROUP RELATIONS AND AMERICAN RACISM

In 1967, following racial disorders in major American cities, President Johnson appointed a Commission on Civil Disorders. The Commission reported that:

> White racism is essentially responsible for the explosive mixture that has been accumulating in our cities since the end of World War II. Race prejudice has shaped our history decisively and it now threatens to affect our future . . . What white America has never fully understood, but what the Negro can never forget, is that white society is deeply implicated in the (black) ghetto. White institutions created it, white institutions maintain it, and white society condones it.

Racism in a major social problem in America today. Although this chapter has illustrated the discussion of social-psychological processes underlying all kinds of intergroup relations with examples of black-white relations in America, the phenomenon of racism and what it entails has not yet been investigated in detail.

The investigation first requires that one distinguish between racist beliefs (attitudes) and racist actions (behavior). Feelings of ill will toward blacks as a group and derogatory stereotypes of Negroes are examples of *prejudice* (attitudes). Barring members of minority groups from restaurants, paying blacks lower wages than whites for equal work, enacting zoning laws to prevent any blacks from living in a particular area are all acts of *discrimination* (behavior). The relationship between attitudes and behavior was discussed in Chapter 26 and is relevant to the distinction between prejudice and discrimination. Although the two often go together, they do not always coincide. When there were laws demanding separate seating for blacks and whites on buses, even people who were not prejudiced against blacks typically complied. In order to avoid causing an embarrassing scene or possibly going to jail, they ignored their personal convictions and engaged in discriminatory behavior. Today, the laws have changed and the situation is reversed. There are undoubtedly prejudiced individuals who continue to ride buses and even to sit next to blacks, despite their personal feelings. They do this to comply with social norms and formal laws, to avoid being conspicuous or incurring social disapproval, and because compliance is necessary if they are to continue to use public transport.

It is commonly believed that behavior reflects attitudes and that in order to change discrimination, one must first eliminate prejudice. The notion that "laws can't change the hearts and minds of men" contains the assumption that although laws might change overt behavior, they cannot reach deeply held attitudes. However, the discussion of intergroup contact in this chapter and of the link between behavior change and attitude change in Chapter 26 suggests that this common-sense notion may be wrong. In situations where whites and blacks are forced to associate because of laws, social convention, or the desire to achieve some valued goal, their attitudes frequently do improve. In the Deutsch and Collins study, many white housewives were initially upset about living with blacks. They had moved to the biracial project because it offered the best available housing and because they valued having a comfortable apartment more than maintaining racial separation. After living in integrated housing, many came to enjoy their interracial contacts. Studies of the desegregation of department stores and hospitals, of housing, public transportation, and schools all demonstrate that when behavior is changed, the "heart and mind" are often subsequently affected. In fact, this strategy may be more effective than trying to eliminate prejudice in the hope of ultimately reducing discrimination. However, for the attitude change to take place, the *conditions of contact must be favorable;* they must follow the guidelines set down earlier in this chapter.

A distinction should be made between individual and institutional racism. *Individual racism* includes both personal prejudice and individual acts of discrimination. *Institutional racism* refers to institutional practices that maintain racial inequality and limit opportunities for blacks and other minorities. Discriminatory hiring practices, restrictive zoning codes, and segregated schools are instances of institutional racism. Although practices such as these are often carried out by a particular

Figure 28.11
An important contributor to recent prison unrest and riots is institutional racist practices. These black inmates of Attica State Prison in New York rebelled in protest of unfair and abominable conditions; one of their complaints was that the institution did not permit them to practice the Black Muslim religion. The institutional racism practiced by prison authorities is only the last instance in a long string of such instances that led to the almost solid mass of black faces in this photograph. Discrimination in many institutions—in schools, in employment practices, in law enforcement, and in the legal system—all contributed to the disproportionate numbers of black men in prisons.

individual, they are controlled by the norms and traditions of some social system, whether an informal group, a city council, a trade union, or the federal government. The person who carries out a racist policy may not always like his task, but he often accepts it because he believes "it's my job to do it," "we've always done it this way," or "you can't buck the system."

Institutional racism is not always intentional. For example, many large universities have adopted objective criteria for hiring professors, an important one being the number of books and articles that the candidate has published. These policies were instituted to ensure fairness and to raise the standards of the university, but they often serve to prevent capable blacks from joining a faculty. For a long time, many black professors taught at small colleges, where they had enormous teaching loads and little, if any, time or resources to conduct research. Thus, even the most competent black professor might not be able to meet criteria considered objective for white professors. Because the perpetuation of institutional racism does not depend on individual prejudice or on deliberate intentions to discriminate, the institutional practices may prove the most difficult barriers to the achievement of racial equality in the United States.

In the field of intergroup relations, the study of social-psychological theory and of social problems like racism often go hand in hand. By applying general principles to the case of American race relations, psychologists can test the validity and usefulness of their theories. In seeking to understand particular social problems, psychologists not only may be able to formulate new principles, they may be able to use theory in suggesting effective strategies for change.

SUGGESTED READINGS

ALLPORT, G. *The Nature of Prejudice.* Garden City, N.Y., Anchor Books, 1958. A classic but still vital analysis of different approaches to the study of prejudice and of the basic psychological processes involved.

GRIER, W. H., and COBBS, P. M. *Black Rage.* New York, Bantam, 1969. Two black psychiatrists present their views of what it means psychologically to be black in America in a book that is liberally sprinkled with details of the life histories of their patients.

KELMAN, H. C. (Ed.). *International Behavior: A Social-Psychological Analysis.* New York, Holt, Rinehart and Winston, 1965. New applications of the social-psychological concepts presented in this chapter—such as stereotypes and the effects of contact—are provided by this collection of articles on international relations.

MACK, R. (Ed.). *Race, Class and Power.* New York, American Book, 1968. A large assortment of short articles, both theoretical and empirical, on aspects of intergroup relations ranging from stereotypes in Brazil to the causes of race riots in America.

MARX, G. T. *Protest and Prejudice.* New York, Harper Torchbook, 1969. A survey of the attitudes of black Americans toward the civil rights movement and black militancy, and toward white Americans.

PETTIGREW, T. *Profile of the Negro American.* New York, Van Nostrand, 1964. A social psychologist discusses racial differences in health, intelligence, and crime, and applies concepts such as social role and relative deprivation to American race relations.

SIMPSON, G. E., and YINGER, J. M. *Racial and Cultural Minorities.* 3rd ed. New York, Harper & Row, 1965. A comprehensive discussion of both prejudice and discrimination that draws from both psychology and sociological theory and research. Examples include not only American race relations but anti-Semitism as well.

VAN DEN BERGHE, P. *South Africa: A Study in Conflict.* Berkeley, University of California Press, 1967. This detailed analysis of race relations in another country provides an interesting comparison with the discussion of American race relations in this chapter.

29
Intensive Groups

LIFE COMES AT DIFFERENT LEVELS of organization. There are viruses, which are rather like independent chromosomes, that get busily to work only after they are inside a cell. There are blue-green algae and bacteria, which have no separate nuclei and which may be rather analogous to independent nuclei. And then, of course, there are nucleated cells, which are most familiar to us—if only because our own bodies are composed of some fifty trillion of them.

Nucleated cells can exist singly, as independent organisms, or as colonies of undifferentiated or scarcely differentiated individuals, each of which can singly start a new colony, if necessary. Finally, cells can drown their individuality and abandon their free-living abilities in order to form a multicellular organism, which may be as simple as a flatworm, or as complicated as a giant sequoia, a whale, or a man.

As multicellular organisms ourselves, we tend to think of that stage as the peak of development, but of course it isn't. A complex organism by itself is scarcely better off than a cell by itself. For any but the simplest multicellular organisms, it takes two to reproduce. Family groupings of one sort or another will form, and larger groupings too: herds, schools, tribes, flocks—call them what you will. In the case of the social insects, such as ants, bees, and termites, the groups are so closely knit, the individuals within them are so specialized and in some cases so incapable of independent life that we seem to be dealing with what we might call a multiorganismic organism.

We would all, as multicellular organisms, readily agree that the complex organization of our fifty trillion cells produces a single whole that is greater than the sum of the individual cells. We would all judge that the individual cells gain more by their association into a human being than they lose by their inability to function independently.

As individual multicellular organisms, however, we would be less willing to agree that a complex society or state is greater than the sum of the individual organisms making it up. We would be less ready to judge that it is a cheap price to give up our individualism to become part of a society.

Yet the tug is there. It is as though we are at some stage of evolution between the multicellular and multiorganismic. We cling to our individuality, to our freedom to go our own way—and at the same time we yearn to belong, to have that special feeling of being part of a group.

I. A.

Somewhere in the United States right now a group of about a dozen or so people, surrounded by overflowing ashtrays and disposable coffee cups, are sitting in a rough circle and talking with each other somewhat like this:

Daphne: (to Jeff, angrily) *You keep patting me on the head. I don't understand how that could be a nice thing. Then you feel I misinterpret everything you do . . . which may be true.*

Jeff: (talking more softly) *I feel an affection for you, but it always seems to lead to difficulties.*

Daphne: *It starts off like I really like it, then I feel like a puppy-dog mascot you're patting on the head. Maybe it's you, maybe it's me.*

Jeff: *Maybe it's me. I've hit every girl in this group on the head. It's just an expression of affection.*

(At the same time, both Dave and Steve speak)

Dave: (with mockery) *Do you make a point of doing it?*

Steve: *Have you hit Cathy on the head?*

Jeff: *Why Cathy specifically?*

Steve: *Because she's the most dominant female in the group.*

Daphne: *All along in the group, I've felt assertive, but on the other hand, I pull back and feel bad for doing so.*

Jim, the Group Leader: *Many people are having a hard time communicating with Jeff. He has pats for everybody's head. He's an expert at disarming people. A number of times . . .*

D. MILLSAP

Members of a group like this one may meet for an hour or ten hours or even as long as thirty hours at a time. Although they probably entered as strangers, each may leave with intimate knowledge of the others' behavior patterns and with insights into their motives that not even their husbands or wives and close friends have. In the situation just described, for example, several people are beginning to realize how Jeff has tried to keep the women in a submissive position with patronizing gestures like pats on the head. Their discussion leads them to an examination of unconscious prejudices against women. Such insights are part of what this and other special groups try to accomplish: to make people more open to one another so that they begin to learn more about their own behavior and the behavior of others. The members hope that this learning process will lead to a richer interpersonal life outside the group, with husbands or wives, children, parents, friends, co-workers, bosses.

These groups differ from the naturally occurring groups discussed in the rest of the unit. The combination of intention and psychological focus differentiate them from all other groups. Although there are other kinds of groups that are deliberately formed—for example, chambers of commerce or chess clubs, which are oriented around tasks or interests—the groups that are examined in this chapter are unique in being intentionally formed to explore the psychological processes of the members.

Figure 29.1 *(opposite)*
The members of the hypothetical weekend group described in this chapter. In this drawing we see the intense interaction between Jeff and Daphne. He patronizingly pats her on the head. This gesture makes Daphne feel belittled and ineffective, and she confronts him angrily. Because Jeff has done this to other women in the group, his pattern is pointed out to him. One of the most beneficial aspects of such groups is that the members' behavior patterns can be examined in a relatively safe atmosphere; Jeff, therefore, has the opportunity to learn about his condescending behavior toward women and its effects upon their reactions to him.

ORIGINS

It was only after World War II that most of the efforts to develop intentional psychological groups began. K. Lewin, who founded the Research Center for Group Dynamics at the Massachusetts Institute of Technology, did much to encourage this work. Lewin initially wanted to change people's attitudes—including a person's attitudes toward himself—and he discovered that group discussions and group decision-making processes were powerful tools in motivating attitude change. During World War II rationing days, for example, Lewin found that group discussions helped persuade people to eat such unpopular foods as turnips, beef hearts, and kidneys.

In 1947, shortly after Lewin's death, his students started the National Training Laboratories (NTL) in Bethel, Maine, and later helped devise the T-group (training group), one of the earliest types of intentional psychological groups. L. Bradford and his colleagues report that in the T-groups organized by NTL for industry and gradually for groups outside of industry, it was found that individuals often had very deep personal experiences of change as a result of the trusting, caring relationship that developed in the group itself.

Another aspect of the movement toward the intentional-group experience was taking place at about the same time at the University of Chicago. Immediately after World War II, C. Rogers and his associates at the university were asked by the Veterans Administration to create a brief but intensive course of training that would prepare men—all of whom had at least a master's degree—to work effectively as personal counselors with returning GIs. The staff felt that no amount of ordinary classroom training would prepare these men, so they experimented with an intensive-group experience in which the trainees met for several hours each day in order to understand themselves better, to become aware of attitudes that might be self-defeating in the counseling relationship, and to relate to each other in ways that would be helpful and that could carry over into their counseling work. This attempt to tie together experiential and cognitive learning in a process that had therapeutic value for the individual provided many deep and meaningful experiences for the trainees and was so successful in a sequence of groups that the staff continued to use this procedure in summer workshops thereafter.

Some psychologists began working with groups of mental patients, using the techniques of intentional groups for therapeutic goals. Others insisted that the group

Figure 29.2
Kurt Lewin was a social psychologist who began his research in Germany and then continued it in America. His pioneering work in group process and outcomes has contributed important theories and research methods to the area known as group dynamics. His influence reaches outside the academic discipline because of his interest in practical applications of his work.

Table 29.1—Types of Groups

Group	Emphasis
T-group	Originally tended to emphasize human relations *skills* but has become much broader in its approach.
Encounter group (or basic encounter group)	Tends to emphasize personal growth and development and improvement in interpersonal communication through the experiencing of these things.
Sensitivity-training group	May resemble either T-group or encounter group.
Task-oriented group	Widely used in industry; focuses on the task of the group in its interpersonal context.
Sensory-awareness group, body-awareness group, body-movement group	Tends to emphasize physical awareness and physical expression through movement, spontaneous dance, and the like.
Creativity workshop	Focuses on creative expression through various art media.
Organizational-development group	Primarily aimed at leadership growth ability.
Team-building group	Used in industry to develop more closely knit and effective working teams.
Gestalt group	Emphasis on a Gestalt therapeutic approach where an expert therapist focuses on one individual at a time but from a diagnostic and therapeutic point of view.
Synanon group or "game"	Developed in the treatment of drug addicts by Synanon; tends to emphasize almost violent attack on the defenses of the participants.

Figure 29.3
Exercises that increase physical sensitivity are often used in groups. In the photograph, the two persons have been asked to touch each other's faces without speaking or seeing. By depriving them of sight and speech, the leader hopes that the people will perceive and react to each other in new ways.

techniques were appropriate only for people free of mental disorder, and in fact the great majority of groups currently in operation are composed of "normal" people.

TYPES OF GROUPS

Table 29.1 describes some of the variations in form and purpose that intentional groups can take. The activities of groups may be very controlled and task-oriented like those at the bottom of the table, or they may be more expressive, spontaneous, and free like those at the top. As their popularity grows, psychological groups proliferate faster than one can categorize them. Each entry in the table actually represents dozens of similar groups going by different names.

Psychological groups vary in the amount of time that people spend together and in the settings in which they take place. Some groups meet for one hour three times a week for a year; some meet only once for four or sixteen or more hours. Groups can meet in a beautiful California redwood forest or in a shabby Manhattan apartment; they may be conducted in "growth centers," businesses, universities, or even agencies of the federal government. In America alone, there are probably hundreds of thousands of people who have found their way into one or more of these several kinds of intentional groups.

Why They Form

What are the reasons for the rapidly increasing popularity of psychological groups? It has been suggested that psychological factors in modern American society have caused people to seek a new way of making sense of their lives and of relating to others. The strong American emphasis on rationality and the achievement of difficult goals through diligent, hard work sets very high standards for individual performance, not only at work but at home as well. As their society becomes increasingly large and complex, people often sense a loss of power and meaning in their lives.

Many people turn to psychological groups to find the security, camaraderie, and love that they miss in daily life. The norms in psychological groups often emphasize feeling and emotion rather than reason, and the group situation encourages each person to look inward and express feelings openly. In the group everyone tries to

Figure 29.4
In this interracial group, white policemen and black militants met in order to encounter each other. The aim was to increase each group's understanding and tolerance of the other, with the ultimate goals of increasing cooperation and reducing tensions in the community. One of the techniques used was to have the members "exchange races" by wearing a white or black mask and role-playing a member of that race. This method gives each person the opportunity to experience, in an immediate fashion, the behavior, attitudes, and self-concept of the other group.

Figure 29.5
Carl Rogers is shown with members of a "basic encounter group," of which he was the leader. Rogers (top left) has adapted his "client-centered" therapy approach to the encounter group situation. He attempts to create a warm, accepting, and safe atmosphere in which the group members can evolve a direction and relate to each other. He avoids the use of techniques and exercises. Instead, he facilitates the communication of feelings and attitudes between members. His chief aim is the personal growth of the members through exploration of the interpersonal relationships within the group.

develop sensibilities, and to do so must put aside striving to achieve and produce. The group situation suspends the norms of the real world, so that people feel free to engage in extreme behaviors or to divulge painful truths.

Ideally, a climate of mutual trust develops out of a sense of mutual freedom—the freedom to express real feelings, whether positive or negative. Each person moves toward greater acceptance of his total being—his emotional, intellectual, and physical being—as it now is, including its potential. The ideal within the group is that everyone is accepted for what he or she is, and group members often feel from the very beginning that the people they are with will not abuse their trust. Although the experience of instant trust can be reassuring, it can also lead occasionally to the betrayal of trust and to misplaced trust.

What They Can Accomplish

Some people have very exaggerated expectations about psychological groups. They may hope in one weekend to buy instant therapy or an instant identity. No group can effect a personality change overnight. Successful groups are often able, however, to develop skills of interpersonal relations for people who have not had the opportunity to interact honestly with others and in turn to get honest feedback about how they appear to others and about the kind of impact they have in interpersonal relationships (see Chapter 23).

A HYPOTHETICAL GROUP

Most of the rest of the chapter traces the development of a typical weekend encounter group that might have occurred near any large city in America. The dialogue at the beginning of the chapter is a sample from this fictional encounter weekend led by a man we shall call Jim Olson. As you read along, you will see that the sections in italics dramatize the kinds of things that happen in psychological

Figure 29.6
Frederick ("Fritz") Perls is portrayed in this photographic essay of a Gestalt group. Perls was the founder and chief developer of Gestalt therapy; he also pioneered its application to groups. In most Gestalt groups, the leader "works" individually with a member who wishes to explore a problem, wish, dream, or other concern. Thus, the group is highly structured, especially compared with Rogers' "basic encounter group." A Gestalt therapist's methods are designed to increase the person's awareness of his own experiencing and behavior and of the behavior of others. He also helps the person deal with unresolved feelings toward significant persons in his life so that he can increase his ability to function effectively in the present, unhampered by "unfinished situations."

groups and illustrate the concepts and processes discussed throughout the chapter. At this point, you may want to read through the italicized excerpts to get the flavor of the group's progress.

The six men and five women—all except one forty-year-old—were between the ages of twenty-four and thirty-five. Each had driven from his own separate niche in an always modernizing world to a rickety wooden house in the country for an "encounter-group weekend." Some had read about the group in a local entertainment weekly; others had heard of it from friends who had previously been to such weekends.

In their suburbs and college towns they had read the advertisement: "Experience the full expression of your human potential!" Who could feel that he had been fully expressing his human potential? So they came, even the skeptics, thinking that it was unlikely a weekend could free their human potential—but it was worth a try.

This group is actually a composite drawn from a number of different types of psychological groups; only some of the events described would typically occur in any given encounter group. In the text, we have tried to describe the general processes that occur in all psychological groups. Many of the explanations given, however, have grown out of extensive research conducted on one special kind of intentional group made up of college students who met several times a week for a semester under the supervision of social psychologists. The groups set up by R. F. Bales at Harvard represent a pioneering effort along these lines. By carefully observing and testing such special groups, psychologists have tried to get a better understanding of general group processes.

LEADERSHIP

All groups have individuals who stand out because of the way they influence group patterns of communication and behavior. In groups with an intentional psychological focus we distinguish between two kinds of leaders. One is the formally ascribed group leader, the person who has been defined at the outset as the person in charge of the group. The second is the emergent leader, the person who gains special prominence in the group and helps determine its direction.

The Ascribed Leader

As the participants entered the cottage, they were greeted by the man designated as group leader for the weekend, a veteran of many encounter groups and marathons. "Call me Jim," he replied, when they asked if he was the Mr. Olson they had spoken to on the phone. Each participant checked into an assigned room for the weekend and handed Jim an envelope containing a check for the cost of room, board, and leader's fee, a total of $115 for the weekend.

They later entered the meeting room for the first session and sat on the chairs arranged around the room. Only Gayle, the older woman, sat on the floor on a large pillow, as if to show that she too was young and with it.

An awkward silence descended as people sat down. Some glanced furtively at the others, but few eyes met. Only Jim smiled back. Others glued their eyes to the floor, or looked off into space, as if thinking deeply.

Gradually everyone shifted his attention to Jim in the hope of getting some clue about how to proceed. Jim began, "This group is yours. The more open and honest you are, the deeper the experience will be. The only rule is that there is to be no physical violence. Also, each person has the right to refuse to do anything asked of him. But remember that your openness determines the worth of this weekend. My job is to help you become more sensitive to yourselves and to encounter each other."

Some group leaders use their role to actively influence the group and may draw out and cajole people to express themselves. The strong trust in the experienced leader, it is argued, can be used to pull people out of their shy, inhibited, or withdrawn states. By drawing upon his own special training and technical expertise, an active leader may suggest exercises of various kinds and tell the group what to do in order

Figure 29.7
The leader of the weekend encounter group greets the members and asks that they call him Jim. By being relaxed and informal, he hopes to promote the members' sense of ease. However, he provides few ground rules, aside from his advice that they be open and his prohibition against physical violence. This minimal structuring means that the members must deal with their anxiety and uncertainty about relating to each other and about giving direction to the group. Out of the resulting interactions, the group's goals and norms and the members' roles begin to emerge.

to help the group move toward its goals. He may offer interpretation of events in the group and of the behavior of some of the members.

At the other extreme are groups that have no ascribed leader at all. Advocates of leaderless groups contend that the imposition of a difference in power and status predetermines the group structure; these believe that the group should create its own structure, based on its goals. They argue that providing the group with a leader may cause it to focus on the leader rather than on the relationships among people in the group. The presence of authority also may inhibit the expressions of true feelings because people in the group feel that the leader is not involved in the group in the same way that they are.

The style that an ascribed group leader adopts depends on his or her conceptions of the best uses of authority. Many leaders disavow the term leadership and think of themselves instead as *facilitators* or *trainers* who help people in the group communicate with one another. They may use their expertise to point to subtle and often hidden issues in a group interaction. Some leaders use their authoritative role in order to understand a person's relationship to authority better. The kinds of attitudes that people in the group express toward the leader often lead to insights about relationships they have had with other authority figures in their lives.

Even when the formal leader tries not to control or direct his group, his special position nevertheless affects people in the group and influences group processes. The group leader may have brought the others together and chosen them from among an indefinite number of applicants. He claims expertise and has had previous experience with the situation in which the others are soon to find themselves; he may be getting paid. These reasons and others make the leader's position in the group fundamentally different from the others'; so his every intervention can direct the group in a new way. Whether by suggestions of exercises or games, by forceful interpretation, or by enforced silence, he affects group processes in ways that are sometimes unnoticed or intentionally ignored by the group.

Emergent Leadership

Jim's opening remarks to the group were followed by another short silence, but Bill jumped in this time, "I'm Bill. I think we should introduce ourselves and say why we came here. Someone should begin, and then we can go around the room."

Some members stirred as if about to speak, but there was no immediate response. "If no one wants to speak, I'll start. As I said, I'm Bill and I'm here because I think today's society is a terrible place to live. You're next, what's your name?"

Daphne glanced at Jim to see if all this was what he meant and began, "I'm Daphne. I'm looking forward to knowing you all, and getting close to you."

As people in the group begin to interact, some of them begin to emerge as central figures; members who gain influence and dominance are called *emergent leaders.* What strengths and abilities does an emergent leader possess? When members of a small group are asked to rate each other on leadership, they most often seem to use three criteria.

The first of these is *power,* and Bill's performance in the group shows how he exercises it. He is verbally active and willing to take the initiative in the discussion right away. This ability makes it possible for him to influence others, and he does in fact influence them—sometimes aginst their will. For example, Bill gets others to talk, even though some of them might prefer to remain silent.

A second important leadership quality is *likeability*—the ability to elicit positive feelings from other people in the group. Likeability follows the same general principle that underlies attraction (see Chapter 27): a person is well-liked to the extent that he is rewarding to others. In the group setting a likeable person is usually one who creates new opportunities for group interaction and who helps to establish a

Figure 29.8
Bill (seated) quickly emerges as a leader. He responds to the uncomfortable initial silence by suggesting introductions; his suggestion turns to a demand, as he introduces himself and then coerces Daphne to be next. He often repeats this pattern in the group; he gains his leadership more through power than through likability.

positive, trusting atmosphere. Daphne seems to have this ability; she may not be as powerful as Bill, but her rewarding qualities make her a leader also.

In assessing leadership qualities, people in the group use a third criterion: the ability of a leader to help the group succeed in its chosen tasks. In intentional groups *task success* means the ability to help others gain insight into themselves and to get the group to reach its goals.

Leadership abilities may be exercised in a number of ways. In a group discussion, for example, the leader may perform a particular task himself, like giving reasons for a particular event, or he may elicit and coordinate the different opinions of the other members. Occasionally one person possesses a combination of power, likeability, and task-success characteristics that makes him a uniquely gifted leader. Perhaps more frequently leadership is exercised by several people in the group, each of whom possesses different leadership qualities. At the same time there may also be considerable conflict among these contending leaders. Even in groups that define themselves as truly egalitarian, one can observe group leaders emerging and attempting to enhance their personal power or control and direct toward themselves the rewards of other people in the group. For example, Daphne's statements show that she may be trying to attract all of the group's feelings of warmth and trust.

ROLES

The members introduced themselves, some using their real names, some using false names. No one gave his surname, nor did anyone describe his occupation or place of residence. A discussion ensued about how to continue. One person spoke after another, often without taking the personal comments of the previous speakers very seriously—everyone was anxious to talk. The middleaged woman, Gayle, told of a group her daughter was in where the people had become very close to each other.

Bill burst out, "Why can't you talk about yourself? It's because of you we're not getting close to each other. Why did you come here? You're older than the rest of us and you insist on sitting on the floor while we're all up here. If you want to be close you'll have to stop avoiding us."

Cathy looked at Gayle, "Gayle really does want to be with us: She's sitting on the floor to show us she's not too old for this or for us. If she talks about her daughter, Bill, it's to do just what you *want.*

The different personality types of people in the group soon become apparent. We have already seen that Bill is dominant and that Daphne is likeable, but now more complex roles are being established. Gayle has been made a target for some

Figure 29.9
Bill's aggressive criticism of Gayle results in the beginnings of a division of members' roles in the group. Cathy quickly becomes a *defender,* while Gayle may become the *scapegoat* for Bill's (and others') anxieties. By adopting a certain behavioral consistency, or role, a person reduces his discomfort and uncertainty over how he should behave in the group. Often, the person is confronted about his role; thus, we should not be surprised to find Bill criticized eventually for his aggressiveness or Gayle confronted for allowing herself to be the scapegoat.

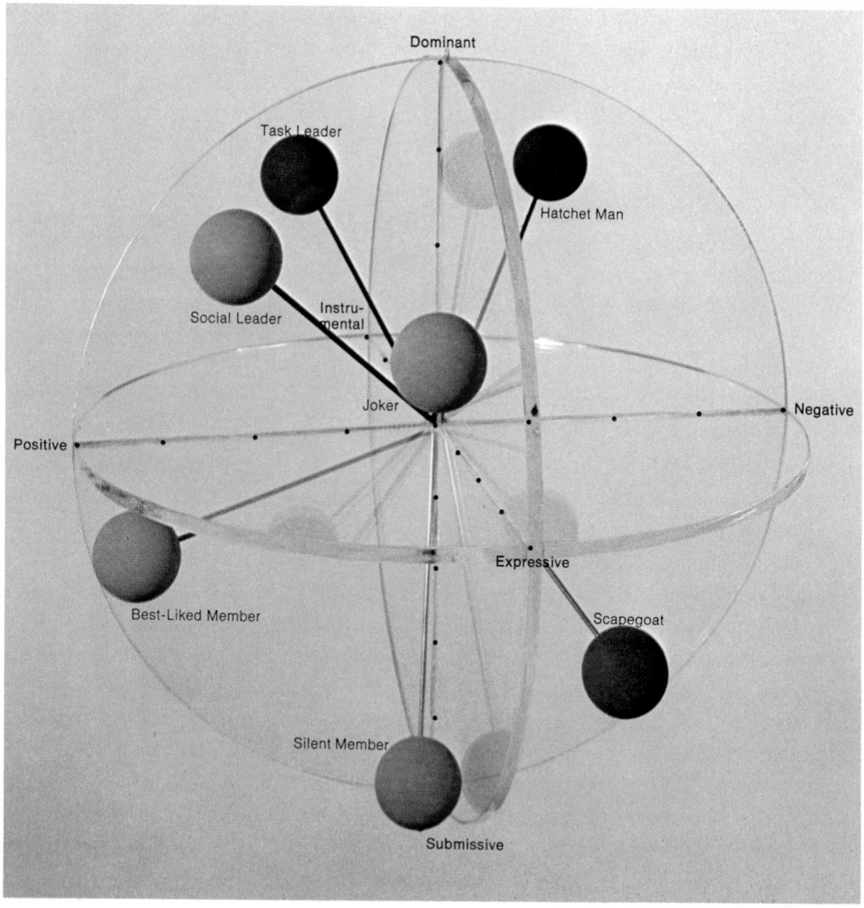

Figure 29.10
Some possible group member's roles are located in a three-dimensional group space; the construction is based on an analysis of small groups by R. F. Bales. The dimensions of the analysis are Dominant-Submissive, Expressive-Instrumental, and Positive-Negative. By focusing upon one role at a time, you can delineate its characteristics. For example, Bill is emerging as a *hatchetman:* according to the diagram, we would expect his behavior to be dominant and instrumental (oriented toward a task or a direction and away from feelings); the group's reaction to him is rather negative. According to Bales, the best-liked member of any group is generally expressive and tends to be somewhat submissive. If you have been in an intensive group and can remember certain people as occupying these roles, determine whether their characteristics on these dimensions correspond to Bales' conceptions.

of the other people's anxiety over the slow progress of the group; Bill has become a moody and aggressive attacker; Cathy has shown herself as a defender.

Several roles are formed during a group, and after many confrontations, like the one between Bill and Gayle, a group structure is established. It is hard for the members of a group to believe, after the slow and painful process of setting up this structure, that theirs is similar to those found in most other groups. Research done by P. E. Slater has shown, however, that there are certain functions within any group that are taken up by its members.

The three aspects of emergent leadership—power, likeability, and task success —are dimensions in this respect. Thus, we have Bill—very dominant, not very likeable, and somewhat task-oriented—whose combination of leadership assets and liabilities contributes to his role as *hatchet man.* Another role is that of the *joker;* he or she is usually very likeable, extremely expressive, and neither very dominant nor submissive. See if you can find the joker in the remaining excerpts.

Major Participants

D. Dunphy has described five different roles that are often observed in groups whose ascribed leader does not directly suggest how the group should behave: the emergent group leader, the aggressor, the scapegoat, the seducer, and the idol. According to Dunphy, a group spends most of its time involved in the dramatic interactions between these major participants. In the preceding excerpt, Gayle has become the scapegoat; Bill, the aggressor. Cathy's conciliatory attitude is part of the role of the idol. We have not yet seen anyone assume the role of the seducer—someone to bring up sex and intimacy as possibilities for conversation or even action. Group roles develop only gradually, and not all roles are necessarily represented in all groups. Some roles emerge just as conspicuously by their absence, like the role of silent person, who is extremely submissive and not highly rated on either likeability or task success. This role does not emerge early in the group because few people have had the opportunity to say anything yet.

Figure 29.11
Rick's suggestion that the members discuss their goals is a good one. By clarifying their aims and expectations, they can help eliminate possible misconceptions about what the group can or will provide. People who are in an intensive group for the first time often have such misconceptions.

Checking on Roles

It is often helpful for the group to spend time becoming aware of its own structure. Checking on group roles must be done periodically because roles can change throughout the group. An illustration of such checking is at the beginning of the chapter, when other persons in the group identify Jeff as a dominating, masculine aggressor, a role relationship that had gone unnoticed until that time.

GOALS

Rick leaned forward and spoke to Cathy, "That's an important problem you refer to. But, let's not go so fast. Let's try to come to a consensus about why we are here in the first place."

Rick is asking about the group's goals. Psychological groups of this sort have many unstated goals—for example, getting closer to each other as individuals and reducing feelings of anger and aggression while expanding feelings of love and empathy.

Goals can also be stated openly. Quite often people in a group will begin by making a kind of contract with the leader, or with one another. The contract sets forth the goals of the group as explicitly as possible and establishes certain basic rules for starting and stopping sessions, acceptable behavior during group time, and so on. Jim's opening remark about fuller experience as a group goal is an example. Rick, however, is eager to be more specific about these vague goals. The kind of discussion Rick wants is often fruitful because people in the group find out that each wants a different reward from the same experience. By openly discussing their wants and expectations, they can agree about what they are trying to do and how they might accomplish it. Or if they cannot agree, they can at least come to understand their disagreements.

Specified Goals

By their nature, special kinds of groups are set up with specifically defined goals. Some intentional groups are formed to render cure through therapy. Some are formed to develop a person's awareness of how he or she is involved in some contemporary issue—such techniques as *consciousness-raising,* for example, may be used for men's and women's groups, for interracial encounter, or even for international encounter. Other groups foster the development of interpersonal skills through concentration on a person's sensitivity to others. Still others try to expand a person's capacity for self-expression by the elicitation of intense *peak experiences,* in which the person feels for a time overwhelmed by psychological input. All of these goals are facilitated by the group's concentration on the psychological processes of the here-and-now.

Evaluation of Success

How does a group evaluate its success in reaching its goals? Groups often develop by themselves an aura of good feeling by the end of the session. The previous chapter's discussion of group-think shows the dangers that may follow from failure to evaluate an aura of good feeling objectively. People in an intentional group can mistake this good feeling for success in the task they set up at the beginning, but they usually find that the feeling is short-lived: only days later they consider their accomplishments and wonder how they could have felt so elated, effective, and satisfied. This is one place where the leader can be useful: he can help the group make a realistic evaluation of its own experience of success.

Norms

People began to talk about previous situations where real intimacy had developed in their lives. They also talked of disappointments in other groups, especially with friends, former schoolmates, and work colleagues. The conversation jumped from one person to another and from one kind of setting to another.

Bill and Jane grew more sullen as the discussion continued. Bill finally spoke, "Listen, this is so disorganized, we're not getting anywhere."

Della, who had just told a personal story of how her family had grown apart, was furious. "You, how can you say that, you're always hogging the group's time."

Cathy agreed, "Yeah, each person has the right to say what he feels."

We have been talking all along about different kinds of norms or standards of behavior. Some norms are stated quite explicitly. At the very beginning, Jim made it clear that everyone should be open and honest and that there should be no physical violence or coercion.

Over time, a set of *emergent norms* will also appear in the group; these are created by the members themselves. When emergent norms are openly stated or otherwise acknowledged by the group, they can be talked about and perhaps be

Figure 29.12
Bill criticizes the group members for their "disorganized" discussion about intimacy and disappointments; his remark is met by Della's and Cathy's strong opposition. He has attempted to oppose the group norm of open discussion about feelings. His power as emergent leader is not as influential as is this group norm, and he is successfully challenged. Norms function as strong guides to group behavior; effective leaders must be aware of the particular group's norms.

changed. In other cases, however, the group norms remain below the surface; precisely because they are unacknowledged, they can be very difficult to change. Whether they are acknowledged or unacknowledged, group norms—like the norms of society at large discussed in Chapter 25—exert powerful controls on behavior in the group. As R. Whitman writes, "The group forms its own history and constructs its own standards and modes of behavior, and once fixed, they are extremely difficult to alter. . . . They have almost the binding effect of laws; for the social punishment when they are broken (such as disapproval, ostracism, and hostility) is as severe as its equivalent prison sentence in Western society."

Group Mind

Sometimes people in the group recognize a norm that they had not recognized before. Perhaps there has been a covert agreement not to talk about certain things; thus, someone might suddenly realize that "we do not talk about sex in this group" or "we always let Gayle say whatever she wants." Sometimes there is a belief in a *group mind* that arranges the events of the group independently. It is spoken of as a single entity with its own life and character—for instance, "what does the group think about . . . ?" or "I wanted to tell something to the group today." Actually, the group mind is nothing more than a set of implicit norms shared by all the members of the group. The norms have not been publicly identified, but they nonetheless play a large part in determining the group's agenda.

Figure 29.13
Patrick is the "silent member" of the group. According to Bales' system (see Figure 29.10, p. 575), his behavior is characterized as submissive; he is neither instrumental nor expressive. Bales' Interaction Process Analysis would show few communications to Patrick, and few from him to group members. In short, he is silent and unknown. In almost all groups, this member becomes conspicuous by his silence, and he becomes the focus of attempts to "get him to open up."

Democratic Ideology

Examples of emergent norms were displayed in Della's angry plea for equal shares of time and in Cathy's insistance on each person's right to say what he feels. These emergent norms derive from the democratic ideology of groups in general. But over time this ideology may change. Group members often want to set up an egalitarian system, but they do not want to be bored by a dull talker, even though he is taking the equal share of the time guaranteed him by a formal democracy. They often settle instead for a system in which the more passive people in the group can interrupt the more dominant and talkative ones when they feel they have something to say. After a time there develops a number of norms concerning who can talk or interrupt —something like a tacitly accepted pecking order.

The norm that members should be spontaneous, like the norm of democracy, can sometimes appear to be operative when it really is not. Some people use "spontaneous" hugs or verbal attacks to mask their real feelings; gestures like these, as Chapter 23 points out, may actually be well-rehearsed maneuvers to avoid a truly honest response to another.

COMMUNICATION PROCESSES

Although the processes of communication that take place in intentional psychological groups may be quite complex, we can begin to understand them by making some systematic observations about verbal and nonverbal communication patterns.

Verbal

We can observe the verbal communication processes by noting how often each person enters the group discussion and how much time he or she spends talking.

Daphne: *Jim, is there something we can do to help Pat? He's always silent.*
Jane: *You always ask Jim everything. I think we could do better ourselves.*
Bill: *That's right, Jane.*
Della: *Daphne raised an important problem. You know I think that Pat is like a sphinx.*
Dave: *And Jim is like a sphincter.* (Group laughs.)

Such data help us understand much about the group's structure. For example, a tabulation of the communication acts of a group might show that those members who seem dominant are the ones who initiate the most acts of communication and whose speeches are longest. We can continue our systematic observation of communication patterns by making a table of who speaks to whom. This information reveals a great deal about the relationships among people in the group. Who addresses the group as a whole rather than individuals? Who is always talking to the leader? Which pairs of members address most of their remarks exclusively to each other? Observing who speaks after whom and who interrupts whom often shows who a person's supporters and challengers are.

A more extensive examination of group communication processes must, of course, take into account the content of people's statements. R. F. Bales developed the Interaction Process Analysis, one popular method of analyzing the communication process. Bales' method is a scheme for categorizing each act of communication not only in terms of who is addressing whom but also in terms of the type of interaction involved, such as asking for a suggestion or giving an opinion. The scheme is presented in Figure 29.14. In the above excerpt, for example, Daphne asks for a suggestion but addresses her question to Jim. Jane's response to Daphne is hostile, and she gives her opinion to the group as a whole. Bill agrees with Jane. Dave's statement addressed to the group as a whole falls into the category of dramatizing, and the group responds by laughing.

Nonverbal

In observing communication processes in a group, psychologists also consider the more subtle, less obvious ways in which people communicate. Some of these were discussed in Chapter 23. For instance, a person's tone of voice or speaking style can communicate meanings and emotions that are not conveyed by his words. Nonverbal behaviors, such as gesture, posture, and position in relation to others, also give information about interpersonal relationships. Often, one can tell that a group is interested and involved in a discussion by the fact that everyone is leaning

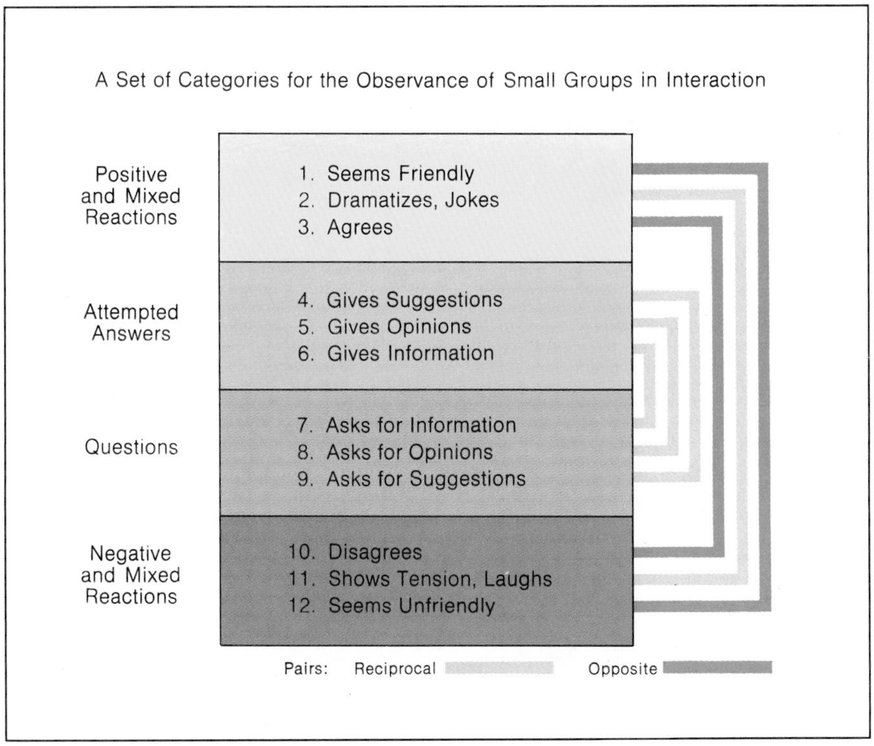

Figure 29.14
R. F. Bales' Interaction Process Analysis method uses the categories shown in this table. This scheme can be used to analyze not only the behavior of intensive groups, such as the hypothetical one in this chapter, but also the behavior of task-oriented groups, such as a team of corporate executives. For each member, a "profile" can be obtained that describes the extent and nature of his participation in the group. Also, the relationship between *pairs* of group members can be analyzed by using these categories to describe the communications between them.

forward. Even the symbolic or metaphorical meaning of statements may be important. Thus, in the last excerpt we might pay special attention to the link between the silence of Pat ("the sphinx") and the reference to Jim ("sphincter"). Those who study groups often analyze metaphors, fantasies, and references to dreams in groups to understand deeper levels of motivation and feeling.

PHASES OF GROUP DEVELOPMENT

Psychological groups pass through five general phases of development. In any one group, some phases may be particularly important while others are hardly noticeable. The experienced group observer can usually find some elements of every phase in all groups.

The group had taken the night before off, saying that the meeting room was not conducive to real intimacy and they would rather go out on the town. The next morning, the group spent the first five minutes in tense silence. Dave coughed. Cathy started tapping her foot on the floor. She was joined by others. They stopped. The following occurred in short, rapid spurts, punctuated by anxious laughter and long silences.

Gayle: *Was it a rough night? . . .* (whispers) *How long are we supposed to be quiet for?*

Rick: *Shh.*

Figure 29.15
The group is moving beyond the phase of testing boundaries and appears to be creating its own unique norm with respect to Jim, the leader. Jane (left), Gayle (center), and Cathy (right) participate in a not-so-gentle discussion of the group's relation to Jim. Jane and Gayle make comments about Jim's "stifling" influence. Although the group members are somewhat uncomfortable during this conversation, they are at an important phase in the group's development: they are dealing with their obstacles to intimacy, and if they can handle this phase successfully, they will be able to share the intimate interactions that they desire.

Jeff: *We're trying to set a record.*
Daphne: *Oh, yeah . . .*
Rick: *How about the days?*
Gayle: *Those too . . . funny thing . . .* (pause)
Della: *Seems like a really long time since yesterday.*
Rick: *Ooh . . .*
Cathy: *Were we here yesterday?*
Della: *Yesterday?* (long pause)
Jane: *Have we revolted yet?*
Gayle: *Of course!* (pause)
Rick: *I was wondering the same thing . . . when I was thinking about calling home.*
Daphne: *Revolted against what?*
Steve: *Against the leader . . . and whether we have gained our independence or not . . . maybe if we decide we have, we have.* (scattered laughter)
Jane: *Pretty revolting group.*
Gayle: *Does anyone feel that Jim is stifling our . . . um . . .* (Dave shakes his head) *. . . No, I didn't think so . . . do you think so?*
Patrick: *That he's what?*
Gayle: *God.* (laughter)
Daphne: *I think you wouldn't have said it if you didn't mean it.*
Gayle: *What?*
Daphne: *You wouldn't have said* that *if you hadn't meant it at the time.*
Gayle: *But . . . I did mean it but I meant it to . . . but then when . . . I meant it if it was agreed with.* (scattered laughter)

Early Phases

Presentation of Self The first phase in the development of any group is the presentation of self. (Chapter 23 discusses research on this topic.) At the very beginning, when the participants meet for the first time, they often try to fashion a favorable image of themselves in the group situation. They have preconceptions about what should happen in a group; they are simultaneously unsure of what to do and eager to do something. Initial attempts to make decisions about group norms fail, and people may for a time become discouraged about the possibilities of ever really getting close to each other.

Testing Boundaries and Modeling Roles The second phase is characterized by testing boundaries and modeling roles. The participants have advanced beyond the original encounter to a point where they can try out new roles for themselves in the group to see how others will react. They now attempt to assess one another's commitments and contributions to the group. The boundaries that restrict behavior, like Jim's rule against coercion, are cautiously tested to see if they are really strong, to see just how far one can go and still be safe. People in the group spend some time at this point challenging the leader's source of power or taking on his functions themselves or trying to force him into acting out their stereotype of a leader's role.

Creation of Norms In the third phase, the group attempts to create its own special set of norms. People attempt to bring to light and challenge the rules and expectations that have governed their previous behavior in the group. Because people see the group as a very special situation that should have its own unique norms, they often reject such outside cultural norms as the dominance of men over women and societal prohibitions about touching people in public. As people in the group question the norms that obstruct progress toward the group goals of intimacy and insight, their expressions of hostility against the ascribed leader may become more extreme; this process seems to be occurring in the preceding excerpt. People in other groups have been known to suggest that the leader leave the room, "just as an experiment," so that they can be alone.

Later in the course of group development, people often show less concern about authority and power issues; instead, they become concerned with one another. This fourth phase of development is *achieving intimacy and insight.* In a sense, this is what the group is for. The final phase is *termination,* where the group comes to terms with its own ending and the separation of the members. The following sections discuss the fourth and fifth phases in greater detail.

Achieving Intimacy and Insight

Daphne and Jeff have been hostile to each other. (See the excerpt at the beginning of the chapter.) *Daphne now tells of the loss of her dearest friend in an auto accident and Jeff comes over to Daphne and hugs her.*

Daphne: *This gesture . . . you don't know how much it means to me. That was the first feeling that I was accepted. Your pats on the head, those were condescending, but now I felt just plain loved.*

As the group members begin to explicitly express their positive and negative feelings and to reveal deeper personal experiences, the work of the group reaches its most difficult and most rewarding phase. People in the group now move between the expression of feelings and the attempt to understand them; the twin products of their efforts are intimacy in group feeling and insight into their own and others' problems.

People in the group often move into this phase with expressions of strong personal hostility to a group member who is perceived as blocking progress or taking too large a share of the group's time. Confrontation among group members increases as they refuse to accept each other's defenses against insight and openness. These strong or gentle attacks can only occur when people have come to feel some security in the situation; they begin to see each confrontation as a step toward intimacy, acceptance of one another, and—for the victim of the attack—self-acceptance.

There is, of course, one danger: The group may overestimate its healing capacity and open wounds it cannot close. People in the group often concentrate heavily on the harmful and annoying aspects of another person's personal style or pattern

Figure 29.16
Jeff is deeply moved by Daphne's sorrow, and expresses his feelings by hugging her. This genuine display of his emotions contrasts markedly with the paternal "pats on the head" he had given Daphne earlier. During the later phases of a group, spontaneous sharing of feelings between members often occurs; this happens only when a climate of sufficient trust has been developed, to allow people to risk such behavior. Sometimes the emerging norm is for only positive emotions or only negative emotions to be expressed. This is unfortunate, in that these norms deny the members the chance to express and understand both types of reactions.

of interaction. In doing so they may fail to see why this style is maintained and the useful function it serves in the individual's life. In the group, Gayle is attacked for being maternal; but in her societal role as mother, the same behavior may be useful, appropriate, and adaptive. A helpful approach is to distinguish between appropriate and inappropriate situations for a particular pattern of behavior. If people in the group are insensitive to this distinction, their attacks can harm the victim by leaving him defenseless and confused.

Most groups cherish especially the moments of *basic encounter* when the actions of one person touch another person in the deepest way, bringing the two people a feeling of oneness. Through such encounters the group moves to a more open and positive expression of feeling. Not everyone in the group experiences the same emotions or has the same reaction to the group itself. There is often a strong norm that inhibits potentially negative comments about the group at this stage; people then pretend that all feelings are good ones. On the other hand, if group members accept mixed or hostile feelings, they succeed in making the group experience more similar to the complexity of life outside the group; in this case, the security of the group setting becomes a situation in which people can learn new and more satisfactory ways to deal with their emotions.

Termination

The last hour after the last coffee break. Lots of laughing that stops abruptly. Steve has not arrived yet and Jeff notices it.

Jeff: *How can someone miss last rites or extreme unction?*

Rick: (counting all the people) *Eleven.*

Patrick: *Once upon a time . . .*

Daphne: *It's like wishing you wouldn't know when you're going to die. Just die one night in your sleep . . . when you're having a good time.*

Steve: (enters) *I just called my mother—she calls herself the old gray-hair—that's why I'm late.*

Rick: *I had a fantasy about the group while I was walking here for this last meeting. Gayle went around to each of us and kissed us. Kissed us good-bye . . . you know, nothing really heavy but . . .* (laughter) *and then somehow we were to be placed in positions in the room that . . . showed how much we got out of the group . . .*

Bill: *That's interesting.*

Gayle: *That's nice.*

Jeff: *That's actually a very nice last sacrament.*

Gayle: *What does it mean?*

Jeff: *We've talked about Jim as father, but then we fantasized about you, Gayle, as mother . . . At the end of the group maybe the mother should kiss everybody good-bye as they leave.*

Patrick: *Doesn't that imply that the mother's going to stay around?*

Rick: *I can just see it. "OK, children, be good now. You're out on your own now. You have to fight for yourselves. But Daddy Jim and I will be here in case you need us . . . Just come back anytime. Remember all we taught you. Be good and remember we love you."*

Gayle: *I do feel that incredible . . . well, I wish I could keep you all together . . . Sounds really maternal . . . that I could do something for all of you and you could do something for each other . . .*

Bill: *It just occurred to me . . . maybe at the last hour it would be a good idea to accept your maternal feelings. You said "I guess that sounds maternal." I feel that's all right. That's OK. Maybe a lot of us, especially me, attacked you for being a mother because we hadn't worked things out with our own mothers.*

Steve: *I think this is a little superficial. We don't need a ritualizing end to the group. I hope each person comes to terms with it in his own way. I hope that I will.*
Dave: *I have two funny thoughts . . . Jim is going to hand us pieces of paper on which he would explain what each of us is really like and tell us truths and we'd leave with understanding and happiness . . . And the other thought . . . what does the end mean to Jim himself, how does he feel about the end of the group . . .*
Jane: *I really don't want to have to hear Jim say, "I think it's time to break up."*
Dave: *So let's go.*

The prospect of separation often generates renewed efforts to grasp some unified meaning from the experience. In the above excerpt, the religious references in Jeff's remarks represent such attempts.

As the ties of group solidarity are threatened, some people withdraw their feelings from the situation; others idealize the group and incorporate its lessons and memories as part of their personal identity. Sometimes there are final hurried attempts to reconcile rivals or to at least establish their differences as legitimate. We can see this in Gayle's acceptance of her maternal feelings and Bill's willingness to say "that's OK."

In some groups a special case of the attempt to reconcile differences becomes the most powerful of termination experiences: this is the attempt to reach the leader, to convince him to be "real" or to reveal all his secret knowledge about the group. Members look to the leader and to others for an outward sign of success and for some pronouncement of the group's achievement. As T. Mills observes, "Yearning for a benediction from some source, the group dies."

HOW EFFECTIVE ARE GROUPS?

Intentional psychological groups set for themselves goals of great difficulty and complexity. It is not easy to develop human sensitivity or to foster personal growth, and it is almost as difficult to assess whether groups have actually achieved their lofty goals. Subtle changes in attitudes and behavior are difficult to measure. Psychologists have often had to rely on the self-reports of people in the group. However, it is difficult to know how to interpret a person's statement that the group experience was "meaningful and rewarding." Does this mean that the group really was a success? Or do glowing reports indicate people's desire to please the leader or to convince themselves that their time and energy have been well-spent? It is often impossible to be sure what self-reports really indicate.

Figure 29.17 *(opposite)*
Termination of the group usually leaves most members with feelings of satisfaction about the experience and sadness because of the ending of the group. Some members regard the experience as very meaningful and may feel changed by some of the events; others may feel despair because their daily existence does not have the relatively high degree of intimacy that the group achieved. Proponents of intensive groups have made strong claims regarding the types of changes such groups can bring about. These claims are being tested through controlled research on group outcomes (both short-term and longer-term effects), but at present no reliable data exist to show what effects group encounters have on their members.

Research Reports

A few studies of group effectiveness have used more reliable tools. For example, B. Meador had people rate film clips of actual group sessions. She discovered that the raters indicated significant increases in group members' abilities to express feelings more spontaneously and to relate more openly to others. Other studies have also found increased sensitivity, flexibility, and self-acceptance as a result of group experiences. On the other hand, studies have also indicated that group experiences can produce psychological casualties, people who may undergo mental crises or breakdowns. A recent study by I. Yalom and M. Lieberman found a casualty rate of 9 percent. For 16 of the 170 students in their study, they found evidence of serious harm resulting from a group experience. In some cases the effect of the group may have been to aggravate or bring to a head previously existing personal problems.

Far too little is known beyond the general conclusions that groups can often have strikingly positive effects and that they also sometimes give rise to casualties. Much more careful research is needed to define precisely the kind of group that will be most effective for a particular individual with a particular goal. At present

our knowledge is based too much on the personal impressions of group proponents, impressions that have not been adequately corroborated by systematic research.

Transfer of Training

How general are the effects of psychological groups? Does the learning that occurs in the group setting carry over to life situations outside the group as well? The general issue underlying the question is *transfer of training.* Some psychological groups create a group setting and group norms that are as different as possible from the person's familiar, everyday environment. Psychologists who think the unfamiliarity of the group setting is needed say that only a radical change in one's social setting can provide the security needed for experimenting with new roles or expressing repressed parts of the self.

On the other hand, the remoteness of these group situations may make appropriate transfer most difficult. "Can I only be open with people I do not know?" is a frequent question after an exciting weekend; this problem plagues people who want to know how to introduce openness into their relationships with wives, husbands, children, or work colleagues. Accounts are common of business executives who are unable to apply their T-group experiences in a work setting that requires emotional detachment. In addition, group members may come to believe that *only* in such special settings can one be open and honest. People may use the weekend group as an escape to which they turn now and then as to a holiday from the pain of everyday relationships. Instead of spurring people on to make changes in their lives, the group situation can thus become a fantasy world with no bridge to the real one.

For this reason, many groups have follow-up sessions that chart the progress of an individual, over time. Unlike one-shot marathons, groups that run over an extended time period (say, six months) and meet once or a few times a week do not often reach high peaks of intensity. The long-term kind of group experience, along with constant evaluation within the group, is more likely to result in the person's ability to apply what he has learned to life outside the group. J. Gibb suggests that the only way to prevent the wearing off of skills learned from group experiences is to have the group itself embedded within a familiar context—like a group of managers in a corporation or a group of neighbors in a community—so that a new level of growth achieved in the group will be supported by people one meets and interacts with every day.

PICKING A GROUP

Many of you may have already participated in or may be thinking of joining an intentional psychological group. You cannot assume that a group you apply to will carefully examine your application and thoroughly investigate the suitability of the group for you. You must do the selecting, and you should not hesitate to ask questions before deciding to apply.

From the welter of claims and advertisements how can you choose the right group? You should address the first question to yourself: What is your *goal?* Desiring a good time for a weekend suggests a different type of group from one designed to give you psychological help in solving personal problems. Pick a group whose goals coincide with your own and one that seems likely to help you reach your goal. If your goal is to learn to release personal inhibitions, you might seek a group that orients itself toward emotional expression. If you are interested in learning about group dynamics and communication, you would find more appropriate a group explicitly concerned with analyzing its own processes. A group that promises to change your whole life in a weekend should raise doubts about the competence of the people running the group.

You may want to inquire about the group norms that you can expect to find. Some leaders encourage aggressive focus on one person; others lead exercises of touching and feeling. Think about what kinds of pressures you would or would not like to be exposed to. If you want a mostly verbal group or a mostly nonverbal group, ask the organizers before joining, so that you will not be surprised, disappointed, or misled. Finally, you would be well advised to look into the credentials of your prospective leader. He should be well-trained and experienced in conducting groups and able to handle crises effectively.

SUGGESTED READINGS

BALES, R. F. *Personality and Interpersonal Behavior.* New York, Holt, Rinehart and Winston, 1970. Probably the best theoretical and methodological system for understanding the interrelationships of members and the internal structure in small groups of all sorts.

GIBB, J. R. "Sensitivity Training as a Medium for Personal Growth and Improved Interpersonal Relationships," *Interpersonal Development,* 1 (1970), 6–31. A recent, comprehensive analysis and review of the research on the effects of experiences in intentional psychological groups.

SCHEIN, E. H. *Process Consultation: Its Role in Organizational Development.* Reading, Mass., Addison-Wesley Publishing Co., Inc., 1969. A practical guide to understanding how the psychological (or form or process) requirements of any group can be recognized to make interaction more effective and to help the group reach its goals.

SLATER, P. E. *Microcosm: Structural, Psychological, and Religious Evolution in Groups.* New York, Wiley, 1966. Slater emphasizes the deep symbolic meanings of group development, relating experiences in modern-day intentional psychological groups to religious myths and primitive societies.

YALOM, I., AND LIEBERMAN, M. "A Study of Encounter Group Casualities," *Archives of General Psychiatry,* 25 (1971), 16–30. An experimental comparison of many different styles of T-groups and some of their unfortunate consequences.

UNIT IX
Behavior Disorders and Therapy

The area of abnormal psychology is undergoing important and far-reaching changes. Not too long ago, the terms "madness" and "insanity" were replaced by the term "mental illness," which represents a medical, or clinical, model of psychological disorder. Although this model still has much currency in the diagnosis and treatment of disorder, it is under attack for a number of reasons. The detailed diagnostic system of the American Psychiatric Association, which is used by many clinicians, contains many medical concepts and terms. It describes "symptoms" of each class of disorder. Yet, studies have shown that different clinicians who interview a certain person

Chapter 30, Adjustment and Disorder, first discusses the various criteria of normality, including the clinical (medical) one, and the concept of adjustment. It then discusses the classification of disorders and describes the behaviors commonly associated with each. Finally, the epidemiology of disorder is analyzed.

Chapter 31, Bases of Disorder, looks at several theoretical explanations of what causes psychological disorder: psychoanalytic, social-learning, and physiological approaches are set out, and complex theories, which combine parts of all these approaches, are discussed.

Chapter 32, Psychotherapy I, after discussing such general aspects of therapy as its history, analyzes the characteristics that all therapies have in common. It describes the various types of practitioners and mental institutions and looks at some data about patients. The chapter then describes at length classical psychoanalytic and psychoanalytically oriented therapies.

3

Conditioning and Learning presents the basic principles of learning of the behaviorist orientation; one theoretical explanation in Chapter 31 of how mental disorder arises is based on those principles—the social-learning approach, which says, essentially, that disorders are maladaptive behaviors that have been learned because they were reinforced. Also, the therapies based on these principles are presented in Chapter 33.

8

Social Development: The Case of Morality presents several theoretical approaches to normal social development, including the psychoanalytic and social-learning views. These views are also presented in Chapter 31's investigation of why psychological disorder occurs.

15

Consciousness and Awareness describes altered states of consciousness that occur in sleep, during meditation, and under hypnosis. These descriptions can be compared to those in Chapter 30 of the alterations in perception, cognition, and consciousness that accompany various kinds of mental disorder. Also, the effects on consciousness of marijuana and LSD, discussed in Chapter 15, can be compared to the effects of other drugs, discussed in Chapter 34.

The Biological Organism describes the normal physiological functions of the nervous system and the glandular system. This discussion underlies the discussion of organically based disorders, in Chapter 30; the analysis of the mechanisms by which drugs work their effects, in Chapter 34; and the discussion of possible biochemical causes of disorder, in Chapter 31. Also, Chapter 16's discussion of behavior genetics is basic to Chapter 31's examination of possible hereditary causes of disorder.

16

17

Emotion presents several ways of analyzing normal emotional behavior; its approach can be compared with Chapter 31's discussion of emotional factors implicated in the development of neuroses and psychoses.

will come up with different diagnoses of what is troubling him. Studies have found that the personal attributes and characteristics of a diagnostician affect the subject's behavior during the diagnostic interview and testing; in turn, then, the patient's behavior affects the diagnosis of his disorder. These effects argue against the equation of medical diagnosis with psychological diagnosis.

Those who disagree with the medical model say that what begins as a descriptive label of a person's behavior—say, paranoia—becomes transformed into an explanation of that behavior. That is, all the person's behavior subsequent to his being labeled is attributed to his paranoia—a kind of circular reasoning that often goes unrecognized.

It is likely that in the future we will see substantial changes in the diagnosis and treatment of psychological disorder, although the exact form of those changes is not yet clear.

Chapter 33, Psychotherapy II, describes several non-psychoanalytic therapies, including client-centered, existential, and Gestalt therapies; behavior therapy (behavior modification techniques); and group therapies of various forms, from marriage counseling to Synanon.

Chapter 34, Drugs and Drug Therapy, discusses not only the drugs used in the treatment of disorder—both those administered to psychotics and those prescribed for anxiety, depression, insomnia, and other less serious disturbances—but also drugs that can create problems, such as alcohol, psychotogenics, and narcotics.

29

Intensive Groups describes and analyzes a growth-oriented group during a weekend encounter; the aims and methods of such groups can be compared to those of the therapy-oriented groups discussed in Chapter 33.

25

Patterns of Social Behavior: The Case of Sex Roles discusses normal role development; Chapter 31 looks at research on families of those with mental disorder to determine what kinds of social interactions could have led to abnormal role development.

21

Freudian Theories of Personality sets out the theories upon which the therapies examined in Chapter 32 are based.

22

Other Theories of Personality contains descriptions of some theories upon which certain of the therapies presented in Chapter 33 are based. For example, Carl Rogers' self theory is discussed in Chapter 22; his client-centered therapy, in Chapter 33.

30 Adjustment and Disorder

I've often wondered about the value of "adjustment." How do you adjust to a bad situation? And if your adjustment is harmful to others, is the fault yours or the situation's? And if the others you harm actually produce the situation . . . But this is growing complicated. Let me explain what I mean by inventing an eighth voyage of the famous Sinbad the Sailor of the Arabian Nights, and imagining a fictitious society.

In his eighth voyage, Sinbad is shipwrecked (he always is) and finds himself on the island of Ticktacktoe. The population of the island, which is highly civilized, consists of two classes of people, the Circles and the Crosses—since each person has either a circle or a cross tattooed on his forehead. The marking cannot be erased, and is imposed at birth in the following manner. Any baby whose ancestors are all Circles is marked with a circle. Any baby whose ancestors include even one Cross is marked with a cross.

The Circles outnumber the Crosses by ten to one, and the Circles control the government, lead society, and own the industries. They have the best jobs, the finest homes, and the most money. As a matter of fact, the Circles don't think much of the Crosses, do not mix with them socially, confine them to menial jobs, and are very little concerned with their living conditions. Even when a Cross manages to get an education, he finds it difficult to get a job that a Circle with similar education would easily get. If a Cross does obtain a worthwhile job, he has great difficulty in obtaining a promotion even when he is qualified for one.

Most Crosses come early to realize that no amount of thrift and industry will get them what Circles would get with similar thrift and industry. They realize that even if some unusual talent will make them economically secure, they will always suffer under a social stigma, and they know that that ineradicable and always visible cross on their foreheads will keep them from being completely accepted by the ruling Circles.

So Crosses "adjust" to the situation. Some turn to alcohol or to drugs to escape from despair. Some steal or engage in violent crimes as their only chance, they think, of getting their fair share—and as one way of getting back at the Circles. Most "adjust" by lapsing into hopelessness and spending their lives just getting by with the least possible effort. The Circles, viewing the situation, point out that the Crosses are clearly a bunch of shiftless ne'er-do-wells, given to drugs and violence, who demonstrate their own inferiority by their actions, and who are therefore justly treated as inferiors. Some of them indignantly point out to Sinbad that the Crosses are a source of crime and of danger to the entire community, and that this requires a rigorous application of the principles of law and order.

To which Sinbad said, "But the situation, to which the Crosses are reacting in this undesirable fashion, is of your making, it seems to me. The best way of solving these ills is to change the situation that produces them. It may mean great sacrifices on the part of you Circles, but since you Circles are responsible for . . ."

At this point, Sinbad was thrown into the sea as a "bleeding-heart liberal." I. A.

A psychiatric social worker sits at her desk reading the file of one of her clients, a man with an IQ of 50. It occurs to her that she considers the client abnormal but would never apply that word to the brilliant doctor down the hall, even though his IQ is 150, equally far from the average IQ of 100. Later, trying to counsel a fifty-five-year-old woman whose son insisted she come to the clinic because she plans to marry a man who is only twenty-three, the social worker recalls that she felt no need to counsel her uncle, who recently married a woman less than half his age. Next, a man diagnosed as schizophrenic is ushered in. His behavior reminds the social worker of that of an Eastern holy man she has read about, and it disturbs her that this one is about to be committed to a mental hospital while the other has followers who worshipfully take down his revelations. She finds that she must stop here in the course of her profession to attempt to reformulate for herself an answer to the fundamental question of normality.

WHAT IS NORMAL?

It stands to reason that an explanation of what is *ab*normal—away from the normal—first requires a definition of normal. In medical science, normal generally means the integrity of structure and function of an organ or other body part. A broken bone, an excess of certain sugars in the blood, an ulcer on the wall of the stomach are all abnormal. For physicians, the line between normal and abnormal is usually easy to draw. For psychologists and psychiatrists, the criteria that divide normal behavior from abnormal are not so easy to define. In fact, there are several definitions of normality within the field of psychology today, each based on a different theoretical orientation. Chapters 32 and 33 present the various kinds of psychotherapies based on these orientations. This chapter presents a discussion of psychological disorder based on current diagnostic practices of psychiatrists and clinical psychologists, after an examination of normality.

Criteria of Normality

The statistical criterion is one possible way to define normality. It says that what most of the people do is normal behavior. Any deviation from the majority behavior,

Figure 30.1
The juxtaposition of the behaviors illustrated in these photographs and the typical reaction to each of them reflect a double standard in American society. If an old man drops his trousers in a public park, he is considered to be a degenerate; if, however, a woman exhibits her body in a nightclub, she is regarded as a star performer.

then, is abnormal. Use of this criterion presents several problems. First, it is specific to particular times and to particular places. For example, wearing a bikini at the beach today is normal; if a woman had worn one even twenty years ago, she would have been considered abnormal—an exhibitionist, perhaps. And in some countries, it is normal for men to kiss each other, whereas in the United States, the majority of men do not exchange kisses. Think of how returning Russian cosmonauts are welcomed: they are given a hug and kiss and a bouquet of flowers by the chief of state. Can you imagine an American president welcoming astronauts like that?

Another problem with the statistical approach is that it does not distinguish between desirable and undesirable deviations from the norm. (See Appendix for a full discussion of statistical methods.) A person with an IQ of 150 must be considered abnormal in the same sense as one with an IQ of 50. And in a society where most people cheated on their income tax, the person who wrote an honest return would have to be considered abnormal. Clearly, the statistical criterion is deficient as a means of distinguishing between normal and abnormal.

Some personality and developmental theorists view normality as a goal, or ideal, that people strive to attain. This kind of definition can be viewed as an *ideal mental health criterion.* Maslow and Rogers call self-actualization that goal; Fromm called it productivity; Erikson, integrity of intra- and interpersonal life. (Fromm's and Erikson's theories are discussed in Chapter 21; those of Maslow and Rogers, in Chapter 22.) In contrast to the statistical criterion, which defines the majority of people as normal, the theories that set up an ideal see few people reaching that standard of "normality." Their usefulness as criteria for separating normal from abnormal is therefore extremely limited.

The *clinical criterion* defines normality as the absence of abnormal symptoms. A clinician—a psychiatrist or clinical psychologist—decides for each of his patients whether the patient's symptoms indicate mental disorder. If one could clearly define the bases on which clinicians make their judgments, it seems that one could arrive at a universal set of criteria of normality. However, the bases for diagnosis—such as amount of subjective unhappiness or degree of social maladjustment—depend greatly on the individual clinician's interpretation. The clinical criterion therefore cannot serve to universally define normality.

Most of the difficulties with the clinical criterion stem from the fact that it treats psychological disorder as if it were analogous to physical disease. Psychological problems are called "mental illness," and psychologists look for symptoms of illness in the same way that doctors look for symptoms of physical disease. In *The Myth of Mental Illness,* T. Szasz suggests that most mental disorders involve *problems in living,* problems that in the final analysis are solvable only by the person who has them. They cannot be cured in the way that a medical doctor cures a disease.

ADJUSTMENT

Adjustment is often used as an alternative to the concept of normality, especially by psychologists with a humanist orientation, like Szasz, who are dissatisfied with the concept of normality. Many psychologists speak of maladjustment rather than of abnormality because decisions about who is maladjusted do not seem to require reference to a fixed moral or evaluative standard. Although adjustment does imply a referent outside the person—adjustment *to* something—the patient himself can choose the standard to which he should adjust (at least sometimes), and his adjustment then can be judged on a range of efficient to inefficient, without the necessity for the therapist's imposing a particular ideal or a particular moral judgment, as he must if he is concerned with normality.

D. Krebs has suggested that there are four main aspects of adjustment with which people are concerned: physical, psychological, social, and moral adjustment. Physically, the goal of adjustment is survival. If a person feels hungry, he eats; if

Figure 30.2
One reason for the low reliability of psychiatric diagnoses is that patients respond differently to different diagnosticians. Controlled laboratory studies have used examiners of different sexes, races, and approaches (for example, warmth versus aloofness) and have measured subjects' psychological performances in interviews, on psychological tests, and on learning tasks. Many of these experiments have shown that the characteristics of examiners significantly influence subjects' behaviors. Thus, the patient behavior on which a psychiatrist or a psychologist bases his diagnosis and treatment is markedly influenced by his own physical and personal characteristics. Although these effects cannot be completely overcome, they can be minimized by the development of more standardized interview procedures and by the use of two or more diagnosticians.

he is attacked by disease-causing germs, his body marshals materials to fight the disease.

At the psychological level, the most basic referent for adjustment is probably pleasure, or subjective happiness. In Freudian and neo-Freudian theory, the ego is the agent of adjustment; it mediates between primitive impulses from the id and the moralistic demands of the superego. The ego protects itself from the anxiety generated by unsatisfied id impulses or threats to its self-esteem from the superego by means of defense mechanisms (see Chapter 21). Learning theory also says that pleasure and the avoidance of pain are the basic goals of adjustment. Responses that bring rewards are repeated, and those that bring punishment are extinguished (see Chapter 3). In some situations, however, specification of a reward is not so simple: hungry people sometimes give their food to others, and some Hindus have chosen to starve to death rather than eat the meat of sacred cows. Thus, although it is probably true that psychological adjustment brings pleasure, it is necessary to consider that, depending on the individual, the pleasure may stem from such different sources as satisfaction of hunger, social approval, or even ethical behavior.

People live with and depend on other people; they cannot survive and be happy without dealing with other people. In other words, physical and psychological adjustment presuppose social adjustment, the third aspect. At the social level, the referent for survival is probably the species. Individuals do not lead isolated lives—in order to survive and maximize their pleasure, they must work together. People form social contracts; they agree to cooperate, and they establish certain rules and regulations to ensure that the social organization runs smoothly.

But it sometimes happens that adjustment to one dimension—say, the social—results in maladjustment to another—say, the psychological. Sociologists have found that delinquency is a normal way of life in certain sections of American society. Stealing is considered necessary for survival by peer groups in certain subcultures, so a young person in that subculture must balance his psychological adjustment (stealing for survival) against his adjustment to the society at large, which proscribes stealing. And different societies have different organizations and rules, so what constitutes adjustment in one society—or even in one subculture—is maladjustment in another. You can see, then, that any talk of adjustment requires referents: adjustment *to* things—a fit between a certain goal, standard, or problem in a specified situation and the behavior that is designed to cope with that goal, standard, or problem.

The final dimension, the moral one, overrides the others in the sense that a person asks: "How can I decide what I *should* adjust to?" Although there is no easy answer to that question, some psychologists have tried to outline a rough hierarchy of bases of moral adjustment. L. Kohlberg, for one, has studied moral adjustment in children and young adults and found that as a person matures, judgments of morality pass through six stages (see Chapter 8). People in the first two stages view adjustment in terms of personal pleasure and pain. At the second two stages the referent for adjustment is the rules and regulations of the person's social system. In the final two stages, the rules of the social system are subordinated to higher ethical principles, and people adjust to the principles.

The question of adjustment, then, is far from simple. Each person weighs and balances the demands of physical, psychological, social, and moral adjustment. Who, then, defines maladjustment? Physicians diagnose physical disorder; courts decide social abnormality, according to the laws of the society; clergymen usually serve as authorities in the moral realm; and, in most Western societies, psychiatrists and clinical psychologists decide about psychological maladjustment. Although the four dimensions of adjustment overlap considerably, this chapter focuses on the psychological dimensions. It attempts to answer the question, "How do psychologists decide what behavior is maladjusted?"

Psychologists' judgments are based on their training—both academic and practical—and on their experience. They interview a prospective patient and discuss his problem. They often administer a battery of tests, such as the Minnesota Multiphasic Personality Inventory, the Thematic Apperception Test, the Rorschach Test, the Wechsler Intelligence Test, and perhaps some personality scales (see Chapter 20). The clinician uses his own conceptual categories of disorder and processes the vast quantity of information he gets from the client. His categories are based on one of the models of normality or on his evaluation of the patient's adjustment or on some combination of normality and adjustment. In general, he will apply the label of abnormal or maladjusted to a person who is uncomfortable, unhappy with his inner life and interpersonal relations, who has difficulty performing the tasks expected of him, or whose actions appear bizarre. More specifically, he will usually try to diagnose the abnormality or maladjustment in terms of the official categories of mental disorder employed by the American Psychiatric Association. As you read about the categories, try to decide for yourself whether they are based on a questionable model of normality. Can they be interpreted instead in terms of a model of psychological adjustment that allows a person the freedom to choose his own criteria of adjustment?

THE CLASSIFICATION OF DISORDERS

Table 30.1 displays the categories of disorder set out by the American Psychiatric Association. The diagnostic categories are based on clinical studies and clinical experience.

The classification scheme is open to criticism on several counts. First, it largely represents a single, psychoanalytic, point of view. Another weakness seems to be that the principles upon which the classifications are based are not consistent. Some disorders are classed together on the basis of cause, or etiology. Most of the organic psychoses and many of the categories of mental retardation (Categories I and II of Table 30.1) are classified by cause. This principle is consistent with the

Table 30.1—Major Categories of Mental Disorder

- I. Mental Retardation
- II. Organic Brain Syndromes (disorders caused by or associated with impairment of brain tissue function, such as senile dementia and alcoholic psychosis)
- III. Psychoses Not Attributed to Physical Conditions Listed Previously
  - Schizophrenia
    - Simple type
    - Hebephrenic type
    - Catatonic type
    - Paranoid type
    - Acute schizophrenic episode
    - Latent type
    - Residual type
    - Schizo-affective type
    - Childhood type
    - Chronic undifferentiated type
    - Other
  - Major affective disorders
    - Involutional melancholia
    - Manic-depressive illness (manic type, depressed type, or circular type)
    - Paranoid states
    - Other
- IV. Neuroses
  - Anxiety neurosis
  - Hysterical neurosis (conversion type or dissociative type)
  - Phobic neurosis
  - Obsessive compulsive neurosis
  - Depressive neurosis
  - Neurasthenic neurosis
  - Depersonalization neurosis
  - Hypochondriacal neurosis
  - Other
- V. Personality Disorders and Certain Other Nonpsychotic Mental Disorders (such as paranoid personality, schizoid personality, and antisocial personality)
  - Sexual deviations (such as homosexuality, fetishism, and sadism)
  - Alcoholism
  - Drug dependence
- VI. Psychophysiologic Disorders (physical disorders, e.g., respiratory or gastrointestinal, of presumably psychogenic origin)
- VII. Special Symptoms (such as speech disturbances, tics, disorders of sleep)
- VIII. Transient Situational Disturbances (during infancy, childhood, adolescence, adult life, or late life)
- IX. Behavior Disorders of Childhood and Adolescence (such as withdrawing reaction, overanxious reaction, and group delinquent reaction)
- X. Conditions Without Manifest Psychiatric Disorder and Nonspecific Conditions (such as marital maladjustment and occupational maladjustment)

Adapted from: American Psychiatric Association. *Diagnostic and Statistical Manual of Mental Disorders*. 2nd ed. Washington, D.C.: American Psychiatric Association, 1968.

model by which medical science classes diseases. Other categories, however, are based on similarities of displayed symptoms. Even here, as E. Zigler and L. Phillips point out, the symptoms are combined in a number of conceptually distinct ways: psychosomatic disorders are considered syndromes—unique clusters of specific physical *symptoms,* whereas psychoses are generally combined into types, with the groupings based on similarity among *persons.*

One further criticism that has been leveled at the classification scheme is that it narrowly channels the conceptions of clinicians. In interviewing and observing a patient, a clinician will look for response patterns with which he is familiar—patterns of behavior characteristic of one of the categories. This criticism says that conceptual channeling prevents the clinician from seeing each patient as an individual.

In defense of the classification system, it can be said that the system permits psychologists and psychiatrists to share information about symptoms and therapies and to compare notes on possible causes. Perhaps the worst that can be said about the present classification system is that it is premature. Because so little is really known with confidence about the causes of nonorganic types of disorders (and because existing therapies are far from certain to produce cures, as discussed in Chapter 32), it may be too early for a rigidly delimited diagnostic system. The most convincing argument for the use of the classification system is that the descriptions of particular disorders and their manifestations are quite consistent in various cultures and even throughout history.

Some of the major types of disorders shown in Table 30.1 are described at length in the remainder of the chapter.

NEUROSES

Everyone fears some things and takes steps to avoid them. A neurotic fears things inside himself—urges, thoughts, and feelings—whose expression may be punished. The steps the neurotic takes to avoid these feelings merely hide them. He is continually anxious that they may reappear. As long as the anxiety is bearable, the neurotic may have no noticeable trouble with life and society. But if the anxiety increases, he must take increasingly severe steps to cope with it. As a result, the neurotic focuses too much on his own internal problems, and his social behavior suffers. His friends recognize that he is anxiously uptight, but they are unable to see inside him to the source of his fears. As the neurotic's social behavior becomes less and less satisfactory, he begins to worry about that, thereby adding to his anxieties. He takes additional steps to cope with both his anxiety and the problems in his social behavior. If these steps fail, the neurotic may suffer a nervous breakdown; if they succeed, he lives on in society, but often with a limited, anxious existence.

Certain basic theoretical premises are needed to explain the source of disordered human behaviors called neuroses. There is, first, Freud's concept of *repression,* one mechanism by which objectionable impulses are removed from consciousness in order to avoid the anxiety they evoke. We learn to be unaware of the thoughts that trouble us. If repression were always successful, there would be no reason for the emotional overreaction we call neurosis. It is when repression fails to be effective and forbidden thoughts and feelings threaten to return to consciousness that neurotic symptoms come into play as a kind of second line of defense against the threat of anxiety. These symptoms become tension-laden, last-ditch efforts that may seem to be desperate maneuvers to normal persons but that are the only defensive compromise with anxiety that the neurotic is capable of making.

Neurosis does not occur suddenly but requires time to develop. During the course of neurotic development, the continual repression of thoughts and impulses is costly. Some part of the psychic energy and attention usually applied to construc-

Figure 30.3
This woodcut by Edvard Munch, called "The Shriek," conveys the subjective experience of an acute anxiety reaction. The dread and horror on the person's face mirror his feeling that some catastrophe, unknown and unnamable, is happening to him. The flood of anxiety immobilizes him physically and psychologically—he cannot marshall either defenses or behaviors that will let him cope with the anxiety and tension.
(Collection, Museum of Modern Art, New York; Mathew T. Mellon Fund.)

tive work and the management of interpersonal relationships is diverted by the neurotic to guarding the many caged impulses he has found necessary to repress throughout life. By adulthood the neurotic does not have as much free psychic energy as most of us and is thus crippled by limited resources in meeting the challenges of living. The neurotic does not deliberately choose this way of life; he is forced into it by his constant battle with anxiety created by painful and negative experiences in the course of growing up.

Unlike the psychotic, the neurotic lives close to reality, but his is a troubled reality; his world is real but painful. He seldom acts in a totally bizarre fashion, but he is discomforted with life and deals with it in an inefficient manner. The anxiety the neurotic experiences may appear intellectually in the form of worry and concern, emotionally in the form of depression or mood swings, and physically in the form of any of a variety of bodily symptoms (headache, sweating, muscle tightness, psychosomatic illness, heart palpitation, or hysteria). The neurotic's anxiety reaction makes him live a life marked by continuous upset and few periods of true tranquility.

Figure 30.4
The two fictional characters pictured here exhibited obsessive thoughts and compulsive behaviors. Captain Ahab (bottom), the captain of the whale-hunting ship in *Moby Dick,* became obsessed by his desire to find and kill the white whale, which had taken off his leg. Because he was obsessed with the idea of killing the whale, all his acts became compulsively directed to that end. Captain Queeg, in *The Caine Mutiny,* was obsessed with order; any disruption of routine (as when the strawberries disappeared) sent him into panic. His continual rolling of some ball bearings in his hand was a compulsive behavior.
(Top, a Stanley Kramer production, © 1953, Columbia Pictures Industries, Inc.; bottom, courtesy of United Artists Corporation.)

Phobias

When this anxiety reaction is focused on a particular object or situation, it is called a *phobia.* Life has many dangers that realistically must be feared, but the victim of a phobia is frightened disproportionately by some aspects of existence. In addition, the phobic may be made anxious by objects or places that seem danger-free to most people (crowds, open spaces, closed areas, heights, school).

Obsessions and Compulsions

When a neurotic's anxiety becomes unbearably painful, he may begin to display an *obsessive-compulsive* reaction. The obsessive neurotic is totally occupied with recurrent thoughts and actions that he cannot banish from his consciousness. The obsessive-compulsive behavior may be unpleasant and painful, such as a recurrent urge to murder one's family, or completely harmless, such as avoiding stepping on the cracks in the pavement.

The obsessive person is regularly laden with worry and doubt. He fears that he has failed to do something that is important to his welfare and to the well-being of his loved ones, and he may devote such an inordinate amount of time to an obsessive-compulsive double-checking of everything he does that he consequently accomplishes very little. He is even more threatened by being forced to make a decision about the future.

Obsessive-compulsive solutions to the problem of anxiety more frequently occur in intelligent persons with relatively high social status. This response to anxiety is intellectual—less direct and primitive than a neurosis such as hysteria.

Hysteria

The form of neurosis characterized by a collection of physical symptoms that exist without an actual organic basis is known as hysteria. The hysterical personality may experience a loss of hearing, speech, touch, or vision or may be the victim of severe pain or muscle weakness. (See the discussion of dissociation phenomena in Chapter 15.) These symptoms appear to be like those caused by organic illness, but they are not quite perfect imitations, for they tend to be greatly exaggerated. Nevertheless, they apparently lessen the individual's anxiety.

The hysteric might awaken one morning paralyzed from the waist down or find himself deaf or blind. A normal reaction to such a traumatic event would be terror, agitation, and violent upset, but the hysteric may placidly lack anxiety about his condition (although this lack of concern is not characteristic of all hysterics). When a hysteric adapts well to such catastrophes, it is thought that the physical symptoms provide freedom from the nagging anxiety that had previously made life miserable for him. Many hysterics live out their lives in doctors' offices, they are frequently hospitalized, and many undergo a number of fruitless surgical explorations.

Neurosis and Depression

When the neurotic fails to solve issues in his life, to cope with the usual conflicts, or to manage disturbed human relationships, the outcome may be an apathetic depression in which he ceases to function effectively. The "advantage" of depression is that it frees the individual from the pace of life, and this total withdrawal from conflict is a measure of the seriousness of the emotional disorder. Bodily movements slow down and become lethargic, a mood of hopelessness and helplessness pervades the person, and even mental and intellectual functions seem to move in slow motion.

When neurotic depressions occur rather suddenly (as in some kinds of nervous breakdowns), they may be a response to a severe personal loss such as losing a job or the death of a loved one. But these depressions differ in intensity and duration from the normal mood changes that most people experience in such situations. Some neurotics seem moderately depressed throughout their lives, and this depression

Figure 30.5
Types of neurotic disorders include (from top to bottom, left to right) hypochondriacal, phobic, obsessive-compulsive, hysterical, neurasthenic, depressive, and anxiety reactions. Classification of the disorder is not always clear or simple because a neurotic person may, in response to an anxiety-producing situation, display more than one defensive reaction. A person may both be depressed and express hypochondriacal concerns.

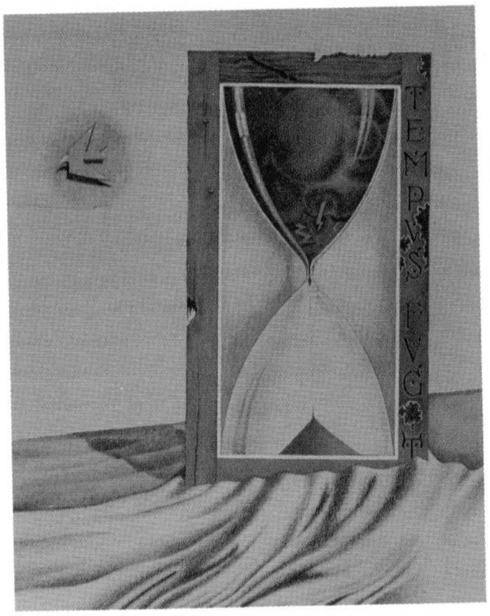

Figure 30.6
The simple type of schizophrenic reaction is characterized by gradual loss of motivation and interest, slow withdrawal from interpersonal relationships, and progressive deterioration. Adjustment is marginal, and the simple schizophrenic is generally considered to be a drifter.

merely deepens in time of crisis. This generalized, daily, depressive outlook on life may be coupled with an oppressive sense of fatigue, lassitude, and irritability.

PSYCHOSES

The neurotic may be handicapped in interpersonal relations, but he continues to slug it out with life, emotionally crippled or not. If a person's psychological distortions and abnormalities of perception and behavior ever reach such an irrational, fantastic, and fear-laden level that the person withdraws completely from normal life, he is labeled *psychotic.* It has been said that the neurotic dreams in an unreal way about life, whereas the psychotic lives life as an unreal dream.

Both neurosis and psychosis appear to have a common base in tension, anxiety, and threat to the self. But the neurotic attempts to deal and cope with these issues with defenses; the psychotic, without the resources available to the neurotic, gives up and withdraws from life altogether.

Psychosis is not a single disease; therefore, it has no single cause or single cure. It is, rather, a collection of symptoms that indicate that the ego or self is in serious trouble trying to meet the demands of life. In some yet unexplained way, biological and psychological forces combine to produce serious disorder. As Chapter 31 points out, inherited genetic bases or biochemical imbalances might account for the disorder, although neither of these factors has been proven absolutely as a cause. Most theorists attribute serious disorder to early childhood experience in which the individual has reacted inadequately to stress, has failed to cope with it constructively, and has been forced to defend himself against the onslaught of anxiety. The defenses he employs may be sufficient to solve immediate problems, but they are disruptive of long-term motivation, perception, action, and thinking.

The individual severely disturbed in most of the dimensions of human existence will probably become psychotic, and this disorder may take the particular form generally called schizophrenia. All schizophrenics have in common severe disturbances in the cognitive, emotional, intellectual, and perceptual sense of the self and of others, but each schizophrenic differs from the other along specific dimensions, as can be noted in a brief examination of the subdivisions of schizophrenia.

Figure 30.7
Inappropriate silliness and irritability, regressive and childlike behavior, and contradictory delusions and hallucinations typically occur in the hebephrenic type of schizophrenia. Thought, speech, and behavior are frequently incoherent and fragmented.

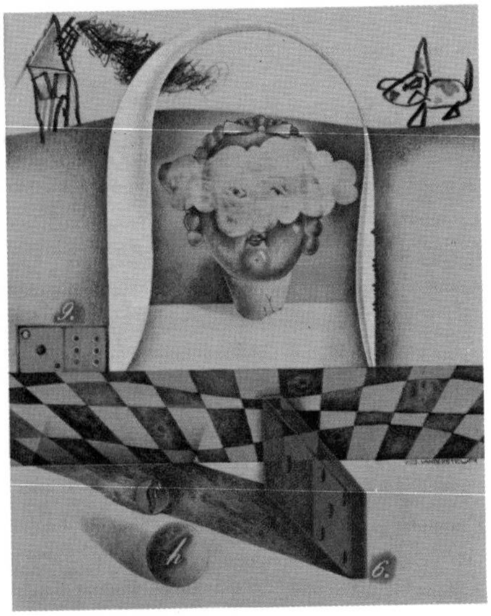

Simple Schizophrenia

Simple schizophrenics are not usually subject to hallucinations or delusions, nor do they commonly act in bizarre ways. Rather, they are apathetic, seclusive human beings whose contact with others is minimal and restrictive. They are dull, unresponsive people who feel insecure in any but an uncomplicated way of life. Some inmates of prisons, prostitutes, and hobos are among such persons—persons who seem unable to make it in life.

Hebephrenic Schizophrenia

The popular stereotype of insanity stems from observing the bizarre behavior of those who undergo this most severe disintegration of personality. In the hebephrenic type of schizophrenia, speech may be incoherent or unintelligible. The hebephrenic may giggle or laugh inappropriately; he lives in a private world dominated by hallucination, delusion, and fantasy; and his behavior is nearly totally unpredictable. One moment he may believe he is a famous person (Napoleon, God); the next, he may be convinced that the world has come to an end and he is its only survivor; and the next, he may lose bowel and bladder control and act like a very young child.

Catatonic Schizophrenia

In the catatonic type of schizophrenia, the patient lives in a stuporous state. The catatonic can hold himself in painful postures for hours on end and not show any response to the physical discomfort that others would find impossible to bear. He

Table 30.2—Distribution of Mental Illness

Diagnostic Category	Public Mental Hospitals, State and County		Private Mental Hospitals		General Hospitals with Psychiatric Facilities	Outpatient Psychiatric Clinics
	First Admissions	Resident Patients	First Admissions	Resident Patients	Discharges	Terminations
Total patients	150,702	452,329	51,104	14,808	446,931	593,000
	Percent	Percent	Percent	Percent	Percent	Percent
All Diagnoses	100.0	100.0	100.0	100.0	100.0	100.0
Total Brain Syndromes	21.8	22.9	7.0	16.8	10.5	3.3
Disorders of Senium	16.5	12.7	3.6	8.2	4.2	0.7
Other Brain Syndromes	5.3	10.2	3.4	8.6	6.3	2.5
Schizophrenic Reactions	18.6	48.3	18.9	26.3	14.9	16.1
Depressive Disorders	9.7	5.1	33.3	19.7	27.4	13.2
Affective Reactions	2.5	4.1	9.1	7.6	6.2	2.1
Psychoneurotic Depressive Reactions	7.2	1.0	24.2	12.1	21.2	11.1
Alcoholic Disorders*	17.8	4.8	7.7	5.3	11.8	3.2
Personality Disorders	11.7	2.2	7.7	8.8	7.0	22.6
Psychoneurotic Disorders	3.7	0.8	10.4	5.1	15.2	11.7
Transient Situational Personality Disorders	3.8	0.8	3.3	2.7	3.4	18.2
Mental Deficiency	2.5	7.9	0.3	2.2	0.8	1.5
All Other Disorders	4.0	5.1	8.8	7.3	7.4	3.2
Undiagnosed	5.0	1.8	2.1	5.5	1.2	5.9
Without Mental Disorder	1.4	0.3	0.5	0.3	0.4	1.1

*Alcoholic Disorders: Includes Brain Syndromes Associated with Alcohol and the category Alcohol (addiction) from the Personality Disorders.

Source: M. Kramer, "Statistics of Mental Disorders in the United States: Some Urgent Needs and Suggested Solutions," *Journal of the Royal Statistical Society. Series A*, 132 (1969), 353–407. Prepared by Biometry Branch, O. P. P. E., National Institute of Mental Health, March 1968.

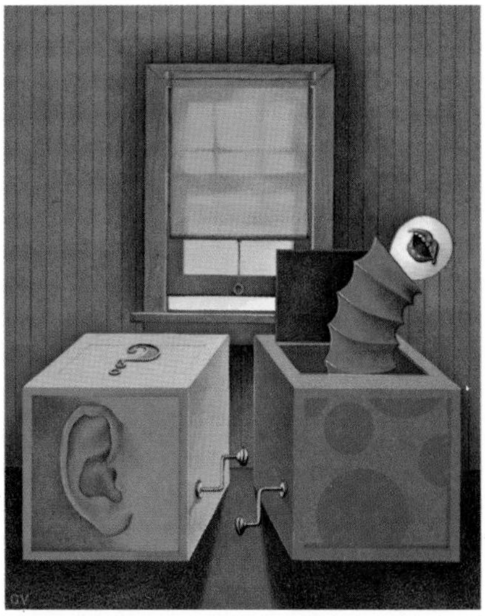

Figure 30.8
Catatonic schizophrenia usually involves motor disturbance in the form of either stupor and mutism or excessive activity and agitation. The latter reaction is often difficult to predict, and the individual appears to "burst" into rage.

may be mute and sit unmoving and unresponsive in the hospital ward. It is as if the catatonic is paralyzed by fear that any action or reaction on his part will jeopardize his already shaky, threatened security. While the patient inhibits his voluntary actions and resists responding to pressure by others, he may be preoccupied with a stream of hallucinations, such as voices that whisper to him of plots against his life. Catatonia is a dramatic, emergency attempt to cope with overwhelming, anxiety-laden experiences; seeing no escape, the patient immobilizes himself for fear of making a wrong move.

Paranoid Schizophrenia

The symptoms of the paranoid schizophrenic are not as visible as the rigid withdrawal of the catatonic or the bizarre behavior of the hebephrenic; the paranoid schizophrenic's difficulty is in the way he views the world and the people in it. He trusts no one and is constantly watchful, for he is convinced others are plotting against him because they are jealous and envious of his superior ability or special status. The combination of these grandiose paranoid delusions of persecution and the emotional and mental disorganization of schizophrenia may make the paranoid dangerous. He may seek to retaliate against his tormentors as he gathers over a

Figure 30.9
Unrealistic thinking, with delusions of persecution and/or grandeur, is characteristic of paranoid schizophrenia. The paranoid individual often distorts new information to accommodate his beliefs. He views the world as hostile and threatening, and is therefore likely to respond with hostility and aggression.

lifetime, his own brand of evidence of suspicious behavior around him. Each one of us draws erroneous conclusions about people and events, but we check the accuracy of our beliefs against the opinions and views of others. The mistrustful, resentful paranoid is isolated from such meaningful contact with others and thus systematically constructs a tangled, distorted view of life that warps his whole existence. (The Diagnostic Manual distinguishes between paranoid schizophrenia and simple paranoia, although the distinction is not always easy to make clinically.)

Affective Reactions

Persons diagnosed as suffering from emotional, or *affective, reactions* experience mood disorders in which they are excessively and inappropriately happy or unhappy, optimistic or pessimistic, manic or depressed. These emotional disorders may be further complicated by the disintegration and disorder of the schizophrenic process.

Manic Reactions The manic patient displays symptoms of increasing agitation, excitement, and deteriorating judgment in relationships with others. The usual history of an expanding manic reaction describes a lightening of mood, a rising level of activity, a subjective sense of accelerated thought processes, and increased alertness and perception. As the mania strengthens, speech and activity speed up, eating and sleeping become annoying interferences, and the victim becomes more agitated and easily irritated by attempts to slow him down. In the final stages of a full-blown manic reaction, the patient may be close to delirium—confused, disoriented, incoherent, and difficult to control. His world is very much like a movie that has been speeded up until the figures and events are no more than a blur of frantic, purposeless movement.

Figure 30.10
The emotional changes associated with depression are extremely compelling to the individual, who feels that his or her sadness, lowered self-regard, failure, and hopelessness can never be alleviated. Although this sense of entrapment (that Vincent Van Gogh captures in his lithograph pictured here entitled *Sorrow*) might seem incomprehensible to an observer, it is actually an intensification of the "down" feeling most people occasionally experience.
(Collection, The Museum of Modern Art, New York.)

Depressive Reactions Depression and mania at first appear to be opposite sides of the same coin of human adjustment. But theorists have suggested that the frantic activity of the manic is a futile attempt to ward off an underlying depression. In some cases, depression and mania may alternate with one another over short or long periods in a person's life.

Depression, like mania, is an exaggeration of the mood that all of us experience for brief periods of time. The person sinking into a deepening depression begins to be preoccupied with feelings of failure, sinfulness, worthlessness, and despair. He cannot be reasoned with or told to cheer up, for his woe is an internal event that does not correspond to reality as others see it. Overcome with his personal hopelessness, the depressive cuts off communication with the outside world, abandons active attempts to help himself, and usually begins to contemplate ending it all by suicide. The depressive may not hallucinate, but he may descend to such a stuporous level of mental and physical inactivity that he may be bed-ridden and require force-feeding.

PERSONALITY DISORDERS

Both neurotic behavior and much psychotic behavior come about through attempts to control anxiety. Other kinds of abnormality are not necessarily based on anxiety; they include such disorders as sexual deviance and antisocial personality. In each case, the person's life style is marked by a limited capacity to adapt to his social environment and an inability to establish a rational, stable, rewarding relationship to the environment and the people who inhabit it. The behavior of such persons appears socially inappropriate and, on closer inspection, is found to be inflexible, self-defeating, unstable, and immature.

Most theorists believe that these disorders are based on anxious and painful childhood experiences that the developing person has not coped with successfully. The adult with a disordered personality acts out his conflicts in ways that bring rejection, censure, and punishment by the better-adjusted members of society. Those with personality disorders have failed to learn socially acceptable ways of resolving conflict and attaining gratification of their needs.

The Antisocial Personality

The antisocial personality has been described as a person who misbehaves socially, is without guilt about his misbehavior, and is incapable of forming lasting affectionate bonds with other human beings. (The terms "psychopath" and "sociopath" have been used to designate persons suffering this personality disorder.)

Some antisocial personalities are irresponsible, emotionally shallow humans who cannot avoid getting into social trouble; some are in aggressive and open rebellion against society; some are criminals that prey on others as a way of life. Yet these types have certain common characteristics: each has failed to develop a conscience; is egocentric, impulsive, and irresponsible; cannot tolerate the normal frustrations usually taken for granted; and exercises poor judgment by seeking immediate gratification for his needs at the expense of more important and valuable long-term goals. The antisocial personality may be intelligent, but his relationships to others are emotionless—without depth, love, or loyalty. He mimics human emotions that he cannot feel, and he cannot organize his life past the pleasures of the moment and the lure of immediate temptation. Moreover, he has little insight about the kind of person he is and seems unable to profit from past errors in his style of life.

Antisocial personalities grow to adulthood relatively free of anxiety and the need for acceptance and support by other persons. People are like objects to them—something to be used for gratification and then cast coldly aside. Some psychopaths find this formula quite workable and rise to eminent positions. Their psychopathy is not recognized as an emotional disorder, and they are envied as ruthless businessmen or realistically tough and calculating politicians. Others, however, continue to get into trouble with social authority and to be rejected by other persons until they finally seek help.

The Sexual Deviant

A deviant is one who departs from accepted standards of proper behavior. Yet it is common knowledge that private sexual behavior regularly differs from the public standards set for it. Normal sexual behavior is relative to what consenting adults agree to in private, but popular opinion labels certain forms of sexual expression as sick or disordered. The professional clinician, in contrast, is concerned about

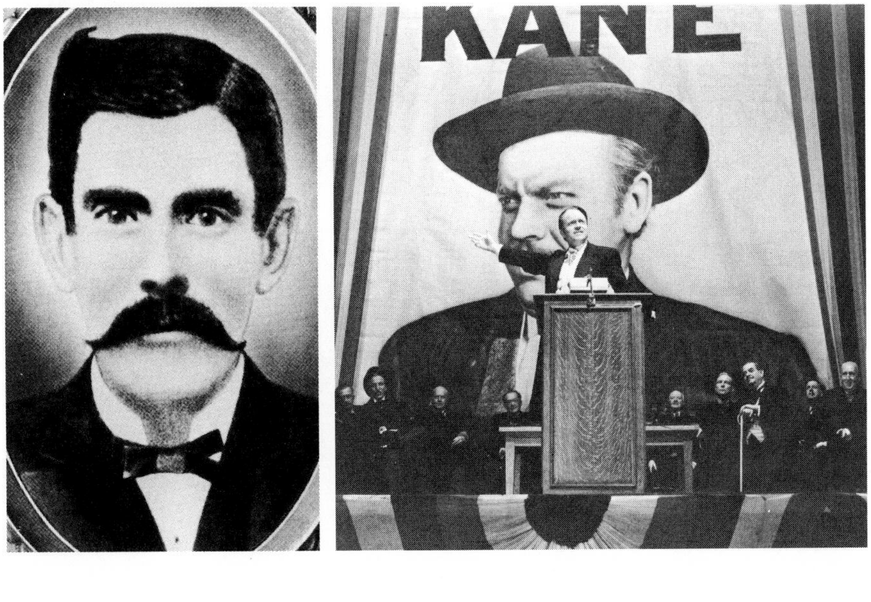

Figure 30.11
Antisocial personality is a diagnostic category reserved for persons whose long-term behavioral patterns include emotional immaturity, inability to follow social or legal standards, poorly developed relationships with others, and disregard for their well-being. Both the men shown here exhibited behaviors that could warrant their diagnosis as antisocial personalities. Doc Holliday (left) was a legendary killer in the American West. In *Citizen Kane,* the film by Orson Welles, the title character climbed to power in American society by using people for his own ends, violating ethical standards, and sacrificing his family and friends. Many theorists argue that psychiatric diagnoses are warranted only when the person's problem behaviors are frequent and intense, and when their effects on the individual or the society are extensive. Both these men qualify for diagnosis under these conditions.

sexual activity primarily when it is disordered by being compulsive, exclusive, destructive, accompanied by great anxiety and guilt, bizarre, inefficient, or the cause of discomfort. In fact, the clinical diagnosis of sexual deviant is not a very common one.

Each of us has a biological sexual identity (we learn to feel, think, and act appropriate masculine or feminine roles, as discussed in Chapter 25). For some, however, the supposedly smooth road to mature sexual adjustment proves to be rocky; fears of normal sexual encounter develop, and socially forbidden sexual activities become more attractive. Thus, sexual satisfaction may be sought exclusively with members of the same sex (homosexuality), with children (pedophilia), with animals (bestiality), with blood relatives (incest), or with inanimate symbolic objects (fetishism). Similarly, satisfaction may be limited to only one form of behavior. If it can be attained *only* by means of oral-genital contact (fellatio, of the penis; cunnilingus, of the female genitalia), anal-genital contact (sodomy, between adult males; ped-

Figure 30.12
Professional female impersonators are considered to have an "acceptable" deviation; this attitude reflects a double standard in American values because a person who dresses in clothing of the opposite sex is, in most other circumstances, labeled a transvestite in need of treatment.

erasty, between man and boy), displaying the genitalia (exhibitionism), observation of the genitalia or sexual activity of others (voyeurism or scopophilia), or wearing the clothing of the opposite sex (transvestism), it is labeled deviant. Further, to be considered normal, sexual pleasure should be attainable without inflicting mental or bodily pain (sadism) or being the victim of such pain (masochism).

Deviation can also take the form of such variations in intensity and frequency of sexual urges as impotence or satyriasis in the male and frigidity or nymphomania in the female.

ORGANIC DISORDERS

Psychoses resulting from acute or chronic brain disorders will become increasingly common as medical technology extends the average life span of human beings. The brain deterioration that may accompany growing old can distort memory, judgment, comprehension, and emotional control.

Patients in their seventies account for as much as 30 percent of all those admitted to mental hospitals each year. These patients not only have cerebral arteriosclerosis (hardening of the brain arteries) and other forms of senile brain disorder, but they also display unmistakable evidence of psychotic disruption of their lives. Controls that these patients were once able to exert over their behavior, emotions, and thoughts seem to deteriorate and become ineffective. However, there is no necessary connection between the amount of damage to the central nervous system and the severity of the psychosis. Brain damage does not produce psychosis as much as it triggers the psychotic process in some persons. For these persons, past, present, and future are jumbled together, conscious and unconscious thoughts merge and mingle, the senses do not function properly, and these events create a psychological crisis great enough to tip the balance of rational adjustment.

Deterioration of the brain and central nervous system in an aging organism is only one of a number of possible causes of organic psychosis. Psychosis can be associated with infection or trauma or with faulty metabolism, nutrition, or growth.

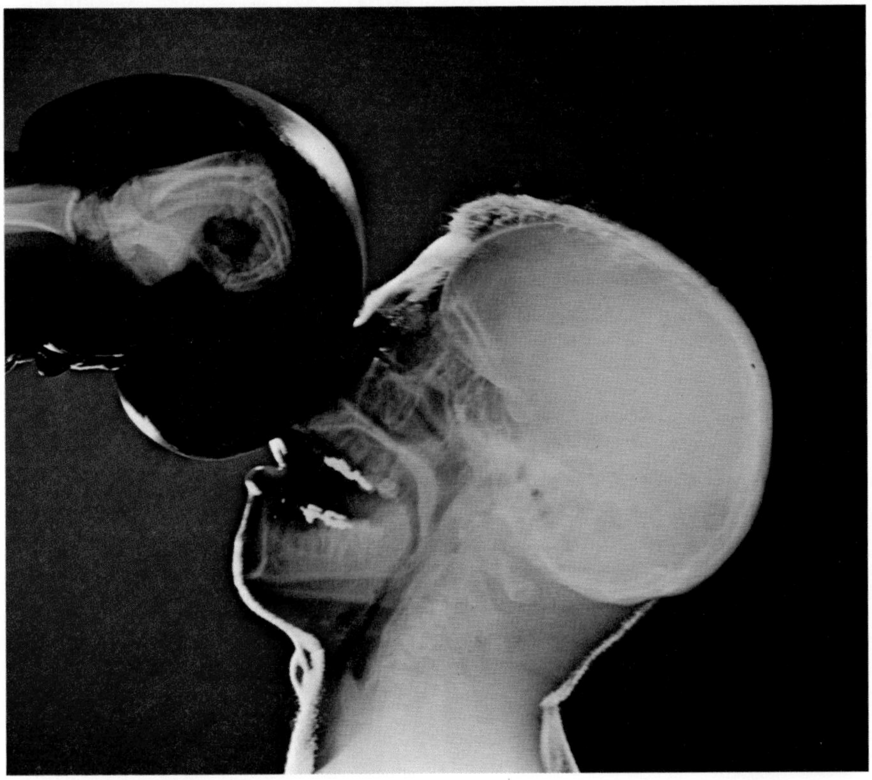

Figure 30.13
This x-ray photograph of a boxer's head at the moment he receives a punch shows that the force of the blow causes the brain to be momentarily displaced toward the back of the skull. Blows like this can produce trauma to the brain. The form of trauma may be a concussion, as in a knockout, when the boxer loses consciousness for a few minutes; he may be dizzy and have headaches for a period following the knockout but sustains no permanent tissue damage. A blow like the one shown may also produce a contusion, actual bruising of the neural tissue of the brain. A series of such traumas could result in personality changes, including organic psychosis.

Of these, a significant contributor will continue to be accidental trauma to the brain. More than 50,000 persons each year are killed in automobile accidents, and a great many more are injured. When brain tissue is cut, torn, crushed, or penetrated in an accident, enough damage may be done to produce a crisis in the person's life.

If the damage is not too severe, it is the patient's response to faulty psychological functioning that determines if he will become psychotic or manage to begin the long road back to a near normal existence. The psychological state of an individual before he has undergone brain damage is a prime determinant of how he will respond to this new event.

EPIDEMIOLOGY OF MENTAL DISORDER

There are many problems in estimating the incidence of mental illness. The number of people admitted to hospitals for mental illness is far smaller than the number of people with mental illness, and the number of hospital admissions probably depends more on the number of beds available than on the number of people who need the beds. Still, admission and residence rates for state hospitals, county hospitals, and outpatient clinics constitute the best available statistics for estimating the prevalence and distribution of mental disorder.

It is estimated that from 6 to 10 percent of the population of the United States will be treated for mental disorder, and that a sizable proportion of the remaining population will suffer from unrecorded maladies. In the famous Midtown Manhattan study, L. Strole and his colleagues categorized a full 81.5 percent of the population they studied as "less than well." And statistics from the military show that during World War II, 15 million, or 12 percent, of the inductees were rejected for psychological disorder. It is possible, however, to question the criteria that were used to make these classifications of disorder, as we saw earlier in the discussion of criteria of normality.

Many investigators have wondered whether our modern environment with all its stresses and strains has resulted in an increase in the incidence of mental disorder. A survey of mental hospitals suggests that it has not. The number of admissions for most disorders peaked in the mid-1950s and has declined steadily since then. Unfortunately, however, this reduction in admissions does not necessarily mean that the actual incidence of mental disorder has declined. It is probably the result of new drug therapies (see Chapter 34) and of the concerted effort of mental health workers to establish community mental health centers, to guide the aged to nursing homes, and to encourage potential patients to enter half-way houses or remain in the community.

Figure 30.14
Results of the Midtown Manhattan study, conducted by L. Strole and his associates. Strole indicated that fully 81.5 percent of those persons studied were "less than well," and 23.4 percent were "impaired."

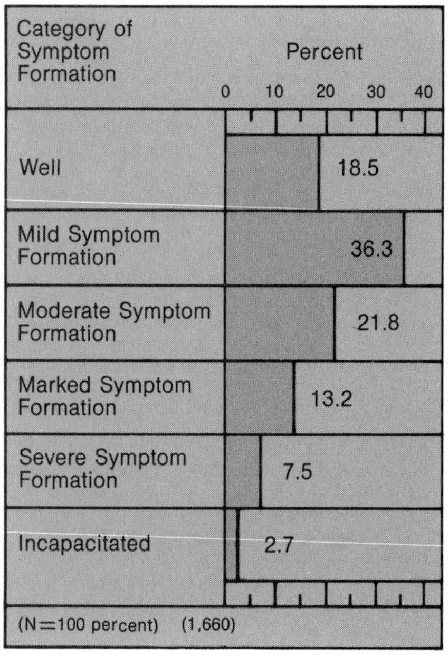

Demographic Variability

In spite of the problems associated with estimating incidence of mental illness, investigators have reached some consensus about the relative proportion of various disorders in the two sexes and among people of various ages, ethnic groups, marital status, religion, and social class. Some of those findings are reported here.

Sex Although there is considerable variability among samples, most researchers have found that there are more males in state, county, and Veterans' Administration hospitals than females, but more females in private mental hospitals and general hospitals. There is a higher incidence of brain syndromes in males but a higher incidence of psychosis and neurosis in females. Males evidence more alcoholism, drug addiction, and sexual deviation than females, but studies have consistently found females to be more generally unhappy with their lives. (See Chapter 25.)

Age Figure 30.15 outlines trends in age for various mental disorders. Neuroses and personality disorders reach a peak in adolescence. Schizophrenia, other psychoses, and alcoholism reach a peak in middle age, and brain syndromes reach a peak in old age.

Ethnic Groups Most studies have found very little difference in the incidence of mental disorder across ethnic groups. Generally speaking, however, rates of mental disorder are higher for foreign-born than for native-born citizens of the United States (probably because of the stress of adjusting to a new culture). The fact that race is highly correlated with occupational group, religion, and social class makes any measurement of strictly racial inputs to mental disorder difficult. Only one thing can be said for sure: there is no evidence of a racially distinct origin for any mental disorder.

Marital Status The highest rates of reported mental illness are found among separated and divorced persons; the next highest, among single persons; the next highest among widows and widowers; and the lowest, among married men and women. As is the case for all demographic trends, there are a number of possible explanations for these differences. One explanation for the greater incidence of disorder in single people may simply be that single people require admittance to hospitals more often than married ones because they have no one to care for them. Another suggestion is that these people have remained single because they have interpersonal problems. A final hypothesis is that being single might involve more stress than being married.

Social Class Social class is a broad category that encompasses such other demographic variables as ethnic group, occupation, marital status, and religion. A clear relationship between social class and reported mental illness has been found. Nineteen of twenty-four studies reviewed by L. C. Kolb, V. N. Bernard, and B. P. Dohinwend in 1969 revealed that the lower the social stratum, the higher the incidence of serious mental disorder. These data are impressive and so raise the question: Why is there a greater incidence of mental illness in the lower social classes?

Two opposing hypotheses have been advanced to explain the phenomenon. The first suggests that people in lower social classes are subject to greater environmental stress than people in higher social classes, and that many succumb to the strain. The second hypothesis says that social class does not determine mental disorder; rather, people who are subject to mental disorder end up in the lower classes. Although there is some evidence of a genetic base for psychosis (see Chapters 16 and 31), the bulk of the evidence suggests that the higher incidence of mental disorder in the lower classes results from continuing stresses—stresses caused by unemployment, relocation, lack of nutrition, experience with divorce. The shorter life expectancy of the lower classes serves as evidence of the existence and effect of these stresses.

Although several researchers have found a higher incidence of psychosis in the lower social strata, several researchers have found a greater incidence of neurosis in the *higher* social strata. W. Hollingshead and W. Redlich, for example, in their famous study of New Haven residents, found the highest rates for neurosis in the social strata with the most expensive residences, the highest levels of education, and the best-paying occupations.

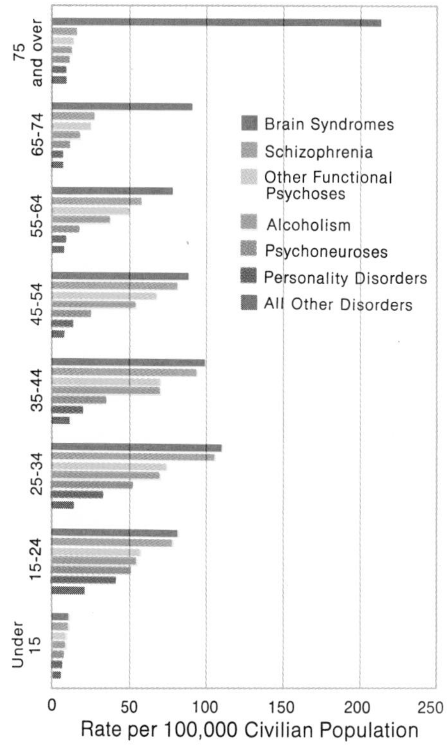

Figure 30.15

Age trends for various psychological disorders in the United States. These data are based on first admissions to state and county mental hospitals in 1965. (After Kramer, 1969)

Cross-Cultural Variability

Psychologists are interested in cross-cultural data about prevalence of mental illness for three reasons: (1) the data can serve to test the universality of the present diagnostic system; (2) they can be used to test theories of etiology, such as those based on defects in family interaction or child-rearing practices; and (3) they can be used in the investigation of the general effect of culture on symptoms of mental disorder. Disorders similar to schizophrenia, manic-depressive psychosis, neurosis, and other disorders are found in other cultures; in fact, some form of most disorders is found in most cultures, but there appear to be important variations in syndromes. For example, H. B. M. Murphy and his colleagues found that social and emotional withdrawal, auditory hallucinations, general delusions, and flatness of effect were common symptoms of schizophrenia in many cultures, but the style of the symptoms varied from one culture to another. For example, Christians and Muslims most frequently showed religious delusions and delusions of destructiveness, but Asians most frequently exhibited delusional jealousy. It is clear that cultures supply the idiom for delusions. For example, delusions about electricity are limited to cultures that have had contact with electricity.

In other cultures symptoms that would be diagnosed as evidence of disorder are part of religious ceremonies or of the cultural ethos. For example, a Hindu Fakir might be diagnosed as catatonic schizophrenic in the United States. The extent to which differences in symptoms can be traced to cultural style is difficult to measure. Many investigators have reported disorders that seem unique to particular cultures. *Arctic hysteria,* a kind of hypnotic condition in which the patient mimics the movements of others, seems unique to the people of Northern Siberia. Members of some Canadian Indian tribes exhibit a condition called *witigo,* in which the victim

Figure 30.16
The standards of beauty and adornment in various cultures can serve to exemplify the widely different standards of normality across cultures. Scarification in Africa, plastic surgery to erase signs of aging in the United States and in Europe, tattooing in Africa and in the United States are acceptable practices to enhance a person's attractiveness to other members of the culture. In other societies, however, these practices are regarded as bizarre, and a person employing them is judged abnormal. All behavior must be understood and judged in the context of what a culture expects, tolerates, and rewards.

becomes agitated, anxious, and nauseous because he thinks he has been bewitched and will become a cannibal. Natives of Malaya are victims of a reaction called *amok* (from which our saying "to run amok" is derived); affected persons are highly agitated and aggressive. Whether these conditions are basically different from conditions in other cultures will not be known until the causes of disorder have been discovered.

The obstacles to cross-cultural comparison are legion. Probably the greatest obstacle is ethnocentrism; people observe things and judge things from their own cultural viewpoint. Consider how you would judge the medicine man of the Nacirema people (described by the anthropologist H. Miner):

There remains one other kind of practitioner, known as a "listener." This witch-doctor has the power to exorcise the devils that lodge in the heads of people who have been bewitched. The Nacirema believe that parents bewitch their own children. Mothers are particularly suspected of putting a curse on children while teaching them the secret body rituals. The countermagic of the witch-doctor is unusual in its lack of ritual. The patient simply tells the "listener" all his troubles and fears, beginning with the earliest difficulties he can remember. The memory displayed by the Nacirema in these exorcism sessions is truly remarkable. It is not uncommon for the patient to bemoan the rejection he felt upon being weaned as a babe, and a few individuals even see their troubles going back to the traumatic effects of their own birth.

Do you recognize them? Spell Nacirema backwards.

SUGGESTED READINGS

ARIETI, S. (Ed.). *American Handbook of Psychology.* 3 vols. New York, Basic Books, Inc., Publishers, 1959. Published in three volumes, the first volume contains papers pertaining to adjustment and disorder and is divided into sections on general psychopathology, neurosis, functional psychosis, psychopathic syndromes, psychosomatic medicine, disorders of childhood and adolescence, and language and speech disorders.

KISKER, G. W. *The Disorganized Personality.* New York, McGraw-Hill, 1964. The best elementary textbook on abnormal psychology. Well-written and well-illustrated, it contains a series of case histories to demonstrate types of disorder and presents an excellent discussion of the history of mental illness. Chapters follow the major categories in the diagnostic manual of the American Psychological Association.

MAHER, B. *Principles of Psychopathology: An Experimental Approach.* New York, McGraw-Hill, 1966. Presents an experimental approach to psychopathology. Contains an excellent discussion of learning theories and the biological basis of psychopathology. Analyzes neurosis in terms of conflict, anxiety, and avoidance. Four chapters deal with theories and research on schizophrenia.

SZASZ, T. *The Myth of Mental Illness: Foundations of a Theory of Personal Conduct.* New York, Dell, 1961. A highly original, extremely stimulating discussion of mental illness. Szasz argues that what is commonly called mental illness really involves only problems in living.

WHITE, R. W. *The Abnormal Personality.* New York, The Ronald Press Company, 1964. A comprehensive, easy-to-read presentation of theories and research on abnormal behavior. Written by one of the pillars of classic personality theory, the book is pervaded by the force of Robert White's own personality. It contains an excellent presentation of psychoanalysis and learning theory.

WOLMAN, B. (Ed.). *Handbook of Clinical Psychology.* New York, McGraw-Hill, 1965. Sections of particular interest are those on diagnostic methods and clinical patterns. Contains a series of papers by experts in the field.

ZILBOORG, G., AND HENRY, G. *A History of Medical Psychology.* New York, Norton, 1941. A fascinating discussion of the history of madness; guaranteed to appall anyone who reads it. A classic in the field.

31
Bases of Disorder

WHO AMONG US can claim freedom from any trace of psychological disorder? Well, maybe the rest of you can, but I can't. I am troubled by a chronic low-grade state of anxiety, which can become acute in certain crises. Kind-hearted friends clap me on the back and tell me that I am "intense," with a tone of voice intended to make me think that this means I am hard-driving, industrious, keen, sharp, and various other complimentary adjectives, but don't you believe it. What I am is "anxious."

One of the things that most sharply activates my capacity for anxiety is my typewriter. After all, I am always typewriting, or getting ready to engage in typewriting, or leaning back to rest preparatory to returning to typewriting. I am told my fingers make typewriting motions when I am sleeping. Naturally, then, any trace of malfunction in my typewriter affects me like a sharp jab to the solar plexus.

I try to guard against this. Not only do I have an electric typewriter of advanced design (since by using electrified keys I can type for eight hours at a time without having both arms fall off at the shoulder), but I have a second electric typewriter of similar design for use in case something happens to the first. I also have a very good manual typewriter in case something happens to the electricity. I also have friends who have promised to make *their* electric typewriters available to me at a moment's notice in case of extreme emergency. But nothing helps. When something goes wrong with one of my typewriters, I am on the phone in an instant, calling the repair shop. They know me, recognize the panic in my voice, and generally have a man at my place well within the hour to prevent complete disintegration on my part.

Last month, something unprecedented happened. My red electric was so seriously off its feed that it had to be carted off, bodily, to the repair shop. I was appalled. My blue electric was still with me, so it was not a question of being unable to work. Yet the thought of the poor red one being away from home for the first time in all the six years I had owned it was a distressing one.

I had been warned that it might take a week or more before it came back, because even after the extensive repairs had been made ("There are many very worn parts, Dr. Asimov," they told me), they would want to keep it and use it several days in order to check it out. That made sense, but as the days passed, I grew more and more anxious—or "intense," if you wish. Finally, I phoned, and got the head of the repair shop on the line. I identified myself and described my typewriter. Yes, he admitted, they had the typewriter in the shop and they were working on it.

"Well, tell me," I said, "did it pass a restful night?"

And instead of answering, he laughed. Some people have no heart. I. A.

Most people, including students of psychology, express a great interest in abnormal behavior and psychological disorder. On the one hand, much of what a mentally ill person says and does is similar to one's own experience; on the other hand, a mentally ill person behaves and reports ideas in perplexing and incomprehensible ways. Mental illness also is associated with great human suffering, and this suffering affects other people, not just the disturbed person; so, emotional concern—as well as curiosity—helps account for the popularity of the subject. The desire to reduce people's suffering and to help solve a problem that is costly to the whole society is an important factor in motivating psychologists to do research in psychopathology—the study of disorder.

This chapter is an introduction to the kinds of thinking and the research strategies used by psychiatrists, clinical psychologists, and researchers to understand the bases of abnormal behavior. The general issues discussed apply to the field of psychopathology as a whole, even though most of the specific examples given deal with schizophrenia, the disorder that has received the most attention by researchers.

DEVELOPMENT

Anyone's personality—the way he thinks, feels, and acts, in short, the kind of person he is—partly reflects the kinds of experiences he has had. As indicated in the chapters in Unit II, the developing child changes somewhat with each new experience. As he encounters new objects and situations, his mental construction of the world becomes more complex. Each interaction with his parents and others allows him to learn a little more about the consequences of his behaviors. At the same time, however, the child is experiencing a range of different emotions, and he is associating these with specific situations, people, and objects. Many researchers have assumed that this period of development contains clues about the bases or causes of psychological disorders.

The idea that mental illness can be traced to the individual's psychological development has been the object of extensive theorizing and research. Two of the most widely accepted theories are the psychoanalytical view of mental illness, which has its basis in the seminal works of Sigmund Freud, and the social-learning, or behaviorist, position, which developed from empirical research in animal laboratories, especially those of Hull, Pavlov, and Skinner. Clinical psychologists and other investigators have also looked for alternative explanations within the family interactions and life histories of disturbed persons.

Psychoanalytic Theory

The psychoanalytic theory of disorder was originally outlined by Freud and was developed, with modification, by subsequent investigators, especially Cameron, Erikson, and Fenichel. It views psychological disorders as rooted in the psychosexual development of the person. According to Freud's theory, which is discussed in greater detail in Chapter 21, there are three kinds of functions or parts of the personality—the *id, ego,* and *superego.*

While the id might be characterized as the "I want" of psychological life, the *ego* might be described as the "how I can get it." The ego operates according to the *reality principle.* Its two functions, the delay of gratification and the use of fantasy substitutes, are important concepts in psychoanalytic theory. The id demands immediate gratification, but the ego recognizes the need to delay satisfaction or to find a substitute. This struggle between id and ego is central to a person's psychodynamics or "inner life." Not only must the ego deal with the unconscious instinctual urges of the id, it also must reconcile these urges with the demands of the superego—the person's internal representation, of right and wrong. And neither the superego's demands nor the id's instinctual urges correspond to the requirements of the external world as perceived by the ego. Consequently the ego is constantly striving to reconcile the id and the superego with the external world.

A person's inner life, then, is characterized by perpetual turbulence and ferment. The person is constantly reconciling instinctual urges, emotionally charged fantasies, and the requirements of his current reality. The terms *psychodynamics* and *psychodynamic processes* describe the psyche's ongoing attempts to integrate these warring forces. Psychological disorders develop when the ego is unable to reconcile the demands of the id and superego without interrupting the person's ability to function in society. Abnormal behavior and other symptoms like extreme anxiety are expressions of the ego's inability to reconcile these conflicts.

In its attempt to resolve the conflicts, the ego translates the conflicts into symbolic substitutes. The person's behavior may therefore express these conflicts symbolically. The symbolic nature of the expression makes it difficult to see the connection between a person's symptoms and the real nature of these basic conflicts. The following example illustrates the point: A twenty-nine-year-old professional woman had recently become engaged. She held a respected position for which she received a high salary, and she had to drive considerable distances several times a week. Two months before her wedding she developed a driving phobia. The psychoanalytically oriented therapist viewed the phobia as rooted in the woman's basic conflicts concerning sexuality. She reported that she usually felt "sort of uncomfortable" during sexual intercourse and that she could not "let go and enjoy it," but she said that she nevertheless felt a strong sexual attraction to her fiancé.

The therapist concluded that her driving represented a fear of losing control. Psychodynamically, the woman's sexual desire was threatening her need for control, and she associated her marriage with a loss of the masculine, controlling role of the professional. The driving phobia symbolically represented both her fear of abandoning herself sexually and her ambivalence about her female sexuality in the roles of wife and professional.

In this way, her inner psychic conflicts account for her experiences of psychological pain or for her inability to function normally. It is important to note this emphasis of psychoanalytic theory. It means that an external, or environmental, situation contributes to a psychological disorder only insofar as it presents a situation that symbolizes an inner conflict.

According to psychoanalytic theory, the nature of the symbolic expression of conflicts and even the nature of the conflicts themselves are a result of a person's development during infancy and childhood. In other words, the type and severity of mental illness is determined by the individual's psychodynamic development. The child passes through a series of psychosexual stages: oral, anal, phallic, oedipal, and genital. As Chapter 21 explained, each stage is characterized by a preoccupation with particular psychoerotic impulses and with certain associated conflicts. At each stage, the person develops ways—sometimes effective and sometimes not—of accommodating divergent psychodynamic impulses. The child who successfully deals with problems at one stage moves to the next with a strong and energetic ego. The child whose ego has been less effective will enter the next stage, but because his ego must continue to expend considerable energy on earlier conflicts, he will be less able to cope effectively with conflicts at later stages.

The later psychodynamic development of a child who has failed to resolve an earlier problem is like a bridge erected on a faulty foundation. The size of the fault will determine how much weight the bridge can withstand; the location of the fault will determine how much of the bridge will crumble if too much strain is applied. The person who experiences great difficulty at some period in his development will be more likely to develop a psychological disorder because there is a major defect in the foundation of his personality. The form and severity of the disorder will be determined to a great extent by the stage at which the fault occurred.

When the bridge begins to crumble, the cracks will extend down to the point of the major defect. This phenomenon is called *regression.* The person who becomes mentally ill experiences a regression, or partial backsliding, to the level or kind of activity that typifies the stage he failed to negotiate. The person's behavior mirrors, to some degree, his way of functioning at the earlier stage. But the *degree of regression*—that is, the extent to which all aspects of a person's functioning revert or regress—depends on the severity of the psychodynamic defect and the nature of the psychologically damaging event, or *trauma*—say, an insult or injury—that triggered the disorder. The term *depth of regression* describes how far back toward birth the person goes in regressing to an early conflict. The psychoanalytic view of schizophrenics and other psychotics, whose behavior appears to be very disturbed and irrational, is that they experienced problems early in their development and that their current behavior reflects an almost total regression to these earlier conflicts. In some cases the person's behavior may literally reflect these conflicts. However, the behavior more commonly expresses the conflicts in symbolic or fantasy representations, as in the case of the woman with the driving phobia.

Psychoanalytic theory views the neurotic disorders as reflecting partial regressions to less primitive stages than those encountered in psychotic disorders. Because the regression is less severe, less of the person's behavior is irrational, and he is better able to cope with the demands of ordinary living. It should be noted that the

Figure 31.1
Psychoanalysts view human life as a continual struggle to reconcile the often-competing demands of id impulses, superego strictures, and objective reality; it is the role of the ego to negotiate this course. Usually the ego handles this task smoothly by delaying gratification and finding fantasied substitutes for id urges. When the components of a conflict (for example, id versus superego) become intensified, or when the ego lacks the capacity to mediate smoothly, defense mechanisms develop, and psychological disorder may result.

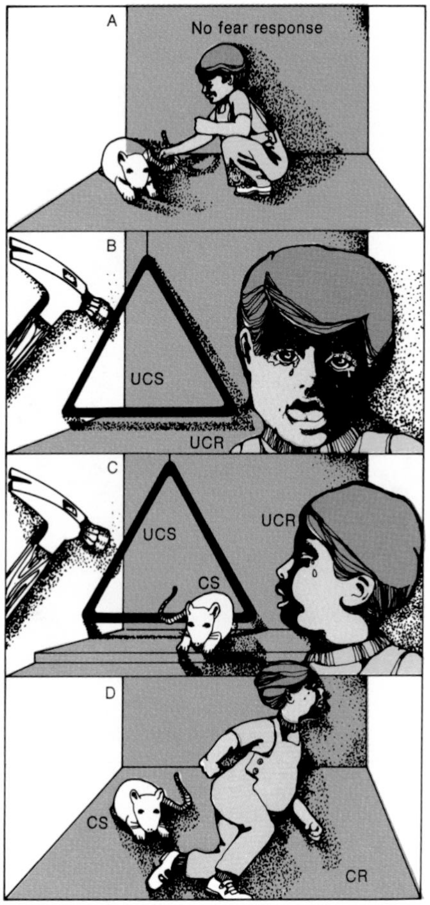

Figure 31.2
The acquisition of a fear response in a child by the process of classical conditioning. In this process, the UCS is a loud noise, the UCR is a fear response, the CS is the white rat (previously neutral), and the CR is the child's avoidance response. The drawing depicts a boy older than the original Little Albert, who cried and crawled away when presented with the rat (or a similar animal or even furry objects) after conditioning.

difference between the psychotic, the neurotic, and the "normal" person is one of degree. It is assumed that everyone responds to irrational impulses. A person is "normal" only insofar as the irrational components of his personality do not prevent him from functioning in society. Some psychoanalysts even believe that everyone is neurotic in one way or another because no one can perfectly resolve all the problems of psychodynamic development (see Chapter 30).

Social-Learning Theory

During the last few decades, social-learning theory has stimulated an increasing amount of research in the area of psychopathology and has yielded several provocative results. Unlike psychoanalytic theory, which attempts to explain all normal and abnormal behavior in terms of a single model of psychodynamic development, social-learning theory has no all-inclusive explanatory model. The learning-theory researcher tries instead to discover how each patient acquired his inappropriate behaviors. He works with the hypothesis that abnormal behavior is learned in much the same way as all other behavior. The person with a disorder is seen as differing from other people because he has *learned inappropriate or maladaptive behaviors* or because he has *failed to learn the adaptive behaviors* that most people acquire. The various learning-theory explanations of abnormal behavior share a number of common assumptions and concepts.

First, learning theorists assume that people learn maladaptive behaviors because the environment in some way rewards or reinforces these behaviors. J. B. Watson and R. Rayner's classic experimental demonstration of how a person learns maladaptive behavior is the case of "Little Albert." Little Albert was a nine-month-old child who, in a classical conditioning experiment, learned a phobia (irrational fear) of furry objects of all sorts. First, a loud noise was paired with each presentation of a white rat. Soon the sight of the rat without the noise was enough to cause a great fear reaction in Albert. This fear rapidly generalized to all sorts of other furry objects, like rabbits and fur pieces, although no noise had been paired with them.

Maladaptive behavior may also result from reinforcement from someone in the person's social environment. For example, a child might develop a fear of horses because his mother encourages his initial fear. A person may also learn behavior that allows him to avoid something aversive or unpleasant. For example, a child who hates going to school might develop hypochondriacal illnesses or learn to behave in ways that cause the school to repeatedly suspend him; either of these behaviors would be reinforced by the fact that they allow him to stay away from school.

Second, learning theorists believe that a given disturbance can result from one or more aspects of the person's learning history. The researcher keeps an open mind when he considers a person with a specific problem; that is, he assumes that there are many different possible explanations for it. When he sees that a person has more than one symptom—for example, a woman has both a driving phobia and an acute fear of heights (acrophobia)—the investigator assumes that the two symptoms may have different origins. Similarly, when he encounters two different people with identical disorders, he assumes that the problem may be rooted in very different histories or sequences of learning. The only similarity that he always assumes is that the disorders reflect the learning of inappropriate responses.

Finally, learning theory views the make-up of psychological disorder as nothing more than a series of maladaptive behaviors. Unlike psychoanalytic theory, which views symptoms of disorder as symbolic expressions of psychodynamic problems or conflicts, the learning-theory view postulates no such underlying process. The person's problem is defined by the symptoms, and when the symptoms have been eliminated, the problem or illness, in most cases, has been eliminated. The psychoanalytic position assumes that if only the symptoms are removed—but the primitive conflict is not resolved—the person will develop new symptoms as alterna-

Figure 31.3
Labeling a person creates serious effects that may perpetuate disorder and make adjustment difficult. The woman in the painting, which is titled "The Madwoman," may have been given this label because she did do some "mad" things. But calling her "madwoman" may have provided her with a social role and a framework for understanding her own behavior. In this way, she can make consistent and predictable the feedback she receives from others, and can purposefully adopt behaviors appropriate to a "madwoman."
(Chaim Soutine, "The Madwoman.")

tive expressions of the conflict. Learning theorists disagree with this tenet of psychoanalytic theory, known as the theory of *symptom substitution.*

The classic example that illustrates the difference between psychoanalytic and learning-theory interpretations of symptoms of disorder is Freud's case of "Little Hans." At the age of five years, Hans developed a horse phobia and was treated by his father, a lay analyst. Freud consulted periodically with the father and subsequently published an analysis of the case. He interpreted the horse phobia as an expression of psychodynamic conflicts with which Hans was then struggling; among these were masturbation, the fear of castration, sibling rivalry with a younger sister,

Figure 31.4
Joseph Wolpe. Wolpe's pioneering work in behavior modification has provided a viable alternative to psychoanalytic formulations of neurosis. Systematic desensitization, described in Chapter 33, is one of the techniques he has developed to alter maladaptive neurotic behavior. Unlike psychoanalysts, Wolpe does not analyze the person's hypothetical psychodynamics as a means of eliminating neurosis; instead, he helps the individual directly to unlearn the neurotic behavior and to replace it with more effective behavior.

Figure 31.5
Theodore Lidz. Lidz and his colleagues were among the first to study schizophrenia in relation to family structure and processes. They concluded that schizophrenic behavior is a response to "disturbed" family processes. This orientation to schizophrenia—as learned social behavior—stands in direct contrast to psychoanalytically-oriented theories.

and the Oedipal desire to seduce the mother and replace the father. Freud thought that what Hans saw—a horse hitched to a milk wagon, slipping on the wet street and falling—symbolically represented Hans' fear of his mother's giving birth to another child (his sister's birth had upset him very much). It also represented his anxiety over his wish that his father would die.

J. Wolpe and S. Rachman critically analyzed Freud's argument and offered a learning-theory explanation of the case. They said that conjecture concerning psychodynamic processes is unnecessary to explain Hans' phobia. Seeing the horse fall was a sufficiently frightening experience to cause the subsequent fear of horses.

In an article they published in 1960, Wolpe and Rachman discuss experimental studies in learning theory. They say that any stimulus that once touches off or is paired with a fear reaction in a person can continue to elicit fear. They say that *neurotic fear* results if the person felt extreme fear with the first experience of the stimulus or if the conditioning is repeated so many times that the fear continues to occur. Wolpe and Rachman note that neurotic fear caused by repeated conditioning may include a generalization of fear to other stimuli that are similar to the original one. Hans can be viewed as having been so frightened by the experience that he was very much afraid of approaching situations in which it might be repeated; he became frightened by the general subject of horses. The case of Little Albert, too, showed this generalization of fear.

Research on Families

Other researchers have examined the life histories and family environments of people with specific psychological disorders and have compared these to similar data from normal control subjects. Their aim has been to isolate factors or processes that are unique to the psychological development of individuals with a given disorder. Two examples of this approach involve research into the family lives of schizophrenic persons.

One group of investigators, headed by T. Lidz, kept contact with schizophrenics and their families over a period of several years. They held weekly interviews with family members, observed the family's interactions with one another and with hospital staff members, visited the person's home, and did diagnostic and other testing. From the findings of their first sixteen cases, these researchers suggested that the families of schizophrenics fall into one of two categories.

The first type of family showed *marital schism.* In the words of Lidz and his associates: "Both spouses were caught up in their own personality difficulties, which were aggravated to the point of desperation by the marital relationship. There was chronic failure to achieve complementarity of purpose or role reciprocity. Neither gained support of emotional needs from the other. . . . These marriages are replete with recurrent threats of separation. . . . Communication consists primarily of coercive efforts and defiance, or of efforts to mask the defiance to avoid fighting. . . . A particularly malignant feature in these marriages is the chronic 'undercutting' of the worth of one partner to the children by the other."

The other group of families was characterized by what the authors call *marital skew.* In these families, "one partner who was extremely dependent or masochistic had married a spouse who had appeared to be a strong and protecting parental figure. The dependent partner would go along with or even support the weaknesses or psychopathological distortions of the parental partner. . . . A striking feature in all cases was the psychopathology of the partner who appeared to be dominant, creating an abnormal environment which, being accepted by the 'healthier' spouse, may have seemed to be a normal environment to the children."

The child faced with the conflict and confusion of either of these two kinds of family situations develops ways of coping that lead to problems later in life. It seems logical to expect that children whose psychological development takes place in such environments would certainly demonstrate atypical behaviors and emotional development.

A second group of investigators, headed by G. Bateson and D. Jackson, examined the family environments of schizophrenics and developed the *double-bind hypothesis.* The basic idea behind their hypothesis is that the mother in these families has great difficulty accepting her child's affection and positive regard for her. She finds it hard to deal with any feelings of anxiety or hostility that she experiences toward

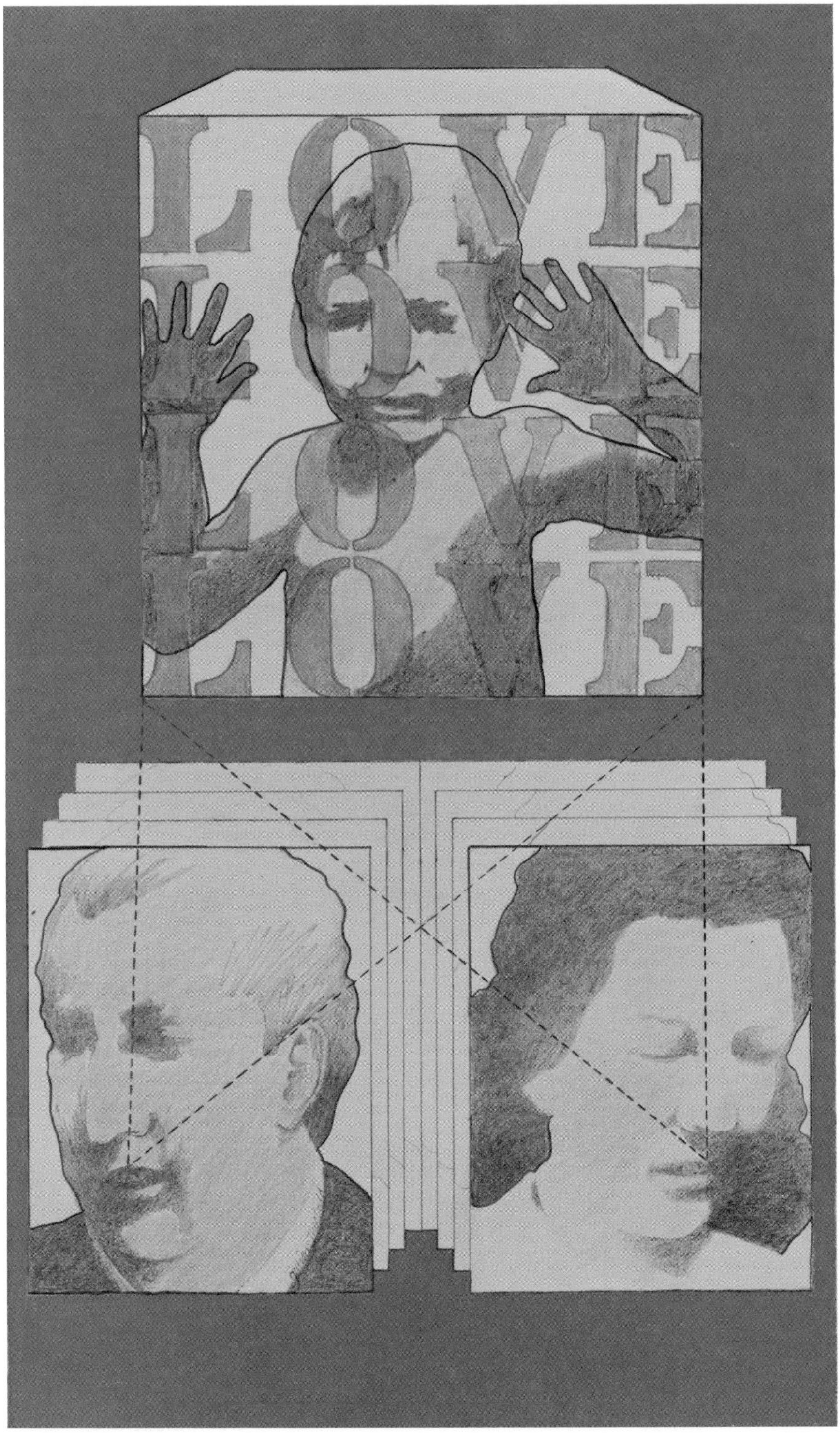

Figure 31.6
The double-bind situation can take several forms. One particularly destructive form is when the child is verbally told that he is loved, and yet all the nonverbal communications he receives tell him that he is not loved. One or both parents, for example, may say, "Of course, we love you," and then recoil at the child's attempt to embrace them. In another type of double-bind situation, one parent contradicts the other's messages to the child, although neither acknowledges a contradiction. In such a situation the child can neither receive nor give effective communication, for if he responds to either parent's message, he incurs the disapproval of the other.

her child. She therefore acts lovingly and correctly toward the child, but the child perceives the discrepancy between her overt actions and her convert feelings and messages—like the mother who tells her child to give her a kiss but stiffens her body when he approaches her. The child repeatedly receives two contradictory messages —one in behavior and one in words—from the most important person in his life. He therefore never learns to understand and make distinctions among the meanings expressed in normal language and behavior. He develops the bizarre language and social ineptness characteristic of schizophrenics.

HEREDITY

Many human characteristics such as eye color and color blindness are inherited as discussed in Chapter 16. Over the years authorities in the field of psychopathology have examined the possible influence of heredity on psychological disorder.

One of the first research strategies used was the so-called *pedigree study*. In this study the researcher examines the family trees of persons who have a specific disorder and compares the number of occurrences of this disorder among the persons' blood relatives with its frequency of occurrence in the general population. The specific hypothesis is, of course, that the disorder occurs at a higher rate among blood relatives. A major inadequacy of pedigree studies is that family members, in addition to being related genetically, have many other things in common; they have, for example, the same physical and social environment. It is therefore possible that exposure to the same kinds of pathogenic environmental influences accounts for the higher rate of mental illness among relatives.

Figure 31.7
Kallman's pioneering research, summarized here, indicated that an individual's chances of becoming schizophrenic are a direct function of how closely he is related to a person already schizophrenic. More recent research, however, indicates that the role of heredity in the etiology of schizophrenia is not totally explained by these data; rather, its role is complex and so has not yet been determined.
(Adapted from Kallman, 1953.)

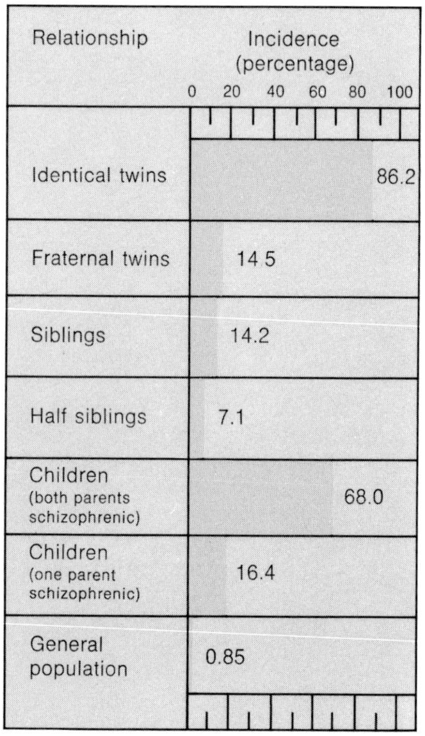

A second research strategy, called the *twin study*, tries to avoid the problems of the pedigree study. This method compares monozygous, or identical, twins, who develop from the splitting of a single fertilized cell and have identical genetic constitutions, with dizygous, or fraternal, twins, who develop from separately fertilized ova and are no more likely to have the same genetic constitution than are any two siblings. With identical twins, the assumption is that the differences in certain behaviors and traits of the two persons can only be attributed to environmental causes. In order to estimate the influence of heredity and environment, the twin study method looks at the resemblance between fraternal twins from similar environments. The researchers' hypothesis is that heredity plays a part in determining the development of a certain characteristic when identical twins show a greater resemblance for that trait than do fraternal twins.

Another type of twin study is also used to examine the role of genetic factors in psychological disorder, and it provides a better control for the effects of the environment during the twins' upbringing. This method examines identical twins who were separated early in life and raised in different environments. If identical twins show very similar traits even when they are reared in different environments, then heredity probably contributes to that trait.

The number of twins with psychological disorder who are available for study, of course, has severely limited the research. However, the information gathered so far has suggested to several researchers, including I. I. Gottesman and F. J. Kallman, that at least one form of disturbance, schizophrenia, has a strong genetic component. Nevertheless, the exact nature of the relationship between schizophrenia and heredity remains unclear. Chapter 16 discusses twin studies in terms of both normal and abnormal behaviors. The most tenable hypothesis is that a person may inherit a predisposition for certain kinds of disorders, but the inheritance of such a predisposition does not guarantee that the person will become mentally ill.

BIOCHEMISTRY

Psychiatrists have found that certain drugs are effective in helping people with certain forms of psychological disorder. For example, chlorpromazine usually reduces the disturbed behavior of a schizophrenic person. Similarly, lithium sometimes reduces the severity of depression. As Chapter 34 points out, the fact that drugs are effective in treating certain psychological disorders does not mean that chemical factors necessarily cause these disorders. However, the use of chemotherapy has led many researchers to conclude that psychopathological behavior may have a biochemical basis.

The way researchers work on this hypothesis—that mental illness is caused by some biochemical pathogen—is to take one group of people with a particular disorder and search for some biochemical difference between them and a control group of nondisturbed people. Although this procedure seems straightforward, it is difficult to carry out. Complications arise in trying to find an appropriate control group. The perfect control group would have to live in an environment identical to the one of the psychiatric patients, so that the only difference between the patients and the control group would be the psychological disorder.

Moreover, the biochemistry of human beings is extremely complex, and our understanding of it is far from complete. The medical and life histories, and even the diets, of psychiatric patients are markedly different from those of normal control subjects. Most hospitalized schizophrenics, for example, eat an institutional diet, smoke incessantly, get little exercise, and have long histories of chemotherapy. Any of these factors can alter a person's biochemistry. Moreover, as S. S. Kety has pointed out, the extreme emotional and physical stresses associated with being mentally ill can also cause changes in biochemical functioning. When the researcher finds differences in the body chemistry of disturbed persons, he must find ways of determining whether these differences are related to the causes of the disorder or whether they are the effects of the person's emotional state or the situation he is living in.

Some progress has been made, especially with schizophrenic disorders. Two major hypotheses have been postulated. R. G. Heath has studied groups of "blue ribbon" schizophrenics—that is, cases where the disorder is specifically definable—and claims to have isolated a protein substance, *tararein,* which forms a compound with other bodily substances. These compounds are toxic and produce functional disturbances in the central nervous system.

A. Hoffer and H. Osmond have advocated the adrenochrome hypothesis. The basic argument is that in all human beings adrenaline is metabolized in a way that produces adrenochrome, which in turn becomes converted in the body into two substances—*adrenolutin* and 5, 6-dihydroxy-N-methylindole. In schizophrenics, the major product will be adrenolutin, which is linked to the occurrence of schizophrenic symptoms; in nonschizophrenic persons, the reaction produces more of the dihydroxy indole. Neither of these hypotheses has been uniformly confirmed or disconfirmed by investigators in other laboratories; however, each has produced enough evidence to justify further research.

GENERAL PSYCHOLOGICAL CONCEPTS

The discussion so far has outlined some methods of investigating the causes and development of psychological disorders. Concepts from other areas of psychology have also stimulated some interesting ideas about the bases of disorder. One such concept is the notion of *conflict.*

Conflict

Conjecture concerning the possible connection between conflict and psychological disorder probably dates back to 1928 when a description of a now-famous experiment conducted in Pavlov's laboratory was first circulated. In this experiment, a dog was conditioned to salivate whenever a circular stimulus was presented but was denied reinforcement whenever an elliptical stimulus was presented. When the dog had learned to discriminate between the two differently shaped stimuli, the second

Figure 31.8
Neal Miller is one of America's foremost psychologists. He has made many contributions to the psychology of learning through his investigations of conflict, drive, fear, and more recently, the autonomic responses, such as visceral and glandular responses.

part of the experiment began. The experimenter presented a series of stimuli that were neither perfectly circular nor perfectly elliptical but somewhere between the two. Gradually, the difference between the circular stimulus and the elliptical one was reduced until it was extremely difficult to discriminate between them. The dog was unable to make a discrimination and began to struggle and howl. Apparently the inability to determine the significance of the stimulus—that is, food to follow or no food to follow—caused the dog's agitation. When they had been subjected to such conflict for a long period, many dogs showed severe psychopathological symptoms—even after they were removed from the stress situation.

Research indicates that when a person encounters two equally attractive but contradictory and mutually exclusive alternatives, he shows extreme agitation, and his normal functioning is disrupted. He may try various ways to escape from the conflict situation. The precise way in which he tries to cope with the conflict situation is determined in part by the type of conflict he is facing. N. E. Miller and others have investigated three logically distinct kinds of conflict situations: the *approach-approach* conflict, in which two equally desirable but mutually exclusive alternatives are presented; the *avoidance-avoidance* conflict, in which two equally aversive alternatives are presented in such a way that one but not both can be avoided; and the *approach-avoidance* conflict, in which a positive alternative is inseparably paired with an equally aversive one. Pavlov's experiment was an example of an approach-avoidance conflict.

The work of Miller and others suggests that the aversiveness or attractiveness of one alternative over another changes with the temporal or spatial distance of the alternative from the individual. For example, a child who must choose between two equally attractive objects but must wait longer to get one of them will take the one that is closer in time. An animal confronted with two equally aversive stimuli would be expected to approach the one slightly farther away if it is impossible to avoid both. However, two alternatives that are not equally aversive will nevertheless be experienced as equal if the person perceiving them is closer to the less aversive one.

The extreme agitation and inability to function that animals show in conflict experiments resembles the behavior of many psychiatric patients. The stress and somatic arousal that conflict situations bring about might be related to the origins of hypochondriacal complaints or even to more far-reaching biochemical changes. (See Chapter 17.) Much of the erratic and irrational behavior of some psychotic patients could reflect the fact that these people are reacting to a complex constellation of conflicting stimuli that other people do not perceive. Schizophrenic behavior does reflect a strategy of withdrawal from an incomprehensible situation, and in a conflict situation, similarly, a person seeks relief and escape. But the exact nature of the connection between conflict and psychological disorder remains unclear.

Figure 31.9 *(opposite)*
Many theories of psychological disorder use the notion of conflict as a central concept. Neal Miller and others have noted three basic types of behavioral conflict: (Top) in an approach-approach conflict, a person is faced with two alternatives of approximately equal desirability; they are mutually exclusive, however, and he must forego the other if he chooses one. (Middle) in a situation in which each alternative is equally unattractive, he is faced with an avoidance-avoidance conflict. He must choose "the lesser of two evils." Typically, the person in such a situation will vacillate, make continual comparisons, and daydream as a means of temporary escape. (Bottom) in an approach-avoidance situation, the person is both attracted to and repelled by the same stimulus. Resolution is difficult because approach means accepting some undesirable aspects, while avoidance means foregoing some things he desires.

Anxiety

Anxiety is another important concept for the understanding of psychological disorder and is of central importance in a number of theories of disorder, including psychoanalysis and social-learning theory. It is also a widely used concept in other areas of psychology. Research has shown a connection between anxiety and both autonomic arousal and task performance. Many students find that if they are anxious about a test, they do poorly even though they are well prepared. Psychologists have found that a high level of anxiety drastically reduces a person's ability to perform complex tasks. Most highly anxious people persist in making a previously learned response and therefore fail to learn new discriminations or to adjust to a change in an experimental task.

Like psychoneurotic people, most highly anxious people are more easily conditioned in classical conditioning experiments. The increased conditionability associated with high levels of anxiety might cause the person to acquire classically

rationalization
PROBABLY
SOUR
ANYWAY!
fixation
projection
WHAT
LION?
denial
displacement
reaction formation
identification
compensation
GV

conditioned responses and associations that make his behavior and thinking different from that of other people who are not highly anxious.

Anxiety can be viewed as an aversive stimulus that causes a person to adopt unusual and maladaptive behaviors as a means of avoiding that stimulus. R. B. Malmo and others have suggested that repeated experiences of extreme anxiety gradually lower a person's tolerance for anxiety-provoking situations. There is relatively little data linking psychotic behavior to heightened anxiety, but most professionals agree that heightened anxiety is an important factor in neurotic disorders.

Figure 31.10 *(opposite)*
According to psychoanalytic theory, when a person cannot directly alleviate anxiety, he may employ defense mechanisms, such as those illustrated, to keep his anxiety at a tolerable level.

Attribution Theory

S. Valins and R. Nisbett have recently attempted to explain some forms of disorder in terms of *attribution theory.* Many of the bizarre thoughts entertained by some psychiatric patients may be caused by their inability to discover the appropriate explanation for a given experience. Valins and Nisbett discuss the example of a forty-four-year-old man who had twitches over his right eye and in the areas of his heart and solar plexus. The man thought that the twitch over his eye was caused by a spirit that was helping him make decisions. The therapist later determined that the twitches occurred in situations of great stress. Valins and Nisbett propose that the individual developed the spirit delusion because he did not understand that the twitches stemmed from an autonomic reaction to stress situations. He had no explanation, so he attributed the twitches to spirit messages.

Valins and Nisbett believe that many disordered thought processes can be completely explained in these terms. They contend, for example, that the arousal and sensory apparatuses of the schizophrenic person are intact. The schizophrenic's disorganized thought stems from the fact that he attributes inappropriate explanations to his experiences.

It is possible, on the other hand, to integrate the attribution concept itself with the view of B. A. Maher and others that schizophrenia and other disorders are associated with atypical autonomic and sensory functioning. A person whose sensory apparatus gives him autonomic and other cues that most people do not get would certainly be expected to develop a most unusual system of cognitions.

COMPLEX THEORIES

The theories and research discussed in the preceding sections are only samples of the relevant material. Although heredity, biochemistry, anxiety, and the other materials in the preceding sections have been treated separately, there are important connections among them. One formulation that integrates different kinds of information is H. J. Eysenck's explanation of psychopathological behavior. It is based on his general theory of personality.

Eysenck thinks that both hereditary factors and the environment in which the person lives affect the development of psychological disorders. An individual inherits a tendency to respond in certain ways, but the exact nature of the behaviors he will learn depends upon the kinds of environmental influences to which he is exposed. The person who inherits a predisposition for neurosis, for example, can be expected to develop a psychoneurotic disorder only in an environment that turns this disposition into maladaptive learning. Learning is viewed as the process that integrates individual and situational factors.

Eysenck believes that most behavior can be understood in terms of two basic dimensions: *neuroticism* and *introversion-extraversion.* He thinks that genetically determined properties of the nervous system are the basis for individual differences along these dimensions. People at the high end of the neuroticism dimension are said to have a labile type of nervous system that causes them to react too strongly and too persistently to strong external stimuli. The nervous systems of people at the introversion end of the introversion-extraversion continuum make these people

Figure 31.11
Hans Eysenck. Eysenck, a British psychologist, has played a large role in the development and growth of the behavior modification movement. In addition to his laboratory research, he has written extensively about the application of learning principles to the understanding and modification of deviant behavior. Eysenck is radically opposed to traditional, psychodynamic psychotherapies. In 1952 he wrote a research review in which he claimed to show that traditional therapies were no more effective than no treatment at all. This claim generated heated replies and counterclaims, and the ensuing controversy resulted in more sophisticated experiments designed to determine the outcomes of psychotherapy.

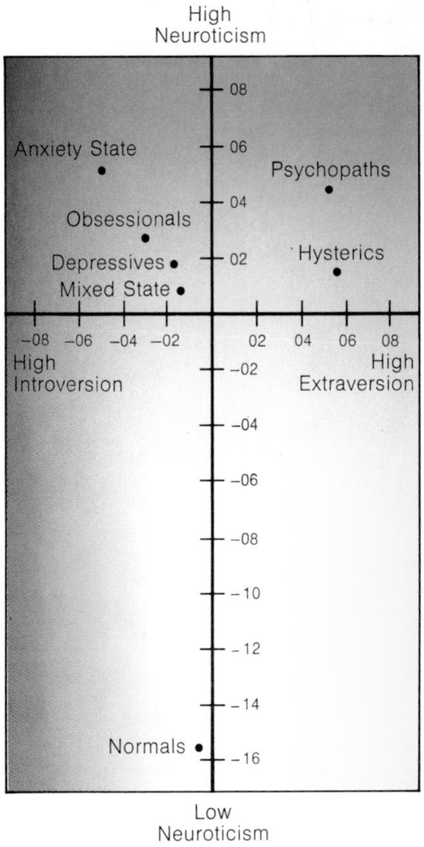

Figure 31.12
The coordinates in Eysenck's classification system upon which normal and neurotic people can be located. The two key dimensions are introversion-extraversion and neuroticism. Normal persons are low in neuroticism, and they show both introverted and extraverted characteristics. Psychopaths, for example, are higher in neuroticism than hysterics and are quite highly extraverted. (After Eysenck, 1957.)

develop conditioned responses more readily than people falling near the middle of this dimension; people at the extraversion end of the continuum condition least easily.

The terms extraversion, introversion, and neuroticism are descriptive of the kinds of behaviors typically shown by people with these kinds of nervous systems. As Figure 31.12 shows, Eysenck's data suggest that most people with highly labile nervous systems learn "neuroticlike" behaviors and concerns; most people who condition very quickly, on the other hand, develop passive and introverted life styles.

Although these dimensions are independent—that is, labile nervous systems are found in both highly conditionable people and people who are less easily conditioned—the influences of these two dimensions interact and cause the person to learn different kinds of behaviors. When a person has a highly labile nervous system and very poor conditionability, he can be expected to develop an extraverted and unrestrained style of behaving. Psychological disorders for people falling at these extremes of the two dimensions typically include assaultive and psychopathic behaviors. On the other hand, when an extremely labile nervous system is combined with high conditionability, the person is likely to become seclusive and obsessed by private fears and anxieties. Eysenck has also postulated a psychotic-nonpsychotic dimension, but there is, at this time, much less information about the possible physiological basis of such a dimension.

The work of J. Dollard and N. E. Miller is another important attempt to explain psychological disorder by drawing together several different concepts. Dollard and Miller have explored the way a person's culture and situation influence his psychosexual development. Their work reflects the assumption that psychoanalytic theory, which describes psychosexual development, provides an accurate picture of a person's psychodynamic development. They say, however, that an adequate explanation of both normal and abnormal behavior requires a more detailed account of external influences. In their attempt to account for environmental influence, they have drawn heavily upon concepts from learning theory.

Dollard and Miller have, for example, substituted the principle of reinforcement for Freud's pleasure principle, which is discussed in Chapter 21. They believe that the person reacts to his psychodynamic conflict with behaviors that are, in some way, reinforced by the environment. This permits them to retain the view that fantasies and other symbolic representations have satisfaction value and even influence motivation, at least on the unconscious level. However, it also allows them to explain why a specific person develops a specific form of disorder or why he chooses to rely upon a particular one of the many behaviors that would be consistent with his own psychodynamic characteristics.

They believe, in short, that it is important to place greater emphasis upon factors in the external environment. They see the psychiatric patient as becoming ill and "getting well in real life." In *Personality and Psychotherapy*, Dollard and Miller say that the concept of "reality"—as in Freud's reality principle—is too ambiguous. They therefore elaborate it in terms of physical and social conditions of learning. They say that understanding behavior requires understanding not only the psychological concepts and principles but also the social conditions—particularly the ones that the structure of society imposes.

PROBLEMS IN RESEARCH

A major methodological problem in psychopathology research is the imprecision of psychodiagnostic categories. The purpose of the classification system, which is described in Chapter 30, is to provide a method of grouping psychologically disturbed people. A category of disorder would include people who are more similar to each other than they are to individuals included in other groups.

Theoretically, the researcher who is familiar with the relevant descriptions and distinctions can diagnose people accordingly and proceed to search for biochemical, psychological, or other differences among groups. But, in fact, most people who suffer from psychological disorders show a variety of symptoms and characteristics that are descriptive of more than one diagnostic category.

This problem could be called the "nectarine dilemma." Just as a nectarine has both peachlike and apricotlike characteristics, most mentally ill individuals have disorders common to more than one diagnostic group. This lack of precision in the diagnostic process makes it difficult for the researcher to create groups of "pure," or blue ribbon, diagnostic types and to interpret research results. For example, a study comparing the biochemistry of schizophrenics with that of normal persons might show a unique biochemical element for some but not all of the schizophrenic persons. How is the investigator to be sure whether there is a real connection between schizophrenia and the isolated element? It might be that such a relationship does exist and that the "schizophrenic" patients who do not have the biochemical element were incorrectly diagnosed. On the other hand, the biochemical difference may indicate a problem that is sometimes, and only peripherally, related to schizophrenia.

Because of this dilemma many researchers try to study only "classic" or "textbook" cases, like the schizophrenics that Heath studied. But these cases are the exception not the rule. Many other researchers have concluded that diagnostic classification is not a useful research tool. They feel that there is no reason to assume that a similarity of overt characteristics necessarily reflects a similarity of underlying causes. They argue against this assumption for two reasons: (1) the diagnostic system is imprecise, and (2) research that tries to find underlying processes of entities like "schizophrenia" has failed continually.

Another difficulty in psychopathology research is that it can be conducted only after a person has become disturbed. This might be called the "chicken or egg" problem. For example, when an investigator finds that factor *X* is almost always present in cases of a given disorder, how does he know whether *X* causes the disorder or the disorder causes *X*?

In the double-bind theory of schizophrenia described earlier, the researchers studied interactions of the families in which a child had already developed a schizophrenic disorder and found that the parents—especially the mother—behaved in ways that simultaneously communicated positive and negative feelings toward the child. Bateson and his colleagues, you will remember, hypothesized that the mother's behavior causes the child's disturbance. However, it is also possible that the mother feels ambivalent and acts in contradictory ways because the child is disturbed, for a disturbed child can be expected to stimulate both compassion and irritation in a parent. Research into either the biochemical or the psychological aspects of abnormal behavior presents this problem of chicken or egg because mental illness may cause changes both in metabolism and in the external environment (the mother's behavior, in this case).

In the short run, at least, researchers will have to depend on their own intelligence and intuition to decide which direction of causality is more likely the real one. Even if the incidence of blue ribbon cases were high—which it is not—it would be almost impossible to completely monitor the lives of enough people for a sufficiently long period of time—say, from birth through forty years—to provide answers to these questions. Experimentation is an ethically unacceptable alternative. If an investigator suspects that some factor, a chemical substance or psychological experience, can trigger a disorder, clearly he cannot expose a person to that factor unless he is quite sure that he can return the person to his preexposed state. Eventually, it may be possible to study from birth certain people whose characteristics would

Figure 31.13
John Dollard. Dollard and Neal Miller helped to bridge the gap between psychoanalysis and learning theory with their book, *Personality Development and Psychopathology.* Their writing provided a discussion of Freudian concepts within the language of Hull's theory of learning. These concepts thus became more understandable to academic psychologists, who could go on to explore psychoanalytic theory through controlled research.

make them likely to develop a psychological disorder. Certainly this strategy would be possible for inherited and physiological factors, but investigators would need strong leads.

A third problem in psychopathology research has to do with *sequential causative factors.* In other words, psychological disorders may be the result of a series of changes or processes in which each step is caused by a different set of circumstances. The following example illustrates the possibility of this kind of causal chain.

Let us assume that one characteristic a person inherits is the high lability of his nervous system, that is, a strong susceptibility to autonomic arousal. Let us also assume that although the person develops ways of accommodating to or channeling this extreme arousal, it can initially produce a temporary biochemical imbalance (before modes of accommodation develop). Therefore, if this type of person should encounter very stressful situations—perhaps situations of extreme conflict—at a very early age, the biochemical imbalance will occur.

During the period of chemical imbalance a person's perceptions and cognitions are distorted. Thus we may have a child in whom heredity and early environment combine to give an altered view of the world. Moreover, because the condition is transient and the child is very young, these occurrences go unnoticed. After the critical period is over the child looks and acts like any other child. He is different only in that he has had and remembers experiences that most children have not had.

Now let us assume that for a considerable length of time the child's psychological development revolves around mastering the current environment, developing language skills, and formulating an understanding of the world. Later, when the child begins to refine his cognitive map or understanding of the world, he compares his memories with his present experiences. The way he integrates these memories of early experiences results in perceptions and attitudes that are very different from other people's. However, the child is not yet mentally ill.

The way his family reacts to him is important. Will they find his uniqueness troublesome and anxiety provoking? The nature of his past learning is a determining

Figure 31.14
A possible set of sequential causative factors might operate as follows. The child is born with a highly labile autonomic nervous system. As an infant, he suffers a temporary chemical change in that system during which the world begins to "spin" and become multicolored; finally, the infant faints. He has no language to communicate what he feels. Between three and five years of age, a period of normal development, the child remembers those early experiences, and tries to understand and interpret them. He associates the spinning feeling and colors with situations in which he was highly stimulated—being tossed in the air, riding in a car. He tries to tell them to others: "Remember, mommy, when we were riding in the car, and the rainbow was going around and Daddy crashed the car?" If his parents assume that this behavior is not extraordinary and say "well, no, maybe you dreamed it," the child will probably go on to something else. However, if the parents become anxious about these "abnormal" images, then it may become important for the child to solve the puzzle. He may think and worry about it continually, daydream, even hallucinate.

factor, too. How will he react to these experiences that produce stress and confusion? What kinds of demands will his future environment make on him? Should the person find himself in a situation where his behaviors are totally inappropriate, he would be unable to function. He would then have a psychological disorder.

The preceding example tries to show how multiple causative factors might operate sequentially and to suggest the almost infinite number of possible causal chains. Like scientists in other areas, the researcher in psychopathology attempts to fully explore a specific phenomenon or set of apparently related phenomena. The questions he can ask—or rather scientifically investigate—and the answers he finds are limited. Much of the material discussed in this chapter will some day be integrated into yet unformulated theories to provide a more comprehensive understanding of psychological disorder. Future research will probably indicate that many factors that now seem related to psychological disorders are, in fact, extraneous.

SUGGESTED READINGS

CAMERON, N. *Personality Development and Psychopathology.* Boston, Houghton Mifflin, 1963. This work provides the reader with an understanding of how the psychoanalytically oriented clinician views psychological development and its relation to psychological disorders. It is a relatively complete presentation but can be easily understood by the unsophisticated reader.

FENICHEL, O. *The Psychoanalytic Theory of Neurosis.* New York, Norton, 1945. This comprehensive and well-written presentation of the psychoanalytic theory of psychological disorder continues to be one of the standard reference books. When used as a text it is most appropriate at the graduate-school level. However, its clear and precise presentation makes it useful for others who wish to thoroughly pursue a specific topic, for example, anxiety.

KAPLAN, B. (Ed.). *The Inner World of Mental Illness.* New York, Harper & Row, 1964. This book contains a collection of descriptions of what it is like to have a psychological disorder. Each is written by the person who experienced the disorder. This volume is invaluable for the student who wants to understand what it is like to have a psychological disorder.

MAHER, B. A. *Principles of Psychopathology: An Experimental Approach.* New York, McGraw-Hill, 1966. This unique volume reviews much of the research in the area of psychopathology. It represents an attempt to provide a basis for understanding and researching psychological disorders in terms of more general psychological processes. It is written for advanced undergraduate-and graduate-level students. However, any student wishing to thoroughly explore specific topics will find this volume to be a valuable source.

SAHAKIAN, W. S. (Ed.). *Psychopathology Today: Experimentation, Theory and Research.* Itasca, Ill., F. E. Peacock, 1970. This volume contains a collection of important research papers concerning psychopathology. The volume is well-organized, and the editor has provided introductory discussions for each section. These introductions allow the reader to understand the individual papers as parts of a comprehensive whole.

ULLMAN, L. P., and KRASNER, L. *A Psychological Approach to Abnormal Behavior.* New York, Holt, Rinehart and Winston, 1970. This volume provides a simply written yet comprehensive understanding of psychological disorders that is based on learning-theory principles. It is useful for students at all levels.

WHITE, R. W. *The Abnormal Personality.* 3rd ed. New York, Ronald Press, 1964. This text provides an excellent introduction to the subject matter of psychopathology. The various forms of psychological disorders are described and a brief discussion of the theories and empirical data concerning each is provided. A wide variety of deviant behaviors are discussed. The reader need not have studied psychology before.

32
Psychotherapy I

The only time I ever felt the need for psychotherapy myself was when I was going through basic training in the army. I don't suppose there was ever a time when I hated anything so much and yet felt so helpless to escape. It seemed to me that if I could at least alter my feelings about the army, that would be something, so I seized the opportunity, now and then, to talk to one of the psychiatrists on the base. I generally felt a little better for doing so—perhaps because it gave me the opportunity to blow off steam and because it gave me the feeling that someone would at least listen.

I must say, though, that I developed a system of practical psychotherapy (so to speak) that enabled me on several occasions to get out of the worst of the army. I was classified as a "critically needed specialist" because I had two degrees in chemistry at that time, but I quickly and sorrowfully learned that a critically needed specialist was not needed at all, critically or otherwise, and that my major jobs consisted of KP and latrine duty. I also noticed, on the other hand, that typists were in great demand and were treated as aristocrats. Yet I could not ask to be a typist for then it would seem, rightly, as though I were gold-bricking, and I would be assigned more KP as punishment.

What I did, then, on more than one occasion when I arrived at a new post was to go to the Orderly Room and ask the First Sergeant, very politely, if I might use a spare typewriter for a few minutes to write a letter to my wife. I would be given permission by an uninterested First Sergeant. I would then sit down, wait for silence, and tear into the letter at top speed (I can go ninety words a minute). Before I had finished a single paragraph, there would be a heavy finger on my shoulder, and the First Sergeant would say, "How would you like to work here as a typist, soldier?" After that there would be no more KP. I would get my food served to me by glowering, critically needed specialists.

In all honesty, though, I must report that my typing once worked out to less than advantage. Before I was drafted into the army, I spent some years at the Navy Yard in Philadelphia. There I worked as a chemist, but it was frequently necessary for me to get material typed. For the purpose, I made use of the secretarial pool. The only trouble was that I was very low down on the chain of command, and it was only rarely that any typist ever managed to filter down to my level. Being young and impatient, I walked into the secretarial pool one day and asked for permission to use a spare typewriter. Glad to have me do my own work, the secretary in charge agreed. So I sat down, typed my report, and left. When I returned some days later to do another job, I was kicked off the premises. Can you guess why? Well, the typists complained that listening to a chemist type at my speed ruined their morale. So from then on, I had to wait till a typist had time for me, which was hardly ever.

I. A.

People change. They change their attitudes, their ways of behaving, and their relations with each other. Some of this change is the result of new learning, but some must be the modification or relearning of attitudes. When the attitudes people hold do not allow constructive functioning in the world, these people may need aid in adjusting their attitudes and behaviors. The task of psychotherapy is to help them do it. This chapter supplies an overview and critical examination of psychoanalytically-oriented psychotherapies; Chapter 33 discusses some newer approaches in psychotherapy.

PSYCHOTHERAPY IN DIFFERENT CULTURES

Wherever you go in the world, you will find that societies, no matter how small or how primitive, have methods for treating psychological disorders. In Western societies the many methods of treatment can be classified under the general heading *psychotherapy.* E. Torrey, a psychiatrist at the National Institute of Mental Health, has suggested that in spite of the apparent differences in methods of treatment across cultures, tribal medicine men and psychiatrists are very similar behind their masks and pipes. They only seem different because their cultural traditions differ. An American psychiatrist for example, might tell an African bushman that his phobia is the result of a bad relationship with his mother, but this analysis would

Figure 32.1
The work of tribal medicine men in nontechnological cultures often parallels the practices of psychotherapists in Western society. (Left) native American medicine man taking part in the Apache Sunrise Dance (a puberty rite for a young girl); (right) Aborigine medicine man (dancing in a corroboree, a nocturnal celebration of an important event). Medicine men like these help their patients partly because of the patient's belief that he will be cured, the patient's suggestibility, and the medicine man's prestige—factors that are important in "sophisticated" psychotherapy as well.

sound incomprehensible to the bushman—approximately as incomprehensible as it would sound to an American if an African medicine man were to tell him that an ancestral spirit was possessing him and causing his phobia.

Methods of psychotherapy in primitive cultures and ancient civilizations have sometimes anticipated the modern techniques of Western society. Drugs were used in West Africa with some effectiveness long before they appeared in Europe. Contemporary shock therapy is reminiscent of the technique of applying electric eels to the heads of "possessed" patients, employed some 4,000 years ago. Many new techniques in psychotherapy are based on principles of learning, but these principles governed practices long ago in Africa. For example, medicine men in western Nigeria cured bed-wetting in boys with a technique based on the principles of classical conditioning. A toad was tied to the penis of a young bed-wetter. When he wet the bed, the toad croaked and woke him up. Modern behavior therapists have invented devices that serve a similar function. In one such device, bed-wetting completes an electric circuit that sets off an electrical alarm and awakens the bed-wetter.

If the psychotherapeutic practices of other societies seem strange to us, it may be because we are unfamiliar with their cultural traditions. The *basic* principles of treatment are often surprisingly alike: The suggestibility of the patient, the authority of the therapist, and the respect each has for the other seem to be basic to treatment in many cultures. There is considerable evidence that, regardless of the particular method of treatment, the personal relationship between the healer and sufferer is the major factor in an effective cure.

Figure 32.2
The Viennese physician, *Anton Mesmer,* is the person who gave hypnosis, or mesmerism, its name. He had a flamboyant personality and liked spectacular happenings. He would "cure" patients by touching their bodies with a wand or by guiding their bodies to the surface of a *Baque,* or large vat that was filled with magnetized water. He was therefore denounced and barred by his fellow physicians, in both Vienna and Paris. His dramatic flair, unfortunately, overshadowed the fact that he was using psychological treatment for psychological disorder.

EARLY PSYCHOTHERAPY

Two traditions of healing have endured throughout mankind's history: the supernatural and the naturalistic. The supernatural tradition viewed mental disorder as caused by supernatural forces and evil spirits; people believed that the mentally ill were "possessed" by demons and devils. Unfortunately for the afflicted ones, it was often thought that evil spirits had invaded their minds and bodies because they did not live properly. As a result, they were often punished or taken to religious men for exorcism and cure.

The naturalistic tradition, on the other hand, related mental disturbance to physical illness and assumed that it was the result of natural causes. The initial effect of the naturalistic tradition was good; it cast mental disorder in a medical rather than a moral idiom and encouraged humane treatment of the mentally disturbed. When the public began to view mental disorder in the same way that it viewed physical illness, treatment also changed—from jail sentences, faith healing, and

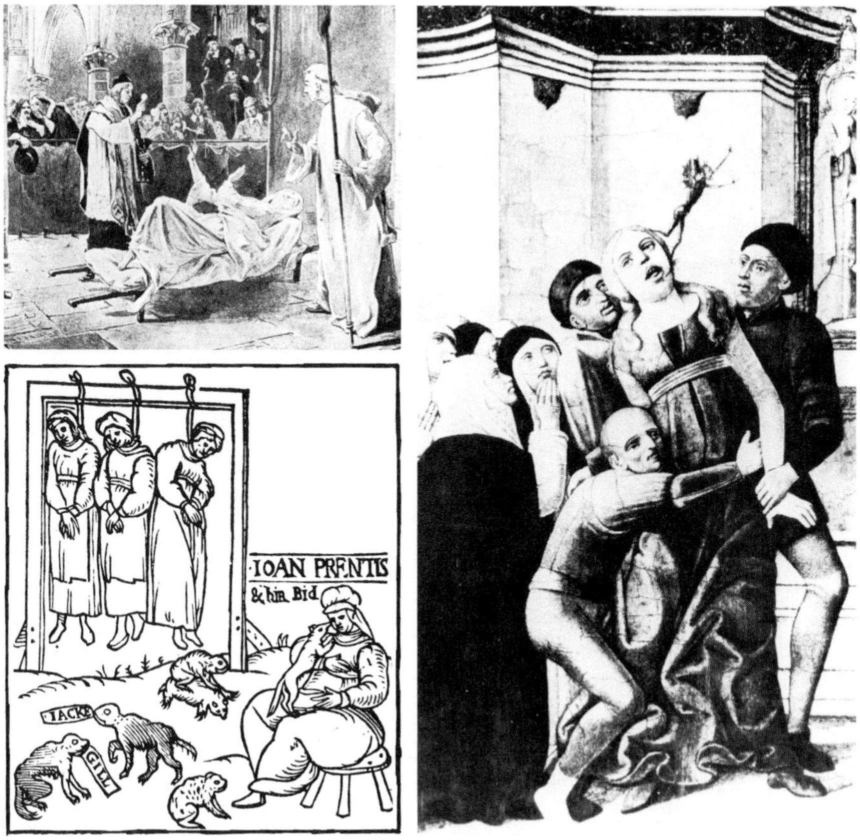

Figure 32.3
Mental disorders were once thought to be caused by evil spirits, and theologians were responsible for detecting and treating those persons possessed by, or in league with, the devil. (Top left), a medieval engraving of a method of exorcism, under the direction of theologians. (Bottom left) a woodcut from the title page of a pamphlet on the third Chelmsford witch trial in 1591 that illustrates the execution of three witches. (Right) a late-fifteenth-century painting that portrays Saint Catherine of Sienna casting the devil out of a possessed woman.

torture to hospitalization and psychotherapy. It followed that therapy was performed by medical men (doctors) and patterned after the cures for physical illness.

In spite of the tremendous benefit of the naturalistic tradition and the medical model of mental illness, recently psychologists such as O. H. Mowrer and T. Szasz have argued that the medical-model approach is deficient. They point out that mental illness *is* different from physical illness and that patients are often less "sick" than they are socially maladjusted. Chapter 30 examines the arguments surrounding the medical model of mental illness in greater detail.

Most types of psychotherapy, primitive and modern, have been influenced by both traditions. In the Western world the emphasis changed from the supernatural to the natural in the late eighteenth and early nineteenth centuries. Prior to this time many disorders, especially those without obvious physical causes, were treated by faith healing. For example, a late eighteenth-century practice that took account of scientific knowledge about physical properties still reflected vestiges of the supernatural approach: a magnet was held to the afflicted parts of a patient's body in an attempt to alter the forces that were causing the affliction. One step away from the supernatural tradition was taken by a Viennese physician, Anton Mesmer, the discoverer of mesmerism, or hypnosis. Mesmer believed that all individuals were under the influence of the stars and that an invisible but powerful force called animal magnetism enveloped all forms of life. When this magnetic force was out of harmony, physical and mental illness occurred. The medical men of Mesmer's day objected to his views and eventually forbade him to practice in France, but mesmerism continued to fascinate thinkers of his time. Mesmer's great contribution was not his theory or even his technique. He is important because he suggested a *psychological* cure for mental disorder. One of the thinkers most influenced by Mesmer was Jean Martin Charcot, a neurologist. Charcot advanced the treatment of mental disorder by applying the technique of hypnotism to the cure of hysteria,

Figure 32.4
O. H. Mowrer has made basic contributions to the psychology of learning, to abnormal psychology, and to the study of psychotherapy. Mowrer has written extensively about the role of personal responsibility in mental disorder. He considers that negative consequences result from considering people "mentally ill"; he believes that persons who require therapy should be held accountable for their behavior, in order that they examine it and learn to behave in a less deviant manner.

Figure 32.5
Charcot at his clinic at Salpetrière. This painting shows him demonstrating hypnosis to his class. He experimented extensively with both the induction and removal of hysterical symptoms under hypnosis. His pioneering work with hysterical neurosis brought Sigmund Freud to study under him.

a neurosis that often produces paralysis in a limb, blindness, or deafness, with no physiological cause (see Chapter 30).

It was while Charcot was practicing in Paris in 1885 that the single most important event in the history of psychotherapy occurred—a young physiologist named Sigmund Freud went to study under him. Freud was basically a medical man, rooted in the naturalistic tradition. He saw merit, however, in the hypnotic techniques of Charcot; after all, they worked! Freud began by using hypnotism to cure hysteric disorders. Then he made a discovery that changed the course of psychotherapy: Patients who were under the influence of a hypnotist could remember early, shocking events in their lives, often of a sexual nature—and after they had remembered them the symptoms of their disorders disappeared or at least diminished. As Freud continued to work with hysterical patients, he discovered that he did not need to hypnotize them in order to make them remember childhood traumas. From these experiences Freud gained the knowledge that started him on the route to the formulation of psychoanalytic theory and the practice of psychoanalysis.

Figure 32.6
Thomas Szasz, a psychiatrist, has argued forcefully that "the myth of mental illness" obscures the true nature of deviant behavior; such behavior, Szasz claims, is the person's attempt to solve a problem in living. This attempted solution, however, may clash with others' interests, and result in the person's being labeled "sick." Szasz has also written extensively on the power of psychiatrists and has argued that psychiatric hospitalization often functions as a means of unjustly depriving people of their freedom.

One of Freud's great contributions was to move the study of mental illness away from the supernatural. Freud's theory is based on a medical model of mental disorder. He thought that traumatic experiences invade the mind and cause mental illness in much the same way that noxious materials invade the body and produce physical illness. The pressure caused by the repression from consciousness of these festering memories, Freud thought, could be relieved by bringing them to consciousness—much as one lances a boil to release the pus.

The creation of the theory of psychoanalysis and psychoanalytic psychotherapy marked the beginning of modern psychotherapy. Psychoanalysis, however, is not strictly scientific—no therapy is. It is a unique combination of art and science; of fact, intuition, and theory; and, in the final analysis, of the supernatural and natural. Not all modern psychotherapies agree with the basic tenets of psychoanalysis, but they have all been influenced by it.

CHARACTERISTICS OF MODERN PSYCHOTHERAPY

There are many kinds or *schools* of psychotherapy in the Western world. By examining some of the characteristics common to all schools of psychotherapy and by noting differences in emphasis among them, we can gain a general understanding of the nature of psychotherapy and an introduction to the different schools of thought. We will later examine the techniques of the various schools in detail.

The most essential characteristic of psychotherapy is its goal: to change the life of the patient for the better. Various schools of psychotherapy interpret this goal in different ways, but they all agree that change is necessary. Some schools hold

Figure 32.7
One patient's progress toward adjustment can be traced through a sequence of pictures he produced in art therapy sessions. He was attempting to copy the painting shown at upper right. The first drawing he produced (middle right) reflects his psychotic state and disturbed perceptions: the form and perspective are markedly distorted, there is an inability to deal with colors, and details are almost entirely omitted. A subsequent drawing done with crayon (large picture) and an even later one done in watercolor (bottom right) show increasing clarity of perception and the ability to organize, plan, and execute a complex task.

that adjustment comes through self-understanding. Others encourage the patient to actively cultivate more satisfying interpersonal relationships in and out of the therapeutic setting. And others attempt to change specific responses like fear of snakes or kleptomania.

In all forms of psychotherapy the relationship between the therapist and the patient influences the patient's potential for change. In most schools of psychotherapy the relationship between patient and therapist is of central importance. A psychoanalyst, for example, will customarily serve as a substitute for his patients' mothers or fathers. He encourages his patients to *transfer* early reactions to their parents to him, so that they and he together can better understand and modify the reactions. In therapy based on principles of learning (that is, behavior therapy) the relationship between the patient and the therapist is less important. Most behavior therapists, however, recognize the fact that changes in behavior are mediated by the relationship between patient and therapist.

Characteristic of this relationship is the unique dependency and suggestibility of the patient. It is no accident that the practice of hypnosis, a technique based on suggestibility, paved the way for modern psychotherapy. Most people seek psychotherapy because they have exhausted their own resources for help. Even though many people have constructed a strong set of barriers and defenses to protect themselves, the fact that they have sought help indicates that their defenses are not working or that they are too costly. The therapist is an expert in psychological health and many patients look to him as their savior.

Although many therapists attempt to be nondirective, all of them exert some influence on the way their patients see the world. Thus, another characteristic of psychotherapy is the tremendous personal power of the psychotherapist. Although many therapists refuse to give advice and insist that the patient must learn to solve his problems for himself, therapists are sometimes induced to help the patient by showing him the way.

People come to psychotherapy because their life experiences are unsatisfactory, but before change can occur, the way for new experiences must be paved. Psychoanalysts typically encourage a person to relive old relationships and work out the problems he has encountered in them. He is encouraged to come to terms with his needs and fantasies and to develop a viable relationship with the therapist. Other types of psychotherapy attempt to create situations in which the patient can develop new ways of dealing with himself and his world—in general, or as relates to a specific troublesome set of behaviors. Masters and Johnson's treatment of sexual problems, discussed in Chapter 33, is an example of this type of therapy.

Another characteristic of successful psychotherapy is that it alters the patient's self-concept, either globally or as it relates to specific responses. One school of therapy, called client-centered therapy, originated from the self theory of Carl Rogers. (See Chapter 21 for a discussion of self theory; client-centered therapy is discussed at length in Chapter 33.)

All schools of psychotherapy attempt to change the feelings, thoughts, and behavior of their patients. Schools differ, however, in the extent to which they focus on feelings, thoughts, or behavior. Psychoanalysis, for example, attempts to help people gain an understanding of their deep underlying conflicts. With understanding, or *insight,* come changes in feelings and behavior. Some other schools of psychotherapy argue that behavior can be changed without regard for the reason it originally occurred. Once a person's behavior is changed, they argue, changes in thoughts and feelings will follow.

By definition, all schools of psychotherapy supply treatment. Some schools attempt to institute major personality changes; other schools attempt to change particular behaviors. Schools of psychotherapy that attempt to make major changes have one general strategy: to work out internal conflicts through conversation. Psychoanalysis is such a therapy. Other schools of psychotherapy focus on *specific* techniques for correcting *specific* behavioral problems.

Psychiatrists are medical doctors who specialize in the treatment of mental illness. They generally take a post-M.D. internship in a mental institution. Because of their medical background, psychiatrists tend to be more biologically oriented than psychologists.

Psychoanalysts are psychiatrists who have taken special training in the theory of personality and techniques of psychotherapy of Sigmund Freud, usually from an established psychoanalyst. They must themselves be psychoanalyzed before they can practice.

Lay Analysts are psychoanalysts who do not have degrees in medicine but who have studied with established psychoanalysts. The most famous lay analysts are Anna Freud and Erik Erikson.

Clinical Psychologists are therapists with a Ph.D. degree. They are the product of a three-to-four-year research-oriented program in the social sciences, plus a one-year predoctoral or postdoctoral internship in psychotherapy and psychological assessment.

Counselors generally have a Master's or Doctor's degree in Counseling Psychology. They usually work in educational institutions where they are available for consultation about personal problems. They customarily refer clients with serious problems to psychiatrists or psychologists.

Psychiatric Social Workers are people with a graduate degree in Psychiatric Social Work. They generally receive supervised practical training coupled with two years of courses in psychology.

Who Are the Therapists?

Every psychotherapist chooses the therapeutic approach that he considers most efficient. Some therapists explicitly and self-consciously align themselves with a formal school of psychotherapy and use only its techniques. Most, however, are *eclectic;* that is, they do not subscribe to one theory but adopt practices employed by the various schools. They select the techniques they consider most appropriate for the particular problems they encounter. On the one hand, their approach is highly flexible and can be beneficially adapted to the requirements of the immediate situation. On the other hand, their approach may be ineffective to the extent that their choices are intuitive or impressionistic rather than based on a well-integrated theory. The effectiveness of an eclectic approach depends on the skill of the therapist who employs it.

In our society there are many people who conduct psychotherapy. Some are highly trained; others have little or no formal training at all. Anyone can administer psychotherapy, but only psychoanalysts, psychiatrists, clinical psychologists, counselors, and psychiatric social workers are trained to do so. (See adjacent margin.)

As a physician, the psychiatrist is the only therapist who can prescribe medicine or electroshock therapy. Clinical psychologists typically administer psychological tests. Counselors are usually affiliated with an institution, like a school or university, and give advice about immediately pressing personal problems. The primary function of the psychiatric social worker is to investigate and modify the home environment of the patient.

When most people think of psychotherapy, they think of psychoanalysts, psychiatrists, or clinical psychologists. It is, however, a fact that if you needed advice about a personal problem, you would be more likely to go to a nonprofessional than a professional. And surprisingly, you would more likely be happy with the advice he gave you. As shown in Figure 32.9, a nationwide survey for the Joint Commission of Mental Illness and Health, conducted by G. Gurin, J. Veroff, and S. Feld, found that most people who needed help went to nonprofessional therapists. As with all surveys, the survey by the Joint Commission is unable to completely explain its findings. It is possible that people who seek professional help are more seriously troubled than those who seek nonprofessional help. Yet the evidence is consistent with the argument advanced by W. Schofield in his book *Psychotherapy, The Purchase of Friendship* that personnel in the outside community can serve a therapeutic function as well as those specially trained to give psychotherapy.

Source of Help	Percent Choosing Source	Percent Satisfied with Help
Clergymen	42	65
Medical Doctors	29	65
Marriage Counselors	10	25
Private Practitioners or Social Agencies	10	39
Psychiatrists or Psychologists	18	46

N=345; percent more than 100 because some people used more than one source.

Figure 32.9
A nationwide survey illustrates that more people seek counseling from nonprofessional therapists (especially doctors and clergymen) than from professional therapists.
(After Gurin, Veroff, and Feld, 1960.)

Who Are the Patients?

At some time in his life everyone wonders if he will need psychotherapy, and if he does, what will happen to him. No one can definitely predict who will need psychotherapy, but research has shown that given the fact that someone does need treatment, his social status will determine whether he receives private individual psychotherapy or is confined to an institution.

S. L. Garfield reported that a disproportionately high percentage of the patients accepted for individual out-patient therapy are young, educated, and of high socioeconomic status, like the therapist. Patients of low socioeconomic status are likely to be assigned to a clinic or hospitalized, and when hospitalized, to be given drug treatment and custodial care rather than psychotherapy.

Most lower-class patients tend to remain in therapy for a shorter period of time than do middle-class patients. Lower-class patients are also less likely than middle-class patients to meet the expectations of (typically middle-class) psychotherapists. They are not as verbal as most members of the middle class, nor are they impressed by the therapist's technical language and theoretical formulations. Unlike the middle-class therapist, these patients are less apt to be concerned with self-actualization and more apt to be concerned with basic survival. In sum, lower-class patients discontinue psychotherapy more frequently than upper-class patients because they understand the middle-class therapist less well. Communication between therapist and patient is hindered by the difference in background experiences, life style, social orientation, and basic values.

Probably the most common reason people in general drop out of psychotherapy is the disparity between their expectations and the initial experience. Garfield found that people who dropped out of psychotherapy often expected to receive specific advice about their problems in the first interview. They also expected a less permissive and more authoritative attitude on the part of the therapist than those who continued therapy. Other research has shown that lower-class patients typically expect a "medical psychiatric interview"; that is, they expect an interview in which the therapist takes the type of active, supportive role routinely attributed to medical practitioners. Most psychotherapists, however, are far more nondirective, noncommittal, and nonauthoritative than people expect them to be.

What Are Mental Institutions?

If a person felt that he had a psychological problem of sufficient severity to see a psychotherapist, the first thing he would have to do is find one. We have seen that people who are relatively well-to-do generally seek out private practitioners; a person who is not well off would probably end up seeing someone associated with an institution—a clinic, psychiatric ward of a general hospital, or a mental hospital. He would be given an initial interview, and if his disturbance was judged sufficiently severe, he might be committed. Some patients commit themselves to mental institutions; most, however, are committed by family, friends, or legal authorities.

Mental Hospitals Most patients in mental hospitals are housed in institutions financed and administered by state governments. The term "state hospital" is often synonymous with mental hospital. Other patients are housed in psychiatric wards of general hospitals, federally operated hospitals such as those run by the Veterans' Administration, in-patient teaching hospitals, or expensive private hospitals.

The quality of treatment and available resources varies tremendously across mental institutions. Some supply adequate care, but all too often they lack sufficient personnel, particularly those expert in psychotherapy. In many cases the day-to-day

Figure 32.10
Conditions in state and county mental institutions are often very poor. Overcrowding, poor facilities, understaffing, and lack of effective therapeutic programs characterize many hospital wards. Much of this difficulty is a function of inadequate funding. Another contributing factor is the heavy influence of institutional tradition; the patients are regarded as "mentally ill," there is sometimes little belief that they can "recover," and the staff reinforces docile and compliant behavior.

care in state hospitals is left to ward staff, and most of the patients' daily routine is irrelevant or even antagonistic to psychotherapy and cure. Patients are rewarded for passive compliance to hospital regulations and cooperation with rules of basic housekeeping. Drugs are commonly used to keep the patients manageable. Occupational therapy (keeping busy by working) is often the major form of rehabilitative effort offered by the institution. Custodial care is the only common, minimal denominator that all hospitals seem to provide.

In his book *Asylums,* E. Goffman shows how patients in mental hospitals become stripped of their identity. First, material possessions relevant to a sense of

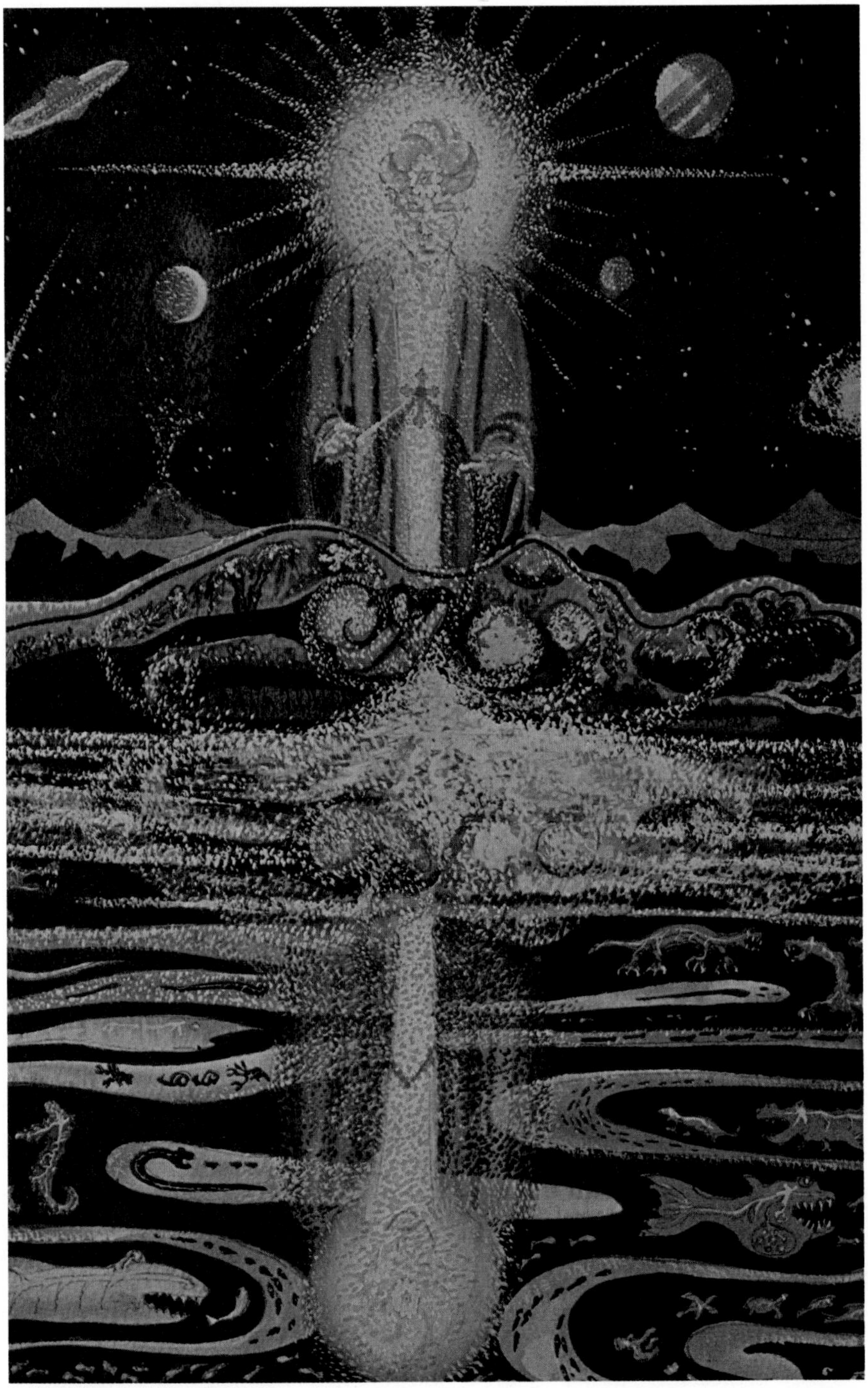

Figure 32.11
In an unstimulating hospital environment, retreating into fantasy may be the only road open to a patient. This retreat serves to increase the person's withdrawal from external reality, and the withdrawal is likely to perpetuate his problems. This painting was created by a hospitalized person preoccupied with religious and aggressive fantasies. A patient's art work may serve as a means for him to express and communicate his fantasies. Discussing his creations with other patients or with a staff member may help him to become more expressive and less withdrawn.

personal identity and individualism are confiscated, and institutional clothes substituted. Patients become molded into a pattern of obedience, dependence, and conformity by the deadening routine of sleep, meals, ping-pong, boring duties, and institutional dress. They are isolated from family and friends, who they often think have abandoned them. As they become increasingly apathetic and resigned, they effectively lose all ties with the outside social world. A reliance upon fantasy may well become their only means of adjusting to this dehumanizing plight. They are seen as crazy, so they act crazy, and eventually they may become crazy.

Whatever the patient's problem upon entering the hospital—be it a personal crisis, a family trauma, or a desire to work things out in a stress-free atmosphere—the effects of institutionalization may well be more noxious than the previous pathology. Research by J. K. Wing indicates that the longer a patient stays in the hospital, the less likely it is that members of the outside community will visit him, and the less likely it is that he will ever want to return to society.

A few hospitals may have some patients assigned to the *day hospital* or *night hospital*. The day-patients come to the hospital for the day's activities, usually including individual or group psychotherapy, but they return to their homes at night. Other patients may feel secure enough to maintain outside jobs and social contacts during the day, yet use the hospital as a reassuring place to sleep at night. In both cases, patients are able to escape the institutionalization syndrome by virtue of their contact with the outside world.

Halfway Houses The term *halfway house* is used to describe institutions that are half way between hospitals and a normal social environment. Halfway houses allow patients more self-regulation than hospitals. Patients typically enter halfway houses when they feel the need for the support of a social community that is more structured than their own and more responsive to their problems but that does not deprive them of their freedom. Patients may enter the halfway house as a transitional way station after leaving the hospital, or they may enter the house directly from the outside community.

Halfway houses vary tremendously in their structure, but all tend to consist of a group of patients living and sharing experiences together in a self-governing community. There are usually relatively few professional staff members present, but the houses are generally quite closely associated with professional workers or a social organization. Unwritten rules and implicit social norms guide the members. Subtle social pressure is brought to bear on the patient to encourage him to continue therapy and solve his problems.

The typical halfway house has around twenty residents, the majority of whom are males between twenty and thirty years of age. Females and males are not segregated, and "normal" people may live in the halfway house with the patients. H. L. Raush and C. L. Raush found the severity of psychological disturbance in halfway houses to be about the same as in hospitals.

Whether psychotherapy is given in an institution, halfway house, or private office, the psychotherapist is guided by a theory or, as stated earlier in the chapter, by a combination of theories, many of which are discussed in Chapters 21 and 22.

PSYCHOANALYSIS

Earlier in this chapter we discussed the great influence of Freudian theory on the treatment of mental disorders, a theory that marked the beginning of modern psychotherapy. The term *psychoanalysis* describes the school and the system of therapy based on the theory of personality and psychopathology that issued from Sigmund Freud's treatment of the Viennese upper class at the beginning of the twentieth century.

In his theory of personality development, Freud assumed that human beings are driven by impulses derived from the biological demands of their bodies—by hunger, thirst, and, most important for the theory, by sex. From infancy, the individual strives for satisfaction of these needs and consequent tension reduction. The kinds and extent of the gratifications and frustrations he meets in his attempts to satisfy these needs are primarily responsible for his personality development. (The psychoanalytical theory of personality development is described at length in Chapter 21, and important aspects of the theory as it relates to moral development are discussed in Chapter 8.)

Neurosis, according to classical psychoanalytic theory, represents a fixation in a person's mental life at an early psychosexual level of development. (See Chapters 21 and 25 for an account of Freud's theory of the psychosexual aspects of sex-role acquisition.) The ego of the neurotic is so preoccupied with warding off impulses from the id and combating unrealistic demands from the superego—that is, with building and maintaining *defenses*—that it does not have time to constructively deal with reality (see Chapter 31). Patients in psychoanalysis are usually neurotics.

People are carefully evaluated before being accepted for psychoanalysis. Psychoanalysts feel that only a person with a relatively strong ego (sense of reality) outside the area affected by his neurosis can benefit from treatment. Once accepted for treatment, the patient is usually expected to come for five hourly visits per week (actually a fifty-minute hour). Such a schedule supposedly motivates the patient—he is required to invest considerable time and considerable money—and supplies the analyst with a great deal of information about his life.

The patient is asked to *free associate*—to say everything that enters his mind without censoring it or attempting to make it seem socially appropriate, logical, consistent, or relevant. The technique of free association is based on the theory that the id (instinctual drives) and repressed memories are dammed up and in search of discharge. The libidinal energy associated with these drives and memories is channelled into various defense mechanisms, but when external pressures become too great, new release mechanisms must be found. By eliminating the social requirements of everyday conversation and interaction, the analyst attempts to encourage the patient to lower his defenses and confront repressed memories. The analysis of defense mechanisms is the chief work of psychoanalytic treatment. (For a description of these mechanisms see Chapter 21.)

During treatment the patient traditionally lies on a couch, a posture that,

Figure 32.12
This painting by Henri Rousseau, called *The Dream,* can be considered a two-dimensional metaphor for the fantasy content of a person's free associations in psychoanalysis. The aim of free association is to encourage the patient to verbalize desires, thoughts, and drives that, according to Freudians, he has repressed. When the "unconscious becomes conscious," the analyst interprets the content in the hope of enabling his patient to take rational (ego) control over his irrational (id) fantasies.
(Collection, The Museum of Modern Art, New York. Gift of Nelson A. Rockefeller.)

because of its relationship to relaxation and sleep, helps bring unconscious processes to the surface. The patient also faces away from the analyst and usually receives few explicit cues from him. He is encouraged to project his fantasies onto a "blank screen"—the unseen, relatively unknown analyst. Through the mechanisms of transference, the patient treats the therapist as if he were his father, mother, or lover and transfers his feelings for that person to the therapist. By doing so, he reexperiences childhood conflicts that are inappropriate in the context of his current life. It is the analyst's task to help make the patient conscious of these transference feelings and fantasies. Any opposition on the patient's part to the goal of the treatment is identified by the analyst as a *resistance*, which represents a behavioral expression of the defenses the patient characteristically employs. The analyst's primary occupation then becomes the recognition of the patient's resistances to the analytic process.

Psychoanalytic treatment is very lengthy, typically on the order of three to five years. Defenses, or their manifestations in the analysis (resistances), have usually proved their usefulness to the patient for years and years. Because they have protected him against pain, acute anxiety, and insecurity for nearly a lifetime, they are quite difficult to alter. They must be interpreted repeatedly and in various contexts before a lasting change in the patient's personality structure can be effected. This process of repeated interpretation of resistance in order to effect lasting change is termed *working through.*

PSYCHOANALYTICALLY-ORIENTED PSYCHOTHERAPY

Many therapists maintain a basic allegiance to the Freudian perspective but have attempted to improve it in several important ways. These therapists collectively are called psychoanalytically-oriented psychotherapists. The two most basic differences between classical psychoanalysis and psychoanalytically-oriented psychotherapy are: (1) Psychoanalytically-oriented therapy takes a much shorter time than psychoanalysis, and (2) psychoanalytically-oriented psychotherapy involves greater direct social interaction between patient and therapist.

Psychoanalytically-oriented therapy typically is given once or twice a week rather than five times a week and lasts from a few months to a few years. The therapist customarily faces the patient (rather than sitting behind him) and assumes an active role in interacting with the patient. He encourages the patient to focus on significant material and to express his thoughts and feelings freely. The entire therapeutic process is more structured than orthodox psychoanalysis; this structure serves to minimize anxiety and speed up the working through of conflicts.

Transference is also an important part of psychoanalytically-oriented psychotherapy. As the patient interacts with the therapist, he inevitably reacts as he has in past relationships, especially early familial relationships. By making the patient aware of the differences between past relationships and his present relationship with the therapist, the therapist attempts to help the patient gain a realistic appraisal of his needs, desires, feelings, and patterns of interaction. Because the therapist is a stranger—a somewhat mysterious and ambiguous figure—he is an ideal object for projection. Ultimately, psychoanalytically-oriented psychotherapists try to provide a corrective relationship, in which the patient learns to understand his behaviors and attitudes toward the therapist. In doing so, the patient learns to understand himself better, and he may be able to form more satisfying relationships with others.

EGO ANALYSTS

Ego analysts also maintain a basic allegiance to classical Freudian theory, but they focus on functions of the ego rather than of the id and its instincts (see Chapter 21). To ego analysts, the behavior that is of major interest is learned in response to the external environment or to promptings of the ego rather than to sexual or aggressive instincts. Ego analysts are concerned with behavior in which the individual consciously, rather than unconsciously, directs his activities and constructively deals with his environment. Among the major figures in this group are Freud's daughter Anna Freud and Erik Erikson.

Classical psychoanalysts contend that all psychic energy must come from the id. Ego analysts, on the other hand, argue that the ego has its own source of energy and that it may perform autonomously. Although ego functions, such as thought, may have originally developed out of pressure from the id, they can become independent from the id and exert control over it.

Ego analysts have attempted to correct Freud's failure to study and emphasize normal or healthy behavior. They argue that because Freud failed to study healthier people, he overestimated the importance of sexual and aggressive instincts. Ego analysts acknowledge the fact that behavior disorders are often the result of pressures from the id and superego, but they say that relatively healthy people are usually guided by the ego.

Whereas Freud gave primary emphasis to the unconscious determination of behavior, the ego analysts lay greater stress on people's conscious planning and control of themselves and their environment. For example, Robert White says that drive reduction in itself cannot account for many of the most important aspects of human behavior. White holds that the pursuit of active contact with and mastery over the environment is as basic a motivation as hunger, thirst, or sex. (White's theory of competence motivation is discussed in Chapter 21.)

The goal of ego analysis is to improve the functioning and organization of the ego, so that the person gains greater control over himself and greater freedom from demands of the id, the superego, and the external environment.

Figure 32.13
Anna Freud, daughter of the founder and developer of psychoanalysis, has herself become a prominent figure in the history of psychoanalysis. She has focused more on ego than on id processes; among her many contributions to psychoanalytic theory is her discussion of the ego's defense mechanisms. She also formulated one of the earliest methods for the psychoanalytic treatment of children.

HOW SUCCESSFUL IS PSYCHOTHERAPY?

Psychoanalysis and the therapies that grew out of it have exerted great influence on modern individual psychotherapy, although the influence has not always generated strict adherence to their methods. Rather, the average psychotherapist, whose practice is essentially eclectic, has adopted some of the points of view and some of the methods. But is there any evidence that traditional individual psychotherapy works?

As we shall see, this important question is extremely difficult to answer. Freud's practices were basically exploratory. It is not enough to accept them on the basis of the genius of their founder; one must subject them to a critical appraisal, and, if they prove faulty, attempt to correct them or search for new techniques. The problem is that it is very difficult to measure the effect of psychotherapy. As was pointed out in Chapter 30, psychologists do not really have a good criterion for mental health. Before we can answer the question, does psychotherapy work, we must supply a criterion for success.

A. P. Goldstein found that people are often much more enthusiastic about their cure than are their therapist or their friends. They feel an increased sense of competence and productivity, but their improvement in work or in interpersonal relations is actually limited. In some cases reviewed by Goldstein, persons reported "highly successful cures" even though they still experienced the general symptoms that had brought them to therapy. Unfortunately for researchers, there are considerable pressures on the patient to report unfounded success in psychotherapy. S. R. Hathaway has discussed the *hello-goodby phenomenon* in psychotherapy. At the beginning of therapy there are pressures on the patient to justify his need for help; therefore, he exaggerates the seriousness of the symptoms. At the end of therapy the patient feels a need to justify the time, money, and energy he has expended

Figure 32.14
A metaphor for the question of therapy's efficacy could be this game of chance. If you pick the correct hand—get the right therapist and the right type of therapy for you—the result could be recovery and a powerful experience for the better. If you pick the wrong hand, it will be empty—you might spend years in therapy and be no better for it, or even be worse.

and to show appreciation toward the therapist, so he exaggerates the extent to which therapy has helped him.

If we cannot depend on the reaction of the patient, maybe we can rely on the judgment of the therapist. He should know whether or not his patients improve. The problem is, of course, that the therapist also has an investment in the outcome of psychotherapy and is not an unbiased observer.

Over the past several decades there have been a large number of psychological studies on the outcome of psychotherapy. In some cases, the criterion of success has been the report of the patient; in others, it has been the report of his therapist; in others it has been the appraisal of another psychologist; and in still others, the presence or absence of the patient in a mental institution. All these criteria are limited, and their limitations have made it difficult to evaluate the consequences of psychotherapy. Meanwhile, the success of psychotherapy is a very important issue in psychology. Discussion and debate about the effect of psychotherapy has become extremely heated, even vitriolic.

Eysenck's Critique

In 1952 H. Eysenck, a psychologist from England, published a critique of psychotherapy based on a statistical analysis of research projects on its success. He compared incidence of cure in psychotherapy with incidence of *spontaneous remission,* or natural cure, usually in patients in mental hospitals. A large proportion of patients (usually around two-thirds) spontaneously lose their symptoms over a period of time, even though they do not undergo psychotherapy. Eysenck's comparison yielded a startling figure: the recovery rate for patients who did not receive psychotherapy was as high as the rate of recovery for patients who actually underwent traditional psychotherapy. Eysenck determined that there was no reason to conclude that psychotherapy had any benefit at all. Psychotherapy had not been demonstrated, by measurable criteria, to be superior to no therapy at all.

The problems inherent in such research are many. As we have mentioned, the precise criteria for improvement—or remission—of symptoms in therapy are hard to define, especially years afterward. And the criteria for remission of symptoms in patients who do not receive psychotherapy are equally difficult to establish. Finally, the two groups that were compared (patients who received therapy and those who did not) may have been different. For example, patients who received psychotherapy, may have been more seriously disturbed than those who did not.

Bergin's Findings

However, Eysenck's critique of psychotherapy sent a shock wave through the ranks of psychotherapists. Following Eysenck, many other outcome studies were done, and most arrived at similar conclusions. One of the outcome researchers was A. E. Bergin. In 1963 he published a review of research on outcomes in psychotherapy that agreed with that of Eysenck. Recently, however, he published a comprehensive and thorough reevaluation of the major outcome studies, studies that ranged from the original articles reviewed by Eysenck in 1952 to studies as recent as 1969—and he came to a different conclusion. Bergin's latest work is quite impressive. It is very carefully prepared and demonstrates a laudatory willingness to recognize prior mistakes.

Bergin's reanalysis of the available data on spontaneous remission rates revealed a very important inconsistency with earlier findings. To begin with, the rates of improvement varied widely across types of disorder; moreover, with use of better statistical tools, it was possible to see that the median rates for remission reported in the literature were actually as low as 30 percent (rather than 60 to 70 percent). Finally, the untreated patients who had served as a comparison were found to have received treatment of various kinds from professional and nonprofessional helpers.

You will remember that people frequently seek the help of such professionals as clergymen and nonpsychiatric physicians whose training is in fields other than psychotherapy but whose assistance in many instances may be as therapeutic as formal psychotherapy.

This comprehensive review of the outcome studies suggested the following conclusion to Bergin:

> [T]here remains some modest evidence that psychotherapy "works." While most studies do not seem to yield very substantial evidence that this is so, the number that do seems to be clearly larger than would be expected by chance. . . . While the average effect is modestly positive, the existence of a substantial improvement, as well as a significant "deterioration effect," suggests that the effects of therapy may be quite powerful indeed. The challenge is to isolate those variables more highly correlated with improvement and to incorporate them into flexible treatment strategies.

If, as Bergin concludes, psychotherapy is a powerful experience for better or for worse, the task of psychologists is to identify ways in which it can be improved. One way of doing this is to examine therapeutic practices, patients, and therapists to see which sorts of experiences benefit what people. L. Luborsky, A. H. Auerbach, M. Chandler, J. Cohen, and H. M. Backrach examined the findings from 166 studies on the effectiveness of psychotherapy. Some of the generalizations they were able to draw are summarized in the adjacent margin.

A detailed discussion of the generalizations adjacent is beyond the scope of this chapter. Several observations, however, are important. First, psychotherapy seems to help those patients most who need it least: middle-class, intelligent, relatively "healthy," educated people. One reason for this phenomenon may be that the more similar a patient is to his therapist, the better his chances for improvement. This second observation shows that the cards are stacked against the person whose social class is different from his therapist's, and most therapists are in the middle class. Third, one school of therapy does not seem inherently superior to another, at least as far as the insight and conversational therapies are concerned. Whatever the source of gain in therapy, the results seem to derive less from a particular theoretical rationale than from more basic aspects of therapy, such as the relationship between patient and therapist. Finally, the longer a patient remains in therapy, the better he feels. This raises the issues of the feasibility of the method of individual psychotherapy and its cost. The question is, are there faster and less expensive ways to complete cures? But these are topics for the following chapter.

Factors Influencing the Outcome of Psychotherapy

1. Initially sicker patients do not improve as much with psychotherapy as the initially healthier do . . . improvement is shown by patients, whatever their initial level of functioning.

2. Patients with higher initial intelligence perform better in psychotherapy.

3. Patients with high anxiety at the initial evaluation or at the beginning of treatment are the ones likely to benefit from psychotherapy. High initial anxiety probably indicates a readiness, or at least an openness, for change . . . almost any affect is better than no affect, and . . . anxiety and depression are probably the two "best" initial affects. The presence of these strong affects may indicate the patient is in pain and asking for help. The absence of affect very likely goes along with a state in which the patient is not reaching out for help, or has given up. . . .

4. Patients with higher social achievements are better suited for psychotherapy.

5. The therapist's empathy (and other related qualities) facilitates the patient's gains from psychotherapy.

6. Greater similarity between therapist and patient is associated with better outcomes . . . The variety of forms of positive similarity includes social class, interests, values, and compatibility or orientation to interpersonal relations. . . .

7. The *combination* of individual and group psychotherapy is better than either individual or group psychotherapy alone.

8. Schools of treatment usually make no measurable difference.

9. In 20 of 22 studies of essentially time-unlimited treatment, the length of treatment was positively related to outcome; the longer the duration of treatment or the more sessions, the better the outcome! Other interpretations: a) Patients who are getting what they need drop out sooner, b) Therapists may overestimate positive change in patients who have been in treatment longer.

10. Psychotherapy with pharmacotherapy tends to be slightly more effective than psychotherapy alone, but in more ways not more effective than pharmacotherapy alone —especially for schizophrenic patients.

Source: L. Luborsky, *et al.* "Factors Influencing the Outcome of Psychotherapy: A Review of Quantitative Research," *Psychological Bulletin,* 75 (1971), 145–185.

SUGGESTED READINGS

BERGIN, A. E., AND GARFIELD, S. L. *Handbook of Psychotherapy and Behavior Change: An Empirical Analysis,* New York, Wiley, 1971. The most comprehensive collection of readings on psychotherapy. It contains sections on experimentation in psychotherapy; analysis of therapies; and papers that discuss therapeutic approaches in the home, family, school, group, organization, and community.

FRANK, J. *Persuasion and Healing: A Comparative Study of Psychotherapy.* Baltimore, Md., The Johns Hopkins Press, 1961. An excellent discussion of the historical roots of psychotherapy and its cross-cultural counterparts.

GOFFMAN, E. *Asylums.* Garden City, N.Y., Doubleday, 1961. A highly original, sociological analysis of institutions that presents mental illness as an act played out to fulfill the expectations of institutional custodians.

HALEY, J. *Strategies of Psychotherapy.* New York, Grune & Stratton, Inc., 1963. Stimulating discussion that argues that one primary goal of the psychotherapist is to help manipulate his patients. Patients' symptoms are analyzed as tactics in human relationships.

SCHOFIELD, W. *Psychotherapy: The Purchase of Friendship.* Englewood Cliffs, N.J., Spectrum Books of Prentice-Hall, 1964. Presents the argument that the primary need of patients is friendship. Suggests that the need for therapists should be filled in the community.

33
Psychotherapy II

THERE WERE GREAT PSYCHOLOGISTS long before the ordered science of psychology existed. For instance, it must be necessary for great generals to understand how to treat their men in such a way as to induce them to do irrational things like facing mutilation and death simply because they are ordered to do so. This is a kind of psychotherapy.

One superb psychologist was Julius Caesar. He was a great general but a reckless one who, on several occasions, would have lost battles through taking too many chances were it not that his men were blindly loyal to him and fought their heads off for him. He understood, for instance, that soldiers who felt confident of victory fought with greater spirit. In 46 B.C., he took an army to north Africa to dispose of enemy forces there. When his ship beached, he leaped to the ground and stumbled, falling to his hands and knees. This was a clear omen of downfall and failure; so a dreadful hush fell over the soldiers who had seen this happen. Caesar was not at a loss, however. He leaped to his feet, clutching a handful of soil. Holding the soil high, he cried, "Thus do I seize thee, O Africa." All the men cheered, for he had converted what had seemed an omen of defeat into one of victory. The result was that when the crucial conflict came at Thapsus some months later, Caesar's men charged into battle even while he himself was still hesitating to give the order—and carried all before them.

Caesar's last battle took place in Munda in southern Spain. One last opposing army faced him. If he could win this battle, he was master of the entire Roman world from end to end. And, as it happened, it was the hardest battle he ever fought. The other army fought stubbornly and valorously and was beginning to drive Caesar's men back. Caesar realized that all his victories might be buried in the ruins of one last defeat. Desperately, he snatched a sword and shield from the nearest soldier and dashed forward toward the enemy, while the men about him were drifting backward. As he ran, he cried, "Soldiers, will you let your general be taken?" The gamble won. To prevent that disgrace, Caesar's soldiers found new courage, turned and surged forward again, winning the last battle for him.

Perhaps Caesar's most remarkable psychological feat came during a hiatus between campaigns, when he was back in Rome. Certain of his army units were grumbling that, after all, they had not been sufficiently rewarded for all their stern fighting on Caesar's behalf. They cried for more pay and grew mutinous, threatening to leave the army if their just demands were not met.

Caesar faced them, and all fell silent to hear what he would say. He didn't say much. He would not give in. If they wanted to leave the army and desert him, that was their affair. "You are dismissed," he called out sternly, then added, with contempt, *"civilians!"* And to avoid the disgrace of that word, men who prided themselves on being professional soldiers all clamored to be accepted back into the army on Caesar's terms. I. A.

The last chapter suggested that psychotherapy is both art and craft. Even if psychotherapy is an art, it needs to find methods of helping more people—methods more reliable and dependable than the interpersonal skills of particular therapists. Expanding the scope of psychotherapy should mean not only establishing new methods of reaching people who need help most but also keeping individual therapeutic methods or schools of psychotherapy from becoming cults.

Most contemporary psychologists recognize the need for new methods in psychotherapy and have responded in a number of ways. Post-Freudian psychoanalysts have observed some of the deficiencies of classical psychoanalytic theory—still the most powerful influence on psychotherapy—and have attempted to improve on it. As the last chapter suggested, psychoanalytically-oriented therapists have made psychoanalytic therapy more practical, and ego analysts have redirected its emphasis from pathology to health.

Several nonpsychoanalytic theories of psychological disorder and personality development have established new schools and methods of therapy. Probably the most influential of these is Carl Rogers' *client-centered* therapy, with its humanistic goals and positive belief in every person's natural ability and right to realize his or her potential. Existential psychology has produced *existential psychotherapy*, which emphasizes the person's actual experiences in the here-and-now and his freedom

Figure 33.1
Good grief! A client-centered psychotherapist would have a much stronger belief in Charlie Brown's potential for self-actualization than Lucy has. Everyone (yes, even Lucy) has a self-actualizing tendency, according to Carl Rogers. In order to realize his potential, however, a person must be free of inside defensiveness and outside threats. Such freedom occurs when one is warmly accepted without being judged by others, and is allowed to experience his own reactions without debilitating self-evaluation. Client-centered therapy is designed to create these conditions.

to change his life. Learning theory, discussed in Chapter 3, has been very influential in psychology. It has given rise to *behavior therapy,* which is based on principles of learning and is one of the most successful as well as controversial schools of therapy in the United States. The *Gestalt* theory of perception has also generated a school of psychotherapy. Gestalt therapists emphasize the importance of perception in the functioning of personality and the need to broaden self-awareness. None of these approaches is necessarily superior to psychoanalysis, but each one has led to new discoveries that have helped expand the scope of psychotherapy.

We have stressed the need for psychotherapy to help a larger number of people who need it. In this respect, *group therapy* has an advantage over individual therapy because it reaches more people in the same amount of time. In this chapter we will examine *psychoanalytically-oriented group therapy,* as well as special forms, such as *psychodrama, Alcoholics Anonymous,* and *Synanon.*

Although group therapy does reach more people who are suffering, it does not always take place in the context of people's lives. As Chapter 29 points out, when the group members are strangers and share no real-life experiences, they may find it difficult once outside the group to apply what they have learned in the group. There are, however, forms of group therapy that are able to work within a person's real-life situation. *Marriage counseling,* for example, brings husband and wife together to work out their problems. *Family therapy* also tries to foster more productive relationships among the most important group in the person's life. *Crisis intervention* is therapy that helps people with particular crises in their lives. Finally, psychologists in *community mental health* are beginning to promote projects to prevent psychological disorder and to make facilities for help easily available.

ROGERIAN OR CLIENT-CENTERED THERAPY

Carl Rogers' theory of personality, his views on disorder, and his techniques of therapy have gained increasing acceptance in the United States. Rogerian treatment was developed primarily with a college population, and until recently, was typically quite brief in duration (usually not exceeding forty weekly visits).

Rogers assumes that people are innately good and that they will become kind, concerned, friendly, and effective in the process of self-actualization if they are not diverted from the course of their normal development. Rogers' views on development are discussed in greater detail in Chapter 22. In the course of normal development the person needs to achieve congruence between his view of himself and his actual experiences. Rogers sees the roots of psychological disorder in incongruence within the person, which generates anxiety, contradictory behaviors, denial of certain thoughts or feelings, and the idea that he cannot control his own behavior. Incongruence occurs because the fundamental desire to actualize the self has been deflected.

The Rogerian therapist tries to reduce conflicts within the person—his client—by showing him what kinds of ideas he expresses about himself and his life. The basic working principle in client-centered therapy is the client's right to and capacity for self-determination. The therapy minimizes the role of special technique, and the therapist tries instead to *reflect back* to the client the feelings the client has expressed. In this way, the client can reevaluate, accept, and finally integrate his own feelings within the self as he works to make his attitudes about himself more congruent with his experiences. Therapy is a continual process of achieving self-awareness and preparing for self-actualization.

The therapist himself must bring two important attitudes to therapy: an *empathetic understanding* of his client's frame of reference and *unconditional positive regard* for him. In this atmosphere of acceptance the client gradually begins to conceptualize experiences that have been out of awareness and to abandon the secondhand values he has taken from others in favor of the self's own natural values.

Figure 33.2
The client-centered therapist attempts to understand what his client is experiencing and then to communicate this understanding to him. Because the therapist often restates what he considers to be the emotional content of the client's communication, he functions as a "mirror of feeling." In this way he provides understanding and positive regard without making value judgments. Feeling safe in such an environment, the client learns to relax the defenses that he has used to deny or distort his experiences and, in turn, to develop a more realistic self-concept and a more accurate perception of events.

Chapter 22 elaborates this point in its discussion of Rogers' concept of the relationship between organism and self.

Client-centered therapy assumes that every person has an innate tendency for self-actualization. Because the client assumes responsibility for his treatment, he is able to continue the process of self-actualization on his own after therapy terminates.

EXISTENTIAL THERAPY

Existential therapy rejects the models of personality structure and functioning that traditional psychological theories, especially psychoanalysis, have postulated. Existential therapists are unwilling to use such unverifiable determiners as id, ego, or superego to account for a person's behavior, and they question the meaning of Freudian concepts like projection and transference. They also suggest that the assumption of an unconscious mind is used as a carte blanche on which almost any causal explanation can be written. It does not explain the facts, they say; it only obscures them.

A person's drives or dynamisms are understandable only in the existential context of the particular person sitting before the therapist. Rather than search for external or internal agents or entities that have determined why the person behaves the way he does, the therapist tries to understand the person as he is in the world in the present and to help him come to terms with his responsibility for his own existence. Only human beings are self-conscious of, and therefore responsible for, the direction of their lives. The freedom to change one's behaviors entails the burden of responsibility, which causes feelings of anxiety in everyone. Freedom is a key concept in existential psychotherapy. The patient is encouraged to exercise will and decision in effecting a change in his life.

The therapist does not try to hide from the person the fact that he too is a real person. The curative factor of the therapy lies in the impingement of the patient's world on the therapist, whose reactions represent the actual world. This encounter in the here-and-now is the medium of change for the person's behaviors and atti-

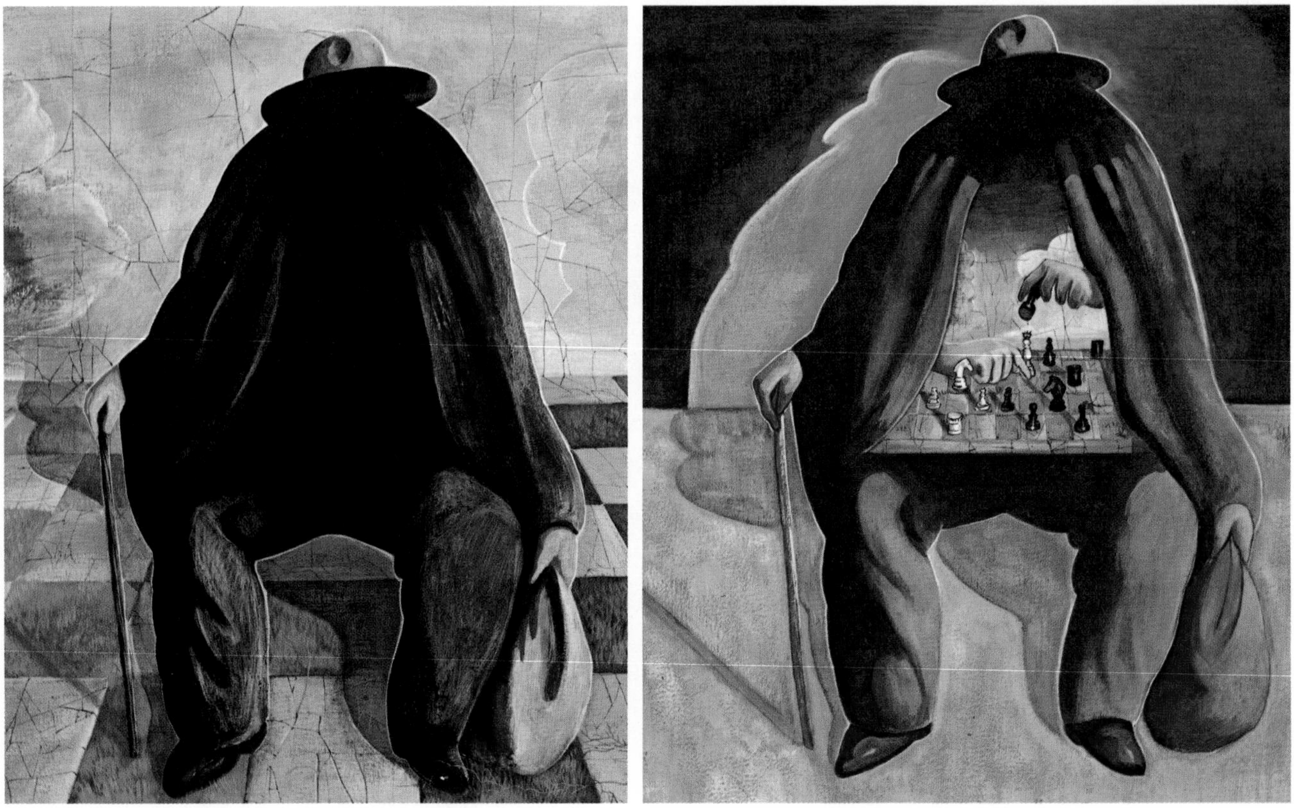

Figure 33.3
One important aim of existential psychotherapy is to help the person assume responsibility for his own actions, because only through accepting responsibility can he create meaning in his own life. Although existential therapists use a variety of methods, they all stress that a person discovers what he *is* by examining what he *does*. The therapist's aim is to help his client "control his own chess board" rather than being one of the pawns.

tudes. Existential therapists do not ignore the past; they assume it will come up in the present. By the same token, they assume that the future will be real to the extent that the person experiences it in his search for meaning and security in the present.

One form of existential psychotherapy is V. Frankl's *logotherapy,* which emphasizes the search for meaning *(logos).* Frankl developed logotherapy as a response to and interpretation of his own attempt to adjust to his experience as #119104 in the Nazi concentration camp of Auschwitz during World War II. Another form of existential psychotherapy is discussed in *Love and Will* by R. May.

Figure 33.4

Victor Frankl. Frankl's existential theory of personality and psychotherapy has been an influential humanistic theory. Frankl stresses man's striving to find meaning in life as being the primary human motivation; psychological disorder is said to result from frustration of this search for meaning. Logotherapy focuses on the person's need to make his life meaningful.

BEHAVIOR THERAPY

Behavior therapy is based on experimentally established principles of learning. This method of treating psychological disorder has presented very strong opposition to Freudian theory and differs radically from psychoanalysis in its definition of disorder and method of cure. The basic assumption of behavior therapy is that disorders are learned phenomena; they are therefore rooted, or at least reflected, in particular behaviors, and they can be changed through the application of behaviorist principles of learning, which are discussed in Chapter 3. Behavior therapists employ such techniques as classical conditioning, operant conditioning, generalization, habituation, and extinction to change a person's behavior. Many of the conditioning paradigms and schedules of reinforcement that have been used in the laboratory have also been used in therapeutic settings. People who are so anxious that they cannot relate to other people—who have trouble, for example, expressing feelings either of aggression or of affection—have been conditioned to *assert* themselves. Behavior therapists have been able to aversively condition (punish) and suppress many behaviors or symptoms of disorder that the person wants to be rid of, including obsessions and attachments to fetishes. They have also successfully extinguished motor responses, such as tics, by eliciting them again and again without reinforcement.

Some of the most valuable applications of behavior therapy have been in areas of severe psychological disorder. Various types of psychoses, including schizophrenia, have been modified through behavior therapy. O. Lindsley and B. F. Skinner first demonstrated that behavior therapy could be used to modify the behavior of severely psychotic patients, and since then many studies have shown that behavior therapy can be effective with many psychotics. Although the psychotics are not really cured, their behavior seems to be altered more than with other therapies.

Behavior therapy has also had success with mentally retarded people, helping them learn to do things previously considered beyond their range of abilities. It is particularly encouraging to observe success with long-term psychotics and mentally retarded people because other therapies had been quite unsuccessful in changing their lives at all.

Behavior therapy has also been used with relatively normal behavior. For example, insomnia, smoking, and obsessive gambling have all been modified with behavior therapy. "Normal pathologies" are extremely widespread, and we may expect much greater application of behavior therapy to them in the future. Behavior therapy has a relatively short history, but it has generated a large number of special techniques. We can examine only a small number of the most important of them here.

Figure 33.5

Rollo May is a psychoanalytically-oriented existential therapist. He is America's foremost writer on existential psychotherapy and helped to arouse interest in existential psychology in the United States through his book (with Angel and Ellenberger), *Existence.*

Token Economies

One major technique of behavior therapy used with hospital patients is to substitute tokens for such specific rewards as food or cigarettes. A token stands for a reinforcer; it could be practically anything—a poker chip, a check mark, a green stamp. The most obvious token in real life is money. Tokens have the advantage of being easy to supply, and patients do not become satiated with them, as they do with food or cigarettes.

A *token economy* program was set up by L. P. Ullmann and L. Krasner in a

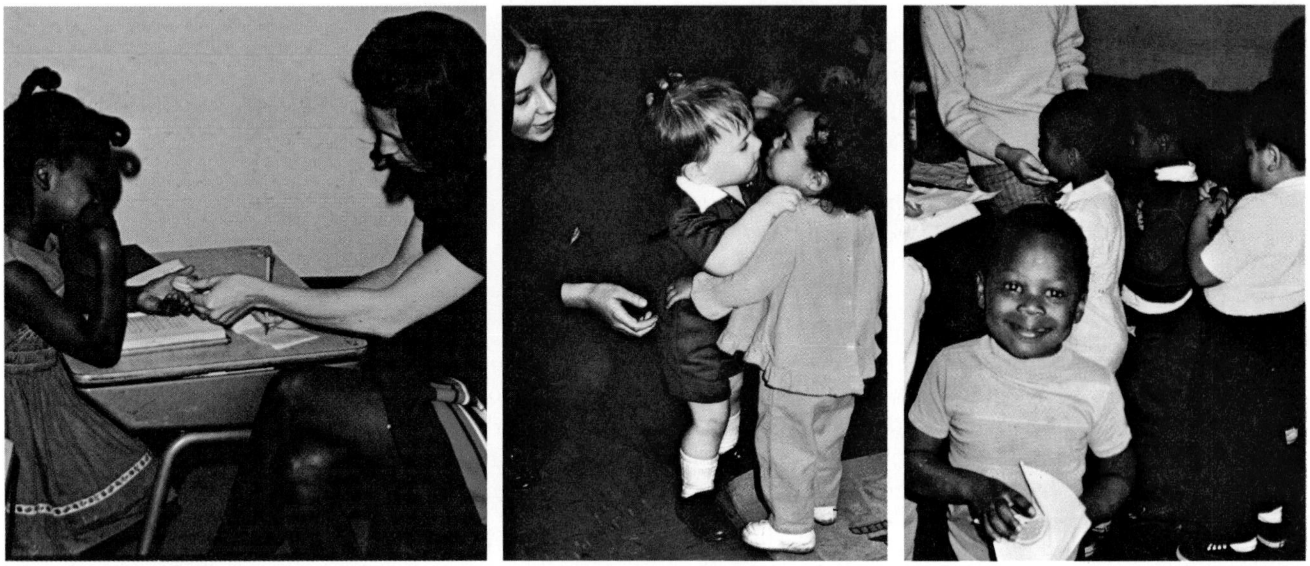

Figure 33.6
Various activities at Learning Village, a school in Michigan that is structured entirely on scientific learning principles. A token economy is used extensively here. (Left) the girl is reinforced with a token for a correct answer. (Middle) two young children are verbally reinforced for an appropriate social interaction. (Right) this happy young fellow has purchased an orange with several tokens that he had earned for good academic performance. Learning Village is a good example of how behaviorist learning principles are applied to nonpsychiatric settings. The number, sophistication, and adoptions of behavior-therapy techniques have increased greatly in the last decade.

Veterans' Administration Hospital in California. Most of the patients in the hospital had been diagnosed as chronic schizophrenics or as having organic brain damage. As a group they were apathetic, indifferent, dependent, and socially isolated. When these patients performed socially desirable behaviors, like attending an occupational therapy session, Ullmann and Krasner reinforced their behavior with tokens that they could cash in for rewards, like candy and cigarettes, or for privileges, like time out of the ward. Before this token economy program, most of the patients had refused to participate in any of the hospital activities available to them. In fact their behavior represented the endpoint of years of compliance and apathy shaped by life in an institution. Token reinforcement sharply reduced the patients' apathy and made them more responsive, active, and productive. Staff morale also improved enormously because the staff felt that they were actually affecting the patients' lives. The patients' improvement made their release from the hospital more likely, but it did not guarantee that they would be able to stay out permanently.

Token economies are still in an early stage of development and must be carefully evaluated by controlled studies, but at this point, it does seem that the application of basic principles of learning through token economies offers considerable hope for severely disturbed individuals.

Systematic Desensitization

In *systematic desensitization,* a person is taught to relax, and while relaxed, to experience a series of increasingly threatening events. All of the situations are frightening to him, but the order is from least frightening to most frightening. In the first step in systematic desensitization, the person constructs an *anxiety hierarchy.* He makes a list of experiences that make him anxious and arranges them in descending order of intensity. For example, a man who cannot stand the sight of blood might go to a behavior therapist for systematic desensitization because his fear reaction is so strong that he faints whenever he sees anyone bleeding. At the bottom of his list he perhaps puts listening to a lecture on first-aid techniques; somewhere near the middle, watching a black-and-white newsreel of a medic dressing a soldier's wounds; and at the top, suddenly finding himself kneeling over a child with an open stomach wound.

After the person completes the list the therapist teaches him to relax, and as he is relaxing, to imagine the least disturbing scene or experience from his anxiety hierarchy. The therapist makes the person repeat his imagined experience of this scene until it fails to generate anxiety, and he follows the same procedure step by step up the list with the other anxiety-arousing events. The person finally reaches a point where he is able to imagine the situations that threaten him most. At that point the therapist actually exposes the person to one of the real-life situations that he is afraid to experience. For example, a therapist might take the man who faints at the sight of blood to a hospital operating room.

Systematic desensitization has worked very effectively in the cure of many phobias, or irrational fears, and the average cure usually takes only about six sessions. The evidence to date indicates that most people do not develop different phobias as alternate expressions of anxiety, contrary to what would be expected according to the psychoanalytic theory of symptom substitution (discussed in Chapter 31).

Figure 33.7
Leonard Krasner. As researcher, author, editor, and teacher, Krasner has been an eloquent and influential proponent of behavior modification. Some of the areas in which he has written include token economies, verbal conditioning of schizophrenic speech, and the role of personal values in the training of persons as behavioral therapists.

Modeling

The idea behind *modeling* is quite simple. When people observe other people—especially people they respect—they tend to imitate them. At Stanford University A. Bandura initiated a program using the principles of modeling to cure fear of snakes. He contacted people whose fear of snakes interfered seriously with their

Figure 33.8
The procedure shown here, known as "modeling with guided participation," has been highly successful for helping a person overcome a fear of snakes. (Top) the young woman observes an attendant who fearlessly handles a snake. (Middle) she gradually approaches the snake, which is kept in an enclosure, until she can touch the snake while remaining calm. (Bottom) she then touches the snake, with far greater comfort than she showed in the top photograph. This behavior modification technique has been used successfully to help people overcome other phobias, such as fear of heights and fear of elevators.

Figure 33.9
Albert Bandura. Bandura's extensive research and theorizing in the area of *imitation* has helped psychologists to become aware of the importance of modeling in the development, maintenance, and modification of behavior, including deviant behavior. Much of Bandura's earlier research focused upon modeling in children; more recently he has investigated the use of imitation in the reduction of intense fears in both children and adults.

everyday lives. Some were anticipating Peace Corps assignments in foreign countries, others were afraid to go hunting, hiking, or camping, and others were in occupations that brought them in contact with snakes. Bandura and his colleagues put people who were afraid of snakes into one of four groups. The first group underwent systematic desensitization. The second watched films of children and adults playing with snakes. The third group watched a therapist through a one-way mirror as he played with a snake; these subjects then entered the room and slowly but surely approached the snake, touched it, and finally held it. The fourth group was a control group, which received no treatment. Each of the three experimental groups received ten treatment sessions.

The results of the experiment were unequivocal: people in group three, who watched the model through the mirror and learned to touch the snake, improved more than people in group two, who watched the film, or people in group one, who engaged in the desensitization procedure but did not ever actually observe a live model handling the snake. All of the people who had observed a live model were able to sit in a chair with their hands at their side and allow a snake to crawl on them for thirty seconds.

After the experiment was over, the experimenters took all the people who had not observed a live model with the snake and had them observe a live model and engage in guided participation with snakes. They succeeded in generating cures in 100 percent of the subjects.

Autonomic Conditioning

Recently, learning experiments have found that heart rate, sweating, and blood pressure, and other responses that are controlled by the autonomic nervous system can be conditioned in much the same way as other behavioral responses. For example, if a patient is rewarded every time his heart rate spontaneously decreases, he will learn to make his heart rate go down, and if he is rewarded when it spontaneously increases, he will learn to make it go up. The techniques of *autonomic conditioning*—or *operant conditioning of autonomic behavior*—hold promise for curing psychosomatic disorders like chronically high heart rate, high blood pressure, gastrointestinal disorders, and other conditions caused by too little or too much activity in the autonomic nervous system.

Although autonomic conditioning has the potential to revolutionize psychosomatic medicine, the procedures do not always work effectively. For the human being, good reinforcers are difficult to find; good reinforcers must be rewarding and must be administered quickly, so that only the desired responses are reinforced. In addition, the reinforcer itself must not cause troublesome unconditioned responses. For example, if you were attempting to lower heart rate, you would not want to use a reinforcer that raises heart rate.

Some experimenters have used money and verbal reinforcement to reward their subjects; others have used purely neutral stimuli as reinforcers but have ascribed to them reinforcing properties. For example, in one experiment, the psychologists presented short bursts of a tone every time the person's heart rate increased; in another experiment, every time the person's heart rate decreased. In each experiment, they asked the person to try to initiate as many tones as possible by changing his heart rate in the appropriate direction.

The most impressive operant conditioning of autonomic behavior has occurred in research with laboratory animals that can be curarized—that is, given a dose of curare, a common South American poison. This poison effectively paralyzes the rat, so that it is unable to move or even breathe. The animal has to receive artificial respiration by machine during curarization, but it will usually recover fully with no adverse effects. Because curarization prevents the rat from making any muscular responses, it helps the experimenters narrow down the source of autonomic conditioning. The experimenter establishes the conditioned autonomic response in the curarized animal by reinforcing it with stimulation to the pleasure center of the brain, a procedure described in Chapter 16. Startling results have been achieved with curarized rats. For example, conditioning procedures have produced 25-percent changes in heart rates. The use of curare has been attempted with a few human subjects, with only limited success. In fact, investigators have found that with or without curare, some people find it difficult to modify their autonomic behavior voluntarily, although others can do so easily.

Autonomic conditioning has not yet been totally successful as a general therapeutic tool, but it promises more success in the future. We have said that it may one day cure disorders associated with faulty heart rate, blood pressure, and digestion; it may also be the therapeutic method that will help cure anxiety, depression, and disorders of attention. Conditioning of brain wave activity (EEG) opens the possibility of modifying a person's state of consciousness. For example, if a person learns to control his alpha activity voluntarily, he may be able also to alter at will and control his states of sleep and attention. Chapter 15 discusses EEG and altered states of consciousness in greater detail.

The Future of Behavior Therapy

Walden Two, a novel B. F. Skinner published in 1948, dramatizes how principles of learning might be used to modify human behavior and shape a future social organization—a utopia governed by laws of reinforcement. Skinner correctly guessed that his principles would be applicable to social, educational, and environmental planning. In his new book, *Beyond Freedom and Dignity,* Skinner carries the argument further. He says that we must sacrifice human freedom in order to control behavior and thereby eliminate social ills. Our ability to control human behavior still has severe limitations, but even if we could totally control it, we would have to answer the real question that is raised by any proposal to control human behavior and eliminate human freedom: What is the desired end of such control, and what *value* will it serve? Principles of learning offer no information to answer the question—in fact, the question cannot even be understood in the light of principles of learning.

Unrestrained control of our behaviors and social institutions would be a great danger—maybe a great tyranny. The goal of behavior therapy is to help the person change maladaptive behaviors and gain some measure of control over his or her own behavior and environment. Whether behavior therapists, as Skinner suggests, will also be able to initiate control over social institutions and extinguish such social evils as war, crime, and poverty is another question.

GESTALT THERAPY

Gestalt therapy is an approach developed by F. Perls, R. Hefferline, and P. Goodman. The principles of Gestalt psychology were originally developed in the study of perception and are described in Chapter 14. Gestalt therapists apply these principles to the study of personality and the treatment of psychological disorder. Gestalt theory suggests that perception is based upon the understanding of meaningful patterns or *Gestalten.* The person perceives one segment of his perceptual field as the *figure* and the remainder as the *ground.* It sees the whole as greater than the sum of its parts; this view of the world applies to the individual personality as well as to the process of perception. Like existential theory, it uses the phenomenological approach, which is discussed at length in Chapter 1. Gestalt therapists suggest that healthy personality functioning occurs when a person's experiences form a meaningful whole, in which there is a fluid alternation between those sets of experiences that are in the focus of awareness (the figure) and those that are in the background. This type of functioning is characterized by liveliness, attention, involvement, excitement, spontaneity, and grace. When a person's experiences of figure and ground are static and when some elements are not in awareness, the person's functioning will be characterized by confusion, boredom, anxiety, compulsion, and self-consciousness.

Gestalt treatment attempts to broaden the person's awareness by the use of graded experiments that are designed to help him remember past experiences and pay attention to sensations in his body. The person may then become conscious of the way he walks, talks, dreams, fantasies, and remembers, but he also may become aware of his inabilities to carry through the suggested experiments fully and successfully. These inabilities are similar to resistances to psychoanalytic therapy, which are discussed in Chapter 32. Gestalt experiments allow the person to see for himself how these inabilities reflect gaps in his experience and awareness. Ideally, the person is then able to reintegrate those missing aspects of awareness into a meaningful whole.

Gestalt theory provided much of the impetus for the encounter movement, in which groups of normal people increase their self-awareness. (A typical group is portrayed in Chapter 29.)

GROUP THERAPY

We have examined several new approaches to psychotherapy that developed in reaction to the varying degrees of unsuccess in traditional forms of individual psychotherapy. Many new approaches have offered promising innovations, but they have not yet proved themselves superior to psychoanalytic or client-centered therapy. One important limitation of individual psychotherapy, whatever school it is based upon, is that it does not reach enough people; group therapy reaches more people in the same amount of time.

Any type of group therapy also has the advantage of supplying a therapeutic context that is more like a real-life situation than is any individual therapy—simply because a group member has to relate to other people in the group, not just to the therapist or group leader. But, as we pointed out earlier in the chapter, the group experience of people who have no interaction outside the group is not as much of real-life experience as is the group therapy experience of family members, colleagues, or spouses. Also, many people feel that group therapy is less threatening than individual therapy, in which the person has to face the therapist alone.

Regardless of the type of group therapy—psychoanalytically-oriented, Rogerian, Gestalt, or any other—group psychotherapies have common pitfalls. If the leader or therapist is not effective, people in the group can become scapegoated, bullied, or otherwise traumatized. Mob psychology of the kind portrayed in William Golding's novel *Lord of the Flies,* in which a group of young schoolboys becomes stranded by themselves on an island, supplies an example of the types of scapegoating, cruelty, and chaos that can develop in uncontrolled groups.

The discussion of group roles, goals, and norms in Chapter 29 makes the point that there are general processes that occur in almost all intentionally formed groups. Psychoanalytically-oriented therapy, as one might expect, brings psychoanalytical concepts to bear on group processes and experiences.

Psychoanalytically-Oriented Group Psychotherapy

In psychoanalytically-oriented group therapy, the concept of *transference,* discussed in the last chapter, is as important as it is in individual psychoanalytic therapy. People must work out their unconscious conflicts through the process of transference, and the group provides the context of a therapeutic relationship. The fact that other people—usually eight to ten—are experiencing similar difficulties helps relieve the person's anxiety and reassure him that he is not alone in his plight. The variety of points of view expressed enables the person to form multiple transferences

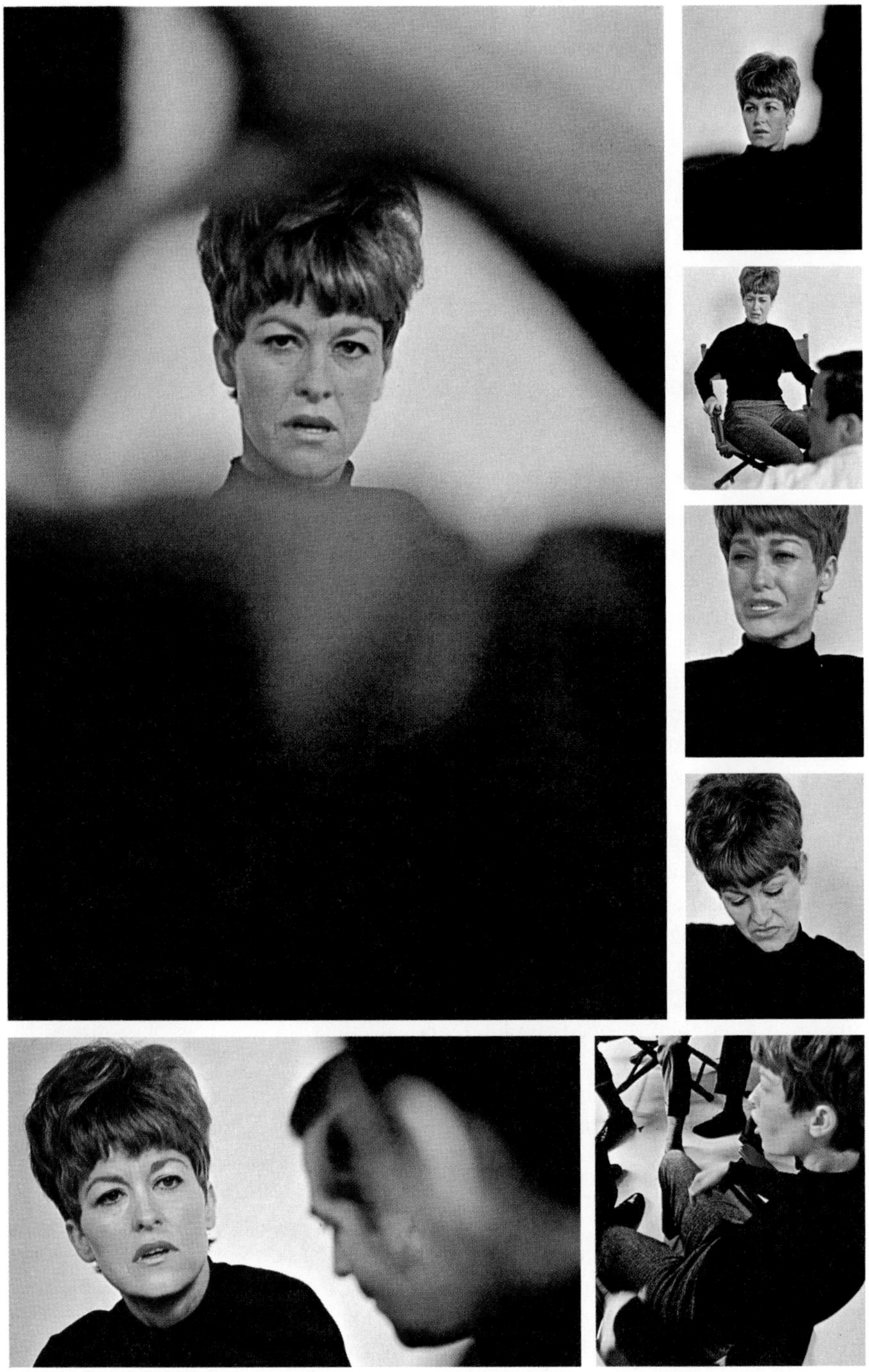

Figure 33.10
This woman is talking about herself to her psychotherapy group. There are many possible ways in which she may benefit from the group's focus on her. If she is discussing a problem that troubles her deeply, she may learn that the group members are not critical of her, as she had expected them to be; some of them may also disclose that they have similar problems, which will reduce her feeling of being "different" and isolated. She may learn a great deal about herself through members' feedback on her characteristics and behaviors—their strengths and weaknesses. If this feedback occurs in a supportive atmosphere, the woman can benefit from it and attempt to adopt more effective behaviors.

and frees him to experiment, in the context of a supportive group atmosphere, with different interaction styles. Finally, the bond that may grow among group members gives him the feeling that he has support in his struggle, especially the struggle with problems of authority that are represented by the therapist.

Special Forms of Group Therapy

Psychodrama is a therapeutic strategy that was developed by J. L. Moreno. Like psychoanalytically-oriented therapy, its goal is to resolve unconscious conflicts. Its medium is a form of improvisational theater in which people are encouraged to act out troublesome emotional situations and interpersonal conflicts. The person is

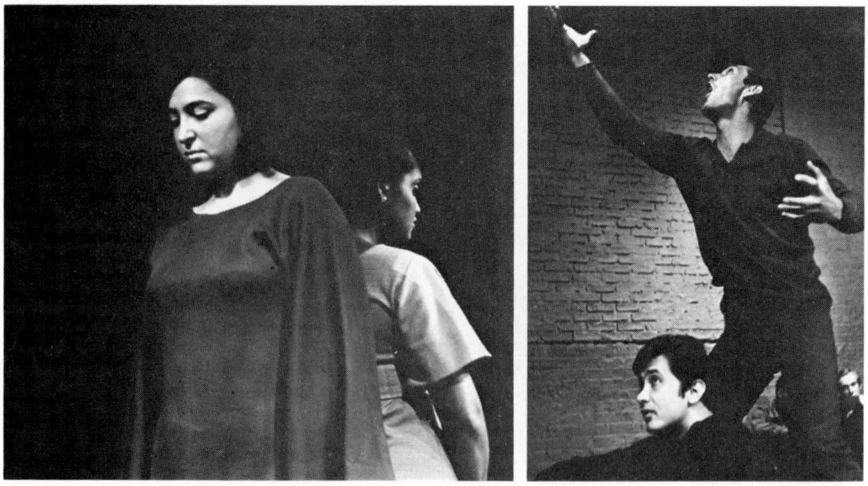

Figure 33.11
Residents of Daytop Village, a center for treatment of drug addiction, perform a scene from their play entitled *The Concept.* Centers such as Daytop and Synanon provide many therapeutic aspects: the live-in arrangement creates a familylike atmosphere that has been missing in most members' lives, and the group therapy sessions give members continual feedback, especially about irresponsible or antisocial behavior. The involvement and concern shown for residents helps them cope with their drug addiction and with the emotional problems that have led them to drug abuse.

asked to play several roles, and the audience is encouraged to participate. The goal is to help the person relive basic conflicts in order to cause in him or her a catharsis of emotion and free him to experiment, at least in fantasy, with more fulfilling and constructive responses to his problems. Members of the group serve as actors in each person's psychodrama. Role switching within each psychodrama occurs frequently as people attempt to increase empathy and intensify the emotional reality of the scene. The person is both observer and participant, and when he is overwhelmed by the trauma of reliving the actual experience—perhaps a past confrontation with his mother that is particularly painful to reenact—he is encouraged to act out the scene as he wished it had occurred. Psychodrama is more successful for the person who can experiment with a number of outcomes and test the benefits and costs associated with each.

Alcoholics Anonymous, a nonprofessional organization with branches in most large cities in America, provides another special form of psychotherapy. Ex-alcoholics meet regularly to give each other support and reinforce successful resolutions of their drinking problems. They give forceful testimonials about the benefits they sustained after they stopped drinking, and in effect, they act as missionaries for abstinence.

Figure 33.12
Jacob L. Moreno, founder and developer of psychodrama. Moreno developed a "Theater of Spontaneity" in Vienna in the 1920s, and his interest in psychodrama grew out of his interest in the theater. In his writings he draws an analogy between the principles of psychodrama and those of classical Greek drama: they both offer the audience opportunity for emotional release and growth through observation.

Synanon, started by C. Dederich, is another nonprofessional organization. Its original goal was to help drug addicts rehabilitate themselves, and it has proved itself to be one of the most successful treatments for drug addiction. Members spend weeks, months, years, and even entire lifetimes living together in an effort to overcome drug addiction, and more recently, other problems. Synanon is a total experience for its participants—and it requires a total commitment. Members are required to play the Synanon Game, a group meeting in which members challenge one another and force one another to account for all the "games" they have been playing in their everyday lives. The Synanon group experience penetrates much deeper than the person's specific problem of drug addiction and intervenes in every aspect of his private life. Some critics have claimed that Synanon leaves the person unprepared for adjustment in the outside world. In response to this, Synanon encourages its members to stay for life and help build a new community.

Encounter groups do not, strictly speaking, constitute a form of psychotherapy for psychological disorder. Rather, they attempt to supply a series of growth experiences for essentially healthy people. Encounter group techniques—which include physical and sensory awareness exercises, role playing, and verbal games—are meant to increase sensitivity to other people and to oneself and to make people aware of their potential for increased growth and self-actualization. As Chapter 29 points out, there are many kinds of encounter groups and many kinds of leaders. The encounter-group experience is often a very enlightening one, but its effects do not necessarily generalize to everyday life. In fact, it is not without its dangers: it can lower the defenses of psychologically vulnerable people and then leave them without means for coping with problems in the group or in their everyday lives.

Family therapy operates on the assumption that disorder must be fed to grow—that behind every person's disorder is a family context that has sustained the person in, or even forced him into, a pathological role. Chapter 31 discusses research on the family environments of schizophrenics.

The orientation of the therapist may be psychoanalytic, humanistic, or behavioristic. A psychoanalytically-oriented family therapist, for example, probably would analyze the individual personality dynamics of each member of the family and show how family members interrelate. Psychoanalytically-oriented therapists are often reluctant to suggest strategies for change and prefer to encourage patients to solve their own problems. More action-oriented family therapists, on the other hand, may actively encourage family members to experiment with different patterns of interaction and ways of resolving basic problems.

Family therapy is sometimes given by cotherapists, one man and one woman who provide a kind of authoritative reference "family" or couple. Other family therapists conduct treatment individually.

Marriage therapy and marriage counseling attempt to help married couples come to terms with their problems. This service is sometimes used by couples who are

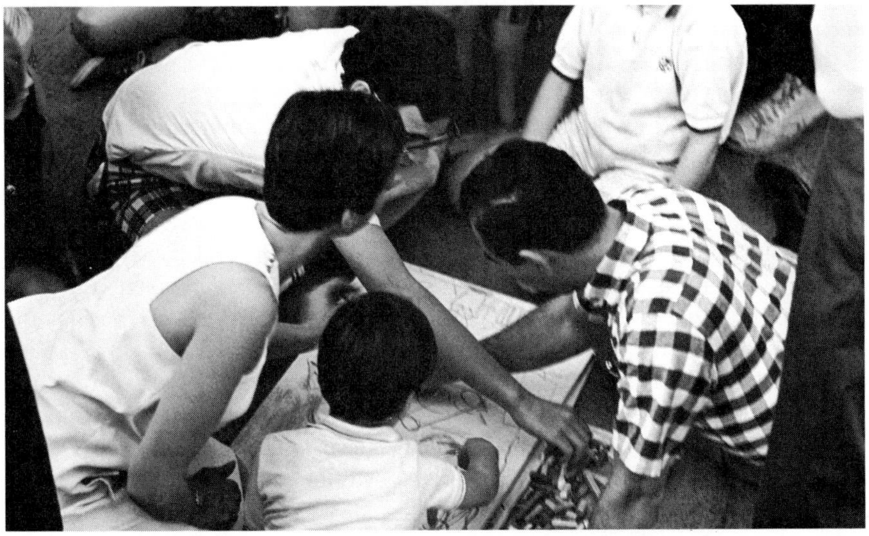

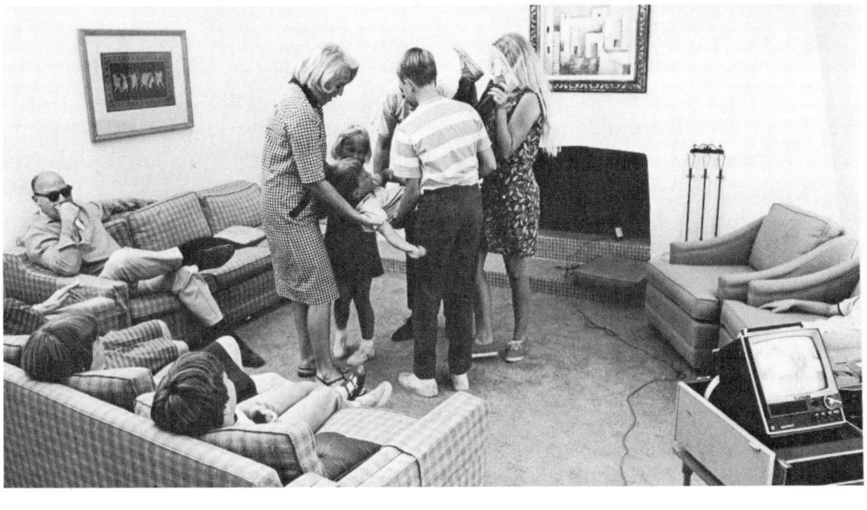

Figure 33.13
This family is engaging in a problem-solving task that will enable them and their therapist to understand some important aspects of their interactions. They can discuss these interactions and begin to experiment with more effective and satisfying behavior. For example, the therapist or another family member may point out that one person has been totally dominant and has not allowed others to state their views. This may lead to the family discussing their feelings about the domination. The emphasis that "the *family* is the patient" helps remove some of the pressure from the "nominal patient," that is, the member whose behavior initially brought the family into psychotherapy. Usually, the family comes to understand that each member's behavior is influenced greatly by the family matrix.

contemplating marriage but who are unsure of their compatibility; at other times, it is used by married people who are contemplating divorce or who want to make a final effort at reconciliation. The focus of the therapeutic endeavor is generally on marital adjustment rather than on the reorganization of the individual personality. The therapist therefore emphasizes interaction patterns rather than individual histories.

An example of a particularly successful form of specialized marriage therapy is the recent treatment of sexual disorders by Masters and Johnson. Masters and Johnson treat individual sexual disorder as a problem in interaction between two sexual partners, a problem that requires mutual cooperation, understanding, and patience. They believe that impotent men and frigid women need practice in sexual relationships. Masters and Johnson help them reach this goal by teaching them to gradually and comfortably relearn sexual behavior. The couple's experiences generalize to their lives outside the therapy situation. The men and women proceed one step at a time, gaining the knowledge and confidence at each step that they need to advance to the next. Masters and Johnson operate as a male-and-female, cotherapist team. Like family therapists, many marriage therapists operate in teams.

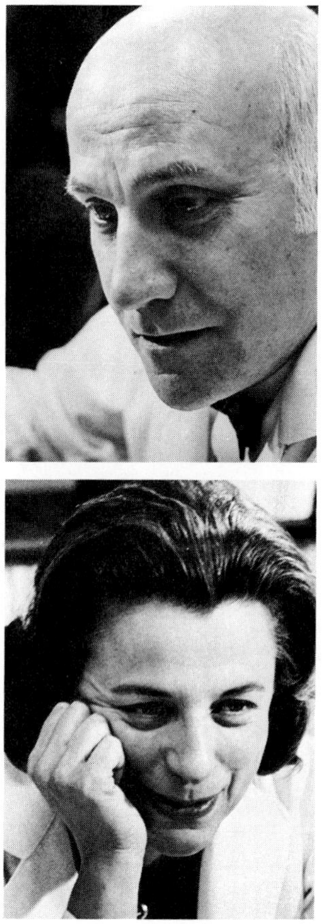

Figure 33.14
The pioneering work of William Masters and Virginia Johnson produced the first basic scientific knowledge about the physiology of human sexual response. This basic understanding enabled them to develop powerful techniques for treating sexual difficulties.

CRISIS INTERVENTION

Psychotherapists may be called upon to help a person over an immediate crisis, such as a suicide attempt, a bad hallucinogenic trip, a major disruption in his family, or the nervous breakdown of a family member. While some clinicians would not call such intervention "therapy," others insist that it is the best kind of therapy.

Many crisis interventionists argue that most people can work out their own adjustment on a day-to-day or year-to-year basis, except at times when a crisis overwhelms them. Crisis periods are thought to be more common at crucial transition points in one's life than at other times. The birth of a child, the death of a family member, the period of adolescence, loss of a job, divorce, the children's moving away from home, menopause, or serious physical illness often produce trauma and precipitate a crisis. Crisis interventionists argue that if they are able to get the person through such a crisis, ideally without resorting to hospitalization, the person can continue as he has in the past. They are skeptical about the success—and discouraged about the high cost—of attempts to reconstruct people's personalities.

A special form of crisis intervention is the telephone hot line, available for people who need help but want to remain anonymous. People who use the hot line are often experiencing a bad drug trip or feeling suicidal. The therapist makes use of people's expectation that they will be helped by calling; he tries to talk the person through his crisis, and when necessary he refers the person to an outside professional for further treatment.

An approach advocated by G. Caplan and others, which is related to crisis intervention, is crisis prevention or preventive psychiatry. In this approach, mental health workers intervene in potentially threatening environments to teach people how to prepare for problems and cope with crises. Preventive psychiatry often creates mock crisis situations for people, so that they can learn, under nonthreatening circumstances, how to react to them. Such experiences supply a kind of immunity to future crises at the same time that they supply training for them.

COMMUNITY MENTAL HEALTH

Community mental health programs intervene in the environments of disadvantaged people and organize facilities to help them combat psychological disorder. Advocates of community mental health argue that the source of disturbance may be less in the person than in his environment. Poor housing, poor food, and poor living standards create priorities for survival that may overshadow a person's intrapsychic conflicts. In helping to improve emotional functioning for disadvantaged people, it makes more sense to improve pathological living conditions first, before trying to "cure" the victims of them.

One of the greatest shortcomings of individual psychotherapy is that even if it does work, there are not enough therapists to meet the need. Community mental health programs encourage the training of nonprofessionals in the community as therapists. W. Schofield has suggested that many people can become therapeutic friends or "invisible therapists," and Caplan has suggested that they can become "care-givers" in preventive psychiatry.

Besides training community residents to offer help, community mental health programs supply professional advice for school counselors, administrators, and teachers; they help organize grass-roots participation in paramedical, recreational, and rehabilitation centers; and they set up sanctuaries for drug addicts and free clinics for street people. Whatever form they take, community mental health programs have one thing in common—they organize facilities that operate on a broad social level. Almost any program designed to promote the goal of community mental health may be a part of this movement if it recognizes the important relation of community environments and resources to the mental health of the people who live there.

SUGGESTED READINGS

ARIETI, S. (Ed.). *American Handbook of Psychiatry.* 3 vols. New York, Basic Books, Inc., Publishers, 1959. Vol. II contains chapters on existential psychotherapy, group psychotherapy, psychodrama, psychoanalytic psychotherapy, and various specific therapies employed in hospitals, such as shock therapy. It also contains a general discussion of the effect of hospitals on patients and community approaches to therapy.

BANDURA, A. *Principles of Behavior Modification.* New York, Holt, Rinehart and Winston, 1969. An extensive discussion of behavior therapy by one of the prime researchers in the field. It contains an especially good discussion of the effect of modeling.

MAY, R., *et al.* (Eds.). *Existence.* New York, Clarion Books of Simon and Schuster, 1967. A series of papers by existential psychologists that captures the core and diversity of their positions.

RAUSH, H. C., AND RAUSH, C. L. *The Halfway House Movement: A Search for Sanity.* New York, Appleton-Century-Crofts, 1968. The most complete discussion of the halfway house movement presently out. Contains an analysis of existing data on halfway houses and argues strongly for increasing their use.

ROGERS, C. *Client Centered Therapy.* Boston, Mass., Houghton Mifflin, 1951. A classic on client-centered therapy. Presents the complete position along with chapters on the applications of client-centered therapy to play therapy, group therapy, and student-centered therapy, and also includes a section on the training of client-centered therapists.

SLATER, P. *Microcosm: Structural, Psychological, and Religious Evaluation in Groups.* New York, Wiley, 1966. A highly engaging discussion on the sensitivity training groups. Slater analyzes self-analytic groups from a sociological, religious, and psychological (mainly psychoanalytic) perspective. Contains ample quotes from self-analytic groups.

KRASNER, L., AND ULLMANN, L. P. *Research in Behavior Modification: New Developments and Implications.* New York, Holt, Rinehart and Winston, 1965. Already a classic in the field. It contains a series of basic positional papers, including Bijou's research on child behavior, Goldiamond's research on stuttering, Matterzao's research on interviews, and Bandura's research on modeling. (The companion volume, Krasner, L. and Ullmann, L., *Case Studies on Behavior Modification,* 1965, presents actual descriptions of successful behavior therapy.)

YABLONSKY, L. *Synanon: The Tunnel Back.* New York, Macmillan, 1965. A somewhat oversimplified discussion of Synanon. However, Yablonsky still supplies a good introduction to the institution.

34
Drugs and Drug Therapy

In writing this particular introduction, I want to advance a suggestion on how to handle the drug problem. I want to do so in all seriousness. First, to be perfectly honest, I want to disclaim any expert knowledge. I have never taken any drugs. I don't even drink or smoke. I don't know any drug addicts; I have no experience in the field at all from any angle. It is just that there is something I don't understand about the drug problem: What is wrong with taking drugs and becoming addicted to them?

I am told, for instance, that drug addicts are a danger to society. But why is that? Because they take drugs? Or because they are kept from taking drugs? It seems to me that all the violent acts attributed to addicts occur when the addict is trying to *get* drugs. In that case, why stop them, I wonder? Why try to keep drugs from them? If we could provide cheap drugs, purchasable legally without prescriptions, one large source of potential violence would be removed.

I am told that drug addicts ruin their lives through their addiction and may even kill themselves through overdoses. Perhaps, but I am also told that it is the uncontrolled variation in strength and purity that does most of the physical damage. If pure drugs in known dosages were supplied, wouldn't drugs become much safer?

I am told that the drug problem is dangerous because it is under the control of criminals. But isn't that because we insist on making drugs illegal? If drugs could be handled legally and honestly, why would criminals get into the act?

I am told that drug addiction is dangerous in the ordinary affairs of life—in driving a car, for instance. True, an addict at the wheel of a car would make me nervous. So would a man under the influence of alcohol who is driving a car. So would a cigarette smoker, with his judgment dulled by chronic hypoxia. So would a man in a haze of anger after a just-concluded argument with his wife.

I am told that drug addiction is simply immoral. Maybe it is, but is it worse than any other addiction; is it worse than alcohol addiction or tobacco addiction or food addiction, all of which are physiologically dangerous?

The United States, back in the 1920s, tried to outlaw alcohol in the thirteen-year experiment of Prohibition. During that time, the attempt to enforce the law brought about the growth of gangsterism, encouraged contempt for the law, led to what some called a general deterioration of moral fiber. One thing it did *not* do. It did *not* succeed in outlawing alcohol.

My suggestion then? Let's consider the possibility of legalizing all drugs and of supervising the production of a cheap and uniform supply. If anyone wants to be an addict—well, it's his life. And, who knows, if we remove the glamour of illegality and danger from the whole thing, perhaps fewer people may be lured into addiction in the first place.

It would also help if we built a society so healthy that few would feel so desperate a need to escape from it.

I. A.

One hot August evening in 1955, Helen Burney sat listlessly on her bed in the violent ward of the large Texas hospital where she had been confined for the past four months. During most of that unhappy time, Helen had been highly vocal, abusive, and overactive. Only the day before she had tried to strike a ward aide, but immediately several burly attendants had grabbed her, roughly tying her into a straitjacket and pinioning her arms against her chest. But today Helen's behavior was very different. Her incessant talking and shouting had stopped; all day long she spoke only when spoken to; most of the time she lay on her bed with her eyes half closed, moving little, and looking rather pale. However, she was unusually cooperative with the nursing personnel, got out of bed when told to, and went to the dining room without resisting. What had happened to bring about this remarkable change?

That morning she had received an injection of a new synthetic drug, *chlorpromazine,* which had been discovered a few years earlier in France. On the same day thousands of mental patients throughout the world were receiving the same drug, many of them for the first time. News of the drug's usefulness had spread rapidly in the preceding months, and it was being tried in mental hospitals throughout the world. Soon it would be difficult to find a psychotic patient who was not receiving a drug of some kind for the treatment of his illness. The era of clinical psychopharmacology had begun, and the new drugs were hailed as the first real breakthrough in the treatment of one of man's most serious and mysterious afflictions—psychosis.

BEFORE PSYCHIATRIC DRUGS

Until it was discovered that drugs could help the severely disturbed, almost the only recourse in the management of such patients was physical restraint. Before 1955 such physical methods as wet-sheet wrapping, "hydrotherapy" (baths), isolation, straitjackets, lobotomy, and electroconvulsive shocks were in relatively common use. So were simple sedation by barbiturates and the not-so-simple—and sometimes fatal—insulin-coma therapy.

Philippe Pinel, the famous French psychiatrist, campaigning for humane treatment of the insane at the end of the eighteenth century, freed the inmates of the grim Bicêtre mental hospital from their iron chains. Unfortunately, other physical restraints had to be substituted when patients became assaultive or destructive, and although the padded cell and the *camisole,* or straitjacket, may have been softer than chains, they allowed no greater freedom.

PSYCHIATRIC DRUGS

Not until the mid-1950s did drugs finally promise emancipation from physical restraint for most patients. Despite the fears of some psychiatrists, psychologists, and social workers that the social and psychological factors contributing to mental illness would be ignored, the use of psychopharmaceuticals radically improved the treatment of the mentally ill within and without the hospital. Indeed, only with their use has it been possible for some families to be held together, for some individuals to be gainfully employed, and for some patients to be reached by psychotherapy. Antipsychotic and antidepressant drugs are easily available and inexpensive compared to classic individual psychotherapy and hospitalization. This form of treatment is more accessible to people of all socioeconomic classes.

Since 1955, psychopharmacology has become an important scientific discipline in its own right, and many new chemical agents have been developed for the treatment of each major category of mental illness. These drugs include phenothiazines (chlorpromazine is an example), rauwolfia alkaloids, butyrophenones, propanediol and benzodiazepine compounds, monoamine oxidase (MAO) inhibitors, dibenzazepine derivatives, and many more. They have been found useful in the treatment of the most severe mental illnesses: schizophrenia, depression, and mania, which are described in Chapter 30. Even autistic behavior, psychopathic behavior, sexual deviation, and mental retardation have been attacked with drugs, but clinical psychopharmacologists feel that the surface has only been scratched in these areas.

It is interesting to note that the total census of patients in public mental hospitals in the United States dropped from 631,503 in 1955 to 549,591 in 1960 and to 399,152 in 1968—in the face of a marked increase in the population of the United States during this time. This striking drop in the number of patients in United States mental hospitals can be ascribed partly to changing attitudes toward the mentally ill and partly to new psychosocial methods for treating patients. For example, group therapy and community psychiatry try to get patients out of hospitals, so that they can return to their families and jobs. But certainly drug therapy has played a vital and central role.

The coming of the psychiatric drugs, however, has not been an entirely unmixed blessing. Many people view psychiatric medicines as magical nostrums, as panaceas

Figure 34.1
Before the advent of psychiatric medication, many procedures in psychiatric institutions centered on physical restraint; therapy for the disorder was most often not even considered. The medications that are described in this chapter, however, provided important breakthroughs. The drugs can control patients' anxiety, cognitive distortions, and assaultiveness so that the patients can make use of whatever therapeutic opportunities exist in their hospital settings. Also, medications often help discharged patients maintain a successful adjustment outside the hospital. One drawback to the use of psychiatric drugs is the tendency to use "chemotherapy" as the only treatment, either because of inadequate therapeutic facilities or the belief that they constitute full treatment. Most authorities agree that such medication arrests symptoms but does not resolve the emotional and interpersonal difficulties that caused the disorder.

for everyone's emotional problems. And with such fanciful attitudes comes the common and sometimes dangerous overuse of these agents.

Major Tranquilizers

The major tranquilizers, or antipsychotic drugs, are so called because they are administered mainly to people with major psychological disorders, or psychoses. They effectively lower a psychotic person's motor activity and responsiveness to external and internal stimuli; these drugs also reduce the hallucinations and delusional behavior of psychotics. There are three basic chemical types of drugs in this class: the phenothiazines, the thioxanthines, and butyrophenones. The phenothiazines, one of the oldest types, often serve as the standard against which other antipsychotic drugs are measured. Schizophrenia and manic psychosis are among the psychoses that are treatable with this group of drugs. Large-scale controlled studies by the United States Veterans' Administration and by the Psychopharmacology Service Center of the National Institute of Mental Health showed chlorpromazine and the related phenothiazines to be useful in the treatment of acute schizophrenia. Other studies show that phenothiazines help discharged mental patients stay out of the hospital.

The results of a study from the Massachusetts Mental Health Center (cited by M. Greenblatt in *Drugs and Social Therapy in Chronic Schizophrenia*) show the effectiveness of the phenothiazines. The study compared four methods of treatment for schizophrenia. People in group one were treated with tranquilizers and psychoso-

Groups	Improvement after 6 Months (percent)	Improvement after 18 Months (percent)
1. Therapy and Drugs (33)	33	48
2. Therapy Only (27)	0	30
3. Drugs Only (35)	23	23
4. Custodial Care Only (20)	10	5

Figure 34.2
The results of the Massachusetts Mental Health Center study on the effectiveness of different forms of treatment.
(After Greenblatt *et al.*, 1965.)

cial therapies, that is, intensive individual psychoanalytically oriented psychotherapy, group, milieu, recreational, and occupational therapies. Group two had only psychosocial therapies; group three, only drugs; and group four, only hospitalization with no specific therapy. The study found that schizophrenics who received custodial care only showed little improvement. The group that received only therapy showed significant improvement only after more than a year of treatment. Although the group that received only drugs showed significant improvement, the group treated with drugs and psychosocial therapies did best of all, especially over a long period of time. The best treatment, then, was the combination of drugs and psychosocial therapy, and of all the single forms of therapy, drugs were by far the most successful.

How do these drugs work biochemically? No one knows, although theories abound. One interesting theory has it that schizophrenia is secondary to abnormal metabolism of the chemical *dopamine*, which is found in the brain, and that the major tranquilizers work by affecting this chemical and its actions. The theory hypothesizes that antipsychotic drugs work by blocking the receptor sites for dopamine, thereby blocking its effects.

The drugs used in the treatment of schizophrenia have numerous side effects, as do many drugs. Although these side effects are bothersome, they are not often serious—certainly not to a degree that would outweigh their therapeutic value in cases of severe mental illness. Some of the common side effects include sedation (which is often a desired side effect, especially in agitated or violent patients), dry mouth, lowered blood pressure, slightly blurred vision, and sometimes abnormal movements or tightness of the muscles. Many of these disturbances fade away if the person remains on the drug for an extended period of time. One puzzling fact about antipsychotic drugs is that some psychotics can take high doses without experiencing the disabling drowsiness and confusion that nonpsychotic people feel on the same doses.

Minor Tranquilizers

Minor tranquilizers, or antianxiety drugs, are so called because they are usually administered to people with minor disorders, where anxiety is the main symptom. But anxiety is not a specific symptom, and it occurs in many states that would not be diagnosed as psychological disorders—for example, the anxiety one feels before a psychology test or a job interview.

Anxiety is such a common experience that everyone has a subjective understanding of the term. It may be defined as an unpleasant state associated with a threatening situation, and it is closely associated with fear. Sedative hypnotic drugs, including alcohol and barbiturates (discussed later in the chapter), have frequently been used to lower anxiety. In 1955 a number of new drugs with properties common to the sedative hypnotics were introduced for the treatment of anxiety, but the most successful of these by far was *meprobamate*, popularly known as Miltown or Equanil. There were many arguments about whether meprobamate was more effective than the barbiturates. Because the properties of the various barbiturates differ, it is not easy to compare the whole class to meprobamate. In any case, meprobamate's standing as the most popular tranquilizer was soon usurped by chlordiazepoxide (Librium). This compound strongly resembles meprobamate and the barbiturates.

Minor tranquilizers, including barbiturates, are ineffective in treating psychoses and other major disorders, but they are effective in treating anxiety and are therefore useful in the treatment of anxiety-related problems like muscular tension and irritability. However, it has not been shown that the new, high-priced minor tranquilizers are any more effective than old-fashioned barbiturates in treating anxiety.

A growing problem with this class of drugs is overuse—they are very seriously abused by large numbers of people who regard them as a cure-all. They are more a danger than a help to a person whose emotional fluctuations are normal but who seeks blissful calm in a troubled world. Unfortunately, physicians all too often promote the overuse of these agents by prescribing too many of them too frequently.

How these drugs work to diminish anxiety is not clear. Probably, the sedative action that they all possess is the major reason for their effect. All of the minor tranquilizers tend to produce sleep when used in large doses; to produce effects reported as pleasant; and to produce convulsive seizures as a consequence of sudden withdrawal after the prolonged administration of large doses. Giving meprobamate to a patient suffering from neurotic anxiety is not quite the same as inserting a nail into a broken bone to hold it together or giving insulin to a diabetic. In giving meprobamate, physicians are employing a drug with a poorly defined action to treat a poorly defined condition.

If the drugs are taken properly, the side effects are few and consist mainly of drowsiness. However, this class of drugs is in fact the most addicting and potentially the most dangerous of any discussed in this chapter, including the narcotics! People often use these drugs to attempt suicide, and many succeed. The withdrawal syndrome—that is, the state that results from discontinuing the use of the drug after the body has become dependent upon it—is especially dangerous. Convulsions are very common, and deaths are not infrequent when people go through an untreated withdrawal from these minor tranquilizers.

Sedatives

Sedatives are a relatively old and widely used class of drugs that cause drowsiness or lowered excitability when taken in low doses. Higher doses produce sleep. Barbiturates are perhaps the best-known sedatives although there are now more expensive chemicals that produce similar effects and similar problems.

Sedatives have two main uses: to treat anxiety and to treat insomnia. The treatment of anxiety was discussed in the preceding section; the similarity of barbiturates to antianxiety drugs like meprobamate was also described.

Insomnia is one of the most common complaints in America, whatever the causes. It is understandable why so many "sleeping pills" are used and abused each year in the United States. Overuse of most sedative drugs can produce psychological and physical addiction. Withdrawal can result in convulsions and sometimes death. Suicide attempts and successful suicide with an overdose of sedatives are common.

Antidepressants

The discovery and development of the *antidepressant* drugs is an especially significant chapter in the history of psychiatry. The chemical mechanisms through which a person's emotional states are mediated are not by any means fully understood, but significant progress is being made with great assistance from these drugs.

Antidepressant drugs should not be confused with *stimulants,* which are discussed in another section. Antidepressants can reverse a state of depression in a mentally ill person but usually have no effect on normal people. Stimulants are not effective in treating depression and can cause a normal person to become excited and euphoric; they produce a stimulation of the autonomic nervous system.

The first observation of a specific antidepressant effect was a beautiful example of serendipity. In 1952 I. J. Selikoff and his colleagues, who were treating patients for tuberculosis with the drug called *iproniazid,* noticed an elevated mood in a number of his patients. This observation led to a period of intense investigation of how *MAO inhibitors* (monoamineoxidase inhibitors, the chemical family to which iproniazid belongs) affect mood and behavior. Now, although some MAO inhibitors are still used clinically, more effective and less toxic drugs—the *tricyclic antidepressants*—are used more often.

The *catecholamine* hypothesis of affective disorders came out of research on how the MAO inhibitors and the tricyclic antidepressants affect chemicals in the brain

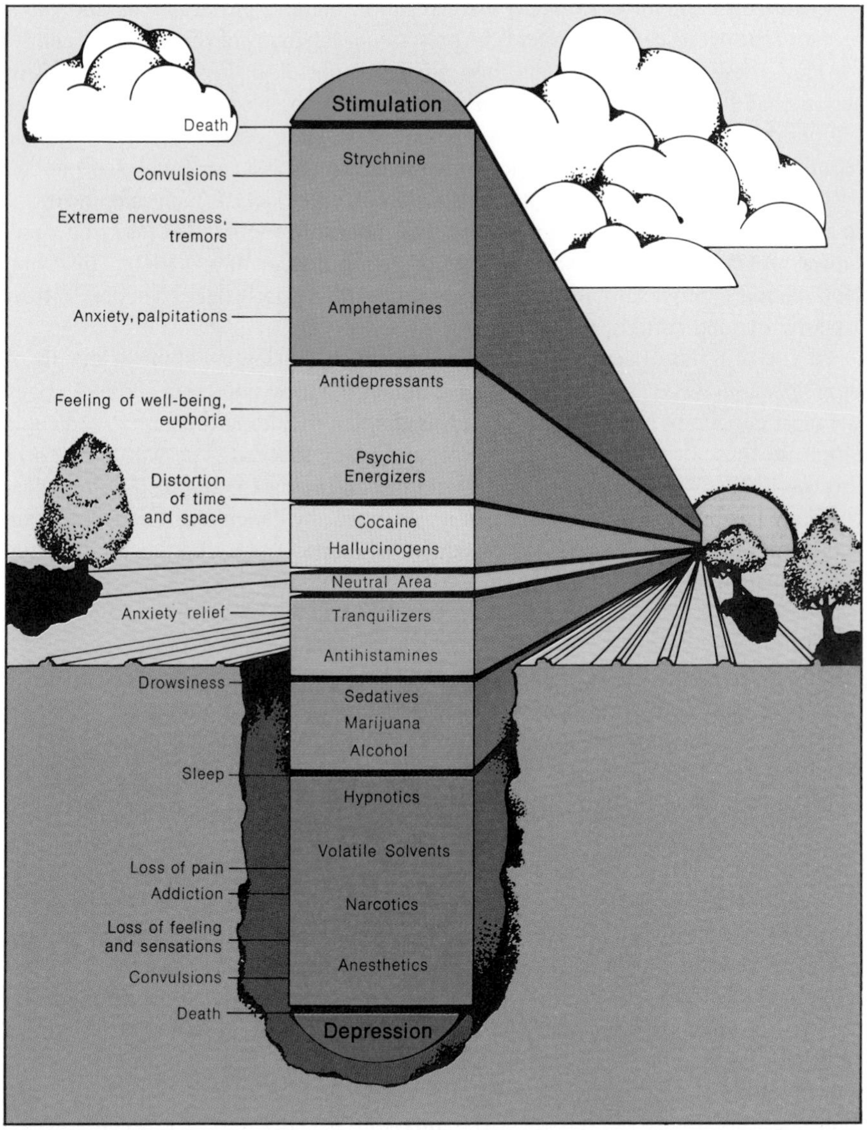

Figure 34.3
The continuum of drug effects, from stimulation to depression, is illustrated in this drawing. Although drugs at different points on the continuum have different effects, convulsions and death can result from overuse of either stimulants or depressants. When used cautiously and realistically, drugs can play a significant role in treating some psychological disorders. The tendency to look for quick and painless solutions to complex problems, however, results in overprescribing and abuse of these drugs, by both professionals and laymen.
(Adapted from a chart by R. W. Earle, Ph.D., Department of Medical Pharmacology and Therapeutics, University of California, Irvine, California College of Medicine.)

called catecholamines—specifically *noradrenaline* (NA), a hormone that is important in the functioning of the autonomic nervous system. (See Chapter 16.) Put very simply, the hypothesis is this: functional deficiencies of NA in the brain are related to the clinical state of depression, and functional excesses of NA are related to mania or excited states. Drugs that increase the availability of NA in the brain, then, might alleviate depression, and drugs that decrease it might cause depression; moreover, drugs that produce an excess of NA might cause excitation or mania, and drugs that decrease the availability or block the effects of NA in the brain might alleviate mania.

As one can see from Figure 34.4, the MAO inhibitors block destruction of NA inside the nerve cell, making more NA available for use. The phenothiazines, on the other hand, which are effective in controlling manic psychosis, may work their actions by blocking the effects of NA.

Antidepressant drugs are usually ineffective if used for the common sadnesses and tragedies of everyday life, like a broken romance or the death of a family member or friend. And they can be effective in increasing drive and elevating mood only for certain types of depression. Studies by L. E. Hollister and others indicate that people with "pure"—that is, specifically definable—depression respond best to MAO

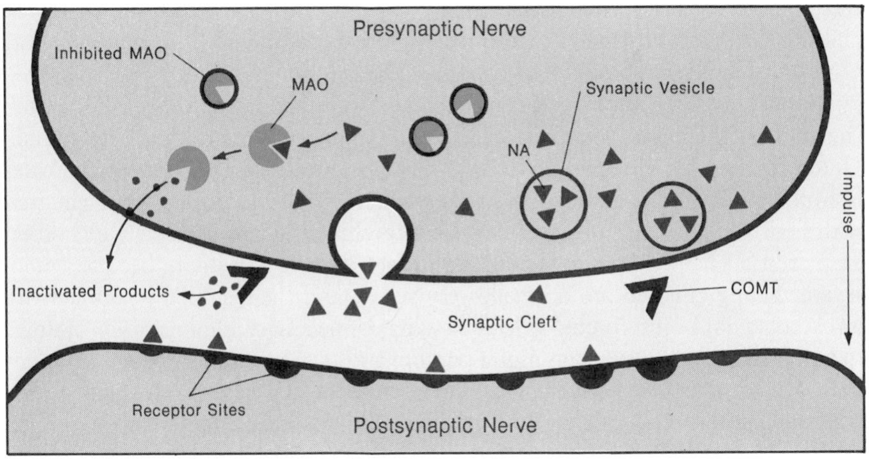

Figure 34.4
Representation of the elements thought to be present in a noradrenaline synapse in the brain. NA is noradrenaline, a substance believed to transmit impulses from one nerve cell to another. MAO is monoamine oxidase, which inactivates NA inside the cell. COMT is catechol-O-methyl transferase, which inactivates NA after it has been released into the synaptic cleft. It is hypothesized that relative or absolute deficiencies of NA in the brain (as occurs after use of the drug reserpine, for example) can produce depression, and that a relative excess or release—or decrease in inactivation—of NA (as with the use of amphetamines) can produce mania or excitement.

inhibitors and tricyclics. These people show severe depressive mood in their slow body movements, reactions, thought, and speech. For a person who also shows anxiety, hostility, or other symptoms that are uncharacteristic of pure severe depression, the antidepressant drugs are less likely to be effective. It has been estimated that only about 10 percent of all people with depressions can benefit from these drugs. The rest respond better to psychosocial therapies.

Lithium

Lithium salts are newcomers among the psychiatric drugs used in the United States, but they have been used for more than fifteen years in Europe. The action of lithium salts was discovered by accident when J. F. Cade, an Australian physician, noticed that they produced drowsiness in guinea pigs. This observation led to the idea that lithium might help alleviate mania in human beings, and at present lithium is used to treat manic psychosis.

The drug seems to be curiously specific for mania, and it often returns severely manic patients—who show hyperactivity, unrealistic euphoria and self-confidence, and other exaggerations of mood—to normal mood states within five to seven days, usually without the side effects of lethargy and drowsiness that major tranquilizers sometimes produce. Some research findings (such as those by H. Corrodi, S. M. Schanberg, and R. W. Coldburn) suggest that the action of lithium salts may be consistent with the catecholamine hypothesis of mood disorders.

Several clinical studies, such as one by A. Coppen and his colleagues, have suggested that lithium administered daily will prevent the recurrent episodes not only of mania but of depression, too, in the mood swings so often seen in people with manic-depressive disorders. There is still not enough research evidence to support these claims. In addition, research by M. Schou indicates that the action of lithium, like that of the antidepressant drugs, is more effective with "pure" mood disorders.

Stimulants

Stimulants include very powerful drugs, like *dextroamphetamine* and *methamphetamine,* and less potent ones, like caffeine and nicotine. All of these agents produce *excitement;* specifically, they can decrease fatigue, increase talkativeness and physical activity, enhance physical performance, produce a state of alertness, diminish appetite, and for a time elevate mood—often to euphoria.

The value of amphetamines in psychiatry is limited. As noted earlier, they are usually not effective in treating depression; actually they can make the disorder worse. However, they can be used to treat a rare condition called *narcolepsy,* in which the person has abnormal fits of sleep, sometimes falling asleep in the middle of a conversation or at other inappropriate times. Amphetamines are also useful in treating the so-called "hyperkinetic," or "hyperactive" child. The hyperkinetic child's overactivity and inability to concentrate are probably secondary to some sort of minimal dysfunction of the brain. This state can sometimes be much improved by stimulants, which in children can act paradoxically and inexplicably as a tranquilizer to calm them and help them concentrate and attend more closely to stimuli. Unfortunately the effectiveness of amphetamines for treating some specific cases of hyperactivity has led to frequent, indiscriminate use of these drugs for all children with high activity levels or other behavioral problems. Many hyperactive children are not at all helped by amphetamines; in fact their hyperactivity becomes more severe. Young children are normally very active, and their naturally high activity level should not be interpreted as hyperactivity. Unnecessary administration of drugs to a normal child can serve no useful purpose and may be harmful. Amphetamines should be administered with great caution because their effects are often unpredictable, and long-term dependency is very dangerous. Use of the drug should be stopped at the first sign that it is adversely affecting a hyperactive child.

The abuse of amphetamines—"speed," "meth," or "ups"—is a very serious problem. A typical example of amphetamine abuse is the thoroughly respectable but obese middle-aged lady who begins taking "diet pills" to lose weight but continues to use them because they give her more energy to face the day. Another is the man who injects large quantities of a stimulant into his veins every three hours for a "run" of sometimes two to three days at a time. Still another is the college student who relies on pills to stay awake all night to write papers or cram for exams. All of these individuals are misusing the drug and are in some way dependent upon it. Society usually ignores the problems of stimulant abusers they think respectable—like the obese lady—but condemns as criminal someone on society's fringe—like the "mainliner."

With continued use of these drugs—for example, dextroamphetamine—anyone will develop tolerance; that is, he or she will need more of the drug to produce the same effect. As a person develops tolerance and needs higher and higher doses, he experiences marked side effects; he may become very suspicious and imagine people are after him or peering at him in a peculiar fashion. He may pick at imaginary objects on his skin, grind his teeth, or get caught up in meaningless, meandering trains of thought. A psychosis, at times indistinguishable from paranoid schizophrenia, may develop. There is no physical withdrawal syndrome like that with narcotics and barbiturates, but there are common reactions after the drug effects wear off—for example, a deep and lasting "rebound" depression, apathy and lethargy lasting many days, and periods of prolonged sleep and increased appetite.

When the drug is injected, the person is subject to a number of very unpleasant additional side effects, like liver disease and local and systemic infections, which occur with the intravenous use of unsterile and impure chemicals.

Figure 34.5 *(opposite)*
Amphetamine misuse constitutes a serious drug problem. Abuse of stimulants occurs in several ways. Young people may use amphetamines for energy, for all-night studying, or to get high. Among older people, amphetamine use may begin as a means of appetite control or to sustain a tolerable mood level. All these uses may lead to drug dependency. Intravenous injection of methamphetamines often creates a dangerous cycle of "speeding"; the person who "runs" speed for days at a time risks disease and even death because of exhaustion and the depletion of bodily resources.

PSYCHOTOGENIC DRUGS

Lysergic acid diethylamide (LSD), psilocybin, dimethyltryptamine (DMT), mescaline (peyote), and "STP" (an amphetamine derivative) are examples of the class of drugs called *psychotogenic* or *psychedelic.* Marijuana and its derivatives are discussed in detail in Chapter 15. Actually, neither these two names nor the multitude of other sobriquets attached to them—including the term "mind-expanding"—adequately describes their main effects on human beings.

The chemical structures of psychotogenic drugs are diverse, and the drugs vary widely in their potency and duration of action as well as in how they are taken—for example, swallowed, smoked, or sniffed. LSD is the most potent of the lot, probably the one most commonly used, and certainly the one most written about. The other psychotogenic drugs, in large enough doses, can produce results similar to those of LSD. LSD is one of the most potent drugs known. It is 100 times stronger than

SPEED KILLS
MARTY GUNSAULLIS

psilocybin, 4,000 times stronger than mescaline, and is effective in doses of millionths of a gram!

LSD has a curious history. In 1943 a Swiss pharmacologist, A. Hoffman, working with ergot drugs (the chemical family of LSD) accidentally ingested the drug and had the first recorded LSD "trip," which, incidentally, he found unpleasant. It became popular in the early and mid-1960s, before its use was made illegal, and it had its boom year in 1967. Since then the use of LSD has diminished significantly, although it is still a rather common drug. The reason for the decrease in use is unknown.

What occurs when LSD is ingested? During the first fifteen to thirty minutes the person is likely to feel physical changes—among them nausea, gooseflesh, dilated pupils, and an increase in heart rate. Within the first three hours there may be changes in mood, perception, and thinking. During a "trip" a person can experience any number of mood states, often quite intense, often rapidly changing. Many users of LSD feel that a person's mood immediately prior to taking the drug determines the kind of experience he will have—enjoyable or frightening.

Perceptual distortions and hallucinations are very common with LSD. A person often has varicolored visual hallucinations; he may find an absence of familiar form in objects, or distortions in form that make familiar objects unrecognizable. For example, a wall may seem to pulsate or breathe; sounds may be "seen," and visual stimuli may be "heard." A person may experience a dissociation of the self into one being who watches the experience and another who feels it (see Chapter 15). He may experience time as slowed down or accelerated. A single stimulus may be the focus of attention for hours, perceived as changing or newly beautiful and fascinating. Such experiences can make a person feel like an explorer among familiar objects.

As measured by the ability to perform simple tests, the LSD user's thinking is impaired; however, he may feel that he is thinking more clearly and logically than ever before. Life-long problems seem suddenly to be resolved, or the need to solve them may seem absurd. The person often experiences the "great truth" phenomenon—that is, he feels that previously hidden and ultimate "inner truths" have been revealed to him. Usually, when the trip is over, the magnitude of these discoveries shrinks, and the solutions turn out to be untenable in reality. After three to five

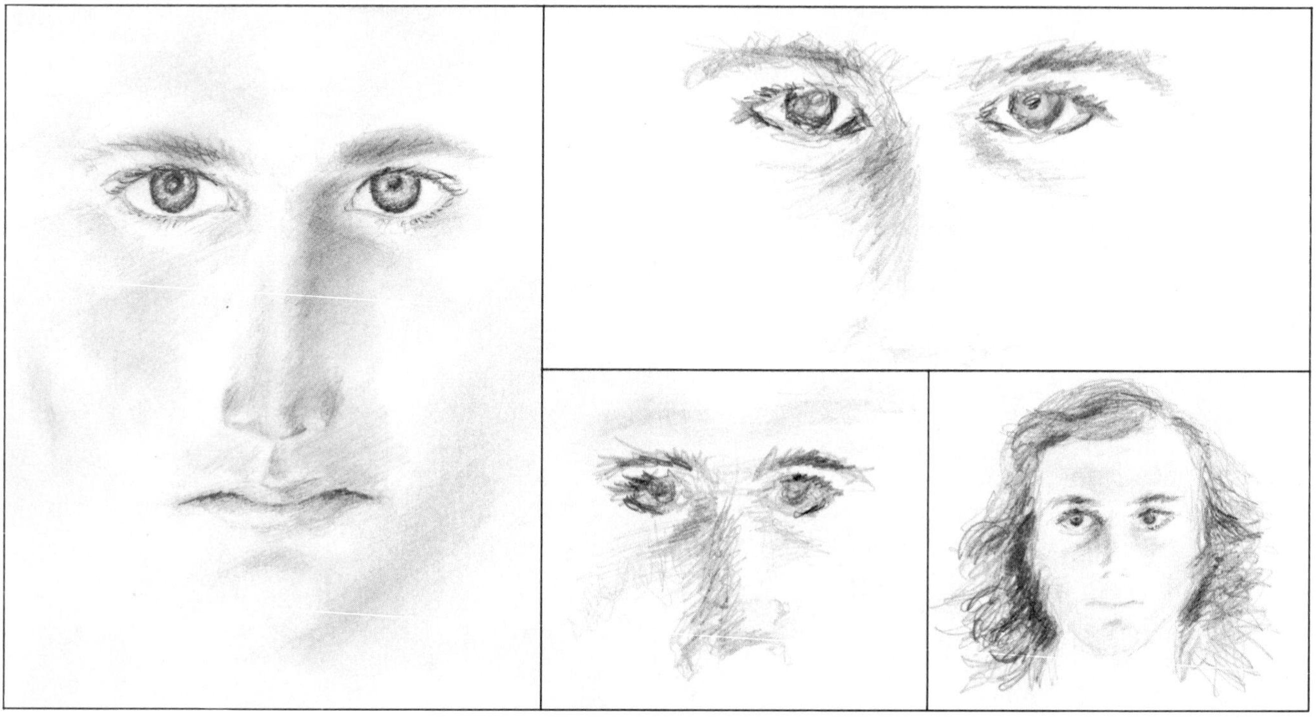

Figure 34.6
This series of self-portraits was drawn by an artist at several points during the course of an LSD experience. (Left) the first self-portrait was completed just prior to taking the drug; he said that this picture reflects his soul, as he saw it. (Top right) the next self-portrait was executed three hours after he had ingested LSD. His desire and ability to concentrate had decreased, and he had begun to "feel paranoid" about his artistic ability. As a result, he frantically sketched this picture "to recapture the person I knew I was." (Bottom left) three hours later the next portrait was attempted. At this point he was almost totally distracted by hallucinations; he could not concentrate, and had no desire to draw. He described this portrait as "a futile attempt." (Bottom right) his final picture of the series was done nine hours after taking the LSD; at this point its effects were wearing off. He diligently attempted a self-portrait, but was less satisfied with this picture than with his initial effort above. He explained that the sketchiness of the drawing "was directly attributable to the paranoia generated by my artistic insecurity."

hours the extreme intensity of the experience begins to dwindle and often stabilizes; the hallucinations and illusions quite frequently disappear after six hours, and the effects of the drug wear off after ten to fourteen hours—if no complications occur.

However, complications do occur and not infrequently. Panic reactions are the most common of the unpleasant side effects, and they may be terrifying. Some users say a panic state, no matter how brief, is a part of every LSD trip. Persons who experience panic and later describe it often say that they felt trapped in the experience and were afraid that they would never get out or that they would go mad. At this point of fear, they try to ignore, change, or otherwise rid themselves of the effects of the drug—and they panic when they cannot succeed. The panic can lead to accidents, even suicide, in attempts to find relief. Reports are common of LSD causing "flashbacks" (or brief recurrences of LSD experiences) even as late as three years after the last dose. Compensated psychotics are described by S. Cohen as relapsing after using LSD. There is no evidence that LSD causes schizophrenia or any lasting psychosis, only that it may make an existing illness more severe.

Persons who take LSD frequently are often said to be passive individuals who avoid active engagements in society. It is doubtful that LSD causes such reactions; in fact it is probably just the reverse: that passive types and "dropouts"—fringe members of active society—are more likely to use LSD frequently. For example, one almost never finds a well-functioning individual, whatever his work, to be a chronic user of LSD.

A "bad trip" usually refers to the panic reaction described earlier. The best treatment, if the panic is not too severe, seems to be the comfort offered by friends and the security of familiar settings. Medical attention is sometimes necessary for very intense reactions. Infrequently, a person will need antipsychotic medications, like the phenothiazines, and even hospitalization.

In the late 1960s there were reports that LSD caused damage to chromosomes, mutation of fetuses, and cancer. Since then, there has been contention among reports. Some reports still find support for these dangers; others refute the findings. From their own work and from their recent review of the literature, N. J. Dishotsky and others state that "pure LSD taken in usual small doses . . . in the human being . . . does not damage chromosomes, cause mutations, or cause cancer."

LSD has been used experimentally by psychiatrists and psychotherapists to determine whether it might be of use in the treatment of behavioral problems. The main theory behind this practice has been that LSD lowers defenses and allows repressed feelings and memories to emerge into consciousness and be dealt with by patient and therapist. LSD has also been used to treat severely withdrawn or autistic children. Although experimental work investigating the use of LSD as a therapeutic agent continues (mainly in Europe), existing evidence, gathered by D. X. Freedman and by A. J. Mandell and L. J. West, among others, suggests that LSD is not a particularly effective psychotherapeutic agent and that in some cases—the borderline schizophrenic, for example—it is potentially harmful.

At one time, especially in the 1950s, excitement in the psychiatric community ran high as LSD was hailed as an agent that produced a "model psychosis"; that is, it induced a psychotic state similar to schizophrenia. It therefore promised to be the key to the biological secrets of schizophrenia. Unfortunately this promise has not been fulfilled; the LSD "psychosis," on closer examination, proves to be quite distinct from schizophrenia.

However, LSD is proving to be a valuable agent in exploring certain of the biochemical and physiological functions of the brain. *Serotonin* is an amine that, like noradrenaline, probably transmits nerve impulses in the brain. Serotonin may have important roles in the regulation of sleep and emotion. This amine is chemically similar to part of the LSD molecule. More important, the fact that LSD blocks the effects of serotonin on tissue may account for some of its effects in human beings.

Figure 34.7
Accurate information is a prerequisite to meaningful communication about drugs, to research, to treatment, and to prevention of their misuse. It is only too easy to be a self-styled "expert" on the basis of rumor and misinformation. The charts on the following pages provide a compendium of information about many commonly used pharmacological agents, and the accompanying photographs illustrate the various substances.

(Adapted from J. Fort, M.D., *The Pleasure Seekers.* Indianapolis: Bobbs-Merrill, 1969, pp. 236-243.)

*Crucial to an evaluation of these drugs is knowledge of the amount consumed, purity, frequency of use, time interval since ingestion and amount of food in the stomach at that time, combinations with other drugs—and, most important, the personality of the individual taking it and the context in which it is taken. The determinations made in this chart are based on evidence with human use of these drugs rather than on isolated experimental situations or animal research.

†Only scattered, inadequate health, education, or rehabilitation programs (usually prison hospitals) exist for narcotic addicts and alcoholics (usually outpatient clinics), with nothing for the others except, sometimes, prison.

Name	Slang Name	Typical Single Adult Dose	Duration of Action (hours)	How Taken	Legitimate Medical Uses (present and projected)	Psychological Dependence Potential	Tolerar Potenti
Alcohol Whisky, gin, beer, wine	Booze Hooch	1½ oz. gin or whisky, 12 oz. beer	2–4	Swallowed	Rare; sometimes used as a sedative	High	Yes
Caffeine Coffee, tea, Coca-Cola, No-Doz, APC	Java	1–2 cups 1 bottle 5 mg.	2–4	Swallowed	Mild stimulant; treatment of some forms of coma	Moderate	Yes
Nicotine (and coal tar) Cigarettes, cigars	Fag	1–2 cigarettes	1–2	Smoked	None	High	Yes
Sedatives Barbiturates Nembutal Seconal Phenobarbital Doriden Chloral hydrate Miltown, Equanil (meprobamate)	 Yellow jackets Red devils Phennies Goofers	 50–100 mg. 500 mg. 500 mg. 400 mg.	4	Swallowed	Treatment of insomnia and tension; induction of anesthesia	High	Yes
Stimulants Amphetamines Benzedrine Methedrine Dexedrine Cocaine	 Bennies Crystal, speed Dexies Coke, snow	 2.5–5.0 mg. Variable	 4	 Swallowed or injected Sniffed or injected	Treatment of obesity, narcolepsy, fatigue, depression Anesthesia of the eye and throat	High	Yes
Tranquilizers Librium Phenothiazines Thorazine Compazine Stelazine Reserpine		 5–10 mg. 10–25 mg. 10 mg. 2 mg. 1 mg.	 4–6	 Swallowed	Treatment of anxiety, tension, alcoholism, neurosis, psychosis, psychosomatic disorders, and vomiting	Minimal	No

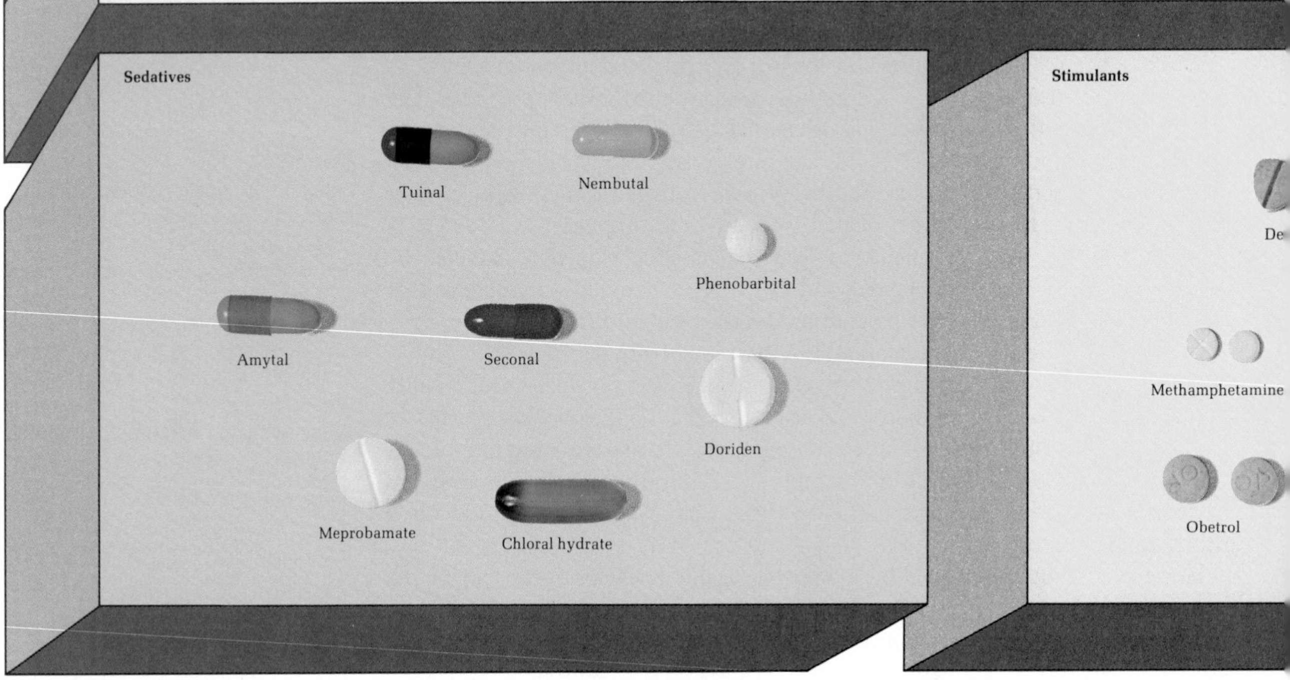

sical endence ntial	Overall Abuse Potential	Reasons for Use	Typical Short-term Effects*	Typical Long-term Effects	Form of Legal Regulation† and Control
	High	To relax; to escape from tensions, problems, and inhibitions; to get "high"	CNS depressant; relaxation; sometimes euphoria; drowsiness; impaired judgment, reaction time, coordination, and emotional control; frequent aggressive behavior and driving accidents	Possible obesity with chronic excessive use; irreversible damage to brain and liver, addiction with severe withdrawal illness (DTs); habituation	Available and advertised without limitation in many forms, with only minimal regulation by age (21 or 18), hours of sale, location, taxation, ban on bootlegging, and driving laws; some "black market" for those under age and those evading taxes; minimal penalties
	None	For a "pickup" or stimulation	CNS stimulant; increased alertness	Sometimes insomnia or restlessness; habituation	Available and advertised without limit, with no regulation for children or adults
	Moderate	For a "pickup" or stimulation	CNS stimulant; relaxation (or distraction) from the process of smoking	Lung (and other) cancer, heart, and blood vessel disease, cough, etc.; habituation	Available and advertised without limit, with only minimal regulation by age, taxation, and labeling of packages
	High	To relax or sleep; to get "high"	CNS depressants; sleep induction; sometimes euphoria; drowsiness; impaired judgment, reaction time, coordination, and emotional control; relief of anxiety-tension	Irritability, weight loss, addiction with severe withdrawal illness (like DTs); habituation, addiction	Available in large amounts by ordinary medical prescription, which can be repeatedly refilled or can be obtained from more than one physician; widely advertised and "detailed" to M.D.s and pharmacists; other manufacture, sale, or possession prohibited under federal drug abuse and similar state (dangerous) drug laws; moderate penalties; widespread illicit traffic
	High	For stimulation and relief of fatigue; to get "high"	CNS stimulants; increased alertness, loss of appetite, insomnia, often euphoria	Restlessness; irritability, weight loss, toxic psychosis (mainly paranoid); habituation; extreme irritability, toxic psychosis	Amphetamines, same as sedatives above; cocaine, same as narcotics below
	Minimal	Medical (including psychiatric) treatment of anxiety or tension states, alcoholism, psychoses, and other disorders	Selective CNS depressants; relief of anxiety-tension; suppression of hallucinations or delusions, improved functioning	Sometimes drowsiness, dryness of mouth, blurring of vision, skin rash, tremor; occasionally jaundice, agranulocytosis	Same as sedatives above, except not usually included under the special federal or state drug laws; negligible illicit traffic

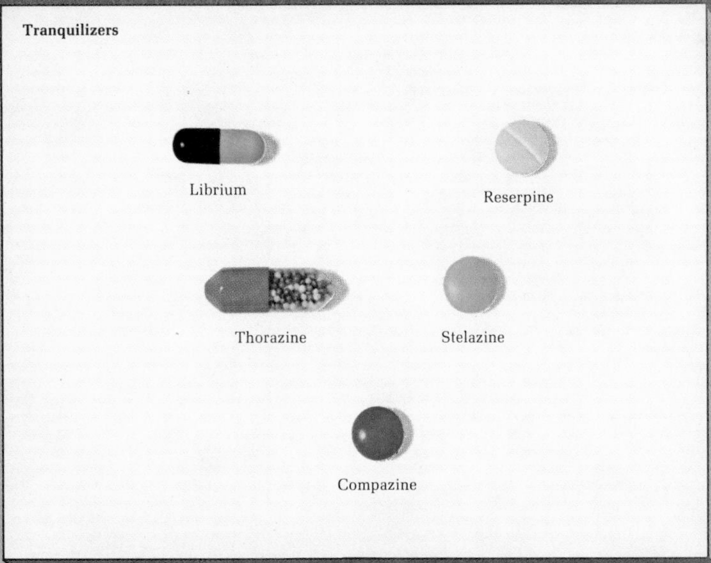

Name	Slang Name	Typical Single Adult Dose	Duration of Action (hours)	How Taken	Legitimate Medical Uses (present and projected)	Psychological Dependence Potential	Toleran Potentia
Cannabis (marijuana)	Pot, grass, tea, weed, stuff	Variable—1 cigarette or 1 drink or cake (India)	4	Smoked Swallowed	Treatment of depression, tension, loss of appetite, sexual maladjustment, and narcotic addiction	Moderate	No
THC (tetra-hydrocannabinol)							
Narcotics (opiates, analgesics)					Treatment of severe pain, diarrhea, and cough	High	Yes
Opium	Op	10-12 "pipes" (Asia)	4	Smoked			
Heroin	Horse, H	Variable—bag or paper with 5-10 percent heroin		Injected			
Morphine		15 mg.					
Codeine		30 mg.					
Percodan		1 tablet					
Demerol		50-100 mg.					
Cough syrups		2-4 oz. (for euphoria)		Swallowed			
Hallucinogens					Experimental study of mind and brain function; enhancement of creativity and problem solving; treatment of alcoholism, mental illness, and the dying person	Minimal	Yes (rare)
LSD	Acid, sugar	150 micrograms	12	Swallowed			
Psilocybin		25 mg.	6				
Mescaline (peyote)	Cactus	350 mg.	12	Chewed			
DMT (dimethyl-tryptamine)		25 mg.		Injected			
Antidepressants					Treatment of moderate to severe depression	Minimal	No
Ritalin		10 mg.	4-6	Swallowed			
Dibenzapines (Tofranil, Elavil)		25 mg., 10 mg.					
MAO inhibitors (Nardil, Parnate)		15 mg., 10 mg.					
Miscellaneous					None except for antihistamines used for allergy and amyl nitrite for some episodes of fainting	Minimal to moderate	?
Glue		Variable	2	Inhaled			
Gasoline							
Amyl nitrite		1-2 ampules					
Antihistamines		25-50 mg.					
Nutmeg		Variable		Swallowed			
Nonprescription "sedatives"							

Marijuana

Narcotics

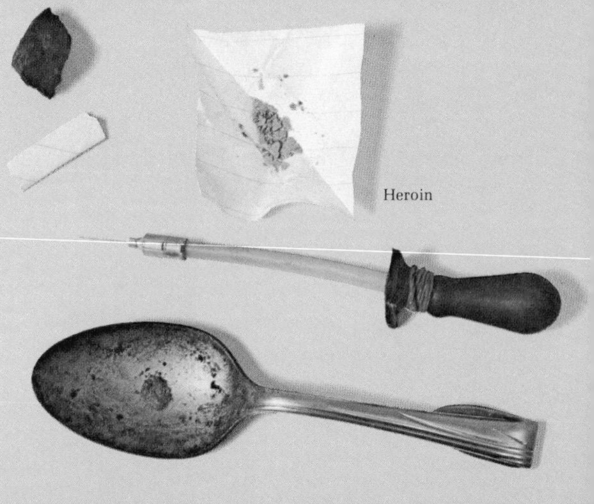

ical endence ntial	Overall Abuse Potential	Reasons for Use	Typical Short-term Effects*	Typical Long-term Effects	Form of Legal Regulation† and Control
	Moderate	To get "high"; as an escape; to relax	Relaxation, euphoria, increased appetite, some alteration of time perception, possible impairment of judgment and coordination; (probable CNS depressant)	Usually none	Unavailable (although permissible) for ordinary medical prescription; possession, sale, and cultivation prohibited by state and federal narcotic or marijuana laws; moderate to severe penalties; widespread illicit traffic
	High	To get "high"; as an escape; to avoid withdrawal symptoms	CNS depressants; sedation, euphoria, relief of pain, impaired intellectual functioning and coordination	Constipation, loss of appetite and weight, temporary impotence or sterility; habituation, addiction with unpleasant and painful withdrawal illness	Available (except heroin) by special (narcotics) medical prescriptions; some available by ordinary prescription or over-the-counter; other manufacture, sale, or possession prohibited under state and federal narcotics laws; severe penalties; extensive illicit traffic
	Moderate	Curiosity created by recent widespread publicity; seeking for meaning and consciousness expansion	Production of visual imagery, increased sensory awareness, anxiety, nausea, impaired coordination; sometimes consciousness expansion	Usually none; sometimes precipitates or intensifies an already existing psychosis; more commonly can produce a panic reaction when person is improperly prepared	Available only to a few medical researchers (or to members of the Native American Church); other manufacture, sale, or possession prohibited by state dangerous drug or federal drug abuse laws; moderate penalties; extensive illicit traffic
	Minimal	Medical (including psychiatric) treatment of depression	Relief of depression; stimulation	Basically the same as tranquilizers above	Same as tranquilizers above
	Moderate	Curiosity; to get "high"	When used for mind alteration, generally produces a "high" (euphoria) with impaired coordination and judgment	Variable—some substances can seriously damage liver or kidney	Generally easily available; some require prescriptions; in several states glue banned for those under 21

llucinogens

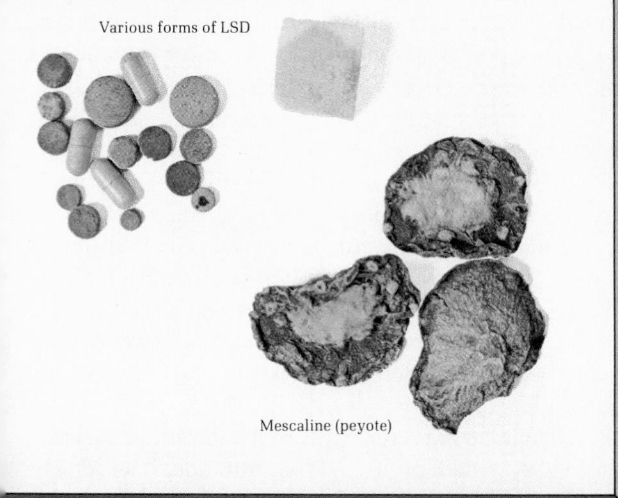

Antidepressants

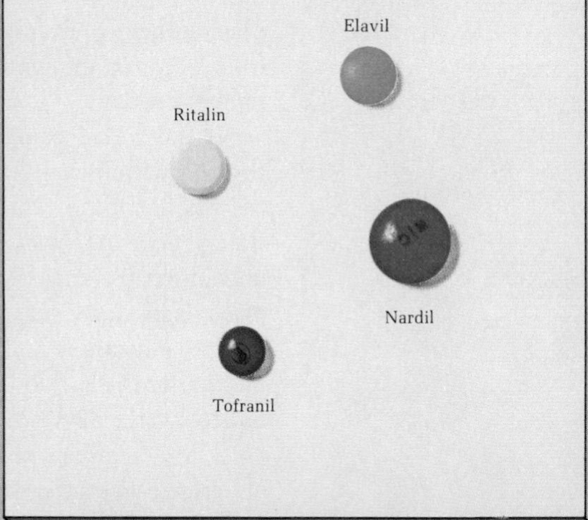

However, the exact mechanism of action of LSD in producing its behavioral effects has yet to be discovered.

NARCOTICS

One of the most serious problems facing this country is the growing abuse of narcotic drugs. Estimates of the number of narcotics addicts in the United States range from 200,000 to 250,000. Twenty years ago, even five years ago, it was easy for most people to ignore narcotics addiction because it was mainly confined to slum and ghetto areas in large cities, like New York, Philadelphia, and Chicago. The larger cities still have the highest number of narcotics addicts, but the problem has spread to the suburbs and rural areas, to colleges and high schools, and even to elementary schools. A recent newspaper report stated that more than 20,000 American soldiers stationed in Vietnam are addicted to heroin. Hard-narcotic trade has long been illegal in the United States, but it is so profitable that it is hard to eliminate.

There is nothing intrinsically evil about narcotics or their effects. Morphine is an old and widely used drug, invaluable in the field of medicine as a potent treatment for pain. Heroin (diacetyl-morphine), a derivative of morphine, was first introduced into this country as a *treatment* for morphine addiction and later declared illegal because it was so often found to be addicting itself. Heroin is abused more than morphine, perhaps because of its greater potency; it is approximately twice as strong as morphine.

There are many psychological reasons given for heroin usage, but none of them adequately explains it. The fact that many heroin users come from the lower classes certainly indicates the significance of social and economic factors. Narcotics addicts frequently say they use heroin because of its euphoriant effect, that it produces a sense of well-being so complete that even the most trying of problems seems no problem at all. In this euphoric but torpid state a person may have no desire to do anything else but remain intoxicated as long as possible. In the acutely intoxicated state, heroin users may also become sleepy ("go on the nod") and feel heavy, exceptionally hot, or itchy. Occasionally there may be nausea or vomiting.

Figure 34.8
An addict "mainlining" heroin. In addition to the risks of physiological addiction, the heroin user is endangered by malnutrition, impure chemicals, contaminated syringes, and the illegal and dangerous circumstances that surround his need to "hustle" to support his habit. Treatment programs for addicts range from those that use synthetic agents, such as methadone, to programs that provide an absorbing and meaningful living arrangement, such as Synanon. Because of the urgency and magnitude of the narcotics problem in the United States, new programs of many types are being explored presently.

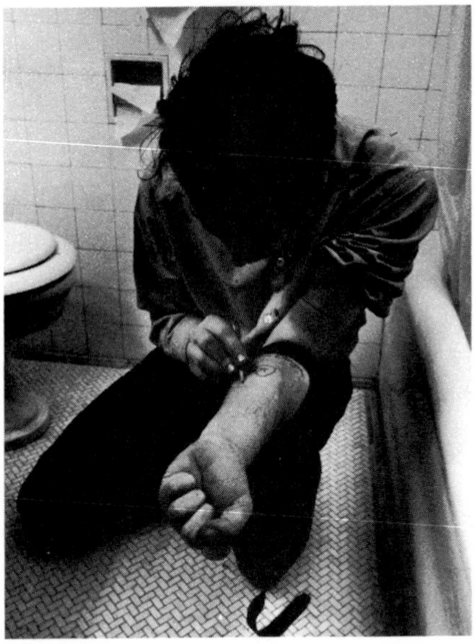

People develop tolerance to the euphoriant effect of heroin. So the person who frequently uses the drug has to continually increase the dose he injects to produce the same "high." He then often becomes physically dependent or addicted; that is, he must continue to use the drug to prevent the ugly and extremely painful experience of a withdrawal syndrome. Addicts can tolerate amazingly high doses of narcotics. For example, the average dose of morphine given for severe pain ranges from 8 to 15 milligrams, but some addicts can use as much as 2,000 to 3,000 milligrams daily.

If the addict cannot get enough heroin to satisfy the body's need, he will go through withdrawal. About ten hours after his last dose the addict will begin to feel the first symptoms and signs of withdrawal. He may perspire, yawn, and have a watery nose and watery eyes. A few hours afterward he may fall into a shallow, uncomfortable state of drowsiness. Even later the addict often has severe cramping pains in his arms, legs, and back, nausea, vomiting, diarrhea, weakness, and gooseflesh ("cold turkey"). The most intense symptoms occur forty-eight to seventy-two hours after the last dose; and with heroin, the syndrome usually runs its course within ten to twelve days.

The side effects of narcotics addiction are severe. It is well known that packets of heroin sold on the street vary widely in their purity and concentration. If an addict accustomed to using four 15-milligram doses ("bags") of heroin per day unknowingly obtains a much purer sample, say, a 70- to a 100-milligram "bag," he may inject it, lapse into coma, and die of an overdose—sometimes within minutes. Also, because heroin is usually administered intravenously without sterile precautions and because the drug often contains gross impurities, abusers of heroin or other injected drugs often develop hepatitis (a type of liver disease), blood-borne bacterial infections, and skin infections, usually at the site of injection; sometimes blood clots collect in the lungs and cause death.

The treatment of severe chronic addiction to narcotics is usually effective only for brief periods. It is estimated that over 90 percent of chronic addicts return to their addiction within a year, whatever the treatment. Self-help groups, like *Synanon,* usually built around a live-in facility, claim that their form of therapy is successful. However, lack of data makes it hard to evaluate such organizations.

In the past few years *methadone* (Dolophine)—a synthetic narcotic with pain-relieving properties similar to those of morphine—has come into wide use. Preliminary studies suggest that it is effective in treating some narcotics addicts. The person under methadone treatment remains an addict, but he is addicted to methadone. Although methadone is addicting, it is not much of a euphoriant; in fact it blocks the euphoriant effects of other narcotics. Methadone supposedly suppresses the "narcotic hunger" that chronic addicts may develop after long experience with the euphoriant effect of heroin. So far, methadone maintenance treatment has been used mainly with impoverished chronic addicts with criminal records. The results are sometimes very encouraging, but the technique is open to many abuses and is difficult to control. Research is now underway to find drugs that can block the effects of narcotics—and so postpone an addict's temptation to resume his "habit"—for longer periods of time.

In Great Britain selected physicians in selected institutions maintain addicts on heroin as a means of coping with the problem. Although the British system is not without its problems, it seems to work reasonably well. It has largely undercut the illicit traffic in narcotics, which is so profitable in this country. Also, the identified number of narcotics addicts in Great Britain is quite small relative to the number in the United States.

ALCOHOL AND ALCOHOLISM

Around five million Americans have a severe drinking problem. That is the recent estimate. About 5 to 10 percent of these—or 250,000 to 500,000 people—eventually become alcoholic derelicts. The cost in human suffering to the alcoholic and his family and the money and the man-hours lost to the country are almost impossible to measure. Alcohol, administered slowly in small doses, is a kind of social wonder drug that loosens inhibitions and makes many people gregarious. Beyond that magic point, it causes disorders of sensation and perception and stimulates behavior that violates common social codes.

Because these effects are characteristic of many drugs besides alcohol, the many who have fallen prey to alcohol in one generation might well have taken to other drugs had they been born at a different time or in another culture.

Many people think of alcohol as a stimulant because drinking is so often followed by loudness and hilarity, but alcohol is really a chemical depressant of the brain—a general anesthetic for those parts of the brain that suppress, control, and inhibit thoughts, feelings, and actions. As the depressant is administered in larger doses and accumulates in the body, there is a steady deterioration in all functions. After enough alcohol has accumulated, it produces a state of unconsciousness. How rapidly this initial stimulation and consequent decline will occur depends on how much and how rapidly alcohol enters the bloodstream.

Three stages of alcoholism have been described by E. M. Jellinek. In the *prealcoholic* stage, the drinker discovers that alcohol reduces his tensions, gives him self-confidence and a sense of courage, and eases psychological and social pressure. In the *prodromal* stage, a beverage is turned into a drug. The drinker drinks heavily and furtively; he may begin to suffer memory blackouts and be unable to recall events during his drinking bouts. In the final, *crucial* stage, he drinks compulsively, begin-

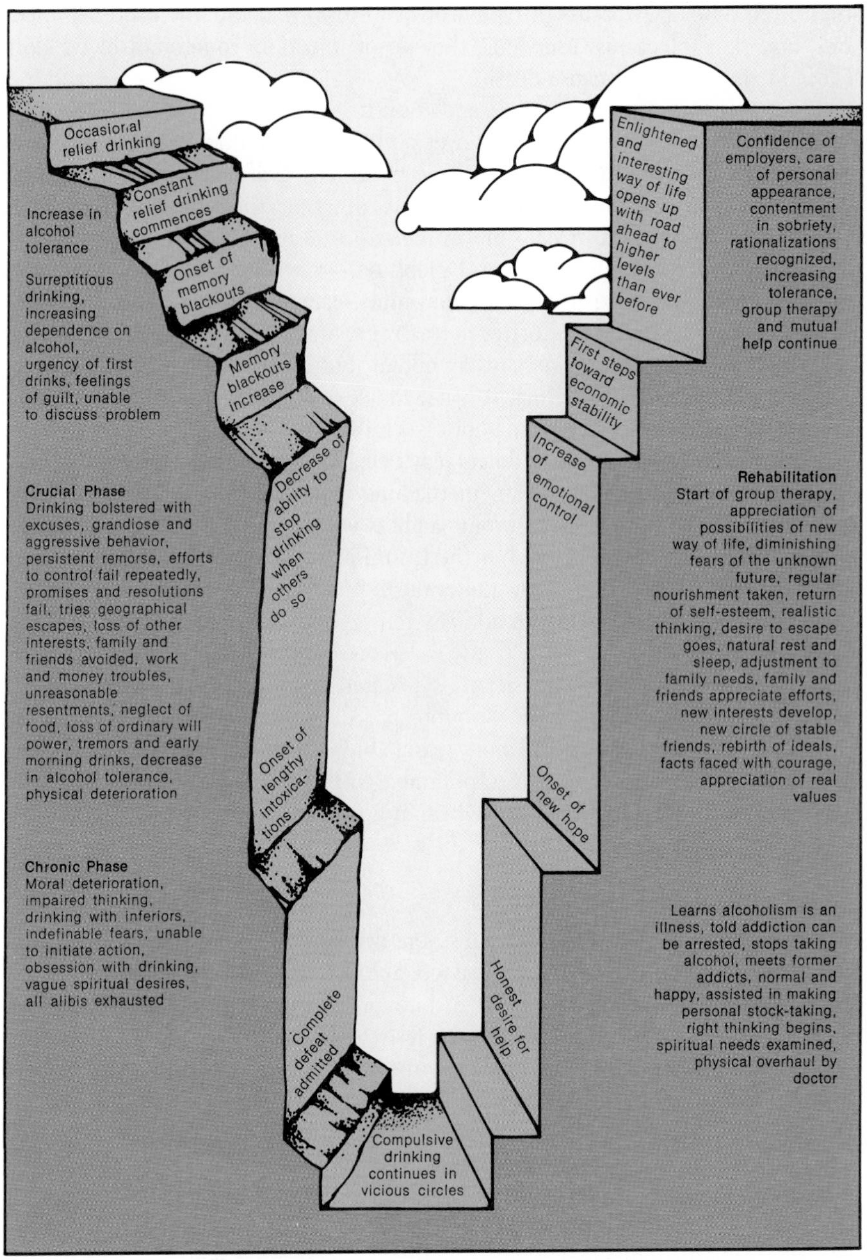

Figure 34.9

Stages of alcohol addiction and steps toward recovery. Many persons who are considered to have "a drinking problem" do not deteriorate to the chronic phase; also, many chronic alcoholics, unfortunately, do not progress through the ideal stages of recovery depicted in the diagram.

ning in the morning; he becomes inefficient in his work and may go on benders that last for weeks. He feels a powerful need for alcohol when he is deprived of it.

By this point, the problem drinker imbibes continuously, eats infrequently, and is unable to alter his compulsive self-drugging despite the anguish he causes others or the obvious destruction of his social life. Each alcoholic has a unique personality and temperament, and the drinking pattern differs accordingly. The so-called periodic alcoholic, for example, may not abide by general social rules of when, where, or how much to drink, yet he is able to stop drinking completely for brief periods of time when he feels it is crucial to do so. He may never progress to the most extreme form of alcoholism even though he bounces in and out of an alcoholic haze most of his life. In the most severe type of alcoholism, the victim's body builds up a tolerance for the drug. He may develop such a psychological dependence on alcohol that he feels normal only when he has been drinking and experiences severe and painful physical symptoms if he stops. Because of the toxic effects of alcohol on the body and the malnutrition that so often occurs with chronic alcoholism, the alcoholic is likely to develop many diseases, especially those affecting the liver and the brain and nervous system.

There are many theories about why some people become alcoholics and others do not. Some theorists suggest that an alcoholic's dependence is part of some biological malfunction of the body. There is as yet, however, no good scientific backing for biological theories of the cause of alcoholism. Other theorists look to the differences in the rate of alcoholism in various cultures and suggest that this problem is a national characteristic related to the family pattern; that is, the family structure of wine-drinking cultures may differ from the family relationships of whiskey-drinking cultures.

A great many attempts have been made to pin down precisely the individual psychodynamics of the alcoholic. Personality theorists have suggested three general characteristics of alcoholics: egocentricity, dependency, and hostility. They say that the alcoholic is immature and more concerned with himself than with others. Like a jealous child, he feels that people pick on him and favor others. He easily feels sorry for himself and justifies his drinking accordingly. As he developed from childhood, he failed to become mature; so he takes the alcoholic escape route from his problems. The alcoholic is a passive person who needs to be cared for by others and cannot manage enough independence to face problems alone. When the necessary protection is not available, he becomes anxious, feels others are more capable, secure, and able, and retreats to the bottle. He is angry and resentful at being thrust into the world unready to face life's problems; he is angry that others do not support him but keep making demands of him. Consciously he feels he loves those close to him, but his hostility lies just below the surface. He does not manage his tensions well and avoids being caught in situations where there might be conflict between people.

A usual first step in treating the alcoholic is to sober him up and try to make him healthier. Once restored to a reasonable state of health, the alcoholic may be exposed to electroshock, tranquilizers, antidepressants, or traditional psychotherapy. These efforts have all been sadly ineffective. Alcoholics Anonymous, essentially a lay group composed mainly of ex-alcoholics, has perhaps had slightly better luck. A variety of techniques have been used in attempts to help the alcoholic, but only a small part of the social resources needed have been devoted to this pursuit. It is as if our culture has, over the years, developed a tolerance for the alcoholic. However, with the establishment of a National Institute for Alcoholism in Washington, the Federal Government has started a trend that, it is hoped, will result in new and more successful methods of dealing with America's number one "drug problem."

SUGGESTED READINGS

FREEDMAN, D. X. "The Use and Abuse of LSD," *Archives of General Psychiatry,* 18 (1968), 300–347. A thorough and complete review of LSD that is scholarly yet readable by a lay audience.

GREENBLATT, M., *et al.* (Eds.). *Drug and Social Therapy in Chronic Schizophrenia.* Springfield, Ill., Charles C Thomas, 1965. Interesting comparisons between the effects of drugs and psychosocial therapies in the treatment of chronic schizophrenia.

GRINSPOON, L. *Marijuana Reconsidered.* Cambridge, Mass., Harvard University Press, 1970. A general but fairly thorough treatment of the subject, written mainly for the lay audience.

KLEIN, D. F., and DAVIS, J. M. *Diagnosis and Drug Treatment of Psychiatric Disorders.* Baltimore, Williams & Wilkins, 1969. A matter-of-fact presentation of the use of medicines in the treatment of mental illness.

SCHILDKRAUT, J. J., and KETY, S. S. "Biogenic Amines and Emotion," *Science,* 156 (1967), 21–30. A review of the catecholamine theory of affective illness.

Appendix: Methodology

Psychology is the study of behavior and its determinants—what people do and why. Several distinctive features make psychological study different from the study of inanimate objects. First, it is hard to look at the phenomena of psychology objectively, simply because everyone's involvement with them is so complete. The involvement of a geologist, say, with rocks, or a botanist with plants is unlikely to be as much affected by his experiences in the past as is the involvement of someone studying human phenomena. All of us have built up hunches and sets of beliefs about people. The psychologist is no exception, yet he has to keep his personal involvement with people from biasing his observations, and he has to make sure that his thinking about human behavior is not distorted by his own intuitive generalizations. Although the psychologist's personal experiences often result in bias, they need not do so. Psychologists can use their experiences as a source of hunches to be confirmed only by carefully controlled observation.

Second, it has been argued that the multiple determinants of behavior make its scientific study more difficult than the study of other phenomena, such as those that follow the laws of physics. Because so many different kinds of factors can operate together to determine a response, psychologists frequently find that they can isolate and identify these factors only under limited conditions—often only in the laboratory. Whether in the laboratory or out, it is their concern to determine what general laws do apply to behavior and under what circumstances each is true or not true.

Third, in looking for general laws, scientists who study *fixed properties* of organisms or elements have the advantage of being able to measure such properties several times to check the accuracy of their first measurements. Some properties, however, cannot be studied more than once in the same object. For example, if you want to see how far a rubber band will stretch before it breaks, you can stretch it only once; to make repeated measurements, you would have to stretch several identical rubber bands. Psychologists often encounter a similar problem: they cannot measure repeatedly the same characteristic in the same organism. The reaction of an organism—whether a laboratory animal or a human being—may change the organism, so that its next reaction to the same stimulus is slower or more rapid, stronger or weaker.

Whatever his special area may be, the psychologist usually finds his task complicated by the multiple factors that influence the behavior he is studying, by the

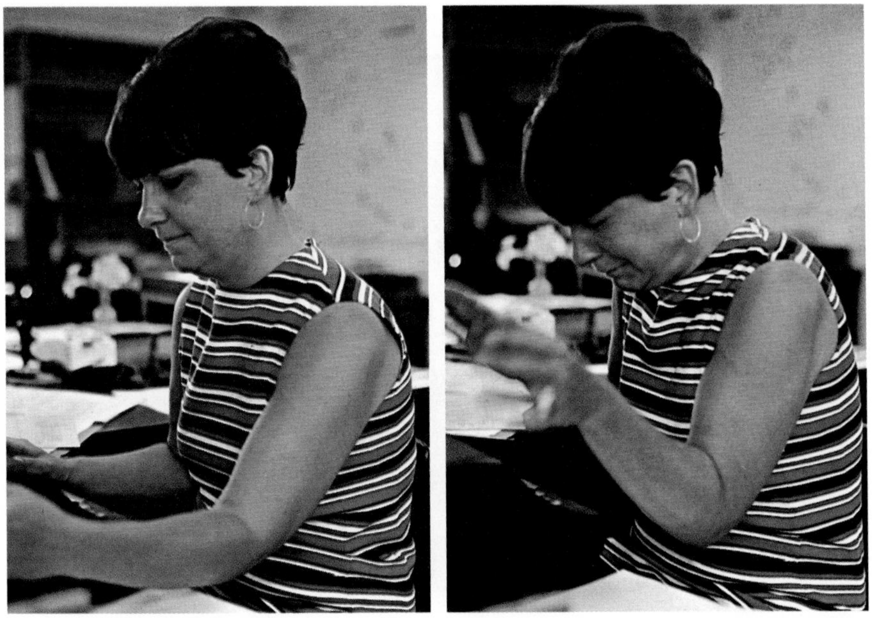

Figure A.1
Human behavior is far more variable than phenomena in sciences such as physics and chemistry. Even reflexive responses, like the startle response, vary with certain conditions; for example, the response changes when it is elicited repeatedly in a brief period of time. The fact that human behavior is so variable, however, necessitates special procedures and caution in designing and analyzing psychological experiments.

changing properties of this behavior, and by the subjective views that he has acquired from his own experiences with people.

METHODS OF OBSERVATION

Psychologists observe behavior in several ways. They may gather data about a person *under natural conditions;* from *ratings* made by others, usually peers or superiors; from the person himself, as in *surveys* of carefully chosen samples of a particular population (public opinion polling, for example); by administering *inventories* and *tests* (see Chapter 20); or by observing the physiological functioning of people. (For example, Figure A.2 shows how changes in pupil size correspond to changes in the emotional content of stimuli.) The critical problem is not in making observations but in making something out of them. The psychologist wants to obtain a reliable estimate of something—say, the average performance of a group of rats in a learning experiment or the types of stimuli that cause people's pupils to dilate. To do so, he has to make a *series of observations.* The human beings or animals that he observes are called the *subjects* of the observations, and the person who carries out the procedures of the experiment is called the *experimenter.*

The Observer's Perspective

One of the major problems of psychology is that its phenomena depend more upon the observer than do the phenomena of other sciences. You have undoubtedly heard about the objectivity of the scientist; you have heard about science's requirement that observers agree on what they see and that scientists must be able to repeat their own experiments and those of other scientists before the findings become accepted as part of scientific knowledge. But there are often discrepancies between phenomena as perceived by different people. You may see a friend as more likable than he

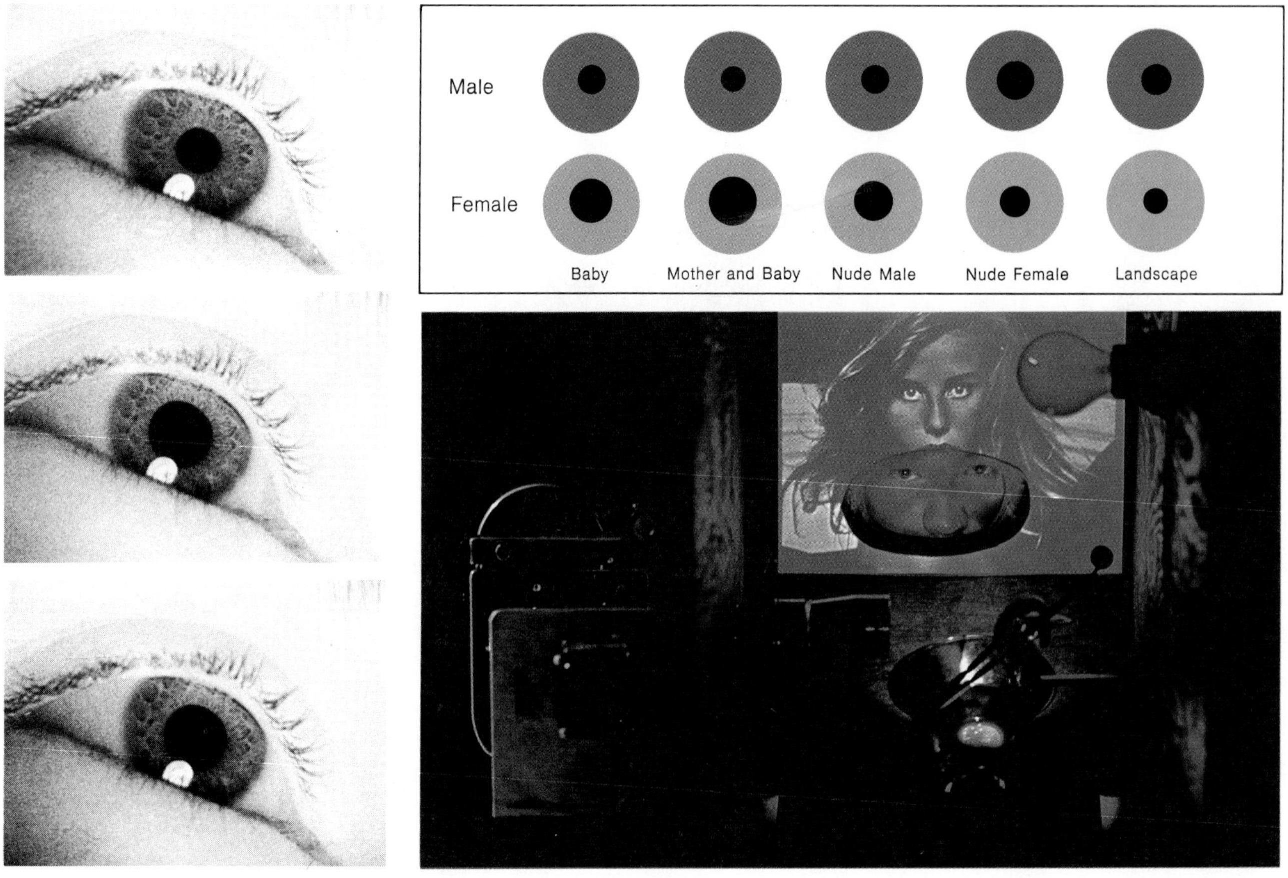

Figure A.2
Psychologists use the apparatus shown in the bottom photograph to study the effects of different types of visual stimuli upon pupil dilation. The series of three photographs shows pupil dilation. The chart to the right indicates the average pupil size of men and women in response to five types of photographs. Do these pupil sizes of men and women conform to what you would predict, based on the content of the material?

sees himself as being, or as less so than his wife sees him. If a psychologist wanted to make a judgment about your friend, he would have to take all these different perspectives into account. Many psychological observations require that many different perspectives be considered. Even more important, the psychologist has to take account of the fact that, when he makes his observations, he is dealing with other human beings. He encounters a number of special problems because he is a member of the species that he is studying. First of all, he has to work especially hard to avoid letting his own personal biases affect his observations. In addition, he must consider the fact that his experiments involve social interaction between his subjects and himself. In this interpersonal interaction he must take extra care to avoid influencing the results of his experiment.

Many of these difficulties that psychologists encounter in making observations are called *observer effects:* an experiment produces a particular finding because the observations are influenced by personal involvement of the experimenter or the subject or because the observers have not been trained to avoid bias. There are several common errors of observation. *Errors of expectation* are errors made because the subject expects specific results; these are especially likely to occur when the experimental instructions in some way suggest a particular expectation to the subject. Another form of bias is the *stimulus error:* when an observer knows something about the stimulus, that knowledge may influence and distort his report of his experience of the stimulus. For example, suppose you are testing a subject's ability to perceive colors in a dimly lit room. The subject is more likely to correctly identify the color yellow if the yellow item is banana-shaped rather than, say, triangular. On the other hand, the color orange in a banana shape would be harder to perceive correctly. The observer's application of past knowledge about the stimulus to the present situation interferes with his judgment of color. (However, under other experimental conditions, a person's accumulated knowledge can aid in correct perception.)

Figure A.3

The observer's perspective will determine, to a great extent, what is observed. The "observer effect" can be illustrated by these four perceptions of this woman.

As she sees herself: ten years younger than her age. Competent yet desirable.

As her husband sees her: older than she actually is.

As the camera sees her: she is thirty-seven and chic but looks inhibited.

As she thinks others see her: sophisticated and sexy, a focus of masculine approval.

Experimenter Effects

The experimenter, too, is fallible. His expectations may influence the outcome of an experiment. For example, if the experimenter is conducting a study in which he has face-to-face interviews with the subject, he may affect the subject's responses by unwittingly communicating positive or negative feelings—by smiling when the subject's statements corroborate his theory and frowning when they disconfirm it. The work of R. Rosenthal of Harvard University shows that such experimenter biases may have profound results. In other situations, an experimenter may communicate his expectations of the outcome of his work to the research assistant or student actually conducting the work. Obviously, the same kinds of biases alluded to above would hold in this situation. The problem may be even more serious here since the assistant may feel pressure to make sure the outcome of the experiment is in line with his superior's expectations.

To guard against the biases that experimenters' expectations can cause in research results, researchers often utilize a *double-blind design.* The subject and the experimenter are "blinded" about the experimental conditions: neither knows, for example, whether the subject got the experimental drug or a placebo (a substance that has no noticeable effect, like sugar pills). Only a third person, perhaps the pharmacist who prepares the pills, holds the secret. Automated procedures may be used also; for example, by recording instructions on tape, the possibilities for subtle communication can be reduced, and the experimenter can make certain that his experimental and control subjects are treated identically in all ways except for the ways that he intends them to be treated differently. In addition, the general scientific community has its own natural system of checks and balances and ways of censoring biased experimental results. The biases of an experimenter may lead to publication

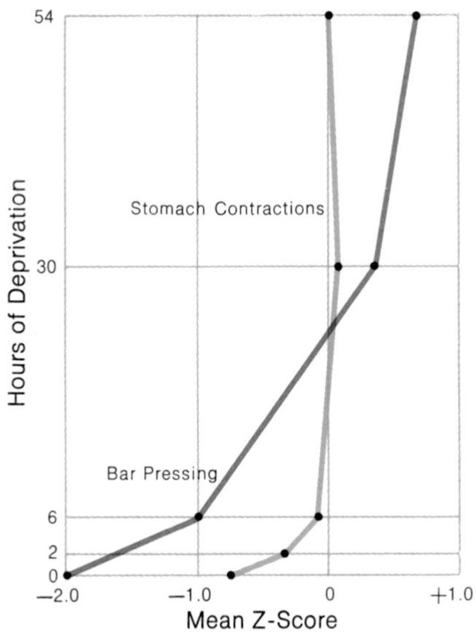

Figure A.4
The graph illustrates the differences between two measures of hunger in a study by Neal Miller. An experimenter who used only one of these measures, say, stomach contractions, might have reached a different and less precise conclusion about the effect of food deprivation over time on hunger.

of an article that contains erroneous conclusions, but if the finding is at all important, other workers—perhaps with different biases—will fail to replicate the findings, and eventually truth will out.

Errors of Measurement

Besides observer bias and experimenter effects, there are two other major types of error in measurement. *Design error* occurs when the experimenter measures something that does not exactly coincide with what he wants to measure. For example, to ask a person to report a dream he had the night before is to measure something that may be very different from the original dream. Simple *imprecision* is lack of agreement among repeated observations. Precision is another word for the concept of reliability, which is discussed in Chapter 20.

AGREEMENT AMONG TYPES OF MEASUREMENT

We have seen that there are problems in observing and that there are many pitfalls awaiting even the best trained and most sincere experimenter. In addition to errors in observation, experimenter effects, and errors of measurement, there is another important source of potential discrepancy between one set of experimental findings and another. The outcome of an experiment may depend critically upon the particular measurement chosen by the experimenter. There are many ways to measure any single variable (for example, anxiety), and different measures may produce different results. It would be ideal but very impractical to use all the possible measures of the variable we are interested in. The sound strategy is to employ at least two or three different measures. If there is rough agreement among the two or three measures, then you can be reasonably confident that your findings have generality.

A series of experiments in the 1950s on hunger demonstrated that the effects of hunger show up differently depending on how you measure them. Figure A.4, adapted from an experiment by N. E. Miller, shows the effects of hunger (defined in terms of hours of food deprivation) upon two measures of hunger: (1) bar-pressing to obtain food and (2) stomach contractions (measured by an inflated balloon permanently implanted in the stomach of a rat). Whereas the stomach contraction measure showed little or no increase after six hours of food deprivation, bar-pressing showed a marked increase.

Different measures, then, may produce different results, and, all things being equal, the psychologist would prefer the response measure that is more sensitive to an experimental manipulation (here, bar pressing); if a variable of interest has only a small effect upon a measure, then it will be more difficult to conduct a conclusive experiment utilizing that measure. As noted earlier, variability and errors of measurement are to a certain extent unavoidable. For example, in comparisons among subjects, individual differences among them on a particular measure will lead to variability in the measure. With a more sensitive measure, it is possible to detect experimental effects despite this variability.

Choice of an *experimental procedure* also may dramatically affect the outcome. C. Catania has noted that investigators concerned with how the duration of a reward—for example, number of seconds of access to food for a deprived organism—affects behavior have generally found that the effect of duration of reward was either small or transient. For example, a hungry pigeon might be required to peck at a key in order to obtain food. By varying how long the pigeon had access to the food after each correct key peck, experimenters were able to observe the effects of duration of the food reward upon the rate of pecking. Catania repeated this procedure, the results of which are shown for each of three pigeons in Figure A.5 (open circles). Catania was able to confirm what previous investigators had found: response strength was relatively insensitive to the duration of food presentation.

Within the same experiment, and with the same three pigeons, Catania also used a *choice procedure:* each pigeon could choose between responding on one key, which provided a shorter duration of food presentation, and responding on a second key, which provided a longer duration of food presentation. The closed circles in Figure A.5 show that for each of the three pigeons the choice procedure was remarkably sensitive to the duration of food presentation. That is, when the pigeon had a choice, it responded more to the key that provided the longer duration of food presentation. Because of this pioneer experiment by Catania, many investigators now utilize choice procedures because of the greater sensitivity to experimental manipulations that they provide. Finally, Catania's results were made more convincing by the fact that he was able to replicate the findings of previous workers (open circles in Figure A.5) within his study, thereby enhancing the likelihood that the choice procedure was indeed responsible for the results represented by the filled circles. This conclusion is further strengthened by the fact that Catania could obtain either effect in a given pigeon.

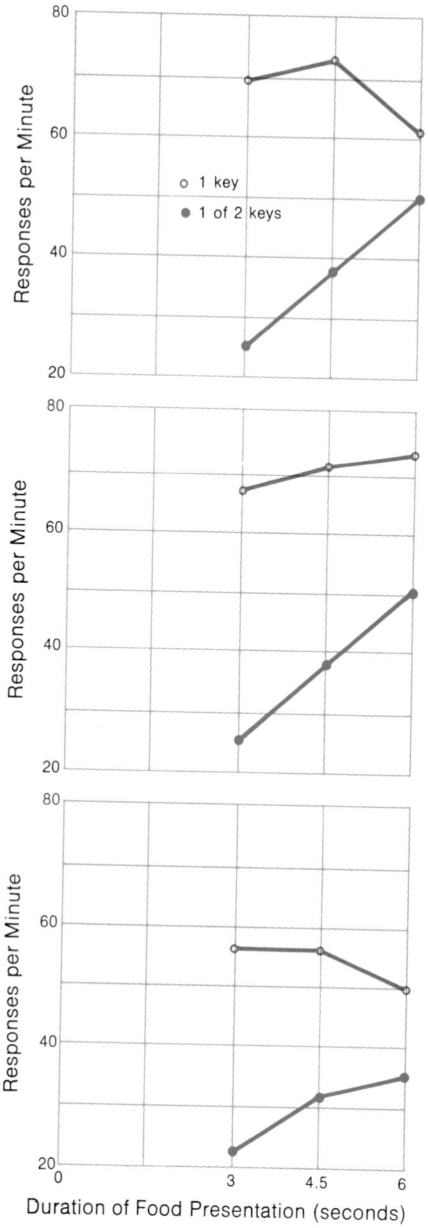

Figure A.5
Catania found two different sets of results by using two different experimental procedures to study the same phenomenon. Catania's discovery that different results occur as a result of using different methods offers a cue to experimenters to examine more carefully the procedures that they take for granted.

SCALES

Measuring is going from observations to indices; it is assigning numbers to things in accordance with certain rules. Psychology uses several number systems, or scales. In the *nominal scale*, numbers are assigned for identification purposes, as license plates are to automobiles. In the *ordinal scale*, numbers are assigned to items ranked in ascending or descending order along a given dimension: for example, you might rank thirty-fifth in a group of eighty people ordered from shortest to tallest. The *interval scale* is made up of units of equal measure but of arbitrary origin: the zero point on centigrade- and fahrenheit-temperature scales is arbitrary, but the difference between, say, 50 and 60 degrees is considered equal to the difference between 60 and 70 degrees. In the *ratio scale* the units are equal as in the interval scale—the difference between $100 and $101 is exactly the same as the difference between $996 and $997, namely $1—but it has an absolute zero point. In weight, for example, the absolute zero point is 0 pounds. Such scales are called ratio scales because their numbers can be used as ratios; a 10-pound weight is twice as heavy as a 5-pound weight.

When we make our measurements with a ratio scale (as scientists almost always prefer to do), we can manipulate the numbers we get in any way we wish—add them, subtract them, or compare them in any way we find meaningful. When we deal with scales other than the ratio, we have to make certain assumptions about the numbers that sometimes are hard to justify. Intelligence and personality tests are often scored like college quizzes—that is, the subject is given one point for each correct answer. Do the items in an intelligence test represent equal units of ability, even though some are easy and some are difficult? Does the difference between IQs of 100 and 110 represent just the same difference in ability as the difference between IQs of 90 and 100? No one really knows. All we can say is that some assumptions usually seem to work and that, at worst, they probably do not lead psychologists too far astray.

RESEARCH DESIGNS

We have considered the kinds of observations made by psychologists and the possible sources of error in them. We have seen that observations are converted into numbers. But what kinds of plans underlie the making of observations and the recording of numbers? There are two major types of research designs: the *correlational* and the *experimental*.

Correlational Analysis

A correlation indicates the degree of relatedness between two things. By knowing that a correlation exists, you could predict the occurrence of one event from the occurrence of the other. In loose terms, a positive correlation between two things merely means that they occur together. A correlation tells nothing about *why* the

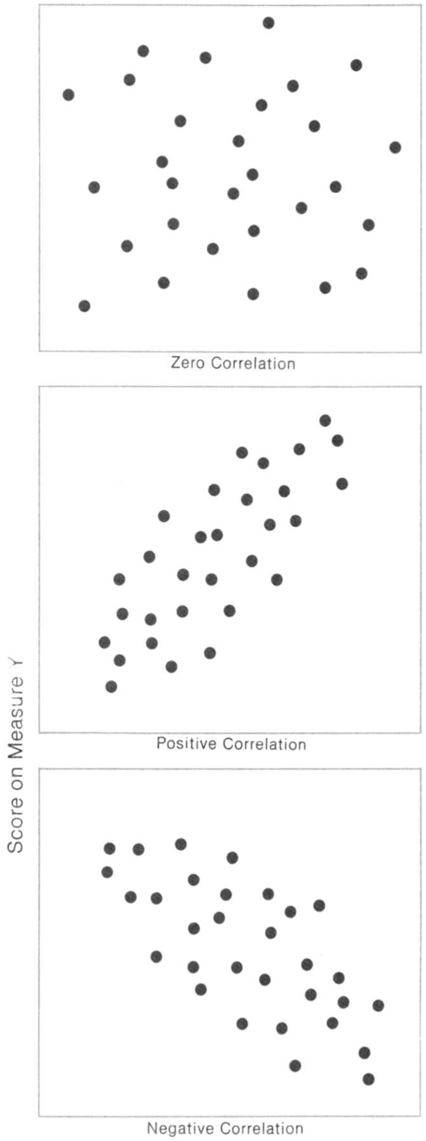

Figure A.6

These scatter diagrams show three types of correlations between Measure X and Measure Y. With a zero correlation, knowing the magnitude of one variable tells nothing about the other. A positive or negative correlation between X and Y indicates that if you know a score on one measure, you can estimate the score on the other measure with better-than-chance accuracy; the higher the correlation, the more likely the estimate is to be correct. A positive correlation indicates that both measures tend to vary in the same direction; a negative correlation indicates that an increase in one measure tends to be associated with a decrease in the other.

two events tend to be associated. For example, there is a well-publicized correlation between cigarette consumption and lung cancer. This correlation does not prove that it is cigarette smoking that is causing the lung cancer. Rather, the correlation is useful for suggesting potential causal factors. It then remains for the medical scientist to actually prove that smoking causes lung cancer. In the meanwhile, of course, a smoker may well be foolhardy to ignore the correlation.

To illustrate correlations, let us take two college students, Mark and Mary. Suppose you happened to notice that, during a certain period of a week or so, almost every time you saw Mark anywhere, you also saw Mary. You saw them together at several parties, at a football game, in the student union, at several meals, and even in a class or two. The appearance of Mark at any given place is obviously correlated with the appearance of Mary; that is, the two events tend to occur together most of the time. If someone told you that he went to a party and saw Mary there, you might be willing to make a strong bet that Mark was there too. Knowing that a correlation exists, you could *predict* the occurrence of one event (seeing Mark) from the occurrence of the other (seeing Mary). Loosely stated, a *positive correlation* between two things merely means that they go together, much as we might presume that Mark and Mary were "going together." A correlation tells us nothing about why the two events tend to be associated, however.

There are *negative correlations* as well as positive ones. If Mark and Mary had been engaged but had had a violent argument and had broken up with great hostility toward each other, you could predict fairly well that if you went to a party and saw Mary, Mark would *not* be there. Negative correlations allow you to predict the *nonoccurrence* of events with just as much accuracy as positive correlations allow you to predict their occurrence. We seldom invite our enemies to dinner.

The single most important thing to remember about correlations is that they tell us nothing about purpose—or, in a loose sense of the word, about causality—although most people intuitively believe that they do. Take Mark and Mary, for example. We automatically assume that if we see them together all the time, they must be going steady; that is, they must be mutually attracted. If Mark's mother looked at the situation, she might imply a different reason for their being together—namely, that Mary was throwing herself at Mark. Mary's mother, of course, might believe that the situation was just the opposite. In point of fact, all these assumptions could be false. It might be that Mark and Mary are not attracted to each other but were in the cast of a play soon to be produced and therefore were thrown together a great deal of the time by factors outside their control.

Mathematically speaking, correlation coefficients run from +1.0 to −1.0, the extreme coefficients indicating either a perfect positive or a perfect negative relationship. A correlation of zero implies that there is no relationship at all between the two variables being measured. A positive correlation of .85 denotes a much stronger relationship between the events than, say, a coefficient of +.35; that is, if the correlation between seeing Mark and also seeing Mary is +.85, you can predict their behavior much more accurately than if the correlation is +.35. To discover why the correlation exists, you must make use of the experimental method.

The Experimental Method

Suppose a psychologist noticed that students who drank a cup of coffee just before taking a long examination seemed to be more alert toward the end of the test than did students who had had nothing to drink. At this point, he has noticed merely a correlation between ingestion of coffee and alertness. If he then performed an experiment in which one group of students (the experimental group) was given coffee while another was given a placebo drink that looked and tasted like coffee (the control group), and subsequently the experimental group was indeed more alert, he would be on the track of a causal connection. He might then assume that it was the caffeine in the coffee that caused the effect and repeat the experiment (giving regular coffee to an experimental group and caffeine-free coffee to the control group). If again the experimental students were more alert, he would be relatively sure that the caffeine did cause the alertness, but he still would not know why.

Next, he might inject caffeine solutions into rats to see if their nervous systems reacted differently than they did when the rats were injected with a control placebo, such as a weak salt solution. If he found that caffeine does indeed act as a neurological excitant, he could safely conclude that the caffeine in coffee causes alertness by exciting the brain in a certain fashion. In all these studies, he would make use of control groups to prove that his results were due to the experimental variable he was manipulating (the coffee or the caffeine) rather than to such extraneous variables as the students' knowing they were participating in an experiment or the rats' becoming excited merely because they had been stuck by a needle. No single part of planning an experiment is more important than the wise selection of control groups. The more an experimenter establishes controls for extraneous variables, the greater faith he can have that his experimental variable is doing what he thinks it is doing.

STATISTICAL ANALYSES

After the experimenter has made his observations on the experimental group and the control group and has collected his data, how does he proceed toward a finding and an interpretation? He uses two kinds of statistics, *descriptive* and *inferential.*

Descriptive Statistics

The psychologist uses descriptive statistics to reduce a mass of data to more manageable terms and to make the data more readily understandable. Suppose a teacher gave a history quiz of 100 questions to a class containing 39 students. Each correct answer receives one point. After grading the quiz, he finds that the highest score was 65, the lowest, 40; the *range* of the scores is therefore 25 (65 − 40 = 25). He can now plot a *frequency distribution* of the scores by laying them out as shown in Figure A.7. The figure shows that one student made a score of 40, no one made scores of 41, 42, 43, or 44, three students made a score of 55, and only one student scored 65. Now, look at the shape of this frequency distribution. It is clear that most students scored about 55, with relatively few scoring at either extreme. In most tests of this type, the scores do tend to pile up in the middle of the distribution. For example, as noted in Chapter 20, roughly two-thirds of the scores on IQ tests fall

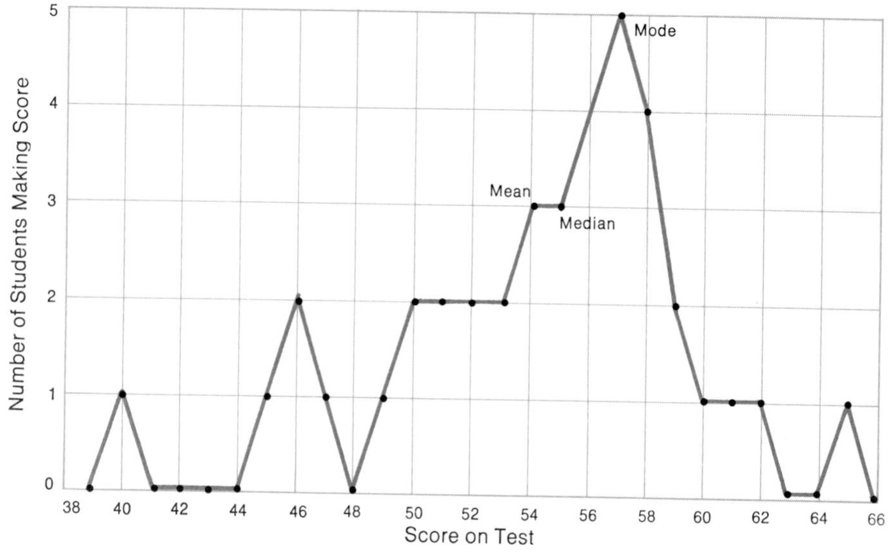

Figure A.7
Frequency distribution of scores on a quiz. Three measures of central tendency are shown. The *mean,* or average, is 54. In this case, the *median* is slightly higher; it is the score on either side of which 50 percent of the scores fall. The *mode,* or the most frequently occurring score, is highest in this case. The mean is the measure of central tendency most often used, and the mode is used least. Each of the three measures, however, has areas of important application.

between 85 and 115, although the range of the test can be as much as 200 points.

Suppose the teacher wanted to compare his class's performance on the quiz with that of another class that took the same test. How could he most meaningfully make such a comparison? A simple way is to find out what the average performance by each group was, then compare the averages. When we seek an average of some kind, we are really looking for what psychologists call a *measure of central tendency.*

One such measure of central tendency is the arithmetic *mean;* to find it, you merely add up all the scores and then divide by the number of people who took the test. For the history test, the mean of the distribution is 54. In order to justify calculating a mean on mathematical terms, you must use a measurement scale that has equal intervals.

Sometimes the scores on a given scale are so oddly distributed that a mean would give a distorted idea of where the center of the distribution actually was. For example, if you went into a large urban ghetto and randomly asked eleven people their annual income, you might accidentally select ten very poor people plus one slum landlord who was in the ghetto to collect rent. The poor people might do well to earn \$1,000 a year each; the landlord might easily make \$1 million. If you added their incomes together and took the arithmetic mean, you would find that their average annual income was about \$92,000. Mathematically, this is a true statement; socially, it is a gross distortion of the facts. In such cases, psychologists make use of a different statistic, the *median,* which is that score in the exact middle of the distribution. In the case of the history class, the median score was 55; in the case of the ghetto dwellers, it was \$1,000. When the data you are gathering come from an ordinal scale, you cannot use the mean; you must make use of the median.

A third measure of central tendency occasionally used by psychologists is the *mode,* which is that score made most frequently in any distribution. In the case of the history class, the modal score was 57. In the distribution of quiz scores, the mean, median, and mode were all different, although closely related to each other. In a perfectly symmetrical distribution, such as the one shown in Figure A.8, the mean, median, and mode would all be perhaps 50. However, compare this distribution with that in Figure A.9, whose mean, median, and mode are also 50. The range of the two distributions is also the same. Yet what a difference between the two in terms of how the scores are dispersed about the center. In Figure A.8, the bulk of the scores is packed tightly about the middle; in Figure A.9, the scores are spread out evenly from one end to the other. It would be misleading to compare these two distributions merely by talking about their similar means or medians; rather, we need

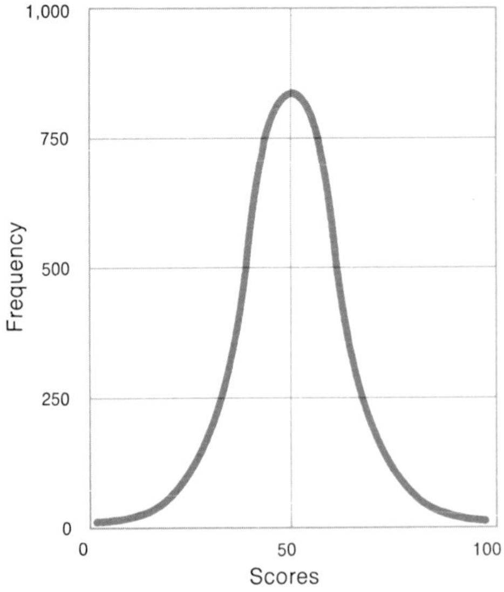

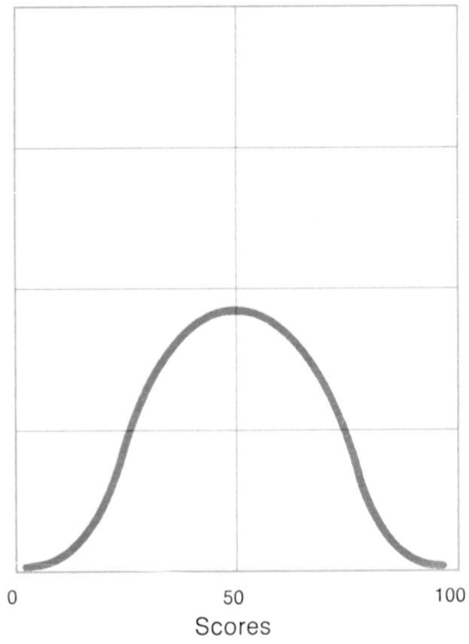

Figure A.8
Compare this distribution, in which the mean, median, and mode are all identical to the distribution in Figure A.9.

Figure A.9
Even though the mean, median, and mode here are also equal, the scores are obviously distributed more widely than those in Figure A.8. A further statistic, the *variance,* is needed to describe both sets of scores.

some additional descriptive statistic that tells us how the scores vary about the center point. One such statistic is the *variance* of the distribution. To find the *variance*, you first calculate the mean, then subtract each score from the mean, square this difference for each score, add all the squares together, then divide by the number of scores you had in the first place. Figure A.10 shows how the variance is calculated for a very small distribution of scores. A more useful statistic for most psychological purposes is the *standard deviation*, which is merely the square root of the variance.

Both the variance and the standard deviation give important information about the shape of the distribution. If they are relatively large, the scores are widely spread out (as in Figure A.9). If they are relatively small (as in Figure A.8), the scores are closely packed about the center of the distribution. To calculate either the variance or the standard deviation, one must use a measurement scale with equal intervals.

Measures of central tendency and of variation are used to describe a set of observations (such as test scores) for a single variable (the history quiz itself) or to compare two sets of observations on the same variable (the test scores of one history class compared to those of another). If one wishes to determine the relationship between two variables (the heights of a team of football players and their test scores on a quiz), we would calculate the mathematical correlation between the two sets of scores. This number, which, as we said earlier, varies from +1.0 to −1.0, is called the *correlation coefficient.*

Scores	Mean = 6	
3	$6 - 3 = 3$	$3^2 = 9$
4	$6 - 4 = 2$	$2^2 = 4$
5	$6 - 5 = 1$	$1^2 = 1$
5	$6 - 5 = 1$	$1^2 = 1$
6	$6 - 6 = 0$	$0^2 = 0$
6	$6 - 6 = 0$	$0^2 = 0$
7	$7 - 6 = 1$	$1^2 = 1$
7	$7 - 6 = 1$	$1^2 = 1$
8	$8 - 6 = 2$	$2^2 = 4$
9	$9 - 6 = 3$	$3^2 = 9$

Sum of Squares = 30

÷

Number of Scores = 10

= 3 (Variance)

$\sqrt{3}$ (Standard Deviation)

Figure A.10

How the variance and standard deviation are calculated for a small number of scores. These measures are used in inferential statistics to help determine whether the findings of an experiment can be considered statistically significant. This determination cannot be made solely on the basis of the measures of central tendency.

Inferential Statistics

Descriptive statistics are important, but inferential statistics—which are based on probability theory—are even more so, for they provide the researcher with ground rules or conventions for determining what conclusion can be drawn from his data. Consider a man tossing a coin 100 times. If it lands heads up 53 times, is the coin biased? What if it lands heads up 79 times? Statisticians have worked out methods for determining the probability of obtaining any given result with any given number of tosses of an unbiased coin. More exactly, if the probability of heads is .50, there are tables to indicate how often in, say, 100 tosses one can expect to obtain 28 heads, 53, 79, or any other number of heads from 0 to 100.

Probability is a complex mathematical area of study; our intuitions about "what the chances are" are not always correct. For example, assume that a coin has been tossed ten times and that it has landed heads up each time. It is about to be tossed once again. Reflect for a moment on what you would predict will occur on this next toss. There are three possible predictions: (1) Another head will turn up. (2) A tail will turn up. Or (3) the odds are still 50/50 (or .50), so there's no way to make a prediction. Which of these three seems intuitively correct to you? If you predicted a tail would turn up, you have committed an extremely common error known as the "gambler's fallacy." The reason it is a fallacy is that there is absolutely no reason to expect that the probability of a tail turning up is any higher than .50 at this point. Indeed, the judgment that has the most merit is that another head will turn up. For it appears by this time that we are dealing with a biased coin. On the other hand, it may be possible that the coin is unbiased and that the ten straight heads we have just witnessed is simply a remarkable chance occurrence. No matter how remarkable the occurrence of ten straight heads may appear, if the coin is fair, the odds on the next trial are precisely .50. If, on the other hand, the coin is not fair, then of course another head is the expectation. But how would one determine whether or not the coin is biased?

The odds of getting a head on any given toss of an unbiased coin are 50/50; that is, a head will turn up half the time. To find the odds of getting two heads in a row, multiply the odds for getting one event (a head) by the odds of getting the second (another head): ½ times ½ is ¼. For four heads in a row, the odds

Figure A.11
Frequency distribution of the outcome of two hundred tosses of ten pennies.

would be $1/16$ that such an event would occur by chance alone (½ times ½ times ½ times ½). At what point would our suspicions become aroused that we were dealing with a biased coin? Psychologists, like most other scientists, have adopted an arbitrary convention for making that decision: If the odds against a given event's occurring are 1 in 20—that is, if the event could be expected to occur by chance alone only 5 percent of the time—then there is a significant likelihood that the results cannot be explained merely in terms of chance variation. If the odds against the event's occurring are 100 to 1—that is, if the event could be expected to occur by chance alone only 1 percent of the time—then something other than chance very probably accounts for the results.

Returning to our example of the coin that came up heads ten times in a row, we can therefore see that the probability of this happening by chance alone is ½ raised to the tenth power, which equals $1/1024$. That means that the odds against it occurring by chance alone (that is, with a fair coin) are better than 1000 to 1. That is why the soundest judgment is to conclude that the coin is, in fact, biased. In the case of coin tossing, it would be a small matter to run some additional trials to test the fairness of the coin. But in many types of scientific research, additional trials may require months or years of further work. Inferential statistics, therefore, help psychologists decide when to stop an unpromising experiment and go on to something else.

Consider the experiment in which an experimental group of rats was injected with caffeine and the control animals were injected with a weak salt solution. The researchers found that the experimental animals learned a maze on the average in 30 trials (that is, the mean number of trials to learn the maze was 30), whereas the control animals on the average took 38 trials. What can the experimenters infer from these means? Does the difference between the two means really make a difference? Or could they have obtained these differences by chance alone?

To test their hypothesis that the caffeine injection enabled the experimental animals to learn faster, the researchers could make use of an inferential statistic called the *t-test.* The t-test allows them to use the means and standard deviation to calculate the odds that such a difference between two means was due to chance alone. If the odds were 1 in 20, they would know that they would obtain such a difference by chance alone only 5 percent of the time, so they could accept their hypothesis that caffeine increases speed of learning a maze at what psychologists call the *5 percent level of confidence* (sometimes also called the *.05 level of significance*). If the odds were 100 to 1, they could accept the hypothesis at what is called the *1 percent level of confidence* (sometimes also called the *.01 level of significance*). In both cases, what the researchers are saying is that they are reasonably confident that their results have some real psychological significance. What this experiment does not tell them, of course, is *how* the caffeine is affecting learning. That is a problem for the physiological psychologist to handle (see Chapter 16).

If their results (using the t-test or perhaps some other inferential statistic) do not reach the .05 level of significance, then by convention the experimenters assume that their hypothesis was not accurate because the odds are too great that the results could be due to chance variation.

As you might guess from the lengthy and rather complicated discussion of descriptive and inferential statistics, they are at the heart of many scientific methods, and anyone wishing to do research in any of the social, behavioral, biological, or physical sciences must have at least a rudimentary understanding of such matters.

Some Problems in the Use of Inferential Statistics

Earlier in the chapter, we discussed some methodological problems dealing primarily with "experimenter effects" and other sources of bias. Unfortunately, there are also problems in the use of inferential statistics. Suppose that you have conducted a study suggesting that a certain drug has a profound effect upon learning. You demonstrate this effect in several rats and are able to conclude at the 5 percent level of confidence that the drug facilitates learning. You have performed the experiment competently; your results are both statistically and conceptually significant and of interest to the scientific community. Consequently, your study is published in a scientific journal. Let us assume further that the drug has no real effect upon learning but that your results were due to chance variation (in other words, to that "one chance in twenty" that you are wrong implied by the 5 percent significance level).

The hypothesis that led you to assume this drug should have an effect upon learning may have led other experimenters around the country to conduct similar experiments. Let us suppose that a large number of competent scientists had performed essentially the same experiment you did but had failed to obtain significant results. In all likelihood they would not have reported their results to a journal. If they had decided to submit the report to a journal, the journal most likely would have rejected the article as failing to make a major contribution. (Journals are able to publish only a minority of the articles they receive and have to exercise certain criteria for selection; they have an understandable bias against negative results, that is, results that indicate some variable does *not* affect performance).

Then your article comes out, and many investigators around the country may be interested in pursuing your research. Indeed, the very experimenters who had failed to obtain your results may be particularly stimulated to reexamine the matter. Eventually, if enough negative results are sent to journals, truth will out, and the results of your original study will be attributed to chance. However, the road toward correcting the erroneous conclusion of a competently done experiment that produced significant results by chance variation is a lengthy and embarrassing one.

THEORIES AND MODELS

No one experiment ever proves anything. A soundly designed and executed experiment can, at best, change the subjective probability that a hypothesis is correct. When one has studied an experiment and found it convincing because its methodology conforms to acceptable scientific standards, one simply has more confidence that some relationship holds or that it does not hold.

Scientific methods are sophisticated common sense. They are the use of rational thinking derived from basic, generally accepted assumptions. One generally accepted assumption is that when a number of independent people make similar observations of a phenomenon, their common description is likely to be accurate. Even if an experiment has been soundly designed and executed, scientists will be skeptical of its validity if its findings cannot be replicated. A finding becomes established when it has been obtained in several experiments conducted by different experimenters in different places but with the same basic methods.

It is much harder to specify when a theory becomes established. No single experiment, even if replicated many times, can provide a definitive test for a theory. As discussed in Chapter 1, a theory assumes a particular viewpoint, and many implications follow from that viewpoint. Often the adoption of a theory involves more than the acceptance of an explanation for a specific set of observations; it involves the adoption of a *paradigm*, an extension of the assumptions behind the theory into many aspects of scientific and professional life. Psychology is a young field, and many psychologists feel that it is not ready for the adoption of a single theory and paradigm, which would be only limiting at this point in its history. In the hope of avoiding the limitations of a prematurely accepted paradigm, many psychologists have limited themselves to the development of more circumscribed theories, often called *models*, which apply only to limited domains like auditory localization, hunger, interpersonal attraction, or moral development. With such models psychologists can stay close to empirical testing, continuously checking the models against their findings; they can make predictions when they are trying to extend the model's applicability and can modify the model when observation has proved their predictions incorrect. Models are much more modest than general theories. They can be easily modified or even abandoned entirely, while general theories tend to be much more intractable. Any science has as its ultimate goal to achieve as thorough an understanding as possible of all the phenomena within its domain—developing general theories when possible but also taking advantage of models when successful general theories are not available.

SUGGESTED READINGS

DOWNIE, N., and HEATH, R. *Basic Statistical Methods* (2nd ed.). New York, Harper & Row, 1965. An excellent, easy-to-read introduction to statistical methods in the social sciences.

HAYS, W. L. *Statistics for Psychologists.* New York, Holt, Rinehart and Winston, 1963. A more advanced treatment of statistical methods and probability theory for the social scientist.

ROSENTHAL, R. "Experimenter Outcome-Orientation and the Results of the Psychological Experiment," *Psychological Bulletin,* Vol. 61, No. 405, 1964. A summary of experimenter-bias effects.

SIDMAN, M. *Tactics of Scientific Research.* New York, Basic Books, 1960. A classic introduction to the strategy and rationale of research with individual organisms and its advantages over group research.

TURNER, M. B. *Philosophy and the Science of Behavior.* New York, Appleton-Century-Crofts, 1967. This prize-winning book is a fascinating discussion of psychological method and theory and their philosophical underpinnings.

Film Appendix

ASPECTS OF BEHAVIOR *(31 minutes, color)*

This film illustrates most of the major approaches to psychology that are discussed in the text. O. Ivar Lovaas represents *behavioral psychology.* The film shows some examples of his behavior-modification program for the treatment of autistic children. Behavior modification is discussed in Chapters 3 and 33 of the text. pp. 44–59

Stanley Milgram introduces the area of *social psychology,* the subject of Unit VIII. As an example of the kinds of issues social psychologists consider, Milgram comments on the impersonality of the social environment in a city: People think of other people as properties of the environment . . . or "familiar strangers." John Darley and Bibb Latané talk about the *bystander phenomenon,* in which numerous unrelated people may observe a crime without making any move to intervene, and they show an experiment they conducted to study it: Students reporting for a "psychological experiment" were asked to wait in a room, which soon began to fill with smoke from a vent. Every one of the twenty-four students who waited in the room alone took some immediate action when smoke began pouring through the vent. But when several students waited together, not one student took any action. Darley and Latané have concluded that the *avoidance of responsibility is made easier by the presence of others* in an emergency situation.

Physiological psychology, the intricacies of which are discussed in Chapter 16, is outlined by J. Anthony Deutsch. Deutsch demonstrates that a rat that has had an electrode inserted in a particular part of its brain will press a bar in order to obtain pleasurable stimulation. pp. 317–321 José Delgado, who has been working with electric stimulation of the brains of bulls and gibbons, comments that the purpose of such studies pp. 318–319 is to determine the *neurophysiological bases of behavior.* A film sequence shows his famous fighting-bull experiment, in which Delgado averts a fighting bull's charge by sending current through electrodes implanted in the bull's brain.

The fact that psychologists do not always agree is exemplified by the area of *abnormal psychology,* the subject of Chapters 30 and 31 in Unit IX. The film points to the great diversity of opinion concerning the causes and treatment of most major p. 600; pp. 611–624 mental disorders, including *schizophrenia.* Silvano Arieti discusses the possibility of a *genetic potentiality,* or predisposition, to schizophrenia; Arnold Friedhoff proposes pp. 326–329 a genetically based *chemical* abnormality as the cause of schizophrenia and discusses the proven usefulness of *drug therapy* in its treatment (see Chapter 34); and Julian pp. 662–664 Silverman discusses the causes of schizophrenia in terms of *existential relating* (see Chapter 33). pp. 648–649

The late Abraham Maslow, whose views are represented in Chapter 22, discusses pp. 444–446 *cultural psychology.* Against a montage of scenes filmed at a commune in the country, a commune member says that the purpose of such a place is to give people a chance to raise their children in an environment that they like and to achieve personal satisfaction in life. The impact of environment on development is discussed pp. 133–147 particularly in Chapters 8, 16, and 25. pp. 324–329 Maslow says that two intertwining questions in any society are how good a society human nature will permit and how good a pp. 490–493 human nature society will permit. Of course, these central questions concern all of psychology; there are, equally, no simple answers.

LEARNING *(30 minutes, color)*

This film shows actual demonstrations and laboratory experiments concerned with both learned and instinctive, or inherited, behavior. For example, *species-specific* pp. 20–21 *behavior,* as defined and explored in Chapter 2, is a behavior that is characteristic of a species. Jack Hailman has been studying the instinctual pecking behavior of young ring-billed gulls. The adults of the species have a characteristic black band,

or ring, around their yellow bills that resembles some of the larger black insects the
pp. 29–30 gulls feed upon. For young gulls, the black ring on the parents' bill is a *sign stimulus*, that is, it elicits the specific instinctual response of pecking. In taking food from the adult's bill, the young gull then learns to feed on the black insects.

pp. 34–35 Eckhard Hess shows experiments on the *critical period* for *imprinting* in young ducklings, which occurs between twelve and sixteen hours after hatching. Once the young duck has imprinted to the model of an adult, it will climb over obstacles in order to follow that adult and will, when grown, attempt to mate with it.

Learning in very young infants is demonstrated by Lewis Lipsitt with a *conjugate reinforcement* procedure. An infant is given a rubber nipple, which is attached by a length of tubing to a doll hanging over the crib; when the infant sucks on the nipple, the doll moves. Lipsitt has found that the rate of sucking increases significantly as the infant learns that his sucking is associated with the doll's movement.

A silent-film sequence demonstrates how a child is *classically* (or Pavlovian)
pp. 41–43 *conditioned* to fear rabbits; how the fear response is *generalized* to all furry objects;
pp. 43–44 and ultimately how it is *extinguished.* These processes are explored in Chapter 3.

pp. 44–45 Richard Mallot discusses *reinforcers* such as money, praise, and attention and
pp. 50–52 their use to change the frequency of a response; discrimination training in pigeons
pp. 45–48 and the process of *shaping* a bar-press response in a rat are demonstrated, as are the applications of such laboratory work on *operant reinforcement* to the development of *behavior-modification* programs for retarded children (see Chapter 33).

Nathan Azrin discusses the use, or misuse, of aversive conditioning, in which
pp. 57–59 reinforcement is in the form of punishment or pain (see Chapter 3). Aversive conditioning is extremely powerful in changing behavior by suppressing particular responses. But experiments with punishment have shown that it also produces aggression, a complex sequence of instinctive behavior, as in demonstrated in the film of Azrin's famous pain-aggression experiment. In this experiment two rats trapped in a cage are repeatedly shocked and eventually turn on each other. The implications of this *pain-aggression relationship* (see Chapter 18) are extensive, particularly with respect to societal use of punitive control in the form of prisons and jails.

B. F. Skinner comments that society is "stuck with punitive control . . . unwilling to change to more successful methods." Skinner also discusses his ideas about Utopian societies against a montage of scenes from a commune.

David McClelland discusses his studies of *motivation training,* which is aimed at teaching people to discriminate among their own motives. For example, as discussed in Chapter 19, the need for power is a motive very different from the
pp. 377–380 need for achievement, although many people cannot discriminate between the two.

DEVELOPMENT *(31¾ minutes, color)*

This film opens with the birth of a child, which is the starting point for the field of *developmental psychology.* Only recently have developmental psychologists become aware of the efficiency of the behavioral equipment with which a newborn child faces his new environment. (Chapters 5, 7, and 16.)

Psychologist Jerome Kagan explains and demonstrates some of the very efficient
pp. 94–95 motor reflexes and complex sensory capacities of the newborn child. Newborn infants, for example, can grasp with surprisingly great force, can suck, can orient themselves in space, and have an innate survival reflex to push away anything that covers their faces. Their sensory capacities allow them to scan a moving stimulus, as is demonstrated in an experiment Kagan carries out with infants between the ages of four and fourteen months. An infant reacts with surprise when a toy car rolls down a ramp and hits but fails to knock over a styrofoam figure it had knocked down several times before. These phenomena are discussed in Chapters 5 and 14.

Mary Ainsworth discusses the relationship between the infant's emotional attachment to the caretaker (usually the mother) and his cognitive development, as well as the possibility of an innate or genetic factor in this emotional attachment. These important facets of social and emotional development are discussed in Chapters 8 and 17.

In the text, cognitive development is the subject of Chapters 5 and 6. In the film, by way of further explanation, Patricia Greenfield discusses the young child's growth away from *egocentrism,* or self-orientation, and growth toward awareness pp. 99–100 of the viewpoint of others and of the environment. She demonstrates the development of this process of *decentration* by interpreting the one-word syntactical expressions of a two-year-old child, which move from self-oriented expression—such as "More!"—to expressions indicating awareness of things other than the self—such as "Mama!"

Rhoda Kellogg speculates on the relationship between a child's development and the institutions to which his development is entrusted, and Jeffrey Travers discusses the development of language in children (see Chapter 7 and listen to Record 2). pp. 135–137

Ross Parke contributes his ideas on behavioral, or obedience, aspects of "morality" in children (as discussed in detail in Chapter 8), and a laboratory study with children of elementary-school age shows that the degree to which a child obeys depends on the rationale given the child for obeying. Such social influence is also pp. 135–136 analyzed in Unit VIII, particularly in Chapter 24.

As he does in Chapter 1 of the text, Charles Hampden-Turner challenges experiments such as the one shown, which was conducted by Dr. Parke; Hampden-Turner charges that hypotheses about human behavior based on experimental or laboratory models are weak because the subject's freedom to act is so narrowly and artificially defined by the situation.

Elizabeth Douvan describes the radical growth that takes place in the period of adolescence. She holds that during adolescence the self is undergoing constant revision as the ego struggles to find stability and deal with the new impulses brought about by sexual maturity.

INFORMATION PROCESSING *(28½ minutes, color)*

Events at a large Hollywood cocktail party illustrate some aspects of human information processing. For example, a mnemonic, or memory device (see Chapter 10), pp. 176–178 makes it possible for a guest to remember easily one of the many telephone numbers he is given at the party. Actor-comedian David Steinberg gives him the word PUSHWOP, each letter of which represents a digit in the telephone number (787-4967).

Donald A. Norman acts as "anchorman" and comments on the action. He notes that the *memory system,* the *sensory system,* and *attention* are the major components of information processing that will be looked for in sequences from the party activities. In another party sequence, a man is confronted with conversation from several people at the same time. His growing confusion is obvious, and Norman comments that the man is experiencing *information overload.* The film shows that pp. 155–157 when two men with similar voices talk on similar topics, a person cannot attend to either conversation. But when two people with dissimilar voices, such as a man and a woman, talk at the same time on dissimilar topics, it is possible to attend to either one or the other of the conversations but not to both. The process of attention is also involved in the performance of a magician. Norman points out that the magician at the party forces his audience's attention to what he *wants* them to see.

In another sequence, the *Stroop phenomenon* is demonstrated as people try to call out the color of the ink in which color names are printed on a chart. Because each color name is printed in a different color (for example, the word "blue" is printed in yellow), the party-goers tend to read the spelled-out names of the colors, no matter how hard they try to call out the ink color. Interference from multiple cues is analyzed from many points of view in the text: Chapters 9 and 10 deal with the phenomena from the same viewpoint as that of the film; the learning-model viewpoint appears in Chapters 2 and 3; and the social perspective appears in Chapters 23 and 28.

pp. 172–173 As in Chapter 10 of the text, two kinds of memory are distinguished: *short-term*
memory, which can usually encompass about seven items in a set that may be
pp. 173–178 remembered for about thirty seconds, and *long-term memory*. As illustrated by a
waitress taking drink orders at the party, the problem is to transfer items from
short-term to long-term memory. This is most easily accomplished through the use
p. 172 of memory devices, or mnemonics. Arthur Bornstein comments that it is the *encod-*
ing of the information that really counts in how it is stored (and therefore retrieved),
and he illustrates devices by which the waitress might remember each person's drink
order.

According to Norman, a person's long-term memory encompasses an enormous
pp. 173–175 amount of information, which is organized around "landmarks," or clusters of things
one remembers well. When he does recall something, a person often can retrieve
only part of what he wishes to recall and must try to piece together the remaining
pp. 178–179 details. To exemplify this phenomenon—called *refabrication* or *confabulation*—the
film returns to the party magician; the audience sees only a partial image of the
magician's actions and so fills in, in what seems to be a logical way, what it did not
see.

People develop working strategies for finding organizational patterns in incom-
ing information. These strategies are important to problem solving. However, strate-
pp. 199–200 gies tend to become "set," and people use them in trying to solve problems that
require new strategies. Problem-solving sets are discussed in Chapter 11 of the text.

THE SENSORY WORLD *(33 minutes, color)*

This film opens with a classic laboratory demonstration, conducted by Charles
Harris of the Bell Telephone Research Laboratories, of the distorting effects and
p. 278 aftereffects of prism goggles on human vision; it explains how the effect of the
goggles is actually caused by confusion in the brain's interpretation of visual stimuli
rather than by any change in the eye itself—and by confusion of the *kinesthetic*
sense. How seeing is aided by the senses of hearing and touch is demonstrated in
a sequence showing a baby playing with a toy.

The film moves on to look at how the senses work. In an animated sequence
pp. 227–236 the mechanics of sight are shown, as described in Chapter 13. Another animated
pp. 246–248 sequence demonstrates the sense of touch, and a third is a voyage through the ear.
pp. 237–244 The processes of the touch and auditory senses are also described in Chapter 13.

As yet, scientists do not know too much about how sensory information is
processed in the brain. What understanding they do have has come from animal
p. 210 experiments such as those conducted by Jerome Lettvin of the Massachusetts
Institute of Technology. In 1959 Lettvin discovered that frogs process some visual
information *before* it reaches the brain. He is now conducting research—a portion
of which is demonstrated in the film—on the optic nerve fibers of the frog in an
attempt to identify and classify fibers according to the kinds of information each
fiber conveys.

At the Montreal Neurological Institute, neurosurgeon Wilder Penfield discusses
pp. 279–280; p. 317 *electrical stimulation* of the human brain. He talks with a woman who had undergone
brain surgery eleven years earlier and asks her about her experiences during the
electrical stimulation experiment he conducted during the surgery.

pp. 236–237 Color blindness may take three forms: dichromatic color blindness involving the
inability to perceive red and green; dichromatic color blindness involving the inability to perceive blue and yellow; and monochromatic color blindness, the most severe form, in which the individual is totally color blind. How the world looks to victims of each form is shown in the film.

The psychological impact of impaired hearing is dramatically described in a statement written by Beethoven after he suffered a total loss of hearing at the age of twenty-eight.

The film concludes with a set of optical illusions, demonstrating how the brain can be tricked by ambiguous or "impossible" visual stimuli, such as the graphics created by M. C. Escher. The psychological reasons behind illusionary effects are explained in Chapter 14. pp. 266–268

PERSONALITY *(29½ minutes, color)*

Martin Facey is a college senior majoring in art. His initial comment on being the subject of this film—an unfolding of many aspects of his individual personality—is "I think I'll learn a lot about myself . . . but if you come too close, I'll close you off."

Important tools in the study of a personality are the reactions of others to the individual. The film presents descriptions of Martin from people who know him well. His parents comment that he is more static than their other son and that he takes things hard and keeps his anger locked inside himself. His girlfriend comments, from her perspective, that "his personality can be seen really well through his art." She describes Martin as a person who has difficulty expressing himself and his emotions verbally, who sometimes won't accept help from others, and who often seems tense in social situations.

Martin talks about himself, his goals in art versus his goals as a person, and his potential as an artist. Self-portraits are accompanied by his own explanations of his mood and thoughts at the time he painted them. He explains that he "needs firm right angles . . . everything needs to be in its place . . . organized," which is a facet of his personality that is particularly evident in several of his self-portraits.

In describing himself, Martin explains that he feels there is something in "the background," something unexpressed that he holds against himself. Martin also feels that he has difficulty verbalizing emotions, which he thinks may stem from his family environment in which emotion was never expressed. He feels that his parents are very goal-oriented, and that their primary goal is to succeed. Martin is also aware that he drinks too much and says that drinking, for him, is a way to relax. Investigations of how people form impressions of others are presented in Chapter 23. Theories of personality against which Martin Facey's personality can be analyzed are presented in Chapters 21 and 22.

Psychologist Douglas Jackson discusses the process of *psychological assessment,* or testing (Chapter 20), and comments that every method by itself is fallible to some degree. But by using a variety of sources of information, including reports by the individual himself and by others, many of the weaknesses can be overcome. Jackson notes that the psychologist who makes the assessment is part of the assessment process, an instrument in the interpretation of data. He also discusses the three major considerations in formulating and designing a psychological test.

Psychologist Ira Nathanson discusses the structure and function of several standard psychological assessment tests—*MMPI, Forer Sentence Completion, WAIS, Draw-a-Person, TAT,* and *Holtzman Inkblot Test*—and administers the test to Martin Facey. pp. 399–400; 406–407 Nathanson interprets the test results for Martin. His initial comment is that he feels Martin would probably have scored at least ten points higher on the IQ portion of the tests if he had been more relaxed. Nathanson feels that Martin's tension and anxiety, which he tends to hold within himself, prevent him from maximizing his potential. The test results also show that Martin uses intellectualization to hide or cover his expression of emotion. Nathanson describes Martin as perfectionistic, with the price of perfectionism being inner tension and worry. This push for unreachable perfection has been internalized from the family background of success as a goal orientation. The interpretation of the results of the projective tests show that Martin faces a conflict between passive dependency, which he equates with femininity, and aggressive independence. Nathanson also comments that Martin sees women mainly as sexual objects, and Martin agrees.

Finally, Martin comments on his test results and assessment and on the filming. He feels that Nathanson's assessment "is pretty accurate"—that he does in fact
pp. 492, 494
associate aggressiveness with masculinity and that he would like to be more aggressive. He considers his lack of aggression to be his only major "sex problem."

SOCIAL PSYCHOLOGY *(32½ minutes, color)*

pp. 561–563
"Prejudice is a way in which human beings betray the fragility of the human ego," says Kenneth Clark, the first black president of the American Psychological Association. Documentary footage of the integration of previously all-white schools in the middle-class suburbs of Westport, Connecticut (accomplished by the busing in of young black children) is accompanied by commentary by Clark and by social psychologists Thomas Pettigrew, David Sears, and Thomas Cottle. Comments from both black and white Westport voters and parents alternate with integrated classroom scenes. (Relations between groups are the concern of Chapter 28; the personalities of the individual people involved, Chapters 21 and 22; and how people form their impressions of others, Chapter 23.)

The documentary footage focuses on a third-grade class in which two black boys show widely differing reactions to their new and alien school situation. The class teacher explains that Leonard is a gregarious, playful youngster who reads at primer level and needs special help in order to catch up with the general class level of academic achievement. Leonard is eager to make friends in his new class and readily accepts help from both his teacher and his white classmates. Derwin, on the other hand, is a moody, withdrawn boy who does second-grade-level work and sometimes rejects help from both his teacher and his white classmates.

Dr. Clark comments that there is a great temptation to interpret Leonard's and Derwin's behavior only in terms of their being aliens, or different, in a setting in
pp. 528–530
which they are not part of the "in" group. However, according to *social comparison theory* (see Chapter 27), people learn most about themselves by comparing themselves with other people who are essentially similar to themselves. In the case of Leonard and Derwin, each boy compares himself to the other because in this situation they are more similar to each other than they are like their white classmates. Thus, Leonard's natural gregariousness and Derwin's natural withdrawal and moodiness are intensified by their appraisals of each other; Leonard sees that he is the more overtly competent of the two and thus feels greater self-confidence, and Derwin's lack of self-confidence and withdrawal are reinforced by what he sees of Leonard's competence and gregariousness. Leonard and Derwin also identify with each other and with the other black children being bused to the school through
pp. 482–483
a phenomenon known as *group identification,* by which they attempt to maintain a positive self-image in the alien situation.

A number of social-psychological principles and concepts are illustrated in a sequence of flashbacks to the documentary portion of the film. For example, parents pass on to their children their own norms and attitudes. It has been found that school integration has been most successful when it is carried out at the elementary levels, before children have completely assimilated and adopted their parents' attitudes. Another flashback shows how the mechanism of *selective perception* (see
p. 523
Chapters 14, 23, and 25) is used to reduce *cognitive dissonance* (which is one special interest of Chapter 26): One white mother says that the reason she feels busing of black children is educationally useless is that one teacher told her that regardless of the quality of teaching during the day, the child still returns to the same deprived home environment each evening. This mother has selectively perceived only that information that is consonant with the attitudes she already held.

Dr. Clark believes that racial prejudice exists because the racially prejudiced
p. 550
person requires such beliefs and attitudes in order to maintain his own positive

self-image and to reinforce his own ego. In order to change prejudiced attitudes, the person must cease to need prejudiced beliefs to confirm his self-image.

ABNORMAL BEHAVIOR *(28¼ minutes, color)*

"We want to show what the modern psychiatric hospital is like, what it feels like, and what it does," says Dr. Zuskin, director of Gateways Mental Hospital in Glendale, California. Throughout the film, Zuskin discusses the problems and intricacies of running a large mental hospital and scheduling the daily activities of a large number of patients of all ages. pp. 635–638

In the text, the question of abnormality is discussed in Chapters 30 and 31. Some of the atmosphere of and problems surrounding care facilities, including mental hospitals, is discussed in Chapters 32 and 33. In the film, a tour of a hospital begins on the grounds and outdoor recreational area. One of the interview rooms is shown. The room has a one-way window through which the patient-therapist interaction can be observed, filmed, and taped. In this hospital, patients are told that the interview will be observed or recorded. Segments of a series of patient-therapist sessions constitute the major part of this film. The first interview is with a young man who has displayed frequent episodes of unprovoked, physically violent, hostile behavior. The therapist comments that the patient has been diagnosed as *schizophrenic* (see Chapters 30 and 31) with mild retardation (see Chapters 16, 20, and 30) and is on drug therapy (Chapter 34). The therapist asks the patient to talk about his own behavior during a recent violent episode, but the young man can explain neither the behavior nor the accompanying feelings. The therapist demonstrates that schizophrenia does not usually interfere with intellectual capacity by having the young man name the last five presidents of the United States. pp. 600–602; 618–619 pp. 661–664

The second interview involves a woman who has been in the hospital for several months. The therapist asks the woman the date she entered the hospital, and after some hesitation she answers. When asked to talk about her "strange experiences," the woman shows slight confusion and hesitation. When she is asked to solve mentally a series of subtraction problems, she becomes very confused and breaks down crying.

A patient-therapist interaction involving a twenty-seven-year-old catatonic woman illustrates the total disorganization and indecision that characterizes *catatonic schizophrenia,* which may occur in both *excited* and *withdrawn* states. The motor behavior of the withdrawn state, the most frequent form, is illustrated as the woman walks down a hallway with her therapist, stopping occasionally and holding a particular posture for several minutes or longer without speaking, moving, or overtly responding to external stimulation. A brief episode of catatonic excitement in this patient is also shown. pp. 600–601

A *paranoid schizophrenic* man is interviewed by his therapist. (Compare his symptoms with those of the woman on Side 1 of Record 1.) The patient claims that he feels much better and is ready to go home. The patient had complained of being watched and filmed through the windows of his home; he says that he knew the phone was tapped but that he felt he was ready to deal with the situation and was no longer fearful. The therapist comments that the patient's *prognosis* is good because he has responded well to drug and *electroconvulsive therapy* and is no longer in a depressed state. The man is shown receiving electroconvulsive therapy. pp. 601–602

An older woman suffering from profound despondency and withdrawal is shown with a therapist. During the interview the woman will say only that she is dead. The therapist feels that the prognosis in this case is good because it is the woman's first psychotic episode and was triggered by a traumatic experience rather than reflecting a long-term form of adjustment.

In closing, Zuskin expresses the opinion that "everyone is a 'carrier' of anxiety, ready to break up as soon as they reach the most traumatic or frustrating part of their life."

Contributing Consultants

R. Arnheim

J. Aronoff

I. Asimov

R. Bales

J. Carlsmith

S. Cohen

M. Deutsch

R. Dominowski

E. Fantino

J. Fentress

K. Fischer

RUDOLF ARNHEIM is a professor of the psychology of art at Harvard University, in the Department of Visual and Environmental Studies. Prior to coming to Harvard, he taught at Sarah Lawrence, New School for Social Research, and Columbia University. He holds a Ph. D. from the University of Berlin. He received a Guggenheim Fellowship in 1942 and was a Fulbright Lecturer at Ochanomizu University, Tokyo, Japan, in 1959. He has written many books on the forms and functions of art, one of the best known being *Toward a Psychology of Art*. Dr. Arnheim is a former President and Trustee of the American Society of Aesthetics and was President of the Division of Psychology and the Arts of the American Psychological Association in 1970.

JOEL ARONOFF is associate professor of psychology at Michigan State University. He received both the B. A. (in history) and the Ph. D. (in psychology) from Brandeis University and has taught at Harvard and Cornell Universities. His contributions to the psychological literature range from studies of human motivation to studies of the influence of motives on the social structure of natural and experimental groups.

ISAAC ASIMOV is a writer of astounding range and volume. He published his first book in 1950 and now has over 100 books to his credit. He is famous for his science fiction, but has done much non-fiction science material, and several distinguished history and geography books. He also writes general fiction such as mysteries. In addition to books he has written hundreds of articles, in publications ranging from Esquire to pamphlets of the Atomic Energy Commission. One of his most recent books is *Asimov on Shakespeare*. Along with this tremendous output, Dr. Asimov has consistently won awards and critical acclaim for his work.

R. FREED BALES, a professor of social relations at Harvard University, has devoted his research effort to the understanding of the processes inherent in the functioning of small groups of individuals. He took the Ph. D. at Harvard in 1945 and, with brief excursions to Yale, RAND Corporation, and Salzburg Summer Seminars, has been there ever since. In addition to innumerable scientific papers over the last twenty-five years, Bales has published several books, two in collaboration with the eminent sociologist Talcott Parsons.

J. MERRILL CARLSMITH, associate professor of psychology at Stanford University, received his Ph. D. from Harvard. He was influential in the early days of the development of dissonance theory in social psychology with Leon Festinger, but his interests now center on more general theories of, and experiments on, interpersonal attraction and attractiveness. Before joining the faculty at his alma mater, he taught for two years at Yale University. Carlsmith is internationally recognized as an authority on experimental social psychology.

STEPHEN PHILIP COHEN is assistant professor of social psychology in the Department of Social Relations at Harvard University. His special interest in the study of small groups developed during his Ph. D. work at Harvard. During undergraduate work at McGill University, he concentrated his efforts in the psychology of language. More recently, he has attempted to adapt group techniques for international conflict resolution.

MORTON DEUTSCH, professor at Teachers College, Columbia University, has a Ph. D. from MIT. He taught at New York University and spent seven years with the Bell Telephone Laboratories before moving to Columbia. He is a social psychologist with broad interests in human groups, their dynamics, and their reconciliation at the personal, national, and international levels.

ROGER L. DOMINOWSKI, associate professor of psychology at the Chicago Circle campus of the University of Illinois, holds the Ph. D. from Northwestern University, where he worked with Carl Duncan. His major interests are in problem solving and thinking, among the most rewarding and productive areas of modern experimental psychology. He is particularly concerned with factors that facilitate or inhibit successful problem solving.

EDMUND J. FANTINO, associate professor of psychology at the University of California, San Diego, has the Ph. D. from Harvard and has taught at Yale. His interests are in animal learning and motivation, and he contributes regularly to the psychological literature on choice, conditioned reinforcement, and aversive control.

JOHN C. FENTRESS, associate professor of psychology and biology at the University of Oregon, holds the Ph. D. from Cambridge University, where he worked under the direction of W. H. Thorpe and R. A. Hinde. His interests are both ethological and physiologically psychological. He has published extensively on ethological problems of animal behavior and motivation, both here and abroad. Among his ethological works has been the taming of a wolf, who, with its wife, lives with him and his wife.

KURT W. D. FISCHER is research psychologist at the Boston Children's Hospital Medical Center and at the Harvard Center for Cognitive Studies. He received both his M. A. and Ph. D. from Harvard in developmental psychology, and his B. A. from Yale University. His major areas of research at present are the organization of simple learning, Piaget's theory of intellectual development, the organization of thinking in infants and preschool children, and the role of motivation and emotion in development. He currently has two books in preparation, *Piaget's Theory of Learning and Cognitive Development* and *The Organization of Simple Learning*.

D. Fiske

S. Glickman

D. Freedman

R. Gregory

C. Hall

C. Hampden-Turner

J. Hirsch

M. Horner

R. Isaacson

D. Jackson

DONALD W. FISKE, professor of psychology at the University of Chicago, received the M. A. from Harvard University and the Ph. D. from the University of Michigan. A lifelong interest in the validity and reliability of human inventories and tests has distinguished his career at Wellesley College, Michigan, and Chicago. He has been active in psychological associations, as well as in the production of books and numerous articles on the theory and practice of measuring the characteristics of people.

DANIEL X. FREEDMAN, chairman and professor of psychiatry at the University of Chicago, holds a B. A. from Harvard and an M. D. from the Yale University School of Medicine (with the Keese Prize for research). He has taught at both Yale and Chicago. His primary interest within psychiatry—apart from schizophrenia, which he believes every psychiatrist sees as primary—is in neuropsychopharmacology, an area almost as intricate as its name is long. A devotee of the experimental method, Freedman has published more than seventy articles of scientific content, as well as a text on psychiatry and a handbook of psychopharmacology.

STEPHEN E. GLICKMAN, professor of psychology at the University of California, Berkeley, followed a Ph. D. from McGill University with teaching and research positions at New Mexico, Northwestern, and Berkeley. His interests are in physiological psychology and in comparative psychology. His primary research thrust is aimed at untangling the brain mechanisms involved in learning, motivation, and emotion.

RICHARD L. GREGORY, of the Brain and Perception Laboratory, the University of Bristol, formerly was director of the Bionics Research Laboratory and chairman of the Department of Machine Intelligence and Perception at the University of Edinburgh. He has received the CIBA Foundation Prize for work on aging; the very prestigious Craik Prize in physiological psychology from St. John's, Cambridge; and the Waverley Prize and gold medal for his solid-image microscope. He has taught at Cambridge, UCLA, MIT, NYU, and Edinburgh. He holds a dozen patents for optical and other devices, and he is a prolific scientific contributor in both apparatus and perception, and his book *Eye and Brain* has appeared in ten languages.

CALVIN S. HALL, the director of the Institute of Dream Research and senior lecturer at the University of California, Santa Cruz, has had a long and distinguished career in teaching and writing. He is coauthor of the widely admired *Theories of Personality* and author of the popular *Primer of Freudian Psychology*. He has taught at Berkeley, the University of Oregon, Western Reserve, Syracuse, and Miami and has held a Fulbright professorship at Nijmegen University, Holland. His abiding interests are in the theory of personality and in the meaning of dreams, about which he has written extensively.

CHARLES M. HAMPDEN-TURNER, a member of the Cambridge Institute, received the M. B. A. and D. B. A. degrees from the Department of Organizational Behavior at Harvard's School of Business Administration, and his B. A. from Cambridge University in England. His awards include the Douglas McGregor Award, for "An Existential Learning Theory . . . ," published in the Fall 1966 issue of the *Journal of Applied Behavioral Science*, and the Columbia University Award fór the Study of the Corporation, which he received for his doctoral thesis. His primary interest is psychosocial development and its ramifications in problem solving, organizational development, conflict resolution, and social structures. He cites as a lifelong ambition the establishment of a national system of psychosocial indicators capable of measuring the process of human emancipation.

JERRY HIRSCH, professor of psychology and of zoology at the University of Illinois, Urbana, holds a Berkeley Ph. D., taught at Columbia, and was fellow at the Center for Advanced Study in the Behavioral Sciences before taking up his present position. His field is behavior-genetic analysis, about which he writes comprehensively and comprehensibly. He has been concerned particularly with geotropism in fruit flies and has successfully demonstrated that tropisms can be transferred genetically and analyzed chromosomally. His broad field of interest is the relations between heredity and behavior in animals and men. He is the editor of *Animal Behavior*.

MATINA HORNER received her B. A. from Bryn Mawr College and her M. S. and Ph. D. from the University of Michigan, where she taught until 1969. She is currently assistant professor in the Department of Social Relations, Harvard. Her research interests are centered in the areas of achievement motivation, the psychology of women, and the psychological impact of internalized sex- and race-role stereotypes.

ROBERT L. ISAACSON, professor of psychology at the University of Florida, has also taught at the University of Michigan, where he took the Ph. D. in 1958. His interests are physiological psychology, with particular emphasis on the contribution of phyletically older brain structures to behavior and the developing nervous system. He has written some sixty technical articles, edited two books, and coauthored two introductory psychology texts.

DOUGLAS N. JACKSON, senior professor of psychology at the University of Western Ontario, has a Ph. D. from Purdue in clinical psychology. He has been associated with the Menninger Foundation, where he pursued research, and with the Veterans Administration, where he pursued clinical work. Jackson taught at the Pennsylvania State University and at Stanford before taking on his current position. He has edited, with Sam Messick, *Problems in Human Assessment* and is a frequent contributor to the scientific literature on the assessment of human characteristics. A major contribution is the Personality Research Form, which brings to bear on assessment problems all the sophistication of both the computer age and the history and experience of assessment tests.

S. Komorita

L. Krasner

D. Krebs

J. Langer

D. Lindsley

J. Lipinski

A. Maslow

R. May

J. McConnell

W. McGuire

A. McLeod

E. McNeil

SAMUEL S. KOMORITA, professor of psychology at Indiana University, holds the Ph. D. from the University of Michigan and has been associated with the RAND Corporation, Vanderbilt University, and Wayne State University. He has been primarily involved with game theory and decision processes. His most recent interest is in the area of bargaining, with particular emphasis on the psychological processes underlying conflict resolution.

LEONARD KRASNER, professor of psychology and director of clinical training at the State University of New York, Stony Brook, obtained the Ph. D. at Columbia University in 1950. His main interest is in clinical psychology, and within the field of psychotherapy, he has become quite closely identified with behavior therapy. He has taught at Massachusetts, Colorado, and Stanford, as well as at SUNY.

DENNIS L. KREBS, an assistant professor of Social Relations at Harvard University, received his B. A. degree in 1967 from the University of British Columbia and went to Harvard as a Woodrow Wilson Fellow. He received his M. A. in 1969 and Ph. D. in 1970. Dr. Krebs is currently Chairman of the Undergraduate Program in Social Relations and is engaged in writing on altruism, theories of moral development, and self in social interaction. He is also interested in educational and social reform, especially reform of prisons.

JONAS LANGER, associate professor of psychology at the University of California, Berkeley, has expressed his abiding interest in *Theories of Development* and has participated in the editing and writing of a collection of original chapters on developmental problems. He holds a classical developmental Ph. D. from Clark University, where he collaborated with Heinz Werner and Seymour Wapner, two of the most distinguished, developmentally oriented psychologists of recent history. His research efforts have spanned the field of development from cognitive considerations to the general theory of the processes of individual development.

DONALD B. LINDSLEY, professor of psychology at the University of California, Los Angeles, holds a Ph. D. from the University of Iowa. His interests are in the electroencephalogram and in physiological processes within psychology. He has held the prestigious William James Lectureship in Psychology at Harvard and has taught at the University of Illinois, Brown, Western Reserve, and Northwestern, as well as at UCLA.

JOSEPH LIPINSKI is presently a Research Fellow in Psychiatry at Harvard Medical School and the Massachusetts General Hospital in Boston. He has studied neurology at the University of Copenhagen, Denmark, and at the National Hospital for Nervous Diseases at Queen Square, London. He received his M. D. from Jefferson Medical College. His general field of interest is behavioral neuroscience, particularly basic neurochemistry, neuropsychopharmacology, and the biological correlates of emotion and behavior.

ABRAHAM H. MASLOW, contributor to the first edition, died June 8, 1970. He was one of the leading spokesmen of humanistic psychology and a major figure in the field of personality theory.

ROLLO MAY, a practicing psychotherapist affiliated with the William Alanson White Institute in New York, holds the Ph. D. from Columbia and has taught and counseled in Greece, at Harvard, and at Princeton. He is also adjunct professor in the graduate school of New York University and lecturer at the New School. His interests are in therapy and personality theory. He is one of the prime American authorities on existential psychotherapy.

JAMES V. MCCONNELL, professor of psychology at the University of Michigan, is best known for his studies of memory transfer at the physiological level and for his abiding interest in the theory and composition of science fiction. With a Ph. D. under Dallenbach at the University of Texas, he has taught at both Texas and Michigan. He is also a research psychologist with the Mental Health Research Institute at Michigan. He has consulted the Departments of Defense and Commerce and the Smithsonian Institution on a variety of problems connected with his interests in motivation and learning. A frequent contributor to the scientific journals, McConnell also edits *The Journal of Biological Psychology* and the popular, though humorously serious, *Worm Runner's Digest*.

WILLIAM J. MCGUIRE is chairman of the Psychology Department at Yale, where he received his Ph. D. He has taught at Yale, Illinois, Columbia, and the University of California, San Diego. He is a social psychologist, primarily concerned with attitude change, selective perception, and psychological implication. Possessed of an extraordinarily classical as well as modern, analytical mind, McGuire has consistently been in the forefront of social psychological debates and issues, not to mention empirical work, for the past decade. He is currently editor of the *Journal of Personality and Social Psychology*.

ALASTAIR MCLEOD earned a B. A. in psychology and philosophy from Queen's University in Canada in 1967 and is now completing his Ph. D. at the University of California, San Diego. While he has been receiving his formal training there in the experimental analysis of behavior, he has also been studying humanism and psychodynamics with Constance Lerner Russell of La Jolla. He plans to work at integrating biological and psychological conceptions of personality with intuitive and spiritual wisdom.

ELTON B. MCNEIL, professor of psychology at the University of Michigan, received his Ph. D. from there in clinical psychology. His interests are too numerous to elaborate upon, for they span the fields of consumer behavior, introspection, mental health, adjustment, education of the gifted, human conflict, sex, subliminal

N. Miller

C. Mueller

E. Murray

H. Murray

D. Norman

R. Ornstein

L. Peplau

H. Pick

N. Reppucci

G. Reynolds

C. Rogers

stimulation, and psychosis. He is a frequent contributor to scholarly journals and is the author of numerous books, including *Human Socialization.*

Neal E. Miller, professor and head of a laboratory of physiological psychology at the Rockefeller University, holds a Ph. D. from Yale, with which he was affiliated for a number of years. From 1952 until assuming his present post, Miller held the James Rowland Angell Professorship. His interests are in learning and motivation and in their physiological basis. He has conducted numerous incisive experiments on motivational mechanisms and continually contributes to the theory of the application of animal studies to the human condition.

Conrad G. Mueller, professor of psychology at Indiana University, took his Ph. D. in 1948 at Columbia, where he also served as chairman of the Psychology Department. He has been visiting professor in biophysics at the Rockefeller Institute. His interests are in sensory processes, particularly visual ones, and in the theory and treatment of data.

Edward J. Murray, professor of psychology at the University of Miami, has pursued his interest in feelings and emotions both with animals and with people since taking a Yale Ph. D. in 1955. He taught at Syracuse before taking up his present post. His interests also include sleep deprivation, and he is now working with emotionally disturbed children and their families.

Harry G. Murray, assistant professor of psychology at the University of Western Ontario, took his Ph. D. at the University of Illinois, where he worked on research projects in both behavior genetics and human learning. His primary field of interest is general experimental psychology. An expert in both learning theory and genetics, Murray attempts in his research to study processes of learning and to show how these combine with hereditary mechanisms in the determination of human and animal behavior.

Donald A. Norman, professor of psychology at the University of California, San Diego, received an M. S. in electrical engineering and the Ph. D. in mathematical psychology from the University of Pennsylvania. He has taught at Harvard, where he was affiliated with the Center for Cognitive Studies. His interests are in understanding computers and human memory, and perhaps simulating one with the other.

Robert E. Ornstein, research psychologist at the Langley Porter Neuropsychiatric Institute in San Francisco, has a Stanford Ph. D. He has written *On the Experience of Time* and is currently interested in sleep, dreaming, and states of consciousness in general.

L. Anne Peplau is a graduate student in social psychology at Harvard University, where she has held NSF and Danforth Fellowships. One of her main interests is in the application of social-psychological theory to the study of social issues such as American race relations. She is currently teaching a seminar on sex roles for Harvard undergraduates.

Herbert L. Pick, Jr., professor of psychology at the University of Minnesota (Institute of Child Development), took the Ph. D. at Cornell University. In 1959–1960, he studied in Russia at the Moscow State University and has visited there since. Pick's interests are in perception generally and in the development of perceptual experience in children.

N. Dickon Reppucci received his Ph. D. at Harvard University in clinical psychology and was a lecturer there for a year. Since 1968 he has been an assistant professor of community/clinical psychology at Yale University. His major areas of interest are community psychology, especially work in correctional facilities and schools, behavior modification as a large-scale rehabilitative tool, and developmental problems of childhood and adolescence. Reppucci has published a number of papers in professional journals and currently has two books in preparation.

G. S. Reynolds, professor of psychology and chairman of the department at the University of California, San Diego, holds the Ph. D. from Harvard University in experimental psychology. His interests are reflected in his *A Primer of Operant Conditioning.* He taught at Harvard and the University of Chicago before taking his present post. As consulting editor to *Psychology Today,* he has contributed surreptitiously to several areas of psychology and has himself published papers in the areas of operant conditioning, human responses to stress, psychoacoustics, psychopharmacology, and physiological psychology. His current interests are schedules of reinforcement and personality theory.

Carl R. Rogers, resident fellow at the Center for Studies of the Person, La Jolla, California, is internationally known as the originator of client-centered psychotherapy, which he developed while head of the Counseling Center at the University of Chicago. For twenty years his research and writing has been in the fields of psychotherapy, personality theory, and education, and increasingly in the last five years he has been involved in both the theory and the practice of encounter groups (sensitivity training). His recent books indicate something of his interest—*On Becoming a Person,* and *Freedom to Learn: A View of What Education Might Become.* He is the only psychologist in the United States to receive from the American Psychological Association both its Scientific Contribution Award and its Award for Professional Contribution. Rogers, the author of many

Z. Rubin

B. Sarata

B. Scharf

D. Slobin

C. Smith

T. Steiner

S. Stevens

D. Tresemer

L. Tyler

R. Watson

R. Watson, Jr.

D. Wood

books and articles, has been a professor at Ohio State University, the University of Chicago, and the University of Wisconsin.

Zick Rubin is assistant professor of social psychology at Harvard University. He received his B. A. from Yale in 1965, and his Ph. D. from the University of Michigan in 1969. His doctoral thesis on "The Social Psychology of Romantic Love" was awarded the 1969 Socio-Psychological Prize of the American Association for the Advancement of Science. Rubin's current research centers on the development of interpersonal bonds, both short-term (among strangers in public places) and long-term (among dating couples). His book *Liking and Loving* is to be published in 1973.

Brian Sarata is now a graduate student at Yale University in clinical psychology. Following undergraduate work at Bowdoin College, he served as a Peace Corps Volunteer in Niger, Africa. He then worked at Connecticut Valley Psychiatric Hospital in Middletown for two years before going into graduate studies. His current research interests include: the work satisfaction of persons working in human service agencies and its relationships to the delivery of services and to characteristics of the work situation; rehabilitation programs for criminal offenders and the need to restructure correctional agencies in line with rehabilitative goals; and the construct of "impulsivity" and its relation to deviant behavior.

Bertram Scharf, professor of psychology at Northeastern University, holds a Ph. D. from Harvard University. His interests are in sensory processes and in psychoacoustics. His particular interests are in masking and in loudness summation. He has served as visiting research associate at both the Technische Hochschule Stuttgart and the Laboratory of Sensory Communication, Syracuse University.

Dan I. Slobin, associate professor of psychology at Berkeley, holds a Ph. D. from Harvard, where he worked with Roger Brown, Jerome Bruner, and George A. Miller on problems of developmental psycholinguistics. His interests cover sociological and anthropological subjects as well as psychology. He edits the translation journal *Soviet Psychology* and is a frequent translator of foreign psychological literature.

Carol L. Smith, a doctoral student in child development at Harvard, received her B. A. in Psychology from Brown University in 1970. Her interests range from the psychology and neurophysiology of vision to the development of social behavior in man and animals in evolutionary perspective.

Theodore E. Steiner, Assistant Professor of Psychology, San Francisco State College, previously taught at the University of Illinois. He received the Ph. D. from Indiana University in 1966. Steiner's main work has been on mathematical models of human learning, with recent emphasis on biofeedback and states of consciousness.

S. S. Stevens, professor of psychophysics at Harvard University, took a Harvard Ph. D. in psychology under E. G. Boring after flirting with both medicine and education. In 1938, he coauthored *Hearing*, a book so thorough in its coverage that it is standard today. Stevens is best known for his recent work on the power law of sensory magnitude.

David Tresemer is a teaching fellow in the Department of Social Relations at Harvard University, where he received an M. A. in social psychology in 1970. He has had widely divergent experiences in the application of various group techniques to different settings, and his current research concerns the dissolution in training groups of gender-role stereotypes and of motivation to inhibit competence in activities normally reserved for the opposite sex.

Leona E. Tyler, professor of psychology and dean of the Graduate School, University of Oregon, received the Ph. D. from the University of Minnesota and has taught at Minnesota, Oregon, Berkeley, and the University of Amsterdam. Her interests are in tests and measurements of the human potential and achievement, areas in which she has published many books and articles.

Robert I. Watson, professor of psychology at the University of New Hampshire, took the Ph. D. at Columbia University. He has served at Dana College, Newark, and Northwestern as well as at New Hampshire, and also Carnegie Institute of Technology and Washington University School of Medicine. His interests are in clinical psychology and particularly the history of psychology.

Robert I. Watson, Jr. is currently a doctoral candidate and teaching fellow and research assistant at Harvard University. He graduated with honors in psychology from the Wesleyan University in 1969, where he received the Wakley prize for excellence in psychological research. His specific interests are motivation, aggression and sex-role stereotyping.

David Wood was educated at the University of Nottingham in the Midlands of England, where he received his B. A. and Ph. D. degrees. His doctoral thesis was concerned with the computer simulation of human reasoning behavior. His interest in the development of problem-solving skills and cognition led him to the Center for Cognitive Studies at Harvard, where he is now a Research Fellow. Dr. Wood's current research work includes studies of imitation in babies, concepts of time in five- to seven-year-olds, and the development of planning skills. He returns to the University of Nottingham in 1971–73 to take a teaching position.

Bibliography

1

Fitzgerald, F. S. *The Crack Up.* New York: New Directions Pub. Corp., 1945.

Kaplan, A. *The Conduct of Inquiry: Methodology for Behavioral Science.* San Francisco: Chandler Publishing Co., 1964.

Koestler, A. *The Act of Creation.* New York: Macmillan, 1966.

Kuhn, T. S. *The Structure of Scientific Revolutions.* Chicago: University of Chicago Press, 1970.

Marcuse, H. *One Dimensional Man.* Boston: Beacon Press, 1964.

Schutz, A. "Concept and Theory Formation in the Social Sciences," in M. Natanson (ed.), *Philosophy of the Social Sciences: A Reader.* New York: Random House, 1963, pp. 231–249.

Winthrop, H. "Cultural Factors Underlying Research Outlooks in Psychology," in J. F. Bugental (ed.), *Challenges of Humanistic Psychology.* New York: McGraw-Hill, 1967.

2

Birch, H. G. "Sources of Order in the Maternal Behavior of Animals," *American Journal of Orthopsychiatry,* 26 (1956), 279–284.

Bowlby, J. *Attachment.* New York: Basic Books, Inc., Publishers, 1969.

Carr, A. *So Excellent a Fische: A Natural History of Sea Turtles.* New York: Doubleday, 1967.

Darwin, C. *Expression of the Emotions in Man and Animals.* Chicago: University of Chicago Press, 1965.

———. *The Origin of the Species by Means of Natural Selection or The Preservation of Favored Races in the Struggle for Life and the Descent of Man and Selection in Relation to Sex.* New York: Modern Library, 1936.

Dethier, V. G. "The Hungry Fly," *Psychology Today,* 1 (1967), 64–72.

———. "Insects and the Concept of Motivation," in D. Levine (ed.), *Nebraska Symposium on Motivation.* Lincoln: University of Nebraska Press, 1966, 105–136.

Eibl-Eibesfelt, I. *Ethology: The Biology of Behavior.* New York: Holt, Rinehart and Winston, 1970.

Fentress, J. C. "Observations on the Behavioral Development of a Hand-Reared Male Timber Wolf," *American Zoologist,* 7 (1967), 339–351.

Frisch, K. von. *Bees: Their Vision, Chemical Senses, and Language.* Ithaca, N.Y.: Cornell University Press, 1950.

———. *The Dance Language and Orientation of Bees.* L. E. Chadwick (tr.), Cambridge, Mass.: Belknap Press of Harvard Univ. Press, 1967.

Hebb, D. O. "Alice in Wonderland or Psychology Among the Biological Sciences," in H. F. Harlow and C. N. Woolsey (eds.), *Biological and Biochemical Bases of Behavior.* Madison: University of Wisconsin Press, 1958, pp. 451–467.

Holst, E. von., and U. von Saint Paul. "Electrically Controlled Behavior," *Scientific American,* 206 (1962), 50–59.

Iersel, J. J. A. van, and A. C. A. Bol. "Preening of Two Tern Species: A Study of Displacement Activities," *Behaviour,* 13 (1958), 1–88.

Konishi, M. "Effects of Deafening on Song Development in Two Species of Juncos," *Condor,* 66 (1964), 85–102.

Lorenz, K. *Evolution and Modification of Behavior.* Chicago: University of Chicago Press, 1965.

———. *King Solomon's Ring.* New York: Crowell, 1952.

———. *Studies in Animal and Human Behavior.* Cambridge, Mass.: Harvard University Press, Vol. I, 1970.

Marler, P. R., and W. J. Hamilton. *Mechanisms of Animal Behavior.* New York: Wiley, 1966.

Marler, P. R., and M. Tamura. "Culturally Transmitted Patterns of Vocal Behavior in Sparrows," *Science,* 146 (1964), 1483–1486.

Matthews, G. V. T. *Bird Navigation.* London: Cambridge University Press, 1955.

Melzack, R. "Irrational Fears in the Dog," *Canadian Journal of Psychology,* 6 (1952), 141–147.

Robert, D., and G. Handel. *Family Worlds: A Psychological Approach to Family Life.* Chicago: University of Chicago Press, 1959.

Schleidt, W. "Reaktionen von Truthühnern auf fliegende Raubvögel und Versuche zur Analyse ihrer AAM's," *Zeitung für Tierpsychologie,* 18 (1961), 534–560.

———. "Über die Auslösung der Flucht vor Raubvögeln bei Truthühnern," *Naturwissenschaften,* 48 (1961), 141–142.

Thorpe, W. H. *Bird Song.* London: Cambridge University Press, 1961.

———. *Learning and Instinct in Animals.* 2nd ed. London: Methuen, 1963.

Tinbergen, N. *The Study of Instinct.* Fairlawn, N. J.: Oxford University Press, 1951.

Uexküll, J. von. *Umwelt und Innenwelt der Tiere.* 2nd ed. Berlin: Springer-Verlag, 1921.

3

Bolles, R. C. "Species-Specific Defense Reactions and Avoidance Learning," *Psychological Review,* 77 (1970), 32–48.

Boring, E. *A History of Experimental Psychology.* New York: Appleton-Century-Crofts, 1950.

Dallenbach, K. M. "Twitmeyer and the Conditioned Response," *American Journal of Psychology,* 72 (1959), 633–638.

Fantino, E., D. Sharp, and M. Cole. "Factors Facilitating Lever-Press Avoidance," *Journal of Comparative and Physiological Psychology,* 62 (1966), 214–217.

Ferster, C. B., and B. F. Skinner. *Schedules of Reinforcement.* New York: Appleton-Century-Crofts, 1957.

Hanson, H. M. "Effects of Discrimination Training on Stimulus Generalization," *Journal of Experimental Psychology,* 58 (1959), 321–334.

Hilgard, E. R., and G. H. Bower. *Theories of Learning.* 3rd ed. New York: Appleton-Century-Crofts, 1966.

Honig, W. H. (ed.). *Operant Behavior: Areas of Research and Application.* New York: Appleton-Century-Crofts, 1966.

Kimble, G. A. *Hilgard and Marquis' Conditioning and Learning.* 2nd ed. New York: Appleton-Century-Crofts, 1961.

Konorski, J., and S. Miller. "On Two Types of Conditioned Reflex," *Journal of General Psychology,* 16 (1937), 264–272.

Lashley, K. S. *The Neuropsychology of Lashley. Selected Papers.* F. A. Beach, *et al.* (eds.). New York: McGraw-Hill, 1960.

Pavlov, I. P. *Conditioned Reflexes.* G. V. Anrep (tr.). London: Oxford University Press, 1927.

Reynolds, G. S. *A Primer of Operant Conditioning.* Glenview, Ill.: Scott, Foresman and Company, 1968.

Schneider, B. A. "A Two-State Analysis of Fixed Interval Responding in the Pigeon," *Journal of the Experimental Analysis of Behavior,* 12 (1969), 677–687.

Skinner, B. F. *The Behavior of Organisms.* New York: Appleton-Century-Crofts, 1961.

———. *Walden Two.* New York: Macmillan, 1948.

Terrace, H. S. "Stimulus Control," in K. W. Honig (ed.), *Operant Behavior: Areas of Research and Application.* New York: Appleton-Century-Crofts, 1966, 271–344.

Watson, J. *Behaviorism.* New York: Norton, 1930.

Wolfe, J. B. "Effectiveness of Token-Rewards for Chimpanzees," *Comparative Psychology Monographs,* Vol. 12, Whole No. 5 (1936).

Woodworth, R. S. *Psychology.* New York: Holt, Rinehart and Winston, Inc., 1921.

4

Azrin, N. H. "Pain and Aggression," *Psychology Today,* 1 (1967), 27–33.

Birch, H. G. "The Relation of Previous Experience to Insightful Problem-Solving," *Journal of Comparative Psychology,* 38 (1945), 367–383.

Bruner, J. S. "The Growth and Structure of Skill," in K. J. Connolly (ed.), *Motor Skills in Infancy.* New York: Academic Press, Inc., 1970.

———. "Origins of Problem-Solving Strategies in Skill Acquisition." Paper presented at Nineteenth International Congress of Psychology, London, 1969.

Darwin, C. *Expression of the Emotions in Man and Animals.* Chicago: University of Chicago Press, 1965.

———. *The Origin of the Species by Means of Natural Selection or The Preservation of Favored Races in the Struggle for Life and the Descent of Man and Selection in Relation to Sex.* New York: Modern Library, 1936.

Fischer, K. W. *The Organization of Simple Learning.* Chicago: Markham Publishing Co., 1973, forthcoming.

Fischer, K. W., and E. Fantino. "The Dissociation of Discriminative and Conditioned Reinforcing Functions of Stimuli with Changes in Deprivation," *Journal of the Experimental Analysis of Behavior,* 11 (1968), 703–710.

Hebb, D. O. "On the Nature of Fear," *Psychological Review,* 53 (1946), 259–276.

———. *The Organization of Behavior. A Neuropsychological Theory.* New York: Wiley, 1949.

Hebb, D. O., and W. R. Thompson. "The Social Significance of Animal Studies," in G. Lindzey (ed.), *Handbook of Social Psychology.* Reading, Mass.: Addison-Wesley Publishing Co., Inc., 1968, Vol. II, 729–774.

Kagan, J. "Attention and Psychological Change in the Young Child," *Science,* 170 (1970), 826–832.

Lashley, K. S. *The Neuropsychology of Lashley. Selected Papers.* F. A. Beach, *et al.* (eds.). New York: McGraw-Hill, 1960.

Mandler, G. "From Association to Structure," *Psychological Review,* 69 (1962), 415–427.

Melzack, R. "Irrational Fears in the Dog," *Canadian Journal of Psychology,* 6 (1952), 141–147.

Neuringer, A. J. "Animals Respond for Food in the Presence of Free Food," *Science,* 166 (1969), 399–401.

Papoušek, H. "Experimental Studies of Appetitional Behavior in Human Newborns and Infants," in H. W. Stevenson, E. H. Hess, and H. L. Rheingold (eds.), *Early Behavior.* New York: Wiley, 1967, 249–277.

Piaget, J. *The Origins of Intelligence in the Child.* New York: International Universities Press, 1952.

Premack, D. "Reinforcement Theory," in D. Levine (ed.), *Nebraska Symposium on Motivation.* Lincoln: University of Nebraska Press, 1965, 123–180.

Sheffield, F. D. "A Drive-Induction Theory of Reinforcement," in R. N. Haber (ed.), *Current Research in Motivation.* New York: Holt, Rinehart and Winston, 1966, 98–111.

———. "New Evidence on the Drive-Induction Theory of Reinforcement," in R. N. Haber (ed.), *Current Research in Motivation.* New York: Holt, Rinehart and Winston, 1966, 111–122.

Sheffield, F. D., and B. A. Campbell. "The Role of Experience in the Spontaneous Activity of Hungry Rats," *Journal of Comparative and Physiological Psychology,* 47 (1954), 97–100.

Tolman, E. C. *Behavior and Psychological Man.* Berkeley: University of California Press, 1961.

———. "Cognitive Maps in Rats and Men," *Psychological Review,* 55 (1948), 189–208.

Wagner, A. R. "Frustration and Punishment," in R. N. Haber (ed.), *Current Research in Motivation.* New York: Holt, Rinehart and Winston, 1966, 229–239.

Zigler, E., J. Levine, and L. Gould. "Cognitive Processes in the Development of Children's Appreciation of Humor," *Child Development,* 37 (1966), 507–518.

5

Baldwin, A. L. *Theories of Child Development.* New York: Wiley, 1967.

Bower, T. G. R. "The Visual World of Infants," *Scientific American,* 215 (1966), 80–92.

———. "The Object in the World of the Infant," *Scientific American,* 225 (1971), 30–38.

Carey-Block, S. "Are Children Little Scientists with False Theories of the World?" (unpublished Ph. D. dissertation, Harvard University, 1971).

Cronbach, L. J. *Essentials of Psychological Testing.* New York: Harper & Row, 1960.

Fischer, K. W. *Piaget's Theory of Learning and Cognitive Development.* Chicago: Markham Publishing Co., 1973, forthcoming.

Furth, H. G. *Piaget and Knowledge.* Englewood Cliffs, N.J.: Prentice-Hall, 1969.

Piaget, J. *Biology and Knowledge.* Chicago: University of Chicago Press, 1971.

———. *The Construction of Reality in the Child.* New York: Basic Books, Inc., Publishers, 1954.

———. *The Origins of Intelligence in the Child.* New York: International Universities Press, 1952.

Piaget, J., and B. Inhelder. *The Psychology of the Child.* New York: Basic Books, Inc., Publishers, 1969.

Smedslund, J. "The Acquisition of Conservation of Substance and Weight in Children. I. Introduction," *Scandinavian Journal of Psychology,* 2 (1961), 11–20.

Tinbergen, N. *The Study of Instinct.* New York: Oxford University Press, 1951.

Wohlwill, J. F. "Perceptual Learning," in P. R. Farnsworth, O. McNeman, and Q. McNeman (eds.), *Annual Review of Psychology,* 17 (1966), 201–232.

6

Baldwin, A. L. *Theories of Child Development.* New York: Wiley, 1967.

Carey-Block, S. "Are Children Little Scientists with False Theories of the World?" (unpublished Ph. D. dissertation, Harvard University, 1971).

Fischer, K. W. *Piaget's Theory of Learning and Cognitive Development.* Chicago: Markham Publishing Co., 1973, forthcoming.

Furth, H. G. *Piaget and Knowledge.* Englewood Cliffs, N.J.: Prentice-Hall, 1969.

Gardner, R. A., and B. T. Gardner. "Teaching Sign Language to a Chimpanzee," *Science,* 165 (1969), 664–672.

Inhelder, B., and J. Piaget. *The Early Growth of Logic in the Child.* New York: Harper & Row, 1964.

Inhelder, B., and J. Piaget. *The Growth of Logical Thinking from Childhood to Adolescence.* New York: Basic Books, Inc., Publishers, 1958.

Lewis, R. *Miracles: Poems by Children of the English-Speaking World.* New York: Simon and Schuster, 1966.

Piaget, J. *Biology and Knowledge.* Chicago: University of Chicago Press, 1971.

Piaget, J., and B. Inhelder. *The Psychology of the Child.* New York: Basic Books, Inc., Publishers, 1969.

Vygotsky, L. *Thought and Language.* Cambridge, Mass.: The MIT Press, 1962.

Werner, H. *Comparative Psychology of Mental Development.* Rev. ed. New York: International Universities Press, 1966.

———. "The Concept of Development from a Comparative and Organismic Point of View," in D. Harris (ed.), *The Concept of Development.* Minneapolis: University of Minnesota Press, 1957, 125–148.

White, S. H. "Some Educated Guesses about Cognitive Development in the Preschool Years," in R. D. Hess and R. M. Baer (eds.), *Early Education: Current Theory, Research, and Practice.* Chicago: Aldine Publishing Company, 1968, 203–214.

White, S. H., and H. D. Fishbein. "Children's Learning," in N. Talbot, J. Kagan, and L. Eisenberg (eds.), *Behavioral Science in Pediatric Medicine.* Philadelphia: W. B. Saunders Company, 1971, 188–227.

7

Bellugi, U. "The Emergence of Inflections and Negative Systems in the Speech of Two Children." Paper presented at the New England Psychological Association, 1964.

Brown, R. *A First Language: The Early Stages.* Cambridge, Mass.: Harvard University Press (forthcoming).

Brown, R., and U. Bellugi. "Three Processes in the Child's Acquisition of Syntax," *Harvard Educational Review,* 34 (1964), 133–151.

Brown, R., and C. Fraser. "The Acquisition of Syntax," in C. N. Cofer and B. S. Musgrave (eds.), *Verbal Behavior and Learning: Problems and Processes.* New York: McGraw-Hill, 1963, 158–209.

Brown, R., and C. Hanlon. "Derivational Complexity and Order of Acquisition in Child Speech," in J. R. Hayes (ed.), *Cognition and the Development of Language.* New York: Wiley, 1970.

Brown, R., *et al. Psycholinguistics: Selected Papers by Roger Brown.* New York: Free Press, 1970.

Cazden, C. "Environmental Assistance to the Child's Acquisition of Grammar" (unpublished Ph. D. dissertation, Harvard University, 1965).

———. "Subcultural Differences in Child Language: An Interdisciplinary Review," *Merrill-Palmer Quarterly,* 12 (1966), 185–219.

Chomsky, N. *Language and Mind.* New York: Harcourt, Brace & World, 1968.

Gardner, R. A., and **B. T. Gardner**. "Teaching Sign Language to a Chimpanzee," *Science,* 165 (1969), 664–672.

Hayes, K. J., and **C. Hayes**. "The Intellectual Development of a Home Raised Chimpanzee," *Proceedings of the American Philosophical Society,* 95 (1951), 105–109.

Kellogg, W. N., and **L. A. Kellogg**. *The Ape and the Child.* New York: McGraw-Hill, 1933.

Kessel, F. "The Role of Syntax in Children's Comprehension from Ages Six to Twelve," *Monographs of the Society for Research in Child Development,* Vol. 35, No. 6 (1970).

Köhler, W. *The Mentality of Apes.* 2nd rev. ed. E. Winters (tr.). New York: Harcourt, Brace & World, 1927.

Lenneberg, E. *The Biological Foundations of Language.* New York: Wiley, 1967.

Premack, D. "A Functional Analysis of Language," *Journal of the Experimental Analysis of Behavior,* 14 (1970), 107–125.

8

Aronfreed, J. *Conduct and Conscience: The Socialization of Internalized Control over Behavior.* New York: Academic Press, Inc., 1968.

———. "The Effects of Experimental Socialization Paradigms upon Two Moral Responses to Transgression," *Journal of Abnormal and Social Psychology,* 66 (1963), 437–448.

Aronfreed, J., and **R. Leff**. "The Effects of Intensity of Punishment and Complexity of Discrimination Upon the Learning of Internalized Suppression" (unpublished manuscript, University of Pennsylvania, 1963).

Bandura, A. "Influence of Models' Reinforcement Contingencies on the Acquisition of Imitative Responses," *Journal of Personality and Social Psychology,* 1 (1965), 589–595.

Bandura, A., and **R. H. Walters**. *Social Learning and Personality Development.* New York: Holt, Rinehart and Winston, 1963.

Freud, S. *The Basic Writings of Sigmund Freud.* A. A. Brill (tr.). New York: Modern Library, 1938.

———. *Collected Papers.* J. Riviere (tr.). New York: Psycho-Analytical Press, 1924–1925.

———. *The Ego and the Id.* Rev. ed. J. Strachey (tr.). New York: Norton, 1962.

———. *An Outline of Psychoanalysis.* J. Strachey (tr.). New York: Norton, 1949.

———. "Some Psychical Consequences of the Anatomical Distinction Between the Sexes," in J. Strachey (ed.), *The Standard Edition of the Complete Psychological Works of Sigmund Freud.* London: Hogarth Press, Vol. 19, 1961, pp. 243–258.

Grinder, R. "Relations Between Behavioral and Cognitive Dimensions of Conscience in Middle Childhood," *Child Development,* 35 (1964), 881–893.

Haan, N., **M. B. Smith**, and **J. Block**. "The Moral Reasoning of Young Adults: Political-Social Behavior, Family Background and Personality Correlates," *Journal of Personality and Social Psychology,* 10 (1968), 183–201.

Hartshorne, H., and **M. A. May**. "Studies in Deceit," in Columbia University, Teachers College, *Studies in the Nature of Character.* New York: Macmillan, Vol. I, 1928–1930.

Hartshorne, H., **M. A. May**, and **F. K. Shuttleworth**. "Studies in the Organization of Character," in Columbia University, Teachers College, *Studies in the Nature of Character.* New York: Macmillan, Vol. III, 1928–1930.

Hartshorne, H., **M. A. May**, and **J. B. Maller**. "Studies in Service and Self Concept," in Columbia University, Teachers College, *Studies in the Nature of Character.* New York: Macmillan, Vol. II, 1928–1930.

Hoffman, M. L., and **H. D. Saltzstein**. "Parent Discipline and the Child's Moral Development," *Journal of Personality and Social Psychology,* 5 (1967), 45–57.

Kohlberg, L. "Development of Moral Character and Moral Ideology," in M. L. Hoffman and L. W. Hoffman (eds.), *Review of Child Development Research.* New York: Russell Sage Foundation, 1964, Vol. I, 383–431.

———. "Moral Development and Identification," in H. Stevenson (ed.), *Child Psychology 62nd Yearbook of the National Society for the Study of Education.* Chicago: University of Chicago Press, 1963, 277–332.

———. "Stage and Sequence: The Cognitive-Developmental Approach to Socialization," in D. A. Goslin (ed.), *Handbook of Socialization Theory and Research.* Chicago: Rand McNally, 1969.

Krebs, D. L. "Altruism, an Examination of the Concept and a Review of the Literature," *Psychological Bulletin,* 73 (1970), 258–302.

Krebs, R. L. "Some Relationships Between Moral Judgment, Attention and Resistance to Temptation" (unpublished Ph. D. dissertation, University of Chicago, 1967).

MacFarlane, J., **L. Allen**, and **M. Honzik**. *A Developmental Study of Behavior Problems of Normal Children Between Twenty-One Months and Four Years.* Berkeley: University of California Press, 1954.

McDougall, W. *An Introduction to Social Psychology.* London: Methuen, 1908.

Miller, N., and **J. Dollard**. *Social Learning and Imitation.* New Haven, Conn.: Yale University Press, 1941.

Mowrer, O. H. *Learning Theory and the Symbolic Processes.* New York: Wiley, 1960.

Piaget, J. *The Child's Conception of the World.* New York: Harcourt, Brace & World, 1928.

Schachter, S. "The Interaction of Cognitive and Physiological Determinants of Emotional State," in L. Berkowitz (ed.), *Advances in Experimental Social Psychology.* New York: Academic Press, Inc., 1964, Vol. 1, pp. 49–80.

Sears, R. R., **E. E. Maccoby**, and **H. Levin**. *Patterns of Child Rearing.* New York: Harper & Row, 1957.

Sears, R. R., **L. Rau**, and **R. Alpert**. *Identification and Child-Rearing.* Stanford, Calif.: Stanford University Press, 1965.

Terman, L. M., and **L. E. Tyler**. "Psychological Sex Differences," in L. Carmichael (ed.), *Manual of Child Psychology.* New York: Wiley, 1946, pp. 1064–1114.

Turiel, E. "Developmental Processes in the Child's Moral Thinking," in P. Mussen, J. Langer, and M. Covington (eds.), *Trends and Issues in Developmental Psychology.* New York: Holt, Rinehart and Winston, 1969.

Whiting, J. W. M. "Resource Mediation and Learning by Identification," in I. Iscoe and H. W. Stevenson (eds.), *Personality Development in Children.* Austin: University of Texas Press, 1960, pp. 112–126.

9

Craik, K. *The Nature of Psychology.* S. L. Sherwood (ed.). London: Cambridge University Press, 1966.

Doyle, W. "Recognition of Sloppy, Hand-Printed Characters," in *Proceedings of the Western Joint Computer Conference.* Palo Alto, Calif.: Western Joint Computer Conference, 1960, 133–142.

Hubel, D. H., and **T. N. Wiesel**. "Receptive Fields, Binocular Interaction and Functional Architecture in the Cat's Visual Cortex," *Journal of Physiology,* 160 (1962), 106–154.

Lettvin, J. Y., *et al.* "What the Frog's Eye Tells the Frog's Brain," *Proceedings of the Institute of Radio Engineers,* 47 (1959), 1940–1951.

Miller, G. "The Magic Number Seven Plus or Minus Two," *Psychological Review,* 63 (1956), 81–97.

Newell, A., **J. C. Shaw**, and **H. A. Simon**. "Elements of a Theory of Human Problem Solving," *Psychological Review,* 65 (1958), 151–166.

Pollack, I. "The Information of Elementary Auditory Displays," *Journal of the Acoustical Society of America,* 24 (1952), 745–749.

Thorpe, W. H. "Talking Birds and Mode of Action of Vocal Apparatus of Birds," *Proceedings of the Zoological Society of London,* 132 (1959), 441–445.

Tinker, M. A. "Recent Studies of Eye Movements in Reading," *Psychological Bulletin,* 54 (1958), 215–231.

Yarbus, A. L. *Eye Movements and Vision.* New York: Plenum, 1967.

10

Adams, J. A. *Human Memory.* New York: McGraw-Hill, 1967.

Bartlett, F. C. *Remembering: An Experimental and Social Study.* London: Cambridge University Press, 1932.

Brown, R. W., and **D. McNeill**. "The 'Tip of the Tongue' Phenomenon," *Journal of Verbal Learning and Verbal Behavior,* 5 (1966), 325–337.

Dallenbach, K. M. "Tables vs. Graphs as Means of Presenting Experimental Results," *American Journal of Psychology,* 76 (1963), 700–702.

De Groot, A. D. *Thought and Choice in Chess.* The Hague: Mouton, 1965.

———. "Perception and Memory Versus Thought: Some Old Ideas and Recent Findings," in B. Kleinmuntz (ed.), *Problem Solving: Research, Method and Theory.* New York: Wiley, 1966.

Ebbinghaus, H. *Memory: A Contribution to Experimental Psychology.* H. A. Ruger and C. E. Bussenius (trs.). New York: Teachers College, Columbia University, 1913.

Haber, R. N. "How We Remember What We See," *Scientific American,* 222 (1970), 104–112.

Haber, R. N., and L. G. Standing. "Direct Measures of Short Term Visual Storage," *The Quarterly Journal of Experimental Psychology,* 21 (1969), 43–54.

Hunter, I. *Memory.* Rev. ed. Baltimore: Penguin, 1964.

Inhelder, B. "Memory and Intelligence in the Child," in D. Elkind and J. H. Flavell (eds.), *Studies in Cognitive Development. Essays in Honor of Jean Piaget.* New York: Oxford University Press, 1969, pp. 337–364.

Kretch, D., R. S. Crutchfield, and **N. Livson.** *Elements of Psychology.* 2nd ed., New York: Knopf, 1969.

McGeoch, J. A. *The Psychology of Human Learning.* New York: Longmans, Green, 1942.

Murdock, B. B. "Serial Position Effect of Free Recall," *Journal of Experimental Psychology,* 64 (1962), 482–488.

Osgood, C. E. "Meaningful Similarity and Interference in Learning," *Journal of Experimental Psychology,* 36 (1946), 277–301.

———. "The Similarity Paradox in Human Learning: A Resolution," *Psychological Review,* 56 (1949), 132–143.

Peterson, L. R., and M. J. Peterson. "Short-Term Retention of Individual Verbal Items," *Journal of Experimental Psychology,* 58 (1959), 193–198.

Sperling, G. "The Information Available in Brief Visual Presentations," *Psychological Monographs,* Vol. 74, Whole No. 498 (1960).

Stromeyer, C. F., III. "Eidetikers," *Psychology Today,* 4 (1970), 76–80.

11

Bloom, B. S., and L. J. Broder. *Problem Solving Processes of College Students.* Chicago: University of Chicago Press, 1950.

Bruner, J. S., and H. J. Kenney. "Representation and Mathematics Learning," *Monographs of the Society for Research in Child Development,* 30 (1965), 50–59.

Chapman, L. J., and J. P. Chapman. "Atmosphere Effect Re-examined," in P. Wason and P. Johnson-Laird (eds.), *Thinking and Reasoning.* Baltimore: Penguin, 1968, pp. 83–92.

De Bono, E. *New Think: The Use of Lateral Thinking in the Generation of New Ideas.* New York: Basic Books, Inc., Publishers, 1968.

De Soto, C., M. London, and S. Handel. "Social Reasoning and Spatial Paralogic," *Journal of Personality and Social Psychology,* 2 (1965), 513–521.

Dominowski, R. L., and C. P. Duncan. "Anagram Solving as a Function of Bigram Frequency," *Journal of Verbal Learning and Verbal Behavior,* 33 (1964), 321–325.

Dunker, C. "On Problem Solving," *Psychological Monographs,* Vol. 58, Whole No. 270 (1945).

Glucksberg, S. "Functional Fixedness: Problem Solution as a Function of Observing Responses," *Psychonomic Science,* 1 (1964), 117–118.

Henle, M. "On the Relation Between Logic and Thinking," in P. Wason and P. Johnson-Laird (eds.), *Thinking and Reasoning.* Baltimore: Penguin, 1968, pp. 93–107.

Luchins, A. S. "Classroom Experiments on Mental Set," *American Journal of Psychology,* 59 (1946), 295–298.

Luchins, A. S., and E. H. Luchins. *Rigidity of Behavior: A Variational Approach to the Effect of Einstellung.* Eugene: University of Oregon Books, 1959.

Mayzner, M. S., and M. E. Tresselt. "Anagram Solution Times: A Function of Multiple Solution Anagrams," in C. P. Duncan (ed.), *Thinking: Current Experimental Studies.* Philadelphia: Lippincott, 1967, pp. 96–106.

Newell, A., J. C. Shaw, and H. A. Simon. "Elements of a Theory of Human Problem Solving," *Psychological Review,* 65 (1958), 151–166.

Scheerer, M. "Problem Solving," *Scientific American,* 208 (1963), 118–128.

Simon, H. A., and A. Newell. "Human Problem Solving: The State of the Theory in 1970," *American Psychologist,* 26 (1971), 145–159.

Staats, A. W. "Verbal and Instrumental Response-Hierarchies and Their Relationship to Problem Solving," *American Journal of Psychology,* 70 (1957), 442–446.

Wason, P. C. "Reasoning About a Rule," *Quarterly Journal of Experimental Psychology,* 20 (1968), 273–281.

12

Blough, D. S. "Animal Psychophysics," *Scientific American,* 205 (1961), 113–122.

Boring, E. G. "Isochromatic Contours," *American Journal of Psychology,* 39 (1937), 130–134.

———. *Sensation and Perception in the History of Experimental Psychology.* New York: Appleton-Century-Crofts, 1942.

Bruner, J. S. "On Perceptual Readiness," *Psychological Review,* 64 (1957), 123–152.

Green, D. M., and J. A. Swets. *Signal Detection Theory and Psychophysics.* New York: Wiley, 1966.

Holway, A. H., and C. C. Pratt. "The Weber-Ratio for Intensive Discrimination," *Psychological Review,* 43 (1936), 322–340.

Lettvin, J. Y., *et al.* "What the Frog's Eye Tells the Frog's Brain," *Proceedings of the Institute of Radio Engineers,* 47 (1959), 1940–1951.

Stevens, S. S. "The Attributes of Tones," *Proceedings of the National Academy of Sciences,* 20 (1934), 457–459.

———. "The Surprising Simplicity of Sensory Metrics," *American Psychologist,* 17 (1962), 29–39.

Swets, J. A. "Is There a Sensory Threshold?" *Science,* 134 (1961), 168–177.

Woodworth, R. S., and H. Schlosberg. *Experimental Psychology.* New York: Holt, Rinehart and Winston, 1954.

13

Bare, J. "The Specific Hunger for Sodium Chloride in Normal and Adrenalectomized White Rats," *Journal of Comparative and Physiological Psychology,* 42 (1949), 242–253.

Beebe-Center, J. G. "Standards for Use of the Gust Scale," *Journal of Psychology,* 28 (1949), 411–419.

Békésy, G. von, and W. A. Rosenblith. "The Mechanical Properties of the Ear," in S. S. Stevens (ed.), *Handbook of Experimental Psychology.* New York: Wiley, 1951, pp. 1075–1115.

Geldard, F. A. *The Human Senses.* New York: Wiley, 1953.

Hecht, S., C. Haig, and G. Wald. "The Dark Adaptation of Retinal Fields of Different Size and Location," *Journal of General Physiology,* 19 (1935), 321–339.

Henning, H. *Der Geruch.* 2nd ed. Leipzig: Barth, 1924.

Hurvich, L. M., and D. Jameson. "Some Quantitative Aspects of an Opponent-Colors Theory: II. Brightness, Saturation, and Hue in Normal and Dichromatic Vision," *Journal of the Optical Society of America,* 45 (1955), 602–616.

Pfaffman, C. "Taste and Smell," in S. S. Stevens (ed.), *Handbook of Experimental Psychology.* New York: Wiley, 1951, pp. 1143–1171.

Ratliff, F., and L. A. Riggs. "Involuntary Motions of the Eye During Monocular Fixation," *Journal of Experimental Psychology,* 40 (1950), 687–701.

Richter, C. P. "Total Self-Regulatory Functions in Animals and Human Beings," *The Harvey Lectures,* 38 (1942), 63–103.

Riggs, L. A., F. Ratliff, J. C. Cornsweet, and T. N. Cornsweet. "The Disappearance of Steadily Fixated Test Objects," *Journal of the Optical Society of America,* 43 (1953), 495–501.

Stevens, S. S. "On the Psychophysical Law," *Psychological Review,* 64 (1957), 153–181.

———. "Volume and Intensity of Tones," *American Journal of Psychology,* 46 (1934), 397–408.

Stevens, S. S., and H. Davis. *Hearing: Its Psychology and Physiology.* New York: Wiley, 1938.

Stevens, S. S., and E. B. Newman. "The Localization of Actual Sources of Sound," *American Journal of Psychology,* 48 (1936), 297–306.

Stuhlman, O., Jr. *An Introduction to Biophysics.* New York: Wiley, 1943.

Valois, R. L de. "Neural Processing of Visual Information," in R. W. Russell (ed.), *Frontiers in Physiological Psychology.* New York: Academic Press, Inc., 1966, pp. 51–91.

Wald, G. "The Receptors of Human Color Vision," *Science,* 145 (1964), 1007–1016.

Wever, E. G. *Theory of Hearing.* New York: Wiley, 1949.

14

Allport, F. H. *Theories of Perception and the Concept of Structure.* New York: Wiley, 1955.

Bower, T. G. R. "The Visual World of Infants," *Scientific American,* 215 (1966), 80–92.

Gelb, A. "Die 'Farbenkonstanz' der Sehdinge," *Handbuch der Normalische und Pathologische Physiologie,* I (1929), 594–678.

Gibson, E. J. *Principles of Perceptual Learning and Development.* New York: Appleton-Century-Crofts, 1969.

Gibson, E. J., and **R. D. Walk.** "The Effect of Prolonged Exposure to Visually Presented Patterns on Learning to Discriminate Them," *Journal of Comparative and Physiological Psychology,* 49 (1956), 239–242.

———. "The Visual Cliff," *Scientific American,* 202 (1960), 64–71.

Gibson, E. J., R. D. Walk, and **T. J. Tighe.** "Enhancement and Deprivation of Visual Stimulation During Rearing as Factors in Visual Discrimination Learning," *Journal of Comparative and Physiological Psychology,* 52 (1959), 74–81.

Gibson, J. J. *The Senses Considered as Perceptual Systems.* Boston: Houghton Mifflin, 1966.

Held, R., and **J. Bossom.** "Neonatal Deprivation and Adult Rearrangement: Complementary Techniques for Analyzing Plastic Sensory-Motor Coordinations," *Journal of Comparative and Physiological Psychology,* 54 (1961), 33–37.

Held, R., J. Bossum, and **A. Hein.** "Movement-Produced Stimulation in the Development of Visually Guided Behavior," *Journal of Comparative and Physiological Psychology,* 56 (1963), 872–876.

Helmholtz, H. von. "Über das Sehan des Menschen," *Vorträge und Reden,* 1 (1884), 365–396.

Hochberg, J. *Perception.* Englewood Cliffs, N.J.: Prentice-Hall, 1964.

Katona, G. "Color-Contrast and Color-Constancy," *Journal of Experimental Psychology,* 18 (1935), 49–63.

Koffka, K. *Principles of Gestalt Psychology.* New York: Harcourt, Brace & World, 1963.

Kohler, I. "Experiment With Goggles," *Scientific American,* 206 (1962), 62–86.

Köhler, W. *Gestalt Psychology.* 2nd ed. New York: Liveright Publishing Corp., 1947.

Lashley, K. S., K. L. Chow, and **J. Semmes.** "An Examination of the Electrical Field Theory of Cerebral Integration," *Psychological Review,* 58 (1951), 123–136.

Perls, F., R. F. Hefferline, and **P. Goodman.** *Gestalt Therapy.* New York: Julian Press Inc., 1951.

Riesen, A. H. "Arrested Vision," *Scientific American,* 183 (1950), 16–19.

———. "The Development of Visual Perception in Man and Chimpanzee," *Science,* 106 (1947), 107–108.

Riesen, A. H., and **L. Aarons.** "Visual Movement and Intensity Discrimination in Cats After Early Deprivation of Pattern Vision," *Journal of Comparative and Physiological Psychology,* 52 (1959), 142–149.

Sperry, R. W., and **N. Miner.** "Pattern Perception Following Insertion of Mica Plates Into Visual Cortex," *Journal of Comparative and Physiological Psychology,* 48 (1955), 463–469.

Stratton, G. M. "Some Preliminary Experiments on Vision Without Inversion of the Retinal Image," *Psychological Review,* 3 (1896), 611–617.

Thiery, A. "Über geometrisch-Optische Tauschungen," *Philosophisches Studien,* 12 (1896), 67–126.

Walk, R. D., and **E. J. Gibson.** "A Comparative and Analytical Study of Visual Depth Perception," *Psychological Monographs,* Vol. 75, Whole No. 519 (1961).

Walk, R. D., E. J. Gibson, and **T. J. Tighe.** "Behavior of Light- and Dark-Reared Rats on a Visual Cliff," *Science,* 126 (1957), 80–81.

Woodworth, R. S., and **H. Schlosberg.** *Experimental Psychology.* 2nd ed. New York: Holt, Rinehart and Winston, 1954.

15

Aserinsky, E., and **N. Kleitman.** "Regularly Occurring Periods of Eye Motility, and Concomitant Phenomena During Sleep." *Science,* 118 (1953), 273–274.

Bexton, W. H., W. Heron, and **T. H. Scott.** "Effects of Decreased Variation in the Sensory Environment." *Canadian Journal of Psychology,* 8 (1954), 70–76.

Current Research on Sleep and Dreams. Washington, D.C.: Government Printing Office. United States Department of Health, Education, and Welfare, Public Health Service Publication No. 1389.

Deikman, A. J. "Experimental Meditation." *Journal of Nervous and Mental Disease,* 136 (1963), 329–373. Reprinted in C. T. Tart, pp. 199–218.

Dement, W. C. "An Essay on Dreams: The Role of Physiology in Understanding Their Nature," in F. Barron *et al., New Directions in Psychology,* Vol. II. New York: Holt, Rinehart and Winston, 1965.

Dunlap, K. "Repetition in the Breaking of Habits." *Science Monographs,* 30 (1930), 66–70.

Erickson, M. H. "An Experimental Investigation of the Hypnotic Subject's Apparent Ability to Become Unaware of Stimuli." *Journal of General Psychology,* 31 (1944), 191–212. Reprinted in R. E. Shor and M. T. Orne, pp. 325–344.

Freeman, T., J. L. Cameron, and **A. McGhie.** *Chronic Schizophrenia.* New York: International Universities Press, 1958.

Freud, S. *The Interpretation of Dreams.* New York: Basic Books, Inc., Publishers, 1955.

Gallup, G. G., Jr. "It's Done with Mirrors—Chimps and Self-Concept." *Psychology Today,* 4 (1971), 58–61.

Galton, F. *Inquiries into Human Faculty and Its Development.* New York: Everyman, 1911. Originally published in 1883.

Gazzaniga, M. S. "The Split Brain in Man." *Scientific American,* 217 (1967), 24–29.

Hall, C. S. "A Cognitive Theory of Dream Symbols." *Journal of General Psychology,* 48 (1953), 169–186.

Hilgard, E. R. *Hypnotic Susceptibility.* New York: Harcourt, Brace & World, 1965.

James, W. *Principles of Psychology.* New York: Dover Publications, Inc., 1950. Originally published in 1890.

Jouvet, M. "Recherches sur les structures nerveuses et les mecanismes responsables de differentes phases du sommeil physiologique." *Archives italiennes de biologie,* 100 (1962), 125–206.

———. "The Stages of Sleep." *Scientific American,* 216 (1967), 62–72.

Kasamatsu, A., and **T. Hirai.** "An Electroencephalographic study on the Zen meditation (Zazen)." *Folia Psychiatrica et Neurologica Japonica,* 20 (1966), 315–336. Reprinted in C. T. Tart, pp. 489–501.

Kleitman, N. *Sleep and Wakefulness,* rev. ed. Chicago: University of Chicago Press, 1963.

Laing, R. D. *The Divided Self.* Baltimore, Penguin, 1965.

Orne, M. T. "The Nature of Hypnosis: Artifact and Essence." *Journal of Abnormal and Social Psychology,* 58 (1959), 277–299. Reprinted also in R. E. Shor and M. T. Orne, pp. 89–123.

Osmond, H. "A Review of the Clinical Effects of Psychotomimetic Agents." *Annals of the New York Academy of Science,* 66 (1957), 418–434.

Pattie, F. A. "A Report of Attempts to Produce Uniocular Blindness by Hypnotic Suggestion." *British Journal of Medical Psychology,* 15 (1935), 230–241. Reprinted in R. E. Shor and M. T. Orne, pp. 69–79.

Penfield, W. *The Excitable Cortex in Conscious Man.* Springfield, Ill.: Charles C Thomas, Publisher, 1958.

———. "Consciousness, Memory, and Man's Conditioned Reflexes," in K. H. Pribram (ed.), *On the Biology of Learning.* New York: Harcourt, Brace & World, 1969.

Shor, R. E., and **M. T. Orne** (eds.). *The Nature of Hypnosis.* New York: Holt, Rinehart and Winston, 1965.

Sperry, R. W. The Great Cerebral Commissure. *Scientific American,* 210 (1964).

———. "Hemisphere Deconnection and Unity in Conscious Awareness." *American Psychologist,* 23 (1968), 723–733.

———. "A Modified Concept of Consciousness." *Psychological Review,* 76 (1969), 532–536.

Tart, C. T. (ed.). *Altered States of Consciousness.* New York: Wiley, 1969.

Thigpen, C. H., and **H. Cleckley.** "A Case of Multiple Personality." *Journal of Abnormal and Social Psychology,* 49 (1954), 135–151. Reprinted in R. E. Shor and M. T. Orne, pp. 407–433.

———. *The Three Faces of Eve.* New York: McGraw-Hill, 1957.

Wallace, R. K., and **H. Benson.** "The Physiology of Meditation." *Scientific American,* 226 (1972), 84–90.

Weil, T., Zinberg, E., and **Nelsen, J. M.** "Clinical and Psychological Effects of Marihuana in Man." *Science,* 162 (1968), 1234–1242.

West, L. J. (ed.). *Hallucinations.* New York: Grune and Stratton, Inc., 1962.

Zuckerman, M., and **N. Cohen.** "Sources of Reports of Visual and Auditory Sensations in Perceptual-Isolation Experiments." *Psychological Bulletin,* 62 (1964), 1–20.

16

Broca, P. "Remarques sur la Siège de la Faculté du Langage Articulé, Suivies d'une Observation d'Amphémie (Perte de la Parole)," *Bulletin de la Société Anatomique de Paris. Série 2,* 6 (1861), 330–357.

Crick, F. H. C. "The Genetic Code," *Scientific American,* 207 (1962), 66–74.

Denny, M. R., and **S. C. Ratner.** *Comparative Psychology: Research in Animal Behavior.* Rev. ed. Homewood, Ill.: Dorsey Press, 1970.

DiCara, L. V., and **J. M. Weiss.** "Effect of Heart-Rate Learning Under Curare on Subsequent Noncurarized Avoidance Learning," *Journal of Comparative and Physiological Psychology,* 69 (1969), 368–374.

Dobzhansky, T. *Genetics and the Origin of Species.* 3rd ed. New York: Columbia University Press, 1951.

Engel, B. T., and **S. P. Hansen.** "Operant Conditioning of Heart Rate Slowing," *Psychophysiology,* 3 (1966), 176–187.

Eysenck, H. J., and **D. B. Prell.** "The Inheritance of Neuroticism: An Experimental Study," *Journal of Mental Science,* 97 (1951), 441–465.

Fuller, J. L., and **W. R. Thompson.** *Behavior Genetics.* New York: Wiley, 1960.

Galambos, R. A. "A Glia-Neural Theory of Brain Function," *Proceedings of the National Academy of Sciences,* 47 (1961), 129–136.

Gottesman, I. I. "Heritability of Personality: A Demonstration," *Psychological Monographs,* Vol. 77, No. 9 (1963).

Grossman, S. P. "Behavioral Effects of Direct Chemical Stimulation of Central Nervous System Structures," *Journal of Neuropharmacology,* 3 (1964), 45–58.

———. "Some Neurochemical Aspects of the Central Regulation of Thirst," in M. J. Wayner (ed.), *Thirst: Proceedings of the First International Symposium on Thirst in the Regulation of Body Water.* New York: Pergamon Press, Inc., 1964, pp. 487–514.

Hagbarth, K. E., and **E. Kugelberg.** Plasticity of the Human Abdominal Skin Reflex," *Brain,* 81 (1958), 305–318.

Hernandez-Péon, R. "Reticular Mechanisms of Sensory Control," in W. A. Rosenblith (ed.), *Sensory Communication.* Cambridge, Mass.: The MIT Press, 1961, pp. 497–520.

Hirsch, J. (ed.). *Behavior-Genetic Analysis.* New York: McGraw-Hill, 1967.

Hodgkin, A. L., and **A. F. Huxley.** "Resting and Action Potentials in Single Nerve Fibers," *Journal of Physiology,* 104 (1945), 176–195.

Hooker, D. *The Prenatal Origin of Behavior.* Hafner, 1969.

Hyden, H., and **E. Egyhazi.** "Glial RNA Changes During a Learning Experiment in Rats," *Proceedings of the National Academy of Sciences,* 49 (1963), 618–624.

Kallman, F. J. *The Genetics of Schizophrenia.* New York: J. J. Augustin, Inc.—Publisher, 1938.

Kandel, E. R. "Nerve Cells and Behavior," *Scientific American,* 223 (1970), 57–70.

Katz, B. "The Nerve Impulse," *Scientific American,* 185 (1952), 55–64.

Kesey, K. *One Flew Over the Cuckoo's Nest.* New York: Viking, 1962.

Moniz, E. *Tentatives Operatoires dans le Traitement de Certaines Psychoses.* Paris: Masson, 1936.

Myers, R. E. "Function of Corpus Callosum in Interocular Transfer," *Brain,* 79 (1956), 358–363.

Newman, H. H., F. N. Freeman, and **K. J. Holzinger.** *Twins: A Study of Heredity and Environment.* Chicago: University of Chicago Press, 1937.

Pavlov, I. P. *Conditioned Reflexes.* G. V. Anrep (tr.). London: Oxford University Press, 1927.

Penfield, W., and **T. Rasmussen.** *The Cerebral Cortex of Man.* New York: Macmillan, 1950.

Penfield, W., and **L. Roberts.** *Speech and Brain Mechanisms.* Princeton, N.J.: Princeton University Press, 1959.

Skodak, M., and **H. M. Skeels.** "A Final Follow-up of One Hundred Adopted Children," *Journal of Genetic Psychology,* 75 (1949), 85–125.

Sokolov, E. N. "Neuronal Models and the Orienting Reflex," in M. A. B. Brazier (ed.), *The Central Nervous System and Behavior.* New York: Josiah Macy, Jr., Foundation, 1960, pp. 187–276.

Watson, J. D. *Double Helix: Being a Personal Account of the Discovery of the Structure of DNA.* New York: Atheneum Publishers, 1968.

Willows, A. O. D. "Giant Brain Cells in Mollusks," *Scientific American,* 224 (1971), 69–75.

17

Arnold, M. *Emotion and Personality.* New York: Columbia University Press, 1960.

Ax, A. F. "The Physiological Differentiation Between Fear and Anger in Humans," *Psychosomatic Medicine,* 15 (1953), 433–442.

Bishop, M. P., S. T. Elder, and **R. G. Heath.** "Intracranial Self-Stimulation in Man," *Science,* 140 (1963), 394–396.

Block, J. "Studies in the Phenomenology of Emotions," *Journal of Abnormal and Social Psychology,* 54 (1957), 358–363.

Brady, J. V. "Ulcers in 'Executive' Monkeys," *Scientific American,* 199 (1958), 95–100.

Cannon, W. B. *Bodily Changes in Pain, Hunger, Fear, and Rage.* 2nd ed. New York: Appleton-Century-Crofts, 1929.

Darwin, C. *The Expression of the Emotions in Man and Animals.* Chicago: University of Chicago Press, 1965.

Delgado, J. M. R. *Physical Control of the Mind.* New York: Harper & Row, 1969.

Delgado, J. M. R., W. W. Roberts, and **N. E. Miller.** "Learning Motivated by Electrical Stimulation of the Brain," *American Journal of Physiology,* 179 (1954), 587–593.

Engen, T., N. Levy, and **H. Schlosberg.** "The Dimensional Analysis of a New Series of Facial Expressions." *Journal of Experimental Psychology,* 55 (1958), 454–458.

Frijda, N. H. "Recognition of Emotion." In L. Berkowitz (ed.), *Advances in Experimental Social Psychology.* New York: Academic Press, Vol. IV, 1969, pp. 167–223.

———. "Emotion and Recognition of Emotion." In M. B. Arnold (ed.), *Feelings and Emotions.* New York: Academic Press, 1970, pp. 241–250.

James, W., and **G. G. Lange.** *The Emotions.* Baltimore: The Williams & Wilkins Co., 1922.

Lazarus, R. S. "Cognitive and Personality Factors Underlying Threat and Coping." In M. H. Appley and R. Trumbull (eds.), *Psychological Stress.* New York: Appleton-Century-Crofts, 1967.

Leventhal, H. "The Emotions: A Basic Issue in Social Psychology." In C. Nemeth (ed.), *Social Psychology.* Chicago: Markham Publishing Co. (in press).

Lindsley, D. B. "Emotion," in S. S. Stevens (ed.), *Handbook of Experimental Psychology.* New York: Wiley, 1951, pp. 473–516.

Lorenz, K. *On Aggression.* New York: Harcourt, Brace and World, 1966.

Mandler, G. "Emotion," in *New Directions in Psychology.* New York: Holt, Rinehart and Winston, Vol. I, 1962, pp. 267–343.

Marañon, G. "Contribution à l'Etude de l'Action Emotive de l'Adrenalin," *Revue Française d'Endocrinologie,* 2 (1924), 301–325.

Miller, N. E. "Central Stimulation and Other New Approaches to Motivation and Reward," *American Psychologist,* 13 (1958), 100–108.

Olds, J. "Physiological Mechanisms of Reward," in M. R. Jones (ed.), *Nebraska Symposium on Motivation.* Lincoln: University of Nebraska Press, 1955, pp. 73–138.

———. "Self-Stimulation of the Brain," *Science,* 127 (1958), 315–323.

Olds, J., and **P. Milner.** "Positive Reinforcement Produced by Electrical Stimulation of the Septal Area and Other Regions of the Rat Brain," *Journal of Comparative and Physiological Psychology,* 47 (1954), 411–427.

Olds, J., and **M. E. Olds.** "Drives, Rewards and the Brain," in F. Barron *et al., New Directions in Psychology.* New York: Holt, Rinehart and Winston, Vol. II, 1965, pp. 327–410.

Osgood, C. E., G. J. Suci, and P. H. Tannenbaum. *The Measurement of Meaning.* Urbana, Ill.: University of Illinois Press, 1957.

Papez, J. W. "A Proposed Mechanism of Emotion," *Archives of Neurology and Psychiatry,* 38 (1937), 725–743.

Plutchik, R. *The Emotions: Facts, Theories, and a New Model.* New York: Random House, 1962.

Roberts, W. W. "Fear-Like Behavior Elicited From Dorsomedial Thalamus of Cat," *Journal of Comparative and Physiological Psychology,* 55 (1962), 191–197.

Schachter, S., and **J. E. Singer.** "Cognitive, Social and Physiological Determinants of Emotional State," *Psychological Review,* 69 (1962), 379–399.

Schachter, S., and **L. Wheeler.** "Epinephrine, Chlorpromazine and Amusement," *Journal of Abnormal and Social Psychology,* 65 (1962), 121–128.

Selye, H. *The Stress of Life.* New York: McGraw-Hill, 1956.

Sem-Jacobsen, C. W., and **A. Torkildsen.** "Depth Recording and Electrical Stimulation in the Human Brain," in E. R. Ramey and D. S. O'Doherty (eds.), *Electrical Studies on the Unanesthetized Brain.* New York: Hoeber Medical Books of Harper & Row, 1960, pp. 275–287.

Watson, J. B., and **R. Rayner.** "Conditional Emotional Reactions," *Journal of Experimental Psychology,* 3 (1920), 1–14.

Weiss, J. M. "Effects of Coping Responses on Stress," *Journal of Comparative and Physiological Psychology,* 65 (1968), 251–260.

Woodworth, R. S., and **H. Schlosberg.** *Experimental Psychology.* Rev. ed. New York: Holt, Rinehart and Winston, 1954. Chapter 5.

18

Andersson, B., and **B. Larsson.** "Influence of Local Temperature Changes in the Preoptic Area and Rostral Hypothalamus on the Regulation of Food and Water Intake," *Acta Physiologica Scandinavica,* 52 (1961), 75–89.

Azrin, N. H., R. Hutchinson, and **R. D. Sallery.** "Pain-Aggression Toward Inanimate Objects," *Journal of the Experimental Analysis of Behavior,* 7 (1964), 223–228.

Coons, E. E. "Motivational Correlates of Eating Elicited by Electrical Stimulation in the Hypothalamic Feeding Area" (unpublished Ph.D. dissertation, Yale University, 1964).

Davis, D. "Self-Selection of Diet by Newly Weaned Infants," *American Journal of Diseases of Children,* 36 (1928), 651–679.

Davis, J. D., and **N. E. Miller.** "A Technique for Mixing the Blood of Unanesthetized Rats," *Journal of Applied Physiology,* 21 (1966), 1873–1874.

Davis, J. D., *et al.* "Disappearance of a Humoral Satiety Factor During Food Deprivation," *Journal of Comparative and Physiological Psychology,* 75 (1971), 476–482.

———. "Inhibition of Food Intake by a Humoral Factor," *Journal of Comparative and Physiological Psychology,* 67 (1969), 407–414.

Delgado, J. M. R. "Aggressive Behavior Evoked by Radio Stimulation in Monkey Colonies," *American Zoologist,* 6 (1966), 669–681.

Ferguson, N. B., and **R. E. Keesey.** "Comparison of Ventromedial Hypothalamic Lesion Effects Upon Feeding and Lateral Hypothalamic Self-Stimulation in the Female Rat," *Journal of Comparative and Physiological Psychology,* 74 (1971), 263–271.

Fisher, A. E. "Maternal and Sexual Behavior Induced by Intracranial Chemical Stimulation," *Science,* 124 (1956), 228–229.

Hebb, D. O. *A Textbook of Psychology.* Philadelphia: W. B. Saunders Company, 1966.

Hellon, R. F., J. D. Hardy, and **K. Sutherland.** "Temperature Sensitive Neurons in the Dog's Hypothalamus," *The Physiologist,* 6 (1963), 199.

Hervey, G. R. "The Effects of Lesions in the Hypothalamus in Parabiotic Rats," *Journal of Physiology,* 145 (1959), 336–352.

Hoebel, B. G. "Feeding and Self-Stimulation," *Annals of the New York Academy of Sciences,* 157 (1969), 758–778.

Miller, N. E. "Learnable Drives and Rewards," in S. S. Stevens (ed.), *Handbook of Experimental Psychology.* New York: Wiley, 1951, pp. 435–472.

———. "Learning and Performance Motivated by Direct Stimulation of the Brain," in D. E. Sheer (ed.), *Electrical Stimulation of the Brain.* Austin: University of Texas Press, 1961, pp. 387–397.

Miller, N. E., C. Bailey, and **J. Stevenson.** "Decreased 'Hunger' But Increased Food Intake Resulting From Hypothalamic Lesions," *Science,* 112 (1950), 256–259.

Miller, N. E., L. V. DiCara, and **G. Wolf.** "Homeostasis and Reward: T-Maze Learning Induced by Manipulating Antidiuretic Hormone," *American Journal of Physiology,* 215 (1968), 684–686.

Moyer, K. E. *The Physiology of Hostility.* Chicago: Markham Publishing Co., 1971.

Nisbett, R. E. "Determinants of Food Intake in Obesity," *Science,* 159 (1968), 1254–1255.

Pavlov, I. P. *Conditioned Reflexes.* G. V. Anrep (tr.). London: Oxford University Press, 1927.

Plotnick, R., D. Mir, and **J. M. R. Delgado.** "Aggression, Noxiousness, and Brain Stimulation in Unrestrained Rhesus Monkeys," in J. P. Scott and B. E. Eleftheriou (eds.), *The Physiology of Aggression and Defeat.* Chicago: University of Chicago Press, 1971, pp. 143–221.

Powley, T. L., and **R. E. Keesey.** "Relationship of Body Weight to the Lateral Hypothalamic Feeding Syndrome," *Journal of Comparative and Physiological Psychology,* 70 (1970), 25–36.

Quartermain, D., and **N. E. Miller.** "Sensory Feedback in Time Response of Drinking Elicited by Carbachol in Preoptic Area of Rat," *Journal of Comparative and Physiological Psychology,* 62 (1966), 350–353.

Rozin, P., and **J. Kalat.** "Specific Hungers and Poison Avoidance as Adaptive Specializations of Learning," *Psychological Review,* 78 (1971), 459–486.

Rozin, P. N., and **J. Mayer.** "Thermal Reinforcement and Thermoregulatory Behavior in the Goldfish, *Carassius Auratus,*" *Science,* 134 (1961), 942–943.

Schachter, S., R. Goldman, and **A. Gordon.** "Effects of Fear, Food Deprivation and Obesity on Eating," *Journal of Personality and Social Psychology,* 10 (1968), 91–97.

Sheffield, F. D., J. J. Wolff, and **R. Backer.** "Reward Value of Copulation Without Sex Drive Reduction," *Journal of Comparative and Physiological Psychology,* 44 (1951), 3–8.

Solomon, R. L., L. J. Kamin, and **L. C. Wynne.** "Traumatic Avoidance Learning: The Outcome of Several Extinction Procedures With Dogs," *Journal of Abnormal and Social Psychology,* 48 (1953), 291–302.

Teitelbaum, P. "Disturbances in Feeding and Drinking Behavior After Hypothalamic Lesions," in M. R. Jones (ed.), *Nebraska Symposium on Motivation.* Lincoln: University of Nebraska Press, 1961, pp. 39–69.

Verney, E. B. "The Antidiuretic Hormone and the Factors Which Determine Its Release," *Proceedings of the Royal Society of London. Series B.* 135 (1947), 25–106.

Wasman, M., and **J. P. Flynn.** "Directed Attack Elicited From Hypothalamus," *Archives of Neurology,* 6 (1962), 220–227.

Weiss, B., and **V. G. Laties.** "Behavioral Thermoregulation," *Science,* 133 (1961), 1338–1343.

Whalen, R. E. "The Concept of Instinct," in J. L. McGaugh (ed.), *Psychobiology: Behavior From a Biological Perspective.* New York: Academic Press, Inc., 1971, pp. 53–72.

Whalen, R. E., and **D. A. Edwards.** "Hormonal Determinants of the Development of Masculine and Feminine Behavior in Male and Female Rats," *Anatomical Record,* 157 (1967), 173–180.

19

Atkinson, J. W. *An Introduction to Motivation.* Princeton, N.J.: Van Nostrand, 1964.

———. (ed.). *Motives in Fantasy, Action, and Society.* Princeton, N.J.: Van Nostrand, 1958.

Atkinson, J. W., and **N. T. Feather.** *A Theory of Achievement Motivation.* New York: Wiley, 1966.

Atkinson, J. W., and **G. H. Litwin.** "Achievement Motive and Test Anxiety Conceived as Motive to Approach Success and Motive to Avoid Failure," *Journal of Abnormal and Social Psychology,* 60 (1960), 52–63.

Atkinson, J. W., and **D. C. McClelland.** "The Projective Expression of Need. II. The Effect of Different Intensities of the Hunger Drive on Thematic Apperception," *Journal of Experimental Psychology,* 38 (1948), 643–658.

Berlyne, D. E. "The Arousal and Satiation of Perceptual Curiosity in the Rat," *Journal of Comparative and Physiological Psychology,* 48 (1955), 238–246.

———. *Conflict Arousal and Curiosity.* New York: McGraw-Hill, 1960.

———. "Novelty and Curiosity as Determinants of Exploratory Behavior," *British Journal of Psychology,* 41 (1950), 68–80.

Brown, J. S. *The Motivation of Behavior.* New York: McGraw-Hill, 1961.

Clark, R. A. "The Projective Measurement of Experimentally Induced Levels of Sexual Motivation," *Journal of Experimental Psychology,* 44 (1952), 391–399.

Cronbach, L. J. "The Two Disciplines of Scientific Psychology," *American Psychologist,* 12 (1957), 671–684.

Dollard, J. L., and **N. E. Miller.** *Personality and Psychotherapy.* New York: McGraw-Hill, 1950.

Feather, N. "Persistance in Relation to Achievement Motivation, Anxiety About Failure and Task Difficulty" (unpublished Ph.D. dissertation, University of Michigan, 1968).

Festinger, L. *A Theory of Cognitive Dissonance.* New York: Harper & Row, 1957.

French, E. G. "Motivation as a Variable in Work Partner Selection," *Journal of Abnormal and Social Psychology,* 53 (1956), 96–99.

French, E. G., and F. H. Thomas. "The Relation of Achievement Motivation to Problem-Solving Effectiveness," *Journal of Abnormal and Social Psychology,* 56 (1958), 45–48.

Freud, S. "Lecture Number Thirty-Three," in S. Freud, *New Introductory Lectures on Psychoanalysis.* J. Strachey (tr.). New York: Norton, 1933, pp. 153–186.

Harlow, H. F. "Motivation as a Factor in the Acquisition of New Responses," in M. R. Jones (ed.), *Current Theory and Research in Motivation: Symposium.* Lincoln: University of Nebraska Press, 1953, pp. 24–49.

Horner, M. "Femininity and Successful Achievement: A Basic Inconsistency," in J. Bardwick, *et al., Feminine Personality and Conflict.* Belmont, Calif.: Brooks/Cole Publishing Co., 1970, pp. 44–75.

———. "Sex Differences in Achievement Motivation and Performance in Competitive and Non-competitive Situations" (unpublished Ph.D. dissertation, University of Michigan, 1968).

Hull, C. L. *Principles of Behavior.* New York: Appleton-Century-Crofts, 1943.

Jones, M. R. (ed.). *Nebraska Symposium on Motivation.* Lincoln: University of Nebraska Press, 1955.

Lewin, K. *Field Theory in Social Science.* D. Cartwright (ed.). New York: Harper & Row, 1951.

Lowell, E. L. "The Effect of Need for Achievement on Learning and Speed of Performance," *Journal of Psychology,* 33 (1952), 31–40.

Maccoby, E. E. *The Development of Sex Differences.* Stanford, Calif.: Stanford University Press, 1963.

Mahone, C. H. "Fear of Failure and Unrealistic Vocational Aspiration," *Journal of Abnormal and Social Psychology,* 60 (1960), 253–261.

Maslow, A. H. *Motivation and Personality.* New York: Harper & Row, 1954.

———. *Toward a Psychology of Being.* Princeton, N.J.: Van Nostrand, 1962.

McClelland, D. C. *The Achieving Society.* Princeton, N.J.: Van Nostrand, 1961.

McClelland, D. C., *et al. The Achievement Motive.* New York: Appleton-Century-Crofts, 1953.

———, *et al.* "The Projective Expression of Need. IV. The Effect of the Need for Achievement on Thematic Apperception," *Journal of Experimental Psychology,* 39 (1949), 242–255.

McDougall, W. *An Introduction to Social Psychology.* Boston: Robert R. Luce, Inc., 1915.

McGregor, D. *The Human Side of Enterprise.* New York: McGraw-Hill, 1960.

Miller, N. E. "Studies of Fear as Acquirable Drive: I. Fear as Motivation and Fear-Reduction as Reinforcement in the Learning of New Responses," *Journal of Experimental Psychology,* 38 (1948), 89–101.

Montgomery, K. C. "The Relation Between Exploratory Behavior and Spontaneous Alternation in the White Rat," *Journal of Comparative and Physiological Psychology,* 44 (1951), 582–589.

Murray, H. *Explorations in Personality.* New York: Oxford University Press, 1938.

Scott, W. "The Avoidance of Threatening Material in Imaginative Behavior," *Journal of Abnormal and Social Psychology,* 52 (1956), 338–346.

Solomon, R. L., and L. C. Wynne. "Traumatic Avoidance Learning Acquisition in Normal Dogs," *Psychological Monographs,* Vol. 67, Whole No. 4 (1953).

Tolman, E. C. *Collected Papers in Psychology.* Berkeley: University of California Press, 1951.

———. *Behavior and Psychological Man.* Berkeley: University of California Press, 1951.

Walker, E., and R. Heyns. *The Anatomy for Conformity.* Englewood Cliffs, N.J.: Prentice-Hall, 1962.

Watson, J. B., and R. Rayner. "Conditioned Emotional Reactions," *Journal of Experimental Psychology,* 3 (1920), 1–14.

White, R. W. "Competence and the Psychosexual Stages of Development," in M. R. Jones (ed.), *Nebraska Symposium on Motivation.* Lincoln: University of Nebraska Press, 1960, pp. 97–144.

———. "Motivation Reconsidered: The Concept of Competence," *Psychological Review,* 66 (1959), 297–333.

20

Allport, G. W., and P. E. Vernon. *Studies in Expressive Movements.* New York: Macmillan, 1932.

Allport, G. W., P. E. Vernon, and G. Lindzey. *Study of Values: Manual.* Boston: Houghton Mifflin, 1960.

American Psychological Association. *Standards for Educational and Psychological Tests and Manuals.* Washington, D.C.: American Psychological Association, 1966.

Beck, S. J. *Rorschach's Test, Basic Processes.* New York: Grune & Stratton, Inc., Vol. I, 1944.

———. *Rorschach's Test, A Variety of Personality Pictures.* New York: Grune & Stratton, Inc., Vol. II, 1945.

———. *Rorschach's Test, Advances in Interpretation.* New York: Grune & Stratton, Inc., Vol. III, 1952.

Buros, O. K. (ed.). *The Fifth Mental Measurement Yearbook.* Highland Park, N.J.: Gryphon Press, 1959.

Cronbach, L. *Essentials of Psychological Testing.* New York: Harper & Row, 1960.

Drake, L. E., and E. R. Oetting. *An MMPI Codebook for Counselors.* Minneapolis: University of Minnesota Press, 1959.

Edwards, A. L. *Manual for the Personal Preference Schedule.* New York: Psychological Corp., 1953.

Hathaway, S. R., and P. E. Meehl. *An Atlas for the Clinical Use of the MMPI.* Minneapolis: University of Minnesota Press, 1951.

Herrnstein, R. "I.Q." *The Atlantic Monthly,* Vol. 228, No. 3 (Sept., 1971), 43–64.

Holtzman, W. H., J. S. Thorpe, J. O. Swartz, and E. W. Herron. *Inkblot Perception and Personality.* Austin: University of Texas Press, 1961.

Jackson, D. N. *Manual for the Personality Research Form.* Goshen, N.Y.: Research Psychologists Press, 1967.

Jensen, A. R. "How Much Can We Boost I.Q. and Scholastic Achievement?" *Harvard Educational Review,* Vol. 39, No. 1 (Winter, 1969), 1–123.

Klopfer, B., and D. M. Kelley. *The Rorschach Technique.* New York: Harcourt, Brace & World, 1946.

Machover, K. *Personality Projection in the Drawing of the Human Figure: A Method of Personality Investigation.* Springfield, Ill.: Charles C Thomas, Publisher, 1949.

Murray, H. A., *et al. Explorations in Personality.* New York: Oxford University Press, 1938.

Office of Strategic Services Assessment Staff. *Assessment of Men.* New York: Holt, Rinehart and Winston, 1948.

Spearman, C. *The Abilities of Man: Their Nature and Measurement.* Providence, R.I.: American Mathematical Society, 1927.

Terman, L. M. *The Measurement of Intelligence.* Boston: Houghton Mifflin, 1916.

Terman, L. M., and M. A. Merrill. *Measuring Intelligence.* Boston: Houghton Mifflin, 1937.

———. *Stanford-Binet Intelligence Scale.* Boston: Houghton Mifflin, 1960.

Wechsler, D. *Wechsler Adult Intelligence Scale Manual.* New York: Psychological Corp., 1955.

———. *The Measurement and Appraisal of Adult Intelligence.* 14th ed. Baltimore: The Williams & Wilkins Co., 1958.

21

Adler, A. "Individual Psychology," in C. Murchinson (ed.), *Psychologies of 1930.* Worcester, Mass.: Clark University Press, 1930, pp. 395–405.

———. *What Life Should Mean to You.* Alan Porter (ed.), Boston: Little, Brown, 1931.

Ansbacher, H. L., and R. Ansbacher. *The Individual Psychology of Alfred Adler.* New York: Basic Books, Inc., Publishers, 1956.

Breuer, J., and S. Freud. *Studies on Hysteria.* J. Strachey (tr.). New York: Basic Books Inc., Publishers, 1957.

Erikson, E. H. *Childhood and Society.* New York: Norton, 1950.

Freud, S. *Civilization and Its Discontents.* J. Strachey (tr.). New York: Norton, 1962.

———. *Collected Papers.* J. Riviere (tr.). New York: Psycho-Analytical Press, 1924–1925.

———. *The Interpretation of Dreams.* J. Strachey (tr.). New York: Science Editions, 1961.

Fromm, E. *Escape From Freedom.* New York: Holt, Rinehart and Winston, 1941.

———. *Man for Himself.* New York: Holt, Rinehart and Winston, 1947.

Hall, C. S., and **G. Lindzey.** *Theories of Personality.* New York: Wiley, 1957.

Jung, C. G. *Collected Works.* Princeton, N.J.: Princeton University Press, 1958–1967.

White, R. W. "Motivation Reconsidered: The Concept of Confidence," *Psychological Review,* 66 (1959), 297–333.

———. "Competence and the Psychosexual Stages of Development," in M. R. Jones (ed.), *Nebraska Symposium on Motivation.* Lincoln: University of Nebraska Press, 1960, pp. 97–144.

———. *Lives in Progress.* 2nd ed. New York: Holt, Rinehart and Winston, 1966.

Terman, L. M. "Were We Born That Way?" *World's Work,* 44 (1922), 655–660.

22

Allport, G. W. *Personality: A Psychological Interpretation.* New York: Holt, 1937.

———. *Becoming: Basic Considerations for a Psychology of Personality.* New Haven: Yale University Press, 1955.

———. *Pattern and Growth in Personality.* New York: Holt, Rinehart and Winston, 1961.

Costa, P. T., and **S. R. Maddi.** *Humanism and Personology: Allport, Maslow, and Murray.* Chicago: Aldine-Atherton (forthcoming).

Hall, C. S., and **G. Lindzey.** *Theories of Personality.* New York: Wiley, 1957.

Kelley, G. A. *The Psychology of Personal Construct.* New York: Norton, Vols. I and II, 1955.

Maslow A. *Motivation and Personality.* New York: Harper & Row, 1954.

———. "Deficiency Motivation and Growth Motivation," in M. R. Jones (ed.), *The Nebraska Symposium on Motivation.* Lincoln: University of Nebraska Press, 1955.

———. *Toward a Psychology of Being.* Princeton, N.J.: Van Nostrand, 1968.

Morgan, C. D., and **H. A. Murray.** "A Method for Investigating Fantasies: The Somatic Apperception Test," *Archives of Neurological Psychiatry,* Vol. 34 (1935), 289–306.

Murray, H. A., *et al. Explorations in Personality.* New York: Wiley, 1938.

Rogers, C. R. *On Becoming a Person.* Boston: Houghton Mifflin, 1961.

Skinner, B. F. *Science and Human Behavior.* New York: Macmillan, 1953.

Sullivan, H. S. *The Interpersonal Theory of Psychiatry.* New York: Norton, 1953.

23

Asch, S. E. "Forming Impressions of Personality," *Journal of Abnormal and Social Psychology,* 41 (1946), 258–290.

Backman, C. W., and **P. F. Secord.** "The Self and Role Selection," in C. Gordon and K. J. Gergen (eds.), *The Self in Social Interaction.* New York: Wiley, Vol. I, 1968, p. 285.

Birdwhistell, R. L. "Background to Kinesics, ETC," *A Review of General Semantics,* 13 (1955).

Bruner, J. S., D. Shapiro, and **R. Tagiuri.** "The Meaning of Traits in Isolation and Combination," in R. Tagiuri and L. Petrullo (eds.), *Person Perception and Interpersonal Behavior.* Stanford, Calif.: Stanford University Press, 1958, pp. 277–288.

Bruner, J. S., and **R. Tagiuri.** "The Perception of People," in G. Lindzey (ed.), *Handbook of Social Psychology.* Reading, Mass.: Addison-Wesley Publishing Co., Inc., Vol. II, 1954, pp. 634–654.

Burns, T. "Non-Verbal Communication," *Discovery,* 25 (1964), 30–37.

Cooley, C. H. *Human Nature and the Social Order.* New York: Scribner, 1922.

Davis, F. "The Cabdriver and His Fare: Facets of a Fleeting Relationship," *American Journal of Sociology,* 65 (1969), 158–165.

Davis, J. A. "Compositional Effects, Role Systems, and the Survival of Small Discussion Groups," in A. P. Hare, E. F. Borgatta, and R. F. Bales (eds.), *Small Groups: Studies in Social Interaction.* Rev. ed. New York: Knopf, 1966, pp. 637–647.

Davis, K. E., and **E. E. Jones.** "Changes in Interpersonal Perception as a Means of Reducing Cognitive Dissonance," *Journal of Abnormal and Social Psychology,* 61 (1960), 402–410.

Dornbusch, S. M., *et al.* "The Perceiver and Perceived: Their Relative Influence on Categories of Interpersonal Perception," *Journal of Personality and Social Psychology,* 1 (1965), 434–440.

Ekman, P., and **W. V. Friesen.** "Constants Across Cultures in the Face and Emotion," *Journal of Personality and Social Psychology,* 17 (1971), 124–129.

Exline, R. V., *et al.* "Visual Interaction in Relation to Machiavellianism and an Unethical Act," *American Psychologist,* 16 (1961), 396.

Exline, R. V., and **L. C. Winters.** "Affective Relations and Mutual Glances in Dyads," in S. S. Tomkins and C. E. Izard (eds.), *Affect, Cognition and Personality: Empirical Studies.* New York: Springer Publishing Co., Inc., 1965, pp. 319–350.

Fast, J. *Body Language.* New York: M. Evans & Co., Inc., 1970.

Gerard, H. B. "Some Determinants of Self-Evaluation," *Journal of Abnormal and Social Psychology,* 62 (1961), 288–293.

Gergen, K. J. "Interaction Goals and Personalistic Feedback as Factors Affecting the Presentation of Self" (unpublished Ph.D. dissertation, Duke University, 1962).

———. *The Psychology of Behavior Exchange.* Reading, Mass.: Addison-Wesley Publishing Co., Inc., 1969.

Gergen, K. J., and **B. Wishnov.** "Others' Self-Evaluations and Interaction Anticipation as Determinants of Self-Presentation," *Journal of Personality and Social Psychology,* 2 (1965), 348–358.

Goffman, E. *The Presentation of Self in Everyday Life.* Garden City, N.Y.: Doubleday, 1959.

———. "Presentation of Self to Others," in J. G. Manis and B. N. Meltzer (eds.), *Symbolic Interaction: A Reader in Social Psychology.* Boston: Allyn & Bacon, Inc., 1967, pp. 220–231.

———. *Stigma: Notes on the Management of Spoiled Identity.* Englewood Cliffs, N.J.: Prentice-Hall, 1963.

Hall, E. T. *The Hidden Dimension.* New York: Doubleday Anchor, 1969.

———*The Silent Language.* New York: Fawcett World Library, 1959.

James, W. *The Principles of Psychology.* New York: Dover, 1890.

Jones, E. E. *Ingratiation: A Social Psychological Analysis.* New York: Appleton-Century-Crofts, 1964.

Jones, E. E., K. J. Gergen, and **K. E. Davis.** "Some Determinants of Reactions to Being Approved or Disapproved as a Person," *Psychological Monographs,* Vol. 76, Whole No. 521 (1962).

Kinsey, A., W. B. Pomeroy, and **C. E. Martin.** *Sexual Behavior in the Human Male.* Philadelphia: W. B. Saunders Company, 1948.

LaBarre, W. "The Cultural Basis of Emotions and Gestures," *Journal of Personality,* 16 (1947), 49–68.

Laing, R. D. *The Divided Self: A Study of Sanity and Madness.* Chicago: Quadrangle Books, Inc., 1960.

Lay, C. H., and **D. N. Jackson.** "Analysis of the Generality of Trait-Inferential Relationships," *Journal of Personality and Social Psychology,* 12 (1969), 12–21.

Mahl, G. F., and **G. Schulze.** "Psychological Research in the Extralinguistic Area," in T. A. Sebeok, A. S. Hayes, and M. C. Bateson (eds.), *Approaches to Semiotics.* The Hague: Mouton, 1964, pp. 51–124.

Mead, G. H. *Mind, Self and Society.* Chicago: University of Chicago Press, 1934.

Milmoe, S., *et al.* "The Mother's Voice: Postdictor of Aspects of Her Baby's Behavior," *Proceedings of the 76th Annual Convention of the American Psychological Association,* 3 (1968), 463–464.

Mitford, N. *Noblesse Oblige: An Inquiry into the Identifiable Characteristics of the English Aristocracy.* London: H. Hamilton, 1956.

Park, R. E. *Race and Culture.* New York: Free Press, 1950.

Rogers, P. L., K. R. Scherer, and **R. Rosenthal.** "Content Filtering Human Speech: A Simple Electronic System," *Behavior Research Methods and Instrumentation,* 3 (1971), 16–18.

Rosenthal, R. *Experimenter Effects in Behavioral Research.* New York: Appleton-Century-Crofts, 1966.

Rosenthal, R., and **L. Jacobson.** *Pygmalion in the Classroom: Teacher Expectation and Pupils' Intellectual Development.* New York: Holt, Rinehart and Winston, 1968.

Rubin, Z. "Measurement of Romantic Love," *Journal of Personality and Social Psychology,* 16 (1970), 265–273.

Scheflen, A. E. *Stream and Structure of Communicational Behavior.* Philadelphia: Eastern Pennsylvania Psychiatric Institute, 1965.

Verplanck, W. S. "The Control of the Content of Conversation: Reinforcement of Statements of Opinion," *Journal of Abnormal and Social Psychology,* 51 (1955), 668–676.

Wiggins, N., P. Hoffman, and T. Taber. "Types of Judges and Cue Utilization in Judgments of Intelligence," *Journal of Personality and Social Psychology,* 12 (1969), 52–59.

Wishner, J. "Reanalysis of 'Impressions of Personality'," *Psychological Review,* 67 (1960), 96–112.

24

Aronson, E., and J. Mills. "Effect of Severity of Initiation on Liking for a Group," *Journal of Abnormal and Social Psychology,* 59 (1959), 177–181.

Asch, S. "Effects of Group Pressure Upon the Modification and Distortion of Judgments," in H. Proshansky and B. Seidenberg (eds.), *Basic Studies in Social Psychology.* New York: Holt, Rinehart and Winston, 1965, pp. 393–401.

Brown, R. *Social Psychology.* New York: Free Press, 1965.

Buss, A. H., and N. W. Portnoy. "Pain Tolerance and Group Identification," *Journal of Personality and Social Psychology,* 6 (1967), 106–108.

Converse, P., and A. Campbell. "Political Standards in Secondary Groups," in D. Cartwright and A. Zander (eds.), *Group Dynamics.* 3rd ed. New York: Harper & Row, 1968, pp. 199–211.

Dunnette, M. D., J. Campbell, and K. Jaastad. "The Effect of Group Participation on Brainstorming Effectiveness for Two Industrial Samples," *Journal of Applied Psychology,* 47 (1963), 30–37.

Festinger, L. *A Theory of Cognitive Dissonance.* Stanford, Calif.: Stanford University Press, 1957.

Illing, H. A. "C. G. Jung on the Present Trends in Group Psychotherapy," *Human Relations,* 10 (1957), 77–84.

Janis, I. L. "Groupthink Among Policy Makers," in N. Sanford and C. Comstock (eds.), *Sanctions for Evil.* San Francisco: Jossey-Bass, Inc., Publishers, 1971, pp. 71–89.

———. *Victims of Groupthink: A Psychological Analysis of Historical Decisions and Fiascos.* Boston: Houghton Mifflin (forthcoming).

Kanter, R. M. "Commitment and Social Organization: A Study of Commitment Mechanisms in Utopian Communities," *American Sociological Review,* 33 (1968), 449–518.

Lambert, W. E., E. Libman, and E. G. Poser. "The Effect of Increased Salience of a Membership Group on Pain Tolerance," *Journal of Personality,* 28 (1960), 350–357.

LeBon, G. *The Crowd.* New York: Viking, 1960.

Newcomb, T. M. "Attitude Development as a Function of Reference Groups: The Bennington Study," in H. Proshansky and B. Seidenberg (eds.), *Basic Studies in Social Psychology.* New York: Holt, Rinehart and Winston, 1965, pp. 215–225.

Osborn, A. F. *Applied Imagination.* Rev. ed. New York: Scribner, 1957.

Piliavin, I., J. Rodin, and J. A. Piliavin. "Good Samaritanism: An Underground Phenomenon?" *Journal of Personality and Social Psychology,* 13 (1970), 289–299.

Raper, A. *The Tragedy of Lynching.* Chapel Hill: University of North Carolina Press, 1933.

Schachter, S. "Deviation, Rejection and Communication," *Journal of Abnormal and Social Psychology,* 46 (1951), 190–207.

Schachter, S., *et al.* "Cross-Cultural Experiments on Threat and Rejection," *Human Relations,* 7 (1954), 403–439.

Schlesinger, A. M., Jr. *A Thousand Days.* Boston: Houghton Mifflin, 1965.

Shaw, M. E. "Comparison of Individuals and Small Groups in the Rational Solution of Complex Problems," *American Journal of Psychology,* 44 (1932), 491–504.

Sorensen, T. *Kennedy.* New York: Harper & Row, 1965.

Taylor, D. W., P. C. Berry, and C. H. Block. "Does Group Participation When Using Brainstorming Facilitate or Inhibit Creative Thinking?" *Administrative Science Quarterly,* 3 (1958), 23–47.

Zimbardo, P. G. "The Human Choice: Individuation, Reason, and Order Versus Deindividuation, Impulse, and Choice," in W. J. Arnold and D. Levine (eds.), *Nebraska Symposium on Motivation.* Lincoln: University of Nebraska Press, 1969, pp. 237–307.

25

Albert, E. "The Roles of Women: A Question of Values," in S. M. Farber and R. H. L. Wilson (eds.), *The Potential of Woman.* New York: McGraw-Hill, 1963, pp. 105–115.

Anonymous. "What is a Flower," *Up from Under,* 1 (1971), 67.

Beller, E. K. "Dependence and Independence in Young Children," *Journal of Genetic Psychology,* 87 (1955), 25–35.

Bird, C. *Born Female: The High Cost of Keeping Women Down.* New York: Pocket, 1969.

Bronfenbrenner, U. "Freudian Theories of Identification and Their Derivatives," *Child Development,* 31 (1960), 15–40.

Broverman, I. K., *et al.* "Sex-Role Stereotypes and Clinical Judgments of Mental Health," *Journal of Consulting and Clinical Psychology,* 34 (1970), 1–7.

Brown, R. *Social Psychology.* New York: Free Press, 1965.

Freud, S. "Female Sexuality," *International Journal of Psychoanalysis,* 13 (1932), 281–297.

———. *New Introductory Lectures on Psychoanalysis.* J. Strachey (tr.). New York: Norton, 1966.

———. "Some Psychological Consequences of the Anatomical Distinction Between the Sexes," *International Journal of Psychoanalysis,* 8 (1927), 133–142.

Goldberg, P. "Are Women Prejudiced Against Women?" *Trans-Action,* 5 (1968), 28–30.

Hall, E. T. *The Hidden Dimension.* Garden City, N.Y.: Anchor Books of Doubleday & Co., Inc., 1966.

———. *The Silent Language.* New York: Fawcett World Library, 1959.

Hartley, R. E. "Children's Concepts of Male and Female Roles," *Merrill Palmer Quarterly,* 6 (1960), 83–91.

———. "Sex Role Pressures and Socialization of the Male Child," *Psychological Reports,* 5 (1959), 457–468.

———. "Sex Roles From a Child's Point of View," in M. B. Sussman (ed.), *Sourcebook in Marriage and the Family.* 3rd ed. Boston: Houghton Mifflin, 1968, pp. 266–275.

Heiss, J. "Degree of Intimacy and Male-Female Interaction," *Sociometry,* 25 (1962), 197–208.

Horner, M. S. "Fail Bright Women," *Psychology Today,* 3 (1969), 36–38, 62.

———. "Femininity and Successful Achievement: A Basic Inconsistency," in J. Bardwick *et al.* (eds.), *Feminine Personality and Conflict.* Belmont, Calif.: Brooks/Cole Publishing Co., 1970, pp. 45–74.

Jourard, S. *The Transparent Self.* Rev. ed. New York: Van Nostrand Reinhold of Litton Educational Publishing, Inc., 1971.

Kagan, J., and H. A. Moss. "The Stability of Passive and Dependent Behavior From Childhood Through Adulthood," *Child Development,* 31 (1960), 577–591.

Kohlberg, L. "A Cognitive Developmental Analysis of Children's Sex-Role Concepts and Attitudes," in E. Maccoby (ed.), *The Development of Sex Differences.* Stanford, Calif.: Stanford University Press, 1966, pp. 82–172.

Komarovsky, M. "Cultural Contradictions and Sex Roles," *American Journal of Sociology,* 52 (1946), 184–189.

Levinger, G. "Task and Social Behavior in Marriage," *Sociometry,* 27 (1964), 433–448.

McKee, J. P., and A. C. Sheriffs. "The Differential Evaluation of Males and Females," *Journal of Personality,* 25 (1957), 356–371.

Mead, M. *From the South Seas: Studies of Adolescence and Sex in Primitive Societies.* New York: William Morrow & Co., Inc., 1939.

Mischel, W. "A Social-Learning View of Sex Differences in Behavior," in E. Maccoby (ed.), *The Development of Sex Differences.* Stanford, Calif.: Stanford University Press, 1966, pp. 56–81.

Mussen, P. "Early Sex-Role Development," in D. Goslin (ed.), *Handbook of Socialization Theory and Research.* Chicago: Rand McNally, 1969, pp. 707–732.

Myrdal, G. *An American Dilemma: The Negro Problem and Modern Democracy.* New York: Harper & Row, 1962.

Remmers, H. H., and **D. H. Radler.** *The American Teenager.* Indianapolis: Bobbs-Merrill, 1957.

Rosenkrantz, P., *et al.* "Sex-Role Stereotypes and Self-Concepts in College Students," *Journal of Consulting and Clinical Psychology,* 32 (1968), 287–295.

Strodtbeck, F. L., and **R. D. Mann.** "Sex Role Differentiation in Jury Deliberations," *Sociometry,* 19 (1956), 3–11.

Strodtbeck, F. L., R. J. Simon, and **C. Hawkins.** "Social Status in Jury Deliberations," in I. D. Steiner and M. Fishbein (eds.), *Current Studies in Social Psychology.* New York: Holt, Rinehart and Winston, 1965, pp. 333–341.

Tiger, L. "The Possible Biological Origins of Sexual Discrimination," *Impact of Science on Society,* 20 (1970), 29–44.

Torok, M. "The Significance of Penis Envy in Women," in J. Chasseguet-Smirgel, *et al., Female Sexuality: New Psychoanalytic Views.* Ann Arbor: University of Michigan Press, 1970, pp. 135–170.

Watson, G. *Social Psychology: Issues and Insights.* Philadelphia: Lippincott, 1966.

26

Abelson, R. P., and **J. C. Miller.** "Negative Persuasion via Personal Insult," *Journal of Experimental Social Psychology,* 3 (1967), 321–333.

Abelson, R. P., and **P. G. Zimbardo.** *Canvassing for Peace: A Manual for Volunteers.* Ann Arbor, Mich.: Society for the Psychological Study of Social Issues, 1970.

Albert, S., and **J. M. Dabbs, Jr.** "Physical Distance and Persuasion," *Journal of Personality and Social Psychology,* 15 (1970), 265–270.

Asch, S. "Effects of Group Pressure Upon the Modification and Distortion of Judgments," in H. Proshansky and B. Seidenberg (eds.), *Basic Studies in Social Psychology.* New York: Holt, Rinehart and Winston, 1965, pp. 393–401.

Bem, D. J. *Beliefs, Attitudes, and Human Affairs.* Belmont, Calif.: Brooks/Cole Publishing Co., 1970.

Brown, R. *Social Psychology.* New York: The Free Press, 1965.

Cohen, A. R. *Attitude Change and Social Influence.* New York: Basic Books, Inc., Publishers, 1964.

———. "Need for Cognition and Order of Communication as Determinants of Opinion Change," in C. I. Hovland, *et al., The Order of Presentation in Persuasion.* New Haven: Yale University Press, 1955.

Deutsch, M., and **H. Gerard.** "A Study of Normative and Informational Influences on Social Judgment," *Journal of Abnormal and Social Psychology,* 51 (1955), 629–636.

Dichter, E. *Handbook of Consumer Motivations.* New York: McGraw-Hill, 1964.

Festinger, L. *A Theory of Cognitive Dissonance.* Stanford, Calif.: Stanford University Press, 1957.

Festinger, L., and **J. M. Carlsmith.** "Cognitive Consequences of Forced Compliance," *Journal of Abnormal and Social Psychology,* 58 (1959), 203–210.

Hovland, C. I., and **W. Weiss.** "The Influence of Source Credibility on Communication Effectiveness," *Public Opinion Quarterly,* 15 (1951), 636–650.

Janis, I. L., and **B. T. King.** "The Influence of Role-Playing on Opinion Change," *Journal of Abnormal and Social Psychology,* 49 (1954), 211–218.

Kelman, H. C. "Processes of Opinion Change," *Public Opinion Quarterly,* 25 (1961), 57–78.

Marlowe, D., and **K. J. Gergen.** "Personality and Social Interaction," in G. Lindzey and E. Aronson (eds.), *Handbook of Social Psychology.* 2nd ed. Reading, Mass.: Addison-Wesley Publishing Co., Inc., Vol. 3, 1969, pp. 590–665.

McGuire, W. J. "A Vaccine for Brainwash," *Psychology Today,* 3 (1970), 36–39, 63–64.

Milgram, S. "Behavioral Study of Obedience," *Journal of Abnormal and Social Psychology,* 67 (1963), 371–378.

———. "Nationality and Conformity," *Scientific American,* 205 (1961), 45–51.

———. "Some Conditions of Obedience and Disobedience to Authority," in I. D. Steiner and M. Fishbein (eds.), *Current Studies in Social Psychology.* New York: Holt, Rinehart and Winston, 1965, pp. 243–262.

Riesman, D., *et al. The Lonely Crowd.* New Haven, Conn.: Yale University Press, 1961.

Shirer, W. L. *The Rise and Fall of the Third Reich.* New York: Simon and Schuster, 1960.

Snow, C. P. "Either-Or," *Progressive,* 25 (1961), 24–25.

Strodtbeck, F. L., R. M. James, and **C. Hawkins.** "Social Status in Jury Deliberations," in E. E. Maccoby *et al., Readings in Social Psychology.* New York: Holt, Rinehart and Winston, 1958, pp. 379–388.

Walster, E., and **L. Festinger.** "The Effectiveness of 'Overheard' Persuasive Communications," *Journal of Abnormal and Social Psychology,* 65 (1962), 395–402.

Worchel, S., and **J. W. Brehm.** "Effects of Threats to Attitudinal Freedom as a Function of Agreement With the Communicator," *Journal of Personality and Social Psychology,* 14 (1970), 18–22.

27

Aronson, E., and **D. Linder.** "Gain and Loss of Esteem as Determinants of Interpersonal Attractiveness," *Journal of Experimental Social Psychology,* 1 (1965), 156–172.

Beyle, Marie-Henri [Stendahl]. *On Love.* New York: Grosset & Dunlap, Inc., 1967.

Brickman, P., and **J. Redfield.** "Drive and Predisposition as Factors in the Attitudinal Effects of Mere Exposure." Paper presented at the 78th Annual American Psychological Association Convention, September, 1970, Miami, Florida.

Byrne, D. *The Attraction Paradigm.* New York: Academic Press, Inc., 1971.

Capellanus, A. *The Art of Courtly Love.* J. J. Parry (tr.). New York: Columbia University Press, 1941.

Disraeli, B. *Lothair.* New York: Appleton-Century-Crofts, 1870.

Evans, R. I. *Conversations with Carl Jung.* New York: Van Nostrand Reinhold, 1964.

Festinger, L. "A Theory of Social Comparison Processes," *Human Relations,* 7 (1954), 117–140.

Festinger, L., S. Schachter, and **K. Back.** *Social Pressures in Informal Groups.* Stanford, Calif.: Stanford University Press, 1963.

Ford, C. S., and **F. A. Beach.** *Patterns of Sexual Behavior.* New York: Harper & Row, 1951.

Fromm, E. *The Art of Loving.* New York: Harper & Row, 1956.

Gerard, H. B. "Emotional Uncertainty and Social Comparison," *Journal of Abnormal and Social Psychology,* 66 (1963), 568–573.

Goldstein, J. W., and **H. Rosenfeld.** "Insecurity and Preference for Persons Similar to Oneself," *Journal of Personality,* 37 (1969), 253–268.

Heron, W. "The Pathology of Boredom," *Scientific American,* 196 (1957), 52–56.

Jones, E. E. *Ingratiation: A Social-Psychological Analysis.* New York: Appleton-Century-Crofts, 1964.

Kerckhoff, A. C., and **K. E. Davis.** "Value Consensus and Need Complementarity in Mate Selection," *American Sociological Review,* 27 (1962), 295–303.

Newcomb, T. M. *The Acquaintance Process.* New York: Holt, Rinehart and Winston, 1961.

Priest, R. F., and **J. Sawyer.** "Proximity and Peership: Bases of Balance in Interpersonal Attraction," *American Journal of Sociology,* 72 (1967), 633–649.

Rubin, Z. "Measurement of Romantic Love," *Journal of Personality and Social Psychology,* 16 (1970), 265–273.

Sarnoff, I., and **P. G. Zimbardo.** "Anxiety, Fear, and Social Affiliation," *Journal of Abnormal and Social Psychology,* 62 (1961), 356–363.

Schachter, S. *The Psychology of Affiliation.* Stanford, Calif.: Stanford University Press, 1959.

Sheatsley, P. B., and **J. J. Feldman.** "The Assassination of President Kennedy: A Preliminary Report on Public Reactions and Behavior," *Public Opinion Quarterly,* 28 (1964), 189–215.

Slocum, J. *Sailing Alone Around the World.* London: Rupert-Hart-Davis, 1948.

Stroebe, W., *et al.* "Effects of Physical Attractiveness, Attitude Similarity, and Sex on Various Aspects of Interpersonal Attraction," *Journal of Personality and Social Psychology,* 18 (1971), 79–91.

Sullivan, H. S. *Conceptions of Modern Psychiatry.* 2nd ed. New York: Norton, 1953.

Wiggins, J. S., N. Wiggins, and **J. C. Conger.** "Correlates of Heterosexual Somatic Preference," *Journal of Personality and Social Psychology,* 10 (1968), 82–90.

Winch, R. F. *Mate Selection: A Study of Complementary Needs.* New York: Harper & Row, 1958.

Wright, P. H. "A Model and a Technique for Studies of Friendship," *Journal of Experimental Social Psychology,* 5 (1969), 295–309.

Zajonc, R. B. "Attitudinal Effects of Mere Exposure," *Journal of Personality and Social Psychology,* 9 (1968), 1–27.

28

Adorno, T. W., *et al. The Authoritarian Personality.* New York: Harper & Row, 1950.

Allport, G. *The Nature of Prejudice.* Garden City, N.Y.: Doubleday, 1958.

Amir, Y. "Contact Hypothesis in Ethnic Relations," *Psychological Bulletin,* 71 (1969), 319–342.

Bayton, J. A., L. B. McAlister, and **J. Hamer.** "Race-Class Stereotypes," *Journal of Negro Education,* 25 (1956), 75–78.

Brown, R. *Social Psychology.* New York: Free Press, 1965.

Davis, J. P. (ed.). *The American Negro Reference Book.* Englewood Cliffs, N.J.: Prentice-Hall, 1966.

Deutsch, M., and **M. Collins.** *Interracial Housing: A Psychological Evaluation of a Social Experiment.* Minneapolis: University of Minnesota Press, 1951.

———. "The Effects of Public Policy in Housing Projects Upon Interracial Attitude," in H. Proshansky and B. Seidenberg (eds.), *Basic Studies in Social Psychology.* New York: Holt, Rinehart and Winston, 1965, pp. 646–657.

Fein, R. "An Economic and Social Profile of the Negro American," in R. Mack (ed.), *Race, Class and Power.* 2nd. ed. New York: Van Nostrand Reinhold, 1968, pp. 6–28.

Gundlach, R. H. "The Effect of On-the-Job Experience With Negroes Upon Social Attitudes of White Workers in Union Shops," *Psychological Reports,* 2 (1956), 67–77.

Harding, J., and **R. Hogrefe.** "Attitudes of White Department Store Employees Toward Negro Co-workers," *Journal of Social Issues,* 8 (1952), 18–28.

Hendrick, C. E., V. E. Bixenstine, and **G. Hawkins.** "Race Versus Belief Similarity as Determinants of Attraction: A Search for a Fair Test," *Journal of Personality and Social Psychology,* 17 (1971), 250–258.

James, H. E. O. "Personal Contact in School and Change in Intergroup Attitudes," *International Social Science Bulletin,* 7 (1955), 66–70.

Karlins, M., T. L. Coffman, and **G. Walters.** "On the Fading of Social Stereotypes: Studies in Three Generations of College Students," *Journal of Personality and Social Psychology,* 13 (1969), 1–16.

Katz D., and **K. W. Braly.** "Racial Stereotypes on One Hundred College Students," *Journal of Abnormal and Social Psychology,* 28 (1933), 280–290.

Merton, R. K. *Social Theory and Social Structure.* Rev. ed. New York: Free Press, 1957.

Minard, R. D. "Race Relations in the Pocahontas Coal Field," *Journal of Social Issues,* 8 (1952), 29–44.

Pettigrew, T. F. *A Profile of the Negro American.* Princeton, N.J.: Van Nostrand, 1964.

Pettigrew, T. F., and **R. T. Riley.** "The Social Psychology of the Wallace Phenomenon," in T. F. Pettigrew (ed.), *Racially Separate or Together?* New York: McGraw-Hill, 1971, pp. 231–256.

Rokeach, M., P. W. Smith, and **R. I. Evans.** "Two Kinds of Prejudice or One?" in M. Rokeach (ed.), *The Open and Closed Mind.* New York: Basic Books, 1960, pp. 132–168.

Sherif, M., *et al. Intergroup Conflict and Cooperation: The Robbers Cave Experiment.* Norman, Okla.: Institute of Group Relations, 1961.

Simpson, G. E., and **J. M. Yinger.** *Racial and Cultural Minorities.* 3rd ed. New York: Harper & Row, 1965.

Sims, V., and **J. Patrick.** "Attitudes Toward the Negro of Northern and Southern College Students," *Journal of Social Psychology,* 7 (1936), 192–203.

Stein, D. "The Influence of Belief Systems on Interpersonal Preference: A Validation of Rokeach's Theory of Prejudice," *Psychological Monographs,* 80 (1966), 1–29.

Triandis, H. C., and **E. E. Davis.** "Race and Belief as Determinants of Behavioral Intentions," *Journal of Personality and Social Psychology,* 2 (1965), 715–725.

U.S. National Advisory Commission on Civil Disorders. *Report of the National Advisory Commission on Civil Disorders.* New York: Bantam, 1968.

U.S. Department of Commerce, Bureau of the Census. *General Population Characteristics.* Washington, D.C.: U.S. Government Printing Office, Final Report No. PC(1)–1B, 1961.

29

Bales, R. F. *Personality and Interpersonal Behavior.* New York: Holt, Rinehart and Winston, 1970.

Bradford, L., J. Gibb, and **K. Benne** (eds.). *T-Group Theory and Laboratory Method.* New York: Wiley, 1964.

Dunphy, D. "Social Change in Self-Analytic Groups," in P. Stone *et al.* (eds.), *The General Inquirer.* Cambridge, Mass.: M.I.T. Press, 1966, pp. 287–340.

Gibb, J. R. "Sensitivity Training as a Medium for Personal Growth and Improved Interpersonal Relationships," *Interpersonal Development,* 1 (1970), 6–31.

Lewin, G. W. (ed.). *Resolving Social Conflict: Selected Papers on Group Dynamics.* New York: Harper & Row, 1948.

Meador, B. "An Analysis of Process Movement in a Basic Encounter Group" (unpublished Ph.D. dissertation, United States International University, 1969).

Mills, T. M. "Toward a Conception of the Life Style of Groups," in T. Mills and S. Rosenberg (eds.), *Readings on the Sociology of Small Groups.* Englewood Cliffs, N.J.: Prentice-Hall, 1970, pp. 238–247.

Rogers, C. *Carl Rogers on Encounter Groups.* New York: Harper & Row, 1970.

Slater, P. E. "Role Differentiation in Small Groups," *American Sociological Review,* 20 (1955), 300–310.

———. *Microcosm: Structural, Psychological, and Religious Evolution in Groups.* New York: Wiley, 1966.

Whitman, R. M. "Psychodynamic Principles Underlying T-Group Processes," in L. Bradford, J. Gibbs, and K. Benne (eds.), *T-Group Theory and Laboratory Method.* New York: Wiley, 1964, pp. 310–335.

Yalom, I., and **M. Lieberman.** "A Study of Encounter Group Casualties," *Archives of General Psychiatry,* 25 (1971), 16–30.

30

Aberle, D. F. "Arctic Hysteria and Latah in Mongolia," *Transactions of the New York Academy of Sciences,* 14 (1952), 291–297.

American Psychiatric Association. *Diagnostic and Statistical Manual of Mental Disorders.* 2nd ed. Washington, D.C.: American Psychiatric Association, 1968.

Al-Issa, I. "Culture and Symptoms," in C. G. Costello (ed.), *Symptoms of Psychopathology: A Handbook.* New York: Wiley, 1970, pp. 27–45.

Beck, A. T. "Reliability of Psychiatric Diagnoses: A Critique of Systematic Studies," *American Journal of Psychiatry,* 119 (1962), 210–216.

Costello, C. G. "Classification and Psychopathology," in C. G. Costello (ed.), *Symptoms of Psychopathology: A Handbook.* New York: Wiley, 1970, pp. 1–26.

Fontana, A. F. "Familial Etiology of Schizophrenia: Is a Scientific Methodology Possible?" *Psychological Bulletin,* 66 (1966), 214–227.

Hollingshead, A. B., and **F. G. Redlich.** *Social Class and Mental Illness.* New York: Wiley, 1958.

Kisker, G. W. *The Disorganized Personality.* New York: McGraw-Hill, 1964.

Kohlberg, L. "Development of Moral Character and Moral Ideology," in M. L. Hoffman and L. W. Hoffman (eds.), *Review of Child Development Research.* New York: Russell Sage Foundation, 1964, Vol. I, pp. 383–431.

Kolb, L. C., V. W. Bernard, and **B. P. Dohinwend** (eds.). *Urban Challenges to Psychiatry: The Case History of a Response.* Boston: Little, Brown, 1969.

Kramer, M. "Statistics of Mental Disorders in the United States: Current Status, Some Urgent Needs and Suggested Solutions," *Journal of the Royal Statistical Society. Series A,* 132 (1969), 353–407.

Loon, F. G. H. Van. "Amok and Latah," *Journal of Abnormal and Social Psychology,* 21 (1927), 434–444.

Lorr, M., and **C. J. Klett.** "Constancy of Psychotic Syndromes in Men and Women," *Journal of Consulting Psychology,* 29 (1965), 309–313.

Lorr, M., and **D. M. McNair.** *Syndromes of Psychosis.* New York: Macmillan, 1963.

Maher, B. *Principles of Psychopathology.* New York: McGraw-Hill, 1966.

Malzberg, B. "New Data Relative to Incidence of Mental Disease Among Jews," *Mental Hygiene,* 20 (1936), 280–291.

Merton, R. K. *Social Theory and Social Structure.* New York: Free Press, 1956.

Miner, H. "Body Ritual Among the Nacirema," in W. Petersen and D. Matza (eds.), *Social Controversy.* Belmont, Calif.: Wadsworth, 1963, pp. 8–12.

Murphy, H. B. M., *et al.* "A Cross-Cultural Survey of Schizophrenic Symptomatology," in *Proceedings of the Third World Congress of Psychiatry.* Toronto: University of Toronto Press, Vol. II, 1961, pp. 1309–1315.

Roberts, G. H., and **J. K. Meyers.** "Religion, National Origin, Immigration and Mental Illness," *American Journal of Psychiatry,* 110 (1954), 759–764.

Stengel, E. "Problems of Nosology and Nomenclature in the Mental Disorders," in J. Zubin (ed.), *Field Studies in the Mental Disorders.* New York: Grune & Stratton, 1961.

Strole, L., *et al. Mental Health in the Metropolis: The Midtown Manhattan Study.* New York: McGraw-Hill, Vol. I, 1962.

Zigler, E., and **L. Phillips.** "Psychiatric Diagnosis: A Critique," *Journal of Abnormal and Social Psychology,* 63 (1961), 607–618.

Zilboorg, G., and **G. W. Henry.** *A History of Medical Psychology.* New York: Norton, 1941.

Zubin, J. "A Cross-Cultural Approach to Psychopathology and Its Implications for Diagnostic Classification," in L. D. Eron (ed.), *The Classification of Behavior Disorders.* Chicago: Aldine, 1966, pp. 43–85.

———. "Classification of the Behavior Disorders," *Annual Review of Psychology,* 18 (1967), 373–401.

Zubin, J., and **M. L. Kietzman.** "A Cross-Cultural Approach to Classification in Schizophrenia and Other Mental Disorders," in P. H. Hoch and J. Zubin (eds.), *Psychopathology of Schizophrenia.* New York: Grune & Stratton, 1966, pp. 482–514.

31

Bandura, A. *Principles of Behavior Modification.* New York: Holt, Rinehart and Winston, 1969.

Bateson, G., *et al.* "Toward a Theory of Schizophrenia," *Behavioral Science,* 1 (1956), 251–264.

Cameron, N. *Personality Development and Psychopathology.* Boston: Houghton Mifflin, 1963.

Dollard, J., and **N. E. Miller.** *Personality and Psychotherapy.* New York: McGraw-Hill, 1950.

Erikson, E. H. "Identity and the Life Cycle," *Psychological Issues,* Vol. I, Monograph No. 1 (1959).

Eysenck, H. J. (ed.). *Handbook of Abnormal Psychology: An Experimental Approach.* New York: Basic Books, 1961.

———. "Reminiscence Drive and Personality—Revision and Extension of a Theory," *British Journal of Social and Clinical Psychology,* 1 (1962), 127–140.

Farber, I. E., and **K. W. Spence.** "Complex Learning and Conditioning as a Function of Anxiety," *Journal of Experimental Psychology,* 45 (1953), 120–125.

Fenichel, O. *The Psychoanalytic Theory of Neurosis.* New York: Norton, 1945.

Freud, S. *Collected Papers.* J. Strachey (tr.). London: Hogarth Press, Vol. III, 1950.

Fuller, J. L., and **W. R. Thompson.** *Behavior Genetics.* New York: Wiley, 1960.

Gottesman, I. I., and **J. Shields.** "Contributions of Twin Studies to Perspectives on Schizophrenia," in B. A. Maher (ed.), *Progress in Experimental Personality Research.* New York: Academic Press, Vol. III, 1966, pp. 1–84.

Heath, R. G. "A Biochemical Hypothesis on the Etiology of Schizophrenia," in D. D. Jackson (ed.), *The Etiology of Schizophrenia.* New York: Basic Books, 1960, pp. 146–156.

Hoffer, A., and **H. Osmond.** "The Adrenochrome Model and Schizophrenia," *Journal of Nervous and Mental Diseases,* 128 (1959), 18–35.

Hull, C. L. *Principles of Behavior.* New York: Appleton-Century-Crofts, 1943.

Kallman, F. J. "The Genetic Theory of Schizophrenia—An Analysis of 691 Twin Index Families," *American Journal of Psychiatry,* 103 (1946), 309–322.

———. *Heredity in Mental Health and Disorder.* New York: Norton, 1953.

Kety, S. S. "Biochemical Hypotheses and Studies," in L. Bellak and L. Loeb (eds.), *The Schizophrenic Syndrome.* New York: Grune & Stratton, 1969, pp. 155–171.

Kringlen, E. "Hereditary and Social Factors in Schizophrenic Twins," in J. Romano (ed.), *The Origins of Schizophrenia.* New York: Excerpta Medica Foundation, 1967, pp. 2–14.

Lidz, T., *et al.* "The Intrafamilial Environment of Schizophrenic Patients: Marital Schism and Marital Skew," *American Journal of Psychiatry,* 114 (1957), 241–248.

Maher, B. A. "The Application of the Approach-Avoidance Conflict Model to Social Behavior," *Journal of Conflict Resolution,* 8 (1964), 287–291.

———. *Principles of Psychopathology: An Experimental Approach.* New York: McGraw-Hill, 1966.

Malmo, R. B. "Anxiety and Behavioral Arousal," *Psychological Review,* 64 (1957), 276–287.

Malmo, R. B., and **P. Amsel.** "Anxiety-Produced Interference in Serial Rote Learning, With Observation on Rote Learning After Partial Frontal Lobectomy," *Journal of Experimental Psychology,* 38 (1948), 440–454.

Miller, N. E. "Liberalization of Basic S-R Concepts: Extensions of Conflict Behavior, Maturation and Social Learning," in S. Koch (ed.), *Psychology: A Study of a Science.* New York: McGraw-Hill, Vol. II, 1958, pp. 196–292.

Osmond, H., and **J. Smithies.** "Schizophrenia: A New Approach," *Journal of Mental Science,* 98 (1952), 309–315.

Pavlov, I. P. *Lectures on Conditioned Reflexes.* W. H. Gantt (tr.). New York: International Publishers, 1928.

Schroder, H. M., and **J. B. Rotter.** "Rigidity as Learned Behavior," *Journal of Experimental Psychology,* 44 (1952), 141–150.

Shields, J. "Twins Brought Up Apart," *Eugenics Review,* 50 (1958), 115–123.

Skinner, B. F. *Science and Human Behavior.* New York: Macmillan, 1953.

———. *The Behavior of Organisms: An Experimental Analysis.* New York: Appleton-Century-Crofts, 1938.

Spence, K. W., and **J. A. Taylor.** "The Relation of Conditioned Response Strength to Anxiety in Normal, Neurotic and Psychotic Subjects," *Journal of Experimental Psychology,* 45 (1953), 265–272.

Strachey, J. (ed.). *The Standard Edition of the Complete Psychological Works of Sigmund Freud.* London: Hogarth Press, 1961.

Taylor, J. A. "The Relationship of Anxiety to the Conditioned Eyelid Response," *Journal of Experimental Psychology,* 41 (1951), 81–92.

Ullman, L. P., and **L. Krasner.** *A Psychological Approach to Abnormal Behavior.* New York: Holt, Rinehart and Winston, 1970.

Valins, S., and **R. Nisbett.** "Attribution Processes in the Development and Treatment of Emotional Disorders," in E. Jones *et al.* (eds.), *Attribution: Perceiving the Causes of Behavior.* Morristown, N.J.: General Learning Press, 1972.

Watson, J. B., and **R. Rayner.** "Conditioned Emotional Reactions," *Journal of Experimental Psychology,* 3 (1920), 1–14.

Wolpe, J., and **S. Rachman.** "Psychoanalytic Evidence: A Critique Based on Freud's Case of Little Hans," *Journal of Nervous and Mental Diseases,* 31 (1960), 134–147.

32

Bergin, A. E. "The Effects of Psychotherapy: Negative Results Revisited," *Journal of Counseling Psychology,* 10 (1963), 244–250.

———. "The Evaluation of Therapeutic Outcomes," in A. E. Bergin and S. L. Garfield (eds.), *Handbook of Psychotherapy and Behavior Change: An Empirical Analysis.* New York: Wiley, 1971, pp. 217–270.

Eysenck, H. J. *The Effects of Psychotherapy.* New York: International Science Press, 1966, pp. 505–510.

Freud, S. *A General Introduction to Psychoanalysis.* Rev. ed. J. Riviere (tr.). New York: Liveright, 1935.

Garfield, S. L. "Research on Client Variables in Psychotherapy," in A. E. Bergin and S. L. Garfield (eds.), *Handbook of Psychotherapy and Behavior Change: An Empirical Analysis.* New York: Wiley, 1971, pp. 271–298.

Goffman, E. *Asylums.* Garden City, N.Y.: Doubleday, 1961.

Goldstein, A. P. "Psychotherapy Research and Psychotherapy Practices: Independence of Equivalence?" in S. Lesse (ed.), *An Evaluation of the Results of the Psychotherapies.* Springfield, Ill.: Charles C Thomas, 1968, pp. 5–17.

Gurin, G., J. Veroff, and **S. Feld.** *Americans View Their Mental Health.* New York: Basic Books, 1960.

Haley, J. (ed.). *Advanced Techniques in Hypnosis and Therapy.* New York: Grune & Stratton, Inc., 1967.

Hathaway, S. R. "Personality Inventories," in B. B. Wolman, *Handbook of Clinical Psychology.* New York: McGraw-Hill, 1965.

Hollingshead, A. B., and **F. C. Redlich.** *Social Class and Mental Illness: A Community Study.* New York: Wiley, 1958.

Luborsky, L., *et al.* "Factors Influencing the Outcome of Psychotherapy: A Review of Quantitative Research," *Psychological Bulletin,* 75 (1971), 145–185.

Masters, W. H., and **V. E. Johnson.** *Human Sexual Inadequacy.* Boston: Little, Brown, 1970.

———. *Human Sexual Response.* Boston: Little, Brown, 1966.

Mowrer, O. H. "Sin: The Lesser of Two Evils," *American Psychologist,* 15 (1960), 301–304.

Raush, H. L., and **C. L. Raush.** *The Halfway House Movement: A Search for Sanity.* New York: Appleton-Century-Crofts, 1968.

Schofield, W. *Psychotherapy: The Purchase of Friendship.* Englewood Cliffs, N.J.: Prentice-Hall, 1964.

Szasz, T. S. "The Myth of Mental Illness," *American Psychologist,* 15 (1960), 113–118.

Wing, J. K. "Institutionalism in Mental Hospitals," *British Journal of Social and Clinical Psychology,* 1 (1962), 38–51.

33

Bandura, A. "Psychotherapy as a Learning Process," *Psychology Bulletin,* 58 (1961), 143–159.

Beck, A. T. *Depression: Clinical, Experimental, and Theroretical Aspects.* New York: Harper & Row, 1967.

Caplan, G. *Principles of Preventive Psychiatry.* New York: Basic Books, 1965.

Ellis, A. "The Effectiveness of Psychotherapy with Individuals Who Have Severe Homosexual Problems," *Journal of Consulting and Clinical Psychology,* 20 (1956), 191–195.

Erikson, E. H. *Childhood and Society.* 2nd ed. New York: Norton, 1963.

Frankl, V. E. *Man's Search for Meaning: An Introduction to Logotherapy.* I. Lasch (tr.). Boston: Beacon Press, 1962.

Freud, A. *The Ego and the Mechanisms of Defense.* New York: International Universities Press, 1946.

Golding, W. *Lord of the Flies.* New York: Coward-McCann, 1962.

Lindsley, O. R., and **B. F. Skinner.** "A Method for the Experimental Analysis of the Behavior of Psychotic Patients," *American Psychologist,* 9 (1954), 419–420.

Masters, W. H., and **V. E. Johnson.** *Human Sexual Inadequacy.* Boston: Little, Brown, 1970.

May, R. *Love and Will.* New York: Norton, 1970.

May, R., *et al. Existential Psychology.* Rev. ed. New York: Random House, 1969.

Moreno, J. L. *Psychodrama.* New York: Beacon House, Vol. I, 1946.

Perls, F., R. F. Hefferline, and **P. Goodman.** *Gestalt Therapy.* New York: Julian Press, 1951.

Schofield, W. *Psychotherapy: The Purchase of Friendship.* Englewood Cliffs, N.J.: Prentice-Hall, 1964.

Schutz, W. *Joy: Expanding Human Awareness.* New York: Grove Press, 1967.

Skinner, B. F. *Beyond Freedom and Dignity.* New York: Knopf, 1971.

———. *Walden Two.* New York: Macmillan, 1948.

Ullman, L. P., and **L. Krasner** (eds.). *Case Studies in Behavior Modification.* New York: Holt, Rinehart and Winston, 1965.

White, R. W. "Motivation Reconsidered: The Concept of Competence," *Psychological Review,* 66 (1959), 297–333.

34

Cade, J. F. "Lithium Salts in the Treatment of Psychotic Excitement," *Medical Journal of Australia,* 2 (1949), 349–352.

Cohen, S. "The Hallucinogens," in W. G. Clark and J. del Giudice (eds.), *Principles of Psychopharmacology.* New York: Academic Press, 1970.

Coldburn, R. W., *et al.* "Effect of Lithium on Uptake of Noradrenaline by Synaptosomes," *Nature,* 215 (1967), 1395–1397.

Cooper, J. R., F. E. Bloom, and **R. H. Roth.** *The Biochemical Basis of Neuropharmacology.* New York: Oxford University Press, 1970.

Coppen, A., *et al.* "Prophylactic Lithium in Affective Disorders," *Lancet,* 2 (1971), 275–279.

Corrodi, H., *et al.* "Effect of Lithium on Cerebral Monoamine Neurons," *Psychopharmacologia,* 11 (1967), 345–353.

Dishotsky, N. J., *et al.* "LSD and Genetic Damage," *Science,* 172 (1971), 431–440.

Freedman, D. X. "The Use and Abuse of LSD," *Archives of General Psychiatry,* 18 (1968), 300–347.

Goodman, L. S., and **A. Gillman.** *The Pharmacological Basis of Therapeutics.* 4th ed. New York: Macmillan, 1970.

Greenblatt, M., *et al.* (eds.). *Drugs and Social Therapy in Chronic Schizophrenia.* Springfield, Ill.: Charles C Thomas, 1965.

Grinspoon, L. *Marijuana Reconsidered.* Cambridge, Mass.: Harvard University Press, 1970.

Hoffman, A. "Psychotomimetic Drugs: Chemical and Pharmacologic Aspects," *Acta Physiologica et Pharmacologica Neerlandica,* 8 (1959), 240–258.

———. "Psychotomimetic Substances," *Indian Journal of Pharmacology,* 25 (1963), 245–256.

Hollister, L. E. *Chemical Psychoses, LSD and Related Drugs.* Springfield, Ill.: Charles C Thomas, 1968.

Jarvik, M. E. "The Psychopharmacological Revolution," *Psychology Today,* 1 (1967), 51–59.

Jellinek, E. M. *The Disease Concept of Alcoholism.* New Haven, Conn.: Hillhouse Press, 1960.

Klein, D. F., and **T. M. Davis.** *Diagnosis and Drug Treatment of Psychiatric Disorders.* Baltimore: Williams & Wilkins, 1969.

Mandell, A. J., and **L. J. West.** "Hallucinogens," in A. M. Freedman and H. I. Kaplan (eds.), *Comprehensive Textbook of Psychiatry.* Baltimore: Williams & Wilkins, 1967.

Schanberg, S. M., *et al.* "Effects of Psychoactive Drugs on Norepinephrine-3H Metabolism in Brain," *Biochemical Pharmacology,* 16 (1967), 393–399.

Schildkraut, J. J., and **S. S. Kety.** "Biogenic Amines and Emotion," *Science,* 156 (1967), 21–30.

Schou, M. "Lithium in Psychiatric Therapy and Prophylaxis," *Journal of Psychiatric Research,* 6 (1968), 67–95.

Selikoff, I. J., E. H. Robitzik, and **G. G. Ornstein.** "Toxicity of Hydrazine Derivatives and Isonicotinic Acid in the Chemotherapy of Human Tuberculosis," *Quarterly Bulletin of Sea View Hospital,* 13 (1952).

Statistical Abstract of the United States. 84th ed. Washington, D.C.: U.S. Government Printing Office, 1963.

Statistical Abstract of the United States. 92nd ed. Washington, D.C.: U.S. Government Printing Office, 1971.

Tinklenberg, J. R., and **R. C. Stillman.** "Drug Use and Violence," in D. N. Daniels, M. F. Gilula, and F. M. Ochberg (eds.), *Violence and the Struggle for Existence.* Boston: Little, Brown, 1970, pp. 327–365.

Weil, A. T. "Adverse Reactions to Marijuana," *New England Journal of Medicine,* 228 (1970), 997–1000.

Weil, A. T., *et al.* "Clinical and Psychological Effects of Marijuana in Man," *Science,* 162 (1968), 1234–1242.

Appendix: Methodology

Catania, A. C. "Concurrent Performances: A Baseline for the Study of Reinforcement Magnitude," *Journal of the Experimental Analysis of Behavior,* 6 (1963), 299–300.

Dawes, R. M. "Letter to the Editor," *American Statistician,* 25 (1971), 56–57.

Miller, N. "Effects of Drugs on Motivation: The Value of Using a Variety of Measures," *Annals of the New York Academy of Science,* 65 (1951), 318–333.

———. "Experiments on Motivation," *Science,* 126 (1957), 1271–1278.

Miller, N., C. J. Bailey, and **J. A. Stevenson.** "Decreased 'Hunger' But Increased Food Intake Resulting From Hypothalamic Lesions," *Science,* 112 (1950), 256–259.

Rosenthal, R. *Experimenter Effects in Behavioral Research.* New York: Appleton-Century-Crofts, 1966.

Glossary

A

ablation. Surgical removal of an organ, bodily part, or growth from the body.

abnormality. The quality or state of deviating from the average, standard, or normal; an extreme or excessive departure from the usual, especially as applies to distorted, morbid, or pathological mental states.

absolute refractory period. A brief interval following the discharge of a neural impulse by a neuron during which the neuron is completely insensitive to further stimulation. See also *relative refractory period.*

absolute threshold. The minimum intensity of a stimulus that is necessary for eliciting a response.

abstraction. The process of drawing out or isolating a general character or particular aspect from an aggregate of elements for the purpose of analysis or communication; a thought that is the result of such a process.

accommodation. In vision, the process whereby the lens of the eye changes its shape in order to focus on the retina objects at various distances from the eye; in social psychology, changes in individual or group habits or customs made to reduce conflict with others; in Piaget's developmental theory, adjustment of one's schemes for understanding the world to the characteristics of the object or event at hand.

acetylcholine (ACh). A chemical believed to transmit nerve impulses across a synapse.

acetylcholinesterase. An enzyme found in the blood that accelerates the destruction of acetylcholine.

ACh. See *acetylcholine.*

achievement, need for. A felt requirement to accomplish or attain goals. The concept figures prominently in the expectancy-value theory of motivation.

achievement test. A measure of how much an individual has learned in a given field or area that is obtained by the assessment of performance in that area.

achromatic. Devoid of color; having no hue; black, gray, or white.

acoustics. The study of the properties of sound; the qualities of a room or area that determine how distinctly sounds can be heard.

acquisition. The stage in which a habit is being learned; the learning stage of memorizing, in which new information is incorporated into long-term memory.

ACTH. See *adrenocorticotrophic hormone.*

action potential. A localized, rapid change in electrical state that travels across the cell membrane of a neuron or muscle fiber at the moment of excitation. Also called a spike.

activation theory of emotion. The theory that emotion results from the stimulation of the reticular activating system of the brain.

actor. In E. Goffman's theory of the presentation of self, a participant in a human interaction.

actualization. See *self-actualization.*

acuity. Perceptual sharpness or keenness. See also *minimum separable acuity; minimum visual acuity; vernier acuity; visual acuity.*

adaptation. The alteration of an organism's structure or functions so that it can survive and reproduce in a changed environment; in perception, adjustment of sensory receptors in response to the increasing or decreasing of stimulation. See also *accommodation; adaptive behavior; cross-adaptation; dark adaptation.*

adaptive behavior. An inherited or acquired mode of behavior that allows an organism to meet the demands of a changed environment.

addiction. Physiological dependence on a substance, especially a drug, often with the result that increased amounts of the substance are required to maintain normal or near-normal bodily functioning. Psychological dependence is sometimes also referred to as addiction. See also *withdrawal syndrome.*

adenohypophysis. See *anterior pituitary.*

ADH. See *antidiuretic hormone.*

adrenal cortex. The external tissue of the adrenal glands that is involved in many physiological and metabolic functions and that secretes steroid compounds. The adrenal cortex is essential to the life of an organism. See also *adrenal gland; adrenal medulla.*

adrenal gland. One of a pair of endocrine glands located above the kidneys that produces epinephrine, norepinephrine, and cortin. See also *adrenal cortex; adrenal medulla.*

adrenal medulla. The inner tissue of the adrenal glands that forms epinephrine and norepinephrine and participates with the sympathetic nervous system in the maintenance of homeostasis. See also *adrenal cortex; adrenal gland.*

adrenalin. See *epinephrine.*

adrenin. See *epinephrine.*

adrenocorticotrophic hormone (ACTH). A hormone secreted by the anterior pituitary gland that stimulates the adrenal cortex to secrete steroid compounds.

affect. A class name for emotion, mood, and feeling; the feeling state that accompanies cognition.

afferent. Carrying inward; in reference to neurons, conducting neural impulses toward the brain and spinal cord. See also *efferent.*

afterimage. A visual image or sense impression that persists after removal of the stimulus.

aggression. Angry, hateful, or destructive behavior; hostile action against another.

albinism. Congenital lack of skin pigmentation.

alcohol. A clear, volatile liquid, capable of being mixed with water, that has an intoxicating effect; a beverage that contains this liquid; any of a certain class of organic compounds.

alcoholism. Addiction to or excessive use of alcohol; a personality disorder in which a person drinks alcoholic beverages in great quantity and is unable to control his drinking; the effects of drinking an excessive amount of alcohol.

alimentary canal. An organ or organ system consisting of a tubular passage that functions in the digestion of food. In humans it includes the esophagus, stomach, and intestines. Also called the alimentary tract.

allele. One of two or more different forms that a gene may take at a given site on a chromosome.

all-or-none law. The principle that a neuron reacts either with full strength or not at all to a stimulus above threshold, regardless of the intensity of the stimulus.

alpha machine. A machine that indicates the occurrence of alpha waves in the brain.

alpha wave. A type of brain wave originating mainly in the occipital lobe of an adult that is typical of a relaxed, waking state. Alpha waves have a large amplitude and an average frequency of ten cycles per second. See also *brain wave.*

American Sign Language (ASL). A system of communication used by the deaf and composed of gestures and hand signs.

Ames room. A room designed to be perceived as rectangular but that is actually a set of trapezoids joined to form acute and obtuse angles; people and objects placed in the Ames room appear to observers to be distorted in size.

amnesia. Complete or partial loss of memory; inability to recall past events, caused by physical injury (*e.g.*, brain damage) or psychic trauma (*e.g.*, death of a loved one).

amok (amuck). A term used by the Malays to describe a state of frenzy that often culminates in homicide. Origin of the phrase "to run amuck."

amphetamine. Any of a group of synthetic drugs that stimulates the central nervous system, suppresses appetite, increases heart rate and blood pressure, and alters sleep patterns. Often used to control appetite, treat narcolepsy, or alleviate depression.

amygdala. A structure of the forebrain located beneath the frontal lobe and connected to the hypothalamus that is partly responsible for the regulation of emotion and motivation.

anagram. A word or sentence formed by transposition of the letters of another word or sentence (*e.g.*, "rate" is an anagram of "tear").

analgesic. Something that eases or alleviates pain; pertaining to an absence of pain.

anal personality. According to Freud, a personality disorder originating in early childhood that is characterized by certain obsessive-compulsive traits, particularly obstinacy, stinginess, and extreme neatness.

anal stage. According to Freud the second psychosexual stage (from approximately one and one-half to three years of age), during which bowel control is accomplished and pleasure is focused on the functions of elimination.

anger. An emotional reaction to frustration, injury, threat, interference, or the like, characterized by displeasure and belligerence. Anger may give rise to overt or concealed aggression and is accompanied by changes in the functioning of the autonomic nervous system.

angstrom. A unit of length (especially wavelength) equal to one ten-billionth of a meter.

animal magnetism. A force hypothesized by F. A. Mesmer that is innate in some people and allows them to hypnotize others.

anorexia. Loss of appetite, especially for a prolonged period of time.

anterior pituitary. The forward part of the pituitary gland. It secretes hormones that stimulate other endocrine glands. Also known as the adenohypophysis.

anthropology. The scientific study of human beings dealing with their origins as a species as well as their physical, cultural, and social evolution; the study of the similarities and differences between humans and other animals.

antianxiety drug. A drug usually given to people with psychological disorders in which anxiety is the main symptom. These drugs, also known as minor tranquilizers, reduce pathological anxiety, tension, and agitation.

antidepressant drug. A drug used in the treatment of pathological depression. Some antidepressant drugs can reverse a state of depression in a person who is pathologically depressed but usually leave normal people unaffected.

antidiuretic hormone (ADH). A hormone probably produced in the hypothalamus and stored in and released by the posterior pituitary, that increases the capacity of kidney tubules to reabsorb water, thereby reducing excretion of water.

antipsychotic drug. A drug used to treat psychoses. Antipsychotic drugs, also known as major tranquilizers, reduce motor activity, responsiveness to stimuli, hallucinations, and delusional behavior.

antisocial. Unwilling to associate with individuals or social groups; opposed to social standards; harmful to society.

anvil. See *incus.*

anxiety. A fearful and apprehensive emotional state, usually in response to unreal or imagined dangers, that interferes with favorable and effective solutions to real problems. Anxiety is typically accompanied by somatic symptoms that leave one in a continuous and physically exhausting state of tension and alertness.

anxiety reaction. Feelings of anxious expectation and accompanying physical symptoms that are characteristic of a state of diffused anxiety.

aplysia. The genus name of a snaillike sea animal.

approach-approach conflict. The conflict that results from a situation in which an organism is drawn toward two gratifying goals that are not compatible.

approach-avoidance conflict. A conflict resulting from a situation in which an organism is both attracted to a stimulus and also motivated to avoid it.

a priori. Knowledge or a type of thinking that exists in the mind prior to and independent of experience; reasoning based on deduction; cause-effect reasoning.

aptitude test. A test in which a person's performance on a standardized group of tasks is used to estimate her or his future abilities in learning specific skills.

aqueous humor. A watery fluid that fills the space between the lens and cornea of the eye and through which light passes.

archetype. A model on which something is based or formed; a prototype; according to Jung, an inherited idea present in the unconscious and based on the experiences of all one's ancestors that regulates one's perceptions of the world.

Arctic hysteria. Behavior that appears to be unique to the population of Northern Siberia, typified by a hypnotic condition during which the patient mimics the movements of others.

arithmetic mean. See *mean, arithmetic.*

artery. A blood vessel that carries blood from the heart to the tissues. See also *vein.*

ASL. See *American Sign Language.*

assimilation. In anatomy, the conversion of substances absorbed by the body into protoplasm; in Piaget's theory of development, the application of a scheme to a particular object, person, or event.

association. The establishment of relationships between ideas or psychological activities so that the occurrence of one evokes the other; the mental bond linking two or more related ideas; bringing two individuals, objects, events, or the like, into relation with each other; a hypothetical neural connection; the relationship between conscious and unconscious ideas.

association value. The relation of one phenomenon to another; in reference to nonsense syllables, a connection between a nonsense syllable and an item already in memory. Items having a high association value are easier to remember than those with a low association value.

associative cell. A neuron that connects nerve centers; a neuron connecting different regions in the cerebral hemispheres.

assortative mating. The selection of a mate who has characteristics similar to one's own.

ataxia. Absence of coordination of voluntary muscular movements. In reference to psychic disorders, the lack of coordination between emotions and thoughts.

atom. The smallest part of an element that retains all the properties of the element. Composed of a nucleus, protons, and electrons.

atomism. The reduction of psychological events to their most elementary stages through analysis.

attention. The selection of and response to a single object or idea from a complex of objects or ideas; mental concentration on a single object or idea or the state of consciousness resulting from such concentration.

attitude. An enduring cognitive predisposition to respond consistently to given objects, events, issues, and the like, assumed to be acquired by learning.

audience. Listeners, viewers, or readers. In the communication process, the person or persons receiving a message.

audition. The sense of hearing.

auditory canal. The tubular passage that extends from the opening of the outer ear to the eardrum. Also known as the external auditory meatus.

auditory cortex. An area located on the surface of the temporal lobe of the brain that is responsible for sensations of hearing.

auditory nerve. Either of a pair of cranial nerves connecting the inner ear with the brain; involved in hearing and balance.

authoritarian personality. A person or personality structure characterized by the following personality traits: rigid and stereotyped thinking; respect for and submission to authority; perception of people as either strong or weak; denial and projection of sexual and aggressive drives; rejection of out-groups; a tendency to perceive the environment and others as hostile; conventionalism; and opposition to psychological analysis or introspection.

authority. A person who is capable of influencing others because of his status, role, or superior knowledge or strength; the credibility attributed to a statement or set of statements issued by a person who is perceived to be a reliable expert in a certain field; a delegated or given power or right.

authority, legitimate. A person who is perceived as being in control of a situation according to law, accepted standards, or principles.

autism. The tendency of a person's thoughts and perceptions to be regulated by his needs and desires as in fantasy, daydreams, delusions; thinking in which objective reality is not apprehended because of the tendency to view the world subjectively; a syndrome thought to be a form of childhood schizophrenia in which the child is withdrawn, unable to relate to people and environmental stimulation in a normal manner, experiences language disturbances, and exhibits compulsive, stereotyped behavior.

autistic behavior. See *autism.*

autoeroticism. Sexual feelings or sexual gratification brought about by one's own acts without the participation of another person.

automatic behavior. Behavior that normally requires, but is performed without, intention or constant attention.

autonomic conditioning. Conditioning designed to achieve conscious control of reflexes regulated by the autonomic nervous system (*e.g.,* involuntary reflexes).

autonomic nervous system. The part of the central nervous system that innervates smooth muscles, heart, blood vessels, viscera, and glands and controls their involuntary function. The autonomic nervous system is evidently only partially independent.

average. The ordinary or typical; a general term for any measure of central tendency; more specifically, the arithmetic mean.

aversion. An unpleasant attitude or feeling of repugnance toward something, accompanied by an impulse to withdraw.

aversive control. Escape or avoidance conditioning achieved by using negative reinforcement.

aversive stimulation. See *aversive stimulus.*

aversive stimulus. Punishment, or a negative or unpleasant stimulus.

avoidance-avoidance conflict. The conflict that results from a situation in which an organism is motivated to avoid two similar stimuli but avoidance of one brings it closer to the other.

avoidance conditioning. A type of operant conditioning in which an organism learns to make the correct response in order to prevent the occurrence of an aversive stimulus. See also *avoidance response.*

avoidance response. Any form of behavior that prevents the occurrence of an aversive stimulus. See also *avoidance conditioning.*

axon. The fiberlike extension of a neuron that transmits impulses away from the cell body.

B

barbiturates. A group of drugs that act as depressants to the central nervous system.

basic needs. In Maslow's theory of personality, those needs whose satisfaction is vital to the normal functioning of the individual. Basic needs form a hierarchy—that is, the needs must be satisfied in a certain order, and higher-level needs cannot be satisfied until lower-level needs are satisfied. *E.g.*, the need for security cannot be satisfied until the hunger need is satisfied. See also *metaneeds.*

basilar membrane. A membrane in the cochlea whose motions stimulate the auditory nerve.

behavior. The activities, responses, or movements of an organism.

behaviorism. A school of psychology based on the contention that only objectively observed behavior can be considered as scientific data. Strict behaviorists exclude consciousness from the study of psychology.

behavior modification. The changing of human behavior, especially by behavior therapy.

behavior pattern. A whole, complex act made up of separate, less complex acts and considered as a functional unit.

behavior therapy. A type of psychotherapy based on the proposition that people have emotional problems because they acquired faulty behavior patterns or failed to learn effective responses. The object of behavior therapy is to change behavior patterns by eliminating symptoms rather than by probing the unconscious or making basic changes in personality.

belongingness, principle of. A Gestalt law of organization proposing that an assemblage of items will be perceived as a whole if the items seem to belong together in some way.

benzodiazepines. A group of antianxiety drugs, or minor tranquilizers.

bestiality. Any type of human behavior resembling that of a beast; most often sexual behavior between humans and animals.

bifurcation. Division into two parts.

binaural differences. The time and intensity differences of a sound as it reaches each of an individual's ears. See also *binaural interaction.*

binaural interaction. The perceptual process by which the input to an organism's two ears are used to determine the location of a sound source. See also *binaural differences.*

binocular disparity. The difference between the retinal images of an object on the two eyes that is the result of the slightly different viewing angles of the eyes.

biofeedback. Information about the correctness of a bodily response reported to the nervous system by the sense or an outside source. This information enables an organism to change its functioning in accordance with changes in the environment.

biology. The scientific study of all forms and phenomena of life.

bipolar cell. A retinal neuron that transmits neural impulses from the rods and cones to the ganglion cells.

bisexuality. Possessing the physical or psychological characteristics of both sexes; sexual responsiveness to both sexes.

bit. In reference to information processing, a single or basic unit of information equivalent to the result of a choice among alternatives. The number of alternatives in a given situation determines the number of bits required to gain all necessary information about the situation.

blind spot. The area of the retina where the optic nerve leaves the eye and that is devoid of rods and cones. The blind spot is relatively insensitive to light.

boomerang effect. A shift in attitude or behavior away from the position advocated by a communication, person, group, or the like.

brain. The primary organ of the nervous system. It is composed of nerve tissue and is encased in the skull. The brain, together with the spinal cord, is vital to life. It regulates bodily functions, sensory experience, intellectual processes, emotional activity, motivation, and so on. The chief divisions of the vertebrate brain are the forebrain, midbrain, and hindbrain.

brain stem. See *diencephalon.*

brain wave. A rhythmic fluctuation of electrical voltage in the brain. See also *alpha wave.*

brainfield. An area of the brain that is excited by activity originating in a receptor.

brainstorming. A technique for fostering creative group problem solving that consists of having group members express ideas freely and without fear of criticism.

brightness. The intensity of light; high degree of intelligence.

brightness constancy. The tendency of objects to retain their apparent brightness under various levels of illumination.

Broca's area. A nerve center located in the frontal lobe of the brain thought to be responsible for the movements necessary for speech.

butyric acid. A liquid compound having a rancid odor.

butyrophenones. A group of antipsychotic drugs.

C

caffeine. A chemical that acts as a stimulant.

camisole. See *straitjacket.*

Cannabis sativa. Indian hemp. The female plant is the source of marijuana and hashish.

cannula. A small tube inserted into the body in order to extract fluid or introduce substances.

cannulation. Insertion of a small tube into the body in order to extract fluid or introduce substances.

carbachol. A chemical that produces thirst when injected into the hypothalamus.

carotid artery. One of two arteries located on either side of the neck that carries blood to the head.

castration. Removal of the testes or of the testes and penis. See also *ovariotomy.*

castration anxiety. Fear of injuring or losing one's genitals; a boy's fear that he will be deprived of his genitals. In Freudian theory castration anxiety develops during the phallic stage and is thereafter repressed in normal individuals.

castration complex. The unconscious affects tied to castration anxiety; the totality of a child's reactions to threats of castration; the sum of the effects experienced by a female when she discovers that she lacks a penis.

catatonic schizophrenia. A psychotic disorder that takes the form of generalized inhibition (catatonic stupor) or excessive, disorganized motor activity (catatonic excitement).

catecholamine. An organic compound possessing certain structural characteristics. Epinephrine, norepinephrine, and dopamine are catecholamines.

catecholamine hypothesis. The proposition that mental depression is related to a deficiency of norepinephrine in the brain and that mania or excited states are related to an excess of norepinephrine.

categorical imperative. A command to act in accordance with a universal moral law. The categorical imperative usually refers to the philosopher Immanuel Kant's formula that one should act only on principles that one could want to become a universal law.

catharsis. The release of emotional tension that follows a strong emotional experience; a form of psychotherapy in which a traumatic experience that has been repressed is brought into the conscious mind, faced, and accepted.

cathexis. The investment of psychic energy in a mental process or representation.

cell. The structural unit (usually microscopic) of plant and animal life composed of cytoplasm and a nucleus surrounded by a semipermeable membrane or cell wall.

cell body. The mass of cytoplasm surrounding the nucleus of a cell not including any projecting fibers; especially the mass of cytoplasm surrounding the nucleus of a neuron exclusive of the axons and dendrites. Also known as the perikaryon.

cell membrane. A semipermeable membrane surrounding an animal cell.

cell wall. The outer boundary of a cell, particularly a plant cell.

central organizing trait. A personality trait that serves to organize other traits.

central nervous system (CNS). In vertebrates, the brain and spinal cord. See also *peripheral nervous system.*

central sulcus. See *fissure of Rolando.*

central tendency, measure of. A single number summarizing a set of scores that reveals the general trend of the scores. See also *mean, arithmetic; median; mode.*

cerebellum. A large, oval structure in the brain made up of neurons and located behind the pons and medulla oblongata that regulates muscle coordination and balance.

cerebral cortex. The layer of nerve cells that forms the outer covering of the cerebral hemispheres and is the primary center for sensory discrimination, motor functions, and intellectual processes. Also known as the neocortex.

cerebral hemispheres. The two symmetrical halves of the cerebrum

cerebrospinal axis. The central nervous system.

cerebrospinal fluid. A secretion containing few cells and nearly devoid of protein that fills the cavity in the interior of the brain, the spinal tract, and the space between certain membranes that cover the central nervous system.

cerebrum. The largest structural division of the vertebrate brain, occupying the entire upper area of the cranium and involved in the regulation of sensory processes, motor activity, and thought formation.

channel. A route; in the communication process, the way in which a message is transmitted from the source to the audience (*e.g.*, by radio, by magazine, by a lecturer).

charge. See *electric charge.*

Chimp-O-Mat. A machine from which a chimp can obtain food by inserting a token; used in experiments on conditioned reinforcers.

chi square. A method, used in statistics, of determining whether the degree to which a given distribution differs from anticipated values indicates the operation of nonchance factors.

chlordiazepoxide. An antianxiety drug, or minor tranquilizer, sold under the trade name Librium.

chlorpromazine. A major tranquilizer, commonly sold under the trade name Thorazine, often used in the treatment of psychoses.

choice study. An experiment in which an organism is required to exhibit a preference for one of several stimuli or make a different prescribed response to each of them.

cholinergic. Pertaining to those nerve fibers that release acetylcholine; referring to the physiological functions of or bodily processes stimulated by acetylcholine.

cholinesterase. An enzyme found in the blood that inactivates acetylcholine and prevents it from accumulating at the nerve endings.

choroid layer. A membrane located behind the retina containing blood vessels and pigment.

chromosome. A thread-shaped body within the nuclei of all plant and animal cells. Chromosomes usually occur in pairs that reproduce and split off during the formation of new cells, and they are the carriers of genes.

cingulate cortex. A structure of the limbic system that lies above the corpus callosum and extends downward to the amygdala and hippocampus. The cingulate cortex is thought to play a part in hunger sensations, learning, and memory retention.

cingulate gyrus. See *cingulate cortex.*

class. A group of people or objects that possess common characteristics distinguishing them from all others; a distribution of people or objects according to rank; a major biological category; a quantitative division of data.

classical conditioning. An experimental learning procedure in which a stimulus that normally evokes a given response is continually presented with a stimulus that does not usually evoke that response, with the result that the latter stimulus will eventually evoke the response when presented by itself. Also known as Pavlovian conditioning or respondent conditioning. See also *conditional stimulus; unconditional stimulus; conditional response; unconditional response.*

classification. The process or result of arranging items into groups or categories on the basis of some predetermined set of characteristics.

client-centered therapy. A type of psychotherapy based on the belief that the client is responsible for his own growth and self-actualization; the therapist creates an atmosphere of acceptance, refrains from directing the client, and reflects back to the client what the client has said.

clinical psychology. The branch of psychology concerned with the prevention, diagnosis, and treatment of personality problems and mental disorders.

closure. A Gestalt law of organization proposing that people tend to perceive incomplete figures as complete.

cluster. A number of similar objects or persons grouped together; a subgroup of variables that are more closely correlated with each other than they are with the variables of the larger group.

CNS. See *central nervous system.*

cochlea. The coiled, bony cavity in the inner ear containing the receptors for hearing.

code. A set of symbols that represents information or converts data into a qualitative or quantitative series; the process of such representation or conversion; a system of rules. See also *encoding.*

coding. See *encoding.*

cognition. The process or processes by which a person acquires knowledge or becomes aware; the product of such a process or processes.

cognitive dissonance, theory of. The theory advanced by L. Festinger that people are motivated to achieve consistency between their attitudes and their behavior.

cognitive map. The mental representation an organism makes of the spatial relationships between parts of a situation and a goal. E. C. Tolman, who hypothesized the cognitive map, believed that a rat learns a cognitive map of a maze rather than a series of movements.

cognitive psychology. See *cognitive theory.*

cognitive scheme. A complex pattern of learned knowledge that influences a person's perception or conceptualization of an object or idea; a set of assumptions and expectancies about the external world.

cognitive theory. A learning theory hypothesizing that cognitive structures, rather than responses to stimuli, are learned and that sees learning as a process resulting from the restructuring of one's perceptions.

cold spot. A pointlike area of the skin that is especially sensitive to cold (*e.g.*, stimuli below 32° C).

collective mind. See *group mind.*

collective unconscious. According to Jung, one of the two parts of an individual's unconscious mind. The collective unconscious is made up of psychic material that is inherited and shared with other members of the species.

color. A visual sensation caused by light of certain wavelengths reflected or radiated from an object; hue; a quality of an object that only the eye can perceive; pigment.

color blindness. Complete or partial inability to distinguish colors. See also *dichromat; monochromat.*

color constancy. The tendency of colors to be perceived as the same regardless of changes in illumination or viewing conditions.

color contrast. The differences in color brought about when two visual stimuli are presented simultaneously or closely together in space (*e.g.*, a gray circle surrounded by a red square will look different from the same gray circle surrounded by a green square).

color mixture. The combined effect of presenting, either simultaneously or in close succession, two or more color stimuli to a specific area of the retina.

color wheel. A circular arrangement of hues in which sectors of complementary colors are opposite to each other. When rotated quickly, the circle produces a mixing of the colors.

coma. A prolonged loss of consciousness, due to injury, disease, poison, or the like, in which there is no voluntary activity.

commissure. A nerve tract that connects corresponding areas of the cerebral hemispheres.

common fate. A Gestalt law of organization proposing that items functioning, changing, or moving in the same direction will be perceived as belonging together.

communication process. The process of transmitting and receiving information. See also *audience; channel; message; source.*

competence motivation. See *effectance motivation.*

complementary color. One of two colors that yield gray or white when mixed.

complex. Related elements or factors grouped together to form a whole; an assemblage of repressed ideas that cause a person to think, feel, and behave in a characteristic or habitual manner (*e.g.*, Oedipus complex); according to Jung, the form into which the contents of the collective unconscious are organized.

compulsion. The state of being forced to do something; a strong impulse to do something contrary to one's will; a stereotyped, repetitive, and insignificant motor activity that a person feels impelled to perform.

computer. A high-speed electronic machine capable of solving problems by receiving information, performing the appropriate operations on the information, and providing the results. Computers can perform repetitious and highly complex mathematical and logical operations.

computer memory. A device or those components of a computer that accept, store, and return data.

concordance rate. In genetics, the proportion of cases in which two individuals show the same expression of a trait.

concurrent validity. With reference to psychological tests, validity as gauged by a comparison with another measure taken at the same time, such as an established test. See also *construct validity; content validity; predictive validity; validity.*

conditional reflex. See *conditional response.*

conditional response. The learned response to a conditional stimulus.

conditional stimulus. A once-neutral stimulus that has come to evoke a given response after a period of training in which it has been paired with an unconditional stimulus.

conditional reinforcer. A stimulus that increases the frequency of a given response because it has become associated with the primary reinforcer of that response.

conditioned response. See *conditional response.* A conditional stimulus.

conditioned stimulus. See *conditional stimulus.*

conditioning. A method of learning responses. The term is often used as a synonym for classical conditioning or operant conditioning or both.

conduction. The act of conveying neural impulses from a neuron's dendrite to its axon termination, from a neuron to an effector organ, or from one neuron to another neuron.

conduction velocity. The speed with which an action potential moves along an axon. The minimum velocity is about 3 meters per second and the maximum 100 meters per second.

cone. One of many cells in the retina that is sensitive to color. The majority of the cones are located in the fovea and are most useful for daytime vision. See also *rod.*

confabulation. The act of filling in memory gaps with statements that make sense but which are in fact untrue. A person who confabulates believes that his statements are true.

confederate. In reference to an experiment, a person who is supposedly a subject in the experiment but who is actually (unknown to the real subjects) an accomplice of the experimenter.

conflict. A struggle or controversy; disagreement of one idea, emotion, action, and so on with another; the mental state that results when mutually exclusive or opposing impulses, drives, wishes, and so on operate at the same time.

conformity. The condition of acting in accordance with or becoming similar to others; a change in attitude or behavior brought about by social pressure to become like one's peers.

conscience. Introjected standards of behavior; an individual's system of moral beliefs or the part of a person that has moral beliefs; one of the functions of the superego.

conscious. Aware or having knowledge of one's feelings, thoughts, environment, and so on; according to psychoanalytic theory, the division of the psyche containing material of which the ego is aware. See also *unconscious.*

consciousness. The totality of a person's mental experiences; the self; that part of the self which is aware of its own ideas, sensations, acts, or surroundings.

conservation. In development, according to Piaget, the ability to comprehend those aspects or relationships of phenomena that remain constant or invariant during and after transformations in appearance, configuration, or state.

conservation of liquid. The principle that a given quantity of liquid is not altered if the shape of its container or containers is changed.

conservation of number. The principle that the number or quantity of items in a set or group is not altered if the configuration of the set is changed.

constancy. The characteristic of being unchanging, stable, or self-identical. See also *object constancy; shape constancy; size constancy.*

construct validity. With reference to psychological tests, the validity of a test as gauged by the degree to which the results of the test conform to results predicted by the constructs of the theory on which the test is based. See also *concurrent validity; content validity; predictive validity; validity.*

content-addressable system. A system in which the properties of an item determine where it is stored. Human memory is thought to be a content-addressable system (*e.g.*, the sound or look of a word determines its position in long-term memory storage).

content validity. With reference to psychological tests, the degree to which a test's items cover material that is actually an example of the performance the test is designed to assess. See also *concurrent validity; construct validity; predictive validity; validity.*

continuity, principle of. A Gestalt law of organization proposing that items will be perceived as belonging together if they appear to continue in the same direction.

continuous reinforcement. A schedule of reinforcement in which every correct response is reinforced. See also *ratio schedule.*

contralateral control. The regulation of the activities of one side of the body by the cortex of the opposite hemisphere of the brain.

control, experimental. Generally, the intentional manipulation of any condition of an experiment, including the independent variable; when referring to a particular experimental control, manipulation of any condition of an experiment except the independent variable.

control, scientific. See *control, experimental.*

control group. In an experiment, a group of subjects having the same characteristics as the experimental group and that experiences the same treatment as the experimental group with the exception that the independent variable is not applied to the control group. See also *experimental group.*

conversion reaction. In psychiatry, the manifestation of abnormal bodily states without any organic pathology; it seems to occur as a neurotic reaction to psychological distress.

convolutions. Irregular folds, such as those in the exterior surface of the cerebrum.

convulsion. A violent and involuntary contraction of the voluntary muscles.

cornea. The transparent outer covering of the lens and iris that admits light into the interior of the eye.

corpus callosum. A band of nerve fibers connecting the two cerebral hemispheres that is thought to help synchronize their activities.

corpus luteum. A yellow mass of progesterone-producing endocrine tissue formed in the ovary from a follicle after it releases an egg. If the egg is not fertilized, the corpus luteum degenerates.

correlation. Reciprocal relation; the degree of relation between two or more variables; the extent to which two or more variables vary together.

correlation coefficient. A number that indicates the extent to which two variables vary together. Correlation coefficients range from +1 (perfect positive correlation) to −1 (perfect negative correlation).

correlational method. In statistics, a method for deriving categories on the basis of correlations between items.

cortex. An outer cell layer or outer covering; the cerebral cortex.

cortin. The collective name for a variety of hormones secreted by the adrenal cortex.

counterconditioning. The extinction of a learned response by the acquisition of a new response that is incompatible with and stronger than the previously learned one.

counterculture. A group of people that actively does not conform to the behavioral norms of the mainstream culture but instead follows its own norms.

cranium. The bony structure enclosing the brain.

critical period. A relatively restricted period of development in which an animal is especially susceptible to particular influences that may bring about enduring behavior changes or behavioral effects.

cross-adaptation. The effect that sensitivity to one stimulus has on other stimuli of the same type (*e.g.*, adjustment of sensory receptors to a certain level of acidity affects their adjustment to other levels). See also *adaptation; dark adaptation.*

cross-cultural study. The acquisition of comparable data from different cultures for the purpose of testing theories about individual and group behavior.

crossing over. The exchange of corresponding segments of a chromosome pair during meiosis.

crucial stage. In the typology of alcoholic behavior proposed by E. M. Jellinek, the final stage of alcoholism in which the individual feels a powerful need for alcohol and drinks compulsively for prolonged periods of time. See also *prealcoholic stage; prodromal stage.*

cue. A stimulus or pattern of stimuli capable of eliciting a particular action or set of actions.

culturally specific symbol. An act or gesture that reflects the learned experiences of a particular culture (*e.g.*, among the Dayak of Borneo, raising the eyebrows indicates agreement, and bringing them together indicates disagreement.)

culture. The established customs, roles, and learned behaviors of a group of people that are passed on from generation to generation.

cumulative record. In operant psychology, a type of graph of an organism's rate of responding in which a recording device automatically plots the number of responses against time.

cunnilingus. Oral stimulation of the external female genitalia.

curve. A line on a graph representing the values of two or more variables.

cutaneous. Pertaining to the skin.

CVC trigram. A nonsense syllable that is composed of a vowel between two consonants (*e.g.*, ZAL). See also *nonsense syllable.*

cytoplasm. The protoplasm of a cell, not including the nucleus.

D

dance. In reference to animals, a characteristic and instinctive series of movements, particularly those of the bee that supply information about a source of food. See also *round dance; wagging dance.*

dark adaptation. The adjustment of the eye to low light intensity by dilation of the pupil; an increase in the number of active rods and a decrease in the number of active cones. Dark adaptation allows objects or weak lights to be seen when illumination is low. See also *adaptation; cross-adaptation.*

data. A collection of statistics, facts, or information obtained by observation, experimentation, or computation.

dB. See *decibel.*

deafness. Partial or complete inability to hear.

decibel (dB). A unit of acoustic measurement based on the ratio between two sound-wave pressures.

defense. A means or method of protecting oneself; a mental activity or a mental structure (*e.g.*, a defense mechanism) that is acquired unintentionally and not subject to voluntary control.

defense mechanism. A structure of the psyche that protects the ego against unpleasant affects or impulses. Defense mechanisms are unconscious and deny, falsify, or distort reality. See also *dissociation; fixation; projection; reaction formation; regression; repression.*

defe
red imitation. The ability to duplicate another's actions long after those actions have been seen.

delirium. A state of temporary mental disorder characterized by confusion, delusions, hallucinations, illusions, and restlessness.

delusion. A false belief that is held despite demonstrable evidence to the contrary.

dendrite. A short, branched extension of a neuron that receives neural impulses from other neurons and conducts them toward the cell body.

density. The degree of concentration of matter as determined by quantity per unit of space; the quality or state of being crowded together; in hearing, the compactness of a tonal sensation.

deoxyribonucleic acid (DNA). An organic molecule composed of subunits consisting of any of several related chemical structures. The particular sequence of these subunits in chromosomal DNA determines the genetic information carried by the chromosome.

dependent variable. A variable that changes in response to changes in an independent variable; the response to an independent variable.

depression. A state of dejection accompanied by lowered sensitivity to certain stimuli, reduction of physical and mental activity, and difficulty in thinking; an unwarranted condition of prolonged sadness or dejection; the state of being sad or downcast.

deprivation. The removal, lack, or loss of something that is wanted or needed.

depth perception. Awareness of the distance between an object and oneself; awareness of the distance from the front to the back of an object, thus making it appear three-dimensional.

dermis. The skin, especially the skin layer below the epidermis.

descriptive statistics. The study of concepts and techniques used to characterize particular groups of data.

design error. In an experiment, a mistake that occurs when the experimenter measures something that does not exactly coincide with what he wants to measure.

desire. A longing for something. Desires are typically thought of as being conscious, although psychoanalytic theory postulates unconscious desires as well.

development. The act, process, or result of bringing something to a more advanced or effective state; a sequence of gradual changes leading to a greater amount of differentiation or complexity within a system or organism; growth.

developmental psychology. The branch of psychology that deals with the sequence of physiological, psychological, and social growth from birth to maturity and is especially concerned with those behaviors characteristic of given ages.

deviation. A departure from what is considered normal, correct, or standard; the amount by which one value of a set differs from a fixed value of the set, such as the mean.

dextroamphetamine. A drug, sold under the name Dexedrine, that acts as a stimulant; often used to control appetite and alleviate mild depression.

diacetylmorphine. See *heroin.*

dibenzazepines. A group of antidepressant drugs.

dichromat. A person who has a form of color blindness in which the retina reacts to only two of the three primary colors.

dichromatic. Possessing or exhibiting two colors.

diencephalon. Brain tissue located in the posterior region of the forebrain, including the thalamus, epithalamus, and hypothalamus. Also known as the brain stem.

differential threshold. The smallest perceptible difference between two stimuli. Also called the *just-noticeable difference.*

digital computer. A computer that functions with numbers represented directly as digits in a binary, decimal, or other system.

dimethyltryptamine (DMT). A psychedelic drug whose effects are similar to but not as long lasting as those of LSD.

discrimination. In sensory psychology, the detection of differences; in learning, responding differently to different objects, events, or individuals; in social psychology, treating people differently on the basis of their race, ethnic group, class, and so on rather than on their relevant traits; acts of discrimination are typically premised upon prejudice. See also *prejudice.*

discrimination training. The training of an organism to respond differently to two or more similar but distinct stimuli by the reinforcement of correct responses.

dishabituation. The process of becoming or the state of being no longer accustomed to something. After dishabituation, an organism will respond to the formerly habituated stimulus as strongly as it did before habituation occurred.

displacement. The process or result of shifting an idea, activity, or emotional attachment from its proper object to another.

displacement activity. In ethology, a seemingly irrelevant fixed action pattern manifested by an animal in a situation in which two other, conflicting fixed action patterns are evoked.

dissociation. The act or process of separating; the state of being disconnected; in psychiatry, a defense mechanism whereby conflicting attitudes, impulses, or parts of personality are separated from one another in order to avoid emotional distress, sometimes manifesting itself as amnesia or multiple personality; a separation of consciousness into two or more seemingly independent or partially independent entities.

dissonance. An incongruity or disagreement. See also *cognitive dissonance, theory of.*

distortion. The process or result of modifying an image so that it no longer correctly resembles the actual object, person, or place it represents; the process by which forbidden or unacceptable unconscious thoughts or impulses are disguised so that they may enter consciousness.

dizygotic (DZ). Of twins, arising from two zygotes and therefore from two fertilized eggs.

DMT. See *dimethyltryptamine.*

DNA. See *deoxyribonucleic acid.*

dominance. A tendency to seek control over or leadership of others, or such control or leadership; the tendency of one hemisphere of the brain or side of the body to take precedence over the other; in genetics, the expression of the characteristics controlled by one of a pair of genes regulating a given trait in an organism and the suppression of the characteristics controlled by the other.

dominance hierarchy. See *hierarchy.*

double-bind theory. In psychiatry, a theory tracing the origin of schizophrenia to a social environment in which an individual receives contradictory messages and cannot either deal with the contradictions or escape from the situation.

double-blind design. A research technique in which neither the subjects nor the experimenter knows which subjects have been exposed to the independent variable. Often used in experiments on drugs.

Draw-a-Person Test (Machover Test). A projective test in which the subject draws a person.

drive. The psychological representation of a physiological need; a complex of internal conditions brought about by sensitivity to certain stimuli that impels an organism to seek a goal.

Drives may be stimulated by internal bodily changes rather than by psychological or social stimuli.

dynamic psychology. Any approach to psychology stressing motives and drives as causes of behavior.

DZ. See *dizygotic.*

E

eardrum. A membrane between the outer and inner ear that is vibrated by sound. Also known as the tympanic membrane.

echolocation. A technique, used by bats and whales, of locating objects by emitting sound waves and monitoring them after reflection from the objects.

ecological niche. An organism's natural habitat and the transactions it has with its environment, especially with reference to its position in the ecological cycle.

ecology. A branch of science that studies the relationships between organisms and their physical environments; the pattern of relationships between organisms and their environments.

EEG. See *electroencephalogram.*

effector. An organ, gland, or muscle that receives and is activated by neural impulses from an effector nerve. See also *receptor.*

efferent. Carrying outward; in reference to neurons, carrying neural impulses away from the central nervous system or cell body. See also *afferent.*

ego. According to Freudian theory, the part of the psyche that handles transactions with the external environment according to the reality principle. The ego mediates between the demands of the id and the superego. See also *id; psyche; superego.*

ego analysis. In psychoanalysis, the exposure of the strengths and weaknesses of the ego in an effort to understand its need to restrain the expressions of the id.

ego strength. The ability of the ego to perform its functions effectively.

egocentrism. The tendency to evaluate objects and events in terms of one's own personal interests and to be relatively insensitive to the concerns of others; especially in Piaget's developmental theory, the inability to understand that others have needs or outlooks different from one's own. Children exhibit literal egocentrism during most of their early lives.

ego-ideal. The image of the self that a person consciously and unconsciously strives to become and against which he judges himself or herself; generally regarded as part of the superego.

eidetic imagery. The formation and reproduction of especially clear and accurate mental images of objects not currently present. People who are capable of eidetic imagery are said to have photographic memories.

Einstellung. A relatively fixed mental predisposition; the mental set predisposing an individual toward a specific type of activity; a particular expectation or set of expectations.

ejaculation. Swift and sudden ejection; the expulsion of semen and seminal fluid from the penis.

Electra complex. According to Freud, the female form of the Oedipus complex; the desire of a girl to possess her father sexually, manifested in the phallic stage and thereafter repressed.

electric charge. The amount of electricity in something, indicating a deficiency or excess of electrons.

electrical potential. See *potential.*

electroconvulsive shock therapy. A form of psychotherapy sometimes used to treat mania, depression, and schizophrenia in which a certain voltage of electric current is passed through the brain for a particular amount of time, causing a convulsion, a temporary suspension of breathing, and a coma lasting from 5 to 30 minutes.

electrode. A conductor that establishes electrical contact with another substance or body part. See also *gross electrode; microelectrode.*

electroencephalogram (EEG). A graphic record of the electrical activity of the brain obtained by electrodes placed on the skull or brain.

electrolysis. The production of chemical changes by the passing of an electric current through an electrolyte.

electrolyte. A substance that, when dissolved in a suitable medium, can conduct electric current by the movement of ions.

electrolytic cell. A device, used either in electrolysis or for generating electricity by chemical action, consisting of electrodes and an electrolyte.

electromagnetic radiation. Waves produced by the periodic variation of electrical and magnetic field intensities, such as radio waves, light, and x-rays. See also *light.*

electron. An elementary particle of matter having a negative electrical charge and existing outside the nucleus of an atom.

electron microscope. A very high-powered microscope that uses a beam of electrons focused by an electron lens to enlarge images of objects. An electron microscope has greater powers of resolution than a light microscope does.

embryo. An organism in the early stages of development; the early stages of development occurring before birth.

Emmert's law. The principle that the perceived size of an afterimage projected onto a ground changes in direct proportion to the distance of the ground from the eye (*e.g.,* the farther away the ground, the larger the afterimage).

emotion. A feeling state of consciousness accompanied by internal bodily changes (*e.g.,* rapid heartbeat, muscular tightening).

emotional disorder. A condition characterized by emotional responses that are too strong or too weak for the actual situation.

empathic accuracy. The accuracy with which an individual can say what another individual's opinion of himself or herself is.

empathy. The condition of understanding another's thoughts or feelings by putting oneself into his or her psychological frame of reference without actually feeling what he or she feels.

empirical. Dependent on observable facts or experience.

empiricism. The belief that knowledge can come only from experience or observable fact.

encoding. The process of transforming data into a code; the process whereby a message is translated into signals that can be carried by a communication channel; the process of transferring information from one communication system to another.

encounter group. A form of group therapy emphasizing personal growth and improvement in interpersonal communication through intensive interpersonal experience in a small group. Encounter groups encourage openness, honesty, emotional expression, and sensitivity and revolve around the feelings and interactions that occur within the group.

endocrine gland. Any one of a group of ductless glands that secrete hormones into the bloodstream or lymph system.

energy. The capacity or available power to act or do work.

engram. A hypothesized physiological change in living tissue that is the physiological correlate of learning. See also *memory trace.*

environment. The sum of external or internal conditions capable of influencing an organism's behavior.

enzyme. Any of various organic compounds that can generate or accelerate chemical changes in organic substances through catalytic action.

epidermis. The outer, epithelial layer of the skin.

epilepsy. A disorder of the nervous system characterized by convulsions usually terminating in loss of consciousness.

epinephrine. A potent hormone released by the adrenal medulla that increases blood pressure, stimulates the cardiac muscle, increases the heart rate, stimulates the conversion of glycogen into glucose, thus increasing the blood-sugar level, and increases muscle sensitivity to neural impulses. Also known as adrenalin or adrenin.

epistemology. Study of the origins, nature, and limitations of knowledge.

epithalamus. Brain tissue located above the thalamus composed of triangular, stalklike ganglia; the pineal body and posterior commissure.

epithelium. Membranous tissue covering bodily surfaces or lining bodily cavities whose functions include protection and secretion.

equilibration. The achievement of a balance between two opposed forces; in Piaget's theory of development, the process by which accommodation and assimilation are brought into balance.

Eros. According to Freud, the life instinct present at birth that includes all drives for self-preservation. See also *Thanatos.*

error of expectation. In an experiment, a mistake made by a subject because he or she anticipates the nature of the stimulus or its time of presentation.

error of habituation. In an experiment, a mistake made by a subject because he or she makes observations based on a previous situation in which those observations were correct.

escape conditioning. A type of operant conditioning in which making the correct response terminates an aversive stimulus or removes the subject from contact with it. See also *escape response.*

escape response. A learned reaction that allows an organism to get away from or terminate an aversive stimulus or an unpleasant situation. See also *escape conditioning.*

estrous cycle. A recurrent series of physiological changes in female mammals, especially in the reproductive organs and endocrine system, that control the degree of sexual receptivity.

estrus. See *estrous cycle.*

ethnic. Pertaining to a group of people who share a common culture, race, nationality, religion, or language.

ethnic group. See *ethnic.*

ethnocentrism. The belief that one's own group or culture is superior to that of others, with accompanying feelings of contempt for different groups and cultures; the tendency to perceive and evaluate other groups or cultures on the basis of one's own group or cultural standards.

ethnography. The branch of anthropology concerned with the description of individual cultures.

ethogram. A complete record of an animal's behavior as it occurs in the animal's natural habitat.

ethology. The comparative study of behavior, usually of animals, with an eye to species-specific and instinctive behavior; the study of human customs, manners, and mores.

euphoria. A general feeling of well-being, often exaggerated and not based on reality.

evolution. A process or product of development; the continuous genetic adaptation of organisms or species to their environment by specialized processes, such as selection, hybridization, and mutation.

excitation. The arousal of activity or the state resulting from such arousal; the stimulation of a nerve, organ, or tissue; a state of emotional agitation.

excitatory potential ($_SE_R$). A construct postulated by C. L. Hull to explain the strength of a response; according to Hull, habit and drive interact to determine the strength of a response.

exhibitionism. Intentional exposure of sexual organs. This behavior is usually compulsive and appears under inappropriate circumstances.

exocrine gland. A gland that secretes fluids through a duct to the outside of the body or to a specific organ.

expectancy. A learned disposition whereby an organism anticipates that a specific situation will be brought about by a given response to a stimulus.

expectancy-value theory. A theory of human motivation that explains human behavior in terms of an individual's expectancy about attaining a goal in a situation in which his or her motives might be aroused and in terms of the incentive value of the goal. See also *motivation; motive.*

experiment. An operation carried out under controlled circumstances for the purpose of testing a hypothesis, proving a law, or discovering unknown relationships, laws, or effects.

experimental condition. A variable, phenomenon, situation, force, or the like manipulated by the experimenter in order to discover relationships or principles; the independent variable.

experimental control. See *control, experimental.*

experimental design. The plan for carrying out an experiment, including the method of subject selection, procedures for administering the independent variable, and the type of statistical analyses required.

experimental extinction. See *extinction.*

experimental group. In an experiment, the group of subjects exposed to the independent variable. See also *control group.*

experimental manipulation. See *control, experimental.*

experimental psychology. The study of psychology by means of experimental investigation.

externalization. The process of regarding one's actions, drives, or images as being caused by forces or objects outside oneself; imagining a mental image to be outside oneself (*e.g.,* hallucinating); ascribing one's own ideas, feelings, or perceptions to others (*i.e.,* projection).

extinction. The act of putting an end to something; the gradual disappearance of a conditioned response, either because of the repeated presentation of the conditioned stimulus without the unconditioned stimulus or because of the withholding of reinforcement for the occurrence of the conditioned response.

extinction, experimental. See *extinction.*

extinction, spontaneous. The disappearance of a response for no apparent reason.

F

fabrication. The process of making up stories and presenting them as the truth.

faith healing. Healing accomplished through the patient's belief or faith in something, *e.g.,* God, the therapist.

false recall. See *intrusion.*

false recognition. A recognition error in which a person claims to recognize an item that he has never seen before.

fantasy. A product of imagination consisting of representations of objects or events that may or may not exist in reality.

farsightedness. The inability to see near objects clearly because the lens focuses light behind the retina instead of on it. Also known as hyperopia.

fashioning effect. The hypothesis that the social role a person assumes helps shape both his behavior and his self-conceptions.

father figure. A person who embodies the characteristics of and who consequently represents a father. Father figures elicit responses that are typically associated with one's actual father.

fear. An emotional response of dread or terror to a real or imagined danger, marked by violent agitation and accompanied by somatic changes (*e.g.,* increased heart rate) and attempts to escape or hide.

Fechner's law. A general law stating that the intensity of a sensation increases proportionately with the magnitude of the stimulus. Fechner's law is a generalization of Weber's law.

feedback. The knowledge a person receives about his past actions or attitudes. See also *biofeedback.*

feedback circuit. See *biofeedback; feedback loop.*

feeling. A physical sensation from the skin and underlying tissues; a vague awareness; an emotional state.

fellatio. Oral stimulation of the external male genitalia.

female hormone. A hormone that regulates the growth and function of the female reproductive organs or stimulates the development of feminine secondary sex characteristics. Both sexes have female hormones, although females have them in greater quantities.

fetish. An unlikely object that is the subject of sexual excitement or excitation. These objects are, for men, ones often used by or associated with females, *e.g.,* nylon stockings, gloves.

fetishism. Attraction to or use of fetishes to attain sexual excitement and gratification.

figure. A written symbol, especially for a number; a graphic representation, outline, or likeness of something, particularly a person; a group of impressions perceived as a whole; a person who represents the essential attributes of a particular role.

figure-ground. The division of the perceptual field into two distinct and interdependent parts, the figure and the background.

filter theory. Kerckhoff and Davis' theory that people select mates by employing a series of "filters" that eliminate certain persons as prospective mates. These filters (in the order in which they occur) are proximity and social background, similarity of attitudes, and need complementarity.

firing. In neurophysiology, the discharge of neural impulses by a neuron.

fissure. A narrow opening occurring from separation of parts; a natural groove in a bodily organ.

fissure of Rolando. The central fissure of each cerebral hemisphere separating the frontal and parietal lobes.

fissure of Sylvius. The groove between the temporal lobe and the parietal and frontal lobes.

fixation. The state of being set or rigid; an arrest in development that continues into later life whereby a person forms an attachment to persons, objects, events, feelings, or attitudes experienced in infancy or early childhood; in psychiatry, a defense mechanism usually implying pathology that prevents a person from forming normal attachments in later life.

fixed action pattern. A relatively stereotyped and frequently repeated pattern of movements that is species-specific, consistent, and resistant to modification.

fixed-interval schedule. A plan of reinforcement in which reinforcement always occurs after a specific amount of time has elapsed.

fixed-ratio schedule. A plan of reinforcement in which a specific number of correct responses are required in order for reinforcement to occur. See also *continuous reinforcement; intermittent reinforcement.*

follicle-stimulating hormone (FSH). A hormone secreted by the anterior pituitary that stimulates the growth of egg-containing sacs in the ovary and the development of sperm in the testis.

forebrain. The area of the brain composed of the thalamus, hypothalamus, and cerebral hemispheres. Also called the prosencephalon.

foregut. The upper part of a vertebrate embryo's alimentary canal from which the rest of the digestive system develops; in the blowfly, the organ that receives food.

forgetting. The inability to recognize or recall something that was previously learned or experienced. See also *interference theory; repression; suppression; trace decay theory.*

formal group. A highly organized group that usually has explicit rules and regulations governing the behavior of group members.

fornix. An arched nerve-fiber tract in the brain located below the corpus callosum that connects the hippocampus and mammillary bodies.

fovea. A small depression near the center of the retina, containing cones but no rods, that is the point of highest visual acuity.

frame of reference. A system of concepts, standards, values, or goals that affects the evaluations or perceptions of an individual or group.

free association. The unrestrained and uncensored expression of thoughts that occur spontaneously; a technique used in psychoanalysis that enables the therapist to explore his patient's unconscious.

frequency. The number of times a phenomenon occurs in a given period of time; the number of occurrences or examples of a given phenomenon in a given sample; the number of electromagnetic or sound waves per second.

frequency distribution. The classification of data by the correlation of a set of frequencies with a set of intervals, categories, or values.

Freudian theory. See *psychoanalytic theory.*

frigidity. Inability of a woman to experience sexual pleasure.

frontal lobe. The foremost lobe of the cerebrum located in front of the fissure of Rolando and above the cerebral fissure and concerned with fine motor activity and speech. See also *Broca's area.*

frustration. Denial of gratification; the hindrance of goal-directed activity; the emotional state resulting from being blocked, disappointed, or defeated.

FSH. See *follicle-stimulating hormone.*

G

galvanic skin resistance. The apparent resistance of the skin to external electric current.

galvanic skin response (GSR). A change in the electrical resistance of the skin indicating emotional change.

gamete. A mature reproductive cell; a sperm or an egg.

ganglion. Nerve tissue lying outside the central nervous system.

ganglion cell. A retinal neuron whose axons form the optic nerve.

Ganzfeld. A completely homogeneous visual field.

gating. See *sensory gating.*

gene. An ultramicroscopic particle considered to be the basic unit for the transmission of hereditary characteristics. Genes are carried by the chromosomes.

general paresis. A psychosis caused by syphilitic infection of the brain and characterized by both neurological and psychological symptoms.

General Problem Solver (GPS). A computer program simulating problem-solving behavior.

generalization. Application of a judgment to a whole class or group after contact with a limited number of members of that class or group; application of an idea or theory to a new object or circumstance.

generalization gradient. The regular variation in the amount of responding an organism makes to stimuli according to their degree of similarity to a particular stimulus to which the organism has been trained to respond. See also *response generalization; stimulus generalization.*

genetics. The scientific study of heredity.

geniculate body. One of four specialized nuclei located in the back of the thalamus that functions in the processing of auditory and visual information before it reaches the cerebral cortex.

genital stage. According to Freud, the final psychosexual stage (beginning with puberty) during which puberty occurs and sexual interest shifts from autoeroticism to heterosexuality.

genotype. The genetic makeup of an individual, either in toto or with respect to a single gene.

germ cell. A gamete or any one of its antecedent cells.

Gestalt. A unified whole or configuration having specific properties that cannot be derived from summing up its separate parts. Usually used with reference to perceptual phenomena.

Gestalt laws of organization. A set of principles put forth by the Gestaltists to explain what determines the perception of Gestalts. See also *belongingness, principle of; closure; common fate; continuity, principle of; proximity; similarity, principle of.*

Gestalt principles of perceptual organization. See *Gestalt laws of organization.*

Gestalt psychology. A school of psychology, concerned primarily with the processes of perception, whose basic premise is that "the whole is greater than the sum of its parts." Gestalt psychology not only contends that stimuli are perceived as whole images rather than as parts built into images, but also maintains that the whole determines the parts instead of the parts determining the whole.

Gestalt psychotherapy. A form of psychotherapy based on the theories of Gestalt psychology. Gestalt treatment attempts to broaden a person's awareness by using experiments that help him to remember past experiences, feel bodily sensations, and so on. Such treatment is intended to enable a person to form meaningful configurations of awareness.

gland. An organ that releases or produces a substance used in or secreted from the body.

glial cell. A neuroglia cell.

goal. The object or event toward which an organism's behavior is directed.

gonad. A sex gland; ovary or testis.

GPS. See *General Problem Solver.*

gradient. Degree of inclination; the progressive differences between two conditions expressed in stages; a variable or dimension that varies from high to low by progressive stages rather than staying constant or changing irregularly.

gratification. The state of having one's desires or needs satisfied.

gross electrode. An electrode approximately .01 inch in diameter that is capable of stimulating thousands of cells. See also *microelectrode.*

ground. Background. See also *figure-ground.*

group acceptance. The positive response of a group to a single or potential member.

group behavior. The collective behavior of several individuals working together; a person's behavior as affected by membership in a certain group.

group mind. The consciousness ascribed to a collection of individuals, and regarded as distinct from the consciousness of any single member of the group, that results in concerted actions, tendencies, and behaviors by the group.

group norm. A standard by which a group judges the behavior of its members.

group psychotherapy. The treatment of several people at the same time, although not always in the same manner.

group structure. The organized pattern of role relationships in a group that establishes a stable set of social relations and status.

group therapy. See *group psychotherapy.*

groupthink. A group decision-making process that results in unrealistic or overly dogmatic group opinion or appraisal. Groupthink presumably occurs when members of a group feel so strong a need for unanimity of thought or expression that they tend to override any realistic appraisal of alternative ideas and, as a result of internalization of group norms, tend to suppress critical thoughts.

grouping. The process of classifying objects into groups.

GSR. See *galvanic skin response.*

guilt. The realization that one has violated legal, moral, ethical, or religious laws, typically accompanied by feelings of lowered self-esteem and regret; pathological, irrational, or neurotic feelings that are not justified by the reasons given for the guilt.

gustation. The sense of taste; the act of tasting.

gyrus. A ridge or fold, especially in the surface of the cerebral cortex. See also *sulcus.*

H

habit. An acquired and consistently manifested behavior; a learned act that has become fixed and relatively automatic through constant repetition.

habituation. Decreased response to a stimulus because it has become familiar or is expected.

hair cell. A cell containing hairlike projections; a receptor for hearing in the organ of Corti.

halfway house. A self-governing living unit of mentally disturbed people who do not generally require hospitalization but do need the support of a social community that can help them with their problems.

hallucination. Perception of an external object by a sense organ when no such object exists in reality.

hallucinogen. See *psychedelic drug.*

halo effect. In ratings by others of a person's characteristics, the influence on those ratings of specific other characteristics or of a general impression of that person.

hammer. See *malleus.*

handedness. The tendency to use either the right or the left hand almost exclusively.

hashish. A gummy powder derived from the resin of Indian hemp (*Cannabis sativa*) that provides an intoxicating effect when smoked or ingested.

hebephrenic schizophrenia. A severe form of schizophrenia characterized by silliness, absurd behavior, shallowness of feelings, and loss of touch with reality.

hedonistic. Motivated by the desire to seek pleasure and avoid pain.

hello-goodbye phenomenon. Hathaway's proposition that a patient exaggerates the seriousness of his symptoms at the beginning of psychotherapy in order to justify his need for help and exaggerates the extent to which he has been helped at the end of psychotherapy in order to justify the time, money, and energy spent.

Henning's smell prism. A smell classification scheme based on human judgments in which six pure odor qualities form the corners of the prism and intermediate qualities lie along the surface.

hepatitis. An inflammation of the liver, one form of which can follow the use of unsterile hypodermic needles and is therefore often contracted by users of illegal drugs injected intravenously.

heredity. The biological transmission of genetic characteristics from parent to offspring.

heritability. Of a trait, the amount of variation in the trait that is due to genotypic differences in individuals.

heroin. A derivative of morphine, diacetylmorphine, that has a euphoriant and sedative effect. Heroin is much stronger than morphine and is one of the most widely used of the illegal addictive drugs.

heterosexuality. Sexual responsiveness to and sexual behavior toward the opposite sex.

heterozygous. Containing two dissimilar alleles of a gene pair. See also *homozygous.*

heuristic. Imprecise in detail but serving to encourage further discovery; a teaching method that encourages students to discover for themselves.

hierarchy. The arrangement of objects, persons, values, or elements in an order based upon criteria such as importance, dominance, or ability.

hindbrain. The area of the brain composed of the medulla, pons, and cerebellum. Also known as the rhombencephalon.

hippocampus. A curved elevation of nerve tissue located in the forebrain below the cerebral cortex, believed to play a part in the regulation of olfaction, sexual activity, and emotional responses.

homeostasis. A state of physiological equilibrium.

homologue. One of a pair of chromosomes, one of maternal, the other of paternal origin, which carry the Mendelian pairs of alleles.

homozygous. Containing two identical alleles of a gene pair. See also *heterozygous.*

homosexuality. The tendency to have sexual desires for or relations with a member of the same sex.

homunculus. A miniature man. Moral behavior was once thought to be governed by a homunculus who inhabited the human body; early theories of reproduction postulated a homunculus located in either sperm or egg.

hormone. A chemical substance produced in the body that is secreted by one organ and carried through the blood or lymph to another. Hormones regulate physiological activity.

hue. Color gradation; the quality of light permitting its classification according to color; color.

hunger. A drive state based on the bodily effects of food deprivation; the need or desire for food. See also *specific hunger.*

hyperactivity. A high degree of physical activity. Used especially of children who are constantly restless and moving. Also known as hyperkinesis.

hyperkinesis. See *hyperactivity.*

hyperopia. See *farsightedness.*

hyperphagia. Habitual overeating.

hyperthyroid. An accelerated metabolic rate caused by excessive secretion of the thyroid gland.

hypnosis. An altered state of consciousness in which a person is very susceptible to suggestion. See also *trance.*

hypophysis. See *pituitary gland.*

hypothalamus. A group of nuclei located below the thalamus that mediate between the brain and the body, helping control many basic drives and emotional processes including hunger, sleep, thirst, body temperature, and sexual behavior. It controls involuntary functions through the autonomic nervous system.

hypothesis. A proposition put forth as an explanation for specific phenomena.

hypothyroidism. A condition marked by a subnormal metabolic rate and caused by a deficiency of thyroid secretions.

hysteria. A mental disorder characterized by many symptoms. The defining symptoms are not universally agreed upon, but dissociation or conversion reactions are usually held to occur. Hysteria is often considered to be a neurotic reaction to an anxiety-provoking situation in which repression is the primary defense. See also *conversion reaction.*

I

icon. An image or pictorial representation of something.

id. According to Freud, the unconscious and most primitive part of the psyche comprising drives, needs, and instinctual impulses. The id operates according to the pleasure principle and is in constant conflict with the superego. See also *ego; psyche; superego.*

idea. The object of mental understanding; an impression, awareness, belief, opinion, or fantasy.

ideal. A mental image of something in its highest degree of excellence; a standard of perfection or a person or object conforming to such a standard; pertaining to perfection.

idealization. The act or result of representing someone or something as perfect or better than she, he, or it actually is; in E. Goffman's theory, the presentation of oneself as fulfilling a socially determined stereotype.

identification. The recognition or verification of a certain person or object; the act or process of responding to a circumstance as if it were the same as a previously experienced one; the act or process of associating oneself with another person or group or of accepting the values and purposes of others for oneself; the perception of oneself as essentially similar to another.

identity. Sameness of basic traits despite superficial differences; a sense of personal sameness and continuity.

illusion. A distorted or incorrect perception of a physically present object; that which produces a false perception.

image. A likeness or representation of a person, place, or thing.

imagination. The process by which mental images are synthesized into new patterns; the process by which mental images are formed.

imitation. The process of duplicating another's actions more or less exactly, or the result of such duplication.

impotence. In the male, the inability to perform sexually during intercourse because of either physical or psychological causes.

impression. The immediate, unanalyzed effect of sensations or perceptions on the mind; an assessment that is not based on thorough investigation or is not firmly maintained; in personality theory, one person's conception of another.

imprinting. In ethology, a social learning mechanism in birds by which attachments are formed to other organisms or to objects. Imprinting occurs very early in life (during a critical period) and is resistant to later modification.

impulse. A stimulus for action; a neural impulse; according to Freudian theory, the upwelling of an instinctive drive in the id, with its subsequent transmission to the ego, where it is either allowed to operate or prevented from operating.

incest. Sexual relations between a male and a female that are socially forbidden by virtue of the family relationship between the participants. The definition of particular relationships that constitute incest varies from culture to culture.

incus. In the middle ear, the middle bone that transmits sound from the eardrum to the cochlea. Commonly known as the anvil. See also *malleus; ossicles; stapes.*

independent variable. A variable that is

manipulated by the experimenter. Changes in an independent variable affect the dependent variable.

individual difference. A trait that distinguishes one species member from another. Used especially when referring to people's performances on tests.

individual racism. Racism originating in a particular person, including personal prejudice and individual acts of discrimination. See also *institutional racism.*

individuation. The process by which an individual part of a whole takes on an identity that is separate from that whole; the process of becoming individualized.

industrial psychology. The application of psychological concepts and methods to the workings and problems of industry, especially to workers in industrial production.

inference. The act or process of making a judgment or coming to a conclusion on the basis of premises or evidence; the judgment or conclusion reached by such a process.

influence. See *social influence.*

informal group. A group that is not highly organized and whose rules and expectations about members' behavior are generally not explicit.

infrahuman. Subhuman.

infrared rays. Electromagnetic radiation whose frequency falls below that of visible red.

in-group. A group of people with common attitudes, concerns, and so on who feel they belong together and consider persons or groups outside their group as inadequate or alien.

inhibition. The process by which an action or response is restrained, stopped, or prevented from starting even though the stimulus that normally elicits the action or response is present; according to Freud, a process of the superego that prevents instinctual impulses from coming into consciousness; a decrease in a neuron's rate of activity.

innate. Existing in an organism from birth; pertaining to characteristics that belong to the essential nature of something.

innate releasing mechanism. A hypothetical construct of an organism's nervous system that elicits a fixed action pattern in response to a particular stimulus; an assumed neural connection between a sign stimulus and a fixed action pattern.

inner ear. The area of the ear comprising the cochlea, vestibular sacs, and semicircular canals.

inoculation. The introduction of a substance, such as microorganisms or serum, into a living organism (or a culturing medium), usually to produce a mild form of disease followed by immunity; a method of developing resistance to persuasion by first exposing a person to an argument challenging one of his beliefs, and then exposing him to a statement that refutes the previous argument and reinforces his belief.

input. Information introduced into a computer; a form of physical energy or a physical event that causes a sense organ to function.

insanity. A relatively permanent state of mental disorder or disease; such unsoundness of mind as excuses a person from legal responsibility.

insight. The understanding and reasonable evaluation of one's own reactions, awareness, and abilities; the degree to which a mentally ill person understands his own mental condition; knowledge of the objective reality of a situation; according to Gestalt psychology, a new understanding that suddenly occurs.

insight learning. Learning in which an organism suddenly perceives the relationships necessary to solve a particular problem; sudden grasp of a problem.

insomnia. An inability to sleep, particularly when habitual or chronic.

instinct. An enduring pattern of behavior that is characteristic of a given species; an inherited, repetitive behavior that is specific to a species; according to Freud, a primal source of energy or an urge that cannot be resolved. The two instincts postulated by Freud are the life instinct (Eros) and the death instinct (Thanatos).

instinctual drive. In some theories, the motivating force behind human behavior; a mental representation of internal, physiological stimuli.

institutional racism. Racism practiced and controlled by an institution or society; includes actions controlled by the norms, rules, or customs of an institution or society. See also *individual racism.*

instrumental activity. Behavior of an animal that alters its environment or its relation to that environment.

instrumental conditioning. See *operant conditioning.*

insulin. A hormone secreted by the pancreas that allows the body to use sugar and other carbohydrates.

insulin coma. A coma produced by the injection of an overdose of insulin into the muscles; sometimes used to treat mental disorders.

intellect. The totality of cognitive processes, especially thought and understanding; the capacity for obtaining knowledge.

intelligence. The ability to deal with abstractions; the capacity to learn; the ability to handle new situations.

intelligence quotient (IQ). Originally, a measure of an individual's mental development obtained by dividing his mental age (the score achieved on a standardized intelligence test) by his chronological age and multiplying the quotient by 100; now any standardized measure of intelligence based on a scale in which 100 is defined to be average.

intelligence test. A standardized series of tasks designed to measure problem-solving ability, intellectual functioning, and/or previously learned concepts or cognitions.

intensity. The strength or magnitude of a behavior; a physical measure of energy or sensory data.

intentional psychological group. A group of people formed for the express purpose of exploring the psychological processes of individual members.

interference. The act of opposing; intervention that hampers actions or procedures; in learning, the hampering of one instance of learning by another.

interference theory. The hypothesis that a person forgets certain material because other material hinders its recall. See also *negative transfer; proactive interference; retroactive interference; serial-position effects.*

intergroup contact. Interaction between groups.

interiorized action. A schema or pattern of behavior carried out mentally but not physically.

intermittent reinforcement. A schedule of reinforcement in which reinforcement is delivered only part of the time regardless of the number of correct responses made by the subject. See also *interval schedule; ratio schedule.*

intermittent schedule. See *intermittent reinforcement.*

internalization. Incorporation into the mind or personality; making the values, ideas, standards, or practices of others a part of oneself.

interneuron. A short neuron whose cell body lies in the spinal cord and that connects other neurons along a neural pathway, such as sensory neurons to motor neurons. Also known as an internuncial neuron.

internuncial neuron. See *interneuron.*

interpersonal space. The spatial relationships between individuals, usually interacting individuals, that are appropriate to the types of encounters between them and the circumstances in which they occur. The distances vary from culture to culture. In general, there are four ranges of distance governing interpersonal space: intimate distance, social distance, personal distance, and public distance.

interval scale. A scale using the differences between two points as a unit of measure and having an arbitrary zero point. Used to determine how many units are contained in a given magnitude.

interval schedule. A plan indicating when an organism is to receive reinforcement, based on the time that elapses between one reinforced response and the next.

intervening variable. An unobservable variable hypothesized to come between a stimulus and a response that influences the response to the stimulus.

intimate distance. The smallest of the four zones of interpersonal space, designated as less than 18 inches.

intoxication. A state produced by ingestion of alcoholic beverages, drugs, or other substances that is characterized by reduced control of physical and mental activity, great excitement and/or stupefaction; a state of elation; poisoning.

intrapsychic feeling. A feeling that originates or takes place within the psyche.

introjection. The incorporation of the image of an object or individual into the psyche; the investment of feeling in an image of an object or person rather than in the actual object or person; taking the demands of an object or individual into the psyche and acting as if they were one's own, whether or not the object or individual is present.

introspection. The contemplation of one's own experiences, behavior, consciousness, or feelings;

the report of one's mental experiences, usually for the purpose of analysis and study.

introspective method. See *introspection.*

intrusion. In reference to memory, a recall error in which a person makes an inappropriate response to a familiar object or memorized set of items; substitution of one part of a list when asked to recall another; substitution of a response from an entirely different set of materials when asked to recall items from a specific list.

intuition. Direct and immediate knowledge obtained without conscious reasoning or reflective thinking; the process of perceiving such knowledge.

involutional melancholia. A depressive psychosis that occurs during the period of decreased reproductive capacity in men (50 to 65 years) and women (40 to 55 years) who have no previous history of mental disorder; characterized by an agitated and dejected state, delusions of sin, guilt, or poverty, an obsession with death, exaggerated concern for the workings of the gastrointestinal tract, and symptoms of paranoia.

ion. An electrically charged atom or group of atoms formed by the loss or gain of one or more electrons.

iproniazid. A toxic drug that belongs to the chemical family of monoamine oxidase (MAO) inhibitors and was formerly used as an antidepressant.

IQ. See *intelligence quotient.*

iris. A circular diaphragm in the eye that expands and contracts to control the amount of light admitted into the retina. The iris contains the pupil and forms the colored part of the eye.

isogenic. Genetically identical.

isomorphic brain field. In Gestalt theory, an electrical field in the brain that corresponds point by point to a perceived object.

JK

jump stand. An experimental device developed by K. S. Lashley to test visual discrimination and discrimination training. The subject (usually a rat) must jump from a platform toward a door with a distinctive mark on it in order to be rewarded.

just-noticeable difference. See *differential threshold.*

key-word system. A mnemonic scheme in which certain words are associated with the items to be remembered and then are worked into a sentence to be remembered. The words and the items often rhyme.

kibbutz. An Israeli collective community that is mainly agricultural.

kinesthesis. The sense of bodily movement. Receptors for kinesthesis are found in muscles, joints, and tendons.

kneecap. The patella.

knee-jerk reflex. See *patellar reflex.*

koan. In Zen, a nonsense question that is used as a focus for meditation.

Korsakoff's syndrome. A brain disorder affecting the memory and usually associated with brain damage. Confabulation is the distinctive mental symptom. Chronic alcoholism is one cause.

L

labyrinth. In reference to the vestibular apparatus, the inner ear.

Landolt ring. A black, incomplete circle used to measure visual acuity. The subject is asked to detect the break in the circle.

language. Communicative behavior, either verbal or nonverbal; an abstract system of symbols and meanings and the rules of grammar that relate them that facilitates communications; system of communication by vocal symbols.

larynx. A structure composed of muscle and cartilage and lined with mucous membrane. The larynx is located at the upper part of the windpipe and houses the vocal cords.

latency period. According to Freud, the period following the phallic stage (from approximately five to twelve years of age) during which social interest is sublimated.

lateral center. See *lateral hypothalamus.*

lateral fissure. See *fissure of Sylvius.*

lateral geniculate body. A nucleus located in the back of the thalamus that transmits impulses from the optic nerve to the occipital lobe.

lateral hypothalamic feeding-drinking area. An area of the hypothalamus located near the ventromedial nucleus thought to regulate feeding and drinking activities. Destruction of the lateral hypothalamic feeding-drinking area causes an animal to completely stop eating and drinking.

lateral hypothalamus. The area of the hypothalamus that helps regulate activities of the sympathetic nervous system.

lateral nucleus. See *lateral hypothalamus.*

lateral preoptic area. See *preoptic area.*

lay analyst. A person who is trained to practice psychoanalysis but who does not have a medical degree.

law of independent assortment. G. Mendel's observation that traits governed by single genes are inherited separately.

law of segregation. G. Mendel's observation that pairs of "elements" (alleles) governing a single trait tend to separate during the production of offspring.

learning. An enduring change in knowledge or behavior resulting from training, experience, or study, or the process that brings about such a change.

learning curve. A graphic representation of performance that depicts learning as a function of time.

learning theory. In general, an attempt to explain learning or account for the acquisition of habits; specifically, the proposition that learning is based on the establishment of stimulus-response relationships.

legitimate authority. See *authority, legitimate.*

Leiter Scale (Leiter International Performance Scale). A series of language-free intelligence tests designed to be free of cultural influences.

lens. In vision, a transparent structure of the eye, covering the iris and pupil, that changes its shape in order to focus images on the retina.

lesion. An injury; a localized, abnormal change in the structure of a bodily organ or tissue due to injury or disease.

level of confidence. In statistics, the probability at which the null hypothesis can be rejected, expressed as the number of times the predicted results would occur by chance. For example, a .01 level of confidence represents the statistical probability that the predicted results would occur by chance one time in a hundred.

LH. See *luteinizing hormone.*

libido. According to Freud, psychic energy. There is some confusion as to whether libido is the energy of the sex drive and the force behind Eros or the energy behind the destructive drives of Thanatos, or both.

light. The visible range of electromagnetic radiation; the part of the electromagnetic spectrum extending from the ultraviolet to the infrared and including the visible range.

limbic system. A set of neural structures bordering the cerebral cortex that are particularly important in emotion, motivation, and some visceral functions. It consists of the amygdala, cingulate gyrus, hippocampus, and septal area.

linguistics. The science of the origin, structure, and effects of language.

lithium. A naturally occurring metallic element whose salts have been used in the treatment of manic-depressive psychosis.

lobotomy. Surgery that cuts across or into a brain lobe. Lobotomies alter brain functions and are sometimes used in the treatment of mental disorders.

localization. The condition of being in a specific area; the perception of a sensory stimulus as being in a certain location; the location of control over certain bodily functions in definite areas of the brain.

locomotion. The ability to move from place to place, especially the power of an organism to move itself.

logic. The branch of philosophy that examines the principles controlling valid and reliable reasoning; a specific manner of reasoning; trustworthy judgment.

logotherapy. A form of psychotherapy based on analysis of the meaning of one's existence.

long-term memory (LTM). "Permanent" memory that has a seemingly unlimited capacity. LTM endures for very long periods of time, if not for the life of an individual.

loudness. The psychological dimension of sound intensity; the subjective magnitude of the strength of a sound.

love object. According to Freud, a person or thing to which the libido attaches itself; any person or object that one feels affection toward.

LSD. See *lysergic acid diethylamide.*

LSD trip. The altered mental state resulting from the ingestion of LSD. Some characteristics are hallucinations, distortion, high suggestibility, ego fragmentation, and other changes in mood, perception, and thought.

LTM. See *long-term memory.*

lumbar. Relating to the middle back.

luteinizing hormone (LH). A hormone secreted by the anterior pituitary that stimulates ovulation and induces the formation of the copus luteum in females and stimulates the testes to produce testosterone in males.

lysergic acid diethylamide (LSD). An extremely potent psychedelic drug that can produce behavior and sensations characteristic of schizophrenia (*e.g.*, hallucinations, perceptual distortions, thinking impairment).

M

Machover test. See *Draw-a-Person Test.*

magazine training. The establishment of conditioned reinforcers by periodic provision of reinforcement no matter what the subject is doing.

major tranquilizer. See *antipsychotic drug.*

male hormone. A hormone (*e.g.* androsterone, testosterone) that regulates the growth and function of the male reproductive organs or stimulates the development of masculine secondary sex characteristics. Both sexes have male hormones, but in different amounts.

malleus. The outermost bone of the middle ear that transmits sound from the eardrum to the cochlea. Commonly known as the hammer. See also *incus; ossicles; stapes.*

mammary gland. A gland found in female mammals that secretes milk.

mammillary body. One of two tiny, spherical structures in the hypothalamus that receive olfactory impulses from the hippocampus and send them to the thalamus, pons, and medulla oblongata.

mandala. A representation of the cosmos made up of concentric shapes that often contain images of deities and that is often used as an aid to meditation; in Jung's theory, a magical circle that represents the effort to unify the self.

mania. An uncontrollable impulse to behave in a particular manner; behavior characterized by agitation, excitement, and violent and unrestrained motor activity; behavior characteristic of the elated phase of manic-depressive psychosis.

manic-depressive psychosis. A severe mental disorder characterized by depressive states or states of elation or periodic shifts from one to the other.

manipulation, experimental. See *control, experimental.*

MAO inhibitors. See *monoamine oxidase (MAO) inhibitors.*

marijuana. The dried leaves and flowers of Indian hemp (*Cannabis sativa*) that provide an intoxicating effect when smoked or ingested.

masculinization. The production of particular male secondary sex characteristics, especially in a female.

masking. The partial or total interference of one type of sensory stimulus with another; genetic dominance.

masochism. A condition in which sexual satisfaction depends upon mental or physical suffering, pain or degradation; gratification obtained from pain inflicted upon oneself by others or by oneself; the seeking of such gratification; turning one's destructive tendencies inward.

masturbation. The achievement of sexual satisfaction by manual or mechanical stimulation of the genitals.

maturation. The process or end result of completing physical growth and development, accompanied by behavioral changes; in genetics, the process by which gametes are produced.

maze. A network of passages, some of which lead to an exit or a reward and some of which do not. Mazes are frequently used in laboratory experiments to test the learning abilities of animals.

mean, arithmetic. A measure of central tendency computed by dividing the sum of a set of scores by the number of scores in the set.

means-end analysis. In the General Problem Solver computer program, a method of problem solving in which the goal is broken down in subgoals.

measure of central tendency. See *central tendency, measure of.*

median. In a set of scores ranked from low to high, the score that has half of the scores above it and half below; a measure of central tendency that separates a set of scores into two groups of equal number.

meditation. Prolonged reflective thought or contemplation.

medulla. The inner part of a bodily organ or plant structure; bone marrow; the medulla oblongata.

medulla oblongata. The lowest and most posterior part of the brain, connected to the spinal cord, containing nerve centers that control breathing, heartbeat, and blood pressure.

meiosis. In gamete formation, the process of cell division resulting in germ cells with half the number of chromosomes present in normal somatic cells (*i.e.*, containing one homologue of each chromosome pair.

membrane. A thin, pliable layer, particularly of animal or plant tissue, that connects bodily parts, lines an organ, or covers a cell or cell part.

memorization. A learning process, typically accomplished by repetition of the material to be learned, that results in the accurate reproduction of images, ideas, or verbal passages.

memory. The complex mental function of recalling what has been learned or experienced; the image of what has been learned or experienced; the physical retention of information. See also *recall; recognition; storage.*

memory aids. See *mnemonics.*

memory image. A mental representation of an object or event that was previously experienced but that is not now present.

memory storage. See *storage.*

memory trace. A hypothesized physiological change in the nervous system that occurs in learning. See also *engram.*

mental disease. See *mental disorder.*

mental disorder. A serious failure to adapt mentally to external conditions that incapacitates a person in some way. Mental disorders can be short-lived or persistent, can be due to somatic or psychic processes, and can manifest themselves by physical or psychological symptoms. Sometimes also called mental or emotional disturbances, emotional disorder, or psychological disorder. See also *neurosis; psychosis;* and the entries listed under the various names of mental disorders.

mental illness. See *mental disorder.*

mental image. A mental representation of something that is not currently being experienced by the senses.

mental retardation. Subnormal intellectual development and functioning accompanied by subsequent impairment of learning, social development, and maturation.

mentalism. The principle that mental processes are distinct from physiological processes; as opposed to behaviorism, the proposition that conscious processes exposed by introspection are the proper study of psychology.

mentalistic psychology. See *mentalism.*

meprobamate. An antianxiety drug and muscle relaxant, marketed as Miltown or Equanil.

mescaline. A psychedelic drug obtained from the round top of the peyote plant. Mescaline is similar to but not as potent as LSD.

mesencephalon. See *midbrain.*

message. The information transmitted in the communication process.

metabolism. The physical and chemical processes occurring within an organism by which energy is provided and protoplasm built up, maintained, and broken down.

metaneeds. In A. Maslow's theory of personality, human needs that are growth needs rather than deficiency needs, are not hierarchically ordered, and are substitutable for one another. Metaneeds cannot be satisfied unless basic needs are satisfied. The satisfaction of metaneeds leads to self-actualization. See also *basic needs; self-actualization.*

methadone. A synthetic narcotic used to treat heroin addicts. Methadone eliminates the heroin withdrawal syndrome and blocks the euphoric effects of other narcotics but is itself an addicting drug.

methamphetamine. A synthetic drug that acts as a stimulant.

method of loci. A mnemonic device in which people or objects to be remembered are imagined as placed in specific spots in a familiar location.

methodology. The procedures, principles, and rules of a given discipline.

microelectrode. An electrode less than .01 inch in diameter that is capable of stimulating a single cell. See also *gross electrode.*

midbrain. One of the two parts of the cerebrum that lie beneath the forebrain and connect the forebrain to the hindbrain. The midbrain, also known as the mesencephalon, is concerned with sight and hearing.

middle ear. A membrane-lined cavity located between the eardrum and and inner ear that contains the malleus, incus, and stapes. Also called the tympanic cavity.

mind. The organized system of all mental activities; all of the structures assumed to account for voluntary behavior or mental processes; intellect; mental processes; the psyche.

minimum separable acuity. The smallest distance between two items at which the eye can discriminate them as two separate items. See also *acuity; minimum visual acuity; vernier acuity; visual acuity.*

minimum visual acuity. The smallest item the eye can perceive. See also *acuity; minimum separable acuity; vernier acuity; visual acuity.*

Minnesota Multiphasic Personality Inventory (MMPI). A test designed to provide a detailed list of a subject's personality traits based on his answers to a series of 500 statements.

minor tranquilizer. See *antianxiety drug.*

miss. A recognition error in which a person fails to recognize an item that is actually in storage; a recall error in which a person fails to recover information.

MMPI. See *Minnesota Multiphasic Personality Inventory.*

mnemonic device. See *mnemonics.*

mnemonics. A method for remembering items that imposes an invented structure on the material being memorized. See also *key-word system; method of loci; number-consonant system; rhyme.*

mob. A disorderly collection of people that stimulate each other to excitement and lose rational control of their activities.

mob psychology. The study of the psychological aspects of mob behavior.

mode. In a set of scores, the score that occurs most frequently. The mode is a measure of central tendency.

model. A representation that serves as a copy of a process, an object, or an event.

modeling. In social-learning theory, a form of learning in which a person learns how to perform an act by watching another person do it.

molecule. The smallest quantity a substance can be divided into without losing its characteristic properties.

mongolism. See *Down's syndrome.*

monoamine oxidase (MAO) inhibitor. Any of a group of substances that inhibit the activity of the enzyme monoamine oxidase (MAO), one important effect of which is to block destruction of norepinephrine in the neurons. One group of antidepressants are MAO inhibitors.

monochromat. A person whose retina fails to react to any color—*i.e.,* a color-blind person who sees only blacks, whites, and grays.

monochromatic. Possessing or composed of only one color.

monozygotic (MZ). Of twins, arising from one zygote, or fertilized egg.

mood. A repetitive and enduring emotional state that is relatively mild.

moon illusion. The visual illusion that the moon appears larger when it is near the horizon than it does when it is overhead.

moral. Pertaining to standards of right and wrong behavior; conforming to personal ethical beliefs or group and social norms.

moral belief. A belief about whether a certain type of behavior is right or wrong.

morals. See *moral belief.*

morbid. Pertaining to, influenced by, producing, or caused by disease; implying an unhealthy mental state characterized by unwholesome and gloomy feelings.

morphine. An addictive drug used medically to relieve pain. The effects of morphine are similar to those of heroin.

motion parallax. The apparent movement of stationary objects that occurs when the position of the observer changes. Near objects seem to move in wider arcs than far objects.

motivation. An organism's tendency toward action in a given situation. See also *drive.*

motivation research. Studies that attempt to discover people's motives for the purpose of appealing to those motives when selling a product.

motive. A stable personality trait that consists of a tendency to perform certain actions or to seek certain goals.

motor activities. Activities involving muscular movement (*e.g.,* walking).

motor cell. See *motor neuron.*

motor cortex. See *precentral gyrus.*

motor nerve. A bundle of nerve fibers extending from motor neurons.

motor neuron. An efferent neuron that carries impulses from the central nervous system to a muscle.

Müller-Lyer illusion. A visual illusion in which two lines of equal length appear unequal because one has acute-angled arrowheads on its ends and the other has obtuse-angled arrowheads on its ends; the angle of the obtuse arrowheads makes the line seem longer.

multiple personality. A form of dissociation in which two or more distinct but not totally autonomous personalities are present in a single person.

myelin sheath. A white, fatty substance covering certain nerve fibers.

myopia. See *nearsightedness.*

muscle. An organ or tissue that functions to produce movement in a bodily part.

mystification. The act or process of attributing special, mysterious, or supernormal powers to oneself or to others. Mystification of oneself usually involves the maintenance of emotional distance from others.

MZ. See *monozygotic.*

N

NA. See *norepinephrine.*

nACh. See *achievement, need for.*

narcissism. Self-love, frequently associated with erotic gratification. According to psychoanalytic theory, a stage of child development in which the child does not differentiate between himself and objects outside himself and in which he perceives himself as the sole source of pleasure.

narcolepsy. A pathological condition in which a person experiences an uncontrollable desire to sleep and has recurrent periods of sleep lasting from a few minutes to several hours.

narcotic. Having the ability to produce a state of depression, sleep, or drowsiness; a drug that dulls the senses, reduces pain, causes drowsiness, and is addictive.

natural selection. A theory of evolutionary change postulated by Darwin asserting that the individuals of a species who are best adapted to the demands of their environment survive and reproduce; in modern genetics, the theory that the makeup of the gene pool of a species depends on the efficacy to the individuals of the traits governed by the genes in the pool.

nearsightedness. The inability to see clearly objects at a distance because the lens focuses images in front of the retina instead of on it. Also known as myopia.

Necker cube. An ambiguous graphic representation of a transparent cube. The drawing has no clear perspective because back and front are equal in size and one cannot determine for certain which face is nearer.

need. The lack of something that is required; a tissue deficiency due to deprivation.

need complementarity. According to Kerckhoff and Davis, the extent to which the two members of a couple in a love or marital relationship can satisfy each other's needs.

need for achievement. See *achievement, need for.*

negative correlation. A correlation indicating that two variables change in opposite directions (*i.e.,* a high value for one variable corresponds with a low value for the other variable). See also *positive correlation.*

negative reinforcer. A stimulus whose removal increases the frequency of a response.

negative transfer. A process of interference in which previously learned material inhibits the learning of a new task. See also *proactive interference.*

neocortex. See *cerebral cortex.*

neophobia. The fear of something new or unknown.

nerve. A bundle of neural fibers, together with connective and supportive tissue, generally located outside the brain or spinal cord.

nerve cell. See *neuron.*

nerve center. Any part of the nervous system where neural impulses change from afferent to efferent; a hypothetical group of interconnected neurons in the brain that perform specific functions.

nerve excitation. See *excitation.*

nerve fiber. A filamentous extension of a neuron covered by a membrane; an axon or dendrite.

nerve impulse. See *neural impulse.*

nerve tissue. An aggregate of neurons having a common developmental history that perform specialized functions. Nerve tissue is sensitive to certain types of physical energy and transmits electrical energy to parts of the body.

nerve tract. A bundle of nerve fibers with a common origin and ending; a nervous pathway of the brain or spinal cord.

nervous discharge. See *firing.*

nervous system. All nerve cells in the body and their associated organs and processes; the brain, spinal cord, and all nerve tissue.

neural. Pertaining to a nerve, a neuron, or the nervous system.

neural coding. The process by which the nervous system transforms information about the environment into a particular pattern of nervous discharge.

neural fiber. See *nerve fiber.*

neural impulse. A temporary physical, chemical, and electrical change in the membrane of a nerve fiber that travels along the fiber to its end, causing excitation in muscles, glands, or other nerves.

neuroglia. Non-neural tissue that probably provides support for the central nervous system.

neurohypophysis. See *posterior pituitary.*

neurological. Pertaining to the nervous system.

neurology. The branch of medicine concerned with the organization, function, and diseases of the nervous system.

neuromuscular. Relating to both nerves and muscles.

neuromuscular junction. The point at which a motor neuron comes in contact with a muscle.

neuron. A specialized cell that transmits neural impulses from one region of the nervous system to another and to muscles and glands. A neuron consists of a soma (cell body), dendrites, and axons.

neurosis. A mental disorder, much milder than psychosis, affecting only part of the personality, often characterized by the following: a chronic state of anxiety; sensory, sexual, motor, or visceral disturbances; inhibition of emotions or instincts; difficulty in sleeping; lack of interest in the environment; and lack of physical energy. See also *hysteria.*

neurotic anxiety. An unjustified and chronic state of general apprehension; exaggerated apprehension associated with certain ideas; unjustified anxiety accompanied by somatic symptoms, as in hysteria.

neutral stimulus. A stimulus that does not elicit the response one is seeking. In classical conditioning, conditioned stimuli are developed out of neutral stimuli.

nicotine. A toxic substance found in tobacco that acts as a stimulant.

night blindness. Lessened visual acuity in dim light, especially at night, often due to lack of vitamin A or rhodopsin.

nominal scale. A scale in which a number is arbitrarily assigned to an item or entity for the purpose of identification.

nondirective therapy. See *client-centered therapy.*

nonsense syllable. A meaningless combination of letters that can be pronounced, such as QUK. See also *CVC trigram.*

noradrenaline (NA). See *norepinephrine.*

norepinephrine. A catecholamine that functions as a neural transmitter substance and that is released at nerve endings of the sympathetic nervous system, as well as from the adrenal medulla into the circulation.

norm. The average performance level of a given group; that which is expected.

normal. Conforming to the average; free from mental disorder.

noxious stimulus. An unpleasant or harmful stimulus.

nucleus. In a cell, a dense specialized mass of protoplasm that is typically round and enclosed by a membrane; a cluster of neurons in the central nervous system thought to have common functions and connections; a positively charged mass within an atom.

null hypothesis. In statistics, the hypothesis that the effect, difference, or relationship in question does not in fact exist.

number-consonant system. A mnemonic device used to remember numbers. Numbers are translated into consonantal sounds (*e.g.*, 4 = *r*, 6 = *s*, 3 = *t*), the consonants are put together to form a syllable, often with vowels added (*e.g.*, *rst*, *roast*), and the word is remembered.

nymphomania. An abnormally strong sexual impulse in women.

nystagmus. Rapid and involuntary movement of the eye, usually from side to side, but occasionally vertical or circular.

O

object constancy. The tendency of objects to be recognizable as the same object regardless of surrounding stimuli or the point of view of the observer; according to Piaget, the knowledge that an object does not cease to exist once it can no longer be perceived.

objective. Actually existing in the world and capable of being observed by physical instruments; independent of an individual observer's emotions or judgments, hence, unbiased. See also *subjective.*

observational learning. See *modeling.*

obsession. An idea, image, emotion, or the like most often very disturbing or disruptive, that dominates one's consciousness.

obsessive-compulsive neurosis. Neurosis characterized by the constant presence of unwanted, anxiety-provoking ideas and the occurrence of impulses to perform certain acts repeatedly.

occipital lobe. The hindmost of the three posterior lobes of the cerebrum. Concerned with the reception and analysis of visual information.

occupational therapy. Psychotherapy whose goal is to help a patient overcome a psychological or physical disability through purposeful work.

odor. The quality of a substance that affects olfaction; one of a class of sensations produced by chemical stimulation of the receptors for olfaction.

Oedipus complex. According to Freud, a boy's desire to possess his mother sexually, manifested in the phallic stage and thereafter repressed. The female form of the Oedipus complex is the Electra complex.

Ohm's acoustic law. The principle that a person can distinguish the individual tones that compose a complex sound, thus hearing a sound as a compound of tones rather than as a single sound.

olfaction. The sense of smell.

olfactory bulb. One of two oval-shaped masses of nerve tissue located above the nasal cavity and extending to the cerebrum.

olfactory epithelium. A membrane in the nasal cavity containing the receptors for smell.

olfactory nerve. Either of a pair of cranial nerves that transmit neural impulses from the mucous membranes in the nose to the brain.

operant behavior. A response not associated with a specific or identifiable stimulus that is defined by its effects on the environment.

operant conditioning. A form of training in which certain of an organism's spontaneous activities are reinforced. Also known as instrumental conditioning.

operant response. See *operant behavior.*

operational thinking. See *operationalism.*

operationalism. The doctrine that scientific concepts derive their meaning from the methods of investigation used to arrive at them. Thus, scientific concepts cannot be separated from the research methods used.

opiate. Any one of a group of drugs containing a form of opium; anything causing inaction or inducing sleep.

opponent cell. A neuron located in the lateral geniculate body that is excited when the eye is stimulated by light at certain wavelengths and inhibited when the eye is stimulated by light at other wavelengths.

opponent-processes theory. The theory that three different systems, composed of three types of cells, are responsible for color vision: In one system, some cells are stimulated by red and inhibited by green and others are stimulated by green and inhibited by red. In another system yellow and blue similarly act in opposition to each other. The third system is achromatic and sensitive to brightness.

optic nerve. One of a pair of cranial nerves that carry neural impulses from the retina to the brain.

optical image. See *retinal image.*

oral impulse. An unconscious drive toward oral gratification that is residual from infancy and unacceptable to the ego; an instinctual drive leading to activities that satisfy aggressive or libidinal needs.

oral stage. According to Freud, the first psychosexual stage (occurring during the first eighteen months of life) in which pleasure is focused on the mouth and oral activities (*e.g.*, eating, sucking).

order. An arrangement of objects, individuals or events; a biological category that is the major subdivision of class.

ordinal scale. A number system in which numbers are assigned to items according to their rank ordering on some dimension.

organ of Corti. A structure in the cochlea containing hair cells that are the receptors for hearing.

organism. A form of life capable of performing specific, coordinated functions and normally capable of maintaining itself as a system; in psychology, usually one of the higher animals, including people.

orientation. The ability to locate onself in reality or one's environment by reference to persons, places, and time; knowledge of where one is in personal relations or perplexing situations; an inclination to particular behavior patterns; direction or position in reference to people, objects, concepts, or principles.

osmoreceptor. A nerve ending in the hypothalamus that responds to changes in osmotic pressure in the blood, two functions of which are the regulation of the emission of antidiuretic hormones and the stimulation of thirst; a sensory nerve ending that functions in the sensation of odor.

osmotic pressure. The force exerted by a dissolved substance on a semipermeable membrane it cannot penetrate when the substance and membrane are separated by a solvent.

ossicles. Three small bones in the middle ear that transmit sound from the eardrum to the cochlea. See also *incus; malleus; stapes.*

other-directed. Tending to underemphasize individual standards and values and overemphasize the expectations and preferences of others.

outer ear. The part of the ear consisting of the pinna and auditory canal.

out-group. A specific group of people, or people in general, who do not belong to an in-group or to one's own group and whom one often considers to be inadequate or alien; a group to which one does not belong.

output. Production; in reference to computers, information that has been transferred from internal to external units.

oval window. A membrane-covered opening between the middle ear and the vestibule that transmits sound from the ossicles to the cochlea. Also known as the fenestra ovalis or fenestra vestibuli.

ovariotomy. Removal of the ovaries by surgery. See also *castration.*

ovary. One of the pair of female reproductive glands in which egg cells and female hormones are produced.

overlearned response. See *overlearning.*

overlearning. Learning in which responses are practiced past the point of apparent mastery.

overt behavior. An act easily observed by others.

ovulation. The maturation and release of an ovum, or egg, from the ovary, or simply the release of the ovum from the ovary.

ovum. An egg, or female germ cell.

oxytocin. A hormone, probably produced in the hypothalamus and stored in the posterior pituitary, that is released during pregnancy and helps induce uterine contractions.

P

pain. An unpleasant and distressing physiological sensation; physiological, mental, or emotional suffering.

paired-associate learning. A method of learning in which items, usually verbal, are presented in pairs so that the learner connects one item with the other. See also *response item; stimulus item.*

papilla. A small, nipple-shaped protuberance; one of a cluster of small bumps located on the surface of the tongue, in hair cells, or on the skin of the hands and feet. There are papillae associated with sensory receptors for smell, taste, and touch.

parabiotic twins. Two organisms parts of whose bodily systems are joined together—*e.g.,* Siamese twins; animals so joined surgically, for the purpose of experimentation.

paradigm. A conceptual model or system depicting some aspect of reality from which one draws conclusions about how to proceed in conducting an investigation.

paradoxical cold. The sensation of cold that results when a cold spot is touched by a stimulus that is very warm (approximately 45° C or above).

paradoxical depth. The perception of a drawn figure as being both two- and three-dimensional.

parallel processing. Categorizing and dealing with several streams of incoming information at one time.

paranoia. A psychosis characterized by the gradual development of systematic persecutory or grandiose delusions that affect only part of the personality and are isolated from intelligence.

paranoid schizophrenia. A psychosis characterized by elaborate and systematic delusions of persecution and grandeur. Paranoid schizophrenia, unlike paranoia, affects the entire personality.

parasympathetic nervous system. The division of the autonomic nervous system in which efferent nerve fibers leave from either the cranium or sacrum and synapse in ganglia located near the muscles to be excited. The parasympathetic nervous system is activated by acetylcholine and conserves body energy by slowing heart rate and aiding digestion.

parietal lobe. One of the three posterior lobes of the cerebrum located behind the fissure of Rolando and concerned with skin senses and detection of bodily position.

patella. The kneecap.

patellar reflex. The involuntary forward extension of the lower leg that occurs when the patellar tendon is tapped. Commonly known as the knee-jerk reflex.

patellar tendon. The tendon connecting the patella to a muscle in the thigh that produces the patellar reflex when tapped.

pathological. Pertaining to diseases or deviations from a normal or healthy state; morbid.

pattern. Anything that serves as a guide for making objects or performing actions; an arrangement of parts forming a unified and characteristic whole.

pattern, behavior. See *behavior pattern.*

pattern, break-and-run. In experimental psychology, a response pattern produced by fixed-interval schedules in which very few responses occur until approximately two-thirds of the way through the interval, when a high response rate suddenly occurs and continues until reinforcement is obtained.

Pavlovian conditioning. See *classical conditioning.*

peak shift. In discrimination training, the movement of the highest point of the curve of responses in a generalization test away from a nonreinforced stimulus. The peak normally occurs on the presentation of the stimulus on which the organism was originally trained (*i.e.,* the reinforced stimulus).

pederasty. Anal intercourse between a man and young boy.

pedophilia. The sexual attraction felt by an adult for a child.

peg system. See *key-word system.*

penis envy. In Freudian theory, a girl's discontent with her genital apparatus accompanied by a desire to possess a penis, which is generally associated with omnipotence. Penis envy develops during the phallic stage and is thereafter repressed in normal individuals.

perception. The process of becoming aware of one's environment through the senses; awareness of the environment obtained through interpretation of sensory data.

perceptual constancy. In perception, the tendency to recognize the characteristics (*e.g.,* size, shape) of a stimulus object as being the same even under highly varied conditions.

perceptual field. That part of the external world an organism perceives and to which it makes a discriminating response.

perceptual judgment. Evaluation made on the basis of sensory processes.

perceptual set. A readiness to perceive or respond to the environment in a particular manner. Perceptual set helps determine what will and will not be perceived, the rapidity of perception, and the vividness of perception.

performance. Any activity that produces a result; the execution of an action or series of actions; the accomplishment of an undertaking; how a person reacts to a task. Often contrasted with learning.

perikaryon. See *cell body.*

peripheral. Relating to the outer or external boundary or surface; referring to the nerves located farthest from the brain and spinal cord; referring to any bodily process that has a direct connection with the external world.

peripheral nervous system. The part of the nervous system that is made up of nerves connecting the central nervous system with the body's receptors and effectors—*i.e.,* all nerve processes and neurons outside the central nervous system.

periphery. The outer boundary of an area or surface; the retina exclusive of the fovea and containing rods but no cones.

pernicious anemia. A blood deficiency characterized by a gradual lessening of the number and increase in the size of the red blood cells. The symptoms of pernicious anemia include paleness, lack of strength, nervous disturbances, and gastrointestinal problems.

personal distance. One of the four regions of interpersonal space, extending from 1½ to 4 feet.

personal front. In E. Goffman's theory of the presentation of self, the sum total of all the impressions that can be gathered about a person from his appearance and manner.

personal stereotype. A stereotype created by an individual on the basis of his or her personal experience.

personality. The distinguishing traits and characteristic behaviors of a person; the sum total of a person's somatic, mental, emotional, and social traits or of those that are commonly perceived as most important.

personality characteristic. See *trait.*

personality disorder. Habitual and rigid patterns of behavior that are maladaptive and restricting although persons affected are relatively free from anxiety, distress, and mental, emotional, and somatic symptoms.

personality problem. An enduring personal characteristic that limits or hinders the attainment of harmonious relations with other people or the environment, *e.g.*, shyness, jealousy, callousness.

personality test. Any device or method used to facilitate the analysis or evaluation of personality.

peyote. A small cactus, eaten by certain native North and South American tribes as part of their religious rituals, that contains a psychedelic. Mescaline is derived from the peyote plant.

phallic stage. According to Freud, the third psychosexual stage (from approximately three to five years of age) during which pleasure is focused on the genitals. Autoeroticism, castration anxiety, penis envy, and the Electra and Oedipus complexes arise during the phallic stage.

phenomenology. The study of objects and events as they are experienced rather than from the view of objectively described reality. Sometimes contrasted with behaviorism.

phenothiazines. A group of antipsychotic drugs, used especially in the treatment of schizophrenia and manic-depressive psychosis.

phenotype. The observable characteristics or constitution of an organism, either in toto or with respect to a single trait.

phi phenomenon. The perception of motion, particularly the illusion of movement of stationary objects when they are presented in quick succession.

phobia. Excessive fear of particular objects or situations, often with no basis in reality; morbid fear and anxiety about something.

photographic memory. See *eidetic imagery.*

photon. A unit of electromagnetic radiation; an elementary particle with no electrical charge; a unit of retinal illumination by a source of light.

photopic threshold curve. A curve showing the weakest light the eye can detect when adapted to strong light.

photopic vision. Vision under illumination that is intense enough to allow complete differentiation of colors. Photopic vision is mediated by the cones.

phylogenetic scale. A scale showing the development and evolution of biological characteristics specific to a species or group.

physiological psychology. The branch of psychology concerned with the relationships between physiological activities and mental processes or behavior.

physiological zero. The temperature at which a stimulus touched to the skin yields no thermal sensations (usually 32° C).

physiology. The study of the organic processes of living beings.

pigment. A substance that colors; a substance found in animal and plant tissues and cells that accounts for their characteristic color; a substance that absorbs some wavelengths of visible light and reflects others.

pineal body. A small, oval glandular outgrowth of the epithalamus that is located above the thalamus in vertebrates having a cranium. The function of the pineal body is unknown.

pinna. The part of the ear not within the head, consisting of a funnel-shaped body composed primarily of cartilage that opens into the auditory canal and serves as a collector of sound. Also called the auricle.

pitch. The subjective highness or lowness of sound determined by sound frequency.

pituitary gland. An endocrine gland located at the base of the brain that consists of anterior and posterior parts. The pituitary gland secretes hormones that regulate metabolism, body growth, sexual maturation, and the activities of other endocrine glands. Also known as the hypophysis. See also *anterior pituitary; posterior pituitary.*

place theory. A theory of hearing hypothesizing that different fibers on the basilar membrane are responsive to different sound frequencies.

placebo. A substance that has no marked pharmacological effect (*e.g.*, a sugar pill) but is given as a control to test the efficacy of another substance or to satisfy a person who wishes to take a remedy for a disorder.

pleasure principle. According to psychoanalytic theory, one of the regulatory principles of mental functioning whereby painful tensions are reduced to the lowest possible level by immediate gratification of instinctual needs. Gratification can either be direct (getting water to satisfy thirst) or by fantasy. See also *reality principle.*

plexus. A network of interrelated parts, especially of nerves or blood vessels.

polarization. A condition, or the creation of a condition, in which light waves oscillate parallel to a single axis; the deposition of gases on an electrolytic cell and the subsequent increase in the cell's resistance; separation into two opposites; an electrical potential or uneven distribution of electrical charge.

polygenic trait. A trait that depends on the combined effects of several or many genes.

pons. A band of nerve fibers located in the hindbrain connecting the lobes of the midbrain, medulla, and cerebrum and controlling facial movements, hearing, and respiration, among other things.

Ponzo illusion. A visual illusion.

population. The number of inhabitants of a place; an assemblage of individuals or items subject to statistical analysis for certain characteristics; all the individuals of a species.

positive correlation. A correlation indicating that two variables change in the same direction —*i.e.*, a high value for one variable corresponds with a high value for the other variable. See also *negative correlation.*

positive reinforcer. A stimulus whose occurrence increases the frequency of a response.

positive transfer. A process whereby previously learned material facilitates the learning of a new task.

postcentral gyrus. A convolution located behind the fissure of Rolando and extending to the fissure of Sylvius. The postcentral gyrus is the primary receiving area of sensations originating in the skin, muscles, tendons, and joints. Also known as the somesthetic cortex.

posterior pituitary. The hind part of the pituitary gland. The posterior pituitary develops from neural tissue and releases hormones that affect blood pressure, the smooth muscles, and excretion of urine. Also known as the neurohypophysis.

potential. Possibility; a latent ability that has the possibility of being developed; something that can become actual; degree of electrification.

pragmatism. The philosophical belief in practical consequences as the standard by which concepts are evaluated.

prealcoholic stage. In E. M. Jellinek's typology of alcoholic behavior, the first stage of alcoholism, in which the drinker discovers that alcohol reduces his tensions, gives him self-confidence and courage, and eases psychological and social pressures. See also *crucial stage; prodromal stage.*

precentral gyrus. A convolution of the cerebrum located in front of the fissure of Rolando and extending to the fissure of Sylvius. The precentral gyrus controls voluntary movements of skeletal muscle. Also known as the motor cortex.

predictive validity. The ability of a test to predict actual performance in the area supposedly assessed by the test. Predictive validity is commonly measured by the correlation of test results with measures of actual performance at a later date. See also *concurrent validity; construct validity; content validity; validity.*

predisposition. The condition of being inclined to something beforehand; an inherited factor that inclines a person to develop certain diseases or morbid traits.

prefrontal area. The foremost region of the frontal lobe of the cerebrum, possibly concerned in the ability to order stimuli and information.

prefrontal lobotomy. A surgical procedure by which the nerve fibers from the frontal lobe to the thalamus are severed.

prejudice. Beliefs or judgments made without sufficient evidence and not easily changed by opposing facts or circumstances; preconceived feelings, opinions, or attitudes about a group or an individual belonging to a certain group (*e.g.*, race, social class); hostile and irrational attitudes about a person made without consideration of his own attributes. See also *discrimination.*

preoptic area. The region of the hypothalamus in which the cells that produce ADH are located.

primacy effect. The principle that items occurring at the beginning of a series are easier to remember than those occurring in the middle.

primary color. One of a small set of colors that yield all other colors when mixed in various combinations. The colors that are called primary differ according to whether colored light or colored pigment is being referred to and also according to the particular color theory being consulted, but the most commonly cited set is red, yellow, and blue.

primary reinforcer. A stimulus that is innately satisfying; a stimulus that strengthens a response without need of prior training (*e.g.*, food).

proactive interference. A process in which previously learned material hampers the recall of newly learned material. See also *negative transfer.*

probability. The quality of being likely to happen; the likelihood that a given phenomenon will occur, expressed as the ratio between the number of times the phenomenon actually occurs and the total number of possible occurrences.

problem. A situation that is uncertain, doubtful, or difficult; a question or statement that requires a solution.

problem solving. The process of resolving a difficulty or task or finding the answer to a question; the process of choosing from a series of alternatives those that lead to the attainment of a specific objective.

proboscis. A feeding organ that is elongated or snoutlike.

prodromal stage. In E. M. Jellinek's typology of alcoholic behavior, the second stage of alcoholism, in which alcohol is turned into a drug upon which the drinker relies; he drinks heavily and furtively, may suffer memory blackouts, and is often unable to recall what happened to him during his drinking bouts. See also *crucial stage; prealcoholic stage.*

projection. The process of ascribing one's own attitudes, feelings, or thoughts to others, especially when those attitudes, feelings, or thoughts are considered as undesirable; regarding objective stimuli subjectively.

projective test. A measure of personality traits that requires a subject to interpret neutral or ambiguous stimuli. The subject responds to the unstructured stimuli according to the dictates of his personality (*e.g.,* his needs, drives, defenses, etc.). The Rorschach test, the TAT, and sentence- or story-completion tests are examples of projective tests.

prolactin. A pituitary hormone that induces the secretion of milk.

propaganda. Information that is deliberately spread by an individual, a group, or an institution for the purpose of influencing the attitudes or behavior of others.

propanediols. A group of antianxiety drugs.

proton. A fundamental particle of the nuclei of atoms, having a positive electric charge of the same magnitude as the negative charge of an electron.

protoplasm. A semifluid, complex substance found in all living cells that is the physical basis of life.

proximity. Nearness in location, time, arrangement, occurrence, or connection; the principle of Gestalt psychology that objects close to each other will tend to be perceived as a whole.

psilocybin. A psychedelic drug obtained from certain mushrooms. The effects of psilocybin are similar to those of LSD.

psyche. According to Freud, the performer of psychological activities, composed of conscious and unconscious divisions; the mind. See also *ego; id; superego.*

psychedelic drug. A group of drugs, also known as hallucinogens or psychotogenic drugs, that produce unusual and exaggerated mental effects, especially in cognition and perception, and often provoke highly imaginative thought patterns.

psychiatric social worker. A person holding a graduate degree in psychiatric social work who is trained to work with and counsel children and adults who seem socially maladjusted because of mental or behavioral problems.

psychiatrist. A medical doctor who specializes in the treatment of mental disorders.

psychiatry. The branch of medicine concerned with the prevention, diagnosis, and treatment of mental disorders.

psychic energy. A postulated force, similar to energy as defined by physical science, originating in the instinctual drives and accompanying all mental activity.

psychoanalysis. The Freudian theory of personality; a type of psychotherapy that utilizes the techniques of transference and free association.

psychoanalyst. Generally, a person trained in the techniques of psychoanalysis (*e.g.,* a lay analyst); a psychiatrist trained in the techniques of psychoanalysis.

psychoanalytic theory. The theory of personality originated by Freud that is based on the unconscious.

psychodrama. The living through or portrayal by a person of certain situations, incidents, or conflicts suggested by a therapist. This technique is used to bring to the surface the real meaning of certain social relationships, as well as to reveal aspects of the person's private personality.

psycholinguistics. The study of the relationships between the mental characteristics of language users and the structure of language.

psychological disorder. See *mental disorder.*

psychological reactance. The underlying principle of J. W. Brehm's theory of persuasion stating that people will either reject a message delivered by a source they perceive as coercive or shift their views in the direction opposite to that of the message.

psychology. The study of the behavior and mental processes of organisms, or the behavior and mental processes themselves.

psychopathy. Mental disorder.

psychopharmaceutical. A drug that affects mental or behavioral functioning.

psychopharmacology. The study of the psychological effects of drugs.

psychophysical experiment. An experiment designed to study the relationships between stimuli and sensations. Typical examples of psychophysical experiments include requiring a subject to determine differences in stimulus intensity and measuring a subject's thresholds for certain stimuli.

psychophysics. The study of the relationships between the physical attributes of stimuli and resulting organismic sensations; the study of the relationships between external stimuli and an organism's behavior or mental processes.

psychosexual stages. According to Freud, the different phases of sexual development, especially the mental aspects of sexual development, occurring between infancy and adolescence. See also *anal stage; genital stage; oral stage; phallic stage.*

psychosis. A severe mental disorder marked by a generalized failure of functioning in all areas of a person's life. Characteristics of psychoses include an inability to maintain effective relationships with the external environment, distortion of objective reality, exaggeration of emotions to the point that they constitute one's entire existence, language and thought disturbance, hallucinations, delusions, and regression. Commonly known as insanity or madness. See also *involutional melancholia; paranoia; paranoid schizophrenia; schizophrenia.*

psychosomatic. Pertaining to the correlation of normal, abnormal, or pathological psychic phenomena with somatic conditions or variations.

psychotherapy. The use of psychological techniques for the treatment of mental disorders or behavioral maladaptations.

psychotogenic drug. See *psychedelic drug.*

PTC. See *phenylthiocarbamide.*

puberty. The period in which a person's reproductive organs first become capable of functioning and in which secondary sex characteristics begin to develop; thought to begin at the age of twelve in females and fourteen in males and to continue for approximately two or three years thereafter.

puberty rite. A formal act or procedure occurring in various cultures that initiates a person who has reached puberty into the adult life of a community.

public distance. One of the four zones of interpersonal space, from 12 to 25 feet.

punisher. A stimulus that decreases the future frequency of occurrence of the behavior it follows.

punishment. The act of imposing a penalty on an animal because it has performed a disapproved action or because it has failed to perform an approved action; it reduces the probability that a given response will occur.

pupil. In reference to vision, the opening in the iris that regulates the amount of light entering the retina.

R

race. A population whose descent can be traced back to a common ancestor; a population related by blood or heredity that forms a relatively isolated mating group with distinctive gene frequencies and physical traits.

racial role. The attitudes and behavior patterns considered by a society to be appropriate to a certain race.

racism. A doctrine emphasizing the importance of race as the foundation of group action and interaction; the assumption that race determines psychological and cultural traits accompanied by the belief that races differ decisively from each other; the belief that a particular race is superior to others and thus has a right to dominate them. See also *individual racism; institutional racism.*

radiation. The process of emitting energy as waves or particles; the energy emitted by this process; diffusion from a center.

random sorting. See *randomize.*

randomize. To select items of a set or persons in a group by chance so that each has the same probability of being chosen; to treat or distribute an experimental population in such a way as to remove experimenter bias or eliminate selective factors.

range. The limits of a series; the difference between the highest and lowest scores in a set of scores.

rapid eye movement (REM). A rapid movement of an organism's eye during sleep. Dreaming appears to take place only during the period of sleep in which rapid eye movements occur.

RAS. See *reticular activating system.*

rating. An evaluation of the characteristics or attributes of a person, place, or thing. In experiments, such evaluation should be made with strict rules for accuracy, completeness, and lack of bias.

ratio scale. A scale based on a unit of measurement that is a fraction of a standard difference between two points, and therefore in which units are equal, and that has an absolute zero point.

ratio schedule. In experimental psychology, a plan indicating when reinforcement is to occur based on the number of correct responses made between reinforcements.

rauwolfia alkaloids. A group of antipsychotic drugs, the most widely used being reserpine, derived from an extract of the roots of certain trees and shrubs.

reaction formation. According to psychoanalytic theory, a form of repression in which conscious traits and patterns of behavior are developed in the ego that are in direct opposition to strong trends within the unconscious. For example, extreme sympathy may be a reaction formation against sadistic impulses.

reality. The state or quality of existing in fact; the totality of objects or conditions in the world that can be perceived by the senses and are independent of imagination or theory.

reality principle. According to Freudian theory, one of the regulatory principles of mental functioning whereby an individual adjusts his behavior to the conditions of real life and the environment by delaying, giving up, inhibiting, or changing drive and need satisfaction. See also *pleasure principle.*

reasoning. The act or process of thinking in a logical way; forming judgments or conclusions on the basis of evidence or premises.

recall. A type of memory retrieval in which a person recovers previously learned information.

recency effect. The principle that items occurring most recently in a series are easier to remember than those that were presented earlier.

receptor. A nerve ending in the skin or a special sense organ that is sensitive to a particular type of stimulus and initiates neural impulses. See also *effector.*

receptor cell. A sensory neuron that is sensitive to particular forms of physical energy and capable of initiating a neural impulse.

recognition. A type of memory retrieval in which a person exhibits an awareness of an object, person, or situation as one that he has experienced before.

recurrent behavior. Behavior patterns that occur repeatedly or periodically.

recurrent nerve. A nerve in the blowfly that receives impulses from receptors measuring distention of the foregut.

reference group. A group with which a person associates or identifies himself. Identification with a reference group often leads to the adoption of the attitudes, standards, and behaviors exhibited by the group.

reflex. An involuntary response to a stimulus due to the transmission of a neural impulse from a receptor to a nerve center and outward to an effector.

reflex arc. A hypothetical pathway, extending from a receptor to an effector, that a neural impulse follows in order to produce a reflex.

regression. According to psychoanalytic theory, a defense mechanism consisting of a return to an earlier stage of development or behavior, particularly when the person is threatened or in a stressful situation.

rehearsal. Repetition of information or behavior to be learned. Rehearsal prolongs the retention of material in short-term memory and helps the transfer of material from short-term memory to long-term memory.

reinforcement. The act or state of strengthening by adding something; any circumstance that increases the possibility that a given response will recur in a similar situation; in operant conditioning, the experimental procedure of immediately following a response with a reinforcer, in order to strengthen the response.

reinforcement schedule. A plan indicating when reinforcement is to occur, in terms of either time intervals or number of correct responses. See also *interval schedule; ratio schedule; continuous reinforcement; intermittent reinforcement; schedule.*

reinforcer. A stimulus that increases the frequency of a response.

rejection. The process of excluding someone or something from one's affections or attention or the state resulting from such exclusion; judging someone or something as having no worth; casting off or putting aside.

relative refractory period. A brief period, following the absolute refractory period, during which a neuron will respond only to relatively strong stimuli.

reliability. The state of being trustworthy and dependable; the dependability and consistency of a measure. A reliable test is one that obtains similar results upon repetition.

REM. See *rapid eye movement.*

REM period. A hypothesized stage of sleep. See *rapid eye movement.*

remembering. The active process of mentally reconstructing previously learned or experienced events. Remembering involves successful acquisition, storage, and retrieval of information. See also *retrieval.*

repression. According to psychoanalytic theory, a defense mechanism that guards against anxiety and guilt by the unconscious exclusion of painful and unacceptable ideas or impulses from consciousness.

resistance. The act of opposing; the opposition given by a substance to the transmission of electric current; the sensation experienced when moving against a force or resting mass. In psychoanalytic theory, the opposition to attempts to bring repressed thoughts into the conscious.

resolving power. The ability of the eye or an optical device to produce separate images of two objects that are close to each other.

respondent conditioning. See *classical conditioning.*

response. An answer; a physiological reaction or process that depends on or is the result of stimulation.

response generalization. The tendency of an organism to make responses that are similar to the specific conditioned responses it has learned. See also *generalization gradient; stimulus generalization.*

response item. In paired-associate learning, the item a subject is to recall when presented with the stimulus item. See also *paired-associate learning; stimulus item.*

response pattern. A particular quantitative and qualitative arrangement of reactions to a stimulus or stimuli.

resting potential. The difference in electrical potential normally maintained between the interior surface and the body fluids just outside the cell membrane of an inactive cell in excitable tissue, such as nerves or muscles. The charge inside is negative with respect to that outside.

restoration of function. A phenomenon occurring after ablation of a part of the brain in which some of an organism's impaired functions recover with time.

reticular activating system (RAS). A network of nerve cells deep in the brain that extends from the upper spinal cord through the medulla and pons and constituting a secondary pathway of nerves over which the senses alert the brain. The RAS regulates wakefulness, alertness, attention, and perceptual association. See also *straight-line sensory system.*

retina. The light-sensitive, innermost coat of the eyeball. The retina is a predominantly neural structure consisting of several layers, including a layer of rods and cones.

retinal image. The representation of an object that is formed on the retina. Also known as optical image or visual image.

retinene. A yellow pigment found in the retina and formed by the breakdown of rhodopsin. A lack of retinene causes night blindness. Also known as retinol or visual yellow.

retrieval. The process of obtaining information that is in storage, *e.g.*, the bringing of memories into consciousness. See also *recall; recognition.*

retroactive interference. A process in which newly learned material hampers the recall of previously learned material.

reward. See *reinforcement.*

rhodopsin. A red, light-sensitive pigment found in the rods that is important for vision in dim light. Also known as visual purple.

rhombencephalon. See *hindbrain.*

rod. One of many cells in the retina that are sensitive to light of low intensity and function primarily in peripheral and nighttime vision. Rods are located in the periphery and are essentially unresponsive to color. See also *cone.*

Rogerian therapy. See *client-centered therapy.*

role. The function of an individual in a group; the pattern of behavior that characterizes and is expected of a person who occupies a particular status or position in a group or social situation.

role playing. The performance of a role; a technique of psychotherapy in which a person acts out a role that is not his own. See also *role taking.*

role portrayal. The particular style in which a person acts out a role that he has selected.

role selection. Choice of a role that allows a person to behave in a manner most consistent with his own self-image.

role taking. Imagining oneself as another person and assuming his attitudes and point of view in order to determine how he would actually behave in given circumstances. See also *role playing.*

Rorschach Inkblot Test. A projective test in which the subject is shown ten inkblots of varying shape and color and asked to give his interpretation of each one.

rote learning. Learning accomplished by memorization of words, symbols, or sequences without regard for their meanings.

round dance. A circular movement performed by bees indicating that a food source is nearby. See also *wagging dance.*

round window. A membrane-covered opening between the middle ear and the cochlea that transmits sound from the ossicles to the cochlea. Also known as the fenestra rotunda or fenestra cochlea.

S

saccule. The smaller of two sacs in the labyrinth of the ear. See also *utricle.*

sacrum. The triangular bone located at the lower end of the spinal column that forms the back of the pelvis.

sadism. A perversion in which sexual pleasure and gratification are derived from inflicting pain, humiliation, or destruction on others.

saliva. A thin, colorless liquid secreted by the salivary glands of the mouth. One of its functions is to aid in the breakdown of food.

salivary gland. One of several glands located in the mouth that secretes saliva.

salivary reflex. Salivation in response to a stimulus.

salivation. The process of producing saliva.

sane. Of sound mind; free from mental disorder; showing good judgment or reasoning.

satiation. The complete gratification of a need or desire.

satyriasis. Excessive sexual desire in the male.

savings score. The difference between the number of trials an organism needs to learn material for the first time and the number of trials it needs to relearn the material after a lapse of time.

scale. A representation of the regular progression of quantities or qualities; a measuring device that provides standards against which other objects, events, or variables can be compared.

scallop pattern. A response pattern produced by fixed-interval schedules in which very few responses occur at the beginning of the interval, but as time passes, responding gradually increases until a large number of responses occur just prior to reinforcement.

schedule. In experimental psychology, a detailed plan of procedure, typically written, indicating time sequences for carrying out operations that lead toward a certain goal. See also *reinforcement schedule.*

schedule of reinforcement. See *reinforcement schedule.*

schema. A number of ideas or concepts combined to form a plan; a framework for showing the relationships of data. See also *scheme.*

scheme. In Piaget's developmental theory, a cognitive and behavioral framework for dealing with experiences.

schizophrenia. Any of a group of psychoses primarily characterized by disturbances in thinking.

scientific control. See *control, experimental.*

scopolamine. A chemical derived from plants that temporarily paralyzes the endings of the parasympathetic nerves. Scopolamine and its derivatives also act as cerebral depressants and are used as sedatives.

scopophilia (scoptophilia). See *voyeurism.*

score. A measure of performance; a numerical value assigned to a particular test response.

scotopic threshold curve. A curve showing the weakest light the eye can detect when adapted to darkness.

scotopic vision. Vision in dim light that is mediated by the rods.

secondary reinforcer. See *conditioned reinforcer.*

secondary sex characteristic. A trait specific to either males or females that begins to appear at or after puberty and is not necessary for reproduction (*e.g.*, beard growth in males and breast development in females).

secretion. The process whereby a cell or gland produces and releases or simply releases a substance that functions in an organism; the product of such a process.

secretory nerve. An efferent neuron ending in a gland. When stimulated, a secretory nerve causes an increase in a gland's activity.

sedative. A substance that causes drowsiness, sleep, or lowered excitability. Sedatives are used mainly to treat insomnia and anxiety.

sedative hypnotic drug. See *sedative.*

seizure. A sudden attack or convulsion as in epilepsy or other diseases.

selection. The act of choosing an object, individual, or phenomenon from a collection of alternatives; that which is chosen. See also *natural selection.*

self. All that a person perceives or believes is true about himself as an individual; the ego; the total person.

self-actualization. The process of fulfilling one's potentials or the state resulting therefrom. According to A. Maslow, self-actualization results from the satisfaction of metaneeds. See also *basic needs; metaneeds.*

self-concept. A person's knowledge and understanding of himself; that which a person conceives himself to be.

self-control. Regulation of one's own behavior.

self-esteem. A favorable impression of oneself.

self-fulfilling prophecy. A belief, prediction, or expectation that operates to bring about its own fulfillment.

self-image. All a person thinks himself to be.

self-perception theory. The theory advanced by D. Bem that people often make inferences about their attitudes by observing their own behavior.

semantics. The scientific study of the meanings of words; the rules describing the relationships between signs and that which they denote.

semicircular canal. Any of three tubular structures in the ear that help maintain body equilibrium and are part of the vestibular apparatus.

senility. Mental and physical degeneration occurring in old age.

sensation. The experience that occurs when a sense organ is stimulated; a feeling resulting from excitation of parts of the nervous system.

sense. A faculty by which organisms perceive stimuli, or the operation of such faculties; a feeling or perception produced through the sense organs; a receptor; apprehension by means of receptors.

sense organ. A bodily part that is sensitive to particular stimuli; a receptor.

sensitive period. See *critical period.*

sensitivity. An organism's ability to respond to stimuli; susceptibility to stimulation; capacity to perceive; the extent to which an apparatus responds to alterations in the phenomena it is measuring.

sensorimotor. Relating to motor activity produced by sensory stimulation; pertaining to actions that depend upon the combined activity of sensory organs and muscles; both motor and sensory.

sensory cell. See *sensory neuron.*

sensory data. See *data.*

sensory deprivation. Minimal stimulation of the sense organs accomplished by the experimental elimination of most, if not all, external stimuli.

sensory gating. A process by which a feedback system between the brain and sensory receptors regulates or dampens sensory activity that is less important at a given time.

sensory information storage (SIS). The momentary storage of sensory information that occurs primarily at the level of the sensory receptors.

sensory input. See *input.*

sensory isolation. See *sensory deprivation.*

sensory-motor. See *sensorimotor.*

sensory neuron. An afferent neuron that carries neural impulses from sense organs to the spinal cord.

sensory pattern. Sensory data perceived as a unit; a Gestalt.

sensory transduction. The conversion of stimulus energy (*e.g.*, light) into neural impulses.

sentence-completion test. A test of ability in which the subject must complete a number of meaningful sentences with an appropriate word or phrase.

septal area. A region of the brain and part of the limbic system located beneath the corpus callosum that is thought to inhibit emotionality

Tell us what you think...

Students today are taking an active role in determining the curricula and materials that shape their education. Because we want to be sure that *Psychology Today: An Introduction* continues to meet student needs and concerns, we would like your opinion of the current edition. We invite you to tell us what you like about the text—as well as where you think improvements can be made. Your opinions will be taken into consideration in the preparation of future editions. Thank you for your help.

Your Name ______________________

City and State ______________________

School ______________________

Course Title ______________________

How does this text compare with texts you are currently using in other courses?

☐ Excellent ☐ Good ☐ Adequate ☐ Poor ☐ Very Poor

Name other texts you consider good and why ______________________

____

Do you plan to sell the text back to the bookstore or to keep it for your library? ☐ Sell it ☐ Keep it

Circle the number of each chapter you read because it was covered by your instructor.

Unit I. Chapters: 2 3 4
Unit II. Chapters: 5 6 7 8
Unit III. Chapters: 9 10 11
Unit IV. Chapters: 12 13 14 15
Unit V. Chapter: 16
Unit VI. Chapters: 17 18 19
Unit VII. Chapters: 20 21 22 23
Unit VIII. Chapters: 24 25 26 27 28 29
Unit IX. Chapters: 30 31 32 33 34

What chapters did you read that were not assigned by your instructor? (Give chapter numbers.) ______________________

Please tell us your overall impression of the text.	Excellent	Good	Adequate	Poor	Very Poor
1. Did you find the text to be logically organized?					
2. Was it written in a clear and understandable style?					
3. Did the graphics enhance readability and understanding of topics?					
4. Did the captions contribute to a further understanding of the material?					
5. Were difficult concepts well explained?					

Can you cite examples that illustrate any of your above comments? ______________________

____

____

Which chapters did you particularly like and why? (Give chapter numbers.) ______________________

____

____

Which chapters did you dislike and why? ______________________

____

____

After taking this course, are you now interested in taking more courses in this field? ☐ Yes ☐ No

Do you feel that this text had any influence on your decision? ☐ Yes ☐ No

General Comments ______________________

____

What topics did the instructor discuss that were not covered in the text? ______________________

____

____

Did you see the Psychology Today films? ☐ Yes ☐ No
Did you read the film appendix? ☐ Yes ☐ No
If yes, did the film appendix aid in the understanding and enjoyment of the films? ☐ Yes ☐ No

Comments____

Did you listen to the CRM Sound Sheet Recordings? ☐ Yes ☐ No

If yes, what did you think of them?	Excellent	Fair	Poor
Adjustment and Disorder			
Language Development			

Comments____

Did you use the Involvement Manual? ☐ Yes ☐ No

Comments____

Did you use the Study Guide? ☐ Yes ☐ No

Comments____

FIRST CLASS
PERMIT NO. 59
DEL MAR, CALIF.

BUSINESS REPLY MAIL
No Postage Necessary if Mailed in the United States

Postage will be paid by

CRM BOOKS
Del Mar, California 92014

Just fold, staple and mail. No stamp necessary.

Q129

and to have a restraining effect on the hypothalamus.

sequential processing. Dealing with one strain or flow of incoming information at a time.

$_{S}E_{R}$. See *excitatory potential.*

serial-position effect. The effect of position on ability to remember an item in a series. Items that occur at the beginning or end of a series are remembered better than those that occur in the middle. See also *primacy effect; recency effect.*

serotonin. A compound found in the brain, intestines, and blood that is thought to transmit neural impulses across synapses in the brain and to play a part in the regulation of sleep and emotion.

set. Items that appear in a group or series; a tendency to continue to use a particular method or type of solution to a problem based on previous experience or instructions; a fixed form of behavior. See also *Einstellung; perceptual set.*

setting. In E. Goffman's theory of the presentation of the self, the environment in which a person presents himself.

sex. The quality of being either male or female; gender; erotic attraction or behavior.

sex hormone. A hormone that regulates the growth and activity of the reproductive organs or stimulates the development of secondary sex characteristics. See also *female hormone; hormone; male hormone.*

sex role. A complex or range of behaviors, attitudes, and social roles that a culture or society considers appropriate to members of one sex but not to those of the other.

sexual behavior. Behavior that relates to reproductive functions or stimulates sensation in receptors located in or about the reproductive organs and erogenous zones.

sexual deviancy. See *sexual deviation.*

sexual deviation. Any departure from what a society considers normal sexual behavior; sexual behavior that is illegal; a personality disorder in which sexual behavior is bizarre, compulsive, exclusive, and accompanied by guilt and anxiety.

shape constancy. The tendency to perceive familiar objects as always having the same shape, regardless of the angle from which they are viewed.

shaping. A form of operant conditioning in which all acts similar to the desired response are reinforced at first, and then acts that are progressively more like the desired response are reinforced until the desired response is attained. Also called method of successive approximations.

shock therapy. See *electroconvulsive shock therapy.*

short-term memory (STM). Memory that has a limited storage capacity (5 to 9 items) and a short duration. Items stored in STM are quickly forgotten if they are not transferred to long-term memory.

sign stimulus. A specific stimulus in the environment that elicits a particular pattern of behavior.

signal. A stimulus or pattern of stimuli capable of eliciting a response from an animal; anything that causes action; a physical entity or impulse used to transmit messages (*e.g.,* electric current, nerve impulse).

similarity, principle of. A Gestalt law of organization proposing that similar items will be perceived as belonging with each other more than with equally near but different items.

simple schizophrenia. A psychotic disorder marked by withdrawal from the external world. A person with this disorder is indifferent and apathetic but can continue to exist in society doing simple routine tasks.

SIS. See *sensory information storage.*

size constancy. The tendency of objects to be perceived as always having the same size, regardless of the distance from which they are viewed.

Skinner box. A compartment designed by B. F. Skinner containing a mechanism that produces reinforcement when operated correctly.

smell prism. See *Henning's smell prism.*

Snellen chart. A chart used to test visual acuity. Each line of the chart contains letters of the same size that the normal eye can read at a specified distance. The letters decrease in size from the top to the bottom of the chart. The Snellen chart is the standard eye chart.

social. Pertaining to relations between people or groups or to the influence of a person or group upon another.

social behavior. Behavior influenced or controlled by other persons or social norms; interpersonal behavior.

social category. An aggregate of people who have similar social traits or statuses but who do not form a social group (*e.g.,* firemen, people over 30, millionaires).

social class. A group of people within a society whose members share economic, cultural, and political characteristics (*e.g.,* education, wealth, and occupation).

social comparison theory. The theory put forth by L. Festinger that a large number of individual beliefs, attitudes, and values can be verified only by comparison with other persons.

social distance. One of the four zones of interpersonal space, from 4 feet to 12 feet.

social group. A collection of people in a cooperative and interdependent relationship who obtain special recognition as a group because of their interdependence. Members of social groups share common norms and have certain roles to perform.

social influence. A force generated by a society that affects a person's attitudes or behaviors; the power to produce a voluntary change in an individual's or a society's attitudes, beliefs, opinions, or practices.

social norm. A standard by which a society judges or regulates behavior.

social psychology. The branch of psychology that studies social behavior. Social psychology is concerned with group behavior and interactions between individuals and groups.

social role. See *role.*

social status. See *status.*

social stereotype. A stereotype held by most of the members of a group.

socialization. The process of learning to behave in a manner appropriate to the values of one's culture.

society. An organized, highly structured community of individuals associated together for specific purposes; a social group.

sociology. The study of the structures and functions of social institutions and social groups.

sodomy. In the broadest sense, culturally proscribed types of sexual relations between humans or between humans and animals; narrowly, anal intercourse.

soma. The body of an organism; all of the cells of the body excluding the germ cells; the cell body.

somesthetic. Pertaining to bodily sensations.

somesthetic cortex. See *postcentral gyrus.*

sound. A longitudinal, vibrational disturbance that occurs in an elastic medium and that is capable of producing an auditory effect.

sound frequency. See *frequency.*

sound pressure. The force per square centimeter that a sound exerts on the eardrum or basilar membrane. Sound pressure level is expressed in decibels.

sound spectrograph. An electronic device that records and graphically represents the intensity, duration, and variation of a sound or series of sounds as a function of time.

source. The place, object, or event from which something originates; the person or institution that delivers a message.

species. A distinct class of individuals having common characteristics; a biological category composed of similar individuals usually able to breed only with each other.

species-specific. Pertaining to behavior that is characteristic of a given species or exhibited by most of the members of a species under the same or very similar circumstances.

specific hunger. A drive toward a particular food, usually because the food contains a substance (*e.g.,* a vitamin) that an organism lacks.

spectrograph. A device that produces and photographs a spectrum of radiation. See also *sound spectrograph.*

spectrum. An array of entities arranged in order of magnitude of a shared physical attribute; a wide range of different but related objects or ideas. See also *visual spectrum.*

speech. Oral communication; language.

spermatozoon. A single sperm, or male germ cell.

spike. An action potential; a sharp rise in a graphic representation of an electrical, magnetic, or bodily process (*e.g.,* in an electroencephalogram).

spinal column. The vertebrae forming the supporting axis of the body and the protective casing of the spinal cord; backbone.

spinal cord. The thick bundle of neurons running vertically along the back through the spinal column.

spinal reflex. A reflex arc that passes through the spinal cord.

spinal reflex arc. See *spinal reflex.*

spontaneous extinction. See *extinction, spontaneous.*

spontaneous recovery. The recurrence of a conditioned response after a rest period following extinction.

spontaneous remission. The unaided disappearance of a pathological condition; the loss, after a time, of symptoms of psychological disturbance in an individual although he or she has not undergone therapy.

standard. Anything considered to be a basis for judgment or comparison; any ethic, belief, habit, etc., established by authority, persons, or custom as acceptable; an established unit of measurement; an average, normal, or expected quality, requirement, quantity, and so on.

standard deviation. In a frequency distribution, a number indicating the extent to which measurements within a set differ from each other, expressed as the square root of the squared differences of each measurement from the mean, divided by the number of measurements.

Stanford-Binet Test. An individually administered intelligence test, devised at Stanford University, that follows Binet's test in grouping tests by age levels. It is the test most frequently used for children.

stapes. The innermost bone of the middle ear that transmits sound from the eardrum to the cochlea. Commonly known as the stirrup. See also *incus; malleus; ossicles.*

statistics. The branch of mathematics or its group of techniques involved with the making of meaningful inferences from collections of data; the numerical data themselves.

status. The position or rank of a person in a group as related to and distinguished from other members of the group; the social position of an individual or group in reference to others; a state of affairs.

stereochemical theory (of odor). The theory that odors can be classified into seven primary categories on the basis of molecular shape.

stereoscope. An optical instrument that allows two flat pictures of the same object to be seen as one three-dimensional picture by presenting one picture to one eye and the other picture, taken from a slightly different viewpoint, to the other eye.

stereoscopic vision. Perception of depth due to the merging of two slightly different retinal images; three-dimensional vision.

stereotype. A preconceived notion about some aspect of reality, particularly people or social groups; a set of oversimplified, rigid, and biased generalizations about a group or category of people.

steroid hormone. Any of various chemically similar hormones. Some of the processes regulated by steroid hormones are water balance, energy expenditure, and sexual processes.

stigma. Any socially undesirable condition or trait.

stimulant. A substance that increases physiological activity, produces a state of alertness, elevates mood, diminishes appetite, and enhances physical performance.

stimulus. Any phenomenon that initiates a response or evokes sensory activity in an organism. A stimulus may be internal or external to an organism and physical or mental in nature.

stimulus control. The regulation of behavior by the stimulus (stimuli) that is (are) present during reinforcement.

stimulus error. In an experiment, a mistake that occurs when the observer fails to report what he actually perceives and instead reports as a perception what he merely believes is there.

stimulus generalization. The tendency of an organism to respond to stimuli that are similar to the conditioned stimulus. See also *generalization gradient; response generalization.*

stimulus item. In paired-associate learning, the item presented to the subject that is supposed to elicit the response item. See also *paired-associate learning; response item.*

stimulus pattern. A relatively stable arrangement of stimuli; a grouping of related stimuli considered as a whole.

stirrup. See *stapes.*

STM. See *short-term memory.*

stopped image. An image fixated on one section of the retina. The receptor cells of the retina adapt to the unchanging pattern within a few seconds and the image quickly disappears.

storage. The physical retention of information in long-term memory. Storage appears to be an automatic process that is not under a person's direct control (*e.g.*, once information is stored in LTM, it does not seem possible to erase it).

STP. A synthetic psychedelic drug whose effects are similar to but last longer than those of LSD.

straight-line sensory system. The main pathway of nerves over which travels physical energy from a sensory stimulus that is transduced into physiological energy and is carried to the brain. The straight-line sensory system is the channel that carries information. See also *reticular activating system.*

strain. In genetics, a population that has been reproductively isolated or the descendants of a common ancestor

straitjacket. A shirt made of very strong material and used to bind the arms and constrict a violent person's movements. Also known as a camisole.

structural psychology. A school of psychology concerned with reducing experience to its basic parts, determining the laws by which the parts are synthesized, and investigating the structure and content of mental states by introspection.

subgoal analysis. A form of problem solving in which the original problem is broken down into a smaller series of problems.

subject. In experiments, an organism to which stimuli are applied and whose responses are observed; the initiator or doer of an action or a process.

subjective. Belonging to the individual observer rather than to the object being observed; not capable of being verified by others; dependent upon an individual observer's emotions or judgments, hence, biased. See also *objective.*

sublimation. In psychoanalytic theory, the unconscious process of redirecting or modifying an instinct or impulse so as to meet the conventional standards of society. Through this modification one is provided with a substitute activity that gives some means to satisfy the original need. Sublimation is an acceptable means of expressing an impulse, rather than a form of repression.

subvocalization. Movements of the lips, tongue, and larynx that do not produce audible sound. Subvocalization was once theorized to be the single vehicle of thinking.

successive approximations, method of. See *shaping.*

sulcus. One of the shallow fissures on the surface of the brain that separates convolutions, or gyri.

superego. According to Freud, the partially unconscious part of the ego that incorporates parental and social standards of morality. The superego inhibits those impulses of the id that are most condemned by society or parents and is thus in constant conflict with the id. See also *ego; id; psyche.*

superstitious behavior. In operant conditioning, responses not necessarily leading to a goal that persist simply because they preceded reinforcement.

suppression. The conscious and intentional process of inhibiting disapproved impulses or ideas.

survey. To investigate in great detail; general or comprehensive examination of something.

sweat gland. One of many tubular glands located in the skin that secrete perspiration.

syllogism. In logic, a formalized argument whose conclusion is based on two premises, the major and minor premises. Example: All *x* is *y.* All *y* is *z.* Therefore all *x* is *z.*

Sylvian fissure. See *fissure of Sylvius.*

sympathetic nervous system. The division of the autonomic nervous system in which nerve fibers leave from either the lumbar region or the thorax and synapse in ganglia located adjacent to the spinal cord. The sympathetic nervous system promotes the expenditure of body energy and mobilizes the body to meet emergencies by increasing blood-sugar level and heart rate, dilating peripheral blood vessels, and inhibiting the digestive process.

Synanon. A self-help, private group organized primarily to aid former narcotics addicts to readjust their social behavior.

synapse. The area of contact between the axon of one neuron and the dendrite or cell body of another, and therefore the point at which a neural impulse is transmitted from the axon of one neuron to the dendrite or cell body of another.

synaptic junction. See *synapse.*

syndrome. A group or pattern of symptoms characterizing a specific disease or condition; a group of related events, actions, objects, etc.

syphilis. An infectious veneral disease that may have many grave physiological effects, including damage to the brain and most other bodily organs.

T

tachistoscope. An instrument that presents visual stimuli for short, regulated periods of time.

tactile. Pertaining to the sense of touch.

taste bud. One of many tiny organs located in

the epithelium of the tongue that are the receptors for taste.

TAT. See *Thematic Apperception Test.*

tectorial membrane. A jellylike membrane that covers the organ of Corti in the ear and in which hair cells are embedded.

telegraphic speech. Patterns manifested in the speech of young children in which certain words that seem minimally related to the message content are omitted (*e.g.*, "Pick glove" instead of "Pick up the glove").

temporal lobe. One of the three posterior lobes of the cerebrum located below the fissure of Sylvius and in front of the occipital lobe and concerned with the sensations of hearing and some visual processing.

tendon. An inelastic, fibrous tissue that connects a muscle to a bone.

test. A measurement technique designed to determine individual differences in knowledge, personality characteristics, etc.; a technique that determines the correctness of a hypothesis and yields quantitative data. See also *achievement test; intelligence test; projective test; Thematic Apperception Test.*

testis. One of the pair of male reproductive glands in which sperm and male hormones are produced.

testosterone. A male sex hormone secreted by the testes.

tetrahydrocannabinol (THC). A complex molecule that is the active ingredient in marijuana and hashish. THC is found naturally in the Indian hemp plant and appears chiefly in the female plant.

T-group. A group technique used by businessmen in an attempt to develop insight and skills in human relations.

thalamus. A group of nuclei located in the forebrain some of which relay information from the sensory organs to the cerebral cortex.

Thanatos. According to Freud, the death instinct—a tendency toward self-destruction that is present at birth. See also *Eros.*

THC. See *tetrahydrocannabinol.*

Thematic Apperception Test (TAT). A projective test in which relatively vague pictures are presented to a subject who is asked to make up stories about them.

theory. A group of principles, generally supported by observable evidence, that explains certain phenomena; a proposed explanation for certain phenomena.

therapy. See *psychotherapy.*

thermal. Pertaining to heat.

thiamine. Vitamin B_1, a substance essential for normal metabolism and nerve function.

thioxanthines. A group of antipsychotic drugs.

thirst. A drive state based on dehydration or loss of water from bodily tissues; the need or desire for water.

thorax. The body cavity located between the neck and abdomen in man and higher vertebrates in which the heart and lungs lie.

thought. The process or product of thinking; a complex idea or mental activity involving symbols.

threshold. The level of intensity at which a stimulus begins to elicit a response.

threshold value. The critical voltage necessary to generate an action potential.

thyroid gland. An endocrine gland composed of two lobes lying on either side of the windpipe whose secretions regulate body growth and rate of metabolism.

thyroid-stimulating hormone (TSH). A hormone secreted by the anterior pituitary that stimulates the thyroid gland to produce thyroxin.

thyroxin. A hormone produced by the thyroid gland or manufactured synthetically that regulates body metabolism.

tissue. An aggregate of cells (usually of the same kind) that performs a common function; one of the structural materials in an organism.

T-maze. A maze in the shape of a T; a maze consisting of several T-shaped sections.

tone. A quality of sound; a sound that has an exact pitch and vibration; vocal accent or inflection; a healthy state of tension and firmness in the bodily organs; a quality of color.

tonoptic organization. The correlation between place and frequency of a sound from the basilar membrane to the auditory cortex.

trace decay theory. The theory that forgetting is a result of the deterioration and eventual disappearance of memory traces.

training. The sum total of instructions, treatments, or manipulations that an animal or person must undergo in order to learn or to become able to perform some role or task.

trait. A distinguishing quality, property, attribute, etc., especially of a person that is consistently displayed, including behavior patterns, physical attributes, and personality characteristics; according to Allport, a predisposition to respond to many types of stimuli in the same manner.

trance. A sleeplike state in which awareness of external stimuli is dulled and the ability to act voluntarily is suspended. Trances are common in hysteria and may be induced by hypnotism. See also *hypnosis.*

tranquilizer. A drug that has a calming effect, reduces anxiety and depression, but does not induce sleep. See also *antianxiety drug; antipsychotic drug.*

transactionalist. A scientist who adheres to the theory that awareness is based on the transactions a person has with his environment and that judgments with respect to ambiguous stimuli depend on the person's assumptions about the world.

transduction. The conversion of one type of energy into another.

transfer. Conveyance from one person, place, etc. to another; a change in ability to perform a certain act as a result of previous learning.

transfer of training. See *negative transfer; positive transfer; transfer.*

transference. The process of shifting affect from one object to another. In psychoanalysis transference occurs when the patient responds to the analyst as though the analyst were some other significant person, usually someone important in the patient's early life.

transmitter substance. A chemical released from an axon into a synapse that carries neural impulses across the synapse and causes changes in the membrane of the receiving cell. Acetylcholine and norepinephrine are transmitter substances.

transvestism. The tendency to dress in the clothing associated with members of the opposite sex or the association of sexual excitement with this behavior.

trauma. An injury; an experience that causes an organism serious physical or psychological damage.

trichromat. A person whose retina responds to all colors.

trichromatic. Pertaining to or consisting of three colors.

trichromatic theory (of color vision). The theory that there are three different types of color receptors in the eye for detecting all hues of each of the three primary colors.

tricyclic antidepressants. A group of antidepressant drugs that block the destruction of norepinephrine in the neurons.

trigram. Any nonsense syllable or word composed of three letters.

trip. See *LSD trip.*

Tritonia diomedia. A sluglike species with especially large brain cells.

TSH. See *thyroid-stimulating hormone.*

tympanic cavity. See *middle ear.*

tympanic membrane. See *eardrum.*

type. An individual, item, or entity, or a group of them, distinguished by certain physiological, morphological, or psychological traits; one or more specimens that form the basis for classifying a species; an individual embodying the characteristics of a group; a kind or class.

typology. A classification made on the basis of types.

U

ultraviolet rays. Radiant energy with a shorter wavelength than that of the violet end of the spectrum. These radiations are shorter than 390 millimicrons and are not directly visible to the human eye.

unconditional reflex. See *unconditional response.*

unconditional response. In classical conditioning, an organism's natural reaction to an unconditional stimulus.

unconditional stimulus. In classical conditioning, a stimulus that evokes a given response without previous training.

unconditioned stimulus. See *unconditional stimulus.*

unconscious. Unaware; marked by an absence of perception, cognition, or sensation; in psychoanalytic theory, the division of the psyche containing material of which the ego is unaware but which is capable of influencing conscious processes or behavior. See also *conscious.*

unconscious inference. A judgment one makes without being aware of a reasoning process but upon which he or she acts. Such a judgment is usually not verbalized.

utricle. The larger of two sacs in the labyrinth of the ear; the part of the vestibular apparatus into which the semicircular canals open. See also *saccule.*

V

vacuum activity. Behavior that occurs even though the appropriate stimuli are not present. Vacuum activity is believed to result from a very high drive state.

validity. Well-foundedness or soundness; the extent to which a test measures what it purports to measure.

value. Worth; a type of belief that concerns how one ought or ought not to act (*e.g.,* with sincerity and honesty) or the goals one is trying to obtain (*e.g.,* happiness, freedom); in mathematics, a number representing magnitude or quantity.

variable. Anything that is capable of change; quantities that can take on more than one mathematical value.

variable-interval schedule. In experimental psychology, a plan of reinforcement in which reinforcement occurs after varying amounts of time have elapsed. Thus, the subject does not know when reinforcement will occur.

variable-ratio schedule. A plan of reinforcement in which a variable number of responses are required in order for reinforcement to occur. Thus, the subject does not know when reinforcement will occur.

variance. The state or quality of being different; the square of the standard deviation.

vein. A relatively large, thin-walled blood vessel that conducts blood away from the tissues back to the heart.

venereal disease. Any of several communicable diseases usually transmitted by sexual intercourse (*e.g.,* gonorrhea, syphilis).

ventral nerve cord. A nerve in the blowfly that receives impulses from receptors that indicate when the fly's body is becoming distended with food.

ventromedial center. See *ventromedial nucleus.*

ventromedial nucleus. The middle area of the hypothalamus that controls hunger. If the ventromedial nucleus is destroyed or inactive, an animal's weight-control mechanism will readjust so that it maintains a higher-than-normal body weight if good-tasting food is easily available or a lower-than-normal weight otherwise.

verbal behavior. Behavior consisting of spoken language—*i.e.,* the act of speech.

vernier acuity. The ability of the eye to detect a break in contour or to discriminate alignment.

vestibular apparatus. The apparatus in the ear for perception of head orientation and bodily acceleration. It includes the area of the labyrinth containing the utricle, saccule, and semicircular canals.

vestibular nerve. A branch of the auditory nerve that transmits neural impulses from the vestibule and semicircular canals to the brain.

vestibular organ. See *vestibular apparatus.*

vestibular sacs. Two baglike structures located in the labyrinth that are part of the vestibular apparatus. See also *saccule; utricle.*

vestibular sense. The sense of balance.

vestibule. Any of several bodily cavities serving as an entrance; the central cavity of the inner ear that forms the entrance to the cochlea.

virtual social identity. In E. Goffman's theory of the presentation of self, the identity that a person seems to have, in contrast to his or her actual identity.

vision. The sense or act of seeing.

visual acuity. Sharpness of sight; ability of the eye to discern spatial separations between points or to distinguish objects at a distance; the ratio between the distance at which a person can see a given object and the distance at which a person with normal vision can see it (*e.g.,* 20/20 vision).

visual cliff. A device designed by E. Gibson and D. Walk to study depth perception. The visual cliff consists of a center board resting on a glass table; on one side of the board a patterned surface is visible directly beneath the glass and on the other side the patterned surface is several feet below the glass.

visual field. Everything perceived by the eye when it is fixed on an object.

visual image. See *retinal image.*

visual purple. See *rhodopsin.*

visual spectrum. The band of colors obtained by the passage of sunlight or white light through a prism.

vitreous humor. A transparent, gelatinous substance occupying the space between the retina and the lens of the eye.

vocal cords. Either of two pairs of mucous membrane folds that protrude into the cavity of the larynx and produce certain vocal sounds when vibrated.

volley theory. The theory that individual nerve fibers do not respond to each sound wave but that a sound wave excites one group of nerve fibers, the second sound wave excites another group of nerve fibers, and so on. The pattern of neural impulses that go to the brain in successive volleys corresponds to the sound frequency.

volume. The amount of space occupied by a substance; a quantity of something; loudness; largeness of a tone.

voyeurism. Sexual gratification achieved by observing the genitals of another or by watching the sexual activities of others. Also known as scopophilia.

W

wagging dance. A sequence of running and turning movements performed by bees indicating the direction and distance of a food source. See also *round dance.*

WAIS. See *Wechsler Adult Intelligence Scale.*

warm spot. A pointlike area on the skin that is especially sensitive to warmth (*e.g.,* stimuli above 32° C).

wavelength. In a wave moving along a medium, the distance between two successive points that are characterized by the same phase of oscillation.

Weber's law. A law formulated by E. Weber that the smallest difference in intensity between two stimuli that can be reliably detected is a constant fraction of the original stimulus. See also *Fechner's law.*

Wechsler Adult Intelligence Scale (WAIS). A widely used battery of intelligence tests for adults combining performance, vocabulary, and verbal tests.

Wechsler Intelligence Scale for Children (WISC). A variation of the WAIS intelligence test that is usable for adolescents and older children. See also *Wechsler Adult Intelligence Scale.*

white noise. The noise that results from sounds of different wavelengths coming together randomly and masking one another.

WISC. See *Wechsler Intelligence Scale for Children.*

withdrawal syndrome. The symptoms that occur after a person discontinues use of a drug he has become addicted to. These include watery nose and eyes, drowsiness, cramps, vomiting, diarrhea, gooseflesh, and general weakness.

witigo. A disorder existing in members of Canadian Indian tribes that is characterized by agitated anxiety and nausea, and an extreme fear of cannibalism fostered by a morbid craving for human flesh. Also known as Wihtiko psychosis.

word-association test. A method of determining a subject's associations with certain stimuli in a verbal stimulus-response exchange. The subject's experience and attitudes determine his responses.

working consensus. In E. Goffman's theory of the presentation of self, the compromise reached between two actors on the nature of the situation in which they are interacting.

working through. In psychoanalysis, the process of having the patient repeatedly face the same conflicts until he can master them; all of the intrapsychic processes that must occur in a patient in order for him to gain insight into and resolve his problems; a period of relative inactivity on the part of a patient in psychoanalysis that occurs spontaneously.

Z

zygote. A single cell resulting from the union of a sperm and an egg and from which an organism develops.

Index

NAME INDEX

UV

W

YZ

SUBJECT INDEX

A

B

Credits and Acknowledgments

CHAPTER 1

2—John Oldenkamp/IBOL; 4–14—Tom Suzuki.

CHAPTER 2

16–17—(photos left to right) George Leavens, Steve McCarroll/IBOL (2); 18—George Leavens; 20—(top) The Granger Collection, (bottom) Courtesy Konrad Lorenz; 21—(top) John C. Fentress, (bottom) John Dawson; 22—(top) Doug Armstrong, (bottom) John C. Fentress; 23—(top) Niko Tinbergen, (bottom) R. F. Head, National Audubon Society; 24—Eadweard Muybridge; 25—(top) John Dawson, (middle) John H. Gerard, National Audubon Society, (bottom) John Dawson; 26—(top) Tony Florio, National Audubon Society, (bottom) George Leavens; 28—(left) Doug Armstrong, (right) John Dawson; 29—(top right) John Dawson, (bottom right) John Dawson, (bottom left) Thomas McEvoy, Life Magazine, © Time, Inc.; 30—From Schleidt, *Naturwissen schaften*, 1961; 31—From *So Excellent a Fishe*, by Archie Carr, © 1957 Archie Carr, reprinted by permission of Doubleday and Company; 32 and 33—Tom Lewis; 34—Steve McCarroll/IBOL; 35—From R. D. Hess and G. Handel, *Family Worlds: A Psychological Approach to Family Life*, University of Chicago Press, 1959; 36—From W. H. Thorpe, *Bird-Song*, Cambridge University Press, 1961.

CHAPTER 3

38—Steve McCarroll/IBOL; 40—(top) The Bettmann Archive, Inc., (center) The Granger Collection, (bottom) Yale University Photographic Services; 41—(top) Ted Polumbaum, (bottom) Gerri Blake; 42—John Dawson; 43—(top right) Shirley Dethloff; 43 (bottom) and 45—Howard Saunders; 46—(top) Steve McCarroll/IBOL, (bottom) John Dawson; 47—(top) Steve McCarroll/IBOL, (bottom) John Dawson; 48—(bottom) After R. S. Woodworth, *Psychology*, Holt, Rinehart and Winston, 1921; 49—(top left) John Dawson, (top right) Fogg Art Museum and Bachrach Studios, (bottom left) Doug Armstrong, (bottom right) Steve McCarroll/IBOL; 50–51—Doug Armstrong; 52—After H. M. Hanson, "Effects of Discrimination Training on Stimulus Generalization," *Journal of Experimental Psychology*, 1959, Vol. 58, pp. 321–334; 53—Steve McCarroll/IBOL; 55–56—Doug Armstrong; 57—Steve McCarroll/IBOL; 58—After E. Fantino, D. Sharp, and M. Cole, "Factors Facilitating Lever-Press Avoidance," *Journal of Comparative and Physiological Psychology*, 1966, Vol. 62, pp. 214–217, © by the American Psychological Association and reproduced by permission.

CHAPTER 4

60—Steve McCarroll/IBOL; 62—(top) Courtesy D. O. Hebb, (bottom) John Dawson; 65—Bill Boyarsky; 66—Werner Kalber/PPS; 67—Courtesy of Jerome Kagan; 71—Doug Armstrong, after Kurt Fischer, 1970; 74—(bottom) John Dawson; 75—(left) Steve McCarroll/IBOL.

CHAPTER 5

78–79—(photos left to right) Bill MacDonald/IBOL, Elizabeth Wilcox, Bill MacDonald/IBOL, Steve McCarroll/IBOL; 80—Bill MacDonald/IBOL; 82—Eric Schaal; 83 and 86—Steve Wells/IBOL; 88—(top) Bill MacDonald/IBOL, (middle) John Oldenkamp/IBOL, (bottom) Mary Potter; 89—(top) Doug Armstrong, (bottom) George Zimbel/Monkmeyer Press Photos; 90—Mary Potter; 91—George Zimbel/Monkmeyer Press Photos; 92—(top) Art by Doug Armstrong, (bottom) Mary Potter; 93—Bill MacDonald/IBOL; 94—(top) Art by Doug Armstrong, (bottom) Mary Potter.

CHAPTER 6

96—Elizabeth Wilcox; 99—Karl Nicholason; 101—(top) David Wood, (bottom) Bill MacDonald/IBOL; 102—Bill MacDonald/IBOL; 103—Steve Wells/IBOL; 104—Bill MacDonald/IBOL; 106—Doug Armstrong; 107—Bill MacDonald/IBOL; 109—(top) Doug Armstrong, 109 (bottom) and 111—From E. R. Emmet, *Brain Puzzler's Delight*, Emerson Books, 1968; 110—Alan Mercer.

CHAPTER 7

112—Bill MacDonald/IBOL; 115—Courtesy R. A. and B. T. Gardner; 117—Steve McCarroll/IBOL; 118—Courtesy Noam Chomsky; 126—Courtesy Jasper Johns; 127—(top) Steve McCarroll/IBOL, (bottom) from E. H. Lenneberg, *Biological Foundations of Language*, Wiley, 1967, pp. 321–323; 129—Photography by Werner Kalber/PPS by permission of the C. H. Stoelting Company.

CHAPTER 8

132—Steve McCarroll/IBOL; 134—The Granger Collection; 135–136—Karl Nicholason; 137–140—Terry Lamb; 142—David Hicks; 144—(top) From L. Kohlberg, "The Development of Children's Orientation Towards a Moral Order," *Vita Humana*, 1963, Vol. 6, S. Karger, Basel, (bottom) from L. Kohlberg, "The Child as a Moral Philosopher," *Psychology Today*, September 1968, p. 27; 147—Moshe Lapidot; 149—From Richard Krebs, "Some Relationships Between Moral Judgment, Attention, and Resistance to Temptation," Ph.D. Dissertation, December 1967.

CHAPTER 9

150–151—(photos left to right) © 1968 Metro-Goldwyn-Mayer, Inc., John Oldenkamp/IBOL, Steve McCarroll/IBOL; 152—© 1968 Metro-Goldwyn-Mayer, Inc.; 154—Shirley Dethloff; 155—Millsap and Kinyon; 156—painting from Novasti Press Agency, courtesy of U.S.S.R. Embassy, data from A. L. Yarbus, *Eye Movements and Vision*, Plenum Press, 1967; 159—Tom Lewis and Doug Armstrong; 160—From W. H. Thorpe, "Talking Birds and the Mode of Action of the Vocal Apparatus of Birds," *Proceedings of the Zoological Society of London*, 1959, Vol. 132, pp. 441–455; 162—Doug Armstrong; 166—Raimondo Borea; 167—Werner Kalber/PPS; 168—(top) From I. Pollack, "The Information of Elementary Auditory Displays," *Journal of the Acoustical Society of America*, Vol. 24, No. 6, p. 746, (bottom) Doug Armstrong.

CHAPTER 10

170—John Oldenkamp/IBOL; 173—After Peterson and Peterson, "Short-Term Retention of Individual Verbal Items," *Journal of Experimental Psychology*, 1959, Vol. 58, pp. 193–198, © 1959 American Psychological Association and reproduced by permission; 176—The Bettmann Archive, Inc.; 177—(bottom right) Doug Armstrong; 179—Gerri Blake; 180—The Bettmann Archive, Inc.; 181—From H. Ebbinghaus, *Memory: A Contribution to Experimental Psychology*, Dover Publications, 1913; 182—Doug Armstrong, after D. Kretch, R. Crutchfield, and N. Livson, *Elements of Psychology*, second ed., Knopf, 1969; 183—Doug Armstrong, after B. Inhelder, "Memory and Intelligence in a Child," in Elkind and Flavell (Eds.), *Studies in Cognitive Development*, Oxford University Press, 1959; 184—Gillian Theobald; 185—(top) After K. M. Dallenbach, "Table vs. Graphs as Means of Presenting Experimental Results," *American Journal of Psychology*, 1963, Vol. 76, pp. 700–702; 186—(bottom) After C. Osgood, *Psychological Review*, 1949, Vol. 56, p. 140, © 1949 American Psychological Association and reproduced by permission; 187—(top) After B. B. Murdock, "Serial Position Effect of Free Recall," *Journal of Experimental Psychology*, 1962, Vol. 64, pp. 482–488, © 1962 American Psychological Association and reproduced by permission, (bottom) Courtesy Charles F. Stromeyer; 188—(top) Werner Kalber/PPS, (bottom) Courtesy Charles F. Stromeyer.

CHAPTER 11

190—Steve McCarroll/IBOL; 192—Werner Kalber/PPS; 193—Shirley Dethloff; 194 and 195—Art by Karl Nicholason, after P. L. Wason, "Reasoning About a Rule," *Quarterly Journal of Experimental Psychology*, 1968, No. 20; 196—Howard Saunders; 199—Shirley Dethloff; 200—Doug Armstrong, after A. S. Luchins and E. H. Luchins, *Rigidity of Behavior: A Variational Approach to the Effect of "Einstellung,"* University of Oregon Books, 1959; 200—(bottom) Werner Kalber/PPS; 201—Inge Bell, *Involvement in Society Today*, CRM BOOKS, 1971; 202—Art by Gillian Theobald; 203—Photography by Werner Kalber/PPS; 201—Inge Bell, *Involvement in Society Today*, CRM BOOKS, 1971; 202—Art by Gillian Theobald; 203—Photography by Werner Kalber/PPS, after J. S. Bruner, *Toward a Theory of Instruction*, Harvard University Press, 1966; 204—(all but bottom right) Werner Kalber/PPS, (bottom right) Gillian Theobald; 205—From *The Meier Art Judgment Test* by permission of The Bureau of Educational Research and Service.

CHAPTER 12

206–207—(photos left to right) Courtesy of NASA, Manned Space Craft Center, Tom Suzuki, William Noonan, Tom Suzuki; 208—Courtesy of NASA, Manned Space Craft Center, Houston; 210—Karl Nicholason; 211—(top) Gerri Blake; 213—(right) Werner Kalber/PPS; 214–216—Doug Armstrong; 216—From S. S. Stevens, "The Attributes of Tones," *Proceedings of the National Academy of Sciences*, 1934, Vol. 20, pp. 457–459; 217—(top and center) The Granger Collection; 219—(top) From S. S. Stevens, "The Surprising Simplicity of Sensory Metrics," *American Psychologist*, 1962, Vol. 17, pp. 29–39, © 1962 American Psychological Association and reproduced by permission; 223—Doug Armstrong; 224—(top) After D. M. Green and J. A. Swets, *Signal Detection Theory and Psychophysics*, Wiley, 1966.

CHAPTER 13

226—Tom Suzuki; 228—(top right) Millsap and Kinyon; 230—(top) From Hecht, Haig, and Wald, "The Dark Adaptation of Retinal Fields of Different Size and Location," *Journal of General Physiology*, 1935, Vol. 19, pp. 321–339; 231—(top) Millsap and Kinyon; 231 (bottom) and 232–235—Doug Armstrong, after R. L. deValois, "Neural Processing of Visual Information," in R. W. Russell (Ed.), *Frontiers in Physiological Psychology*, Academic Press, 1966; 237—From the Dvorine Pseudo-Isochromatic Plates; 238–239—Steve McCarroll/IBOL; 240–242—Millsap and Kinyon; 244—From S. S. Stevens and E. B. Newman, "Localization of Actual Sources of Sound," *American Journal of Psychology*, 1936, Vol. 48, pp. 297–300; 245—(right) Millsap and Kinyon; 246—From C. Pfaffmann, "Taste and Smell," in S. S. Stevens (Ed.), *Handbook of Experimental Psychology*, Wiley, 1951; 247–248—Millsap and Kinyon.

CHAPTER 14

250—William Noonan; 255—Tom Suzuki; 258—(top) Courtesy Lawrence Roberts, (bottom) Steve McCarroll/IBOL; 259—(top) Bill MacDonald/IBOL; 260—(bottom) The Granger Collection; 262—Steve McCarroll/IBOL; 263—(top) Werner Kalber/PPS, (bottom left) Tom Suzuki; 264—(top) Bob Ward/IBOL, (bottom left) John Oldenkamp/IBOL, (bottom right) Academia, Venice/Scala, New York and Florence; 265—(top) Steve McCarroll/IBOL; 266—(top) Doug Armstrong, (bottom center) Philip Clark, (bottom right) Bob Ward/IBOL; 267—(left) Photo by Robert Berger, reprinted with permission of *Science Digest*, © The Hearst Corporation; 269–270—Steve McCarroll/IBOL; 273—John Dawson, after R. Held and A. Hein, "Movement-Produced Stimulation in the Development of Visually Guided Behavior," *Journal of Comparative and Physiological Psychology*, 1963, Vol. 56, pp. 872–876, © 1963 American Psychological Association and reproduced by permission; 277—Courtesy Dr. B. L. White; 278—(top) John Oldenkamp/IBOL; (bottom) William Noonan.

CHAPTER 15

276—Tom Suzuki; 278—Steve McCarroll/IBOL; 280—John Dawson; 282—Art by Karl Nicholason, adapted from L. J. Karnosh and F. M. Zucker, *Handbook of Psychiatry*, Mosby, 1945; 283—After F. A. Pattie, "A Report of Attempts to Produce Uniocular Blindness by Hypnotic Suggestion," *British Journal of Medical Psychology*, 1936, Vol. 15, p. 236; 284—Steve McCarroll/IBOL; 285—(top) From P. Naitoh and L. C. Johnson, "Sleep Patterns of Aquanauts During Tektite I," Navy Medical Neuropsychiatric Research Unit Report; 288—Jerry Uelsmann; 289—Courtesy Mrs. Ettilie Wallace, from Dr. Craig W. Carter; 290—Philip Daly; 291—King Features Syndicate; 293—Yale Joel, Life Magazine, © Time, Inc.

CHAPTER 16

299–300—Rowland Scherman; 303—(top) Lester V. Bergman & Associates, (center) John Dawson, (bottom) Plate I from *Journal of Physiology*, 1965, Vol. 104, pp. 176–195, by A. L. Hodgkin and A. F. Huxley; 304—Millsap and Kinyon; 306—(top left) UPI, Compix, (right and bottom left) John Dawson; 307–309—Millsap and Kinyon; 310—From W. Penfield and L. Roberts, *Speech and Brain Mechanisms*, Princeton University Press, 1959; 311—Millsap and Kinyon, after W. Penfield and T. Rasmussen, *The Cerebral Cortex of Man*, Macmillan, 1950; 312–315—Millsap and Kinyon; 317—Steve McCarroll/IBOL; 318—John Dawson; 320—Courtesy A. O. D. Willows; 321—After H. Curtis, *Biology*, Worth Publishers, 1968, p. 433; 323–324—Art by Doug Armstrong; 328—(top) Doug

Armstrong, adapted from L. B. Arey, *Developmental Anatomy,* 6th ed., Saunders, 1954; 329—From M. P. Honzik, "The Development of Parent-Child Resemblance in Intelligence," *Child Development,* 1957, Vol. 28, pp. 219–222, © 1957, Society for Research in Child Development. All Rights reserved.

CHAPTER 17

330–331—(photos left to right) Courtesy NASA, Manned Space Craft Center, Steve McCarroll/IBOL, Bob Van Doren; 332—Courtesy NASA; 335—Lorenzo Gunn/Gordon Menzie Studio; 336–337 (top)—Millsap and Kinyon; 337—(bottom) Dr. James Olds; 339—(top) The Granger Collection, (bottom) Steve McCarroll/IBOL; 340—Arlene Thompson; 341—(top) Courtesy Charles Osgood, (bottom) Steve McCarroll/IBOL; 342—(top) John Dawson, (bottom left) Steve McCarroll/IBOL, (bottom center and right) Bill MacDonald/IBOL; 343—(center) From *Mirror of Venus* by Wingate Paine, (bottom) Courtesy Midas, Inc.; 344—From H. Schlosberg, "The Description of Facial Expressions in Terms of Two Dimensions," *Journal of Experimental Psychology,* 1952, Vol. 44, © 1952 American Psychological Association, and reprinted by permission; 347—Shirley Dethloff; 348—Karl Nicholason.

CHAPTER 18

350 and 355—Steve McCarroll/IBOL; 356—Courtesy Neal Miller; 357—Millsap and Kinyon; 358—From N. Ferguson and R. Keesey, "Comparison of Ventromedial Hypothalamic Lesion Effects Upon Feeding and Lateral Hypothalamic Self-Stimulation in the Female Rat," *Journal of Comparative and Physiological Psychology,* 1971, Vol. 74, pp. 263–271, © 1971 American Psychological Association, and reprinted by permission; 359—John Dawson; 361 and 364—Steve McCarroll/IBOL; 365—(top) After N. Miller, from S. S. Stevens (Ed.), *Handbook of Experimental Psychology,* Wiley, 1951, (bottom) Courtesy José Delgado; 366—Steve McCarroll/IBOL.

CHAPTER 19

368—Bob Van Doren; 370—Alan Mercer; 371—(top) Courtesy Regional Primate Center, (bottom) Courtesy R. A. Butler; 373—Rowland Scherman; 375—Henri Cartier Bresson/Magnum Photos; 376—Jane Cowles; 378—Henri Cartier Bresson/Magnum Photos; 379—Karl Nicholason; 380—Dennis Stock/Magnum Photos; 381—Charles Harbutt/Magnum Photos; 384—(top) Robert A. Isaacs, (bottom) Jane Bown.

CHAPTER 20

386–387—(photos left to right) Construction Tom Gould, photography Steve McCarroll/IBOL, Phillip Kirkland (2), John Oldenkamp/IBOL; 388—Construction Tom Gould, photography Steve McCarroll/IBOL; 390—The Granger Collection; 391—Photography John Oldenkamp by permission of Houghton Mifflin Co. from Terman and Merrill, Stanford Binet Intelligence Scale; 392—Werner Kalber/PPS; 393—(left) Reproduced by permission of Cooperative Test Division of Educational Testing Service, (right) from the *Army General Classification Test,* First Civilian Division, Form AH, © 1947 Science Research Associates, Inc. Reprinted by permission; 394—(top) Ted Polumbaum, (bottom) Karl Nicholason; 396—Adrian Dove; 397—Robert A. Isaacs; 398—(top) Sheridan Psychological Services, (bottom) Courtesy U.S. Department of Labor; 399—(top) Courtesy Stanford University Press, (bottom) from *Strong Vocational Interest Blank Manual,* 1966 and 1969 revision, by permission of Stanford University Press; 400—Reproduced by permission, © 1943, renewed 1970, by the University of Minnesota. Published by the Psychological Corporation, New York. All rights reserved; 401—From Allport, Vernon, and Lindzey, *Psychological Testing,* 3rd ed., Houghton Mifflin, 1968; 403–404—From Douglas N. Jackson, © 1967 by Research Psychologists Press, Goshen, New York; 405—Tom Gould; 406—(top) Karl Nicholason, (bottom) The Granger Collection.

CHAPTER 21

410—Phillip Kirkland; 416—(top) Joyce Kitchell, after S. Freud, *New Introductory Lectures on Psychoanalysis,* newly translated by James Strachey, Norton, 1965, (bottom) Edmund Engleman; 417—Phillip Kirkland; 419 and 421—Edmund Engleman; 423—Phillip Kirkland; 424—The Granger Collection; 425—(left) From R. Kellogg, *The Psychology of Children's Art,* CRM BOOKS, 1967, (right) Pamela Morehouse; 426—(top) The Granger Collection; 427—(bottom) Clemens Kalischer; 428—Courtesy Robert White; 429—(bottom) Courtesy Erich Fromm; 430—Phillip Kirkland.

CHAPTER 22

432—Phillip Kirkland; 436—Karl Nicholason; 437—Phillip Kirkland; 438—Robert A. Mamis; 441—Courtesy Gordon Allport; 442—John Oldenkamp/IBOL; 443 and 445—Phillip Kirkland; 446—Ted Polumbaum; 447—Courtesy George Kelly; 448—Ted Polumbaum.

CHAPTER 23

450—John Oldenkamp/IBOL; 452—Photo by Karl Heider; 453—(bottom) Edward Hall; 454—Karl Nicholason after A. E. Sheflin; 455—Doug Armstrong after T. Burns, "Non Verbal Communication," *Science Journal,* 1964; 456—Art by Karl Nicholason, text from *Collected Poems* by Sara Teasdale, © 1915 The Macmillan Co., renewed 1943 by Mamie T. Wheless; 462—W. Gordon Menzie; 463—Steve McCarroll/IBOL; 464—UPI, Compix; 466–467—Art by Karl Nicholason.

CHAPTER 24

468–469—(photos left to right) Nancy Chase, John Oldenkamp/IBOL, Michael Alexander, John Oldenkamp/IBOL, construction Joyce Fitzgerald, photography Steve McCarroll and John Oldenkamp/IBOL, Steve McCarroll/IBOL; 470—Nancy Chase; 473—Steve McCarroll/IBOL; 475—(top) Cornell Capa/Magnum Photos, (bottom) UPI, Compix; 477—John Oldenkamp/IBOL; 478—(bottom) Courtesy Roger Brown; 480—Courtesy Leon Festinger; 481—The Bettmann Archive, Inc.; 483—(top) After A. Buss and N. Portnoy, "Pain Tolerance and Group Identification," *Journal of Personality and Social Psychology,* 1967, Vol. 6, p. 107, (bottom) courtesy Theodore Newcomb; 484—Karl Nicholason.

CHAPTER 25

486—John Oldenkamp/IBOL; 488—Ken Regan/Camera 5; 489—(top) Courtesy The White House, (bottom) Doug Armstrong; 490—Karl Nicholason; 492—Jane Cowles; 495—(top and center right) Bill MacDonald/IBOL, (bottom left) Leon Bolognese, (bottom right) Jane Cowles; 498—(top) Jane Bown, (bottom left) Michael Alexander, (bottom center) Reginald Jones, (bottom right) John Oldenkamp/IBOL; 500—*Up From Under,* 1971, Vol. 1, Jan.-Feb.; 502—Gillian Theobald.

CHAPTER 26

506—Michael Alexander; 509—Karl Nicholason; 511—Art by Karl Nicholason; 512—Courtesy Medical World News; 513—Courtesy Life Magazine; 514—Courtesy Department of the Army; 516—Art by Karl Nicholason; 518—From S. Milgram, "Some Conditions of Obedience to Authority," *Human Relations,* 1965, Vol. 18, p. 63; 519—(top) Courtesy Solomon Asch; 519—(bottom) Doug Armstrong; 520—William Vandivert; 522—From *Tootle* by Gertrude Crampton, illustrated by Tibor Gergeby, © 1945 by Western Publishing Co., Inc., reprinted by permission of the publisher; 523—Doug Armstrong after R. Brown, *Social Psychology,* The Free Press, 1965; 524—Marc Riboud/Magnum Photos.

CHAPTER 27

526—John Oldenkamp/IBOL; 528—Friends of American Art Collection, courtesy Art Institute of Chicago; 529—(top) Art by Karl Nicholason, (bottom) courtesy Stanley Schachter; 530—Arthur Sirdofsky; 531—Doug Armstrong, after I. Sarnoff and P. Zimbardo, "Anxiety, Fear, and Social Affiliation," *Journal of Abnormal and Social Psychology,* 1961, Vol. 62, © 1961 American Psychological Association, and reprinted by permission; 532—(top) Pete Robinson, (bottom) John Oldenkamp/IBOL; 536—Art by Karl Nicholason; 538—Harry Crosby; 541—(top) Doug Armstrong, after W. Stroebe *et al.,* "Effects of Physical Attractiveness, Attitude Similarity, and Sex on Various Aspects of Interpersonal Attraction," *Journal of Personality and Social Psychology,* 1971, Vol. 18, © 1971 American Psychological Association, and reprinted by permission; 541–542—(bottom) Art by Karl Nicholason.

CHAPTER 28

544—Construction Joyce Fitzgerald, photography Steve McCarroll and John Oldenkamp/IBOL; 547—From M. Sherif and C. W. Sherif, *Social Psychology,* Harper and Row, 1969; 549—(top and center) by permission of Metro-Goldwyn-Mayer, (bottom left) © Warner Bros. 1945, (bottom right) by permission of Twentieth Century Fox; 551—Art by Karl Nicholason, after The Thematic Apperception Test; 552—Art by Karl Nicholason; 554—Norris McNamara/Nancy Palmer Photo Agency; 557—(top) Courtesy Antelope Valley Press, Lancaster, California; 558—Karl Nicholason; 560—Tom Lewis; 562—UPI, Compix.

CHAPTER 29

564—Steve McCarroll/IBOL; 566—Darrel Millsap/Millsap and Kinyon; 567—Courtesy Alfred Marrow; 568—Michael Alexander; 569—CBS Television Network; 570—H. Lee Pratt; 571—(top left) Hugh Wilkerson, (top right and bottom) Michael Alexander; 572–585—Darrel Millsap/Millsap and Kinyon.

CHAPTER 30

588–589—(photos left to right) John Oldenkamp/IBOL; Bob Van Doren, John Oldenkamp/IBOL, Bob Van Doren (2); 590—John Oldenkamp/IBOL; 592—(top) Alan Mercer, (bottom) Bruce Davidson/Magnum Photos; 594—Karl Nicholason; 599—Ignacio Gomez; 600–601—Gary Vandersteur; 603—(left) The Bettmann Archive, Inc., (right) © 1941 RKO Radio Pictures, a division of RKO General; 604—Mary Ellen Mark; 605—Howard Sochurek; 606—Doug Armstrong, adapted from Srole *et al., Mental Health in the Metropolis,* McGraw-Hill, 1964; 607—From M. Kramer, "Statistics of Mental Disorders in the United States: Current Status, Some Urgent Needs and Suggested Solutions," *Journal of the Royal Statistical Society,* Series A, 1969, Vol. 132; 608—(top left) Courtesy Dr. Kurt Wagner, (bottom left) George Rodger/Magnum Photos, (right) Robert Isaacs.

CHAPTER 31

610—Bob Van Doren; 613—Phillip Kirkland; 614—Joyce Kitchell; 615—The National Museum of Western Art, Tokyo; 616—(top) Courtesy Joseph Wolpe, (bottom) courtesy Theodore Lidz; 617—Gillian Theobald; 618—Adapted from F. J. Kallman, *Heredity and Health and Mental Disorder,* Norton, 1953; 620—Raimondo Borea; 621—Joyce Kitchell; 622—Gary Vandersteur; 623—Courtesy Hans Eysenck; 624—(top) From H. J. Eysenck, "Classification and the Problem of Diagnosis," in H. J. Eysenck (Ed.), *Handbook of Abnormal Psychology,* Basic Books, 1961, (bottom) courtesy John Dollard; 626—Karl Nicholason.

CHAPTER 32

628—John Oldenkamp/IBOL; 630—(top left) Arthur Sirdofsky, (top right) John Carnemolla/Photographic Library of Australia, (bottom) The Granger Collection; 631—(top left) The Granger Collection, (right and bottom left) The Bettmann Archive, Inc., (bottom) courtesy O. H. Mowrer; 632—(top) The Granger Collection, (bottom) courtesy Thomas Szasz; 633—Courtesy Al Vercoutere, Camarillo State Hospital; 635—From G. Gurin, J. Veroff, and S. Feld, "Americans View Their Mental Health," *Joint Commission on Mental Illness and Health, Monograph Series,* No. 4, p. 307, Basic Books, 1960; 636—Eric Aerts; 637—Courtesy Al Vercoutere, Camarillo State Hospital; 641—Edmund Engleman; 642—Bob Van Doren.

CHAPTER 33

644—Bob Van Doren; 647—Cliff McReynolds; 648—Karl Nicholason; 649—(top) Courtesy Viktor Frankl, (bottom) courtesy Rollo May; 650—Kalamazoo Learning Village; 651—(top) Courtesy Leonard Krasner, (bottom) Steve McCarroll/IBOL; 652—Courtesy Albert Bandura; 655—John Oldenkamp/IBOL; 656—(top) Raimondo Borea, (bottom) courtesy Jacob Moreno; 657—John Oldenkamp/IBOL; 658—Robert LaRoche.

CHAPTER 34

660—Bob Van Doren; 663—G. William Holland; 664—From M. Greenblatt *et al., Drug and Social Therapy in Chronic Schizophrenia,* Charles C Thomas, 1965; 666—Joyce Kitchell, adapted from R. W. Earle, Department of Medical Pharmacology and Therapeutics, University of California, Irvine; 667—Doug Armstrong; 669—Marty Gunsaullus; 672–675—Photography by Werner Kalber/PPS; 676—Michael Hanulack/Magnum Photos; 678—Joyce Kitchell, adapted from H. M. Glatt, "Group Therapy in Alcoholism," *British Journal of Addiction,* 1957, Vol. 54.

Appendix: Methodology

681—Tom Suzuki; 682—(left) Courtesy Dr. Eckhard H. Hess, (right) Steve McCarroll; 683—Steve McCarroll/IBOL; 684—From N. E. Miller, "Effects of Drugs on Motivation: The Value of Using a Variety of Measures," *Annals of the New York Academy of Sciences,* 1956, Vol. 65, pp. 318–333; 685—From A. C. Catania, "Concurrent Performances: A Baseline for the Study of Reinforcement Magnitude," *Journal of Experimental Analysis of Behavior,* 1963, Vol. 6, pp. 299–300; 700–704—Karl Nicholason.

If we have unwittingly omitted acknowledgment of ownership or have been unable to obtain permissions for usage of any material in this book, we sincerely apologize. We will be most happy, however, upon being presented with proof of ownership, to pay an appropriate fee as if we had been able to obtain permission prior to publication.

Psychology Today: An Introduction, Second Edition, Book Team
Arlyne Lazerson, *Senior Editor*
Catherine Caldwell, Martha Rosler, *Editors*
Cindi Farden, *Associate Editor*
Susan Orlofsky, *Editorial Assistant*
Patricia Campbell, *Research Assistant*
Sally Collins, Tom Suzuki, *Designers*
Kurt Kolbe, *Art Assistant*
Pat Bouchard, *Production Supervisor*
Vickie Self, *Production Assistant*
Richard Holme, *Publisher*
Jeffrey Eisen, Phillip M. Whitten, *Associates*
Barbara Rose, *Publishing Coordinator*

John Ochse, *Sales Manager*
David Phanco, Roger Romito, John Staley, *Sales Representatives*
Christine Condon, Leslie Wahl, LaDelle Willett, *Sales Coordinators*
Howard Smith, *Social Science Marketing Manager*
Nancy Hutchison Sjöberg, *Rights and Permissions Supervisor and Graphics Researcher*

CRM BOOKS
Richard Holme, *President and Publisher*
John H. Painter, Jr., *Publisher, Life and Physical Sciences*
Roger E. Emblen, *Publisher, Social Sciences*
Tom Suzuki, *Director of Design*
Charles Jackson, *Managing Editor*
Henry Ratz, *Director of Production*

Officers of Communications Research Machines, Inc.
Charles C. Tillinghast III, *President*
Richard Holme, *Vice-President*
James B. Horton, *Vice-President*
Paul N. Lazarus III, *Vice-President*
Wayne E. Sheppard, *Vice-President*